HANDBOOK OF PERSONALITY DEVELOPMENT

Also Available

Handbook of Temperament
Edited by Marcel Zentner and Rebecca L. Shiner

Power, Intimacy, and the Life Story:
Personological Inquiries into Identity
Dan P. McAdams

The Art and Science of Personality Development
Dan P. McAdams

The Stories We Live By:
Personal Myths and the Making of the Self
Dan P. McAdams

HANDBOOK OF PERSONALITY DEVELOPMENT

edited by
Dan P. McAdams
Rebecca L. Shiner
Jennifer L. Tackett

THE GUILFORD PRESS
New York   London

Library of Congress Cataloging-in-Publication Data

Names: McAdams, Dan P., editor. | Shiner, Rebecca L., editor. | Tackett,
  Jennifer L., editor.
Title: Handbook of personality development / edited by Dan P. McAdams,
  Rebecca L. Shiner, Jennifer L. Tackett.
Description: New York : Guilford Press, [2019] | Includes bibliographical
  references and index.
Identifiers: LCCN 2018004957 | ISBN 9781462536931 (hardcover : alk. paper) |
  ISBN 9781462547739 (paperback)
Subjects: LCSH: Personality development. | Developmental psychology.
Classification: LCC BF698 .H3344 2018 | DDC 155.2/5—dc23
LC record available at https://lccn.loc.gov/2018004957

About the Editors

Dan P. McAdams, PhD, is the Henry Wade Rogers Professor of Psychology and Professor of Education and Social Policy at Northwestern University. Past president of the Association for Research in Personality, he is a recipient of the Henry A. Murray Award for the study of lives and the Jack Block Award for career contributions from the Society for Personality and Social Psychology, Division 8 of the American Psychological Association (APA); the Theodore Sarbin Award from APA Division 24 (Theoretical and Philosophical Psychology); and the William James Book Award from APA Division 1 (General Psychology). Dr. McAdams's research focuses on concepts of self and identity in contemporary American society and on themes of power, intimacy, redemption, and generativity across the adult life course. He has published nearly 300 scientific articles and chapters and numerous books, including, most recently, *The Art and Science of Personality Development*.

Rebecca L. Shiner, PhD, is Professor of Psychology at Colgate University. Her research centers on temperament and personality trait development in children, adolescents, and young adults, including structure, stability and change, and links to positive life outcomes and the emergence of psychopathology. She was a consultant to the DSM-5 Personality Disorders Work Group, served as Executive Officer of the Association for Research in Personality, and is a past associate editor of the *Journal of Personality and Social Psychology* and the *Journal of Personality*. Dr. Shiner has held many leadership roles at Colgate University, including Psychology Department Chair and Director of the Residential Commons.

Jennifer L. Tackett, PhD, is Associate Professor of Psychology and Director of Clinical Training at Northwestern University. Her research focuses on child and adolescent personality and externalizing and disinhibitory psychopathology in youth. Much of her work emphasizes assessment, measurement, and construct validation approaches. Dr. Tackett is a recipient of early career awards from the Society for Personality Assessment, the Society for Research in Psychopathology, and the Ontario Ministry of Research and Innovation. She is currently a senior editor of the journal *Collabra: Psychology* and an associate editor of the *Journal of Abnormal Psychology* and *Advances in Methods and Practices in Psychological Science*.

Contributors

Jonathan M. Adler, PhD, Department of Psychology, Olin College of Engineering, Needham, Massachusetts

Timothy A. Allen, PhD, Campbell Family Mental Health Institute, Centre for Addiction and Mental Health, Toronto, Ontario, Canada

Berenice Anaya, MS, Department of Psychology, The Pennsylvania State University, University Park, Pennsylvania

Wiebke Bleidorn, PhD, Department of Psychology, University of California, Davis, Davis, California

Jordan A. Booker, PhD, Department of Psychology, University of Missouri, Columbia, Missouri

Daniel A. Briley, PhD, Department of Psychology, University of Illinois at Urbana–Champaign, Champaign, Illinois

Kristin A. Buss, PhD, Department of Psychology, The Pennsylvania State University, University Park, Pennsylvania

Andrew M. Chanen, PhD, Orygen, National Centre of Excellence in Youth Mental Health, Parkville, Victoria, Australia; Centre for Youth Mental Health, University of Melbourne, Parkville, Victoria, Australia

Marco Del Giudice, PhD, Department of Psychology, University of New Mexico, Albuquerque, New Mexico

Colin G. DeYoung, PhD, Department of Psychology, University of Minnesota, Minneapolis, Minnesota

Michele Dillon, PhD, Department of Sociology, University of New Hampshire, Durham, New Hampshire

M. Brent Donnellan, PhD, Department of Psychology, Michigan State University, East Lansing, Michigan

C. Emily Durbin, PhD, Department of Psychology, Michigan State University, East Lansing, Michigan

Amanda M. Durik, PhD, Department of Psychology, Northern Illinois University, DeKalb, Illinois

Nancy Eisenberg, PhD, Department of Psychology, Arizona State University, Tempe, Arizona

Dan Farina, BA, Department of Psychology, Hamilton College, Clinton, New York

Robyn Fivush, PhD, Department of Psychology, Emory University, Atlanta, Georgia

Alexandra M. Freund, PhD, Department of Psychology, University of Zurich, Zurich, Switzerland

Maria A. Gartstein, PhD, Department of Psychology, Washington State University, Pullman, Washington

Gary S. Gregg, PhD, Department of Psychology, Kalamazoo College, Kalamazoo, Michigan

Phillip L. Hammack, PhD, Department of Psychology, University of California, Santa Cruz, Santa Cruz, California

Sarah E. Hampson, PhD, Oregon Research Institute, Eugene, Oregon

Maciel M. Hernández, PhD, Department of Psychology, Portland State University, Portland, Oregon

Patrick L. Hill, PhD, Department of Psychological and Brain Sciences, Washington University in St. Louis, St. Louis, Missouri

Christopher J. Hopwood, PhD, Department of Psychology, University of California, Davis, Davis, California

Nathan W. Hudson, PhD, Department of Psychology, Southern Methodist University, Dallas, Texas

Joshua J. Jackson, PhD, Department of Psychological and Brain Sciences, Washington University in St. Louis, St. Louis, Missouri

Rachael E. Jones, BA, Department of Psychology, University of Minnesota, Minneapolis, Minnesota

Ruthellen Josselson, PhD, School of Psychology, Fielding Graduate University, Santa Barbara, California

Margaret L. Kern, PhD, Centre for Positive Psychology, Melbourne Graduate School of Education, University of Melbourne, Melbourne, Australia

Christine A. Lee, MS, Department of Psychology, University of Kentucky, Lexington, Kentucky

Liliana J. Lengua, PhD, Department of Psychology, University of Washington, Seattle, Washington

Jacqueline V. Lerner, PhD, Department of Applied Developmental and Educational Psychology, Boston College, Chestnut Hill, Massachusetts

Richard M. Lerner, PhD, Eliot-Pearson Department of Child Study and Human Development and Institute for Applied Research in Youth Development, Tufts University, Medford, Massachusetts

Jennifer P. Lilgendahl, PhD, Department of Psychology, Haverford College, Haverford, Pennsylvania

Richard E. Lucas, PhD, Department of Psychology, Michigan State University, East Lansing, Michigan

Michelle M. Martel, PhD, Department of Psychology, University of Kentucky, Lexington, Kentucky

Dan P. McAdams, PhD, Department of Psychology and School of Education and Social Policy, Northwestern University, Evanston, Illinois

Kate C. McLean, PhD, Department of Psychology, Western Washington University, Bellingham, Washington

Christopher M. Napolitano, PhD, Department of Educational Psychology, University of Illinois at Urbana–Champaign, Champaign, Illinois

Darcia Narvaez, PhD, Department of Psychology, University of Notre Dame, Notre Dame, Indiana

Ulrich Orth, PhD, Department of Psychology, University of Bern, Bern, Switzerland

Koraly Pérez-Edgar, PhD, Department of Psychology, The Pennsylvania State University, University Park, Pennsylvania

Peter Prinzie, PhD, Department of Pedagogical Sciences, Erasmus University Rotterdam, Rotterdam, The Netherlands

Elaine Reese, PhD, Department of Psychology, University of Otago, Dunedin, New Zealand

K. Ann Renninger, PhD, Department of Educational Studies, Swarthmore College, Swarthmore, Pennsylvania

Richard W. Robins, PhD, Department of Psychology, University of California, Davis, Davis, California

Joshua L. Rutt, PhD, Department of Psychology, University of Zurich, Zurich, Switzerland

Julia Schüler, PhD, Department of Sports Science, University of Kostanz, Kostanz, Germany

Ted Schwaba, MA, Department of Psychology, University of California, Davis, Davis, California

Jennifer M. Senia, PhD, Department of Psychology, Michigan State University, East Lansing, Michigan

Kennon M. Sheldon, PhD, Department of Psychological Sciences, University of Missouri, Columbia, Missouri

Rebecca L. Shiner, PhD, Department of Psychology, Colgate University, Hamilton, New York

Jeffry A. Simpson, PhD, Department of Psychology, University of Minnesota, Minneapolis, Minnesota

Helena R. Slobodskaya, MD, PhD, Institute of Physiology and Basic Medicine, Novosibirsk State University, Novosibirsk, Russia

Luke D. Smillie, PhD, Melbourne School of Psychological Sciences, University of Melbourne, Melbourne, Australia

Tess E. Smith, MS, Department of Psychology, University of Kentucky, Lexington, Kentucky

Jennifer L. Tackett, PhD, Department of Psychology, Northwestern University, Evanston, Illinois

Katherine N. Thompson, PhD, Orygen, National Centre of Excellence in Youth Mental Health, Parkville, Victoria, Australia; Centre for Youth Mental Health, University of Melbourne, Parkville, Victoria, Australia

Erin E. Toolis, MS, Department of Psychology, University of California, Santa Cruz, Santa Cruz, California

Elliot M. Tucker-Drob, PhD, Department of Psychology, University of Texas at Austin, Austin, Texas

Mirko Uljarevic, PhD, Department of Psychology and Counseling, La Trobe University, Melbourne, Australia

Alicia Vallorani, MS, Department of Psychology, The Pennsylvania State University, University Park, Pennsylvania

Paul Wink, PhD, Department of Psychology, Wellesley College, Wellesley, Massachusetts

Preface

The fields of personality psychology and developmental psychology have historically followed different paths. Personality psychologists have traditionally examined broad and purportedly stable individual differences in thought, emotion, motivation, and behavior, typically as these differences (often called *traits*) manifest themselves in adult lives. The emphasis has been on *stability* in individual differences over the adult life course. By contrast, developmental psychologists have traditionally studied growth and *change* in psychological characteristics in the early years of life (infancy through adolescence). The distinction has never been completely sharp, however, in that some researchers focus on "child personality" (especially those who study "temperament") and an entire field of lifespan developmental psychology pays as much attention to adulthood as it does to the early years. Nonetheless, the terms *personality* and *development* tend to suggest different emphases. Therefore, the term *personality development* has historically represented a problematic juxtaposition.

There is strong reason today to believe that things are changing. The two fields of personality and developmental psychology now appear to be moving toward each other at a rapid clip. Personality variables are increasingly featured in studies of children and adolescents, and scientific journals given over to developmental psychology routinely feature personality constructs, often as expressed in adulthood. In 2014, for example, an entire issue of the journal *Developmental Psychology* (Vol. 50, No. 5) spotlighted the personality trait of "conscientiousness," presenting a 16-article special section on the role of conscientiousness in healthy aging. In a parallel fashion, journals in personality psychology—such as the *Journal of Personality and Social Psychology* and the *Journal of Personality*—often examine both stability and change over the human life course, frequently feature studies of children and adolescents, routinely incorporate developmental ideas such as "temperament" in their published studies, and often feature lifespan developmental frameworks and developmental methodologies. In 2014, an entire issue of the *European Journal of Personality* was given over to the question of how personality *develops* during the adult years. Foreshadowing the coming together of two fields, the first ever "handbook" of "personality development" appeared in 2006, edited by Dan K. Mroczek and Todd Little. More recently, Dan P. McAdams published a new synthesis of theory and research on personality development, in *The Art and Science of Personality Development* (2015).

It is with great excitement, therefore, that we introduce you to our new and innovative *Handbook of Personality Development*. Forgive our immodesty, but we coeditors believe that this is a groundbreaking work. We have brought together top scholars who work at the interface of personality and developmental psychology to write integrative chapters that are both *authoritative* and *accessible*.

We have asked the authors to provide a broad-based and up-to-date review of theoretical ideas, empirical findings, methodological conventions, and emerging trends in the study of personality development, from a broad range of angles and with respect to a diverse set of topics and goals. We have endeavored to produce a unique and uniquely valuable resource for faculty, researchers, students, practitioners, and even educated laypersons who wish to learn more about the development of personality across the human life course. Let us, then, highlight four features of the *Handbook of Personality Development* that, we believe, make it unique and uniquely valuable:

1. Our volume adopts a *lifespan perspective* throughout, with respect to both how the entire book is organized and to individual chapters. To the extent possible, each author considers his or her topic from the standpoint of the full human life course.

2. Our aim is that each chapter be as broad-based as possible, giving the reader the *big-picture overview* rather than zeroing in on a particular line of research. Most of the chapters provide *historical context* for the topics covered and feature the particular research *methodologies* that are most germane to the inquiry.

3. Most chapters feature a specific *case study* to illustrate the main ideas in the chapter—an examination of a single human life in context—and/or the chapters provide vivid illustrations and concrete examples in order to enliven the presentation and ground fundamental ideas about personality development in flesh-and-blood human lives. We asked our authors to avoid the conventions of the predictable, and sometimes predictably boring, research literature review. No need to be 100% comprehensive—as if such a thing were possible anyway. The primary goal is to engage the reader. We believe that many of the chapters have accomplished this goal admirably, and in ways that do not compromise the science and the sophistication of the material.

4. We have organized the book around an emerging three-layer conception of personality development (McAdams, 2015) that considers the development of the person as (a) a social *actor*, (b) a motivated *agent*, and (c) an autobiographical *author*. As has become clear over the past three decades, personality is about the dispositional traits that we as social actors display, conveyed, for example, in the well-known Big Five conception and in models of childhood temperament. But it has also become increasingly clear that personality and personality development are about more than traits, encompassing the emergence and articulation of motives, goals, values, personal ideologies, strategies, scripts, narratives, and a wide range of other phenomena and processes that are conveyed through conceiving of psychological individuality from the standpoints of personal agency and authorship as well. There are surely many alternative ways to conceptualize personality development as a whole. But we believe that the three-layer conception we use herein enables us to portray the development of personality in its most inclusive and dynamic sense and through its most nuanced manifestations.

REFERENCES

McAdams, D. P. (2015). *The art and science of personality development*. New York: Guilford Press.
Mroczek, D. K., & Little, T. (Eds.). (2006). *The handbook of personality development*. Mahwah, NJ: Erlbaum.

Contents

Contents

PART III. MOTIVATED AGENTS: THE DEVELOPMENT OF GOALS AND VALUES

PART IV. AUTOBIOGRAPHICAL AUTHORS: LIFE STORIES AND THE SEARCH FOR MEANING

PART V. APPLICATIONS AND INTEGRATIONS

PART I

PERSONALITY DEVELOPMENT
AND HUMAN NATURE

Each person is a once-in-eternity variation on the general design of human nature, a never-to-be-replicated experiment, wherein a singular genetic mash-up encounters, and participates in, a particular sequence of environmental events spread across time. A gene-carrying member of the species *Homo sapiens,* each person must be like all other members of the species in certain foundational ways, and yet unique, too, like no other person who ever was or will be—unique from the very beginning, and unique in the trajectory of change that will ultimately characterize the person's life. Laypeople and scientists alike use the term *personality* to capture aspects of that psychological uniqueness, and the term *development* to convey how that uniqueness changes (and remains the same) over time. In this opening section of the *Handbook of Personality Development,* we consider the broad relationship between the development of an individual person on the one hand, and the nature of what it means to be an individual person, a unique instantiation of *Homo sapiens,* on the other.

In Chapter 1, Dan P. McAdams provides some historical context for understanding the recent convergence of personality studies and developmental science, and he lays out the conceptual model that organizes this volume. He argues that when it comes to personality, each person's unique variation on the general theme of human nature follows three different (though interacting) lines of development: from infant temperament to adult personality traits (the social actor), from childhood theory of mind to the articulation of life values and goals (the motivated agent), and from the emergence of autobiographical memory to the construction of a self-defining life story (the autobiographical author). In Chapter 2, Marco Del Giudice steps back from the individual life to consider in detail the broad outlines of human nature, the template against which every life reveals its uniqueness. In discussing topics such as human ecology and adaptation, inclusive fitness, intragenomic conflict, differential susceptibility to environmental influences, developmental switch points, and life-history strategies, Del Giudice shows that evolutionary frameworks for understanding personality development are foundational rather than discretionary. In that members of the species *Homo sapiens* evolved to meet the challenges that our ancestors have confronted for millions of years, it simply makes no scientific sense to consider the development of personality outside the ultimate context of human evolution.

Chapters 3 and 4 pick up the conversation regarding the ultimate determinants of and contexts for personality development by considering, in broad terms, the interaction of genotypes and environments in the development of the person. Elliot M. Tucker-Drob and Daniel A. Briley

1

(Chapter 3) examine how models and methods derived from behavioral genetics help us understand the ways in which genetic and environmental factors combine to produce consequential individual differences. They review many of the well-documented descriptive results from studies in behavior genetics, such as those regarding the heritability of dispositional personality traits and the lack of empirical support for shared-environment influences. Then, they describe exciting new findings and insights that paint a nuanced and intricate portrait of how genes and environments interact, combine, and collude in the making of personality, and how these dynamics appear to change markedly over the course of development. Taking a sharply different tack, Richard M. and Jacqueline V. Lerner (Chapter 4) caution against the kind of conceptual essentializing that sometimes results from inquiries into the genetics of personality traits. They offer a relational developmental systems model for personality development. From their perspective, genes are only one part of the holistic and dynamically integrated ecology of human development, which itself encompasses the biological, psychological, behavioral, social, community, institutional, economic, ideological, and cultural systems into which each child is born and lives across the course of life.

CHAPTER 1

The Emergence of Personality

Dan P. McAdams

How do we become who we are? This is the question of personality development. If there is a more compelling question in all of psychological science, I cannot think of it.

The phrase "who we are" pertains to personality itself, which may be conceived as those socially consequential features of a person's psychological makeup that distinguish him or her from other human beings—the psychological differences that make the biggest difference in adaptation to human life. The phrase "how do we become" pertains to development. How does a person's characteristic psychological makeup come to be? How does it emerge, how does it change, and in what ways does it—personality itself—demonstrate continuity over developmental time?

In this opening chapter for the *Handbook of Personality Development,* I consider the *emergence* of personality in two very different senses. The first is signaled by my opening question, the developmental question around which the *Handbook* is constructed. I argue that personality development may be usefully construed from three different standpoints. These are the standpoints of the person as (1) a social actor, (2) a motivated agent, and (3) an autobiographical author (McAdams, 2015a, 2015b; McAdams & Olson, 2010). Each standpoint corresponds to a line of personality development running across the human life course, from infancy

through old age. This tripartite conception of personality development provides an organizing framework for the *Handbook.*

The second sense of emergence refers to the emergence of personality studies as a legitimate and powerful intellectual movement in psychological science. Personality psychology has endured a conflicted history within the broad discipline of psychology. While all fields of study are shaped by their history, personality psychology has an especially notable story to tell, I think, for the field has struggled mightily over the past 40 years to *emerge* from a difficult past. Let's just say that, beginning in the 1960s, personality psychology went through a tumultuous adolescence, filled with *Sturm und Drang* (Barenbaum & Winter, 2008; McAdams, 1997). And the field still bears the psychological scars to prove it. While some observers of this history argue that trauma ultimately produced resilience (Kenrick & Funder, 1988), the insecurities and confusions that plagued the field during its protracted adolescence for decades made it nearly impossible to address seriously the topic of personality *development.* In a nutshell, it was extraordinarily difficult to think systematically about how personality itself might develop when it was not clear what personality itself was, or even if such a thing existed.

Personality psychology finally emerged as a mature and confident scientific discipline over the past two decades. Its emergence enables us now to consider the question of how indeed the phenomenon of personality itself emerges, and how it develops over the human life course. Therefore, current developmental conceptions derive from a historical legacy. In what follows, I consider both senses of the word *emergence* as applied to personality, then I end with a case example of personality development in one life of substantial historical significance: the life of former U.S. President Barack Obama. Our understanding of the emergence and development of personality across the human life course, shaped as it is by the history of our science, comes fully alive in the close examination of a real human being developing over time.

Struggling to Emerge as a Field: A Brief (and Troubled) History

Early Promise

The future looked bright when Gordon Allport and Henry Murray first carved out an intellectual space for the field of personality psychology in the mid-1930s. In the field's first authoritative text, *Personality: A Psychological Interpretation,* Allport (1937) brought together British and American research on individual differences, German studies of character, and investigations into abnormal psychology and mental hygiene to create a new subdiscipline in psychology. In *Explorations in Personality,* Murray (1938) took a slightly different tack, drawing more from the psychoanalytic tradition (Freud and Jung, mainly), cultural anthropology, and the case studies he and his colleagues assembled at the Harvard Psychological Clinic; but his take-home message was very similar to Allport's. Both men envisioned an integrative field of psychological study aimed at understanding the whole person. Whereas 1930s experimental psychology dissected persons into their component pieces (sensation, perception, habit, and conditioning) in order to generate universal laws of animal behavior, personality psychology should aim instead to synthesize the psychological pieces, Allport and Murray argued, and to bring inquiry to bear upon the individual human life.

Allport (1937, 1961) was especially sensitive to the tension inherent in such an enterprise, for personality psychology would need to launch *nomothetic* investigations to examine psychological variation across different human beings, while also conducting *idiographic* studies that aimed to examine personality structure, dynamics, and development within the single case. In Allport's view, the central construct to be employed in this endeavor was the dispositional personality *trait*—a position that anticipated the seminal contributions of Cattell (1943), Eysenck (1952), Guilford (1959), and the many personality psychologists who contributed to the formulation of the Big Five trait taxonomy (e.g., Goldberg, 1993; McCrae & Costa, 1987). For Murray (1938), motivational constructs (needs, motives, goals, complexes), rather than traits per se, were deemed to be the most important variables for conceptualizing psychological variation between persons, and the key to understanding the individual life. As such, Murray's perspective anticipated the seminal contributions of McClelland (1961) on need for achievement, Winter (1973) on the power motive, Deci and Ryan (1991) on intrinsic motivation and self-determination, and motivational approaches espoused by Cantor (1990), Emmons (1986), and Sheldon (2004), among others.

The early promise of the field was also captured in the grand theories of personality proposed in the first half of the 20th century, systematized and collated in personality textbooks, such as that of Hall and Lindzey (1957). Broad theoretical conceptions offered by Freud, Jung, Adler, Rogers, Maslow, Kelly, and others, as well as by Allport and Murray themselves, provided integrative conceptual frameworks for understanding the whole person, and for specifying the most important individual differences to be studied. In the years immediately following World War II, personality researchers mined these theories for their most valuable constructs, launching innovative research programs to assess and elaborate phenomena such as authoritarianism (Adorno, Frenkel-Brunswik, Levinson, & Sanford, 1950), achievement motivation (McClelland, 1961), anxiety (Taylor, 1953), extraversion (Eysenck, 1952), and identity (Marcia, 1966). During the same period, methodologists published a series of classic papers that extended and refined the science of personality measurement (e.g, Campbell & Fiske, 1959; Cronbach & Meehl, 1955; Loevinger, 1957). Blessed with integrative theories, provocative constructs, and increasingly sophisticated assessment methods, postwar personality psychology seemed destined for success.

Trouble

But rumblings of discontent could be heard by the early 1960s. A surprisingly contentious debate arose regarding the meaning of self-report items commonly used on personality scales. Many items held a social desirability bias, critics observed. Regardless of the content of the item, some respondents may simply rate themselves in an especially positive and socially desirable manner (Crowne & Marlow, 1960), potentially undermining the validity of self-report scales. Similarly, some respondents may tend to agree with nearly any statement about the self (yea-sayers), while others may tend to disagree (nay-sayers), suggesting that test-taking styles (rather than trait-specific content) may ultimately determine people's scores on trait scales. After the publication of hundreds of articles and monographs on the subject, personality psychologists seemed to exhaust the issue, ultimately concluding the following: (1) The problem of test-taking styles is technically real, but mainly trivial and (2) minor tweaks to existing scales can resolve the issue well enough (Block, 1965).

The decade-long debate over response styles foreshadowed the course of future controversies in the field of personality psychology: First, a plausible critique is levied, but in exaggerated terms; second, those who perceive themselves to be targets of the critique respond with fierce counterattack; third, a protracted battle ensues, filling up countless pages in journals and books while spreading a sense of discord and confusion; and fourth, the combatants finally run out of energy, or others run out of patience, and reasonable people conclude that the original critics may have had a point, but they took it way too far.

The 1960s and 1970s witnessed a number of trends, both in science and in society, that challenged basic assumptions of personality psychology. The dramatic, and sometimes counterintuitive, findings of experimental social psychology (e.g., iconic studies by Asch [1955] and Milgram [1974] on conformity and on obedience to authority) illustrated the power of situational variables to shape behavior, over and against individual differences in personality. Social upheavals cast serious doubt on the adequacy of frameworks for identifying "types" or "kinds" of people and stable individual differences. Both in clinical work and in the study of normal persons, personality diagnosis and as-

sessment came to be viewed in some circles as nothing more than "labeling," promulgated by an establishment interested in retaining its own power, or by small-minded observers under the sway of stereotypes (Goffman, 1961; Rosenhahn, 1973). The antiwar, civil rights, and women's movements all sensitized Americans to the pervasive influence of culture and environment on human behavior and experience—influence experienced in the contexts of family, class, ethnicity, race, and nation-state. The implicit message was this: The person is a product—even a victim—of social context; therefore, one should focus on context rather than the person—on social influence rather than individuality. In addition, some came to see personality psychology as dominated by an Anglo-masculine viewpoint. One could reasonably argue in 1970 that the only whole persons whom personality psychologists ever studied anyway were upper-middle-class white males.

The field of personality psychology endured a number of devastating critiques around this time: Carlson (1971) chastised the field for ignoring Allport's original call for idiographic studies; Fiske (1974) despaired that personality constructs were hopelessly imprecise, impossible to pin down with concrete behaviors; Shweder (1975) suggested that behavioral scientists abandon all efforts to study stable individual differences; and Sechrest (1976) wondered whether there was really a "there" there when it came to the so-called "field" of personality psychology, joking that there are two ways to spell it: *c-l-i-n-i-c-a-l* and *s-o-c-i-a-l*.

But the strongest critique came from Mischel (1968), who best captured the cultural ethos of the late 1960s. Based on a highly selective review of the empirical literature, Mischel concluded that personality dispositions, typically measured via paper-and-pencil questionnaires, account for very little of the variance in human behavior. For the most part, there is little cross-situational generality for human thought, feeling, and action, Mischel argued. Instead, what human beings do (and feel and think) tends to be dictated mainly by factors specific to the given situational context. Individual differences in situations are more effective predictors of behavior than are individual differences in personality variables (e.g., traits), which are essentially nothing more than stereotypic labels. Mischel suggested that the only place traits may truly exist is in the minds of personality psychologists. Thus, personality psychologists may be guilty of committing a fundamental attribution error by invoking broad categories concerning internal dispositions to explain (and predict) the behavior of others, labels that they are probably loath to apply to themselves.

Mischel's critique ignited an internecine feud in personality psychology—what came to be called the *person–situation debate*. Which is more important in the prediction of behavior: the person (e.g., his or her traits) or the situation? Defenders of the trait position viewed the situationist critique as an indictment on the entire field of personality psychology. They had a point: If psychologists could not even concede that individual differences in basic traits predicted, or at least were associated with, corresponding behavioral trends, then the very existence of personality itself must be called into question (Hogan, DeSoto, & Solano, 1977). From the beginning, the trait advocates were on the defensive.

Following Mischel (1968, 1973), the advancing forces for situationism found intellectual sustenance in social learning theory (Bandura, 1971), and they found ideological allies among many social psychologists who tended then to be (by either training or disposition) suspicious of dispositional explanations in psychology. In an ironic turn, the term *trait psychologist* became a label of ill repute in many circles of psychological science during the 1970s and early 1980s. Jackson and Paunonen (1980) wryly observed that "trait psychologists" seemed then to be viewed "like witches of 300 years ago. . . . [T]here is confidence in their existence, and even possibly their sinister properties, although one is hard pressed to find one in the flesh or even meet someone who has" (p. 523). As if to save the field's founder from eternal damnation, Zuroff (1986) went to great lengths to prove that Allport himself was *not* a trait psychologist. Allport never claimed that behavior was perfectly consistent from one situation to the next, Zuroff showed. Nor did he ever claim that individual differences in trait scores perfectly predict individual differences in behavior. But of course, no credible personality psychologist had ever claimed these things!

The debate raged on for at least 15 years, dominating the discourse in journals and books published in personality psychology. The controversy produced important conceptual papers, and it led to refinements in research methodology. Nonetheless, it is difficult to argue with Rorer and Widiger's (1983) assessment, when they concluded, "a great deal of nonsense has been written on the trait–situation topic" (p. 446). By the mid-1980s, both sides in the conflict seemed to settle on the compromise position of *interactionism*—behavior is a function of the *interaction* of the person and the situation, a position that each side claimed it had held all along (Maddi, 1984).

(Re-)Emergence

When the dust finally settled on the person–situation debate, the field of personality psychology began to make notable progress in fulfilling some of the promise that Allport (1937) and Murray (1938) envisioned half a century earlier. By the mid-1990s, signs of the field's vigorous (re-)emergence were everywhere to be seen.

Most important, the field's cardinal construct—the idea of a basic personality trait—began to receive overwhelming empirical support. For example, longitudinal studies began to show that individual differences in dispositional personality traits are highly stable over long periods of time (Roberts & DelVecchio, 2000). Studies of twins suggested substantial heritability for personality traits (Tellegen et al., 1988). In light of such findings, it is difficult now to argue that traits are merely attributional fictions residing in the heads of personality psychologists.

Importantly, studies wherein behavior is aggregated across many situations and over time show again and again that individual differences on trait scores are significantly, and often robustly, associated with summary behavioral trends (Fleeson & Gallagher, 2009), even as it remains difficult to predict exactly what a person will do in any single situation. Trait scores, moreover, are powerful predictors of many of the most consequential outcomes in human life, including psychological well-being, occupational success, marital stability, health, and mortality (Ozer & Benet-Martinez, 2006; Roberts, Kuncel, Shiner, Caspi, & Goldberg, 2007). Forging a much-needed consensus in the 1980s, the Big Five framework now provides an elegant and heuristically powerful scheme for organizing the many dispositional traits that might be invoked to describe and explain variation in human behavior (McCrae & Costa, 1987), and a few rival schemes have also enjoyed significant notice (Ashton et al., 2004). And neuroscientists have made important advances in identifying the cortical reward circuits and control systems that constitute the biological bases of traits (DeYoung et al., 2010).

With the consolidation of the trait concept, personality psychologists have moved vigorously into other important domains to explore features of psychological individuality that go well beyond traits. In the tradition of Murray (1938), motivational approaches to personality have flourished in the past few decades. Drawing from theoretical sources as diverse as evolutionary theory, lifespan developmental psychology, self-determination theory, Maslow's (1968) theory of needs, McClelland's (1961) theory of social motives, and many other sources, personality psychologists have examined the manifestations, dynamics, and development of people's life goals and strivings, generally conceiving of this domain as separate from but complementary to the domain of dispositional personality traits (e.g., Freund & Riediger, 2006; Hofer & Bush, 2011; Kenrick, Griskevicius, Neuberg, & Schaller, 2011; Sheldon & Schuler, 2011). Researchers have also redoubled their efforts to understand the role of ideological beliefs and values in personality (Graham, Haidt, & Nosek, 2009; Schwartz, 2009).

Over the past two decades, narrative perspectives on human lives have gained increasing favor among personality psychologists (McAdams & Manczak, 2015). In terms of methodology, researchers have demonstrated growing interest in assessing features of human personality as they are revealed in autobiographical memories and other storied accounts of human experience (Baddeley & Singer, 2007). With respect to theory, McAdams (1996) and others (e.g., McLean, Pasupathi, & Pals, 2007) have formulated new conceptions of personality that feature the role of life stories in the construction of the self. A central concept in this literature is *narrative identity,* which refers to a person's internalized story of his or her reconstructed past and imagined future, the narrative of how "I came to be the person I am becoming" (McAdams & McLean, 2013). Variations in structural and content features of life narratives constitute important individual differences in personality itself, separate from dispositional traits and predictive of important life outcomes above and beyond traits (Adler, Lodi-Smith, Philippe, & Houle, 2016).

In the Meantime . . .

During the decades of crisis and revival in personality psychology, researchers in *developmental* psychology were articulating new theoretical frameworks and empirical agendas for the study of meaningful and orderly psychological change over time. Just a year after Mischel (1968) threw the field of personality psychology into turmoil, Bowlby (1969) published one of the game-changing psychological books of the 20th century: *Attachment and Loss, Volume 1.* Almost half a century later, attachment theory continues to stimulate exciting research in developmental psychology, much of which would seem to have direct bearing on the issue of personality development. Surprisingly few explicit connections have been made, however, between personality psychology and the traditions of research that have grown up around attachment theory—often grouped by developmentalists under the rubric of *socioemotional development.*

Going back to Thomas, Chess, and Birch (1970), developmental scientists have examined the early-emerging trends in behavior, emotion, and attention that fall under the category of infant *temperament.* Important advances in this research domain were made throughout the 1980s and 1990s, but it is only within the last decade or so that researchers have systematically considered the relationship between early temperament and adult personality traits (Rothbart, 2007; Shiner & DeYoung, 2013). Many other important trends in developmental psychology have, until quite recently, barely registered a signal in the mainstream literature on personality psychology. These include the study of childhood agency and the development of competence (Walls & Kollat, 2006), emotion regulation in the family (Thompson & Meyer, 2007), moral development (Narvaez & Lapsley, 2009), the dynamics of emerging adulthood (Arnett, 2000), parenting and caregiving through midlife (Lachman, 2001), and the architecture of development in old age (Baltes, 1997). Moreover, personality psychologists are just beginning to take seriously the lessons of the *life-course* developmental tradition (Elder, 1995), with its emphasis on linked lives, social convoys, social class, and the exigencies of the historical moment within which a developing human life is situated.

Links between the study of personality and the study of human development should have been made decades ago, I would argue. But for their part, personality psychologists were unable to make them. They were unable to make them because for many years the concept of personality itself was not secure enough to warrant expansion into the developmental domain. During the dark days of the person–situation debate, situationists constructed an image of human life that privileged the influences of short-term effects and constantly changing environments. Therefore, it was incumbent on personality psychologists to show that dispositional traits were stable enough and efficacious enough to resist the forces of instability, change, and flux. Sure, contexts change by the moment, but personality perseveres, to some extent at least. Yet the study of human development is fundamentally about *change*—change over the long haul, rather than from one situation to the next, but change nevertheless. Personality psychologists were unable to embrace fully this kind of change—the kind of change that goes under the title of *personality development*—until they had achieved a suitable level of confidence in the solidity and stability of their own pet constructs and, by extension, the legitimacy of the very idea of human personality.

After an extended adolescence, personality psychology has finally emerged as a confident and mature discipline, well positioned to pursue generative collaborations with many different fields in psychology and the behavioral sciences. At this moment in history, then, one of the brightest prospects on the horizon is the pursuit of a rich scientific understanding of personality development over the human life course.

Personality Development: A Conceptual Itinerary

If every human being on the planet were exactly the same, psychological science could still examine fundamental laws of human sensation, perception, emotion, cognition, and social relations. But there would be no field of personality psychology, for personality is fundamentally about *difference*. Going back to Allport (1937) and Murray (1938), personality psychologists have typically focused less on human nature per se and rather more on *variations* on the broad theme of human nature—how one person is demonstrably and consequentially different from another. Thus, the fact that human beings evolved to live in social groups is a feature of human nature; the fact that some human beings are more sociable than others, by contrast, is a feature of personality. Personality is about the psychological differences that make the biggest difference for adaptation to social life. Personality *development*, then, is about the temporal course of emergence, growth, change, and continuity as it pertains to these consequential psychological differences.

In what follows, I briefly sketch a conceptual itinerary for the development of personality over the human life course. An itinerary is like a schedule or guidebook; it labels the main topics that will be addressed, and it organizes them into a meaningful sequence. Synthesizing traditional and emerging trends in personality psychology and the study of human development, the itinerary I propose identifies three *lines* of personality development in human beings, each following a sequence from infancy or childhood through late life (McAdams, 2015a, 2015b; McAdams & Olson, 2010).

Describing the sense in which a person develops as a *social actor,* the first traces the line of development running from the emergence of temperament differences in infancy to the maturation of dispositional personality traits in the adult years. Depicting a related but different sense whereby a person becomes a *motivated agent* over time, the second line runs from the childhood apprehension of intentionality through the establishment of life goals and values. Finally, a third line—tracking the development of the person as an *autobiographical author*—runs from the emergence of autobiographical memory to the construction of a self-defining life story in the adult years.

Each of the three lines, then, tracks the development of characteristic differences among human beings—differences in traits, goals (and values), and narratives, respectively (McAdams & Pals, 2006). Moreover, there is a sense in which the features of the developing social actor emerge first in developmental time, apparent even in temperament dimensions of infancy, whereas features of motivated agency become psychologically apparent later on, and features of autobiographical authorship after that. In other words, the rough contours of traits may emerge first, followed next by goals and values, and finally by the stories people create to make sense of their lives. As suggested in Figure 1.1, the author's developing stories layer over the agent's developing goals and values, which in turn layer over the actor's developing traits. Personality thickens over time.

Becoming a Social Actor: From Temperament to Traits

The primal arena wherein consequential psychological differences between human beings are expressed and observed is *the group.* Human beings evolved to live in complex social

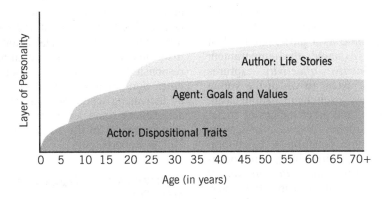

FIGURE 1.1. Three layers of personality development.

groups, striving to get along and to get ahead so as to garner the resources that are needed for survival and reproduction. Within the group, each individual is like an actor on the theatrical stage, performing roles in ways that reflect both situational demands and dispositional tendencies. In all human groups, social actors observe each other and observe themselves. Over time, observations coalesce into social reputations (Hogan, 1982): Actor *A* comes to be seen (by others and by the self) as an especially cooperative person on whom group members can count; Actor *B* exudes energy and confidence; Actor *C* avoids the limelight; and Actor *D* is perceived to be unreliable and even malicious, and comes to occupy a marginalized status in the group.

Personality begins, then, with the different reputational signatures that social actors achieve as they jockey for status and acceptance in the group. Reputational signatures are the shorthand mental representations that observers formulate in their minds regarding the dispositional traits of the social actors they observe, including even their own. While people's dispositional traits arise from genetic and experiential factors that reside within the actor, there is still a basic human sense in which the traits live in the group, and are dependent on the group's imprimatur for their very psychological existence. If a tree falls in the forest and nobody hears it, we still must concede that the tree fell. But personality traits, like extraversion and conscientiousness, have no meaning outside a social context. Not only do other actors need to be present on stage to take part in the performances wherein these traits are expressed, but others need to observe the performance if the traits are to become known to the group, and thereby captured in social reputations. Ultimately, reputational advantages lead to greater acceptance and status in the group, which promote survival and reproductive success. There are few things more important in life than developing personality traits that promote the kind of social reputations that maximize the chances for success in human groups.

Young children first recognize themselves in mirrors and other reflecting objects around age 2 years (Povinelli, 2001). What they literally see is an actor who moves through physical and social space. However, infants are viewed to be social actors by others long before they recognize themselves as such—from the first few weeks of life onward. Like audience members in the front row of the theater, parents and other observers watch the baby's every move, ready to assign initial reputational signatures based on the infant's characteristic emotional and behavioral displays. *Here we have a fussy baby. There we have a smiley baby. Here is one who seems to be afraid of people.* Formalized in observational protocols and rating scales, developmental psychologists call these differences *temperament*.

Temperament refers mainly to broad individual differences in behavioral and emotional style, and in emotion regulation, manifest early on in human development. Assumed by some researchers to be inborn or (at minimum) strongly driven by constitutional factors, and assumed by others to be a product of interactions between genes and early experience even at this early age, temperament establishes an early style of attending, feeling, and behaving, through which observers come to recognize the young child as a particular kind of social actor. For example, the temperament dimension of *positive affectivity* captures differences in the extent to which the young child exhibits joy, excitement, enthusiasm, positive approach, and other indices of social and emotional surgency. *Negative affectivity* tracks differences in fearfulness, behavioral inhibition, avoidance, irritability, and negative response to frustration. *Effortful control* refers to the child's voluntary capacity to override momentary impulse in order to attend to the environment in a sustained manner and to enact a more deliberate and reasoned response to situational demands (Rothbart, 2007; Shiner & DeYoung, 2013).

Personality and developmental psychologists have recently found common cause in the realization that early temperament provides some of the socioemotional material out of which the full-fledged dispositional traits comprising the Big Five framework are formed. Indeed, Shiner (2015) has concluded that temperament and personality traits should "be seen as the same basic set of traits, one manifested early in the life and thus somewhat more limited in scope (temperament) and one manifested a little later in life and broader in scope" (p. 87). A growing number of longitudinal studies document significant continuities between childhood temperament dimensions and dispositional features of personality that social actors display later in life (e.g., Moffitt et al., 2011).

Still, the road from early temperament to the dispositional traits of adulthood is not smooth and perfectly predictable (e.g., Hampson & Goldberg, 2006). Even though temperament differences may predispose a person to exhibit a particular style of socioemotional performance, a wide range of external factors—from accidents to family dynamics to the macro effects of culture and history—will invariably shape the actor's development (Bleidorn, Kandler, & Caspi, 2014). For example, research shows that the influence of social roles becomes increasingly important in the development of personality traits as social actors move into and through adulthood (Specht et al., 2014). Studies have shown that taking on normative roles in family life, work, and community appears in some cases to promote (and partially mediate) the well-documented developmental trend toward increasing conscientiousness and agreeableness

and declining neuroticism across the adult life course. Becoming a parent or a paid employee may require that the social actor demonstrate instrumental competence, commitment, social responsibility, self-control, cooperation, and other signs of psychosocial maturity, indexed by increasing scores on conscientiousness and agreeableness and decreasing scores on the trait of neuroticism in the adult years (Donnellan, Hill, & Roberts, 2015).

Becoming a Motivated Agent: From Intentionality to Life Goals

Going back to Murray (1938), many personality psychologists have made a sharp distinction between personality traits and motives. If traits pertain to the *means* people employ in thought, feeling, and behavior, motives typically refer to the *ends*—the valued goals and strivings people pursue (Winter, John, Stewart, Klohnen, & Duncan, 1998). According to some theorists, basic motives and goals derive from fundamental human needs (Sheldon & Schuler, 2011). *Motivation,* then, refers to what people want in life, what they desire, what they hope and plan to attain, as well as what they do not want and thereby seek to avoid. While some personality psychologists argue that traits themselves hold motivational power (Allport, 1961) and that traits imply certain social (and nonsocial) goals (DeYoung, 2015), there exists in personality psychology a vast array of constructs that are fundamentally not about *how* social actors perform their roles (traits) but instead address specifically *what* valued goals human beings aim to achieve in life. As such, constructs related to human goals, strivings, and values explicitly conceive of the human being as a motivated agent—a forward-looking decision maker who articulates plans in order to achieve valued ends (Martin, Sugarman, & Thompson, 2003; Mischel, 1973).

How do a person's characteristic motives, goals, strivings, and values come to be? Some clues may reside in studies of how young children apprehend and come to understand the issue of human intentionality. By age 1 year, children show a marked interest in intentional, goal-directed action (Woodward, 2009). They turn their attention toward, and sometimes seek to imitate, goal-directed behaviors of others, more so than random behaviors. They even adjust their own activities and reactions to take into consideration what they perceive to be another agent's intentionality. But it is not until the third or fourth year of life that most children develop an explicit understanding of their own and others' motivated agency. With the consolidation of what developmental psychologists call *theory of mind,* prekindergarten children come to understand that human agents have *desires* and *beliefs* in their minds, and that they *act upon* these desires and beliefs in a goal-directed manner (Apperly, 2012). This developmental landmark paves the way for the explicit articulation of personal goals and plans in the minds of young agents. The effects of parents, schooling, and other socializing factors strongly shape the nature of children's developing motivational agendas.

Variation in the kinds of motivational agendas children develop in their daily lives—the characteristic suites of short-term and long-term goals and plans that children articulate in their minds, and the strategies they develop to achieve their goals—marks the emergence of a second layer of personality development. The child's motivational agenda eventually layers over his or her dispositional traits. The personality of a 10-year-old, therefore, is *thicker* than the personality of a 3-year-old. The younger child is mainly a social actor whose temperament traits comprise the main stuff of personality. The older child is both a social actor and a motivated agent, revealing two different layers or lines of personality development. To comprehend how the 10-year-old is psychosocially similar to and different from other 10-year-olds, the psychologist must consider constructs that are drawn from both the trait and the motivational domains. Three-year-old Sally is endowed with high levels of positive affectivity and shows moderate levels of effortful control. Ten-year-old Maria is also endowed with high levels of positive affectivity (we are starting to call it extraversion at this point) and shows moderate levels of conscientiousness and agreeableness. But Maria also *wants* to be the best math student in her class, *hopes* that her divorcing parents will reconcile, *plans* to quit attending her mother's church as soon as she is confirmed, *fears* she will never be popular with the other Latina girls because her skin is darker, and *values* domestic harmony in her life ("Why do my parents have to fight so much?!") more than nearly anything else. More so than Sally, furthermore, Maria is a *moral* agent (Gray, Young, & Waytz, 2012). She has an explicit understanding of what is right and wrong, she has a developing moral

ideology or value system, and other people hold her accountable for her moral choices.

How do people's motivational agendas develop over the course of life? Research from lifespan developmental psychology documents important shifts in the kinds of goals people set forth and their modes of goal engagement. In young adulthood, promotion goals (approaching rewards) may prevail over prevention goals (avoiding punishments) as motivated agents vigorously pursue competence (achievement) and relatedness (affiliation) agendas that prioritize education, job training, friendship, love, and marriage (Freund & Riediger, 2006). Goals in early adulthood often focus on expanding the self and gaining new information. Young adults are often comfortable with motivational agendas that contain variegated and even conflicting aims. They frequently employ primary control strategies (Heckhausen, 2011), actively striving to change their environments to fit their goal pursuits.

By midlife, however, motivated agents seek to manage their goals so as to minimize conflict. What Baltes (1997) described as the processes of selection, optimization, and compensation come into major play in the management of goal agendas. Midlife adults pursue a wide range of goals, from running a household to passing on cultural traditions. Goals aimed at making positive contributions to the next generation become more pronounced (McAdams, de St. Aubin, & Logan, 1993). In later adulthood, prevention focused goals may come to predominate. With increasing age, adults rely more and more on secondary control strategies in goal pursuit, which involve adjusting expectations and changing the self in order to adapt to mounting constraints. There is also some evidence to suggest that older adults may invest more heavily in intrinsically valued ends, while pulling back from goals that promote future rewards, fame, money, and the like (Morgan & Robinson, 2013).

Throughout the life course, individual differences in goal pursuit are contoured by gender, race, social class, and other demographic variables (Elder, 1995). Goals and values may also relate in interesting ways to individual differences in dispositional personality traits (Roberts & Robins, 2000). As such, lines of personality development may run together at times. It is one integrated person, after all, even if that one person operates both as a social actor and a motivated agent.

Becoming an Autobiographical Author: From Episodic Memory to Narrative Identity

The past two decades have witnessed an upsurge of interest among social and behavioral scientists in the role of *narrative* in human behavior and development. Within personality and developmental psychology, research and theory have identified a third line of personality development, running from the emergence of episodic autobiographical memory in early childhood to the development of a full life story in adulthood (Fivush & Haden, 2003; McAdams & McLean, 2013). Early on, children encode, store, and retrieve memories of particular episodes in their lives. Encouraged by parents at first and later by peers, children tell stories about these events to others. By the time they are 5 or 6 years of age, children implicitly understand that such stories conform to a narrative grammar (Mandler, 1984). Story plots begin in a particular time and place, and involve characters (agents) who act on their desires and beliefs over time. Children expect stories to evoke suspense and curiosity, and sometimes humor, and they dismiss as "boring" a narrative account that fails to live up to these emotional standards.

It is one thing to tell personal stories about discrete episodes in life—a day at the zoo, a visit to Grandma's house, a mishap on the playground. It is quite another to fashion a narrative for one's life in full. Narrative identity is the story that a person composes about how he or she came to be the person he or she is becoming—a selective reconstruction of the past integrated with the imagined future, providing a life in full, with some sense of meaning, purpose, and temporal continuity (McAdams, 1996; McAdams & McLean, 2013). In adolescence and the emerging adult years, people typically take on the psychological perspective of an autobiographical author, endeavoring to tell and internalize an evolving story for their lives in full. The stories they create and continue to work on throughout the adult years ultimately become an integral part of personality itself. Personality, therefore, thickens again in adolescence and emerging adulthood as the autobiographical author's narrative identity layers over the goals and values of the motivated agent, which layer over the social actor's dispositional traits. In a temporal sense, personality also broadens: Dispositional traits speak mainly to the performative present; goals and values project the agent from the present into the future; and life stories

ideally integrate the reconstructed past, experienced present, and imagined future into a coherent narrative identity.

Building on memory and storytelling skills developed in childhood, the cognitive aptitudes and personal experiences required for the development of a full narrative identity begin to come online in adolescence. A key factor is the emergence of *autobiographical reasoning,* which refers to a wide set of interpretive operations through which people derive personal meanings from their own autobiographical memories (Habermas & Bluck, 2000). Through autobiographical reasoning, people may derive an organizing theme to summarize an important feature of their life experience, or string together multiple events from the past in order to explain the development of a particular self characteristic, or derive lessons and insights from negative scenes in life, searching for redemptive meanings in suffering (McAdams, 2013; McLean & Pratt, 2006). From the early teens through the 20s, furthermore, autobiographical authors develop a more detailed understanding of the typical or expected events and transitions that mark the human life course as it plays out in their own culture—when, for example, a person leaves home, how schooling and work are sequenced, the expected progressions of marriage and family formation, how careers develop, what people do when they retire, and so on (Thomsen & Berntsen, 2008). These expectations provide an overall developmental/cultural script for the life story, within which—or sometimes against which—the author may construct his or her own personalized narrative identity.

Authoring a self-defining life narrative is a process embedded in the social ecology of everyday life (McLean et al., 2007). Narrative identity emerges gradually through daily conversations and social interactions, through introspection, through decisions young people make regarding work and love, and through normative and serendipitous passages in life, such as when a student meets with a vocational counselor to discuss "What do I want to do with my life?" or a young couple sits down to write wedding vows. The story continues to develop across the lifespan, incorporating expected developmental milestones and the many unexpected turns that a life may take.

Life stories are profoundly shaped by history and culture. Culture provides a menu of plots, images, characters, and themes for living a human life, and autobiographical authors appropriate those features from the menu that seem best to convey their own lived experience (McAdams, 2013). Culture, moreover, may exert more hegemonic and marginalizing effects on the construction of narrative identity as authors run up against the constraints to self-definition that societal institutions and cultural meaning systems apply to particular demographic groups—to women as opposed to men, for example, to ethnic minorities, or to those who deviate in some way from the favored narratives for living a good life (Hammack, 2008). As such, a life story sometimes says as much about the culture within which a person's life is embedded as it does about the person's life itself.

A growing body of research examines age differences in life narration (e.g., Baddeley & Singer, 2007; McAdams & Olson, 2010; Pasupathi & Mansour, 2006). Overall, middle-aged adults tend to construct life stories that show more sophisticated forms of autobiographical reasoning compared to younger adults. Their stories may be more complex, more coherent, and more psychologically nuanced. Life stories also seem to warm up as people age. Older narrators give more emphasis to positive events and tend to downplay the conflicts and struggles they have experienced, at least through late midlife. As autobiographical authors grow older, their life stories show a warmer glow, even as the vivid details of what they have experienced in their lives begin to fade.

Three Lines of Personality Development in a Single Human Life

Ever since Allport (1937) set forth the distinction between nomothetic and idiographic approaches to research, personality psychologists have struggled to reconcile investigations of individual differences with the intensive examination of the single case (Barenbaum & Winter, 2008). Although the respective demands of nomothetic and idiographic approaches seem to compete with each other (Holt, 1962), the two derive from a common wellspring: the need to understand *variation* among persons. Nomothetic research examines variation on personality dimensions—dispositional traits, goals and values, and life stories, for example—across many different persons. Idiographic case studies take the idea of variation to the extreme, treating an individual human life as a unique

variant on the general design of human nature. The intensive study of the individual case can serve many functions (McAdams & West, 1997). In the scientific context of *discovery,* for example, case studies can generate new ideas and insights that subsequently may be examined in more systematic ways through hypothesis-testing, nomothetic research. Cases may also serve the purpose of *exemplification*—illustrating how principles and ideas examined in nomothetic studies manifest themselves in the individual human life, or how they don't.

In this last section of the chapter, my brief commentary on the life and personality of Barack Obama, 44th President of the United States, serves the purpose of exemplification. The idiographic examination of the individual life illustrates the utility of conceiving of personality development from the three standpoints of the social actor, motivated agent, and autobiographical author. How, then, might the three lines of personality development play out in Obama's life?

The Actor's Developing Traits

Psychological portraits of notable lives often begin with broad trait attributions regarding a person's unique style of socioemotional performance. Among U.S. presidents, for example, historians routinely remark upon Abraham's Lincoln's "melancholy," John F. Kennedy's "charm" and "wit," Richard M. Nixon's "insecurity," and Ronald Reagan's "sunny optimism." While each of these men exhibited a complex psychological makeup, simple trait attributions are often the first things that come to mind in characterizing the broad contours of their social reputations.

Reading through representative sources in the historical record, teams of psychologists and historians have rated all of the U.S. chief executives on the Big Five personality traits (Rubenzer & Faschingbauer, 2004; Simonton, 2006). The scores turn out to exhibit strong interrater reliability, suggesting substantial consensus among independent observers. The rank-order list for the broad trait of extraversion runs from Theodore Roosevelt at the top (followed closely by Bill Clinton and George W. Bush) to Calvin Coolidge at the bottom. (In the 1920s, it was reported that a woman seated at a dinner party next to the introverted President Coolidge said to him, "Mr. Coolidge, I've made a bet against a fellow who said it was impossible to get more than two words out of you." His famous reply: "You lose.")

In a psychological biography I wrote on President George W. Bush, I argued that his high ratings on extraversion and his very low standing on the trait of openness to experience were consistent with his general decision-making style, as somebody willing to take big risks for positive emotion payoffs while remaining steadfast in the belief that the decisions he did make were categorically right and justified (McAdams, 2011). In the case of Barack Obama, by contrast, ratings on extraversion would surely be much lower than those for Bush, and ratings on openness to experience much higher. The one Big Five trait that stands out the clearest for Obama, however, may be neuroticism. Known for his legendary "cool," even as a teenager, Barack Obama appears to exhibit an emotional and behavioral style suggestive of unusually *low* levels of neuroticism (N), when compared to other U.S. presidents, and probably when compared as well to today's American adult population. As evidenced in biographical sources (e.g., Remnick, 2011) and his own autobiographical writings (Obama, 1995), Obama has been consistently described as especially calm, emotionally tranquil, even-keeled, deliberate, and dispassionate. His friends and supporters view these characteristics as indications of emotional stability, which they are. But his detractors may also have a point when they suggest that his dispositional style of social and emotional performance can seem overly detached and even bloodless.

Tracking the development of any dispositional trait over the life course entails (1) weighing evidence for the trait attribution in the first place (Is Obama really low on N?), (2) searching for temperament precursors early in life (Where did his low N come from?), and (3) tracing the idiographic path whereby the early form or manifestation gradually morphed into the recognizable disposition of the adult social actor (How did his low N develop over time? What were the experiences, environments, and social roles that ultimately contributed to the development of his low N?). A full analysis of Barack Obama's personality from the standpoint of a social actor would therefore call upon family members' and teachers' descriptions of the young Barry Obama as an especially even-tempered child, rarely subject to strong emotions of anxiety, sadness, or shame. It would examine his mother's, stepfather's, and grandparents' ef-forts to regulate and socialize the young boy's temperament. It might also pay special attention to Obama's own strategies of emotion regulation, especially during periods of emotional turmoil surrounding his conflicted relationship with his absent father and his struggles to reconcile his mixed racial heritage.

The Agent's Goals and Values

As do many children, Barry Obama began to develop explicit goals for his life in the elementary school years. In an essay he wrote in the third grade, he announced that he planned to be President of the United States one day. But most of his goals were rather more humble and mundane. For example, when he switched schools at age 10, he worried about fitting into the new environment, and he developed plans to make new friends. Throughout middle childhood and into his adolescence, the young boy experienced strong desires regarding the biological father who had abandoned him and his mother shortly after Barry was born. He peppered his mother with questions about the man, whom he came to imagine as a great scholar and statesman. When Barack Obama, Sr. did indeed return to Hawaii, ever so briefly, to meet his son for the first and only time, Barry reacted with profound disappointment and confusion. His father did not seem to be the great man that he had imagined. Yet he held on to the goal to learn more about his father—a goal he eventually achieved as a young adult when he visited his (now deceased) father's homeland. Barry Obama's motivational agenda changed substantially as he moved through high school. The issue of his mixed-race heritage became especially fraught. "Am I black or am I white?" he asked. Finding an answer became a salient personal goal:

> I learned to slip back and forth between my black and white worlds, understanding that each possessed its own language and customs and structures of meaning, convinced that with a bit of translation on my part the two worlds would eventually cohere. Still, the feeling that something wasn't quite right stayed with me, a warning that sounded whenever a white girl mentioned in the middle of a conversation how much she liked Stevie Wonder; or when a woman in the supermarket asked me if I played basketball; or when the school principal told me that I was cool. I did like Stevie Wonder, I did love basketball, and I tried my best to be cool at all times. So why did such comments set me on edge? (Obama, 1995, p. 82)

Obama's goal to integrate the two sides of his racial nature dovetailed with his developing personal ideology. A young man who lived in two different worlds and who experienced the stark contrasts of a mixed heritage came to prioritize the values of tolerance, diversity, and personal exploration. Adopting a thoroughly humanistic ideological perspective (Tomkins, 1987), Obama came to believe that human beings should continue to grow and learn and to strive to actualize their potential. And he came to believe that he himself possessed tremendous potential, and that he was destined to achieve great things.

The Author's Story

When he enrolled in Occidental College, Obama took classes in politics, history, and literature mainly, and he made friends with the more politically active black students on campus. He wore leather jackets, drank beer, and smoked marijuana. He began to use the name "Barack" to signify a stronger identification with his mythic father and a newfound sense of worldliness and sophistication. After 2 years, he transferred to Columbia University, embarking on an especially intense period of social isolation, introspection, and identity search. In an interview with Remnick (2011), a middle-aged Obama looks back on this critical period in his life:

> [At Columbia] a whole bunch of stuff that had been inside of me—questions of identity, questions of purpose, questions of, not just race, but also the international nature of my upbringing—all those things [were] converging in some way. And so there's this period of time when I move to New York and go to Columbia where I pull in and wrestle with that stuff, and do a lot of writing and a lot of reading and a lot of thinking and a lot of walking through Central Park. And somehow I emerge on the other side to that ready and eager to take a chance in what was a pretty unlikely venture: moving to Chicago and becoming an organizer. So I would say that's a moment in which I gain a seriousness of purpose that I had lacked before. Now, whether it is just a matter of, you know, me hitting a certain age when people start getting a little more serious—whether it was some combination of factors—my father dying, me realizing I had never known him, me moving from Hawaii to a place like New York that stimulates a lot of new ideas—you know, it's hard to say what exactly prompted that. (in Remnick, 2011, p. 114)

At age 24, Obama moved to Chicago to take a position as a community organizer. After 3 years in Chicago, he enrolled in law school, at Harvard. Upon completion of his legal studies, he returned to Chicago, where he worked briefly as a lawyer, taught classes at University of Chicago law school, met and married Michelle Robinson, and launched a political career. In *Dreams from My Father,* Obama (1995) tells the story of his personal development from his early years in Hawaii to the consolidation of his vocation in his early 30s. The book explores his developing understanding of his father, his choice of black over white in developing a racial identity (solidified in his marriage to an African American woman from the South Side of Chicago), and his ultimate embrace of community organizing as an arena for actualizing his values and as a launching pad for a political career. The book is essentially a *testament of narrative identity*—one man's story (written down and published to wide acclaim) of how he came to be the person he is becoming.

As conveyed in *Dreams,* Obama's (1995) story is a narrative of ascent and redemption (McAdams, 2013; Remnick, 2011). On a personal level, the story tracks the protagonist's development from relatively humble beginnings, and through a protracted period of confusion and identity search, to the realization of a generative vocation in life. A growing body of nomothetic research on narrative identity shows that redemptive stories like these tend to be associated with high levels of psychological well-being and generativity, especially among midlife American adults (McAdams, 2013; McAdams & Guo, 2015).

In Obama's case, furthermore, the narrative appropriates a strong line of African American storytelling, both personal and cultural, that chronicles the liberation of the oppressed and the hope for a more just society. The story's theme is captured in the hallowed words of Martin Luther King, Jr.: The arc of history is long, but it bends toward justice. Although Obama never experienced the horrors of slavery and the indignities of Jim Crow racism, he identified strongly with those who have and with those heroes who dedicated their lives to liberation. In the narrative identity he constructed for his own life, Obama plays the Old Testament role of Joshua to Martin Luther King, Jr.'s Moses. King famously proclaimed, "I might not see the Promised Land," referencing the biblical story of Moses, who led the Israelites for decades but died before they reached the Promised Land. Joshua was his successor.

But Obama's story suggests that he might indeed see it, as Joshua did, or at least move things forward such that a full sighting might be not too far in the future. Given the ambiguities of history, we may never know whether Obama's presidency helped moved the country forward in the way he imagined. But it is nonetheless rather remarkable that Barack Obama authored this audacious and quintessentially redemptive life story when he was in his mid-30s, long before anybody (except Obama himself) imagined he might become President of the United States.

Conclusion

The emergence of personality may be construed in both historical and developmental terms. With respect to history, how did the field of personality psychology come to be? On the topic of development, how does personality itself emerge and develop across the human life course?

As the scientific study of psychological individuality, the field of personality psychology has experienced a difficult and conflicted history, reaching something of a nadir in the 1970s. During that decade, many psychologists came to question the scientific credibility of the very concept of personality, focusing their critique mainly on the legitimacy of dispositional personality traits. The protracted crisis in the field delayed for decades any serious consideration of how personality itself develops. Until relatively recently, therefore, the fields of personality psychology and developmental psychology traveled on separate tracks. With the reemergence of a revitalized and robust science of personality psychology over the past couple of decades, the time is now right for a systematic examination of personality development.

How, then, should personality development be conceived? I offer a conceptual itinerary for approaching the topic of personality development. My central thesis is that personality develops along three separate but related lines: (1) from infant temperament to the articulation of adult personality traits (personality from the standpoint of the social actor), (2) from childhood intentionality to the development of life goals and values (personality from the standpoint of the motivated agent), and (3) from the emergence of episodic memory in childhood to

the construction of narrative identity (personality from the standpoint of the autobiographical author). Over the course of human development, people's life stories layer over their characteristic goals and values, which in turn layer over their developing dispositional traits. The tripartite framework helps to organize and make sense of the many different programs of research and theory that prevail today in the burgeoning field of personality development, much of which is featured in the chapters to follow. And it provides a powerful heuristic, I believe, for tracing lines of personality development in the individual human life, as briefly illustrated in the case of Barack Obama.

REFERENCES

Adler, J. M., Lodi-Smith, J., Philippe, F. L., & Houle, I. (2016). The incremental validity of narrative identity in predicting well-being: A review of the field and recommendations for the future. *Personality and Social Psychology Review, 20,* 142–175.

Adorno, T. W., Frenkel-Brunswik, E., Levinson, D. G., & Sanford, R. N. (1950). *The authoritarian personality.* New York: Harper & Brothers.

Allport, G. W. (1937). *Personality: A psychological interpretation.* New York: Holt, Reinhart & Winston.

Allport, G. W. (1961). *Pattern and growth in personality.* New York: Holt, Reinhart & Winston.

Apperly, I. A. (2012). What is "theory of mind"?: Concepts, cognitive processes, and individual differences. *Quarterly Journal of Experimental Psychology, 65,* 825–839.

Arnett, J. J. (2000). Emerging adulthood: A theory of development from the late teens through the twenties. *American Psychologist, 55,* 469–480.

Asch, S. E. (1955). Opinions and social pressure. *Scientific American, 19,* 31–35.

Ashton, M. C., Lee, K., Perguini, M., Szarota, P., de Vries, R. E., DiBlas, L., et al. (2004). A six-factor structure of personality descriptor adjectives: Solutions from psycholexical studies in seven languages. *Journal of Personality and Social Psychology, 86,* 356–366.

Baddeley, J., & Singer, J. A. (2007). Charting the life story's path: Narrative identity across the life span. In J. Chandinin (Ed.), *Handbook of narrative research methods* (pp. 177–202). Thousand Oaks, CA: SAGE.

Baltes, P. B. (1997). On the incomplete architecture of human ontogeny: Selection, optimization, and compensation as foundation for developmental theory. *American Psychologist, 52,* 366–380.

Bandura, A. (1971). *Social learning theory.* Morristown, NJ: General Learning Press.

Barenbaum, N. B., & Winter, D. G. (2008). History of

modern personality theory and research. In O. P. John, R. W. Robins, & L. A. Pervin (Eds.), *Handbook of personality: Theory and research* (3rd ed., pp. 3–26). New York: Guilford Press.

Bleidorn, W., Kandler, C., & Caspi, A. (2014). The behavioural genetics of personality development in adulthood: Classic, contemporary, and future trends. *European Journal of Personality, 28,* 244–255.

Block, J. (1965). *The challenge of response sets: Unconfounding meaning, acquiescence, and social desirability in the MMPI.* New York: Appleton-Century-Crofts.

Bowlby, J. (1969). *Attachment and loss: Vol. 1. Attachment.* New York: Basic Books.

Campbell, D. T., & Fiske, D. W. (1959). Convergent and discriminant validity by the multitrait–multimethod matrix. *Psychological Bulletin, 56,* 81–105.

Cantor, N. (1990). From thought to behavior: "Having" and "doing" in the study of personality and cognition. *American Psychologist, 45,* 735–750.

Carlson, R. (1971). Where is the person in personality research? *Psychological Bulletin, 75,* 203–219.

Cattell, R. B. (1943). The description of personality: Basic traits resolved into clusters. *Journal of Abnormal and Social Psychology, 38,* 476–506.

Cronbach, L. J., & Meehl, P. E. (1955). Construct validity in personality tests. *Psychological Bulletin, 52,* 281–302.

Crowne, D. P., & Marlow, D. (1960). A new scale of social desirability independent of psychopathology. *Journal of Consulting Psychology, 24,* 349–354.

Deci, E. L., & Ryan, R. M. (1991). A motivational approach to self: Integration in personality. In R. Dienstbier & R. M. Ryan (Eds.), *Nebraska Symposium on Motivation* (Vol. 38, pp. 237–288). Lincoln: University of Nebraska Press.

DeYoung, C. G. (2015). Cybernetic Big Five theory. *Journal of Research in Personality, 56,* 33–58.

DeYoung, C. G., Hirsch, J. B., Shane, M. S., Papademetris, X., Rajeevan, N., & Gray, J. R. (2010). Testing predictions from personality neuroscience: Brain structure and the Big Five. *Psychological Science, 21,* 820–828.

Donnellan, M. B., Hill, P. L., & Roberts, B. W. (2015). Personality development across the life span: Current findings and future directions. In M. Mikulincer & P. Shaver (Eds.), *APA handbook of personality and social psychology: Vol. 4. Personality processes and individual differences* (pp. 107–126). Washington, DC: American Psychological Association Press.

Elder, G. H., Jr. (1995). The life course paradigm: Social change and individual development. In P. Moen, G. H. Elder, Jr., & K. Lusher (Eds.), *Examining lives in context: Perspectives on the ecology of human development* (pp. 101–139). Washington, DC: American Psychological Association Press.

Emmons, R. A. (1986). Personal strivings: An approach to personality and subjective well-being. *Journal of Personality and Social Psychology, 51,* 1058–1068.

Eysenck, H. J. (1952). *The scientific study of personality.* London: Routledge & Kegan Paul.

Fiske, D. W. (1974). The limits of the conventional science of personality. *Journal of Personality, 42,* 1–11.

Fivush, R., & Haden, C. (Eds.). (2003). *Autobiographical memory and the construction of a narrative self: Developmental and clinical perspectives.* Mahwah, NJ: Erlbaum.

Fleeson, W., & Gallagher, P. (2009). The implications of Big Five standing for the distribution of trait manifestations of behavior: Fifteen experience-sampling studies and a meta-analysis. *Journal of Personality and Social Psychology, 97,* 1097–1114.

Freund, A. M., & Riediger, M. (2006). Goals as building blocks of personality and development in adulthood. In D. K. Mroczek & T. D. Little (Eds.), *Handbook of personality development* (pp. 353–372). Mahwah, NJ: Erlbaum.

Goffman, E. (1961). *Asylums.* Garden City, NY: Doubleday.

Goldberg, L. R. (1993). The structure of phenotypic personality traits. *American Psychologist, 48,* 26–34.

Graham, J., Haidt, J., & Nosek, B. A. (2009). Liberals and conservatives rely on different sets of moral foundations. *Journal of Personality and Social Psychology, 96,* 1029–1046.

Gray, K., Young, L., & Waytz, A. (2012). Mind perception is the essence of morality. *Psychological Inquiry, 23,* 101–124.

Guilford, J. P. (1959). *Personality.* New York: McGraw-Hill.

Habermas, T., & Bluck, S. (2000). Getting a life: The emergence of the life story in adolescence. *Psychological Bulletin, 126,* 748–769.

Hall, C. S., & Lindzey, G. (1957). *Theories of personality.* New York: Wiley.

Hammack, P. L. (2008). Narrative and the cultural psychology of identity. *Personality and Social Psychology Review, 12,* 222–247.

Hampson, S. E., & Goldberg, L. R. (2006). A first large cohort study of personality trait stability over the 40 years between elementary school and midlife. *Journal of Personality and Social Psychology, 91,* 763–779.

Heckhausen, J. (2011). Agency and control striving across the life span. In K. L. Fingerman, C. A. Berg, J. Smith, & T. Antonucci (Eds.), *Handbook of life-span development* (pp. 183–212). New York: Springer.

Hofer, J., & Bush, H. (2011). When the needs for affiliation and intimacy are frustrated: Envy and indirect aggression among German and Cameroonian adults. *Journal of Research in Personality, 45,* 219–228.

Hogan, R. (1982). A socioanalytic theory of personality. In M. Paige (Ed.), *Nebraska Symposium on Motivation* (Vol. 29, pp. 58–89). Lincoln: University of Nebraska Press.

Hogan, R., DeSoto, C. B., & Solano, C. (1977). Traits, tests, and personality research. *American Psychologist, 32,* 255–264.

Holt, R. R. (1962). Individuality and generalization in the psychology of personality: An evaluation. *Journal of Personality, 30,* 377–402.

Jackson, D. N., & Paunonen, S. V. (1980). Personality structure and assessment. In M. R. Rosenzweig & L. W. Porter (Eds.), *Annual review of psychology* (Vol. 31, pp. 503–552) Palo Alto, CA: Annual Reviews.

Kenrick, D. T., & Funder, D. C. (1988). Profiting from controversy: Lessons from the person–situation debate. *American Psychologist, 43,* 23–34.

Kenrick, D. T., Griskevicius, V., Neuberg, S. L., & Schaller, M. (2011). Renovating the pyramid of needs: Contemporary extensions built upon ancient foundations. *Perspectives on Psychological Science, 5,* 292–314.

Lachman, M. (Ed.). (2001). *Handbook of midlife development.* New York: Wiley.

Loevinger, J. (1957). Objective tests as instruments of psychological theory. *Psychological Reports, 3,* 635–694.

Maddi, S. (1984). Personology for the 1980s. In R. A. Zucker, J. Aronoff, & A. I. Rabin (Eds.), *Personality and the prediction of behavior* (pp. 7–41). New York: Academic Press.

Mandler, J. M. (1984). *Stories, scripts, and scenes: Aspects of schema theory.* Hillsdale, NJ: Erlbaum.

Marcia, J. E. (1966). Development and validation of ego identity status. *Journal of Personality and Social Psychology, 3,* 551–558.

Martin, J., Sugarman, J., & Thompson, J. (2003). *Psychology and the question of agency.* Albany: State University of New York Press.

Maslow, A. H. (1968). *Toward a psychology of being* (2nd ed.). New York: Van Nostrand.

McAdams, D. P. (1996). Personality, modernity, and the storied self: A contemporary framework for studying persons. *Psychological Inquiry, 7,* 295–321.

McAdams, D. P. (1997). A conceptual history of personality psychology. In R. Hogan, J. Johnson, & S. Briggs (Eds.), *Handbook of personality psychology* (pp. 3–39). San Diego, CA: Academic Press.

McAdams, D. P. (2011). *George W. Bush and the redemptive dream: A psychological portrait.* New York: Oxford University Press.

McAdams, D. P. (2013). *The redemptive self: Stories Americans live by* (expanded and rev. ed.). New York: Oxford University Press.

McAdams, D. P. (2015a). *The art and science of personality development.* New York: Guilford Press.

McAdams, D. P. (2015b). Three lines of personality development: A conceptual itinerary. *European Psychologist, 20,* 252–264.

McAdams, D. P., de St. Aubin, E., & Logan, R. L. (1993). Generativity among young, midlife, and older adults. *Psychology and Aging, 8,* 212–230.

McAdams, D. P., & Guo, J. (2015). Narrating the generative life. *Psychological Science, 26,* 475–483.

McAdams, D. P., & Manczak, E. (2015). Personality and the life story. In M. Mikulincer & P. R. Shaver (Eds.), *APA handbook of personality and social psychology:* *Vol. 4. Personality processes and individual differences* (pp. 425–446). Washington, DC: American Psychological Association Press.

McAdams, D. P., & McLean, K. C. (2013). Narrative identity. *Current Directions in Psychological Science, 22,* 233–238.

McAdams, D. P., & Olson, B. D. (2010). Personality development: Continuity and change. In S. Fiske, D. Schacter, & R. Sternberg (Eds.), *Annual review of psychology* (Vol. 61, pp. 517–542). Palo Alto, CA: Annual Reviews.

McAdams, D. P., & Pals, J. L. (2006). A new Big Five: Fundamental principles for an integrative science of personality. *American Psychologist, 61,* 204–217.

McAdams, D. P., & West, S. G. (1997). Introduction: Personality psychology and the case study. *Journal of Personality, 65,* 757–783.

McClelland, D. C. (1961). *The achieving society.* New York: Van Nostrand.

McCrae, R. R., & Costa, P. T., Jr. (1987). Validation of the five-factor model of personality across instruments and observers. *Journal of Personality and Social Psychology, 52,* 81–90.

McLean, K. C., Pasupathi, M., & Pals, J. L. (2007). Selves creating stories creating selves: A process model of self-development. *Personality and Social Psychology Review, 11,* 262–278.

McLean, K. C., & Pratt, M. W. (2006). Life's little (and big) lessons: Identity statuses and meaning-making in the turning point narratives of emerging adults. *Developmental Psychology, 42,* 714–722.

Milgram, S. (1974). *Obedience to authority: An experimental view.* New York: Harper & Row.

Mischel, W. (1968). *Personality and assessment.* New York: Wiley.

Mischel, W. (1973). Toward a cognitive social learning reconceptualization of personality. *Psychological Review, 80,* 252–283.

Moffitt, T. E., Arseneault, L., Belsky, D., Dickson, N., Hancox, R. J., Harrington, H., et al. (2011). A gradient of childhood self-control predicts health, wealth, and public safety. *Proceedings of the National Academy of Sciences of the USA, 108,* 2693–2698.

Morgan, J., & Robinson, O. (2013). Intrinsic aspirations and personal meanings across adulthood: Conceptual interrelationships and age/sex differences. *Developmental Psychology, 49,* 999–1010.

Murray, H. A. (1938). *Explorations in personality.* New York: Oxford University Press.

Narvaez, D., & Lapsley, D. K. (Eds.). (2009). *Personality, identity, and character: Explorations in moral psychology.* New York: Cambridge University Press.

Obama, B. (1995). *Dreams from my father.* New York: Three Rivers Press.

Ozer, D. J., & Benet-Martinez, V. (2006). Personality and the prediction of consequential outcomes. In S. T. Fiske, A. E. Kazdin, & D. L. Schacter (Eds.), *Annual review of psychology* (Vol. 57, pp. 401–421). Palo Alto, CA: Annual Reviews.

Pasupathi, M., & Mansour, E. (2006). Adult age differences in autobiographical reasoning in narratives. *Developmental Psychology, 42,* 798–808.

Povinelli, D. (2001). The self: Elevated consciousness and extended in time. In C. Moore & K. Lemmon (Eds.), *The self in time: Developmental perspectives* (pp. 75–95). Mahwah, NJ: Erlbaum.

Remnick, D. (2011). *The bridge: The life and rise of Barack Obama.* New York: Vintage.

Roberts, B. W., & DelVecchio, W. (2000). The rank-order consistency of personality from childhood to old age: A quantitative review of longitudinal studies. *Psychological Bulletin, 126,* 3–25.

Roberts, B. W., Kuncel, N. R., Shiner, R. L., Caspi, A., & Goldberg, L. (2007). The power of personality: The comparative validity of personality traits, socioeconomic status, and cognitive ability for predicting important life outcomes. *Perspectives on Psychological Science, 2,* 313–342.

Roberts, B. W., & Robins, R. W. (2000). Broad dispositions, broad aspirations: The intersection of personality traits and major life goals. *Personality and Social Psychology Bulletin, 26,* 1284–1296.

Rorer, L. G., & Widiger, T. A. (1983). Personality structure and assessment. In M. R. Rosenzweig & L. W. Porter (Eds.), *Annual review of psychology* (Vol. 34, pp. 431–463). Palo Alto, CA: Annual Reviews.

Rosenhahn, D. L. (1973). On being sane in insane places. *Science, 179,* 250–258.

Rothbart, M. K. (2007). Temperament, development, and personality. *Current Directions in Psychological Science, 16,* 207–212.

Rubenzer, S. J., & Faschingbauer, T. R. (2004). *Personality, character, and leadership in the White House: Psychologists assess the presidents.* Washington, DC: Brassey's.

Schwartz, S. H. (2009). Basic values: How they motivate and inhibit prosocial behavior. In M. Mikulincer & P. R. Shaver (Eds.), *Proscial motives, emotions, and behavior* (pp. 221–241). Washington, DC: American Psychological Association Press.

Sechrest, L. (1976). Personality. In L. W. Porter & M. R. Rosenzweig (Eds.), *Annual review of psychology* (Vol. 27, pp. 1–27). Palo Alto, CA: Annual Reviews.

Sheldon, K. M. (2004). *Optimal human being: An integrated, multi-level perspective.* Mahwah, NJ: Erlbaum.

Sheldon, K. M., & Schuler, J. (2011). Wanting, having, and needing: Integrating motive disposition theory and self-determination theory. *Journal of Personality and Social Psychology, 101,* 1106–1123.

Shiner, R. L. (2015). The development of temperament and personality traits in childhood and adolescence. In M. Mikulincer & P. R. Shaver (Eds.), *APA handbook of personality and social psychology: Vol. 4. Personality processes and individual differences* (pp. 85–105). Washington, DC: American Psychological Association Press.

Shiner, R. L., & DeYoung, C. G. (2013). The structure of temperament and personality traits: A developmental perspective. In P. D. Zelazo (Ed.), *Handbook of developmental psychology* (pp. 113–141). New York: Oxford University Press.

Shweder, R. A. (1975). How relevant is an individual difference theory of personality? *Journal of Personality, 43,* 455–484.

Simonton, D. K. (2006). Presidential IQ, openness, intellectual brilliance, and leadership: Estimates and correlations for 42 U.S. chief executives. *Political Psychology, 27,* 511–526.

Specht, J., Bleidorn, W., Denissen, J. J. A., Hennecke, M., Hutteman, R., Kandler, C., et al. (2014). What drives adult personality development?: A comparison of theoretical perspectives and empirical evidence. *European Journal of Personality, 28,* 216–230.

Taylor, J. (1953). A personality scale of manifest anxiety. *Journal of Abnormal and Social Psychology, 48,* 285–290.

Tellegen, A., Lykken, D. J., Bouchard, T. J., Jr., Wilcox, K. J., Segal, N. L., & Rich, S. (1988). Personality similarity in twins raised apart and together. *Journal of Personality and Social Psychology, 54,* 1031–1039.

Thomas, A., Chess, S., & Birch, H. G. (1970). The origins of personality. *Scientific American, 223,* 102–109.

Thompson, R. A., & Meyer, S. (2007). Socialization of emotion regulation in the family. In J. J. Gross (Ed.), *Handbook of emotion regulation* (pp. 249–268). New York: Guilford Press.

Thomsen, D. K., & Berntsen, D. (2008). The cultural life script and life story chapters contribute to the reminiscence bump. *Memory, 16,* 420–435.

Tomkins, S. S. (1987). Script theory. In J. Aronoff, A. I. Rabin, & R. A. Zucker (Eds.), *The emergence of personality* (pp. 147–216). New York: Springer.

Walls, T. A., & Kollat, S. H. (2006). Agency to agentic personalities: The early to middle childhood gap. In D. K. Mroczek & T. D. Little (Eds.), *Handbook of personality development* (pp. 231–244). Mahwah, NJ: Erlbaum.

Winter, D. G. (1973). *The power motive.* New York: Free Press.

Winter, D. G., John, O. P., Stewart, A. J., Klohnen, E. C., & Duncan, L. E. (1998). Traits and motives: Toward an integration of two traditions in personality research. *Psychological Review, 105,* 230–250.

Woodward, A. L. (2009). Infants' grasp of others' intentions. *Current Directions in Psychological Science, 18,* 53–57.

Zuroff, D. C. (1986). Was Gordon Allport a trait theorist? *Journal of Personality and Social Psychology, 51,* 993–1000.

CHAPTER 2

The Evolutionary Context of Personality Development

Marco Del Giudice

Studying the development of personality means grappling with some of the deepest and most fundamental questions about human nature. Why are we so different from one another? Where do our desires, goals, and values come from? Is our development shaped by external forces or guided by internal dispositions? And what does it mean to be an individual in the first place? To answer these questions we need the most powerful tools we can find, and when the goal is to understand biological organisms like ourselves, no single tool has proven more powerful than evolutionary theory.

Traditionally, psychology has sought to describe the neural and mental mechanisms that control behavior, understand how they work, and track their development across the life course. Questions that focus on mechanism and development are of the *proximate* kind—they describe organisms as we see them in the present, and deal with the immediate causes and consequences of behavior. While the proximate view is extremely important, it fails to address another, equally important question: *Why* do those mechanisms work and develop the way they do? Or, why did the version we observe today win out in the perpetual game of variation and selection that drives evolutionary change? Evolutionary theory provides an "ultimate" perspective on psychological mechanisms by focusing on their *adaptive* function, that is,

their eventual contribution to genetic replication (see below). In addition, *phylogenetic* questions address the emergence and transformation of those mechanisms over deep evolutionary time, including their variation between closely and distantly related species. The ultimate level of analysis complements and illuminates the proximate one; the four questions of biology—mechanism, development, adaptation, and phylogeny—must be asked in combination if we seek to fully explain a biological system (Scott-Phillips, Dickins, & West, 2011).

The application of evolutionary concepts to the human mind and behavior is the domain of *evolutionary psychology* (see Buss, 2015a, for an introduction and Buss, 2015b, for an in-depth account). Properly understood, evolutionary psychology is a general framework for the study of behavior rather than a specific set of models and hypotheses. If one accepts the idea that humans and their brains are biological entities produced by natural selection, then any realistic science of behavior *has* to be grounded in evolutionary principles. This is why evolutionary psychology is not just another item in the familiar menu of psychological "schools," but a genuine *metatheory* for the discipline as a whole (Durrant & Ellis, 2012; Tooby & Cosmides, 2015).

Unfortunately, the two subdisciplines of personality and developmental psychology—the main tributaries of personality development—have been particularly reluctant to embrace evolutionary thinking, as compared, for example, with social and cognitive psychology. To compound the problem, evolutionary psychology throughout the 1990s had a strong emphasis on universal mechanisms—the invariant "design specs" of the human mind—and a tendency to neglect individual differences or regard them as relatively unimportant. In addition, most researchers paid relatively little attention to developmental issues and focused on the adaptive problems of adult individuals, such as foraging and mate selection. The good news is that things have changed rapidly and dramatically over the last two decades. The evolution of personality has become a major focus of interest in both biology and psychology (Buss & Hawley, 2011; Carere & Maestripieri, 2013). At the same time, more researchers have started to integrate the evolutionary and developmental levels of analysis, and evolutionary–developmental psychology is now a thriving subfield (Bjorklund & Ellis, 2014; Ellis & Bjorklund, 2005). While there is still much work to do, the foundation is solid enough to support a biologically informed science of personality development.

In this chapter, I set the development of personality in the broader context of human evolution, and show how an evolutionary approach illuminates important questions and helps integrate findings across disciplines and levels of analysis. In doing so, I aim to convey a sense of the big picture, stimulate reflection, and provide pointers to the literature for the interested reader. I begin the chapter by introducing key evolutionary concepts and outlining some important aspects of the ecology of our species, the ape *Homo sapiens*. I then apply those concepts to three foundational issues: the nature of motivation, the nature of variation, and the nature of development. For each of these topics I present a selection of notable contributions and insights, and discuss their implications for the study of personality development.

Key Evolutionary Concepts

Natural Selection and Adaptation

The concept of natural selection lies at the core of evolutionary biology. Simply stated, Darwin's insight was that organisms compete for reproduction in a world of limited resources, so that the traits of those organisms who leave more descendants spread in the population and eventually replace other variants. As long as new variation is produced (e.g., by genetic mutations), this selection process results in organisms that are increasingly better adapted to their environment—for example, more capable of surviving (at least until reproduction); harvesting energy; and outcompeting other organisms, including conspecifics, prey, predators, and pathogens. Evolution never stops because the environment does not remain static and includes other organisms that also keep changing via selection. A trait can be *adaptive, maladaptive,* or *neutral* depending on whether its net effect on an individual's relative reproductive success (*fitness*) is positive, negative, or null. Over many generations, natural selection results in the gradual evolution of complex mechanisms—organs such as the eye or the liver, behaviors such as predation strategies and mating rituals. In this way, biological mechanisms acquire the appearance of being designed in order to serve specific functions (e.g., pumping blood is the key function of the heart), even though they have been produced by a fundamentally blind and impersonal process. Mechanisms that evolved because of their positive effects on fitness are labeled *adaptations* (Durrant & Ellis, 2012; Tooby & Cosmides, 2015).

The ultimate currency of Darwinian selection is an organism's number of descendants (relative to others in the population): thus, the function of traits and adaptations can be ultimately linked—even if indirectly—to the organism's reproduction. Survival is often emphasized in popular discussions of evolution; however, surviving is only useful insofar it leads to reproduction, and many organisms forgo survival in exchange for reproductive opportunities (the male praying mantis offers a memorable example). In organisms that reproduce sexually, there is strong selection for traits that increase mating success by making individuals more attractive or more able to compete with rivals (*sexual selection*). Sexual selection may produce traits that are costly and extravagant (e.g., the peacock's tail), and often drives the evolution of morphological and behavioral differences between males and females (Stanyon & Bigoni, 2014).

Adaptations, Byproducts, and Noise

While selection is the main driver of evolution and adaptation is ubiquitous in nature, it is important to stress that not all traits are adaptive. Many traits are byproducts of adaptations—for example, the white color of bones is not an adaptive feature but a byproduct of the chemical composition of bone tissue. Other traits may be neutral or arise from random "noise." Under certain conditions, even maladaptive traits can spread, especially in small populations. Finally, selection always interacts with all sorts of constraints, from the laws of physics and chemistry to trade-offs between competing functions and adaptations (e.g., lighter bones help an animal move faster but are also more fragile).

Inclusive Fitness

The classic Darwinian account of natural selection is based on an individual's relative number of descendants. While this approach can explain a lot about the design of organisms, it cannot explain the evolution of altruistic behaviors that reduce an individual's reproductive success while increasing that of another. From the standpoint of individual fitness, true altruism of the fitness-reducing kind should never evolve, although there is still room for cooperation and *reciprocal altruism*—that is, behaviors that ultimately increase the fitness of both actors involved (e.g., teaming up to hunt bigger prey; exchanging favors). The solution to this thorny problem was provided by William Hamilton (1964), whose crucial insight was that individuals do not replicate across generations—instead, what is ultimately replicated is their *genes,* defined broadly as units of inheritance rather than segments of DNA. Genes within an individual can maximize their own replication (i.e., their share of *descendants* in the population gene pool) by improving not only the reproductive success of that particular individual but also that of other individuals who are likely to carry the same genes. The probability of carrying the same genes is instantiated by the *relatedness* between two individuals, which is highest between close relatives but can vary systematically across different groups of people within a population (e.g., one's own tribe vs. neighboring tribes).

The implication of Hamilton's work is that natural selection does not maximize individual fitness, but a more complex quantity called *inclusive fitness.* Inclusive fitness reflects the joint effects of an organism's behavior on its own reproduction *and* the reproduction of related individuals. The framework of inclusive fitness accommodates all sorts of social interactions between individuals: selfishness and competition, reciprocal cooperation, altruism, and even *spite*—actions that reduce one's reproductive success but impose an even larger penalty on that of other, negatively related individuals. Selection can favor any of these social patterns depending on the exact balance of costs, benefits, and relatedness that applies to a given situation (Bourke, 2011). Inclusive fitness theory (also known by the less accurate label of *kin selection*) lies at the foundation of the modern understanding of social evolution. When populations include multiple groups that compete with one another for resources and (ultimately) reproduction, another way to understand the logic of social evolution is to separate the individual consequences of behavior from those that impact the entire group. In general, selection between groups favors altruism between group members, but this force is opposed by selection for individual selfishness within each group. This approach is known as *multilevel* or *group selection.* Since inclusive fitness theory centers on the individual and does not explicitly consider the hierarchical structure of the population, multilevel selection is often presented as an alternative theory of evolution. In fact, inclusive fitness and multilevel selection are two equivalent ways to describe the same underlying theory—a theory that provides an elegant, powerful explanation of the interplay between cooperation and competition in the biological world (West & Gardner, 2013).

Parent–Offspring Conflict

An especially striking illustration of this interplay is *parent-offspring conflict* (Trivers, 1974), which arises because siblings in sexual species are only moderately related (i.e., genetically similar) to one another. This basic fact limits the optimal degree of biological altruism between siblings; each offspring should try to obtain a larger share of the parents' investment of food, protection, and other resources, whereas parents benefit by distributing their investment equally among their offspring (all else being equal). As a result, the amount of investment in each offspring that would maximize the parents' inclusive fitness is lower than the amount that would maximize the offspring's fitness. Selection then acts on offspring so they will try to obtain more investment for themselves, and on parents, so that they will curtail their altruistic investment to some extent. These divergent selection pressures create a cascade of systematic tensions in family relations and counter their inherently altruistic quality. Parent–offspring conflict has far-reaching implications for many aspects of development, from physiological interactions between mother and fetus during pregnancy to differences between parents and adult offspring in the characteristics they value most in the offspring's romantic partners (see Schlomer, Del Giudice, & Ellis, 2011).

The Gene's-Eye View of Evolution

Arguably, the most important implication of inclusive fitness theory is that selection favors traits that maximize the replication of an organism's genes (Grafen, 2007). This makes it possible to understand the evolution of individual and social behavior by taking the "gene's-eye view," that is, by considering the impact of behavior on the replication of genes rather than on the reproduction of individuals. This hugely counterintuitive perspective shift is the rationale for Richard Dawkins's much misunderstood point that genuinely altruistic behavior between *individuals* can emerge from the competition between *genetic variants* that are selected to replicate as much as possible within the population, and for this reason can be figuratively described as "selfish" (Dawkins, 1976).

Intragenomic Conflict

The ramifications of the gene's-eye view of evolution extend beyond social interactions. As a rule, genes within an individual have the same biological interest because they share a common destiny—that is, they have the same chance of ending up in that individual's offspring. This rule is sufficiently valid that one can calculate a single fitness for the individual as a whole; however, this approximation hides a lot of interesting detail and some important exceptions. Sex chromosomes, for instance, replicate at different rates depending on the sex of the offspring. Moreover, some genes are expressed only (or at higher rates) if they are inherited from a specific parent, the father or the mother. Differential expression is achieved through an epigenetic mechanism known as *genomic imprinting*. Imprinted genes have different coefficients of relatedness with paternal versus maternal relatives, and their interest may diverge quite a bit from that of the individual. For example, paternal genes (or, more precisely, imprinted genes that are expressed when they are inherited from one's father) are predicted to "side" with the offspring and against the mother in parent–offspring conflict, whereas maternal genes should evolve so as to counteract this effect (Kramer & Bressan, 2015; Schlomer et al., 2011). These and other cases of *intragenomic conflict* make it clear that from the standpoint of natural selection, individuals are not unitary but represent a compromise among a multitude of genetic factions engaged in various forms of cooperation and conflict. What's more, conflicts within the genome are likely to translate into conflicts for the control of the individual's behavior—and, not coincidentally, many imprinted genes are highly expressed in the brain.

In total, the picture painted by modern evolutionary theory is one in which conflict, cooperation, and altruism evolve in a complex and shifting interplay, which can be ultimately understood through the lens of genetic replication. With few and unusual exceptions, evolution does not lead to purely cooperative relationships; conflicts of interest easily creep in—even between parents and their offspring, and even between cells and genes of the same individual.

Testing Evolutionary Hypotheses

When researchers formulate hypotheses about the adaptive function of a trait (or the lack thereof), they inevitably make inferences about the past history of that trait and its contribution to fitness—often in environments that have long disappeared. It follows that, generally speaking, evolutionary hypotheses cannot be tested directly but only through the accumulation of convergent indirect evidence from multiple sources. This does not mean that adaptive hypotheses are unfalsifiable. To begin, they can be used to derive novel predictions that can then be tested with standard psychological methods. In addition, researchers can use mathematical models of the evolutionary process to gain insight into the plausibility of alternative hypotheses and work out their assumptions and implications. Other common sources of evidence employed by evolutionary scholars include cross-cultural research (including studies of forager populations), phylogenetic comparisons with other species, and genetic studies. Researchers may also attempt to measure the fitness contribution of a trait, although past effects on survival and reproduction may be obscured by recent social and technological changes (e.g., contraception). The methodology of evolutionary psychology is a complex topic that defies a short summary; for more in-depth discussion, see Andrews, Gangestad, and Matthews (2002), Schmitt and Pilcher (2004), and Simpson and Campbell (2015).

Human Ecology

Humans separated from the lineage of chimpanzees 5–7 million years ago and evolved as hunters and gatherers for the past few million years, until the invention of agriculture around 12,000 years ago. Our distant ancestors migrated out of Africa in multiple waves, adapting to a striking range of environments and ultimately settling the entire planet. The behavioral flexibility of our species and its capacity to generate complex, divergent cultural traditions clearly played a major role throughout its evolutionary history. Without any pretense of completeness, in this section, I introduce two related ideas that illuminate important aspects of human nature and are particularly relevant to personality development: the concept of the *human adaptive complex* and that of the *cognitive niche*.

The Human Adaptive Complex

The human adaptive complex, shorthand for a unique set of interlocking traits that evolved in our species (Kaplan, Gurven, & Lancaster, 2007; Kaplan, Hill, Lancaster, & Hurtado, 2000), is founded on the sophisticated foraging techniques that enabled us to exploit high-quality, energy-rich food sources such as large game, shellfish, and roots. These techniques involve the use of manufactured tools (cutting and excavation tools, bows and arrows, fishing nets, etc.), learning-intensive skills, and sustained cooperation between group members. The key requirements for such intensive learning are a large brain and a long, slow developmental trajectory, with an extended phase of dependence before sexual maturity. At the same time, large, slow-developing brains require massive amounts of energy, which is provided by high-quality food items and buffered by a multigeneration system in which resources flow from grandparents to parents to children. The economics of human development is also highly dependent on the shared contribution of mothers and fathers, which in turn is supported by long-term bonds between sexual partners (typi-

cally in the form of marriage). Finally, protection by parents and food sharing between kin and cooperative partners contribute to substantially reduce child mortality, thus making slow development and extended dependency viable options. The traits that make up this complex enable and reinforce each other, and could not have evolved in isolation.

The human adaptive complex paints a picture of unusually high cooperation at multiple levels, from parental couples to extended kin networks to broader social groups (Bowles & Gintis, 2011). Indeed, the social organization of our species for the last 200,000 years—and before the demographic explosion kickstarted by agriculture—was defined by a hierarchy of social units nested within each other, from small bands of 30–50 people to tribes of perhaps 1,000 or 2,000 individuals with various degrees of relatedness (Dunbar, 1993). The scale and quality of human cooperation have far-reaching implications for psychological evolution. To begin, our social life involves a delicate and complex balance between "getting ahead" and "getting along"—between gaining individual power and advantages on the one hand, and avoiding rejection and ostracism on the other. Also, getting to the top of social hierarchies—whether peacefully or by force—is rarely possible without building alliances and reciprocal exchanges. This dynamic tension between cooperation and competition sets the stage for the evolution of our sophisticated social intelligence, which in turn depends on a multitude of psychological processes and adaptations, from empathy and "theory of mind" to Machiavellian strategizing (Dunbar & Schultz, 2007).

Dual-Status Hierarchies and Social Selection for Altruism

The ubiquity of reciprocity and cooperation also explains the dual nature of human competition for status. In many animals, status is mainly determined by *dominance*—the ability to control others with the threat of physical force. In cooperative species, however, status can also be gained by possessing skills, abilities, and knowledge that make one a valuable social partner. This kind of freely conferred status based on admiration rather than fear is captured by the term *prestige* (Henrich & Gil-White, 2001). The duality of dominance and prestige means that human groups allow for multiple kinds of potentially successful social roles. In turn, a multiplicity of social roles creates divergent selection pressures for a broad range of personalities, as well as different combinations of prosocial and coercive strategies for competition (Hawley, 2014). The evolutionary dynamics set in motion by extended cooperation include the possibility of self-reinforcing *social selection* for altruistic traits. Social selection, a process analogous to sexual selection, depends on being chosen as a social partner rather than a sexual one. If people rely on credible displays of altruism and generosity when they select their cooperation partners, these traits will spread in the population and become more common, in spite of their costs for the individual. Social selection likely contributes to explain our partial but still remarkable disposition to behave altruistically toward other group members (Nesse, 2007). It also provides another striking illustration of how selfish selection processes can drive the evolution of genuinely altruistic behaviors. Finally, one should not neglect the dark side of cooperation and altruism: Aggression and war between enemy groups—which are sustained by extensive cooperation and even self-sacrifice within each group—have been a constant of human societies since the dawn of time (Pinker, 2011).

The Cognitive Niche

The evolution of language—another defining adaptation of our species—permits the exchange and transmission of information on an unprecedented scale. Language and the cooperative exchange of information have entrenched humans in the cognitive niche: a unique foraging niche in which problem solving based on cause–effect reasoning, transmitted information, and social coordination are used to overcome other organisms' defenses in order to feed on them (e.g., building traps and weapons for hunting; cooking and processing plants to detoxify them; Pinker, 2010). As inhabitants of the cognitive niche, we depend critically on the transmission and accumulation of massive amounts of information and know-how. Over time, we have evolved a truly amazing range of information-sharing devices, from innate mechanisms, such as imitation, to recent technological innovations, such as drawing and writing. These devices sustain the creation of cultures—cumulative repositories of knowledge, behavioral rules, norms, and institutions. In traditional societies, a great deal of this transmission work is accomplished by storytelling, a biologically based ability whose importance is hard to overstate (Scalise Sugiyama, 2011). As discussed in Part IV of this volume, our propensity to organize the world into memorable narratives has wide-ranging implications for the way we think about our own lives and present ourselves to others.

Recent Social Evolution

The evolutionary dynamics that accompanied our entrance in the cognitive niche have undergone a sudden acceleration with the invention of agriculture and the emergence of large-scale, stratified societies over the past few thousand years. Among the many consequences of the agricultural revolution, one is especially important from the standpoint of personality development: the explosive increase in the number of highly specialized social, technological, and cognitive roles within a society—farmers, herders, merchants, soldiers, priests, artists, builders, teachers, and so forth. Each social niche in this ever-expanding menu entails not only a particular set of skills but also a best-fitting range of interests and personality traits. The demands of farming have likely amplified selection for average levels of conscientiousness and self-control (Cochran & Harpending, 2009). However, our recent social evolution may have had an even more important outcome, namely, a marked increase in the *diversification* of individual personalities (Figueredo et al., 2005). Intriguingly, the only detailed study of personality in a population of foragers who practice low-level agriculture—the Tsimane of Bolivia—has found evidence of two broad personality factors of "prosociality" and "industriousness" instead of the customary Big Five. These factors are largely composed of agreeableness and conscientiousness items, mixed with facets of extraversion and openness to experience (Gurven, von Rueden, Massenkoff, Kaplan, & Lero Vie, 2013). There is also cross-cultural evidence that correlations among the Big Five decrease as societies become more complex, consistent with the idea that individual personalities become more diversified (Lukaszewski, Gurven, von Rueden, & Schmitt, 2017).

The Nature of Motivation

Functional Specialization

While maximizing inclusive fitness can be legitimately described as the ultimate biological goal of all organisms, it is impossible for individuals to *directly* increase their fitness. Instead, what organisms face is a set of basic tasks—surviving, growing, reproducing—that in turn have to be met by successfully solving a host of narrower problems: finding and choosing food, avoiding parasites and pathogens, securing suitable sexual partners, feeding and protecting the offspring, and so on. In highly social species, these problems are compounded by other unique challenges—for example, improving and defending one's status, finding and choosing cooperation partners, and avoiding exploitation by other individuals. Living in the cognitive niche, humans must deal with still other tasks that have to do with gathering and transmitting information, learning and teaching one's culture, and negotiating the difficult balance between conformity and innovation.

Each of the adaptive problems I just listed implies a different set of goals and requires a different type of solution. A good food item and a good partner have totally different characteristics; the behavioral strategies that work best to become a dominant individual are not helpful in avoiding infectious diseases. Whereas some domains (e.g., mating and courtship) admit a large amount of trial-and-error learning, others (e.g., avoiding toxic foods and deadly predators) are much less forgiving of mistakes. For all these reasons, selection tend to favors the evolution of multiple mechanisms for the control of behavior—much like distinct mental "organs," each specialized for dealing with a certain kind of domain. Functional specialization (often discussed as *modularity* or *domain specificity*) promotes efficiency in dealing with the environment, confers robustness on the mind as a whole, and allows selection to fine-tune each mechanism without affecting the functionality of the others (Barrett, 2015; Tooby & Cosmides, 2015). While some general-purpose processes such as reinforcement learning or working memory can be shared or reused by multiple psychological mechanisms, each mechanisms is specifically attuned to a certain kind of input (e.g., potential sexual partners) and employs criteria and rules of operation that are at least in part innate. From another perspective, evolved mechanisms incorporate implicit knowledge that has been accumulated over millions of years, and that in many cases would be too hard, too costly, or too dangerous to relearn from scratch in each new generation. Of course, innate predisposition are often supplemented, refined, and modified by learning: Infants react automatically to bitter flavors (i.e., potentially toxic foods) with intense disgust, even if later on they learn to enjoy many of the same flavors. Specialization and learning are not antithetical—on the contrary, they are both the product of natural selection and represent two sides of successful adaptation.

Motivational Systems

Motivational systems are the specialized systems that regulate goal-directed behavior. A vital motivational system is the one that controls the intake of energy and nutrients through hunger and eating; other systems of this kind regulate water intake (thirst and drinking), body temperature (seeking colder or warmer places), and so on. Survival-related motivations include *fear* and *aggression* systems designed to escape imminent threats and/or fight back against attackers; *behavioral inhibition* and *security* systems designed to deal with potential danger, with anxiety rather than fear as their core emotion; and a *disgust* system, whose main goal is avoidance of pathogens and toxic substances (Corr, DeYoung, & McNaughton, 2013; Curtis, 2011; Woody & Szechtman, 2011). Each of these systems is defined by not only a set of goals but also specific inputs that assess the organism's state (e.g., blood glucose, stomach fullness), sensations and emotions that signal success or failure (e.g., satiety vs. hunger), and specific physiological and behavioral outputs designed to reach the system's goals and overcome potential obstacles. Motivational systems depend on specialized neural circuits; however, the neural pathways that serve different systems often overlap to some extent (e.g., sensors of stomach fullness provide inputs to both the hunger and thirst systems). Crucially, biological goals do not have to be consciously represented for the system to work. A person disgusted by rotten food does not need to know anything about microbes; a distressed infant does not need to know in any conscious sense that the function of crying is to maintain proximity with the mother. In this sense, the implicit goals of motivational systems are distinct from the deliberate, planful goals emphasized in McAdams's model of personality development (McAdams, 2015, and Chapter 1, this volume).

The logic of functional specialization applies just as well to social adaptive problems. Evolutionary psychologists and neurobiologists have described a variety of motivational systems that regulate social interactions. These include an *attachment* system that promotes contact with (and availability of) one's caregivers and a complementary *caregiving* system that promotes nurturance and protection of one's offspring; a *mating* system that regulates sexual attraction and courtship; a *status* system that mediates interactions based on dominance and prestige; a *reciprocity* system that deals with reciprocal exchanges and the risk of cheating; and *affiliation* and *pair-bonding* systems that underlie close relationships with long-term sexual partners, friends, and select group members. Other likely candidates for autonomous motivations are *play, curiosity,* and *acquisition* (Aunger & Curtis, 2013; Del Giudice, 2018; Toronchuk & Ellis, 2013).

Note that different authors in this area may use somewhat different labels to describe the same system; also, there are often multiple ways to draw the boundaries between functionally related systems, as their behavioral and neural correlates overlap to a significant degree. For example, one can legitimately distinguish between a fear and aggression system, but also frame them as part of a unitary "fight-or-flight" system. Similarly, attachment, affiliation, and pair-bonding share many of the same emotions, behaviors, and neurobiological substrates (e.g., molecules such as oxytocin, dopamine, and endogenous opioids) (Feldman, 2017; Machin & Dunbar, 2011). This is not a limitation of the model but a predictable consequence of the evolutionary process—new mechanisms are not built from scratch but emerge as modified and differentiated versions of existing ones (Barrett, 2015). For example, affiliative behaviors seem to ultimately originate from mother–infant bonds but have been adapted and differentiated over time to serve a multiplicity of relationships with other social partners. The result is an organic network of partially overlapping systems rather than a rigid division between independent, self-contained units.

The model of motivation I just sketched is remarkably rich, especially compared with alternative accounts that depend on domain-general processes (e.g., reinforcement learning) or focus on a small set of abstract, general goals. A notable example of the latter is *self-determination theory* (Deci & Ryan, 2000; Sheldon & Schüler, Chapter 16, this volume), a model that explains psychological motivation in terms of three universal needs—competence, autonomy, and relatedness—and frames the ultimate goal of be-

havior in terms of subjective well-being rather than biological fitness. While concepts such as autonomy and self-determination are psychologically meaningful, one can debate whether they represent specific evolved goals, or rather emerge from more fundamental biological motivations (e.g., status, mating) in combination with the human capacity for deliberate self-regulation and self-representation—including the ability to mentally simulate oneself in future scenarios (see Kenrick, Griskevicius, Neuberg, & Schaller, 2010). Clearly, there is still much work to do before we fully understand how motivational systems interact with other psychological mechanisms to construct our multifaceted sense of identity. Still, analyzing human motivation from the standpoint of multiple fitness-relevant goals can yield many fascinating insights, as illustrated by Kenrick and colleagues' evolutionary revision of Maslow's classic "pyramid of needs."

Motivation, Values, and Self-Esteem

An important implication of adopting a rich model of motivation is that moral values can be framed naturally as extensions of basic motivational goals. When people reason about moral problems they typically rely not on abstract principles, but on a set of emotionally charged intuitions that revolve around a small number of fundamental themes (Haidt, 2007). For example, Jonathan Haidt (2012) has identified six such themes: fairness, avoidance of harm and pain, respect of authority, loyalty to the ingroup, and spiritual purity. It is easy to see how moral themes are rooted in particular motivational systems—reciprocity for fairness-based morality, caregiving for harm prevention, status for authority, affiliation for ingroup loyalty, and disgust for purity concerns. These functional links bring the study of motivation and that of morality under the same theoretical framework. Even more importantly, they suggest ways in which considerations of fitness costs and benefits can be used to illuminate the deeper logic of moral behavior. (For a detailed example, see Baumard, André, & Sperber's [2013] analysis of the evolution of fairness.)

From a similar perspective, self-esteem can be understood as the output of evolved assessment mechanisms that gauge the person's effectiveness in achieving key goals such as affiliation, status, mating, and reproduction (Kavanagh, Robins, & Ellis, 2010; Kirkpat-

rick & Ellis, 2001). By extending the sociometer theory (Leary, 2005) in light of functional
specialization, this approach explains not only
the multidimensional nature of self-esteem but
also the existence of a global sense of value that
may summarize the individual's overall fitness
prospects (necessarily estimated from his or her
success in pursuing narrow biological tasks).
On this point, it is crucial to remember that selection maximizes *inclusive* fitness, and that inclusive fitness can be increased by helping relatives, providing benefits to group members, and
so on. The fact that altruistic pursuits can boost
self-esteem is definitely not in contrast with a
sophisticated biological view of motivation.

Cooperation and Conflict

The interplay of cooperation and conflict pervades motivation at all levels of analysis. To
begin, cooperation and conflict with social
partners shape the design of motivational systems and associated cognitive processes. For
example, evolutionary psychologists have documented how successful reciprocal exchanges
require the ability to detect, avoid, and remember cheaters, and how these tasks rely on
specialized mechanisms (Cosmides & Tooby,
2015). Different settings of these mechanisms
carry different costs and benefits: A suspicious
individual who responds to the slightest sign of
exploitation will effectively avoid cheaters but
also miss many opportunities for fruitful cooperation. Individual differences in the settings
of motivational systems contribute to define
broad personality traits such as the Big Five—
for example, high trust and forgiving responses
to exploitation are key aspects of agreeableness (Denissen & Penke, 2008). Motivational
systems should also respond to differences in
relatedness, systematically tilting the cost–benefit balance in favor of more closely related individuals. The same variables can be expected
to indirectly influence moral judgments and
decisions. Patterns of nepotism and ingroup
favoritism are well documented in human societies; more subtly, our sensitivity to indicators of relatedness is revealed in the tendency
to behave more altruistically with people who
physically resemble us (e.g., DeBruine, Jones,
Little, & Perrett, 2008). On an even broader
scale, some evolutionary scholars have argued
that morality itself can be understood as an
evolved mechanism of conflict resolution and
group coordination. Specifically, moral judg-

ments allow people to choose sides in disputes
without forming rigid alliances and compromising the integrity of the group (DeScioli &
Kurzban, 2013).

An evolutionary perspective highlights the
fact that conflict plays a role not only in interactions with strangers, but also in the context of
close family relationships. In particular, parent-
offspring conflict inevitably shapes the functioning of the attachment and caregiving systems. Insecure attachment styles (Simpson &
Jones, Chapter 15, this volume) are typically understood as responses to parents' sensitivity and
emotional availability. From a complementary
perspective, the behaviors of insecure children
(e.g., clinginess, controlling aggression) can be
seen as attempts to obtain more investment and
care, even against the parent's best interest (see
Simpson & Belsky, 2016).

In the model of motivation I sketched earlier,
behavior is energized and controlled by a large
number of goal-directed mechanisms, each
with its own rules and priorities; this leads to
the problem of how to manage the resulting patterns of cooperation and competition between
different motivational systems. In many ways,
how the brain arbitrates between multiple and
often contradictory goals is still an open question. Motivational systems can achieve a certain
degree of self-regulation by directly activating
or inhibiting one another; for example, sexual
arousal temporarily suppresses hunger, whereas
extreme fear can trigger explosive aggression.
However, the complexity of human behavior
requires more sophisticated mechanisms of
top-down control, including those known as *executive functions,* which range from relatively
simple processes such as motor inhibition to
high-level abilities such as planning and mental simulation. Executive functions play a crucial role in both cooperation and competition.
For example, the ability to suppress immediate
impulses is a requisite for all kinds of long-
term cooperation; at the same time, inhibition
is extremely useful to successfully manipulate
others and avoid being manipulated (Barkley,
2012).

Conflict shapes motivational systems not
only from the outside but also from within. Because of intragenomic conflicts, different sets
of genes (e.g., maternal vs. paternal) may have
divergent interests when it comes to the regulation of behavior. Hunger provides a simple but
striking example of this dynamics. Since a hungry infant extracts more energy and nutrients

from the mother, one can predict that paternal genes expressed in the infant should evolve so as to increase hunger, whereas maternal genes should suppress it. This invisible tug-of-war should be played within the brain mechanisms that control the motivation to eat and the relevant behaviors (e.g., suckling). And indeed, infants who lack paternal genes because of chromosomal abnormalities (e.g., Prader–Willi syndrome) have very little appetite and are often unable to suckle (Haig & Wharton, 2003). We still know little about the ways in which genomic conflicts affect other motivational systems such as attachment and mating, but their impact is likely to be profound and extend well beyond infancy and childhood (Kramer & Bressan, 2015; Úbeda & Gardner, 2011).

The Nature of Variation

The Origin of Individual Differences

Genetic Variation

A century of twin studies has shown conclusively that personality traits and attitudes are strongly influenced by a person's genotype. Genetic factors account for about 50% of the variance in adult personality, and likely contribute to the remaining variation through genotype-by-environment (G × E) interactions (Knopik, Neiderhiser, DeFries, & Plomin, 2017; see Tucker-Drob & Briley, Chapter 3, this volume). For the most part, this genetic component consists of extremely small effects distributed across thousands of DNA regions (Chabris, Lee, Cesarini, Benjamin, & Laibson, 2015; Penke & Jokela, 2016).

From an evolutionary point of view, there are three main explanations for the existence of genetic differences in personality (Gangestad, 2011). The simplest possibility is that such differences are neutral with respect to fitness and are maintained in the population by fundamentally random processes (*genetic drift*). This hypothesis is not very likely given that personality traits systematically predict key biological outcomes such as mating, reproduction, and mortality (see Ashton, 2013). It is also possible for selection to favor a particular level of a personality trait, for example, an intermediate level of neuroticism or a high level of extraversion. In this scenario, random mutations typically cause maladaptive deviations from the optimal trait level. Selection can take

a long time to eliminate deleterious mutations from the gene pool; the equilibrium between the constant generation of new mutations and their elimination (*mutation–selection balance*) can maintain a considerable amount of genetic variation in a population. While mutation–selection balance is probably not a major source of variation for personality as a whole, there is some evidence that it may play a role in extraversion. High extraversion in men predicts enhanced reproductive success across cultures and is associated with indicators of low "mutation load" (e.g., Alvergne, Jokela, & Lummaa, 2010; Berg, Lummaa, Lahdenperä, Rotkirch, & Jokela, 2014; Gangestad, 2011). Importantly, the genetic variants that influence extraversion need not act directly on brain functioning. An intriguing possibility—for which there is mixed evidence—is that extraversion is calibrated to one's physical characteristics, so that stronger and more attractive individuals tend to become more extraverted as a result (Lukaszewski & von Rueden, 2015; Zietsch, 2016).

While neutral variants and deleterious mutations may contribute to individual differences in some personality traits, the evidence so far is most consistent with a third type of process, namely, *balancing selection* (Penke & Jokela, 2016), which occurs when the fitness contribution of a certain genetic variant is not fixed but changes across different times, places, or individuals. Each personality profile has both benefits and costs: For example, highly extraverted people not only tend to be more successful in social and mating competition but are also at higher risk of accidents and sexually transmitted diseases. Stable social arrangements may select for lower extraversion, dangerous and unpredictable environments may select for higher neuroticism, and so on (Denissen & Penke, 2008; Nettle, 2011). Many different aspects of the social environment can drive balancing selection, including some nonobvious candidates. For example, the proportion of males to females in a population, or *sex ratio,* has a cascade of remarkable consequences for social behavior. When men are scarce relative to women, and thus in higher demand in the mating "market," the dynamics of sexual competition shift toward the (average) male preference for short-term sexual relations and delayed commitment. As a result, aggressive sexual competition becomes more intense, violent crime increases, and couple relationships become less stable. In contrast, a preponderance of men shifts competition toward long-term commitment, monogamous relationships, and earlier marriage. As sex ratios fluctuate across time and place, they create the opportunity for variable selection on multiple personality traits at once (see Del Giudice, 2012). Finally, some genetic variation in personality may arise as a side effect of intragenomic conflicts—as, for example, when maternal and paternal imprinted genes "pull" behavioral traits in opposite directions. This type of genetic effect is adaptive from the perspective of individual genes but can be quite maladaptive for the person as a whole.

The Role of the Environment

All in all, the effects of the environment (including potential G × E interactions) account for about as much variation in personality as those of the genotype. In biological terms, the fact that the same genotype may give rise to different behavioral profiles depending on the environmental context is an example of *developmental plasticity* (West-Eberhard, 2003). Plastic organisms can adapt to rapid fluctuations in the environment, which would be impossible through genetic evolution alone. In order to be biologically adaptive, developmental plasticity cannot be unconstrained or arbitrarily flexible; on the contrary, natural selection often produces finely tuned plastic responses that attempt to "match" present or future conditions so as to maximize the organism's fitness. In addition to learning processes, organisms possess evolved *epigenetic* mechanisms that regulate genetic expression based on inputs and cues from the external environment (Ledón-Rettig, Richards, & Martin, 2013; Meaney, 2010). Epigenetic mechanisms are likely to be involved in the long-term development of personality, even though the details of how they operate are still mostly unknown.

Twin studies consistently show that environmental effects on personality are largely or completely nonshared; that is, they act independently on siblings within the same family (Knopik et al., 2017). The predominance of nonshared effects is a developmental and evolutionary puzzle, since many aspects of the environment that may plausibly affect the development of personality—from adversity and socioeconomic status to the quality of family relationships—are shared between siblings. In principle, a child's personality could shaped by his or her particular niche within the family, as

determined, for example, by birth order; however, the existence of systematic birth order effects is not supported by the evidence (see Ashton, 2013). Experiences with peers are another plausible source of nonshared environmental influences, but they are hard to disentangle from the indirect influence of genetic factors. In general, a person's activities and experiences are influenced by his or her preexisting personality; in many cases, those activities and experiences reinforce the initial personality traits and stabilize them even further (Specht et al., 2014). Another possible explanation for the predominance of nonshared effects is the existence of pervasive G×E interactions. In this scenario, genetic differences between siblings moderate the effects of shared experiences, so that the same event may have different consequences for the development of personality in different siblings (Duncan, Pollastri, & Smoller, 2014; Knopik et al., 2017; see Tucker-Drob & Briley, Chapter 3, this volume).

Differential Susceptibility

A particularly interesting model of G × E interactions is the theory of *differential susceptibility* (Belsky, 1997; Belsky & Pluess, 2009; Ellis, Boyce, Belsky, Bakermans-Kranenburg, & van IJzendoorn, 2011). According to this theory, the same genetic variants that make children more susceptible to negative aspects of the environment, such as stress and harsh parenting (and would be traditionally regarded as vulnerability factors), also make them more open to positive aspects such as safety, social support, and positive interactions with parents. In other words, some children are more plastic in response to both types of environmental input ("for better *and* for worse"). The evolutionary rationale is that the early environment is an imperfect predictor of what will happen later in life; children who are shaped by early experiences not only benefit from enhanced plasticity when cues correctly predict the future but also risk developing maladaptive (mismatched) traits when early cues are misleading. Differences in susceptibility between offspring evolve as a form of "insurance" against such prediction errors. Another version of this idea focuses less strongly on genetic factors and postulates that early experiences shape subsequent plasticity, increasing susceptibility in both adverse and protected environments and giving rise to a U-shaped curve (Boyce & Ellis, 2005).

There is some evidence that infants and young children who are more irritable and higher in negative emotionality are also more susceptible to environmental influences (Slagt, Dubas, Deković, & van Aken, 2016). Other candidate plasticity factors are elevated physiological reactivity to stress and individual differences in various neurotransmitter systems, including serotonin, dopamine, and oxytocin (see Moore & Depue, 2016). However, the role of specific genetic variants is still difficult to assess because of the formidable methodological challenges in this type of study (Del Giudice, 2017; Duncan et al., 2014; Ellis & Del Giudice, 2019). Another limitation of current models of differential susceptibility is that they do not consider the possible effects of parent–offspring conflict. Given that highly susceptible offspring are also easier to influence, it is reasonable to expect that the optimal level of plasticity will differ between parents and offspring. This additional layer of conflict might contribute to shape the development of individual differences in plasticity (Del Giudice, 2015c).

Life-History Strategies

Individual differences in behavior can be described at various levels of detail and potentially comprise hundreds or even thousands of specific traits and dispositions. Models of personality organize those traits into a manageable hierarchy, with a few broad factors at the top and dozens of narrow facets at the bottom. Crucially, behavioral traits are not independent from one another but tend to covary in clusters. There are also correlations between behavioral traits and individual differences in physiology (e.g., sex and stress hormones), physical and sexual maturation (e.g., timing of puberty), health, and so on. To understand these large-scale patterns from a functional perspective, evolutionary researchers have increasingly drawn on *life-history theory* (see Del Giudice, Gangestad, & Kaplan, 2015; Ellis, Figueredo, Brumbach, & Schlomer, 2009). Life-history theory is a branch of biology that seeks to understand how organisms allocate time and energy to the various activities that comprise their life cycle—chiefly growth, bodily maintenance, and reproduction. Since all these activities ultimately contribute to fitness, organisms face a number of inevitable trade-offs: for instance, there is a general trade-off between growth and reproduction, as both require substantial energetic investment. When resources are directed toward reproduction, devoting more time and energy to parenting (e.g., by maintaining stable pair-bonds) leaves one with fewer opportunities for mating (e.g., in the form of short-term sexual relations).

Natural selection favors organisms that schedule developmental tasks and activities so as to optimize resource allocation; this chain of resource allocation decisions—expressed in the development of an integrated suite of physiological and behavioral traits—constitutes the individual's life-history strategy. At the level of behavior, individual differences in life-history strategy are reflected in patterns of self-regulation and motivation, with implications for aggression, cooperation, sexuality, and pair-bonding (among others). While life-history strategies are partly determined by genetic factors, they also show a degree of plasticity in response to key dimensions of the environment that include danger, unpredictability, and availability of adequate nutritional resources. In a nutshell, dangerous and unpredictable environments tend to favor "fast" strategies characterized by early maturation and reproduction (especially in females), sexual promiscuity, relationship instability, impulsivity, risk taking, aggression, and exploitative tendencies. Safe and predictable environments tend to entrain "slow" strategies characterized by late reproduction, stable pair-bonds, high self-control and future orientation, risk aversion, and prosociality. Slow strategies are also favored by nutritional scarcity in the absence of high levels of danger (Del Giudice et al., 2015; Ellis et al., 2009).

Life-history theory can inform the study of personality development in two ways. First, life-history models point to broader patterns of covariation—not only among personality traits but also with maturation and physiology—and help make sense of their functional underpinnings. Second, they single out some aspects of the environment (e.g., unpredictability) as potentially important for the coordinated development of individual differences. Note that different authors approach the relations between life-history strategies and personality in somewhat different ways. Some focus on specific traits such as agreeableness, conscientiousness, and impulsivity (e.g., Del Giudice, 2014a, 2018; Del Giudice et al., 2015), whereas others look for superfactors that may be as broad as a "general factor of personality" (e.g., Figueredo, Woodley of Menie, & Jacobs, 2015; Olderbak,

Gladden, Wolf, & Figueredo, 2014). Beyond the Big Five, life-history concepts have been used to explain the evolution of "dark" traits such as psychopathy and narcissism, autistic-like traits, and other dimensions of personality at the interface with psychopathology (e.g., Del Giudice, Klimczuk, Traficonte, & Maestripieri, 2014; Jonason, Koenig, & Tost, 2010).

Sex Differences in Personality

Throughout our evolutionary history, males and females have faced different challenges in their quest for survival and reproduction. Because of childbearing and lactation, women are the default caregivers for infants and children; from a fitness standpoint, they have more to lose from physical damage, which can severely reduce their ability to bear offspring. Women also depend more on family ties and social networks for successful reproduction, and female competition focuses heavily on exclusion and less on overt dominance. In contrast, men have been engaging in more physical aggression and violence for millions of years, both within their group (dominance contests) and between rival groups. Sexual selection also follows different criteria when males and females choose their mates. Men universally prefer cues of youth and fertility, and can increase their fitness by having children from multiple partners. While women can get some benefits from multiple sexual relationships, they can only bear one child at a time (barring twin pregnancies); moreover, they benefit more from choosing higher-status partners than younger ones given that male fertility decreases much less steeply with age. Historically, most human societies have been polygynous to various degrees—socially imposed monogamy is a recent cultural innovation that originated in ancient Greece and Rome and began to spread during the Middle Ages (see Benenson, 2014; Geary, 2010).

In short, human males and females differ in their mating and social strategies, have engaged in sexual division of labor for millions of years (e.g., hunting and fighting vs. caregiving), and experience different costs and benefits from a wide range of behaviors and life-history decisions. In light of all these facts, it would be truly surprising if men and women had not evolved some robust differences in their typical personalities. Yet the consensus view in psychology since the 1970s has been that sex differences in personality are small and inconsequential—the

main exception being that men show moderately higher levels of physical and verbal aggression (Hyde, 2014). As it turns out, this view is vitiated by two methodological problems: (1) a focus on broad personality traits when sex differences mainly emerge at the level of narrower facets and (2) a failure to aggregate differences across multiple traits (Del Giudice, 2015b).

When men and women are compared on Big Five domains, differences tend to be small—from less than 0.1 standard deviations in conscientiousness and openness to about 0.4 standard deviations in agreeableness and neuroticism (both higher in women). However, this is probably not the best level of analysis for sex differences. Natural and sexual selection should lead to sexually differentiated patterns of motivation (e.g., mating, affiliation, caregiving) and self-regulation (e.g., risk taking). While motivational tendencies do not map in a straightforward fashion on broad, multifaceted traits such as the Big Five, they can often be recovered more directly by zooming in to the level of narrower traits such as dominance and trust. This is also where sex differences become stronger and more meaningful. For example, some facets of neuroticism (e.g., anxiety and vulnerability) show much larger effects than others (e.g., angry hostility). Not infrequently, sex differences of opposite sign cancel each other out when one only considers the broader level of analysis: Despite scoring similar to women in overall extraversion, men are lower in sociability but higher in dominance and sensation seeking. Other narrow traits that are not well represented in the five-factor model show extremely large differences; in particular, women score more than two standard deviations higher than men on the personality dimension of *sensitivity* (aesthetic, intuitive, and tender-minded vs. utilitarian, objective, and tough-minded; Del Giudice, Booth, & Irwing, 2012). On top of these average differences, personality traits tend to be somewhat more variable in men than in women (Del Giudice, 2015b). This is a common outcome of sexual selection when males compete more strongly than females for mating and reproductive success (Archer & Mehdikhani, 2003).

When sex differences across multiple traits are combined using multivariate statistical methods and corrected for measurement error, the global difference between the average profiles of men and women is remarkably large (2.7 standard deviations in Del Giudice et al., 2012). This means that the personality distributions of males and females overlap by about 10%, which is close to the anatomical overlap between male and female faces (Del Giudice, 2013). The comparison between faces and personality profiles is illuminating: While the sexes look fairly similar if one considers one anatomical feature at a time (e.g., the size of the eyes, the length of the nose), the difference becomes obvious as soon as one starts looking at whole faces of men and women.

Common Misconceptions

An evolutionary approach to sex differences in personality tends to evoke two kinds of misconceptions. The first is that large differences imply a categorical, all-or-none separation between males and females and a disregard for the variability that exist *within* each sex. This is definitely not the case. Both males and females exhibit an enormous variety of personalities and combinations of traits; moreover, about 10% of men have a personality profile that is more typical of women (and vice versa). Again, the analogy with faces can be helpful: While each person has a unique face with a peculiar combination of features, there is still a clear-cut difference between the average face of a woman and that of a man. The second misconception concerns developmental timing and holds that evolved traits should already be present at birth or in early infancy. When differences appear later in development, they are often explained with socialization and regarded as not "biological." It is true that many sex differences in personality emerge or intensify between middle childhood and late adolescence (Soto, John, Gosling, & Potter, 2011); however, this is irrelevant to the question of their evolutionary origin and biological basis. It is quite possible for sex-specific adaptations to be absent at birth and only develop when they become useful to the organism. To cite just one example, breasts in girls do not develop until puberty, but it would be absurd to argue that they are a product of learning or socialization.

The Nature of Development

Evolution and development are more than deeply connected—they are inseparable. Organs and behaviors do not just appear from nowhere but develop over time, ultimately from a single cell; indeed, selection can only modify the traits of an organism by acting on the developmental processes that build them. At the same time, developmental mechanisms are shaped by selection as adaptations in their own right (West-Eberhard, 2003). An evolutionary perspective can illuminate human development in myriad different ways (see Bjorklund & Ellis, 2014; Ellis & Bjorklund, 2005). In addition to models of G × E interactions and differential susceptibility, the last few years have seen tremendous progress in our understanding of sensitive periods and functionally specialized learning processes (Barrett, 2015; Frankenhuis & Fraley, 2017). In this section, I briefly focus on the stages and transitions that make up the life cycle.

Human Life Stages

The trajectory of human development can be segmented into a small number of relatively well-defined stages: fetal life, infancy, early childhood (about 3–7 years), middle childhood (about 7–11 years in modern societies), adolescence, and adulthood. In women, postmenopausal life can also be regarded as a distinct stage. Life stages are characterized by clusters of physical, cognitive, and behavioral features, and are joined to one another by phases of rapid change (transitions), usually mediated by specific hormonal mechanisms. The key biological function of stages is to organize life-history tasks into an optimal sequence. Most organisms go through at least two stages: An initial phase of growth is followed by the transition to reproductive maturity, after which energy is diverted from growth and used to produce offspring. From the standpoint of motivation, each life stage corresponds to the activation of particular biological goals and a rearrangement of the organism's priorities (Del Giudice et al., 2015).

To illustrate these concepts, consider the critical but often neglected stage of middle childhood (Del Giudice, 2014b), which roughly corresponds to *juvenility*, a life stage found in primates and other mammals in which the young are still sexually immature, yet no longer dependent on adults for feeding and protection. Middle childhood starts around age 6–8 years with the eruption of the first permanent teeth and the awakening of the adrenal gland (*adrenarche*), which begins to secrete increasing amounts of androgens. Adrenal androgens promote neural plasticity, and shift the allocation of energy away from the brain and toward the accumulation of muscle and fat in preparation for puberty. They can also be converted to testosterone and estrogens in the brain, activating sexually differentiated pathways and regulating brain development in a sex-specific manner (Campbell, 2011; Del Giudice, 2014b; Del Giudice, Angeleri, & Manera, 2009). The changes of middle childhood include dramatic increases in self-control and motor skills, enabling juveniles to help with domestic tasks—foraging, preparing food, taking care of younger siblings, and so on. Overall, middle childhood combines intensive social learning and *integration* into one's group and culture with the emergence of social *competition* for status among peers.

Middle childhood is marked by the onset or intensification of sex differences in aggression, social play, attachment styles, and some personality traits (mainly agreeableness and facets of conscientiousness and openness; Soto et al., 2011). The mating system also becomes activated, as reflected in the first sexual and/or romantic attractions. The initial activation of mating and status goals not only prepares children for competition in adolescence but also provides them with important feedback on their attractiveness, competence, dominance, and overall desirability as social partners. Not coincidentally, individual differences in self-esteem are virtually absent in young children but emerge rapidly with the transition to middle childhood (Harter, 2012). With the eruption of permanent teeth and the maturation of fine motor skills, children become capable of feeding themselves; this exposes them to new threats from rotten or poisonous food, and likely explain the sudden increase in disgust sensitivity that is observed at this age (see Del Giudice, 2014b).

The middle childhood stage ends with the transition to adolescence, marked by a characteristic growth spurt and the onset of sex hormones production by the gonads (*gonadarche*). Adolescence completes physical growth and transform children into sexually mature adults. Predictably, sexual and competitive motivations become even more salient to adolescents; this motivational shift is paralleled by enhanced sensitivity to social cues and social evaluation, and by a dramatic increase in risk-taking behavior (especially in boys; Ellis et al., 2012). During adolescence, sex differences in conscientiousness and agreeableness show a temporary decline, whereas those in neuroticism and extraversion appear for the first time (Soto et al., 2011). This pattern of sex differences matches the different social styles of males and females,

and reflects the changing cost–benefit balance of physical aggression, social exclusion, and so on (Benenson, 2014; Del Giudice, 2015b).

Developmental Switch Points

The nature of transitions between life stages can be illuminated by the concept of developmental switch points, a modern extension of the classic idea of sensitive periods (West-Eberhard, 2003). A *developmental switch* is a regulatory mechanism that activates at a specific point in development, collects input from the external environment and/or the internal state of the organism, and shifts the individual along alternative pathways that result in different outcomes. For example, a switch may regulate the development of aggressive behavior so that safe conditions entrain the development of low levels of aggression, whereas threatening environments trigger high levels of aggression. Developmental switches are often implemented through hormonal signals; their activation controls the coordinated expression of multiple sets of genes—both those involved in the regulatory mechanism itself and those involved in the expression of the new traits. The transition to middle childhood and the onset of puberty are two crucial switch points in human development; they are mediated by the hormonal mechanisms of adrenarche and gonadarche, respectively (Del Giudice et al., 2009; Ellis, 2013). Other, less studied but potentially critical switch points are pregnancy and childbirth—which trigger hormonal changes in both mothers and fathers—and the onset of menopause (Del Giudice & Belsky, 2011).

A key feature of developmental switches is that they integrate environmental information with variation in the genes that regulate the switch; for example, genetic factors may partly determine the threshold for switching between alternative developmental pathways. The embodied effects of past experiences may also modulate the switch (e.g., via epigenetic mechanisms), allowing the organism to integrate information over time and across life stages. Like a sensitive period, a developmental switch point implies heightened sensitivity to the environment, but with a crucial difference: Since genetic and environmental inputs converge in the same regulatory mechanism, a developmental switch can not only amplify the individual's susceptibility to some aspects of the environment but also reveal the effects of genetic factors that were previously hidden from view. Accordingly, twin studies of traits as disparate as aggression, prosociality, and language skills consistently show the emergence of substantial new genetic factors during the transition from early to middle childhood (see Del Giudice, 2014b).

Ontogenetic and Deferred Adaptations

Looking at developmental stages through the lens of biological function suggests a useful distinction between two kinds of adaptations that are often observed in early life. *Ontogenetic adaptations* are designed to serve their fitness-enhancing function at a specific time in development, and often disappear as soon as they are no longer needed. Examples include the placenta (a fetal organ that provides nourishment and other vital functions during the fetal stage and is discarded immediately after birth) and infantile reflexes, such as the suckling reflex. *Deferred adaptations* are traits that appear in childhood but function—at least in part—to prepare children for adult behavior (Bjorklund & Ellis, 2014). Play is a paramount example of a deferred adaptation; in humans and other mammals, playing trains youngsters to deal with unexpected events and, at the same time, paves the way to the acquisition of specialized adult skills (e.g., foraging, fighting, parenting) (Geary, 2010; Spinka, Newberry, & Bekoff, 2001).

The concept of an ontogenetic adaptation is particularly useful to understand the limits of early experiences in shaping adult personality. Some behavioral traits expressed in childhood serve important functions in the context of family life but may cease to be useful as the child turns into an independent adult. These traits may either disappear or get repurposed in a different form in the service of new developmental goals. For example, attachment styles in infancy are largely determined by the parents' caregiving styles and show negligible genetic effects. In middle childhood, attachment styles start to become differentiated by sex, possibly under the influence of adrenal androgens; adults' attachment styles to romantic partners are only weakly correlated with those of infancy, and reflect a sizable contribution of genetic factors (Barbaro, Boutwell, Barnes, & Shackelford, 2017; Del Giudice, 2009, 2015a). At an even deeper level, the existence of parent–offspring conflict implies that the parents' behavior is not *completely* in the best interest of their children.

For this reason, children should not passively accept the influence of parents; instead, they should show a certain amount of developmental "resistance" to parental shaping. While it is difficult to directly test this hypothesis, parent–offspring conflict may well contribute to explain why family experiences have only small and inconsistent effects on the development of adult personality.

Conclusion

At the beginning of this chapter, I argued that evolutionary psychology offers an integrative theoretical framework for personality development and a wealth of insights into the nature of motivation, variation, and developmental processes. On the one hand, the evolutionary approach solidifies some long-standing, even commonsense intuitions—for example, about the ubiquity of social conflicts and the importance of sex differences. On the other hand, it drastically restructures previously familiar ideas, and introduces notions that are often counterintuitive and sometimes unsettling. Philosopher Daniel Dennett (1995) likened this effect of evolutionary theory to that of a "universal acid"—it eats through every traditional concept it touches and leaves in its wake something that is still recognizable but transformed in fundamental ways. In addition to summarizing basic ideas and findings, I hope I have succeeded in conveying some of the excitement that permeates the field, and sparked the reader's curiosity about what lies ahead.

REFERENCES

Alvergne, A., Jokela, M., & Lummaa, V. (2010). Personality and reproductive success in a high-fertility human population. *Proceedings of the National Academy of Sciences of the USA, 107,* 11745–11750.

Andrews, P. W., Gangestad, S. W., & Matthews, D. (2002). Adaptationism—how to carry out an exaptationist program. *Behavioral and Brain Sciences, 25,* 489–504.

Archer, J., & Mehdikhani, M. (2003). Variability among males in sexually selected attributes. *Review of General Psychology, 7,* 219–236.

Ashton, M. C. (2013). *Individual differences and personality* (2nd ed.). New York: Academic Press.

Aunger, R., & Curtis, V. (2013). The anatomy of motivation: An evolutionary–ecological approach. *Biological Theory, 8,* 49–63.

Barbaro, N., Boutwell, B. B., Barnes, J. C., & Shackelford, T. K. (2017). Rethinking the transmission gap: What behavioral genetics and evolutionary psychology mean for attachment theory: A comment on Verhage et al. (2016). *Psychological Bulletin, 143,* 107–113.

Barkley, R. A. (2012). *Executive functions: What they are, how they work, and why they evolved.* New York: Guilford Press.

Barrett, H. C. (2015). *The shape of thought: How mental adaptations evolve.* New York: Oxford University Press.

Baumard, N., André, J.-B., & Sperber, D. (2013). A mutualistic approach to morality: The evolution of fairness by partner choice. *Behavioral and Brain Sciences, 36,* 59–122.

Belsky, J. (1997). Variation in susceptibility to rearing influences: An evolutionary argument. *Psychological Inquiry, 8,* 182–186.

Belsky, J., & Pluess, M. (2009). Beyond diathesis–stress: Differential susceptibility to environmental influences. *Psychological Bulletin, 135,* 885–908.

Benenson, J. F. (2014). *Warriors and worriers: The survival of the sexes.* New York: Oxford University Press.

Berg, V., Lummaa, V., Lahdenperä, M., Rotkirch, A., & Jokela, M. (2014). Personality and long-term reproductive success measured by the number of grandchildren. *Evolution and Human Behavior, 35,* 533–539.

Bjorklund, D. F., & Ellis, B. J. (2014). Children, childhood, and development in evolutionary perspective. *Developmental Review, 34,* 225–264.

Bourke, A. F. G. (2011). *Principles of social evolution.* New York: Oxford University Press.

Bowles, S., & Gintis, H. (2011). *A cooperative species: Human reciprocity and its evolution.* Princeton, NJ: Princeton University Press.

Boyce, W. T., & Ellis, B. J. (2005). Biological sensitivity to context: I. An evolutionary–developmental theory of the origins and functions of stress reactivity. *Development and Psychopathology, 17,* 271–301.

Buss, D. M. (2015a). *Evolutionary psychology: The new science of the mind* (5th ed.). New York: Routledge.

Buss, D. M. (Ed.). (2015b). *The handbook of evolutionary psychology* (2nd ed.). New York: Wiley.

Buss, D. M., & Hawley, P. H. (2011). *The evolution of personality and individual differences.* New York: Oxford University Press.

Campbell, B. C. (2011). Adrenarche and middle childhood. *Human Nature, 22,* 327–349.

Carere, C., & Maestripieri, D. (2013). *Animal personalities: Behavior, physiology, and evolution.* Chicago: University of Chicago Press.

Chabris, C. F., Lee, J. J., Cesarini, D., Benjamin, D. J., & Laibson, D. I. (2015). The fourth law of behavior genetics. *Current Directions in Psychological Science, 24,* 304–312.

Cochran, G., & Harpending, H. (2009). *The 10,000 year explosion: How civilization accelerated human evolution.* New York: Basic Books.

Corr, P. J., DeYoung, C. G., & McNaughton, N. (2013). Motivation and personality: A neuropsychological perspective. *Social and Personality Psychology Compass, 7,* 158–175.

Cosmides, L., & Tooby, J. (2015). Adaptations for reasoning about social exchange. In D. M. Buss (Ed.), *The handbook of evolutionary psychology: Vol. 2. Integrations* (2nd ed., pp. 625–668). New York: Wiley.

Curtis, V. (2011). Why disgust matters. *Philosophical Transactions of the Royal Society of London B, 366,* 3478–3490.

Dawkins, R. (1976). *The selfish gene.* Oxford, UK: Oxford University Press.

DeBruine, L. M., Jones, B. C., Little, A. C., & Perrett, D. I. (2008). Social perception of facial resemblance in humans. *Archives of Sexual Behavior, 37,* 64–77.

Deci, E. L., & Ryan, R. M. (2000). The "what" and "why" of goal pursuits: Human needs and the self-determination of behavior. *Psychological Inquiry, 11,* 227–268.

Del Giudice, M. (2009). Sex, attachment, and the development of reproductive strategies. *Behavioral and Brain Sciences, 32,* 1–21.

Del Giudice, M. (2012). Sex ratio dynamics and fluctuating selection on personality. *Journal of Theoretical Biology, 297,* 48–60.

Del Giudice, M. (2013). Multivariate misgivings: Is *D* a valid measure of group and sex differences? *Evolutionary Psychology, 11,* 1067–1076.

Del Giudice, M. (2014a). An evolutionary life history framework for psychopathology. *Psychological Inquiry, 25,* 261–300.

Del Giudice, M. (2014b). Middle childhood: An evolutionary–developmental synthesis. *Child Development Perspectives, 8,* 193–200.

Del Giudice, M. (2015a). Attachment in middle childhood: An evolutionary–developmental perspective. *New Directions for Child and Adolescent Development, 148,* 15–30.

Del Giudice, M. (2015b). Gender differences in personality and social behavior. In J. D. Wright (Ed.), *International encyclopedia of the social and behavioral sciences* (2nd ed., pp. 750–756). New York: Elsevier.

Del Giudice, M. (2015c). Plasticity as a developing trait: Exploring the implications. *Frontiers in Zoology, 12*(Suppl. 1), S4.

Del Giudice, M. (2017). Statistical tests of differential susceptibility: Performance, limitations, and improvements. *Development and Psychopathology, 29*(4), 1267–1278.

Del Giudice, M. (2018). *Evolutionary psychopathology: A unified approach.* New York: Oxford University Press.

Del Giudice, M., Angeleri, R., & Manera, V. (2009). The juvenile transition: A developmental switch point in human life history. *Developmental Review, 29,* 1–31.

Del Giudice, M., & Belsky, J. (2011). The development of life history strategies: Toward a multi-stage theory. In D. M. Buss & P. H. Hawley (Eds.), *The evolution of personality and individual differences* (pp. 154–176). New York: Oxford University Press.

Del Giudice, M., Booth, T., & Irwing, P. (2012). The distance between Mars and Venus: Measuring global sex differences in personality. *PLOS ONE, 7,* e29265.

Del Giudice, M., Gangestad, S. W., & Kaplan, H. S. (2015). Life history theory and evolutionary psychology. In D. M. Buss (Ed.), *The handbook of evolutionary psychology: Vol 1. Foundations* (2nd ed., pp. 88–114). Hoboken, NJ: Wiley.

Del Giudice, M., Klimczuk, A. C. E., Traficonte, D. M., & Maestripieri, D. (2014). Autistic-like and schizotypal traits in a life history perspective: Diametrical associations with impulsivity, sensation seeking, and sociosexual behavior. *Evolution and Human Behavior, 35,* 415–424.

Denissen, J. J., & Penke, L. (2008). Motivational individual reaction norms underlying the Five-Factor model of personality: First steps towards a theory-based conceptual framework. *Journal of Research in Personality, 42,* 1285–1302.

Dennett, D. C. (1995). *Darwin's dangerous idea: Evolution and the meanings of life.* New York: Simon & Schuster.

DeScioli, P., & Kurzban, R. (2013). A solution to the mysteries of morality. *Psychological Bulletin, 139,* 477–496.

Dunbar, R. I. M. (1993). Co-evolution of neocortex size, group size and language in humans. *Behavioral and Brain Sciences, 16,* 681–735.

Dunbar, R. I. M., & Shultz, S. (2007). Evolution in the social brain. *Science, 317,* 1344–1347.

Duncan, L. E., Pollastri, A. R., & Smoller, J. W. (2014). Mind the gap: Why many geneticists and psychological scientists have discrepant views about gene–environment interaction (G×E) research. *American Psychologist, 69,* 249–268.

Durrant, R., & Ellis, B. J. (2012). Evolutionary psychology. In I. B. Weiner, R. J. Nelson, & S. Mizumori (Eds.), *Handbook of psychology: Vol. 3. Behavioral neuroscience* (2nd ed., pp. 26–51). Hoboken, NJ: Wiley.

Ellis, B. J. (2013). The hypothalamic–pituitary–gonadal axis: A switch-controlled, condition-sensitive system in the regulation of life history strategies. *Hormones and Behavior, 64,* 215–225.

Ellis, B. J., & Bjorklund, D. F. (Eds.). (2005). *Origins of the social mind: Evolutionary psychology and child development.* New York: Guilford Press.

Ellis, B. J., Boyce, W. T., Belsky, J., Bakermans-Kranenburg, M. J., & van IJzendoorn, M. H. (2011). Differential susceptibility to the environment: An evolutionary–neurodevelopmental theory. *Development and Psychopathology, 23,* 7–28.

Ellis, B. J., & Del Giudice, M. (2019). Developmental adaptation to stress: An evolutionary perspective. *Annual Review of Psychology, 70.* [EPub ahead of print]

Ellis, B. J., Del Giudice, M., Dishion, T. J., Figueredo, A. J., Gray, P., Griskevicius, V., et al. (2012). The evolutionary basis of risky adolescent behavior: Im-

plications for science, policy, and practice. *Developmental Psychology, 48,* 598–623.

Ellis, B. J., Figueredo, A. J., Brumbach, B. H., & Schlomer, G. L. (2009). The impact of harsh versus unpredictable environments on the evolution and development of life history strategies. *Human Nature, 20,* 204–268.

Feldman, R. (2017). The neurobiology of human attachments. *Trends in Cognitive Sciences, 21,* 80–99.

Figueredo, A. J., Sefcek, J. A., Vasquez, G., Brumbach, B. H., King, J. E., & Jacobs, W. J. (2005). Evolutionary personality psychology. In In D. M. Buss (Ed.), *The handbook of evolutionary psychology* (pp. 851–877). Hoboken, NJ: Wiley.

Figueredo, A. J., Woodley of Menie, M. A., & Jacobs, J. (2015). The General Factor of Personality: A hierarchical life history model. In D. M. Buss (Ed.), *The handbook of evolutionary psychology: Vol 2. Integrations* (2nd ed., pp. 943–967). Hoboken, NJ: Wiley.

Frankenhuis, W. E., & Fraley, R. C. (2017). What do evolutionary models teach us about sensitive periods in psychological development? *European Psychologist, 22,* 141–150.

Gangestad, S. W. (2011). Evolutionary processes explaining the genetic variance in personality: An exploration of scenarios. In D. M. Buss & P. H. Hawley (Eds.), *The evolution of personality and individual differences* (pp. 338–375). New York: Oxford University Press.

Geary, D. C. (2010). *Male, female: The evolution of human sex differences* (2nd ed.). Washington, DC: APA Press.

Grafen, A. (2007). The formal Darwinism project: A mid-term report. *Journal of Evolutionary Biology, 20,* 1243–1254.

Gurven, M., von Rueden, C., Massenkoff, M., Kaplan, H., & Lero Vie, M. (2013). How universal is the Big Five?: Testing the five-factor model of personality variation among forager-farmers in the Bolivian Amazon. *Journal of Personality and Social Psychology, 104,* 354–370.

Haidt, J. (2007). The new synthesis in moral psychology. *Science, 316,* 998–1002.

Haidt, J. (2012). *The righteous mind: Why good people are divided by politics and religion.* New York: Pantheon.

Haig, D., & Wharton, R. (2003). Prader–Willi syndrome and the evolution of human childhood. *American Journal of Human Biology, 15,* 320–329.

Hamilton, W. D. (1964). The genetical evolution of social behavior. *Journal of Theoretical Biology, 7,* 1–52.

Harter, S. (2012). *The construction of the self: Developmental and sociocultural foundations.* New York: Guilford Press.

Hawley, P. H. (2014). Ontogeny and social dominance: A developmental view of human power patterns. *Evolutionary Psychology, 12,* 318–342.

Henrich, J., & Gil-White, F. J. (2001). The evolution of

prestige: Freely conferred deference as a mechanism for enhancing the benefits of cultural transmission. *Evolution and Human Behavior, 22,* 165–196.

Hyde, J. S. (2014). Gender similarities and differences. *Annual Review of Psychology, 65,* 373–398.

Jonason, P. K., Koenig, B. L., & Tost, J. (2010). Living a fast life: The Dark Triad and life history theory. *Human Nature, 21,* 428–442.

Kaplan, H. S., Gurven, M., & Lancaster, J. B. (2007). Brain evolution and the human adaptive complex: An ecological and social theory. In S. W. Gangestad & J. A. Simpson (Eds.), *The evolution of mind: Fundamental questions and controversies* (pp. 269–279). New York: Guilford Press.

Kaplan, H. S., Hill, K., Lancaster, J. B., & Hurtado, A. M. (2000). A theory of human life history evolution: Diet, intelligence, and longevity. *Evolutionary Anthropology, 9,* 156–185.

Kavanagh, P. S., Robins, S. C., & Ellis, B. J. (2010). The mating sociometer: A regulatory mechanism for mating aspirations. *Journal of Personality and Social Psychology, 99,* 120–132.

Kenrick, D. T., Griskevicius, V., Neuberg, S. L., & Schaller, M. (2010). Renovating the pyramid of needs: Contemporary extensions built upon ancient foundations. *Perspectives on Psychological Science, 5,* 292–314.

Kirkpatrick, L. A., & Ellis, B. J. (2001). An evolutionary–psychological approach to self-esteem: Multiple domains and multiple functions. In G. Fletcher & M. Clark (Eds.), *The Blackwell handbook of social psychology: Vol. 2. Interpersonal processes* (pp. 411–436). Oxford, UK: Blackwell.

Knopik, V. S., Neiderhiser, J. M., DeFries, J. C., & Plomin, R. (2017). *Behavioral genetics* (7th ed.). New York: Worth.

Kramer, P., & Bressan, P. (2015). Humans as superorganisms: How microbes, viruses, imprinted genes, and other selfish entities shape our behavior. *Perspectives on Psychological Science, 10,* 464–481.

Leary, M. R. (2005). Sociometer theory and the pursuit of relational value: Getting to the root of self-esteem. *European Review of Social Psychology, 16,* 75–111.

Ledón-Rettig, C. C., Richards, C. L., & Martin, L. B. (2013). Epigenetics for behavioral ecologists. *Behavioral Ecology, 24,* 311–324.

Lukaszewski, A. W., Gurven, M., von Rueden, C. R., & Schmitt, D. P. (2017). What explains personality covariation?: A test of the socioecological complexity hypothesis. *Social Psychological and Personality Science, 18,* 943–952.

Lukaszewski, A. W., & von Rueden, C. R. (2015). The extraversion continuum in evolutionary perspective: A review of recent theory and evidence. *Personality and Individual Differences, 77,* 186–192.

Machin, A. J., & Dunbar, R. I. (2011). The brain opioid theory of social attachment: A review of the evidence. *Behaviour, 148,* 985–1025.

McAdams, D. P. (2015). *The art and science of personality development.* New York: Guilford Press.

Meaney, M. J. (2010). Epigenetics and the biological definition of gene × environment interactions. *Child Development, 81,* 41–79.

Moore, S. R., & Depue, R. A. (2016). Neurobehavioral foundations of environmental reactivity. *Psychological Bulletin, 142,* 107–164.

Nesse, R. M. (2007). Runaway social selection for displays of partner value and altruism. *Biological Theory, 2,* 143–155.

Nettle, D. (2011). Evolutionary perspectives on the Five Factor model of personality. In D. M. Buss & P. H. Hawley (Eds.), *The evolution of personality and individual differences* (pp. 5–28). New York: Oxford University Press.

Olderbak, S., Gladden, P., Wolf, P. S. A., & Figueredo, A. J. (2014). Comparison of life history strategy measures. *Personality and Individual Differences, 58,* 82–88.

Penke, L., & Jokela, M. (2016). The evolutionary genetics of personality revisited. *Current Opinion in Psychology, 7,* 104–109.

Pinker, S. (2010). The cognitive niche: Coevolution of intelligence, sociality, and language. *Proceedings of the National Academy of Sciences of the USA, 107,* 8993–8999.

Pinker, S. (2011). *The better angels of our nature: Why violence has declined.* New York: Viking.

Scalise Sugiyama, M. (2011). The forager oral tradition and the evolution of prolonged juvenility. *Frontiers in Psychology, 2,* 133.

Schlomer, G. L., Del Giudice, M., & Ellis, B. J. (2011). Parent–offspring conflict theory: An evolutionary framework for understanding conflict within human families. *Psychological Review, 118,* 496–521.

Schmitt, D. P., & Pilcher, J. J. (2004). Evaluating evidence of psychological adaptation: How do we know one when we see one? *Psychological Science, 15,* 643–649.

Scott-Phillips, T. C., Dickins, T. E., & West, S. A. (2011). Evolutionary theory and the ultimate–proximate distinction in the human behavioral sciences. *Perspectives on Psychological Science, 6,* 38–47.

Simpson, J. A., & Belsky, J. (2016). Attachment theory within a modern evolutionary framework. In J. Cassidy & P. R. Shaver (Eds.), *Handbook of attachment: Theory, research, and clinical applications* (3rd ed., pp. 91–116). New York: Guilford Press.

Simpson, J. A., & Campbell, L. (2015). Methods of evolutionary sciences. In D. M. Buss (Ed.), *The handbook of evolutionary psychology: Vol 1. Foundations* (2nd ed., pp. 115–135). Hoboken, NJ: Wiley.

Slagt, M., Dubas, J. S., Deković, M., & van Aken, M. A. G. (2016). Differences in sensitivity to parenting depending on child temperament: A meta-analysis. *Psychological Bulletin, 142,* 1068–1110.

Soto, C. J., John, O. P., Gosling, S. D., & Potter, J. (2011). Age differences in personality traits from 10 to 65: Big Five domains and facets in a large cross-sectional sample. *Journal of Personality and Social Psychology, 100,* 330–348.

Specht, J., Bleidorn, W., Denissen, J. J., Hennecke, M., Hutteman, R., Kandler, C., et al. (2014). What drives adult personality development?: A comparison of theoretical perspectives and empirical evidence. *European Journal of Personality, 28,* 216–230.

Spinka, M., Newberry, R. C., & Bekoff, M. (2001). Mammalian play: Training for the unexpected. *Quarterly Review of Biology, 76,* 141–168.

Stanyon, R., & Bigoni, F. (2014). Sexual selection and the evolution of behavior, morphology, neuroanatomy and genes in humans and other primates. *Neuroscience and Biobehavioral Reviews, 46,* 579–590.

Tooby, J., & Cosmides, L. (2015). The theoretical foundations of evolutionary psychology. In D. M. Buss (Ed.), *The handbook of evolutionary psychology: Vol 1. Foundations* (2nd ed., pp. 3–87). Hoboken, NJ: Wiley.

Toronchuk, J. A., & Ellis, G. F. (2013). Affective neuronal selection: The nature of the primordial emotion systems. *Frontiers in Psychology, 3,* 589.

Trivers, R. L. (1974). Parent–offspring conflict. *American Zoologist, 14,* 249–264.

Úbeda, F., & Gardner, A. (2011). A model for genomic imprinting in the social brain: Adults. *Evolution, 65,* 462–475.

West, S. A., & Gardner, A. (2013). Adaptation and inclusive fitness. *Current Biology, 23,* r577–r584.

West-Eberhard, M. J. (2003). *Developmental plasticity and evolution.* New York: Oxford University Press.

Woody, E. Z., & Szechtman, H. (2011). Adaptation to potential threat: The evolution, neurobiology, and psychopathology of the security motivation system. *Neuroscience and Biobehavioral Reviews, 35,* 1019–1033.

Zietsch, B. P. (2016). Individual differences as the output of evolved calibration mechanisms: Does the theory make sense in view of empirical observations? *Current Opinion in Psychology, 7,* 71–75.

CHAPTER 3

Theoretical Concepts in the Genetics of Personality Development

Elliot M. Tucker–Drob
Daniel A. Briley

How do genetic and environmental factors combine to give rise to individual differences in personality? How do such factors operate over time to give rise to individual differences in personality development and change? These are some of the most fundamental questions within differential psychology. However, the answers to these questions are not straightforward. Individual differences may arise, persist forward, and decay over time by way of a complex system of endogenous and contextual influences that themselves come to be correlated with and interact with one another over time. In this chapter we review several classes of developmental mechanisms that may influence the course of personality stability and change. We begin by describing behavioral genetic methodology and some of the key descriptive findings that such methodology has produced. We then describe and illustrate several theoretical mechanisms of the genetics of personality development, and consider how such mechanisms may combine and interact.

Developmental Behavioral Genetic Methods and Key Descriptive Findings

Standard behavioral genetic methods provide a descriptive account of the extent to which individual differences in personality are sta-

tistically associated with genetic differences between people, the extent to which individual differences in personality are associated with the rearing environment that individuals share with their siblings (the *shared environment*), and the extent to which individual differences in personality persist after accounting for these two factors (the *nonshared environment*). When appropriately applied to longitudinal data, behavioral genetic methods can also provide a descriptive account of the extent to which rank-order stability and individual differences in change are associated with genetic, shared environmental, and nonshared environmental factors. Just as is the case for descriptive information regarding phenotypic (i.e., observed) age trends in the mean, variability, and rank-order stability of personality traits, such descriptive information regarding genetic and environmental components of individual differences can be highly valuable for distinguishing between alternative theories of personality development, constraining theories of personality development, and generating new mechanistic theories of personality development. For instance, phenotypic trends have served as the basis for foundational principles in lifespan personality psychology (Roberts, Wood, & Caspi, 2008), such as the cumulative continuity principle (that the rank-order stability of personality increases with age), the maturity principle (that people, on average, become more dominant, agreeable, conscientious, and emotionally stable, from adolescence forward), and the corresponsive principle (that the typical effect of life experience on personality is to magnify the characteristics that led to those experiences); however, empirical work to identify the precise contexts and life experiences that undergird these processes is still preliminary (Bleidorn, Hopwood, & Lucas, 2018). Similarly, standard behavioral genetic methods provide key information about how latent genetic and environmental sources of variation contribute to individual differences in personality variation, stability, and change that can be used to construct, develop, and test theory, but they do not by themselves provide direct empirical information about how specific genes, contexts, or life experiences combine and interact over development to shape personality. As we discuss at the end of this chapter, we believe that a more complete understanding of how individual differences in personality arise and develop over time can be achieved through careful integration of behavioral genetic theory, methods, and results into ongoing theoretical and empirical work in mainstream personality psychology.

Conventional work in the behavioral genetics of personality largely focused on single point estimates of heritability of personality. For instance, point estimates for the heritability of all of the Big Five personality traits have been reported to be approximately .40–.60 (for a review, see Bouchard & McGue, 2003), with no consistent differences reported across different Big Five traits (Turkheimer, Pettersson, & Horn, 2014). Evidence for genetic influences on personality are derived from the observation that genetically more related individuals (e.g., identical twins) are more similar in their personality traits than genetically less related individuals (e.g., fraternal twins), even when researchers hold shared rearing environment constant across relationship types. Also of note is that after accounting for genetic relatedness, individuals reared together are no more similar to one another in their personalities than would be expected for individuals chosen at random out of the population. Nongenetic factors that differentiate individuals regardless of whether they shared a rearing environment with one another are termed the *nonshared environment*. These two important and interesting observations, that the heritability of personality is approximately 40–60% at the population level

and that nongenetic variation in personality is attributable to nonshared environmental factors, are the primary findings from behavioral genetics that inform conventional personality theories. Yet they do not do justice to the important developmental patterns in the genetics of personality.

The relative influence of genetic and environmental effects may shift across the lifespan rather than remain static. Age trends in the heritability of personality have been reported in quantitative syntheses by Kandler (2012) for neuroticism and extraversion, and Briley and Tucker-Drob (2014) for all of the Big Five. In both syntheses, age trends have been very similar across each of the Big Five traits. We therefore consider the aggregate trend reported by Briley and Tucker-Drob. Figure 3.1 presents the main findings. It can be seen that the heritability of personality (left panel) is highest in early life, decreasing most precipitously in childhood and adolescence, and far more gradually in adulthood, with a countervailing trend for environmentality (right panel). Heritability of personality is estimated at approximately 70% in early childhood, declines to approximately 50% by late adolescence, and subsequently declines to approximately 35% by late adulthood. Nonshared environmentality increases from approximately 30–50% to 65% from infancy to late adolescence, to late adulthood. However, at least some of this trend may reflect method bias, as nearly all of the effect sizes for very young children come from parent reports. These ratings may exaggerate differences between siblings and thus inflate heritability.

Behavioral genetic methods have also been applied to probe the role of genetic and environmental factors in the rank-order stability of personality over time. Rank-order stability refers to the correlation between individual differences in personality at one point in time and a later point in time. As patterns for rank-order stability are very similar across Big Five traits, we focus on the aggregate pattern here. Two major research syntheses have described the overall phenotypic pattern of age trends in rank-order stability that behavioral genetic research has gone on to probe. As displayed in the top two panels of Figure 3.2, results from both Roberts and DelVecchio (2000) and Ferguson (2010) have indicated that the rank-order stability of personality (over an average time interval of approximately 6.6 years) increases relatively monotonically over the first 30 years of life,

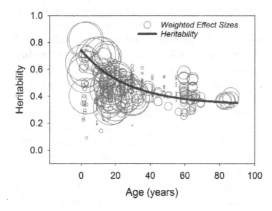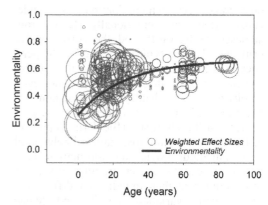

FIGURE 3.1. Genetic and (nonshared) environmental influences on individual differences in personality across the lifespan. Shared environmental influences on personality tend to be absent at all ages and are therefore not modeled. Meta-analytic results from longitudinal behavioral genetic studies. Adapted from Briley and Tucker-Drob (2014).

after which point it remains very high. Roberts and DelVecchio reported increases in rank-order stability from approximately .35 in infancy to .65 by age 30 years. Ferguson, who disattenuated stability coefficients for unreliability, reported somewhat higher stability coefficients, with rank-order stability increasing from approximately .50 to .90 over this same age range. Briley and Tucker-Drob (2014), Kandler (2012), and Turkheimer and colleagues (2014) have all examined meta-analytically the role of genetic and environmental factors in rank-order stability. Results from Briley and Tucker-Drob, who provide the most comprehensive treatment of the topic, are represented in the bottom two panels of Figure 3.2. These plots indicate the genetic (circles and solid line in bottom left panel) and nonshared environmental (circles and solid line in bottom right panel) contributions to overall phenotypic stability (dashed line) as a function of age, over an average longitudinal time lag of approximately 5.6 years. First, it can be seen that the overall trend in phenotypic stability closely matches the trend reported by Roberts and DelVecchio, with rank-order stability increases from approximately .35 in infancy to .65 by age 30 years. Behavioral genetic decomposition indicates that stability in infancy is exclusively driven by genetic factors, and that the genetic contribution remains at the same level (~.35) for the entirety of the lifespan. A *genetic contribution* to stability refers to the extent to which the correlation between the same personality trait across two points in

time is statistically accounted for by the influence of overlapping sets of genetic variants on that trait at both time points. (Genetic factors would not contribution to stability, even if personality were heritable at both time points, if different sets of genes were responsible for individual differences in personality at the two time points.) Increasing phenotypic stability with age is driven exclusively by an increase in the nonshared environmental contribution to stability from no contribution in infancy to approximately .35 correlation units by late adulthood, such that the overall phenotypic stability increases from approximately .35 to .70 during this time. A *nonshared environmental contribution to stability* refers to the extent to which the correlation between the same personality trait across two points in time is statistically accounted for by the influence of overlapping or covarying nonshared environmental factors at both points in time. (If entirely different and uncorrelated environmental factors, e.g., adolescent peer group and adult occupational stress, are responsible for individual differences in personality at two different time points in time, then environmental factors will not contribute to stability, even though they contribute to individual differences at each time point.)

How can a researcher or student without a strong background in behavioral genetics make intuitive sense of these findings? For instance, what is the meaning of the finding that the overwhelming majority of stable variance in personality at early ages (e.g., age 5 years) is driven by

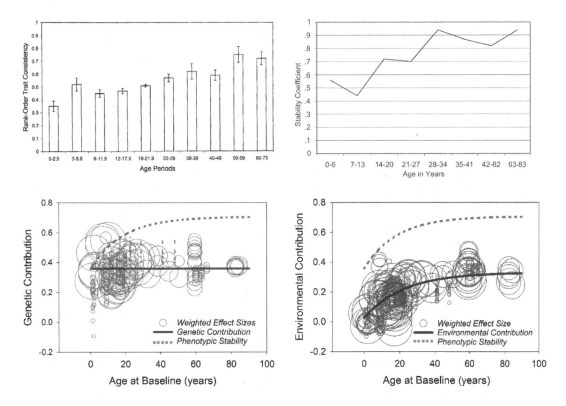

FIGURE 3.2. *Top left panel*: Longitudinal rank-order (test–retest) stability of personality. From Roberts and DelVecchio (2000). Copyright 2000 by the American Psychological Association. Reprinted with permission. *Top right panel*: Disattenuated longitudinal rank-order (test–retest) stability of personality. From Ferguson (2010). Copyright 2000 by the American Psychological Association. Reprinted with permission. *Bottom left panel*: Genetic contribution to longitudinal rank-order (test–retest) stability of personality adapted from Briley and Tucker-Drob (2014) meta-analysis. *Bottom right panel*: Environmetnal contribution to longitudinal rank-order (test–retest) stability of personality adapted from Briley and Tucker-Drob (2014) meta-analysis.

genetic factors? One way to describe this finding is that if each person in the population were raised together with an identical twin (with whom he or she has 100% of DNA in common), then the level of a personality trait (e.g., extraversion) for a given person at age 5 would be nearly as predictive as his or her cotwin's score on that personality trait at age 15 as it was of his or her own score at age 15. Alternatively, if each person in the population were raised together with a fraternal twin (with whom he or she shares only 50% of the DNA variation that differs within humans), then the level of a personality trait for a given person at age 5 would be less predictive of his or her cotwin's score on that personality trait at age 15 than it was of his or her own score at age 15. This knowledge, that stability of earlier personality is mediated by genetic factors,

can help us to reduce the possible set of causal mechanisms for personality stability to a subset that is most plausible. For example, on the basis of this result, it might be fruitful to examine how DNA sequence variation relates to the efficiency of hormonal production, brain structure, or some other biological process. It may be similarly fruitful to examine how individuals evoke or actively create environmental experiences that are in some way linked to their temperaments. (We discuss below why this seemingly environmentally mediated process is relevant in the context of large or total genetic influence on stability.) However, the finding that environmental factors contribute negligibly to stability of early personality rules out major roles for random sorts of environmental experiences (e.g., car crashes, illnesses, uncontrollable family events) in early life in the stability of personality in the population at large. Moreover, that the shared environment does not account for personality variation further reduces the viability of examining differences in experience that cluster within families as systematic correlates of personality variation. In other words, the behavioral genetic results constrain the types of likely explanatory mechanisms that warrant further investigation.

Now, let's turn to another classic empirical problem: What drives personality development during emerging adulthood? The meta-analytic findings described earlier indicate that the nonshared environment plays an emerging and increasing role in personality stability in adolescence through middle adulthood. In other words, superimposed on a backdrop of genetically mediated stability, the nonshared environment plays an increasing role in the longitudinal stability of personality traits over the life course. This finding suggests a number of promising sources of stable variation in personality in adolescent and young adulthood warranting further investigation. For instance, researchers may do well to examine effects of peer groups, social clubs, occupational roles, and the general social niches that individuals adopt as they become adults. As we discuss later, the nonshared environment also includes potential interactions between environmental experiences and genetics. For instance, genetic differences between people may predict how they respond to unique environmental experiences. For instance, it is possible that some individuals may experience social rejection by withdrawing from further social interactions, while others may redouble their efforts to integrate themselves socially. Drawing these sorts of insights is not obvious or straightforward from the results we presented earlier. We suggest that before such quantitative genetic results can be integrated more fully into personality theory, it is useful to articulate the sorts of empirical patterns that would result from different mechanisms of personality development.

Mechanisms of Personality Development

Several theoretical perspectives have proposed developmental processes that give rise to individual differences in personality, and their stability and change over time. Here we attempt to articulate the sorts of empirical patterns that

each of several archetypical theoretical processes would be expected to produce.

Genetic Set Point

One of the most long-standing perspectives on the basis of individual differences of personality holds that endogenous genetic factors determine each individual's level of each personality trait, and that experiential factors have only transient, short-lived effects on personality. Under this perspective, perturbations in trait levels result from exposure to novel environmental experiences, but these perturbations rapidly decay over time such that individual personality levels regress back toward their person-specific genetic set points. For example, someone may be more open to new experiences when traveling abroad for a summer, but levels of openness to experience would be expected to return to a set point shortly after returning home. Under this *genetic set-point* hypothesis (Figure 3.3, left panel), even if exposure to the novel environment persists over time—either through repeated exposure or via permanent wholesale change in environmental context—individuals acclimate to the novelty and traits regress back to their genetic set points. For instance, faced with the challenge of making new friends, an individual may increase in extraversion shortly after moving permanently to a new city. However, after a few months of establishing a routine, the genetic set point would predict that his or her extraversion levels would return to a preexisting set point.

According to early theoretical work (e.g., Waddington, 1942), individuals evolved to have buffered responses to environmental variability, such that each genotype would produce a relatively constant ultimate phenotype. Conley (1984) hypothesized that "the heritabilities of intelligence and personality would produce innate individual differences which could to a greater or lesser degree resist the destructuring, randomizing influence of the environment" (p. 22). Scarr (1992) speculated that "ordinary differences between families have little effect on children's development, unless the family is outside of a normal, developmental range" (p. 15), and that "fortunately, evolution has not left development of the human species, nor any other, at the easy mercy of variations in their environments. We are robust and able to adapt to wide-ranging circumstances. . . . If we were so vulnerable as to be led off the normal develop-

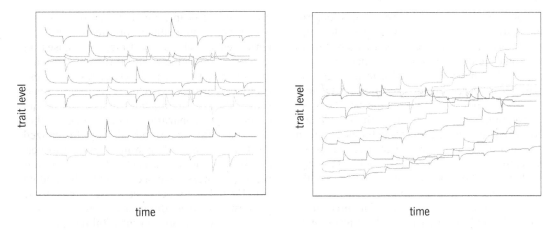

FIGURE 3.3. Genetic set point (left) and moving genetic set point (right). Randomly experienced environmental events cause short-term perturbations in trait levels that decay over time, such that individuals return to their genetic set point. *Left panel*: The set point remains constant over development for each person. *Right panel*: Genetically influenced individual differences exist in both the initial set point and the linear rate of change in the set point over development. On average, the genetic set point for the trait increases with development. Each individual randomly experiences different short-term events that perturb trait levels. Following perturbations, trait levels regress back to the person-specific, age-specific set point.

mental track by slight variations in our parenting, we should not long have survived" (p. 16). Indeed, some degree of *penetrance* of genetic variability into phenotypic variability is necessary for natural selection to occur (Falconer & Mackay, 1996).

Support for a genetic set-point understanding of personality comes from several sources. Theoretically, genetic set points are included in many models of personality development. For example, Fraley and Roberts (2005) include a form of genetic set point as a "constancy factor" due to the fact that DNA sequence variation remains unchanged across the lifespan (importantly, the authors build several other developmental processes on top of this set point). In the behavioral genetic literature, a classic piece of evidence comes from the Minnesota Study of Twins Reared Apart (Bouchard, Lykken, McGue, Segal, & Tellegen, 1990). This study tracked identical and fraternal twins put up for adoption and placed in different homes weeks after their birth. Apart from their time together in the womb, these twins shared none of the same upbringing, but they did share DNA. Bouchard and colleagues (1990) reported, remarkably, that the reared apart identical twins correlated at .50, only slightly lower than the expected differential stability of personality in

adulthood. More recently, Kandler, Bleidorn, Riemann, Angleitner, and Spinath (2012) used a sophisticated longitudinal behavioral genetic design to test for a genetic set point. Their impressive model incorporated three waves of self- and informant reports of personality to alleviate concerns about measurement error. Although their results were complicated (we return to this study below), they found some support for a genetic set point. Specifically, variance that was stable across all three waves of data collection was solely associated with genetic effects, and they found that variance specific to a measurement occasion decreased, consistent with the idea that individuals shift in personality but return to a genetically influenced set point.

Moving Set Point (Genetic Influences on Developmental Change)

A slightly more nuanced version of the genetic set-point hypothesis does not require that person-specific genetic set points remain fixed over development. Proponents of this hypothesis have suggested that developmental changes in genetic set points may result from "biologically based intrinsic maturation" (Costa & McCrae, 2006). Under this *moving set-point* hypothesis (Figure 3.3, right panel), genetic factors are thought to determine the longitudinal trajectory of trait levels over development, such that each person's set point moves with age, and environmental experiences are expected to have short-lived effects, such that trait levels regress to the person-specific, age-specific set point postinitial exposure. Such an elaboration helps to account for the sizable and consistent developmental trajectories of mean levels of personality traits (Roberts, Walton, & Viechtbauer, 2006; Srivastava, John, Gosling, & Potter, 2003). The moving set-point hypothesis is also somewhat consistent with findings of moderate-to-large genetic influences on individual differences in long-term (e.g., 5 or more years) changes in personality traits (e.g., Bleidorn, Kandler, Riemann, Angleitner, & Spinath, 2009; Harden, Quinn, & Tucker-Drob, 2012), although, in its purest form, it would incorrectly predict very minimal environmental influences on such changes. Indeed, although Kandler and colleagues (2012) found some evidence for genetic influences on personality maturation (consistent with a moving set point), they also found substantial environmental variance in personality development, much of which was stable and carried forward across time (contrary to a strict interpretation of a moving set point). The moving set-point hypothesis is also consistent with the moderate heritability and robust genetic contributions to longitudinal stability of personality traits across the lifespan. Environmental influences on personality are expected to occur at all phases of development, but they are expected to be short-lived over time: New environmental influences are expected to arise as old environmental influences dissipate. Thus, the (moving) genetic set-point hypothesis by itself is not well equipped to account for decreasing heritability and increasing environmentality of personality with age, or the increasing contribution of environmental factors on longitudinal stability of individual differences in personality across the lifespan.

Random Walk

Random walk mechanisms (Figure 3.4) contrast starkly with genetic set-point mechanisms, in that they predict that trait-level change in response to environmental experiences persist forward in time such that trait levels at a given point in time constitute a random deviation from the trait level at the immediately preceding point in time. This can occur either because environmental events are randomly experienced at each point in time, or because trait levels change as the result of randomly behaving intrinsic processes. In either respect, these trait levels are not expected to regress to a person-specific set point, and changes are instead expected to haphazardly build on one another over time. Taking a step back from formalized mechanisms, a random walk approach to personality has intuitive aspects. How many of our life experiences have seemed entirely random but affected us for better or worse? Some of the greatest scientific discoveries have occurred through such random events. Taking just one example, penicillin was discovered due to a messy laboratory and a holiday break (Fleming, 1929). More generally, some of life's most important moments appear to happen seemingly at random: the chance encounter with a stranger who turns into a spouse, being in the wrong place at the wrong time while a drunk driver is on the road, or saying just the right thing in a job interview that speaks to the interviewer's past. Each of these random coincidences has the possibility to influence personality development. Using the behavioral genetic framework, we can anticipate the expected effects of random walks for empirical findings.

Random walk models provide some appealing mechanistic accounts of certain developmental patterns. For instance, they easily account for the increasing nonshared environmentality of personality with age, in that accumulating variation resulting from random walks—if truly random—will be unrelated to either genetic variation or the family environment. As Turkheimer (2000) wrote, "Nonshared environmental variability predominates . . . because of the unsystematic effects of all environmental events, compounded by the equally unsystematic process that expose us to environmental events in the first place" (p. 163). Additionally, under simple random walk models, between-person variability of personality would be expected to increase with age, the stability of personality would be expected to increase with age (because of increasing between-person variability with age, the same magnitude of random deviation from the previous trait level will shift the rank order of individuals to a lesser extent with increasing age), and the increasing stability with age would be expected to be mediated by the nonshared environment. Empirical evidence supports each of these expectations.

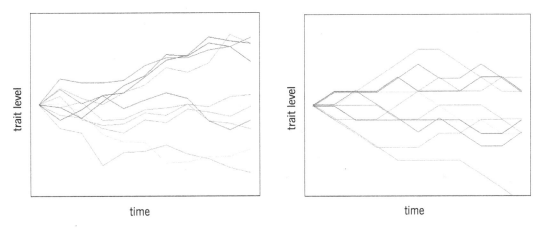

FIGURE 3.4. Random walk. Each participant's trait level at a given time point is a random deviation from his or her trait level at the preceding point in time. *Left panel*: The deviation is randomly drawn from a continuous normal distribution. *Right panel*: The deviation is drawn from a two-trial binomial distribution, generating three discrete levels (increase, decrease, stay).

The stability of personality increases across the lifespan (Roberts & DelVecchio, 2000) primarily due to the nonshared environment (Briley & Tucker-Drob, 2014). Furthermore, the variance of personality also increases in childhood and early adolescence (Mõttus, Soto, & Slobodskaya, 2017; Mõttus et al., in press). Random walk processes will, of course, yield incomplete accounts of personality development, insofar as (1) personality is genetically influenced, (2) environmental experiences are nonrandomly experienced on the basis of preexisting individual differences (an issue to which we return to in subsequent sections), and (3) even those environmental experiences that are initially experienced for random reasons tend to recur or shape the profile of other future environments that an individual experiences.

One interesting elaboration of the random walk process would hold that the range of possible changes (i.e., the variance the random walk distribution from one time point to the next) decreases over development as individuals form social, educational, and professional niches; as individuals form roles and identities; and as personality traits crystallize and become resistant to change (Caspi, Roberts, & Shiner, 2005; McCrae & Costa, 1994). This elaboration is not necessary to account for increasing nonshared, environmentally mediated rank-order stability with age, but it would accentuate this process. It would also predict a slowing of increases in

between-person variability in personality with age.

Heterogeneity in (Near-Universal) Transition Points

An additional mechanism that may contribute to the differentiation of individual differences in personality traits with age involves social or biological transitions that are nearly universally experienced, but experienced according to different developmental schedules. Even in a simplified scenario in which each transition has the exact same effect on personality traits for each individual (Figure 3.5), variability in the timing of developmental milestones across individuals will result in same-age individuals being at different developmental "stages," and thus evincing different trait levels. Examples of near-universal social transitions include leaving the parental household, completing education, and establishing an occupation, for which timing varies markedly across individuals and has been implicated in personality development (e.g., Bleidorn et al., 2013). Another example is the pubertal transition, for which individual differences in timing are also marked (Mendle, Harden, Brooks-Gunn, & Graber, 2010) and implicated in the development of both personality and psychopathology (Harden et al., 2015; Kretsch, Mendle, & Harden, 2016; Mendle, Moore, Briley, & Harden, 2016). More gener-

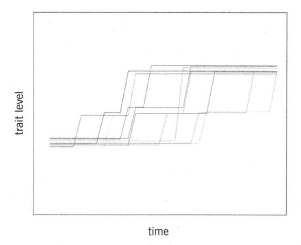

FIGURE 3.5. Heterogeneity in transition points. In this stylized example, all individuals go through two developmental transitions. Each transition has the exact same influence on personality trait levels for all people, but individuals differ from one another in the timing of these transitions (some individuals may even experience both transitions concurrently). Heterogeneity in timing could be attributable to differences in genetically programmed maturational processes (e.g., pubertal development) and/or to differences in the timing of social transitions (children leaving their parents' home, marriage, parenthood). We allow for individual differences in preexisting trait levels.

ally, individual differences in timing and pace of psychological and social development have been a focus of considerable attention in life-history theory, a "theory from evolutionary biology that describes the strategic allocation of bioenergetic and material resources among different components of fitness" (Figueredo et al., 2006, p. 244).

Individual differences in timing of transitions may not, by themselves, be particularly useful in accounting for established patterns of personality development. Such mechanisms may, however, be a key element in the wider constellation of co-occurring processes that underlie personality development. They are particularly valuable for highlighting that, regardless of the extents to which variations in timing are themselves attributable to genetic and environmental factors, there may be some circumstances in which individual differences in personality traits are better conceptualized as reflective of a particular point in a maturational process rather than a characteristic or chronic trait level.

"Learning" Curves with Decay (Genetic Reaction Norms to Environmental Experiences)

So far, we have been discussing stylized examples of processes in which personality trait changes in response to environmental experience are either entirely random (set-point theory and random walk) or entirely fixed (transition point). Our examples have also treated experience-related changes in personality traits as either entirely ephemeral (set-point theory) or entirely lasting (random walk and transition point). In reality, however, individuals may systematically differ in how their personality trait levels change in response to environmental experiences. Moreover, the durability of these changes may be intermediate along the continuum from short-lived to permanent, with individuals potentially differing from one another in trait change durability.

The panels in Figure 3.6 represent stylized versions of a very general pattern that has been observed in many different realms of psychological research, in which levels of a psychological, behavioral, or biological phenotype change (in this case, increase) systematically over time in response to the initial introduction of an environmental experience, after which point, levels recover to some degree, regressing partly back to their preexposure levels either as a result of adaptation to the previously novel situation, removal of the experiential stimulus, or some combination of the two. Lucas, Clark, Georgellis, and Diener (2003), for instance, characterized individual differences in life satisfaction over the period leading up to and following marriage, in terms of a baseline phase, a reaction phase, and an adaptation phase. The overall trend generally resembles aggregate trends observed in Figure 3.6, in which life satisfaction increases leading up to and until marriage, then partly regresses back to lower levels after marriage, with individual differences in both the reaction and adaptation changes. Lucas (2007) surveyed several experiences that conform to this general pattern, including divorce, widowhood, unemployment, and disability (for which life satisfaction decreases during the reaction phase, then partly regresses back to baseline levels during that adaptation phase), with the specific shape of the response pattern differing both as a function of the specific event under study and individual differences. Another, very different example of the general pattern observed in the panels of Figure 3.6 is the salivary cortisol response to a challenging situation or stressor, such as the Trier Social Stress Test. Cortisol, a stress hormone that is produced in response to psychological and physiological threats to homeostasis, has been postulated to influence behavior, including personality and psychopathology (Tucker-Drob et al., 2017). In stressful situations (e.g., public speaking under high-pressure evaluative situations), cortisol levels increase substantially and, shortly after removal of the stressful situation, begin to return back to basal levels. Ram and Grimm (2007) modeled cortisol levels according to baseline, production/response, and dissipation phases, with the overall profile closely paralleling that observed in Figure 3.6. They further documented individual differences in changes across each of the phase transitions. Finally, the general patterns observed in panels in Figure 3.6 are consistent with the widely known patterns observed in cognitive and educational psychology (Ebbinghaus, 1885), in which material is learned with continued studying, repetition, or practice over time, and is partly forgotten over time.

The top two panels of Figure 3.6 represent examples in which individuals differ from one another in their response to and recovery from an experience. In the upper left panel of Figure 3.6, individuals differ from one another in the magnitude of initial response to the experience. When between-person heterogeneity in response to environmental input varies as a systematic function of between-person genetic

variation, this phenomenon is a G × E interaction. Put differently, individual differences in development may emerge from a genetically influenced "norm of reaction" to the environment (Dobzhansky, 1955; Gottesman, 1963; Turkheimer & Gottesman, 1991). Using occupational stress as an example, the upper left panel of Figure 3.6 could represent increases in neurotic thinking and behaving following a harsh interaction with a supervisor. All individuals in this hypothetical example experience the same event, but some individuals react to the experience more dramatically than do others. In the upper right panel of Figure 3.6, everyone initially responds identically to the experience, but some individuals are better able to cope and show greater recovery to baseline levels than do others. In both of these situations, individuals follow different reaction norms due to genetic differences in sensitivity to the environment.

In conceptualizing the relations between differential response curves and lifespan behavioral genetic trends in personality, it is important to consider the nature of the relevant environments in question, and whether they are necessarily objectively shared by twins within a given pair. For instance, if the G × E interaction is not explicitly modeled, a standard behavioral genetic model will attribute individual differences in response to an objectively shared family-level environment to the genetic factor (Purcell, 2002; Turkheimer, 2000). This is because, in the context of such a G × E interaction, the shared environment will differentiate the phenotypes of children raised together as a function of their genetic relatedness. However, if individuals respond differentially to an objectively nonshared environment, and the G × E interaction is not explicitly modeled, a standard behavioral genetic model will attribute this interaction to the nonshared environmental factor (Purcell, 2002; Turkheimer, 2000) because when individuals differentially respond to different experiences as a function of genotype, their phenotypes will become differentiated, even if they share the same genotype.

More concretely, let's assume that the effect of parental warmth on child agreeableness differs across children on the basis of their genotypes: Some children become more agreeable when treated warmly by their parents (as we might intuitively expect), whereas others respond to parental warmth by becoming less agreeable (perhaps they feel smothered). Because these responses are associated with

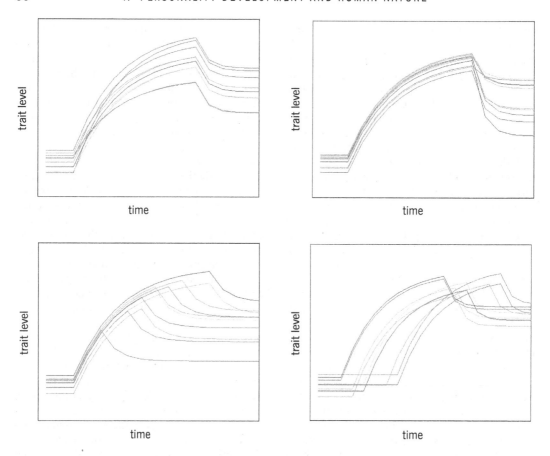

FIGURE 3.6. (Genetically influenced) individual differences in response to experience, and postexperience decay/acclimation. *Upper left panel*: Individual differences in response to experience. Decay parameters held constant. *Upper right panel*: Individual differences in and postexperience decay. Response parameters held constant. *Lower left panel*: Individual Differences in timing of experience offset. Learning and decay parameters held constant. *Lower right panel*: Individual differences in timing of experience onset. Learning and decay parameters held constant. In all panels, we allow for preexisting individual differences in trait levels.

genetic differences between people, identical twins (who share all of their DNA) will respond more similarly to warm parents than will fraternal twins (who share only 50% of DNA that varies within humans). As heritability is estimated as the extent to which more genetically similar individuals are more similar on the phenotype, this G × shared environment interaction will be reflected in the heritability estimate for agreeableness. Now, let's complicate this example by no longer assuming that parents have a set level of warmth that is applied equally across siblings. Parents can play favorites. This elaboration moves in the direction of G × nonshared environment interaction. Again, children may respond differently to levels of warmth based on their genetically influenced levels of agreeableness. To make things easier, we can consider two types of parental warmth applied to siblings: consistent across siblings and inconsistent. Here, because we are focusing on the nonshared aspect of the interaction, it is most relevant to consider the inconsistent parenting type. Identical twins would respond similarly if they received similar parenting, but if parenting differs across identical twins, this may further exaggerate dissimilarity because the difference in environmental treatment is magnified by the genetically influenced difference in response. When differences between identical twins are maintained or magnified, the result is nonshared environmental variance.

At first glance, this sort of logic may seem a bit strange. Why can we make such broad statements about psychological development just by looking at similarity among twins? Behavioral geneticists are trained to think in terms of sibling comparisons or other family-based contrasts, whereas typical psychological scientists are trained to think about how individuals or groups behave. The same sorts of mechanisms described earlier are certainly at work outside of twin pairs; the rationale can be drawn out for single individuals. Assuming complete knowledge of the genetic architecture of agreeableness, researchers would be able to create agreeableness profiles for individuals based solely on their DNA sequence. Then, one could test whether individuals who score a standard deviation above the mean on this genetic agreeableness scale respond more positively to parental warmth. This sort of interaction and study design is common and the logic is straightforward. Twin- and family-based studies use a slightly more complicated rationale to get to the same inferential endpoint.

Ideally, a researcher would be interested in comprehensively modeling all these sorts of interactions using measured variables, so as to produce an accurate representation of genetic and environmental influence across all observed levels of all moderators. In reality, however, if G × E interactions occur pervasively, in response to daily interactions, with a nearly infinite range of different environmental experiences, comprehensively modeling all possible G × E interactions may be an unobtainable goal. Indeed, the capability of behavioral genetic modeling to represent latent variance components representing the total aggregation of all genetic and environmental effects may be viewed as an advantage, so long as the variance components are properly interpreted.

An additional consideration concerns the durability of the interaction effect on behavior. Trait levels may respond instantaneously to an environmental experience but quickly and entirely return to the origin point (as in the genetic set-point model). Alternatively, some portion of the environmental effect (and the differential response) may persist across time. Returning to our earlier example of parental warmth and child agreeableness, durability of the effect entails whether warm parenting instills a lasting sense of positivity and friendliness or fades away as soon as the child encounters a stressful social experience in school. The durability of

the genetically differentiated response may also differ as a function of age (e.g., Fraley & Roberts, 2005) and history of previous experiences. Thus, many of the same key issues surrounding the action of environmental main effects also apply to G × E interactions. If interactions between genetic factors and unique life experiences have lasting effects, these could serve as the basis for the increasing nonshared environmentality and increasing contribution of the nonshared environment to stability with age. However, to our knowledge, such interactions have yet to be consistently tested. Thus, the roles of G × E interaction in lifespan trends in personality development are currently unclear and in need of further investigation.

The magnitude and timescale of the environmental exposure is also important to consider. If the stylized curves depicted in the top panels of Figure 3.6 are taken as representing reactions to major life changes with consequences for long-term quality of life (e.g., marriage, divorce, job loss), it is plausible for their effects on personality to be appreciable and lasting. However, if the curves are taken as representing reactions to a single, seemingly trivial experience (e.g., a negative interaction at the office), the psychological reaction may likely receive the label of "state" rather than "trait," as in our Figure 3.6. Indeed, personality trait development is conventionally thought to be slow, gradual, and not due to "one-off" environmental exposures. However, it is important to keep in mind that the lifespan comprises small units of time that sum to the whole. It may be that short-term psychological reactions to seemingly trivial experiences, when taken in aggregate, provide the foundation for lasting personality change (Roberts & Jackson, 2008; Wrzus & Roberts, 2017). Indeed, this basic principle may be clearly observed in the work on multitrial learning dating back to the late 19th century (Ebbinghaus, 1885). As displayed in Figure 3.7, information retention after a single initial learning trial quickly fades over time, with ultimately little appreciable effect. However, with each successive trial, the rate of decay becomes shallower, such that after a sufficiently large number of trials, information is retained at near maximum for very long periods of time. We suspect that this pattern may apply to not only cognitive and educational contexts but also a broad array of contexts in which the behavioral repertoire (i.e., personality) is affected by environmental experience. Moreover, as we discuss next, indi-

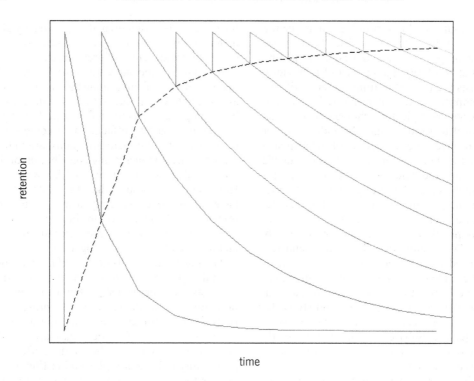

FIGURE 3.7. Ebbinghaus's (1885) learning and decay curve over repeated trials of exposure to a learning experience. Retention decays postexposure, but overall memory trace increases with repeated exposures, such that the rate of decay becomes shallower with increasing repetitions of exposure. The dashed line represents retention after the constant interval between exposures, after which the subsequent repetition commences. Different trials of exposure for a single individual are represented.

vidually varying endogenous factors may guide the timing and duration of personality-relevant environmental exposures, such that exposures differentially aggregate across individuals over time.

Selecting and Sorting Experiences (Gene–Environment Correlations)

Gene–environment correlation (rGE) refers to the tendency for individuals to encounter environmental experiences nonrandomly as a systematic function of their genetically influenced characteristics (Plomin, DeFries, & Loehlin, 1977; Scarr & McCartney, 1983). Evidence for rGE comes from subjecting measures of the environment to behavioral genetic models, as if they were phenotypes. For instance, just as a behavioral genetic model of personality infers heritability by determining whether (holding shared rearing experience constant) more genetically related individuals tend to be more

similar in their personality than less related individuals, rGE can be inferred from determining whether more genetically related individuals tend to experience more similar environments than less genetically related individuals. Active rGE occurs when individuals actively select their experiences on the basis of their genetically influenced interests, proclivities, personality, and aptitudes. Evocative rGE occurs when individuals are selected into different environments on the basis of others' observations of their genetically influenced traits. For example, active rGE occurs when individuals interested in pursuing ideas have greater motivation to pursue postsecondary education, and evocative rGE occurs when colleges select individuals for admission on the basis of their high school performance (which is itself influenced by traits such as organization, self-discipline, and intelligence).

Putting these textbook definitions of rGE aside, a vivid experimental demonstration of rGE can be found in the VH1 show *Twinning*. The concept of the show is to take a group of identical twins and separate each pair into separate, mirror-image houses. The show is a behavioral geneticist's dream: Place incredibly complex human beings into a social situation to see what happens; then do it again with genetically identical individuals with no knowledge of what happened. Similarities in behavior abound. The somewhat nerdy twins both fall into socially awkward positions of trying to figure out whether boys and girls are sleeping throughout the house or are segregating by gender. Subsequently, a different twin pair independently bullies each of the nerdy twins. The muscle-bound twins each notice the gym equipment immediately upon entering the house and comment identically. Most interestingly, peer groups form, based on the same group members while performing the same behaviors. In one house, four men take turns playing pool and commenting on how crazy the situation is. One twin hypothesizes that their co-twins are probably having the same conversation. Cut to the other house, where, as predicted, the co-twins of the four men are all standing around the pool table discussing their co-twins. This is rGE in action. The somewhat diminished social graces of the nerdy twin pair evoke a similar response from the environment in the form of bullying. Meanwhile, other twins actively form similar peer groups, likely because each individual looks for somewhat similar qualities and attributes in potential friends. Of course, some video editing magic may have enhanced these similarities.

Returning to empirical work with somewhat larger sample sizes, rGE for important environmental experiences, such as stressful life events and social support, appears to be widespread; genetic factors have been estimated to account for a relatively large portion of variation in these experiences (roughly 30%; Kendler & Baker, 2007). The empirical implications of this finding for personality development are displayed graphically in the bottom two panels of Figure 3.6. In the lower left panel, all individuals encounter an environmental experience at the same point in time, but some individuals leave the environment more quickly. In the context of the harsh supervisor example, the lower left panel of Figure 3.6 predicts that everyone will get into an argument at some point in time, but that some individuals are able to resolve the disagreement more quickly than others. These

more conciliatory workers may therefore experience a less steep increase in neurotic behaving and thinking in response to the experience. In the lower right panel, individuals differ in the timing of the event. Some workers may be more pleasant or diligent in their work, pushing back a negative encounter with their supervisor for a longer period of time. Again, this process means that measures of personality capture a cross-section of people at different points of the dynamic interplay between genetic influences, environmental experiences, and the mutual control of the expression of one over the other. If genetically influenced traits guide the timing, duration, and frequency of small, neuroticism-inducing experiences on an everyday basis, these individually trivial encounters may aggregate over time to have lasting effects on personality.

Gene–environment correlations have potentially widespread theoretical implications for personality development following environmental exposures and life events. As Lüdtke, Roberts, Trautwein, and Nagy (2011, p. 622) have written, "Life events were originally construed as random—a position that has long been abandoned given that putatively random life events are both heritable and partially explained by personality traits." To the extent that life events are heritable and have causal effects on personality development, this process should lead more genetically related individuals to be more psychologically similar than less genetically related individuals. Put differently, genetic effects on personality may not exclusively flow through purely inside-the-skin biological pathways; they may also occur through outside-the-skin environmental pathways. For example, if bullying or peer groups have some causal effect on personality development, then the results of VH1's experiment with *Twinning* indicates that such rGE may be not just be a consequence, but a mechanism of genetic influences on personality. Genetic effects on personality may be environmentally mediated. More generally, evidence of rGE should temper strong interpretations of heritability as supporting a purely biological model of personality development.

The existence of rGE implies that individuals tend to select or evoke environments on the basis of genetically influenced characteristics, such that the effects of environmental experience magnify the initially small genetic influences (Briley & Tucker-Drob, 2013; Dickens

& Flynn, 2001). If rGE guides personality development, then one would expect increases in heritability and that phenotypic stability would be increasingly mediated by genetic variance components. However, the lifespan behavioral genetic trends highlighted in Figures 3.1 and 3.2 are inconsistent with this prediction. It may be the case that, absent rGE, genetic effects on personality would fade even more precipitously with age, and that rGE largely maintains, but does not strengthen, genetic influences on personality. It is also possible that rGE processes operate in conjunction with other processes (e.g., random walk processes), such that any magnification of genetic influences produced is diluted by variation that arises over development through nongenetic pathways.

Putting It All Together

In the previous sections, we pulled apart many different mechanisms of personality development to identify their unique components individually. However, many of these different mechanisms may simultaneously act to shape personality development. Rather than seeking to identify the "true" or "more correct" mechanisms of personality development, we believe that ongoing work in personality development research will do well to empirically delineate the circumstances under which aspects of each of the aforementioned are most relevant. This involves identifying specific measurable experiences that are relevant for personality change, measuring them intensively and repeatedly over time, and charting how they dynamically relate to the development of different personality traits. In this final section, we outline some important unanswered questions and reflect on why the questions have remained unanswered throughout the history of personality psychology.

Personality psychology has undergone several historical transitions, from periods in the early 20th century, during which personality was viewed as fixed and highly relevant to an individual's behavioral interactions and social and economic standing, to periods in the 1970s, during which it was viewed as impotent and easily overwhelmed by the demands of situational contexts. In the 1990s, the pendulum largely swung back, and personality was again seen as a relatively stable, enduring feature of an individual's psychology that was largely un-

touched by the external world. This aspect of personality was particularly useful from a persuasion perspective because it allowed personality researchers to argue in favor of causality. According to this thinking, if personality is correlated with some outcome, it must be the case that personality is the cause. However, as personality psychology has again come to be accepted within the mainstream, current personality psychology may be going through some of the pains of a shift in thinking on these issues. For example, growing evidence is emerging that cross-cultural differences in social roles shape trajectories of personality development. For instance, Bleidorn and colleagues (2013) reported that in cultures where people tend to take on occupational roles at an earlier age, the normative age trends in conscientiousness and neuroticism are accelerated relative to cultures in which social roles are adopted later. These broad-band culture effects may act on individuals by way of day-to-day social influences that aggregate over time. Other work has identified more specific social pressures, such as joining the military (Jackson, Thoemmes, Jonkmann, Lüdtke, & Trautwein, 2012) and preparing for transition to postsecondary education (Bleidorn, 2012). These studies have been instrumental in establishing that enduring changes in social roles and environmental contexts can have appreciable effects on personality development, presumably because they gradually and incrementally accrue over time. Recent work, however, suggests that personality changes may in some cases be more abrupt (as in Figure 3.5). Roberts and colleagues (2017) documented large ($d = 0.37$) changes in personality development over a short period of time (4 weeks) in response to an intervention. These changes held in observational and experimental studies and lasted over long periods of time. The results raise the intriguing possibility that classic reports of slow, steady changes in personality over the entire lifespan (e.g., Roberts et al., 2006) may in fact smooth over exaggerated and discontinuous periods of personality change occurring at the individual level.

A number of central questions in personality development remain unanswered. We view the following questions as most pertinent.

• *How do people engage the environment?* The assortment of specific environmental experiences known to correlate with personality development is rather limited. Part of the issue may reflect our lack of knowledge concerning why people enter into certain environments, such as stressful life events. To what extent do specific life events occur at random, occur via social stratification, occur via active selection and evocation on the basis of genetically influenced factors, or occur as consequences of past personality development? Others factors that seem logically related to personality maturation but typically go unmeasured include details on the intensity, frequency, duration, timing, and consistency of exposures across time. One of the best examples of work attempting to answer these questions comes from Kandler, Bleidorn, Riemann, Angleitner, and Spinath (2012). The study was a genetically informative, three-wave longitudinal study measuring both personality and life events. This design allowed for disentangling the extent to which individuals selected into environments on the basis of genetically influenced characteristics and whether the life events, in turn, had effects on personality development. Furthermore, the authors distinguished between controllable and uncontrollable life events, positive and negative life events, and measured the intensity of the experience. However, the temporal resolution of the design, roughly 5 years between waves, leaves uncertain the specific engagement of the environment (e.g., would the effect have been different if the participant was a year younger? Or if the participant was fired from work before or after having a child?).

• *What is the shape and time course of environmental effects on personality?* Studies of personality tend to focus on enduring effects. For example, a strength of the 5-year interval between assessments in the Kandler and colleagues (2012) study is that associations between a life event and personality are known to endure over a long period of time. However, it may be that after a 5-year interval, the effect of life events on personality has already decayed somewhat, and may be near a lower asymptote. Shorter interval, higher frequency longitudinal approaches may offer opportunities for mapping dynamic changes of the sort represented by the stylized reaction curves in Figures 3.6 and 3.7.

• *Do individuals differ in their response to the environment on the basis of genotype?* A defining feature of modern conceptions of personality is that some dimensions confer differential

response to the same environment (Denissen & Penke, 2008). An environment that is stimulating to someone high on extraversion may be overwhelming to someone low on extraversion. Given this, it is surprising that there are relatively few examples of studies examining G × E interaction in the development of personality. Some evidence comes from Krueger, South, Johnson, and Iacono (2008), who demonstrated shifts in heritability and environmentality across different levels of parenting variables. However, this finding has not been replicated to the best of our knowledge, and follow-up work for other sorts of environmental variables is lacking. One explanation is that researchers are looking in the wrong place for such interactions. We highlighted two ways that genotype could interact with environmental experiences: by moderating the initial response to the environment or by moderating the recovery from the response (Figure 3.6, top two panels). Whereas some teens may respond well to instances of parental control, the same experience may lead others to rebel. Or perhaps all teens respond initially to the enforcement of parental control and reduce risk taking, but for some this effect is only short lived, whereas it sets setting others on the straight and narrow path. Ultimately, if these sorts of parent–child interactions are stable and recurrent, then one might expect this phenomenon to accumulate in systematic G × E interaction that is measurable by aggregate measures of parenting and adolescent behavior, thus partially obviating the need to measure specific instances of parent–child interaction. That said, much may be learned from the measurement of differential responsivity to specific episodes of experience, such as whether and how individual responses aggregate over time.

• *How does personality development build on itself?* Moving beyond specific behavioral instances, it will also be important to accumulate information about how previous developmental history might also impact the response or decay of environmental effects. More generally, it may not be necessary to delineate how differential responses relate to both genotype (as in the previous question) and environmental history. It is possible that differential response is best accounted for by individual differences in the observable personality phenotype, such that identifying separate sources of variance may not be necessary (Turkheimer et al., 2014). Of course, whether developmental links among personality, genetic variation, and environmental variation occur through a unified (i.e., phenotypic) path or a specialized (i.e., showing preference for genetic or environmental processes) path is an empirical question yet to be sufficiently addressed.

Several existing personality theories may provide useful conceptual frames for ongoing empirical research to address these questions. For example, the sociogenomic model of personality (Roberts & Jackson, 2008) articulates how small-scale changes in states, such as those depicted in Figure 3.6, can accumulate into personality development. Similarly, whole trait theory (Fleeson & Jayawickreme, 2015) is premised on the idea that individual differences in personality constitute differences in density distributions of behaviors that are elicited from continuously changing situations. Finally, the network perspective on personality (Cramer et al., 2012) moves away from the latent trait concept in favor of personality dimensions as systems of discrete, causally interconnected behaviors. Each model has it strengths. The sociogenomic model highlights ways in which genes and environments are mutually interdependent; whole trait theory draws on the most compelling work on short-term fluctuations in behavior (e.g., Fleeson, 2004; Fleeson & Gallagher, 2009); the network perspective refines the locus of personality development away from the latent trait toward specific, narrow aspects of personality that more accurately reflect how the environment affects behavioral development (e.g., is it more plausible that getting a promotion at work activates general conscientiousness, including whether one's desk is clean, or, more specifically, achievement striving?).

In conclusion, we anticipate a bright future for genetically informative research in personality. We believe that we have the tools necessary to make substantial progress on how genetic and experiential inputs combine and interact over the course of development to affect individual differences in repertoires of thinking, feeling, and behaving.

ACKNOWLEDGMENTS

During the writing this chapter, Elliot M. Tucker-Drob's research was supported by National Institutes of Health (NIH) Grant Nos. R01HD083613 and R21HD081437. Dr. Tucker-Drob is a member of the Population Research Center at the University of Texas at Austin, which is supported by NIH Grant No. R24HD042849. During the writing this chapter, Daniel A. Briley's research was supported by a grant from the John Templeton Foundation (No. JTF58792).

REFERENCES

Bleidorn, W. (2012). Hitting the road to adulthood short-term personality development during a major life transition. *Personality and Social Psychology Bulletin, 38*(12), 1594–1608.

Bleidorn, W., Hopwood, C. J., & Lucas, R. E. (2018). Life events and personality trait change. *Journal of Personality, 86*(1), 83–96.

Bleidorn, W., Kandler, C., Riemann, R., Angleitner, A., & Spinath, F. M. (2009). Patterns and sources of adult personality development: Growth curve analyses of the NEO PI-R scales in a longitudinal twin study. *Journal of Personality and Social Psychology, 97*(1), 142–155.

Bleidorn, W., Klimstra, T. A., Denissen, J. J., Rentfrow, P. J., Potter, J., & Gosling, S. D. (2013). Personality maturation around the world a cross-cultural examination of social-investment theory. *Psychological Science, 24*, 2530–2540.

Bouchard, T. J., Lykken, D. T., McGue, M., Segal, N. L., & Tellegen, A. (1990). Sources of human psychological differences: The Minnesota Study of Twins Reared Apart. *Science, 250*, 223–228.

Bouchard, T. J., & McGue, M. (2003). Genetic and environmental influences on human psychological differences. *Journal of Neurobiology, 54*(1), 4–45.

Briley, D. A., & Tucker-Drob, E. M. (2013). Explaining the increasing heritability of cognition over development: A meta-analysis of longitudinal twin and adoption studies. *Psychological Science, 24*, 1704–1713.

Briley, D. A., & Tucker-Drob, E. M. (2014). Genetic and environmental continuity in personality development: A meta-analysis. *Psychological Bulletin, 140*(5), 1303–1331.

Caspi, A., Roberts, B. W., & Shiner, R. L. (2005). Personality development: Stability and change. *Annual Review of Psychology, 56*, 453–484.

Conley, J. J. (1984). The hierarchy of consistency: A review and model of longitudinal findings on adult individual differences in intelligence, personality and self-opinion. *Personality and Individual Differences, 5*(1), 11–25.

Costa, P. T., McCrae, R. R. (2006). Age changes in personality and their origins: Comment on Roberts, Walton and Viechtbauer (2006). *Psychological Bulletin, 132*(1), 26–28.

Cramer, A. O., Sluis, S., Noordhof, A., Wichers, M., Geschwind, N., Aggen, S. H., et al. (2012). Dimensions of normal personality as networks in search of equilibrium: You can't like parties if you don't like people. *European Journal of Personality, 26*(4), 414–431.

Denissen, J. J., & Penke, L. (2008). Motivational individual reaction norms underlying the Five-Factor model of personality: First steps towards a theory-based conceptual framework. *Journal of Research in Personality, 42*(5), 1285–1302.

Dickens, W. T., & Flynn, J. R. (2001). Heritability estimates versus large environmental effects: The IQ paradox resolved. *Psychological Review, 108*(2), 346–369.

Dobzhansky, T. (1955). *Evolution, genetics, and man.* New York: Wiley.

Ebbinghaus, H. (1885). *Memory: A contribution to experimental psychology.* New York: Dover.

Falconer, D. S., & Mackay, T. F. C. (1996). *Introduction to quantitative genetics* (4th ed.). Harlow, UK: Longmans Green.

Ferguson, C. J. (2010). A meta-analysis of normal and disordered personality across the life span. *Journal of Personality and Social Psychology, 98*(4), 659–667.

Figueredo, A. J., Vásquez, G., Brumbach, B. H., Schneider, S. M., Sefcek, J. A., Tal, I. R., et al. (2006). Consilience and life history theory: From genes to brain to reproductive strategy. *Developmental Review, 26*(2), 243–275.

Fleeson, W. (2004). Moving personality beyond the person–situation debate the challenge and the opportunity of within-person variability. *Current Directions in Psychological Science, 13*(2), 83–87.

Fleeson, W., & Gallagher, P. (2009). The implications of Big Five standing for the distribution of trait manifestation in behavior: Fifteen experience-sampling studies and a meta-analysis. *Journal of Personality and Social Psychology, 97*(6), 1097–1114.

Fleeson, W., & Jayawickreme, E. (2015). Whole trait theory. *Journal of Research in Personality, 56,* 82–92.

Fleming, A. (1929). On the antibacterial action of cultures of a penicillium, with special reference to their use in the isolation of *B. influenzae. British Journal of Experimental Pathology, 10*(3), 226–236.

Fraley, R. C., & Roberts, B. W. (2005). Patterns of continuity: A dynamic model for conceptualizing the stability of individual differences in psychological constructs across the life course. *Psychological Review, 112*(1), 60–74.

Gottesman, I. I. (1963). Genetic aspects of intelligent behavior. In N. Ellis (Ed.), *The handbook of mental deficiency: Psychological theory and research* (pp. 253–296). New York: McGraw-Hill.

Harden, K. P., Patterson, M. W., Briley, D. A., Engelhardt, L. E., Kretsch, N., Mann, F. D., et al. (2015). Developmental changes in genetic and environmental influences on rule-breaking and aggression: Age and pubertal development. *Journal of Child Psychology and Psychiatry, 56*(12), 1370–1379.

Harden, K. P., Quinn, P. D., & Tucker-Drob, E. M. (2012). Genetically influenced change in sensation seeking drives the rise of delinquent behavior during adolescence. *Developmental Science, 15*(1), 150–163.

Jackson, J. J., Thoemmes, F., Jonkmann, K., Lüdtke, O., & Trautwein, U. (2012). Military training and personality trait development: Does the military make the man, or does the man make the military? *Psychological Science, 23*(3), 270–277.

Kandler, C. (2012). Nature and nurture in personality development: The case of Neuroticism and Extraversion. *Current Directions in Psychological Science, 21*(5), 290–296.

Kandler, C., Bleidorn, W., Riemann, R., Angleitner, A., & Spinath, F. M. (2012). Life events as environmental states and genetic traits and the role of personality: A longitudinal twin study. *Behavior Genetics, 42*(1), 57–72.

Kendler, K. S., & Baker, J. H. (2007). Genetic influences on measures of the environment: A systematic review. *Psychological Medicine, 37*(5), 615–626.

Kretsch, N., Mendle, J., & Harden, K. P. (2016). A twin study of objective and subjective pubertal timing and peer influence on adolescent risk-taking. *Journal of Research on Adolescence, 26,* 45–59.

Krueger, R. F., South, S., Johnson, W., & Iacono, W. (2008). The heritability of personality is not always 50%: Gene–environment interactions and correlations between personality and parenting. *Journal of Personality, 76*(6), 1485–1522.

Lucas, R. E. (2007). Adaptation and the set-point model of subjective well-being: Does happiness change after major life events? *Current Directions in Psychological Science, 16*(2), 75–79.

Lucas, R. E., Clark, A. E., Georgellis, Y., & Diener, E. (2003). Reexamining adaptation and the set point model of happiness: Reactions to changes in marital status. *Journal of Personality and Social Psychology, 84*(3), 527–539.

Lüdtke, O., Roberts, B. W., Trautwein, U., & Nagy, G. (2011). A random walk down university avenue: Life paths, life events, and personality trait change at the transition to university life. *Journal of Personality and Social Psychology, 101*(3), 620–637.

McCrae, R. R., & Costa, P. T. (1994). The stability of personality: Observations and evaluations. *Current Directions in Psychological Science, 3*(6), 173–175.

Mendle, J., Harden, K. P., Brooks-Gunn, J., & Graber, J. A. (2010). Development's tortoise and hare: Pubertal timing, pubertal tempo, and depressive symptoms in boys and girls. *Developmental Psychology, 46*(5), 1341–1353.

Mendle, J., Moore, S. R., Briley, D. A., & Harden, K. P. (2016). Puberty, socioeconomic status, and depression in girls: Evidence for gene × environment interactions. *Clinical Psychological Science, 4,* 3–16.

Mõttus, R., Briley, D. A., Mann, F. D., Tackett, J. L., Harden, K. P., & Tucker-Drob, E. M. (in press). Kids becoming less alike: A behavioral genetic decomposition of developmental increases in personality variance from childhood to adolescence. *Journal of Personality and Social Psychology.*

Mõttus, R., Soto, C. J., & Slobodskaya, H. J. (2017). Are all kids alike?: The magnitude of individual differences in personality characteristics tends to increase from early childhood to early adolescence. *European Journal of Personality, 31*(4), 313–328.

Plomin, R., DeFries, J. C., & Loehlin, J. C. (1977). Genotype–environment interaction and correlation in the analysis of human behavior. *Psychological Bulletin, 84*(2), 309–322.

Purcell, S. (2002). Variance components models for gene–environment interaction in twin analysis. *Twin Research and Human Genetics, 5*(6), 554–571.

Ram, N., & Grimm, K. (2007). Using simple and complex growth models to articulate developmental change: Matching theory to method. *International Journal of Behavioral Development, 31*(4), 303–316.

Roberts, B. W., & DelVecchio, W. F. (2000). The rank-order consistency of personality traits from childhood to old age: A quantitative review of longitudinal studies. *Psychological Bulletin, 126*(1), 3–25.

Roberts, B. W., & Jackson, J. J. (2008). Sociogenomic personality psychology. *Journal of Personality, 76*(6), 1523–1544.

Roberts, B. W., Luo, J., Briley, D. A., Chow, P. I., Su, R., & Hill, P. L. (2017). A systematic review of personality trait change through intervention. *Psychological Bulletin, 143*, 117–141.

Roberts, B. W., Walton, K. E., & Viechtbauer, W. (2006). Patterns of mean-level change in personality traits across the life course: A meta-analysis of longitudinal studies. *Psychological Bulletin, 132*(1), 1–25.

Roberts, B. W., Wood, D., & Caspi, A. (2008). The development of personality traits in adulthood. *Handbook of Personality: Theory and Research, 3*, 375–398.

Scarr, S. (1992). Developmental theories for the 1990s: Development and individual differences. *Child Development, 63*(1), 1–19.

Scarr, S., & McCartney, K. (1983). How people make their own environments: A theory of genotype greater than environment effects. *Child Development, 54*, 424–435.

Srivastava, S., John, O. P., Gosling, S. D., & Potter, J. (2003). Development of personality in early and middle adulthood: Set like plaster or persistent change? *Journal of Personality and Social Psychology, 84*(5), 1041–1053.

Tucker-Drob, E. M., Grotzinger, A., Briley, D. A., Engelhardt, L. E., Mann, F. D., Patterson, M., et al. (2017). Genetic influences on hormonal markers of chronic hypothalamic–pituitary–adrenal function in human hair. *Psychological Medicine, 47*, 1389–1401.

Turkheimer, E. (2000). Three laws of behavior genetics and what they mean. *Current Directions in Psychological Science, 9*(5), 160–164.

Turkheimer, E., & Gottesman, I. I. (1991). Individual differences and the canalization of human behavior. *Developmental Psychology, 27*, 18–22.

Turkheimer, E., Pettersson, E., & Horn, E. E. (2014). A phenotypic null hypothesis for the genetics of personality. *Annual Review of Psychology, 65*, 515–540.

Waddington, C. H. (1942). Canalization of development and the inheritance of acquired characters. *Nature, 150*, 563–565.

Wrzus, C., & Roberts, B. W. (2017). Processes of personality development in adulthood: The TESSERA framework. *Personality and Social Psychology Review, 21*(3), 253–277.

CHAPTER 4

The Development of a Person
A Relational–Developmental Systems Perspective

Richard M. Lerner
Jacqueline V. Lerner

Isla Terese Lerner, our fourth grandchild and second granddaughter, was born early on the morning of October 3, 2017 (Figure 4.1). When we met Isla later that morning, we behaved as we imagine all grandparents do—with immediate love for our new grandchild and with feelings of being blessed by having a healthy and beautiful new granddaughter, a wonderful daughter-in-law, Danni, and an equally wonderful son, Jarrett. We were thrilled that the family members were all doing well, and that Danni and Jarrett were exuberant, albeit understandably quite tired (especially Danni, who had had a long labor). We chatted about Isla's bountiful crop of black hair, reminding us of Jarrett's hair at birth, and about how the baby's nose and eyes looked like those of Danni.

However, and perhaps unlike at least some other grandparents, we did not talk about other things that Isla might "get" from her parents;

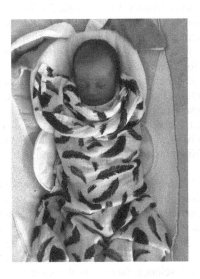

FIGURE 4.1. Isla Terese Lerner, October 3, 2017.

for instance, we did not speculate about whether Isla would have her dad's artistic abilities or her mom's entrepreneurial skills. We also did not make predictions about the baby's temperament—for instance, the rhythmicity of her sleep–wake cycles or the quality of her mood—based on our recollection of how Jarrett or his older brother and sister had manifested these attributes during their respective neonatal periods.

Because we are both developmental scientists and, even more, because of our approach to the study of human development, we know that there is no necessary connection between the genetic inheritance of a child and the characteristics of psychological and behavioral individuality that will develop across his or her lifespan. Genes are only one part of the holistic and dynamically integrated system of biological, psychological, behavioral, social, community, institutional, and designed and natural ecological relations within which each child is born and lives across the course of life. The arrow of time—history or temporality—runs through this system; therefore, changes in the dynamics of the relations that Isla will have within and across the levels of this system will make any specific feature of her development, at any specific time in her life, probabilistic and not fixed or certain. Temporality involves both stochastic and systematic, normative and non-normative life and historical events (Baltes, Lindenberger, & Staudinger, 2006; Elder, Shanahan, & Jennings, 2015), and, of course, temporality involves as well a person's unique history of relations with the people, settings, and events that occur day after day, and year after year in the person's life. Each human life is marked by the potential for change, and for specific patterns of change, because of the specificity of the life course of these encounters (Bornstein, 2017; Rose, 2016). Some of these changes may be short lived and transitory but, as well, there may be systematic change, there may be relative plasticity (Lerner, 1984, 2018), across the lifespan.

Therefore, as developmental scientists, we see Isla as developing in probabilistic ways within this ecology, and not as merely following an inevitable pathway set by her genetic inheritance. Not all developmental scientists would agree with us.

The history of developmental science has been plagued by accounts of human life that are actually adevelopmental, in that they have posited that *genes*—the genotype received at conception—determine all that is essential in the composition of a person (e.g., Belsky, Steinberg, & Draper, 1991; Bjorklund, 2016; Bjorklund & Ellis, 2005; Costa & McCrae, 1980; Dawkins, 1976; Freedman, 1979; McCrae et al., 2000; Plomin, DeFries, Knopik, & Neiderhiser, 2016; Rushton, 2000). Such nature-reductionist accounts make development across life secondary in importance, in that the accounts suggest that experiences encountered across the lifespan can at best only actualize (or not) primarily intrinsic trends (see Witherington & Lickliter, 2016, for a very detailed discussion of this point).

However, we envision Isla as developing within a dynamic individual–context system—through mutually influential relations that may be represented an individual ↔ context relations—and therefore acting on her world at the same time her world is acting on her (Lerner, 1982; Overton, 2015). As depicted in Figure 4.2, Isla will develop across her life within this dynamic, relational developmental system (Bronfenbrenner, 2005; Bronfenbrenner & Morris, 2006). The dynamics of this system mean that Isla—like all humans—will develop as a consequence of the specific individual ↔ context relations she has at specific points in her life, in specific settings, and at specific points in history. In principle, the specificity of Isla's pathway through life means that her development will be *idiographic*; it will be individually distinct (Bornstein, 2017; Molenaar & Nesselroade, 2014, 2015; Nesselroade & Molenaar, 2010; Rose, 2016).

Neither *nomothetic phenomena* (i.e., phenomena that pertain to all humans and/or to a purported generic human being; Rose, 2016) nor *group differential norms or averages* (phenomena that pertain to subgroups of people; e.g., to women, but not to men, or to adolescents but not to adults) will suffice to denote who Isla is as a person. Although she will, of course, have attributes shared by all humans (e.g., a respiratory system, a circulatory system, and a digestive system) and attributes shared by only members of specific groups (e.g., she will have a female reproductive system, and therefore the primary and secondary sexual characteristics of females), she will also have attributes shared by no other person. For instance, she will have a unique genotype, which, in fact, is the case for all humans. Even monozygotic (MZ) twins do not have the same complement of DNA; they share nuclear DNA attributes, but

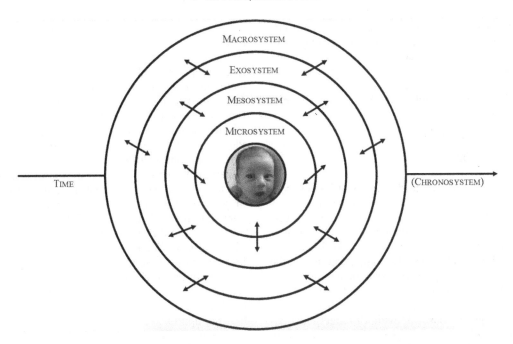

FIGURE 4.2. Isla Terese Lerner and her world. Isla develops within a dynamic developmental system. Using Urie Bronfenbrenner's (1979, 2005) model for such a system, Isla is bidirectionally engaged within a microsystem (the setting within which she is developing at a given moment—e.g., her home, the home of her grandparents and her parents' friends, or the office of the pediatrician), a mesosystem (the set of microsystems constituting Isla's developmental niche at each period across her lifespan), an exosystem (contexts that, although not directly involving Isla—e.g., the workplace of one of her parents—nevertheless have an influence on her behavior and development, as may occur when her mom or dad has had a stressful day at work and, as a result, has a reduced capacity to provide quality caregiving to her at a specific time, an unlikely event in Isla's case, of course, given the excellence of her parents [i.e., our son and daughter-in-law]), and a macrosystem (the superordinate level of the system, which involves culture, macroinstitutions, such as the federal government, and public policy). Isla coacts with all levels of her developmental system across time (the chronosystem).

their mitochondrial DNA is different (Joseph, 2015; Richardson, 2017). In addition, her history of individual ↔ context relations will also be singular to her. Therefore, neither typologies nor a fixed set of trait-like attributes, especially those claimed to be the product of genes that are impregnable to experiential influences (e.g., McCrae et al., 2000), will encompass the individual features of her psychological characteristics. Indeed, although developmental scientists are still fighting to eliminate genetic reductionist, essentialist, and mechanist formations (e.g., those noted earlier) from their field (e.g., see Lerner, 2018; Lickliter & Witherington, 2017; Moore, 2015, 2017a, 2017b; Richardson, 2017), the claims of these reductionists have been shown to be counterfactual in the face of the burgeoning evidence of developmental plastici-

ty provided by epigenetics research (e.g., Lester, Condrat, & Marsit, 2016; Meaney, 2010; Moore, 2015, 2017a, 2017b).

In short, we believe that any attempt to describe, explain, or optimize Isla's development will have to begin by understanding her specific, idiographic characteristics (Bornstein, 2017; Rose, 2016). In addition to specificity and idiography, we also believe that accounts of development of a person should eschew reductionist and essential formulations—and, perhaps especially, genetic reductionist ones—and, instead, as illustrated by the dynamic relations that Isla will encounter as she moves across life (Figure 4.2), should use theoretical models that emphasize holism and integrative person–context relational processes. These concepts (specificity, idiography, holism, and the dynamic, systems character of person ↔ context relations) frame what, at this writing, is the key metatheory of development—termed *relational developmental systems* (RDS; Overton, 2015); that is, at this writing, RDS metatheory is at the cutting edge of theory and research in developmental science.

RDS Metatheory

The study of human development has evolved from a field dominated by reductionist (psychogenic or biogenic) approaches to a multidisciplinary scholarly domain that seeks to integrate variables from biological through cultural and historical levels of organization across the lifespan into a synthetic, coactional system (e.g., Elder, 1998; Ford & Lerner, 1992; Gottlieb, 1997, 1998; Lerner, 2012). This approach to human development contrasts with all reductionist accounts of change across the lifespan, which in the main have been shaped by the philosophical ideas of Descartes. Cartesian conceptions split reality into purported fundamental or essential phenomena and derivative or secondary phenomena (Overton, 2015). Reductionist views in social and behavioral science elevated the salience to researchers of split formulations such as nature versus nurture, continuity versus discontinuity, stability versus instability, or basic versus applied science (Lerner, 2002, 2006).

These split formulations are essentialist in character. *Essentialism* may be defined as a doctrine holding that there are necessary properties of things, and that these properties are logically prior to the existence of the individuals which instantiate them. Essentialism may also be conceptualized as the doctrine that essence is prior to existence and/or as the practice of regarding something as having innate existence (Lerner, 2018). Complexity is in essence explained away through ideas that reduce higher (and more complex) levels of organization to a fundamental level (in the case of an essential, nature position, a gene). The essentialist proposal is that the to-be-reduced-to element comprises the unit of analysis existing at the fundamental or ultimate level of analysis (i.e., the one that explains development or, perhaps better, that explains it away or, at the least, that assigns to development a secondary or trivial role in providing a foundation for key features of human structure or function).

Examples of such formulations in developmental science are the stimulus–response (S-R) connections to which complex human behavior (e.g., cognitive development, language development, moral development) was said to be reducible (e.g., Bijou & Baer, 1961; Skinner, 1971), fixed action patterns (FAPs; Lorenz, 1965) of specific species, genes per se (e.g., Belsky, 2014; Plomin et al., 2016; Rimfeld, Ayorech, Dale, Kovas, & Plomin, 2016; Rushton, 2000), or constructions termed *evolved probabilistic cognitive mechanisms* (ECPMs) that are said to reside in genes by proponents of evolutionary developmental psychology (EDP) (e.g., Bjorklund, 2015; Bjorklund & Ellis, 2005; Del Giudice & Ellis, 2016; see Witherington & Lickliter, 2016, for a review of these ideas).

In addition, a classic instance of such essentialist, reductionist, and split conceptions pertinent to the study of personality involves the trait approach to understanding human development, as exemplified by the five-factor theory (FFT) championed by Costa, McCrae, and their colleagues (e.g., Costa & McCrae, 1980, 2006; McCrae et al., 2000) for more than four decades at this writing. The Big Five traits (conscientiousness, agreeableness, neuroticism, openness to experience, and extraversion) are held to be fixed, stable, and biologically-set fundamental facets of individual functioning. For instance, McCrae and colleagues (2000, pp. 175–176) believe that personality traits reflect "nature over nurture" and that "personality traits are more or less immune to environmental influences. . . . Significant variations in life experiences have little or no effect on measured personality traits." They argue that, "barring interventions or catastrophic events, personality traits appear to be essentially fixed after age 30" (Costa, McCrae, & Siegler, 1999, p. 130). Costa and McCrae (2006) continue to maintain this view, despite the fact that a meta-analysis has provided strong evidence that personality traits change in adulthood past the age of 30 (Roberts, Walton, & Viechtbauer, 2006; also see John & Naumann, 2010).

At this writing, interest in the purported "Big Five" personality traits that form the FFT is still very much in use in the literature of developmental science. For instance, the Big Five typology is used as a standard against which some models of character development (most often, the model of 24 character strengths proposed by Peterson & Seligman, 2004) are compared, frequently in an attempt to identify whether attributes of character can be reduced to the purportedly nature-based FFT typology (e.g., McGrath, Hall-Simmonds, & Goldberg, 2017; McGrath & Walker, 2016; Noftle, Schnitker, & Robins, 2011; Park & Peterson, 2006).

In our view, the continuing presence of the FFT model in developmental science signifies not so much an interest in the particular substance of this theory (there is not a lot of developmental science research about the five attributes proposed in the model), but rather the continuing presence of what is now a minority "voice" in the field—that of genetic reductionism. Despite its egregious flaws, including counterfactual conceptions of genes and their role in development, this minority voice has remarkable persistence. For example, as we mentioned earlier in this chapter, the growth in epigenetics research and, specifically, evidence about the developmental character of the genome (e.g., Ho, 2010; 2013; Lester et al., 2016; Lickliter & Witherington, 2017; Meaney, 2010; Moore, 2015, 2017a, 2017b; Moore & Shenk, 2016; Richardson, 2017; Witherington & Lickliter, 2016), points to the fact that the plasticity of epigenetic change occurs as a consequence of coactions with the within- and the outside-the-organism context of human development (Cole, 2014; Slavich & Cole, 2013). This literature, as well as the literature underscoring the host of methodological problems associated with genetic reductionist accounts of human development (e.g., see Charney, 2017; Joseph, 2015; Moore & Shenk, 2016; Richardson, 2017; Wahlsten, 2012) have been decisive in making genetic reductionism a minority approach within developmental science. As well, the burgeoning of theoretically predicated and methodologically rigorous research framed by RDS metatheory (e.g., see the almost 100 chapters across the four volumes of the seventh edition of the *Handbook of Child Psychology and Developmental Science* [Lerner, 2015b] for numerous examples) has diminished interest, in and scientific regard for, nature–reductionist approaches.

Across the past four plus decades, several scholars have provided ideas contributing to the evolution of this RDS metatheory (e.g., Baltes, 1997; Brandtstädter, 1998; Bronfenbrenner, 1979, 2005; Bronfenbrenner & Morris, 2006; Elder, 1998; Elder et al., 2015; Ford & Lerner, 1992; Nesselroade, 1988; Overton, 1973; Overton & Reese, 1981; Riegel, 1975, 1976; and even earlier, see von Bertalanffy, 1933). However, Overton (e.g., 2013, 2015) has been the key

scholar integrating and extending this scholarship.

Overton (2015) explains that compared to a Cartesian worldview involving splits, reductionism, essentialism, positivism, and mechanism, RDS metatheory is associated with a superordinate process–relational paradigm. The ideas within this paradigm focus on process (systematic changes in the developmental system), becoming (moving from potential to actuality; seeing a developmental process as having a past, present, and future; Whitehead, 1929/1978), holism (the meanings of entities and events derive from the context in which they are embedded), relational analysis (assessment of the mutually influential relations within the developmental system), and the use of multiple perspectives and explanatory forms (employment of ideas from multiple theory-based models of change within and of the developmental system). Within the process–relational paradigm, the organism is seen as inherently active, self-creating, self-organizing, self-regulating (agentic), nonlinear and complex, and adaptive (Overton, 2015; see also Sokol, Hammond, Kuebli, & Sweetman, 2015).

Theoretical models derived from this paradigm therefore emphasize that development involves mutually influential relations within a dynamic system. This idea frames RDS metatheory. Within the RDS approach to theory, split conceptions are, then, obviously eschewed in favor of a metatheory that emphasizes the study and integration of different levels of organization, ranging from biology and physiology to culture and history, as a means to understand lifespan human development (Lerner, 2006; Overton, 2013, 2015). Accordingly, the conceptual emphasis in RDS theories is placed on mutually influential relations between individuals and contexts, which we have noted are represented as individual ↔ context relations.

This representation of the coactions between person and setting within RDS-based models is not meant to convey a person–context interaction (which is typically represented in the developmental literature as "person × context"). An interaction connotes that the entities involved in the relation are separate and independent (as in a statistical interaction) and that, as such, their association involves a linear combination of discrete and separate variables. Both before and after the interaction, these entities (variables) are independent and unchanged by each other.

The bidirectional arrow used in the RDS illustration of person–context relations is intended to emphasize that the coaction of individual and context involves the entire developmental system (Lerner, 2018; Moore, 2017a, 2017b). As such, the relations among levels of the self-constructing system, and not independent linear combinatorial attributes, are the focus in such a model. Indeed, the fusion of individual and context within the developmental system means that any portion of the system is inextricably embedded with—or, in Overton's (2013, 2015) conceptualization, embodied by—all other portions of the developmental system. *Embodiment* refers to the way individuals behave, experience, and live in the world by being active agents with particular kinds of bodies; the body is integratively understood as form (a biological referent), as lived experience (a psychological referent), and as an entity in active engagement with the world (a sociocultural referent) (Overton, 2015). Of course, a simple bidirectional arrow is a less-than-ideal figural representation of the embodied relations between an individual

and his or her context within the dynamic developmental system.

Figure 4.3, which depicts the integrated, multilevel relations we describe, shows the bidirectional influences between the environment (physical, social, and cultural), behavior, neural activity, and genetic activity, and it depicts these influences coacting across individual development. The use of such a representation within textual material in not efficient, however, so we use the symbol ↔ to evoke such multilevel, bidirectional relations. These relations are nonrecursive across ontogenetic, family, and historical time and place (Elder et al., 2015); thus, they do not connote interaction but rather coaction.

The individual ↔ context relations depicted in Figure 4.3 are, of course, identical to the relations depicted in Figure 4.2. Again, then, whether referring to the development of humans in general (Figure 4.3), or to the development of Isla Lerner in particular (Figure 4.2), the view of proponents of RDS models is that the systematic and successive changes that are involved in the life course of an individual involve mutually

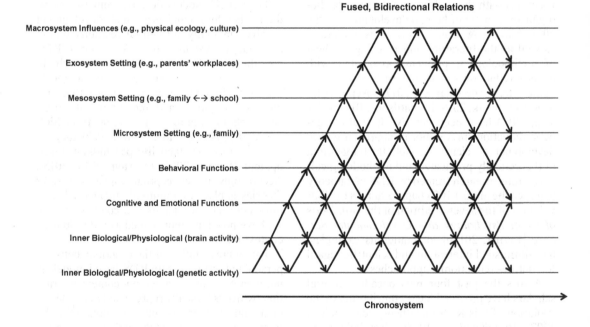

FIGURE 4.3. A relational developmental systems-based representation of the fused (coacting) relations among levels of organization within the ecology of human development. Only a subset of the relations (involving adjacent levels) is illustrated. This figure was inspired by Bronfenbrenner (e.g., 1979, 2005), Gottlieb (e.g., 1992, 1997, 1998), and Lerner (2002, 2004; Ford & Lerner, 1992) and is adapted from Lerner, Johnson, and Buckingham (2015).

influential coactions among all levels of organization integrated within the holistic, dynamic, and self-constructing developmental system.

Within the context of such a bidirectional relational system, the embeddedness within history (temporality) is of fundamental significance (Elder, 1998; Elder et al., 2015). Simply, the developmental system is embedded in history (temporality). One implication of this embeddedness is that Isla and her cohort of 2017 neonates will have paths through life that are different (in substance, events, and outcomes) than those of her grandparents and parents, and, in turn, different than those of her future children and grandchildren. Time and, as well, place are fundamental moderators of the life course and, in this case, regulators, of the substance, pace, direction, and outcome of the development of individuals. The embeddedness of the dynamic system within time also means that change is constant in the developmental system and that, as such, there may be either stochastic or systematic changes in person ↔ context relations across time and place (Elder, 1998; Elder et al., 2015; Misteli, 2013). The presence of such temporality in the developmental system means that there always exists some potential for systematic change and, thus, for (relative) plasticity in human development. In short, potential plasticity in individual ↔ context relations derives from the "arrow of time" (Lerner, 1984; Lerner & Benson, 2013; Overton, 2013, 2015) running through the integrated (relational) developmental system.

In summary, the assumption within an RDS approach to the development of a person is that the specific features that define his or her set of attributes are at least relatively plastic. The presence of such plasticity provides a rationale for enacting programs that are aimed at enhancing attributes of the individual across the lifespan. For example, in our own field of developmental research (i.e., adolescent development), it is possible to view character education programs, ones aimed at character promotion or optimization, or youth development programs, ones aimed at enhancement of thriving among diverse individuals, as examples of such work (Lerner & Callina, 2014; Lerner, Lerner, Urban, & Zaff, 2016). In such RDS-inspired programs, and in RDS theory and research that seeks to provide the evidence base for programs aimed at enhancing the life course of diverse people, the focus on the individuality of the individual is of fundamental importance.

RDS Metatheory and the Promotion of Person-Centered, Idiographic Models and Methods

The substantive foci of developmental science research emphasize the primacy in empirical analysis of the changes *within* a person across developmental periods, indeed across the lifespan (e.g., Molenaar, 2010, 2014; Molenaar & Nesselroade, 2015; Nesselroade & Molenaar, 2010). As such, within developmental science, variable-centered assessments are not relevant to person-centered analyses of intraindividual change; that is, to study intraindividual change—to study the development of a person—developmental scientists must assess how variables covary within an individual across time and *not* how variables covary across individuals within points in time. Such variable-centered analyses, even if conducted at successive points in time for a data set involving repeatedly studied participants, reveal nothing about development (Molenaar & Nesselroade, 2014, 2015; Rose, 2016)! Such analyses have no relevance to changes within an individual. As such, across the past 30 years, developmental science has increasingly emphasized that the study of the individual, and of his or her potentially and, in fact, likely, individually distinct pathway across life (Rose, 2016), requires methods that *begin* with a concern for the idiographic features of human development.

Of course, developmental scientists certainly agree with Kluckhohn and Murray (1948, p. 35) that every person is

1. *Like all other people.* There are *nomothetic* characteristics, that is, as noted earlier in the chapter, characteristics shared by all individuals. For instance, Isla shares with her parents, grandparents, cousins and, indeed, all humans, morphological attributes that exist in everyone, for instance, respiratory, circulatory, and digestive systems. There are also attributes of development that are nomothetic. For example, in developmental science, Werner (1957) and Raeff (2016) have presented a principle (termed *orthogenesis*) that stipulates that whenever development occurs, it involves changes from globality to differentiation and hierarchical organization. The orthogenetic principle is regarded as applicable to each individual, each process, and in fact any variable (e.g., relationships, families, institutions) that are regarded as developing (Lerner, 2018; Raeff, 2011, 2016). Nomothetic

characteristics are therefore held to be general to all humanity.

2. *Like only some other people.* As also noted earlier, there are group *differential* characteristics, that is, attributes shared by some people but not others. For example, we indicated that Isla has a reproductive system and internal and external anatomical features that correspond to those of other females. Males have another, different reproductive and anatomical system. In turn, attributes assessed in studies of human development may be organized into subgroupings on the basis of the sex, race, ethnicity, childrearing experiences, cultural groups, character attributes, interests, cognitive skills, behavioral styles, and so forth, of the sample being assessed (Block, 1971; Emmerich, 1968; Feldman, 1980; Lerner, 2002).

3. *Like no other person.* There are *idiographic* characteristics of every person, that is, attributes that are specific to him or her. For instance, Isla has a unique complement of genes, that is, a genotype. We have already explained that no two people share the same complement of DNA—including MZ twins (Joseph, 2015; Richardson, 2017). Accordingly, because of such facts of genetic diversity, Hirsch (1997, 2004) explained that the course of gene–context relations of every person will be unique because each person has a unique genotype and a unique set of environmental experiences across his or her life; each person will therefore have a unique phenotype. In addition, across life, individuals acquire specific epigenetic markers (Moore, 2015). Therefore, in addition to their nomothetic and group–differential characteristics, every person has idiographic characteristics that define him or her as unique.

Although there is no theoretical or empirical controversy about the fact that each person possesses nomothetic, differential, and idiographic characteristics, there has been considerable controversy about which, if any, of these domains of characteristics should take precedence in the conceptualization and empirical elucidation of development within and across periods of life. Developmental science has had a long history of focusing on theories that emphasize the generic, or nomothetic, facets of human development (e.g., as instantiated by an interest in universal stage theories of development; e.g., Freud, 1954; Piaget, 1970) and, as such, interest in such nomothetic ideas was coupled with min-

imal interest in individual differences, whether at the level of group differences or idiographic characteristics (Lerner, 2018).

For instance, in both the socioemotional and cognitive areas of adolescent development, classical stage theorists (e.g., Erikson, 1959; Freud, 1954; Kohlberg, 1978; Piaget, 1970) have emphasized that all people pass through a series of qualitatively different stages in a fixed, invariant sequence; people cannot skip or reorder stages. The only conceptualization of individual diversity offered in these stages pertained to the rate of development through stages, the final level of stage development reached, or sex differences in some stage models. For example, both Freud (1954) and Erikson (1968) claimed that anatomy was destiny, and posited that the substantive characteristics of universal stage progression of males and females differed. For instance, Erikson argued that women were oriented to inner space, that is, to the "space" inside of their bodies. Men, in turn, were oriented to the space outside of their bodies.

Similarly, some researchers assessing adolescent development focused on differential patterns of youth development (e.g., Block's 1971 classic study, *Lives through Time*). However, as with stage theorists, the nature of individual differences in youth development was restricted to the several clusters of groups or subgroups into which people could be assorted within and across time. Block differentiated between males and females, and he indicated that adolescent and young adult males could be differentiated into five subgroups, whereas adolescent and young adult females could be differentiated into six subgroups.

In contrast to the theoretical and empirical scholarship about nomothetic and differential patterns of adolescent development that have marked, and that continue to mark, the adolescent development literature, there has been no theoretical model offered about the idiographic patterns of adolescent development. Thomas, Chess, and their colleagues (e.g., Chess & Thomas, 1999; Thomas, Chess, Birch, Hertzig, & Korn, 1963) suggested that nine attributes of temperament create individual clusters of attributes for all children, but their actual research focused on only three clusters of temperament (i.e., difficult, easy, and slow-to-warm-up temperament types) that pertained to the majority of youth they studied (about 65% of participants).

However, the emergence of RDS-based theory and method has moved the field to emphasize beginning developmental analysis by placing at the forefront of programmatic research the assessment of the individual; that is, despite the recognition that all humans possess features of their structure and function that reflect nomothetic (like all other people), differential (like only some other people), and idiographic (like no other person) attributes (Emmerich, 1968), in contemporary developmental science, RDS-based theory and method point to *beginning* developmental analysis with a focus on the idiographic.

Rose (2016) has explained why the "assess (the individual first) before aggregating (to the differential or nomothetic level)" approach should be followed in the study of human development, and that three principles capture the individuality of people. First, every person has a jagged individual set of attributes; that is, no person falls at the mean (no individual is "average") for all attributes of physical or functional attributes assessed in the biomedical or the social/behavioral sciences. Second, context matters for all people; that is, time and place shape the specific set of attributes an individual develops across his or her life, and this role of the context occurs through the fundamental developmental process of individual ↔ context relations (Elder et al., 2015). Third, every individual walks the road less traveled; that is, no two people—even identical twins (Joseph, 2015)—have the same trajectory of intraindividual change across the lifespan.

Molenaar and Nesselroade (2015) and Rose (2016) agree that the penchant in psychological science to begin with aggregate data, then assess how a given individual may vary from "the average," is both conceptually and empirically wrong given the evidence that jaggedness, context, and idiographic trajectories across life are fundamental features of human development. As such, these scholars recommend that developmental scientists should analyze and then aggregate; that is, in developmental science, the first step in exploring a data set should be to assess the patterns of intraindividual change involved with each person in a sample; then, after such analyses are completed, developmental scientists should determine whether and how aggregation might proceed (Molenaar & Nesselroade, 2015).

However, the methodology of developmental science has privileged the study of groups (either purportedly universal/nomothetic or group-differential ones) to the exclusion of a focus on the idiography of human development. Molenaar and Nesselroade (e.g., 2014, 2015) and Rose (2016) have pointed to the shortcomings of this focus. For instance, as explained by Rose, Rouhani, and Fischer (2013), individual ↔ context relations are the fundamental process of living organisms. As such, to understand and empirically examine fruitfully the course of individual development, researchers must use two concepts integral to dynamic systems models—individual in context and variability (across individuals and across individual–context relations) as information (not as error variance). "Behavior is not something that a person 'has'—instead, it emerges from interactions between the individual and his or her contexts. . . . [T]he dynamic systems approach starts by assuming individuals vary, and seeks to identify stable patterns within that variability" (Rose et al., 2013, p. 153).

When the specific course of individual ↔ context relations is beneficial to both individual and context, it is termed adaptive. "Individual variability is the essence of adaptive behavior, whether we are talking about a person or a cell" (Rose et al., 2013, p. 153). Specific adaptive individual ↔ context relations are the fundamental process involved in the positive development of individual ↔ context relations (Lerner, Lerner, Bowers, & Geldhof, 2015). Moreover, these relations are a key feature of dynamic, relational developmental systems-based models of human development. The concepts and associated methods of these models should frame research on the course of individual development (Lerner, 2018; Rose, 2016; Rose et al., 2013). This emphasis on the idiographic features of youth development is based on an understanding of the dynamic system of relations linking people to their context.

Human Development Is Nonergodic

The process of individual development involves specific instances across the life of individual ↔ context relations. In other words, development happens because of specific individual ↔ context relations at specific times and in specific places (Elder et al., 2015). As a consequence, human development is fundamentally *idiographic* (Molenaar & Nesselroade, 2015; Rose, 2016). Therefore, within dynamic systems models focused on an individual's specific relations with the other components of his or her specific ecology of human development (e.g., Mascolo

& Fischer, 2015; Overton, 2015; Rose, 2016), the individuality of all humans, and the diversity of human development are of primary substantive significance. This conception of diversity has important implications for developmental methodology and for the questions asked in developmental research.

The standard approach to statistical analysis in the social and behavioral sciences is not focused on change but is instead derived from mathematical assumptions regarding the constancy of phenomena across people and, critically, time (Molenaar, 2014). These assumptions are based on the ergodic theorems. To explain these theorems, consider as a sample case Gaussian (normally distributed) processes. Molenaar noted that any ergodic Gaussian process has to obey the following two necessary conditions:

1. The Gaussian process has to be *stationary* (this condition indicates that the mean of the process has to be constant in time, the variance of the process has to be constant in time, and the sequential dependencies characterizing the process only depend on the relative distance, or lag, between time points).
2. The Gaussian process also has to be *homogeneous* across individuals (indicating that each participant in the population or group has to obey the same dynamic model).

Simply, the assumption used when framing statistical analysis through the use of the ergodic theorem is that the structure of interindividual variation of a developmental process at the population level is equivalent to the structure of intraindividual variation at the individual level (Molenaar, 2014; Molenaar & Nesselroade, 2015). These ideas lead, then, to statistical analyses placing prime interest on the population level. Interindividual differences, rather than intraindividual change, are the source of this population information (Molenaar & Nesselroade, 2015).

If the concept of ergodicity is applied to the study of human development, then within-person variation across time would either be ignored or treated as error variance. In addition, any sample (group) differences would be held to be invariant across time and place. However, from the previously noted relational and dynamic developmental systems perspective, develop-

ment varies across people and across contexts. These facts violate the ideas of ergodicity; that is, developmental processes have time-varying means, variances, and/or sequential dependencies. The structure of interindividual variation at the population level is therefore not equivalent to the structure of intraindividual variation at the level of the individual (Molenaar & Nesselroade, 2015). Simply, developmental processes are nonergodic.

As a consequence, to obtain valid information about developmental processes, it is necessary to study intraindividual variation within single individuals. Molenaar and Nesselroade (2015; Nesselroade & Molenaar, 2010) have developed statistical procedures for such analyses. An example is the idiographic filter (IF), which involves use of the dynamic factor model at the level of the individual but then generates group–differential or nomothetic latent constructs to enable generalization across participants. Through use of procedures such as the IF, developmental scientists can capture the nonergodic nature of intraindividual change and, as well, produce generalities about groups that apply as well to the individuals within them. As such, differences between people in developmental trajectories (i.e., in the course of within-person changes) are important foci for research and, as well, for program and policy applications aimed at enhancing development across time and place.

These implications arise because the focus in dynamic developmental systems models is on the specificity of individual ↔ context relations and, as a result, on the fundamental idiographic nature of human development (Rose et al., 2013). These ideas provide a rationale for a distinct approach to diversity, one that has implications for the description, explanation, and optimization of human development.

How, then, may research proceed? Bornstein (2006, 2017) has presented a *specificity principle* that focuses on the idiographic character of individual ↔ context relations. The principle delineates the way research questions should be posed. In addition, this phrasing has implications for applications of research intended to be sensitive to the idiographic character of human development; that is, addressing a multipart "what" question is the key to conducting programmatic research about the function, structure, and content of development across the lifespan and to applying knowledge from this research to applications aimed at enhancing the development of each individual in a program. For instance, researchers might undertake programs of research to gain answers to the following multipart "what" question:

1. What structure–content relations emerge; that are linked to
2. What antecedent and consequent adaptive developmental regulations (to what trajectory of individual ↔ context relations); at
3. What points in development; for
4. What individuals; living in
5. What contexts; across
6. What historical periods?

In summary, RDS-based theoretical and methodological ideas enable developmental scientists interested in the defining features of individuals to view every individual as, at least in part, systematically unique, as possessing attributes of individuality that are plastic and that, through planned attempts to alter the structure or function of these attributes, through changes in the pathways of individual ↔ context relations traversed by an individual across his or her life, may help optimize the course of individual development across the lifespan. Accordingly, as we have noted, an RDS-based approach to the development of an individual has important implications for the application of developmental science.

Applications of RDS-Based Research on the Development of an Individual

The Bornstein (2017) specificity principle can guide the generation of research and application that might uniquely promote health and positive development of individuals across the lifespan. Consider, the recent statement by Shonkoff and his colleagues at the Harvard University Center on the Developing Child (2017). In their paper, "Protected: A System for Science-Based R&D That Achieves Breakthrough Outcomes at Scale for Young Children Facing Adversity," Shonkoff (the director of the Center) and his colleagues ask how their approach to early childhood research and development is different from current best practices. Reflecting the nonergodic and idiographic approach involved in the Bornstein specificity principle, they write:

The conventional definition of an "evidence-based" program is met by a statistically significant difference on average between a measured outcome in a group that received an intervention (which typically includes multiple components that are not defined precisely) and that same outcome assessed in a control or comparison group. Frontiers of Innovation challenges this approach. We believe that assessing program effects on average misses what may work exceptionally well for some and poorly (or not at all) for others. Moreover, attempting to create a single "did it work?" test for a multi-faceted intervention obscures its active ingredients, leaving only a "black box" that must be adopted in its entirety. We pose a new set of questions, whose answers require a higher level of precision in program design, implementation, and measurement:

- What about the program works? If we understand the active ingredients, we are better able to replicate and scale them.
- How does it work? Being specific about the underlying mechanisms can help us increase the impacts and assure they will be sustained when we transport the program to other contexts.
- For whom does it work and for whom does it not work? When we know more about who is and isn't responding, we can scale what works for the former and make changes for the latter.
- Where does it work? If we specify and understand the relevant contextual factors, then we are better able to make adaptations so it will also work in a multitude of diverse settings" (p. 4).

Accordingly, through conducting programmatic research addressing such specificity-based questions, the particular ontogenetic sets of individual ↔ context relations involved in a person's life may be identified and, as well, the specific relations associated with his or her positive development may be discovered (e.g., see Rose, 2016). Therefore, one key outcome of such specificity principle-framed research can be the identification of the diverse ways in which specific individual ↔ context relations may capitalize on the potential for plasticity in human life and result in adaptive, healthy, or positive development for specific youth developing in specific settings (Spencer, Swanson, & Harpalani, 2015).

In essence, then, nonergodic, specificity principle-framed research focusing on the diversity of human development may be able to identify the specific individual ↔ context relations linked to positive development for specific individuals or groups of individuals. If so, then, developmental scientists could capitalize on the relative plasticity of human development and assess whether, by creating the conditions for such relations among other, similar individuals, more general positive development could be promoted. The key idea here is that developmental scientists should forego beginning their developmental study with the overall (nomothetic) group or the subgroup or differential group, and then looking at individuality (either in a restricted way or, even more problematically, as error variance—as in standard ergodic-theorems-based methods—for instance, in procedures that compare averages, such as analyses of variance). Instead, developmental scientists should begin to assess human development at the individual level, *then* assess whether it is legitimate to aggregate developmental phenomena at the differential or nomothetic level.

With such an approach, developmental science could gain the knowledge to contribute to thriving across the life of our granddaughter and, as well, to the diverse children and grandchildren of the world in present and future generations. Such contributions would enable developmental scientists to be part of a multisector network of people enhancing equity and social justice for the diverse people of our world.

Idiography and the Promotion of Social Justice

Developmental scientists have in the repertoire of models and methods in their intellectual "toolbox" the means to work to promote a better life for all people, to give diverse individuals the requisite chances needed to maximize their aspirations and actions aimed at being active producers of their positive development, and to promote a more socially just world (Lerner, 2002, 2004; Lerner & Overton, 2008). In this regard, Lerner and Overton noted that theoretically predicated changes in the RDS need to be evaluated with regard to how the promotion of positive development may be enhanced among individuals whose ecological characteristics (e.g., socioeconomic circumstances or educational opportunities) lower the probability of such development.

To contribute significantly to creating a developmental science aimed at promoting social justice, scholars need to identify the means to change individual ↔ context relations in manners that enhance the probability that all individuals, no matter their individual characteristics or contextual circumstances, have greater opportunity to experience positive development (e.g., see Fisher, Busch-Rossnagel, Jopp, & Brown, 2012). Indeed, Fisher and Lerner (2013) noted that social justice focuses on the rights of all groups in a society to have fair access to and a voice in policies governing the distribution of resources essential to their physical and psychological well-being. Social justice focuses also on social inequities, characterized as avoidable and unjust social structures and policies that limit access to resources based solely on group or individual characteristics such as race/ethnicity, age, gender, sexual orientation, physical or developmental ability status, and/or immigration status, among others.

Developmental science framed by the process–relational paradigm has a clear agenda involving such scholarship. For instance, Fisher and colleagues (2012) provided a vision for social justice-relevant research in developmental science. Some of the research foci they discuss include addressing the pervasive systemic disparities in opportunities for development; investigating the origins, structures, and consequences of social inequities in human development; identifying societal barriers to health and well-being; identifying barriers to fair allocation and access to resources essential to positive development; identifying how racist and other prejudicial ideologies and behaviors develop in majority groups; studying how racism, heterosexism, classism, and other forms of chronic and acute systemic inequities and political marginalization may have a "weathering" effect on physical and mental health across the lifespan; enacting evidence-based prevention and policy research aimed at demonstrating whether systemic oppression can be diminished and psychological and political liberation can be promoted; taking a systems-level approach to reducing unjust institutional practices and to promoting individual and collective political empowerment within organizations, communities, and local and national governments; evaluating programs and policies that alleviate developmental harms caused by structural injustices; and, creating and evaluating empirically based interventions that promote a just society that nurtures lifelong healthy development in all of its members.

Conclusions

The embodied developmental changes that characterize individual ↔ context relations within the self-constructing and self-organizing autopoietic relational developmental system (Overton, 2015; Witherington & Lickliter, 2016), and that provide a rationale for and optimism about applying developmental science in the service of promoting thriving and social justice for all people, requires "a theoretical framework more akin to current dynamic systems models than to traditional conceptions of either behavioral development or evolution" (Harper, 2005, p. 352). Overton (2013, 2015) has provided much of this theoretical framework.

Derived from a process–relational paradigm, the RDS metamodel that Overton has forwarded explains why the essentialist and Cartesian-split–mechanistic scientific paradigm, that until recently functioned as the standard conceptual framework for subfields of developmental science (including inheritance, evolution, and organismic—prenatal, cognitive, emotional, motivational, sociocultural—development) has been progressively failing as a scientific research program (Overton, 2013). He noted:

> An alternative scientific paradigm composed of nested metatheories with relationism at the broadest level and relational developmental systems as a midrange metatheory is offered as a more progressive conceptual framework for developmental science. Termed broadly the relational developmental systems paradigm, this framework accounts for the findings that are anomalies for the old paradigm; accounts for the emergence of new findings; and points the way to future scientific productivity. (p. 22)

In this chapter, we have argued that the old paradigm—the Cartesian–split, reductionist, essentialist one—that Overton discusses has been the frame for essentialist formulations in the study of the person and, in particular, the ideas associated with genetic reductionist models. In addition to the myriad empirical shortcoming of genetic reductionism, the conceptual flaws of this approach to describing, explaining, and optimizing an individual obviate its use in a developmental science that emphasizes nonergodicity and the ideas of jaggedness, context, and idiographic developmental pathways (Lerner, 2015a, 2016, 2018; Rose, 2016). To the extent that scholars interested in personality, in the attributes that constitute an individual's personological "signature," seek to inform and enhance the goals of developmental science—to describe, explain, and optimize intraindividual change and interindividual differences in intraindividual change—it will be incumbent on them to use key ideas associated with RDS metatheory. These ideas include ones such as plasticity, embodiment, and the fundamental importance of mutually influential individual ↔ context relations.

Such work will enable the stories of individual lives in context to be more fully, more richly, and more accurately told than in past work framed by essentialist formulations. The greater ecological validity of these accounts will further understanding of the process of individual development and, as such, may provide a potentially more useful evidence base for enhancing policies and programs aimed at promoting pathways to thriving for Isla Terese Lerner, for our other grandchildren, Harper Rose Ramsey, Dylan Maxwell Ramsey, and Bodie Anthony Ramsey, and as well all the diverse individuals around the world.

ACKNOWLEDGMENTS

The preparation of this chapter was supported in part by grants from the John Templeton Foundation and the Templeton Religion Trust.

REFERENCES

Baltes, P. B. (1997). On the incomplete architecture of human ontogeny: Selection, optimization, and compensation as foundations of developmental theory. *American Psychologist, 52,* 366–380.

Baltes, P. B., Lindenberger, U., & Staudinger, U. M. (2006). Life span theory in developmental psychology. In R. M. Lerner (Ed.), *Handbook of child psychology: Vol. 1. Theoretical models of human development* (6th ed., pp. 569–664). Hoboken, NJ: Wiley.

Belsky, J. (2014, November 30). The downside of resilience. *New York Times, Sunday Review,* p. SR4.

Belsky, J., Steinberg, L., & Draper, P. (1991). Childhood experience, interpersonal development, and reproductive strategy: An evolutionary theory of socialization. *Child Development, 62,* 647–670.

Bijou, S. W., & Baer, D. M. (1961). *Child development: A systemic and empirical theory* (Vol. 1). New York: Appleton-Century-Crofts.

Bjorklund, D. F. (2015). Developing adaptations. *Developmental Review, 38,* 13–35.

Bjorklund, D. F. (2016). Prepared is not preformed: Commentary on Witherington and Lickliter. *Human Development, 59,* 235–241.

Bjorklund, D. F., & Ellis, B. J. (2005). Evolutionary psychology and child development: An emerging synthesis. In B. J. Ellis & D. F. Bjorklund (Eds.), *Origins of the social mind: Evolutionary psychology and child development* (pp. 3–18). New York: Guilford Press.

Block, J. (1971). *Lives through time*. Berkeley, CA: Bancroft.

Bornstein, M. H. (2006). Parenting science and practice. In K. A. Renninger & I. E. Sigel (Vol. Eds.) W. Damon, & R. M. Lerner (Eds.-in-Chief), *Handbook of child psychology: Vol. 4. Child psychology in practice* (6th ed., pp. 893–949). Hoboken, NJ: Wiley.

Bornstein, M. H. (2017). The specificity principle in acculturation science. *Perspectives in Psychological Science, 12*(1), 3–45.

Brandtstädter, J. (1998). Action perspectives on human development. In W. Damon & R. M. Lerner (Eds.), *Handbook of child psychology: Vol. 1. Theoretical models of human development* (5th ed., pp. 807–863). New York: Wiley.

Bronfenbrenner, U. (1979). *The ecology of human development: Experiments by nature and design*. Cambridge, MA: Harvard University Press.

Bronfenbrenner, U. (2005). *Making human beings human: Bioecological perspectives on human development*. Thousand Oaks, CA: SAGE.

Bronfenbrenner, U., & Morris, P. A. (2006). The bioecological model of human development. In W. Damon & R. M. Lerner (Eds.), *Handbook of child psychology: Vol. 1. Theoretical models of human development* (6th ed., pp. 793–828). Hoboken, NJ: Wiley.

Center on the Developing Child. (2017). *Building a system for science-based R&D that achieves breakthrough outcomes at scale for young children facing adversity*. Cambridge, MA: Harvard University Press.

Charney, E. (2017, January). Genes, behavior, and behavior genetics. *Wiley Interdisciplinary Reviews: Cognitive Science, 8*(1–2), e1405.

Chess, S., & Thomas, A. (1999). *Goodness of fit: Clinical applications from infancy through adult life*. Philadelphia: Brunner/Mazel.

Cole, S. W. (2014). Human social genomics. *PLOS Genetics, 10*(8), 1–7.

Costa, P. T., Jr., & McCrae, R. R. (1980). Still stable after all these years: Personality as a key to some issues in adulthood and old age. In P. B. Baltes & O. G. Brim, Jr. (Eds.), *Life span development and behavior* (Vol. 3, pp. 65–102). New York: Academic Press.

Costa, P. T., Jr., & McCrae, R. R. (2006). Age changes in personality and their origins: Comment on Roberts, Walton, and Viechtbauer (2006). *Psychological Bulletin, 132*, 28–30.

Costa, P. T., Jr., McCrae, R. R., & Siegler, I. C. (1999). Continuity and change over the adult life cycle: Personality and personality disorders. In C. R. Cloninger (Ed.), *Personality and psychopathology* (pp. 129–154). Washington, DC: American Psychiatric Press.

Dawkins, R. (1976). *The selfish gene*. New York: Oxford University Press.

Del Giudice, M., & Ellis, B. J. (2016). Evolutionary foundations of developmental psychopathology. In D. Cicchetti (Ed.), *Developmental psychopathology: Vol. 12. Developmental neuroscience* (3rd ed., pp. 1–58). New York: Wiley.

Elder, G. H., Jr. (1998). The life course and human development. In W. Damon (Series Ed.) & R. M. Lerner (Vol. Ed.), *Handbook of child psychology: Vol. 1. Theoretical models of human development* (5th ed., pp. 939–991). New York: Wiley.

Elder, G. H., Jr., Shanahan, M. J., & Jennings, J. A. (2015). Human development in time and place. In M. H. Bornstein & T. Leventhal (Eds.), *Handbook of child psychology and developmental science: Vol. 4. Ecological settings and processes* (7th ed., pp. 6–54). Hoboken, NJ: Wiley.

Emmerich, W. (1968). Personality development and concepts of structure. *Child Development, 39*, 671–690.

Erikson, E. H. (1959). *Identity and the life cycle*. New York: International Universities Press.

Erikson, E. (1968). *Identity, youth, and crisis*. New York: Norton.

Feldman, D. H. (1980). *Beyond universals in cognitive development*. Norwood, NJ: Ablex.

Fisher, C. B., Busch-Rossnagel, N. A., Jopp, D. S., & Brown, J. L. (2012). Applied developmental science, social justice, and socio-political well-being. *Applied Developmental Science, 16*(1), 54–64.

Fisher, C. B., & Lerner, R. M. (2013). Promoting positive development through social justice: An introduction to a new ongoing section of *Applied Developmental Science. Applied Developmental Science, 17*(2), 57–59.

Ford, D. H., & Lerner, R. M. (1992). *Developmental systems theory: An integrative approach*. Newbury Park, CA: SAGE.

Freedman, D. G. (1979). *Human sociobiology: A holistic approach*. New York: Free Press.

Freud, S. (1954). *Collected works: Standard edition*. London: Hogarth Press.

Gottlieb, G. (1992). *Individual development and evolution: The genesis of novel behavior*. New York: Oxford University Press.

Gottlieb, G. (1997). *Synthesizing nature–nurture: Prenatal roots of instinctive behavior*. Mahwah, NJ: Erlbaum.

Gottlieb, G. (1998). Normally occurring environmental and behavioral influences on gene activity: From central dogma to probabilistic epigenesis. *Psychological Review, 105*, 792–802.

Harper, L. V. (2005). Epigenetic inheritance and the intergenerational transfer of experience. *Psychological Bulletin, 131*, 340–360.

Harvard University Center on the Developing Child. (2017, April). Protected: A system for science-based R&D that achieves breakthrough outcomes at scale for young children facing adversity. Retrieved from https://developingchild.harvard.edu/concept-paper-feature/.

Hirsch, J. (1997). Some history of heredity-vs-environment, genetic inferiority at Harvard (?), and The (incredible) Bell Curve. *Genetica, 99*, 207–224.

Hirsch, J. (2004). Uniqueness, diversity, similarity, repeatability, and heritability. In C. Garcia Coll, E. Bearer, & R. M. Lerner (Eds.), *Nature and nurture: The complex interplay of genetic and environmental influences on human behavior and development* (pp. 127–138). Mahwah, NJ: Erlbaum.

Ho, M. W. (2010). Development and evolution revisited. In K. E. Hood, C. T. Halpern, G. Greenberg, & R. M. Lerner (Eds.), *Handbook of developmental systems, behavior and genetics* (pp. 61–109). Malden, MA: Wiley-Blackwell.

Ho, M. W. (2013). No genes for intelligence in the fluid genome. In R. M. Lerner & J. B. Benson (Eds.), *Advances in child development and behavior: Embodiment and epigenesis: Theoretical and methodological issues in understanding the role of biology within the relational developmental system: Part B. Ontogenetic dimensions* (pp. 67–92). London: Elsevier.

John, O. P., & Naumann, L. P. (2010). Surviving two critiques by Block?: The resilient Big Five have emerged as the paradigm for personality trait psychology. *Psychological Inquiry, 21*(1), 44–49.

Joseph, J. (2015). *The trouble with twin studies: A reassessment of twin research in the social and behavioral sciences.* New York: Routledge.

Kluckhohn, C., & Murray, H. A. (1948). *Personality in nature, society, and culture.* New York: Knopf.

Kohlberg, L. (1978). Revisions in the theory and practice of moral development. *New Directions for Child Development, 2*, 93–120.

Lerner, R. M. (1982). Children and adolescents as producers of their own development. *Developmental Review, 2*, 342–370.

Lerner, R. M. (1984). *On the nature of human plasticity.* New York: Cambridge University Press.

Lerner, R. M. (2002). *Concepts and theories of human development* (3rd ed.). Mahwah, NJ: Erlbaum.

Lerner, R. M. (2004). *Liberty: Thriving and civic engagement among America's youth.* Thousand Oaks, CA: SAGE.

Lerner, R. M. (Ed.). (2006). *Handbook of child psychology: Vol. 1. Theoretical models of human development* (6th ed.). Hoboken, NJ: Wiley.

Lerner, R. M. (2012). Essay review: Developmental science: Past, present, and future. *International Journal of Developmental Science, 6*(1–2), 29–36.

Lerner, R. M. (2015a). Eliminating genetic reductionism from developmental science. *Research in Human Development, 12*, 178–188.

Lerner, R. M. (Ed.). (2015b). *Handbook of child psychology and developmental science* (7th ed.). Hoboken, NJ: Wiley.

Lerner, R. M. (2016). Complexity embraced and complexity reduced: A tale of two approaches to human development. *Human Development, 59*, 242–249.

Lerner, R. M. (2018). *Concepts and theories of human development* (4th ed.). New York: Routledge.

Lerner, R. M., & Benson, J. B. (Eds.). (2013). *Embodiment and epigenesis: Theoretical and methodological issues in understanding the role of biology within the relational developmental system: Vol. 1. Philosophical, theoretical, and biological dimensions.* London: Elsevier.

Lerner, R. M., & Callina, K. S. (2014). The study of character development: Towards tests of a relational developmental systems model. *Human Development, 57*(6), 322–346.

Lerner, R. M., Johnson, S. K., & Buckingham, M. H. (2015). Relational developmental systems-based theories and the study of children and families: Lerner and Spanier (1978) revisited. *Journal of Family Theory and Review, 7*, 83–104.

Lerner, R. M., Lerner, J. V., Bowers, E., & Geldhof, G. J. (2015) Positive youth development and relational developmental systems. In W. F. Overton & P. C. Molenaar (Eds.), *Handbook of child psychology and developmental science: Vol. 1. Theory and method* (7th ed., pp. 607–651). Hoboken, NJ: Wiley.

Lerner, R. M., Lerner, J. V., Urban, J. B., & Zaff, J. (2016). Evaluating programs aimed at promoting positive youth development: A relational developmental systems-based view. *Applied Developmental Science, 20*(3), 175–187.

Lerner, R. M., & Overton, W. F. (2008). Exemplifying the integrations of the relational developmental system: Synthesizing theory, research, and application to promote positive development and social justice. *Journal of Adolescent Research, 23*(3), 245–255.

Lester, B. M., Conradt, E., & Marsit, C. (2016). Introduction to the special section on epigenetics. *Child Development, 87*, 29–37.

Lickliter, R., & Witherington, D. C. (Eds.). (2017). Transcending the nature–nurture debate through epigenetics: Are we there yet? *Human Development, 60*(2–3), 61–140.

Lorenz, K. (1965). *Evolution and modification of behavior.* Chicago: University of Chicago Press.

Mascolo, M. F., & Fischer, K. W. (2015) Dynamic development of thinking, feeling, and acting. In W. F. Overton & P. C. Molenaar (Eds.), *Handbook of child psychology and developmental science: Vol. 1. Theory and method* (7th ed., pp. 113–161). Hoboken, NJ: Wiley.

McCrae, R. R., Costa, P. T., Hrebickova, M., Ostendord, F., Angleitner, A., Avia, M. D., et al. (2000). Nature over nurture: Temperament, personality, and life span development. *Journal of Personality and Social Psychology, 78*(1), 173–186.

McGrath, R. E., Hall-Simmonds, A., & Goldberg, L. R. (2017). Are measures of character and personality distinct?: Evidence from observed-score and true-score analyses. *Assessment.* [Epub ahead of print]

McGrath, R. E., & Walker, D. I. (2016). Factor structure of character strengths in youth: Consistency across ages and measures. *Journal of Moral Education,* *45*(4), 400–418.

Meaney, M. (2010). Epigenetics and the biological definition of gene × environment interactions. *Child Development, 81,* 41–79.

Misteli, T. (2013). The cell biology of genomes: Bringing the double helix to life. *Cell, 152,* 1209–1212.

Molenaar, P. C. M. (2010). On the limits of standard quantitative genetic modeling of inter-individual variation: Extensions, ergodic conditions and a new genetic factor model of intro-individual variation. In K. E. Hood, C. T. Halpern, G. Greenberg, & R. M. Lerner (Eds.), *Handbook of developmental systems, behavior and genetics* (pp. 626–648). Malden, MA: Wiley-Blackwell.

Molenaar, P. C. M. (2014). Dynamic models of biological pattern formation have surprising implications for understanding the epigenetics of development. *Research in Human Development, 11*(1), 50–62.

Molenaar, P. C. M., & Nesselroade, J. R. (2014). New trends in the inductive use of relational developmental systems theory: Ergodicity, nonstationarity, and heterogeneity. In P. C. M. Molenaar, R. M. Lerner, & K. M. Newell (Eds.), *Handbook of developmental systems theory and methodology* (pp. 442–462). New York: Guilford Press.

Molenaar, P. C. M., & Nesselroade, J. R. (2015). Systems methods for developmental research. In W. F. Overton & P. C. Molenaar (Eds.), *Handbook of child psychology and developmental science: Vol. 1. Theory and method* (7th ed., pp. 652–682). Hoboken, NJ: Wiley.

Moore, D. S. (2015). *The developing genome: An introduction to behavioral epigenetics.* New York: Oxford University Press.

Moore, D. S. (2017a). Behavioral epigenetics. *WIREs Systems Biology and Medicine, 9*(1), e1333.

Moore, D. S. (2017b). The potential of epigenetics research to transform conceptions of phenotype development. *Human Development, 60,* 69–80.

Moore, D. S., & Shenk, D. (2016). The heritability fallacy. *WIREs Cognitive Science, 8*(1–2), e1400.

Nesselroade, J. R. (1988). Some implications of the trait–state distinction for the study of development over the life-span: The case of personality. In P. B. Baltes, D. L. Featherman, & R. M. Lerner (Eds.), *Life-span development and behavior* (Vol. 8, pp. 163–189). Hillsdale, NJ: Erlbaum.

Nesselroade, J. R., & Molenaar, P. C. M. (2010). Emphasizing intraindividual variability in the study of development over the life span. In W. F. Overton (Ed.), *The handbook of life-span development: Vol. 1. Cognition, biology, methods* (pp. 30–54). Hoboken, NJ: Wiley.

Noftle, E., Schnitker, S., & Robins, R. (2011). Character and personality: Connections between positive psychology and personality psychology. In K. M. Sheldon, T. B. Kashdan, & M. F. Steger (Eds.), *Designing positive psychology: Taking stock and moving for-*

ward (pp. 207–227). New York: Oxford University Press.

Overton, W. F. (1973). On the assumptive base of the nature–nurture controversy: Additive versus interactive conceptions. *Human Development, 16,* 74–89.

Overton, W. F. (2013). Relationism and relational developmental systems: A paradigm for developmental science in the post-Cartesian era. *Advances in Child Development and Behavior, 44,* 21–64.

Overton, W. F. (2015). Processes, relations, and relational developmental systems. In W. F. Overton & P. C. M. Molenaar (Vol. Eds.) & R. M. Lerner (Ed.-in-Chief), *Handbook of child psychology and developmental science: Vol. 1. Theory and method* (7th ed., pp. 9–62). Hoboken, NJ: Wiley.

Overton, W. F., & Reese, H. W. (1981). Conceptual prerequisites for an understanding of stability–change and continuity–discontinuity. *International Journal of Behavioral Development, 4,* 99–123.

Park, N., & Peterson, C. (2006). Moral competence and character strengths among adolescents: The development and validation of the Values in Action Inventory of Strengths for Youth. *Journal of Adolescence, 29,* 891–909.

Peterson, C., & Seligman, M. E. (2004). *Character strengths and virtues: A handbook and classification.* Washington, DC: American Psychological Association.

Piaget, J. (1970). Piaget's theory. In P. H. Mussen (Ed.), *Carmichael's manual of child psychology* (3rd ed., Vol. 1, pp. 703–723). New York: Wiley.

Plomin, R., DeFries, J. C., Knopik, V. S., & Neiderhiser, J. M. (2016). Top 10 replicated findings from behavioral genetics. *Perspectives on Psychological Science, 11*(1), 3–23.

Raeff, C. (2011). Distinguishing between development and change: Reviving organismic-developmental theory. *Human Development, 54*(1), 4–33.

Raeff, C. (2016). *Exploring the dynamics of human development: An integrative approach.* New York: Oxford University Press.

Richardson, K. (2017). *Genes, brains and human potential: The science and ideology of human intelligence.* New York: Columbia University Press.

Riegel, K. F. (1975). Toward a dialectical theory of human development. *Human Development, 18,* 50–64.

Riegel, K. F. (1976). The dialectics of human development. *American Psychologist, 31,* 689–700.

Rimfeld, K., Ayorech, Z., Dale, P. S., Kovas, Y., & Plomin, R. (2016). Genetics affects choice of academic subjects as well as achievement. *Scientific Reports, 6,* Article No. 26373.

Roberts, B. W., Walton, K. E., & Viechtbauer, W. (2006). Patterns of mean-level change in personality traits across the life course: A meta-analysis of longitudinal studies. *Psychological Bulletin, 132*(1), 1–25.

Rose, L. T., Rouhani, P., & Fischer, K. W. (2013). The

science of the individual. *Mind, Brain, and Education, 7*(3), 152–158.

Rose, T. (2016). *The end of average: How we succeed in a world that values sameness.* New York: HarperCollins.

Rushton, J. P. (2000). *Race, evolution, and behavior* (2nd ed., special abridged). New Brunswick, NJ: Transaction.

Skinner, B. F. (1971). *Beyond freedom and dignity.* New York: Knopf.

Slavich, G. M., & Cole, S. W. (2013). The emerging field of human social genomics. *Clinical Psychological Science, 1,* 331–348.

Sokol, B. W., Hammond, S., Kuebli, J., & Sweetman, L. (2015). The development of agency. In W. F. Overton & P. C. Molenaar (Eds.), *Handbook of child psychology and developmental science: Vol. 1. Theory and method* (7th ed., pp. 284–322). Hoboken, NJ: Wiley.

Spencer, M. B., Swanson, D. P., & Harpalani, V. (2015). Development of the self. In M. E. Lamb (Vol. Ed.) & R. M. Lerner (Ed.-in-Chief), *Handbook of child psychology and developmental science: Vol. 3. Socio-*

emotional processes (7th ed., pp. 750–793). Hoboken, NJ: Wiley.

Thomas, A., Chess, S., Birch, H. G., Hertzig, M. E., & Korn, S. J. (1963). *Behavioral individuality in early childhood.* New York: New York University Press.

von Bertalanffy, L. (1933). *Modern theories of development.* London: Oxford University Press.

Wahlsten, D. (2012). The hunt for gene effects pertinent to behavioral traits and psychiatric disorders: From mouse to human. *Developmental Psychobiology, 54,* 475–492.

Werner, H. (1957). The concept of development from a comparative and organismic point of view. In D. B. Harris (Ed.), *The concept of development* (pp. 125–148). Minneapolis: University of Minnesota Press.

Whitehead, A. N. (1978). *Process and reality: Corrected edition.* New York: Free Press. (Original work published 1929)

Witherington, D. C., & Lickliter, R. (2016). Integrating development and evolution in psychological science: Evolutionary developmental psychology, developmental systems, and explanatory pluralism. *Human Development, 59,* 200–234.

PART II

SOCIAL ACTORS

From Temperament to Personality Traits

Personality begins with the inborn differences in attention, emotional response, and social demeanor that human infants show in the first few months of life. Long before these new members of the *Homo sapiens* species have a clear sense of themselves in a social world, they are *social actors,* displaying different styles in their interactions with other members of the species. And certain other members are especially keen to observe the infant's displays, like the mother and father, other members of the extended kin network, nurses and health care professionals who monitor new human beings as they burst forth into the birthing rooms of modern societies, and other significant people in the infant's environment. For all of them, the infant is first and foremost an actor on the social stage of life, performing emotion for an audience that alternates between rapt attention and exhaustion. What kind of an actor will the baby turn out to be? A smiley baby? A fussy baby? An outgoing and gregarious person? An introvert? An angry young man? A pensive, thoughtful, deliberate young lady? How will this person play his roles in life? Will she eventually turn out to be generally nice, mean, angry, calm, enthusiastic, dominant, anxious, depressive, or conscientious? Nobody knows for sure, but we watch our babies closely in search of clues.

Going back to the observations of Thomas, Chess, and Birch in the 1960s, developmental psychologists have expressed strong interest in the temperament differences that appear very early in the human life course. In more recent years, personality and developmental psychologists have theorized that these early differences may lay the groundwork for the articulation of full-fledged personality dispositions in adulthood. Perhaps early differences in positive emotionality, detectable in the first year of life, represent temperamental precursors of what may eventually develop into the trait of extraversion. Childhood effortful control may be a harbinger of later conscientiousness. Or maybe not. Perhaps continuity is the exception rather than the rule. This is a wide-open area of contemporary research in the study of personality development. The research explores a fundamental layer of human uniqueness, a line of personality development that may track the move from early temperament dimensions to the eventual elaboration of more complex and fully articulated dispositional traits.

The chapters gathered together in Part II of this volume focus on the nature, origins, and development of dispositional personality traits over the human life course. For the most part, the chapters' authors consider the kinds of traits that are typically grouped within such well-known trait taxonomies as the Big Five framework. In Chapter 5, Colin G. DeYoung and Timothy A. Allen lay the neuroscience groundwork for conceptualizing dispositional dimensions of personality.

Surveying a rapidly growing body of empirical research and theorizing, they aim to identify stable patterns of brain functioning that are proximally responsible for individual differences in personality traits and to understand how these patterns are shaped by more distal causal factors in the genome and the environment. In Chapter 6, Kristin A. Buss, Koraly Pérez-Edgar, Alicia Vallorani, and Berenice Anaya trace links between temperament and personality through the lens of emotional reactivity and regulation. They argue that by examining early reactivity and regulation, researchers may maximize the probability of understanding developmental trajectories to specific traits in adulthood.

Chapters 7–11 consider, in turn, each of the broad clusters of dispositional dimensions that group together under the Big Five categories of traits. In Chapter 7, Luke D. Smillie, Margaret L. Kern, and Mirko Uljarevic examine the broad family of traits that fall within the extraversion domain, including inclinations toward positive emotionality, surgency, gregariousness, assertiveness, sociability, social vitality, and the like. Rebecca L. Shiner casts a developmental eye on the many facets and features of negative emotionality/neuroticism in Chapter 8. In Chapter 9, Joshua J. Jackson and Patrick L. Hill take up conscientiousness and related constructs, such as effortful control. Jennifer L. Tackett, Marcel M. Hernández, and Nancy Eisenberg explore in Chapter 10 the development of agreeableness, a dimension whose common name is surely too anemic to capture the positive emotional pole of love and compassion and the mean-spirited negative pole of cruelty, hostility, and aggression. Finally, in Chapter 11, Ted Schwaba considers the curious trait of openness to experience, sometimes viewed to be the odd man out in the Big Five. Openness is as much about cognition as it is about the social–emotional performance of the actor. What exactly is this trait? Where does it come from?

Chapters 12 and 13 take a closer look at the complex interrelationships that develop between environmental factors and the development of temperament and personality traits. In Chapter 12, Liliana J. Lengua, Maria A. Gartstein, and Peter Prinzie synthesize the burgeoning research literature regarding the effects of parenting on the development of children's and adolescents' traits, and the reciprocal effect of their traits on parenting. A powerful message from their review is that there is no one-size-fits-all when it comes to parenting and traits. The influence of parenting factors in the family typically depends on the particular traits that children and adolescents possess, as well as other factors, such as the age of the child. In Chapter 13, Helena R. Slobodskaya considers the broad cultural factors that may shape the development of dispositional personality traits. She views culture as the organization of the developmental environment, like a garden where conditions for growth are created. Switching metaphors, Slobodskaya discusses the nested nature of cultural contexts, whereby the proximal influences of childrearing patterns and regular social interactions are subsumed within the more distal environments of school, work, and the broad cultural ethos of a given society. Distal forces may exert their important effects on the development of personality traits through mediating proximal mechanisms located in the family and peer group.

Finally, in Chapter 14, Wiebke Bleidorn and Christopher J. Hopwood review the literature on stability and change in personality traits over the human lifespan. They evaluate some of the most celebrated findings in the study of personality development, including (1) the remarkable rank-order stability of individual differences, especially in the middle-adult years; (2) the prevalence of a maturity principle in trait development (which predicts mean-level increases in conscientiousness and agreeableness from adolescence through late midlife, and corresponding declines in neuroticism); and (3) the rapidly growing body of evidence for the influence of discrete live events in adulthood (e.g., marriage, employment) on personality change.

CHAPTER 5

Personality Neuroscience
A Developmental Perspective

Colin G. DeYoung
Timothy A. Allen

From birth through old age, individual human beings are at least somewhat predictable. Some 5-year-olds are consistently more fearful or more talkative than others, and so are some 75-year-olds. People exhibit clear consistencies in their thoughts, emotions, motivations, and behaviors. Individual differences between people in these consistent patterns are sufficiently reliable that the concept of "personality" is self-evident to most people, and it has been well established scientifically, too. But where do differences in personality come from? This is one of the major questions that personality psychology aims to answer, and it is also one of the most difficult. Most research on this question has focused on what can be called the *distal causes* of personality, trying to determine to what extent differences in personality traits are caused by genetic versus environmental forces, then trying to understand how specific genes and specific environmental forces shape personality. In contrast, in this chapter, we focus on the *proximal causes* of personality in the brain.

Researchers have begun to make substantial progress toward understanding the neurobiological systems underlying personality only in the last two decades. Nonetheless, the field of personality neuroscience is growing quickly, and its findings are beginning to have important implications for understanding personality development over the life course. Such research is crucial for a full understanding of where personality comes from because all behavior and experience, aside from the simplest spinal reflexes, is generated by the brain. Thus, even environmental influences on personality are "biological," in the sense that the environment must have a lasting effect on the brain in order to influence personality. When personality changes, whether at age 5, 35, or 75, the brain necessarily changes, too. In this chapter, we go beyond previous summaries of personality neuroscience research by attempting to link what is known about the neural correlates of personality to what is known about brain development.

Before attempting to understand the sources of personality from a developmental perspective, one needs to have a reasonably robust picture of the structure of personality across the life course and how it changes over time. By "structure," we mean the patterns of traits that tend to appear together in individuals; this is interpersonal structure, in contrast to the intrapersonal structure of one individual's personality. By early childhood, personality appears to have roughly the same interpersonal structure that it does in adulthood, with most individual differences well captured by one of five broad trait dimensions known as the "Big Five": extraversion, neuroticism, conscientiousness, agreeableness, and openness/intellect (Caspi &

Shiner, 2006; Mervielde, De Clerq, De Fruyt, & Van Leeuwen, 2005). The Big Five show increasing rank-order stability from childhood to old age, when they finally begin to become less stable again, but even in adulthood they are not immune to change or disruption (Roberts & DelVecchio, 2000; Roberts, Walton, & Viechtbauer, 2006; Soto, John, Gosling, & Potter, 2011; Specht et al., 2014). In addition to increasing rank-order stability, they show normative patterns of mean-level change, with particularly large changes in adolescence and young adulthood followed by more gradual changes over the rest of the lifespan. These patterns of stability and change can be meaningfully linked to brain development.

Personality neuroscience has two main goals: (1) to identify stable patterns of brain functioning that are proximally responsible for personality and (2) to understand how those patterns are shaped by more distal causal factors in the genome and the environment. Both goals have important connections to development. By understanding the maturation of biological systems, personality researchers will be better equipped to explain the patterns of continuity and change in personality that occur over the course of development. Additionally, the reverse may be true as well: Understanding how personality changes may help guide hypotheses about neural processes. Research on personality development has already provided a wealth of data showing how developmental factors (e.g., stress and adversity, life transitions) are related to personality functioning (e.g., Shiner, Allen, & Masten, 2017; Specht, Egloff, & Schmukle, 2011). Adding a neuroscience perspective allows us to better understand the mechanisms involved in these transactions.

As with all scientific endeavors, personality neuroscience is likely to be most effective in pursuing its goals when guided by sound theory. A number of theories have attempted to identify the psychological mechanisms underlying each of the Big Five (Denissen & Penke, 2008; DeYoung, 2015; Nettle, 2006, 2007; Van Egeren, 2009), and they are sufficiently similar to suggest that we can identify the general type of mechanism involved in each trait dimension. This perspective has two implications that are particularly useful for a developmental approach to personality neuroscience. First, once the psychological functions underlying traits are made explicit, existing knowledge about how those functions are carried out by the brain,

and how the relevant brain systems develop, can be used to form neuroscientific hypotheses. Importantly, any given psychological function is likely to be affected by many different neural parameters. Further, a given neural parameter, such as the density of a particular neurotransmitter receptor, may influence multiple psychological functions. Hence, the mapping of traits to their neurobiological sources is likely to be many-to-many, not one-to-one (Allen & DeYoung, 2017; Yarkoni, 2015).

Second, identifying the psychological functions underlying traits helps to account for *heterotypic continuity,* in which the same traits have different manifestations at different times during development. Many of the patterns of behavior and experience that the Big Five describe in adulthood may not be applicable in childhood; nonetheless, the same underlying psychological functions may be at work across the lifespan. For example, the interest in poetry or philosophy that is characteristic of adults high in openness/intellect is unlikely to be apparent in childhood, but the underlying mechanisms of this trait are nonetheless likely to be apparent in the child's curiosity and imaginative play. Thus, theories that identify the mechanisms underlying traits are crucial for a lifespan developmental perspective on personality. Additionally, heterotypic continuity may be a useful guide to personality neuroscientists, as traits reflecting the same psychological mechanism are likely to have considerable continuity in their biological mechanisms as well.

Developmental Origins of Personality

Personality can be considered to encompass all reasonably persistent psychological individual differences, incorporating not just broad traits such as the Big Five but also specific goals, beliefs, skills, and roles that people acquire through experience, and even conscious identity or life narrative (DeYoung, 2015; McAdams & Pals, 2006). Because most of these latter constructs have received little attention from a neurobiological perspective, we focus exclusively on traits. Research on psychological traits has historically been conducted under two distinct headings, temperament and personality, depending on the age of the individuals under study. "Temperament" has typically been used by developmental psychologists to refer to early-emerging, genetically influenced individual differences in emotional reactivity and self-regulation (Rothbart & Derryberry, 1981), whereas research on "personality" has more often focused on adolescent and adult populations. Despite emerging from different research traditions, however, constructs described as temperament or personality traits appear to describe the same phenomena. Behavioral genetics studies indicate that traits are subject to substantial genetic influences, regardless of whether they were initially labeled "temperament" or "personality" (Krueger & Johnson, 2008; Saudino & Wang, 2012). Trait measures from both traditions show both stability and change over the life course. Contrary to some early perspectives, neither temperament nor personality is immune to environmental influence during development, though both become more consistent over time (Roberts & DelVecchio, 2000; Specht et al., 2014). Perhaps most convincingly, conceptual and empirical investigations show that temperament and personality trait models exhibit a high degree of structural similarity, despite being developed independently (Caspi & Shiner, 2006; De Pauw & Mervielde, 2010; De Pauw, Mervielde, & Van Leeuwen, 2009; Shiner & DeYoung, 2013; Soto & Tackett, 2015).

Our perspective is that temperament traits are personality traits, and that we can reconcile traditional usages in developmental and personality psychology by considering the usual conception of childhood temperament to describe the early basis of personality, which becomes broader and more differentiated as the developing child acquires new tendencies and competencies through both genetically programmed maturation and environmentally mediated learning (Shiner & DeYoung, 2013). We organize our review from the perspective of the Big Five personality model because the five factors appear able to capture the most important individual differences in both children and adults. (Activity level often appears as a separate, sixth dimension in childhood, but it is clearly incorporated within extraversion during adolescence; Soto & Tackett, 2015.)

Nonetheless, we recognize that the Big Five are not the only trait dimensions of interest. For one thing, personality is structured hierarchically. Traits at higher levels of the hierarchy describe real patterns of covariation among traits at lower levels of the hierarchy, but, at every level of the hierarchy, traits also have their own unique, valid variance. In other words, for each trait, some variance is shared with others at its own level, giving rise to the traits at the next higher level of the hierarchy, but some variance is unique. Thus, traits at any level of the hierarchy may be important for understanding a given phenomenon. The bottom level of the hierarchy contains relatively narrow traits traditionally described as "facets." Between the Big Five and their facets, an intermediate level of traits has been described as "aspects" (DeYoung, Quilty, & Peterson, 2007). Each of the Big Five contains two aspects that represent the major empirical subdimensions of each Big Five domain, often demonstrating discriminant validity (DeYoung, 2015). The discovery of the aspects may be useful in unifying child and adult personality research, as many of the aspect-level traits map onto distinctions that have been made in childhood personality research as well (Shiner & DeYoung, 2013).

One additional level of the trait hierarchy exists above the Big Five. Though they were originally thought to be orthogonal, the Big Five in fact covary in a consistent pattern that indicates the existence of two overarching metatraits, stability and plasticity, which have been demonstrated in children as well as adults (DeYoung, 2006; Digman, 1997; Slobodskaya, 2011; Wang, Chen, Petrill, & Deater-Deckard, 2013). *Stability* comprises the shared variance of neuroticism (reversed), agreeableness, and conscientiousness and appears to reflect the tendency to maintain stable, goal-directed functioning without disruption by emotions, impulses, doubts, and distractions. *Plasticity* comprises the shared variance of extraversion and openness/intellect, and appears to capture variation in a broad tendency toward exploration, through which people generate new interpretations of the world, and new goals and strategies for acting in it (DeYoung, 2015).

The importance of the metatraits can potentially be seen very early in life. Abe and Izard (1999) found that 18-month-olds' facial expressions of emotion in the Strange Situation Paradigm predicted parent ratings of Big Five traits at 3.5 years, with the following pattern: Negative emotional expression predicted neuroticism, agreeableness, and conscientiousness, whereas strong positive emotional expression predicted extraversion and openness/intellect. It seems that even the earliest emotional regularities are related to the basic functions of maintaining stability and engaging flexibly with the world.

The metatraits allow a reasonably succinct summary of many of the normative changes observed in the Big Five over the course of the lifespan. Neuroticism, agreeableness, and conscientiousness tend to change at the same time within individuals, as do extraversion and openness/intellect, a phenomenon known as *correlated change* (Klimstra, Bleidorn, Asendorpf, van Aken, & Denissen, 2013). On average, people decrease in the stability traits during early adolescence, and then increase at the end of adolescence and into early adulthood (Soto et al., 2011; Van den Akker, Deković, Asscher, & Prinzie, 2014). Further increases in stability are gradual throughout adulthood, and some evidence suggests a decline begins in old age (Mõttus, Johnson, & Deary, 2012; Roberts et al., 2006; Wagner, Ram, Smith, & Gerstorf, 2016). In contrast, plasticity tends to decrease from middle age through old age (Specht et al., 2011; Srivastava, John, Gosling, & Potter, 2003).

We do not focus on the metatraits in our review of personality neuroscience because most research that is potentially relevant to their biological substrates has been carried out at the Big Five level. However, it is worth noting that our theory identifies general levels of serotonin and dopamine in the brain as likely substrates of stability and plasticity, respectively (Allen & DeYoung, 2017; DeYoung, 2006). A recent study provided the first direct test of the stability hypothesis, showing that people high in stability have greater serotonergic function than those moderate or low in stability (Wright, Creswell, Flory, Muldoon, & Manuck, 2018). The decline in plasticity in adulthood is consistent with known declines in dopaminergic function during adulthood, but direct evidence of a causal relation is lacking (Bäckman, Lindenberger, Li, & Nyberg, 2010; Erixon-Lindroth et al., 2005). Indeed, most inferences regarding links between personality development and brain development are still indirect at this point. Before moving to a review of direct evidence in personality neuroscience, therefore, we discuss some additional core findings from personality development and their parallels in brain development.

Remarkably, individual differences in behavior are apparent even prior to birth (e.g., DiPietro, Hodgson, Costigan, & Johnson, 1996; Eaton & Saudino, 1992), and many more emerge rapidly postnatally. Within the first year of life, infants begin to show reliable differences in their tendencies toward positive and negative affect, interest, and attention (Gartstein & Rothbart, 2003; Rothbart & Bates, 2006). As infants gain new capabilities, personality becomes more expansive, and new traits begin to emerge. During this early period, spanning the first 3 years of life, personality is at its most changeable (Roberts & DelVecchio, 2000).

This early flexibility reflects rapid brain development, mediated by *experience-expectant* and *experience-dependent* processes involved in *synaptogenesis,* or synapse formation (Greenough, Black, & Wallace, 1987). *Synapses* are the tiny gaps between neurons, where the axon of one neuron meets the dendrite of another. Neurotransmitters are released across this gap to transform electrical signaling within neurons into chemical signaling between neurons. During prenatal development and infancy, synaptogenesis occurs rapidly, as new dendrites and axons sprout and the brain's wiring becomes more and more intricate. Interestingly, the brain becomes more highly wired than it ultimately needs to be, with more synapses being made than will survive. In experience-expectant development, environmental inputs dictate which synapses are necessary for maximizing the brain's efficiency, and these synapses are retained and strengthened. Conversely, unnecessary synapses are destroyed in a process called *synaptic pruning,* which continues well into adolescence. Though much of the brain is wired in an experience-expectant manner, experience-dependent processes are important as well. In this type of development, new synapses are created in response to specific environmental inputs, allowing the brain to respond flexibly to the unique input of each developing person's context. Thus, both experience-dependent development (via synaptogenesis) and experience-expectant development (via pruning) are important mechanisms by which environmental factors shape long-term individual differences in human behavior.

Another important mechanism of brain development is *myelination,* in which glial cells wrap neuronal axons in a sheath of fatty tissue (called *myelin*) that serves to insulate the electrical impulses transmitted down the axon, greatly increasing the speed of neural transmission. Myelination typically begins in the third trimester and continues through adolescence, proceeding from the brainstem toward the cortex and from the rear of the brain (primarily responsible for processing sensory information) to the front (primarily responsible for organizing thought and action around complex goals) (Inder & Huppi, 2000; Webb, Monk, & Nelson, 2001). This trajectory of myelination has potentially important implications for personality. Because neurons in the prefrontal cortex (PFC) are typically last to be myelinated, traits most influenced by this region are likely to be slower to develop and subject to greater developmental change when myelination does occur. This may be one reason why extraversion and neuroticism—traits that reflect differences in positive and negative emotional systems based primarily in subcortical regions—are typically identified earlier than traits such as conscientiousness or openness/intellect, which rely more heavily on prefrontal regions.

The PFC undergoes extensive and rapid maturation in the period from 2 to 5 years of age, but there is another very important period of prefrontal maturation in adolescence and young adulthood (Bunge & Zelazo, 2006; Somerville, Jones, & Casey, 2010) Studies of normative mean-level trait change show more pronounced shifts during adolescence and young adulthood than at any other time during the lifespan (De Fruyt et al., 2006; Roberts et al., 2006; Soto et al., 2011; Van den Akker et al., 2014), and these changes are likely to reflect the underlying dynamics of brain maturation. Studies of brain structure in adolescents show an initial increase in gray matter (which is correlated with the number of synapses) early in puberty, followed by a subsequent decline thought to be mediated by additional synaptic pruning (Giedd et al., 1999). At the same time, myelination continues throughout the brain, leading to linear increases in white matter (bundles of axons) and advances in network efficiency (Lenroot & Giedd, 2006). The PFC matures at a slower rate than the subcortical structures that drive motivation, leading adolescents to become more impulsive and prone to externalizing problems such as antisocial behavior and drug abuse, as their reactions to potential rewards and punishments reach adult levels of sensitivity before the full maturation of the cortical systems that will constrain and regulate those reactions in adulthood (Casey, 2015). The stability traits—conscientiousness, agreeableness, and (low) neuroticism—which dip sharply in adolescence, are the major correlates of impulsivity and externalizing behavior in the Big Five (DeYoung, Peterson, Séguin, & Tremblay, 2008; DeYoung & Rueter, 2016).

Neural Correlates of the Big Five

In the rest of this chapter, we provide an overview of the biological systems that are most central to personality differences, focusing on the neural correlates of the Big Five. We rely on methodologically rigorous research as much as possible, typically avoiding, or at least offering caveats when citing, studies conducted in small samples. We are somewhat limited by the paucity of personality neuroscience studies conducted in child samples. Nonetheless, as much as possible, we discuss neural mechanisms in a developmental context.

Extraversion

Most theories of the Big Five posit that extraversion reflects variation in the biological systems governing sensitivity to reward, which causes characteristics as diverse as being talkative, sociable, physically active, joyful, and assertive to covary within a single broad trait dimension. Reward systems can be divided into those governing *incentive rewards,* which are cues that a reward may be obtained in the future and which involve desire, and those governing *consummatory or hedonic rewards,* which occur when a reward is achieved in the present and involve pleasure.

Individual differences in these systems are present within the first few months of life, evidenced by variation in the degree to which babies smile, laugh, or otherwise express positive affect (Gartstein & Rothbart, 2003). Early positive emotionality can be considered both a sign of infants' hedonic enjoyment and an incentive-motivated attempt to prolong an interaction with rewarding stimuli. The behaviors infants use to pursue rewards become more complex and refined over the course of development, as they attain new competencies—for example, the emergence of motor skills in the first year of life that allows for increased exploration of the environment and more vigorous pursuit of potential rewards (Rothbart, 2007). The emergence of language abilities in toddlerhood allows for even further expansion of extraversion, as children become more talkative and expressive. During the school years, children's sociability takes on growing import, as children gain greater exposure to peers. Thus, extraversion expands and grows more differentiated throughout the childhood years.

The heterotypic continuity of extraversion during this developmental period has been demonstrated empirically. Infant activity level, sociability, and positive emotionality all predict individual differences in facets of extraversion later in childhood (Caspi & Shiner, 2006; Hagekull & Bohlin, 2003; Rothbart, Derryberry, & Hershey, 2000), and early facets of the trait often predict *other* facets later on (e.g., Durbin, Hayden, Klein, & Olino, 2007; Dyson et al., 2015). Studies by Fox and colleagues have found that both motor activity and positive emotionality at 4 months of age predict increased approach behavior and higher levels of sociability throughout the first 4 years of life (Calkins, Fox, & Marshall, 1996; Fox, Henderson, Rubin, Calkins, & Schmidt, 2001; Hane, Fox, Henderson, & Marshall, 2008).

Personality neuroscience sheds light on the mechanisms likely to underlie and unify these changing manifestations of extraversion. One of the most robust findings in personality neuroscience to date is that extraversion is associated with the the neurotransmitter dopamine, which is the core of the brain's incentive reward system (Depue & Collins, 1999; DeYoung, 2013; Wacker & Smillie, 2015). The most direct evidence comes from studies indicating that extraversion moderates the effect of pharmacological manipulations of the dopaminergic system. In these studies, researchers administer a drug known to modulate the dopaminergic system, and effects of the drug are then assessed via behavioral measures or a neurobiological assay. If a personality trait moderates the drug's effect on the outcome of interest, one can be reasonably sure that the trait is linked to the system targeted by the drug. For example, Depue and Fu (2013) found that those high in extraversion were more sensitive to the rewarding properties of a *dopamine agonist* (a drug that increases dopaminergic function), leading them to develop preferences for the context in which the drug was administered that introverts did not develop.

Additional evidence linking the incentive reward system to extraversion comes from studies using electroencephalography (EEG), which is a noninvasive method of monitoring the brain's electrical activity using electrodes placed along the scalp. EEG has excellent temporal resolution, at the level of milliseconds; it is highly effective at tracking *when* things happen in the brain. One important EEG finding involves a waveform known as the *reward positivity* (confusingly, this waveform is more commonly known as the "feedback-related negativity," but Proudfit [2015] has convincingly demonstrated that it is best viewed as a positivity related to reward, occuring 200–350 milliseconds after receiving feedback about an outcome). A recent meta-analysis examining studies of the reward positivity found that it is best considered a prediction error signal; it spikes in response to better-than-expected outcomes and declines below baseline in response to worse-than-expected outcomes (Sambrook & Goslin, 2015). Importantly, dopaminergic neurons projecting from the midbrain to the anterior cingulate cortex (ACC) show this same pattern of firing (Bromberg-Martin, Matsumoto, & Hikosaka, 2010), supporting the theory that the reward positivity is dopaminergically mediated. Adult studies have indicated repeatedly that extraversion is associated with reward positivity amplitudes following feedback about reward (Bress & Hajcak, 2013; Cooper, Duke, Pickering, & Smillie, 2014; Lange, Leue, & Beauducel, 2012; Smillie, Cooper, & Pickering, 2011).

The relation between extraversion and the reward positivity in EEG is one of the few findings in personality neuroscience that has been replicated in a study of child development. Kujawa and colleagues (2015) examined the association in 381 children assessed at ages 3 and 9 years. Positive emotionality measured through behavioral observation at age 3 and self-reported positive emotionality at age 9 were both significantly related to reward positivity amplitudes following monetary gains and losses at age 9. Considered with adult research on the reward positivity, these findings indicate that dopaminergically mediated responses to reward are likely to play an important role in the neurobiological basis of extraversion throughout the lifespan.

As noted earlier, dopamine is the main neurotransmitter in the incentive reward system. An *incentive reward* is a cue that one is moving toward a valued goal, whereas a *hedonic reward* involves the actual attainment of a goal. Both types of reward are present throughout the lifespan; the child who earns a star on a "star chart" at school has earned an incentive reward, a sign that progress toward a larger goal is underway. The child who completes the star chart and cashes in on the reward of an ice-cream sundae revels in the enjoyment of a hedonic reward. The distinction between *incentive* and *hedonic* has been described as the difference between "wanting" and "liking" (Berridge, Robinson, & Aldridge, 2009), and the two processes are governed by different neurotransmitter systems. Whereas dopamine produces desire and approach behavior, it is the opioid system that produces pleasure.

The distinction between these two neurotransmitter systems has been linked to the difference between extraversion's two aspects, assertiveness and enthusiasm (Allen & DeYoung, 2017; DeYoung, 2013). Assertiveness, sometimes referred to as *agentic extraversion,* reflects individual differences in traits such as drive, activity, and decisiveness. It is also closely related to dominance and leadership, traits that become more salient as children are increasingly integrated into peer environments. Assertiveness seems likely to be driven primarily by desire and, hence, dopamine. Indeed, studies employing pharmacological manipulations typically find that measures of assertiveness are more strongly related to dopaminergic functioning than are measures of enthusiasm (Mueller et al., 2014; Wacker, Mueller, Hennig, & Stemmler, 2012). Enthusiasm, in contrast, includes lower-order traits related to positive emotionality and sociability, and appears to reflect not only incentive motivation but also the hedonic enjoyment of reward. At this point, very limited evidence links enthusiasm to the opioid system. In one study, social closeness, a good marker of the enthusiasm aspect, moderated the effects of an opiate manipulation (Depue & Morrone-Strupinsky, 2005; DeYoung, 2013).

Our hypothesis that enthusiasm reflects variation in both dopaminergic and opioid function has to do with the fact that rewards are often simultaneously incentive and hedonic, due to the nested nature of goals. To achieve complex goals, we must break them down into various subgoals. Achieving one of those subgoals thus represents simultaneously the pleasurable consummation of one goal and a cue of progress toward a larger goal. Using our classroom example, one can easily imagine that completing the star chart and receiving the ice-cream sundae is experienced by the child as not only a hedonic reward, pleasing to the taste buds, but also a sign of progress toward even larger goals, such as earning the esteem of peers, finishing at the head of the class, or making his or her parents proud. Similarly, it is likely that receiving each individual star, before the chart is complete, causes the child to experience momentary pleasure (opiate-mediated), as well as increased

desire to earn more stars and progress toward receiving the sundae (dopaminergically mediated). It seems likely, therefore, that individual differences in dopaminergic function and incentive reward sensitivity are the dominant force underlying extraversion in general, whereas individual differences in opioid function and hedonic reward sensitivity make a more specific contribution to its enthusiasm aspect.

The importance of the distinction between assertiveness and enthusiasm is highlighted by developmental research finding that mean-level changes in extraversion during late adolescence and young adulthood vary according to the facet of extraversion being investigated (Roberts et al., 2006). A look at the facets discussed in Roberts and colleagues' meta-analysis reveals that they largely resemble the two aspects; what they called "social vitality" (sociability, gregariousness, and positive emotionality) aligns with enthusiasm, whereas what they called "social dominance" (assertiveness and independence) aligns with assertiveness. Dominance increases more during adolescence and young adulthood than does vitality, which increases briefly in adolescence before declining in young adulthood (Roberts et al., 2006; Urošević, Collins, Muetzel, Lim, & Luciana, 2012).

Whereas the neurobiological research we have so far examined for extraversion has been based in EEG and pharmacological manipulation, a number of neuroimaging studies have also provided evidence that extraversion reflects variation in the brain's reward system. The most common neuroimaging technique, magnetic resonance imaging (MRI), allows noninvasive scanning of both the structure and functioning of the brain. Dopaminergic neurons in the midbrain send axons to both cortical and subcortical regions involved in response to reward, including the medial orbitofrontal cortex (mOFC), ventral and dorsal striatum (including the nucleus accumbens and caudate, respectively), the ACC, and the amygdala. Studies have indicated that individual differences in extraversion are related to either the structure or function of nearly all of these regions in adults (Cremers et al., 2011; DeYoung et al., 2010; Grodin & White, 2015; Lewis et al., 2014; Passamonti et al., 2015; Wu, Samanez-Larkin, Katovich, & Knutson, 2014).

Urošević and colleagues (2012) extended these findings in a developmental context, using MRI to investigate longitudinal changes in reward sensitivity and related neural parameters among 149 9- to 23-year-olds assessed at two time points, 2 years apart. To measure reward sensitivity, they used a behavioral approach system (BAS) sensitivity questionnaire that is a reasonably good proxy for extraversion (Quilty, DeYoung, Oakman, & Bagby, 2014). Developmental changes in reward sensitivity were mirrored by structural findings in the reward system. Increases in a Drive subscale (which is a marker of assertiveness; Quilty et al., 2014) during adolescence and young adulthood were positively associated with increases in the volume of the left nucleus accumbens during the same period. Thus, structural changes to the ventral striatum may help explain why many youth become increasingly motivated to attain rewards during the adolescent and young adult years. Interestingly, the study also found that baseline volumes of the nucleus accumbens and mOFC were positively correlated with increases in reward sensitivity during adolescence, suggesting that a higher density of synapses within these regions may be associated with increased susceptibility to the environmental rewards that become available in adolescence.

Neuroticism

Neuroticism, or *negative emotionality,* reflects individual differences in the biological systems governing defensive responses to threat, punishment, and uncertainty (Allen & DeYoung, 2017; Shackman et al., 2016). Individuals high in neuroticism experience more negative affect of all sorts, such as sadness, anxiety, fear, anger, irritability, and insecurity. These emotions emerge very early in life. Anger, frustration, and distress are present within the first 2–4 months of life, and anxiety, sadness, and fear emerge later in the first year, as the infant undergoes further maturation and socialization (Lewis, 2000). Variation in these early negative emotions serves as an important developmental precursor to later neuroticism. For instance, infant expressions of negative emotion observed at 18 months predicted individual differences in neuroticism during early childhood (Abe & Izard, 1999). Over time, neuroticism is differentiated and refined, spurred along by cognitive development that enables the developing child to represent both the self and the external world. For children high in neuroticism, their early representations are likely to be colored by negative affect, leading to low self-worth and more pessimistic views about the future.

Neural correlates of neuroticism can be divided into three major groupings: (1) medial temporal lobe structures, including the amygdala and hippocampus; (2) the hypothalamic–pituitary–adrenal (HPA) axis; and (3) frontal lobe structures, including the ACC, insula, and medial PFC. The structure most frequently linked to neuroticism is the amygdala, which is centrally involved in the coordination of response to threat (Shackman et al., 2016). Functional MRI (fMRI) studies in adults have indicated that neuroticism is positively associated with amygdala activation during tasks involving threatening or ambiguous stimuli (Everaerd, Klumpers, van Wingen, Tendolkar, & Fernández, 2015; Schuyler et al., 2014). In one developmental study of 165 adults, males (but not females) who had been classified as highly reactive infants (defined as high levels of motor activity accompanied by crying and fretting during a laboratory task) at age 4 months displayed heightened amygdala activation in response to neutral faces as adults (Schwartz et al., 2012).

In a structural MRI study of over 1,000 adults, neuroticism was positively correlated with the volume of both the amygdala and the hippocampus (Holmes et al., 2012). The hippocampus is particularly implicated in anxiety and, in one meta-analysis (Gray & McNaughton, 2000), neuroticism was positively associated with hippocampal activation during fear learning, the process by which an individual learns to predict threats from environmental cues (Servaas, Riese, et al., 2013). Very little research on children has examined the link between neuroticism and the amygdala or hippocampus. In one study of 89 adolescents, neuroticism was *negatively* correlated with amygdalar volumes (Dennison et al., 2015).

One of the main targets of amygdalar outputs is the hypothalamus, which forms the top of the HPA axis that controls the body's response to stress. The HPA cascade begins with the release of corticotropin-releasing hormone (CRH) and vasopressin from the paraventricular nucleus of the hypothalamus. A number of studies have linked variation in the CRH receptor 1 gene to neuroticism in individuals with a history of childhood maltreatment, though the effects sometimes vary by race or type of maltreatment (Bradley et al., 2008; DeYoung, Cicchetti, & Rogosch, 2011; Grabe et al., 2010; Kranzler et al., 2011; Polanczyk et al., 2009). Neuroticism has been more convincingly associated with the terminal result of HPA activation, release of the stress hormone cortisol. In adults, Neuroticism is positively associated with baseline cortisol levels (Garcia-Banda et al., 2014; Gerritsen et al., 2009; Miller, Cohen, Rabin, Skoner, & Doyle, 1999; Nater, Hoppman, & Klumb, 2010; Polk, Cohen, Doyle, Skoner, & Kirschbaum, 2005). Studies of children also seem to support a positive association between cortisol levels and early neuroticism. Behaviorally inhibited and highly emotional children have higher levels of baseline cortisol (Kagan, Reznick, & Snidman, 1987; Schmidt et al., 1997; Tyrka et al., 2010). Remarkably, it may even be the case that exposure to cortisol in breast milk leads to increased neuroticism, as level of cortisol in breast milk has been shown to predict infant negative emotionality, and maternal cortisol levels predicted negative emotion in breast-fed but not formula-fed infants (Glynn et al., 2007; Grey, Davis, Sandman, & Glynn, 2013). Longitudinal studies provide evidence for prospective links between these two constructs as well, as neuroticism measured in the preschool years predicts cortisol levels later in childhood (Dougherty et al., 2013; Mackrell et al., 2014).

Somewhat surprisingly, however, this association does not appear to be present in adolescence. Two longitudinal studies of adolescents found no prospective associations between cortisol levels and neuroticism (Evans et al., 2016; Shoal, Giancola, & Kirillova, 2003). If it is indeed the case that the association between neuroticism and cortisol temporarily vanishes in adolescence, this could be related to the relatively large shifts in personality traits, including neuroticism, that occur in adolescence (Soto et al., 2011; Van den Akker et al., 2014). On the other hand, even the adult literature is not entirely consistent here: In a study of 490 adults, Miller and colleagues (2016) found no link between cortisol and neuroticism, but did find an association between cortisol function and extraversion. More large studies are needed at all ages.

Individuals high on neuroticism are prone to negative affect in part because they have difficulty regulating emotions. While variation in structures such as the amygdala and hypothalamus is likely to explain neuroticism's relation to emotion generation, cortical structures are more likely to be involved in problems of emotion regulation. In the frontal lobe, the rostral/subgenual ACC and adjacent medial PFC have been heavily implicated in emotion regulation (Etkin, Egner, & Kalisch, 2011), and several lines of evidence link neuroticism to this region and its connections to the threat system. For instance, in the study of over 1,000 adults mentioned earlier, neuroticism was negatively correlated with cortical thickness in a region of the medial PFC that encompassed the rostral/subgenual ACC (Holmes et al., 2012).

More direct studies of connectivity, both structural and functional, also support this idea. The brain's white matter consists of bundles of axons that connect regions of gray matter to each other, and the coherence or integrity of these white-matter tracts can be measured through diffusion tensor imaging (DTI), an MRI technique that detects the diffusion of water molecules along axons. Several DTI studies have shown that neuroticism is negatively associated with white-matter integrity in axons connecting cortical and subcortical regions (Bjørnebekk et al., 2013; Taddei, Tettamanti, Zanoni, Cappa, & Battaglia, 2012; Westlye, Bjørnebekk, Grydeland, Fjell, & Walhovd, 2011; Xu & Potenza, 2012). This pattern is consistent with results from two fMRI studies examining functional connectivity in adults. (*Functional connectivity* refers to synchrony between the activity of brain regions over time, which implies that they are causally linked in their operations—though it cannot indicate direct cause or causal direction.) Both studies found that neuroticism was associated with reduced connectivity between the amygdala and prefrontal regions, including the dorsomedial and dorsolateral PFC (Mujica-Parodi et al., 2009; Servaas, van der Velde, et al., 2013). Similarly, in a study of adolescents, Davey and colleagues (2015) found that functional connectivity between the amygdala and subgenual ACC was positively correlated with neuroticism at baseline and 2 years later. Further, change in the amygdala–ACC connectivity over this 2-year period was positively correlated with change in neuroticism.

Shifting from our discussion of global neuroticism to traits beneath it in the hierarchy, we note that two forms of neuroticism, dubbed *anxious distress* and *irritable distress,* have received special attention during early development (Caspi & Shiner, 2006; John, Caspi, Robins, Moffitt, & Stouthamer-Loeber, 1994; Rothbart & Bates, 1998). Whereas anxious distress involves inwardly directed forms of negative affect, including anxiety, sadness, guilt, and insecurity, irritable distress encompasses tendencies toward more externalized negative affect, including anger, frustration, and labile mood. Evidence from studies of youth suggests these two subdimensions of neuroticism may have different developmental correlates, leading some theorists to recommend measuring them separately in research on child personality (Caspi & Shiner, 2006; Shiner & Caspi, 2003).

Anxious distress and irritable distress appear to be developmental antecedents to neuroticism's two aspects in adults, withdrawal and volatility (DeYoung, 2015; DeYoung et al., 2007). *Withdrawal* reflects anxiety, depression, and insecurity, whereas *volatility* reflects irritability, anger, labile mood, and the tendency to get upset easily. In parsing the distinction between withdrawal and volatility, we refer to Gray and McNaughton's (2000) theory that neuroticism reflects the joint sensitivity of two underlying brain systems, the behavioral inhibition system (BIS) and the fight–flight–freeze system (FFFS). The BIS, centered around the amygdala and hippocampus, governs response to threats in the form of conflicts between goals, most often approach–avoidance conflicts (e.g., wanting to impress one's peers in a class presentation, but dreading the embarrassment that might accompany a mistake). In situations in which conflict or uncertainty is detected, the BIS increases passive avoidance, leading to heightened anxiety, increased vigilance and rumination, and inhibition of approach behavior; all of these effects are characteristic of both anxious distress and withdrawal. The label "Withdrawal" does not refer specifically to being socially withdrawn (which could be a function of low extraversion), but rather to the partial or complete withdrawal of effort from a goal, which is the core of all forms of passive avoidance.

Whereas the BIS responds to situations involving conflict between goals, in which one is uncertain about whether to continue to approach, the FFFS, centered around the hypothalamus and periaqueductal gray (a region of midbrain below the hypothalamus), is sensitive to situations in which one's only motivation is to escape or eliminate a threat. In these instances, the FFFS triggers active defensive responses, such as panicked flight or defensive anger. The anger component, at least, is clearly reflected in volatility. Many general neuroticism scales are weighted toward withdrawal rather than volatility, and the biological correlates of irritable dis-

tress and volatility are much less well studied than those of anxious distress and withdrawal. One area in which the distinction between withdrawal and volatility is important is in EEG research, which has consistently found that neuroticism predicts a pattern of increased activity in right, relative to the left, prefrontal regions both when viewing stimuli and while at rest (for meta-analyses, see Thibodeau, Jorgensen, & Kim, 2006; Wacker, Chavanon, & Stemmler, 2010). Developmental research examining this rightward pattern of EEG asymmetry has shown that the effect is present as early as 6 months of age (Buss et al., 2003). Other methods also seem to point to increased activity of the right frontal lobe as a potential substrate of neuroticism. In adults, blood flow to this region is positively associated with neuroticism during anticipation of an aversive stimulus (Morinaga et al., 2007). Focal damage to the left frontal lobe (leaving function biased toward the right hemisphere) is also associated with higher neuroticism scores (and specifically the anxiety facet; Forbes et al., 2014).

Importantly, the relation between rightward EEG asymmetry and neuroticism appears to be confined specifically to the withdrawal aspect (which, as noted, tends to be emphasized in global assessments of neuroticism). Traits related to volatility, especially anger, are associated with a pattern of leftward frontal EEG asymmetry instead (Everhart, Demaree, & Harrison, 2008; Harmon-Jones, 2004; Harmon-Jones & Allen, 1998). This differential asymmetry appears to stem from the fact that avoidance and approach behavior are differentially related to the right and left hemispheres, respectively (Davidson, 1992; Fox, 1991). Anger is an approach-oriented negative emotion that facilitates approach to threats when aggression is used as an active defense or when effort is needed to overcome frustration. (Consistent with the link between the left hemisphere and approach, there is also some evidence of a relation between leftward frontal EEG asymmetry and extraversion as well; Wacker et al., 2010; Wacker, Mueller, Pizzagalli, Hennig, & Stemmler, 2013).

The link between withdrawal and rightward asymmetry is consistent with research on a related early childhood trait known as *behavioral inhibition*. The origin of this label comes from descriptions of childhood temperament, not from Gray's theory of the BIS, but the evidence is consistent with the hypothesis that the BIS is an important contributor to this form of behavioral inhibition. "Behavioral inhibition" was originally used by Kagan and colleagues to describe a group of shy toddlers who became withdrawn and inhibited when confronted with novel or unfamiliar situations (Garcia-Coll, Kagan, & Reznick, 1984; Kagan, Reznick, Snidman, Gibbons, & Johnson, 1988). Since then, considerable research has examined the biological basis of behavioral inhibition, its continuity over time, and its relation to important developmental outcomes, including psychopathology (Fox, Henderson, Marshall, Nichols, & Ghera, 2005). Investigations of its relations to other personality traits in youth suggest it is a blend of neuroticism and extraversion. Despite being most similar in theory to the withdrawal aspect of neuroticism, some studies suggest that it predicts low extraversion even more strongly than neuroticism (Muris et al., 2009; Vreeke & Muris, 2012). In general, withdrawal and related problems such as anxiety and depression are negatively correlated with extraversion, which is not surprising given that a primary function of the BIS is to inhibit approach behavior (DeYoung, 2015; DeYoung et al., 2007; Naragon-Gainey, Watson, & Markon, 2009).

Research on the the neurobiological correlates of behavioral inhibition shows considerable overlap with the literature on neuroticism and withdrawal, including the links to rightward frontal EEG asymmetry (Fox, Calkins, & Bell, 1994; Fox et al., 2001) and increased cortisol (Kagan et al., 1987; Schmidt et al., 1997). Behavioral inhibition in childhood has been linked to amygdala activation and connectivity in both adolescents and adults, although mostly in studies with small samples (Blackford, Allen, Cowan, & Avery, 2013; Pérez-Edgar et al., 2007; Roy et al., 2014). Some studies on behavioral inhibition seem to be more reflective of its relation to extraversion. In particular, several fMRI studies have found that a history of behavioral inhibition in childhood is associated with alterations in the structure and function of both the nucleus accumbens and striatum, regions strongly involved in reward (Bar-Haim et al., 2009; Clauss et al., 2014; Guyer et al., 2006; Lahat, Benson, Pine, Fox, & Ernst, 2016). The neural evidence on behavioral inhibition is consistent with its ties to both neuroticism and low extraversion, and future research would benefit from examining these two components of behavioral inhibition separately.

Conscientiousness

As any parent knows, the gradual (and sometimes downright plodding) emergence of self-regulatory capacities is a defining feature of development. The behavior and emotions of young children are often chaotically buffeted by the impulses to approach or avoid that are associated with extraversion and neuroticism. Nonetheless, from early childhood onward, humans show reliable individual differences in their persistence, planfulness, distractibility, and orderliness. Within the Big Five, variation in these regulatory characteristics is reflected primarily in conscientiousness. The mechanisms associated with conscientiousness function to facilitate nonimmediate goal pursuit and promote rule-based behavior, which requires avoiding distractions and suppressing disruptive impulses (DeYoung, 2015). Conscientiousness is closely aligned with the temperament trait *effortful control,* which Rothbart and colleagues (Rothbart, Ellis, Rueda, & Posner, 2003; Rothbart & Rueda, 2005) have defined as the ability to inhibit or suppress a dominant response in favor of a subdominant response. Although very little research has examined the developmental origins of conscientiousness specifically, much research has examined the foundations of effortful control.

Whereas variation in positive and negative emotionality is present within the first few months of life, regulatory capacities related to effortful control appear slightly later, typically emerging only toward the end of the first year (Posner & Rothbart, 1998). Differences in attentional processes during infancy predict the development of effortful control in toddlerhood (Bridgett et al., 2011; Gartstein, Slobodskaya, Putnam, & Kinsht, 2009; Kochanska, Murray, & Harlan, 2000; Putnam, Rothbart, & Gartstein, 2008). Additionally, high early emotionality is associated with lower effortful control in childhood, which is consistent with the adult correlation between neuroticism and conscientiousness, and also suggests that the intensity and frequency of early emotions may complicate the normative development of regulatory systems (Caspi & Shiner, 2006; Kochanska & Knaack, 2003; Putnam et al., 2008). Though effortful control may be measured during the toddler years, it remains very much a developing construct during this period. Indeed, children show considerable mean-level increases in effortful control in early childhood (Carlson,

2005). Despite these normative mean-level in- creases, however, the rank-order stability and internal consistency of effortful control are similar to those of most other trait constructs from the age of 3 years onward (Kochanska & Knaack, 2003).

Neurobiological research on effortful control and conscientiousness suggests that these traits are strongly linked to the frontal lobes. In par- ticular, Posner and colleagues have posited that effortful control is associated with the develop- ment of brain regions known to be involved in the control of attention, including the ACC and a number of lateral prefrontal regions (Posner & Fan, 2008; Posner & Rothbart, 2007; Rothbart & Posner, 2006). Indeed, the dorsolateral pre- frontal cortex (DLPFC), which is crucial for the ability to maintain nonimmediate goals, flexi- bly modulate attention, and follow complex rule systems (Bunge, 2004; Bunge & Zelazo, 2006), has repeatedly been linked to conscientiousness. In adults, several structural imaging studies have revealed that conscientiousness is positive- ly associated with volume of regions in DLPFC (DeYoung et al., 2010; Jackson, Balota, & Head, 2011; Kapogiannis, Sutin, Davatzikos, Costa, & Resnick, 2013). Another study found that, in a large sample of patients with brain damage (N = 199), focal damage to the left DLPFC was as- sociated with lower scores on conscientiousness (Forbes et al., 2014). However, some structural studies have failed to replicate the link between the DLPFC and conscientiousness (Bjørnebekk et al., 2013; Liu et al., 2013).

In adults, functional connectivity studies in- dicate that the lateral prefrontal regions involved in controlling attention encompass nodes of two broad networks that are extensively inter- twined—these are the frontoparietal or cogni- tive control network and what we have called the *goal priority network* (Rueter, Abram, Mac- Donald, Rustichini, & DeYoung, 2018; Yeo et al., 2011). (Yeo and colleagues referred to the latter network as the "ventral attention net- work," but the network they identified in a sam- ple of 1,000 subjects is larger than the standard ventral attention network and comprises an amalgamation of networks traditionally labeled "ventral attention" and "salience.") Functional- ly, the frontoparietal network is strongly linked to working memory and intelligence, abilities that are primarily related to the openness/intel- lect domain within the Big Five (DeYoung, Pe- terson, & Higgins, 2005; DeYoung et al., 2009;

Taki et al., 2013). In contrast, the goal priority network, which includes regions of the middle frontal gyrus, ACC, right inferior frontal gyrus, temporoparietal junction, and anterior insula, is specifically associated with conscientiousness (Allen & DeYoung, 2017; Rueter et al., 2018). Broadly, the function of this network seems to be to prioritize goals based on motivationally salient stimuli and maintain focus on the select- ed goal. The prefrontal components of this net- work appear especially responsible for direct- ing attention away from distracting stimuli and back to the task at hand (Fox, Corbetta, Snyder, Vincent, & Raichle, 2006).

One study of 200 healthy adults applied graph theory analysis to resting functional connectiv- ity data (Davis et al., 2013). In highly impulsive individuals, medial and lateral regions of the PFC broke off into a distinct module from sub- cortical regions, including the amygdala, hip- pocampus, thalamus, and brainstem, suggest- ing that high impulsivity reflects a breakdown between top-down control structures and those governing more immediate emotional respons- es. A conceptually related study found that ef- fortful control in 3- to 5-year-olds was positively associated with integration, differentiation, and efficiency of functional networks in lateral PFC (Fekete, Beacher, Cha, Rubin, & Mujica-Paro- di, 2014). Finally, Rueter and colleagues (2018) found that conscientiousness predicted both increased functional connectivity within the frontal portion of the goal priority network, en- compassing DLPFC, anterior insula, and dorsal ACC, as well as increased connectivity of these regions with other more posterior parts of the network. Thus, it seems plausible that an impor- tant basis of conscientiousness is the ability of the goal priority network to control the brain's lower-level emotional and motivational systems.

Beyond the DLPFC, other regions of the ventral attention network also seem to be as- sociated with conscientiousness, although the literature is still relatively sparse and conflict- ed (Allen & DeYoung, 2017). Multiple studies have found measures of conscientiousness or effortful control (or impulsivity, which often reflects the low pole of conscientiousness and effortful control) to be associated with struc- tural variation in the ACC and adjacent medial cortex (mainly the supplementary motor area), insula and adjacent ventrolateral PFC, and puta- men (Liu et al., 2013; Nouchi et al., 2016; Sakai et al., 2012). One study exploring the relation between the insula and conscientiousness in a sample spanning ages 10–22 years, found that planning (vs. impulsivity) was negatively correlated with cortical thickness in the anterior insula, and that age was associated with higher levels of planning and lower cortical thickness (Churchwell & Yurgelun-Todd, 2013). Functional studies have also reported associations in these regions, typically between conscientiousness and activation during response inhibition tasks (Brown, Manuck, Flory, & Hariri, 2006; Farr, Hu, Zhang, & Li, 2012).

Some developmental evidence exists for a link between the ACC and conscientiousness. A study following participants over the course of adolescence found that greater thinning of the ACC was associated with smaller reductions in effortful control between ages 12 and 16 (Vijayakumar et al., 2014). This finding may be relevant to studies showing mean-level decreases in conscientiousness during adolescence (Soto et al., 2011; Van den Akker et al., 2014), and to the pattern of brain development in which prefrontal development catches up to subcortical development only toward the end of adolescence (Casey, 2015; Somerville, Jones, & Casey, 2010). Cortical thinning of the ACC during this period may reflect synaptic pruning of overabundant synapses, with greater pruning leading to more efficient cognitive control. If this is the case, one might expect that structural changes to the ACC would be associated with greater regulation of impulses later in development. Indeed, Vijayakumar and colleagues (2014) found that cortical thinning of the ACC was associated with reductions in both internalizing and externalizing psychopathology, and this relation was mediated by changes in effortful control.

An additional region that has repeatedly been associated with conscientiousness and effortful control is the orbitofrontal cortex (OFC), especially lateral areas of the orbital surface (Jackson et al., 2011; Matsuo et al., 2009; Nouchi et al., 2016). One longitudinal study of 107 adolescents assessed effortful control and OFC volume at 12 years, then assessed substance use and abuse at 15, 16, and 18 years (Cheetham et al., 2017). Effortful control at age 12 predicted both OFC volume and the severity of substance problems over the three later assessments. Further, OFC volume could account statistically for the covariance between effortful control and substance problems.

Agreeableness

As a social species, human beings must navigate the needs and goals of others in order to achieve their own goals. This requires willingness to accommodate and even work for the needs and goals of others. Variation in traits involved in cooperation and altruism is reflected in the personality trait of agreeableness (DeYoung, 2015; Graziano & Tobin, 2013). Less is known about the developmental origins of agreeableness than some of the other Big Five traits, in part because most measures of temperament have not included a trait comparable to agreeableness, although *affiliativeness* has been suggested as a component of temperament and included in some more recently developed instruments (Rothbart & Bates, 2006). Nonetheless, developmental antecedents of agreeableness, including individual differences in aggression, empathy, and prosocial behavior, are evident quite early in life.

Aggression, falling at the low pole of agreeableness, emerges during the first year of life and increases into toddlerhood, peaking sometime between 24 and 42 months after birth, before decreasing steadily throughout the rest of childhood (Côté, Vaillancourt, LeBlanc, Nagin, & Tremblay, 2006; Tremblay et al., 2004). The emerging ability to restrain aggressive impulses can be considered a key component of agreeableness from then on. Empathy and concern for others likewise emerge in the first year, increasing in frequency over the course of infancy and early childhood (for a review, see Davidov, Zahn-Waxler, Roth-Hanania, & Knafo, 2013). The capacities associated with agreeableness gradually come online over the course of infancy, leading to decreases in aggression and increases in empathy, prosociality, and compliance as children age. By early childhood, most temperament and personality models yield an agreeableness factor similar to the one found in the Big Five (De Pauw et al., 2009).

Nonetheless, there are some subtle differences between childhood and adulthood agreeableness. In youth, compared to adulthood, agreeableness is even more closely tied to the two other traits, neuroticism and conscientiousness, that constitute the broader metatrait stability (Tackett et al., 2012). Both low agreeableness and high neuroticism are consistently associated with elevated levels of physical aggression, relational aggression, and rule-breaking behavior throughout childhood and adolescence

(Becht, Prinzie, Deković, Van Den Akker, & Shiner, 2016; Tackett, Daoud, De Bolle, & Burt, 2013). These types of antagonistic behaviors are more central to the childhood variant of agreeableness than to its adult counterpart (De Pauw et al., 2009; Digman & Shmelyov, 1996; Tackett et al., 2012). Adult studies of the Big Five indicate that, although aggression remains an important component of low agreeableness, traits reflecting politeness and compassion are emphasized more. Additionally, in adults, the facet-level traits of irritability and anger have their primary loading on neuroticism (though they also show a strong secondary loading on agreeableness), but in childhood some ambiguity remains regarding whether they are more closely aligned with neuroticism or agreeableness (De Pauw et al., 2009). Brain development may offer one explanation for the age-related shift in agreeableness content away from anger and aggression. In childhood, the presence or absence of cooperative and altruistic behavior is likely to be more strongly determined by angry and aggressive impulses because the prefrontal brain systems that come to inhibit those impulses (and to promote emotion regulation, empathy, and concern for others) are still maturing.

The closer link between agreeableness and conscientiousness in childhood is consistent with Ahadi and Rothbart's (1994) proposal that early individual differences in effortful control may underlie the development of both agreeableness and conscientiousness. Effortful control is positively associated with agreeableness in both childhood and adulthood (Cumberland-Li, Eisenberg, & Reiser, 2004; Jensen-Campbell et al., 2002), but it nonetheless appears to become more differentiated over time, leading to increasingly distinct agreeableness and conscientiousness factors in later childhood and adolescence (Soto, John, Gosling, & Potter, 2008; Tackett et al., 2012). Again, we may trace this differentiation back to the relatively late development of the PFC.

The two aspects of agreeableness are compassion and politeness (DeYoung et al., 2007). Compassion encompasses empathic concern about others, whereas politeness reflects tendencies to conform to social norms and avoid belligerent and exploitative behavior. Both compassion and politeness can be identified in childhood, and longitudinal studies show that the two traits differentially predict adult outcomes (Kern et al., 2013). Compassion, in particular,

is likely to be strongly related to the development of theory of mind or "mentalizing" abilities, which reflect one's capacity to understand the mental states of others (Premack & Woodruff, 1978). Meta-analysis of theory-of-mind tests showed that mentalizing ability is positively associated with prosocial behaviors such as helping, cooperation, and comforting others (Imuta, Henry, Slaughter, Selcuk, & Ruffman, 2016). This is not surprising given the difficulty of coordinating one's goals with those of others if one cannot understand others' intentions and desires. Research on the development of theory of mind suggests that it follows a similar trajectory to agreeableness, increasing during late adolescence and adulthood (Dumontheil, Apperly, & Blakemore, 2010). Performance on theory of mind tasks has been positively related to agreeableness and to compassion more specifically (Allen, Rueter, Abram, Brown, & DeYoung, 2017; Nettle & Liddle, 2008). This link between theory of mind and compassion is consistent with studies showing high correlations between theory of mind and questionnaire measures of empathy (Baron-Cohen & Wheelwright, 2004) given that empathy falls within compassion rather than politeness. Indeed, a recent structural study found that compassion was positively correlated with gray matter volume in the bilateral ACC and anterior insula, and meta-analyses have linked both of these regions to empathy as well (Hou et al., 2017).

To the extent that agreeableness is associated with mentalizing capabilities, it is likely to be associated with regions of the so-called "default network" that are involved in decoding the mental states of others (Andrews-Hanna, Smallwood, & Spreng, 2014). (The "default network" got its name because it tends to be active when people are engaged in self-directed thought, such as daydreaming, but it appears to be crucial for any simulation of experience, including imagining the experience of others.) Though relatively little research has examined the neurobiological correlates of agreeableness specifically, several studies have examined the neural substrate of individual differences in empathy using questionnaire measures that are good indicators of compassion. A structural MRI study of 567 adults indicated that empathy was negatively correlated with gray-matter volume in various regions of the default network, including the medial PFC, precuneus, temporal pole, and superior temporal sulcus (STS) (Takeuchi et al., 2014). Two other studies have reported negative correlations between agreeableness and volume in the posterior STS, a region that is important for interpreting the actions and intentions of others by decoding biological motion (DeYoung et al., 2010; Kapogiannis et al., 2013). A recent resting functional connectivity study found that empathy was associated with greater connectivity between medial PFC, precuneus, and left STS (Takeuchi et al., 2014).

A longitudinal neuroimaging study relevant to the neural substrates of agreeableness examined the structural development of brain regions implicated in social cognition, beginning in late childhood and extending into young adulthood. Gray-matter volume and cortical thickness of regions including the medial PFC and posterior STS peaked in late childhood or early adolescence, before declining over the course of adolescence (Mills, Lalonde, Clasen, Giedd, & Blakemore, 2014). These findings are consistent with studies of personality suggesting that agreeableness falls in early adolescence and then rises again in late adolescence and early adulthood (Soto et al., 2011; Van den Akker et al., 2014).

Finally, the hormone testosterone appears to be negatively associated with agreeableness, and its politeness aspect specifically, based on research relating it to interpersonal behavior and aggression (DeYoung, Weisberg, Quilty, & Peterson, 2013; Montoya, Terburg, Box, & Van Honk, 2012; Turan, Guo, Boggiano, & Bedgood, 2014). More complexly, two studies found that agreeableness moderated the association between testosterone and externalizing behavior problems, such that high testosterone was associated with externalizing only when agreeableness was low (Reardon, Herzhoff, Tackett, 2015; Tackett, Herzhoff, Harden, Page-Gould, & Josephs, 2014). Finally, in a longitudinal study of 216 individuals between ages 6 and 22 years, Nguyen and colleagues (2016) found that, independent of age and sex, testosterone levels, aggression, and the covariance of amygdala volume and cortical thickness in the medial PFC were all mutually interrelated. Such a complex finding needs replication, of course, but the overlap with the substrates of neuroticism in the amygdala and medial PFC is notable and may speak to the connection between aggression and failure to suppress angry or hostile impulses. Testosterone may suppress that inhibitory control.

Openness/Intellect

The last Big Five trait, openness/intellect, reflects individual differences in imagination, creativity, innovation, curiosity, and aesthetic and intellectual interests and abilities. The tendency toward cognitive exploration appears to be what unifies these traits (DeYoung, 2014, 2015). Of all the Big Five, openness/intellect has been the least studied in a developmental context, largely due to the fact that most models of child temperament have not included a dimension similar to openness/intellect (Caspi & Shiner, 2006; De Pauw et al., 2009; Shiner & DeYoung, 2013). Direct research on the developmental precursors of openness/intellect is scarce, although conceptually it is clearly linked to early behaviors such as imaginative play and curious exploration. In adults, openness/intellect incorporates perceived intelligence and is the one Big Five trait to be substantially associated with IQ (DeYoung, 2014). The fact that curiosity, stimulation seeking, and exploration of new situations in early childhood have been found to predict IQ later in life (Caspi & Shiner, 2006; Raine, Reynolds, Venables, & Mednick, 2002) therefore suggests patterns of heterotypic continuity for openness/intellect.

One adult temperament model includes a factor of orienting sensitivity that corresponds well empirically to openness/intellect (Evans & Rothbart, 2007), and a similar factor has been found in a large study of 5-year-old children, marked by scales measuring *low-intensity pleasure* and *perceptual sensitivity,* which include items such as "Enjoys looking at picture books" and "Notices the smoothness or roughness of objects he or she touches" (De Pauw et al., 2009). By the preschool years, researchers have been able to measure openness/intellect directly, but the reliability of these measures has not always been very high (Abe, 2005; Gjerde & Cardilla, 2009; Halverson et al., 2003). Beginning around age 6 or 7 years, however, studies consistently recover a robust openness/intellect factor that is reliable and structurally stable over time (Herzhoff & Tackett, 2012; Soto & John, 2014).

The two aspects of openness/intellect are readily apparent in its compound label: *openness to experience* and *intellect* (DeYoung, 2014; DeYoung et al., 2007). Whereas openness to experience encompasses tendencies to engage with sensory and perceptual information— through art or fantasy, for example—intellect primarily reflects engagement with abstract or intellectual material through reasoning. Broadly, both of these tendencies serve to generate new interpretations of experience, but openness more in terms of sensory patterns and intellect more in terms of causal or logical patterns (DeYoung, 2014, 2015). We use the compound label "openness/intellect" to refer to the Big Five domain and "openness" or "intellect" to refer to one aspect specifically.

Very little personality neuroscience research has examined correlates of openness/intellect in childhood or adolescence, presumably due to its exclusion from most temperament models. Nonetheless, existing adult research may inform future developmental work. One promising hypothesis is that dopamine is involved, which may help to explain why openness/intellect shows a regular correlation with extraversion. Given dopamine's role in positive affect and approach, the fact that high-intensity pleasure in childhood predicts later openness/intellect as well as extraversion is suggestive (Abe & Izard, 1999). Whereas global levels of dopamine may influence both extraversion and openness/intellect, we have argued that the distinction between two different types of dopaminergic neuron is relevant to differentiating the two traits (Allen & DeYoung, 2017; DeYoung, 2013). As noted earlier, the type of neuron linked to extraversion encodes the value of stimuli, increasing its firing rate to positive stimuli and decreasing to negative. In contrast, the type proposed to be linked to openness/intellect encodes salience, becoming more active in response to both better- and worse-than-expected outcomes and triggering cognitive processing to explore these potentially meaningful events (Bromberg-Martin et al., 2010). Thus, differences in dopaminergic function may explain why those high in openness/intellect are curious and find information rewarding.

Most evidence supporting this hypothesis is indirect and stems from correlations between openness/intellect and variables known to be influenced by dopamine (e.g., working memory capacity; DeYoung, 2013). More direct evidence comes from a recent fMRI study that examined functional connectivity between the small area of the midbrain where dopaminergic neurons originate and other parts of the brain to which they send axons and hence dopamine. While viewing images of food, smelling pleasant odors, or even just at rest, individuals high in openness/intellect showed more synchrony between the dopaminergic region and areas of the DLPFC involved in attention (Passamonti et al., 2015). This finding suggests greater dopaminergic influence on information processing in those high in openness/intellect and is consistent with the fact that salience-coding dopamine neurons preferentially project to the DLPFC (Bromberg-Martin et al., 2010).

The association of openness/intellect and functioning of the DLPFC is consistent with findings to which we alluded while discussing conscientiousness—namely, that openness/intellect is associated with intelligence and working memory (which is the ability to manipulate and rapidly update information in short-term memory). Both working memory and intelligence appear to rely heavily on the DLPFC and the broader frontoparietal network (Jung & Haier, 2007). Studies in children, adolescents, and adults have shown that variation in the functioning of this network is consistently associated with individual differences in working memory (Darki & Klingberg, 2015; Klingberg, 2006). Working memory is the cognitive function that appears to contribute most to intelligence (Conway, Kane, & Engle, 2003). It is intellect specifically, not openness, that is related to working memory and intelligence (DeYoung, Quilty, Peterson, & Gray, 2014; DeYoung, Shamosh, Green, Braver, & Gray, 2009). One study of the neural basis of this association found that intellect, but not openness, predicted neural activity in regions of the DLPFC and medial PFC that supported accurate performance on a difficult working memory task performed during fMRI (DeYoung et al., 2009). Thus, one's tendency toward intellectual confidence and engagement is, not surprisingly, linked to one's actual cognitive abilities. (Openness may nonetheless be related to DLPFC function, but presumably more in the context of directing attention toward sensory stimuli of interest.)

Although little developmental research has been done on openness/intellect, an expanding body of literature examines the neural development of working memory and intelligence, and this is informative regarding the trait of intellect. Working memory capacity increases during childhood and adolescence, a developmental trend consistent with the late cortical maturation of the frontal lobes, involving synaptic pruning and cortical thinning (Conklin, Luciana, Hooper, & Yarger, 2007; Finn, Sheridan, Kam, Hinshaw, & D'Esposito, 2010). In one longitudinal study, Tamnes and colleagues (2013) found that improvement in working memory in children and adolescents over a span of 2.5 years was related to reduction of cortical volume in PFC and parietal cortex. Similarly, multiple studies have found that intelligence is associated with greater rates of cortical thinning, especially in PFC during late childhood and adolescence, once again suggesting the importance of relatively late pruning processes for cognitive abilities (Schnack et al., 2015; Shaw et al., 2006; Tamnes et al., 2011).

As mentioned earlier, the frontoparietal network is extensively intertwined with the ventral attention network that has been linked to conscientiousness, and the close proximity of these two networks, in conjunction with the late development of the PFC, may help to explain developmental changes in the covariance structure of personality traits. Measures of intellect (but not openness) are more strongly correlated with conscientiousness in childhood than they are later in life (Mervielde, Buyst, & De Fruyt, 1995; Mervielde & De Fruyt, 2000). Furthermore, childhood measures of openness/intellect tend to emphasize intellect content (Gjerde & Cardilla, 2009; Herzhoff & Tackett, 2012), which may account for the occasional difficulty of identifying an openness/intellect factor in childhood. In the study of 5-year-olds mentioned earlier, measures of intellect loaded on the conscientiousness factor rather than on the factor resembling openness that included measures of perceptual and sensory engagement (De Pauw et al., 2009).

Functional connectivity research shows that, over the course of development, the correlations between regions of the brain that are anatomically close lessens, whereas the correlations between more distal regions within networks increases (Fair et al., 2009). It may be that during childhood, individual differences in overall development of the PFC are more important in determining which traits appear together in an individual than are individual differences in the more specific networks that underlie each trait. Later in development, the different networks in PFC that are associated with conscientiousness and intellect presumably become more functionally differentiated, and intellect becomes more closely aligned with the other forms of cognitive exploration reflected in openness.

One neural substrate common to both intellect and openness may be found in parameters of the default network, which we have already discussed in relation to agreeableness. The default network is extensive, contains at least three subnetworks, and is likely to be involved in multiple important personality traits. Areas of this network, especially in the left temporal lobe, are linked to intelligence, probably because of their involvement in language (Choi et al., 2008; Jung & Haier, 2007). However, the default network is better known for its role in imagination, which is so central to openness/intellect that "imagination" was proposed as an alternative label for the domain (Saucier, 1992). In keeping with this fact, a resting-state fMRI study using two indpendent samples found that openness/intellect was positively associated with information-processing efficiency in the default network (Beaty et al., 2016). The default network seems to be a particularly promising target for research on the development of openness/intellect in children given that imagination is one component of the trait that is evident at an age long before appreciation of art or philosophy might be relevant.

Conclusion

Having reviewed neurobiological research pertaining to each of the Big Five and their development, it should be obvious that, whereas personality neuroscience is a still young field, *developmental* personality neuroscience is still in its infancy. Nonetheless, we hope that our endeavor has provided some insight into the underlying biological systems that shape the patterns of behavior and experience described by the major dimensions of personality. For each of the Big Five, and often at the level of narrower traits below them, we can point to evidence consistent with the idea that numerous biological parameters contribute to trait variation, but that these parameters are reasonably coherent in being linked to a particular function that seems to unify the trait in question. For example, extraversion appears to be associated with a number of neural parameters involved in processing information about rewards and motivating approach toward them.

It is one thing to identify the neural systems involved in a personality trait and another to understand how those systems develop and how their development is linked to changes in the content and level of that trait. Neuroscience is beginning to reveal a great deal about the way that the brain develops across the lifespan, but we still know very little about how individual differences fit into this story. We can be reasonably confident that the child who is energetic and expressive and then becomes an adolescent who loves parties and excitement has a dopaminergic system that is more sensitive to cues of reward than the child (and adolescent) who is reserved and introverted. We can even say that the proneness of extraversion to be expressed in riskier behavior during adolescence than at other ages is due, at least in part, to the relatively late development of the PFC. However, we have no direct evidence regarding how changes in dopaminergic function might be linked to changes in personality in an extraverted child versus an introverted child. Providing this evidence, for extraversion and also for other traits, will require extensive additional research, and developmental personality neuroscience is the field that will carry it out.

REFERENCES

Abe, J. A. A. (2005). The predictive validity of the Five-Factor Model of personality with preschool age children: A nine year follow-up study. *Journal of Research in Personality, 39*(4), 423–442.

Abe, J. A. A., & Izard, C. E. (1999). A longitudinal study of emotion expression and personality relations in early development. *Journal of Personality and Social Psychology, 77*(3), 566–577.

Ahadi, S. A., & Rothbart, M. K. (1994). Temperament, development, and the Big Five. In C. F. Halverson, Jr., G. A. Kohnstamm, & R. P. Martin (Eds.), *The developing structure of temperament and personality from infancy to adulthood* (pp. 189–207). Hillsdale, NJ: Erlbaum.

Allen, T. A., & DeYoung, C. G. (2017). Personality neuroscience and the five factor model. In T. A. Widiger (Ed.), *Oxford handbook of the five factor model* (pp. 319–352). New York: Oxford University Press.

Allen, T. A., Rueter, A. R., Abram, S. V., Brown, J. S., & DeYoung, C. G. (2017). Personality and neural correlates of mentalizing ability. *European Journal of Personality, 31*(6), 599–613.

Andrews-Hanna, J. R., Smallwood, J., & Spreng, R. N. (2014). The default network and self-generated thought: Component processes, dynamic control, and clinical relevance. *Annals of the New York Academy of Sciences, 1316,* 29–52.

Bäckman, L., Lindenberger, U., Li, S. C., & Nyberg, L. (2010). Linking cognitive aging to alterations in dopamine neurotransmitter functioning: Recent data and future avenues. *Neuroscience and Biobehavioral Reviews, 34*(5), 670–677.

Bar-Haim, Y., Fox, N. A., Benson, B., Guyer, A. E., Williams, A., Nelson, E. E., et al. (2009). Neural correlates of reward processing in adolescents with a history of inhibited temperament. *Psychological Science, 20*(8), 1009–1018.

Baron-Cohen, S., & Wheelwright, S. (2004). The empathy quotient: An investigation of adults with Asperger syndrome or high functioning autism, and normal sex differences. *Journal of Autism and Developmental Disorders, 34*(2), 163–175.

Beaty, R. E., Kaufman, S. B., Benedek, M., Jung, R. E., Kenett, Y. N., Jauk, E., et al. (2016). Personality and complex brain networks: The role of openness to experience in default network efficiency. *Human Brain Mapping, 37*(2), 773–779.

Becht, A. I., Prinzie, P., Deković, M., Van den Akker, A. L., & Shiner, R. L. (2016). Child personality facets and overreactive parenting as predictors of aggression and rule-breaking trajectories from childhood to adolescence. *Development and Psychopathology, 28*(2), 399–413.

Berridge, K. C., Robinson, T. E., & Aldridge, J. W. (2009). Dissecting components of reward: "Liking," "wanting," and learning. *Current Opinion in Pharmacology, 9*(1), 65–73.

Bjørnebekk, A., Fjell, A. M., Walhovd, K. B., Grydeland, H., Torgersen, S., & Westlye, L. T. (2013). Neuronal correlates of the Five Factor Model (FFM) of human personality: Multimodal imaging in a large healthy sample. *NeuroImage, 65,* 194–208.

Blackford, J. U., Allen, A. H., Cowan, R. L., & Avery, S. N. (2013). Amygdala and hippocampus fail to habituate to faces in individuals with an inhibited temperament. *Social Cognitive Affective Neuroscience, 8*(2), 143–150.

Bradley, R., Binder, E., Epstein, M., Tang, Y., Nair, H., Liu, W., et al. (2008). Influence of child abuse on adult depression: Moderation by the corticotropin-releasing hormone receptor gene. *Archives of General Psychiatry, 65*(2), 190–200.

Bress, J. N., & Hajcak, G. (2013). Self-report and behavioral measures of reward sensitivity predict the feedback negativity. *Psychophysiology, 50*(7), 610–616.

Bridgett, D. J., Gartstein, M. A., Putnam, S. P., Lance, K. O., Iddins, E., Waits, R., et al. (2011). Emerging effortful control in toddlerhood: The role of infant orienting/regulation, maternal effortful control, and maternal time spent in caregiving activities. *Infant Behavior and Development, 34*(1), 189–199.

Bromberg-Martin, E. S., Matsumoto, M., & Hikosaka, O. (2010). Dopamine in motivational control: Rewarding, aversive, and alerting. *Neuron, 68*(5), 815–834.

Brown, S. M., Manuck, S. B., Flory, J. D., & Hariri, A. R. (2006). Neural basis of individual differences in impulsivity: Contributions of corticolimbic circuits for behavioral arousal and control. *Emotion, 6*(2), 239–245.

Bunge, S. A. (2004). How we use rules to select actions: A review of evidence from cognitive neuroscience. *Cognitive, Affective, and Behavioral Neuroscience, 4*(4), 564–579.

Bunge, S. A., & Zelazo, P. D. (2006). A brain-based

account of the development of rule use in childhood. *Current Directions in Psychological Science, 15*(3), 118–121.

Buss, K. A., Schumacher, J. R. M., Dolski, I., Kalin, N. H., Goldsmith, H. H., & Davidson, R. J. (2003). Right frontal brain activity, cortisol, and withdrawal behavior in 6-month-old infants. *Behavioral Neuroscience, 117*(1), 11–20.

Calkins, S. D., Fox, N. A., & Marshall, T. R. (1996). Behavioral and physiological antecedents of inhibited and uninhibited behavior. *Child Development, 67*(2), 523–540.

Carlson, S. M. (2005). Developmentally sensitive measures of executive function in preschool children. *Developmental Neuropsychology, 28*(2), 595–616.

Casey, B. J. (2015). Beyond simple models of self-control to circuit-based accounts of adolescent behavior. *Annual Review of Psychology, 66*, 295–319.

Caspi, A., & Shiner, R. L. (2006). Personality development. In W. Damon & R. Lerner (Series Eds.) & N. Eisenberg (Vol. Ed.), *Handbook of child psychology: Vol. 3. Social, emotional, and personality development* (6th ed., pp. 300–365). New York: Wiley.

Cheetham, A., Allen, N. B., Whittle, S., Simmons, J., Yücel, M., & Lubman, D. I. (2017). Orbitofrontal cortex volume and effortful control as prospective risk factors for substance use disorder in adolescence. *European Addiction Research, 23*(1), 37–44.

Choi, Y. Y., Shamosh, N. A., Cho, S. H., DeYoung, C. G., Lee, M. J., Lee, J. M., et al. (2008). Multiple bases of human intelligence revealed by cortical thickness and neural activation. *Journal of Neuroscience, 28*(41), 10323–10329.

Churchwell, J. C., & Yurgelun-Todd, D. A. (2013). Age-related changes in insula cortical thickness and impulsivity: Significance for emotional development and decision-making. *Developmental Cognitive Neuroscience, 6*, 80–86.

Clauss, J. A., Seay, A. L., VanDerKlok, R. M., Avery, S., Cao, A., Cowan, R. L., et al. (2014). Structural and functional bases of inhibited temperament. *Social Cognitive and Affective Neuroscience, 9*(12), 2049–2058.

Conklin, H. M., Luciana, M., Hooper, C. J., & Yarger, R. S. (2007). Working memory performance in typically developing children and adolescents: Behavioral evidence of protracted frontal lobe development. *Developmental Neuropsychology, 31*(1), 103–128.

Conway, A. R., Kane, M. J., & Engle, R. W. (2003). Working memory capacity and its relation to general intelligence. *Trends in Cognitive Sciences, 7*(12), 547–552.

Cooper, A. J., Duke, E., Pickering, A. D., & Smillie, L. D. (2014). Individual differences in reward prediction error: Contrasting relations between feedback-related negativity and trait measures of reward sensitivity, impulsivity and extraversion. *Frontiers in Human Neuroscience, 8*, 248.

Côté, S., Vaillancourt, T., LeBlanc, J. C., Nagin, D. S., & Tremblay, R. E. (2006). The development of physical aggression from toddlerhood to pre-adolescence: A nation wide longitudinal study of Canadian children. *Journal of Abnormal Child Psychology, 34*(1), 68–82.

Cremers, H., van Tol, M. J., Roelofs, K., Aleman, A., Zitman, F. G., van Buchem, M. A., et al. (2011). Extraversion is linked to volume of the orbitofrontal cortex and amygdala. *PLOS ONE, 6*(12), e28421.

Cumberland-Li, A., Eisenberg, N., & Reiser, M. (2004). Relations of young children's agreeableness and resiliency to effortful control and impulsivity. *Social Development, 13*(2), 193–212.

Darki, F., & Klingberg, T. (2015). The role of fronto-parietal and fronto-striatal networks in the development of working memory: A longitudinal study. *Cerebral Cortex, 25*, 1587–1595.

Davey, C. G., Whittle, S., Harrison, B. J., Simmons, J. G., Byrne, M. L., Schwartz, O. S., et al. (2015). Functional brain-imaging correlates of negative affectivity and the onset of first-episode depression. *Psychological Medicine, 45*(5), 1001–1009.

Davidov, M., Zahn-Waxler, C., Roth-Hanania, R., & Knafo, A. (2013). Concern for others in the first year of life: Theory, evidence, and avenues for research. *Child Development Perspectives, 7*(2), 126–131.

Davidson, R. J. (1992). Emotion and affective style: Hemispheric substrates. *Psychological Science, 3*(1), 39–43.

Davis, F. C., Knodt, A. R., Sporns, O., Lahey, B. B., Zald, D. H., Brigidi, B. D., et al. (2013). Impulsivity and the modular organization of resting-state neural networks. *Cerebral Cortex, 23*(6), 1444–1452.

De Fruyt, F., Bartels, M., Van Leeuwen, K. G., De Clercq, B., Decuyper, M., & Mervielde, I. (2006). Five types of personality continuity in childhood and adolescence. *Journal of Personality and Social Psychology, 91*, 538–552.

De Pauw, S. S., & Mervielde, I. (2010). Temperament, personality and developmental psychopathology: A review based on the conceptual dimensions underlying childhood traits. *Child Psychiatry and Human Development, 41*(3), 313–329.

De Pauw, S. S., Mervielde, I., & Van Leeuwen, K. G. (2009). How are traits related to problem behavior in preschoolers?: Similarities and contrasts between temperament and personality. *Journal of Abnormal Child Psychology, 37*(3), 309–325.

Denissen, J. J., & Penke, L. (2008). Motivational individual reaction norms underlying the Five-Factor model of personality: First steps towards a theory-based conceptual framework. *Journal of Research in Personality, 42*(5), 1285–1302.

Dennison, M., Whittle, S., Yücel, M., Byrne, M. L., Schwartz, O., Simmons, J. G., et al. (2015). Trait positive affect is associated with hippocampal volume and change in caudate volume across adolescence. *Cognitive, Affective, and Behavioral Neuroscience, 15*(1), 80–94.

Depue, R. A., & Collins, P. F. (1999). Neurobiology of the structure of personality: Dopamine, facilitation of incentive motivation, and extraversion. *Behavioral and Brain Sciences, 22*(3), 491–517.

Depue, R. A., & Fu, Y. (2013). On the nature of extraversion: Variation in conditioned contextual activation of dopamine-facilitated affective, cognitive, and motor processes. *Frontiers in Human Neuroscience, 7,* 288.

Depue, R. A., & Morrone-Strupinsky, J. V. (2005). A neurobehavioral model of affiliative bonding: Implications for conceptualizing a human trait of affiliation. *Behavioral and Brain Sciences, 28*(3), 313–349.

DeYoung, C. G. (2006). Higher-order factors of the Big Five in a multi-informant sample. *Journal of Personality and Social Psychology, 91*(6), 1138–1151.

DeYoung, C. G. (2013). The neuromodulator of exploration: A unifying theory of the role of dopamine in personality. *Frontiers in Human Neuroscience, 7,* 762.

DeYoung, C. G. (2014). Openness/intellect: A dimension of personality reflecting cognitive exploration. In M. L. Cooper & R. J. Larsen (Eds.), *APA handbook of personality and social psychology: Vol. 4. Personality processes and individual differences* (pp. 369–399). Washington, DC: American Psychological Association.

DeYoung, C. G. (2015). Cybernetic Big Five theory. *Journal of Research in Personality, 56,* 33–58.

DeYoung, C. G., Cicchetti, D., & Rogosch, F. A. (2011). Moderation of the association between childhood maltreatment and neuroticism by the corticotropin-releasing hormone receptor 1 gene. *Journal of Child Psychology and Psychiatry, 52*(8), 898–906.

DeYoung, C. G., Hirsh, J. B., Shane, M. S., Papademetris, X., Rajeevan, N., & Gray, J. R. (2010). Testing predictions from personality neuroscience: Brain structure and the Big Five. *Psychological Science, 21*(6), 820–828.

DeYoung, C. G., Peterson, J. B., & Higgins, D. M. (2005). Sources of openness/intellect: Cognitive and neuropsychological correlates of the fifth factor of personality. *Journal of Personality, 73*(4), 825–858.

DeYoung, C. G., Peterson, J. B., Séguin, J. R., & Tremblay, R. E. (2008). Externalizing behavior and the higher order factors of the Big Five. *Journal of Abnormal Psychology, 117*(4), 947–953.

DeYoung, C. G., Quilty, L. C., & Peterson, J. B. (2007). Between facets and domains: 10 aspects of the Big Five. *Journal of Personality and Social Psychology, 93*(5), 880–896.

DeYoung, C. G., Quilty, L. C., Peterson, J. B., & Gray, J. R. (2014). Openness to experience, intellect, and cognitive ability. *Journal of Personality Assessment, 96*(1), 46–52.

DeYoung, C. G., & Rueter, A. R. (2016). Impulsivity as a personality trait. In K. D. Vohs & R. F. Baumeister (Eds.), *Handbook of self-regulation: Research, theory, and applications* (3rd ed., pp. 345–363). New York: Guilford Press.

DeYoung, C. G., Shamosh, N. A., Green, A. E., Braver, T. S., & Gray, J. R. (2009). Intellect as distinct from openness: Differences revealed by fMRI of working memory. *Journal of Personality and Social Psychology, 97*(5), 883–892.

DeYoung, C. G., Weisberg, Y. J., Quilty, L. C., & Peterson, J. B. (2013). Unifying the aspects of the Big Five, the interpersonal circumplex, and trait affiliation. *Journal of Personality, 81*(5), 465–475.

Digman, J. M. (1997). Higher-order factors of the Big Five. *Journal of Personality and Social Psychology, 73*(6), 1246–1256.

Digman, J. M., & Shmelyov, A. G. (1996). The structure of temperament and personality in Russian children. *Journal of Personality and Social Psychology, 71*(2), 341–351.

DiPietro, J. A., Hodgson, D. M., Costigan, K. A., & Johnson, T. R. (1996). Fetal antecedents of infant temperament. *Child Development, 67*(5), 2568–2583.

Dougherty, L. R., Smith, V. C., Olino, T. M., Dyson, M. W., Bufferd, S. J., Rose, S. A., et al. (2013). Maternal psychopathology and early child temperament predict young children's salivary cortisol 3 years later. *Journal of Abnormal Child Psychology, 41*(4), 531–542.

Dumontheil, I., Apperly, I. A., & Blakemore, S. J. (2010). Online usage of theory of mind continues to develop in late adolescence. *Developmental Science, 13*(2), 331–338.

Durbin, C. E., Hayden, E. P., Klein, D. N., & Olino, T. M. (2007). Stability of laboratory-assessed temperamental emotionality traits from ages 3 to 7. *Emotion, 7*(2), 388–389.

Dyson, M. W., Olino, T. M., Durbin, C. E., Goldsmith, H. H., Bufferd, S. J., Miller, A. R., et al. (2015). The structural and rank-order stability of temperament in young children based on a laboratory-observational measure. *Psychological Assessment, 27*(4), 1388–1401.

Eaton, W. O., & Saudino, K. J. (1992). Prenatal activity level as a temperament dimension?: Individual differences and developmental functions in fetal movement. *Infant Behavior and Development, 15*(1), 57–70.

Erixon-Lindroth, N., Farde, L., Wahlin, T. B. R., Sovago, J., Halldin, C., & Bäckman, L. (2005). The role of the striatal dopamine transporter in cognitive aging. *Psychiatry Research: Neuroimaging, 138*(1), 1–12.

Etkin, A., Egner, T., & Kalisch, R. (2011). Emotional processing in anterior cingulate and medial prefrontal cortex. *Trends in Cognitive Sciences, 15*(2), 85–93.

Evans, B. E., Stam, J., Huizink, A. C., Willemen, A. M., Westenberg, P. M., Branje, S., et al. (2016). Neuroticism and extraversion in relation to physiological stress reactivity during adolescence. *Biological Psychology, 117,* 67–79.

Evans, D. E., & Rothbart, M. K. (2007). Developing a model for adult temperament. *Journal of Research in Personality, 41*(4), 868–888.

Everaerd, D., Klumpers, F., van Wingen, G., Tendolkar, I., & Fernández, G. (2015). Association between neuroticism and amygdala responsivity emerges under stressful conditions. *NeuroImage, 112,* 218–224.

Everhart, D. E., Demaree, H. A., & Harrison, D. W. (2008). The influence of hostility on electroencephalographic activity and memory functioning during an affective memory task. *Clinical Neurophysiology, 119*(1), 134–143.

Fair, D. A., Cohen, A. L., Power, J. D., Dosenbach, N. U., Church, J. A., Miezin, F. M., et al. (2009). Functional brain networks develop from a "local to distributed" organization. *PLOS Computational Biology, 5*(5), e1000381.

Farr, O. M., Hu, S., Zhang, S., & Li, C. S. R. (2012). Decreased saliency processing as a neural measure of Barratt impulsivity in healthy adults. *NeuroImage, 63*(3), 1070–1077.

Fekete, T., Beacher, F. D., Cha, J., Rubin, D., & Mujica-Parodi, L. R. (2014). Small-world network properties in prefrontal cortex correlate with predictors of psychopathology risk in young children: A NIRS study. *NeuroImage, 85,* 345–353.

Finn, A. S., Sheridan, M. A., Kam, C. L. H., Hinshaw, S., & D'Esposito, M. (2010). Longitudinal evidence for functional specialization of the neural circuit supporting working memory in the human brain. *Journal of Neuroscience, 30*(33), 11062–11067.

Forbes, C. E., Poore, J. C., Krueger, F., Barbey, A. K., Solomon, J., & Grafman, J. (2014). The role of executive function and the dorsolateral prefrontal cortex in the expression of neuroticism and conscientiousness. *Social Neuroscience, 9*(2), 139–151.

Fox, M. D., Corbetta, M., Snyder, A. Z., Vincent, J. L., & Raichle, M. E. (2006). Spontaneous neuronal activity distinguishes human dorsal and ventral attention systems. *Proceedings of the National Academy of Sciences of the USA, 103*(26), 10046–10051.

Fox, N. A. (1991). If it's not left, it's right: Electroencephalograph asymmetry and the development of emotion. *American Psychologist, 46*(8), 863–872.

Fox, N. A., Calkins, S. D., & Bell, M. A. (1994). Neural plasticity and development in the first two years of life: Evidence from cognitive and socioemotional domains of research. *Development and Psychopathology, 6*(4), 677–696.

Fox, N. A., Henderson, H. A., Marshall, P. J., Nichols, K. E., & Ghera, M. M. (2005). Behavioral inhibition: Linking biology and behavior within a developmental framework. *Annual Review of Psychology, 56,* 235–262.

Fox, N. A., Henderson, H. A., Rubin, K. H., Calkins, S. D., & Schmidt, L. A. (2001). Continuity and discontinuity of behavioral inhibition and exuberance: Psychophysiological and behavioral influences across the first four years of life. *Child Development, 72*(1), 1–21.

Garcia-Banda, G., Chellew, K., Fornes, J., Perez, G., Servera, M., & Evans, P. (2014). Neuroticism and cortisol: Pinning down an expected effect.

International Journal of Psychophysiology, 91(2), 132–138.

Garcia-Coll, C., Kagan, J., & Reznick, J. S. (1984). Behavioral inhibition in young children. *Child Development, 55*(3), 1005–1019.

Gartstein, M. A., & Rothbart, M. K. (2003). Studying infant temperament via the revised infant behavior questionnaire. *Infant Behavior and Development, 26*(1), 64–86.

Gartstein, M. A., Slobodskaya, H. R., Putnam, S. P., & Kinsht, I. A. (2009). A cross-cultural study of infant temperament: Predicting preschool effortful control in the United States of America and Russia. *European Journal of Developmental Psychology, 6*(3), 337–364.

Gerritsen, L., Geerlings, M., Bremmer, M., Beekman, A., Deeg, D., Penninx, B. W. J. H., et al. (2009). Personality characteristics and hypothalamic–pituitary–adrenal axis regulation in older persons. *American Journal of Geriatric Psychiatry, 17*(12), 1077–1084.

Giedd, J. N., Blumenthal, J., Jeffries, N. O., Castellanos, F. X., Liu, H., Zijdenbos, A., et al. (1999). Brain development during childhood and adolescence: A longitudinal MRI study. *Nature Neuroscience, 2*(10), 861–863.

Gjerde, P. F., & Cardilla, K. (2009). Developmental implications of openness to experience in preschool children: Gender differences in young adulthood. *Developmental Psychology, 45*(5), 1455–1464.

Glynn, L. M., Davis, E. P., Schetter, C. D., Chicz-DeMet, A., Hobel, C. J., & Sandman, C. A. (2007). Postnatal maternal cortisol levels predict temperament in healthy breastfed infants. *Early Human Development, 83*(10), 675–681.

Grabe, H., Schwahn, C., Appel, K., Mahler, J., Schulz, A., Spitzer, C., et al. (2010). Childhood maltreatment, the corticotropin-releasing hormone receptor gene and adult depression in the general population. *American Journal of Medical Genetics B: Neuropsychiatric Genetics, 153*(8), 1483–1493.

Gray, J. A., & McNaughton, N. (2000). *The neuropsychology of anxiety: An enquiry into the function of the septo-hippocampal system.* New York: Oxford University Press.

Graziano, W. G., & Tobin, R. M. (2013). The cognitive and motivational foundations underlying Agreeableness. In M. D. Robinson, E. R. Watkins, & E. Harmon-Jones (Eds.), *Handbook of cognition and emotion* (pp. 347–364). New York: Guilford Press.

Greenough, W. T., Black, J. E., & Wallace, C. S. (1987). Experience and brain development. *Child Development, 58*(3), 539–559.

Grey, K. R., Davis, E. P., Sandman, C. A., & Glynn, L. M. (2013). Human milk cortisol is associated with infant temperament. *Psychoneuroendocrinology, 38*(7), 1178–1185.

Grodin, E. N., & White, T. L. (2015). The neuroanatomical delineation of agentic and affiliative extraversion. *Cognitive, Affective, and Behavioral Neuroscience, 15*(2), 321–334.

Guyer, A. E., Nelson, E. E., Pérez-Edgar, K., Hardin, M. G., Roberson-Nay, R., Monk, C. S., et al. (2006). Striatal functional alteration in adolescents characterized by early childhood behavioral inhibition. *Journal of Neuroscience, 26*(24), 6399–6405.

Hagekull, B., & Bohlin, G. (2003). Early temperament and attachment as predictors of the Five Factor Model of personality. *Attachment and Human Development, 5*(1), 2–18.

Halverson, C. F., Havill, V. L., Deal, J., Baker, S. R., Victor, J. B., Pavlopoulos, V., et al. (2003). Personality structure as derived from parental ratings of free descriptions of children: The Inventory of Child Individual Differences. *Journal of Personality, 71*(6), 995–1026.

Hane, A. A., Fox, N. A., Henderson, H. A., & Marshall, P. J. (2008). Behavioral reactivity and approach–withdrawal bias in infancy. *Developmental Psychology, 44*(5), 1491–1496.

Harmon-Jones, E. (2004). Contributions from research on anger and cognitive dissonance to understanding the motivational functions of asymmetrical frontal brain activity. *Biological Psychology, 67*(1–2), 51–76.

Harmon-Jones, E., & Allen, J. J. B. (1998). Anger and frontal brain activity: EEG asymmetry consistent with approach motivation despite negative affective valence. *Journal of Personality and Social Psychology, 74*(5), 1310–1316.

Herzhoff, K., & Tackett, J. L. (2012). Establishing construct validity for Openness-to-Experience in middle childhood: Contributions from personality and temperament. *Journal of Research in Personality, 46*(3), 286–294.

Holmes, A. J., Lee, P. H., Hollinshead, M. O., Bakst, L., Roffman, J. L., Smoller, J. W., et al. (2012). Individual differences in amygdala–medial prefrontal anatomy link negative affect, impaired social functioning, and polygenic depression risk. *Journal of Neuroscience, 32,* 18087–18100.

Hou, X., Allen, T. A., Wei, D., Huang, H., Wang, K., DeYoung, C. G., et al. (2017). Trait compassion is associated with the neural substrate of empathy. *Cognitive, Affective, and Behavioral Neuroscience, 17*(5), 1018–1027.

Imuta, K., Henry, J. D., Slaughter, V., Selcuk, B., & Ruffman, T. (2016). Theory of mind and prosocial behavior in childhood: A meta-analytic review. *Developmental Psychology, 52*(8), 1192–1205.

Inder, T. E., & Huppi, P. S. (2000). In vivo studies of brain development by magnetic resonance techniques. *Developmental Disabilities Research Reviews, 6*(1), 59–67.

Jackson, J., Balota, D. A., & Head, D. (2011). Exploring the relationship between personality and regional brain volume in healthy aging. *Neurobiology of Aging, 32*(12), 2162–2171.

Jensen-Campbell, L. A., Rosselli, M., Workman,

K. A., Santisi, M., Rios, J. D., & Bojan, D. (2002). Agreeableness, conscientiousness, and effortful control processes. *Journal of Research in Personality, 36*(5), 476–489.

John, O. P., Caspi, A., Robins, R. W., Moffitt, T. E., & Stouthamer-Loeber, M. (1994). The "Little Five": Exploring the five-factor model of personality in adolescent boys. *Child Development, 65,* 160–178.

Jung, R. E., & Haier, R. J. (2007). The Parieto-Frontal Integration Theory (P-FIT) of intelligence: Converging neuroimaging evidence. *Behavioral and Brain Sciences, 30*(2), 135–154.

Kagan, J., Reznick, J. S., & Snidman, N. (1987). The physiology and psychology of behavioral inhibition in children. *Child Development, 58*(6), 1459–1473.

Kagan, J., Reznick, J. S., Snidman, N., Gibbons, J., & Johnson, M. O. (1988). Childhood derivatives of inhibition and lack of inhibition to the unfamiliar. *Child Development, 59*(6), 1580–1589.

Kapogiannis, D., Sutin, A., Davatzikos, C., Costa, P., & Resnick, S. (2013). The five factors of personality and regional cortical variability in the Baltimore longitudinal study of aging. *Human Brain Mapping, 34*(11), 2829–2840.

Kern, M. L., Duckworth, A. L., Urzúa, S. S., Loeber, R., Stouthamer-Loeber, M., & Lynam, D. R. (2013). Do as you're told!: Facets of agreeableness and early adult outcomes for inner-city boys. *Journal of Research in Personality, 47*(6), 795–799.

Klimstra, T. A., Bleidorn, W., Asendorpf, J. B., Van Aken, M. A., & Denissen, J. J. (2013). Correlated change of Big Five personality traits across the lifespan: A search for determinants. *Journal of Research in Personality, 47*(6), 768–777.

Klingberg, T. (2006). Development of a superior frontal–intraparietal network for visuo-spatial working memory. *Neuropsychologia, 44*(11), 2171–2177.

Kochanska, G., & Knaack, A. (2003). Effortful control as a personality characteristic of young children: Antecedents, correlates, and consequences. *Journal of Personality, 71*(6), 1087–1112.

Kochanska, G., Murray, K. T., & Harlan, E. T. (2000). Effortful control in early childhood: Continuity and change, antecedents, and implications for social development. *Developmental Psychology, 36*(2), 220–232.

Kranzler, H. R., Feinn, R., Nelson, E. C., Covault, J., Anton, R. F., Farrer, L., et al. (2011). A CRHR1 haplotype moderates the effect of adverse childhood experiences on lifetime risk of major depressive episode in African-American women. *American Journal of Medical Genetics B: Neuropsychiatric Genetics, 156*(8), 960–968.

Krueger, R. F., & Johnson, W. (2008). Behavioral genetics and personality: A new look at the integration of nature and nurture. In O. P. John, R. W. Robins, & L. A. Pervin (Eds.), *Handbook of personality: Theory and research* (3rd ed., pp. 387–287). New York: Guilford Press.

Kujawa, A., Proudfit, G. H., Kessel, E. M., Dyson, M., Olino, T., & Klein, D. N. (2015). Neural reactivity to monetary rewards and losses in childhood: Longitudinal and concurrent associations with observed and self-reported positive emotionality. *Biological Psychology, 104,* 41–47.

Lahat, A., Benson, B., Pine, D. S., Fox, N. A., & Ernst, M. (2018). Neural responses to reward in childhood: Relations to early behavioral inhibition and social anxiety. *Social Cognitive and Affective Neuroscience, 13*(3), 281–289.

Lange, S., Leue, A., & Beauducel, A. (2012). Behavioral approach and reward processing: Results on feedback-related negativity and P3 component. *Biological Psychology, 89*(2), 416–425.

Lenroot, R. K., & Giedd, J. N. (2006). Brain development in children and adolescents: Insights from anatomical magnetic resonance imaging. *Neuroscience and Biobehavioral Reviews, 30*(6), 718–729.

Lewis, G. J., Panizzon, M. S., Eyler, L., Fennema-Notestine, C., Chen, C. H., Neale, M. C., et al. (2014). Heritable influences on amygdala and orbitofrontal cortex contribute to genetic variation in core dimensions of personality. *NeuroImage, 103,* 309–315.

Lewis, M. (2000). The emergence of human emotions. In M. Lewis & J. Haviland (Eds.), *Handbook of emotions* (pp. 265–280). New York: Guilford Press.

Liu, W.-Y., Weber, B., Reuter, M., Markett, S., Chu, W.-C., & Montag, C. (2013). The Big Five of personality and structural imaging revisited: A VBM-DARTEL study. *NeuroReport, 24*(7), 375–380.

Mackrell, S. V., Sheikh, H. I., Kotelnikova, Y., Kryski, K. R., Jordan, P. L., Singh, S. M., et al. (2014). Child temperament and parental depression predict cortisol reactivity to stress in middle childhood. *Journal of Abnormal Psychology, 123*(1), 106–116.

Matsuo, K., Nicoletti, M., Nemoto, K., Hatch, J. P., Peluso, M. A., Nery, F. G., et al. (2009). A voxel-based morphometry study of frontal gray matter correlates of impulsivity. *Human Brain Mapping, 30*(4), 1188–1195.

McAdams, D. P., & Pals, J. L. (2006). A new Big Five: Fundamental principles for an integrative science of personality. *American Psychologist, 61*(3), 204–217.

Mervielde, I., Buyst, V., & De Fruyt, F. (1995). The validity of the Big-Five as a model for teachers' ratings of individual differences among children aged 4–12 years. *Personality and Individual Differences, 18*(4), 525–534.

Mervielde, I., De Clercq, B., De Fruyt, F., & Van Leeuwen, K. (2005). Temperament, personality, and developmental psychopathology as childhood antecedents of personality disorders. *Journal of Personality Disorders, 19*(2), 171–201.

Mervielde, I., & De Fruyt, F. (2000). The Big Five personality factors as a model for the structure of children's peer nominations. *European Journal of Personality, 14*(2), 91–106.

Miller, G., Cohen, S., Rabin, B., Skoner, D. P., & Doyle, W. J. (1999). Personality and tonic cardiovascular, neuroendocrine, and immune parameters. *Brain, Behavior, and Immunity, 13*(2), 109–123.

Miller, K. G., Wright, A. G., Peterson, L. M., Kamarck, T. W., Anderson, B. A., Kirschbaum, C., et al. (2016). Trait positive and negative emotionality differentially associate with diurnal cortisol activity. *Psychoneuroendocrinology, 68,* 177–185.

Mills, K. L., Lalonde, F., Clasen, L. S., Giedd, J. N., & Blakemore, S. J. (2014). Developmental changes in the structure of the social brain in late childhood and adolescence. *Social Cognitive and Affective Neuroscience, 9*(1), 123–131.

Montoya, E. R., Terburg, D., Bos, P. A., & Van Honk, J. (2012). Testosterone, cortisol, and serotonin as key regulators of social aggression: A review and theoretical perspective. *Motivation and Emotion, 36*(1), 65–73.

Morinaga, K., Akiyoshi, J., Matsushita, H., Ichioka, S., Tanaka, Y., Tsuru, J., et al. (2007). Anticipatory anxiety-induced changes in human lateral prefrontal cortex activity. *Biological Psychology, 74*(1), 34–38.

Mõttus, R., Johnson, W., & Deary, I. J. (2012). Personality traits in old age: Measurement and rank-order stability and some mean-level change. *Psychology and Aging, 27*(1), 243–249.

Mueller, E. M., Burgdorf, C., Chavanon, M. L., Schweiger, D., Wacker, J., & Stemmler, G. (2014). Dopamine modulates frontomedial failure processing of agentic introverts versus extraverts in incentive contexts. *Cognitive, Affective, and Behavioral Neuroscience, 14*(2), 756–768.

Mujica-Parodi, L. R., Korgaonkar, M., Ravindranath, B., Greenberg, T., Tomasi, D., Wagshul, M., et al. (2009). Limbic dysregulation is associated with lowered heart rate variability and increased trait in healthy adults. *Human Brain Mapping, 30*(1), 47–58.

Muris, P., Bos, A. E., Mayer, B., Verkade, R., Thewissen, V., & Dell'Avvento, V. (2009). Relations among behavioral inhibition, Big Five personality factors, and anxiety disorder symptoms in non-clinical children. *Personality and Individual Differences, 46*(4), 525–529.

Naragon-Gainey, K., Watson, D., & Markon, K. E. (2009). Differential relations of depression and social anxiety symptoms to the facets of extraversion/positive emotionality. *Journal of Abnormal Psychology, 118*(2), 299–310.

Nater, U. M., Hoppmann, C., & Klumb, P. L. (2010). Neuroticism and conscientiousness are associated with cortisol diurnal profiles in adults—role of positive and negative affect. *Psychoneuroendocrinology, 35*(10), 1573–1577.

Nettle, D. (2006). The evolution of personality variation in humans and other animals. *American Psychologist, 61*(6), 622–631.

Nettle, D. (2007). *Personality: What makes you the way you are.* New York: Oxford University Press.

Nettle, D., & Liddle, B. (2008). Agreeableness is related to social-cognitive, but not social-perceptual, theory of mind. *European Journal of Personality, 22*(4), 323–335.

Nguyen, T. V., McCracken, J. T., Albaugh, M. D., Botteron, K. N., Hudziak, J. J., & Ducharme, S. (2016). A testosterone-related structural brain phenotype predicts aggressive behavior from childhood to adulthood. *Psychoneuroendocrinology, 63,* 109–118.

Nouchi, R., Takeuchi, H., Taki, Y., Sekiguchi, A., Kotozaki, Y., Nakagawa, S., et al. (2016). Neuroanatomical bases of effortful control: Evidence from a large sample of young healthy adults using voxel-based morphometry. *Scientific Reports, 6,* Article No. 31231.

Passamonti, L., Terracciano, A., Riccelli, R., Donzuso, G., Cerasa, A., Vaccaro, M. G., et al. (2015). Increased functional connectivity within mesocortical networks in open people. *NeuroImage, 104,* 301–309.

Pérez-Edgar, K., Roberson-Nay, R., Hardin, M. G., Poeth, K., Guyer, A. E., Nelson, E. E., et al.(2007). Attention alters neural responses to evocative faces in behaviorally inhibited adolescents. *NeuroImage, 35*(4), 1538–1546.

Polanczyk, G., Caspi, A., Williams, B., Price, T. S., Danese, A., Sugden, K., et al. (2009). Protective effect of CRHR1 gene variants on the development of adult depression following childhood maltreatment: Replication and extension. *Archives of General Psychiatry, 66*(9), 978–985.

Polk, D., Cohen, S., Doyle, W., Skoner, D. P., & Kirschbaum, C. (2005). State and trait affect as predictors of salivary cortisol in healthy adults. *Psychoneuroendocrinology, 30*(3), 261–272.

Posner, M. I., & Fan, J. (2008). Attention as an organ system. In J. R. Pomerantz (Ed.), *Topics in integrative neuroscience* (pp. 31–61). New York: Cambridge University Press.

Posner, M. I., & Rothbart, M. K. (1998). Attention, self-regulation, and consciousness. *Philosophical Transactions of the Royal Society of London B, 353,* 1915–1927.

Posner, M. I., & Rothbart, M. K. (2007). Research on attention networks as a model for the integration of psychological science. *Annual Review of Psychology, 58,* 1–23.

Premack, D., & Woodruff, G. (1978). Does the chimpanzee have a theory of mind? *Behavioral and Brain Sciences, 1*(4), 515–526.

Proudfit, G. H. (2015). The reward positivity: From basic research on reward to a biomarker for depression. *Psychophysiology, 52*(4), 449–459.

Putnam, S. P., Rothbart, M. K., & Gartstein, M. A. (2008). Homotypic and heterotypic continuity of fine-grained temperament during infancy, toddlerhood, and early childhood. *Infant and Child Development, 17*(4), 387–405.

Quilty, L. C., DeYoung, C. G., Oakman, J. M., & Bagby, R. M. (2014). Extraversion and behavioral activation: Integrating the components of approach. *Journal of Personality Assessment, 96*(1), 87–94.

Raine, A., Reynolds, C., Venables, P. H., & Mednick,

S. A. (2002). Stimulation seeking and intelligence: A prospective longitudinal study. *Journal of Personality and Social Psychology, 82*(4), 663–674.

Reardon, K. W., Herzhoff, K., & Tackett, J. L. (2015). Adolescent personality as risk and resiliency in the testosterone–externalizing association. *Journal of Research on Adolescence, 26*(3), 390–402.

Roberts, B. W., & DelVecchio, W. F. (2000). The rank-order consistency of personality traits from childhood to old age: A quantitative review of longitudinal studies. *Psychological Bulletin, 126*(1), 3–25.

Roberts, B. W., Walton, K. E., & Viechtbauer, W. (2006). Patterns of mean-level change in personality traits across the life course: A meta-analysis of longitudinal studies. *Psychological Bulletin, 132*(1), 1–25.

Rothbart, M. K. (2007). Temperament, development, and personality. *Current Directions in Psychological Science, 16*(4), 207–212.

Rothbart, M. K., & Bates, J. E. (1998). Temperament. In W. Damon (Series Ed.) & N. Eisenberg (Vol. Ed.), *Handbook of child psychology: Vol. 3. Social, emotional, and personality development* (5th ed., pp. 105–176). New York: Wiley.

Rothbart, M. K., & Bates, J. E. (2006). Temperament. In W. Damon & R. Lerner (Series Eds.) & N. Eisenberg (Vol. Ed.), *Handbook of child psychology: Vol. 3. Social, emotional, and personality development* (6th ed., pp. 99–166). New York: Wiley.

Rothbart, M. K., & Derryberry, D. (1981). Development of individual differences in temperament. In M. E. Lamb & A. L. Brown (Eds.), *Advances in developmental psychology* (Vol. 1, pp. 37–86). Hillsdale, NJ: Erlbaum.

Rothbart, M. K., Derryberry, D., & Hershey, K. (2000). Stability of temperament in childhood: Laboratory infant assessment to parent report at seven years. In V. J. Molfese & D. L. Molfese (Eds.), *Temperament and personality development across the life span* (pp. 85–119). Mahwah, NJ: Erlbaum.

Rothbart, M. K., Ellis, L. K., Rueda, M. R., & Posner, M. I. (2003). Developing mechanisms of temperamental effortful control. *Journal of Personality, 71*(6), 1113–1144.

Rothbart, M. K., & Posner, M. I. (2006). Temperament, attention, and developmental psychopathology. In D. Cicchetti & D. J. Cohen (Eds.), *Developmental psychopathology: Vol. 2. Developmental neuroscience* (2nd ed., pp. 450–465). Hoboken, NJ: Wiley.

Rothbart, M. K., & Rueda, M. R. (2005). The development of effortful control. In U. Mayr, E. Awh, & S. W. Keele (Eds.), *Developing individuality in the human brain: A tribute to Michael I. Posner* (pp. 167–188). Washington, DC: American Psychological Association.

Roy, A. K., Benson, B. E., Degnan, K. A., Pérez-Edgar, K., Pine, D. S., Fox, N. A., et al. (2014). Alterations in amygdala functional connectivity reflect early temperament. *Biological Psychology, 103,* 248–254.

Rueter, A. R., Abram, S. V., MacDonald, A. W., Rustichini, A., & DeYoung, C. G. (2018). The goal priority network as a neural substrate of conscientiousness. *Human Brain Mapping.* [Epub ahead of print]

Sakai, H., Takahara, M., Honjo, N. F., Doi, S. I., Sadato, N., & Uchiyama, Y. (2012). Regional frontal gray matter volume associated with executive function capacity as a risk factor for vehicle crashes in normal aging adults. *PLOS ONE, 7*(9), e45920.

Sambrook, T. D., & Goslin, J. (2015). A neural reward prediction error revealed by a meta-analysis of ERPs using great grand averages. *Psychological Bulletin, 141*(1), 213–235.

Saucier, G. (1992). Openness versus intellect: Much ado about nothing? *European Journal of Personality, 6,* 381–386.

Saudino, K. J., & Wang, M. (2012). Quantitative and molecular genetic studies of temperament. In M. Zentner & R. L. Shiner (Eds.), *Handbook of temperament* (pp. 315–346). New York: Guilford Press.

Schmidt, L. A., Fox, N. A., Rubin, K. H., Sternberg, E. M., Gold, P. W., Smith, C. C., et al. (1997). Behavioral and neuroendocrine responses in shy children. *Developmental Psychobiology, 30*(2), 127–140.

Schnack, H. G., Van Haren, N. E., Brouwer, R. M., Evans, A., Durston, S., Boomsma, D. I., et al. (2015). Changes in thickness and surface area of the human cortex and their relationship with intelligence. *Cerebral Cortex, 25*(6), 1608–1617.

Schuyler, B. S., Kral, T. R., Jacquart, J., Burghy, C. A., Weng, H. Y., Perlman, D. M., et al. (2014). Temporal dynamics of emotional responding: Amygdala recovery predicts emotional traits. *Social Cognitive and Affective Neuroscience, 9*(2), 176–181.

Schwartz, C. E., Kunwar, P. S., Greve, D. N., Kagan, J., Snidman, N. C., & Bloch, R. B. (2012). A phenotype of early infancy predicts reactivity of the amygdala in male adults. *Molecular Psychiatry, 17*(10), 1042–1050.

Servaas, M. N., Riese, H., Renken, R. J., Marsman, J.-B. C., Lambregs, J., Ormel, J., et al. (2013). The effect of criticism on functional brain connectivity and associations with neuroticism. *PLOS ONE, 8*(7), e69606.

Servaas, M. N., van der Velde, J., Costafreda, S. G., Horton, P., Ormel, J., Riese, H., et al. (2013). Neuroticism and the brain: A quantitative meta-analysis of neuroimaging studies investigating emotion processing. *Neuroscience and Biobehavioral Reviews, 37*(8), 1518–1529.

Shackman, A. J., Tromp, D. P., Stockbridge, M. D., Kaplan, C. M., Tillman, R. M., & Fox, A. S. (2016). Dispositional negativity: An integrative psychological and neurobiological perspective. *Psychological Bulletin, 142*(12), 1275–1314.

Shaw, P., Greenstein, D., Lerch, J., Clasen, L., Lenroot, R., Gogtay, N., et al. (2006). Intellectual ability and cortical development in children and adolescents. *Nature, 440,* 676–679.

Shiner, R. L., Allen, T. A., & Masten, A. S. (2017). Adversity in adolescence predicts personality trait change from childhood to adulthood. *Journal of Research in Personality, 67,* 171–182.

Shiner, R. L., & Caspi, A. (2003). Personality differences in childhood and adolescence: Measurement, development, and consequences. *Journal of Child Psychology and Psychiatry, 44,* 2–32.

Shiner, R. L., & DeYoung, C. (2013). The structure of temperament and personality traits: A developmental perspective. In P. D. Zelazo (Ed.), *The Oxford handbook of developmental psychology: Vol. 2. Self and other* (pp. 113–141). New York: Oxford University Press.

Shoal, G. D., Giancola, P. R., & Kirillova, G. P. (2003). Salivary cortisol, personality, and aggressive behavior in adolescent boys: A 5-year longitudinal study. *Journal of the American Academy of Child and Adolescent Psychiatry, 42*(9), 1101–1107.

Slobodskaya, H. R. (2011). Two superordinate personality factors in childhood. *European Journal of Personality, 25*(6), 453–464.

Smillie, L. D., Cooper, A. J., & Pickering, A. D. (2011). Individual differences in reward–prediction–error: Extraversion and feedback-related negativity. *Social Cognitive and Affective Neuroscience, 6*(5), 646–652.

Somerville, L. H., Jones, R. M., & Casey, B. J. (2010). A time of change: Behavioral and neural correlates of adolescent sensitivity to appetitive and aversive environmental cues. *Brain and Cognition, 72*(1), 124–133.

Soto, C. J., & John, O. P. (2014). Traits in transition: The structure of parent-reported personality traits from early childhood to early adulthood. *Journal of Personality, 82*(3), 182–199.

Soto, C. J., John, O. P., Gosling, S. D., & Potter, J. (2008). The developmental psychometrics of Big Five self-reports: Acquiescence, factor structure, coherence, and differentiation from ages 10 to 20. *Journal of Personality and Social Psychology, 94*(4), 718–737.

Soto, C. J., John, O. P., Gosling, S. D., & Potter, J. (2011). Age differences in personality traits from 10 to 65: Big Five domains and facets in a large cross-sectional sample. *Journal of Personality and Social Psychology, 100*(2), 330–348.

Soto, C. J., & Tackett, J. L. (2015). Personality traits in childhood and adolescence structure, development, and outcomes. *Current Directions in Psychological Science, 24*(5), 358–362.

Specht, J., Bleidorn, W., Denissen, J. J., Hennecke, M., Hutteman, R., Kandler, C., et al. (2014). What drives adult personality development?: A comparison of theoretical perspectives and empirical evidence. *European Journal of Personality, 28*(3), 216–230.

Specht, J., Egloff, B., & Schmukle, S. C. (2011). Stability and change of personality across the life course: The impact of age and major life events on mean-level and rank-order stability of the Big Five. *Journal of Personality and Social Psychology, 101*(4), 862–882.

Srivastava, S., John, O. P., Gosling, S. D., & Potter, J.

(2003). Development of personality in early and middle adulthood: Set like plaster or persistent change? *Journal of Personality and Social Psychology, 84*(5), 1041–1053.

Tackett, J. L., Daoud, S. L., De Bolle, M., & Burt, S. A. (2013). Is relational aggression part of the externalizing spectrum?: A bifactor model of youth antisocial behavior. *Aggressive Behavior, 39*(2), 149–159.

Tackett, J. L., Herzhoff, K., Harden, K. P., Page-Gould, E., & Josephs, R. A. (2014). Personality × hormone interactions in adolescent externalizing psychopathology. *Personality Disorders: Theory, Research, and Treatment, 5*(3), 235–246.

Tackett, J. L., Slobodskaya, H. R., Mar, R. A., Deal, J., Halverson, C. F., Baker, S. R., et al. (2012). The hierarchical structure of childhood personality in five countries: Continuity from early childhood to early adolescence. *Journal of Personality, 80*(4), 847–879.

Taddei, M., Tettamanti, M., Zanoni, A., Cappa, S., & Battaglia, M. (2012). Brain white matter organisation in adolescence is related to childhood cerebral responses to facial expressions and harm avoidance. *NeuroImage, 61*(4), 1394–1401.

Takeuchi, H., Taki, Y., Sassa, Y., Hashizume, H., Sekiguchi, A., Fukushima, A., et al. (2014). Regional gray matter volume is associated with empathizing and systemizing in young adults. *PLOS ONE, 9*(1), e84782.

Taki, Y., Thyreau, B., Kinomura, S., Sato, K., Goto, R., Wu, K., et al. (2013). A longitudinal study of the relationship between personality traits and the annual rate of volume changes in regional gray matter in healthy adults. *Human Brain Mapping, 34*(12), 3347–3353.

Tamnes, C. K., Fjell, A. M., Østby, Y., Westlye, L. T., Due-Tønnessen, P., Bjørnerud, A., et al. (2011). The brain dynamics of intellectual development: Waxing and waning white and gray matter. *Neuropsychologia, 49*(13), 3605–3611.

Tamnes, C. K., Walhovd, K. B., Grydeland, H., Holland, D., Østby, Y., Dale, A. M., et al. (2013). Longitudinal working memory development is related to structural maturation of frontal and parietal cortices. *Journal of Cognitive Neuroscience, 25*(10), 1611–1623.

Thibodeau, R., Jorgensen, R. S., & Kim, S. (2006). Depression, anxiety, and resting frontal EEG asymmetry: A meta-analytic review. *Journal of Abnormal Psychology, 115*(4), 715–729.

Tremblay, R. E., Nagin, D. S., Séguin, J. R., Zoccolillo, M., Zelazo, P. D., Boivin, M., et al. (2004). Physical aggression during early childhood: Trajectories and predictors. *Pediatrics, 114*(1), e43–e50.

Turan, B., Guo, J., Boggiano, M. M., & Bedgood, D. (2014). Dominant, cold, avoidant, and lonely: Basal testosterone as a biological marker for an interpersonal style. *Journal of Research in Personality, 50*, 84–89.

Tyrka, A. R., Kelly, M. M., Graber, J. A., DeRose, L., Lee, J. K., Warren, M. P., et al. (2010). Behavioral adjustment in a community sample of boys: Links with basal and stress-induced salivary cortisol concentrations. *Psychoneuroendocrinology, 35*(8), 1167–1177.

Urošević, S., Collins, P., Muetzel, R., Lim, K., & Luciana, M. (2012). Longitudinal changes in behavioral approach system sensitivity and brain structures involved in reward processing during adolescence. *Developmental Psychology, 48*(5), 1488–1500.

Van den Akker, A. L., Deković, M., Asscher, J., & Prinzie, P. (2014). Mean-level personality development across childhood and adolescence: A temporary defiance of the maturity principle and bidirectional associations with parenting. *Journal of Personality and Social Psychology, 107*(4), 736–750.

Van Egeren, L. F. (2009). A cybernetic model of global personality traits. *Personality and Social Psychology Review, 13*(2), 92–108.

Vijayakumar, N., Whittle, S., Dennison, M., Yuecel, M., Simmons, J., & Allen, N. B. (2014). Development of temperamental effortful control mediates the relationship between maturation of the prefrontal cortex and psychopathology during adolescence: A 4-year longitudinal study. *Developmental Cognitive Neuroscience, 9*, 30–43.

Vreeke, L. J., & Muris, P. (2012). Relations between behavioral inhibition, Big Five personality factors, and anxiety disorder symptoms in non-clinical and clinically anxious children. *Child Psychiatry and Human Development, 43*(6), 884–894.

Wacker, J., Chavanon, M. L., & Stemmler, G. (2010). Resting EEG signatures of agentic extraversion: New results and meta-analytic integration. *Journal of Research in Personality, 44*(2), 167–179.

Wacker, J., Mueller, E. M., Hennig, J., & Stemmler, G. (2012). How to consistently link extraversion and intelligence to the catechol-*O*-methyltransferase (COMT) gene: On defining and measuring psychological phenotypes in neurogenetic research. *Journal of Personality and Social Psychology, 102*(2), 427–444.

Wacker, J., Mueller, E., Pizzagalli, D. A., Hennig, J., & Stemmler, G. (2013). Dopamine-D2-receptor blockade reverses the association between trait approach motivation and frontal asymmetry in an approach-motivation context. *Psychological Science, 24*(4), 489–497.

Wacker, J., & Smillie, L. D. (2015). Trait extraversion and dopamine function. *Social and Personality Psychology Compass, 9*(6), 225–238.

Wagner, J., Ram, N., Smith, J., & Gerstorf, D. (2016). Personality trait development at the end of life: Antecedents and correlates of mean-level trajectories. *Journal of Personality and Social Psychology, 111*(3), 411–429.

Wang, Z., Chen, N., Petrill, S. A., & Deater-Deckard, K. (2013). Observed personality in childhood: Psychometric and behavioural genetic evidence of two broad personality factors. *European Journal of Personality, 27*(1), 96–105.

Webb, S. J., Monk, C. S., & Nelson, C. A. (2001). Mechanisms of postnatal neurobiological development: Implications for human development. *Developmental Neuropsychology, 19*(2), 147–171.

Westlye, L. T., Bjørnebekk, A., Grydeland, H., Fjell, A. M., & Walhovd, K. B. (2011). Linking an anxiety-related personality trait to brain white matter microstructure: Diffusion tensor imaging and harm avoidance. *Archives of General Psychiatry, 68*(4), 369–377.

Wright, A. G., Creswell, K. G., Flory, J., Muldoon, M., & Manuck, S. B. (2018). Neurobiological functioning and the personality trait hierarchy: Central serotonergic responsivity and the stability meta-trait. Retrieved from *https://osf.io/ru9ve*.

Wu, C. C., Samanez-Larkin, G. R., Katovich, K., & Knutson, B. (2014). Affective traits link to reliable neural markers of incentive anticipation. *NeuroImage, 84,* 279–289.

Xu, J., & Potenza, M. N. (2012). White matter integrity and Five-Factor personality measures in healthy adults. *NeuroImage, 59*(1), 800–807.

Yarkoni, T. (2015). Neurobiological substrates of personality: A critical overview. In M. Mikulincer & P. R. Shaver (Eds.), *APA handbook of personality and social psychology: Vol. 4. personality processes and individual differences* (pp. 61–84). Washington, DC: American Psychological Association.

Yeo, B., Krienen, F., Sepulcre, J., Sabuncu, M., Lashkari, D., Hollinshead, M., et al. (2011). The organization of the human cerebral cortex estimated by intrinsic functional connectivity. *Journal of Neurophysiology, 106*(3), 1125–1165.

CHAPTER 6

Emotion Reactivity and Regulation

A Developmental Model of Links between Temperament and Personality

Kristin A. Buss
Koraly Pérez-Edgar
Alicia Vallorani
Berenice Anaya

Case Study 1: A Behaviorally Inhibited Child

A 2-year-old boy, Bobby, sits on his mother's lap in the laboratory patiently waiting for the next "game" to start. He just finished playing with a basket full of toys with his mother, so today has been a pretty good visit to the lab so far. Across the room from Bobby and his mother stands a small puppet theater. After a short delay, two animal puppets appear, greet each other, and introduce themselves to Bobby. The puppets want Bobby to join them in their fun games. As is typical for most 2-year-olds, Bobby sits and watches the puppets interact. However, as the puppets continue, he does not warm up and approach to play with the puppets. Instead, Bobby is frozen on his mother's lap and becomes increasingly nervous, showing signs of muscle tension and mildly fearful facial expressions. Bobby strongly resists his mother's efforts to get him to approach. He becomes fussy, cries, and clings to her when she attempts to put him down so he can go get a sticker from the puppets. He never warms up, which is an extreme response relative to most 2-year-olds.

The rest of the visit to the laboratory is very stressful for Bobby, and this pattern of fearful,

avoidant, and distress behavior is repeated across most of the tasks, including interactions with friendly strangers and novel objects (e.g., large mechanical spider). Bobby's pattern of fearful behavior and avoidance is particularly interesting because it is highly stable, as is evident when he returns to the laboratory at age 5 to interact with unfamiliar people. For instance, when interacting with an unfamiliar male research assistant, Bobby is very hesitant to speak, speaks very quietly, fails to make eye contact, and even turns his back to the stranger during the conversation. In another stranger encounter later in the visit, Bobby is so afraid of a female research assistant trying on a Halloween mask that he leaves the room. His behavior with unfamiliar peers in the laboratory is equally stressful for him. He spends most of the time either sitting by himself (while the other boys play) or stands across the room and watches them play but remains unoccupied and appears anxious.

Reflecting the behavioral descriptions, Bobby's parents and teachers also rate him very high on wariness, avoidance, and social anxiety measures in preschool and kindergarten. He and his mother both note that he is still very socially anxious 10 years later, and this anxiety is starting to interfere with his ability to make friends now that he is in middle school.

Case Study 2: An Exuberant Child

Two-year-old Torrie begins the first portion of the visit on her mom's lap, where she immediately becomes aware of the stage and puppets on the opposite side of the room. Unlike most toddlers, who may naturally stay with mom as they enter a novel setting, Torrie runs out to meet the puppets as soon as they introduce themselves and announce they will play games. As the puppets engage Torrie in a series of tasks (e.g., throwing a ball), she is very open and happy to interact with them and help when needed. Although she initially returns to her mom's proximity frequently, as the episode unfolds, Torrie becomes more immersed in playing with the puppets and seems less and less dependent on her mom for reassurance.

Throughout the rest of the visit, Torrie's high approachability is evident in her resistance to staying on her mom's lap when presented with novel toys (e.g., talking robot in the corner) and her impulse to touch the toys and interact with them even before she receives any instructions. Her desire to approach and interact is also evident in social circumstances. In fact, when a stranger enters the room, Torrie greets him and stays engaged and close in proximity for the extent of the task. Furthermore, in a usually fearful episode in which a large, mechanical black spider sits in a corner of the room, Torrie's immediate response upon entering is to run toward the spider and touch it.

Similar to Bobby's fearful behavioral pattern, Torrie's pattern of high approach and positive affect seems to show considerable stability. Although at age 5 she no longer has problems waiting for instructions or impulsively running into the experimental room for every episode, she is happy to engage a stranger even when alone in the room. For example, Torrie not only responds happily to the stranger's questions but also initiates lively conversations on new topics, and actually becomes the active leader of the social dyad. She also displays this pattern of high engagement and social interaction when interacting with peers of the same age, as well as the experimenter during other episodes in the visit. Torrie's parents and teachers rate her as a very sociable, outgoing child, albeit somewhat impulsive and easily frustrated when things don't go her way. Although Torrie

doesn't self-report any difficulties, her mother notes that the transition to middle school has been challenging, with a few episodes of acting out and some minor conflicts with peers at school.

These case studies highlight the individual differences in behavior, reflecting the perspective that underlying temperamental biases, as marked by variation in emotion reactivity and regulation, shape personality development (Rothbart, 2011). Particularly, we argue that by examining early reactivity and regulation, we may maximize the probability of understanding developmental trajectories to specific personality traits in adulthood.

Although myriad potential temperamental profiles likely exist, we focus on two that have received the greatest attention in the literature: fearful temperament, most often studies of behavioral inhibition (Kagan, Reznick, Clarke, Snidman, & Garcia-Coll, 1984), and exuberance or surgency (Fox, Henderson, Rubin, Calkins, & Schmidt, 2001). Fearful and exuberant temperaments have been linked to distinct personality traits in adulthood, neuroticism (Muris et al., 2009) and extraversion (Grist & McCord, 2010), respectively. As such, these temperamental profiles allow us to best illustrate how emotional reactivity and regulation during childhood may constrain eventual personality development.

Prior to delving into the specifics of particular temperamental profiles and personality outcomes, we feel it is important to discuss the trajectories of temperament to personality as a whole. Thus, this chapter comprises three central sections. First, we examine how temperamental profiles may be linked to later personality traits. Second, we describe early-emerging temperamental fear and exuberance. Finally, we address the role that emotion regulation plays in bridging early temperament to later personality.

Temperamental Links to Personality

We take the perspective that early temperament alone does not determine developmental outcomes. Rather, temperament traits interact with internal (e.g., neural processes and cognitive control functions) and external (e.g., parenting and family environment) factors to influence an individual's risk and resilience to events and contexts that shape developmental trajectories. Particular temperaments are therefore likely to lead to specific personality profiles. In attempting to link early temperament to later personality, the field must initially deal with two main concerns: (1) long-rooted differences in methodology and procedure and (2) assessment of the developmental appropriateness of some central personality constructs (e.g., openness to experience).

With respect to methodology, there are two central traditions in the temperament literature: direct observation of behavior and measurement of biological substrates. Together, these sources of information have been used to create typologies that are then observed over time. As we note below, these information streams, when coupled together, are particularly useful in trying to tease apart the role of emotional processes in current behavior and later outcomes. However, this general approach is quite different from the traditional, self-report model used in personality psychology. Here, individuals are typically asked to report across a broad set of behaviors and motivations (Zuckerman, Kuhlman, Joireman, Teta, & Kraft, 1993).

When bridging the gap between temperament typologies and personality traits, much of the initial work drew conceptual or theoretical links (Chen & Schmidt, 2015). For example, Caspi and Shiner (2008) suggested that temperament traits can be linked to later personality in the Big Five umbrella, such that positive emotionality would lead to extraversion, negative emotionality to neuroticism, effortful control to conscientiousness, and sociability to agreeableness. In this formulation, openness to experience would have a less direct link to early traits. Children high in negative affect may also rank high in neuroticism as adults, without assuming that the expression of a single, stable latent construct has led to this relation (Kandler, 2012).

The earliest manifestations of temperament are thought to be reactive, unconscious, and typically out of the child's control. In this case, genetics and neural maturation may be the driving force in observed behavior and underlying physiology. Of course, with time, more complex and conscious temperament traits emerge, along with the temperament-based tools needed to regulate initial reactivity. However, again, these constructs can sometime be crude (e.g., visual orienting) (Sheese, Rothbart, Posner, White, & Fraundorf, 2008; Sheese, Voelker, Posner, & Rothbart, 2009). In contrast, many personality traits emerge from sophisticated cognitive and emotional processes that consolidate after so-cial experiences (Briley & Tucker-Drob, 2014). Thus, young children have neither the capacity nor the opportunity to display the rich personality traits seen in adults.

And yet, with a nod to rank-order stability and developmental considerations, recent work has made progress toward bridging the divide between temperament and personality. In this regard, the work of Rothbart (2011) has been at the vanguard. At a methodological level, Rothbart and colleagues have designed and validated a comprehensive set of parental- and self-report measures designed to capture variations in reactivity and regulation across the lifespan. The set of six questionnaires, spanning infancy to adulthood, share a broad three-construct structure, reflecting temperamental negative affect, positive affect, and effortful control, that modulates with development.

The Infant Behavior Questionnaire (IBQ; Gartstein & Rothbart, 2003; Rothbart, 1981), for example, uses early markers of negative affect (crying, vocal reactivity), positive affect (smiling, cooing) and effortful control (visual orienting). By childhood, the Children's Behavior Questionnaire (CBQ; Rothbart, Ahadi, Hershey, & Fisher, 2001) assesses variation in sadness and fear, smiling and laughter, and inhibitory control. Finally, the Adult Temperament Questionnaire (ATQ; Evans & Rothbart, 2007) most closely resembles the factors seen in the personality literature, with superordinate constructs of negative affect, extraversion/surgency, effortful control, and orienting sensitivity. In parallel, social behavior morphs from cuddliness (IBQ) to sociability (ATQ). In this way, the Rothbart model stretches across the affect-laden Big Five structure and the regulatory focus of the Big Three model.

Muris, Meesters, and Blijlevens (2007) had adolescents (ages 9–13) self-report on individual traits using both the Early Adolescent Temperament Questionnaire (EATQ; Capaldi & Rothbart, 1992) and the Junior version of the Eysenck Personality Questionnaire (EPQ-J; Eysenck, Eysenck, & Barrett, 1985). They found strong relations between Rothbart's three high-order factors and the Big Three model, such that negative affect and extraversion were highly and positively correlated with neuroticism and extraversion, respectively. By the same token, effortful control showed a negative association with neuroticism and psychoticism. This is in line with Rothbart's own work (Rothbart, Ahadi, & Evans, 2000), showing a link between temperament traits (shyness, self-regulation, and positive affect) with later personality profiles.

While promising, there is of course the concern that similarities emerge from a simple methodological artifact—that the instruments used to measure temperament and personality rely on overlapping items, thereby creating a shared construct; that is, there are only so many ways we can distinguish temperamental sociability (e.g., "I often enjoy talking to strangers" from the ATQ) and the personality trait of extraversion (e.g., "Do you enjoy meeting new people?" from the EPQ). Direct observation of behavior, coupled with biomarkers, can help address this methodological and conceptual concern.

A prominent example comes from the work of Caspi and Moffitt. The Dunedin Multidisciplinary Health and Development Study (Silva, 1990) has followed a full cohort of infants born in the early 1970s through today. Temperament was assessed at age 3 via direct observation in the laboratory. Cluster-analytic methods were used to characterize children based on three behavioral styles marked by lack of control, approach, and sluggishness (Caspi & Silva, 1995). Then, using a typological approach and cluster analysis, profiles were created based on patterns across behavioral styles. Five groups emerged: Undercontrolled, Inhibited, Confident, Reserved, and Well-Adjusted.

At age 18, the same individuals self-reported on their personality using the Multidimensional Personality Questionnaire (MPQ; Tellegen, 1982). While the effect sizes were small (Caspi & Silva, 1995), connections between observed behavior and self-report were evident across the 15-year span. As young adults, Undercontrolled children scored high on measures of impulsivity, danger seeking, aggression. In contrast, Inhibited children scored low on measures of impulsivity, danger seeking, aggression, and social potency; Confident children scored high on impulsivity; Reserved children scored low on social potency; and Well-Adjusted children presented as "typical" young adults.

Eight years later, the same individuals reported on their perceived personality traits (Caspi et al., 2003), and close "informants" rated the cohort members. As they note, the intervening time represents a marked change in the environmental demands place on individuals and the social relationships they were likely to take on. Undercontrolled children were nega-

tive, unreliable, and also more likely to show anti-social behavior (Moffitt, Caspi, Dickson, Silva, & Stanton, 1996). In contrast, Inhibited children were overcontrolled, nonassertive, and more likely to show internalizing difficulties as young adults (Caspi, Moffitt, Newman, & Silva, 1996).

Even with the descriptive links between temperament and personality, we are still left with open questions regarding the mechanisms by which these relations emerge. In this next section, we focus on the two best-supported temperamental markers of later personality, fear and exuberance, with an eye to potential processes that shape developmental trajectories.

Early Temperament, as Illustrated by Fear and Exuberance

The most obvious, and earliest, markers of temperament are evident in the infant's response to environmental triggers. Some infants, when confronted with a new object or person, respond with acute negative affect—crying, arching the back, and thrashing limbs (Kagan & Snidman, 1991). If capable, the next response is often to withdraw, either as reflex or in an active attempt to regulate their initial emotional response (Buss, 2011). In contrast, when presented with the identical stimulus, another infant might display a starkly different result, often characterized as positive affect, if not glee (Hane, Fox, Henderson, & Marshall, 2008). The next step, in line with the initial reactivity, is often to approach and engage. In our typological approach, one infant would be characterized with a fearful temperament, while his or her counterpart would have an exuberant temperament. In our opening case study, Bobby's behavior reflects underlying mechanisms of a fearful temperament, while Torrie is his exuberant, nonfearful, counterpart.

Fearful temperament is marked by a unique neural, physiological, and cognitive profile that is readily differentiated from an exuberant temperament. Fearful temperament is most evident in response to environmental and social stressors. For example, one form of fearful temperament, behavioral inhibition (BI), is characterized by hypervigilant and withdrawal behavior in response to unfamiliar people and situations in toddlerhood and childhood (Garcia-Coll, Kagan, & Reznick, 1984; Kagan et al., 1984). Kagan and colleagues (1984) suggested that BI is rooted in individual differences that are evident in early infancy as elevated negative affective and motor reactivity in response to unfamiliar stimuli. These characteristics, in turn, increase the likelihood that the infant will show BI in childhood. Dysregulated fear (DF), another form of fearful temperament, is marked by a profile of heightened fear responses in both high- and low-threat contexts (Buss, 2011).

Unlike the traditional personality literature, temperament research has specifically focused on underlying biological substrates. As such, fearful temperament, although initially characterized via direct behavioral observation, is accompanied by distinct biological profiles as well. Rooted in the limbic response to novelty and threat (Fu, Taber-Thomas, & Pérez-Edgar, 2017), the profile is marked by distinct patterns of functioning across multiple systems, both at rest and in response to environmental probes. Fearful temperament is reflected in an initial hyperactive response in the amygdala to novelty and threat, evident in both childhood and adulthood (Pérez-Edgar et al., 2007; Schwartz, Wright, Shin, Kagan, & Rauch, 2003). The temperament profile is also marked by distinct patterns of functioning across multiple systems, both at rest and in response to environmental probes (Guyer et al., 2006). In addition, there are variations in the functional connectivity of neural regions, supporting distinct network profiles that extend across cortical and subcortical regions, encompassing fear, reward, and regulatory systems (Roy, Dennis, & Warner, 2015; Taber-Thomas & Pérez-Edgar, 2015). Building on this foundation, temperamentally fearful children show right-frontal electroencephalographic (EEG) asymmetry (Fox, 1992) that appears to be relatively stable, which is accompanied by withdrawal responses (Buss et al., 2003) and indicative of future internalizing behaviors (Smith & Bell, 2010) and personality (Jones & Fox, 1992).

Physiological indicators can be used throughout childhood to help define the fearful temperament profile, allowing for comparisons into adulthood. For example, Garcia-Coll and colleagues (1984) demonstrated that fearful infants exhibited higher heart rates when presented with novel stimuli than when presented with familiar stimuli. Similarly, Kagan and colleagues (1984) showed that young children, labeled as reactive during infancy, exhibited consistently high heart rate during peer interactions, unlike their nonreactive peers who displayed lower heart rates. Similarly, markers of respiratory sinus arrhythmia (RSA) reflect the individual's attempt to regulate in the face of threat and mount an appropriate response. Prior work suggests that RSA may be either suppressed (Buss, Goldsmith, & Davidson, 2005; Calkins, 1997; Stifter & Fox, 1990) or augmented (Buss, Davis, Ram, & Coccia, 2017) in fearful temperament, depending on the environmental context the child is navigating. Specifically, Buss and colleagues (2017) have shown that infants displaying high fear exhibited higher RSA (i.e., consistent with a failure to suppress). However, this only held true when the infants were high in fear during low-threat situations (Buss et al., 2017), suggesting the importance of context for understanding physiological patterns underlying BI and future personality development.

Distinct profiles are also evident in the electrophysiological response to errors (McDermott et al., 2009) and novel stimuli (Marshall, Reeb, & Fox, 2009; Reeb-Sutherland et al., 2009), the hormonal response to stress (Kertes et al., 2009; Mackrell et al., 2014), and the individual's automatic response to unexpected events (Barker et al., 2015; Barker, Reeb-Sutherland, & Fox, 2014; Schmidt, Fox, Rubin, & Sternberg, 1997). Thus, there is an emergent and coherent profile that encompasses cascading processes from the central nervous system to the periphery. Given that the fearful profile involves both overt behavior and underlying biology, it is not surprising that variations in cognitive mechanisms are often evident, bridging biology and behavior.

Attention is the most studied cognitive marker of fearful temperament. Particularly, researchers have shown that BI in toddlerhood, coupled with a bias toward threat in childhood, leads to greater social withdrawal during early childhood and adolescence (Pérez-Edgar et al., 2010, 2011; White et al., 2017). Similarly, Morales, Pérez-Edgar, and Buss (2015) showed that young children who showed high fear in low-threat situations during infancy (DF) exhibited social withdrawal only when also displaying a bias toward threat. The same relation is evident even when examining temperamental traits, such as negative affect, in isolation (Cole, Zapp, Fettig, & Pérez-Edgar, 2016). These findings suggest that cognitive processes may work to tether initial temperamental profiles into adolescence (Pérez-Edgar et al., 2010), thus impacting emergent personality.

If fearful temperament grows out of an initial withdrawal response when novelty is taken as a marker of threat (e.g., Bobby), then exuberant temperament reflects approach to novelty as a marker of opportunity (e.g., Torrie). Early positive affect and approach is later associated with boldness and sociability into childhood (Fox et al., 2001; Putnam & Stifter, 2005). Exuberance remains relatively stable overtime (Degnan et al., 2011; Stifter, Putnam, & Jahromi, 2008) and can be measured by distinctive neural, physiological, and cognitive outcomes.

Neural markers for later exuberance are first apparent in infancy and include left-frontal EEG asymmetry (Davidson & Fox, 1989; Fox et al., 2001) and increased electrophysiological responses to novelty (Marshall et al., 2009). Additionally, researchers have suggested that these biological markers are related to consistency in exuberant temperament throughout development (Coan & Allen, 2003). For example, Degnan and colleagues (2011) showed that exuberant infants with left frontal EEG asymmetry, but not right frontal EEG asymmetry, showed increased social competence in early childhood. This early foundation may then set the stage for the adult profile of extraversion. Again, in parallel with fearful temperament, RSA in response to environmental triggers is associated with positive reactivity and affect (Calkins, 1997), linking early exuberance to patterns of externalizing behaviors for some children (Morales, Beekman, Blandon, Stifter, & Buss, 2015). This pattern suggests that for both fearful temperament and temperamental exuberance, RSA marks the child's response to the environment and his or her allostatic load (Buss, Davis, & Kiel, 2011). The specific developmental manifestation, however, is rooted in the child's initial temperament-linked idiosyncratic biases.

Cognitive markers of exuberance have been less studied; however, recent research from Morales, Pérez-Edgar, and Buss (2016) suggests that attention to reward may be important to the developmental trajectory of exuberant temperament. Specifically, they found that exuberance during infancy predicted attention bias to reward and externalizing behaviors during early childhood. Additional research is needed to examine how attention bias to reward predicts personality outcomes later in life. For example, attention to reward may shape differential trajectories to adult personality, in the context of foundational temperamental profiles; that is, while attention to reward may buffer fearful children from negative affect (Forbes et al.,

2010), and perhaps neuroticism, the same attention pattern may exacerbate initial profiles in exuberant children (Morales et al., 2016).

Emotion Regulation Shapes the Transition from Temperament to Personality

Across measures and constructs, the available data suggest that continuities are identifiable between early temperament and later personality (Caspi & Shiner, 2008; Chen & Schmidt, 2015). At the same time, by no means do we find easy one-to-one correlations across development. As we discuss, the noted relations seem to hold for broad constructs (e.g., positive affect to exuberance), rather than more fine-grain behaviors. In addition, our strongest data point is to rank-order stability, rather than homotypic continuity.

This pattern of findings suggests that additional individual difference and context measures are likely to impact and modulate early temperament. Social and contextual factors play a large role, often crossing broad levels of analysis to incorporate culture, parenting, and socialization (Chen & Schmidt, 2015). Indeed, there is the suggestion that personality is, at its core, the profile that emerges when temperament confronts the environment (Rothbart et al., 2000). Emotion regulation, one facet of temperament, may be particularly relevant for understanding how these temperament–environment interactions constrain personality development.

Emotion regulation is a complex and varied construct in the literature. Here we define how emotions both are regulators and are regulated (Cole, Martin, & Dennis, 2004), and how these variations in emotion experience may cue researchers into important individual temperament differences that may lead to particular personality traits. When we say emotions are regulators, we are describing a set of relatively automatic processes deployed to elicit changes in internal or external states, whereas when we say emotions are regulated, we are suggesting more controlled processes designed to alter emotional states. For example, a baby's continuous negative affect driving a mother to address the baby's needs would be emotion as regulator, whereas a child acting grateful when a research assistant gives him or her a broken toy to play with would be an example of emotion as regulated. Importantly, both types of emotion regulation are related to temperamental profiles and personality outcomes.

During infancy, we expect to see more instances of emotion as regulator than emotion as regulated. Infants are born with preorganized and innate emotions, believed to be triggered by an array of environmental stimulation (Damasio, 1994). The temperament literature additionally suggests that infants display biologically based or genetically influenced individual differences in levels of reactivity for basic systems of functioning, one of these systems being emotion (Kagan & Fox, 2006; Rothbart & Bates, 2006). From very early on (1–3 months), infants also develop what seem to be innate or reflexive mechanisms to regulate their emotional reactivity, such as sucking, head turning, and self-soothing (Kopp, 1989). During early infancy, the role of emotions as regulating seems to be more prevalent, perhaps because higher-order mechanisms such as attention and behavior have yet to emerge (Rothbart, Ziaie, & O'Boyle, 1992) as sources of regulatory strategies.

That is, emotions may act as regulators of arousal levels more than being regulated by organism-initiated strategies. Additionally, emotions also trigger external regulation by signaling adults to intervene (Cole, Michel, & Teti, 1994). For example, when highly aroused, an infant may express negative affect through crying, which will trigger maternal responsivity to sooth and down-regulate the infant's high arousal. According to some researchers (Cole et al., 1994, 2004), the elicited emotion and its expression modulate the mother's behavior and emotional responding. Based on this interpretation, infants' use of external sources (e.g., maternal behavior) as a means to emotion regulation represents direct support for the role of emotions as regulating. Similarly, the role of emotions as regulating could also serve to explain the influence that mother–child interactions have on later patterns of observed behaviors across contexts (Morris et al., 2011).

These interactions have been widely studied through caregiver–child dyads, in which infants are thought to synchronize with their mothers in cuing and being cued for emotional expressions and the regulation of emotional states (Beebe et al., 2011; Feldman, 2012; Gianino & Tronick, 1988; MacLean et al., 2014). Parent–child dyads promote socialization of emotion regulation, contributing to development of adaptive strategies and increases in initiation and modulation of emotions (Cole et al., 1994). However, other researchers (Eisenberg & Spinrad, 2004) argue that these external sources of regulation may not entirely fit the definition of *emotion regulation,* and should be differentiated from emotion regulation that is internally initiated by the organism.

Across infancy, behavioral and attentional mechanisms allow for higher-order and more refined mechanisms of emotion regulation (Buss & Goldsmith, 1998; Mangelsdorf, Shapiro, & Marzolf, 1995). During this time, infants consistently grow more sophisticated and effective in their emotion regulation capabilities, from directing attention away from emotional stimulus (3-month-olds), to more readily sustaining attention allocation or withdrawal once fixated (9-month-olds), and engaging in behavioral strategies such as physically moving object of distress or seeking information (e.g., facial cues) from the caregiver.

More sophisticated regulatory mechanisms, typically placed under the umbrella of executive functions, emerge and strengthen throughout childhood and adolescence. Executive functions are often thought of as top-down mechanisms that modulate initial reactivity in order to maintain goal-directed functioning (Diamond, 2013; Zelazo et al., 2003). For example, one component of executive functioning, effortful control, can be defined as the ability to inhibit a dominant response in the service of performing a subdominant response (Rothbart & Rueda, 2005). A child playing Simon Says must carefully regulate his or her behavior in order to perform (or avoid performing) as needed. Effortful control is also invoked when individuals must detect errors during, or must engage in planning in anticipation of, performance. Effortful control, which is seen as a core tool in the child's arsenal, is needed to both self-regulate and integrate oneself as an adaptive member of the larger social environment. Thus, individual differences in effortful control have been associated with the emergence of conscience and empathy (Kochanska, Barry, Jimenez, Hollatz, & Woodard, 2009; Kochanska, Murray, & Coy, 1997), levels of academic success (Checa & Rueda, 2011), and the quality and quantity of peer relationships (Valiente, Lemery-Chalfant, Swanson, & Reiser, 2008). These profiles have, in turn, been linked to variations in personality (Kochanska et al., 2009). Thus, any stability in Bobby's and Torrie's initial emotional responses to the laboratory experience is in part due to their ability to regulate initial responses and conform to contextual expectations for emotional expression and social behavior.

Often, discussions of executive functioning and emotion regulation hold closely to the proposition that higher levels of control and regulation, and the underlying skills leading to regulation, are necessarily positive influences on the course of development. This, indeed, is generally the case. However, as with most aspects of development, the impact of a particular skill or trait must be assessed within the context in which it is manifested (Pérez-Edgar, 2015). This is seen in the previously discussed profiles that noted both overcontrolled and undercontrolled patterns of functioning, which each lead to difficulties in personality and adjustment (Caspi et al., 2003).

For example, infants selected for increased temperamental negative reactivity (Fox et al., 2001) and at increased risk for fearful temperament show increased error monitoring (McDermott et al., 2009) and rigid attention Henderson (2010) in adolescence. These data suggest that temperamentally fearful children may demonstrate an overcontrolled behavioral style. Here, the subcomponents of effortful control, rather than freeing the child to flexibly and nimbly respond to environmental demands, may lock the child into a rigid response pattern (Henderson & Wilson, 2017; Wong et al., 2006). Over time, early fearful temperament, coupled with overcontrol, may increase the probability of heightened levels of neuroticism and less openness to experience as adults (Caspi et al., 2003).

Levels of effortful control are also associated with broad patterns of exuberance, leading to high levels of sociability and extraversion when deftly regulated, or externalizing behavior, such as aggression, when undercontrolled (Degnan et al., 2011); that is, low levels of effortful control are associated with greater reactive aggression, particularly in children prone to high levels of anger (Eisenberg, Champion, & Ma, 2004). This may be due to poor emotional regulation and the inability to inhibit initial reactive tendencies. In contrast, high levels of effortful control are associated with proactive aggression, when coupled with contextual factors that encourage aggressive behavior (Rathert, Fite, & Gaertner, 2011). Here, goal setting, planning, and performance monitoring are drawn in support of planful acts of aggression. Finally, in a powerful demonstration of the long-term effects of regulation on personality development and a range of outcomes, Moffitt, Poulton, and Caspi (2013; Moffitt et al., 2011) found that childhood self-control continues to predict variation in adult outcomes approximately 25 years later.

In summary, both emotion as regulator and emotion as regulated create individualized patterns of responses that reflect both the immediate circumstances and the individual's history of interactions. In this sense, emotion as regulator and emotion as regulated are partners in the evolution from initial temperament to personality. Regulation, in reflecting the slow accumulation of new modulatory processes, is often more sensitive to environmental constraints; that is, the environment can dictate what behaviors and emotions need to be regulated and why. As an intermediary between reactivity and the environment, regulatory mechanisms may translate temperament into personality—for better and for worse.

Conclusions and Next Steps

In this chapter, we have discussed the broad literature of two temperaments, exuberance and BI, in order to articulate the development of personality. We make the argument that temperament constrains personality development. BI and exuberance are defined by both reactive and regulatory processes (Rothbart et al., 2000); are relatively stable (Degnan et al., 2011; Stifter et al., 2008); can be delineated through neural, physiological, and cognitive mechanisms (Fox, Henderson, Marshall, Nichols, & Ghera, 2005); and often lead to externalizing and internalizing behaviors later in life (Buss et al., 2013; Chronis-Tuscano et al., 2009; Degnan et al., 2011; Morales et al., 2016; Pérez-Edgar & Fox, 2005). Specifically, many but not all infants exhibiting high BI, and even some infants exhibiting low BI, go on to have social anxiety disorder later in life (Schwartz, Snidman, & Kagan, 1999). Similarly, many, but not all, children displaying high levels of exuberance go on to show conduct issues later in life (López-Romero, Romero, & Luengo, 2012).

Some of these differences in trajectories are likely due to environmental and contextual factors interacting with variations in neural, physiological, and cognitive profiles within individual temperaments; however, it is also important to consider regulatory difference within individuals. Although particular regulatory strategies have been related to both externalizing and internalizing behaviors, understanding variations in regulatory capacity within the temperamental profiles that lead to externalizing and internalizing behaviors is important in understanding specific personality outcomes. In the chapter, we have described how regulatory capacities within the confines of temperament protect against, or enhance, the probability of developing internalizing or externalizing behaviors later in life, thereby affecting future personality development.

REFERENCES

Barker, T. V., Reeb-Sutherland, B., Degnan, K. A., Walker, O. L., Chronis-Tuscano, A., Henderson, H. A., et al. (2015). Contextual startle responses moderate the relation between behavioral inhibition and anxiety in middle childhood. *Psychophysiology, 52*(11), 1544–1549.

Barker, T. V., Reeb-Sutherland, B. C., & Fox, N. A. (2014). Individual differences in fear potentiated startle in behaviorally inhibited children. *Developmental Psychobiology, 56*(1), 133–141.

Beebe, B., Steele, M., Jaffe, J., Buck, K. A., Chen, H., Cohen, P., et al. (2011). Maternal anxiety symptoms and mother–infant self- and interactive contingency. *Infant Mental Health Journal, 32*(2), 174–206.

Briley, D. A., & Tucker-Drob, E. M. (2014). Genetic and environmental continuity in personality development: A meta-analysis. *Psychological Bulletin, 140*(5), 1303–1331.

Buss, K. A. (2011). Which fearful toddlers should we worry about?: Context, fear regulation, and anxiety risk. *Developmental Psychology, 47*(3), 804–819.

Buss, K. A., Davis, E. L., & Kiel, E. J. (2011). Allostatic and environmental load in toddlers predicts anxiety in preschool and kindergarten. *Development and Psychopathology, 23*(4), 1069–1087.

Buss, K. A., Davis, E. L., Kiel, E. J., Brooker, R. J., Beekman, C., & Early, M. C. (2013). Dysregulated fear predicts social wariness and social anxiety symptoms during kindergarten. *Journal of Clinical Child and Adolescent Psychology, 42*(5), 1–14.

Buss, K. A., Davis, E. L., Ram, N., & Coccia, M. (2017). Dysregulated fear, social inhibition, and RSA: A replication an extension. *Child Development.* [Epub ahead of print]

Buss, K. A., & Goldsmith, H. H. (1998). Fear and anger regulation in infancy: Effects on the temporal dynamics of affective expression. *Child Development, 69*(2), 359–374.

Buss, K. A., Goldsmith, H. H., & Davidson, R. J. (2005). Cardiac reactivity is associated with changes in negative emotion in 24-month-olds. *Developmental Psychobiology, 46*(2), 118–132.

Buss, K. A., Schumacher, J. R. M., Dolski, I., Kalin, N. H., Goldsmith, H. H., & Davidson, R. J. (2003).

Right frontal brain activity, cortisol, and withdrawal behavior in 6-month-old infants. *Behavioral Neuroscience, 117*(1), 11–20.

Calkins, S. D. (1997). Cardiac vagal tone indices of temperamental reactivity and behavioral regulation in young children. *Developmental Psychobiology, 31*(2), 125–135.

Capaldi, D. M., & Rothbart, M. K. (1992). Development and validation of an early adolescent temperament measure. *Journal of Early Adolescence, 12*(2), 153–173.

Caspi, A., Harrington, H., Milne, B., Amell, J. W., Theodore, R. F., & Moffitt, T. E. (2003). Children's behavioral styles at age 3 are linked to their adult personality traits at age 26. *Journal of Personality, 71*(4), 495–513.

Caspi, A., Moffitt, T. E., Newman, D. L., & Silva, P. A. (1996). Behavioral observations at age 3 years predict adult psychiatric disorders: Longitudinal evidence from a birth cohort. *Archives of General Psychiatry, 53*(11), 1033–1039.

Caspi, A., & Shiner, R. (2008). Temperament and personality. In M. Rutter, D. V. M. Bishop, D. S. Pine, S. Scott, J. Stevenson, E. Taylor, et al. (Eds.), *Rutter's child and adolescent psychiatry* (5th ed., pp. 182–199). Hoboken, NJ: Wiley.

Caspi, A., & Silva, P. A. (1995). Temperamental qualities at age three predict personality traits in young adulthood: Longitudinal evidence from a birth cohort. *Child Development, 66*(2), 486–498.

Checa, P., & Rueda, M. R. (2011). Behavioral and brain measures of executive attention and school competence in late childhood. *Developmental Neuropsychology, 36*, 1018–1032.

Chen, X., & Schmidt, L. A. (2015). Temperament and personality. In M. E. Lamb (Ed.), *Handbook of child psychology and developmental science: Vol. 3. Socioemotional processes* (7th ed., pp. 152–200). Hoboken, NJ: Wiley.

Chronis-Tuscano, A., Degnan, K. A., Pine, D. S., Pérez-Edgar, K., Henderson, H. A., Diaz, Y., et al. (2009). Stable early maternal report of behavioral inhibition predicts lifetime social anxiety disorder in adolescence. *Journal of the American Academy of Child and Adolescent Psychiatry, 48*(9), 928–935.

Coan, J. A., & Allen, J. J. (2003). Frontal EEG asymmetry and the behavioral activation and inhibition systems. *Psychophysiology, 40*(1), 106–114.

Cole, C., Zapp, D. J., Fettig, N. B., & Pérez-Edgar, K. (2016). Impact of attention biases to threat and effortful control on individual variations in negative affect and social withdrawal in very young children. *Journal of Experimental Child Psychology, 141*, 210–221.

Cole, P. M., Martin, S. E., & Dennis, T. A. (2004). Emotion regulation as a scientific construct: Methodological challenges and directions for child development research. *Child Development, 75*(2), 317–333.

Cole, P. M., Michel, M. K., & Teti, L. O. D. (1994). The development of emotion regulation and dysregulation: A clinical perspective. *Monographs of the Society for Research in Child Development, 59*(2–3), 73–100, 250–283.

Damasio, A. R. (1994). *Descartes' error: Emotion, rationality and the human brain.* New York: Putnam.

Davidson, R. J., & Fox, N. A. (1989). Frontal brain asymmetry predicts infants' response to maternal separation. *Journal of Abnormal Psychology, 98*(2), 127–131.

Degnan, K. A., Hane, A. A., Henderson, H. A., Moas, O. L., Reeb-Sutherland, B. C., & Fox, N. A. (2011). Longitudinal stability of temperamental exuberance and social–emotional outcomes in early childhood. *Developmental Psychology, 47*(3), 765–780.

Diamond, A. (2013). Executive functions. *Annual Review of Psychology, 64,* 135–168.

Eisenberg, N., Champion, C., & Ma, Y. (2004). Emotion-related regulation: An emerging construct. *Merrill–Palmer Quarterly, 50,* 236–259.

Eisenberg, N., & Spinrad, T. L. (2004). Emotion-related regulation: Sharpening the definition. *Child Development, 75*(2), 334–339.

Evans, D. E., & Rothbart, M. K. (2007). Developing a model for adult temperament. *Journal of Research in Personality, 41*(4), 868–888.

Eysenck, S. B., Eysenck, H. J., & Barrett, P. (1985). A revised version of the Psychoticism scale. *Personality and Individual Differences, 6*(1), 21–29.

Feldman, R. (2012). Parent–infant synchrony: A biobehavioral model of mutual influences in the formation of affiliative bonds. *Monographs of the Society for Research in Child Development, 77*(2), 42–51.

Forbes, E. E., Olino, T. M., Ryan, N. D., Birmaher, B., Axelson, D., Moyles, D. L., & Dahl, R. E. (2010). Reward-related brain function as a predictor of treatment response in adolescents with major depressive disorder. *Cognitive, Affective, and Behavioral Neuroscience, 10*(1), 107–118.

Fox, N. A. (1992). Frontal brain asymmetry and vulnerability to stress: Individual differences in infant temperament. In T. M. Field, P. M. McCabe, & N. Schneiderman (Eds.), *Stress and coping in infancy and childhood* (pp. 83–100). Hillsdale, NJ: Erlbaum.

Fox, N. A., Henderson, H. A., Marshall, P. J., Nichols, K. E., & Ghera, M. M. (2005). Behavioral inhibition: Linking biology and behavior within a developmental framework. *Annual Review of Psychology, 56,* 235–262.

Fox, N. A., Henderson, H. A., Rubin, K. H., Calkins, S. D., & Schmidt, L. A. (2001). Continuity and discontinuity of behavioral inhibition and exuberance: Psychophysiological and behavioral influences across the first four years of life. *Child Development, 72*(1), 1–21.

Fu, X., Taber-Thomas, B. C., & Pérez-Edgar, K. (2017). Frontolimbic functioning during threat-related attention: Relations to early behavioral inhibition and anxiety in children. *Biological Psychology, 122,* 98–109.

Garcia-Coll, C., Kagan, J., & Reznick, J. S. (1984). Behavioral inhibition in young children. *Child Development, 55,* 1005–1019.

Gartstein, M. A., & Rothbart, M. K. (2003). Studying infant temperament via the Revised Infant Behavior Questionnaire. *Infant Behavior and Development, 26*(1), 64–86.

Gianino, A., & Tronick, E. (1988). The mutual regulation model: The infant's self and interactive regulation and coping and defensive capacities. In T. M. Field, P. M. McCabe, & N. Schneiderman (Eds.), *Stress and coping across development* (pp. 47–68). Hillsdale, NJ: Erlbaum.

Grist, C. L., & McCord, D. M. (2010). Individual differences in preschool children: Temperament or personality? *Infant and Child Development, 19*(3), 264–274.

Guyer, A. E., Nelson, E. E., Pérez-Edgar, K., Hardin, M. G., Roberson-Nay, R., Monk, C. S., et al. (2006). Striatal functional alteration in adolescents characterized by early childhood behavioral inhibition. *Journal of Neuroscience, 26*(24), 6399–6405.

Hane, A. A., Fox, N. A., Henderson, H. A., & Marshall, P. J. (2008). Behavioral reactivity and approach–withdrawal bias in infancy. *Developmental Psychology, 44*(5), 1491–1496.

Henderson, H. A. (2010). Electrophysiological correlates of cognitive control and the regulation of shyness in children. *Developmental Neuropsychology, 35,* 177–193.

Henderson, H. A., & Wilson, M. J. G. (2017). Attention processes underlying risk and resilience in behaviorally inhibited children. *Current Behavioral Neuroscience Reports, 4*(2), 99–106.

Jones, N. A., & Fox, N. A. (1992). Electroencephalogram asymmetry during emotionally evocative films and its relation to positive and negative affectivity. *Brain and Cognition, 20*(2), 280–299.

Kagan, J., & Fox, N. A. (2006). Biology, culture, and temperamental biases. In N. Eisenberg, W. Damon, & R. M. Lerner (Eds.), *Handbook of child psychology: Vol. 3. Social, emotional, and personality development* (6th ed., pp. 167–225). Hoboken, NJ: Wiley.

Kagan, J., Reznick, J. S., Clarke, C., Snidman, N., & Garcia-Coll, C. (1984). Behavioral inhibition to the unfamiliar. *Child Development, 55,* 2212–2225.

Kagan, J., & Snidman, N. (1991). Infant predictors of inhibited and uninhibited profiles. *Psychological Science, 2*(1), 40–44.

Kandler, C. (2012). Nature and nurture in personality development: The case of neuroticism and extraversion. *Current Directions in Psychological Science, 21*(5), 290–296.

Kertes, D. A., Donzella, B., Talge, N. M., Garvin, M. C., Van Ryzin, M. J., & Gunnar, M. R. (2009). Inhibited temperament and parent emotional availability differentially predict young children's cortisol responses to novel social and nonsocial events. *Developmental Psychobiology, 51*(7), 521–532.

Kochanska, G., Barry, R. A., Jimenez, N. B., Hollatz, A. L., & Woodard, J. (2009). Guilt and effortful control:

Two mechanisms that prevent disruptive developmental trajectories. *Journal of Personality and Social Psychology, 97*(2), 322–333.

Kochanska, G., Murray, K., & Coy, K. C. (1997). Inhibitory control as a contributor to conscience in childhood: From toddler to early school age. *Child Development, 68,* 263–277.

Kopp, C. (1989). Regulation of distress and negative emotions: A developmental view. *Developmental Psychology, 25,* 343–354.

López-Romero, L., Romero, E., & Luengo, M. A. (2012). Disentangling the role of psychopathic traits and externalizing behaviour in predicting conduct problems from childhood to adolescence. *Journal of Youth and Adolescence, 41*(11), 1397–1408.

Mackrell, S. V., Sheikh, H. I., Kotelnikova, Y., Kryski, K. R., Jordan, P. L., Singh, S. M., et al. (2014). Child temperament and parental depression predict cortisol reactivity to stress in middle childhood. *Journal of Abnormal Psychology, 123*(1), 106–114.

MacLean, P. C., Rynes, K. N., Aragón, C., Caprihan, A., Phillips, J. P., & Lowe, J. R. (2014). Mother–infant mutual eye gaze supports emotion regulation in infancy during the still-face paradigm. *Infant Behavior and Development, 37*(4), 512–522.

Mangelsdorf, S. C., Shapiro, J. R., & Marzolf, D. (1995). Developmental and temperamental differences in emotion regulation in infancy. *Child Development, 66*(6), 1817–1828.

Marshall, P. J., Reeb, B. C., & Fox, N. A. (2009). Electrophysiological responses to auditory novelty in temperamentally different 9-month-old infants. *Developmental Science, 12*(4), 568–582.

McDermott, J. M., Pérez-Edgar, K., Henderson, H. A., Chronis-Tuscano, A., Pine, D. S., & Fox, N. A. (2009). A history of childhood behavioral inhibition and enhanced response monitoring in adolescence are linked to clinical anxiety. *Biological Psychiatry, 65*(5), 445–448.

Moffitt, T. E., Arseneault, L., Belsky, D., Dickson, N., Hancox, R. J., Harrington, H., et al. (2011). A gradient of childhood self-control predicts health, wealth, and public safety. *Procedings of the National Academy of Sciences of the USA, 108*(7), 2693–2698.

Moffitt, T. E., Caspi, A., Dickson, N., Silva, P., & Stanton, W. (1996). Childhood-onset versus adolescent-onset antisocial conduct problems in males: Natural history from ages 3 to 18 years. *Development and Psychopathology, 8*(02), 399–424.

Moffitt, T., Poulton, R., & Caspi, A. (2013). Lifelong impact of early self-control: Childhood self-discipline predicts adult quality of life. *American Scientist, 101*(5), 352–359.

Morales, S., Beekman, C., Blandon, A. Y., Stifter, C. A., & Buss, K. A. (2015). Longitudinal associations between temperament and socioemotional outcomes in young children: The moderating role of RSA and gender. *Developmental Psychobiology, 57*(1), 105–119.

Morales, S., Pérez-Edgar, K., & Buss, K. (2015). Attention biases towards and away from threat mark the relation between early dysregulated fear and the later emergence of social withdrawal. *Journal of Abnormal Child Psychology, 43*(6), 1067–1078.

Morales, S., Pérez-Edgar, K., & Buss, K. (2016). Longitudinal relations among exuberance, externalizing behaviors, and attentional bias to reward: the mediating role of effortful control. *Developmental Science, 19,* 853–862.

Morris, A. S., Silk, J. S., Morris, M. D., Steinberg, L., Aucoin, K. J., & Keyes, A. W. (2011). The influence of mother–child emotion regulation strategies on children's expression of anger and sadness. *Developmental Psychology, 47*(1), 213–235.

Muris, P., Bos, A. E., Mayer, B., Verkade, R., Thewissen, V., & Dell'Avvento, V. (2009). Relations among behavioral inhibition, Big Five personality factors, and anxiety disorder symptoms in non-clinical children. *Personality and Individual Differences, 46*(4), 525–529.

Muris, P., Meesters, C., & Blijlevens, P. (2007). Self-reported reactive and regulative temperament in early adolescence: Relations to internalizing and externalizing problem behavior and "Big Three" personality factors. *Journal of Adolescence, 30*(6), 1035–1049.

Pérez-Edgar, K. (2015). Effortful control in adolescence: Individual differences within a unique developmental window. In G. Oettingen & P. M. Gollwitzer (Eds.), *Self-regulation in adolescence* (pp. 78–100). New York: Cambridge University Press.

Pérez-Edgar, K., Bar-Haim, Y., McDermott, J. M., Chronis-Tuscano, A., Pine, D. S., & Fox, N. A. (2010). Attention biases to threat and behavioral inhibition in early childhood shape adolescent social withdrawal. *Emotion, 10*(3), 349–357.

Pérez-Edgar, K., & Fox, N. A. (2005). Temperament and anxiety disorders. *Child and Adolescent Psychiatric Clinics of North America, 14*(4), 681–706.

Pérez-Edgar, K., Reeb-Sutherland, B. C., McDermott, J. M., White, L. K., Henderson, H. A., Degnan, K. A., et al. (2011). Attention biases to threat link behavioral inhibition to social withdrawal over time in very young children. *Journal of Abnormal Child Psychology, 39*(6), 885–895.

Pérez-Edgar, K., Roberson-Nay, R., Hardin, M. G., Poeth, K., Guyer, A. E., Nelson, E. E., et al. (2007). Attention alters neural responses to evocative faces in behaviorally inhibited adolescents. *NeuroImage, 35*(4), 1538–1546.

Putnam, S. P., & Stifter, C. A. (2005). Behavioral approach–inhibition in toddlers: Prediction from infancy, positive and negative affective components, and relations with behavior problems. *Child Development, 76*(1), 212–226.

Rathert, J., Fite, P. J., & Gaertner, A. E. (2011). Associations between effortful control, psychological control and proactive and reactive aggression. *Child Psychiatry and Human Development, 42,* 609–621.

Reeb-Sutherland, B. C., Vanderwert, R. E., Degnan, K. A., Marshall, P. J., Pérez-Edgar, K., Chronis-Tuscano, A., et al. (2009). Attention to novelty in behaviorally inhibited adolescents moderates risk for anxiety. *Journal of Child Psychology and Psychiatry, 50*(11), 1365–1372.

Rothbart, M. K. (1981). Measurement of temperament in infancy. *Child Development, 52,* 569–578.

Rothbart, M. K. (2011). *Becoming who we are: Temperament and personality in development.* New York: Guilford Press.

Rothbart, M. K., Ahadi, S. A., & Evans, D. E. (2000). Temperament and personality: Origins and outcomes. *Journal of Personality and Social Psychology, 78*(1), 122–135.

Rothbart, M. K., Ahadi, S. A., Hershey, K. L., & Fisher, P. (2001). Investigations of temperament at three to seven years: The Children's Behavior Questionnaire. *Child Development, 72*(5), 1394–1408.

Rothbart, M. K., & Bates, J. E. (2006). Temperament. In N. Eisenberg (Ed.), *Handbook of child psychology: Social, emotional, and personality development* (6th ed., pp. 99–166). Hoboken, NJ: Wiley.

Rothbart, M. K., & Rueda, M. R. (2005). The development of effortful control. In U. Mayr, E. Awh, & S. Keele (Eds.), *Developing individuality in the human brain: A tribute to Michael I. Posner* (pp. 167–188). Washington, DC: American Psychological Association.

Rothbart, M. K., Ziaie, H., & O'Boyle, C. G. (1992). Self-regulation and emotion in infancy. *New Directions for Child and Adolescent Development, 55,* 7–23.

Roy, A. K., Dennis, T. A., & Warner, C. M. (2015). A critical review of attentional threat bias and its role in the treatment of pediatric anxiety disorders. *Journal of Cognitive Psychotherapy, 29*(3), 171–184.

Schmidt, L. A., Fox, N. A., Rubin, K. H., & Sternberg, E. M. (1997). Behavioral and neuroendocrine responses in shy children. *Developmental Psychobiology, 30*(2), 127–140.

Schwartz, C. E., Snidman, N., & Kagan, J. (1999). Adolescent social anxiety as an outcome of inhibited temperament in childhood. *Journal of the American Academy of Child and Adolescent Psychiatry, 38,* 1008–1015.

Schwartz, C. E., Wright, C. I., Shin, L. M., Kagan, J., & Rauch, S. L. (2003). Inhibited and uninhibited infants "grown up": Adult amygdalar response to novelty. *Science, 300*(5627), 1952–1953.

Sheese, B. E., Rothbart, M. K., Posner, M. I., White, L. K., & Fraundorf, S. H. (2008). Executive attention and self-regulation in infancy. *Infant Behavior and Development, 31*(3), 501–510.

Sheese, B. E., Voelker, P., Posner, M. I., & Rothbart, M. K. (2009). Genetic variation influences on the early development of reactive emotions and their regulation by attention. *Cognitive Neuropsychiatry, 14*(4–5), 332–355.

Silva, P. A. (1990). The Dunedin Multidisciplinary Health and Development Study: A 15-year longitudinal study. *Paediatric and Perinatal Epidemiology, 4,* 96–127.

Smith, C. L., & Bell, M. A. (2010). Stability in infant frontal asymmetry as a predictor of toddlerhood internalizing and externalizing behaviors. *Developmental Psychobiology, 52*(2), 158–167.

Stifter, C. A., & Fox, N. A. (1990). Infant reactivity: Physiological correlates of newborn and 5-month temperament. *Developmental Psychology, 26*(4), 582–588.

Stifter, C. A., Putnam, S., & Jahromi, L. (2008). Exuberant and inhibited toddlers: Stability of temperament and risk for problem behavior. *Development and Psychopathology, 20*(2), 401–421.

Taber-Thomas, B., & Pérez-Edgar, K. (2015). Emerging adulthood brain development. In J. J. Arnett (Ed.), *The Oxford handbook of emerging adulthood* (pp. 126–141). New York: Oxford University Press.

Tellegen, A. (1982). *Brief manual for the Multidimensional Personality Questionnaire.* Unpublished manuscript, University of Minnesota.

Valiente, C., Lemery-Chalfant, K., Swanson, J., & Reiser, M. (2008). Prediction of children's academic competence from their effortful control, relationships, and classroom participation. *Journal of Educational Psychology, 100,* 67–77.

White, L. K., Degnan, K. A., Henderson, H. A., Pérez-Edgar, K., Walker, O. L., Schechner, T., et al. (2017). Developmental relations between behavioral inhibition, anxiety, and attention biases to threat and positive information. *Child Development, 88,* 141–155.

Wong, M. M., Nigg, J. T., Zucker, R. A., Puttler, L. I., Fitzgerald, H. E., Jester, J. M., et al. (2006). Behavioral control and resiliency in the onset of alcohol and illicit drug use: A prospective study from preschool to adolescence. *Child Development, 77,* 1016–1033.

Zelazo, P. D., Müller, U., Frye, D., Marcovitch, S., Argitis, G., Boseovski, J., et al. (2003). The development of executive function in early childhood: I. The development of executive function. *Monographs of the Society for Research in Child Development, 68,* vii–137.

Zuckerman, M., Kuhlman, D. M., Joireman, J., Teta, P., & Kraft, M. (1993). A comparison of three structural models for personality: The Big Three, the Big Five, and the Alternative Five. *Journal of Personality and Social Psychology, 65*(4), 757–768.

CHAPTER 7

Extraversion

Description, Development, and Mechanisms

Luke D. Smillie
Margaret L. Kern
Mirko Uljarevic

One morning, Erika has arranged to meet her new colleague, Tom, to walk with him to a team meeting. As he approaches, she immediately notices the bounce in his step. He displays a bright, wide smile. He introduces himself with a firm handshake and a warm tone in his voice, which he projects well. She is reminded of a *Seinfeld* episode about the "low talker," whose quiet voice creates social mishaps. Tom is the polar opposite of a low talker—his booming voice causes Erika to take a step back as he dispenses enthusiastic pleasantries punctuated by cheerful laughter. As they walk to the meeting, Erika's impression of Tom forms rapidly: He is gregarious, assertive, energetic, confident, and full of mirth. He eagerly fills any silences with bright conversation and expansive gestures. He is, she surmises, a classic extravert.

In this (fictitious) story, we need not assume that Erika's identification of Tom's extraversion stems from any expertise in psychology. Laypeople asked to describe their own personalities will often refer to the extraversion–introversion continuum, and lay understanding of extraversion is relatively accurate (e.g., Semin, Rosch, & Chassein, 1981). In psychological science, this continuum has appeared in some form in virtually all taxonomic systems developed to organize major individual differences. Variations in extraversion have been observed in many human cultures (Allik, 2005), as well as in several nonhuman species, including dogs, birds, and fish (Gosling & John, 1999). Key elements of extraversion, especially positive emotionality, are detectable in infants and children, and remain relatively stable over much of the lifespan. In short, extraversion appears to capture one of the most fundamental and enduring features of our individuality.

This chapter provides a broad overview of trait extraversion from a lifespan perspective. We begin by providing a conceptual and definitional overview of extraversion, before tracing the evolution of this construct, which stretches back to some of the earliest known writings on personality. We discuss various methods that have been used to assess extraversion in infants, children, and adults. We outline current understanding of the role that genes and the environment—especially early life experiences—may play in the development of extraversion. We describe the currently dominant reward processing theory of extraversion, and chart the developmental course of extraversion across the lifespan.

Finally, we provide a snapshot of the extraverted life, drawing on a rich literature that shows us what extraverts are like and how they experience the world.

Conceptual and Historical Overview

Extraversion is a broad trait "domain" subsuming a cluster of interrelated characteristics and tendencies, including talkativeness, boldness, dominance, sociability, outgoingness, enthusiasm, and positive emotionality (Smillie, 2013; Wilt & Revelle, 2017). Partly because extraversion is strongly characterized by the tendency to experience positive emotion (Lucas & Fujita, 2000; Smillie, DeYoung, & Hall, 2015), especially as it manifests during early childhood (Caspi & Shiner, 2006), some personality researchers have preferred labels such as *positive emotionality* (e.g., Tellegen & Waller, 2008). Alternatively, within one of the most influential models of childhood temperament, *surgency* is the preferred label to describe children's tendencies toward behavioral activity and outgoingness, positive emotions, and enjoyment of socialization (Evans & Rothbart, 2007; Rothbart & Bates, 2006). While categorical terms such as 'extravert' and 'introvert' are often used as shorthand, most individuals lie somewhere between these bipolar extremes, scattered along a relatively normally-distributed continuum. Also, in line with the view that personality traits are *probabilistic* descriptions of behavior and experience, all individuals act and feel more or less extraverted at different times and in different situations (Breil et al., 2016; Fleeson, Malanos, & Achille, 2002).

Traits comprising the extraversion domain can be structured hierarchically, with broader constructs at higher levels subsuming progressively narrower dimensions at lower levels (DeYoung, Quilty, & Peterson, 2007; Markon, Krueger, & Watson, 2005; Soto & John, 2017). Lower-level traits provide increasingly specific concrete descriptions of extraversion, manifesting as different behavioral patterns in various contexts (DeYoung, 2015; McCabe & Fleeson, 2016). The number of levels within the hierarchy, and the number of traits subsumed by any higher order factor such as extraversion, is indeterminate, and depends, in part, upon which trait descriptors are included in any analysis. Table 7.1 provides examples of the variety of different extraversion traits that have been dis-

cussed and assessed in the literature, clustered in terms of their approximate location in the trait hierarchy. Note that some traits do not fall squarely within a single trait domain, such as *trait affiliation* (i.e., the tendency to seek and maintain close social bonds), which combines extraversion and agreeableness (DeYoung, Weisberg, Quilty, & Peterson, 2013). Similarly, some measures of positive emotionality, including traits such as "cheerful," "happy," "friendly," "vibrant," and "sociable," can also be considered a combination of extraversion and high agreeableness (Hofstee, de Raad, & Goldberg, 1992). Thus, although the sociable tendencies of the extravert might suggest that extraversion primarily entails seeking and maintaining close social bonds with others, such tendencies in fact lie at the fringes of extraversion. Indeed, extraversion is just as concerned with enjoying social power and behaving dominantly toward others as it is about acting affiliatively toward and feeling closely connected to others.

Although Table 7.1 is an attempt to capture modern conceptualizations of extraversion and its psychometric structure, many of the characteristics listed have been discussed and examined for thousands of years (see Revelle, Wilt, & Condon, 2011, for a review). Around 300 B.C., philosopher Theophrastus of Lesbos wrote *The Characters,* in which he described 30 human archetypes, some of which epitomized extraverted qualities such as talkativeness and gregariousness (e.g., "The Chatty Man"). Around the same period, Hippocrates (460–370 B.C.) proposed four "humors" (blood, yellow bile, black bile, and phlegm), or bodily fluids, whose balance shaped an individual's physical health and temperament. Galen of Pergamon developed this idea further by linking the four humors with four temperaments, one of which was the sanguine person—described as lively, talkative, optimistic, and outgoing. The Galen–Hippocrates model of temperament resonated with many thinkers over the centuries, including H. J. Eysenck (1967), who noted its heuristic similarity to his own model of extraversion and neuroticism.

In the late 1800s and early 1900s, several theorists attempted to classify features of personality into different types and dimensions (see Millon, 2012, for a review). Ribot (1890) combined sensitivity and activity to suggest different characters, such as the "humble character" (high sensitivity, low activity), and the "contemplative character" (moderate

TABLE 7.1. Extraversion at Different Levels of the Personality Trait Hierarchy

Level of hierarchy	Examples of traits, grouped by model/framework
Domain level	• Extraversion (e.g., BFAS; NEO-PI-R, BFI-2; HEXACO, Little Six, EPQ-R, AB5C) • Positive emotional temperament (e.g., MPQ; Tellegen, 1982) • Surgency (e.g., CBQ; Rothbart, Ahadi, Hershey & Fisher, 2001)
Intermediate level(s)	• Assertiveness and enthusiasm (BFAS; DeYoung et al., 2007) • Sociability and impulsivity (see Rocklin & Revelle, 1981) • Social dominance and social vitality (see Helson & Kwan, 2000) • Assertiveness, sociability, and activity level (BFI-2; Soto & John, 2016) • Assertiveness, enthusiasm, and sensation seeking (see Quilty, DeYoung, Oakman, & Bagby, 2014) • Sociability, social boldness, social self-esteem, and liveliness (HEXACO-100; Lee & Ashton, 2018) • Social potency, achievement, social closeness, and well-being (MPQ; Tellegen, 1982)
Facet level	• Assertiveness, activity, gregariousness, warmth, excitement seeking, and positive emotions (NEO-PI-R; Costa & McCrae, 1995) • Assertiveness, activity, sociability, expressiveness, ambition, dogmatism, and aggression (EPP; Eysenck, Barrett, Wilson, & Jackson, 1991) • Assertiveness, poise, leadership, gregariousness, sociability, talkativeness, friendliness, self-disclosure, and provocativeness (AB5C; Goldberg, 1999)
Nuance level	• Indexed by individual items of the NEO-PI-R (e.g., "Likes attending games"; see Mõttus, Kandler, Bleidorn, Riemann, & McCrae, 2017)

Note. AB5C, Abridged Big Five–Dimensional Circumplex; BFAS, Big Five Aspects Scales; BFI-2, Big Five Inventory–2; EPP, Employee Personality Profile; EPQ-R, Eysenck Personality Questionnaire—Revised; HEXACO, Honesty–Humility, Emotionality, eXtraversion, Agreeableness, Conscientiousness, Openness to experience; MPQ, Multidimensional Personality Questionnaire; NEO-PI-R, NEO Personality Inventory—Revised.

sensitivity, low activity). Heymans and Wiersma (1906–1909) identified dimensions of activity, emotionality, and susceptibility to internal versus external stimulation. McDougall (1908) suggested eight "tempers," or personality types, stemming from intensity, persistency, and affectivity dimensions. The "hopeful" temper, characterized by high intensity, high persistence, and high affectivity, resembles the modern conceptualization of extraversion. Ivan Pavlov, famous for his work on classical conditioning, also posited three personality traits accounting for individual differences in conditioning processes—strength of excitation, strength of inhibition, and mobility (see Gray, 1964, for an overview). In all of this early taxonomic work, activity and emotionality—both salient features of extraversion—were recurrent themes.

By the middle of the 20th century, theorists turned to quantitative approaches to identify personality dimensions. Raymond Cattell (1957), H. J. Eysenck (1947, 1967), and others used *factor analysis*—a family of statistical techniques used to reduce a larger set of variables to a smaller set of dimensions, or "factors"—to aid in the development of personality taxonomies. Many were guided by an assumption, now known as the "lexical hypothesis," that the most fundamental features of human personality will, over time, become encoded into the language we use to describe ourselves and others (Goldberg, 1982, 1993). Based on many decades of work, across multiple languages and cultures, a broad consensus has emerged that five (John, Naumann, & Soto, 2008), or perhaps six (Ashton, Lee, & de Vries, 2014) factors describe the patterns of covariance among responses to questionnaire items and lexical descriptors. Such taxonomic work has consistently yielded an Extraversion–Introversion factor.

Although our understanding of extraversion has mainly emerged from studies of adult populations, there are clear parallels in the study of childhood personality within developmental psychology. Most models of temperament have included analogues of extraversion, including surgency, positive emotionality, and activity level (e.g., Buss & Plomin, 1975; Rothbart, Ahadi, Hershey, & Fisher, 2001; Rothbart & Bates, 2006; Tellegen & Waller, 2008; Thomas & Chess, 1977). For instance, in one study, a factor analysis of trait descriptors by over 50,000 parents identified 14 trait dimensions evident from age 3, including sociability, positive emotions, and activity level (Halverson et al., 2003). In a more recent study of parent ratings of over 3,500 children across five countries, features of extraversion again were evident as early as age 3, as captured by indicators such as energetic, outgoing, sociable, lively, makes friends easy, and loves to be with people (Tackett et al., 2012). In an integrative review of temperament models, Zentner and Bates (2008) suggested positive emotionality as a core temperament dimension, evident even in infants through behaviors such as smiling, laughing, clapping hands, and playfulness, and which appears to be relatively stable throughout early childhood (also see Lemery, Goldsmith, Klinnert, & Mrazek, 1999; Putnam, Gartstein, & Rothbart, 2006; Rothbart, Derryberry, & Hershey, 2000). This literature has also shown that aspects of extraversion appearing from a young age are predictive of important outcomes across the lifespan (Friedman & Martin, 2011).

More recent attempts to integrate the temperament and personality literatures show that childhood temperament can be usefully described in terms of the same Big Five personality dimensions that characterize adult populations (Tackett, Krueger, Iacono, & McGue, 2008). However, it appears that a sixth dimension, representing overall levels of behavioral activity and energy, is also required to comprehensively describe personality in early childhood (Caspi & Shiner, 2006; Soto & John, 2014). By adolescence and throughout adulthood, this activity dimension becomes subsumed partly within extraversion and partly within conscientiousness (Costa & McCrae, 1995; Shiner & DeYoung, 2013). This provides a glimpse of the broadening of the extraversion spectrum throughout childhood. Research into the so-called "Little Six" model of childhood personality is still emerging (see Soto, 2016; Soto & John, 2014), and it remains to be seen whether it will achieve the status that the Big Five has reached in the adult literature. Nevertheless, given its recurrent appearance in the literature, it seems likely that any compre-

hensive model of childhood personality will include extraversion, positive emotionality or other, analogous dimensions.

Individual differences in extraversion are also discussed in other literatures, though this fact is obscured by the use of different terminology across disciplines (i.e., the "jangle fallacy"). Within social psychology, for instance, constructs such as "power" (Keltner, Gruenfeld, & Anderson, 2003) and "dominance" (Wiggins, 1979) are virtually indistinguishable from aspects of extraversion relating to boldness and assertiveness. But it is also crucial to note that the term *extraversion* has been used in different ways over the years (i.e., the "jingle fallacy"). Swiss psychiatrist Carl Jung (1921) originally coined the labels *extraversion* and *introversion* to describe orientations toward the external versus the internal world (from the Latin terms *extra,* meaning "outside," *intro,* meaning "inside," and *verte,* meaning "to turn").[1] For Jung, the extravert was motivated to explore the objects and experiences of the outside world, while the introvert was motivated to explore the inner mental life of thoughts, ideas, and fantasies. This conceptualization was swiftly challenged by early research into the structure of personality (e.g., Guilford & Guilford, 1934), and it turns out that nonextraverted individuals are not necessarily more reflective, ideas-focused, or "turned inward." Thus, the term *introversion* is something of a misnomer for the low pole of extraversion, and continues to cause confusion—especially in popular spheres, where the Jungian notion of introversion continues to reverberate (e.g., Cain, 2012). Seeking greater clarity, some have suggested more etymologically appropriate labels for the low pole of extraversion (e.g., "detachment"; Krueger & Markon, 2014), but it seems likely that Jung's labels are here to stay.

Methods for Assessing Extraversion

Almost all research from the adult personality literature assesses levels of extraversion using

---

[1] Extraversion has been chronically misspelt as *extroversion,* presumably due to the assumption that Jung had intended the word to mirror the spelling of introversion. Jung himself is said to have dismissed this as "bad Latin," and his original spelling is preserved within academic psychology. However, the misspelling has been so widely adopted that it is now the preferred spelling in major English-language dictionaries.

self-report questionnaires. These comprise either lexical terms (e.g., "assertive," "talkative"), or more elaborate descriptions of behavior and experience (e.g., "knows how to captivate people," "warms up quickly to others"), to which a person responds by indicating the accuracy to which the person feels that the item describes him or her (e.g., Goldberg, 1999; Lee & Ashton, 2018; Soto & John, 2017). Use of informant ratings is also common, and research demonstrates that extraverted behaviors and experiences are highly visible to others—it is literally easy to *see* when a person is bold, talkative, and cheerful (Funder & Colvin, 1988; Funder & Sneed, 1993; McCrae, 1982; Vazire, 2010). Self–other agreement for ratings of extraversion exceeds chance levels even among complete strangers within a 5-minute interaction (Funder & Colvin, 1988) or a single photograph (Naumann, Vazire, Rentfrow, & Gosling, 2009). Above chance-levels of self–other agreement have also been reported when judges viewed a photograph of a target individual for just 50 milliseconds (Borkenau, Brecke, Mottig, & Paelecke, 2009)—close to the "speed of sight."

Accurate informant ratings of extraversion are critical for assessing extraversion early in life, given the limited capacity of young children to introspect and report on their own behaviors and experiences. A plethora of questionnaires has been developed specifically for parents, teachers, and other adults to provide ratings of childhood personality (see Shiner & DeYoung, 2013, for a recent review), but perhaps the most widely used are those based on Rothbart's temperament model. Item content for measures of surgency changes slightly from measures focused on infancy and toddlerhood (Infant Behaviour Questionnaire—Revised; Gartstein & Rothbart, 2003) through those intended for early (Early Childhood Behavior Questionnaire; Putnam et al., 2006) and middle childhood (Children's Behavior Questionnaire; Rothbart et al., 2001). Nevertheless, they all include ratings of expression of positive emotions, such as smiling and laughter during interactions with caregiver and play, as well as seeking and taking pleasure in interactions with others. More recently, questionnaires for assessing the Little Six factors of childhood personality have been developed using brief sentence descriptions, such as "is a talkative person, talks a lot" for extraversion and "is energetic and full of life" for the activity factor (Soto, 2016; Soto & John, 2014).

Traditional personality questionnaires, whether completed by a subject or an informant/observer, require respondents to retrospect on previous behaviors and experiences, and to make generalizations across multiple times and situations. An alternative approach is to use *experience sampling methods (ESMs),* which involve repeated sampling of *momentary* behaviors and experiences throughout daily life via a mobile device (Conner & Mehl, 2015). In one of the first ESM studies focused on extraversion, Fleeson and colleagues (2002) assessed participants' momentary "extraverted states" multiple times per day for 2 weeks. Each assessment involved the same lexical terms used in traditional questionnaires (e.g., *bold, talkative,* and *assertive*), but for ratings of *current,* rather than typical or average, behavior and experience. The authors found that participants' average levels of *state* extraversion were highly stable from one week to the next and, in a later meta-analysis (Fleeson & Gallagher, 2009), moderately to strongly correlated with traditional questionnaire measures of *trait* extraversion. This finding not only speaks to the promise of ESMs as an alternative means to assess personality, but also confirms that traditional personality questionnaires, despite their limitations, do at least a reasonable job of capturing regularities in behavior and experience across time and space (see also Conner & Barrett, 2012; Finnigan & Vazire, 2017).

An interesting insight from the ESM literature concerns the coherence of different elements of personality expressed in the moment. Extensive research now shows that the behaviors and experiences that characterize *between-person* differences in trait extraversion also cohere *with persons* over time; that is, whenever people display some features of extraversion (e.g., talkativeness) they also tend to display other features of extraversion (e.g., positive emotion),[2] as shown in both correlational (Fleeson et al., 2002; Heller, Komar, & Lee, 2007; Sun, Stevenson, Kabbani, Richardson, & Smillie, 2017; Wilt, Noftle, Fleeson, & Spain, 2012) and experimental (e.g., Smillie et al., 2015; Sun et al., 2017; Zelenski, Santoro, & Whelan, 2012) studies. In a recent ESM study, Wilt, Bleidorn, and Revelle (2017) found that the tendency to pursue rewarding goals predicted extraverted

---

[2]It is important to note that this particular convergence of between-person and within-person coherence may be the exception rather than the rule within personality psychology (Cervone, 2005).

behavior, which in turn predicted perceptions of successful goal progress, which in turn predicted positive emotion. As the authors observed, this provides one perspective on why particular affects (positive emotion), behaviors (outgoingness, boldness), cognitions (perceptions of goal progress), and motivations (reward goals) may cohere together within the extraversion domain.

Moving entirely beyond self- and other-ratings, observational methods provide greater objectivity in the assessment of extraversion. Developmental psychologists have developed several rigorous protocols for this purpose, such as the Laboratory Temperament Assessment Battery (LAB-TAB; Goldsmith & Rothbart, 1991), a standardized, behaviorally based assessment that presents a series of tasks to elicit differential responses organized along nine trait dimensions (anger, sadness, fear, shyness, positive affect, approach, activity level, persistence, and inhibitory control). Each assessed dimension is based on a range of facial, vocal, motor, and behavioral responses elicited by the specific episode. Factor-analytic studies (e.g., Dyson, Olino, Durbin, Goldsmith, & Klein, 2012; Kotelnikova, Olino, Mackrell, Jordan, & Hayden, 2013) show that the LAB-TAB temperament dimensions interface well with Rothbart's psychobiological temperamental framework and the Big Five, and yield at least one factor analogous to extraversion. For example, Dyson and colleagues (2012) identified "Sociability," which subsumed sociability, initiative, and dominance, as well as variables related to positive affect and interest.

There is also a small but growing number of observational approaches to assessing adult extraversion. One dramatic example is work showing that personality can be predicted with reasonable accuracy from "digital footprints," such as one creates when using social media (e.g., Kosinski, Stillwell, & Graepel, 2013; Park et al., 2015). For instance, using only "Likes" from the social media service Facebook, machine-learning algorithms can predict extraversion with similar accuracy to that based on 1–3 weeks of experience sampling data (Kosinski et al., 2013). It is also possible to capture elements of personality through audio recordings, which, like ESMs, take advantage of mobile technology. Mehl, Gosling, and Pennebaker (2006) developed the electronically activated recorder (EAR), which uses mobile devices to record 30-second snippets of sound in participants' environment at random intervals across a speci-

fied period, and can capture how personality appears through verbal behaviors. For instance, over a 2-day period, Mehl and colleagues found that extraverted students spent more time talking and less time alone. These methods can be complemented with wearable cameras that add information about the environment in which behaviors occur (Brown, Blake, & Sherman, 2017), although this technology has not yet been incorporated into personality research. As is the case for ESMs, these novel measures may not turn out to be "better" than traditional questionnaires, but they nevertheless offer another window onto extraverted personality.

As technology continues to advance, alternative approaches for assessing extraversion will continue to be designed and evaluated, and best-practice approaches for processing and analyzing the resulting data will be developed. An important question that arises is which measure should serve as the "gold standard" for personality assessment. Agreement across different methods is often moderate at best, which may suggest that different approaches reveal different aspects of the person (Conner & Barrett, 2012). Multimethod approaches may therefore be necessary to fully capture the complexity of extraversion and other aspects of personality.

The Origins of Extraversion

As is the case with all aspects of personality, variation in extraversion can be attributed to both genetic and environmental influences (Bouchard & McGue, 2003; Krueger & Johnson, 2008). In line with the rising prominence of theories linking extraversion with dopamine-mediated reward processes (discussed below), molecular genetics studies of extraversion have targeted specific gene variants linked with dopamine function. However, this approach has proven largely unsuccessful (Chabris, Lee, Cesarini, Benjamin, & Laibson, 2015), and most candidate gene studies of extraversion fail to replicate (Munafo, Yalcin, Willis-Owen, & Flint, 2008; Wacker & Smillie, 2015). Even genomewide association studies (GWAS), in which hundreds of thousands of gene–trait associations are examined simultaneously, and studies of genomic-relatedness-matrix residual maximum likelihood (GREML), in which estimation of the heritability of personality and other traits is based on genetic similarities of unrelated individuals, have so far failed to paint a coherent picture of the molecular genetics of extraversion (e.g., de Moor et al., 2012; Power & Pluess, 2015). This failure reveals the complexity of the genetic architecture of personality, and the fact that extraversion is subject to hundreds or even thousands of tiny genetic influences.

There has also been relatively little progress in identifying the specific environmental factors that influence the development of extraversion. Most studies that attempt to identify such factors are completely vulnerable to rival hypotheses. Consider the popular belief—reinforced by much theory and research in psychology (e.g., Sulloway, 1996)—that personality is influenced by birth order. Firstborn children are often found to be more extraverted than their siblings, especially in terms of traits concerned with dominance and assertiveness (Beck, Burnet, & Vosper, 2006; Sulloway, 1996). This has been attributed to, for example, the greater capacity of firstborns to establish dominance over their physically smaller siblings throughout childhood. However, recent attempts to confirm birth order effects in very large (Damian & Roberts, 2015a) and multinational (Rohrer, Egloff, & Schmukle, 2015) samples find essentially no relation with personality. Many spurious factors may explain the birth order effects reported in earlier studies (see Damian & Roberts, 2015b). For example, because firstborns may be found in families of any size, while fourth-borns can only be found in families with at least four children, family size is a potentially confounding factor in this research. Additionally, parental ratings of multiple siblings are confounded by age (i.e., the firstborn will always be the eldest), and biased by the parental tendency to either exaggerate (i.e., the contrast effect) or underestimate (i.e., the assimilation effect) differences between their children by evaluating them relative to one another (see Majdandžić, van den Boom, & Heesbeen, 2008).

The causal ambiguity inherent in correlational data further obscures our view of the early life experiences that shape the development of extraversion. For example, Nakao and colleagues (2000) found that extraverted children were less likely to have overprotective parents. Similarly, Kochanska, Friesenborg, Lange, Martel, and Kochanska (2004) explored relationships among LAB-TAB-assessed child temperament (joy, anger, fear), parental personality (Big Five traits), and the quality of parent–child relationships. This revealed an association of infants' joy—a key marker of extraversion—with both maternal openness to experience and parent–child relationship quality. Many have concluded that such findings reveal how parenting styles and the family environment shape a child's personality, but an alternative explanation is that the child's personality triggers different parenting styles, thereby driving parent–child relationship dynamics. Shiner and Caspi (2012) suggested that childhood temperament influences and shapes the subsequent personality development through processes such as *environmental elicitation* (i.e., trait expressions that trigger particular responses from peers and caregivers), and *situation perception* (i.e., experiencing the world through the lenses of one's personality). Similarly, in adult populations, our level of extraversion can influence how others behave toward us and how we perceive that behavior—among other complex person–situation transactions (Eaton & Funder, 2002; Friedman, 2000; Furr & Funder, in press).

Genetic confounding also complicates studies of the influence that parental behavior may have on child personality (see Bouchard & McGue, 2003). For instance, it is possible that genetic factors shared among family members influence both the child's level of extraversion and the parent's approach to childrearing, creating an illusory correlation between parental behavior and child personality. This seems a plausible explanation for the link between child extraversion and maternal openness identified by Kochanska and colleagues (2004), given that both openness and extraversion have been linked with overlapping neural processes (DeYoung, 2013). Such confounds become even more complex as genetic structures interact with early environmental experiences. Overall, the identification of family environment influences on personality has proven extremely difficult, and for this reason the early experiences that impact on one's level of extraversion remain essentially unknown.

In summary, identifying the sources of major personality traits is one of the biggest challenges for personality theory and research. In the case of extraversion, both genetic and environmental factors explain why some of us are bolder and more outgoing than others, but the identification of these factors is a formidable and elusive puzzle.

Reward Processing: The Engine of Extraversion?

Genetic and environmental factors have *distal* influences on our personalities; they exert their effects via brain functions that produce emergent psychological processes—the *proximal* mechanisms underlying personality. Research on proximal mechanisms has been guided by a family of theories in personality neuroscience (see Allen & DeYoung, 2017), positing that traits within the extraversion domain result from differential function in the reward processing regions of the brain (Depue & Collins, 1999; Pickering & Gray, 1999; Rammsayer, 1998). Reward information is signaled by midbrain dopamine neurons projecting to the striatum, nucleus accumbens, and prefrontal regions. Evidence linking this system with extraverted personality has drawn on a range of neuroscience methods, including neuroimaging of dopamine-rich brain areas and manipulation of dopamine levels via pharmacological agents (see Wacker & Smillie, 2015, for a review). For example, extraversion has been found to predict neural activity in the nucleus accumbens during the anticipation of financial gains (Wu, Samanez-Larkin, Katovich, & Knutson, 2014), and to facilitate the effects of dopamine on the association of contextual stimuli with reward (Depue & Fu, 2013). These neural-level findings fit well with research into the hierarchical structure of extraversion, discussed earlier, which suggests that purpose-built measures of trait reward sensitivity and incentive motivation can be considered intermediate-level traits within the extraversion domain (Quilty, DeYoung, Oakman, & Bagby, 2014; see also Table 7.1).

An important finding within the neuroscience literature is that midbrain dopamine neurons show a phasic increase in firing following an unpredicted reward, and a phasic decrease following unpredicted nonreward (Schultz, 1998). This suggests that dopaminergic activity can be modeled in terms of "reward prediction error" signals, which are postulated to drive reinforcement learning, and also energize and direct behavior toward rewarding outcomes (see Holland & Schiffino, 2016, for a review). A number of studies reveal an association between extraversion and a peripheral index of reward prediction error signaling derived from EEG (e.g., Cooper, Duke, Pickering & Smillie, 2014; Smillie, Cooper, & Pickering, 2011; Smillie et al., 2017). This association has also been found to be stopped by the administration of a dopamine blocker, providing some credibility for the view that it is, at least in part, dopamine-driven (Mueller et al., 2014). This latter finding mirrors a number of other pharmacological

studies demonstrating extraversion-dependent effects of dopamine on other neural indices of reward processing (e.g., Wacker, Chavanon, & Stemmler, 2006; Wacker, Mueller, Pizzagalli, Hennig, & Stemmler, 2013). Overall, these studies suggest that extraverted individuals are more sensitive, at the level of neural processing, to motivationally salient signals of reward.

A link between extraversion and behavioral indicators of reward processing has also been supported by researchers using a range of simple cognitive tasks. For example, Rusting (1999) found that extraversion predicts the tendency to identify the more positively valenced word of an aurally presented homophone pair (e.g., hearing *won* rather than *one*). In a second study, when presented with an ambiguous sentence, such as "Linda is looking out at the sunset," and instructed to write a short story based on the sentence, extraversion predicted the tendency to generate narratives that were more positively valenced. Finally, in a free-recall task, extraversion predicted recall accuracy for positively valenced words but not for negatively valenced words. Rusting interpreted all three of these findings in relation to reward processing theories of extraversion—in each instance, extraverts appeared to be more attuned to semantically positive information. More recently, Robinson, Moeller, and Ode (2010) examined extraversion in relation to *positive affective priming,* which refers to the facilitative effect that a positively valenced stimulus will have on the processing of a subsequently presented stimulus that is also positively valenced. Across four experiments, this priming effect was more pronounced for those higher in extraversion. Again, these effects were interpreted in terms of reward processing theories of extraversion.[3]

Mood induction paradigms have also proven valuable for testing the link between extraversion and reward processing. The basic prediction here is that the pleasurable impact of rewarding stimuli should be more pronounced in extraverted individuals. Despite support from early tests of this hypothesis (e.g., Larsen & Ketelaar, 1991), clear replication of this finding proved to be elusive (Lucas & Baird, 2004). However, this inconsistency may have resulted

---

[3] We are aware that priming effects have come under scrutiny in recent years due to several well-publicized replication failures. For a recent discussion of different kinds of priming effects, particularly in relation to so-called "social priming" (which seem particularly fragile), see Payne, Brown-Iannuzzi, and Loersch (2016).

from the variety of mood induction paradigms and measures of affective states that researchers in this area had used. Over five experiments and a meta-analysis, Smillie, Cooper, Wilt, and Revelle (2012) demonstrated that extraverts reliably show a stronger response to mood inductions with salient rewards or appetitive stimuli, in terms of increases in highly activated/aroused positive affect (e.g., feelings of excitement and energy). On the other hand, they do not differ markedly from introverts in terms of their responses to merely pleasantly valenced mood inductions, or when responses are measured in terms of medium or low activated/aroused positive affect (e.g., feelings of pleasure and contentment). This divergent pattern of findings appears to fit well with research suggesting that dopamine is more strongly implicated in feelings of vigor and energy associated with reward pursuit than with pleasant feelings surrounding reward consummation (Berridge, 2007).

In contrast with the adult literature, the relation between reward sensitivity and extraversion during childhood remains largely unexplored. One study that was originally designed to assess behavioral inhibition revealed a subset of children expressing key characteristics of extraversion (i.e., positive emotionality), together with behavioral approach of rewarding social and nonsocial stimuli, but unfortunately did not include any measures of temperament or personality (Fox, Henderson, Rubin, Calkins, & Schmidt, 2001). More recently, Simonds (2006) found some support for a relation between extraversion and reward processing, as indexed by performance on an incentivized reaction time task, in that extraverted children (ages 8–10 years) performed significantly better during a gain condition compared to a loss condition (in which stickers were used as the incentive rewards). It should be noted, however, that a number of other behavioral indices of reward processing were examined in this study and yielded mainly mixed results, potentially owing to logistical problems arising from the young age of the participants.

One appeal of the reward processing theory is its apparent ability to account for the coherence of different elements of extraversion. For instance the previously described study by Wilt and colleagues (2017) shows how affective, behavioral, and cognitive components of extraversion (e.g., positive emotion, assertive behavior) may be understood as a cascade of processes arising from the motivation to pur-

sue rewarding goals. Similarly, the experience of enthusiasm and excitement in response to rewarding events is both a hallmark of extraversion and central to the concept of something being "rewarding" (Smillie et al., 2012; Smillie, Wilt, Kabbani, Garratt, & Revelle, 2015). Sociability, perhaps the most salient feature of extraversion, may also be understood in terms of reward-directed processes given that status and affiliation are potent rewards embedded in social structures, and we obtain many other rewards (e.g., resources, safety) via other human beings (DeYoung, 2010). In this way, sensitivity to rewards may help to explain why the various components of extraversion cohere as a robust cluster of characteristics (Smillie, 2013).

Despite its influence, there is not a complete consensus regarding the reward processing theory of extraversion. An alternative perspective is that extraverts are particularly sensitive to social rewards. For example, Fishman and Ng (2013) suggest that extraverts' neural responses to social rewards are stronger than their responses to financial rewards. Ashton, Lee, and Paunonen (2002) offered a similar perspective, theorizing that extraversion emerges from a set of mechanisms designed to attract (presumably rewarding) social attention. The view that there is something "special" about social rewards is less parsimonious than the more basic reward processing view, but it seems plausible that some rewards will be more potent for extraverts than others. Indeed, if a reward can be defined as anything for which an individual will work, or expend effort, then there are likely many rewards to which extraverts are not especially responsive, such as the reward of helping someone (related to agreeableness) or the reward of learning something new (related to openness/intellect). There is currently a dearth of research able to clearly indicate which rewards—social or otherwise—are especially potent for extraverted individuals. Thus, further work is needed to clarify and sharpen the boundaries of the reward processing mechanisms underlying extraversion.

Extraversion throughout Development and across the Lifespan

Stability is inherent to the notion of any personality trait, and individuals who score above average on extraversion in their youth are likely to remain at least relatively extraverted throughout their adult lives (Costa & McCrae, 1994; Roberts, Walton, & Viechtbauer, 2006; Roberts, Wood, & Caspi, 2008). Even throughout early development, extraversion demonstrates clear patterns of stability and continuity. For example, in a longitudinal study, Neppl, Donnellan, Scaramella, Widaman, and Spilman (2010) found evidence for continuity of positive emotionality from toddlerhood (age ~2 years) through early childhood (ages 3–5 years) to middle childhood (ages 6–10 years). Similarly, Putnam, Rothbart, and Gartstein (2008) found evidence for continuity of surgency from infancy through toddlerhood to early childhood using age-appropriate versions of Rothbart's temperament scales.

At the same time, changes in extraversion do occur over the lifespan. First, complex changes in the *composition* of extraversion occur throughout the childhood years. From infancy, there are visible individual differences in the expression of positive emotions, manifested as pleasure, joy, and laughter in response to caregiver interactions (Gartstein & Rothbart, 2003; Rothbart & Bates, 2006). From infancy and toddlerhood to early and middle childhood, this cluster of traits becomes broader, as positive emotions combine with motivation to engage socially, and to approach a range of rewarding stimuli and situations (Olino, Klein, Durbin, Hayden, & Buckley, 2005; Shiner & DeYoung, 2013). Interestingly, this childhood dimension of surgency/positive emotionality does not seem to include assertiveness, a core component of extraversion in adults (Shiner & Caspi, 2012; see also Table 7.1).

There are also changes in in *mean levels* of extraversion from infancy through toddlerhood to the preschool years. For example, expressions of positive emotionality (i.e., smiling and vocalizations) increases steadily from birth through the first year of life (Bates, Schermerhorn, & Goodnight, 2010), and social behaviors increase during the toddlerhood and early childhood years (Eisenberg, Fabes, & Spinrad, 2006). From childhood through early adolescence, extraversion and positive emotionality tend to decrease (Lamb, Chuang, Wessels, Broberg, & Hwang, 2002; Prinzie & Deković, 2008; Sallquist et al., 2009). For example, a recent study employing parent reports of the Little Six dimensions in cross-sectional data for 16,000 individuals between ages 3 and 20 found that both extraversion and activity decreased as age increased (Soto, 2016). Overall, these studies indicate that extraversion declines throughout childhood before leveling off in late adolescence.

Throughout adulthood, most of the Big Five traits show some pattern of mean-level change. Several studies in multiple cultures have found evidence of a progressive decline in extraversion as individuals age (Allik et al., 2004; Costa & McCrae, 1994; McCrae et al., 2000, 2004). However, other researchers have suggested that changes in Extraversion over the lifespan diverge for two major components of extraversion: social dominance and social vitality (Helson & Kwan, 2000; see also Table 7.1). The former comprises traits such as assertiveness, confidence, and independence, and appears to increase throughout the lifespan. The latter comprises traits such as sociability, enthusiasm, and energy level, and shows a modest decline (Roberts et al., 2006). This pattern of change may fit with the notion that personality changes generally trend toward increasing "psychosocial maturity" across the lifespan (Greenberger & Sørensen, 1974; Roberts et al., 2008).

There has been some disagreement in the literature regarding the causes of mean-level shifts in extraversion throughout adulthood (see Roberts & Caspi, 2001). Behavioral genetic (McCrae et al., 2000; see also Buss, 1991), nonhuman primate (e.g., Weiss & King, 2014), and cross-cultural (e.g., McCrae et al., 2004) studies point to an evolved, genetically controlled maturation sequence. But numerous environmental influences—such as developmental tasks that require greater sociability and authority—are also at work. For example, most humans face the task of developing a career, which often involves taking on various social roles and responsibilities (e.g., working in a team, rising to leadership and management positions). In a longitudinal study following women from age 21 through age 43, Roberts (1997) found that women who involved themselves more in the world of work experienced increases in components of extraversion associated with assertiveness and social boldness, compared to those who worked less. Similar changes were observed in a subsequent study of young adults, proportional to the levels of power and authority they experienced in their work roles (Roberts, Caspi, & Moffitt, 2003). Such experiences potentially contribute to the mean-level increases observed for the social dominance component of extraversion throughout adult life (Roberts et al., 2006). Conversely, settling down and starting a family may narrow social circles, and aging often brings declines in physical energy and increased risk of morbidities and functional limitations (e.g., House,

Lantz, & Herd, 2005; Rowe & Kahn, 1987). These factors may contribute to the mean-level decreases in the social vitality component of extraversion.

Change may also come from people purposefully altering their personality trajectory (Hudson & Frayley, 2015). For many, the notion that we can shape our own personality at will is a powerful one—powerful enough to drive a worldwide multibillion-dollar self-help industry. It is easy to imagine why one might have the goal to become more outgoing or talkative, as part of what has been referred to as one's "personal projects" (Little, 2008). For example, many job roles involve leading others and demonstrating ambition, and many social situations create pressure to be talkative, enthusiastic, and gregarious. These pressures may lead more introverted people to desire increases in their levels of extraversion, and to actively work toward this goal. Evidence from ESM studies suggest that, on a moment-to-moment basis, we alter our expressed level of extraversion depending on the goal we are currently pursuing (McCabe & Fleeson, 2012, 2016). When people are trying to connect with or lead others, to attract attention, make a positive impression, or simply "get things done," they increase their levels of extraverted behavior. Over time, cultivation of the habit of enacted extraversion may coalesce into a more extraverted personality (Hudson & Frayley, 2015).

In summary, amid moderate rank-order stability across the lifespan, extraversion is also pliable. The very nature of extraversion shifts and evolves throughout the early years of life, with some aspects of personality emerging at the core of this domain (e.g., assertiveness), while others drift to the periphery (e.g., activity). Following a general decline in mean levels of extraversion throughout childhood, we then see a general leveling off in adolescence, following by diverging trajectories for different components of extraversion throughout adulthood. These changes appear to be driven partly by genetic factors, partly by environmental factors, and may even be shaped by the goals we set for ourselves.

"La Vida Extravertida"

We set the scene for this chapter by describing a fictitious extravert, Tom, as viewed through the eyes of a new coworker, Erika, as she pieced together a first impression of him. How might this initial impression broaden and deepen over time as she gets to know Tom better? What are extraverts really like? What is it like to be extraverted? And how do extraverts experience and create their worlds? In this final section, we describe some examples of how extraversion manifests in everyday behavior and experience, with the aim of painting a broad picture of the extraverted life.

The levels of gregariousness, dominance, and social engagement that mark extraverted individuals color their behavioral landscapes. In video recordings of social interactions, extraverts have been found to show more enthusiasm and energy, to speak in a loud voice, and to be more verbally and nonverbally expressive than introverts (Funder & Sneed, 1993). In everyday life, extraverts engage in more conversations, say more words, express a greater amount of positive emotion, and spend less time alone (Mehl, Gosling, & Pennebaker, 2006). In a fascinating series of studies, Gosling, Ko, Mannarelli, and Morris (2002) demonstrated that ratings of personality based on the spaces that individuals inhabit (e.g., university dormitory rooms, workplace offices) corresponded with their self-reported extraversion. Cues of extraversion included a room being decorated, cheerful, cluttered, distinctive, and perceived as unconventional. Ratings were even more accurate for websites ($r = .38$), showing that even online "spaces" are shaped by our personality (Vazire & Gosling, 2004). Extraversion also manifests physically, in peoples' stance (energetic), clothing (stylish), facial expressions (smiling), and basic appearance (neat, healthy) (Nauman et al., 2009).

Positivity and sociability also permeate the content of extraverts' linguistic behaviors. In self-narratives, extraverts express a greater amount of positive emotion and use more social words than their introverted counterparts (e.g., Hirsh & Peterson, 2009; Pennebaker & King, 1999). Online, they talk about themselves more and document their lives in greater detail (Gill, Nowson, & Oberlander, 2009). A study of nearly 70,000 Facebook users provides a linguistic snapshot of how extraversion manifests in everyday life (Kern et al., 2014). As depicted in Figure 7.1, the words that were most strongly correlated with extraversion are clearly dominated by expressions of enthusiasm (e.g., "so excited," "can't wait," "sooo," "!!!," "love my

FIGURE 7.1. The top 100 words and phrases most strongly correlated with extraversion, based on 452 million word and phrases across 69,792 Facebook users. Adapted from Kern et al. (2014). Larger words are more strongly correlated with extraversion.

life," and "great night") and sociability ("bestie," "fam," "party," "we," and "text me").

The behavioral manifestations of extraversion shape the way that extraverted individuals experience their world, as well as the impressions that others form of them. As Eaton and Funder (2003) explain, the interpersonal behaviors that mark a prototypical extravert have consequences for how others behave toward them, which in turn reinforces their own personality. These feedback-loops may explain, for example, why extraverts—who typically behave toward others in ways that are more bold, assertive, and dominant—perceive themselves to have more power and influence in their social circles (Anderson, John, & Keltner, 2012), believe they make stronger contributions to their social affairs (Smillie, Wilt, et al., 2015; Sun et al., 2017), and attain social positions with higher status or authority (Roberts et al., 2003). It may likewise explain why friends of extraverts describe the development of those friendships using "force–impact" metaphors (e.g., "We *hit it off*"; "He *blew me away*"). On the other hand, the tendencies of extraverts toward interpersonal warmth and affiliation may account for their propensity for developing larger social circles (Lönnqvist & Itkonen, 2014), more active social lives (e.g., Lucas, Le, & Dyrenforth, 2008; Watson, Clark, McIntyre, & Hamaker, 1992), as well as closer and more satisfying friendships (Berry, Willingham, & Thayer, 2000; Festa, McNamara Barry, Sherman, & Grover, 2012; Wilson, Harris, & Vazire, 2015).

One of the most robustly established insights into the extraverted life is evidence that extraverts may generally be happier than their introverted counterparts. To some extent, this follows from the fact that positive emotionality, one of the key ingredients of well-being (e.g., Butler & Kern, 2016; Diener, 1984), is one of the defining features of extraversion (see Table 7.1). However, extraversion is also a robust correlate of multiple aspects of well-being beyond positive emotion, such as measures of life satisfaction and happiness (see Steel, Schmidt, & Shultz, 2008, for a meta-analytic review). Substantial positive correlations between extraversion and over a dozen well-being dimensions were observed in a more recent study by Sun, Kaufman, and Smillie (2018), but with an interesting caveat: The higher level of well-being enjoyed by extraverts is almost entirely driven by aspects of extraversion concerning enthusiasm and sociability, and is largely unrelated to aspects concerned with assertiveness and dominance. Another important caveat to note is that the happiness of extraverts does not entail the misery of introverts. Indeed, introverts generally self-report being happy, but simply do not score quite as high as extraverts on measures of well-being (Zelenski, Sobocko, & Whelan, 2014). Moreover, if we shift the focus to physical well-being, we find that extraversion may be a mixed blessing: On the one hand, extraverts have strong social systems, which are health protective (Taylor, 2011), but their propensity toward impulsive or risky behaviors may place them at greater risk for accidents and early mortality (Chapman, Roberts, & Duberstein, 2011; Nettle, 2005).

Overall, how can we describe the extraverted life? Research shows that the typical extravert experiences a life filled with friendship, laughter, thrilling experiences, and joy. Extraverts are zestful, dominate the room with their presence, fill the silence in conversation, and exude enthusiasm and charm. Such characteristics are apparent in how a person speaks, writes, behaves, dresses, and interacts with others. These characteristics appear in the activities that the extravert chooses and the social interactions they create, how other people interact with them, and how they perceive themselves and experience the world. Of course, this does not mean that all extraverted individuals are always this way. Rather, the average extravert is simply more likely to express such behaviors than the average introvert. And as most people fall somewhere between these two extremes, we may all identify with facets of the extraverted life at different times and across different circumstances.

Concluding Remarks

Throughout history, extraversion has repeatedly emerged from the efforts of philosophers and psychologists to identify and understand the fundamental psychological axes along which people differ. This domain of personality reflects our level of positivity, sociability, energy, and dominance, and may have a common underlying basis in our sensitivity to rewarding stimuli. Traits within the extraversion domain appear very early in life, and their development across the life course is shaped both by genetics and life experiences. In turn, they shape individuals' experiences through the social interactions and situations toward which extraverts are drawn, and through extraverts' impact on the environments they inhabit. Extraversion has implications for one's well-being, social relationships, and everyday behaviors. Of course, many of the strands of literature that we have reviewed are obscured by inconsistent findings, most causal pathways are extremely ambiguous, and the full implications of the extraversion continuum remain to be discovered. But there are also facts about extraversion that have been reinforced over time by steadily mounting evidence. And as extraversion continues to

captures the interest of researchers and general audiences alike, it will continue to play an important role in personality theory and research for many years to come.

ACKNOWLEDGMENTS

We are grateful to Nicholas Tan for his assistance in our literature review for this chapter, and to the editorial team for constructive feedback on the first draft.

REFERENCES

Allen, T. A., & DeYoung, C. G. (2017). Personality neuroscience and the Five Factor model. In T. A. Widiger (Ed.), *Oxford handbook of the Five Factor model* (pp. 319–352). New York: Oxford University Press.

Allik, J. (2005). Personality dimensions across cultures. *Journal of Personality Disorders, 19*(3), 212–232.

Allik, J., Laidra, K., Realo, A., & Pullman, H. (2004). Personality development from 12 to 18 years of age: Changes in mean levels and structure of traits. *European Journal of Personality, 18,* 445–462.

Anderson, C., John, O. P., & Keltner, D. (2012). The personal sense of power. *Journal of Personality, 80*(2), 313–344.

Ashton, M. C., Lee, K., & de Vries, R. E. (2014). The HEXACO Honesty–Humility, Agreeableness, and Emotionality Factors: A review of research and theory. *Personality and Social Psychology Review, 18,* 139–152.

Ashton, M. C., Lee, K., & Paunonen, S. V. (2002). What is the central feature of extraversion?: Social attention versus reward sensitivity. *Journal of Personality and Social Psychology, 83,* 245–252.

Bates, J. E., Schermerhorn, A. C., & Goodnight, J. A. (2010). Temperament and personality through the lifespan. In R. M. Lerner, M. E. Lamb, & A. M. Freund (Eds.), *The handbook of life-span development: Vol. 2. Social and emotional development* (pp. 208–253). Hoboken, NJ: Wiley.

Beck, E., Burnet, K. L., & Vosper, J. (2006). Birth-order effects on facets of extraversion. *Personality and Individual Differences, 40*(5), 953–959.

Berridge, K. C. (2007). The debate over dopamine's role in reward: the case for incentive salience. *Psychopharmacology, 191,* 391–431.

Berry, D. S., Willingham, J. K., & Thayer, C. A. (2000). Affect and personality as predictors of conflict and closeness in young adults' friendships. *Journal of Research in Personality, 34*(1), 84–107.

Borkenau, P., Brecke, S., Mottig, C., & Paelecke, M. (2009). Extraversion is accurately perceived after a 50-ms exposure to a face. *Journal of Research in Personality, 43*(4), 703–706.

Bouchard, T. J., Jr., & McGue, M. (2003). Genetic and

environmental influences on human psychological differences. *Developmental Neurobiology, 54,* 4–45.

Breil, S. M., Geukes, K., Wilson, R. E., Nestler, S., Vazire, S., & Back, M. D. (2016*). Zooming into real-life extraversion—How personality and situation shape sociability in social interactions.* Retrieved from *https://osf.io/w96mv.*

Brown, N. A., Blake, A. B., & Sherman, R. A. (2017). A snapshot of the life as lived: Wearable cameras in social and personality psychology science. *Social Psychological and Personality Science, 8*(5), 592–600.

Buss, A., & Plomin, R. (1975). *A temperament theory of personality development.* New York: Wiley.

Buss, D. M. (1991). Evolutionary personality psychology. *Annual Review of Psychology, 42,* 459–491.

Butler, J., & Kern, M. L. (2016). The PERMA-Profiler: A brief multidimensional measure of flourishing. *International Journal of Wellbeing, 6,* 1–48.

Cain, S. (2012). *Quiet: The power of introverts in a world that can't stop talking.* New York: Crown.

Caspi, A., & Shiner, R. L. (2006). Personality development. In W. Damon & R. Lerner (Series Eds.) & N. Eisenberg (Vol. Ed.), *Handbook of child psychology: Vol. 3. Social, emotional, and personality development* (6th ed., pp. 300–365). New York: Wiley.

Cattell, R. B. (1957). *Personality and motivation structure and measurement.* New York: World Book Company.

Cervone, D. (2005). Personality architecture: within-person structures and processes. *Annual Review of Psychology, 56,* 423–452.

Chabris, C. F., Lee, J. J., Cesarini, D., Benjamin, D. J., & Laibson, D. I. (2015). The Fourth Law of Behavior Genetics. *Current Directions in Psychological Science, 24,* 304–312.

Chapman, B. P., Roberts, B., & Duberstein, P. (2011). Personality and longevity: Knowns, unknowns, and implications for public health and personalized medicine. *Journal of Aging Research, 2011,* Article No. 759170.

Conner, T. S., & Barrett, L. F. (2012). Trends in ambulatory self-report: The role of momentary experience in psychosomatic medicine. *Psychosomatic Medicine, 74,* 327–337.

Conner, T. S., & Mehl, M. R. (2015). Ambulatory assessment: Methods for studying everyday life. In R. A. Scott, S. M. Kosslyn, & N. Pinkerton (Eds.), *Emerging trends in the social and behavioral sciences* (pp. 1–13). Hoboken, NJ: Wiley.

Cooper, A. J., Duke, E., Pickering, A. D., & Smillie, L. D. (2014). Individual differences in reward prediction error: Contrasting relations between feedback-related negativity and trait measures of reward sensitivity, impulsivity and extraversion. *Frontiers in Human Neuroscience, 8,* 248.

Costa, P. T., Jr., & McCrae, R. R. (1994). Set like plaster?: Evidence for the stability of adult personality. In T. F. Heatherton & J. L. Weinberger (Eds.), *Can personality change?* (pp. 21–40). Washington, DC: American Psychological Association.

Costa, P. T., Jr., & McCrae, R. R. (1995). Domains and facets: Hierarchical personality assessment using the Revised NEO Personality Inventory. *Journal of Personality Assessment, 64,* 21–50.

Damian, R. I., & Roberts, B. W. (2015a). The associations of birth order with personality and intelligence in a representative sample of U.S. high school students. *Journal of Research in Personality, 58,* 96–105.

Damian, R. I., & Roberts, B. W. (2015b). Settling the debate on birth order and personality. *Proceedings of the National Academy of Sciences of the USA, 112,* 14119–14120.

de Moor, M. H. M., Costa, P. T., Terracciano, A., Krueger, R. F., de Geus, E. J. C., Toshiko, T., et al. (2012). Meta-analysis of genome-wide association studies for personality. *Molecular Psychiatry, 17,* 337–349.

Depue, R. A., & Collins, P. F. (1999). Neurobiology of the structure of personality: Dopamine, facilitation of incentive motivation, and extraversion. *Behavioral and Brain Sciences, 22,* 491–569.

Depue, R. A., & Fu, Y. (2013). On the nature of extraversion: Variation in conditioned contextual activation of dopamine-facilitated affective, cognitive, and motor processes. *Frontiers in Human Neuroscience, 7,* 288.

DeYoung, C. G. (2010). Personality neuroscience and the biology of traits. *Social and Personality Psychology Compass, 4,* 1165–1180.

DeYoung, C. G. (2013). The neuromodulator of exploration: A unifying theory of the role of dopamine in personality. *Frontiers in Human Neuroscience, 7,* 762.

DeYoung, C. G. (2015). Cybernetic Big Five theory. *Journal of Research in Personality, 56,* 33–58.

DeYoung, C. G., Quilty, L. C., & Peterson, J. B. (2007). Between facets and domains: 10 aspects of the Big Five. *Journal of Personality and Social Psychology, 93*(5), 880–896.

DeYoung, C. G., Weisberg, Y. J., Quilty, L. C., & Peterson, J. B. (2013). Unifying the aspects of the Big Five, the interpersonal circumplex, and trait affiliation. *Journal of Personality, 81*(5), 465–475.

Diener, E. (1984). Subjective well-being. *Psychological Bulletin, 95,* 542–575.

Dyson, M. W., Olino, T. M., Durbin, C. E., Goldsmith, H. H., & Klein, D. N. (2012). The structure of temperament in preschoolers: A two-stage factor analytic approach. *Emotion, 12,* 44–57.

Eaton, L. G., & Funder, D. C. (2003). The creation and consequences of the social world: An interactional analysis of extraversion. *European Journal of Personality, 17*(5), 375–395.

Eisenberg, N., Fabes, R. A., & Spinrad, T. L. (2006). Prosocial development. In N. Eisenberg, W. Damon, & R. M. Lerner (Eds.), *Handbook of child psychology: Vol. 3. Social, emotional, and personality development* (pp. 646–718). Hoboken, NJ: Wiley.

Evans, D. E., & Rothbart, M. K. (2007). Developing a

model for adult temperament. *Journal of Research in Personality, 41,* 868–888.

Eysenck, H. J. (1947). *Dimensions of personality.* New York: Praeger.

Eysenck, H. J. (1967). *The biological basis of personality.* London: Thomas.

Eysenck, H., Barrett, P., Wilson, G., & Jackson, C. (1992). Primary trait measurement of the 21 components of the P-E-N system. *European Journal of Psychological Assessments, 8,* 109–117.

Festa, C. C., McNamara Barry, C., Sherman, M. F., & Grover, R. L. (2012). Quality of college students' same-sex friendships as a function of personality and interpersonal competence. *Psychological Reports, 110*(1), 283–296.

Finnigan, K. M., & Vazire, S. (2017). The incremental validity of average state self-reports over global self-reports of personality. *Journal of Personality and Social Psychology.* [Epub ahead of print]

Fishman, I., & Ng, R. (2013). Error-related brain activity in extraverts: Evidence for altered response monitoring in social context. *Biological Psychology, 93*(1), 225–230.

Fleeson, W., & Gallagher, P. (2009). The implications of Big Five standing for the distribution of trait manifestation in behavior: Fifteen experience-sampling studies and a meta-analysis. *Journal of Personality and Social Psychology, 97*(6), 1097–1114.

Fleeson, W., Malanos, A. B., & Achille, N. M. (2002). An intraindividual process approach to the relationship between extraversion and positive affect: Is acting extraverted as "good" as being extraverted? *Journal of Personality and Social Psychology, 83,* 1409–1422.

Fox, N. A., Henderson, H. A., Rubin, K. H., Calkins, S. D., & Schmidt, L. A. (2001). Continuity and discontinuity of behavioral inhibition and exuberance: Psycho-physiological and behavioral influences across the first four years of life. *Child Development, 72,* 1–21.

Friedman, H. S. (2000). Long-term relations of personality and health: Dynamisms, mechanisms, tropisms. *Journal of Personality, 68,* 1089–1107.

Friedman, H. S., & Martin, L. R. (2011). *The longevity project: Surprising discoveries for health and long life from the landmark eight-decade study.* New York: Hudson Street Press.

Funder, D. C., & Colvin, C. R. (1988). Friends and strangers: Acquaintanceship, agreement, and the accuracy of personality judgment. *Journal of Personality and Social Psychology, 55,* 149–158.

Funder, D. C., & Sneed, C. D. (1993). Behavioral manifestations of personality: An ecological approach to judgmental accuracy. *Journal of Personality and Social Psychology, 64,* 479–490.

Furr, R. M., & Funder, D. C. (in press). Persons, situations, and person–situation interactions. In O. P. John & R. W. Robins (Eds.), *Handbook of personality: Theory and research* (4th ed.). New York: Guilford Press.

Gartstein, M. A., & Rothbart, M. K. (2003). Studying infant temperament via the Revised Infant Behavior Questionnaire. *Infant Behavior and Development, 166,* 1–23.

Gill, A. J., Nowson, S., & Oberlander, J. (2009, May). *What are they blogging about?: Personality, topic and motivation in blogs.* Presented at the proceedings of the Third International ICWSM Conference, San Jose, CA.

Goldberg, L. R. (1982). From Ace to Zombie: Some explorations in the language of personality. In C. D. Spielberger & J. N. Butcher (Eds.), *Advances in personality assessment* (Vol. 1, pp. 203–234). Hillsdale, NJ: Erlbaum.

Goldberg, L. R. (1993). The structure of phenotypic personality traits. *American Psychologist, 4,* 26–34.

Goldberg, L. R. (1999). A broad-bandwidth, public-domain, personality inventory measuring the lower-level facets of several five-factor models. In I. Mervielde, I. Deary, F. De Fruyt, & F. Ostendorf (Eds.), *Personality psychology in Europe* (Vol. 7, pp. 7–28). Tilburg, The Netherlands: Tilburg University Press.

Goldsmith, H. H., & Rothbart, M. K. (1991). Contemporary instruments for assessing early temperament by questionnaire and in the laboratory. In A. Angleitner & J. Strelau (Eds.), *Explorations in temperament* (pp. 249–272). New York: Plenum Press.

Gosling, S. D., & John, O. P. (1999). Personality dimensions in non-human animals: A cross-species review. *Current Directions in Psychological Science, 8,* 69–75.

Gosling, S. D., Ko, S. J., Mannarelli, T., & Morris, M. E. (2002). A room with a cue: Judgments of personality based on offices and bedrooms. *Journal of Personality and Social Psychology, 82,* 379–398.

Gray, J. A. (1964). *Pavlov's typology: Recent theoretical and experimental developments from the laboratory of B. M. Teplov.* Oxford, UK: Pergamon.

Greenberger, E., & Sørensen, A. B. (1974). Toward a concept of psychosocial maturity. *Journal of Youth and Adolescence, 3,* 329–358.

Guilford, J. P., & Guilford, R. B. (1934). An analysis of the factors in a typical test of introversion–extroversion. *Journal of Abnormal and Social Psychology, 28,* 377–399.

Halverson, C. F., Havill, V. L., Deal, J., Baker, S. R., Victor, J. B., Pavlopoulos, V., et al. (2003). Personality structure as derived from parental ratings of free descriptions of children: The inventory of child individual differences. *Journal of Personality, 71,* 995–1026.

Heller, D., Komar, J., & Lee, W. B. (2007). The dynamics of personality states, goals, and well-being. *Personality and Social Psychology Bulletin, 33,* 898–910.

Helson, R., & Kwan, V. S. Y. (2000). Personality development in adulthood: The broad picture and processes in one longitudinal sample. In S. Hampson (Ed.), *Advances in personality psychology* (Vol. 1, pp. 77–106). London: Routledge.

Heymans, G., & Wiersma, E. (1906–1909). Beitrage zur speziellen psychologie auf grundeiner massenunter-suchung [Contributions to specialist psychology on the basis of a large investigation]. *Zeitschrift für Psychologie, 42,* 46, 49, 51.

Hirsh, J. B., & Peterson, J. B. (2009). Personality and language use in self-narratives. *Journal of Research in Personality, 43,* 524–527.

Hofstee, W. K. B., de Raad, B., & Goldberg, L. R. (1992). Integration of the Big Five and circumplex approaches to trait structure. *Journal of Personality and Social Psychology, 63,* 146–163.

Holland, P. C., & Schiffino, F. L. (2016). Mini-review: Prediction errors, attention and associative learning. *Neurobiology of Learning and Memory, 131,* 207–215.

House, J. S., Lantz, P. M., & Herd, P. (2005). Continuity and change in the social stratification of aging and health over the life course: Longitudinal study from 1986 to 2001/2002 [Special issue II]. *Journals of Gerontology B: Psychological Sciences and Social Sciences, 60,* 15–26.

Hudson, N. W., & Fraley, R. C. (2015). Volitional personality trait change: Can people choose to change their personality traits? *Journal of Personality and Social Psychology, 109,* 490–507.

John, O. P., Naumann, L. P., & Soto, C. J. (2008). Paradigm shift to the integrative Big Five trait taxonomy: History: measurement, and conceptual issues. In O. P. John, R. W. Robins, & L. A. Pervin (Eds). *Handbook of personality: Theory and research* (3rd ed., pp. 114–158). New York: Guilford Press.

Jung, C. G. (1921). *Psychologische typen [Psychological types].* Zurich, Switzerland: Rascher & Cie.

Keltner, D., Gruenfeld, D. H., & Anderson, C. (2003). Power, approach, and inhibition. *Psychological Review, 110,* 265–284.

Kern, M. L., Eichstaedt, J. C., Schwartz, H. A., Dziurzynski, L., Ungar, L. H., Stillwell, D. J., et al. (2014). The online social self: An open vocabulary approach to personality. *Assessment, 21,* 158–169.

Kochanska, G., Friesenborg, A. E., Lange, L. A., Martel, M. M., & Kochanska, G. (2004). Parents' personality and infants' temperament as contributors to their emerging relationship. *Journal of Personality and Social Psychology, 86,* 744–759.

Kosinski, M., Stillwell, D., & Graepel, T. (2013). Private traits and attributes are predictable from digital records of human behavior. *Proceedings of the National Academy of Sciences of the USA, 110,* 5802–5805.

Kotelnikova, Y., Olino, T. M., Mackrell, S. V., Jordan, P. L., & Hayden, E. P. (2013). Structure of observed temperament in middle childhood. *Journal of Research in Personality, 47,* 1–19.

Krueger, R. F., & Johnson, W. (2008). Behavioral genetics and personality: A new look at the integration of nature and nurture. In L. A. Pervin, O. P. John, & R. W. Robins (Eds.), *Handbook of personality: Theory and research* (3rd ed., pp. 287–310). New York: Guilford Press.

Krueger, R. F., & Markon, K. E. (2014). The role of the DSM-5 personality trait model in moving toward a quantitative and empirically based approach to classifying personality and psychopathology. *Annual Review of Clinical Psychology, 10,* 477–501.

Lamb, M. E., Chuang, S. S., Wessels, H., Broberg, A. G., & Hwang, C. P. (2002). Emergence and construct validation of the Big Five factors in early childhood: A longitudinal analysis of their ontogeny in Sweden. *Child Development, 73,* 1517–1524.

Larsen, R. J., & Ketelaar, T. (1991). Personality and susceptibility to positive and negative emotional states. *Journal of Personality and Social Psychology, 61,* 132–140.

Lee, K., & Ashton, M. C. (2018). Psychometric properties of the HEXACO-100. *Assessment, 25*(5), 543–556.

Lemery, K. S., Goldsmith, H. H., Klinnert, M. D., & Mrazek, D. A. (1999). Developmental models of infant and childhood temperament. *Developmental Psychology, 35,* 189–204.

Little, B. R. (2008). Personal projects and free traits: Personality and motivation reconsidered. *Social and Personality Psychology Compass, 2/3,* 1235–1254.

Lönnqvist, J., & Itkonen, J. V. A. (2014). It's all about extraversion: Why Facebook friend count doesn't count towards well-being. *Journal of Research in Personality, 53,* 64–67.

Lucas, R. E., & Baird, B. M. (2004). Extraversion and emotional reactivity. *Journal of Personality and Social Psychology, 86,* 473–485.

Lucas, R. E., & Fujita, F. (2000). Factors influencing the relation between extraversion and pleasant affect. *Journal of Personality and Social Psychology, 79,* 1039–1056.

Lucas, R. E., Le, K., & Dyrenforth, P. S. (2008). Explaining the extraversion/positive affect relation: Sociability cannot account for extraverts' greater happiness. *Journal of Personality, 76*(3), 385–414.

Majdandžić, M., van den Boom, D. C., & Heesbeen, D. G. (2008). Peas in a pod: Biases in the measurement of sibling temperament? *Developmental Psychology, 44*(5), 1354–1368.

Markon, K. E., Krueger, R. F., & Watson, D. (2005). Delineating the structure of normal and abnormal personality: An integrative hierarchical approach. *Journal of Personality and Social Psychology, 88*(1), 139–157.

McCabe, K. O., & Fleeson, W. (2012). What is extraversion for?: Integrating trait and motivational perspectives and identifying the purpose of extraversion. *Psychological Science, 23*(12), 1498–1505.

McCabe, K. O., & Fleeson, W. (2016). Are traits useful?: Explaining trait manifestations as tools in the pursuit of goals. *Journal of Personality and Social Psychology, 110,* 287–301.

McCrae, R. R. (1982). Consensual validation of personality traits: Evidence from self-reports and ratings. *Journal of Personality and Social Psychology, 43,* 293–303.

McCrae, R. R., Costa, P. T., Jr., Ĥrebíĉková, M., Ur-bánek, T., Martin, T. A., Oryol, V. E., et al. (2004). Age differences in personality traits across cultures: Self-report and observer perspective. *European Journal of Personality, 18,* 143–157.

McCrae, R. R., Costa, P. T., Jr., Ostendorf, F., Anglei-tner, A., Ĥrebíĉková, M., Avia, M. D., et al. (2000). Nature over nurture: Temperament, personality, and lifespan development. *Journal of Personality and Social Psychology, 78,* 173–186.

McDougall, W. (1908). *Introduction to social psychol-ogy.* London: Methuen.

Mehl, M. R., Gosling, S. D., & Pennebaker, J. W. (2006). Personality in its natural habitat: Manifesta-tions and implicit folk theories of personality in daily life. *Journal of Personality and Social Psychology, 90,* 862–877.

Millon, T. (2012). On the history and future study of personality and its disorders. *Annual Review of Clin-ical Psychology, 8,* 1–19.

Mõttus, R., Kandler, C., Bleidorn, W., Riemann, R., & McCrae, R. R. (2017). Personality traits below facets: The consensual validity, longitudinal stability, heri-tability, and utility of personality nuances. *Journal of Personality and Social Psychology, 112*(3), 474–490.

Mueller, E. M., Burgdorf, C., Chavanon, M. L., Schwei-ger, D., Hennig, J., Wacker, J., et al. (2014). Dopa-mine modulates frontomedial failure processing of agentic introverts versus extraverts in incentive con-texts. *Cognitive, Affective, and Behavioural Neuro-science, 14*(2), 756–768.

Munafo, M. R., Yalcin, B., Willis-Owen, S. A., & Flint, J. (2008). Association of the dopamine D4 recep-tor (DRD4) gene and approach-related personality traits: Meta-analysis and new data. *Biological Psy-chiatry, 63,* 197–206.

Nakao, K., Takaishi, J., Tatsuta, K., Katayama, H., Iwase, M., Yorifuji, K., et al. (2000). The influences of family environment on personality traits. *Psychi-atry and Clinical Neurosciences, 54,* 91–95.

Naumann, L. P., Vazire, S., Rentfrow, P. J., & Gosling, S. D. (2009). Personality judgements based on physi-cal appearance. *Personality and Social Psychology Bulletin, 35,* 1661–1671.

Neppl, T. K., Donnellan, M. B., Scaramella, L. V., Wi-daman, K. F., & Spilman, S. K. (2010). Differential stability of temperament and personality from tod-dlerhood to middle childhood. *Journal of Research in Personality, 44,* 386–396.

Nettle, D. (2005). An evolutionary approach to the ex-traversion continuum. *Evolution and Human Behav-iour, 26,* 363–373.

Olino, T. M., Klein, D. N., Durbin, C. E., Hayden, E. P., & Buckley, M. E. (2005). The structure of extra-version in preschool aged children. *Personality and Individual Differences, 39,* 481–492.

Park, G., Schwartz, H. A., Eichstaedt, J. C., Kern, M. L., Kosinski, M., Stillwell, D. J., et al. (2015). Automatic personality assessment through social media lan-guage. *Journal of Personality and Social Psychol-ogy, 108,* 934–952.

Payne, B. K., Brown-Iannuzzi, J. L., & Loersch, C. (2016). Replicable effects of primes on human be-havior. *Journal of Experimental Psychology: Gen-eral, 145*(10), 1269–1279.

Pennebaker, J. W., & King, L. A. (1999). Linguistic styles: Language use as an individual difference. *Journal of Personality and Social Psychology, 77,* 1296–1312.

Pickering, A. D., & Gray, J. A. (1999). The neuroscience of personality. In L. A. Pervin & O. P. John (Eds.), *Handbook of personality: Theory and research* (2nd ed., pp. 277–299). New York: Guilford Press.

Power, R. A., & Pluess, M. (2015). Heritability estimates of the Big Five personality traits based on common genetic variants. *Translational Psychiatry, 14,* e604.

Prinzie, P., & Deković, M. (2008). Continuity and change of childhood personality characteristics through the lens of teachers. *Personality and Indi-vidual Differences, 45*(1), 82–88.

Putnam, S. P., Gartstein, M. A., & Rothbart, M. K. (2006). Measurement of fine-grained aspects of toddler temperament: The early childhood behavior questionnaire. *Infant Behavior and Development, 29,* 386–401.

Putnam, S. P., Rothbart, M. K., & Gartstein, M. A. (2008). Homotypic and heterotypic continuity of fine-grained temperament during infancy, toddler-hood, and early childhood. *Infant and Child Devel-opment, 17,* 387–405.

Quilty, L. C., DeYoung, C. G., Oakman, J. M., & Bagby, R. M. (2014). Extraversion and behavioral activation: Integrating the components of approach. *Journal of Personality Assessment, 96,* 87–94.

Rammsayer, T. H. (1998). Extraversion and dopamine: Individual differences in responsiveness to changes in dopaminergic activity as a possible biological basis of extraversion. *European Psychologist, 3,* 37–50.

Revelle, W., Wilt, J., & Condon, D. (2011). Individual differences and differential psychology: A brief his-tory and prospect. In T. Chamorro-Premuzic, A. Furnham, & S. von Stumm (Eds.), *The Wiley-Black-well handbook of individual differences* (pp. 3–38). Oxford, UK: Wiley-Blackwell.

Ribot, T. (1890). *Psychologie des sentiments [Psychol-ogy of feelings].* Paris: Delahaye & Lecrosnier.

Roberts, B. W. (1997). Plaster or plasticity: Are adult work experiences associated with personality change in women? *Journal of Personality, 65*(2), 205–232.

Roberts, B. W., & Caspi, A. (2001). Personality develop-ment and the person–situation debate: It's déjà vu all over again. *Psychological Inquiry, 12*(2), 104–109.

Roberts, B. W., Caspi, A., & Moffitt, T. E. (2003). Work experiences and personality: Development in young adulthood. *Journal of Personality and Social Psy-chology, 84*(3), 582–593.

Roberts, B. W., Walton, K., & Viechtbauer, W. (2006).

Patterns of mean-level change in personality traits across the life course: A meta-analysis of longitudinal studies. *Psychological Bulletin, 132,* 1–25.

Roberts, B. W., Wood, D., & Caspi, A. (2008). The development of personality traits in adulthood. In L. A. Pervin, O. P. John, & R. W. Robins (Eds.), *Handbook of personality: Theory and research* (3rd ed., pp. 287–310). New York: Guilford Press.

Robinson, M. D., Moeller, S. K., & Ode S. (2010). Extraversion and reward-related processing: Probing incentive motivation in affective priming tasks. *Emotion, 10*(5), 615–626.

Rocklin, T., & Revelle, W. (1981). The measurement of extraversion: A comparison of the Eysenck Personality Inventory and the Eysenck Personality Questionnaire. *British Journal of Social Psychology, 20,* 279–284.

Rohrer, J. M., Egloff, B., & Schmukle, S. C. (2015). Examining the effects of birth order on personality. *Proceedings of the National Academy of Sciences of the USA, 112,* 14224–14229.

Rothbart, M. K., Ahadi, S. A., Hershey, K., & Fisher, P. (2001). Investigations of temperament at 3 to 7 years: The Children's Behavior Questionnaire. *Child Development, 72,* 1394–1408.

Rothbart, M. K., & Bates, J. E. (2006). Temperament. In W. Damon & R. Lerner (Series Eds.) & N. Eisenberg (Vol. Ed.), *Handbook of child psychology: Vol. 3. Social, emotional, and personality development* (6th ed., pp. 99–166). Hoboken, NJ: Wiley.

Rothbart, M. K., Derryberry, D., & Hershey, K. (2000). Stability of temperament in childhood: Laboratory infant assessment to parent report at seven years. In V. J. Molfese & D. L. Molfese (Eds.), *Temperament and personality development across the life span* (pp. 85–119). Mahwah, NJ: Erlbaum.

Rowe, J. W., & Kahn, R. L. (1987). Human aging: Usual and successful. *Science, 237,* 143–149.

Rusting, C. L. (1999). Interactive effects of personality and mood on emotion-congruent memory and judgment. *Journal of Personality and Social Psychology, 77*(5), 1073–1086.

Sallquist, J. V., Eisenberg, N., Spinrad, T. L., Reiser, M., Hofer, C., Zhou, Q., et al. (2009). Positive and negative emotionality: Trajectories across six years and relations with social competence. *Emotion, 9*(1), 15–28.

Schultz, W. (1998). Predictive reward signal of dopamine neurons. *Journal of Neurophysiology, 80,* 1–27.

Semin, G. R., Rosch, E., & Chassein, J. (1981). A comparison of the common-sense and "scientific" conceptions of extroversion–introversion. *European Journal of Personality, 11,* 77–86.

Shiner, R. L., & Caspi, A. (2012). Temperament and the development of personality traits, adaptations, and narratives. In M. Zentner & R. L. Shiner (Eds.), *Handbook of temperament* (pp. 497–516). New York: Guilford Press.

Shiner, R. L., & DeYoung, C. (2013). The structure of

temperament and personality traits: A developmental perspective. In P. D. Zelazo (Ed.), *The Oxford handbook of developmental psychology: Vol. 2. Self and other* (pp. 113–141). New York: Oxford University Press.

Simonds, J. (2006). *The role of reward sensitivity and response: Execution in childhood extraversion.* Unpublished doctoral dissertation, University of Oregon, Eugene, OR.

Smillie, L. D. (2013). Extraversion and reward processing. *Current Directions in Psychological Science, 22,* 167–172.

Smillie, L. D., Cooper, A., & Pickering, A. D. (2011). Variation in event related potential (ERP) index of dopamine signalling as a function of extraverted personality. *Social Cognitive and Affective Neuroscience, 6,* 646–652.

Smillie, L. D., Cooper, A., Wilt, J., & Revelle, W. (2012). Do extraverts get more bang for the buck?: Refining the affective-reactivity hypothesis of extraversion. *Journal of Personality and Social Psychology, 103,* 306–326.

Smillie, L. D., DeYoung, C. G., & Hall, P. J. (2015). Clarifying the relation between extraversion and positive affect. *Journal of Personality, 83,* 564–574.

Smillie, L. D., Jach, H. K. M., Hughes, D. M., Wacker, J., Cooper, A. J., & Pickering, A. D. (2018). *Extraversion and reward-processing: Consolidating evidence from an electroencephalographic index of reward-prediction-error.* Manuscript under review.

Smillie, L. D., Wilt, J., Kabbani, R., Garratt, C. L., & Revelle, W. (2015). Quality of social experience explains the relation between extraversion and positive affect. *Emotion, 15,* 339–349.

Soto, C. J. (2016). The Little Six personality dimensions from early childhood to early adulthood: Mean-level age and gender differences in parents' reports. *Journal of Personality, 84,* 409–422.

Soto, C. J., & John, O. P. (2014). Traits in transition: The structure of parent-reported personality traits from early childhood to early adulthood. *Journal of Personality, 82,* 182–199.

Soto, C. J., & John, O. P. (2017). The next Big Five Inventory (BFI-2): Developing and assessing a hierarchical model with 15 facets to enhance bandwidth, fidelity, and predictive power. *Journal of Personality and Social Psychology, 113,* 117–143.

Steel, P., Schmidt, J., & Shultz, J. (2008). Refining the relationship between personality and subjective well-being. *Psychological Bulletin, 134,* 138–161.

Sulloway, F. (1996). *Born to rebel: Birth order family dynamics, and creative lives.* New York: Pantheon.

Sun, J., Kaufman, S. B., & Smillie, L. D. (2018). Unique associations between Big Five personality aspects and multiple dimensions of well-being. *Journal of Personality, 86*(2), 158–172.

Sun, J., Stevenson, K., Kabbani, R., Richardson, B., & Smillie, L. D. (2017). The pleasure of making a difference: Perceived social contribution explains the relation between extraverted behavior and positive affect. *Emotion, 17*(5), 794–810.

Tackett, J. L., Krueger, R. F., Iacono, W. G., & McGue, M. (2008). Personality in middle childhood: A hierarchical structure and longitudinal connections with personality in late adolescence. *Journal of Research in Personality, 42,* 1456–1462.

Tackett, J. L., Slobodskaya, H. R., Mar, R. A., Deal, J., Halverson, C. F., Jr., Baker, S. R., et al. (2012). The hierarchical structure of childhood personality in five counties: Continuity from early childhood to early adolescence. *Journal of Personality, 80,* 847–879.

Taylor, S. E. (2011). Social support: A review. In H. S. Friedman (Ed.), *The Oxford handbook of health psychology* (pp. 189–214). New York: Oxford University Press.

Tellegen, A. (1982). *Brief manual for the Multidimensional Personality Questionnaire.* Unpublished manuscript, University of Minnesota, Minneapolis, MN.

Tellegen, A., & Waller, N. G. (2008). Exploring personality through test construction: Development of the Multidimensional Personality Questionnaire. In G. J. Boyle, G. Matthews, & D. H. Saklofske (Eds.), *The SAGE handbook of personality theory and assessment: Vol 2. Personality measurement and testing* (pp. 261–292). Thousand Oaks, CA: SAGE.

Thomas, A., & Chess, S. (1977). *Temperament and development.* New York: Brunner/Mazel.

Vazire, S. (2010). Who knows what about a person?: The self–other knowledge asymmetry (SOKA) model. *Journal of Personality and Social Psychology, 98,* 281–300.

Vazire, S., & Gosling, S. D. (2004). E-perceptions: Personality impressions based on personal websites. *Personality and Individual Differences, 87,* 123–132.

Wacker, J., Chavanon, M.-L., & Stemmler, G. (2006). Investigating the dopaminergic basis of extraversion in humans: A multilevel approach. *Journal of Personality and Social Psychology, 91,* 171–187.

Wacker, J., Mueller, C. J., Pizzagalli, D. A., Hennig, J., & Stemmler, G. (2013). Dopamine D2 receptor blockade reverses the association between trait BAS and frontal asymmetry in an approach motivational context. *Psychological Science, 24,* 489–497.

Wacker, J., & Smillie, L. D. (2015). Trait extraversion and dopamine function. *Social and Personality Psychology Compass, 9*(6), 225–238.

Watson, D., Clark, L. A., McIntyre, C. W., & Hamaker, S. (1992). Affect, personality, and social activity. *Journal of Personality and Social Psychology, 63,* 1011–1025.

Weiss, A., & King, J. E. (2014). Great ape origins of personality maturation and sex differences: A study of orangutans and chimpanzees. *Journal of Personality and Social Psychology, 108,* 648–664.

Wiggins, J. S. (1979). A psychological taxonomy of trait-descriptive terms: The interpersonal domain. *Journal of Personality and Social Psychology, 37,* 395–412.

Wilson, R. E., Harris, K., & Vazire, S. (2015). Personality and friendship satisfaction in daily life: Do everyday social interactions account for individual differences in friendship satisfaction? *European Journal of Personality, 29*(2), 173–186.

Wilt, J. A., Bleidorn, W., & Revelle, W. (2017). Velocity explains the links between personality states and affect. *Journal of Research in Personality, 69,* 86–95.

Wilt, J., Noftle, E. E., Fleeson, W., & Spain, J. S. (2012). The dynamic role of personality states in mediating the relationship between extraversion and positive affect. *Journal of Personality, 80*(5), 1205–1236.

Wilt, J., & Revelle, W. (2017). Extraversion. In T. A. Widiger (Ed.), *Oxford handbook of the Five Factor Model* (pp. 57–82). New York: Oxford University Press.

Wu, C. C., Samanez-Larkin, G. R., Katovich, K., & Knutson, B. (2014). Affective traits link to reliable neural markers of incentive anticipation. *NeuroImage, 84,* 279–289.

Zelenski, J. M., Santoro, M. S., & Whelan, D. C. (2012). Would introverts be better off if they acted more like extraverts?: Exploring emotional and cognitive consequences of counterdispositional behavior. *Emotion, 12*(2), 290–303.

Zelenski, J. M., Sobocko, K., & Whelan, D. C. (2014). Introversion, solitude, and subjective well-being. In R. J. Coplan & J. C. Bowker (Eds.), *The handbook of solitude: Psychological perspectives on social isolation, social withdrawal, and being alone* (pp. 184–201). Chichester, UK: Wiley.

Zentner, M., & Bates, J. E. (2008). Child temperament. *European Journal of Developmental Science, 2,* 2–37.

CHAPTER 8

Negative Emotionality and Neuroticism from Childhood through Adulthood

A Lifespan Perspective

Rebecca L. Shiner

Negative emotions—anxiety, irritation, sadness, vulnerability, insecurity, moodiness—are a universal aspect of human experience. Most people experience at least some of these emotions every day of their lives. Yet people vary widely in how often and how intensely they experience negative emotions. The trait of *neuroticism* reflects individual differences in people's predispositions to experience and express such negative emotions. This trait is typically called *negative emotionality* in early childhood rather than neuroticism, but its core is the same. From infancy through adulthood, compared to people who are more emotionally stable, people who score high on trait neuroticism experience larger fluctuations in their mood, higher levels of fear and anxiety in stressful situations, more irritation and frustration when their desires are thwarted, and greater sadness over losses, both large and small.

The comedian, actor, and podcast host Marc Maron has made his high levels of negative emotions the foundation for much of his work; neuroticism is his trademark. Now, at age 54, he has achieved considerable success; he has starred in two television shows and regularly tours doing stand-up comedy. He has been re-

cording his successful podcast *WTF* since 2009; every week, Maron sits down in his garage to interview other comedians and actors, as well as artists, musicians, authors, and other well-known creative people, and he typically manages to get even the most recalcitrant guests to open up about their struggles and triumphs. Maron's guests are not just people in the entertainment industry; he has interviewed journalists, public intellectuals, and politicians as well. Even Barack Obama made his way to Maron's garage in 2015 for a moving interview about his perspectives on family, race, the Presidency, and the possibilities for large-scale societal change.

Maron's story is one of both triumphing over his high levels of negative emotions and using them as a source for good things in his life. He was born in 1963 into an upper-middle-class Jewish family, with a distant, bipolar orthopedic surgeon for a father and a narcissistic, weight- and-appearance-obsessed real estate broker for a mother. Marc grew up with his father, mother, and younger brother in Albuquerque, New Mexico, where he was often left to his own devices because his parents were too focused on their own lives to pay much attention to him. He looked to people like Keith Richards and Woody Allen to develop his identity. Maron describes his childhood as follows:

> When I was a kid I loved to talk to people. . . . I wanted to be engaged by people who had interesting lives, thoughts, ideas, and information. I needed it. I think part of my compulsion was because I didn't feel whole. My dad wasn't around much and my mother was into herself. I didn't feel like I fit in. I was an overly sensitive, creative kid. I didn't feel comfortable in my body, and I was angry. I was painfully insecure, and being part of someone else's life for a while always felt like a relief. As long as I was talking to people, I wasn't lost in my own fear, pain, and dark thoughts. It was like I was using them as a battery for my own soul (Maron & McDonald, 2017, p. 1)

After graduating in 1986 from Boston University with a degree in English, Maron began trying his hand at stand-up comedy, and he eventually started doing radio shows and spots on television. But over the next two decades, professional success eluded him, as he bounced from one venture to the next. Romantic success eluded Maron as well; he married and divorced twice and struggled to establish a stable, positive romantic relationship. Maron also developed serious addictions to cocaine and alcohol, and his addictions worsened his underlying struggles with anxiety and despair. At one point, he contemplated suicide.

Maron finally got sober in 1999, after coming to realize that he would likely die early if he didn't, but he continued to struggle in his personal and professional life. At a particularly low point in 2009, he decided to start his podcast. He began inviting guests to his garage for long, rambling, vulnerable conversations that opened up their lives in ways that touched a chord with listeners. As comedian John Oliver has put it, "An unremarkable garage took a very funny, very broken man into its wooden womb and helped him create one of the most recognizable podcasts in the world" (in Maron & McDonald, 2017, p. ix). It turned out that Maron's lifelong knack for engaging people as a means of coping with his own distress made him a terrific interviewer; he used his honesty about his own suffering, mistakes, and struggles to draw his guests into genuine and frank conversations about their own lives. Maron's success at his podcast gave him a platform to launch his career as an actor and revived his stand-up comedy career. Over the last several years, he seems to be constantly working on himself, finding ways to better manage and cope with his still-present anxiety, anger, envy, and general existential despair. And he has reached some kind of self-acceptance as well:

> After years of talking to people, I can honestly say that I have learned to accept myself for who I am and accept my issues and problems for what they are. If you learn to shut up and listen and empathize with others, your emotions start to regulate a bit, your problems become manageable, and your issues become tedious to you, and maybe you can let them go for a while, or temper them. (Maron & McDonald, 2017, p. 232)

Maron remains far higher than average on the trait of neuroticism, but he seems to be okay with that. He has achieved career success in a way that he finds deeply satisfying, and he has achieved a kind of peace with himself.

Maron's story offers important insights into the ways that negative emotionality and neuroticism develop and change; affect coping, relationships, and daily functioning; and both shape and are shaped by challenging and stressful life experiences. In this chapter, I review recent research investigating the nature and development of trait neuroticism from early childhood through adulthood. The common theme running through this chapter is that trait neuroticism indexes individual differences in an underlying biological system that equips people to detect and respond to threat, punishment, and uncertainty (DeYoung & Allen, Chapter 5, this volume; Shackman, Tromp, et al., 2016; Shiner & DeYoung, 2013). According to this model, levels of negative emotionality reflect variations in two biological systems: a *behavioral inhibition system* (BIS) that prompts people to respond to situations containing both rewards and threats with avoidance, vigilance, and rumination, and a *fight–flight–freeze system* (FFFS) that activates an anger (fight) or avoidance (flight or fear) response in the face of immediate threat, frustration, or punishment (Gray & McNaughton, 2000; see also DeYoung & Allen, Chapter 5, this volume; Shiner & DeYoung, 2013). In the face of uncertain and ambiguous situations, the BIS prompts avoidance, anxiety, vigilance, inhibition, and rumination, whereas the FFFS prompts fear, panic, or anger in the face of imminent threats that one must escape or eliminate. This model accounts well for the patterns of findings for negative emotionality and neuroticism described in this chapter, including the consistent finding that threatening or stressful experiences increase levels of neuroticism, and that neuroticism increases the likelihood of having such experiences.

The review of neuroticism in this chapter is necessarily selective because the literature on this trait is vast. I have chosen to focus on four fundamental issues regarding the trait. The first section of the chapter describes what researchers have learned about the components of the trait—from negative emotionality in infancy through neuroticism in later childhood, adolescence, and adulthood, as well as mean-level changes in each stage of life. The second section addresses the cognitive, motivational, and regulatory processes that accompany and affect the outcomes of neuroticism. The third section looks at what is known about the interplay among neuroticism, stress, and adversity, including the findings that neuroticism predicts increases in stressful experiences, and threatening and stressful experiences predict increases in neuroticism. In the final section, I briefly summarize the chapter, make suggestions for future research, and conclude with a more positive perspective on neuroticism, showing that this trait in particular seems to be malleable in response to positive, supportive, secure life experiences. Throughout, I highlight the different insights that come from research on the trait in youth versus adults, as well as the ways that we may develop a more seamless lifespan perspective on this important trait.

The Fundamentals of Neuroticism: What Is It "Made of" and How Does It Change across the Lifespan?

The core makeup of the traits of negative emotionality or neuroticism remains remarkably similar across the lifespan, perhaps more so than for any other Big Five trait: At every point in the life course, the core of this trait remains the experience and expression of negative emotions. Table 8.1 provides examples of temperament and personality questionnaire items used to measure negative emotionality, negative affectivity, and neuroticism in infancy, preschool, middle childhood and adolescence, and adulthood. These items help illustrate both commonalities and changes in the makeup of this trait over time. It is notable that there are fewer descriptors for the low end of this trait than there

are descriptors for the high end; the low end includes stability, self-confidence, and effective coping with stress.

Although the heart of this trait remains a predisposition toward negative emotionality from infancy through adulthood, neuroticism broadens with age in in ways that reflect children's and adolescents' increasingly complex capacities for cognition and self-awareness. Infants vary greatly in their typical negative emotions—including frustration, fear, discomfort, and sadness—and individual differences in these negative emotions form an overarching negative affectivity trait in the first year of life (Gartstein & Rothbart, 2003; Rothbart, 2011). Research on temperament makes it clear that these same aspects of the trait—frustration, fear, sadness, and difficulties with settling and being soothed—continue to be important throughout the toddler, preschool, and middle childhood years (Rothbart, 2011). Behavior observations of preschoolers likewise provide evidence of an overarching negative emotionality trait that includes sadness and depression, anger and irritability, and lability of mood (Buckley, Klein, Durbin, Hayden, & Moerk, 2002). Experimenter ratings of 3- to 7-year old children's behavior during a set of laboratory tasks likewise reveal a higher-order negative emotionality trait (Vroman, Lo, & Durbin, 2014). Across all of the temperament measures of negative affectivity, the focus tends to be on children's negative emotional reactions to threatening situations they face *in the moment.*

By around the age of 3 (and perhaps even earlier), children begin to show an even broader range of negative emotional tendencies than are captured in temperament research. Young children begin to vary in the extent to which they feel insecure, vulnerable, jealous, fearful of failing, incapable of coping with stress and uncertainty, sensitive to criticism, and concerned about acceptance (Shiner & DeYoung, 2013); these more complex emotions are captured in the Big Five questionnaire items in Table 8.1. For children to display these characteristics, they need to be able to think about the future and to have self-awareness that enables them to see themselves in relation to others. In other words, at some point in early childhood, negative emotionality and neuroticism expand to include children's negative emotional responses to future threats and uncertainty, and to more complex threats to children's sense of value and place in the social sphere. These more complex

TABLE 8.1. Measuring Neuroticism: Sample Questionnaire Measures, Items, and Lower-Order Components in Childhood, Adolescence, and Adulthood

Period of life, measure, and scale name	Sample items	Lower-order components
Infancy Revised Infant Behavior Questionnaire[a]: Negative Affectivity	How often in the last week did the baby . . . Fuss or protest when placed on his or her back Calm down within 5 minutes when frustrated with something Seem sad when the caregiver was away for an unusually long time Startle to a sudden or loud noise	Distress to limitations Falling reactivity/rate of recovery from distress Sadness Fear
Preschool to early middle childhood Children's Behavior Questionnaire[b]: Negative Affectivity	Gets quite frustrated when prevented from doing something he or she wants to do Is very difficult to soothe when he or she has become upset His or her feelings are easily hurt by what parents say Is afraid of the dark Is quite upset by a little cut or bruise	Anger/frustration Falling reactivity/ soothability Sadness Fear Discomfort
Preschool, middle childhood, adolescence California Child Q-Set[c]: Neuroticism	Worries about things for a long time Needs to have people encourage him or her. Is not very sure of him- or herself Tends to go to pieces under stress; gets rattled when things are tough Has hurt feelings if he or she is made fun of or criticized	None
Adulthood Big Five Inventory–2[d]: Negative Emotionality	Can be tense Is relaxed, handles stress well (rev) Tends to feel depressed, blue Feels secure, comfortable with self (rev) Is moody, has up and down mood swings Is temperamental, gets emotional easily	Anxiety Depression Emotional volatility
Adulthood Big Five Aspects Scale[e]: Neuroticism	Feels threatened easily Worries about things Changes mood a lot Gets upset easily	Withdrawal Volatility

Note. rev, item is scored in the reversed direction.

[a]Revised Infant Behavior Questionnaire—items defining the factor in a study of infants 3–12 months of age (Gartstein & Rothbart, 2003). Items are from the Revised Infant Behavior Questionnaire (Rothbart, 1996).

[b]Children's Behavior Questionnaire—items defining the factor in several studies of children ages 3–7 (Rothbart, Ahadi, Hershey, & Fisher, 2001). Items are from the Children's Behavior Questionnaire (Rothbart, 1996).

[c]California Child Q-Set—items defining the trait in adult caregiver online reports of 16,000 youth ages 3–20. Presented in Soto and John (2013, Table 4, p. 193).

[d]Big Five Inventory–2—items defining neuroticism trait across four samples: (1) 1,137 community adults, (2) and (3) two samples of 1,000 online adults, and (4) 470 students. Presented in Soto and John (2017, Appendix, pp. 142–143).

[e]Big Five Aspect Scales—items defining the Big Five trait across two samples: (1) 481 community adults and (2) 480 undergraduates. Presented in DeYoung, Quilty, and Peterson (2007, Table 4, pp. 887–888).

manifestations of neuroticism remain a central aspect of the trait in adolescence and adulthood. Research from the personality tradition thus reveals aspects of the trait that may be overlooked in temperament research on negative affectivity.

What are the underlying components or lower-order traits that make up this more general predisposition toward negative emotionality? There is no clear consensus about this issue across the lifespan. However, there is some evidence for at least two basic components of negative emotionality in both early childhood and adulthood: one involving withdrawal, fear, and anxiety, and the other involving irritability and emotional volatility (for examples, see Table 8.1). In young children, *fear* and *irritability/anger* have received especially intensive study (Rothbart, 2011; Shiner & DeYoung, 2013). Fear measures children's tendencies to express fear and exhibit withdrawal and avoidance in the face of stressful or novel situations. Irritability/anger taps children's propensities toward outer-directed, hostile emotions such as anger, frustration, and irritation, sometimes in response to limits set by adults. These same two components appear to be distinctive aspects of negative affectivity that can be observed in laboratory tasks with young children (Dyson et al., 2015). Two similar components of neuroticism have been identified in adults: one labeled *withdrawal* that encompasses anxiety, depression, and self-consciousness, and one labeled *volatility* that encompasses irritability, unstable moods, and the tendency to get upset or panicky (DeYoung, Quilty, & Peterson, 2007). At least in children, the irritability component may be as related to low agreeableness as to high neuroticism (De Pauw, 2017). A third likely component is *sadness,* which appears as a separate dimension from fear and anger/disinhibition in task-based measures in childhood (Kotelnikova, Olino, Mackrell, Jordan, & Hayden, 2013) and questionnaire measures in adulthood (Soto & John, 2017).

People show typical mean-level changes in negative emotionality and neuroticism across the lifespan. Across infancy and early childhood, average levels of negative emotionality and its components of fear and irritability/anger increase, as the biological systems underlying these tendencies come on line, and means levels for this family of traits continue to increase across the preschool and early school-age years (Shiner, 2018). Relative to preschool-age children, elementary school-age children are better at regulating their emotions; therefore, mean levels of intense negative emotions such as irritability and anger may stabilize in elementary school (De Haan, De Pauw, van den Akker, Deković, & Prinzie, 2017; Shiner, 2018), but there is also evidence that anxiety may increase and self-confidence decline across the elementary school years (De Haan et al., 2017). Findings for mean levels of neuroticism are not fully consistent, and this in part may be because different measures of the trait assess different components (e.g., some emphasize anxiety and self-confidence more than others), and some aspects of neuroticism may decline or remain stable, while others increase. Although findings are not entirely consistent across studies in middle childhood, a meta-analysis of the Big Five traits in adolescence (Denissen, Van Aken, Penke, & Wood, 2013) suggests that neuroticism may increase during early adolescence, although there is more evidence that paths may diverge for girls and boys in adolescence, with boys decreasing or remaining stable on neuroticism later in adolescence and girls continuing to increase in neuroticism in adolescence (Borghuis et al., 2017; De Haan et al., 2017).

On average, people decline in neuroticism from their later adolescent years through their middle adult years. An extensive meta-analysis of mean-level changes in personality traits found that neuroticism decreased in late adolescence and continued to decrease for people on average during their 20s, 30s, and 40s (Roberts, Walton, & Viechtbauer, 2006). More recent studies have confirmed this general pattern of declines in neuroticism in the transition to adulthood and adult years across a variety of measures (reviewed in Costa, McCrae, & Lockenhoff, in press). There are some caveats to this general pattern, however. The rates of decline vary by culture, and the declines may begin earlier in countries in which people complete their education and enter the workforce earlier (Bleidorn et al., 2013). Furthermore, not all countries show a decline in neuroticism at all across the adult years (Costa et al., in press). In addition, a smaller number of studies suggest that neuroticism may increase during extreme old age (Costa et al., in press), but the reasons for this increase are not yet clear.

The Psychological Processes Accompanying Neuroticism

I don't make pretty pictures. Sometimes I wish my imagination were fueled by something other than panic and dread. But I don't have control over my gift. It has control over me, and I am dragged by it more often than not, away from the idyllic land of normal and onto the jagged shores of self-destruction. Imagining the worst has always been a great comfort to me. If there is a turbulence, there is an immediate crash. . . . If there is a lump, it is a tumor. By thinking like this, I protect myself from disappointment. And if anything other than

the worst-case scenario unfolds, what a pleasant surprise! The problem is that I am always walking around preparing for and reacting to the horrors of what my brain is making up, living as if every potential terror and every defeat were already happening—because in my mind, it always is.
—MARON (2014, pp. 7–8)

What psychological processes accompany and fuel negative emotionality and neuroticism? Marc Maron describes the role that thinking plays in his experience of negative emotionality—the ways that he consistently assumes the worst in order to be ready for whatever negative thing may come. In this section, I review research evidence for neuroticism's links with attentional and interpretive biases toward threat, problems with cognitive control, and difficulties with emotion regulation and coping.

Childhood negative emotionality and adult neuroticism are associated with attentional and interpretive biases toward threat, as well as with difficulties with cognitive control. Both children and adults who score higher on anxiety show a biased tendency to direct their attention toward threatening stimuli; more anxious adults also have more trouble disengaging with these threatening cues once they fixate on them (Shackman, Stockbridge, et al., 2016). Children, adolescents, and adults with greater anxiety or negative emotionality likewise show a bias toward interpreting ambiguous information in a negative or threatening way (Barlow, Sauer-Zavala, Carl, Bullis, & Ellard, 2014; Stuijfzand, Creswell, Field, Pearcey, & Dodd, 2017); it is notable that the relationship between anxiety and such biases is stronger among adolescents than among children, suggesting that interpretative biases may become more linked with anxiety with age (Stuijfzand et al., 2017). In an interesting recent study, college students' self-reported neuroticism predicted their tendencies to experience mind wandering in a (presumably stressful) laboratory setting and predicted, in daily life, more racing thoughts, less clear thinking, and more negative thought content in their mind wandering (Kane et al., 2017). Finally, neuroticism in adulthood predicts instability in cognitive processing (e.g., alternating between rapid and atypically slow response rates to stimuli; Robinson & Wilkowski, 2014). Taken together, these studies suggest that negative emotionality (including trait anxiety) is associated with negative processing of information and difficulties with cognitive control.

Neuroticism may undermine people's motivation and capacities to cope in a positive way when they encounter stress and difficulty. This may occur in part because neuroticism is associated with tendencies toward avoidance, inaction, and various forms of disengagement coping. A meta-analysis of personality traits and coping in youth and adults revealed a modest to moderate relationship between neuroticism and various types of disengagement coping (denial, withdrawal, wishful thinking, and substance abuse; Connor-Smith & Flachsbart, 2007). Neuroticism predicts preferences for inaction across many different cultures (Ireland, Hepler, Li, & Albarracin, 2015) and appears to reduce people's willingness to exert effort when they are alone and therefore not motivated by the need for approval by others (Uziel, 2016). Neuroticism is linked with avoidance, even including tendencies to perceive nonthreatening stimuli as being further away from the self (Robinson & Wilkowski, 2014). Already in infancy, infants' temperamental negativity predicts more avoidance and fewer attentional regulation strategies several months later (Thomas et al., 2017). These findings are consistent with the model of neuroticism as a manifestation of a threat-detection system: Neuroticism likely increases perceptions of threats and therefore leads to avoidance, inactivity, and low effort in the face of potentially distressing situations.

Neuroticism is associated with a number of other problematic patterns of emotion regulation and coping as well. The cognitive and emotional processes associated with neuroticism may lead to impulsive action (Selby, Kranzler, Panza, & Fehling, 2016), rather than simply avoidance. In addition, the previously noted meta-analysis of personality traits and coping strategies revealed that neuroticism has negative relationships with three positive means of coping—problem solving, cognitive restructuring, and acceptance (Connor-Smith & Flachsbart, 2007). Acceptance of negative emotions and thoughts promotes well-being and psychological health (Ford, Lam, John, & Mauss, 2017), so people who experience high negative emotions that they cannot accept or reinterpret may miss out on the benefits that come from those more engaged forms of coping.

Given all the negative experiences associated with trait neuroticism, one may reasonably expect that individuals who are high on this trait would want to tamp down their negative emotions or their propensity to detect threats in order to feel better. Yet, surprisingly, there may be times in which highly neurotic people prefer to feel negative emotions. It turns out that when people who are high on neuroticism want to perform effectively, they prefer to experience worry, and they may even perform better when in a worried state (Tamir, 2005). Similarly, highly neurotic people prefer to worry before doing a challenging creative task and demonstrate greater creativity and cognitive flexibility when they feel worried, in part because such worry seems to strengthen their intrinsic motivation for the task (Leung et al., 2014). In short, in a performance setting, highly neurotic people perform better when their emotional state (worry, or an activated avoidance system) matches their trait (neuroticism, or motivation toward avoidance). Another interesting pattern that emerges is consistent with the idea that highly neurotic people are motivated to avoid threats: Highly neurotic people experience fewer negative emotions and more life satisfaction in their daily lives when they are cognitively skilled at detecting threats that are present (Tamir, Robinson, & Solberg, 2006), presumably because their strong threat-detection skills allow them to do what they are motivated to do, which is to detect and avoid threats.

Taken together, the relationship between neuroticism and cognitive processing, coping, and emotion regulation has turned out to be complex. The relationships between neuroticism and the various cognitive styles, coping mechanisms, and means of emotion regulation are often only modest to moderate in size, so neuroticism cannot simply be reduced to patterns of cognition, motivation, or coping. Rather, neuroticism may increase the likelihood that people develop certain negative patterns of thinking or styles of coping, but the ultimate effects of neuroticism on people's well-being may depend on its interaction with those other processes. For example, a study that tracked a group of fearful, inhibited young children into adolescence found not only that the inhibited children showed greater attentional bias to threat as adolescents, but also that early inhibition only predicted social withdrawal in those adolescents with the biased attention to threat (Pérez-Edgar et al., 2010). Thus, it is possible that neuroticism may be most problematic for people who struggle with both high levels of negative emotions and negative methods of handling such negative emotions. And at times, the experience of trait-consistent negative emotions that more highly neurotic people

accept and feel capable of regulating may even prove beneficial for performance.

The quote from Marc Maron illustrates well these complex patterns of cognition and motivation underlying neuroticism. Maron is biased toward thinking about his experiences in a negative way, but he is content with that cognitive bias (it is a "great comfort") because it helps protect him from negative outcomes and disappointment. And his panic and dread help fuel his "gift"—his great capacity for creativity and imagination.

Neuroticism in Interaction with Stress, Threatening Experiences, and Adversity: A Vicious Cycle

When life is scary and chaotic, I like to make it more so.
—Maron (2014, p. 53)

There are a lot of kinds of relationships. I've ruined all kinds. I've ruined marriages, friendships, relationships with siblings and parents, pets, business partners, plants, etc. Relationships with pets are the easiest to repair. It usually just takes a few hours and a fun snack and you're back on track. It's harder with humans, but sometimes snacks still work.
—Maron (in Maron & McDonald, 2017, p. 107)

In this section, I present a cyclical model for the ways that neuroticism shapes developmental outcomes and day-to-day experience by increasing adverse experiences, and the ways that adverse experiences in turn lead to increases in neuroticism. Neuroticism leads to a greater number of threatening, adverse, or stressful experiences through at least two processes. First, neuroticism and negative emotionality increase exposure to negative life events, broadly construed. As Maron suggests, neuroticism may increase the extent to which "life is scary and chaotic" by increasing individuals' exposure to life stressors. Second, neuroticism has negative effects on the mastery of developmental tasks that are important at each stage of development—including relationships with peers and romantic partners, and the development of effectiveness at work. As Maron notes, he has "ruined all kinds" of relationships as a result of high neuroticism, and these kinds of negative experiences in important domains of life are stressful.

In turn, stressful life experiences lead to increases in neuroticism. Evidence for this claim comes from research across the lifespan. In many cases, the adversity may come from life experiences that are independent of the person's own behavior; for example, as I review, adverse and stressful family experiences (which may be shaped by children and adolescents themselves but may also arise independently of the youths' behavior) predict increases in youths' negative emotionality. In other cases, the adversity may arise as a result of the person's own behavior, but this stress and adversity, too, leads to increases in neuroticism.

In this section, I review evidence for both parts of this model—that neuroticism heightens exposure to stressful experiences and that stressful and threatening experiences predict increases in neuroticism.

Neuroticism Increases Exposure to Stress and Adversity

Converging evidence from research with children, adolescents, and adults supports the claim that negative emotionality and neuroticism predict increases in stressful life events (for reviews, see Jeronimus, Riese, Sanderman, & Ormel, 2014; Laceulle, van Aken, Ormel, & Nederhof, 2015; Stroud, Sosoo, & Wilson, 2015). For example, a study of late adolescents and adults followed over 16 years revealed that participants with higher neuroticism experienced consistently higher levels of several different kinds of negative experiences, including negative life events, long-term life difficulties lasting 2+ months, and decreased quality of life (Jeronimus et al., 2014). Similarly, a study of young adolescent girls revealed that the girls' negative emotionality predicted increases in both acute and chronic interpersonal stress (Stroud et al., 2015). There is some evidence that shyness may actually *decrease* exposure to stressful life events (Laceulle et al., 2015), but other aspects of neuroticism, particularly more outwardly directed negative emotions such as anger and alienation, are more consistently associated with life stress (Stroud et al., 2015).

Other work supporting the claim that negative emotions lead to increases in stressful life events comes from research on psychopathology demonstrating that depression and anxiety disorders contribute to increases in stress generation over time. For example, in a sample of adolescents, youth who experienced anxiety disorders or depression generated more stressful life events for themselves, and this occurred in part because the youth with anxiety or depression were higher on neuroticism, which in turn predicted increases in episodes of stressful life events (Uliaszek et al., 2012). Negative cognitive styles—for example, tendencies to see the causes of negative life events as internal, stable, and global, and to be highly self-critical—also predict increases in interpersonal stress over time (Auerbach, Ho, & Kim, 2014), a finding that is important given that negative cognitive styles often accompany neuroticism. Taken together, it is clear that adolescents and adults who score higher on negative emotionality and neuroticism experience greater numbers of stressful life events, particularly negative interpersonal events, than do adolescents and adults who are more emotionally stable.

Another piece of evidence that neuroticism increases stressful experiences comes from the extensive literature showing that negative emotionality and neuroticism are associated with difficulties in a number of important life tasks, including social relationships and work.

In childhood, adolescence, and adulthood, neuroticism predicts difficulties in establishing positive relationships. In terms of children's peer relationships, more shy and inhibited children have fewer friendships and poorer quality friends, and may not benefit as much from the close relationships that they do have (Coplan & Bullock, 2012). Children who are higher on the volatility components of negative emotionality (irritability, frustration, anger) experience more conflict and rejection from peers, as well as fewer high-quality friendships (Coplan & Bullock, 2012). Higher neuroticism at the time of high school graduation predicts more negative relationship functioning in relationships with romantic partners, friends, and family members during the transition to adulthood (Deventer, Wagner, Lüdtke, & Trautwein, 2018). Neuroticism in adulthood also predicts more negative relationships with romantic partners (Senia & Donnellan, Chapter 33, this volume), as well as heightened risks for divorce (Roberts, Kuncel, Shiner, Caspi, & Goldberg, 2007).

Neuroticism is also predictive of more negative developmental outcomes in the domains of work. Child and adolescent neuroticism predicts lower occupational attainment in adulthood (Roberts et al., 2007) and less competent work performance (Shiner & Masten, 2012), and neuroticism likewise is associated with lower work satisfaction, organizational commitment, and financial security (Ozer & Benet-Martinez, 2006). As Freud (1930/1962) famously noted, "Love and work are the cornerstones of our humanness" (p. 42). Neuroticism likely leads to greater day-to-day stress because it makes the developmental tasks of both love and work more challenging. Given that more neurotic people perceive their experiences more negatively and have more difficulty coping, they are less equipped to handle these stresses effectively.

Adverse and Threatening Experiences Increase Negative Emotionality and Neuroticism

As reviewed previously in this chapter, people who are higher on negative emotionality/ neuroticism tend to respond more strongly to threat, punishment, and uncertainty with distress, avoidance, irritability, vigilance, and rumination. These responses to adverse and stressful experiences may in turn lead to increases in negative emotionality/neuroticism. Thus, it is not surprising that adverse life experiences of many different kinds predict increases in neuroticism over time. The potential role of adversity in shaping personality change has been investigated in multiple longitudinal studies that have assessed changes in neuroticism by controlling for earlier levels of the trait. In thinking about adversity, it is helpful to distinguish two categories of stressful experiences: (1) *independent adversity* that arises for reasons other than the person's own behavior (e.g., children's exposure to poverty in childhood, having a good friend move away in adolescence) and (2) *dependent adversity* that is the result of the person's own behavior (Gest, Reed, & Masten, 1999). The stressful life events described in the previous section are nearly all examples of dependent adversity because they result from the person's own behavior. For example, if an adolescent boy gets into frequent conflicts with his parents and friends because he is irritable and insecure in those relationships, his experience of conflict in those relationships would be an example of dependent adversity.

The first line of research suggesting a role for adversity in the development of negative emotionality comes from studies examining the effects of the broader social environment on the development of youths' traits. Children and adolescents who experience more adverse environments tend to develop higher levels of

negative emotionality and more problems with regulating negative emotions over time. Specifically, youth who are exposed to more stressful, rejecting, punitive, or insensitive family environments increase in negative emotionality during childhood and adolescence (Caspi & Shiner, 2008; Lengua, Gartstein, & Prinzie, Chapter 12, this volume; Lengua & Wachs, 2012). Infants' and toddlers' negative emotionality seems to be worsened by disorganized, chaotic, and noisy home environments (Matheny & Phillips, 2001). Research on the effects of poverty and low socioeconomic status (SES) has not examined directly the effects on youths' negative emotionality, but it has examined effects on youths' capacities for regulating their negative emotions, yielding evidence that poverty and low SES do undermine children's capacities for emotion regulation (Conger & Donnellan, 2007; Evans & Kim, 2013). A study of adolescents found that parental hostility and low warmth predicted increases in an overarching trait made up of emotional stability (or low neuroticism), conscientiousness, and agreeableness (Schofield et al., 2012). Behaviorally inhibited children receiving intrusive or rejecting parenting remain more consistently inhibited across time than inhibited children receiving other parenting (though it should be noted that overly warm or overprotective parenting may have similar negative effects; Fox, Henderson, Marshall, Nichols, & Ghera, 2005; Lengua et al., Chapter 12, this volume). Across all of these studies, increases in children's negative emotionality were predicted by negative life experiences that posed threats to children's emotional well-being—for example, hostility and rejection from parents, chaos in the home, or lack of family resources.

Adolescents and adults likewise may experience increases in neuroticism in the face of stressful life experiences. In many studies on negative life events, life stress is assessed by creating an overall index of how many negative life events participants experienced during a particular stretch of time; it is important to note that such life events may be independent or dependent on participants' own behaviors. Across a number of studies, a higher number of stressful life events was associated with increases in neuroticism over time (Jeronimus, Ormel, Aleman, Penninx, & Riese, 2013; Jeronimus et al., 2014; Lüdtke, Roberts, Trautwein, & Nagy, 2011; Riese et al., 2014; Vaidya, Gray, Haig, & Watson, 2002). In a study of adolescents followed from ages 11–19, Laceuelle and colleagues (2015) found that stressful life experiences predicted increases in the lower-order traits of fear and frustration. Changes in neuroticism may even occur over longer spans of time as a result of adverse experiences. For example, Shiner, Allen, and Masten (2017) found that both independent and dependent negative life events during adolescence predicted increases in neuroticism from childhood through adulthood 20 years later. Youths' difficulties in mastering developmental tasks may also lead to increases in neuroticism; for example, problems in the life tasks of childhood (peer relationships, academic achievement, learning to follow rules) predicted increases in negative emotionality from childhood to late adolescence (Shiner, Masten, & Tellegen, 2002). In some cases, increases in neuroticism may simply reflect relatively more short-term increases in negative affect away from people's more typical set points for negative affect (Ormel, Riese, & Rosmalen, 2012), but in other cases, the increases in neuroticism may be more long-lasting (Jeronimus et al., 2014; Ormel et al., 2012).

Finally, neuroticism may increase in response to particular traumatic or otherwise negative specific life events. It is easy to imagine how a traumatic event might lead to an increase in neuroticism. Traumatic events may be particularly difficult to manage for youth and adults who are prone to negative emotions; these experiences require an unusually high degree of coping, and they may confirm a neurotic person's sense that the world is full of potential threats. In several studies looking at all of the Big Five traits, only neuroticism was found to increase following traumatic events, such as natural disasters (Boals, Southard-Dobbs, & Blumenthal, 2015; Milojev, Osborne, & Sibley, 2014; Ogle, Rubin, & Siegler, 2014). Other negative events in adulthood also predict increases in neuroticism, such as getting fired (Costa, Herbst, McCrae, & Siegler, 2000), trying drugs (Leikas & Salmela-Aro, 2015), and experiencing the onset of a chronic disease (Leikas & Salmela-Aro, 2015). It is important to note that these single events are a mixture of both independent events (e.g., natural disasters) and dependent events (e.g., getting fired).

Consistent with a model of neuroticism as a "threat-detection system," threatening experiences seem to lead to increases in people's predispositions toward negative emotions. These threatening experiences may be chronic

negative events or single, more severe events. In childhood, the adverse experiences that increase negative emotionality seem more likely to be independent negative experiences, given that children have less control over their environments and experiences; thus, family effects on neuroticism may predominate in childhood. But, as people get older, they have increasing control over their day-to-day lives; thus, by adolescence and adulthood, the negative experiences that worsen neuroticism may be a mixture of both independent and dependent stressors. Given that neuroticism increases the risks for experiencing dependent negative life events, a cycle of neuroticism ⇒ stressful life events ⇒ increased neuroticism may become more entrenched in adulthood. Such a pattern emerged in Marc Maron's life in late adolescence and adulthood. Maron sought refuge from his chronic neurotic distress by abusing drugs and alcohol, which led to failures in work and relationships, which only served to increase his sense of desperation, anxiety, and despair, and the cycle continued.

It is important to recognize, however, that such a cycle is not inevitable. Indeed, the associations between neuroticism and life adversity are only modest, or at most moderate in size. The same is true for the links between neuroticism and difficulties in relationships and work, and for the effects of life adversity on increases in neuroticism. If adversity leads to increases in neuroticism, the increases are typically small. There is reason to be hopeful that people can change and escape a negative cycle of stress and increasing neuroticism, a point to which I now turn.

Conclusions, Directions for Future Research, and Reasons to Be Hopeful: Neuroticism Can Change, Be Managed Effectively, or Even Offer Benefits

We're built to deal with death, disease, failure, struggle, heartbreak, problems. It's what separates us from the animals and why we envy and love animals so much. We're aware of it all and have to process it. The way we each handle being human is where all the good stories, jokes, arts, wisdom, [and] revelations . . . come from.
                                    —MARON (2014, p. xviii)

In this chapter, I have presented research that supports the model of neuroticism as a threat-detection system. The trait begins with an emotional core of distress, fear, discomfort, sadness and frustration in infancy and expands over time to include a more complex set of negative emotions, thoughts, and behaviors. By the preschool and school-age years, children who score high on this trait feel insecure, vulnerable, jealous, fearful of failing, and sensitive to criticism; they are less capable of coping with stress and uncertainty and more concerned about acceptance. Although the content of the trait is reasonably well understood in adulthood, there is still much to explore in terms of the nature of negative emotionality in childhood. It is not yet clear how the more complex cognitive and social aspects of the trait emerge over time; for example, do the negative patterns of thinking associated with negative emotionality result directly from youths' chronic experience of negative emotions, or do they arise as a consequence of encountering difficulties in daily life? The structure of the trait in childhood is also not yet clear. Temperament and personality measures each seem to add additional information in predicting children's outcomes (De Pauw, 2017); in other words, personality measures do not simply subsume temperament measures in childhood. To better understand the breadth of negative emotionality in childhood, it will be important to draw from both the temperament and personality traditions.

In terms of mean-level change, negative emotionality seems to increase from infancy through the preschool years, as the systems for the various negative emotions come online. The nature of mean-level change in middle childhood remains unclear because studies have yielded contradictory results, likely because different components of neuroticism (e.g., anxiety vs. irritability) may have different patterns of mean-level change. However, there is more consistent evidence that, on average, girls increase in neuroticism in adolescence, whereas boys show less or no mean-level change. Then, across adulthood, neuroticism decreases as adults establish greater stability and security in their lives. More work is needed to understand mean-level change in childhood and the causes of increasing neuroticism in adolescence for girls, as well as the cross-cultural replicability of these patterns. It is important to note that although many people may exhibit these mean-level patterns of change as they get older, not everyone does. For example, Marc Maron's history suggests that rather than decreasing in neuroticism in late adolescence and early adulthood, he may have maintained or even increased his high levels of neuroticism. These kinds of non-normative change are worthy of more intensive study, especially for the trait of neuroticism, because of its profound importance for well-being and adaptation.

Neuroticism is associated with negative processing of information and difficulties with cognitive control. Neuroticism also seems to pose challenges for coping and self-regulation given that it is linked with tendencies toward avoidance, inaction, and a variety of less effective emotion regulation strategies. However, the negative effects of neuroticism on information processing and coping vary, depending on whether people have good strategies for managing their propensities for experiencing high levels of negative emotions. At present, very little is known about the processes underlying neuroticism in older children and adolescents, compared to what is known about the processes in adults. We also know very little about the circumstances in which the cognitive and coping biases associated with neuroticism are problematic, versus neutral, versus positive in either children or adults. These processes may be helpful in some circumstances, and this topic is worthy of further study. Another helpful angle for looking at processes underlying neuroticism would be to examine whether changes in these processes lead to decreases in neuroticism over time. For example, there is evidence that, when people in romantic relationships decrease in their tendencies to interpret ambiguous information through a biased lens, they experience long-term decreases in neuroticism (Finn, Mitte, & Neyer, 2015). It is possible to examine the effects of such processes on neuroticism in nonexperimental studies (as in the Finn et al. study), or by experimentally manipulating the processes and observing whether they affect neuroticism.

It is important to note that it may not be necessary to have exceptionally high levels of self-regulation to manage high levels of neuroticism. Interesting evidence for this comes from a study by Shiner and Masten (2012) that examined predictors of resilience and maladaptation in the face of significant life adversity. In a sample of 205 participants, a tiny group of six was identified as "turnaround" cases—namely, people who had experienced high levels of adversity during childhood and adolescence, and who were faring poorly at age 20 but turned their lives around by age 30. These dramatic cases all turned out to be women, and they all turned out to have exhibited levels of childhood neuroticism a full standard deviation higher than the rest of the sample. Interestingly, however, they showed levels of self-regulation that were typical for the sample as a whole. Although they may have struggled to manage their high neuroticism effectively while they were growing up, their average capacities for self-regulation and autonomy seem to have enabled them to cope better as adults. Such a finding offers hope for other young people who might have especially high levels of neuroticism in childhood.

Neuroticism has important transactions with life stress and adversity. Children, adolescents, and adults alike experience more negative life events the higher they score on negative emotionality or neuroticism. Conversely, stressful and adverse life experiences lead to increases in negative emotionality or neuroticism; this is true for events that are independent of individuals' own behaviors, as well as for events that are the result of their own behaviors. It will be important for future research to probe the processes through which these transactions occur: What are the microprocesses through which neuroticism leads to negative events, and through which adversity leads to increases in neuroticism? A recent study of a sample of preschoolers over the course of a year offers a helpful example of how to examine the effects of negative emotionality at a fine-grained level (Neal, Durbin, Gornik, & Lo, 2017). This study tracked the emergence of the children's social play networks over time and found that children exhibiting high negative emotionality were less likely to develop consistent social play relationships with other children over the course of that year; this finding offers insights into the way that early negative emotionality reduces children's social resources early in life. Studies with a variety of methods will be able to investigate more fine-grained processes in the transactions between neuroticism and stressful experiences. It will also be helpful for more studies to test for bidirectional effects of neuroticism and negative life events in the same samples; at least two studies have done so thus far (Jeronimus et al., 2014; Laceulle et al., 2015), but more of such work is needed. Finally, it will be important to look at the meaning of negative events to individuals to determine whether it is the interpretation of the experience or simply the experience itself that is most important in shaping its effects on neuroticism.

Finally, it will be important to examine more thoroughly the life experiences and psychological processes that help people to reduce their tendencies toward neuroticism, effectively cope with or manage their neuroticism (without necessarily reducing it), or even benefit in some circumstances from it. As Maron notes in the quotation at the start of this section, "We're built to deal with death, disease, failure, struggle, heartbreak, problems. . . . We're aware of it all and have to process it." People can and do find ways to reduce or manage their neuroticism. Out of all the Big Five traits, neuroticism is the trait that the most people want to change (Hudson & Fraley, 2016; Robinson, Noftle, Guo, Asadi, & Zhang, 2015). Fortunately, there is good reason to believe that negative emotionality and neuroticism are changeable through intervention. A recent meta-analysis of clinical interventions, mostly therapy, revealed that, of all the Big Five traits, neuroticism was the most substantially changed as a result of therapy (Roberts et al., 2017). In fact, after only about a month of therapy, people on average experienced as much of a decline in neuroticism as is typically seen across decades of adulthood in the studies of mean-level change. Interventions targeting children's high levels of negative emotionality likewise result in significant positive changes (McClowry & Collins, 2012).

Life experiences, especially social relationships, that promote a greater sense of security likewise predict decreases in neuroticism and prevent neuroticism from having deleterious effects. Children whose parents approach them in a sensitive and warm way experience decreases in negative emotionality (Bates, Schermerhorn, & Petersen, 2012). Entering into a romantic relationship in young adulthood and experiencing secure, positive relationships with partners, family, and friends all lead to decreases in neuroticism over time (Deventer et al., 2018; Mund, Finn, Hagemeyer, & Neyer, 2016). Inhibited children are able to stave off the risk for anxiety disorders in adulthood if they develop strong social relationships in adolescence (Frenkel et al., 2015). In fact, people who score particularly high on neuroticism might receive the most benefit from feeling accepted and connected (Shackman et al., 2017). By developing a sense of security, safety, and support, youth and adults who score high on neuroticism may find that their sensitivity to threat and propensity toward negative emotions decrease over time.

Finally, it is important to focus on research that will yield a better understanding of how people like Marc Maron, with high levels of neuroticism, often thrive in spite of, or even because of, their high levels of neuroticism. There are gifts that negative emotions might offer; people may rightly recognize injustice and wrongs in the world because of their sensitivity to threats. They might produce excellent work because of their worries that they might not reach their goals or meet their expectations. They may be able to offer empathy for others' experiences of distress because they are so sensitive to their own distress. As Maron notes, "The way we each handle being human is where all the good stories, jokes, arts, wisdom, [and] revelations . . . come from" (2014, p. xviii). Grappling with our negative emotions may be a source for all kinds of good stories, jokes, arts, wisdom, and revelations if we can do it well.

REFERENCES

Auerbach, R. P., Ho, M.-H. R., & Kim, J. C. (2014). Identifying cognitive and interpersonal predictors of adolescent depression. *Journal of Abnormal Child Psychology, 42*(6), 913–924.

Barlow, D. H., Sauer-Zavala, S., Carl, J. R., Bullis, J. R., & Ellard, K. K. (2014). The nature, diagnosis, and treatment of neuroticism: Back to the future. *Clinical Psychological Science, 2*(3), 344–365.

Bates, J. E., Schermerhorn, A. C., & Petersen, I. T. (2012). Temperament and parenting in developmental perspective. In M. Zentner & R. L. Shiner (Eds.), *Handbook of temperament* (pp. 425–441). New York: Guilford Press.

Bleidorn, W., Klimstra, T. A., Denissen, J. J. A., Rentfrow, P. J., Potter, J., & Gosling, S. D. (2013). Personality maturation around the world: A cross-cultural examination of social-investment theory. *Psychological Science, 24*, 2530–2540.

Boals, A., Southard-Dobbs, S., & Blumenthal, H. (2015). Adverse events in emerging adulthood and associated with increases in neuroticism. *Journal of Personality, 83*(2), 202–211.

Borghuis, J., Denissen, J. J. A., Oberski, D., Sijtsma, K., Meeus, W. H. J., Branje, S., et al. (2017). Big Five personality stability, change, and codevelopment across adolescence and early adulthood. *Journal of Personality and Social Psychology, 113*(4), 641–657.

Buckley, M. E., Klein, D. N., Durbin, C. E., Hayden, E. P., & Moerk, K. C. (2002). Development and validation of a Q-sort procedure to assess temperament and behavior in preschool-age children. *Journal of Clinical Child and Adolescent Psychology, 31*, 525–539.

Caspi, A., & Shiner, R. L. (2008). Temperament and personality. In M. Rutter, D. Bishop, D. Pine, S. Scott, J. Stevenson, E. Taylor, et al. (Eds.), *Rutter's child and adolescent psychiatry* (5th ed., pp. 182–199). London: Blackwell.

Conger, R. D., & Donnellan, M. B. (2007). An interactionist perspective on the socioeconomic context of human development. *Annual Review of Psychology, 58,* 175–199.

Connor-Smith, J. K., & Flachsbart, C. (2007). Relations between personality and coping: A meta-analysis. *Journal of Personality and Social Psychology, 93*(6), 1080–1107.

Coplan, R. J., & Bullock, A. (2012). Temperament and peer relationships. In M. Zentner & R. L. Shiner (Eds.), *Handbook of temperament* (pp. 442–461). New York: Guilford Press.

Costa, P. T., Jr., Herbst, J. H., McCrae, R. R., & Siegler, I. C. (2000). Personality at midlife: Stability, intrinsic maturation, and response to life events. *Assessment, 7*(4), 365–378.

Costa, P. T., Jr., McCrae, R. R., & Lockenhoff, C. E. (in press). Personality across the lifespan. *Annual Review of Psychology.*

De Haan, A., De Pauw, S., van den Akker, A., Deković, M., & Prinzie, P. (2017). Long-term developmental changes in children's lower-order Big Five personality facets. *Journal of Personality, 85*(5), 616–631.

De Pauw, S. S. W. (2017). Childhood personality and temperament. In T. A. Widiger (Ed.), *The Oxford handbook of the Five-Factor Model* (pp. 243–280). New York: Oxford University Press.

Denissen, J. J. A., van Aken, M. A. G., Penke, L., & Wood, D. (2013). Self-regulation underlies temperament and personality: An integrative developmental framework. *Child Development Perspectives, 7*(4), 255–260.

Deventer, J., Wagner, J., Lüdtke, O., & Trautwein, U. (2018). Are personality traits and relationship characteristics reciprocally related?: Longitudinal analyses of co-development in the transition out of high school and beyond. *Journal of Personality and Social Psychology.* [Epub ahead of print]

DeYoung, C. G., Quilty, L. C., & Peterson, J. B. (2007). Between facets and domains: 10 aspects of the Big Five. *Journal of Personality and Social Psychology, 93*, 880–896.

Dyson, M. W., Olino, T. M., Durbin, C. E., Goldsmith, H. H., Bufferd, S. J., Miller, A. R., et al. (2015). The structural and rank-order stability of temperament in young children based on a laboratory-observational measure. *Psychological Assessment, 27*(4), 1388–1401.

Evans, G. W., & Kim, P. (2013). Childhood poverty, chronic stress, self-regulation, and coping. *Child Development Perspectives, 7,* 43–48.

Finn, C., Mitte, K., & Neyer, F. J. (2015). Recent decreases in specific interpretation biases predict decreases in neuroticism: Evidence from a longitudinal study with young adult couples. *Journal of Personality, 83*(3), 274–286.

Ford, B. Q., Lam, P., John, O. P., & Mauss, I. B. (2017). The psychological health benefits of accepting negative emotions and thoughts: Laboratory, diary, and longitudinal evidence. *Journal of Personality and Social Psychology.* [Epub ahead of print]

Fox, N. A., Henderson, H. A., Marshall, P. J., Nichols, K. E., & Ghera, M. M. (2005). Behavioral inhibition: Linking biology and behavior within a developmental framework. *Annual Review of Psychology, 56,* 235–262.

Frenkel, T. I., Fox, N. A., Pine, D. S., Walker, O. L., Degnan, K. A., & Chronis-Tuscano, A. (2015). Early childhood behavioral inhibition, adult psychopathology and the buffering effects of adolescent social networks: A twenty-year prospective study. *Journal of Child Psychology and Psychiatry, 56*(10), 1065–1073.

Freud, S., & Sigmund Freud Collection (Library of Congress). (1962). *Civilization and its discontents.* New York: Norton. (Original work published 1930)

Gartstein, M. A., & Rothbart, M. K. (2003). Studying infant temperament via the Revised Infant Behavior Questionnaire. *Infant Behavior and Development, 26,* 64–86.

Gest, S. D., Reed, M.-G., & Masten, A. S. (1999). Measuring developmental changes in exposure to adversity: A Life Chart and rating scale approach. *Development and Psychopathology, 11,* 171–192.

Gray, J. A., & McNaughton, N. (2000). *The neuropsychology of anxiety: An enquiry into the functions of the septo-hippocampal system* (2nd ed.). New York: Oxford University Press.

Hudson, N. W., & Fraley, R. C. (2016). Do people's desires to change their personality traits vary with age?: An examination of trait change goals across adulthood. *Social Psychological and Personality Science, 7*(8), 847–856.

Ireland, M. E., Hepler, J., Li, H., & Albarracin, D. (2015). Neuroticism and attitudes toward action in 19 countries. *Journal of Personality, 83*(3), 243–250.

Jeronimus, B. F., Ormel, J., Aleman, A., Penninx, B. W., & Riese, H. (2013). Negative and positive life events are associated with small but lasting changes in neuroticism. *Psychological Medicine, 43*(11), 2403–2415.

Jeronimus, B. F., Riese, H., Sanderman, R., & Ormel, J. (2014). Mutual reinforcement between neuroticism and life experiences: A five-wave, 16-year study to test reciprocal causation. *Journal of Personality and Social Psychology, 107*(4), 751–764.

Kane, M. J., Gross, G. M., Chun, C. A., Smeekens, B. A., Meier, M. E., Silvia, P. J., et al. (2017). For whom the mind wanders, and when, varies across laboratory and daily-life settings. *Psychological Science, 28*(9), 1271–1289.

Kotelnikova, Y., Olino, T. M., Mackrell, S. V., Jordan, P. L., & Hayden, E. P. (2013). Structure of observed temperament in middle childhood. *Journal of Research in Personality, 47*(5), 524–532.

Laceulle, O. M., van Aken, M. A. G., Ormel, J., & Nederhof, E. (2015). Stress-sensitivity and reciprocal associations between stressful events and adolescent temperament. *Personality and Individual Differences, 81,* 76–83.

Leikas, S., & Salmela-Aro, K. (2015). Personality trait changes among young Finns: The role of life events and transitions. *Journal of Personality, 83*(1), 117–126.

Lengua, L. J., & Wachs, T. D. (2012), Temperament and risk: Resilient and vulnerable responses to adversity. In M. Zentner & R. L. Shiner (Eds.), *Handbook of temperament* (pp. 519–540). New York: Guilford Press.

Leung, A. K.-Y., Qui, L., Chiu, C.-y., Liou, S., Kwan, L. Y.-Y., & Young, J. C. (2014). The role of instrumental emotion regulation in the emotions–creativity link: How worries render individuals with high neuroticism more creative. *Emotion, 14*(5), 846–856.

Lüdtke, O., Roberts, B. W., Trautwein, U., & Nagy, G. (2011). A random walk down university avenue: Life paths, life events, and personality trait change at the transition to university life. *Journal of Personality and Social Psychology, 101*(3), 620–637.

Maron, M. (2014). *Attempting normal.* New York: Spiegel & Grau.

Maron, M., & McDonald, B. (2017). *Waiting for the punch.* New York: Flatiron Books.

Matheny, A. P., & Phillips, K. (2001). Temperament and context: Correlates of home environment with temperament continuity and change, newborn to 30 months. In T. D. Wachs & G. A. Kohnstamm (Eds.), *Temperament in context* (pp. 81–101). Mahwah, NJ: Erlbaum.

McClowry, S. G., & Collins, A. (2012). Temperament-based intervention: Reconceptualized from a response-to-intervention framework. In M. Zentner & R. L. Shiner (Eds.), *Handbook of temperament* (pp. 607–626). New York: Guilford Press.

Milojev, P., Osborne, D., & Sibley, C. G. (2014). Personality resilience following a natural disaster. *Social Psychological and Personality Science, 5*(7), 760–768.

Mund, M., Finn, C., Hagemeyer, B., & Neyer, F. J. (2016). Understanding dynamic transactions between personality traits and partner relationships. *Current Directions in Psychological Science, 25*(6), 411–416.

Neal, J. W., Durbin, C. E., Gornik, A. E., & Lo, S. L. (2017). Codevelopment of preschoolers' temperament traits and social play networks over an entire school year. *Journal of Personality and Social Psychology, 113*(4), 627–640.

Ogle, C. M., Rubin, D. C., & Siegler, I. C. (2014). Changes in neuroticism following trauma exposure. *Journal of Personality, 82*(2), 93–102.

Ormel, J., Riese, H., & Rosmalen, J. G. M. (2012). Interpreting neuroticism scores across the adult life course: Immutable or experience-dependent set points of negative affect? *Clinical Psychology Review, 32,* 71–79.

Ozer, D. J., & Benet-Martinez, V. (2006). Personality and the prediction of consequential outcomes. *Annual Review of Psychology, 57,* 401–421.

Pérez-Edgar, K., McDermott, J. M., Pine, D. S., Bar-Haim, Y., Chronis-Tuscano, A., & Fox, N. A. (2010). Attention biases to threat and behavioral inhibition in early childhood shape adolescent social withdrawal. *Emotion, 10*(3), 349–357.

Riese, H., Snieder, H., Jeronimus, B. F., Korhonen, T., Rose, R. J., Kaprio, J., et al. (2014). Timing of stressful life events affects stability and change of neuroticism. *European Journal of Personality, 28,* 193–200.

Roberts, B. W., Kuncel, N. R., Shiner, R. L., Caspi, A., & Goldberg, L. R. (2007). The power of personality: The comparative validity of personality traits, socioeconomic status, and cognitive ability for predicting important life outcomes. *Perspectives in Psychological Science, 2,* 313–345.

Roberts, B. W., Luo, J., Briley, D. A., Chow, P. L., Su, R., & Hill, P. L. (2017). A systematic review of personality trait change through intervention. *Psychological Bulletin, 143*(2), 117–141.

Roberts, B. W., Walton, K. E., & Viechtbauer, W. (2006). Patterns of mean-level change in personality traits across the life course: A meta-analysis of longitudinal studies. *Psychological Bulletin, 132*(1), 1–25.

Robinson, M. D., & Wilkowski, B. (2014). Personality processes and processes as personality: A cognitive perspective. In M. Mikulincer & P. Shaver (Eds.), M. L. Cooper, & R. Larsen (Assoc. Eds.), *APA handbook of personality and social psychology: Vol. 3. Personality processes and individual differences* (pp. 129–145). Washington, DC: American Psychological Association.

Robinson, O. C., Noftle, E. E., Guo, J., Asadi, S., & Zhang, X. (2015). Goals and plans for Big Five personality trait change in young adults. *Journal of Research in Personality, 59,* 31–43.

Rothbart, M. K. (1996). *Revised Infant Behavior Questionnaire.* Unpublished manuscript, University of Oregon, Eugene, OR.

Rothbart, M. K. (2011). *Becoming who we are: Temperament and personality in development.* New York: Guilford Press.

Rothbart, M. K., Ahadi, S. A., Hershey, K. L., & Fisher, P. (2001). Investigations of temperament at three to seven years: The Children's Behavior Questionnaire. *Child Development, 72,* 1394–1408.

Schofield, T. J., Conger, R. D., Donnellan, M. B., Jochem, R., Widaman, K. F., & Conger, K. J. (2012). Parent personality and positive parenting as predictors of positive adolescent personality development over time. *Merrill–Palmer Quarterly, 58,* 255–283.

Selby, E. A., Kranzler, A., Panza, E., & Fehling, K. B. (2016). Bidirection-compounding effects of rumination and negative emotion in predicting impulsive behavior: Implications for emotional cascades. *Journal of Personality, 84*(2), 139–153.

Shackman, A. J., Stockbridge, M. D., Tillman, R. M., Kaplan, C. M., Tromp, E. P. M., Fox, A. S., et al. (2016). The neurobiology of dispositional negativity and attentional biases to threat: Implications for understanding anxiety disorders in adults and youth. *Journal of Experimental Psychopathology, 7*(3), 311–342.

Shackman, A. J., Tromp, D. P. M., Stockbridge, M. D., Kaplan, C. M., Tillman, R. M., & Fox, A. S. (2016). Dispositional negativity: An integrative psychological and neurobiological perspective. *Psychological Bulletin, 142*(12), 1275–1314.

Shackman, A. J., Weinstein, J. S., Hudja, S. N., Bloomer, C. D., Barstead, M. G., Fox, A. S., et al. (2017). Dispositional negativity in the wild: Social environment governs momentary emotional experience. *Emotion.* [Epub ahead of print]

Shiner, R. L. (2018). What develops in emotional development? In R. Davidson, A. Hackman, A. Fox, & R. Lapate (Eds.), *The nature of emotion* (2nd ed.). New York: Oxford University Press.

Shiner, R. L., Allen, T. A., & Masten, A. S. (2017). Adversity in adolescence predicts personality trait change from childhood to adulthood. *Journal of Research in Personality, 67,* 171–182.

Shiner, R. L., & DeYoung, C. G. (2013). The structure of temperament and personality traits: A developmental perspective. In P. Zelazo (Ed.), *Oxford handbook of developmental psychology* (pp. 113–141). New York: Oxford University Press.

Shiner, R. L., & Masten, A. S. (2012). Childhood personality as a harbinger of competence and resilience in adulthood. *Development and Psychopathology, 24*(2), 507–528.

Shiner, R. L., Masten, A. S., & Tellegen, A. (2002). A developmental perspective on personality in emerging adulthood: Childhood antecedents and concurrent adaptation. *Journal of Personality and Social Psychology, 83,* 1165–1177.

Soto, C. J., & John, O. P. (2013). Traits in transition: The structure of parent-reported personality traits from early childhood to early adulthood. *Journal of Personality, 82*(3), 182–199.

Soto, C. J., & John, O. P. (2017). The next Big Five Inventory (BFI-2): Developing and assessing a hierarchical model with 15 facets to enhance bandwidth, fidelity, and predictive power *Journal of Personality and Social Psychology, 113,* 117–143.

Stroud, C. B., Sosoo, E. E., & Wilson, S. (2015). Normal personality traits, rumination and stress generation among early adolescent girls. *Journal of Research in Personality, 57,* 131–142.

Stuijfzand, S., Creswell, C., Field, A. P., Pearcey, S., & Dodd, H. (2017). Is anxiety associated with negative interpretations of ambiguity in children and adolescents?: A systematic review and meta-analysis. *Journal of Child Psychology and Psychiatry.* [Epub ahead of print]

Tamir, M. (2005). Don't worry, be happy?: Neuroticism, trait-consistent affect regulation, and performance.

Journal of Personality and Social Psychology, 89(3), 449–461.

Tamir, M., Robinson, M. D., & Solberg, E. C. (2006). You may worry, but can you recognize threats when you see them?: Neuroticism, threat identifications, and negative affect. *Journal of Personality, 74*(5), 1481–1506.

Thomas, J. C., Letourneau, N., Campbell, T. S., Tomfohr-Madsen, L., Giesbrecht, G. F., & APrON Study Team. (2017). Developmental origins of infant emotion regulation: Mediation by temperamental negativity and moderation by maternal sensitivity. *Developmental Psychology, 53*(4), 611–628.

Uliaszek, A. A., Zinbarg, R. E., Mineka, S., Craske, M. G., Griffith, J. W., Sutton, J. M., et al. (2012). A longitudinal examination of stress generation in de-

pressive and anxiety disorders. *Journal of Abnormal Psychology, 121*(1), 4–15.

Uziel, L. (2016). Alone, unhappy, and demotivated: The impact of an alone mind-set on neurotic individuals' willpower. *Social Psychological and Personality Science, 7*(8), 818–827.

Vaidya, J. G., Gray, E. K., Haig, J., & Watson, D. (2002). On the temporal stability of personality: Evidence for differential stability and the role of life experiences. *Journal of Personality and Social Psychology, 83,* 469–484.

Vroman, L. N., Lo, S. L., & Durbin, C. E. (2014). Structure and convergent validity of children's temperament traits as assessed by experimenter ratings of child behavior. *Journal of Research in Personality, 52,* 6–12.

CHAPTER 9

Lifespan Development of Conscientiousness

Joshua J. Jackson
Patrick L. Hill

Hard work, discipline, and initiative—along with a level playing field—are often said to be prerequisites necessary to obtain the American dream, a life of prosperity and freedom for oneself and one's family. In grappling with the question of how to obtain a life of prosperity, most policy discussion focus on leveling societal barriers related to ethnicity, gender, race, socioeconomic status, region of residence, and religion. Once these societal barriers to success are leveled, the thinking goes, then anyone with enough gumption and dedication can get a degree, own a home, raise a family, and establish a lucrative career—all markers of prosperity. Assuming it is possible to level the playing field by having these barriers vanquished, would everyone be able to obtain prosperity? Or would the supposed meritocracy that ensues result in sustained inequality, a by-product of the natural distribution of individual talents in which some are able to work harder, are naturally smarter, or have skills others do not? In other words, is everyone capable of the hard work, dedication, and initiative necessary to obtain successful outcomes?

In this chapter, we examine personality traits such as self-control, responsibility, and effortful control, which are important individual characteristics that yield prosperity and success in a multitude of domains. We argue that these characteristics are key components in obtaining a broad swath of successful life outcomes, outcomes that are invoked by the ideal of the American Dream. In reviewing the literature on the development of these characteristics we discuss typical developmental trends, the reasons why these characteristics are so helpful in yielding lifelong success, and what factors are related to growth in these domains.

Conscientiousness and Effortful Control

Two of the most discussed characteristics related to lifelong success are effortful control and conscientiousness. However, the two are often not discussed together, as effortful control is measured almost exclusively in childhood, whereas conscientiousness is more often assessed in adolescent and adult samples. Further complicating matters is that characteristics related to effortful control often are referred to with other names, such as self-regulation. Together, however, effortful control and conscientiousness capture characteristics across the lifespan that relate to behaviors linked to positive outcomes such as paying attention, showing up on time, following through with commitments, and hard work (Jackson et al., 2009).

Effortful control broadly refers to self regulatory abilities whereby one inhibits a dominant response in favor of a subdominant response

(Rothbart & Bates, 2006). This process results in sustained attention and persistence across tasks, planning behavior, and task persistence (Kochanska, Murray, & Harlan, 2000; Rothbart & Rueda, 2005). Effortful control is considered intentional and is therefore done with regard to goal-directed processes (Eisenberg, Smith, Sadovsky, & Spinrad, 2004). These self-regulatory abilities allow children to temper emotional responses, which results in associations between effortful control and affective personality traits such as neuroticism and extraversion. However, both definitionally and empirically, effortful control is most strongly related to later measures of conscientiousness (Halverson et al., 2003), though attention is more central to the concept of effortful control than to conscientiousness (Eisenberg, Duckworth, Spinrad, & Valiente, 2014).

The personality trait of *conscientiousness* refers to a broad number of constructs that describe individual differences in the propensity to be self-controlled, responsible to others, hardworking, orderly, and rule abiding (Jackson & Roberts, 2017). As with all personality traits, conscientiousness can be broken down into narrower traits referred to as *facets.* Depending on how broad or narrow one wants to split conscientiousness up, there may be as few as two facets to as many as 14 identifiable subcomponents. Commonly assessed facets of conscientiousness include orderliness, industriousness, responsibility, self-control, and formality (for a more thorough discussion of the subcomponents of conscientiousness and common measures used to assess facets, see Jackson & Roberts, 2017; Roberts, Lejuez, Krueger, Richards, & Hill, 2014).

Typically, conscientiousness is thought of as primarily a behavioral trait (Jackson, Wood, Bogg, Walton, Harms, & Roberts, 2010), often the direct result of some motivated or goal-directed behavior. As with all personality traits, the manifest behaviors associated with the trait alone do not describe what it means to be conscientiousness. In addition to the behavioral side of conscientiousness, the emotional and cognitive components of conscientiousness play an important role. In terms of the emotional side of conscientiousness, guilt is central. Conscientious individuals are less likely to report feeling guilt but are *more* prone to experiencing guilt in a given situation (Fayard, Roberts, Robins, & Watson, 2012); that is, they act in ways that avoid guilt-provoking situations, for example, by being responsible and hardworking to meet deadlines. Moreover, they are helped in meeting these deadlines by anticipating the negative consequences that would weigh on them if they did not accomplish their goal, and using this as a motivating factor. Furthermore, because of the productive behaviors they exhibit, conscientious individuals tend to have higher levels of subjective well-being and positive affect.

In terms of the cognitive side of personality, conscientiousness individuals may be best described with respect to their decision-making tendencies, especially with regard to time preference (Daly, Harmon, & Delaney, 2009). In general, conscientious individuals are future-oriented, thinking about the consequences of their actions (Mahalingam, Stillwell, Kosinski, Rust, & Kogan, 2014). These thoughts are often goal and achievement focused (Costantini et al., 2015).

Effortful control and *conscientiousness* are not the only terms used to refer to these suites of characteristics. *Self-regulation* (which captures even more constructs; see Nigg, 2017), *undercontrolled* and *overcontrolled* (Block & Block, 1980), *behavioral inhibition, impulsivity, cognitive control, delay of gratification,* and *willpower,* among many others, all capture some aspects that fall under the broad umbrella of conscientiousness or relate to effortful control. While each term has utility in certain contexts, we prefer to use the term *conscientiousness,* using more specific terms when warranted. First, it (or a very closely related construct such as constraint) is part of all the main taxonomies of individual differences (e.g., the Big Three, the Big Five, the Big Six), whereas other terms are omitted or constitute a smaller subcomponent of the taxonomy. Second, conscientiousness was initially developed to assess and is predominantly discussed with regard to individual differences, as opposed to describing general process (e.g., cognitive control). As a result, there are clear ways and enough literature to report on the nomological net of conscientiousness. Third, conscientiousness is broad by definition, with many of the other characteristics serving as facets of the overarching latent trait. For example, in addition to being thought as a developmental precursor to conscientiousness, effortful control may be thought of as constituting an inhibitive component, similar to the self-control facets of conscientiousness (Carver, Johnson, & Joormann, 2008).

The Importance of Conscientiousness for Future Life Outcomes

The importance of conscientiousness as a psychological construct is indisputable when considering the ability to predict many important life outcomes, such as health and longevity (Jackson, Connolly, Garrison, Levine, & Connolly, 2015; Moffitt et al., 2011), occupational success (Dudley, Orvis, Lebiecki, & Cortina, 2006), marital stability (Solomon & Jackson, 2014b), academic achievement (Noftle & Robins, 2007), wealth (Moffitt et al., 2011), criminality (Moffitt et al., 2011), and social networks (Van der Linden, Scholte, Cillessen, te Nijenhuis, & Segers, 2010). Unsurprisingly, accumulation of these positive outcomes results in conscientious individuals being happier (DeNeve & Cooper, 1998). Given the associations with almost any life outcome that can be deemed significant, it is important to understand how conscientious individuals obtain a healthy, wealthy, and happy life. Through uncovering pathways between conscientiousness and significant life outcomes, we can better understand how conscientious individuals behave throughout their lifespan. Moreover, these associations may also provide insights on how the trait of conscientiousness remains stable or changes across the lifespan.

For example, these predictive associations are found across decades, such as with childhood and young adult personality predicting longevity up to 80 years later (Friedman et al., 1995; Jackson et al., 2015). The long-term predictive ability for personality suggests that many life outcomes are built on cumulative processes that take years or decades to emerge, such as continually smoking for decades. An alternative hypothesis is that the long-term stability of personality (Roberts & DelVeccio, 2000) is responsible for the predictive associations between childhood personality and late-life outcomes rather than a cumulative process. The predictive validity of neuroticism may especially be likely due to the long-term stability of neuroticism. Neurotic tendencies such as being overly stressed in childhood likely do not directly influence current stressors within a romantic relationship, even if neuroticism in childhood predicts divorce in adulthood. Here, the association between early personality and a later-life outcome is driven by the mediating variable of neuroticism in adulthood, which is associated with childhood neuroticism. The

mechanism responsible for predicting divorce via early neuroticism is (likely) the consistency of neuroticism across the lifespan, not that neuroticism in childhood set forth a causal pathway of cascading influences that reached past childhood into adulthood.

Conscientiousness, on the other hand, is associated with many outcomes because of cumulative processes that reach across decades. Recently, we described this cumulative process through the invest and accrue model of conscientiousness (Hill & Jackson, 2016). Briefly, conscientious individuals may be thought of as operating, consciously or not, to discount present desires relative to the future goals, and to establish positive, foundation-building behaviors within particular domains (e.g., exercise, study). Often this process corresponds with disregarding short-term gains that may also be considered more enjoyable in the present (e.g., relaxing in front of the TV or going out with friends). For example, resources such as time, energy, and even money, are used by conscientious individuals to study longer and harder, to be more likely to go to a top college, all in the effort to obtain some positive, long-term outcome. We view this as a tendency to "invest" in one's future, similar to how one would invest money instead of letting it burn a hole in one's pocket (Hill & Jackson, 2016). As most broad life outcomes such as good health and a successful job are not something one can accomplish in a short period, conscientious individuals discount short-term payouts—neglect fun parties to study, work late nights instead of hanging out with friends, exercise instead of relaxing—and put time and effort in the hope for a positive payout in the future. Here are the ingredients of the American dream, which are built from the ground up, a process that takes time and effort.

Time, energy, and money are not infinite, so where should one invest one's limited resources and when? Conscientious individuals invest their energies toward success in a given domain, depending on the goals of the developmental period. Using lifespan theories of development (e.g., Hutteman, Hennecke, Orth, Reitz, & Specht, 2014), each developmental period of life is characterized by challenges and obstacles that one needs to address. These typically take the path of friendship development and education in adolescence and young adulthood, to family and career in adulthood, and finally to retirement, broadening family roles and increased societal and health concerns in later life. These are rough developmental milestones with respect to when and whether they occur for every person, but they roughly characterize what domains conscientious individuals emphasize over other choices. We do not want to say that investment behaviors must occur during these time periods, nor do we suggest that people should invest in their careers and neglect to start a family. Instead, these milestones guide what goals or motivations drive the broad actions of conscientious individuals during different life domains.

In financial investing, the returns of one's investment multiply via compound interest. In lifespan investment, a similar cumulative benefit occurs when success in one domain spills over into another. A good education leads to a good job, which helps with securing a good job, which assists in marriage market, as well as the knowledge, ability, and desire to stay fit and healthy. Furthermore, the cumulative advantage that conscientious individuals get from success within one domain means that they are more likely to be able to weather a storm in another domain. For example, if dealing with job loss, a conscientious individual should be better able to find another job due to his or her higher levels of education, and may already have several contacts in the field given his or her greater entrenchment and connection to the community. Also, he or she may have greater levels of savings and better credit to ease the way during this transition period (Bernerth, Taylor, Walker, & Whitman, 2012; Webley & Nyhus, 2006). There are a number of instances in which an unforeseen event (job loss, long-term illness, divorce) may send shockwaves throughout a person's life domains. Being conscientious means that there is a scaffolding—via educational degrees, social networks, savings, advantageous work policies and insurance—that prevents these storms from wreaking havoc on multiple domains. Importantly, this scaffolding cannot be built quickly; it is the result of long-term dedication to accruing skills and resources.

The scaffolding safeguards are often invoked as privileges afforded to those with higher levels of socioeconomic status and higher levels of cognitive ability (Herrnstein & Murray, 2010). We do not want to imply that scaffolding in terms of social networks and monetary resources can only accrue via conscientiousness or that everyone with these safeguards is high in conscientiousness. Instead, we want to highlight that safeguards to unforeseen life events may

accrue through hard work if one is not already born into the upper social strata.

In addition to scaffolding to fall back on in the case of an unforeseen life event, disrupting life events are less likely to affect conscientious individuals. In addition to direct pathways between conscientiousness and life events reviewed earlier, there are synergistic pathways in which beneficial behaviors within a particular domain are also beneficial across multiple domains. Think of the characteristics that make a good romantic partner, friend, or employee; being dependable, organized, and self-controlled would yield greater success in each of these domains. Once someone is proficient at organization within his or her work, for example, other domains are likely to benefit because the person can use the same resources across different life domains. In contrast, a person who is low on conscientiousness may see escalating problems when problems in his or her home life seep into work performance. There is some evidence for this cross-domain effect. For example, being able to rely on a conscientious spouse allows one to work more successfully in terms of obtaining a higher salary and job satisfaction (Solomon & Jackson, 2014a). These effects are largely mediated through the conscientious spouse's ability to mitigate additional household chores. In short, being conscientious means that a person doesn't make extra work for him- or herself, leading to intertwined success and failure in life domains.

To highlight cross-domain synergistic effects, it is helpful to look at those low in conscientiousness who are most in need of a safety net. Cases have been documented in which people who lost their job faced additional crises concerning paying for and finding shelter, caring for their children, and even getting enough sleep to fully function due to the need to take on multiple part time jobs to make ends meet. Losing one's job (or spouse, or contracting a severe illness) is stressful and costly, and without a social network or excess funds, it may be difficult to climb out of the hole. And this has nothing to say about the negative coping mechanisms (e.g., drinking or other drug use) that often come with unexpected life events such as these. Again, it is not the case that everyone who is in this situation is low in conscientiousness because those who are younger and female are more likely to be in perilous situations in which one setback could cause a series of additional setbacks. The difficulties faced by those low in conscientiousness stem partly from the growing chasm between those with and without education, which results in fewer resources for those low in conscientiousness.

In summary, the invest and accrue model of conscientiousness provides a lifespan perspective on how to think about the tasks that are relevant for conscientiousness and how early transactions can form pathways that shape the outcomes of conscientious individuals. Below we further describe the life tasks across each age period that are indicative of investing in one's future success and thus influencing the development of conscientiousness. During each life period, we discuss the descriptive patterns of development and the mechanisms likely to shape the development of conscientiousness.

Conscientiousness in Childhood and Adolescence

As mentioned earlier, conscientiousness in childhood takes a different form than conscientiousness as assessed in adulthood. Partly this is due to the difficulties of assessing standard conscientiousness item content within children. Most children do not have many opportunities to work hard, show up to places on time, or meet deadlines given that much of their life is controlled by their parents. Furthermore, most children are quite disorganized and impulsive due to lack of brain maturation and motivation. Moreover, the standard measures of conscientiousness that were initially developed for adults are self-reports, which present numerous problems for adolescents, let alone children. As a result of these difficulties, the assessment of constructs such as effortful control is preferred over conscientiousness proper.

Given assessment difficulties, it is amazing that starting at approximately 3 years of age, the test–retest consistency of effortful control is roughly between .2 and .5 during childhood, depending on the time in between assessments and age at assessment (Eisenberg et al., 2004; Kochanska et al., 2000). Clearly, these levels of consistency are a far cry from unity, but they are suggestive of meaningful consistency across childhood from an early age, especially in light of assessment difficulties in children.

In addition to measures of effortful control, numerous studies employ a typology approach to personality assessment of children (Block & Block, 1980; Robins, John, Caspi, Moffitt, & Stouthamer-Loeber, 1996). Personality types related to effortful control and conscientiousness have been replicated in child (e.g., Asendorpf & van Aken, 1999) and adolescent samples (e.g., Robins et al., 1996), as well as older samples (Specht, Luhmann, & Geiser, 2014). However, like effortful control measures, these scales do not have a one-to-one correspondence with conscientiousness in older adulthood. While personality types can be characterized by taxonomies such as the Big Five (Klimstra, Luyckx, Teppers, Goossens, & De Fruyt, 2011), most types are associated with conscientiousness. For example, resilient youth have higher than average levels of emotional stability, extraversion, openness, agreeableness, and conscientiousness; undercontrolled youth are characterized by lower than average levels of those domains (outside of extraversion), and overcontrolled youth tend to exhibit the lowest scores on extraversion and emotional stability (Klimstra et al., 2011; Robins et al., 1996). These type studies again point to the difficulty of measuring a construct commensurate with conscientiousness in childhood. Despite this, personality types are relatively consistent across time, with little change in types, suggesting that the characteristics related to conscientiousness in childhood are modestly consistent through adolescence and young adulthood (Klimstra, Hale, Raaijmakers, Branje, & Meeus, 2009). For example, types in childhood as young as age 3 show consistency into adulthood (Caspi, 2000).

One difficulty in assessing the development of conscientiousness from childhood into adolescence and beyond is the variety of methods used to assess conscientiousness. Assessments of conscientiousness and related constructs in childhood mainly feature parent or observer reports, whereas starting in adolescence, one may be able to utilize self-reports. Furthermore, there are additional concerns related to potential structural changes in personality constructs across development. Adolescence represents a time when cognitive faculties, linguistic abilities, and metacognitive perspectives, including identity development and self-concept, may all affect the validity of ratings. Shifts in the construct coherence and age-appropriate expression of traits further complicate trait assessment (Caspi & Shiner, 2008). Adolescence then represents a unique measurement scenario, as it straddles the space between self-ratings in adulthood and observer rating methods in childhood.

Conscientiousness is seen to decrease, sometimes dramatically, starting around age 10, before beginning to increase in late adolescence and young adulthood (De Fruyt et al., 2006; Heaven & Ciarrochi, 2008; Soto, John, Gosling, & Potter, 2011; Van den Akker, Deković, Asscher, & Prinzie, 2014). Some of these declines are related to the onset of puberty, which, beyond a number of biological changes, also thrusts a number of new social experiences and expectations into the lives of adolescents. Notably, during this time, there appear to be steep declines in the self-control facet of conscientiousness (Harden & Tucker-Drob, 2011). These declines in conscientiousness, however, are not always seen in both teacher- and self-reports. For example, teacher- and self-reports of conscientiousness over a 2-year period were found to show opposite trends and were not correlated with one another (Jackson, 2017a).

Mechanisms of Change

What are the experiences responsible for driving these changes? The most important social experience during this time period is the educational context. Here, children are exposed to new ideas and interact with different people, and form peer groups. It is during school time that children are able to separate themselves from their family life and differentiate themselves. Relative to later adolescence, there is some work suggesting that success in school is related to positive conscientiousness development (Brandt, Mike, & Jackson, 2018). For example, increases in conscientiousness are related to increases in achievement behavior, such as good study habits (Bleidorn, 2012), academic performance (Heaven & Ciarrochi, 2008), and doing one's homework (Göllner et al., 2017). In other words, while most individuals decline in conscientiousness around adolescence, those who perform well in school demonstrate fewer declines.

Why would school experiences shift conscientiousness? Based on a number of personality development theories (Roberts & Jackson, 2008; Specht, Bleidorn, et al., 2014; Wrzus & Roberts, 2017), most of the changes that occur are due to long-term shifts in behavior. School systems ultimately shift behavior by promoting certain expectations for behavior, and setting up consequences when students fall outside expectations. By encouraging skills that lead to success, such as being responsible, paying attention in class, and resisting impulses, schools are rewarding students to modify their motivations, goals, and behaviors. The end result is that spending a significant amount of time immersed in environments that promote changes in behavior may lead to enduring, prolonged changes in one's identity and ultimately in conscientiousness. These processes may be particularly relevant during adolescence, when personality is especially receptive to outside influences, considering that it is a key period of identity formation (Hampson, 2008; Steinberg & Morris, 2001).

A recent study has explored the specific experiences within school environments and how they influenced the development of conscientiousness during adolescence (Brandt et al., 2018). They found that positive student–teacher relationships, positive peers, parents who are involved in school, positive feelings about school, finding school and classes engaging, and putting effort into one's schoolwork are associated with increases in conscientiousness. Especially important appear to be parental relationships and overall feelings of school satisfaction. Earlier levels of impulse control may influence future levels of school satisfaction by setting up positive pathways and habits that make school a more enjoyable experience. For example, conscientious students may have a better understanding of school rules and expectations, causing them to more easily integrate into the school schedule and environment from year to year, and making them less likely to get in trouble. Students who are conscientious may also encourage more productive parental involvement by being willing to have discussions about academic topics, goals, and values, whereas parents whose students are highly impulsive may spend more time admonishing and disciplining their children rather than discussing academic choices (Brandt et al., 2018).

In addition to these individual-level school experiences, there are a number of programs that attempt to foster a more effective school environment, with the ultimate goal to produce widespread positive outcomes. These programs (e.g., Head Start) do not seem to affect cognitive ability, but they do affect outcomes linked to conscientiousness, such as fewer school absences, higher graduation rates, higher rates of college attendance, higher employment rates, and higher earnings (Kautz, Heckman, Diris, Ter Weel, & Borghans, 2014). As a result, there has been a suggestion that these early school programs have their effect through fostering skills related to conscientiousness. Despite these suggestions, almost no studies have systematically tested whether these school programs yield changes in conscientiousness or other related traits. A recent study tested whether entry into Head Start (a long running program that promotes school readiness and cognitive and noncognitive skills in children ages 3–5 from low-income families) would lead to increased levels conscientiousness during adolescence, roughly 10 years after the Head Start experience. Those involved in Head Start were lower or equivalent in conscientiousness to matched controls, indicating no long-term effects of Head Start for conscientiousness (Jackson, Beck, & Weston, 2017). These findings are consistent with those from adolescence, suggesting that programs such as these have few widespread positive effects on character traits or important outcomes (Hill, Turiano, Hurd, Mroczek, & Roberts, 2011).

Conscientiousness in Adulthood

Across a number of cross-sectional and longitudinal studies, conscientiousness tends to increase from young adulthood up to the age of 60 (Allemand, Zimprich, & Hendriks, 2008; Roberts, Walton, & Viechtbauer, 2006; Soto & John, 2012; Terracciano, McCrae, Brant, & Costa, 2005). This normative pattern of development replicates across a number of different cultures and countries, including Germany, Italy, Portugal, Croatia, South Korea (McCrae et al., 1999), and Vietnam (Walton et al., 2013). Most of the increases in conscientiousness occur during young adulthood, with the increases tapering off during middle age (Roberts, Walton, et al., 2006). Out of all of the Big Five traits, conscientiousness is the trait that evidences the largest absolute increase across the lifespan, mostly during the adulthood years.

Viewing conscientiousness at a facet level reveals a more nuanced developmental story. The facets of self-control and responsibility increase in young adulthood and continue to increase into old age, mirroring the trends found at the broad trait level (Jackson et al., 2009; Soto et al., 2011). Industriousness tends to change the most during young adulthood, with some evidence of increases continuing to occur throughout the lifespan (Jackson et al., 2009; Soto & John, 2012; Terracciano et al.,

2005). Two facets prove unique: Conventionality does not change from young adulthood to middle adulthood, but it appears to change during older adulthood (Jackson et al., 2009). Orderliness, on the other hand, undergoes limited change across the lifespan compared to the other facets (Jackson et al., 2009; Soto et al., 2011; Soto & John, 2012). Overall, increases in conscientiousness earlier in life can be thought of as mainly resulting from increases in impulse control, responsibility, and industriousness, while increases in later adulthood are driven by changes in impulse control, reliability, and conventionality.

Most of these findings have relied on self-reports of change. Looking at observer reports of change paints a different picture of development. A number of studies using observer reports generally replicate the pattern of change for conscientiousness found using self-reports (Jackson et al., 2009; Jackson, Beck, & Weston, 2017; McCrae et al., 2004, 2005). There are, nonetheless, some subtle, but important, differences between the patterns of change based on self and observer ratings. For example, the magnitude of change tends to be lower when using observer-reports compared to self-reports (McCrae et al., 2004; McCrae & Terracciano, 2005). In addition, greater changes in observer-reported personality are found later in the life course compared to more stability in self-reports (Jackson et al., 2009). These findings suggest that genuine personality trait change may be difficult for observers to detect and may take time to become integrated into the observer's assessment. Alternatively, these findings could imply that changes in conscientiousness are more behaviorally observable in older adulthood.

While observer reports of conscientiousness sometimes converge with self-ratings, studies in which the informants are romantic partners find declines in conscientiousness, the opposite of increases found in self-reports (Costa & McCrae, 1988; Watson & Humrichouse, 2006). Are romantic partners, who should be close and confide in one another, unable to see eye-to-eye with their spouse, not only missing changes felt in the self but finding change in the opposite direction? A recent study indicated that these declines are driven primarily by declines in relationship satisfaction and study characteristics such as participant age and study length (Jackson, 2017b). These disparate self–other findings are mostly a result of using relationship satisfaction as a heuristic for romantic partners rating their spouses' personalities. Given that relationships tend to decline in relationship satisfaction over the course of a partnership, the decline also results in romantic partners seeing their spouses less favorably in terms of conscientiousness as time goes on. Importantly, however, informant-reported declines in conscientiousness were not found when the study was over a long period of time (20 years) or with older couples who have been together for decades (Jackson, 2017b). Presumably, the normative changes in relationship satisfaction occur mostly earlier on in a relationship, when people are transitioning out of the honeymoon period. As such, the conditions that result in opposite patterns of development from self- and observer reports appear to be short-lived, mostly happening earlier in the lifespan.

Do these opposite trends mean that informant reports of development are not valid in some circumstances or that change in conscientiousness based on self-reports are biased in some way? No. Regardless of whether normative changes match across method, changes in self are modestly correlated with informant-based changes at the individual level (Jackson, 2017b); that is, if someone has greater than average self-reported change, this is likely to correspond with a partner who reports that his or her spouse increased in conscientiousness. While the two perspectives do not see eye-to-eye, the correlated changes between methods suggest that these changes are not solely in the eye of the beholder.

Mechanisms of Change

As with all personality traits, not everyone experiences the same normative development— some people do not increase in conscientiousness and others even decline. Much of the work explaining these individual differences in change focuses on the roles occupied during adulthood, notably, one's occupation and one's family life. To expand on the findings from childhood school success, some of the most influential experiences in adulthood relate to achievement settings. For example, students tend to increase in conscientiousness during the final year of high school, likely in preparation for the new responsibilities they anticipate taking on in college or in the workforce (Bleidhorn, 2012). However, individual experiences are important, as not everyone follows this pattern. Those who are not invested in school tend

to change less compared to those who do invest in school (Bleidhorn, 2012; Brandt et al., 2018).

Leaving school and obtaining one's first job is also associated with increases in conscientiousness (Specht, Egloff, & Schmukle, 2011). Presumably, these changes are due to the increased responsibilities, demands, and expectations associated with one's first job. In line with this idea, individuals who invest in and are satisfied with their occupation evidence increases in conscientiousness (Roberts, Caspi, & Moffitt, 2003), whereas people who deinvest in work, such as committing counterproductive work behaviors, demonstrate declines (Hudson, Roberts, & Lodi-Smith, 2012; Roberts, Walton, Bogg, & Caspi, 2006). Responsibilities and demands for one's job could continue to ratchet up throughout midlife as people are promoted and placed in new work roles, continuing the processes likely to increase levels of conscientiousness. However, there is also a lot of stagnation during this time period, when people get settled in their work roles, do not take on new opportunities, and merely punch the clock and work for the weekend. It is likely partly due to this middle to late career phenomenon that we do not see as many increases in conscientiousness during this point in the lifespan compared to earlier adulthood.

The other major role during adulthood is the romantic relationships and family life. There appears to be some evidence that becoming involved in one's first romantic relationship is associated with increases in conscientiousness (Neyer & Asendorpf, 2001; Neyer & Lehnart, 2007). Similarly, the length of a relationship is also associated with increases in conscientiousness, such that women who were married longer increased more in conscientiousness (Roberts & Bogg, 2004). Such increases in conscientiousness likely reflect the maintenance of daily behaviors that keep a relationship healthy, given that conscientiousness influences the quality romantic relationships (Solomon & Jackson, 2014b). It should be noted, however, that in a number of studies, investment in romantic relationships was not associated with changes in conscientiousness (Jackson, 2017b). It may be the case that those who enter into relationships and have longer relationships are different in other regards, and that it is these differences that are driving changes in conscientiousness, not the relationship experiences per se. While it is well known that being conscientious is important for a successful relationship, it is less understood whether these interactions facilitate growth in conscientiousness.

Ending a long-term relationship has also been associated with changes in conscientiousness, though evidence suggests the effects depend on gender. Specht and colleagues (2011) found that conscientiousness increases after a divorce, whereas Roberts and Bogg (2004), in a study consisting solely of women, found that women decreased in conscientiousness after a divorce. Though further research is needed to determine the nature of these findings, one possible explanation is that divorced women may have fewer responsibilities because they no longer have to take care of their husbands, resulting in lower levels of conscientious, whereas men's responsibilities may increase after a divorce.

A major life event during this time period is having a child. Despite being a relatively normative event that is indicative of investment in one's relationship, there is little evidence that having a child is associated with changes in conscientiousness. Specht and colleagues (2011) found declines in women's conscientiousness after experiencing childbirth. Presumably, declines could result from an overloaded schedule, one with increased responsibilities and less time to take care of previous obligations. Neglecting work, cleanliness and organization, and even self-control to cope with a new child would be almost expected from new parents. However, the increased responsibility that a new life in one's care entails would, perhaps, be associated with increases in conscientiousness over the long haul. In line with a number of theories, this idea of increased commitment to one's family by having a child, and the daily obligations to successfully raise the child, should ultimately yield increases in conscientiousness (Roberts, Wood, & Caspi, 2008). A recent study over 5 years in length attempted to address some of the shortcomings of previous studies, namely, the differences in personality of people who have children versus those that choose not to (van Scheppingen et al., 2016). Interestingly, no long-term changes in conscientiousness were associated with having a child, despite all of the increased responsibilities that go into parenting. Thus, it appears that some of the previously reported effects of childbirth were due to differences in the types of people who have children versus those that do not.

After spending years in education and establishing one's career, family life, and friends, individuals find themselves channeled toward the status quo during the middle adult years. During this time, changes in conscientiousness may not be as prevalent due to the scaffolding that has been built up to complete many of these life goals. As a result, conscientious individuals may be less willing to take a new job, return to school for additional degrees, or to move to a new job or disengage from a dysfunctional family life. The lack of action likely results in fewer changes in personality, especially if the comfort of the current situation results in less investment within a particular domain. In this light, fewer novel experiences are the reward for the years of building and investing in one's career and social life. Accordingly, being overly conscientious could lead individuals to avoid taking the risks necessary to get ahead or to try new things. In summary, a calm life in terms of having a job, family, and housing situation set up prior to retirement age bodes well for the transition into retirement, but it does not necessarily prompt further change.

Conscientiousness in Older Adulthood

The transition into older adulthood is more tumultuous than that in the later years of adulthood. Retirement is a time for new social activities, for potentially moving to a new home and maybe to a new region, for the broadening of grandparent or lessening of parental roles, and an increased focus on health. Given the associations between conscientiousness and critical issues facing older adults, such as onset of chronic conditions (Weston, Hill, & Jackson, 2015), Alzheimer's disease (Wilson, Schneider, Arnold, Bienias, & Bennett, 2007), and even mortality risk (Hill, Turiano, et al., 2011; Kern & Friedman, 2008), older adulthood may be viewed as a period during which stability, or even normative increases, in conscientiousness may be particularly valuable.

In terms of rank-order consistency, the consistency of conscientiousness increases steadily with age until it plateaus between ages of 50 and 70 (Roberts & DelVecchio, 2000), and then declines in old-old age (Lucas & Donnellan, 2011). Earlier meta-analytic work suggested that the potential for increases in stability during the seventh decade, with relative stability occurring after age 70 (Roberts, Walton, & Viechtbauer, 2006). Though this early work was limited by the relatively few longitudinal studies available for the meta-analysis, research into normative trajectories on conscientiousness has been bolstered in recent years by the increasing inclusion of personality measures into large-scale longitudinal studies of aging. While some investigations have supported the claims of mean-level stability in older adulthood (Hill, Weston, & Jackson, 2018), other recent studies have suggested modest, mean-level declines in conscientiousness into older adulthood (Lucas & Donnellan, 2011; Specht et al., 2011; Wortman, Lucas, & Donellan, 2012).

While cross-sectional research has shown that the facets of conscientiousness (e.g., industriousness, orderliness, self-control) show differential patterns of change during adulthood (Jackson et al., 2009), further work is needed to test these claims in longitudinal samples as well. In summary, the longitudinal evidence paints a picture of either relative stability or potential mean-level declines on the trait during older adulthood. While some may be disheartened to hear that older adults' conscientiousness typically does not increase, particularly during a period of greater health concerns, it may be reassuring for some that even in older adulthood, studies have demonstrated consistent evidence for interindividual variability in change in conscientiousness (e.g., Hill et al., 2018; Small, Hertzog, Hultsch, & Dixon, 2003; Specht et al., 2011). The question then becomes which factors are influential in predicting who is more likely to experience declines rather than stability (or even increases) of conscientiousness during older adulthood.

Mechanisms of Change

One potential catalyst for declines may be exiting the workplace and entering retirement. Indeed, previous work suggests that retired individuals decline in conscientiousness compared to those who are still working (Specht et al., 2011). While retirement may bestow several positives for individuals, such as greater opportunities for leisure and/or declines in work-related stress, it is associated with a decreased sense of purpose and direction in life (Pinquart, 2002). With the loss of structure provided by work, older adults may feel more disorganized or have fewer daily pressures for orderliness. Conscientious individuals may be especially effected by the transition to retirement given that they tend to invest a lot into work, as well as excel at it (Lodi-Smith & Roberts, 2005). While retired individuals tend to spend more time doing enjoyable activities compared to full-time

employees, they have less variety in their daily tasks, do less problem solving, are less likely to learn new things, and have significantly fewer positive social interactions (Ross & Drentea, 1998)—all of which make the transition to retirement especially difficult. While engaging in new activities such as volunteering and spending more time with one's family makes the transition easier (Kaskie, Imhof, Cavanaugh, & Culp, 2008; Potocnik & Sonnentag, 2013; Wang & Shi, 2014), these activities may be especially important for the highly conscientious, who likely desire more structured, goal-oriented activities to fill their time (Jackson et al., 2010). In line with this, conscientious individuals report having more aspirational motivations for retiring, such as wanting to pursue new opportunities outside of work rather than retiring because they have reached the appropriate age to do so (Robinson, Demetre, & Corney, 2010). In line with this, Mike, Jackson, and Oltmanns (2014) found that conscientious retired individuals were more likely to volunteer than conscientious, working individuals. This implies that the utility of volunteering changes during the transition into retirement for conscientious individuals, replacing the occupational role with a new role that offers many of the same features as work.

A smooth transition into retirement may be accomplished through other means. In contrast to filling out one's time by contributing to society (i.e., volunteering), a natural tendency during retirement is to invest more in social ties of family and friends. In midlife, social well-being has been shown to change in tandem with conscientiousness (Hill, Turiano, Mroczek, & Roberts, 2012), and similar correlated changes have been shown for perceived support and conscientiousness in middle-to-older adults (Hill et al., 2018). Moreover, research also suggests that perceived social support may longitudinally predict changes in conscientiousness in older adulthood (Hill, Payne, Jackson, Stine-Morrow, & Roberts, 2014). One possible reason for these connections is that social networks provide pressures for organization and structure, which decline following retirement.

Older adulthood is also a time when health becomes more important given the rapid changes that start to occur during this age period. There is evidence that health behaviors are associated with changes in conscientiousness. For example, substance abuse is associated with non-normative decreases in conscientiousness (Roberts & Bogg, 2004). In contrast, those that demonstrate the normative increases in conscientiousness have better self-reported health and report fewer sick days at work (Magee, Heaven, & Miller, 2013; Takahashi, Edmonds, Jackson, & Roberts, 2013; Turiano et al., 2012). Conscientiousness plays an important role in the declining health period because conscientiousness is associated with the tendency to take care of oneself. Consistent with this notion, increases in conscientiousness are associated with increases in preventive health behaviors such as healthy eating, exercising, and safe driving (Takahashi et al., 2013). Similarly, decreases in alcohol usage are related to increases in conscientiousness (Littlefield, Sher, & Wood, 2009, 2010). Moreover, physical fitness in older adults was associated with increases in conscientiousness during this time span (Mõttus, Johnson, Starr, & Deary, 2012). Older adults differ from younger adults with an increased focus on health and health behaviors, with the goal to mitigate further declines in health. These adaptation processes could constrain the number of places one may demonstrate behaviors associated with conscientiousness. Together these findings indicate that behaving in a healthy manner is associated with more positive development of conscientiousness.

If poorer health is causally associated with declines in conscientiousness, then the onset of major diseases should be associated with change. In one of the few studies to examine this question, Jokela, Hakulinen, Singh-Manoux, and Kivimäki (2014) investigated whether personality traits change after the onset of a particular disease or illness (e.g., diabetes, heart disease, cancer). Across four large samples spanning 4–10 years in length, pooled analyses revealed that conscientiousness was associated with the onset of disease. Compared to participants who did not develop a major illness, those who did tended to decline in conscientiousness. However, a reanalysis of the some of the studies with an added wave of data and accounting for selection bias—as initial levels of health and personality are associated with the onset of many diseases (Weston et al., 2015)—complicates this interpretation. Results indicated fewer associations between health events and changes in conscientiousness, indicating that personality traits are highly resistant to change even in the face of life-altering events such as being diagnosed with cancer (Jackson, Weston, & Schultz, 2017). These results are in line with those of Sutin, Zonderman, Ferrucci, and Terracciano (2013), who examined personality develop-

ment within the Baltimore Longitudinal Study of Aging across 10 years. Increases in illness burden, as assessed by the Charlson Comorbidity Index, a weighted sum of 19 conditions (e.g., congenital heart failure, diabetes), were not associated with the development of conscientiousness. Similarly, Human and colleagues (2013) found that changes in conscientiousness were not related to various health markers. Collectively, these studies, and other studies in the health domain (see Jackson, Weston, & Schulz, 2017) suggest that health events do not lead directly to changes in conscientiousness.

Cultivating Conscientiousness?

If conscientiousness is associated with lifelong success, can these characteristics be taught or trained? Questions like this are routinely asked outside of traditional psychology departments, within economics (Heckman, 2007), education (Duckworth, 2016) and even public health (Caspi et al., 2016), as an avenue to impact major life outcomes. While there are indications that interventions could change personality traits (Chapman, Hampson, & Clarkin, 2014), the evidence on just how to do so is relatively weak at the moment, especially for conscientiousness (Jackson, Beck, & Mike, in press; Magdison, Roberts, Collado-Rodriguez, & Lejuez, 2014; Roberts, Hill, & Davis, 2017).

In an effort to describe what it would look like to change conscientiousness, we describe five conditions necessary for changing trait levels of conscientiousness. Most of the research on cultivating conscientiousness is derived from passive longitudinal designs rather than intervention work; thus, these preconditions are derived from longitudinal work and/or are testable hypotheses waiting to be applied to interventions. Most of these conditions are not specific to conscientiousness and could generalize to broader personality traits (see Wrusz & Roberts, 2017, for overlapping perspectives). In addition to shaping what an intervention for conscientiousness might look like, these preconditions also serve as general processes that may create stability and or change in conscientiousness across the lifespan.

• *Changes in conscientiousness take time to occur.* In general, we rely on the long-standing test–retest reliability of personality traits (Roberts & DelVecchio, 2000), along with the relatively modest mean-level changes across the lifespan (Roberts, Walton, & Viechtbauer, 2006), to indicate that personality traits do not drastically change over the life course. Thus, personality trait change typically unfolds relatively slowly, likely the result of an accumulation of experiences, but with a number of mechanisms to prevent change from occurring rapidly. To see why personality trait develops slowly, it helps to view conscientiousness through two different levels of analysis: (1) a broad, latent personality trait level, where conscientiousness is typically discussed and measured, and (2) a state level, which reflects the manifestations of personality that occur moment to moment in particular situations (Fleeson, 2001). Together these two levels help integrate conflicting theories about personality continuity and change (Roberts, 2009) and can help us visualize how environmental experiences impact personality. For example, the environment directly impacts state-level manifestations (e.g., one is more likely to work hard at school), but broad personality traits also impact state-level manifestations (e.g., industrious individuals work harder than do lazy individuals). When describing the development of conscientiousness, it is necessary to take into account the existence of both a relatively stable trait that may change slowly across time and state-level manifestations that can fluctuate depending on the environment. Viewed in this manner, short-term shifts in state-level conscientiousness will likely not lead to lasting changes in conscientiousness because the external stimulus impacts the state-level manifestation, not latent conscientiousness. A direct consequence of this view is that it is unlikely that short-term or one-shot interventions, such as those that assert personality characteristics are malleable (Yeager & Dweck, 2012), would be effective at providing long-term change in characteristics related to conscientiousness.

• *Conscientiousness changes when conscientious states are shifted.* The environment most directly impacts state-level, not trait-level, manifestations. Thus, for the environment to engender changes in latent personality traits, shifts in states beyond what is typical for a person are necessary (Chapman et al., 2014; Magidson et al., 2014; Wrusz & Roberts, 2017). For example, getting into the habit of filling out a daily planner may immediately shift state-level behaviors related to conscientiousness (e.g., showing up for meetings on time). Done over a long enough time period, filling out one's planner may become an engrained habit, one that no longer takes effort and would make one feel odd not to do so. This feeling may spread into a general desire and need for organization beyond having timely meetings, to having a clean work space and household, for example. Thus, experiences that lead to shifts in states related to conscientiousness beyond a person's typical repertoire are necessary for long-term change to occur. A caveat is that not all long-term shifts in states lead to changes in traits. Change will likely be mediated via a number of identity-related processes, such as whether changes in behavior are internalized, how pleasurable these changes are, and whether there are short- or long-term rewards associated with changes.

• *Experiences most likely to shape conscientiousness are not isolated life events.* A direct consequence of the previously described condition is that the experiences that change personality are not likely to be single life events such as getting divorced or having a child. Or at least not in the way that many people think about life events causing a fork in a road that leads to a drastic change or a "grand awakening" (Miller & C'deBaca, 1994) that occurs quickly. These significant life events may be relevant to one's life story and to changes in other levels of one's personality (McAdams & Olson, 2010)— and may even be statistically associated with changes in conscientiousness (e.g., Specht et al., 2011), but the event itself likely did not create an instantaneous change for someone. Instead, experiences related to the event that occur prior to and after the event are likely responsible for change. For example, the lead-up to a divorce involves more independence in each member, along with new responsibilities and taking on new roles. These new behaviors and roles that lead up to and extend after the divorce are more likely to prompt change rather than the life event itself. One difficulty with looking at whether life events such as divorce are related to the development of conscientiousness is that everyone interprets them differently and may need to take on many new responsibilities or may be able to outsource them to new partners. As a result, life events likely have idiosyncratic effects on personality, similar to the effects of life events in developmental twin studies. The experiences one has in the daily grind of life are more likely to change conscientiousness than major life events. The peaks and valleys are memorable, but it is likely that the mundane, day-to-day experiences have a greater impact, as those are the experiences we encounter the most.

• *Changes in behavior must be internalized.* State-related changes in conscientiousness need to be internalized in some manner, such that people see differences as being due to them, not some external force. Typically, this is conceptualized as a change in one's self-concept. For example, a self-control app on a computer that prevents someone from checking a website to safeguard against distraction from his or her writing may be too external to meaningfully change the person's behavior into a long-formed habit. The ability not to check Twitter or Facebook may be seen by a person as entirely due to the app and not as any intrinsic part of the person, much the same way a person knows he or she is a horrible speller but is saved by spellcheck. Without spellcheck maybe the person would be more diligent about spelling correctly, but with this nifty feature he or she doesn't need to be a good speller.

The change to one's self concept as a precondition to personality trait change has been discussed for some time, as a means to create lasting change (Roberts et al., 2008). This concept is also related to a number of preconditions that are common to therapeutic interventions (Grawe, 2004). For example, it is considered necessary to have insight into the problem that one wants to solve before change can occur. Reflective processes, such as insight, therefore serve as a means to make sense of the need to change, as does the realization that one has the ability to change. For example, if a person is only able to avoid distractions because of an app, then that person may think he or she does not have the ability to change. Similarly, seeing changes as desirable may also greatly impact one's ability to change, with undesirable changes occurring less frequently than desirable (Hudson & Fraley, 2015).

• *Experiences responsible for change and continuity in conscientiousness are related to age graded life tasks.* If major life event are not the major factors of change then *what types* of experiences matter? Would any environments that shift state-level personality ultimately change conscientiousness? This question is more difficult to answer but a good first pass would be experiences within the major life roles one inhabits (Roberts, Wood, & Caspi, 2008). Unfortunately, major life roles cover almost the entire lived experience of one's life, providing little to the narrowing of the types of experiences associated with change. The invest and accrue model of conscientiousness (Hill & Jackson, 2016) helps to narrow the focus on life roles by emphasizing two points. First, roles cannot be evaluated in isolation and must be considered in the perspective of one another. This may work across both time and contexts. For example, someone who wants to be a physician must work hard in school contexts and must therefore devote a number of hours at the expense of direct time with his or her romantic partner. Here investment in the occupational domain, but not the romantic partner domain, may be enough to increase levels of conscientiousness. If viewed on the aggregate, many people may be investing in one of these two roles, diluting the effect of the overall role. Second, the model offers a time when these roles may be most important. Starting a new career during midlife may not engender the same change, being driven partly by the off-time experience, as well as the fact that changes typically attributed to occupational experiences may have already occurred due to previous experiences, such as family investment.

One complication for deriving interventions to change personality is that the life experiences responsible for changes are not random. Specifically, the experiences most likely to change personality traits are associated with the trait in the first place, known as the *cumulative continuity principle* (Roberts et al., 2008). This association creates difficulties in intervention design because it is not clear whether the experiences are responsible for changes in personality or whether the characteristics the person brought into the experience in the first place are responsible for the change. This is referred to as *selection bias,* or to put it another way, the people who have the experience are not the same as those who did not. Thus, despite the promise of interventions for conscientiousness, or personality more broadly (e.g., Roberts et al., 2017), it is unclear whether utilizing experiences from passive lifespan studies will identify experiences capable of cultivating conscientiousness.

Conclusion

The American dream is built on individual character traits such as conscientiousness. Personality traits under the umbrella of conscientiousness, such as self-control, responsibility, and effortful control, yield prosperity and success across a number of life domains. Fostering these traits should be a greater emphasis of public policy given that conscientiousness emerges early in the lifespan, is not only relatively stable but also open to change, and has broad associations with life outcomes. In contrast to targeting more narrow behaviors, as is typical of behavioral interventions (which are often the focus of public policy), we suggest that attempting to change conscientiousness would provide greater overall impact. An intervention built on fostering conscientiousness is preferred given that a personality intervention targets a stable trait associated with many outcomes as opposed to a narrow behavior that may be associated with only a single outcome. Despite this promise, however, the best way to go about purposely developing the trait of conscientiousness is still unclear.

REFERENCES

Allemand, M., Zimprich, D., & Hendriks, A. A. (2008). Age differences in five personality domains across the lifespan. *Developmental Psychology, 44,* 758–770.

Asendorpf, J. B., & van Aken, M. A. (1999). Resilient, overcontrolled, and undercontrolled personality prototypes in childhood: Replicability, predictive power, and the trait-type issue. *Journal of Personality and Social Psychology, 77,* 815–832.

Bernerth, J. B., Taylor, S. G., Walker, H., & Whitman, D. S. (2012). An empirical investigation of dispositional antecedents and performance-related outcomes of credit scores. *Journal of Applied Psychology, 97*(2), 469–478.

Bleidorn, W. (2012). Hitting the road to adulthood: Short-term personality development during a major life transition. *Personality and Social Psychology Bulletin, 38*(12), 1596–1608.

Block, J. H., & Block, J. (1980). The role of ego-control and ego-resiliency in the organization of behavior. In W. A. Collins (Ed.), *Development of cognition, affect, and social relations: The Minnesota Symposia on Child Psychology* (Vol. 13, pp. 39–101). Mahwah, NJ: Erlbaum.

Brandt, N. D., Mike, A., & Jackson, J. J. (2018). *Do school experiences impact personality?: Selection and socialization effects of impulse control across high school years.* Manuscript under review.

Carver, C. S., Johnson, S. L., & Joormann, J. (2008). Serotonergic function, two-mode models of self-regulation, and vulnerability to depression: What depression has in common with impulsive aggression. *Psychological Bulletin, 134*(6), 912–943.

Caspi, A. (2000). The child is father to the man: Personality continuities from childhood to adulthood. *Journal of Personality and Social Psychology, 78,* 158–172.

Caspi, A., Houts, R. M., Belsky, D. W., Harrington, H., Hogan, S., Ramrakha, S., et al. (2016). Childhood forecasting of a small segment of the population with large economic burden. *Nature Human Behaviour, 1,* Article No. 0005.

Caspi, A., & Shiner, R. L. (2008). Temperament and personality. In M. Rutter, D. Bishop, D. Pine, S. Scott, J. S. Stevenson, E. Taylor, et al. (Eds.), *Rutter's child and adolescent psychiatry* (5th ed.. pp. 251–270). Oxford, UK: Wiley-Blackwell.

Chapman, B. P., Hampson, S., & Clarkin, J. (2014). Personality-informed interventions for healthy aging: Conclusions from a National Institute on Aging work group. *Developmental Psychology, 50*(5), 1426–1441.

Costa, P. T., & McCrae, R. R. (1988). Personality in adulthood: A six-year longitudinal study of self-reports and spouse ratings on the NEO Personality Inventory. *Journal of Personality and Social Psychology, 54*(5), 853–863.

Costantini, G., Richetin, J., Borsboom, D., Fried, E. I., Rhemtulla, M., & Perugini, M. (2015). Development of indirect measures of conscientiousness: Combining a facets approach and network analysis. *European Journal of Personality, 29*(5), 548–567.

Daly, M., Harmon, C. P., & Delaney, L. (2009). Psychological and biological foundations of time preference. *Journal of the European Economic Association, 7,* 659–669.

De Fruyt, F., Bartels, M., Van Leeuwen, K. G., De Clercq, B., Decuyper, M., & Mervielde, I. (2006). Five types of personality continuity in childhood and adolescence. *Journal of Personality and Social Psychology, 91,* 538–552.

DeNeve, K. M., & Cooper, H. (1998). The happy personality: A meta-analysis of 137 personality traits and subjective well-being. *Psychological Bulletin, 124*(2), 197–229.

Duckworth, A. (2016). *Grit: The power of passion and perseverance.* New York: Simon & Schuster.

Dudley, N. M., Orvis, K. A., Lebiecki, J. E., & Cortina, J. M. (2006). A meta-analytic investigation of conscientiousness in the prediction of job performance: Examining the intercorrelations and the incremental validity of narrow traits. *Journal of Applied Psychology, 91,* 40–57.

Eisenberg, N., Duckworth, A. L., Spinrad, T. L., & Valiente, C. (2014). Conscientiousness: Origins in childhood? *Developmental Psychology, 50*(5), 1331–1349.

Eisenberg, N., Smith, C. L., Sadovsky, A., & Spinrad, T. L. (2004). Effortful control. In K. D. Vohs & R. F. Baumeister (Eds.), *Handbook of self-regulation: Research, theory, and applications* (pp. 259–282). New York: Guilford Press.

Fayard, J. V., Roberts, B. W., Robins, R. W., & Watson, D. (2012). Uncovering the affective core of conscientiousness: The role of self-conscious emotions. *Journal of Personality, 80*(1), 1–32.

Fleeson, W. (2001). Toward a structure- and process-integrated view of personality: Traits as density distributions of states. *Journal of Personality and Social Psychology, 80*(6), 1011–1027.

Friedman, H. S., Tucker, J. S., Schwartz, J. E., Martin, L. R., Tomlinson-Keasey, C., Wingard, D. L., et al. (1995). Childhood conscientiousness and longevity: Health behaviors and cause of death. *Journal of Personality and Social Psychology, 68*(4), 696–703.

Göllner, R., Damian, R. I., Rose, N., Spengler, M., Trautwein, U., Nagengast, B., et al. (2017). Is doing your homework associated with becoming more conscientious? *Journal of Research in Personality, 71,* 1–12.

Grawe, K. (2004). *Psychological psychotherapy.* Cambridge, MA: Hogrefe & Huber.

Halverson, C. F., Havill, V. L., Deal, J., Baker, S. R., Victor, J. B., Pavlopoulos, V., et al. (2003). Personality structure as derived from parental ratings of free descriptions of children: The Inventory of Child Individual Differences. *Journal of Personality, 71*(6), 995–1026.

Hampson, S. E. (2008). Mechanisms by which childhood personality traits influence adult well-being. *Current Directions in Psychological Science, 17*(4), 264–268.

Harden, K. P., & Tucker-Drob, E. M. (2011). Individual differences in the development of sensation seeking and impulsivity during adolescence: Further evidence for a dual systems model. *Developmental Psychology, 47*(3), 739–746.

Heaven, P. L., & Ciarrochi, J. (2008). Parental styles, conscientiousness, and academic performance in high school: A three-wave longitudinal study. *Personality and Social Psychology Bulletin, 34*(4), 451–461.

Heckman, J. J. (2007). The economics, technology, and neuroscience of human capability formation. *Proceedings of the National Academy of Sciences of the USA, 104,* 13250–13255.

Herrnstein, R. J., & Murray, C. (2010). *Bell curve: Intelligence and class structure in American life.* New York: Simon & Schuster.

Hill, P. L., & Jackson, J. J. (2016). The invest-and-accrue model of conscientiousness. *Review of General Psychology, 20,* 141–154.

Hill, P. L., Payne, B. R., Jackson, J. J., Stine-Morrow, E. A., & Roberts, B. W. (2014). Perceived social support predicts increased conscientiousness during older adulthood. *Journals of Gerontology B: Psychological Sciences and Social Sciences, 69*(4), 543–547.

Hill, P. L., Turiano, N. A., Hurd, M. D., Mroczek, D. K., & Roberts, B. W. (2011). Conscientiousness and longevity: An examination of possible mediators. *Health Psychology, 30*(5), 536–541.

Hill, P. L., Turiano, N. A., Mroczek, D. K., & Roberts, B. W. (2012). Examining concurrent and longitudinal relations between personality traits and social well-being in adulthood. *Social Psychological and Personality Science, 3,* 698–705.

Hill, P. L., Weston, S., & Jackson, J. J. (2018). The joint development of social support and personality in older adulthood. *International Journal of Behavioral Development, 42*(1), 26–33.

Hudson, N. W., & Fraley, R. C. (2015). Volitional personality trait change: Can people choose to change their personality traits? *Journal of Personality and Social Psychology, 109*(3), 490–507.

Hudson, N. W., Roberts, B. W., & Lodi-Smith, J. (2012). Personality trait development and social investment in work. *Journal of Research in Personality, 46*(3), 334–344.

Human, L. J., Biesanz, J. C., Miller, G. E., Chen, E., Lachman, M. E., & Seeman, T. E. (2013). Is change bad?: Personality change is associated with poorer psychological health and greater metabolic syndrome in midlife. *Journal of Personality, 81*(3), 249–260.

Hutteman, R., Hennecke, M., Orth, U., Reitz, A. K., & Specht, J. (2014). Developmental tasks as a framework to study personality development in adulthood and old age. *European Journal of Personality, 28,* 267–278.

Jackson, J. J. (2017a). *Do teachers see what students see?: Development of personality from multiple perspectives.* Unpublished manuscript, Washington University at St. Louis, St. Louis, MO.

Jackson, J. J. (2017b). *Multiple perspectives of personality development* Unpublished manuscript, Washington University at St. Louis, St. Louis, MO.

Jackson, J. J., Beck, E. D., & Mike, A. (in press). Personality interventions. In O. P. John & R. W. Robins (Eds.), *Handbook of personality: Theory and research* (4th ed.). New York: Guilford Press.

Jackson, J. J., Beck, E. D., & Weston, S. J. (2017). *Does early childhood education cultivate personality?: A 20-year longitudinal study of Head Start.* Unpublished manuscript, Washington University in St. Louis, St. Louis, MO.

Jackson, J. J., Bogg, T., Walton, K. E., Wood, D., Harms, P. D., Lodi-Smith, J., et al. (2009). Not all conscientiousness scales change alike: A multimethod, multisample study of age differences in the facets of conscientiousness. *Journal of Personality and Social Psychology, 96,* 446–459.

Jackson, J. J., Connolly, J. J., Garrison, M., Levine, M., & Connolly, S. L. (2015). Your friends know how long you will live: A 75 year study of peer-rated personality traits. *Psychological Science, 26,* 335–340.

Jackson, J. J., & Roberts, B. W. (2017). Conscientiousness. In T. A. Widiger (Ed.), *The Oxford handbook of the Five Factor Model of personality* (pp. 133–150). New York: Oxford University Press.

Jackson, J. J., Weston, S. J., & Schultz, L. H. (2017). Personality development and health. In J. Specht (Ed.), *Personality development across the lifespan* (pp. 371–384), San Diego, CA: Elsevier.

Jackson, J. J., Wood, D., Bogg, T., Walton, K. E., Harms, P. D., & Roberts, B. W. (2010). What do conscientious people do?: Development and validation of the behavioral indicators of conscientiousness (BIC). *Journal of Research in Personality, 44*(4), 501–511.

Jokela, M., Hakulinen, C., Singh-Manoux, A., & Kivimäki, M. (2014). Personality change associated with chronic diseases: Pooled analysis of four prospective cohort studies. *Psychological Medicine, 44*(12), 2629–2640.

Kaskie, B., Imhof, S., Cavanaugh, J., & Culp, K. (2008). Civic engagement as a retirement role for aging Americans. *The Gerontologist, 48,* 368–377.

Kautz, T., Heckman, J. J., Diris, R., Ter Weel, B., & Borghans, L. (2014). *Fostering and measuring skills: Improving cognitive and non-cognitive skills to promote lifetime success* (NBER Working Paper No. 20749). Cambridge, MA: National Bureau of Economic Research.

Kern, M. L., & Friedman, H. S. (2008). Do conscientious individuals live longer?: A quantitative review. *Health Psychology, 27*(5), 505.

Klimstra, T. A., Hale, W. W., III, Raaijmakers, Q. A., Branje, S. J., & Meeus, W. H. (2009). Maturation of personality in adolescence. *Journal of Personality and Social Psychology, 96,* 898–912.

Klimstra, T. A., Luyckx, K., Teppers, E., Goossens, L., & De Fruyt, F. (2011). Congruence between adolescent personality types based on the Big Five domains and the 30 NEO-PI-3 personality facets. *Journal of Research in Personality, 45,* 513–517.

Kochanska, G., Murray, K. T., & Harlan, E. T. (2000). Effortful control in early childhood: Continuity and change, antecedents, and implications for social development. *Developmental Psychology, 36*(2), 220–232.

Littlefield, A. K., Sher, K. J., & Wood, P. K. (2009). Is "maturing out" of problematic alcohol involvement related to personality change? *Journal of Abnormal Psychology, 118*(2), 360–374.

Littlefield, A. K., Sher, K. J., & Wood, P. K. (2010). A personality-based description of maturing out of alcohol problems: Extension with a five-factor model and robustness to modeling challenges. *Addictive Behaviors, 35,* 948–954.

Lodi-Smith, J., & Roberts, B. W. (2005). Social investment and personality: A meta-analysis of the relationship of personality traits to investment in work, family, religion, and volunteerism. *Personality and Social Psychology Review, 11*(1), 68–86.

Lucas, R. E., & Donnellan, M. B. (2011). Personality development across the life span: Longitudinal analyses with a national sample from Germany. *Journal of Personality and Social Psychology, 101,* 847–861.

Magee, C. A., Heaven, P. C. L., & Miller, L. M. (2013). Personality change predicts self-reported mental and physical health. *Journal of Personality, 81*(3), 324–334.

Magidson, J. F., Roberts, B. W., Collado-Rodriguez, A., & Lejuez, C. W. (2014). Theory-driven intervention for changing personality: Expectancy value theory, behavioral activation, and conscientiousness. *Developmental Psychology, 50*(5), 1442–1450.

Mahalingam, V., Stillwell, D., Kosinski, M., Rust, J., & Kogan, A. (2014). Who can wait for the future?: A personality perspective. *Social Psychological and Personality Science, 5*(5), 573–583.

McAdams, D. P., & Olson, B. D. (2010). Personality development: Continuity and change over the life course. *Annual Review of Psychology, 61,* 517–542.

McCrae, R. R., Costa, P. T., Jr., Hrebicková, M., Urbánek, T., Martin, T. A., Oryol, V. E., et al. (2004). Age differences in personality traits across cultures: Self-report and observer perspectives. *European Journal of Personality, 18*(2), 143–157.

McCrae, R. R., Costa, P. T., Pedroso de Lima, M., Simões, A., Ostendorf, F., Angleitner, A., et al. (1999). Age differences in personality across the adult life span: Parallels in five cultures. *Developmental Psychology, 35*(2), 466–477.

McCrae, R. R., & Terracciano, A. (2005). Universal features of personality traits from the observer's perspective: Data from 50 cultures. *Journal of Personality and Social Psychology, 88*(3), 547–561.

Mike, A., Jackson, J. J., & Oltmanns, T. F. (2014). The conscientious retiree: The relationship between conscientiousness, retirement, and volunteering. *Journal of Research in Personality, 52,* 68–77.

Miller, W. R., & C'deBaca, J. (1994). Quantum change: Toward a psychology of transformation. In T. Heatherton & J. Weinberger (Eds.), *Can personality change?* (pp. 253–280). Washington, DC: American Psychological Association Books.

Moffitt, T. E., Arseneault, L., Belsky, D., Dickson, N., Hancox, R. J., Harrington, H. L., et al. (2011). A gradient of childhood self-control predicts health, wealth, and public safety. *Proceedings of the National Academy of Sciences of the USA, 108,* 2693–2698.

Mõttus, R., Johnson, W., Starr, J. M., & Deary, I. J. (2012). Correlates of personality trait levels and their changes in very old age: The Lothian Birth Cohort 1921. *Journal of Research in Personality, 46*(3), 271–278.

Neyer, F. J., & Asendorpf, J. B. (2001). Personality-relationship transaction in young adulthood. *Journal of Personality and Social Psychology, 81*(6), 1190–1204.

Neyer, F. J., & Lehnart, J. (2007). Relationships matter in personality development: Evidence from an 8-year longitudinal study across young adulthood. *Journal of Personality, 75,* 535–568.

Nigg, J. T. (2017). Annual research review: On the relations among self-regulation, self-control, executive functioning, effortful control, cognitive control, impulsivity, risk-taking, and inhibition for developmental psychopathology. *Journal of Child Psychology and Psychiatry, 58*(4), 361–383.

Noftle, E. E., & Robins, R. W. (2007). Personality predictors of academic outcomes: Big Five correlates of GPA and SAT scores. *Journal of Personality and Social Psychology, 93*(1), 116–130.

Pinquart, M. (2002). Creating and maintaining purpose in life in old age: A meta-analysis. *Ageing International, 27*(2), 90–114.

Potocnik, K., & Sonnentag, S. (2013). A longitudinal study of well-being in older workers and retirees: The role of engaging in different types of activities. *Journal of Occupational and Organizational Psychology, 86,* 497521.

Roberts, B. W. (2009). Back to the future: Personality and assessment and personality development. *Journal of Research in Personality, 43*(2), 137–145.

Roberts, B. W., & Bogg, T. (2004). A longitudinal study of the relationships between conscientiousness and the social-environmental factors and substance-use behaviors that influence health. *Journal of Personality, 72*(2), 325–354.

Roberts, B. W., Caspi, A., & Moffitt, T. E. (2003). Work experiences and personality development in young adulthood. *Journal of Personality and Social Psychology, 84*(3), 582–593.

Roberts, B. W., & DelVecchio, W. F. (2000). The rank-order consistency of personality traits from childhood to old age: A quantitative review of longitudinal studies. *Psychological Bulletin, 126*(1), 3–25.

Roberts, B. W., Hill, P. L., & Davis, J. P. (2017). How to change conscientiousness: The sociogenomic trait intervention model. *Personality Disorders: Theory, Research, and Treatment, 8*(3), 199–205.

Roberts, B. W., & Jackson, J. J. (2008). Sociogenomic personality psychology. *Journal of Personality, 76*(6), 1523–1544.

Roberts, B. W., Lejuez, C., Krueger, R. F., Richards, J. M., & Hill, P. L. (2014). What is conscientiousness and how can it be assessed? *Developmental Psychology, 50*(5), 1315–1330.

Roberts, B. W., Luo, J., Briley, D. A., Chow, P. I., Su, R., & Hill, P. L. (2017). A systematic review of personality trait change through intervention. *Psychological Bulletin, 143*(2), 117–141.

Roberts, B. W., Walton, K., Bogg, T., & Caspi, A. (2006). De-investment in work and non-normative personality trait change in young adulthood. *European Journal of Personality, 474,* 461–474.

Roberts, B. W., Walton, K., & Viechtbauer, W. (2006). Patterns of mean-level change in personality traits across the life course: A meta-analysis of longitudinal studies. *Psychological Bulletin, 132,* 3–27.

Roberts, B. W., Wood, D., & Caspi, A. (2008). The development of personality traits in adulthood. In O. P. John, R. W. Robins, & L. A. Pervin (Eds.), *Handbook of personality: Theory and research* (3rd ed., pp. 375–398). New York: Guilford Press.

Robins, R. W., John, O. P., Caspi, A., Moffitt, T. E., & Stouthamer-Loeber, M. (1996). Resilient, overcontrolled, and undercontrolled boys: Three replicable personality types. *Journal of Personality and Social Psychology, 70,* 157–171.

Robinson, O. C., Demetre, J. D., & Corney, R. (2010). Personality and retirement: Exploring the links between the Big Five personality traits, reasons for retirement and the experience of being retired. *Personality and Individual Differences, 48,* 792–797.

Ross, C. E., & Drentea, P. (1998). Consequences of re-tirement activities for distress and the sense of personal control. *Journal of Health and Social Behavior, 39,* 317–334.

Rothbart, M. K., & Bates, J. E. (2006). Temperament. In W. Damon & R. Lerner (Series Eds.) & N. Eisenberg (Vol. Ed.), *Handbook of child psychology: Vol. 3. Social, emotional, and personality development* (6th ed., pp. 99–166). Hoboken, NJ: Wiley.

Rothbart, M. K., & Rueda, M. R. (2005). The development of effortful control. In U. Mayr, E. Awh, & S. W. Keele (Eds.), *Developing individuality in the human brain: A tribute to Michael I. Posner* (pp. 167–188). Washington, DC: American Psychological Association.

Small, B. J., Hertzog, C., Hultsch, D. F., & Dixon, R. A. (2003). Stability and change in adult personality over 6 years: findings from the Victoria Longitudinal Study. *Journals of Gerontology B: Psychological Sciences and Social Sciences, 58*(3), P166–P176.

Solomon, B. C., & Jackson, J. J. (2014a). The long reach of one's spouse: Spouses' personality influences occupational success. *Psychological Science, 25,* 2189–2198.

Solomon, B. C., & Jackson, J. J. (2014b). Why do personality traits predict divorce?: Multiple pathways through satisfaction. *Journal of Personality and Social Psychology, 106,* 978–996.

Soto, C. J., & John, O. P. (2012). Development of Big Five domains and facets in adulthood: Mean-level age trends and broadly versus narrowly acting mechanisms. *Journal of Personality, 80*(4), 881–914.

Soto, C. J., John, O. P., Gosling, S. D., & Potter, J. (2011). Age differences in personality traits from 10 to 65: Big Five domains and facets in a large cross-sectional sample. *Journal of Personality and Social Psychology, 100*(2), 330–348.

Specht, J., Bleidorn, W., Denissen, J. J., Hennecke, M., Hutteman, R., Kandler, C., et al. (2014). What drives adult personality development?: A comparison of theoretical perspectives and empirical evidence. *European Journal of Personality, 28*(3), 216–230.

Specht, J., Egloff, B., & Schmukle, S. C. (2011). Stability and change of personality across the life course: The impact of age and major life events on mean-level and rank-order stability of the Big Five. *Journal of Personality and Social Psychology, 101*(4), 862–882.

Specht, J., Luhmann, M., & Geiser, C. (2014). On the consistency of personality types across adulthood: Latent profile analyses in two large-scale panel studies. *Journal of Personality and Social Psychology, 107*(3), 540–556.

Steinberg, L., & Morris, A. S. (2001). Adolescent development. *Annual Review of Psychology, 52*(1), 83–110.

Sutin, A. R., Zonderman, A. B., Ferrucci, L., & Terracciano, A. (2013). Personality traits and chronic disease: Implications for adult personality development. *Journals of Gerontology B: Psychological Sciences and Social Sciences, 68*(6), 912–920.

Takahashi, Y., Edmonds, G. W., Jackson, J. J., & Roberts, B. W. (2013). Longitudinal correlated changes in conscientiousness, preventative health-related behaviors, and self-perceived physical health. *Journal of Personality, 81*(4), 417–427.

Terracciano, A., McCrae, R. R., Brant, L. J., & Costa, P. T. (2005). Hierarchical linear modeling analyses of the NEO-PI-R scales in the Baltimore Longitudinal Study of Aging. *Psychology and Aging, 20*(3), 493–506.

Turiano, N. A., Pitzer, L., Armour, C., Karlamangla, A., Ryff, C. D., & Mroczek, D. K. (2012). Personality trait level and change as predictors of health outcomes: Findings from a national study of Americans (MIDUS). *Journals of Gerontology B: Psychological Sciences and Social Sciences, 67*(1), 4–12.

Van den Akker, A. L., Deković, M., Asscher, J., & Prinzie, P. (2014). Mean-level personality development across childhood and adolescence: A temporary defiance of the maturity principle and bidirectional associations with parenting. *Journal of Personality and Social Psychology, 107*(4), 736–750.

Van der Linden, D., Scholte, R. H., Cillessen, A. H., te Nijenhuis, J., & Segers, E. (2010). Classroom ratings of likeability and popularity are related to the Big Five and the general factor of personality. *Journal of Research in Personality, 44*(5), 669–672.

van Scheppingen, M. A., Jackson, J. J., Specht, J., Hutteman, R., Denissen, J. J. A., & Bleidorn W. (2016). Personality development during the transition to parenthood: A test of social investment theory. *Social Personality and Psychological Science, 7*(5), 452–462.

Walton, K. E., Huyen, B. T. T., Thorpe, K., Doherty, E. R., Juarez, B., D'Accordo, C., et al. (2013). Cross-sectional personality differences from age 16–90 in a Vietnamese sample. *Journal of Research in Personality, 47*(1), 36–40.

Wang, M., & Shi, J. (2014). Psychological research on retirement. *Annual Review of Psychology, 65,* 209–233.

Watson, D., & Humrichouse, J. (2006). Personality development in emerging adulthood: Integrating evidence from self-ratings and spouse ratings. *Journal of Personality and Social Psychology, 91*(5), 959–974.

Webley, P., & Nyhus, E. K. (2006). Parents' influence on children's future orientation and saving. *Journal of Economic Psychology, 27,* 140–164.

Weston, S., Hill, P. L., & Jackson, J. J. (2015). Personality traits predict the onset of major disease. *Social Personality Psychological Science, 6,* 309–317.

Wilson, R. S., Schneider, J. A., Arnold, S. E., Bienias, J. L., & Bennett, D. A. (2007). Conscientiousness and the incidence of Alzheimer disease and mild cognitive impairment. *Archives of General Psychiatry, 64*(10), 1204–1212.

Wortman, J., Lucas, R. E., & Donnellan, M. B. (2012). Stability and change in the Big Five personality domains: Evidence from a longitudinal study of Australians. *Psychology and Aging, 27,* 867–874.

Wrzus, C., & Roberts, B. W. (2017). Processes of personality development in adulthood: The TESSERA framework. *Personality and Social Psychology Review, 21*(3), 253–277.

Yeager, D. S., & Dweck, C. S. (2012). Mindsets that promote resilience: When students believe that personal characteristics can be developed. *Educational Psychologist, 47*(4), 302–314.

CHAPTER 10

Agreeableness

Jennifer L. Tackett
Maciel M. Hernández
Nancy Eisenberg

INTERVIEWER: Imagine you are in a situation where someone is bothering you. What did you do?

12-YEAR-OLD BOY RATED HIGH ON AGREEABLENESS: . . . There was this girl in grade 2 and . . . I walked by and she kicked me in the shins. And, the principal was on duty so I told him that and . . . I talked to her and I said this wasn't good because it hurt me, and it's not nice first of all and it's just mean to do. . . . I felt kinda like, what should I do, there's so much options, and I felt kind of nervous to make the right choice.

13-YEAR-OLD BOY RATED LOW ON AGREEABLENESS: I'm not sure. I'm not sure, like, it would be appropriate. . . . I once punched a person pretty hard in the face and then I kinda beat the person up after he beat me up first. There was a lot of bleeding. Yes, I actually did. I'm not lying. It actually did all help.

Children, adolescents, and adults differ in many ways, including their approach to handling interpersonal situations and their tendencies to show concern for others' feelings. Such interpersonal manifestations—including empathy, compassion, altruism, and love—are inherently interesting to and consequential for everyone. We focus in this chapter on the personality trait of *agreeableness*, including how this trait manifests in children, adolescents, and adults, and is related to behavioral outcomes across the lifespan. In addition to being intrinsically interesting and consequential, agreeableness is multifaceted. It intersects with self-regulation, including negative self-regulation (e.g., aggression, anger, hostility) and self-discipline and order (e.g., agreeable compliance and cooperation). Moreover, developmental research suggests that these distinct aspects of agreeableness are highly overlapping early in the lifespan

(e.g., toddlerhood and early childhood), and become increasingly distinct from one another over the course of middle childhood and adolescence. Notably, these time periods are also when major social and academic changes are taking place, as well as emotional, cognitive, and biological changes within the individual, offering many possible mechanisms to potentially explain such changes. We first discuss definitions and measurement approaches for trait agreeableness, then turn to reviewing associations between agreeableness and psychological and social functioning.

Defining and Measuring Agreeableness

Trait Agreeableness

Agreeableness is a trait that typically indexes characteristics such as compassion, compliance, politeness, empathy, and modesty (e.g., Caprara, Alessandri, Di Giunta, Panerai, & Eisenberg, 2010; Soto & John, 2017; Tackett, Kushner, De Fruyt, & Mervielde, 2013). Like the other traits in the five-factor model (FFM; Soto, John, Gosling, & Potter, 2008), agreeableness is a bipolar trait. Low levels of agreeableness reflect tendencies to be aggressive, hostile, manipulative, callous, oppositional, and strong-willed. As agreeableness is often missing or otherwise less consistently conceptualized in early taxonomies of personality traits, many questions remain about what early agreeableness looks like, how best it may be measured, and how early in life it manifests as a clearly differentiated trait.

It is now well established that five broad factors of personality traits can be measured in valid and reliable ways from very early in life, at least by early childhood (Goldberg, 2001; Halverson et al., 2003; Mervielde & De Fruyt, 1999). Yet, these traits are only analogous, not identical, to the established FFM in adulthood. Importantly, trait agreeableness appears to be one of the more inconsistent traits across child and adult measures, and between different child personality and temperament measures.

Fairly consistent emergent evidence has indicated that agreeableness in childhood more strongly reflects willing compliance and low antagonism, in comparison with agreeableness conceptualizations in adults, which focus more on empathic and compassionate tendencies (De Pauw & Mervielde, 2010; Digman & Shmelyov, 1996; Goldberg, 2001; Tackett, Krueger, Iacono, & McGue, 2008; Tackett et al., 2012). An important remaining question is the extent to which this reflects a measurement artifact, as opposed to an actual difference in developmental conceptualization of the substantive nature of the trait. Measurement of agreeableness is discussed in more depth below. Although agreeableness does tend to show gender differences favoring girls, these differences tend to be quite small—but fairly consistent from childhood to adulthood (Soto, 2016).

Developmentally, higher-order trait agreeableness appears to increase during early/middle childhood, decline slightly during the transition to adolescence, but then increase again in later adolescence to adulthood (Slobodskaya & Akhmetova, 2010; Soto, 2016; Van den Akker, Deković, Asscher, & Prinzie, 2014). At the facet-level, developmental patterns appear

more complex. In one recent study, de Haan, De Pauw, van den Akker, Deković, and Prinzie (2017) found that agreeableness facets increased across early childhood, but they found divergent patterns for different agreeableness facets during pre-adolescence and adolescence. Specifically, altruism increased during the adolescent transition, but only in girls. On the other hand, whereas compliance decreased into adolescence, dominance showed a particular decrease in girls during the adolescent transition. Finally, egocentrism and irritability showed little developmental change in preadolescence and adolescence. Thus, it is reasonable to expect developmental trends for higher-order agreeableness to mask more complicated developmental patterns among relevant facets. There is also some empirical evidence to suggest that changes in *effortful control* (a self-regulatory temperament trait akin to conscientiousness) and agreeableness in later adolescence may promote increases in agreeableness-relevant behaviors such as prosociality (Alessandri, Kanacri, et al., 2014; Caprara, Alessandri, & Eisenberg, 2012).

A small body of literature speaks to the differential instantiation of trait agreeableness across countries and cultures. Comparing parental free descriptions of their children in a sample of parents from many countries, researchers found that Greek parents generated the greatest proportion of agreeable phrases in their descriptions, and Chinese parents generated that smallest proportion (Havill, Besevegis, & Mouroussaki, 1998). These researchers also found that German and Greek parents were more likely to use negative descriptors of agreeableness (e.g., argumentative, mean) than were parents from the United States. In a study of children and early adolescents, a "pure" agreeableness trait (i.e., that does not contain substantial negative affectivity or antagonism variance) emerged for Canadian, Chinese, and Russian children, but not for Greek and American children (for whom a negative affect-laden antagonism trait did emerge; Tackett et al., 2012). These differences may reflect differing cultural values, if parents (who reported on their children's characteristics) tend to show heightened differentiation of those traits most valued, or salient, to them. Specifically, values that parents hope to instill in their children do appear to show cultural differences, and many prioritized values appear to tap agreeableness content (e.g., honesty, good manners, assertiveness, and compassion; Tamis-LeMonda, Wang, Koutsouvanou, & Albright, 2002).

Agreeableness Covariation

Fairly robust evidence indicates that agreeableness covaries most highly with two traits: negative affectivity/neuroticism (NA/N) and effortful control/conscientiousness (EC/C; e.g., Martel, Nigg, & Lucas, 2008; Soto & Tackett, 2015; Tackett et al., 2008, 2012). An understanding of trait covariation patterns is important because it helps us to identify the position of a given trait in broader personality space, more clearly delineate the substantive nature of each trait, and understand how traits are hierarchically related; it facilitates connections between empirical researchers using different trait measures and models.

The close connections with trait agreeableness and NA/N also show some evidence of developmental specificity. Although aspects of agreeableness (i.e., aggression) are modeled directly with NA/N in prominent temperament models, this close association in childhood appears to be more than a measurement artifact. In an investigation of trait covariation across development (ages 3–14), using a child personality measure (which identifies a distinct agreeableness trait), a clear agreeableness trait (distinguishable from negative affect) did not emerge until early adolescence (ages 12–14; Tackett et al., 2012). This might indicate an unusually close association between these traits in childhood, which becomes more differentiated as children age into adolescence. By adulthood, even three-factor temperament models show differentiated variance between aggressive negative affect (which correlates more highly with agreeableness) and nonaggressive negative affect (which correlates more highly with neuroticism; Evans & Rothbart, 2007), suggesting that agreeableness and neuroticism show greater differentiation across development.

On the other hand, positive aspects of agreeableness (e.g., compliance) also seem to covary with EC/C more tightly in childhood than is evidenced in adult research. However, "pure" conscientiousness (as differentiated from agreeableness/agreeable compliance) appears to emerge by ages 6–8 and differentiates further by ages 9–11 (Tackett et al., 2012). This differentiation between agreeableness/agreeable compliance and "pure" conscientiousness

potentially coincides with school entry and increased environmental demands for structured and self-regulated behaviors, offering some hint of an environmental mechanism driving this increased differentiation.

Agreeableness Facets

Facets, or lower-order traits, show even greater variability between measures, both within measures intended for younger populations and across measures for children versus those for adults. Examining facets of agreeableness in different measures is pragmatically important because it allows us to better understand differences between measures and draw stronger connections across studies using different measures. It is also helpful theoretically because it offers a deeper understanding of the psychological content that trait agreeableness comprises. Specific agreeableness facets typically reflect both researchers' expectations of agreeableness content (because researchers often offer their perspective on which items to include in a measure and make decisions about label names for facets) and empirical evidence for them (because facet formation, and connection to higher-order agreeableness, typically results from factor-analytic and other quantitative efforts).

Given this context, we can briefly review those agreeableness facets that are measured in a variety of common dispositional models. Common measures of child personality include the Hierarchical Personality Inventory for Children (HiPIC; Mervielde & De Fruyt, 1999) and the Inventory for Child Individual Differences (ICID; Halverson et al., 2003). A common measure of youth temperament is the Revised Early Adolescent Temperament Questionnaire (EATQ-R; Ellis & Rothbart, 2001). The HiPIC higher-order trait is labeled Benevolence and consists of five facets: Egocentrism, Irritability, Compliance, Dominance, and Altruism. The ICID higher-order trait is labeled Antagonism or Agreeableness, and various scoring systems are sometimes used in the literature. The simple structure outlined by Halverson and colleagues (2003) identifies two facets of Agreeableness: Antagonism and Strong-Willed. The EATQ-R, as with most temperament measures (described in more depth below), does not include a specific higher-order agreeableness trait. However, it does assess a lower-order Affiliation trait, which indexes desires toward warmth and social closeness.

We can compare these facet-level taxonomies with those in adult measures. Two common measures in adults (both used frequently in adolescence as well) are the Big Five Inventory (BFI; Soto et al., 2008) and the NEO Personality Inventory—Revised (NEO-PI-R; Costa & McCrae, 1992). Although previous versions of the BFI did not include well-developed facet-level measurement, the most recent version (BFI-2) does incorporate facets (Soto & John, 2017). Specifically, the BFI-2 Agreeableness domain comprises three facets: Compassion, Respectfulness, and Trust. On the other hand, NEO-PI-R Agreeableness comprises six facets: Warmth, Modesty, Trust, Tender-Mindedness, Compliance, and Straightforwardness. Comparing across all these measures, we see some common themes emerging—particularly to the extent that trait agreeableness often indexes both tendencies to get along well with others and follow interpersonal "rules," and the ability and motivation to empathize with and care for others.

Temperament and Other Approaches

As previously noted, temperament approaches typically do not define a higher-order factor of agreeableness (e.g., Rothbart, Ahadi, Hershey, & Fisher, 2001). Instead, these measures converge on three higher-order dispositional traits and, alongside popular three-factor measures used for adults (Tellegen & Waller, 1992), higher-order traits in these models include one indexing positive affectivity/sociability (which in children often also includes activity level), another indexing negative affectivity, and still another indexing self-control. An important remaining question is where agreeableness-relevant variance populates such three-factor models. In both temperament and adult personality models, agreeableness variance appears to load on both self-control (i.e., effortful control, constraint) and negative affectivity traits (Caspi, Roberts, & Shiner, 2005; Tackett et al., 2012). This makes some sense, given that agreeableness can reflect both self-regulation (i.e., the ability to inhibit behavior in social adaptive and compassionate ways) and negative emotions (particularly low levels of interpersonal negativity such as anger and hostility). These distinctions have been discussed in developmental terms, with researchers suggesting that broadly defined self-regulatory traits (e.g., effortful control) may bifurcate into more narrowly defined interpersonal and intrapersonal aspects of self-regulation later in development (Rothbart, Ahadi, & Evans, 2000; Rothbart & Bates, 2006; Shiner & Caspi, 2003). This hypothesis has not undergone rigorous empirical scrutiny to date, although hierarchical analyses offer some indication that agreeableness may "break off" from conscientiousness, albeit with later agreeableness drawing from earlier negative affect tendencies as well (Tackett et al., 2012).

Although a higher-order agreeableness trait is not measured in popular temperament models, trait affiliativeness, which is somewhat analogous, does appear in adolescent and adult measures, as also described in the previous section (Evans & Rothbart, 2009). These differences are particularly salient in a developmental context because temperament measures are very frequently used in studies of infants, children, and adolescents. Thus, this creates a more fragmented literature when seeking to understand the early emergence and development of agreeableness and related characteristics.

Measuring Agreeableness

Measuring personality traits across the lifespan encounters numerous challenges (De Pauw & Mervielde, 2010; Tackett et al., 2013). In particular, the field suffers from a lack of psychometrically sound measurement tools that span wide age ranges (De Pauw & Mervielde, 2010), and can therefore be used in samples with a wide variety of participant ages or longitudinal studies spanning many years and/or major developmental epochs. An understanding of measurement of trait agreeableness, given its omission in many early temperament measures, particularly suffers from the consequences of these limitations. Of course, it is also important to acknowledge that trait manifestations may meaningfully differ across developmental stages, such that widely used trait measures (e.g., popular adult questionnaires) may not be ideal for younger age groups (Caspi et al., 2005; De Fruyt, Mervielde, Hoekstra, & Rolland, 2000).

Measurement of early personality traits similarly faces barriers due to methodological limitations and constraints. The use of parent-report questionnaires is likely the most common, but not without limitations (Rothbart & Bates, 2006; Tackett, Herzhoff, Kushner, & Rule, 2016). Self-report questionnaires are often not feasible to use in young children, and when they are given to children, they typically demonstrate lower reliability and higher acquiescence (e.g., Rothbart & Bates, 2006; Soto et al., 2008). Other measures are often used, including interviews or the use of behavioral tasks, but each approach includes substantial limitations (Rothbart & Bates, 2006). In addition, many established protocols for laboratory tasks to measure early dispositions are formulated on popular measures of temperament and therefore do not include tasks specifically designed to measure agreeableness. Recent research indicates that laboratory tasks may contain just as much information about other traits as the ones they were designed to tap (Tackett et al., 2016), however. Although agreeableness information likely was not coded in previously collected laboratory tasks designed to assess temperament, this suggests that it could potentially be added to coding protocols moving forward. This would greatly enhance our existing literature base regarding early agreeableness measurement and conceptualization.

Given these limitations in measuring personality traits more generally, as well as specific challenges for agreeableness, it is critically important to understand what any given measure is tapping into it. One way to do this is by examining the facets, or lower-order traits, indexing agreeableness (or its analogues) in a specific measure. This level of analysis may be impeded by instances of the jingle-jangle fallacy, if trait labels are not always adequate in delineating overlapping and unique variance. Thus, it is also important to draw on empirical investigations seeking to define the specific agreeableness variance captured as it overlaps with and is distinguished from that in other measures.

Some such investigations have been conducted, although more empirical work is sorely needed. For example, one study by Tackett and colleagues (2013) compared two measures of child personality (the ICID [Halverson et al., 2003] and the HiPIC [Mervielde & De Fruyt, 1999]), as well as a popular measure of youth temperament (the EATQ-R; Ellis & Rothbart, 2001). The authors found HiPIC Benevolence and ICID-S (short form) Agreeableness correlated quite highly ($r = .89$), and showed superior unique prediction of one another when entered into a regression simultaneous with other higher-order traits from each measure. In other words, despite fairly different approaches to the agreeableness content in each measure (see previous delineation of agreeableness facets in both measures), they appear to capture very highly overlapping content. However, the authors found some differentiation in their measurement when examining associations with EATQ-R temperament traits. Although both HiPIC Benevolence and ICID-S Agreeableness showed substantial overlapping variance with EATQ-R Negative Affectivity, ICID-S Agreeableness overlapped more with EATQ-R Surgency and Effortful Control than did HiPIC Benevolence. These differentiated patterns offer some hints as to their different coverage of the broader trait.

Agreeableness and Psychological and Social Functioning

Agreeableness and Psychopathology

Given the various definitions and components of agreeableness discussed previously, there are strong conceptual reasons to expect agreeableness to relate negatively to psychopathology. In general, the research supports this expectation, especially for externalizing-type disorders (e.g., disinhibitory forms of psychopathology) and psychopathic traits.

Externalizing Problems

Almost by definition, agreeable people are positive and cooperative rather than aggressive with others, and they are indeed more prosocial and empathic (Caprara et al., 2010; Graziano, Habashi, Sheese, & Tobin, 2007; Habashi, Graziano, & Hoover, 2016). Moreover, agreeable people tend to be lower in impulsivity and higher in self-regulation (e.g., Cumberland-Li, Eisenberg, & Reiser, 2004; Hagekull & Bohlin, 1998; Laursen, Pulkkinen, & Adams, 2002; McCrae & Löckenhoff, 2010), prone to positive rather than negative emotion (Tackett et al., 2012; Zhang & Tsingan, 2013), and do not exhibit an undercontrolled personality (Alessandri, Vecchione, et al., 2014; Oshri, Rogosch, & Cicchetti, 2013)—all characteristics expected to relate to lower levels of externalizing problems (Eisenberg, Spinrad, & Eggum, 2010; Robins, John, Caspi, Moffitt, & Stouthamer-Loeber, 1996).

Considerable research supports a negative relation between agreeableness and externalizing behaviors. Most of the existing findings are derived from studies using FFM operationalizations of agreeableness. In various meta-analyses, agreeableness has been negatively related to antisocial behavior (broadly defined) (apparently mostly studies with adults; Miller & Lynman, 2001), psychopathy or antisocial personality according to DSM-4 criteria (with adolescents and adults; Decuyper, De Pauw, De Fruyt, De Bolle, & De Clercq, 2009), children's externalizing problems and adults' alcohol and drug usage (Malouff, Thorsteinsson, & Schutte, 2005), and adults' substance use disorders (Kotov, Gamez, Schmidt, & Watson, 2010). Moreover, in a meta-analysis including children and adults, agreeableness was negatively related to components of attention-deficit/hyperactivity disorder (ADHD), with a small relation for inattention and a stronger relation for impulsivity/hyperactivity (Gomez & Corr, 2014).

Some researchers have examined specific facets of agreeableness. In the Decuyper and colleagues (2009) meta-analysis, negative relations were found for both antisocial personality disorders and psychopathy for all facets of agreeableness (trust, straightforwardness, compliance, altruism, modesty, tender-mindedness), although psychopathy was characterized by stronger negative associations with agreeableness and straightforwardness, compliance, and modesty compared to antisocial personality. In the Jones, Miller, and Lynam (2011) meta-analysis (in which it was unclear how young participants were), antisocial personality and aggression were significantly related to all facets of agreeableness and were more strongly related to agreeableness than were other Big Five personality traits; however, positive relations with the straightforwardness, compliance, and altruism factors were considerably stronger than for trust, modesty, and tender-mindedness.

In addition, agreeableness (or disagreeableness) tends to relate to the specific types of externalizing problems examined in children. For example, Tackett, Herzhoff, Reardon, De Clercq, and Sharp (2014) found that disagreeableness (characterized by antagonism and difficulty getting along with others) was positively associated with both relational aggression and physical aggression, and weakly (and inconsistently) with rule breaking. Of interest, the relation of disagreeableness with rule breaking was higher in adolescence than in childhood, whereas the relation of disagreeableness with relational aggression was highest in middle childhood. In a longitudinal study including maltreated and nonmaltreated youth, Oshri and colleagues (2013) found that agreeableness at ages 10–12 predicted externalizing problems, cannabis use, and alcohol symptoms at ages 15–18 years. Thus, findings linking agreeableness to low levels of multiple types of externalizing problems are relatively robust and have been found for both children and adults. However, it is unclear to what degree agreeableness and externalizing problems affect one another across time, and to what degree genetics account for the relation.

Internalizing Problems

Given that agreeable people tend to get along well with others (see below) and are high in personality resiliency (Cumberland-Li et al., 2004; also see Oshri et al., 2013), they are expected to be less likely than nonagreeable people to be prone to social withdrawal, social anxiety, or depression. However, internalizing problems have been less consistently and less strongly related to agreeableness. In a meta-analysis, Kotov and colleagues (2010) found that agreeableness was not related to an array of diagnosed internalizing disorders (e.g., major depression, panic disorder, major depressive disorder; unipolar depression; generalized anxiety disorder; posttraumatic stress disorder, or obsessive–compulsive disorder), apparently assessed primarily in adults. Hakulinen and colleagues (2015), in a meta-analysis of 10 prospective community cohort studies, also found no relation of agreeableness to depression concurrently. However, prospectively, depressive symptoms were negatively related to personality change in agreeableness, albeit not vice versa. In a third meta-analysis, Zaninotto and colleagues (2016) found a negative relation between adults' mood disorders and cooperativeness, a personality trait operationalized as highly similar to agreeableness.

In a meta-analysis of research with children and adolescents, Malouff and colleagues (2005) found a substantial negative relation between agreeableness and children's internalizing problems. Moreover, disagreeableness has been associated with internalizing problems in children and adolescents in studies since the 2005 meta-analysis (e.g., De Clercq, Van Leeuwen, De Fruyt, Van Hiel, & Mervielde, 2008; Laursen, Hafen, Rubin, Booth-LaForce, & Rose-Krasnor, 2010). In studies with adults, mood disorders, including depression, have often been the measure of internalizing problems, whereas in studies with children, internalizing problems sometimes include behaviors such as social withdrawal, as well as anxiety and depressive symptoms, which might affect the strength of the negative relation with agreeableness.

Agreeableness likely is sometimes *positively* related to youths' internalizing symptoms: Overcontrolled youth, who tend to have internalizing problems (Oshri et al., 2013), tend to be high in agreeableness (Robins et al., 1996). Overcontrolled youth likely are high in compliance and regulated behaviors such as politeness and altruism (see Alessandri, Vecchione, et al., 2014), which could partly account for this relation. Thus, it may be that some aspects of agreeableness are positively related to internalizing problems (or some types of internalizing problems), whereas other aspects (e.g., trust) are negatively related.

Consequently, the relation between agreeableness and internalizing problems may vary as a function of age, as well as the facet of agreeableness and type of internalizing problems examined. In addition, it is quite possible that internalizing problems often have an effect on individual differences in agreeableness across time rather than low agreeableness increasing internalizing problems (Hakulinen et al., 2015).

Agreeableness and Quality of Relationships

Graziano and Eisenberg (1997) suggested that *agreeableness* refers to the motivation to accommodate to others, with the goal of maintaining smooth interpersonal relationships. Consistent with this view, individual differences in agreeableness have been associated with the quality of social relationship with peers, family, and romantic partners. Individuals who have agreeable personalities likely enjoy the company of others and are better able to relate to others, which make it easier to build and maintain relationships.

For example, agreeableness has been associated with greater peer acceptance and decreased victimization from peers across the school years in childhood (Jensen-Campbell et al., 2002), better peer relations in adolescence (Laursen et al., 2010), and higher social competence in emerging and later adulthood (Shiner, 2000; Shiner & Masten, 2012). Similarly, agreeableness was concurrently associated with higher peer closeness, but not with change in relationships with peers, in a German young adult sample (Neyer & Lehnart, 2007). Thus, although agreeableness has generally been associated with peer competence, there are some measures of social competence

that may be more (or less) often predicted by agreeableness.

Consistent with the transactional model of development (Sameroff, 2009), parents' and children's personalities also have implications for parent–child interactions and relationship quality in the family. For example, Denissen, van Aken, and Dubas (2009) found that Dutch adolescents' agreeableness was positively associated with parent–child relationship warmth (e.g., quality of information, warmth, acceptance). Consistent with these findings, Parker, Ludtke, Trautwein, and Roberts (2012) found that an increase in agreeableness from high school to adulthood was associated with declines in conflictual relationships with parents, siblings, and friends. Among adults in Germany, agreeableness was concurrently associated with lower family conflict (but not significantly associated with change in relationships with family members because there was no significant variability in change across 8 years; Neyer & Lehnart, 2007). In regard to parents, fathers' agreeableness was positively associated with more positive observed interactions with their infant children (Kochanska, Friesenborg, Lange, Martel, & Kochanska, 2004). Similarly, in a meta-analysis, Prinzie, Stams, Deković, Reijntjes, and Belsky (2009) found that parental agreeableness was positively associated with parental warmth (especially among younger children), negatively associated with parental control, and positively associated with autonomy support. Thus, both child (Denissen et al., 2009; Parker et al., 2012) and parent (Kochanska et al., 2004; Prinzie et al., 2009) agreeableness have been positively associated with parent–child relationship quality, highlighting how parents and children jointly shape their relationship with each other.

Agreeableness also has implications for romantic relationships. Based on a review of longitudinal studies, Roberts, Kuncel, Shiner, Caspi, and Goldberg (2007) concluded that agreeableness is negatively related to divorce and positively related to the number of years married. Similarly, in meta-analyses, agreeableness was positively associated with relationship satisfaction (Malouff, Thorsteinsson, Schutte, Bhullar, & Rooke, 2010) and family life social investments (e.g., commitment to family, investment in family) and marital status (i.e., length and status of marriage; Lodi-Smith & Roberts, 2007). Other findings suggest bidirectional effects: Mund and Neyer (2014) found that change in prosociality (a facet of agreeableness) was positively related to change in adults' romantic relationship closeness across 15 years, and vice versa.

Conflict in relationships is expected, and appropriately managing conflict is key to relationship stability. Agreeableness has been negatively associated with aggressive tendencies in childhood and adulthood (Caprara et al., 2013; de Haan, Prinzie, & Deković, 2010; Shiner, Masten, & Roberts, 2003), which also has implications for how individuals resolve conflict with others. Agreeable adolescents tend to be more likely to endorse negotiation resolution strategies (e.g., third-party mediation, stepping down from argument) and less likely to endorse power assertion resolution strategies (e.g., physical action, criticism, threats, low compromise) as acceptable ways to deal with conflict with parents, siblings, and friends (Jensen-Campbell, Graziano, & Hair, 1996). Similarly, children's agreeableness was positively associated with constructive conflict resolutions (including submission, disengagement, third-party intervention), and negatively associated with destructive resolutions (including manipulation, guilt, physical force; Jensen-Campbell, Gleason, Adams, & Malcolm, 2003). These resolution strategies inevitably affect social relationship formation and maintenance, for which power assertion resolution strategies may be perceived as threatening to others.

The underlying mechanisms facilitating constructive resolutions appear to have an automatic cognitive component. When adults were presented with an emotion attribution task (i.e., attributing positive or negative causes to happy or sad faces, respectively, vs. a control task), agreeableness was associated with greater right temporoparietal junction activity when making emotion attribution decisions, which suggests that agreeableness was positively related to a person's perspective taking (given higher activity in the temporoparietal junction) during emotional attribution decisions (Haas, Ishak, Denison, Anderson, & Filkowski, 2015). These findings align with studies pointing to a positive relation between agreeableness and prosocial behaviors (e.g., Caprara et al., 2010; Graziano et al., 2007; Habashi et al., 2016).

Numerous mechanisms that have been identified may explain the association between agreeableness and social relationships. In two meta-analyses, agreeableness was positively associated with forgiveness tendencies among adults (Balliet, 2010; Riek & Mania, 2012), which has implications for the maintenance of social relationships. In another meta-analysis, Sibley and Duckitt (2008) found that agreeableness is negatively associated with a social dominance orientation (i.e., the belief that one's group is more dominant than other groups), which is associated with prejudice and may be counterproductive to forming positive relationships with outgroup members. There is also some evidence that agreeableness is a resilience-promoting factor. For example, among adolescents from the United States and China, rejection sensitivity predicted higher social withdrawal and lower friendship satisfaction for those low—but not high—in agreeableness (Wang, Hartl, Laursen, & Rubin, 2017); that is, it is likely that agreeableness helped reduce the negative effects of rejection sensitivity on social relationships. Similarly, the associations between a series of behavioral factors (e.g., internalizing, physical weakness, prosocial skills) and peer victimization were moderated by agreeableness among children in the United States (Jensen-Campbell et al., 2002). Specifically, the negative associations between prosocial skills or physical strength and peer victimization, and the positive association between child internalizing symptoms and peer victimization, were significant only for children low in agreeableness; among those with medium or high agreeableness, peer victimization was low and not predicted by the behavioral factors examined (Jensen-Campbell et al., 2002). These findings indicate that agreeableness mitigates the negative effects that risk factors might be expected to have on social relationships, and that those high in agreeableness are able to sustain quality social relationships despite difficult circumstances (e.g., internalizing symptoms, rejection sensitivity, low prosocial skills).

Agreeableness and Academic Competence

Academic competence is multifaceted and involves regulation and cooperation in both academic and social tasks in school. Although conscientiousness has been more consistently associated with academic achievement (O'Connor & Paunonen, 2007), agreeableness likely also plays a role in children's everyday experiences in school, in both academic and social capacities. Individuals who are more agreeable tend to be better regulated (McCrae & Löckenhoff, 2010). Thus, in school, agreeable individuals may adjust better to school demands and excel in academic tasks, as well as build positive relationships with teachers and peers in school.

There have been a number of studies examining the associations between agreeableness and academic adjustment, albeit a majority of studies have been conducted with college students. Meta-analyses indicate that agreeableness has a small positive relation to academic achievement among mostly college-age participants (McAbee & Oswald, 2013; O'Connor & Paunonen, 2007; Vedel, 2014), children in elementary school (Poropat, 2014), and students from elementary school to college levels (Poropat, 2009). There is also compelling longitudinal evidence; Shiner (2000), for example, found that agreeableness in childhood predicted with academic attainment 10 and 20 years later in adulthood (see also Shiner & Masten, 2012; Shiner et al., 2003).

However, some research findings do not support the significance of agreeableness relative to academic achievement. In one meta-analysis, Trapmann, Hell, Hirn, and Schuler (2007) did not find that agreeableness predicted academic success in college. Various researchers have also reported null findings (Barthelemy & Lounsbury, 2009; Caprara, Barbaranelli, Pastorelli, & Cervone, 2004; Smrtnik-Vitulić & Zupančič, 2011; Spengler, Lüdtke, Martin, & Brunner, 2013; Trapmann et al., 2007; Zuffianò et al., 2013). Some researchers have found that agreeableness, at best, has small effects on some academic measures. For instance, Barthelemy and Lounsbury (2009) found that agreeableness was associated with adolescents' grades, but when they controlled for adolescent aggression, agreeableness was no longer a significant predictor of grades. Correspondingly, although agreeableness was positively associated with high school grade point averages (GPAs) in one sample of undergraduate students, agreeableness was negatively associated with standardized achievement test (SAT) scores and college GPA (Noftle & Robins, 2007). Similar results have been reported among adolescents; Spengler, Lüdtke, Martin, and Brunner (2013) found that agreeableness was unrelated to academic grades and negatively associated with achievement in standardized tests. Together, these studies suggest that the association between agreeableness and academic achievement may be more nuanced, partly based on what measure of academic competence is being considered.

Regulatory, motivational, and relationship factors have been implicated as mechanisms for the association between agreeableness and academic achievement (Komarraju, Karau, & Schmeck, 2009). For example, among undergraduate students in the United States, agreeableness was associated with GPA via effort regulation during academic tasks (e.g., persistent effort at tasks, dealing with failure in learning; Bidjerano & Dai, 2007). Relatedly, agreeableness was associated with academic adaptability among high school students (adaptability resembles resilience and coping in academic settings of novelty; Martin, Nejad, Colmar, & Liem, 2013). Regarding motivational processes, agreeableness was positively associated with commitment to education among college students (Klimstra, Luyckx, Germeijs, Meeus, & Goossens, 2012). Furthermore, agreeableness was negatively associated with teacher–student dependence and conflict, and positively associated with teacher–student closeness, which predicted higher motivational beliefs and achievement among children in the Netherlands (Zee, Koomen, & Van der Veen, 2013). Teacher-student relationship quality and motivational beliefs mediated the association between agreeableness and academic achievement. Although the aforementioned researchers tested mediation, Zhou (2015) found that autonomous motivation was a significant moderator: Agreeableness positively predicted academic performance for Chinese children low in autonomous motivation, whereas, highly motivated students were academically adjusted regardless of their agreeableness levels.

Some of the disparate findings between agreeableness and academic achievement may also be due to varying assessments of agreeableness and not accounting for underlying facets of agreeableness that may promote or hinder academic achievement. For example, McAbee, Oswald, and Connelly (2014) estimated a bifactor model of agreeableness based on the HEXACO (Honesty–Humility, Emotionality, eXtraversion, Agreeableness, Conscientiousness, Openness to Experience) scale and found that among college students in the United States, agreeableness was positively associated with GPA, adaptability, and life skills (e.g., balance in personal, academic, and professional priorities), and persistence (e.g., pursuing goals despite difficulties), all of which are key to academic achievement. However, some facets of agreeableness were either positively or negatively associated with academic outcomes. Flexibility and patience both uniquely predicted higher continuous learning (e.g., seeking opportunities to learn new ideas or skills). Notably, gentleness, another subfactor of agreeableness, was negatively associated with GPA, adaptability and life skills, and persistence (McAbee et al., 2014), echoing findings on academic achievement among adolescents (Spengler et al., 2013) and college students (Noftle & Robins, 2007). Similarly, among inner-city boys, compassion in preadolescence negatively predicted total years of schooling in adulthood even though compliance was associated with more years of schooling and a lower likelihood of dropping out or being expelled from school by adulthood (Kern et al., 2013). These findings highlight the nuanced role that agreeableness may have on academic outcomes, with attention to both broad and narrow personality traits, as well as different definitions of agreeableness (e.g., Big Five vs. HEXACO). Furthermore, specific aspects of agreeableness (e.g., gentleness, compassion) may have negative effects on achievement, perhaps because these are more subtly associated with meek or compliant behaviors and relate less to assertive agreeableness features. Future research examining both broad and narrow aspects of agreeableness will help clarify the role of agreeableness in academic achievement.

One notable limitation in this research area is that most of the empirical findings have been based on college students and rarely on children and adolescents, perhaps because earlier temperament measures do not correspond well with agreeableness (Tackett et al., 2013). Thus, we know less about how agreeableness in childhood and adolescence relates to school functioning. Given that early markers of school functioning are strong predictors of academic attainment, examining early precursors of agreeableness and school functioning could clarify mediating and moderating mechanisms that link agreeableness to later academic achievement.

Conclusion

In summary, agreeableness is a personality trait that clearly emerges by childhood, yet it has elicited less empirical attention earlier in life. When agreeableness has been studied in children, measurements often emphasize compliance and (reverse-coded) antagonism more heavily than do adult measures (although child measures frequently include aspects of prosocial functioning as well). When agreeableness has been measured in children, it often demonstrates psychometric properties equivalent to other major personality traits, indicating that it can be validly and reliably measured from childhood. Furthermore, agreeableness demonstrates robust associations with a host of relevant consequential behavioral constructs, including psychopathology, relational functioning, and academic performance. In particular, agreeableness emerges as a very strong indicator of (low) externalizing psychopathology from childhood to adulthood. Similarly, agreeableness in children and adolescents is associated with higher relational functioning (e.g., with parents and peers) and lower levels of conflict. Although much less studied in childhood and early adolescence, there is some indication that agreeableness is associated with indicators of academic competence, although findings are mixed and more developmental research is needed. Overall, agreeableness is a robust and widely studied personality trait in adults, but the lack of empirical attention to early agreeableness points to many areas for future research development. The potential predictive value of early agreeableness for many life outcomes, including mental health and relational function, underscore the need for more research on agreeableness and related behaviors across the lifespan.

REFERENCES

Alessandri, G., Kanacri, B. P. L., Eisenberg, N., Zuffianò, A., Milioni, M., Vecchione, M., et al. (2014). Prosociality during the transition from late adolescence to young adulthood: The role of effortful control and ego-resiliency. *Personality and Social Psychology Bulletin, 40*, 1451–1465.

Alessandri, G., Vecchione, M., Donnellan, B. M., Eisenberg, N., Caprara, G. V., & Cieciuch, J. (2014). On the cross-cultural replicability of the resilient, undercontrolled, and overcontrolled personality types. *Journal of Personality, 82*, 340–353.

Balliet, D. (2010). Conscientiousness and forgivingness: A meta-analysis. *Personality and Individual Differences, 48*, 259–263.

Barthelemy, J. J., & Lounsbury, J. W. (2009). The relationship between aggression and the Big Five personality factors in predicting academic success. *Journal of Human Behavior in the Social Environment, 19*, 159–170.

Bidjerano, T., & Dai, D. Y. (2007). The relationship between the Big-Five model of personality and self-regulated learning strategies. *Learning and Individual Differences, 17,* 69–81.

Caprara, G. V., Alessandri, G., Di Giunta, L., Panerai, L., & Eisenberg, N. (2010). The contribution of agreeableness and self-efficacy beliefs to prosociality. *European Journal of Personality, 24,* 36–55.

Caprara, G. V., Alessandri, G., & Eisenberg, N. (2012). Prosociality: The contribution of traits, values, and self-efficacy beliefs. *Journal of Personality and Social Psychology, 102,* 1289–1303.

Caprara, G. V., Alessandri, G., Tisak, M. S., Paciello, M., Caprara, M. G., Gerbino, M., et al. (2013). Individual differences in personality conducive to engagement in aggression and violence. *European Journal of Personality, 27,* 290–303.

Caprara, G. V., Barbaranelli, C., Pastorelli, C., & Cervone, D. (2004). The contribution of self-efficacy beliefs to psychosocial outcomes in adolescence: Predicting beyond global dispositional tendencies. *Personality and Individual Differences, 37,* 751–763.

Caspi, A., Roberts, B. W., & Shiner, R. L. (2005). Personality development: Stability and change. *Annual Review of Psychology, 56,* 453–484.

Costa, P. T., & McCrae, R. R. (1992). *Neo PI-R professional manual.* Odessa, FL: Psychological Assessment Resources.

Cumberland-Li, A., Eisenberg, N., & Reiser, M. (2004). Relations of young children's agreeableness and resiliency to effortful control and impulsivity. *Social Development, 13,* 193–212.

De Clercq, B., Van Leeuwen, K., De Fruyt, F., Van Hiel, A., & Mervielde, I. (2008). Maladaptive personality traits and psychopathology in childhood and adolescence: The moderating effect of parenting. *Journal of Personality, 76,* 357–383.

De Fruyt, F., Mervielde, I., Hoekstra, H. A., & Rolland, J. P. (2000). Assessing adolescents' personality with the NEO PI-R. *Assessment, 7,* 329–345.

de Haan, A., De Pauw, S., van den Akker, A., Deković, M., & Prinzie, P. (2017). Long-term developmental changes in children's lower-order Big Five personality facets. *Journal of Personality, 85,* 616–631.

de Haan, A. D., Prinzie, P., & Deković, M. (2010). How and why children change in aggression and delinquency from childhood to adolescence: Moderation of overreactive parenting by child personality. *Journal of Child Psychology and Psychiatry, 51,* 725–733.

De Pauw, S. S. W., & Mervielde, I. (2010). Temperament, personality and developmental psychopathology: A review based on the conceptual dimensions underlying childhood traits. *Child Psychiatry and Human Development, 41,* 313–329.

Decuyper, M., De Pauw, S., De Fruyt, F., De Bolle, M., & De Clercq, B. J. (2009). A meta-analysis of psychopathy-, antisocial PD- and FFM associations. *European Journal of Personality, 23,* 531–565.

Denissen, J. J., van Aken, M. A., & Dubas, J. S. (2009). It takes two to tango: How parents' and adolescents' personalities link to the quality of their mutual relationship. *Developmental Psychology, 45,* 928–941.

Digman, J. M., & Shmelyov, A. G. (1996). The structure of temperament and personality in Russian children. *Journal of Personality and Social Psychology, 71,* 341–351.

Eisenberg, N., Spinrad, T. L., & Eggum, N. D. (2010). Emotion-related self-regulation and its relation to children's maladjustment. *Annual Review of Clinical Psychology, 6,* 495–525.

Ellis, L. K., & Rothbart, M. K. (2001, April). *Revision of the early adolescent temperament questionnaire.* Poster presented at the biennial meeting of the Society for Research in Child Development, Minneapolis, MN.

Evans, D. E., & Rothbart, M. K. (2007). Developing a model for adult temperament. *Journal of Research in Personality, 41,* 868–888.

Evans, D. E., & Rothbart, M. K. (2009). A two-factor model of temperament. *Personality and Individual Differences, 47,* 565–570.

Goldberg, L. R. (2001). Analyses of Digman's child-personality data: Derivation of Big-Five factor scores from each of six samples. *Journal of Personality, 69,* 709–743.

Gomez, R., & Corr, P. J. (2014). ADHD and personality: A meta-analytic review. *Clinical Psychology Review, 34,* 376–388.

Graziano, W. G., & Eisenberg, N. (1997). Agreeableness: A dimension of personality. In R. Hogan, J. Johnson, & S. Briggs (Eds.), *Handbook of personality psychology* (pp. 795–824). San Diego, CA: Academic Press.

Graziano, W. G., Habashi, M. M., Sheese, B. E., & Tobin, R. M. (2007). Agreeableness, empathy, and helping: A person × situation perspective. *Journal of Personality and Social Psychology, 93,* 583–599.

Haas, B. W., Ishak, A., Denison, L., Anderson, I., & Filkowski, M. M. (2015). Agreeableness and brain activity during emotion attribution decisions. *Journal of Research in Personality, 57,* 26–31.

Habashi, M. M., Graziano, W. G., & Hoover, A. E. (2016). Searching for the prosocial personality: A Big Five approach to linking personality and prosocial behavior. *Personality and Social Psychology Bulletin, 42,* 1177–1192.

Hagekull, B., & Bohlin, G. (1998). Preschool temperament and environmental factors related to the five-factor model of personality in middle childhood. *Merrill–Palmer Quarterly, 44,* 194–215.

Hakulinen, C., Elovainio, M., Pulkki-Råback, L., Virtanen, M., Kivimäki, M., & Jokela, M. (2015). Personality and depressive symptoms: Individual participant meta-analysis of 10 cohort studies. *Depression and Anxiety, 32,* 461–470.

Halverson, C. F., Havill, V. L., Deal, J., Baker, S. R., Victor, J. B., Pavlopoulous, V., et al. (2003). Personality structure as derived from parental ratings of free descriptions of children: The Inventory of Child Individual Differences. *Journal of Personality, 71,* 995–1026.

Havill, V. L., Besevegis, E., & Mouroussaki, S. (1998).

Agreeableness as a diachronic human trait. In G. A. Kohnstamm, C. F. Halverson, Jr., I. Mervielde, & V. L. Havill (Eds.), *Parental descriptions of child personality: Developmental antecedents of the Big Five* (pp. 49–64). Mahwah, NJ: Erlbaum.

Jensen-Campbell, L. A., Adams, R., Perry, D. G., Workman, K. A., Furdella, J. Q., & Egan, S. K. (2002). Agreeableness, extraversion, and peer relations in early adolescence: Winning friends and deflecting aggression. *Journal of Research in Personality, 36,* 224–251.

Jensen-Campbell, L. A., Gleason, K. A., Adams, R., & Malcolm, K. T. (2003). Interpersonal conflict, agreeableness, and personality development. *Journal of Personality, 71,* 1059–1086.

Jensen-Campbell, L. A., Graziano, W. G., & Hair, E. C. (1996). Personality and relationships as moderators of interpersonal conflict in adolescence. *Merrill–Palmer Quarterly, 42,* 148–164.

Jones, S. E., Miller, J. D., & Lynam, D. R. (2011). Personality, antisocial behavior, and aggression: A meta-analytic review. *Journal of Criminal Justice, 39,* 329–337.

Kern, M. L., Duckworth, A. L., Urzua, S., Loeber, R., Stouthamer-Loeber, M., & Lynam, D. R. (2013). Do as you're told!: Facets of agreeableness and early adult outcomes for inner-city boys. *Journal of Research in Personality, 47,* 10.

Klimstra, T. A., Luyckx, K., Germeijs, V., Meeus, W. H., & Goossens, L. (2012). Personality traits and educational identity formation in late adolescents: Longitudinal associations and academic progress. *Journal of Youth and Adolescence, 41,* 346–361.

Kochanska, G., Friesenborg, A. E., Lange, L. A., Martel, M. M., & Kochanska, G. (2004). Parents' personality and infants' temperament as contributors to their emerging relationship. *Journal of Personality and Social Psychology, 86,* 744–759.

Komarraju, M., Karau, S. J., & Schmeck, R. R. (2009). Role of the Big Five personality traits in predicting college students' academic motivation and achievement. *Learning and Individual Differences, 19,* 47–52.

Kotov, R., Gamez, W., Schmidt, F., & Watson, D. (2010). Linking "big" personality traits to anxiety, depressive, and substance use disorders: A meta-analysis. *Psychological Bulletin, 136,* 768–821.

Laursen, B., Hafen, C. A., Rubin, K. H., Booth-LaForce, C., & Rose-Krasnor, L. (2010). The distinctive difficulties of disagreeable youth. *Merrill–Palmer Quarterly, 56,* 80–103.

Laursen, B., Pulkkinen, L., & Adams, R. (2002). The antecedents and correlates of agreeableness in adulthood. *Developmental Psychology, 38,* 591–603.

Lodi-Smith, J., & Roberts, B. W. (2007). Social investment and personality: A meta-analysis of the relationship of personality traits to investment in work, family, religion, and volunteerism. *Personality and Social Psychology Review, 11,* 68–86.

Malouff, J. M., Thorsteinsson, E. B., & Schutte, N.

S. (2005). The relationship between the five-factor model of personality and symptoms of clinical disorders: A meta-analysis. *Journal of Psychopathology and Behavioral Assessment, 27,* 101–114.

Malouff, J. M., Thorsteinsson, E. B., Schutte, N. S., Bhullar, N., & Rooke, S. E. (2010). The Five-Factor Model of personality and relationship satisfaction of intimate partners: A meta-analysis. *Journal of Research in Personality, 44,* 124–127.

Martel, M. M., Nigg, J. T., & Lucas, R. E. (2008). Trait mechanisms in youth with and without attention-deficit/hyperactivity disorder. *Journal of Research in Personality, 42,* 895–913.

Martin, A. J., Nejad, H. G., Colmar, S., & Liem, G. A. D. (2013). Adaptability: How students' responses to uncertainty and novelty predict their academic and non-academic outcomes. *Journal of Educational Psychology, 105,* 728–746.

McAbee, S. T., & Oswald, F. L. (2013). The criterion-related validity of personality measures for predicting GPA: A meta-analytic validity competition. *Psychological Assessment, 25,* 523–544.

McAbee, S. T., Oswald, F. L., & Connelly, B. S. (2014). Bifactor models of personality and college student performance: A broad versus narrow view. *European Journal of Personality, 28,* 604–619.

McCrae, R. R., & Löckenhoff, C. E. (2010). Self-regulation and the five-factor model of personality traits. In R. H. Hoyle (Ed.), *Handbook of personality and self-regulation* (pp. 145–168). Oxford, UK: Wiley-Blackwell.

Mervielde, I., & De Fruyt, F. (1999). Construction of the Hierarchical Personality Inventory for Children (HiPIC). In I. Mervielde, I. Deary, F. De Fruyt, & F. Ostendorf (Eds.), *Proceedings of the Eighth European Conference on Personality Psychology* (pp. 107–127). Tilburg, The Netherlands: Tilburg University Press.

Miller, J. D., & Lynman, D. (2001). Structural models of personality and their relation to antisocial behavior: A meta-analytic review. *Criminology, 39,* 765–798.

Mund, M., & Neyer, F. J. (2014). Treating personality-relationship transactions with respect: Narrow facets, advanced models, and extended time frames. *Journal of Personality and Social Psychology, 107,* 352–368.

Neyer, F. J., & Lehnart, J. (2007). Relationships matter in personality development: Evidence from an 8-year longitudinal study across young adulthood. *Journal of Personality, 75,* 535–568.

Noftle, E. E., & Robins, R. W. (2007). Personality predictors of academic outcomes: Big Five correlates of GPA and SAT scores. *Journal of Personality and Social Psychology, 93,* 116–130.

O'Connor, M. C., & Paunonen, S. V. (2007). Big Five personality predictors of post-secondary academic performance. *Personality and Individual Differences, 43,* 971–990.

Oshri, A., Rogosch, F. A., & Cicchetti, D. (2013). Child maltreatment and mediating influences of childhood personality types on the development of adolescent psychopathology. *Journal of Clinical Child and Adolesc Psychology, 42,* 287–301.

Parker, P. D., Ludtke, O., Trautwein, U., & Roberts, B. W. (2012). Personality and relationship quality during the transition from high school to early adulthood. *Journal of Personality, 80,* 1061–1089.

Poropat, A. E. (2009). A meta-analysis of the five-factor model of personality and academic performance. *Psychological Bulletin, 135,* 322–338.

Poropat, A. E. (2014). A meta-analysis of adult-rated child personality and academic performance in primary education. *British Journal of Educational Psychology, 84,* 239–252.

Prinzie, P., Stams, G. J., Deković, M., Reijntjes, A. H., & Belsky, J. (2009). The relations between parents' Big Five personality factors and parenting: A meta-analytic review. *Journal of Personality and Social Psychology, 97,* 351–362.

Riek, B. M., & Mania, E. W. (2012). The antecedents and consequences of interpersonal forgiveness: A meta-analytic review. *Personal Relationships, 19,* 304–325.

Roberts, B. W., Kuncel, N. R., Shiner, R., Caspi, A., & Goldberg, L. R. (2007). The power of personality: The comparative validity of personality traits, socioeconomic status, and cognitive ability for predicting important life outcomes. *Perspectives on Psychological Science, 2,* 313–345.

Robins, R. W., John, O. P., Caspi, A., Moffitt, T. E., & Stouthamer-Loeber, M. (1996). Resilient, overcontrolled, and undercontrolled boys: Three replicable personality types. *Journal of Personality and Social Psychology, 70,* 157–171.

Rothbart, M. K., Ahadi, S. A., & Evans, D. E. (2000). Temperament and personality: Origins and outcomes. *Journal of Personality and Social Psychology, 78,* 122–135.

Rothbart, M. K., Ahadi, S. A., Hershey, K. L., & Fisher, P. (2001). Investigations of temperament at three to seven years: The Children's Behavior Questionnaire. *Child Development, 72,* 1394–1408.

Rothbart, M. K., & Bates, J. E. (2006). Temperament. In N. Eisenberg (Vol. Ed.) & W. Damon & R. M. Lerner (Eds.), *Handbook of child psychology: Vol. 3. Social, emotional, and personality development* (6th ed., pp. 105–176). Hoboken, NJ: Wiley.

Sameroff, A. (2009). The transactional model. In A. Sameroff (Ed.), *The transactional model of development: How children and contexts shape each other* (pp. 3–21). Washington, DC: American Psychological Association.

Shiner, R. L. (2000). Linking childhood personality with adaptation: Evidence for continuity and change across time into late adolescence. *Journal of Personality and Social Psychology, 78,* 310–325.

Shiner, R., & Caspi, A. (2003). Personality differences in childhood and adolescence: Measurement, development, and consequences. *Journal of Child Psychology and Psychiatry, 44,* 2–32.

Shiner, R. L., & Masten, A. S. (2012). Childhood personality as a harbinger of competence and resilience in adulthood. *Development and Psychopathology, 24,* 507–528.

Shiner, R. L., Masten, A. S., & Roberts, J. M. (2003). Childhood personality foreshadows adult personality and life outcomes two decades later. *Journal of Personality, 71,* 1145–1170.

Sibley, C. G., & Duckitt, J. (2008). Personality and prejudice: A meta-analysis and theoretical review. *Personality and Social Psychology Review, 12,* 248–279.

Slobodskaya, H. R., & Akhmetova, O. A. (2010). Personality development and problem behavior in Russian children and adolescents. *International Journal of Behavioral Development, 34,* 441–451.

Smrtnik-Vitulić, H., & Zupančič, M. (2011). Personality traits as a predictor of academic achievement in adolescents. *Educational Studies, 37,* 127–140.

Soto, C. J. (2016). The little six personality dimensions from early childhood to early adulthood: Mean-level age and gender differences in parents' reports. *Journal of Personality, 8,* 409–422.

Soto, C. J., & John, O. P. (2017). The next Big Five Inventory (BFI-2): Developing and assessing a hierarchical model with 15 facets to enhance bandwidth, fidelity, and predictive power. *Journal of Personality and Social Psychology, 113*(1), 117–143.

Soto, C. J., John, O. P., Gosling, S. D., & Potter, J. (2008). The developmental psychometrics of Big Five self-reports: Acquiescence, factor structure, coherence, and differentiation from ages 10 to 20. *Journal of Personality and Social Psychology, 94,* 718–737.

Soto, C. J., & Tackett, J. L. (2015). Personality traits in childhood and adolescence: Structure, development, and outcomes. *Current Directions in Psychological Science, 24,* 358–362.

Spengler, M., Lüdtke, O., Martin, R., & Brunner, M. (2013). Personality is related to educational outcomes in late adolescence: Evidence from two large-scale achievement studies. *Journal of Research in Personality, 47,* 613–625.

Tackett, J. L., Herzhoff, K., Kushner, S. C., & Rule, N. (2016). Thin slices of child personality: Perceptual, situational, and behavioral contributions. *Journal of Personality and Social Psychology, 110,* 150–166.

Tackett, J. L., Herzhoff, K., Reardon, K. W., De Clercq, B., & Sharp, C. (2014). The externalizing spectrum in youth: Incorporating personality pathology. *Journal of Adolescence, 37,* 659–668.

Tackett, J. L., Krueger, R. F., Iacono, W. G., & McGue, M. (2008). Personality in middle childhood: A hierarchical structure and longitudinal connections with personality in late adolescence. *Journal of Research in Personality, 42,* 1456–1462.

Tackett, J. L., Kushner, S. C., De Fruyt, F., & Mervielde, I. (2013). Delineating personality traits in childhood and adolescence: Associations across measures, temperament, and behavioral problems. *Assessment, 20,* 738–751.

Tackett, J. L., Slobodskaya, H. R., Mar, R. A., Deal, J.,

Halverson, C. F., Baker, S. R., et al. (2012). The hierarchical structure of childhood personality in five countries: Continuity from early childhood to early adolescence. *Journal of Personality, 80,* 847–879.

Tamis-LeMonda, C. S., Wang, S., Koutsouvanou, E., & Albright, M. (2002). Childrearing values in Greece, Taiwan, and the United States. *Parenting: Science and Practice, 2,* 185–208.

Tellegen, A., & Waller, N. G. (1992). *Exploring personality through test construction: Development of the Multi-Dimensional Personality Questionnaire (MPQ).* Minneapolis: Department of Psychology, University of Minnesota.

Trapmann, S., Hell, B., Hirn, J. W., & Schuler, H. (2007). Meta-analysis of the relationship between the Big Five and academic success at university. *Zeitschrift für Psychologie, 215,* 132–151.

Van den Akker, A. L., Deković, M., Asscher, J., & Prinzie, P. (2014). Mean-level personality development across childhood and adolescence: A temporary defiance of the maturity principle and bidirectional associations with parenting. *Journal of Personality and Social Psychology, 107,* 736–750.

Vedel, A. (2014). The Big Five and tertiary academic performance: A systematic review and meta-analysis. *Personality and Individual Differences, 71,* 66–76.

Wang, J. M., Hartl, A. C., Laursen, B., & Rubin, K. H. (2017). The high costs of low agreeableness: Low agreeableness exacerbates interpersonal consequences of rejection sensitivity in U.S. and Chinese adolescents. *Journal of Research in Personality, 67,* 36–43.

Zaninotto, L., Solmi, M., Toffanin, T., Veronese, N., Cloninger, C. R., & Correll, C. U. (2016). A meta-analysis of temperament and character dimensions in patients with mood disorders: Comparison to healthy controls and unaffected siblings. *Journal of Affective Disorders, 194,* 84–97.

Zee, M., Koomen, H. M., & Van der Veen, I. (2013). Student–teacher relationship quality and academic adjustment in upper elementary school: The role of student personality. *Journal of School Psychology, 51,* 517–533.

Zhang, R., & Tsingan, L. (2013). Extraversion and neuroticism mediate associations between openness, conscientiousness, and agreeableness and affective well-being. *Journal of Happiness Studies, 15,* 1377–1388.

Zhou, M. (2015). Moderating effect of self-determination in the relationship between Big Five personality and academic performance. *Personality and Individual Differences, 86,* 385–389.

Zuffianò, A., Alessandri, G., Gerbino, M., Luengo Kanacri, B. P., Di Giunta, L., Milioni, M., et al. (2013). Academic achievement: The unique contribution of self-efficacy beliefs in self-regulated learning beyond intelligence, personality traits, and self-esteem. *Learning and Individual Differences, 23,* 158–162.

CHAPTER 11

The Structure, Measurement, and Development of Openness to Experience across Adulthood

Ted Schwaba

What I have is a malevolent curiosity. That's what drives my need to write and what probably leads me to look at things a little askew.

—DAVID BOWIE

Openness to experience is a fundamental and universal personality trait (McCrae & Costa, 1997). Forty years of research have substantiated that this trait captures individual differences in motivation to explore and tendency to think in ways both broad and deep (DeYoung, 2014; McCrae & Costa, 1997; McCrae & Sutin, 2009). Of the Big Five personality traits, however, openness to experience has always been the least understood. There is still much to learn about the structure of this trait (DeYoung, 2014) and its development across the lifespan (Schwaba, Luhmann, Denissen, Chung, & Bleidorn, 2017). Even the label that best summarizes the diverse contents of this trait is still a subject of debate: Should this trait be called openness to experience, intellect, or open-mindedness (Soto & John, 2017)? Here, I refer to the trait by the term *openness,* for the sake of simplicity. Perhaps the most intuitive way to understand this broad personality trait is through profiling a single paragon of openness. The musician, actor, and iconoclast David Bowie is one such paragon.

Bowie, in Brief

David Bowie is perhaps as close as one can come to the living embodiment of a personality trait. The man was defined by his openness to experience. An examination into the childhood of Bowie, born David Jones in 1947 in South London, reveals first and foremost an insatiable desire to consume and create art. By age 10, Bowie was playing piano, bass, and ukulele in a local rock 'n' roll band. At age 14, he had become enamored with jazz and took up the saxophone. At age 17, he released his first single, "Liza Jane," as part of a short-lived blues quintet (Sandford, 1998). By all accounts, these initial musical attempts were rather dismal, especially compared to the remarkable stage presence that Bowie displayed. Bowie's feel for the stage and improvisational dance ability led him to study avant-garde theater and appear in a few TV commercials (Sandford, 1998). While none of these initial musical and theatrical ventures amounted to much, they reveal an adolescent with an insatiable hunger to consume and produce art, regardless of genre or mode of expression.

Bowie's breakthrough came in spurts, first with the well-timed rock opera single "Space Oddity," which was released just before the *Apollo 11* lunar landing (Wolk, 2016), and then, a few years later, with the psychedelic album *Ziggy Stardust and the Spiders from Mars.* While touring for the latter album, Bowie assumed the character of Ziggy Stardust, an androgynous rock star in contact with aliens. Bowie's decision (and ability) to remain in character during the entirety of the tour speaks to his uniquely vivid fantasy life and capability to be absorbed into his own art.

Bowie's superstardom brought him to Los Angeles, where he assumed another alter ego, the Thin White Duke, for his chart-topping albums *Young Americans* and *Station to Station.* As the Duke, Bowie saw great commercial success, but his personal life fell apart. He became addicted to cocaine and made a bizarre series of fascist comments and gestures during his concerts (Sandford, 1998). Bowie's inability to separate the Duke character from his own identity reveals a maladaptive quality of his high openness—it was unclear whether Bowie controlled his art or his art controlled him. In 1976, Bowie left Los Angeles for Berlin, leaving the Duke behind.

Bowie's move to Europe allowed him to showcase his creativity in a new, healthier way. Rhythmic music by German bands such as Neu! and Kraftwerk, which made use of the recently invented synthesizer keyboard, enraptured Bowie. Bowie incorporated this sound into his next three albums, *Low, Heroes,* and *Lodger.* These three albums eschewed the qualities that made Bowie famous and instead focused on rather eccentric ideas, such as playing the chord structure from an earlier Bowie composition backwards (*Lodger*'s "Move On") and incorporating white noise into compositions (*Low*'s "Always Crashing in the Same Car"). These albums, predictably, did not sell very well compared to his previous efforts, but this did not matter much to Bowie. Bowie's eye was always on innovation and creativity, and his stardom followed almost incidentally.

Defining Openness

When distilling his biography, a few key components to David Bowie's personality emerge. Bowie was constantly creating art, seemingly driven by near-obsessive intrinsic motivation.

He was readily absorbed into fantasy and reflection, especially when it came to alternative identities he assumed. Bowie was always exploring, making art that was somehow both easily accessible and complexly layered. In each of these cognitive, behavioral, and motivational aspects, Bowie was an exemplar of openness to experience.

Departing from the life of Bowie, I define *openness to experience* as follows: Openness to experience captures individual differences in the motivation to approach and create novel stimuli, as well as in patterns of convergent and divergent thought. This definition draws heavily on conceptions of openness provided by DeYoung (2015) and McCrae and Costa (1997). *Motivation to approach novel stimuli* is seen in the goal-directed and presumably evolved tendency for open people to prefer the new over the familiar, and for open people to approach rather than avoid unfamiliar concepts and experiences (DeYoung, 2015). *Motivation to create novel stimuli* captures the drive that highly open people have to make art and "think outside the box" (McCrae & Costa, 1997). *Patterns of convergent thought* are seen in openness's associations with intelligence, and perhaps at a more fundamental level, individual differences in the ability to learn from patterns (DeYoung, Grazioplene, & Peterson, 2012). And finally, *patterns of divergent thought* are made apparent through openness's associations with breadth of thought (McCrae, 1987), fantasy and daydreaming, and, at the clinical extremes, with the false pattern perception more commonly seen in highly open people (DeYoung et al., 2012).

This definition delineates the four ingredients that I believe lie at the core of openness to experience, but the trait itself contains many intriguing emergent properties that merit further discussion. The rest of this chapter is divided into two main sections. First, I detail the history and structure of openness. I review how the trait was and is conceptualized, commonly used measures of openness, and how and why openness is associated with creativity, culture, intelligence, and political orientation. Second, I describe and explain the development of openness across adulthood. This section follows openness from emerging adulthood, through midlife, and into old age.[1] Beyond age, however,

---

[1] In this chapter, I exclusively discuss openness to experience across adulthood. For an extensive review of the emergence of openness and its structure in childhood, I refer readers to De Pauw (2017).

recent research has implicated other important experiences in the development of an individual's openness. I review those experiences in the final section.

Throughout this chapter, I go beyond description and into explanation, and attempt to explain why open people do what they do and what mechanisms may drive changes in openness. There are ample reasons to stick to description and prediction when it comes to personality; the two are difficult enough as is (Yarkoni & Westfall, 2017). But I believe that explaining and theorizing, in measured doses, makes for an interesting and thought-provoking chapter.

The History and Structure of Openness

Long before a critical mass of studies identified openness as a major dimension of personality, researchers theorized about the importance of other, roughly similar constructs to personality. A first line of research that came to influence our understanding of openness to experience was motivated by the atrocities of World War II. Investigations into the personality underpinnings of authoritarianism and fascism led to research that sought to measure and understand fascist personality traits (Adorno, Frenkel-Brunswik, Levinson, & Sanford, 1950) and dogmatism (Rokeach, 1960). Rokeach's writings were particularly useful to the concept of openness, as his book *The Open and Closed Mind* provided the trait's eventual name.

A separate line of research investigated how people's patterns of thinking color how they perceive the world. Tellegen and Atkinson (1974) developed an absorption scale that measured hypnotic sensitivity and other perceptual components of openness. Furthermore, research into field independence demonstrated associations between the way in which people make sense of an ambiguous figure and their cognitive styles and social preferences (Witkin & Goodenough, 1977).

A final thread that would be spun into the cloth of openness was done by researchers seeking to understand optimal human functioning. The clinical psychologist Carl Rogers (1961) asserted that openness to inner experience must be regarded as a criterion of good mental health. Coan (1972) sought to understand optimal cognitive functioning in college students, examining concepts such as aesthetic sensitivity and constructive utilization of fantasy. Finally, Loevinger (1979) developed an ego development scale aimed at identifying individuals who had rich and varied inner lives.

These research traditions were eventually united by researchers who sought to understand the structure of adult personality *in toto* (Digman, 1990; John, Naumann, & Soto, 2008). They used a statistical technique called *factor analysis* to partition many correlated questionnaire responses into a smaller set of underlying dimensions. For example, people who respond "yes" to the item "I tend to daydream" also tend to respond "yes" to the item "I like art." However, these two responses are unrelated to whether a person responds "yes" to "I keep my things organized" or "I arrive on time to meetings." Factor analysis would indicate that two dimensions underlie these four questions, one that captures the associations between the first two questions (we might term this dimension *openness*) and another that captures the associations between the latter two questions (we might term this dimension *conscientiousness*). While researchers agreed that factor analysis was an appropriate tool to understand the dimensions underlying personality, they were divided on the question of where to gather the material for an omnibus questionnaire that measured all of the important dimensions (John et al., 2008). Some researchers, the lexical group, believed that all important descriptors of individual differences would be found in natural language (Allport & Odbert, 1936); that is, the omnibus personality questionnaire should be built by consulting the dictionary. Other researchers, the questionnaire group, believed that that the lexical group was too restrictive because sometimes entire phrases are needed to capture an important individual difference (McCrae, 1990). This group believed that the omnibus personality questionnaire should be built by combing through existing questionnaires and selecting from them a diverse set of questions.

Both the lexical and questionnaire groups, following their preferred methodology, found that human personality was best described by five factors (neuroticism, extraversion, conscientiousness, agreeableness, and openness to experience), and that this five-dimension solution replicated across multiple samples in the United States and Europe (Digman, 1990). The fifth and final dimension to emerge was termed *openness to experience* (by the questionnaire group) and *intellect* (by the lexical group; McCrae & Costa, 1997). After the resolution of disagreements between these two camps (McCrae, 1990; Saucier, 1992), the term *openness to experience* eventually gained traction as the de facto descriptor of the various affective, behavioral, and cognitive tendencies that comprise the fifth personality factor.

Modern Conceptualizations of Openness to Experience

Despite agreeing in principle on naming the trait openness to experience, the actual content of the trait differs depending on what measurement instrument one uses to assess the trait. Openness measures derived using the questionnaire methodology, such as the NEO Five-Factor Inventory (NEO-FFI), emphasize the importance of motivational and experiential components in the trait (McCrae & Costa, 1997). Openness measures derived using the lexical methodology, such as the International Personality Item Pool (IPIP) inventory, emphasize the importance of intellectual, cultural, and cognitive components in the trait. Differences between questionnaire-derived and lexically derived openness scores are more substantial than those for the other four Big Five traits; NEO openness and IPIP openness only correlate about .5 (Goldberg, 1992). There is therefore value in reviewing the specific content of the most commonly used openness questionnaires, as doing so allows us to better understand the current resting place of the questionnaire and lexical conceptualizations of openness, as well as the construct of openness as a whole.

NEO Inventories

The flagship openness measures from the questionnaire tradition are the NEO series of inventories, developed by Costa and McCrae (1992). These inventories measure a broad and motivationally inclined latent openness construct. Costa and McCrae believed that the measurement of personality should, as best as possible, exclude measurement of ability. Therefore, the NEO asks whether the respondent is curious about, for example, theories and abstract ideas, but purposefully avoids interrogating respondents about their ability to understand these theories and abstract ideas. The NEO Personality Inventory—Revised (NEO-PI-R) investigates six particular openness facets identified by Costa and McCrae: openness to aesthetics and fantasy, which comprises the center of the trait; openness to ideas, which relates more

closely to the psycholexical conceptualization of openness as intellect; openness to values, which measures political orientation; openness to feelings, which measures breadth and depth of emotion; and openness to actions, which measures a blend of openness and extraversion (DeYoung et al., 2012). In abridged versions of the 240-item NEO-PI-R, the intellect and aesthetic facets are retained, along with a blended "unconventionality" facet that contains a mixture of values and fantasy (Saucier, 1998).

IPIP Inventories

The flagship openness measures of the lexical tradition come from the IPIP Project (Goldberg, 1992; Goldberg et al., 2006). Goldberg and colleagues (2006) were less averse about including ability in their measurement of openness, perhaps because words such as *thoughtful, smart,* and *bright* are commonly used trait descriptors in the English language. Lexically derived openness questionnaires therefore hew closer to the measurement of ability and are more highly correlated with intelligence tests than the NEO inventories (DeYoung et al., 2012). The most extensive version of the IPIP openness inventory also distinguishes six trait facets: intellect, imagination, artistic interests (which is highly associated with NEO openness), emotionality, adventurousness, and liberalism. A further contrast between the IPIP and the NEO is their ease of use by researchers. While use of the NEO inventories requires written permission, the IPIP inventories are freely available for use by interested researchers at *ipip.ori.org.*

Other Measures of Openness: The Big Five Inventory and Big Five Aspect Scales

While the discrepancies between lexically derived openness and questionnaire-derived openness are the most compelling and illustrate stark differences in trait conceptualization, there are a few other openness measures in common use today. These measures tend to conceptualize openness as somewhere in between. One commonly used inventory is the Big Five Inventory (BFI), developed at the University of California, Berkeley (John et al., 2008). The BFI, in its initial form, did not have a clear lower-order facet structure, which was addressed in the creation of the recent BFI-2 (Soto & John, 2017). The BFI-2 takes an ideological stance on the naming of openness, reterming it *open-mindedness.*

Furthermore, while each of the other four traits in the BFI-2 have a "central facet" that best describes the trait, openness's three facets are given equal importance, reflecting the authors' opinion that there is no "center" to openness. These facets are creative imagination, aesthetic sensitivity, and intellectual curiosity.

A final omnibus personality measure commonly used in the assessment of openness is the Big Five Aspect Scales (BFAS; DeYoung, Quilty, & Peterson, 2007). The BFAS explicitly acknowledges the discrepancies between the lexical and questionnaire traditions by terming the trait *openness/intellect*. Rather than facets, BFAS openness measures two interstitial "aspects" of the trait: openness, which is more associated with aesthetic sensitivity, fantasy, and reflection, and intellect.

Correlates of Openness

To better understand the construct of openness, researchers have examined the associations between openness measures and various other measures of emotional, behavioral, and cognitive tendencies, goals, abilities, and values. These associations allow researchers to refine and revise theories about what openness is, and what it isn't. Some associations are rather intuitive. People who report that they are intellectually curious also report that they tend to speculate on the nature of the universe (McCrae & Costa, 1997). Other associations, however, are thought provoking. People who enjoy abstract art also tend to vote for liberal political candidates (McCrae, 1996). In this section, I describe and explain four major correlates of openness: creativity, intelligence, culture, and political views.

Openness and Creativity

Although the lexical and questionnaire groups disagree on many of the finer points about openness, both agree that creativity is a major component of the trait. Indeed, according to Saucier (1992), *creativity* may be the best summary term for the common space shared between lexically derived openness and questionnaire-derived openness. Open people tend to be creative, in both senses of the word (Kandler et al., 2016); that is, creative people *create* cultural products, such as pop songs, and come up with *creative,* innovative ideas, such as pretending to be an alien while on tour. A plethora of research over the years has investigated associations between personality and performance in creativity tasks, such as writing down all the uses one can think of for a brick in a span of 5 minutes. This research has consistently found that openness is the strongest predictor of creativity test performance (McCrae, 1987; Silvia, Nusbaum, Berg, Martin, & O'Connor, 2009). (Extraversion also tends to predict performance, but less strongly.) Additionally, people who score high in different aspects of openness tend to be creative in different ways. Kaufman and colleagues (2016) measured openness with the BFAS and split the trait into its openness and intellect aspects. Across four samples, they found that when both of these facets were entered simultaneously into a predictive model, the aspect of openness predicted creative achievement in the arts, while the aspect of intellect predicted creative achievement in the sciences.

To explain these associations between openness and creativity, Kaufman and colleagues (2016) put forth a compelling dual-process model. They theorize that people who are open to experience may possess a combination of divergent and convergent thinking skills that allow them to access and select semantically distant concepts. Asked to name a four-legged animal, a person who is not very open to experience may bring to mind the concepts of "dog" and "cat," while a person scoring high on openness may bring to mind "dog" and "cat," but also the more divergent answer "buffalo." Furthermore, this highly open person may possess the convergent thinking ability to override the predominant feline and canine responses, providing an out-of-the box answer of "buffalo." Beyond this, Kaufman and colleagues suggest that different facets of openness may be differentially associated with these two modes of thought. The facet of intellect may be particularly relevant to convergent thinking, while the facet of aesthetic sensitivity may be particularly relevant to divergent thinking. This hypothesis is intriguing but has yet to be seriously tested. One roadblock that prevents easy testing of this theory is that even common "divergent" thinking tasks, such as thinking of multiple uses for a brick, require convergent thinking to some extent, because participants must select particular answers (convergently) from all that come to mind (divergently). To better understand the mechanisms that connect openness with convergent thinking, and divergent thinking, researchers must get creative with their assessment of creativity.

Openness and Intelligence

There has been long-standing interest in the associations between personality and intellectual ability (Cattell, 1943). This research has found evidence that openness, more than any other Big Five trait, is associated with the general factor of intelligence, *g,* and its major subcomponents, fluid intelligence and crystallized intelligence (Ashton, Lee, Vernon, & Jang, 2000; DeYoung, Peterson, & Higgins, 2005). These correlations vary by study but are typically in the range of .2 to .4, which is as high or higher than the correlation between intelligence test scores and self-reported intelligence (Gignac, Stough, & Loukomitis, 2004). Fluid intelligence, which measures reasoning *ability* (e.g., whether participants can correctly solve a novel puzzle that they have encountered before) is more highly associated with the intellect pole of openness, while crystallized intelligence, which measures accumulated reasoning *knowledge* (e.g., vocabulary) is associated with both intellect and openness (DeYoung et al., 2005, 2012). Interestingly, these associations between openness and intelligence seem to be confined to the domains of semantic, logical, and visuospatial knowledge. Openness is not highly associated with mathematics ability (Ashton et al., 2000) or mathematics SAT scores (Noftle & Robins, 2007).

One partial explanation for the associations between openness and intellectual abilities is differential investment (Ackerman, 1996; Cattell, 1943). Open people enjoy learning and more commonly engage in educational activities such as reading and attending museums (Schwaba et al., 2017). As open people spend time learning, their intelligence may increase. Simply put, open people want to learn and like to learn, so they learn a lot, and they become smart.

One recent study that provided an interesting test of this differential investment hypothesis examined the links between openness and musical discrimination ability (Thomas, Silvia, Nusbaum, Beaty, & Hodges, 2016). In this study, people who scored higher on openness were better at discriminating between similar-sounding tones, but this effect was only found because those who scored higher on openness also tended to have more formal musical training. People who scored high on openness but who were musical novices were no better at the tone discrimination task than those who scored low on openness. These findings and others suggest that investing in enriching environments indeed drives associations between openness and intelligence (Ziegler, Danay, Heene, Asendorpf, & Bühner, 2012; but see Soubelet & Salthouse, 2010, for a contrasting perspective).

Openness and Culture

Openness and the production and consumption of culture are highly intertwined, to the extent that some inventories measure openness through items that explicitly assess a person's artistic preferences (cf. Soto & John, 2017). As exemplified by David Bowie, highly open people tend to enjoy art, music, reading, and the theater (Kraaykamp & Van Eijck, 2005). And, within these modes of cultural expression, openness predicts specific cultural taste. For example, open people tend to enjoy abstract art more than their closed-to-experience peers, who prefer representational art (Belke, Leder, Strobach, & Carbon, 2010). These interests also extend to real-world behavior—open people are more likely to visit cultural institutions such as museums, the theater, and concerts (Kraaykamp & Van Eijck, 2005; Schwaba et al., 2017).

A recent model of aesthetic preferences, developed without openness in mind, may partially explain why open people gravitate toward culture. Graf and Landwehr (2015), in their pleasure–interest model of aesthetic liking, posit that aesthetic appreciation is driven by two processes. First, immediately after seeing an aesthetic object, people make a snap decision about how fluently the stimulus as a whole can be processed and this determines how much they like the object. This fluency "sweet spot" differs from person to person. Highly open people, who prefer complexity and novelty, may enjoy art that is relatively disfluent. After this first judgment, people who process the aesthetic object more fully then judge it based on the extent to which they understand the art and it remains interesting to them. If the art remains confusing (is too disfluent) or is boring (isn't disfluent enough), they like it less. Highly open people may be more motivated to process the aesthetic object more deeply, and they may subsequently derive more meaning from it than do people who are less open. However, because of their high tolerance for disfluency, open people may grow bored more easily. This relatively simple model may explain, at least in part, why open people tend to engage with complex culture. An obtuse Bowie song may appear dense and confusing at first listen. But highly open people enjoy this difficulty, find motivation to engage with it further, appreciate the difficulty in understanding the song, and eventually come to understand and enjoy it.

Openness and Political Views

A final correlate of openness that merits discussion is between openness and political views. Specifically, open people tend to be politically liberal: They advocate for social change and they reject inequality, and these correlations are substantial (r = about .35) and greater than for other Big Five personality traits (Jost, Glaser, Kruglanski, & Sulloway, 2003). As with culture, political views are central enough to the construct of openness that openness questionnaires often include items measuring political orientation. But political preference correlates highly with openness even if one omits this facet (McCrae, 1996).

The attitudinal qualities associated with openness may explain these associations. Highly open people tend to believe strongly that diversity of opinion is a good thing, and they tend to distrust groups that appeal to authority as a source of truth (McCrae, 1996). When open people apply these attitudes to form political preferences, they are attracted to the liberal ideals of progress and equality and repelled by the conservative ideals of tradition and respect for authority.

However, there is still much work to be done to fully understand associations between openness and politics. In particular, the extent to which these associations generalize to other political systems remains unclear. One study that compared measurement properties of the NEO-PI-R across U.S., Mexican, and Filipino samples found that the political values facet of openness was the *least* culturally comparable of any Big Five personality facet (Church et al., 2011). If political values are indeed so central to openness that they can be used to measure levels of the trait, one would hope that these associations remain invariant across cultures.

Interim Summary

At this point in the chapter, we have synthesized a common definition of openness, reviewed the trait's structure, and outlined some important trait associations. In other words, we've described open people as they are at a single point in time. But to truly understand openness, the trait must be considered longitudinally. For the remainder of this chapter, I focus on describing and explaining the development of openness at the population and individual levels.

Ch-Ch-Changes: The Development of Openness to Experience across Adulthood

An early tenet in psychology was that personality tends to be set like plaster around age 30 (Allport, 1961; Block, 1971; McCrae et al., 2000). At this point in time, however, a massive body of collected research definitively overturns this position. Personality can, and does, change throughout the lifespan (Roberts & DelVecchio, 2000; Roberts, Walton, & Viechtbauer, 2006). These changes come in three important types (Schwaba & Bleidorn, 2017).

The first type of change is mean-level change, which measures the average amount of *absolute* change in a personality trait across time. Mean-level change addresses the question, "How does the average person tend to change in openness over time?" Second, and independent of mean-level change, are individual differences in change. An estimate of individual differences in change quantifies the amount of heterogeneity around the mean-level change trajectory. It addresses the question, "To what extent are people changing differently than the mean-level trend?" Finally, rank-order change measures the average amount of *relative* change in a sample over time. It addresses the question, "If we were to order a sample of people from most open to least open, wait an amount of time, and measure their openness again, how different would the order be?" For a more detailed explanation of these three measures of change, I direct the interested reader to Schwaba and Bleidorn (2017). In the next section, I summarize the current state of research on mean-level, individual-level, and rank-order change in openness across the adult lifespan, focusing on three particular life stages: emerging adulthood, midlife, and older age.

Emerging Adulthood

When I was 18, I thought that, to be a romantic, you couldn't live past 30.

—DAVID BOWIE

Emerging adulthood is a life stage characteristic of modern, developed societies (Arnett, 2007). It describes the ages between roughly 18 and 30, when young adults typically explore in the domains of work and love, before they commit to adult identities (Arnett, 2000; Erikson, 1959). The mean-level development of openness to experience across emerging adulthood is a research question that is still under investigation. Some research has found mean-level increases in openness during emerging adulthood (Roberts et al., 2006). Other research has found mean-level stability (Schwaba et al., 2017; Specht, Egloff, & Schmukle, 2011; Wortman, Lucas, & Donnellan, 2012). One hypothesis that accounts for these interstudy differences is that increases in openness during emerging adulthood are driven by the identity exploration central to this life stage. If different samples of emerging adults are differentially engaged in identity exploration, openness changes will vary from sample to sample (Bleidorn & Schwaba, 2017). Bleidorn and colleagues (2013) provided an initial investigation into this hypothesis using cross-sectional data from over 800,000 participants in 62 nations. They found that in nations such as Pakistan, where the average age of marriage and entering the workforce is earlier, age-related increases in openness were less strong. In nations such as the Netherlands, however, where people tend to delay marriage and entrance into the workforce, increases in openness during emerging adulthood were steeper.

Beyond these mean-level increases in openness, emerging adulthood also appears to be the life stage with the most substantial individual differences in openness development (Schwaba & Bleidorn, 2017) and the most rank-order change in openness (Roberts & DelVecchio, 2000); that is, during emerging adulthood, there are many people who are becoming much more open to experience and much less open to experience, making it more difficult to predict a person's future openness during emerging adulthood than at any other point in adulthood. These findings are also consistent with the notion of emerging adulthood as a period of identity exploration. Within a particular nation, not everyone follows the same progression and timing of life events. Americans who spend their 20s pursuing graduate education, dating around, and moving from place to place may increase in openness, and those who marry immediately after high school may decrease in their levels of the trait.

Overall, openness development during this stage is best understood as a time of relative heterogeneity in development. People take many paths through emerging adulthood, and the development of openness appears to be similarly variable.

Middle Adulthood

I had such a struggle letting go of youthful things and learning how to exist and have enthusiasm while settling into the comfort of an older age.
—DAVID BOWIE

Middle adulthood, which I define as ages 30–60, is a relatively placid time in the development of openness. Mean levels of the trait appear to be relatively stable during this period, and there are fewer individual differences in openness development during this life stage than during emerging adulthood (Schwaba et al., 2017; Schwaba & Bleidorn, 2017). Rank-order change decreases throughout middle adulthood, reaching its lowest point at around age 60 (Roberts & DelVecchio, 2000; Wortman et al., 2012).

One common explanation for stability in openness across midlife, which appears across the Big Five personality traits, has been termed the *cumulative continuity principle of personality development* (Caspi & Roberts, 2001; but see Costello, Srivastava, & Saucier, 2017). As they navigate midlife, people reach the peak of their ability and motivation to create stability in their environments. A person's week-to-week environment across midlife may be remarkably repetitive, and with few environmental pressures rewarding increases or decreases in openness, the trait may tend to remain stable (Caspi & Moffitt, 1993). This stability may be adaptive for those committed to adult roles. Sticking to a single career allows one to develop steady sources of income. With children, one cannot easily move residences, and changing core beliefs and behaviors in one's mid-50s may strain a person's social life, and potentially their marriage. This is not to say that openness cannot change in midlife (as we see later), but for most people, it tends not to do so.

Older Adulthood

It's the lack of years left that weighs far heavier on me than the age that I am.
—DAVID BOWIE

Ages 60 and up are a time of resumed openness development at the population level. Across all large, nationally representative longitudinal studies of openness, mean levels of the trait decline increasingly rapidly across old age (Schwaba et al., 2017; Specht et al., 2011; Wortman et al., 2012). In terms of absolute magnitude, these changes of .5 to 1.5 standard deviations from age 60 until about 90 are the largest of any mean-level Big Five personality changes at any point in the lifespan. Further, during older adulthood there is the least heterogeneity in openness development—most people develop according to this decreasing trajectory (Schwaba et al., 2017).

Socioemotional selectivity theory (*SST*; Carstensen, Fung, & Charles, 2003), developed to explain affective processing and motivational changes in older adults, fits well as a partial explanation for mean-level openness decreases across older adulthood. SST posits that as people near the end of their lives, they become less motivated to explore new domains and more motivated to savor what (and who) they already know. SST makes the claim that exploring is rewarding mostly because doing so offers extrinsic rewards such as social and cultural capital that can prove valuable in the future (see also DeYoung, 2015, on the value of exploration). For older adults, who are nearer to death and have already invested in exploration throughout their lives, trying new things and meeting new people is less valuable. Retirees don't need to build skills or social networks for future career success—their careers are over. And given the choice between spending their last years alive with loved ones or with strangers, the choice for most older adults is obvious.

However, SST does not effectively explain openness declines found among highly open people. For people like David Bowie, exploration is most likely an intrinsically rather than extrinsically motivated behavior. To accompany the theoretical propositions made by SST, I posit that declines in intelligence and physical ability that come with old age may lead older adults to decline in openness.

Earlier in this chapter, I reviewed the cross-sectional associations between openness and both fluid and crystallized intelligence. A wealth of research has shown that mean levels of fluid intelligence peak in emerging adulthood and decline afterward, while mean levels of crystallized intelligence peak later, around the mid-60s, and decline afterward (Rönnlund,

Nyberg, Bäckman, & Nilsson, 2005; Salthouse, 2010). Furthermore, research has demonstrated that openness and intelligence tend to codevelop (Ziegler et al., 2012; Zimprich, Allemand, & Dellenbach, 2009) As aging older adults decline in intelligence, particularly crystallized intelligence, they may become less creative, less imaginative, and have fewer novel ideas; that is, the ability of people to be open may decline in older adulthood, spurring openness decreases.

Additionally, although openness has been conceptualized as primarily a cognitive construct, physical functioning plays a role in the trait's development as well. In a particularly dramatic example, a shoulder injury forced Bowie to end his touring career—his body was no longer capable of performing for nights on end. In more quotidian cases, arthritis, declines in vision, and mobility problems may prevent people from attending Bowie tribute band concerts, using the computer, or reading the newspaper. People who are forced to divest from high-openness behaviors due to physical decline may subsequently decline in openness (Wrzus & Roberts, 2017).

In summary, older adulthood is a time of mean-level openness decreases. These changes may be driven by normative declines in both the extrinsic and intrinsic value of openness, as well as decreases in mental and physical functioning that come with old age.

Explaining an Individual's Openness Trajectory

As I have just shown, age is a major factor in the development of openness. If we know a person's age, we can predict how they may change in openness in the future. But, as there are substantial individual differences in openness change throughout the lifespan, age-graded experiences cannot be the only factor driving openness development (Allemand, Zimprich, & Hertzog, 2007; Robins, Fraley, Roberts, & Trzesniewski, 2001; Schwaba & Bleidorn, 2017). In the following section, I investigate how genes and environment contribute to individual differences in openness development, as well as specific "candidate environments" that have been associated with the development of openness.

Nature and Nurture

At the most fundamental level, explaining individual differences in openness development is a matter of nature versus nurture. Behavioral genetics studies have tracked sets of twins across their lives to understand the relative contributions of genetics and environment to personality development (Briley & Tucker-Drob, 2014). Because identical twins share the same set of genes and fraternal twins share, on average, 50% of their genes, estimates of personality development that take this genetic similarity into account can partition change and stability into genetic and environmental components. Behavioral genetics studies have indicated that change in openness is roughly driven by half genetic influences and half environmental influences, and that environmental influences tend to make people different from one another rather than similar (Bleidorn, Kandler, Riemann, Angleitner, & Spinath, 2009; Briley & Tucker-Drob, 2014).

After finding that personality development is guided substantially by genetics, a logical next step is to identify the specific genes that guide development. Unfortunately, researchers' lack of success in identifying particular genes associated with personality traits in cross-sectional research has precluded research into developmental "candidate genes" (Chabris, Lee, Cesarini, Benjamin, & Laibson, 2015); personality traits instead appear to be driven by a combination of very many genetic variants, which each exert a small effect. It makes intuitive sense that a single gene could not code for a behavioral pattern as broad as "creativity." However, even molecular genetics techniques such as genome-wide association studies, which investigate the entire sequenced genome instead of a few candidate genes, have only been able to predict about 10% of the observed variability in openness, to date (Lo et al., 2017). While genetics clearly plays a substantial role in openness development, asking "which genes matter?" is, at least as of now, a dead-end question.

A similar line of questioning can be applied to understand how the environment drives openness development. Because about half of the variance in openness development is due to the effects of the environment, researchers have begun to identify candidate experiences that may reliably affect openness development. Compared to a single gene, a single experience (e.g., studying abroad) often encapsulates a broad set of environments that puts many points of pressure on personality development. In the next section, I describe and explain the candidate experiences that have been associated with

change in openness. These experiences fall into three broad categories. First, events in the domains of work and love have been associated with openness development (cf. Bleidorn, Hopwood, & Lucas, 2018). Second, changes in mental and physical functioning have been associated with changes in openness to experience. Third, a collection of "mind-expanding" experiences have been associated with increases in openness.

Events in the Domains of Work and Love

Commonly experienced life events, such as entering college, having children, and retiring, may be catalysts for personality development, in part due to their wide-reaching consequences. As people anticipate, experience, and adapt to major life events, they make lasting changes to their behavioral repertoires, and they reconfigure their identity to conform to a new role with different expectations (Roberts, Wood, & Caspi, 2008; Wood & Roberts, 2006; Wrzus & Roberts, 2017). These changes may coalesce into lasting personality trait change.

In the domain of work, promotion, involuntary job loss, and retirement have been associated with changes in openness. With respect to promotion, in a recent study of Australian workers, Neiss and Zacher (2015) found that people scoring high on openness were more likely to be promoted into managerial and professional positions at their jobs, and that these promotions corresponded to subsequent increases in openness measured 4 years later. After a promotion, managers may be thrust into a set of novel environments that prioritize learning: They must learn to work with new people and grapple with new ideas, and they often move to new locations for their new job. To the extent that recently promoted persons adapt to this new environment, they are rewarded with success in their new job role, offering powerful incentives to increase in openness.

Beyond this, openness has also been shown to increase after a person is involuntarily laid off from his or her job. In a clever epidemiological study, Anger, Camehl, and Peter (2017) examined changes in personality among workers who were unemployed due to a manufacturing plant closure. Because plant closure is almost entirely out of employees' control, this study allowed the authors to better disentangle cause and effect than in previous studies. Those who were unemployed for short amounts of time tended to increase in openness in the following years. The mechanism behind openness increases in unemployed workers may be similar to that driving openness increases following promotion. As people find and adapt to new jobs, they must adapt to a novel work environment and learn the tools of the trade.

Finally, a recent study that investigated personality trait development across the transition to retirement found abrupt increases in openness corresponding to the month after retirement (Schwaba & Bleidorn, 2018). During the 5 years before they retired, people tended to decrease in openness, consistent with the age-graded mean-level trends in older adulthood. But in the month after they retired, people showed rapid increases in openness that were gradually counteracted over the following 5-year period. This study was one of the first to investigate temporal patterns of personality development in response to an event. Openness increases appeared to evaporate with time, suggesting that the event-occasioned changes are impermanent and eventually overridden by other age-graded developmental influences. This short-lived increase in openness may reflect a brief exploratory period accompanying retirement. After leaving work, retirees must refill their day-to-day schedule, and this rebuilding process may initiate a period of identity and behavioral exploration that soon ceases as retirees settle into their new role.

Moving from the domain of work to the domain of love, both marriage and divorce have been associated with changes in openness. With respect to marriage, Specht and colleagues (2011) studied a large, nationally representative sample of Germans and found that in the years after they married, both men and women tended to become less open to experience. For many people, marriage may signal the end of emerging adulthood and a conclusion to identity exploration. In the same study, Specht and colleagues also found that men, but not women, who divorced from their partner tended to increase in openness in the following years. The authors termed this finding the "dirty diapers effect," implying that divorced men may have a lot to learn in terms of childrearing once their spouse leaves, and this rapid accumulation of knowledge may lead to changes in openness. An alternative explanation for this finding is that men who are divorced often reenter the dating world and begin to reexplore their interpersonal identity, leading to increases in openness.

Changes in Functioning

Changes in cognitive and physical functioning have also been associated with changes in openness to experience. Earlier in the chapter, I briefly reviewed two studies that found codevelopment between openness and intelligence in older adulthood (Ziegler et al., 2012; Zimprich et al., 2009). Beyond these observational studies, two additional studies have taken an experimental approach to better understand how increases in cognitive functioning may cause increases in openness (Jackson et al., 2012; Sander, Schmiedek, Brose, Wagner, & Specht, 2017). The first study (Jackson et al., 2012) followed 78 older adults who were part of a 16-week sudoku-and-crossword brain training program and 88 who were part of a waitlist control group. Across a period of 30 weeks, the experimental group increased in openness compared to the control group. This difference emerged gradually across the training sessions and generalized to each facet of openness. The second study (Sander et al., 2017) measured 167 adults who participated in a 100-day-long cognitive training intervention that consisted of 1 hour daily of basic perceptual speed, episodic memory, and working memory tasks. Development in this group was compared to a 71-adult control group. This study provided a rather stringent test of whether cognitive training causes openness increases, as personality was measured 2 years after the intervention concluded. In this study, no between-group differences in openness development were found.

Time may be the moderating factor that explains why Jackson and colleagues (2012) found openness increases, whereas Sander and colleagues (2017) did not. It may be that cognitive training regimens can bring about changes in identity such that someone sees him- or herself as more curious, intellectual, and creative in the short term, but these changes may eventually wear off rather than metastasize into lasting openness trait change. Indeed, a large body of research has failed to identify a single "brain training" game that builds broader cognitive skills (Simons et al., 2016). In other words, doing crossword puzzles may make people better at crossword puzzles, and they may think of themselves as more open because of this, but this practice won't actually make them any better at solving math problems, and as soon as they stop solving crossword puzzles, their openness may return to what it was.

Change in physical functioning, and exercise in particular, may also be relevant to the development of openness. Open people tend to be more physically active, possibly through a common link between openness and extraversion (Sutin et al., 2016). And, as people exercise more frequently, they tend to become more open than their sedentary peers (Stephan, Sutin, & Terracciano, 2014). In an aerobic exercise intervention targeted at sedentary older adults (N = 40), those who exercised rather than stretched over a period of 3 months exhibited greater levels of regional cerebral blood flow and volume, as well as improvement on recognition memory tasks (Maass et al., 2015). This study, though it had a small sample size, provides a potential mechanism that explains the associations between exercise and openness. Exercise both spurs neurogenesis and improves blood flow to the brain, and these biological changes may lead to cognitive benefits that spill over into a broader increase in openness.

Overall, decreases in mental and physical functioning have been associated with decreases in openness, but whether interventions can cause increases in mental functioning that may lead to lasting increases in openness remains an open question.

Mind-Expanding Experiences

A final set of experiences associated with changes in openness includes those that fall under the loose umbrella of "mind-expanding," such as engaging in cultural activity, studying abroad, and using hallucinogenic drugs.

As I mentioned earlier, openness and cultural experiences are closely related (Kraaykamp & van Eijck, 2005). On a longitudinal scale as well, openness and cultural activity tend to codevelop. People who begin to attend more concerts, museums, and art galleries tend to become more open in the future, and vice versa (Jackson, 2011; Schwaba et al., 2017). What may be more surprising is that this association is found across the lifespan—openness and cultural activity were found to codevelop similarly in emerging adults (ages 16–26), in midlife (ages 26–65) and in older age (ages 65+) (Schwaba et al., 2017). Although older adults show fewer individual differences in openness development than do younger adults, changes in cultural activity appear to be related to individual differences in openness development at all ages. These changes may be due to changes in

exploratory tendencies. For people who want to explore and be intellectually engaged, a perfect outlet may be a trip to the theater or a museum.

Studying abroad is another cultural experience that may provide a heavy and sustained dose of mind expansion, especially for those who immerse themselves in the local culture. In a quasi-experiment, Zimmermann and Neyer (2013) measured personality change in a sample of college students who studied abroad and compared it to change in those who signed up to study abroad but were put on a waitlist instead. Those who studied abroad tended to become more open to experience compared to the control group. The mechanism behind this change may be, in part, engaging with the mind-expanding novel environments, new people, and unique cultural experiences made possible by studying abroad. Additionally, in mediation analyses, Zimmermann and Neyer found that people who made many friends while abroad tended to increase more on openness than those who did not. This provides evidence for a social mechanism in openness change. Perhaps meeting and befriending people from different backgrounds is a particularly horizon-broadening experience.

Open people also appear to be more attracted to mind-expanding drug experiences. While openness is not associated with alcohol, cigarette, cocaine, or heroin use, people scoring higher on openness are more likely to use marijuana (Ruiz, Pincus, & Dickinson, 2003; Terracciano, Löckenhoff, Crum, Bienvenu, & Costa, 2008). Use of marijuana, and other psychoactive drugs such as psilocybin mushrooms and lysergic acid diethylamide (LSD), appears to boost state openness, and a compelling area of research has begun investigating how use of these drugs may occasion openness change (Lebedev et al., 2016; MacLean, Johnson, & Griffiths, 2011).

In one provocative study, people who had a "mystical experience" during guided mediation sessions on psilocybin mushrooms displayed a 1.5 standard deviation increase in openness 1 year later, an effect that generalized across openness facets. This effect is one of the largest ever found in the personality change literature. In a similar study that took place across a shorter timescale, those who took LSD increased on openness over a period of 2 weeks, and this increase was proportional to the amount of entropic brain activity measured via functional magnetic resonance imaging (fMRI) (Lebedev et al., 2016).

These findings are particularly intriguing and merit further investigation. In particular, it is unclear whether these changes were brought about via top-down processes of identity reconfiguration following drug use or bottom-up processes of biological change caused by the drug use. Beyond questions of mechanism, two important limitations of these studies are that that the sample size was relatively small for both studies and that those who signed up to participate were already quite high in openness at baseline. Future research is needed to understand whether increases in openness following psychoactive drug use are contingent on baseline levels of openness, and whether these effects extend to the use of marijuana, a much more commonly used but much less psychoactively potent drug.

Interim Summary

A review of the past research on candidate experiences in openness development suggests two common mechanisms underlying individual differences in openness change. First and foremost, changes in exploration may drive changes in openness. Specifically, changes in employment, marital status, cultural experience, and health may encourage or halt the motivation to explore and exploratory behavior, leading to downstream changes in openness. Second, changes in a person's neurobiology may drive changes in openness. Specifically, changes in intelligence, exercise, and psychoactive drug use may alter a person's patterns of thought and ability to think, leading to downstream changes in openness.

Conclusion

This chapter has examined the history, structure, and development of openness to experience. As the last of the Big Five traits to emerge from factor analysis, openness has always held the distinction of being the most difficult of the Big Five to conceptualize and measure. Fundamental differences in trait conceptualization persist to this day, as different openness inventories measure slightly different openness constructs. Regardless of measurement instrument, however, openness has unique and intriguing associations with intelligence, political attitudes, culture, and creativity. Across the lifes-

pan, openness follows an inverted-U-shaped mean-level developmental trajectory, increasing slightly in emerging adulthood, remaining stable throughout midlife, and decreasing across old age. At each of these ages, and especially in emerging adulthood, there are substantial individual deviations from the mean-level developmental trajectory, which may be spurred by changes in exploration and neurobiology.

While openness is the last of the Big Five traits, it is by no means the least important. The construct's breadth and complexity are what make it so compelling to study. Perhaps this is also why figures like David Bowie are so captivating.

Coda

For a final episode in the life of David Bowie, consider the circumstances surrounding his last album, *Blackstar*. Two days after the album was released, Bowie died of cancer, a disease he had not made publicly known. Even a cursory listen to this last album reveals that Bowie positioned his death as a work of art. On the album's lead single, "Lazarus" (named after the biblical figure raised from the dead), Bowie opens with the lyrics, "Look up here, I'm in heaven." The cover art of the album simply features a black star, the only one of Bowie's 25 studio albums to not feature him on the front. And as for the album's title, it is a reference to any and all of a particular type of cancer lesion, an Elvis song about death (Elvis and Bowie share a birthday), and a collapsed star(man). That Bowie invested his final months on Earth into creating a work of art about his own death puts a capstone on his legacy as a man defined by his openness to experience.

ACKNOWLEDGMENTS

I would like to thank Louisa Ashford, Wiebke Bleidorn, Ryan Hutchings, and Sarah S. W. De Pauw for comments on previous drafts of this chapter.

REFERENCES

Ackerman, P. L. (1996). A theory of adult intellectual development: Process, personality, interests, and knowledge. *Intelligence, 22,* 227–257.

Adorno, T. W., Frenkel-Brunswik, E., Levinson, D. J., & Sanford, R. N. (1950). *The authoritarian personality.* New York: Harper.

Allemand, M., Zimprich, D., & Hertzog, C. (2007). Cross-sectional age differences and longitudinal age changes of personality in middle adulthood and old age. *Journal of Personality, 75,* 323–358.

Allport, G. W. (1961). *Pattern and growth in personality.* New York: Holt, Rinehart & Winston.

Allport, G. W., & Odbert, H. S. (1936). Trait-names: A psycho-lexical study. *Psychological Monographs, 47,* i–171.

Anger, S., Camehl, G., & Peter, F. (2017). Involuntary job loss and changes in personality traits. *Journal of Economic Psychology, 60,* 71–91.

Arnett, J. J. (2000). Emerging adulthood: A theory of development from the late teens through the twenties. *American Psychologist, 55,* 469–480.

Arnett, J. J. (2007). Emerging adulthood: What is it, and what is it good for? *Child Development Perspectives, 1,* 68–73.

Ashton, M. C., Lee, K., Vernon, P. A., & Jang, K. L. (2000). Fluid intelligence, crystallized intelligence, and the openness/intellect factor. *Journal of Research in Personality, 34,* 198–207.

Belke, B., Leder, H., Strobach, T., & Carbon, C. C. (2010). Cognitive fluency: High-level processing dynamics in art appreciation. *Psychology of Aesthetics, Creativity, and the Arts, 4,* 214–222.

Bleidorn, W., Hopwood, C. J., & Lucas, R. E. (2018). Life events and personality trait change. *Journal of Personality, 86,* 83–96.

Bleidorn, W., Kandler, C., Riemann, R., Angleitner, A., & Spinath, F. M. (2009). Patterns and sources of adult personality development: Growth curve analyses of the NEO PI-R scales in a longitudinal twin study. *Journal of Personality and Social Psychology, 97,* 142–155.

Bleidorn, W., Klimstra, T. A., Denissen, J. A., Rentfrow, P. J., Potter, J., & Gosling, S. D. (2013). Personality maturation around the world: A cross-cultural examination of social-investment theory. *Psychological Science, 24,* 2530–2540.

Bleidorn, W., & Schwaba, T. (2017). Personality development in emerging adulthood. In J. Specht (Ed.), *Personality development across the lifespan* (pp. 39–52). Amsterdam, The Netherlands: Elsevier.

Block, J. (1971). *Lives through time.* Berkeley, CA: Baucroft.

Bowie, D. (n.d.). Quotations. Retrieved November 26, 2017, from *www.brainyquote.com/authors/david_bowie.*

Briley, D. A., & Tucker-Drob, E. M. (2014). Genetic and environmental continuity in personality development: A meta-analysis. *Psychological Bulletin, 140,* 1303–1331.

Carstensen, L. L., Fung, H. H., & Charles, S. T. (2003). Socioemotional selectivity theory and the regulation of emotion in the second half of life. *Motivation and Emotion, 27,* 103–123.

Caspi, A., & Moffitt, T. E. (1993). When do individual differences matter?: A paradoxical theory of personality coherence. *Psychological Inquiry, 4,* 247–271.

Caspi, A., & Roberts, B. W. (2001). Personality development across the life course: The argument for change and continuity. *Psychological Inquiry, 12*(2), 49–66.

Cattell, R. B. (1943). The measurement of adult intelligence. *Psychological Bulletin, 40,* 153–193.

Chabris, C. F., Lee, J. J., Cesarini, D., Benjamin, D. J., & Laibson, D. I. (2015). The fourth law of behavior genetics. *Current Directions in Psychological Science, 24,* 304–312.

Church, A. T., Alvarez, J. M., Mai, N. T., French, B. F., Katigbak, M. S., & Ortiz, F. A. (2011). Are cross-cultural comparisons of personality profiles meaningful?: Differential item and facet functioning in the Revised NEO Personality Inventory. *Journal of Personality and Social Psychology, 101,* 1068–1089.

Coan, R. W. (1972). Measurable components of openness to experience. *Journal of Consulting and Clinical Psychology, 39,* 346.

Costa, P. T., & McCrae, R. R. (1992). *NEO PI-R professional manual.* Odessa, FL: Psychological Assessment Resources.

Costello, C., Srivastava, S., & Saucier, G. (2017). Stability and change in the Big Five and Big Six: New tests of the maturity and cumulative continuity principles. Retrieved from *https://psyarxiv.com/b36tv.*

De Pauw, S. S. W. (2017). Childhood personality and temperament. In T. A. Widiger (Ed.), *Oxford handbook of the Five Factor Model* (pp. 243–280). Oxford, UK: Oxford University Press.

DeYoung, C. G. (2014). Openness/intellect: A dimension of personality reflecting cognitive exploration. In M. L. Cooper & R. J. Larsen (Eds.), *APA handbook of personality and social psychology: Personality processes and individual differences* (Vol. 4, pp. 369–399). Washington, DC: American Psychological Association.

DeYoung, C. G. (2015). Cybernetic Big Five theory. *Journal of Research in Personality, 56,* 33–58.

DeYoung, C. G., Grazioplene, R. G., & Peterson, J. B. (2012). From madness to genius: The Openness/intellect trait domain as a paradoxical simplex. *Journal of Research in Personality, 46,* 63–78.

DeYoung, C. G., Peterson, J. B., & Higgins, D. M. (2005). Sources of openness/intellect: Cognitive and neuropsychological correlates of the fifth factor of personality. *Journal of Personality, 73,* 825–858.

DeYoung, C. G., Quilty, L. C., & Peterson, J. B. (2007). Between facets and domains: 10 aspects of the Big Five. *Journal of Personality and Social Psychology, 93,* 880–896.

Digman, J. M. (1990). Personality structure: Emergence of the five-factor model. *Annual Review of Psychology, 41,* 417–440.

Erikson, E. H. (1959). Identity and the life cycle: Selected papers. *Psychological Issues, 1,* 1–171.

Gignac, G. E., Stough, C., & Loukomitis, S. (2004). Openness, intelligence, and self-report intelligence. *Intelligence, 32,* 133–143.

Goldberg, L. R. (1992). The development of markers for

the Big-Five factor structure. *Psychological Assessment, 4*, 26–42.

Goldberg, L. R., Johnson, J. A., Eber, H. W., Hogan, R., Ashton, M. C., Cloninger, C. R., et al. (2006). The international personality item pool and the future of public-domain personality measures. *Journal of Research in Personality, 40*, 84–96.

Graf, L. K., & Landwehr, J. R. (2015). A dual-process perspective on fluency-based aesthetics the pleasure-interest model of aesthetic liking. *Personality and Social Psychology Review, 19*, 395–410.

Jackson, J. J. (2011). *The effects of educational experiences on personality trait development.* Unpublished doctoral dissertation, University of Illinois at Urbana–Champaign, Urbana, IL.

Jackson, J. J., Hill, P. L., Payne, B. R., Roberts, B. W., & Stine-Morrow, E. A. (2012). Can an old dog learn (and want to experience) new tricks?: Cognitive training increases openness to experience in older adults. *Psychology and Aging, 27*, 286–292.

John, O. P., Naumann, L. P., & Soto, C. J. (2008). Paradigm shift to the integrative Big Five trait taxonomy: History, measurement, and conceptual issues. In O. P. John, R. W. Robins, & L. A. Pervin (Eds.), *Handbook of personality: Theory and research* (pp. 114–158). New York: Guilford Press.

Jost, J. T., Glaser, J., Kruglanski, A. W., & Sulloway, F. J. (2003). Political conservatism as motivated social cognition. *Psychological Bulletin, 129*, 339–375.

Kandler, C., Riemann, R., Angleitner, A., Spinath, F. M., Borkenau, P., & Penke, L. (2016). The nature of creativity: The roles of genetic factors, personality traits, cognitive abilities, and environmental sources. *Journal of Personality and Social Psychology, 111*, 230–249.

Kaufman, S. B., Quilty, L. C., Grazioplene, R. G., Hirsh, J. B., Gray, J. R., Peterson, J. B., et al. (2016). Openness to experience and intellect differentially predict creative achievement in the arts and sciences. *Journal of Personality, 84*, 248–258.

Kraaykamp, G., & Van Eijck, K. (2005). Personality, media preferences, and cultural participation. *Personality and Individual Differences, 38*, 1675–1688.

Lebedev, A. V., Kaelen, M., Lövdén, M., Nilsson, J., Feilding, A., Nutt, D. J., et al. (2016). LSD-induced entropic brain activity predicts subsequent personality change. *Human Brain Mapping, 37*, 3203–3213.

Lo, M. T., Hinds, D. A., Tung, J. Y., Franz, C., Fan, C. C., Wang, Y., et al. (2017). Genome-wide analyses for personality traits identify six genomic loci and show correlations with psychiatric disorders. *Nature Genetics, 49*, 152–156.

Loevinger, J. (1979). Construct validity of the Sentence Completion Test of Ego Development. *Applied Psychological Measurement, 3*, 281–311.

Maass, A., Düzel, S., Goerke, M., Becke, A., Sobieray, U., Neumann, K., et al. (2015). Vascular hippocampal plasticity after aerobic exercise in older adults. *Molecular Psychiatry, 20*, 585–593.

MacLean, K. A., Johnson, M. W., & Griffiths, R. R. (2011). Mystical experiences occasioned by the hallucinogen psilocybin lead to increases in the personality domain of openness. *Journal of Psychopharmacology, 25*, 1453–1461.

McCrae, R. R. (1987). Creativity, divergent thinking, and openness to experience. *Journal of Personality and Social Psychology, 52*, 1258–1265.

McCrae, R. R. (1990). Traits and trait names: How well is Openness represented in natural languages? *European Journal of Personality, 4*, 119–129.

McCrae, R. R. (1996). Social consequences of experiential openness. *Psychological Bulletin, 120*, 323–337.

McCrae, R. R., & Costa, P. T., Jr. (1997). Conceptions and correlates of openness to experience. In R. Hogan, J. A. Johnson, & R. Stephen (Eds.), *Handbook of personality psychology* (pp. 825–847). San Diego, CA: Academic Press.

McCrae, R. R., Costa, P. T., Jr., Ostendorf, F., Angleitner, A., Hřebíčková, M., Avia, M. D., et al. (2000). Nature over nurture: Temperament, personality, and life span development. *Journal of Personality and Social Psychology, 78*(1), 173–186.

McCrae, R. R., & Sutin, A. R. (2009). Openness to experience. In M. R. Leary & R. H. Hoyle (Eds.), *Handbook of individual differences in social behavior* (pp. 257–273). New York: Guilford Press.

Niess, C., & Zacher, H. (2015). Openness to Experience as a predictor and outcome of upward job changes into managerial and professional positions. *PLOS ONE, 10*(6), e0131115.

Noftle, E. E., & Robins, R. W. (2007). Personality predictors of academic outcomes: Big Five correlates of GPA and SAT scores. *Journal of Personality and Social Psychology, 93*, 116–130.

Roberts, B. W., & DelVecchio, W. F. (2000). The rank-order consistency of personality traits from childhood to old age: A quantitative review of longitudinal studies. *Psychological Bulletin, 126*(1), 3–25.

Roberts, B. W., Walton, K. E., & Viechtbauer, W. (2006). Patterns of mean-level change in personality traits across the life course: A meta-analysis of longitudinal studies. *Psychological Bulletin, 132*(1), 1–25.

Roberts, B. W., Wood, D., & Caspi, A. (2008). The development of personality traits in adulthood. In O. P. John, R. W. Robins, & L. A. Pervin (Eds.), *Handbook of personality: Theory and research* (3rd ed., pp. 375–398). New York: Guilford Press.

Robins, R. W., Fraley, R. C., Roberts, B. W., & Trzesniewski, K. H. (2001). A longitudinal study of personality change in young adulthood. *Journal of Personality, 69*(4), 617–640.

Rogers, C. R. (1961). The process equation of psychotherapy. *American Journal of Psychotherapy, 15*, 27–45.

Rokeach, M. (1960). *The open and closed mind.* Oxford, UK: Basic Books.

Rönnlund, M., Nyberg, L., Bäckman, L., & Nilsson, L.-G. (2005). Stability, growth, and decline in adult life span development of declarative memory: Cross-sectional and longitudinal data from a population-based study. *Psychology and Aging, 20,* 3–18.

Ruiz, M. A., Pincus, A. L., & Dickinson, K. A. (2003). NEO PI-R predictors of alcohol use and alcohol-related problems. *Journal of Personality Assessment, 81,* 226–236.

Salthouse, T. A. (2010). Selective review of cognitive aging. *Journal of the International Neuropsychological Society, 16,* 754–760.

Sander, J., Schmiedek, F., Brose, A., Wagner, G. G., & Specht, J. (2017). Long-term effects of an extensive cognitive training on personality development. *Journal of Personality, 85,* 454–463.

Sandford, C. (1998). *Bowie: Loving the alien.* New York: Da Capo Press.

Saucier, G. (1992). Openness versus intellect: Much ado about nothing? *European Journal of Personality, 6,* 381–386.

Saucier, G. (1998). Replicable item-cluster subcomponents in the NEO Five-Factor Inventory. *Journal of Personality Assessment, 70,* 263–276.

Schwaba, T., & Bleidorn, W. (2017). Individual differences in personality change across the adult lifespan. *Journal of Personality.* [Epub ahead of print]

Schwaba, T., & Bleidorn, W. (2018). Personality trait change across the transition to retirement. *Journal of Personality and Social Psychology.* [Epub ahead of print]

Schwaba, T., Luhmann, M., Denissen, J. J. A., Chung, J. M., & Bleidorn, W. (2017). Openness to Experience and Culture-Openness transactions across the lifespan. *Journal of Personality and Social Psychology.* [Epub ahead of print]

Silvia, P. J., Nusbaum, E. C., Berg, C., Martin, C., & O'Connor, A. (2009). Openness to experience, plasticity, and creativity: Exploring lower-order, high-order, and interactive effects. *Journal of Research in Personality, 43,* 1087–1090.

Simons, D. J., Boot, W. R., Charness, N., Gathercole, S. E., Chabris, C. F., Hambrick, D. Z., et al. (2016). Do "brain-training" programs work? *Psychological Science in the Public Interest, 17*(3), 103–186.

Soto, C. J., & John, O. P. (2017). The next Big Five Inventory (BFI-2): Developing and assessing a hierarchical model with 15 facets to enhance bandwidth, fidelity, and predictive power. *Journal of Personality and Social Psychology, 113,* 117–143.

Soubelet, A., & Salthouse, T. A. (2010). The role of activity engagement in the relations between Openness/Intellect and cognition. *Personality and Individual Differences, 49,* 896–901.

Specht, J., Egloff, B., & Schmukle, S. C. (2011). Stability and change of personality across the life course: The impact of age and major life events on mean-level and rank-order stability of the Big Five. *Journal of Personality and Social Psychology, 101,* 862–882.

Stephan, Y., Sutin, A. R., & Terracciano, A. (2014). Physical activity and personality development across adulthood and old age: Evidence from two longitudinal studies. *Journal of Research in Personality, 49,* 1–7.

Sutin, A. R., Stephan, Y., Luchetti, M., Artese, A., Oshio, A., & Terracciano, A. (2016). The five-factor model of personality and physical inactivity: A meta-analysis of 16 samples. *Journal of Research in Personality, 63,* 22–28.

Tellegen, A., & Atkinson, G. (1974). Openness to absorbing and self-altering experiences ("absorption"), a trait related to hypnotic susceptibility. *Journal of Abnormal Psychology, 83,* 268–277.

Terracciano, A., Löckenhoff, C. E., Crum, R. M., Bienvenu, O. J., & Costa, P. T. (2008). Five-Factor Model personality profiles of drug users. *BMC Psychiatry, 8,* 22.

Thomas, K. S., Silvia, P. J., Nusbaum, E. C., Beaty, R. E., & Hodges, D. A. (2016). Openness to experience and auditory discrimination ability in music: An investment approach. *Psychology of Music, 44,* 792–801.

Witkin, H. A., & Goodenough, D. R. (1977). Field dependence and interpersonal behavior. *Psychological Bulletin, 84,* 661–689.

Wolk, D. (2016, November). David Bowie's "Space Oddity": How "2001"-inspired hit led to rushed 1969 LP. *Rolling Stone.* Retrieved from *www.rollingstone. com/music/news/david-bowies-space-oddity-how-hit-song-led-to-rushed-lp-w448220.*

Wood, D., & Roberts, B. W. (2006). Cross-sectional and longitudinal tests of the Personality and Role Identity Structural Model (PRISM). *Journal of Personality, 74*(3), 779–810.

Wortman, J., Lucas, R. E., & Donnellan, M. B. (2012). Stability and change in the Big Five personality domains: Evidence from a longitudinal study of Australians. *Psychology and Aging, 27*(4), 867–874.

Wrzus, C., & Roberts, B. W. (2017). Processes of personality development in adulthood: The TESSERA Framework. *Personality and Social Psychology Review, 23,* 253–277.

Yarkoni, T., & Westfall, J. (2017). Choosing prediction over explanation in psychology: Lessons from machine learning. *Perspectives on Psychological Science, 12,* 1100–1122.

Ziegler, M., Danay, E., Heene, M., Asendorpf, J., & Bühner, M. (2012). Openness, fluid intelligence, and crystallized intelligence: Toward an integrative model. *Journal of Research in Personality, 46,* 173–183.

Zimmermann, J., & Neyer, F. J. (2013). Do we become a different person when hitting the road?: Personality development of sojourners. *Journal of Personality and Social Psychology, 105,* 515–530.

Zimprich, D., Allemand, M., & Dellenbach, M. (2009). Openness to experience, fluid intelligence, and crystallized intelligence in middle-aged and old adults. *Journal of Research in Personality, 43,* 444–454.

CHAPTER 12

Temperament and Personality Trait Development in the Family

Interactions and Transactions with Parenting from Infancy through Adolescence

Liliana J. Lengua
Maria A. Gartstein
Peter Prinzie

A parent was sharing a problem she was having with one of her daughters, Elizabeth, one of dizygotic, or fraternal, twins, who could not seem to get her school projects done in a timely, organized way. The other daughter, Catherine, was able to plan, organize, and stay focused on getting her work done. When describing how their family scheduled and structured work time, it was clear that this family had a busy and complicated schedule. With three children in sports and two parents working full time, afterschool schedules and weekends with family members coming and going, getting rides with fellow teammates, meals on the run, and one parent often traveling for work, much of the task of keeping everyone organized fell on the other parent during the week.

This parent was struggling to understand how Catherine could be so organized and focused, while Elizabeth was not, not recognizing that their busy, complicated family schedule might not be workable for Elizabeth, who was less organized and persistent. It is a sentiment we hear often from parents, how the things that work well with one child do not work with another, and how puzzling it is that their children could be so different. These individual differ-

ences are the focus of this chapter: how family relationships and parenting can influence and be influenced by children's personality traits.

It is widely understood that parents and families have a marked impact on their children's social, emotional, and behavioral development and mental well-being throughout childhood and into adulthood. One mechanism of these long-term effects of parent and family influences is through their role in shaping an individual's enduring personality characteristics, including capacities for attention, behavior and emotion regulation, persistence, navigating social contexts and weathering stress, and continued capacities to grow and learn from experiences. Beginning in infancy with the earliest emerging signs of personality, referred to as temperament, individual differences both shape and are shaped by parent behaviors and family context. Parenting and family factors play a role in children's developing personality through several mechanisms, including shaping, socialization, modeling, transactional, person–environment fit, and moderating mechanisms, and each of which is defined below. This chapter reviews the evidence for family influences, particularly parenting, on children's personality traits from infancy to adolescence using a developmental perspective, relating these processes to child personality development. Because individual differences in younger children are framed as temperament, whereas many studies with preadolescent and adolescent samples focus on personality characteristics as captured by the five-factor model (FFM), we review evidence for both. First, we discuss the impact of family context and parent personality on parenting behaviors. Second, we review the evidence for the influence of parenting on the development of children's temperament and personality traits. Third, we discuss the impact of children's traits on parenting. Fourth, we review conceptual models and evidence for how parenting might operate differently for different children depending on their individual temperament or personality characteristics. Finally, we discuss the implications and future directions of the research on the interaction and transaction between children's personality and parenting.

Temperament and the FFM of Personality

In this chapter, we focus on traits that can be conceptualized as relatively enduring, automatic dispositions, and individual differences in tendencies to behave, think, and feel in consistent patterns that may change over time (e.g., Caspi & Shiner, 2006). Most often individual differences in early and middle childhood have been characterized as temperament, and in later childhood and adolescence are represented by the FFM of personality. These two models are discussed briefly.

Temperament

Temperament is generally defined as biologically based individual differences in reactivity and self-regulation, including motivation, affect, activity, and attention characteristics (Rothbart & Bates, 2006). *Reactivity* refers to responsiveness to change in the external and internal environments, includes physiological and emotional reactions, and is detectable early in the first year of life. Frustration or anger, and fear or inhibition have been shown to form an overarching temperament factor of *negative emotionality*. Another factor characterizes expressions of approach, joy and pleasure, and has been labeled *surgency, exuberance,* or *positive affectivity,* and incorporates characteristics of

activity, enthusiasm and impulsivity. The third factor, *self-regulation or effortful control,* refers to orienting and executive control of attention and behavior that operates to modulate reactivity, facilitating or inhibiting physiological, affective, or behavioral responses. Temperament is genetically based and relatively stable. Nonetheless, there is considerable evidence for experience and context playing a role in shaping the expression of temperament (Rothbart & Bates, 2006). Thus, temperament represents characteristics present early in life that shape and are shaped within the context of social and environmental interactions and that result in differential responsiveness to socialization experiences.

The FFM

The FFM (or Big Five) is a comprehensive model of personality that identifies five basic dimensions of personality often labeled as extraversion, agreeableness, conscientiousness, emotional stability, and openness to experience. The *extraversion* dimension contrasts emotional, social, and verbal expressiveness with shyness, inhibition, withdrawal, and nonassertiveness. *Agreeableness* describes the degree to which individuals are equipped to maintain close and reciprocal relationships, or the broad area of prosocial versus antisocial interactions. The *conscientiousness* dimension refers to a concentrated, reliable, and achievement-oriented attitude in work-like situations, with high levels of involvement and perseverance. *Emotional stability* (the inverse of *neuroticism*) refers to self-reliance, emotional balance, self-esteem, and being easygoing as opposed to being fearful, anxious, and emotionally disorganized under stress. *Openness to experience* represents openness to new ideas, experiences, or the general richness and complexity of a person's mental life.

Linking Temperament and the FFM

How temperament and the FFM are related to each other has been the topic of much investigation and some debate. While some view FFM dimensions as encompassing temperament, others consider temperament as representing a developmentally different set of dimensions, and still others view temperament as the developmental precursor and core of later emerging FFM characteristics (cf. De Pauw, 2016, for overview).

One model of their association is that there is a progression from early childhood temperament characteristics to FFM characteristics. Temperament represents a specific set of core, biologically based individual differences in reactivity and regulation characteristics, whereas personality represents a broader set of constructs that may encompass temperament and also includes cognitive and social components that elaborate or are "layered around" core temperament characteristics (e.g., Rothbart & Bates, 2006). Starting early in life, individual differences, most commonly viewed as temperament, both shape and are shaped by socialization and contextual experiences that contribute to an individual's cognitive and behavioral styles or personality traits. For example, negative reactivity might contribute to challenging interpersonal interactions, which together shape later emerging cognitive styles to be more negatively biased (e.g., a "glass half-empty" view of the world), contributing to neuroticism. Conversely, early effortful control likely facilitates engagement in supported learning experiences that enhance a sense of efficacy and agency, perhaps leading to greater conscientiousness and openness to experiences. As a result, early emerging individual differences might shape the manifestation of subsequent personality characteristics in transaction with key relationships, interactions, and socialization experiences. This chapter focuses on evidence for parenting and family relationships influencing the development of personality traits from infancy through adolescence, and the role that these play in altering trajectories of growth. Not surprisingly, the research is stratified by age, with most studies examining temperament from infancy to middle childhood and the FFM in preadolescence and adolescence. We focus on the traits that are most common across these models.

Parenting, Family Relationships, and Family Context

Family factors such as family relationships, family contextual factors, parent personality, and parenting predict children's temperament and personality, and these factors are related in complex ways with each other. For example, parent–child communication (Manders, Scholte, Janssens, & De Bruyn, 2006), family conflict (e.g., Davies, Cicchetti, & Martin, 2012), negative discipline and warmth (Van den Akker, Deković, Asscher, & Prinzie, 2014), and chaos (Vernon-Feagans, Willoughby, Garrett-Peters, & the Family Life Project Key Investigators, 2016) were all shown to predict children's personality, often through their effects on parenting and the parent–child relationship (e.g., Vernon-Feagans et al., 2016); that is, factors such as chaos or conflict negatively impact parenting behaviors or the parent–child relationship, causing it to deteriorate. Interactions between child temperament or personality and family relationships have also been noted. For example, difficult temperament and negative mood interacted with family conflict in increasing children's risk for adjustment problems (e.g., Tschann, Kaiser, Chesney, Alkon, & Boyce, 1996; Whiteside-Mansell, Bradley, Casey, Fussell, & Conners-Burrow, 2009), and effortful control altered the association between marital satisfaction and parenting, such that families showed more positive involvement and communication with children who were higher in effortful control regardless of level of marital satisfaction, whereas those aspects of parenting were seen less when marital satisfaction and child effortful control were low (Ato, Galian, & Fernandez-Vilar, 2015).

Parental personality also plays a role in parenting and family relationships. A meta-analysis revealed that more responsive parenting and behavioral control are related to higher levels of parental extraversion, agreeableness, conscientiousness, emotional stability, and openness, whereas more autonomy support is related to higher levels of agreeableness and emotional stability (Prinzie, Stams, Deković, Reijntjes, & Belsky, 2009). Parents' emotional stability emerged as the most important personality trait in contributing to good parenting overall. In addition, parents who manifest greater extraversion, agreeableness, conscientiousness, and openness, and lower levels of neuroticism, may be better able to initiate and maintain positive interactions, to respond appropriately to their child's signals, and to provide a more consistent and structured childrearing environment. The associations of parent personality with parenting may also depend on child personality. For example, lower parental optimism and openness were associated with lower positive parenting when their children were higher in anger-proneness (Koenig, Barry, & Kochanska, 2010). Some child characteristics may be a source of stress for parents, and challenges resulting from children's personality characteristics seem to amplify associations between parental personality and parenting (Prinzie et al., 2012).

Consistent with a bioecological model of development (Bronfenbrenner & Morris, 2006), the associations we summarized earlier point to complex nested and reciprocal systems in which children develop, with parent personality and family context influencing parenting and children's traits, with children's traits also altering the impact of these factors. Importantly, numerous studies demonstrate the central role parenting plays in accounting for or buffering the effects of other family factors. For example, parenting accounts for the effects of marital hostility on child problems (e.g., Stover et al., 2016), and it can mitigate or exacerbate the effects of family risk factors, such as family conflict (Manning, Davies, & Cicchetti, 2014). Therefore, our focus in this chapter is on the effects of parenting on children's temperament and personality development.

Methodological and Design Issues

Complex associations among individual characteristics, family relationships, and family context are often proposed. Bidirectional or transactional effects suggest that parenting and child characteristics influence each other over time. Moderation or interaction effects suggest that parenting or family factors have different implications or effects on child outcomes depending on children's characteristics. Efforts to investigate these complex associations require particular care in selecting study design and quantitative methods. Studies that utilize longitudinal or intervention designs along with analytic techniques that clarify directions of effects facilitate conclusions regarding relations among family context, parenting and personality. Longitudinal studies clarify direction of effects between parenting and personality by providing time precedence of the predictor, the ability to examine change over time, and the opportunity to predict subsequent levels of parenting or personality after controlling for prior levels of each. Thus, effects beyond shared genetics and stability of a particular characteristic can be estimated. The latter is particularly important for transactional models, with the goal of specifying the degree to which parenting shapes personality and vice versa. Intervention or prevention studies offer particular methodological rigor and internal validity, as such trials include

experimental manipulation of the purported mechanisms to test the assumed underlying etiological processes. A small number of studies test parenting interventions in relation to child characteristics and provide rigorous evidence concerning links between parenting and personality. Finally, advanced quantitative methods, such as autoregressive latent trajectory, latent profile analyses, and latent difference scores (Selig & Preacher, 2009) make important contributions to understanding the predictors of development of personality, processes underlying the relations of temperament and FFM, and the combinations of characteristics that contribute to mental health. The few studies that utilize these quantitative advances capture the complexity in relations of temperament to personality and the role of family context and parenting in the development of personality.

Socialization, Transactional, and Moderated Associations between Personality and Parenting

As already noted, links between personality and parenting are expected to be complex. Parents directly influence children's personality through shaping and socialization of emotions, behavior, and cognitions. Children also have eliciting effects, shaping parenting behaviors through their behavioral and emotional responding, and later cognitive styles. Furthermore, children with different characteristics experience their contexts and relationships differently, responding in distinct ways. We discuss these direct, bidirectional, and moderated relations between personality and parenting (see Figure 12.1).

Shaping and Socialization Effects of Parenting on Personality

A mother wanted to help her son, Dylan, be less afraid of dogs because she noticed that he was starting to decline opportunities to go to friends' houses when the friends had a dog. The mother was concerned that Dylan's fear of dogs would start having a broader impact on him. She talked to Dylan about safe ways to approach dogs, and how it was unlikely that his friends' dogs would hurt him. However, when the family came near a dog, particularly if it was barking or jumping, the mother would shield Dylan from the dog, tell him not to worry, that she wouldn't let the dog hurt him, then ask if the dog could be re-

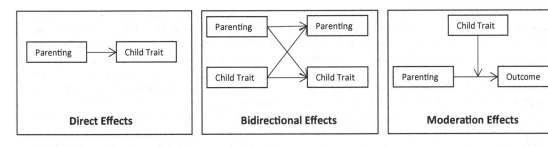

FIGURE 12.1. Direct effects represent parent socialization or shaping of children's traits; bidirectional effects represent transactional or mutual influences between parents and children; and moderated effects represent parent influences having different impact or meaning depending on children's traits.

moved. Although following her natural instinct to protect her son, the mother might inadvertently have been increasing Dylan's fear of dogs by modeling fearful behaviors, protecting him, thereby communicating threat, and by not giving him opportunities for exposure, reinforcing his sense that dogs were dangerous. Children often take their cues from parents in terms of how to behave in fear-eliciting situations, and in this case, available information indicated it would be appropriate to display fearfulness around dogs.

Socialization includes parents' efforts to impart social, emotional, and cognitive skills or habits necessary for successful participation in society (e.g., toilet training), and it implies efforts on parents' part to provide experiences that alter an individual's behavior, emotions, or thoughts. *Shaping* occurs through the application of reinforcement or consequences to increase or decrease a behavior, whether those are applied intentionally or as a reactive process. *Modeling* involves parents displaying behaviors, emotions, or cognitive styles that their children then adopt. For example, children who show high conscientiousness might be reflecting conscientious behaviors modeled by their parents, even if parents did not engage in any intentional socialization or reinforcement of those behaviors. These processes are supported by research with longitudinal designs in which parenting practices predict changes in child personality, taking into account both initial levels of child personality and relative changes or growth in these characteristics. The effect that parents and parenting have on children's developing temperament and personality has received substantial attention in early and middle childhood, with the most extensive body

of literature examining the effects of parenting on children's negative reactivity and emotional stability. However, there has been less attention paid to the effects of parenting on adolescent personality, perhaps as a result of the peer group exerting a greater influence at this later point in development, or due to the fact that personality is mistakenly viewed as "having developed" by adolescence.

Negative Reactivity, Neuroticism, and Emotional Stability

There is consistent evidence that children's negative affect and difficult temperament are shaped by parenting, although the pattern differs across frustration and fear reactivity. When examining negative emotionality or difficult temperament broadly, harsh parenting predicted increases in toddlers' negative emotionality (Scaramella, Sohr-Preston, Mirabile, Callahan, & Robison, 2008), and higher maternal controlling behavior and parental punitive discipline predicted increases in negative reactivity and difficult temperament in older children (Bezirganian & Cohen, 1992; Eisenberg et al., 1999). Higher levels of sensitive and warm parenting predicted later decreases in child negative reactivity (Bates, Schermerhorn, & Petersen, 2012). However, these associations were less consistent when examining fearful reactivity. In several studies, disengaged, insensitive, or rejecting parenting predicted sustained or increased levels of fearfulness (e.g., Belsky, Fish, & Isabella, 1991; Lengua, 2006; Pauli-Pott, Mertesacker, & Beckmann, 2004), but in other studies, parental warmth and acceptance maintained or engendered fearfulness (Arcus, 2001; Kochanska, Friesenborg, Lange, & Martel,

2004). These findings suggest that warmth and sensitivity solicitous of fearful behaviors (e.g., Rubin, Burgess, & Hastings, 2002) and some types of overcontrol or intrusive control behaviors may sustain fearfulness (e.g., Chronis-Tuscano et al., 2015; Coplan, Reichel, & Rowan, 2009; Kiff, Lengua, & Bush, 2011; Kochanska et al., 2004), perhaps through limiting exposure to experiences that may enhance children's confidence and help them overcome fears (Bayer, Sanson, & Hemphill, 2006; Kiel & Buss, 2011).

Effortful Control and Conscientiousness

Parenting consistently predicts the development of effortful control and conscientiousness. Clear, consistent limit setting and nonpunitive discipline relate to higher effortful control (e.g., Karreman, van Tuijl, van Aken, & Deković, 2008; Lengua, Honorado, & Bush, 2007; Lengua et al., 2015; Olson, Bates, & Bayles, 1990), whereas, power assertion, coercion, rejection, and punitive discipline correlate with lower effortful control (Colman, Hardy, Albert, Raffaelli, & Crockett, 2006; Karreman et al., 2008; Kochanska, Askan, Prisco, & Adams, 2008; Kochanska & Knaack, 2003; Taylor, Eisenberg, Spinrad, & Widaman, 2013). In addition, maternal warmth, sensitivity, responsiveness, and scaffolding predict increases in effortful control in early childhood (Colman et al., 2006; Kochanska, Murray, & Harlan, 2000; Lengua et al., 2007; Olson et al., 1990). Maternal overreactivity predicted decreases in conscientiousness in late adolescence (Van den Akker et al., 2014). A randomized controlled study of a parenting intervention decreased conduct problems and enhanced effortful control, with changes accounted for by declines in negative, inconsistent parenting (Elizur, Somech, & Vinokur, 2017). Such experimental evidence speaks to links between parenting and effortful control in a particularly conclusive manner.

Surgency and Extraversion

Effects of parenting on child surgency or extraversion have not been widely examined, although specific aspects of surgency have been considered, with an emerging distinction between positive affectivity aspects of this factor (i.e., propensity to experience joy/pleasure) and those facets reflecting approach tendencies (i.e., impulsivity and exuberance). In a longitudinal study of children ages 4–7 years, de-creases in surgency were predicted by positive parenting behaviors (Blandon, Calkins, Keane, & O'Brien, 2010). Other studies examined the positive affect component of surgency, with one study showing that positive parental involvement was related to increases in infant positive emotionality across 6 months (Belsky et al., 1991), whereas another study found no effect of parenting on positive emotionality (Bates et al., 2012). A longitudinal study of preschool-age children indicated that parental warmth, scaffolding, and low negativity were related to lower levels of observed child positive affect, which the authors suggested might have been tapping child exuberance more than simply positive affectivity (Klein et al., 2016).

Studies of the effects of parenting on impulsivity, another component of surgency, show that power-based control, including strictness and intrusiveness, predicted lower delay of gratification or greater impulsivity in young children (Houck & Lecuyer-Maus, 2004), whereas children whose mothers used relatively nonrestrictive clear, consistent, and nonpunitive discipline when children were 2 years of age demonstrated better behavioral control and delay of gratification when they were 6 and 8 years (Olson et al., 1990; Olson, Bates, Sandy, & Schilling, 2002). It is possible that parenting predicts impulsivity only in children with a genetic predisposition for this trait. Specifically, polymorphic variations in the 7-repeat allele of the dopamine D4 receptor gene (7-repeat DRD4 polymorphism) have been associated with attention-deficit/hyperactivity disorder (ADHD) and attention-related outcomes. For children with the 7-repeat allele of the DRD4, low-quality parenting was correlated with higher levels of sensation seeking, a variable closely associated with impulsivity. Conversely, parenting was unrelated to children's sensation seeking in those classified as 7-repeat absent (Sheese, Voelker, Rothbart, & Posner, 2007). In an intervention study, intervention-related changes in maternal competence-promoting parenting predicted increases in youth self-control that included aspects of impulsivity (Brody et al., 2005).

There is little evidence regarding the effects of parenting on child extraversion. One study showed that warm parenting predicted membership in a resilient personality profile that included higher extraversion, emotional stability, conscientiousness, benevolence, and imagination (de Haan, Deković, van den Akker, Stoltz, & Prinzie, 2013). In another study, overprotective, interfering parenting was correlated negatively with extraversion (Nakao et al., 2000).

Summary

Taken together, parenting appears to alter children's negative emotionality or emotional stability, and their effortful control and conscientiousness, with effects that are fairly consistent across childhood. The effects of parenting on child surgency or extraversion are less well defined, with mixed findings for positive affectivity and approach tendencies.

Bidirectional or Transactional Relations of Parenting and Personality

The parents of a boy, Marco, were seeking help with dealing with his intense and out-of-control anger. They reported that he would react with intense anger when they set limits or gave him directives. He would yell at them, refuse to do what they asked, and sometimes his anger escalated into throwing or slamming things or hitting walls. The father acknowledged that he would often react to his son's anger by yelling back, threatening punishments, and slamming doors. They noted that their son's behavior was in contrast to that of their other son, Paolo, who was just 1 year older, and tended to be more calm and responsive to directives, and who would disagree respectfully with his parents. They did not have challenges with Paolo's behaviors, so he was less often in trouble. They could not figure out how to manage the differences between their sons in a fair and equal manner, and in particular, they did not know how to help Marco react less intensely when he was angry.

As reviewed in the previous section, there is clear evidence of parenting altering aspects of child personality. However, children also have effects on their parents and the parent–child relationship, resulting in transactional associations between child personality and parenting. In a transactional model, parenting and child personality are expected to mutually influence each other over time (Wachs & Kohnstamm, 2001; see Figure 12.1). Key to a transactional relation between children's personality and parenting is the evocative effects of child characteristics on parent behaviors, which in turn might increase or decrease those very child attributes through shaping and socialization processes described earlier. In the transactional

context, parents' efforts aimed at reducing child negative affect and dysregulated behaviors are themselves affected by those very child behaviors. Parenting efforts also encourage positive characteristics such as effortful control, which in turn might elicit more acceptance and appropriate control strategies that further engender adaptive emotional and behavioral responses. We now turn to evidence for the bidirectional or transactional relations between child personality and parenting, noting that we have already discussed the effects of parenting on children's traits.

It is important to acknowledge that the effects of child personality on parenting behaviors described below might be complicated and dependent on other aspects of the family context and relationships. Caregivers may differ in their susceptibility to individual differences in child temperament depending on context. For example, mothers described as having access to "abundant individual and family resources" by the virtue of being less depressed, highly self-efficacious, reporting few marital conflicts, and having a high co-parenting alliance with their spouse, demonstrated an interaction style that varied in accordance with the child's temperament. On the other hand, mothers with access to fewer resources interacted with their children in a less warm and responsive manner, regardless of the child's temperament, thus demonstrating lower susceptibility to child effects noted earlier (Lee, 2013). Future research on child evocative effects or transactional processes between parents and children should consider such potential contextual moderators.

Negative Reactivity, Neuroticism, and Emotional Stability

Children high in negative reactivity tend to become overaroused, may be difficult to sooth, and likely engender frustration, harsh responses, or disengagement from parents. As these children get older, they often direct angry and oppositional behaviors toward parents, which in turn increase parental attempts to control children's affect and behavior in more negative ways. These transactional processes can be expected to lead to low emotional stability or greater neuroticism over time. Indeed, infants and toddlers higher in negative reactivity or "difficult temperament" evoke more parenting stress (e.g., Oddi, Murdock, Vadnais, Bridgett, & Gartstein, 2013) and negative parenting behaviors (Bridgett et al., 2009; Calkins, 2002), such as parenting that is hostile, power assertive, coercive, and controlling (Boivin et al., 2005; Clark, Kochanska, & Ready, 2000), and decreases in positive parenting behaviors, such as responsiveness and sensitivity (Mertesacker, Bade, Haverkock, & Pauli-Pott, 2004). Low parental responsiveness predicted decreases in infant soothability and increases in infant negative reactivity, which in turn, led to further decreases in maternal sensitivity (Ghera, Hane, Malesa, & Fox, 2006). In a study that rigorously tested bidirectional relations between children's negative emotionality and parenting, child negative reactivity had differential effects on various parenting behaviors. Toddlers' negative emotionality predicted lower parental support, but not vice versa, and toddlers' negative reactivity did not predict harsh parenting, whereas harsh parenting predicted increases in child negative affect (Scaramella et al., 2008). In middle childhood, child negative reactivity predicted parental self-reported punitive discipline and distress reactions 2 years later, which were associated with increased child negative emotions 2 years after that (Eisenberg et al., 1999).

A similar pattern emerged for the FFM neuroticism or emotional stability dimension. Low emotional stability in adolescents predicted lower parental warmth above the effects of parent personality and demographics (de Haan, Deković, & Prinzie, 2012), and it predicted a high or increasing pattern of mother–adolescent hostile and aggressive conflict (Castellani et al., 2014). Similarly, the parent–child relationship mediated the association of emotional stability and externalizing problems, with low emotional stability relating to poorer quality relationships (Manders et al., 2006). In a study examining the effects of emotional stability on parental sense of competence, warmth, overreactivity, and psychological control, youth low emotional stability was related to lower warmth but not to other parenting dimensions (Egberts, Deković, Van den Akker, De Haan, & Prinzie, 2015).

Overall, it appears that negative emotionality or neuroticism and parenting have reciprocal effects. However, in some cases, negative reactivity has also been linked with greater maternal sensitivity or responsiveness (Paulussen-Hoogeboom, Stams, Hermanns, Peetsma, & van den Wittenboer, 2008) or has been unrelated to parenting over time (Van den Akker et al., 2014). These inconsistent results may be a func-

tion of the fact that various components of negative emotionality are emphasized across studies, and these are not associated with uniform effects on parenting, as discussed more below. Another possibility has to do with individual differences moderating links between negative emotionality and parenting. For example, infant negative emotionality was positively related to maternal sensitivity if mothers perceived their infants as highly soothable, but negatively related to sensitivity when infant soothability was low (Ghera et al., 2006). This pattern of results highlights the need to consider multiple temperament or personality characteristics simultaneously when examining their effects on parents.

In temperament studies, aspects of negative emotionality are often studied separately, and different patterns of associations with parenting have been identified for fear and frustration reactivity. For the most part, the pattern of findings for frustration reactivity mirrors the findings for the broader dimension of negative emotionality. Child frustration, irritability, and anger predict parental negative behaviors, such as anger, rejection, hostility, and intrusiveness (e.g., Calkins, Hungerford, & Dedmon, 2004; Kochanska et al., 2004), which in turn, predict increasing child anger and frustration (Eisenberg et al., 1999). For instance, irritability in infants predicted decreases in maternal responsiveness, and simultaneously, maternal responsiveness predicted decreases in infant irritability (van den Boom & Hoeksma, 1994). In middle childhood, child irritability predicted increases in maternal inconsistent discipline, while inconsistent discipline and maternal rejection predicted increases in irritability (Calkins, 2002; Lengua, 2006; Lengua & Kovacs, 2005).

Fear reactivity has a complicated association with parenting, at times evoking more warm, supportive, sensitive parenting (e.g., Belsky, Rha, & Park, 2000; Lengua & Kovacs, 2005), but at other times predicting less supportive, less responsive parenting (e.g., Wilson & Durbin, 2012). It may be important to distinguish between the impact of fearfulness on control versus affective aspects of parenting. Fearfulness in young children seems to elicit more protective and accommodating responses and less encouragement of autonomy (Belsky et al., 2000; Martini, Root, & Jenkins, 2004; Rubin, Nelson, Hastings, & Asendorpf, 1999). In longitudinal tests of bidirectional relations, child fearfulness elicited greater acceptance and less rejection from parents (Lengua, 2006; Lengua & Kovacs, 2005). The child's age appears to play an important role in relations between fear and parenting, as inconsistent limit setting, solicitousness, sensitivity, and protective behaviors during infancy and early childhood served to maintain or increase fear (Arcus, 2001; Park, Belsky, Putnam, & Crnic, 1997; Rubin et al., 1999), and rejection, and consistent limit setting predicted increases in fear in preadolescents (Lengua, 2006). The different needs and abilities of children at different developmental stages might account for these differences. Younger children require parents' facilitation of emotion regulation and adaptive responses. However, older children are more autonomous and might require a sense of their parents' acceptance and support of their independence.

Effortful Control and Conscientiousness

Effortful control and conscientiousness consistently relate to more positive or effective parenting behaviors, and there is evidence of bidirectional effects (Tiberio et al., 2016). Since effortful control emerges in the toddler years, other indicators of temperament self-regulation and potential precursors of effortful control are often examined in infants. Greater regulatory capacity, examined via parasympathetic nervous system indicators, was associated with more maternal supportive parenting (Kennedy, Rubin, Hastings, & Maisel, 2004), and higher infant and toddler regulation predicted lower hostile and coercive parenting (Bridgett et al., 2009; Morrell & Murray, 2003). In preschool-age children, effortful control predicted decreases in maternal negative, harsh behaviors, whereas maternal warmth and scaffolding predicted increases in effortful control (Klein et al., 2016). Preschool-age children higher in effortful control demonstrated fewer negative bids for maternal attention and more effort to influence parent–child interactions, predicting higher-quality parental responsiveness (Wilson & Durbin, 2012).

FFM conscientiousness was shown to predict parental sense of competence, but it was not related to parental warmth, overreactivity, or psychological control (de Haan et al., 2012; Egberts et al., 2015), or to changes in warmth or overreactivity over time (Van den Akker et al., 2014). However, in a cross-sectional study of adolescents, conscientiousness predicted

higher quality of parent–adolescent relationship, which mediated the effects of conscientiousness on lower externalizing behavior problems (Manders et al., 2006). Low conscientiousness predicted an increasing trajectory of hostile, aggressive conflict between mothers and adolescents, which predicted more depressive problems (Castellani et al., 2014). Thus, it appears that in adolescence, conscientiousness may have an impact on the quality of the parent–child relationship, but not necessarily on parental warmth or control.

Surgency and Extraversion

Few studies have examined the broad surgency factor in relation to parenting. In one study, infant surgency predicted decreased caregiving and play across infancy (Planalp, Braungart-Rieker, Lickenbrock, & Zentall, 2013), whereas in another, infant surgency did not predict parenting stress (Oddi et al., 2013). The discrepant findings in the relation of surgency to parenting might point to a complex and nuanced role that child surgency or extraversion may play. For example, Planalp and colleagues (2013) noted that infant surgency emerged as a significant predictor of caregiver involvement and sensitivity trajectories, albeit in divergent directions; that is, mothers engaged highly surgent infants in more play activities, yet these babies received less caregiving, and their mothers displayed less sensitivity in interactions over time. These findings provide an indication of caregivers making adjustments to their approach to parent–infant interactions as a result of infant temperament (e.g., increasing the amount of play with a more playful infant). A distinction between positive affect and approach aspects of surgency noted earlier may be important to consider in this context as well.

Effects of FFM extraversion on parenting parallel those of surgency. Extraversion was shown to predict not only increases in parental warmth but also more overreactive discipline (Van den Akker et al., 2014), above the effects of parent personality and demographic variables (de Haan et al., 2012). It may seem counterintuitive that higher levels of extraversion would predict increases in both overreactivity and warmth. However, extraverted children are optimistic and sociable, which may elicit warmth; at the same time, they are energetic and expressive, which may create more challenges for parents. Along these lines, Egberts and colleagues (2015) reported that extraversion predicts not only higher parental competence but also higher overreactivity and psychological control, despite parental competence being related to lower levels of these. These results highlight the fact that youth characteristics evoke complex responses from parents.

The pattern of inconsistent relations between extraversion and parenting parallels findings with younger children that suggest a differentiation between positive emotions and exuberance in terms of related parenting effects, with only the latter posing a challenge to caregivers. In a study of infants, higher levels and growth of smiling and laughter were related to less negative parental control (Bridgett et al., 2009). Preschool-age children who demonstrated higher positive emotionality made more social bids toward their parents, which predicted parental interaction bids and responsiveness (Wilson & Durbin, 2012). The FFM dimension of agreeableness, which entails a tendency toward cooperation, cheerfulness, and being easygoing and compliant, may operate in a manner similar to temperament positive affect. Greater agreeableness was related to a decreasing trajectory of hostile, aggressive conflict between mothers and adolescents, which predicted lower depressive problems in youth (Castellani et al., 2014). Agreeableness also predicted higher-quality parent–adolescent relationships, which mediated the association of agreeableness with lower externalizing problems (Manders et al., 2006). When taking into account the impact of all FFM traits, adolescent agreeableness was consistently related to less overreactive discipline and greater warmth (de Haan et al., 2012). The parent–adolescent relationships of agreeable individuals were characterized by more support and less overreactive discipline (O'Connor & Dvorak, 2001; Prinzie et al., 2003, 2009).

Summary

There is substantial prospective, longitudinal evidence for bidirectional relations between parenting and child characteristics in early and middle childhood, particularly for evocative and transactional effects of negative affect/ emotional stability and effortful control/conscientiousness (Bates et al., 2012; Kiff, Lengua, & Bush, 2011). Fewer rigorous examinations of bidirectional effects for other aspects of personality in adolescence have been conducted.

Goodness of Fit, Differential Responsiveness, and Sensitivity to Context Models

A father was sharing his frustration with the parenting advice he was reading on the Internet. He was trying to implement the idea of providing learning experiences instead of punitive ones with his son, Daniel. These approaches to parenting encourage parents to give children options for choosing acceptable behaviors instead of unacceptable ones, and redirect them to alternatives by explaining why their behavior is inappropriate, how it impacts others, and how to handle it differently. These approaches encourage ignoring misbehaviors and avoiding saying "no" or "stop." The father indicated that these approaches worked really well with his daughter, who would pause, listen and reflect when she was being addressed by her parents in these situations. However, with Daniel, who was rather impulsive, he found that there was no opportunity for these kinds of parenting efforts because Daniel would so quickly begin engaging in inappropriate behaviors that there was no chance to get him to pause and discuss it. Daniel didn't seem to remember from one time to the next what the rules and implications were for his behaviors, and sometimes if the father didn't yell to stop, Daniel would end up in dangerous situations without pausing to think (like running into the street or running off in a crowd). Although the strategies he was trying to implement worked perfectly well with his daughter, the father felt like he was getting nowhere with Daniel.

Another role of temperament and personality is as a moderator of the effects of parenting and family factors (Rothbart & Bates, 2006), such that they may not uniformly influence development depending on child personality. Rather, the effect varies, based on children's characteristics. Theories explaining how and why temperament may interact with parenting include goodness of fit, differential responsiveness, and sensitivity to context models.

Goodness-of-fit models consider the fit between an individual and the environment (Lerner & Lerner, 1994), suggesting that a good match between a child's characteristics and the demands of his or her context (parenting in particular) leads to more positive adjustment, whereas a poor fit leads to problematic outcomes. Variations on goodness-of-fit models include the organismic specificity accounts in which the impact of environmental factors varies with individual differences in temperament or personality (Wachs, 1991). Tests of these models highlighted diathesis–stress and vulnerability patterns of interactions between temperament and parenting, such that temperament may render someone more vulnerable to the effects of a negative or stressful context, in this case, negative parenting. For example, a child high in negative emotionality would be expected to demonstrate less optimal adjustment in a stressful context (e.g., parental divorce) compared to a child lower in negative emotionality. Newer theoretical accounts build on earlier efforts and propose a deviation from vulnerability models. Biological sensitivity to context and differential susceptibility frameworks suggest that individuals vary in the degree to which the environment affects their development, with some individuals being highly permeable or susceptible to environmental conditions and others largely unaffected (Boyce & Ellis, 2005). Focusing on parental influence, Belsky and others have offered the *differential susceptibility hypothesis* (Belsky, Bakermans-Kranenburg, & van IJzendoorn, 2007; Belsky & Pluess, 2009), which proposes that children's individual characteristics, particularly negative reactivity or difficult temperament, increase their responsiveness to parenting, both positive and negative. Thus, instead of casting difficult temperament or reactivity as uniformly leading to poor outcomes, the differential susceptibility framework predicts outcomes superior to those of children who are low in reactivity under optimal environmental circumstances, emphasizing the positive side of the interaction—the response of temperament outliers to good environments and to interventions (Pluess & Belsky, 2013). A recent meta-analysis provided qualified support for differences in sensitivity to parenting such that infants with a more difficult temperament (compared with those with an easy temperament) were more vulnerable to negative parenting and benefited more from positive parenting (Slagt, Dubas, Deković, & van Aken, 2016). However, differential susceptibility was not supported for older children, nor were the patterns of interactions for surgency or effortful control consistent with the biological sensitivity of differential susceptibility models. Differential sensitivity represents a special case of moderation, with a variety of moderation models supported by the literature, predominantly demonstrating negative emotionality/neuroticism as a risk factor. We

discuss next a variety of moderation scenarios involving temperament and personality.

Negative Reactivity and Emotional Stability Moderating Effects

Children higher in negative affect or difficult temperament demonstrate an increased risk for adjustment problems in the presence of poor parenting. However, in infancy, negative reactivity or difficult temperament might also render children more responsive to positive parenting, as noted in the meta-analysis mentioned earlier (Slagt et al., 2016). Several longitudinal studies show that infants high in negative reactivity benefit from parenting that is sensitive (Leerkes, Blankson, & O'Brien, 2009; van IJzendoorn & Bakermans-Kranenburg, 2006), emotionally supportive (Stright, Gallagher, & Kelley, 2008) and synchronous (Feldman, Greenbaum, & Yirmiya, 1999). In particular, children high in negative reactivity are more sensitive to the affective qualities of parenting. For example, negative parenting predicted externalizing problems and inhibition at age 3 for children who were high in negative emotionality as infants, whereas infants high in negative emotionality benefited from parenting that was more positive and supportive (Belsky, Hua Hsieh, & Crnic, 1998). However, other studies do not support interactions of parental warmth, support, or rejection with negative emotionality (Hastings et al., 2008; Paterson & Sanson, 1999; Vitaro, Barker, Boivin, Brendgen, & Tremblay, 2006), which suggests these associations may be most relevant in early childhood. Tests of interactions of parental control and children's negative reactivity suggest that children high in negative reactivity have more problem outcomes in relation to parental use of physical punishment (Lahey et al., 2008; Paterson & Sanson, 1999), overprotection, intrusiveness, or overcontrol (Hastings et al., 2008; Maziade et al., 1990), consistent with a diathesis–stress model.

Some inconsistency in findings related to interactions between negative reactivity and parenting may result from aspects of negative reactivity, frustration, and fearfulness operating differently. Child frustration interacts with parenting behaviors, such that negative parenting is more strongly related to adjustment problems for children who are higher in frustration compared to those lower in frustration. Children high in frustration or irritability are particularly adversely affected by parenting that is overprotective or high in psychological control (Calkins, 2002; Degnan, Calkins, Keane, & Hill-Soderlund, 2008), showing higher externalizing (Kiff, Lengua, & Zalewski, 2011; Sentse, Veenstra, Lindenberg, Verhulst, & Ormel, 2009) and internalizing problems (Morris et al., 2002; Oldehinkel, Veenstra, Ormel, de Winter, & Verhulst, 2006) from early childhood through preadolescence. Children high in frustration might react with anger and distress to intrusiveness, inconsistency, or physical discipline, which could interfere with internalization of rules or expectations. Children high in frustration or irritability are also particularly adversely affected by parenting that is low in warmth or high in hostility and rejection, showing increases in externalizing problems (Lengua, 2008; Morris et al., 2002; Oldehinkel et al., 2006; Sentse et al., 2009). The effects of parental hostility and rejection may be more pronounced for children who are easily frustrated, possibly producing anger, resentment, and distress that can impede prosocial development.

The patterns of interaction effects between parenting and fear are complicated and depend on whether children are fearful or fearless, and on whether affective or control aspects of parenting are considered. It is interesting to note that fear is unique, in that both high and low levels are vulnerabilities for the development of problems, with fearfulness consistently linked to anxiety (Schwartz, Snidman, & Kagan, 1999) and low fear being a risk factor for externalizing symptoms (Kochanska, Aksan, & Joy, 2007). The impact of parental control behaviors appears to be particularly dependent on levels of child fearfulness. The pattern of findings for interactions between parental control and children's fear are complex, with evidence suggesting on the one hand that optimal levels of parental control versus over- or undercontrol are most effective with fearful children (e.g., Kiel, Premo, & Buss, 2016). Fearful children are sensitive to cues of negative consequences, so that consequences applied even gently or inconsistently effectively reduce problem behaviors. On the other hand, fearful temperament exacerbated the negative effects of power assertive or harsh parenting (Kochanska et al., 2007; Leve, Kim, & Pears, 2005), which may produce high levels of child distress that impede the ability to internalize rules, increasing behavior problems. Conversely, low-fear children do not seem to be adversely impacted by harsh or power assertive

parenting (Kochanska et al., 2007). For children low in fear, gentle discipline may be ineffective for eliciting compliance, as it does not result in an "optimal" level of arousal, and inconsistent discipline appears to increase adjustment problems, particularly for low-fear boys (Lengua, 2008). In fact, for children low in fear, negative control seems to have a counterintuitive association, relating to lower problems (e.g., Hastings, Rubin, & DeRose, 2005; Kiff et al., 2011; Rubin et al., 2002), perhaps because fearless children benefit from more strongly and consistently enforced boundaries.

For affective aspects of parenting, it appears that fearful children are more susceptible to the adverse effects of negative parenting, but they do not necessarily benefit more from positive relationship qualities. For example, toddler inhibition predicted later reticence only if mothers exhibited derisive comments (Rubin et al., 2002). In preadolescents, parental rejection was related to increasing internalizing symptoms in fearful children (Kiff, Lengua, & Bush, 2007; Sentse et al., 2009). However, these associations appear to be conditioned by child gender, with fear and shyness in 18-month-old boys, but not girls, predicting greater shyness at 30 months when mothers were insensitive (Eggum et al., 2009). Maternal rejection was more strongly related to adjustment problems in preadolescent girls who were high in fear compared to girls low in fear or boys (Oldehinkel et al., 2006). The effects of parental rejection or insensitivity may be pronounced for highly fearful children, who may internalize parental rejection and criticism more readily and perceive their relationship with parents as threatened. Interestingly, fearful children, at least in preadolescence, do not seem to be particularly sensitive to parental warmth (Kiff et al., 2007; Oldehinkel et al., 2006; Sentse et al., 2009). Conversely, fearless children benefit from parenting that is warm, responsive, and positive (e.g., Hastings et al., 2005; Lahey et al., 2008; Leve et al., 2005). Perhaps this difference in sensitivity to parental warmth due to fearful temperament occurs as a function of differences in behavioral activation and inhibition system engagement; that is, being more sensitive to cues of danger and nonreward as a function of greater relative behavioral inhibition system (BIS) engagement, fearful children are not as responsive to positive (or rewarding) aspects of parenting. On the other hand, children presenting with low levels of fear can be expected to experience underactivity in the BIS, coupled with overactivity of the behavioral activation system (Fox, 1994), thus demonstrating greater sensitivity to rewarding aspects of parenting (e.g., maternal warmth and affection).

Effortful Control and Conscientiousness

Children who are higher in effortful control may require less external regulation of their emotions and behavior, and appear to be less adversely affected by negative or ineffective parenting. However, for children lower in effortful control, the associations of parental negativity and ineffective control with adjustment problems, particularly externalizing, tend to be more pronounced. Children low in effortful control benefit from parenting that is higher in control, guidance, and lower in autonomy granting (Kiff et al., 2007; Van Leeuwen, Mervielde, Braet, & Bosmans, 2004; Xu, Farver, & Zhang, 2009). Hostility (Morris et al., 2002), inconsistent discipline, and physical punishment (Lengua, 2008) predicted externalizing problems in school-age children with low effortful control, but not those with high effortful control. Similarly, parental overreactivity predicted externalizing difficulties in the transition from childhood to adolescence for youth who were lower on conscientiousness (de Haan, Prinzie, & Deković, 2010; cf. Prinzie et al., 2003; Van Leeuwen et al., 2004). It is interesting to note that tests for interactions between effortful control and indicators of a positive parent–child relationship, such as warmth, have generally been nonsignificant (Kiff et al., 2007; Lengua, 2008; Van Leeuwen et al., 2004; Veenstra, Oldehinkel, de Winter, Lindenberg, & Ormel, 2006). However, some evidence suggests that children lower in effortful control seem to benefit from parenting that is high in support or positive affect (Hastings et al., 2008; Rabinowitz, Drabick, Reynolds, Clark, & Olino, 2016; Van Leeuwen et al., 2004), and they are more adversely affected by maternal hostility (Morris et al., 2002) and negative affect (Kiff et al., 2007). Similar patterns were seen in youth low in conscientiousness, suggesting that less conscientious children may be less able to control the way they initially react to harshness, and are more likely to demonstrate externalizing behaviors (Van Zeijl et al., 2007). It appears that maternal positive affect and consistent limit setting promotes emotional and behavioral control in children who are less self-regulated, whereas mothers' expression of negative affect and criticism serves to further dysregulate these youngsters.

Surgency and Extraversion

Across early childhood to adolescence, children high in impulsivity have been shown to benefit from parenting that is high in appropriate control (Rubin, Hastings, Chen, Stewart, & McNichol, 1998; Stice & Gonzales, 1998; Xu et al., 2009) and consistency (Lengua, Wolchik, Sandler, & West, 2000) that is not harsh (Leve et al., 2005; Rubin, Burgess, Dwyer, & Hastings, 2003; Xu et al., 2009). For example, parental negative control was related to more aggression and externalizing problems for toddler boys high in behavioral undercontrol (Rubin et al., 1998) and school-age children high in resistant temperament, reflective of impulsivity (Bates, Pettit, Dodge, & Ridge, 1998). In adolescence, perceptions of parental control were related to antisocial behavior for adolescents high, but not low, in behavioral undercontrol (Stice & Gonzales, 1998). Impulsive children also benefit from warm, supportive, and sensitive parenting. High maternal sensitivity predicted fewer externalizing problems for school-age children with genetic risk for impulsivity (presence of the 7-repeat *DRD4* polymorphism, associated with decreased dopamine receptor efficiency), a pattern consistent with the differential susceptibly hypothesis (van IJzendoorn & Bakermans-Kranenburg, 2006). Furthermore, exuberant toddlers demonstrated increases in effortful control when discipline practices were characterized by a positive and warm emotional tone (Cipriano & Stifter, 2010). However, in adolescence, there is mixed support for substantial benefits of a supportive parent–child relationship for children high in impulsivity. High parental support was related to lower antisocial problems for children high in undercontrol (Stice & Gonzales, 1998), yet supportive parenting predicted lower substance use in youth low in impulsivity (King & Chassin, 2004). When examining the FFM dimension of extraversion, children who were lower in extraversion were more affected by parent overreactivity in their development of externalizing problems (de Haan et al., 2010) and by inconsistent discipline in developing physical aggression (Smack, Kushner, & Tackett, 2015). It appears that approach-tendency-related aspects of surgency have been primarily examined in this context, and additional research is required. The mixed pattern of results for impulsivity or undercontrol may be a function of developmental differences, as the role of impulsivity and its associations with parenting may differ in adolescence.

Summary

Tests of interactions between parenting and temperament have been used to address a variety of conceptual models, including goodness of fit, diathesis–stress, biological sensitivity to context, or differential susceptibility. Overall, evidence indicates that children respond differently to parenting based on their own temperament or personality, and the observed patterns of interaction provide support for multiple models. Most findings suggest that children with certain characteristic, particularly negative emotionality or low emotional stability, impulsive aspects of surgency or extraversion, and low effortful control, show greater problems in the presence of negative parenting, supporting the diathesis–stress or vulnerability interpretation. Other findings, particularly for low or high fearfulness, are consistent with goodness of fit in that children may experience benefit or detriment from the same parenting behaviors depending on their personality. Evidence for differential susceptibility appears to be most consistent for negative affect or difficult temperament in infants, showing that those characteristics confer more vulnerability in response to negative parenting but greater benefit from positive interactions with caregivers. Infant negative affect can represent a variety of motivational and emotional states or responses, including fear, frustration, hunger, discomfort, and tiredness, and negative affectivity becomes more differentiated across development, with evidence that fear and frustration operate differently in relation to parenting supporting this conjecture.

Conclusions and Future Directions

In considering personality within the family context, we have focused on the relations between parenting and children's personality traits, as parenting represents a key conduit through which family relationships and family context impact children's development. Furthermore, we have elaborated on a variety of ways in which parenting and child personality relate to each other. Traditionally, temperament and personality traits have been seen as representing "nature," and parenting as representing "nurture," and research focused on the independent contribution of each, individually or in conjunction, forecasts developmental outcomes. However, more recent theoretical models and research reviewed in this chapter highlight that these concepts can better be seen as developmentally intertwined. Temperament and parenting are dynamic, mutually influencing each other and interacting over time. We have examined the role parents play in shaping or socializing children's personality, the eliciting effects children's personality has on parents, with children's and parents' behaviors influencing each other, and how child personality moderates or alters the effects of parenting on developmental outcomes. Taking these interactions and transactions into account can help parents and families more effectively respond to their children's individual differences. These interrelations are also important to professionals to tailor or personalize parenting advice and validate parents' and families' challenges in interacting with their children, facilitating the delivery of child and family interventions that are sensitive to children's individual differences.

Both researchers and practitioners could benefit from an elaborated understanding of the relations of temperament and personality dimensions, and from clarification of the developmental relevance of different parenting behaviors. For example, more research that explicitly models the developmental associations of temperament and FFM traits is needed. These studies should move beyond factor-analytic approaches mapping temperament and FFM dimensions onto converging latent factors, working toward articulating the developmental course from early temperament characteristics, through socialization and contextual influence, to the emergence of FFM characteristics. From a bioecological perspective, youth personality is influenced by the interplay of biologically based characteristics such as temperament, proximal interpersonal experiences, and broader contextual factors. Future research might examine how temperament and parenting transactions and interactions in early childhood predict the emergence of FFM characteristics later.

It will also be valuable to examine more explicitly the relative importance of different parenting and family relationship factors at different developmental stages. Evidence for parenting and temperament–personality interactions and transactions emerges at every developmental stage, but different parenting dimensions are studied at each of these stages. For example, parental sensitivity and responsiveness are most often examined in infants (De Wolff & van IJzendoorn, 1997; Fearon & Belsky, 2016), whereas parental warmth, rejection, overreactivity, emotion socialization, and limit setting are studied during middle childhood (e.g., Collins, Maccoby, Steinberger, Hetherington, & Bornstein, 2000), and parent–child communication, autonomy support, and conflict are studied during adolescence (de Haan, Soenens, Deković, & Prinzie, 2013; Smetana, Robinson, & Rote, 2015). Longitudinal developmental research could elucidate the relative importance of different parenting behaviors at different stages. For example, sensitive and responsive parenting appears most relevant during infancy; however, it is possible that sensitive, responsive parenting is relevant in adolescence as well, but it is rarely studied. A comprehensive examination of parenting behaviors across developmental stages would be valuable in understanding interaction and transactions between parenting and personality, providing developmentally informed guidance to parents, parenting educators, and clinicians.

Finally, long-term longitudinal and intervention research is needed. Most studies in this area are cross-sectional, with longitudinal investigations typically covering only short periods. More long-term longitudinal efforts could clarify the relations of temperament and FFM development, predictors of their development, and their role in differentiating the influences of parenting and family factors. Such long-term developmental research would also serve to provide rigorous tests of differential effects of parenting at various developmental periods, and needed replication of observed patterns of results. In addition, intervention studies that demonstrate the effects of altering parenting on temperament or personality will provide more definitive evidence of the role that parenting plays in shaping children's personalities. Such research could also investigate how children's temperament or personality might lead to differential responsiveness to parental intervention, further clarifying the moderating role of personality on developmental influences.

REFERENCES

Arcus, D. (2001). Inhibited and uninhibited children: Biology in the social context. In T. D. Wachs & G. A. Kohnstamm (Eds.), *Temperament in context* (pp. 43–60). Mahwah, NJ: Erlbaum.

Ato, E., Galian, M. D., & Fernandez-Vilar, M. A. (2015). The moderating role of children's effortful control in the relation between marital adjustment and parenting. *Journal of Child and Family Studies, 24,* 3341–3349.

Bates, J. E., Pettit, G. S., Dodge, K. A., & Ridge, B. (1998). Interaction of temperamental resistance to control and restrictive parenting in the development of externalizing problems. *Developmental Psychology, 34,* 982–995.

Bates, J. E., Schermerhorn, A. C., & Petersen, I. T. (2012). Temperament and parenting in developmental perspective. In M. Zentner & R. L. Shiner (Eds.), *Handbook of temperament* (pp. 425–441). New York: Guilford Press.

Bayer, J. K., Sanson, A. V., & Hemphill, S. A. (2006). Parent influences on early childhood internalizing difficulties. *Journal of Applied Developmental Psychology, 27,* 542–559.

Belsky, J., Bakermans-Kranenburg, M. J., & van IJzendoorn, M. H. (2007). For better and for worse: Differential susceptibility to environmental influences. *Association for Psychological Science, 16,* 300–305.

Belsky, J., Fish, M., & Isabella, R. A. (1991). Continuity and discontinuity in infant negative and positive emotionality: Family antecedents and attachment consequences. *Developmental Psychology, 27*(3), 421–431.

Belsky, J., Hua Hsieh, K., & Crnic, K. (1998). Mothering, fathering, and infant negativity as antecedents of boys' externalizing problems and inhibition at age 3 years: Differential susceptibility to rearing experience? *Development and Psychopathology, 10,* 301–319.

Belsky, J., & Pluess, M. (2009). Beyond diathesis stress: Differential susceptibility to environmental influences. *Psychological Bulletin, 135,* 885–908.

Belsky, J., Rha, J., & Park, S. (2000). Exploring reciprocal parent and child effects in the case of child inhibition in US and Korean samples. *International Journal of Behavioral Development, 24,* 338–347.

Bezirganian, S., & Cohen, P. (1992). Sex differences in the interaction between temperament and parenting. *Journal of the American Academy of Child and Adolescent Psychiatry, 31,* 790–801.

Blandon, A. Y., Calkins, S. D., Keane, S. P., & O'Brien, M. (2010). Contributions of child's physiology and maternal behavior to children's trajectories of temperamental reactivity. *Developmental Psychology, 46,* 1089–1102.

Boivin, M., Pérusse, D., Dionne, G., Saysset, V., Zoccolillo, M., Tarabulsy, G. M., et al. (2005). The genetic–environmental etiology of parents' perceptions and self-assessed behaviours toward their 5-month-old infants in a large twin and singleton sample. *Journal of Child Psychology and Psychiatry, 46,* 612–630.

Boyce, W. T., & Ellis, B. J. (2005). Biological sensitivity to context: I. An evolutionary–developmental theory of the origins and functions of stress reactivity. *Development and Psychopathology, 17,* 271–301.

Bridgett, D. J., Gartstein, M. A., Putnam, S. P., McKay, T., Iddins, E., Robertson, C., et al. (2009). Maternal and contextual influences on the effect of temperament development during infancy on parenting in toddlerhood. *Infant Behavior and Development, 32,* 103–116.

Brody, G. H., Murry, V. M., McNair, L., Chen, Y.-F., Gibbons, F. X., Gerrard, M., et al. (2005). Linking changes in parenting to parent–child relationship quality and youth self-control: The strong African American families program. *Journal of Research on Adolescence, 15,* 47–69.

Bronfenbrenner, U., & Morris, P. A. (2006). The bioecological model of human development. *Handbook of child psychology: Vol. 1. Theoretical models of human development* (6th ed., pp. 793–828). Hoboken, NJ: Wiley.

Calkins, S. D. (2002). Does aversive behavior during toddlerhood matter?: The effects of difficult temperament on maternal perceptions and behavior. *Infant Mental Health Journal, 23,* 381–402.

Calkins, S. D., Hungerford, A., & Dedmon, S. E. (2004). Mothers interactions with temperamentally frustrated infants. *Infant Mental Health Journal, 25,* 219–239.

Caspi, A., & Shiner, R. L. (2006). Personality development. In W. Damon & R. Lerner (Series Eds.) & N. Eisenberg (Vol. Ed.), *Handbook of child psychology: Vol. 3. Social, emotional, and personality development* (6th ed., pp. 300–365). Hoboken, NJ: Wiley.

Castellani, V., Pastorelli, C., Eisenberg, N., Gerbino, M., Di Giunta, L., Ceravolo, R., et al. (2014). Hostile, aggressive family conflict trajectories during the transition to adulthood: Associations with adolescent FFM and emerging adulthood adjustment problems. *Journal of Adolescence, 37,* 647–658.

Chronis-Tuscano, A., Rubin, K. H., O'Brien, K. A., Coplan, R. J., Thomas, S. R., Dougherty, L. R., et al. (2015). Preliminary evaluation of a multimodal early intervention program for behaviorally inhibited preschoolers. *Journal of Consulting and Clinical Psychology, 83,* 534–540.

Cipriano, E. A., & Stifter, C. A. (2010). Predicting preschool effortful control from toddler temperament and parenting behavior. *Journal of Applied Developmental Psychology, 31,* 221–230.

Clark, L. A., Kochanska, G., & Ready, R. (2000). Mothers' personality and its interaction with child temperament as predictors of parenting behavior. *Journal of Personality and Social Psychology, 79,* 274–285.

Collins, W. A., Maccoby, E. E., Steinberger, L., Hetherington, E. M., & Bornstein, M. H. (2000). Contemporary research on parenting: The case for nature and nuture. *American Psychologist, 55,* 218–232.

Colman, R. A., Hardy, S. A., Albert, M., Raffaelli, M., & Crockett, L. (2006). Early predictors of self-regulation in middle childhood. *Infant and Child Development, 15,* 421–437.

Coplan, R. J., Reichel, M., & Rowan, K. (2009). Exploring the associations between maternal personality, child temperament and parenting: A focus on emotions. *Personality and Individual Differences, 46,* 241–246.

Davies, P. T., Cicchetti, D., & Martin, M. J. (2012). Toward greater specificity in identifying associations among interparental aggression, child emotional reactivity to conflict, and child problems. *Child Development, 83,* 1789–1804.

de Haan, A. D., Deković, M., & Prinzie, P. (2012). Longitudinal impact of parental and adolescent personality on parenting. *Journal of Personality and Social Psychology, 102,* 189–199.

de Haan, A. D., Deković, M., van den Akker, A. L., Stoltz, S. E. M. J., & Prinzie, P. (2013). Developmental personality types from childhood to adolescence: Associations with parenting and adjustment. *Child Development, 84,* 2015–2030.

de Haan, A. D., Prinzie, P., & Deković, M. (2010). How and why children change in aggression and delinquency from childhood to adolescence: Moderation of overreactive parenting by child personality. *Journal of Child Psychology and Psychiatry, 51,* 725–733.

de Haan, A. D., Soenens, B., Deković, M., & Prinzie, P. (2013). Effects of childhood aggression on parenting during adolescence: The role of parental psychological need satisfaction. *Journal of Clinical Child and Adolescent Psychology, 42,* 393–404.

De Pauw, S. S. W. (2016). Childhood personality and temperament. In T. Widiger (Ed.), *The Oxford handbook of the five-factor model of personality* (pp. 243–280). New York: Oxford University Press.

De Wolff, M. S., & van IJzendoorn, M. H. (1997). Sensitivity and attachment: A meta-analysis on parental antecedents of infant attachment. *Child Development, 68,* 571–591.

Degnan, K. A., Calkins, S. D., Keane, S. P., & Hill-Soderlund, A. L. (2008). Profiles of disruptive behavior across early childhood: Contributions of frustration reactivity, physiological regulation, and maternal behavior. *Child Development, 79,* 1357–1376.

Egberts, M., Deković, M., Van den Akker, A. L., de Haan, A. D., & Prinzie, P. (2015). The prospective relationship between child personality and perceived parenting: Mediation by parental sense of competence. *Personality and Individual Differences, 77,* 193–198.

Eggum, N. D., Eisenberg, N., Spinrad, T. L., Reiser, M., Gaertner, B. M., Sallquist, J., et al. (2009). Development of shyness: Relations with children's fearfulness, sex, and maternal behavior. *Infancy, 14,* 325–345.

Eisenberg, N., Fabes, R. A., Shepard, S., Guthrie, I., Murphy, B., & Reiser, M. (1999). Parental reactions to children's negative emotions: Longitudinal relations to quality of children's social functioning. *Child Development, 70,* 513–534.

Elizur, Y., Somech, L. Y., & Vinokur, A. D. (2017). Effects of parent training on callous–unemotional traits, effortful control, and conduct problems: Mediation by parenting. *Journal of Abnormal Child Psychology, 45,* 15–26.

Fearon, R. M. P., & Belsky, J. (2016). Precursors of attachment security. In J. Cassidy & P. R. Shaver (Eds.), *Handbook of attachment: Theory, research, and clinical applications* (3rd ed., pp. 291–313). New York: Guilford Press.

Feldman, R., Greenbaum, C. W., & Yirmiya, N. (1999). Mother-infant affect synchrony as an antecedent of the emergence of self-control. *Developmental Psychology, 35,* 223–231.

Fox, N. A. (1994). Dynamic cerebral processes underlying emotion regulation. *Monographs of the Society for Research in Child Development, 59,* 152–166, 250–283.

Ghera, M. M., Hane, A. A., Malesa, E. E., & Fox, N. A. (2006). The role of infant soothability in the relation between infant negativity and maternal sensitivity. *Infant Behavior and Development, 29,* 289–293.

Hastings, P. D., Rubin, K. H., & DeRose, L. (2005). Links among gender, inhibition, and parental socialization in the development of prosocial behavior. *Merrill–Palmer Quarterly, 51,* 467–493.

Hastings, P. D., Sullivan, C., McShane, K. E., Coplan, R. J., Utendale, W. T., & Vyncke, J. D. (2008). Parental socialization, vagal regulation, and preschoolers' anxious difficulties: Direct mothers and moderated fathers. *Child Development, 79,* 45–64.

Houck, G. M., & Lecuyer-Maus, E. A. (2004). Maternal limit setting during toddlerhood, delay of gratification, and behavior problems at age five. *Infant Mental Health Journal, 25,* 28–46.

Karreman, A., van Tuijl, C., van Aken, M. A. G., & Deković, M. (2008). Parenting, coparenting, and effortful control in preschoolers. *Journal of Family Psychology, 22*(1), 30–40.

Kennedy, A. E., Rubin, K. H., Hastings, P. D., & Maisel, B. A. (2004). The longitudinal relations between child vagal tone and parenting behavior: 2 to 4 years. *Developmental Psychobiology, 45,* 10–21.

Kiel, E. J., & Buss, K. A. (2011). Prospective relations among fearful temperament, protective parenting, and social withdrawal: The role of maternal accuracy in a moderated mediation framework. *Journal of Abnormal Child Psychology, 39,* 953–966.

Kiel, E. J., Premo, J. E., & Buss, K. A. (2016). Maternal encouragement to approach novelty: A curvilinear relation to change in anxiety for inhibited toddlers. *Journal of Abnormal Child Psychology, 44,* 433–444.

Kiff, C. J., Lengua, L. J., & Bush, N. R. (2007). *Temperament variations in sensitivity to parenting: Predict-ing changes in depression and anxiety.* Unpublished master's thesis.

Kiff, C., Lengua, L. J., & Bush, N. (2011). Temperament variation in sensitivity to parenting: Predicting changes in depression and anxiety. *Journal of Abnormal Child Psychology, 39,* 1199–1212.

Kiff, C., Lengua, L. J., & Zalewski, M. (2011). Nature and nurturing: Parenting in the context of children's temperament. *Journal of Clinical Child and Family Review, 14,* 251–301.

King, K. M., & Chassin, L. (2004). Mediating and moderated effects of adolescent behavioral undercontrol and parenting in the prediction of drug use disorders in emerging adulthood. *Psychology of Addictive Behaviors, 18,* 239–249.

Klein, M., Lengua, L. J., Thompson, S., Kiff, C., Ruberry, E., Moran, L., et al. (2016). Bidirectional relations between temperament and parenting predicting preschool-age children's adjustment. *Journal of Clinical Child and Adolescent Psychology.* [Epub ahead of print]

Kochanska, G., Aksan, N., & Joy, M. (2007). Children's fearfulness as a moderator of parenting in early socialization: Two longitudinal studies. *Developmental Psychology, 43,* 222–237.

Kochanska, G., Askan, J., Prisco, T. R., & Adams, E. E. (2008). Mother–child and father–child mutually responsive orientation in the first 2 years and children's outcomes at preschool age: Mechanisms of influence. *Child Development, 79,* 30–44.

Kochanska, G., Friesenborg, A. E., Lange, L. A., & Martel, M. M. (2004). Parents' personality and infants' temperament as contributors to their emerging relationship. *Journal of Personality and Social Psychology, 86,* 744–759.

Kochanska, G., & Knaack, A. (2003). Effortful control as a personality characteristic of young children: Antecedents, correlates, and consequences. *Journal of Personality, 71,* 1087–1112.

Kochanska, G., Murray, K. T., & Harlan, E. T. (2000). Effortful control in early childhood: Continuity and change, antecedents and implications for social development. *Developmental Psychology, 36,* 220–232.

Koenig, J. L., Barry, R. A., & Kochanska, G. (2010). Rearing difficult children: Parents' personality and children's proneness to anger as predictors of future parenting. *Parenting: Science and Practice, 10,* 258–273.

Lahey, B. B., Van Hulle, C. A., Keenan, K., Rathouz, P. J., D'Onofrio, B. M., Rodgers, J. L., et al. (2008). Temperament and parenting during the first year of life   predict future child conduct problems. *Journal of Abnormal Child Psychology, 36,* 1139–1158.

Lee, E. J. (2013). Differential susceptibility to the effects of child temperament on maternal warmth and responsiveness. *Journal of Genetic Psychology, 174,* 429–449.

Leerkes, E. M., Blankson, A. N., & O'Brien, M. (2009). Differential effects of maternal sensitivity to infant distress and nondistress on social–emotional functioning. *Child Development, 80,* 762–775.

Lengua, L. J. (2006). Growth in temperament and parenting as predictors of adjustment during children's transition to adolescence. *Developmental Psychology, 42*(2), 819–832.

Lengua, L. J. (2008). Anxiousness, frustration, and effortful control as moderators of the relation between parenting and adjustment problems in middle-childhood. *Social Development, 17,* 554–577.

Lengua, L. J., Honorado, E., & Bush, N. R. (2007). Contextual risk and parenting as predictors of effortful control and social competence in preschool children. *Journal of Applied Developmental Psychology, 28*(1), 40–55.

Lengua, L. J., & Kovacs, E. A. (2005). Bidirectional associations between temperament and parenting, and the prediction of adjustment problems in middle childhood. *Journal of Applied Developmental Psychology, 26,* 21–38.

Lengua, L. J., Moran, L. R., Zalewski, M., Ruberry, E., Kiff, C., & Thompson, S. (2015). Relations of growth in effortful control to family income, cumulative risk, and adjustment in preschool-age children. *Journal of Abnormal Child Psychology, 43,* 705–720.

Lengua, L. J., Wolchik, S., Sandler, I., & West, S. (2000). The additive and interactive effects of parenting and temperament in predicting adjustment problems of children of divorce. *Journal of Clinical Child Psychology, 29,* 232–244.

Lerner, J. V., & Lerner, R. M. (1994). Explorations of the goodness-of-fit model in early adolescence. In W. B. Carey & S. C. McDevitt (Eds.), *Prevention and early intervention: Individual differences as risk factors for the mental health of children: A festschrift for Stella Chess and Alexander Thomas* (pp. 161–169). Philadelphia: Brunner/Mazel.

Leve, L. D., Kim, H. K., & Pears, K. C. (2005). Childhood temperament and family environment as predictors of internalizing and externalizing trajectories from ages 5 to 17. *Journal of Abnormal Child Psychology, 33,* 505–520.

Manders, W. A., Scholte, R. H., Janssens, J. M. A. M., & De Bruyn, E. E. J. (2006). Adolescent personality, problem behaviour and the quality of the parent–adolescent relationship. *European Journal of Personality, 20,* 237–254.

Manning, L. G., Davies, P. T., & Cicchetti, D. (2014). Interparental violence and childhood adjustment: How and why maternal sensitivity is a protective factor. *Child Development, 85,* 2263–2278.

Martini, T. S., Root, C. A., & Jenkins, J. M. (2004). Low and middle income mother's regulation of negative emotion: Effects of children's temperament and situational emotional responses. *Social Development, 13,* 515–530.

Maziade, M., Caron, C., Cote, R., Merette, C., Bernier, H., Laplante, B., Boutin, P., et al. (1990). Psychiatric status of adolescents who had extreme temperaments at age 7. *American Journal of Psychiatry, 147,* 1531–1536.

Mertesacker, B., Bade, U., Haverkock, A., & Pauli-Pott, U. (2004). Predicting maternal reactivity/sensitivity: The role of infant emotionality, maternal depressiveness/anxiety, and social support. *Infant Mental Health Journal, 25,* 47–61.

Morrell, J., & Murray, L. (2003). Parenting and the development of conduct disorder and hyperactive symptoms in childhood. *Journal or Child Psychology and Psychiatry, 44,* 489–508.

Morris, A. S., Silk, J. S., Steinberg, L., Sessa, F. M., Avenevoli, S., & Essex, M. (2002). Temperamental vulnerability and negative parenting as interacting predictors of child adjustment. *Journal of Marriage and Family, 64,* 461–471.

Nakao, K., Takaishi, J., Tatsuta, K., Katayama, H., Iwase, M., Yorifuji, K., et al. (2000). The influence of family environment on personality traits. *Psychiatry and Clinical Neurosciences, 54,* 91–95.

O'Connor, B. P., & Dvorak, T. (2001). Conditional associations between parental behavior and adolescent problems: A search for personality–environment interactions. *Journal of Research in Personality, 35,* 1–26.

Oddi, K. B., Murdock, K. W., Vadnais, S., Bridgett, D. J., & Gartstein, M. A. (2013). Maternal and infant temperament characteristics as contributors to parenting stress in the first year postpartum. *Infant and Child Development, 22,* 553–579.

Oldehinkel, A. J., Veenstra, R., Ormel, J., de Winter, A. F., & Verhulst, F. C. (2006). Temperament, parenting, and depressive symptoms in a population sample of preadolescents. *Journal of Child Psychology and Psychiatry, 47,* 684–695.

Olson, S. L., Bates, J. E., & Bayles, K. (1990). Early antecedents of childhood impulsivity: The role of parent–child interaction, cognitive competence, and temperament. *Journal of Abnormal Child Psychology, 18,* 317–334.

Olson, S. L., Bates, J. E., Sandy, J. M., & Schilling, E. M. (2002). Early developmental precursors of impulsive and inattentive behavior: From infancy to middle childhood. *Journal of Child Psychology and Psychiatry, 43,* 435–447.

Park, S. Y., Belsky, J., Putnam, S., & Crnic, K. (1997). Infant emotionality, parenting, and 3-year inhibition: Exploring stability and lawful discontinuity in a male sample. *Developmental Psychology, 33,* 218–227.

Paterson, G., & Sanson, A. (1999). The association of behavioral adjustment to temperament, parenting, and family characteristics among 5-year-old children. *Social Development, 8,* 293–309.

Pauli-Pott, U., Mertesacker, B., & Beckmann, D. (2004). Predicting the development of infant emotionality from maternal characteristics. *Development and Psychopathology, 16,* 19–42.

Paulussen-Hoogeboom, M. C., Stams, G. J., Hermanns, J. M., Peetsma, T. T., & van den Wittenboer G. L.

(2008). Parenting style as a mediator between children's negative emotionality and problematic behavior in early childhood. *Journal of Genetic Psychology, 169,* 209–226.

Planalp, E. M., Braungart-Rieker, J. M., Lickenbrok, D. M., & Zentall, S. R. (2013). Trajectories of parenting during infancy: The role of infant temperament and marital adjustment for mothers and fathers. *Infancy, 18,* E16–E45.

Pluess, M., & Belsky, J. (2013). Vantage sensitivity: Individual differences in response to positive experiences. *Psychological Bulletin, 139,* 901–916.

Prinzie, P., Deković, M., van den Akker, A. L., de Haan, A. D., Stoltz, S. E. M. J., & Hendriks, A. A. J. (2012). Fathers' personality and its interaction with children's personality as predictors of perceived parenting behavior six years later. *Personality and Individual Differences, 52,* 183–189.

Prinzie, P., Onghena, P., Hellinckx, W., Grietens, H., Ghesquière, P., & Colpin, H. (2003). The additive and interactive effects of parenting and children's personality on externalising behaviour. *European Journal of Personality, 17,* 95–117.

Prinzie, P., Stams, G. J., Deković, M., Reijntjes, A. H. A., & Belsky, J. (2009). The relations between parents' Big Five personality factors and parenting: a meta-analytic review. *Journal of Personality and Social Psychology, 97,* 351–362.

Prinzie, P., Van der Sluis, C. M., de Haan, A. D., & Deković, M. (2010). The mediational role of parenting on the longitudinal relation between child personality and externalizing behavior. *Journal of Personality, 78,* 1301–1324.

Rabinowitz, J. A., Drabick, D. A. G., Reynolds, M. D., Clark, D. B., & Olino, T. M. (2016). Child temperamental flexibility moderates the relation between positive parenting and adolescent adjustment. *Journal of Applied Developmental Psychology, 43,* 43–53.

Rothbart, M. K., & Bates, J. E. (2006). Temperament. In N. Eisenberg, W. Damon, & R. M. Lerner (Eds.), *Handbook of child psychology: Vol. 3. Social, emotional, and personality development* (6th ed., pp. 99–166). Hoboken, NJ: Wiley.

Rubin, K. H., Burgess, K. B., Dwyer, K. M., & Hastings, P. D. (2003). Predicting preschoolers' externalizing behaviors from toddler temperament, conflict, and maternal negativity. *Developmental Psychology, 39,* 164–176.

Rubin, K. H., Burgess, K. B., & Hastings, P. D. (2002). Stability and social–behavioral consequences of toddlers' inhibited temperament and parenting behaviors. *Child Development, 73,* 483–495.

Rubin, K. H., Hastings, P. D., Chen, X., Stewart, S. L., & McNichol, K. (1998). Intrapersonal and maternal correlates of aggression, conflict, and externalizing problems in toddlers. *Child Development, 69,* 1614–1629.

Rubin, K. H., Nelson, L. J., Hastings, P., & Asendorpf, J. (1999). The transaction between parent's percep-

tions of their children's shyness and their parenting styles. *International Society for the Study of Behavioural Development, 23,* 937–957.

Scaramella, L. V., Sohr-Preston, S. L., Mirabile, S. P., Callahan, K. L., & Robison, S. (2008). Parenting and children's distress reactivity during toddlerhood: An examination of direction of effects. *Social Development, 17,* 578–595.

Schwartz, C. E., Snidman, N., & Kagan, J. (1999). Adolescent social anxiety as an outcome of inhibited temperament in childhood. *Journal of the American Academy of Child and Adolescent Psychiatry, 38,* 1008–1015.

Selig, J. P., & Preacher, K. J. (2009). Mediation models for longitudinal data in developmental research. *Research in Human Development, 6,* 144–164.

Sentse, M., Veenstra, R., Lindenberg, S., Verhulst, F. C., & Ormel, J. (2009). Buffers and risks in temperament and family for early adolescent psychopathology: Generic, conditional or domain-specific effects?: The TRAILS study. *Developmental Psychology, 45,* 419–430.

Sheese, B. E., Voelker, P. M., Rothbart, M. K., & Posner, M. I. (2007). Parenting quality interacts with genetic variation in dopamine receptor D4 to influence temperament in early childhood. *Development and Psychopathology, 19,* 1039–1046.

Slagt, M., Dubas, J. S., Deković, M., & van Aken, M. A. G. (2016). Differences in sensitivity to parenting depending on child temperament: A meta-analysis. *Psychological Bulletin, 142,* 1068–1110.

Smack, A. J., Kushner, S. C., & Tackett, J. L. (2015). Child personality moderates associations between parenting and relational and physical aggression. *Journal of Aggression, Maltreatment and Trauma, 24,* 845–862.

Smetana, J. G., Robinson, J., & Rote, W. M. (2015). Socialization in adolescence. In J. E. Grusec & P. D. Hastings. (Eds.), *Handbook of socialization: Theory and research* (2nd ed., pp. 60–84). New York: Guilford Press.

Stice, E., & Gonzales, N. (1998). Adolescent temperament moderates the relation of parenting to antisocial behavior and substance use. *Journal of Adolescent Research, 13,* 5–31.

Stover, C. S., Zhou, Y., Kiselica, A., Leve, L. D., Neiderhise, J. M., Shaw, D. S., et al. (2016). Marital hostility, hostile parenting, and child aggression: Associations from toddlerhood to school age. *Journal of the American Academy of Child and Adolescent Psychiatry, 55,* 235–242.

Stright, A., Gallagher, K., & Kelley, K. (2008). Infant temperament moderates relations between maternal parenting in early childhood and children's adjustment in first grade. *Child Development, 79,* 186–200.

Taylor, Z. E., Eisenberg, N., Spinrad, T. L., & Widaman, K. F. (2013). Longitudinal relations of intrusive parenting and effortful control to ego-resiliency during early childhood. *Child Development, 84,* 1145–1151.

Tiberio, S. S., Capaldi, D. M., Kerr, D. C. R., Bertrand, M., Pears, K. C., & Owen, L. (2016). Parenting and the development of effortful control from early childhood to early adolescence: A transactional developmental model. *Development and Psychopathology, 28,* 837–853.

Tschann, J. M., Kaiser, P., Chesney, M. A., Alkon, A., & Boyce, W. T. (1996). Resilience and vulnerability among preschool children: Family functioning, temperament, and behavior problems. *Journal of the American Academy of Child and Adolescent Psychiatry, 35,* 184–192.

Van den Akker, A. L., Deković, M., Asscher, J., & Prinzie, P. (2014). Mean-level personality development across childhood and adolescence: A temporary defiance of the maturity principle and bidirectional associations with parenting. *Journal of Personality and Social Psychology, 107,* 736–750.

van den Boom, D. C., & Hoeksma, J. B. (1994). The effect of infant irritability on mother–infant interaction: A growth-curve analysis. *Developmental Psychology, 30,* 581–590.

van IJzendoorn, M., & Bakermans-Kranenburg, M. (2006). *DRD4* 7-repeat polymorphism moderates the association between maternal unresolved loss or trauma and infant disorganization. *Attachment and Human Development, 8,* 291–307.

Van Leeuwen, K. G., Mervielde, I., Braet, C., & Bosmans, G. (2004). Child personality and parental behavior as moderators of problem behavior: Variable- and person-centered approaches. *Developmental Psychology, 40,* 1028–1046.

van Zeijl, J., Mesman, J., Stolk, M. N., Alink, L. R. A., & van IJzendoorn, M. H. (2007). Differential susceptibility to discipline: The moderating effect of child temperament on the association between maternal discipline and early childhood externalizing problems. *Journal of Family Psychology, 21,* 626–636.

Veenstra, R., Oldehinkel, A. J., de Winter, A. F., Lindenberg, S., & Ormel, J. (2006). Temperament, environment, and antisocial behavior in a population sample of preadolescent boys and girls. *International Journal of Behavioral Development, 30,* 422–432.

Vernon-Feagans, L., Willoughby, M., Garrett-Peters, P., & the Family Life Project Key Investigators. (2016). Predictors of behavioral regulation in kindergarten: Household chaos, parenting, and early executive functions. *Developmental Psychology, 52,* 430–441.

Vitaro, F., Barker, E. D., Boivin, M., Brendgen, M., & Tremblay, R. (2006). Do early difficult temperament and harsh parenting differentially predict reactive and proactive aggression? *Journal of Abnormal Child Psychology, 34,* 685–695.

Wachs, T. D. (1991). Synthesis: Promising research designs, measures, and strategies. In T. D. Wachs & R. Plomin (Eds.), *Conceptualization and measurement of organism–environment interaction* (pp. 162–182). Washington, DC: American Psychological Association.

Wachs, T. D., & Kohnstamm, G. A. (2001). The bidirectional nature of temperament–context links. In T. D. Wachs & G. A. Kohnstamm (Eds.), *Temperament in context* (pp. 201–222). Mahwah, NJ: Erlbaum.

Whiteside-Mansell, L., Bradley, R. H., Casey, P. H., Fussell, J. J., & Conners-Burrow, N. A. (2009). Triple risk: Do difficult temperament and family conflict increase the likelihood of behavioral maladjustment in children born low birth weight and preterm? *Journal of Pediatric Psychology, 34,* 396–405.

Wilson, S., & Durbin, C. E. (2012). Dyadic parent–child interaction during early childhood: Contributions of parental and child personality traits. *Journal of Personality, 80,* 1313–1338.

Xu, Y., Farver, J. M., & Zhang, Z. (2009). Temperament, harsh and indulgent parenting, and Chinese children's proactive and reactive aggression. *Child Development, 80,* 244–258.

CHAPTER 13

Culture, Context, and the Development of Traits

Helena R. Slobodskaya

The topic of culture and personality is controversial, since *culture* refers to mindsets and patterns of behavior that are similar within groups of people and different between groups, and *personality* refers to patterns of thoughts, feelings, ančd behaviors in which individuals differ from others within a group of people. The systematic study of personality and culture dates from the early 20th century. Anthropological research described a profound impact of culture on personality development (e.g., Mead, 1947), but individual differences within cultures were largely neglected until the wave of interest in temperament and personality in the second half of the 20th century. Most research on the development of traits has been conducted in Westernized, educated, industrialized, rich and democratic (WEIRD) countries. Therefore, it is crucial to consider whether and to what extent the same findings would apply to other cultures. This chapter reviews research on the development of temperament and personality traits in cultural context. The first section presents cultural context of the developing individual and explores what is known about the processes through which both cultural and individual differences are elaborated. The second section describes cultural differences and similarities in trait structure across the life course and ad-

dresses culture-level associations of traits. The third section reviews cross-cultural research on continuity and developmental trends for temperament and personality traits from infancy to old age. The fourth and final section summarizes key research findings and indicates future directions for the study of the development of traits in cultural context.

The Dynamic Interaction between Personality and Culture

Cross-cultural quantitative research on temperament and personality traits has generated considerable debate about the direction of effects: Does culture make people similar or do similar people create their culture? (Hofstede & McCrae, 2004). Like the well-known nature versus nurture debate, this controversy has given way to questions about the mechanisms by which personality and culture interact. A cultural–contextual approach to the study of development (e.g., van de Vijver & Poortinga, 2002) emphasizes a dynamic interaction between person and environment. This section addresses cultural context in the developmental perspective, focusing on interactions between personality and culture across the life course.

Cultural Context

The broad definition of *culture* encompasses patterns of physical and psychosocial environment shared by a group of people. Physical aspects of culture include geography, architecture, clothing, and other objective elements; psychosocial aspects include worldviews (e.g., beliefs, values, attitudes) and practices (Matsumoto, 2007). An important feature of the cultural context is its *hierarchical structure,* with different levels that vary in proximity and breadth. At the lowest level, we have *proximal situations,* such as everyday settings or social interactions. At the medium level, we have *wider contexts,* such as school, work, and family relationships, and at the highest level, we have *broad cultural dimensions,* such as individualism–collectivism (Bronfenbrenner, 1999; Roberts & Pomerantz, 2004). Cultural context can and does exert an influence on the individual (Wachs & Kohnstamm, 2001), providing the rearing environment in the first years of life, socialization experiences in later childhood, and other environmental experiences across the life course. However, it is important to recognize that personality and culture influence one another in a bidirectional manner.

Personality Influences on Cultural Context

Individuals are not only the products but also the producers of their developmental context. Across the life course, individuals modify, select, and create their environments in accordance with their personality; these processes were described by Caspi and Roberts (2001) as *developmental elaboration* of personality traits. Early temperament differences elicit different reactions from other people, beginning in the first days of life. For example, young children with "difficult" temperaments have negative effects on proximal family environment and evoke negative parental practices (Kiff, Lengua, & Zalewski, 2011). Older children become increasingly able to choose their activities and settings. Thus, whereas some adolescents spend much time at parties, others spend much time alone, and still others engage in volunteer work or caring for animals. Young people and adults make choices about education, occupation, and social relationships. Making these choices, they also begin to modify and create their everyday environments. Overall, these processes are likely to promote the development of early-emerging individual differences, in accordance with a *corresponsive principle* of personality development (Roberts & Wood, 2006).

Cultural Influences on Personality

Numerous behavioral genetics studies document that about half of the variance in personality traits is influenced by environmental experiences (e.g., Krueger, South, Johnson, & Iacono, 2008). However, nearly all environmental influences on personality are *nonshared;* that is, they make people different from each other. Thus, genetic and environmental effects on individual differences within single populations cannot explain how culture exerts an influence on personality traits and why people within the same culture are somewhat similar to each other and different from people in other cultures. One suggestion was that culture may primarily influence behavioral manifestations of basic traits. These are called *characteristic adaptations* or *surface traits* and include attitudes, values, beliefs, goals, and habits (McCrae & Costa, 2008). However, a recent review suggests that basic traits and characteristic adaptations are more alike than different in terms of stability and heritability (Kandler, Zimmermann, & McAdams, 2014).

Clearly, more research is needed to determine how cultural context affects the development of temperament and personality traits. There are promising research designs and statistical techniques that may help to resolve this question. For example, in one study of adolescent twins using newer statistical modeling, Krueger and colleagues (2008) found that shared environmental effects on personality in the domains of positive and negative emotionality varied from minimal to moderate, depending on an adolescent's perceived relationship with his or her parents. Thus, the individual's experience of the environment may influence personality development by acting as a moderator of genetic effects.

Social personality models developed by Roberts and colleagues (e.g., Roberts & Wood, 2006) emphasize cultural effects on adult personality development. They suggested that *social investment,* or making commitments to social institutions, such as work and family, is one of the driving mechanisms of personality development toward greater maturation, leading to the increases in agreeableness, conscientiousness, and emotional stability. A recent study of young adults from 62 nations found support for these models, showing that cultures with an earlier onset of job-role responsibilities were marked by earlier personality maturation (Bleidorn et al., 2013). However, effects of marriage and parenthood were inconsistent with the prediction, which suggests that it is not the formal social role that matters so much, but the individual's internalized investment in social roles.

Thus, although there is still more evidence on how early temperament and later personality can and do affect developmental context than on how cultural context affects traits, the pathways work in both directions. More work is needed to unravel the processes through which both cultural and individual differences are elaborated.

The Developmental Niche

The ways culture interacts with the developing child can be understood within the *developmental niche* framework provided by Super and Harkness (1986). The developmental niche has three components operating together: (1) settings of daily life; (2) customs and practices related to childrearing; and (3) the psychology of caregivers. All three components of the developmental niche are influenced by culture and may cause children to acquire similar characteristics in the process of their development. *Settings* of children's daily life may differ markedly across cultures. One good example is sleeping arrangements: Western middle-class infants in the 20th century generally slept through the night alone in their own bed, often in a separate room, whereas in other parts of the world, babies generally slept with their mothers (Keller, 2008). *Customs and practices* of child care and childrearing are inherently incorporated into culture; some are institutionalized. One example is child care arrangements: Whereas in many traditional cultures young children were cared for by several members of the household, in many Western countries in the 1950s and 1960s, young children were cared for principally by their mothers at home, and in the former Soviet Union, children from early infancy onward were brought up in public nurseries and kindergartens (Bronfenbrenner, 1970; Keller, 2008).

The third component of the developmental niche, the psychology of caregivers, includes *parental ethnotheories*—cultural beliefs regarding children, development, and parenting.

These are particularly important because they set goals for development, organize parental strategies of childrearing, and may shape socialization practices (Super & Harkness, 1986). All components of the developmental niche are interrelated. For example, separate sleeping arrangements for infants in Western middle-class cultures were accompanied by a highly valued socialization goal of early independence, whereas mother–infant co-sleeping arrangements are common in the communities that value interdependence and connectedness (Greenfield, Keller, Fuligni, & Maynard, 2003). Overall, the settings and practices are in accord with cultural beliefs about what is and is not "good" for child development. For example, in cultures with co-sleeping arrangements, "the idea that infants would sleep separate from the mother or other family members or, even worse, in a separate room is regarded as child abuse" (Keller, 2008, p. 672). Still, cultural values are not always congruent with everyday settings and practices, and the coherence of the developmental niche framework does not in any way imply that each culture produces specific personality type, as earlier cultural psychology theories suggested.

Interaction between Childhood Temperament and Culture

From early in life, children react differently to the same setting and caregiving, as every parent knows after the birth of the second child. To date, there is convincing evidence that infant temperamental reactivity moderates family influences on child development (Parade, McGeary, Seifer, & Knopik, 2012). For example, Odden (2009) described two distinct types of infant and toddler developmental niche in a Samoan rural community in Western Polynesia: one for fearless, uninhibited, and assertive children, and the other for fearful, inhibited, and restrained children. Odden's longitudinal observations clearly showed how temperamentally different children were differentially treated by caretakers and members of the household. They initiated rough, playful interactions with assertive infants, "faking a punch, pushing them away, running at them aggressively, speaking in an abnormally deep voice, staring at them with crossed eyes, and so forth" (pp. 170–171). When infants responded "aggressively or violently by slapping, striking, or yelling at the adult," this was met with "laughter and amusement from the audience of adult observers" (p. 171), and the interaction escalated in intensity. The restrained children were treated in a highly affectionate manner; they maintained physical proximity with their caretakers and received extensive cuddling and holding. Children with more moderate temperament characteristics occupied "a more normative or modal form of the developmental niche" (p. 171). Thus, individuals with different temperaments may actually live in markedly different contexts within the same culture (Wachs & Kohnstamm, 2001).

Childhood Temperament and Parenting across Cultures

A number of researchers reported that parenting of children with different temperaments differed across cultures. For example, Chen and colleagues (1998) found that Chinese toddlers were more behaviorally inhibited than Canadian toddlers, and that Chinese and Canadian mothers differed in their childrearing attitudes. Chinese mothers of more inhibited children were less punitive and rejecting, and more accepting and encouraging than mothers of less inhibited toddlers, while Canadian mothers of more inhibited children were less accepting and encouraging, and more punitive than mothers of less inhibited toddlers. Although most cross-cultural research on the links between childhood temperament and parenting has focused on Asian–North American comparisons (e.g., Louie, Oh, & Lau, 2013), a few studies have provided evidence from other parts of the world. For example, Cervera and Méndez (2006) examined temperament in Yucatec Mayan infants and toddlers from two rural villages, one with traditional agriculture, and the other with more Westernized commercial production, and found significant differences in traits, as well as in parents' beliefs and perceptions of their children's behavior.

Another study examined the development of toddler self-regulation in Israel and Palestine (Feldman, Masalha, & Alony, 2006). The two cultures differed in patterns of parents' interaction with their children at 5 months of age. Israeli families used more distal face-to-face contact, showed more positive affect, and more often touched, looked at, and presented toys to their infants. Palestinian parents used more close contact, putting infants on their laps and in their arms, and more often exhibited gaze aversion. There were also cultural differences

in parents' teaching strategies at 33 months: In Israel, both fathers and mothers provided more verbal directions, suggestions, and reinforcement, whereas in Palestine, parents provided more concrete help. This study revealed two fascinating phenomena. First, although Israeli toddlers were better able to mobilize actions in response to adult requests, whereas Palestinian toddlers were better able to inhibit action in response to prohibitions, there were no cultural differences in overall levels of toddler self-regulation. Second, predictors of toddler self-regulation were culture-specific, face-to-face interaction and indirect teaching in Israel, and physical contact and concrete help in Palestine.

Overall, research has revealed many similarities and remarkable differences in childrearing settings and practices, and in parental beliefs regarding child development both between and within cultures. Although the findings do not provide strong evidence on the direction of effects, they suggest universal developmental processes and culture-specific pathways to emerging personality traits (Greenfield et al., 2003). These different pathways are often explained by more broad dimensions of culture.

Dimensions of Culture

One of the most influential studies of cultural differences in basic values and situational attitudes is that of Hofstede (2001), who conducted multivariate analyses of 117,000 questionnaires collected by a multinational corporation in 75 countries. This study identified four dimensions of national culture. *Power distance* refers to the extent to which the less powerful members of organizations and institutions expect and accept inequality and status differences. Cultural differences on this dimension are most evident in family customs and organizational practices, in the relations between youngsters and older adults. *Uncertainty avoidance* refers to culture's tolerance for ambiguity. Uncertainty-avoiding cultures minimize the possibility of novel and unstructured situations, relying on strict rules and routines. Uncertainty-accepting cultures are tolerant of varying opinions, taking risks and trying new things; they try to have as few rules as possible. *Masculinity–femininity* refers to the degree to which a culture values behaviors such as assertiveness, achievement, and acquisition of wealth or caring for others, social support, and quality of life. In feminine cultures, both males and females have the same modest and caring values, and there is ambiguity about gender roles. In masculine cultures, males are very assertive and competitive, and there are large gender differences in values.

Individualism–collectivism refers to the degree to which individuals are integrated into groups. In individualist cultures, the ties between individuals are loose, everyone is expected to look after him- or herself, and people value self-expression, independence, and uniqueness. In collectivist cultures, people are integrated from birth onward into strong, cohesive ingroups, such as extended families, they are expected to have unquestioning loyalty to their group, and there is a large psychological distance between ingroup and outgroup members. Individualism–collectivism has been the most popular cultural dimension in cross-cultural studies (Triandis & Suh, 2002). There is evidence for two very different cultural pathways of individual development: one emphasizing uniqueness and independence, the other emphasizing group membership and interdependence (Greenfield et al., 2003). In collectivist cultures, caregiving and socialization center on close body contact and emotional warmth that foster interdependence, and anticipatory responses to children's needs blur the self–other distinction. In individualist cultures, caregivers promote autonomy, encourage exploration, respond to children's signals contingently, and foster assertivenesss and independence (Greenfield et al., 2003).

Hofstede (2001) rated countries on relative scores for each dimension. For power distance, Latin, Asian, and African countries score relatively high, whereas Germanic countries score relatively low. For uncertainty avoidance, scores are relatively high in Latin countries, German-speaking countries, and Japan, and relatively low in Anglo, Nordic, and Chinese cultures. Developed and Western countries score relatively high on individualism, whereas less developed and Eastern countries are high on collectivism. Masculinity is relatively high in Japan and in some European countries, such as Germany, Austria, and Switzerland, whereas femininity is high in Nordic countries and the Netherlands. Dimensions of culture are related to other nationwide variables; for example, power distance is correlated with income inequality, and individualism is correlated with national wealth (Hofstede & McCrae, 2004). However, there is limited agreement about the number and nature of the major culture dimensions (Triandis & Suh, 2002). To make things more complicated, culture is not static, but developing, and may change over time.

Cultural Change

Although dimensions of culture may be relatively stable, cultures have undergone profound changes worldwide. Most recent changes are likely to stem from ongoing *globalization,* the process of interaction and integration among the people of different cultures (Arnett, 2002; Chiu, Gries, Torelli, & Cheng, 2011). Globalization involves access to information about every part of the world; communication with other people worldwide; the spread of global goods, services, and technologies; and international trade, travel, and migration. As a result, there are global trends from rural and agricultural ways of life to urban and commercial; from larger to smaller families and households; from less to more technology, education, competence, equality, competition, wealth, and consumerism; and from collectivism to individualism. In many countries, cultural values and practices have become more westernized, but there are also processes that preserve the integrity of the local culture (Arnett, 2002; Chiu et al., 2011). For example, there is a revival of interest in traditional culture in Russia following a period of westernization after the fall of communism. Another example of preserving a local culture is the closedown of the Starbucks coffee shop in Beijing's Forbidden City in 2007, driven by the following considerations: "The Forbidden City is a symbol of China's cultural heritage. Starbucks is a symbol of lower middle class culture in the west. We need to embrace the world, but we also need to preserve our cultural identity" (Rui, 2007, cited in Chiu et al., 2011).

It is important to remember that all cultures have undergone historical changes. Fortunately, the World Values Survey (2016) nowadays explores people's values and beliefs in more than 90 societies, representing more than 90% of the world population, and allows direct measurement of cultural change since 1981 (Inglehart & Welzel, 2005). There are few quantitative measures of cultural change in earlier times. One example is a secular trends index, which can be derived from any personality questionnaire that has been administered widely for a decade or more (Caspi & Roberts, 2001). It is also possible to study the effect of important historical events and social transformations on personality development in cultures where these changes have taken place. World War II in the countries involved, the fall of communism in Eastern Europe, and the Great Depression and 9/11 in the United States are obvious examples.

Cultural Change and Personality Traits

It seems reasonable to expect that people living through periods of cultural change will show change in personality traits that reflects changing values and social settings in the culture. And indeed, Roberts and Helson (1997) showed that young adults living through the 1960s and 1970s in the United States became more self-focused and less respectful of social norms, which was consistent with increasing individualism in the U.S. culture during this historical period. A more recent study from the Netherlands examined cohort differences in mean levels of the Big Five and found that 18- to 25-year-old students became a little bit more agreeable, conscientious, and extraverted and less neurotic between 1982 and 2007 (Smits, Dolan, Vorst, Wicherts, & Timmerman, 2011). At the same time, however, Japanese 12- to 18-year-old adolescents became less sociable and more neurotic (Kawamoto & Endo, 2015). Although most large-scale studies come from the United States, the findings on cohort-related personality change over the last decades in this country are inconsistent. Terracciano (2010) reviewed a range of longitudinal and cross-cultural studies, and found most support for the secular trend of increasing competence and assertiveness and declining personal relations and trust. These findings suggest that broad cultural context may affect personality traits, although what accounts for heterogeneity in outcome is not at all clear.

Migration and Acculturation

Many people experience profound cultural change as a result of *migration*. Despite popular stereotypes, most migrants in the world do not go abroad at all, but move within their own country; only about one-third of international migrants have moved from a developing to a developed country, and most migrants are happy and tend to be successful (Human Development Report, 2009). Still, migration is a stressful life event and may lead to substantial changes in individuals' values, beliefs, feelings, and behaviors. The processes through which these changes occur have been described as *accul-*

turation. In a broader sense, acculturation is the process of cultural change that occurs when an individual, a group, or an entire culture comes into continuous and intensive contact with another culture. In this broad sense, the processes of change occur at both the individual and the group level (Nauck, 2008). Migration and acculturation provide a natural experiment and an effective test of cultural effects on the development of traits; however, the relevant evidence remains scarce.

One study comparing mother reports of toddler temperament in Italians, Anglo-Australians, and Italo-Australians (Italian mothers living in Australia) found that mean trait levels in the Italians and the Australians were the most different, with the Italo-Australians in between (Axia, Prior, & Carelli, 1992). Findings from later studies, however, are not entirely consistent. For example, Bornstein and Cote (2009) found only few significant differences in temperament of Latin American, Japanese American, and European American 20-month-olds. In a study of infant temperament in Russians and Russian immigrants in Israel and the United States, Gartstein, Peleg, Young, and Slobodskaya (2009) found some differences in mean trait levels and a different pattern of links between temperament and acculturation in Russian–Israeli and Russian–American samples, but the results have been more complex than anticipated.

In summary, cross-cultural developmental research has highlighted the bidirectional relationships between personality and context. It also suggests that from early in life, cultural context affects different individuals in different ways, leading to both individual and cultural differences in thoughts, feelings, and behaviors. To understand fully cross-cultural similarities and differences in the development of traits, it is necessary first to consider whether the same traits and the same structure can be found across ages and cultures.

Trait Structure and Levels across Cultures

In the past two decades, researchers have largely agreed about the hierarchical structure of individual differences (Markon, Krueger, & Watson, 2005). At the first level, we have specific thoughts, feelings, and behaviors in response to everyday situations. At the second level, we have habitual responses that can be measured by inventory items, and at the third level, we have traits that are theoretical and statistical constructs based on intercorrelations of items (e.g., Roberts & Pomerantz, 2004). Traits describe individual differences that are relatively stable over time and across situations, and are themselves intercorrelated. At the higher levels, we have the Big Traits; the best known are domains of the five-factor model—extraversion, neuroticism, agreeableness, conscientiousness, and openness (McCrae & Costa, 2008). Temperament models comprise three broad dimensions of positive emotionality, negative emotionality, and effortful control (Rothbart, 2007). At the two-factor level, we have the metatraits of alpha/stability and beta/plasticity (Shiner & DeYoung, 2013). The reader can also consult previous chapters in this volume for fuller details on the structure of individual differences across the life course. This section examines trait structure across ages and cultures.

Cross-Cultural Structural Research

Top-Down and Bottom-Up Approaches

Two main approaches are used to examine trait structure in different cultures. The *etic* or *top-down* approach takes the existing personality model as the basis for measurement. This approach usually relies on translating and adapting questionnaires developed in the West. For example, much recent research on early individual differences has been conducted using temperament model and questionnaires developed by Rothbart and colleagues (Putnam, Ellis & Rothbart, 2001; Rothbart, 2007). This approach has many advantages over other methods (natural observations or laboratory assessments) because parents observe their children in a wide range of everyday situations; a major limitation is that parent reports include subjective component representing evaluative biases. Rothbart and colleagues' questionnaires partly overcome this problem, focusing on clearly defined child's behaviors in specific situations instead of asking parents to make global judgments or to compare their child to other children. They also use simple and straightforward wording (e.g., "While at home, how often did your child seem afraid of the dark?") and relatively short timeframe (1–2 weeks for infants and toddlers) to ensure accurate recollection (Putnam et al., 2001). These methodological strengths, along with a coherent conceptual framework, make

the temperament model developed by Rothbart and colleagues a promising approach for cross-cultural research on the development of traits. However, a top-down approach may overlook culture-specific or indigenous dimensions.

The *emic* or *bottom-up* approach starts with empirical descriptions of individual differences in thoughts, feelings, and behaviors; evidence for traits derives from factor analysis of the representative set of personality descriptions (Triandis & Suh, 2002). Emic lexical research uses trait descriptors extracted from dictionaries to examine indigenous structures of personality in different languages. Examples of such descriptors in English include *talkative, shy, affectionate, selfish, responsible, lazy, irritable, creative,* and so forth. Lexical studies have found the Big Five in English and Germanic languages. Indigenous structures resembling the Big Five emerged in Slavic languages. The replication of the Big Five has been more problematic in Romance languages. Finally, the structures derived from non-Indo-European languages (Hebrew, Hungarian, Turkish, Korean, and Filipino) only partly reproduced the Big Five traits (Saucier, Hampson, & Goldberg, 2000). Reviewing studies of personality in 13 languages, Saucier and colleagues suggested that one-, two-, and three-factor structures may be more generalizable cross-culturally than the Big Five. More recently, De Raad and colleagues (2010) found that only three factors—extraversion, agreeableness, and conscientiousness—are fully replicable across 12 different languages.

Probably the best way to understand personality structure across diverse cultures is to combine both approaches by adding information from one approach that is not captured by the other. For example, an international research team used a bottom-up approach to identify lower-order traits from free parental descriptions of children. As a result, over 50,000 free parental descriptions of 2- to 13-year-old children have been collected in seven cultures: Belgium, China, Germany, Greece, the Netherlands, Poland, and the United States (Kohnstamm, Halverson, Mervielde, & Havill, 1998). The subsequent factor analyses selected a culturally and age-decentered set of 141 personality descriptors that map onto the Big Five to measure 15 robust traits (Halverson et al., 2003). Combining etic and emic approaches, researchers have found a number of indigenous traits, such as interpersonal relatedness or relationship harmony in South Africa and East Asia (Church, 2008), but the evidence for most culture-specific dimensions is still inconclusive.

Cultural Equivalence

Although research suggests that cross-cultural comparisons of personality may be meaningful, several methodological issues need to be considered. The most important is the *equivalence* of data obtained in the different cultures. This means that personality constructs, such as extraversion or agreeableness, should have the same meaning and should be measured identically across cultures. For example, comparing Big Five traits in Italian and Dutch adolescents ages 11–14 and 15–19, Klimstra, Crocetti, Hale, Fermani, and Meeus (2011) found that although personality structure was roughly similar, full measurement invariance across culture and age was not supported. The authors concluded that traits may have slightly different meanings for Dutch and Italian adolescents. Thus, for Italian adolescents, "agreeable" is being "cooperative" in the first place, while for Dutch adolescents, "agreeable" is more like being "pleasant."

There are different kinds of cultural bias that may potentially distort the findings. There may be cultural differences in response styles, such as *extreme responding,* a tendency to select the endpoints of a response scale (e.g., *strongly agree* or *never*) when answering questions, or *acquiescence,* the tendency to agree with all items, regardless of their content. Additionally, there may be the tendency for respondents to rate traits in comparison to cultural norms (Church, 2008). For example, parents' answers to a temperament questionnaire tend to be influenced by cultural beliefs regarding children. The sensible way to avoid these kinds of biases is to be aware of them and to establish measurement invariance prior to interpretation of cross-cultural differences. It is also helpful to remember that the more replicable the trait structure, the less susceptible it will be to method biases (Saucier et al., 2000). Cross-cultural replicability of the trait structure is discussed next.

The Structure of Childhood Temperament

The findings have supported the three-factor structure of childhood temperament, including positive affectivity, negative affectivity, and regulatory capacity/effortful control, in widely different countries, including Chile, China, Curaçao, Germany, Japan, Korea, Netherlands, Poland, Suriname, and Taiwan (Majdandžić et al., 2009; Maller et al., 2009; Rothbart, Ahadi, Hershey, & Fisher, 2001).

Infancy and Toddlerhood

A more rigorous analysis of trait structure in infancy and toddlerhood has demonstrated measurement equivalence of Rothbart and colleagues' questionnaires in Dutch, Italian, and Russian languages (Casalin, Luyten, Vliegen, & Meurs, 2012; Gartstein, Knyazev, & Slobodskaya, 2005; Montirosso, Cozzi, Putnam, Gartstein, & Borgatti, 2011). There were also cross-cultural differences in the structure of temperament. In infancy, positive affectivity and regulatory capacity were more closely associated in the Russian sample than in the U.S. sample (Gartstein et al., 2005). In toddlerhood, positive affectivity and effortful control were relatively less differentiated in the Japanese sample than in the U.S. sample (Nakagawa, Sukigara, & Mizuno, 2007). The three higher-order factors demonstrated more overlap in Chile than in five other countries (Maller et al., 2009). One possible explanation for these differences is that in more collectivist cultures, such as Chile, Japan, and Russia, traits may be less salient than in more individualist cultures, such as the United States (Church, 2008). It has been found that people from collectivist cultures describe themselves more in terms of social roles and less in terms of traits, and tend to explain behavior by referring to context rather than traits.

Later Childhood

Although the structure of temperament in later childhood was generally similar across cultures, in one study the trait structure in Japan was similar to that in the United States, but different from that in China. Specifically, Smiling and Laughter was primarily associated with effortful control in the U.S. and Japanese samples and with positive affectivity in the Chinese sample (Rothbart et al., 2001). Given that both Japan and China are more collectivist cultures, while the United States is more individualist (Hofstede, 2001), these results are somewhat surprising. A later study revealed notable cross-cultural differences that could not be explained in terms of individualism–collectivism (Majdandžić et al.,

2009). Approach was primarily associated with positive affectivity in the United States and Taiwan, with negative affectivity in Germany, and with both of these factors in the Netherlands and Suriname. Cross-cultural differences in the relationships between higher-order temperament traits suggest different cultural pathways to the development of traits. For example, effortful control was negatively related to positive affectivity in China and to negative affectivity in the United States (Rothbart, 2007).

In summary, the growing body of structural research supports cross-cultural replicability of early temperament traits from infancy to later childhood. The three-factor structure emerged from parent ratings obtained with Rothbart and colleagues' (2001) measures in a wide variety of cultures around the world. Although notable differences await further investigation and explanation, finding a replicable structure of childhood temperament across ages and countries allows researchers to examine differences in mean trait levels.

The Structure of Personality Traits

The Five-Factor Structure

The five-factor structure of personality first received widespread recognition and cross-cultural support. Schmitt and colleagues (2007) provided evidence for the Big Five traits in 56 countries, using 17,837 self-reports on the Big Five Inventory, translated from English into 28 different languages. McCrae and colleagues (2005b) replicated the five-factor structure in 50 nations using 11,985 observer ratings of young people ages 18–21 and adults over age 40. To date, empirical support for the Big Five traits has come from major regions of the world, including North and South America, Europe, South and East Asia, the Middle East, Africa, and Oceania. Two higher-order factors of the Big Five, alpha comprising agreeableness, conscientiousness and neuroticism (reversed), and beta comprising extraversion and openness, have been confirmed in studies with children, adolescents, and adults from the United States (Shiner & DeYoung, 2013) and replicated in Russia (Slobodskaya, 2011).

Evidence from the large-scale study of adolescents indicates that the structure of personality is nearly identical in younger (ages 12–14 years) and older (ages 15–17) adolescents from 24 cultures, including African, Asian, European, and North and South American cultures (De Fruyt et al., 2009). Still, there were minor differences, for example, openness was not replicated in adolescents from Malaysia, Peru, Uganda, South Korea, Slovak Republic, China, and Puerto Rico. Because this trait was clearly identified in adults in most of these countries, it is possible that openness was not fully developed in adolescents in these cultures. However, this research has relied on translations of instruments created in Western countries and may overlook culture-specific or indigenous dimensions.

Childhood Personality

Tackett and colleagues (2012) examined the hierarchical structure of childhood personality in five countries: Canada, China, Greece, Russia, and the United States, and found more similarities than differences across both countries and ages. For all countries and age groups from 2 to 14 years, the Big Traits and their relationships were very similar to established patterns for adults. Cross-cultural differences in this study were mainly explained in terms of individualism–collectivism. Thus, in Canada, Greece, Russia, and the United States, openness emerged as a separate dimension at the five-factor level, although in Russia, openness features played a smaller role. In China, by contrast, openness did not emerge as a separate dimension. This is consistent with previous research that has often failed to find a robust openness dimension in non-Western samples. In another study, Knyazev, Zupančič, and Slobodskaya (2008) used the same personality measure in Slovenia and Russia, and established full measurement invariance of the five-factor structure across culture and ages 2–15.

In summary, cross-cultural research on temperament and personality structure in different age groups indicates that although there are intriguing differences in the hierarchical relationships and the content of traits, to be sure, there are considerable similarities in trait structures from infancy through adulthood across the globe. This suggests that the structural hierarchy of personality is universal. If this is true, then the next question is whether mean trait levels differ across countries, and if so, whether these differences are related to other culture-level variables such as geographical features and Hofstede's (2001) dimensions of culture (Allik & McCrae, 2004).

Aggregate Traits and Dimensions of Culture

The Personality Profiles of Cultures Project examined geographical patterns in mean trait levels across 51 cultures and showed that cultures similar in personality profiles tended to be geographically, historically, and ethnically related (McCrae & Terracciano, 2005a). These findings, together with a previous study of 27,965 self-reports of young people and adults from 36 cultures (Allik & McCrae, 2004), suggest that European and American cultures are higher in extraversion and openness and lower in agreeableness than Asian and African cultures. In another large-scale study, Schmitt and colleagues (2007) showed that people from African regions tended to be low in neuroticism and high in conscientiousness, and that people from East Asia reported less conscientiousness than people from other world regions. These findings are interesting indeed, but they should be viewed with caution because the samples used in the studies were not representative, and there were discrepancies between the results obtained with self- and observer ratings.

The Adolescent Personality Profiles of Cultures Project found that the geographical distribution of personality traits was similar to the adult pattern. There was one notable exception: Whereas adult Russians were relatively low in extraversion and high in neuroticism, and their personality profile was close to that in Asian and African cultures, Russian adolescents appeared to be more extraverted and less neurotic, and their profile was close to that in the United States (McCrae et al., 2010). One possible explanation for this discrepancy between adult and adolescent personality profiles in Russia is that a profound cultural change in Russia has affected personality development in younger age groups.

A recent meta-analysis of temperament data from 18 countries showed a consistent pattern of cross-cultural differences in aggregate trait levels: East Asian cultures were relatively high in negative affectivity and low in positive affectivity and regulatory capacity, whereas Northern European cultures were relatively high in regulatory capacity and low in negative affectivity (Putnam & Gartstein, 2017). It is also notable that negative emotionality was higher in poorer countries, and effortful control was higher in wealthier countries. In this study, cultures high on positive affectivity were also high on extraversion, negative affectivity was consistent with neuroticism, and regulatory capacity with agreeableness.

Hofstede and McCrae (2004) examined the links between the Big Five and dimensions of culture in 33 countries. They found that extraversion was related to individualism and low power distance; neuroticism was associated with uncertainty avoidance and masculinity; agreeableness was related to femininity and uncertainty acceptance; conscientiousness was linked to power distance; and openness was associated with masculinity and low power distance. Putnam and Gartstein (2017) found that temperamental positive emotionality was associated with low power distance; negative emotionality was related to uncertainty avoidance, masculinity, and collectivism; and effortful control was associated with low power distance and femininity. Findings from these two studies are mostly but not completely consistent. Because effortful control is conceptually related to conscientiousness (Rothbart, 2007), one would expect that these two traits should be similarly linked to dimensions of culture. However, the correlation of effortful control with power distance was opposite in direction than that of conscientiousness, suggesting that the relations between temperament and personality at the cultural level may differ from those at the individual level.

In summary, there are meaningful differences in mean trait levels among countries. These differences are related to geography and dimensions of culture, such as individualism, power distance, uncertainty avoidance, and masculinity. Two contrasting explanations for these relations have been proposed: biological and cultural. Current evidence suggests that both biological and contextual influences are relevant. The next challenge is to understand how developmental trajectories of traits differ across countries.

Age Differences in Traits across Cultures

Ideally, cross-cultural comparisons of mean trait levels at different ages should be based on longitudinal data. However, to date, there are only a few cross-cultural longitudinal studies, and evidence from many parts of the world is lacking. Moreover, because most longitudinal studies assess members of a single birth cohort, it is unclear to what extent knowledge about personality development derived from longitudinal studies is historically specific (Caspi &

Roberts, 2001). On the other hand, age differences obtained in cross-sectional studies confound developmental effects with cohort effects of growing up in a particular historical period. This makes it difficult to disentangle three types of effects: age, cohort, and period (time of measurement). More sophisticated research designs and statistical techniques can overcome some of these difficulties (Caspi & Roberts, 2001; Terracciano, 2010); however, one should bear in mind that, in reality, the effects of age, culture, and time co-occur and interact with one another.

Development of Childhood Temperament across Cultures

In a cross-cultural longitudinal study of temperament in 3-, 6-, and 9-month-old infants from China, Spain, and the United States, Gartstein and colleagues (2006) found differences in mean levels, stability, and developmental trajectories of traits across the three cultures. For example, Smiling and Laughter were more stable in the United States than in Spain, Distress to Limitations and Duration of Orienting were more stable in the United States than in China, and Fear was more stable in China than in Spain. Notably, cross-cultural differences in some traits, such as Smiling and Laughter and Activity Level, emerged at 3 months, but disappeared at 9 months, whereas in others, such as Distress to Limitations and Duration of Orienting, they were not observed at 3 months but appeared later. Overall, infants from Spain and the United States were more similar to one another and different from infants from China, suggesting that an Eastern–Western distinction, rather than individualism–collectivism, played a major role in predicting cross-cultural differences in this study.

More recently, Sung, Beijers, Gartstein, de Weerth, and Putnam (2015) compared the development of infant temperament in two Western cultures, the Netherlands and the United States, and found cross-cultural differences in mean levels and stability of traits from ages 6–12 months. For example, although Dutch infants showed higher regulatory capacity and U.S. infants were more fearful, cultural difference on regulatory capacity decreased with age, whereas cultural difference on fear increased. Another study compared the development of toddler effortful control in the United States and Russia (Gartstein, Slobodskaya, Putnam, & Kinsht, 2009) and found that it was predicted

by infant regulatory capacity in both cultures. Positive affectivity also played a role, but only in the U.S. children. Thus, there are both similarities and differences in the developmental trajectories of traits in different countries.

Cross-sectional studies of early temperament traits also suggest that their developmental trajectories may differ across cultures. Two studies comparing early temperament in Italy and the United States found that although the majority of traits showed a consistent pattern of age differences across cultures, developmental course for some traits was different. For example, in Italy, 3- to 6-month-olds showed less smiling and laughter than 6- to 9-month-olds, whereas 3- to 6-month-olds and 6- to 9-month-olds did not differ in the United States (Montirosso et al., 2011). In Italy, soothability increased from 18 to 38 months of age, whereas in the United States, mean levels of this trait did not differ significantly (Cozzi et al., 2013). Another study of early temperament in Japan, Russia, and the United States also found that the pattern of age differences for some traits varied across cultures. For example, from 3 months to 3 years of age children from Japan, Russia, and the U.S. became more alike in their expression of positive affect (Slobodskaya, Gartstein, Nakagawa, & Putnam, 2013).

The question of whether there is a consistent pattern of cultural differences in the development of childhood temperament remains unanswered by the relatively few cross-cultural studies involving different age groups. Existing evidence does suggest, however, that there are more similarities than differences across countries. It also appears that cross-cultural differences in developmental trajectories are trait-specific: In some domains, they decrease with age, whereas in others, they increase.

Development of Personality Traits across Cultures

Childhood Personality

The study of free parental descriptions of 2- to 13-year-old children found very similar age differences across seven countries (Slotboom, Havill, Pavlopolus, & De Fruyt, 1998). These similarities are remarkable when we consider the large geographic, cultural, and language differences between the samples involved. For example, China and Greece have ancient histories while the United States is relatively young. Recent history in the countries also differed dramatically: Poland and China shared

Communist political rule, while other cultures were more liberal and egalitarian. Chinese culture has been shaped by Buddhist and Confucian traditions; the dominant religion in Poland and Greece is Orthodox Christianity, and other cultures are predominately Protestant. Still, there were notable cultural differences in parental descriptions of children of different ages. For example, in all countries, parents of older children more often used conscientiousness descriptors (e.g., good concentration, reliable, and hardworking or forgetful, careless, and lazy) than parents of younger children, but from age 6, Chinese parents described their children as "easily distracted," "not motivated enough," and "indolent" much more often than did parents from other countries. The authors suggested that this might reflect the importance of high achievement and effortful self-improvement in China based on the Confucian doctrine.

A later study found that cultural differences in personality traits of 3- to 14-year-olds in two Slavic countries, Slovenia and Russia, do not tend to increase with age, but developmental trends for some traits went in the opposite direction (Slobodskaya & Zupančič, 2010). For example, neuroticism and negative affect decreased with age in Slovenians, and increased in Russians, whereas positive emotionality increased in Slovenians and decreased in Russians. These two cultures are largely similar to one another in terms of language, religion, and recent history; however, there may be considerable differences in children's developmental niche and their biological characteristics. The Adolescent Personality Profiles of Cultures Project compared mean levels of the Big Five in 12- to 14- and 15- to 17-year-olds from 24 cultures (McCrae et al., 2010). Culture accounted for 3.5% of variance; cultural differences were largest for extraversion and smallest for agreeableness. Although age accounted for less than 1.5% of variance, age differences in neuroticism and openness varied across cultures. Thus, the findings suggest that childhood personality traits change in similar, but not identical, ways in different cultures.

Personality Development in Adulthood

A cross-cultural comparison suggested similar levels of personality stability in North America, Europe, and the South Pacific, although personality traits in people from the South Pacific (Australia and New Zealand) were somewhat less stable than in other cultures (Ferguson, 2010). The Personality Profiles of Cultures Project compared mean levels of 30 personality traits comprising the Big Five in young people ages 18–21 years and adults ages 40–98 years from 50 cultures representing six continents (McCrae & Terracciano, 2005b). The effects of culture were similar to those seen in adolescents (about 4%), but in adults, cultural differences were largest for openness and smallest for neuroticism and conscientiousness. Age accounted for about 3% of variance in the Big Five. In general, conscientiousness and agreeableness increased with age, while extraversion, openness, and neuroticism declined. However, age differences in all traits varied across cultures. For example, adults were more agreeable than young people in 10 cultures, and more disagreeable in Japan and Portugal. Neuroticism declined in six cultures and increased in two cultures—Estonia and Slovakia (McCrae & Terracciano, 2005b). The authors note that there are no obvious explanations for these discrepancies. Still, similarities are more remarkable than differences when we consider geographic, cultural, and language differences between the samples.

A later study examined Big Five traits in 884,328 individuals ages 16–40 years from 62 countries (Bleidorn et al., 2013) and found strong evidence for universal personality maturation from early to middle adulthood and slight but significant cultural differences in age effects on personality traits. Examining the links between age differences in adult personality traits and cultural dimensions, McCrae and Terracciano (2005a) found that age-related increases in conscientiousness were larger and age-related declines in extraversion were smaller in cultures higher in individualism and national wealth, and lower in power distance. Age differences in agreeableness and openness were positively related to individualism. Why? Perhaps some features of more proximal context could explain these links, but this has not yet been investigated.

In summary, evidence from large-scale studies strongly suggests that the development of traits follows a universal pattern. Still, there are notable cultural differences in age-related changes in personality. These differences may be caused by biological predispositions or cultural context, or both. Cross-cultural research has shown that age differences in personality are related to cultural dimensions; however, the nature of this relationship is not well understood. It is also important to remember that the effects of culture on traits are not large, and that most of the variance in personality arises in the differences among individuals, not in the differences among cultures.

Conclusion and Future Directions

This chapter is a review of the relations between cultural context and personality traits in the developmental perspective. Culture is viewed here as the organization of the developmental environment, like a garden in which conditions for growth are created (Super & Harkness, 2002; van de Vijver & Poortinga, 2002). As such, it is important to consider different levels of cultural context. It is reasonable to expect that proximal situations, such as childrearing practices and social interactions, would be more closely related to individual's thoughts, feelings, and behaviors than more distal environments, such as school, work, climate, or cultural dimensions, and that the effects of cultural dimensions may be mediated by more proximal settings.

This understanding has been supported by empirical evidence. Many studies have demonstrated the links between parenting and childhood traits. There is also evidence that the parenting of children with similar personalities differs across cultures, and that people from different cultures hold very different views on caregiving and parenting. These findings suggest that the developmental niche may lead to cross-cultural differences in the development of traits, although the underlying causal mechanisms are still unclear. Research on the development of traits in childhood and adulthood confirms cultural influences on personality stability and change, suggesting that universal processes of maturation may be affected by the timing of family and job transitions. These findings also indicate that more distal influences, such as cultural dimensions, are mediated by more proximal contexts of family or work, which, in turn, should be mediated by the individual's values and attitudes.

As seen in this chapter, it is also important to consider different levels of personality constructs. Most research on the links between personality and culture has focused on the Big Five traits, while cross-cultural studies of early temperament have mainly utilized age-specific measures of lower-order traits, and more recently, three higher-order dimensions. The evidence on the universality of the hierarchical structure of personality and temperament (Markon et al., 2005; Tackett et al., 2012) across ages and cultures may help to organize and to make sense of the existing data. Following Roberts and Pomerantz's (2004) conclusion, I suggest in this chapter that making the person–culture hierarchies explicit would provide insights into the understanding of the cultural pathways of the development of traits.

The dynamic interaction between personality and culture creates, in effect, different developmental contexts for different children. While prescribing broad guidelines for acceptable conduct, every culture allows a wide range of specific behaviors in everyday situations (Matsumoto, 2007), guiding the development of early temperament and later personality. This understanding of how the dynamic interaction between person and culture leads to the development of both individual and cultural differences in traits helps to resolve a controversy surrounding the relationship between personality and culture. However, the specific mechanisms of personality development in cultural context await further research. Wrzus and Roberts (2017) recently proposed a theoretical framework for explaining how long-term personality development can occur as a result of daily experiences that cumulate over time, but this model needs to be tested empirically. Ongoing globalization provide a natural experiment and an opportunity to relate cultural change to the development of traits, and new communication technologies provide the means to conduct large-scale longitudinal studies all over the world. It is my hope that the near future will bring great advances in our knowledge of the relations between culture and the development of traits.

ACKNOWLEDGMENTS

Preparation of this chapter was supported by grants from the Russian Scientific Foundation (No. 16-18-00003) and Russian Foundation for Basic Research (No. 16-06-00022).

REFERENCES

Allik, J., & McCrae, R. R. (2004). Toward a geography of personality traits: Patterns of profiles across 36 cultures. *Journal of Cross-Cultural Psychology,* *35*(1), 13–28.

Arnett, J. J. (2002). The psychology of globalization. *American Psychologist, 57*(10), 774–783.

Axia, G., Prior, M., & Carelli, M. G. (1992). Cultural influences on temperament: A comparison of Italian, Italo-Australian, and Anglo-Australian toddlers. *Australian Psychologist, 27*(1), 52–56.

Bleidorn, W., Klimstra, T. A., Denissen, J. J. A., Rentfrow, P. J., Potter, J., & Gosling, S. D. (2013). Personality maturation around the world: A cross-cultural examination of social-investment theory. *Psychological Science, 24*(12), 2530–2540.

Bornstein, M. H., & Cote, L. R. (2009). Child temperament in three U.S. cultural groups. *Infant Mental Health Journal, 30*(5), 433–451.

Bronfenbrenner, U. (1970). *Two worlds of childhood: U.S. and USSR.* New York: Sage.

Bronfenbrenner, U. (1999). Environments in developmental perspective: Theoretical and operational models. In S. L. Friedman, & T. D. Wachs (Eds.), *Measuring environment across the life span: Emerging methods and concepts* (pp. 3–28). Washington, DC: American Psychological Association Press.

Casalin, S., Luyten, P., Vliegen, N., & Meurs, P. (2012). The structure and stability of temperament from infancy to toddlerhood: A one-year prospective study. *Infant Behavior and Development, 35*(1), 94–108.

Caspi, A., & Roberts, B. W. (2001). Personality development across the life course: The argument for change and continuity. *Psychological Inquiry, 12*(2), 49–66.

Cervera, M. D., & Méndez, R. M. (2006). Temperament and ecological context among Yucatec Mayan children. *International Journal of Behavioral Development, 30*(4), 326–337.

Chen, X., Hastings, P. D., Rubin, K. H., Chen, H., Cen, G., & Stewart, S. L. (1998). Child-rearing attitudes and behavioral inhibition in Chinese and Canadian toddlers: A cross-cultural study. *Developmental Psychology, 34*(4), 677–686.

Chiu, C. Y., Gries, P., Torelli, C. J., & Cheng, S. Y. (2011). Toward a social psychology of globalization. *Journal of Social Issues, 67*(4), 663–676.

Church, A. T. (2008). Current controversies in the study of personality across cultures. *Social and Personality Psychology Compass, 2*(5), 1930–1951.

Cozzi, P., Putnam, S. P., Menesini, E., Gartstein, M. A., Aureli, T., Calussi, P., et al. (2013). Studying cross-cultural differences in temperament in toddlerhood: United States of America (U.S.) and Italy. *Infant Behavior and Development, 36*(3), 480–483.

De Fruyt, F., De Bolle, M., McCrae, R. R., Terracciano, A., Costa, P. T., & 43 Collaborators of the Adolescent Personality Profiles of Cultures Project. (2009). Assessing the universal structure of personality in early adolescence: The NEO-PI-R and NEO-PI-3 in 24 cultures. *Assessment, 16*(3), 301–311.

De Raad, B., Barelds, D. P., Levert, E., Ostendorf, F., Mlačić, B., Blas, L. D., et al. (2010). Only three factors of personality description are fully replicable across languages: A comparison of 14 trait taxonomies. *Journal of Personality and Social Psychology, 98*(1), 160–173.

Feldman, R., Masalha, S., & Alony, D. (2006). Micro-regulatory patterns of family interactions: Cultural pathways to toddlers' self-regulation. *Journal of Family Psychology, 20*(4), 614–623.

Ferguson, C. J. (2010). A meta-analysis of normal and disordered personality across the life span. *Journal of Personality and Social Psychology, 98*(4), 659–667.

Gartstein, M. A., Gonzalez, C., Carranza, J. A., Ahadi, S. A., Ye, R., Rothbart, M. K., et al. (2006). Studying cross-cultural differences in the development of infant temperament: People's Republic of China, the United States of America, and Spain. *Child Psychiatry and Human Development, 37*(2), 145–161.

Gartstein, M. A., Knyazev, G. G., & Slobodskaya, H. R. (2005). Cross-cultural differences in the structure of infant temperament: United States of America (U.S.) and Russia. *Infant Behavior and Development, 28,* 54–61.

Gartstein, M. A., Peleg, Y., Young, B. N., & Slobodskaya, H. R. (2009). Infant temperament in Russia, United States of America, and Israel: Differences and similarities between Russian-speaking families. *Child Psychiatry and Human Development, 40*(2), 241–256.

Gartstein, M. A., Slobodskaya, H. R., Putnam, S. P., & Kinsht, I. A. (2009). A cross-cultural study of infant temperament: Predicting preschool effortful control in the United States of America and Russia. *European Journal of Developmental Psychology, 6*(3), 337–364.

Greenfield, P. M., Keller, H., Fuligni, A., & Maynard, A. (2003). Cultural pathways through universal development. *Annual Review of Psychology, 54*(1), 461–490.

Halverson, C. F., Havill, V. L., Deal, J., Baker, S. R., Victor, J., Pavlopoulos, V., et al. (2003). Personality structure as derived from parental ratings of free descriptions of children: The Inventory of Child Individual Differences. *Journal of Personality, 71*(6), 995–1026.

Hofstede, G. (2001). *Culture's consequences: Comparing values, behaviors, institutions and organizations across nations* (2nd ed.). Beverly Hills, CA: SAGE.

Hofstede, G., & McCrae, R. R. (2004). Personality and culture revisited: Linking traits and dimensions of culture. *Cross-Cultural Research, 38*(1), 52–88.

Human Development Report. (2009). *Overcoming barriers: Human mobility and development.* Basingstoke, UK: Palgrave Macmillan.

Inglehart, R., & Welzel, C. (2005). *Modernization, cultural change and democracy: The human development sequence.* New York: Cambridge University Press.

Kandler, C., Zimmermann, J., & McAdams, D. P. (2014). Core and surface characteristics for the description and theory of personality differences and development. *European Journal of Personality, 28*(3), 231–243.

Kawamoto, T., & Endo, T. (2015). Personality change in adolescence: Results from a Japanese sample. *Journal of Research in Personality, 57,* 32–42.

Keller, H. (2008). Culture and biology: The foundation of pathways of development. *Social and Personality Psychology Compass, 2*(2), 668–681.

Kiff, C. J., Lengua, L. J., & Zalewski, M. (2011). Nature and nurturing: Parenting in the context of child temperament. *Clinical Child and Family Psychology Review, 14*(3), 251–301.

Klimstra, T. A., Crocetti, E., Hale, W. W., III, Fermani, A., & Meeus, W. H. (2011). Big Five personality dimensions in Italian and Dutch adolescents: A cross-cultural comparison of mean-levels, sex differences, and associations with internalizing symptoms. *Journal of Research in Personality, 45*(3), 285–296.

Knyazev, G. G., Zupančič, M., & Slobodskaya, H. R. (2008). Child personality in Slovenia and Russia: Structure and mean level of traits in parent and self-ratings. *Journal of Cross-Cultural Psychology, 39*(3), 317–334.

Kohnstamm, G. A., Halverson, C. F., Jr., Mervielde, I., & Havill, V. L. (Eds.). (1998). *Parental descriptions of child personality: Developmental antecedents of the Big Five?* Mahwah, NJ: Erlbaum.

Krueger, R. F., South, S., Johnson, W., & Iacono, W. (2008). The heritability of personality is not always 50%: Gene–environment interactions and correlations between personality and parenting. *Journal of Personality, 76*(6), 1485–1522.

Louie, J. Y., Oh, B. J., & Lau, A. S. (2013). Cultural differences in the links between parental control and children's emotional expressivity. *Cultural Diversity and Ethnic Minority Psychology, 19*(4), 424–434.

Majdandžić, M., Putnam, S. P., Siib, F., Kung, J.-F., Lay, K.-L., van Liempt, I., et al. (2009, April). *Cross-cultural investigation of temperament in early childhood using the Children's Behavior Questionnaire.* Paper presented at the biennial meeting of the Society for Research in Child Development, Denver, CO.

Maller, R. D., Nakagawa, A., Slobodskaya, H. R., Ogura, T., Lee, J., Park, C., et al. (2009, April). *Mean-level and structural comparisons of fine-grained temperament attributes in toddlers from multiple countries.* Paper presented at the biennial meeting of the Society for Research in Child Development, Denver, CO.

Markon, K. E., Krueger, R. F., & Watson, D. (2005). Delineating the structure of normal and abnormal personality: An integrative hierarchical approach. *Journal of Personality and Social Psychology, 88*(1), 139–157.

Matsumoto, D. (2007). Culture, context, and behavior. *Journal of Personality, 75*(6), 1285–1320.

McCrae, R. R., & Costa, P. T., Jr. (2008). Empirical and theoretical status of the five-factor model of personality traits. In G. Boyle, G. Matthews, & D. Saklofske (Eds.), *SAGE handbook of personality theory and assessment* (Vol. 1, pp. 273–294). Los Angeles: SAGE.

McCrae, R. R., & Terracciano, A. (2005a). Personality profiles of cultures: Aggregate personality traits. *Journal of Personality and Social Psychology, 89*(3), 407–425.

McCrae, R. R., & Terracciano, A. (2005b). Personality profiles of cultures: Universal features of personality traits from the observer's perspective: Data from 50 cultures. *Journal of Personality and Social Psychology, 88*(3), 547–561.

McCrae, R. R., Terracciano, A., De Fruyt, F., De Bolle, M., Gelfand, M. J., & Costa, P. T., Jr., et al. (2010). The validity and structure of culture-level personality scores: Data from ratings of young adolescents. *Journal of Personality, 78*(3), 815–838.

Mead, M. (1947). The implications of culture change for personality development. *American Journal of Orthopsychiatry, 17*(4), 633–646.

Montirosso, R., Cozzi, P., Putnam, S. P., Gartstein, M. A., & Borgatti, R. (2011). Studying cross-cultural differences in temperament in the first year of life: United States and Italy. *International Journal of Behavioral Development, 35*(1), 27–37.

Nakagawa, A., Sukigara, M., & Mizuno, R. (2007, April). *Cultural effects reflected in the Early Childhood Behavior Questionnaire for Japanese toddlers: Psychometrics and factor structure.* Paper presented at the biennial meeting of the Society for Research in Child Development, Boston, MA.

Nauck, B. (2008). Acculturation. In F. J. R. Van de Vijver, D. A. van Hemert, & Y. H. Poortinga (Eds.), *Multilevel analysis of individuals and cultures* (pp. 249–283). Mahwah, NJ: Erlbaum.

Odden, H. L. (2009). Interactions of temperament and culture: The organization of diversity in Samoan infancy. *Ethos, 37*(2), 161–180.

Parade, S. H., McGeary, J., Seifer, R., & Knopik, V. (2012). Infant development in family context: Call for a genetically informed approach. *Frontiers in Genetics, 3,* 167.

Putnam, S. P., Ellis, L. K., & Rothbart, M. K. (2001). The structure of temperament from infancy through adolescence. In A. Eliasz & A. Angleitner (Eds.), *Advances/proceedings in research on temperament* (pp. 165–182). Lengerich, Germany: Pabst Scientist.

Putnam, S. P., & Gartstein, M. A. (2017). Aggregate temperament scores from multiple countries: Associations with aggregate personality traits, cultural dimensions, and allelic frequency. *Journal of Research in Personality, 67,* 157–170.

Roberts, B. W., & Helson, R. (1997). Changes in culture, changes in personality: The influence of individualism in a longitudinal study of women. *Journal of Personality and Social Psychology, 72*(3), 641–651.

Roberts, B. W., & Pomerantz, E. M. (2004). On traits, situations, and their integration: A developmental perspective. *Personality and Social Psychology Review, 8*(4), 402–416.

Roberts, B. W., & Wood, D. (2006). Personality development in the context of the neosocioanalytic model of personality. In D. Mroczek & T. D. Little (Eds.),

Handbook of personality development (pp. 11–39). Mahwah, NJ: Erlbaum.

Rothbart, M. K. (2007). Temperament, development and personality. *Current Directions in Psychological Science, 16,* 207–212.

Rothbart, M. K., Ahadi, S. A., Hershey, K. L., & Fisher, P. (2001). Investigations of temperament at three to seven years: The Children's Behavior Questionnaire. *Child Development, 72*(5), 1394–1408.

Saucier, G., Hampson, S. E., & Goldberg, L. R. (2000). Cross-language studies of lexical personality factors. In S. E. Hampson (Ed.), *Advances in personality psychology* (Vol. 1, pp. 1–36). East Sussex, UK: Psychology Press.

Schmitt, D. P., Allik, J., McCrae, R. R., Benet-Martinez, V., Alcalay, L., Ault, L., et al. (2007). The geographic distribution of Big Five personality traits: Patterns and profiles of human self-description across 56 nations. *Journal of Cross-Cultural Psychology, 38*(2), 173–212.

Shiner, R. L., & DeYoung, C. G. (2013). The structure of temperament and personality traits: A developmental perspective. In P. Zelazo (Ed.), *Oxford handbook of developmental psychology* (pp. 113–141). New York: Oxford University Press.

Slobodskaya, H. R. (2011). Two superordinate personality factors in childhood. *European Journal of Personality, 25*(6), 453–464.

Slobodskaya, H. R., Gartstein, M. A., Nakagawa, A., & Putnam, S. P. (2013). Early temperament in Japan, the United States, and Russia: Do cross-cultural differences decrease with age? *Journal of Cross-Cultural Psychology, 44*(3), 438–460.

Slobodskaya, H. R., & Zupančič, M. (2010). Development and validation of the Inventory of Child Individual Differences—Short version in two Slavic countries. *Studia Psychologica, 52,* 23–39.

Slotboom, A.-M., Havill, V. L., Pavlopulos, V., & De Fruyt, F. (1998). Developmental changes in personality descriptions of children: A cross-national comparison of parental descriptions of children. In G. A. Kohnstamm, C. F. Halverson, Jr., I. Mervielde, & V. L. Havill (Eds.), *Parental descriptions of child personality: Developmental antecedents of the Big Five?* (pp. 155–168). Mahwah, NJ: Erlbaum.

Smits, I. A., Dolan, C. V., Vorst, H., Wicherts, J. M., & Timmerman, M. E. (2011). Cohort differences in Big Five personality factors over a period of 25 years. *Journal of Personality and Social Psychology, 100*(6), 1124–1138.

Sung, J., Beijers, R., Gartstein, M. A., de Weerth, C., & Putnam, S. P. (2015). Exploring temperamental differences in infants from the USA and the Netherlands. *European Journal of Developmental Psychology, 12*(1), 15–28.

Super, C. M., & Harkness, S. (1986). The developmental niche: A conceptualization at the interface of child and culture. *International Journal of Behavioral Development, 9*(4), 545–569.

Super, C. M., & Harkness, S. (2002). Culture structures the environment for development. *Human Development, 45*(4), 270–274.

Tackett, J. L., Slobodskaya, H. R., Mar, R. A., Deal, J., Halverson, C. F., Baker, S. R., et al. (2012). The hierarchical structure of childhood personality in five countries: Continuity from early childhood to early adolescence. *Journal of Personality, 80,* 847–879.

Terracciano, A. (2010). Secular trends and personality: Perspectives from longitudinal and cross-cultural studies—Commentary on Trzesniewski and Donnellan. *Perspectives on Psychological Science, 5*(1), 93–96.

Triandis, H. C., & Suh, E. M. (2002). Cultural influences on personality. *Annual Review of Psychology, 53*(1), 133–160.

van de Vijver, F. J., & Poortinga, Y. H. (2002). On the study of culture in developmental science. *Human Development, 45*(4), 246–256.

Wachs, T. D., & Kohnstamm, G. A. (Eds.). (2001). *Temperament in context.* Mahwah, NJ: Erlbaum.

World Values Survey. (2016). Retrieved August 28, 2016, from *www.worldvaluessurvey.org.*

Wrzus, C., & Roberts, B. W. (2017). Processes of personality development in adulthood: The TESSERA framework. *Personality and Social Psychology Review, 21*(3), 253–277.

CHAPTER 14

Stability and Change in Personality Traits over the Lifespan

Wiebke Bleidorn
Christopher J. Hopwood

Dodge Morgan's exciting, eccentric lifestyle provides a rich opportunity for considering factors that might impact personality stability and change. As a young Air Force pilot, Dodge had narrowly escaped death in a jet in an emergency crash landing. Having earned his journalism degree in Massachusetts, he and his family moved to remote Alaska, only to return by sailboat several years later to start a company producing radar detectors. During middle age, he sold his tremendously successful company and used the profits to fulfill a lifelong dream: Dodge sailed around the world alone in a record 150 days, without stopping or replenishing his supplies.

Extensive multimethod data had been collected before, during, and after Dodge's journey. Four months prior and following the trip, Dodge was administered measures of personality traits, needs, motives, and cognitive abilities. During the voyage, he completed daily assessments of emotions and cognition, as well as a narrative log of his experiences. In 1997, Nasby and Read, and a number of eminent personality psychologists, analyzed, synthesized, and presented these data in a special issue of the *Journal of Personality.*

Results illuminated both stability and change in Dodge's personality. Pre–post questionnaire data suggested a substantial degree of consistency in Dodge's personality despite this dra-

matic event: He remained fiercely independent, autonomous, and relatively uninterested in close relationships. At the same time, there was evidence of a softening of his personality traits in the direction of an increased desire for nurturance and interest in social recognition.

This case study touched on a number of interesting questions about personality trait stability and change. How stable are our personality traits, in general? When, why, and how much do personality traits change? Do our struggles and triumphs in life leave a permanent mark on our personality, or are we impervious to such influences? Are we more or less susceptible to personality change at different points in our life? To what degree does nature or nurture influence personality stability and change? This case also highlighted a number of thorny methodological issues, such as issues related to sampling, measurement, and conceptualizations of stability and change.

In this chapter, we review the current state of scientific evidence regarding stability and change in personality traits from late childhood to old age. In order to balance the complexity of this topic against brevity constraints of a single chapter, our review focuses on the "Big Five" domains of *neuroticism, extraversion, openness to experience, agreeableness,* and *conscientiousness* (John, Naumann, & Soto, 2008). Although there are many potential broader and narrower traits to consider (Markon, Krueger, & Watson, 2006), the Big Five traits represent a viable balance among conceptual breadth, descriptive fidelity, and generalizability across samples and measures (Soto & Tackett, 2015).

We begin by describing some methodological issues to consider when studying personality stability and change, with an emphasis on the most common research designs and statistical approaches in the existing literature. We next move to a description of four major stages of the lifespan in which different patterns of stability and change might be anticipated: *late childhood and adolescence, emerging and young adulthood, middle adulthood,* and *old age* (cf. Tackett, Balsis, Oltmanns, & Krueger, 2009). In reviewing this literature, we focus on three sets of questions. First, how stable are traits within each life stage and across the lifespan? Second, when and how do traits change? Third, what are the causes and conditions of stability and change? We conclude by outlining important areas for future research on personality stability and change.

Methodological Considerations

Questions about personality trait stability can be answered using different research designs and statistical approaches. A basic distinction involves the type of stability and change under consideration. Although there are various ways to conceptualize stability and change (De Fruyt et al., 2006), we focus on the two that have been examined most often in the literature. *Rank-order stability* reflects the degree to which the relative ordering of individuals maintains over time. The test–retest correlation (r) across two assessment waves is the simplest way to quantify rank-order stability. Cohen (1988) classified correlations around .10 as small, .30 as medium, and .50 as large. By this standard, personality is relatively but not perfectly stable across the lifespan, as described in detail below. Whereas rank-order stability indicates the degree to which different people experience more or less change relative to one another, *mean-level change* reflects the degree to which a trait decreases or increases among all people in a population, on average. The simplest estimate of mean-level change is the standardized mean difference across two assessments (e.g., Cohen's d). Cohen classified d values of .20 (meaning that two means differed by .20 standard

deviations) as small, .50 as medium, and .70 as large. As described below, mean-level changes in personality traits tend to be relatively small, although this depends on sampling interval and varies across different life stages.

Another consideration has to do with how personality data are sampled to examine stability and change. In *cross-sectional* designs, people are compared at different ages at a single point in time and within-person variation is not evaluated. There are two main limitations to cross-sectional designs. First, because there is only one assessment for each person, it is not possible to examine rank-order stability. Second, it is possible that mean-level differences across ages reflect birth-cohort effects rather than, or in addition to, aging effects (Schaie, 1977). For example, if baby boomers were more strongly socialized to be self-centered and hedonistic than older generations, negative cross-sectional age differences in agreeableness could be observed across these baby boomer and older cohorts, even if individuals from each group did not become more agreeable as they aged. Nevertheless, cross-sectional designs can be informative about mean-level differences in personality traits at different ages, particularly when samples are large and a wide age range is covered (e.g., Bleidorn et al., 2013; Soto, John, Gosling, & Potter, 2008, 2011; Srivastava, John, Gosling, & Potter, 2003).

In *longitudinal designs,* the same people are assessed multiple times over the course of their development. Longitudinal studies are ideal for examining stability and change; however, they are resource intensive and not always feasible. When using longitudinal designs, a number of issues need to be considered. The first issue involves how often to sample individuals in longitudinal designs. Although early studies that focused on retest correlations and mean differences across two time points provided a rich foundation for understanding stability and change, researchers have increasingly recognized the limitations of examining personality development using only two waves of data. Estimates of rank-order stability across multiple ages and varying time intervals can reveal the enduring nature of personality traits and identify phases of more or less stability, with greater nuance and flexibility than retest correlations from two waves of data (Fraley & Roberts, 2005). Likewise, multiple time points permit the use of more advanced statistical approaches, such as latent growth curve modeling, to model stability and change in personality traits (e.g., Bleidorn, Kandler, Riemann, Angleitner, & Spinath, 2009; Hopwood et al., 2011). Such approaches also provide more reliable estimates than retest correlations from two waves of data, and allow for a more flexible modeling of the shape of mean-level change (e.g., linear, quadratic, cubic) in personality traits (Luhmann, Orth, Specht, Kandler, & Lucas, 2014).

A second issue concerns the timing of assessments in longitudinal designs. Frequent assessments within and across each life stage are ideal for examining developmental processes. Frequent assessments not only permit more flexibility with data analysis, as described earlier, but they also enable the observation of more nuanced levels of stability and change across the lifespan and in response to certain life events. In general, more confident conclusions can be drawn from studies in which large samples of people are assessed relatively often, using frequent assessments across the lifespan.

In what follows, we review the findings of cross-sectional and longitudinal studies on personality rank-order stability and mean-level change in Big Five personality traits across late childhood/adolescence, emerging/early adulthood, middle adulthood, and old age. By integrating the results of studies with different research designs and statistical approaches to stability and change, we hope to provide a more complete picture of stability and change in Big Five traits across different life stages.

Late Childhood and Adolescence

Scholars have historically distinguished child temperament and adult personality traits, leading to relatively nonoverlapping literatures on developmental patterns in childhood and adulthood (Shiner & Caspi, 2003). This distinction has been challenged in more recent theoretical and empirical work that emphasizes the overlap between temperament and personality (e.g., Caspi, Roberts, & Shiner, 2005). Given that respondents as young as age 10 can provide reliable information about their own Big Five personality traits (Soto et al., 2008, 2011), we focus here on studies that examined personality stability and change in Big Five personality traits from late childhood (age ~10) through late adolescence (age ~18) (for a review of research on stability and change in child temperament, see Tucker-Drob & Briley, Chapter 3, this volume).

A range of important physical, social, and psychological changes that may relate to personality development occurs during late childhood and adolescence. In addition to physical growth and body changes, there are significant changes in brain anatomy and chemistry (e.g., Blakemore, 2008; Casey, Jones, & Hare; 2008; Keating, 2004). In the social sphere, peer relationships become increasingly important (Reitz, Zimmermann, Hutteman, Specht, & Neyer, 2014), attitudes toward social norms change (e.g., Eisenberg & Morris, 2004), and romantic relationships emerge (Collins, 2003). Important psychological changes include substantial gains in youths' cognitive, emotional, and behavioral skills, and the development of a more coherent, abstract, and differentiated self-concept (Erikson, 1968; Harter, 2006; Inhelder & Piaget, 1958; Soto et al., 2008; Soto & Tackett, 2015). Several cross-sectional and longitudinal studies have begun to map the stability and change in personality traits across childhood and adolescence to examine the degree to which these rapid developmental changes likely have implications for youths' personality trait development (Denissen, van Aken, Penke, & Wood, 2013; Soto & Tackett, 2015).

Rank-Order Stability

Theory and research suggest that some of the aforementioned developmental changes during late childhood and adolescence may contribute to increases in personality trait stability. For instance, the development of a more coherent, stable, and differentiated identity should provide youth with a schema through which behaviors and life experiences can be organized, leading to more consistent patterns of trait-relevant behavior (Roberts & DelVecchio, 2000). The formation of relatively stable peer and romantic relationships may also have stabilizing effects on youths' personality traits (Harris, 1995; Hartup, 1996; Reitz et al., 2014).

Meta-analytic findings support this hypothesis (Briley & Tucker-Drob, 2014; Roberts & DelVecchio, 2000). For example, in an influential meta-analysis of test–retest data from 152 longitudinal studies of personality, Roberts and DelVecchio found increases in 7-year stability coefficients from ~.40 in late childhood to ~.50 by late adolescence. Notably, these results held across genders, different methods of assessment (i.e., self-report, observer report, and performance-based methods), and trait domains.

A potential limitation of existing meta-analytic studies on rank-order stability concerns their focus on relatively wide test–retest intervals (5–7 years), which prevents a more fine-grained analysis of rank-order changes across shorter time lags. This may be a particular limitation during childhood and adolescence, when changes are relatively pronounced and rapid.

More recently, researchers have attempted to provide a more nuanced description of the rank-order stability in personality throughout early, middle, and late adolescence (Borghuis et al., 2017; Klimstra, Hale, Raaijmakers, Branje, & Meeus, 2009). Using data from two large and overlapping cohorts of Dutch adolescents containing up to seven waves of longitudinal data ($N = 2,230$), Borghuis and colleagues (2017) examined the 1-year rank-order stability of the Big Five from ages 12 to 22. Consistent with previous meta-analytic findings, this study found increases in stability from early to late adolescence. Again, there were no differences between genders and results were similar across Big Five trait domains, suggesting a universal trend toward more personality stability throughout late childhood and adolescence.

Mean-Level Change

While some of the normative developments associated with adolescence may stabilize personality, other age-graded changes may trigger mean-level shifts in youths' traits. The *disruption hypothesis* posits that adolescents tend to experience temporal dips in socially relevant traits such as conscientiousness and agreeableness due to biological, social, and psychological transitions from childhood to adolescence (Soto & Tackett, 2015). In contrast to younger children, who tend to accept values and norms, adolescents seek greater autonomy by challenging or repelling adult norms (Eisenberg & Morris, 2004). This tendency is reflected in a normative increase in deviant behavior during early adolescence (Allen, Porter, & McFarland, 2006; Moffitt, 1993). During late adolescence, youth increasingly internalize moral principles that promote responsible behaviors, their self-regulatory capacities improve, and they become better at avoiding risky behaviors (Casey et al., 2008; Denissen et al., 2013). In terms of the Big Five, these normative changes should result in a curvilinear U-shaped pattern of mean-level changes in conscientiousness and agreeableness (Soto et al., 2011).

Recent cross-sectional and longitudinal research supports the disruption hypothesis. Soto and colleagues (2011) analyzed cross-sectional Big Five self-report data of more than 1,000,000 participants and found that mean levels of agreeableness, conscientiousness, and openness to experience declined from late childhood into early adolescence, then increased again from late adolescence into early adulthood. These trends have been replicated in a large cross-sectional study of parents' reports (Soto, 2016), longitudinal studies of both self-reports and parents' reports (Borghuis et al., 2017; Van den Akker, Deković, Asscher, & Prinzie, 2014), and a meta-analysis that integrated the results of 14 earlier longitudinal studies (Denissen et al., 2013). These studies provided strong support for a significant mean-level decrease in extraversion during late childhood and adolescence. Most youth seem to become considerably less sociable and active over the course of adolescence (e.g., Borghuis et al., 2017; Branje, van Lieshout, & Gerris, 2007; Soto, 2016; Soto et al., 2011).

Recent research has also identified marked differences in the personality trajectories of adolescent girls and boys. In both cross-sectional and longitudinal studies, girls experienced more pronounced mean-level increases in neuroticism over the course of adolescence than did boys (Borghuis et al., 2017; Soto, 2016; Soto et al., 2011). Several lines of research in clinical, developmental, and social psychology have shown that girls are more likely than boys to encounter various psychological difficulties, including body image concerns (Carlson Jones, 2004), negative self-perceptions (Moksnes & Espnes, 2013), and a heightened risk for mood disorders (Wichstrøm, 1999). These gender disparities seem to be reflected in normative gender differences in adolescents' neuroticism trajectories.

Emerging and Young Adulthood

Emerging adulthood, a life stage between adolescence and full-fledged adulthood, refers to people roughly between the ages of around 18 and 30 years (Arnett, 2000, 2007). The term describes young adults in Western cultures who do not have children, do not live in their own home, or do not have sufficient income to become fully independent. This period allows for identity exploration more than any other time in the adult life course because emerging adults have generally not yet made strong commitments to roles or to a particular identity (Arnett, 2000; see Erikson's [1959] concept of moratorium). In contrast, individuals begin to adopt more stable social roles and responsibilities during *young adulthood,* which generally lasts until around age 40. It is difficult to provide a definitive set of indicators that mark the transition from emerging adulthood to young adulthood. However, the experience of normative life transitions and the commitment to adult social roles, such as spouse, professional, or parent, are typically seen as markers of young adulthood (Arnett, 2000, 2007).

The conceptions of emerging adulthood and young adulthood outlined earlier suggest that these periods are characterized by distinct developmental challenges that may have different implications for personality trait stability and change. In particular, while developmental trajectories in young adulthood may be shaped by commitment to and investment in adult social roles, developmental changes in emerging adults who have not yet committed to these responsibilities may be a product of exploration and a lack of commitments (Bleidorn & Schwaba, 2017).

During the past two decades, a large number of studies have examined the stability and change of Big Five traits throughout emerging and young adulthood (for reviews, see Bleidorn, 2015; Bleidorn & Schwaba, 2017; Roberts & Mroczek, 2008). However, most of these studies have examined personality development over the all-embracing period of early adulthood (age ~18 to 40) rather than treating emerging and young adulthood as discrete developmental periods with distinct tasks and themes. Here, we review the findings of studies that have examined the rank-order stability and mean-level changes in Big Five personality traits over the course of emerging and/or young adulthood. When possible, we highlight similarities and differences between the findings for emerging versus young adulthood.

Rank-Order Stability

The specific developmental tasks and themes that characterize emerging and young adulthood likely have implications for the rank-order stability of personality traits. The normative shift from exploring different lifestyles to committing to stable adult roles should result in an increase in personality stability over the course of this life stage. Consistent with this hypothesis, meta-analytic findings by Roberts and DelVecchio (2000) suggest that the rank-order stability of personality traits increases from $r = .51$ at age 18 to $r = .62$ at age 39. A large number of follow-up studies have found that these results hold across genders, different assessment methods, and different trait domains. More recent large-scale longitudinal studies and meta-analyses have replicated this finding across different samples, measures, and cohorts (Briley & Tucker-Drob, 2014; Ferguson, 2010; Lucas & Donnellan, 2011; Specht, Egloff, & Schmuckle, 2011).

Mean-Level Change

Consistent with the conception of emerging adulthood as a time of exploration, both cross-sectional and longitudinal studies have found that this period is characterized by mean-level increases in openness to experience (Bleidorn, 2012; Bleidorn et al., 2013; Roberts, Walton, & Viechtbauer, 2006; Robins, Fraley, Roberts, & Trzesniewksi, 2001; Schwaba et al., 2017; Soto et al., 2011). These increases were particularly pronounced between ages 18 and 22, a time that seems particularly important for exploration in multiple domains (Arnett, 2007). Lüdtke, Roberts, Trautwein, and Nagy (2011) examined more specific hypotheses about the links between openness and exploration in a longitudinal study of approximately 2,000 students who were tracked from high school to university, vocational training, or work. The findings indicated that high school graduates with higher initial levels of openness were more likely to enter college. Yet, independent of their particular career path, all participants reported significant mean-level increases in openness to experience, with the most pronounced changes occurring between ages 19 and 22. Zimmerman and Neyer (2013) provided more evidence for a potential effect of exploration on changes in openness to experience in a study of personality trait changes among college students who spent time studying abroad. Compared to students who did not travel during the research period, students who spent time abroad experienced greater increases in their openness to experiences.

Whereas identity exploration in emerging adulthood may lead to increases in openness, the transition to young adulthood and committing to adult social roles may lead to changes in other trait domains. In particular, *social investment theory* (Roberts, Wood, & Smith, 2005) proposes that the transition to adult social roles, such as entering the labor force, marrying, or becoming a parent, stimulates increases in traits that reflect greater social maturity in the form of higher emotional stability (the opposite pole of neuroticism), conscientiousness, and agreeableness. Consistent with this hypothesis, a large number of cross-sectional and longitudinal studies indicate that young adults experience substantial normative gains in these three trait domains (Bleidorn, 2012; Neyer & Lehnart, 2007; Roberts & Mroczek, 2008; Roberts et al., 2006; Robins et al., 2001; Soto et al., 2011; Specht et al., 2011). These mean-level trends generalize across cohorts, genders, and, to a certain extent, samples from different cultures (Bleidorn et al., 2013; Roberts et al., 2006; Wortman, Lucas, & Donnellan, 2012). Alluding to young adults' seemingly increasing capacity to become productive contributors to society, this pattern has become known as the *maturity principle* of personality development (Roberts & Mroczek, 2008).

Less consistent results have been reported for mean-level changes in extraversion during emerging and young adulthood. Some researchers reported increases in extraversion (e.g., Neyer & Lehnart, 2007), others reported decreases (e.g., Wortman et al., 2012), and still others found extraversion to be mostly stable during this life stage (e.g., Cobb-Clark & Schurer, 2012). One potential explanation for this mixed pattern of findings has been that different facets of extraversion show distinct developmental patterns. Supporting this hypothesis, Roberts and colleagues (2006) found that two facets of extraversion—social vitality and social dominance—have different trajectories during emerging and young adulthood. Specifically, social vitality increased during emerging adulthood (between ages 18 and 22) but decreased during the following years, whereas social dominance underwent pronounced gradual increases until age 40.

Middle Adulthood

Middle-aged adults (ages 40–65) typically need to negotiate a broad spectrum of roles, such as parent, grandparent, child of aging parents, provider, colleague, neighbor, friend, and so on

(Lachman, 2001; McAdams & Olson, 2010). Key developmental themes center around generativity, caring, and concern for others (McAdams, 2001), as well as the mastery and maintenance of established social roles (Huttemann, Hennecke, Orth, Reitz, & Specht, 2014). Middle adulthood is also a period during which people typically confront the onset of physical challenges associated with the aging process (Lachman, 2001).

Despite these social responsibilities, pressures, and stressors, middle-aged adults usually experience a high sense of mastery and reach the peak of control over their environment (e.g., Baltes, 1987; Wrosch & Heckhausen, 1999). According to Neugarten (1968), increased levels of self-awareness, competence, and a wide array of coping strategies that are characteristic for this life stage improve middle-aged adults' capacity to handle stressors in both personal and interpersonal spheres.

The overall emphasis on consistency and maintenance of established lifestyles and roles implies that personality trait development in middle adulthood should be characterized by a high degree of rank-order stability. Moreover, the developmental tasks of middle adulthood would suggest increases in mean levels of socially relevant traits that are related to generativity and interpersonal behavior.

Rank-Order Stability

Consistent with the description of middle adulthood as a period of consistency and maintenance (e.g., Hutteman et al., 2014), there is strong evidence that the rank-order stability of personality traits peaks during this life stage. Several meta-analyses (Ardelt, 2000; Roberts & DelVecchio, 2000), as well as recent large-scale longitudinal studies of nationally representative samples (Specht et al., 2011; Wortman et al., 2012), indicate that the rank-order stability of personality traits increases in a monotonic fashion throughout middle adulthood, until it reaches a plateau around age 50. This finding holds for both men and women across all Big Five traits and may reflect the fact that middle-aged adults tend to live in relatively stable environments. In addition, improved coping strategies and increases in perceived competence may buffer middle-aged adults from the impact of stressors that would otherwise trigger personality changes (cf. Lachman, 2001; Neugarten, 1968).

Although rank-order stability is higher during middle adulthood than during any other life stage, the empirical literature also makes clear that it is still not perfectly stable. Retest correlation estimates range between .70 and .80 during this period, leaving room for change in individual trajectories that affects rank ordering over time. This finding provides strong evidence for the claim that personality traits can and do change throughout the lifespan (Roberts, Wood, & Caspi, 2008).

Mean-Level Change

Both cross-sectional and longitudinal research suggests that the mean levels of conscientiousness, agreeableness, and emotional stability continue to increase during middle age (e.g., Allemand, Zimprich, & Hendriks, 2008; Allemand, Zimprich, Hertzog, 2007; Soto et al., 2011; Roberts et al., 2006; Specht et al., 2011), albeit at a somewhat lower rate than during young adulthood. Mean-level increases in agreeableness, however, seem to be most pronounced in middle-aged adults (Allemand et al., 2008; Roberts et al., 2006). The relatively strong age-graded increase in agreeableness might reflect enhanced concerns with generativity and the welfare of loved ones during midlife (McAdams & Olson, 2010).

Research on mean-level changes in openness to experience and extraversion during middle adulthood has yielded less consistent results. While some studies have found that the mean levels of openness and extraversion remain fairly stable over the course of middle adulthood (Bleidorn et al., 2009; Roberts et al., 2006), others have found significant decreases, in particular for middle-aged adults' openness to experience (Lucas & Donnellan, 2011; Specht et al., 2011; Wortman et al., 2012). Recently, Schwaba and colleagues (2018) examined the lifespan trajectory of openness to experience in a nationally representative sample of more than 7,000 Dutch participants across five assessment waves. Consistent with previous findings of decreases in openness during middle adulthood, this study also found gradual mean-level decreases in openness to experience between ages 40 and 60.

Old Age

Old age (65 and older) can be a period of wisdom, enhanced respect from others, and opportunities to enjoy the fruits of one's life work (Erikson, 1959). For individuals who successfully navigated previous life stages, common experiences include spending more time with family, pursuing hobbies, and various other behaviors that can deepen meaning in life. At the same time, the transition from midlife to old age comes with appreciable challenges. Aging adults tend to disengage from social roles as they move out of the labor force, and lose relationships as their partners, loved ones, and friends move or pass away. In addition, old age is characterized by diminished physical and cognitive functioning.

These challenges and changes may entail significant adjustments in older adults' thoughts, feelings, and behavior, which may result in personality trait changes. The probability that old age may be more "golden" for some people than others would suggest decreased rank-order stability of personality traits relative to the highly stable period of middle adulthood. With respect to mean-level change, normative declines in physical health and cognitive functioning have been hypothesized to constitute important triggers of personality trait change in old age (Specht et al., 2014). Health problems and impaired cognitive functioning may disrupt an acquired lifestyle and force older adults to be more selective in the activities and social relationships in which they engage (Wrzus, Hänel, Wagner, & Neyer, 2013). Disengagement from social roles, activities, and relationships may lead to decreases in traits such as conscientiousness and agreeableness. Physical and cognitive declines may further limit older individuals' capacity to engage in intellectually demanding activities or to seek out novel experiences, which might contribute to decreases in older adults' openness to experiences and extraversion (Mueller et al., 2016; Schwaba et al., 2018).

Rank-Order Stability

Compared to the large number of studies on personality development in young and middle adulthood, considerably fewer studies have investigated the rank-order stability of personality traits in old age. These studies have provided mixed evidence for the proposition that rank-order stability decreases during old age. Two meta-analyses, both published in the same year, yielded opposite results. Whereas Roberts and DelVecchio (2000) found that that the rank-order stability is relatively stable throughout late adulthood and old age, Ardelt (2000) reported significant decreases in rank-order stability after age 50. Notably, both meta-analyses included relatively few longitudinal studies that covered older age groups, and the sample sizes of these studies were relatively small.

More recently, several large-scale longitudinal studies have examined the rank-order stability of personality traits throughout the adult lifespan. These studies provided more evidence for a significant decrease in personality rank-order stability in old age (Lucas & Donnellan, 2011; Specht et al., 2011; Wortman et al., 2012). Overall, the weight of evidence suggests that the stability of personality decreases during old age relative to the highly stable period of middle age.

Mean-Level Change

A large body of longitudinal research has shown that personality traits continue to show normative trends in older adults (Kandler, Kornadt, Hagemeyer, & Neyer, 2015; Mõttus, Johnson, & Deary, 2012; Mueller et al., 2016; Roberts et al., 2006; Schwaba & Bleidorn, 2018; Specht et al., 2011; Wagner, Ram, Smith, & Gerstorf, 2016; Wortman et al., 2012). Reversing the *personality maturation* trends that characterize young and middle adulthood, old adults experience mean-level decreases in traits that reflect social maturity and interpersonal functioning (Kandler, Bleidorn, Riemann, Angleitner, & Spinath, 2012). In particular, aging adults tend to decrease in emotional stability, agreeableness, extraversion, and conscientiousness, with the most pronounced changes occurring during very old age (> 80 years). For example, Mõttus and colleagues (2012) found only small mean-level changes in a cohort of 69- to 72-year-olds but more significant decreases in extraversion, emotional stability, openness, agreeableness, and conscientiousness in an older cohort of 81- to 87-year-olds. Similarly, in a nationally representative sample of Australians, Wortman and colleagues (2012) found that declines in agreeableness, emotional stability, and extraversion occurred mainly in individuals older than 80.

These trends may reflect a continued disengagement from social roles, activities, and relationships, as well as normative declines in older adults' cognitive and physical functioning (Kandler et al., 2016; Mueller et al., 2016; Stephan, Sutin, & Terracciano, 2014; Wrzus et al., 2013). Consistent with this notion, Schwaba and colleagues (2017) found that older adults who disengage from cultural activities, such as attending concerts or visiting museums, showed accelerated decreases in openness to experience. In a similar vein, Stephan and colleagues (2014) reported that more physically active older adults showed less pronounced decreases in conscientiousness, extraversion, openness, and agreeableness.

Underscoring the importance of physical health for older adults' personality development, recent research has shown that individuals become less emotionally stable, extraverted, open, and conscientious after the onset of a chronic disease (Jokela, Hakulinen, Singh-Manoux, & Kivimäki, 2014). Moreover, higher illness burden (i.e., the onset of an additional chronic disease) further accelerated the average age-related changes in these personality traits. Similarly, Wagner and colleagues (2016) found that poor physical health predicts declines in extraversion and openness in late life.

Summary: Is Personality Stable or Does It Change?

In this chapter, we have reviewed rank-order stability and mean-level change in Big Five personality traits across late childhood/adolescence, early/emerging adulthood, middle age, and old age. One broad conclusion from this review is that, their relatively stable nature notwithstanding, personality traits can and do change across the entire lifespan. The rank-order stability of all Big Five traits is far from perfect over moderately long intervals, and the majority of people experience medium-size to large changes in their Big Five personality traits across the lifespan. However, this review also makes it clear that several factors prohibit simple answers to the question: Are personality traits stable or do they change?

First, it is important to be specific about which type of stability or change is being considered, as patterns are somewhat different for rank-order and mean-level stability. For example, whereas relatively similar patterns of rank-order stability emerge across all Big Five traits, there are marked differences in the trajectories of mean-level change in the different domains of personality.

Second, patterns of stability and change in personality seem to track with the needs and presses of different life stages (Table 14.1).

There is a curvilinear relationship between age and rank-order stability, suggesting that personality traits are most prone to change at the beginning (before age 30) and the end of life (after age 70). This pattern tracks well with the expectations and experiences linked to these life stages. Children and adolescents undergo dramatic social and physical developments. Their lives lie in front of them, which makes possibilities exciting but difficult to predict. The dynamic nature of this period leaves a wide range of possibilities for personality development. During emerging and young adulthood, young people try out different roles and select into the environments that will largely determine their life course. For most people, the focus is not so much on figuring out who to be during middle age, but on being who you are in order to fulfill relevant personal and professional goals. It follows that personality should be relatively stable during this period. Uncertainty returns during old age, when responsibilities related to work and parenting remit and losses accumulate.

The normative direction of mean-level changes also fits with the dynamics of different life stages. Puberty and adolescence are associated with a more antagonistic, neurotic, and impulsive personality changes that may be driven by hormonal undercurrents and connected to individuation processes. Some aspects of personality maturation appear to be gender-linked during this period, as are other aspects of development and socialization that makes adolescence for boys and girls a somewhat different experience. After a temporal disruption during adolescence, the average young person increases in traits that reflect greater social maturity, improved interpersonal functioning, and openness to experience. These changes help young people get along, get ahead, and explore the options before them. This normative pattern of personality maturation peaks and consolidates in middle adulthood, during which time most people are cementing their identity and roles. Old age seems to be characterized by a return to less adaptive personality features, perhaps in connection with a loss of responsibilities, relationships, and functioning.

Causes and Correlates of Personality Trait Change

The lifelong plasticity of personality and the observed increases and decreases in particular trait domains during different life stages have led to a great deal of speculation about the conditions and causes of these changes. All major theories of personality development acknowledge that personality development reflects age-graded influences of both genetic and environmental factors. Accounts differ in the relative importance given to these two factors, with some emphasizing the role of genetic influences and intrinsic biological processes (*ontogenetic*

TABLE 14.1. Normative Patterns of Stability and Change in Big Five Traits across Life Stages

Life stage	Rank-order stability	Mean-level change
Late childhood and adolescence (10–18)	All traits are moderately stable and stability increases.	Increases in N, particularly for girls Decreases in E Initial increases followed by decreases in O, A, and C
Emerging and early adulthood (18–40)	All traits are stable and stability continues to increase.	Decreases in N Increases in O, A, and C
Middle adulthood (40–65)	All traits are very stable.	Continued decreases in N Decreases in O More pronounced increases in A Continued increases in C
Old age (65 and after)	All traits are stable but stability decreases.	Increases in N (particularly in very old age) Decreases in E, O, A, and C (particularly in very old age)

Note. N, neuroticism; E, extraversion; O, openness to experience; A, agreeableness; C, conscientiousness.

approaches) and others stressing the importance of environmental influences and major life events (*sociogenic approaches*).

Ontogenetic approaches argue that personality trait development is largely controlled by genetically determined biological influences, with only a negligible role for environmental influences. For example, five-factor theory (McCrae & Costa, 2008) defines personality traits as "endogenous dispositions that follow intrinsic paths of development essentially independent of environmental influences" (McCrae et al., 2000, p. 173). Proponents of five-factor theory have compared personality traits with height, a characteristic that depends on environmental inputs (e.g., nutrition), but whose development is largely determined by a genetically predisposed program when sufficient environmental resources are available.

In contrast, *sociogenic* approaches emphasize the impact of environmental influences (Roberts et al., 2005). These accounts highlight the role of major life events for the observed mean-level changes in personality traits at different life stages (e.g., Bleidorn, 2015; Roberts et al., 2005; Roberts & Wood, 2006; Specht et al., 2014). Life events, such as graduation from school, marriage, parenthood, or retirement, are theorized to have lasting effects on personality traits because they modify, interrupt, or redirect life trajectories by altering individuals' feelings, thoughts, and behavior (Bleidorn, Hopwood, & Lucas, 2018; Pickles & Rutter, 1991).

Several studies have attempted to test the differential influences of nature and nurture on personality development. Longitudinal behavioral genetics models are a particularly useful approach to understanding the relative importance of genetic and environmental influences for personality trait change throughout the lifespan (Bleidorn, Kandler, & Caspi, 2014; Briley & Tucker-Drob, 2014; Kandler, 2012). In a recent meta-analysis, Briley and Tucker-Drob (2014) integrated the results of 24 longitudinal behavioral genetics studies to examine the extent to which genetic and environmental factors contribute to the stability of personality traits. The results of this study suggested that genetic factors exert a relatively constant influence on personality trait stability across the lifespan. In contrast, environmental contributions to stability were relatively small in childhood but increased substantially throughout adolescence and young, and middle adulthood, continuing even into old age. These findings indicate that

in addition to continuous genetic influences, a substantial proportion of variance in personality stability and change in young and middle adulthood is associated with environmental factors. Which environmental factors matter, however, remains a mostly open question.

To begin to address this question, several longitudinal studies have examined the impact of life events on personality trait change (e.g., Denissen, Luhmann, Chung, & Bleidorn, 2018; Schwaba & Bleidorn, 2018; Specht et al., 2011; van Scheppingen et al., 2016; for a review, see Bleidorn et al., 2018). This research suggests that life events may lead to changes in personality traits, and that different life events may be differentially related to specific trait domains. However, a more general conclusion emerging from this literature is that evidence for the nature, shape, and timing of personality trait change in response to life events is still preliminary (Bleidorn et al., 2018). Whereas some studies reported evidence for personality change during life transitions (e.g., Specht et al., 2011), others found no effect of life events on personality trait change (van Scheppingen et al., 2016). The most cohesive findings seem to emerge for two life events that typically occur in young adulthood. First, studies consistently find that the transition to the first romantic relationship is related to increases in agreeableness and extraversion (e.g., Neyer & Lehnart, 2007). Second, the transition from school to college or work has been associated with increases in agreeableness, conscientiousness, openness, and decreases in neuroticism (e.g., Bleidorn, 2012; Lüdtke et al., 2011). The evidence for the impact of other life events, such as marriage, divorce, unemployment, or retirement, is more mixed than one would expect given the apparent emotional and behavioral relevance of these life events.

There are several possible explanations for the finding that romantic relationships and graduation from school have a stronger impact on personality trait change than other life events. First, as outlined earlier, young adulthood is a period in life when personality traits seem to be highly malleable and therefore open to change and external influences (Bleidorn, 2015; Roberts et al., 2006; Specht et al., 2014). Hence, life events that normatively occur during this life stage may be particularly likely to trigger personality change because personality traits are more sensitive to environmental influences in early adulthood than in middle adulthood, and perhaps also in late adulthood. Second, graduation from school and the first partnership may have a relatively strong influence on personality traits because they are normative experiences in Western societies. In contrast to other non-normative or less scripted life events, such as divorce, unemployment, or retirement, these two life events are characterized by transparent behavioral scripts and relatively clear affective reactions and cognitive demands. For example, expectations associated with graduation from school include being task- and goal-directed, organized, delaying gratification, and following prescribed norms. To the extent that these behaviors can be translated into trait terms (e.g., increases in conscientiousness), graduation from school should form a strong reward structure for personality trait change (Roberts & Wood, 2006). A third explanation for the mixed results concerning the impact of life events on personality trait change focuses on the scope and quality of previous studies, many of which were not explicitly designed to investigate the nature and correlates of personality trait change (Bleidorn et al., 2018).

In summary, longitudinal behavioral genetics research shows that both genetic and environmental factors influence the stability and change of personality traits over the lifespan. Whereas genetic influences are relatively more important early in life, environmental influences become increasingly important over the course of early and middle adulthood. An important question is which environmental influences matter the most, and for which traits? Previous research provides some evidence that major life events can be catalysts for personality trait change, in particular those life events that normatively occur in young adulthood. However, more research is needed to investigate the conditions, timing, and underlying processes of personality trait stability and change across the lifespan.

Future Directions

In view of both the recent accomplishments and the enduring challenges in the field of personality trait development, we conclude with several recommendations and open questions for future research on personality trait stability and change.

First, studies are needed that sample personality more frequently than in most previous research. A general conclusion from past studies is that stability decreases with longer intervals between measurements (for meta-analyses/reviews, see Ardelt, 2000; Ferguson, 2010; Roberts & Del Vecchio, 2000; Specht et al., 2014). However, it is possible that short-term changes to personality may not be observable in designs with relatively long assessment intervals. Longitudinal studies with frequent and well-timed assessments before and after the occurrence of life events would be especially valuable for answering this question (Luhmann, Orth, Specht, Kandler, & Lucas, 2014).

Second, most previous studies have assessed personality traits via self-report instruments that may be prone to biases that distort conclusions regarding the stability and change of personality traits. Multimethod approaches using informant reports, behavioral data, or other kinds of assessments might stimulate research on personality trait stability and change (Eid & Diener, 2006). Discontinuities in the patterns observed across assessment methods might also be illuminating and help explaining some of the inconsistencies among different studies.

Third, as mentioned earlier, most studies on personality trait development have focused on estimates of rank-order stability and/or mean-level change. These two parameters describe changes in individual personality traits at the population level. However, changes at the population level may not mirror changes at the individual level (Roberts et al., 2008). In particular, more research is needed to understand when and how (1) individuals deviate from the general population trends (i.e., individual-level change) and (2) how the configuration of traits within an individual changes across time (i.e., ipsative personality change).

Fourth, virtually all previous studies on personality trait development have examined samples from the United States or other Western, educated, industrialized, rich, and democratic (WEIRD) nations (Henrich, Heine, & Norenzayan, 2010). A systematic examination of stability and change in personality traits across a large and diverse set of cultures has yet to be undertaken. Such an analysis is needed to test whether the reported age trends in personality traits are cross-cultural universals or culture-specific phenomena (Henrich et al., 2010). Moreover, a cross-cultural examination can provide important information about the universal and culture-specific mechanisms that might drive the age-graded changes in personality (Bleidorn et al., 2013; Costa, Terracciano, & McCrae, 2001).

Fifth, we have limited our review to studies on personality stability and change in late childhood and older samples. Few studies have examined personality trait stability and change in earlier life stages, such as infancy or toddlerhood. More research on younger samples using behavioral trait measures and parent report instruments is needed to extend our review to these early life stages and to gain a better understanding of the relationship between temperament and personality traits (De Pauw, Mervielde, & Van Leeuwen, 2009; Tackett, Kushner, De Fruyt, & Mervielde, 2013).

Sixth, very little is known about the underlying genetic and environmental processes that drive personality trait development. A particularly important issue concerns the interplay between genes and environmental factors in personality trait development (Bleidorn et al., 2014; Briley & Tucker-Drob, 2014). For example, the occurrence of certain life events is not necessarily random nor is it always independent of an individual's personality. Individuals often evoke, select, or create environmental experiences based on their genetically influenced preferences, motives, and traits (e.g., Plomin, DeFries, & Loehlin, 1977). Such environmental experiences may then have a reinforcing influence on those traits that have led to these experiences in the first place (person-environment transactions, cf. Neyer & Lehnart, 2007; Schwaba et al., 2018). Longitudinal behavioral genetic studies that include measures of putative environmental influences on personality (e.g., life events) would provide a powerful tool to examine such person-environment transactions in order to disentangle the joint and unique contributions of genetic and environmental factors to personality trait change (Kandler et al., 2012).

Seventh, this chapter has focused exclusively on the broad Big Five domains. Personality psychology involves more concepts than these broad personality traits. Possible discontinuities in stability and change at narrower levels of the personality hierarchy merit closer examination. Developmental patterns of other important aspects of personality, such as goals, interests, values, problems, or narratives, are less well understood than patterns of traits and also deserve greater attention (Hopwood et al., 2013; McAdams & Olson, 2010; Roberts et al., 2008).

Conclusion

Dodge Morgan was 53 when he began his solo voyage around the world. He was in the middle of middle age, a peak period for personality stability and maturity according to the contemporary literature on personality development. In light of this review, it should not be surprising that a major life event did not have a profound impact on his personality. At the same time, changes that were observed in the direction of social maturation could also be anticipated, as current research makes it clear that personality can change even during periods of significant stability, and changes tend to be in the direction of maturation through middle adulthood.

It would be interesting to have had personality assessment data from Dodge Morgan in earlier and later periods of life, to see whether his personality development tracked with normative trends. He endured appreciable family disruption early in life, and selected relatively isolating yet interesting environments that provided room for his free spirit. For instance, he dropped out of college to become a pilot in the U.S. Air Force as a young man. He lived in a variety of remote places, such as Alaska and the Caribbean, and endured two divorces prior to his voyage. Dodge ended his life on an island, where he moored several sailboats and remained largely protected from social interaction. He spent most of his time alone or in the company of the few people he liked most. His life story suggests that his low agreeableness and high openness were enduring aspects of his personality throughout, but it also tantalizingly implies more specific dynamics as a function of some of the very interesting twists and turns during his life.

Unfortunately, the current body of knowledge is not sufficient to explain why Dodge, in particular, experienced the specific changes he did in response to his voyage or other idiographic events. Indeed, relatively little is known about the exact conditions and correlates of personality change, beyond the general conclusion that heredity drives stability and change, but environmental influences matter, too. Questions such as which traits affect personality development, what environmental factors matter, and how do these factors lead to lasting personality trait changes remain largely unanswered. Having described patterns of rank-order and mean-level stability relatively well, addressing these questions is the next frontier in the field personality development.

REFERENCES

Allemand, M., Zimprich, D., & Hendriks, A. A. (2008). Age differences in five personality domains across the life span. *Developmental Psychology, 44*, 758–770.

Allemand, M., Zimprich, D., & Hertzog, C. (2007). Cross-sectional age differences and longitudinal age changes of personality in middle adulthood and old age. *Journal of Personality, 75*, 323–358.

Allen, J. P., Porter, M. R., & McFarland, F. C. (2006). Leaders and followers in adolescent close friendships: Susceptibility to peer influence as a predictor of risky behavior, friendship instability, and depression. *Development and Psychopathology, 18*, 155–172.

Ardelt, M. (2000). Still stable after all these years?: Personality stability theory revisited. *Social Psychology Quarterly, 63*, 392–405.

Arnett, J. J. (2000). Emerging adulthood: A theory of development from the late teens through the twenties. *American Psychologist, 55*, 469–480.

Arnett, J. J. (2007). Emerging adulthood: What is it, and what is it good for? *Child Development Perspectives, 1*, 68–73.

Baltes, P. B. (1987). Theoretical propositions of life-span developmental psychology: On the dynamics between growth and decline. *Developmental Psychology, 23*, 611–626.

Blakemore, S. J. (2008). The social brain in adolescence. *Nature Reviews Neuroscience, 9*, 267–277.

Bleidorn, W. (2012). Hitting the road to adulthood: Short-term personality development during a major life transition. *Personality and Social Psychology Bulletin, 38*, 1594–1608.

Bleidorn, W. (2015). What accounts for personality maturation in early adulthood? *Current Directions in Psychological Science, 24*, 245–252.

Bleidorn, W., Hopwood, C. J., & Lucas, R. E. (2018). Life events and personality trait change. *Journal of Personality, 86*, 83–96.

Bleidorn, W., Kandler, C., & Caspi, A. (2014). The behavioral genetics of personality development in adulthood—Classic, contemporary, and future trends. *European Journal of Personality, 28*, 244–255.

Bleidorn, W., Kandler, C., Riemann, R., Angleitner, A., & Spinath, F. M. (2009). Patterns and sources of adult personality development: Growth curve analyses of the NEO-PI-R scales in a longitudinal twin study. *Journal of Personality and Social Psychology, 97*, 142–155.

Bleidorn, W., Klimstra, T. A., Denissen, J. J. A., Rentfrow, P. J., Potter, J., & Gosling, S. D. (2013). Personality maturation around the world: A cross-cultural examination of social investment theory. *Psychological Science, 24*, 2530–2540.

Bleidorn, W., & Schwaba, T. (2017). Personality development in emerging adulthood. In J. Specht (Ed.), *Personality development across the lifespan* (pp. 39–52). Amsterdam, The Netherlands: Elsevier.

Borghuis, J., Denissen, J. J. A., Sijtsma, K., Meeus, W. H. J., Branje, S. J. T., & Bleidorn, W. (2017). Big Five personality stability, change, and co-development across adolescence and early adulthood. *Journal of Personality and Social Psychology, 113*, 641–657.

Branje, S. J., Van Lieshout, C. F., & Gerris, J. R. (2007). Big Five personality development in adolescence and adulthood. *European Journal of Personality, 21*, 45–62.

Briley, D. A., & Tucker-Drob, E. M. (2014). Genetic and environmental continuity in personality development: A meta-analysis. *Psychological Bulletin, 140*, 1303–1331.

Carlson Jones, D. (2004). Body image among adolescent girls and boys: A longitudinal study. *Developmental Psychology, 40*, 823–835.

Casey, B. J., Jones, R. M., & Hare, T. A. (2008). The adolescent brain. *Annals of the New York Academy of Sciences, 1124*, 111–126.

Caspi, A., Roberts, B. W., & Shiner, R. L. (2005). Personality development: Stability and change. *Annual Review of Psychology, 56*, 453–484.

Cobb-Clark, D. A., & Schurer, S. (2012). The stability of Big Five personality traits. *Economic Letters, 115*, 11–15.

Cohen, J. (1988). *Statistical power analysis for the behavioral sciences* (2nd ed.). Hillsdale, NJ: Erlbaum.

Collins, W. (2003). More than myth: The developmental significance of romantic relationships during adolescence. *Journal of Research on Adolescence, 13*, 1–24.

Costa, P., Jr., Terracciano, A., & McCrae, R. R. (2001). Gender differences in personality traits across cultures: Robust and surprising findings. *Journal of Personality and Social Psychology, 81*, 322–331.

De Fruyt, F., Bartels, M., Van Leeuwen, K. G., De Clercq, B., Decuyper, M., & Mervielde, I. (2006). Five types of personality continuity in childhood and adolescence. *Journal of Personality and Social Psychology, 91*, 538–552.

De Pauw, S. S., Mervielde, I., & Van Leeuwen, K. G. (2009). How are traits related to problem behavior in preschoolers?: Similarities and contrasts between temperament and personality. *Journal of Abnormal Child Psychology, 37*, 309–325.

Denissen, J. J. A., Luhmann, M., Chung, J. M., & Bleidorn, W. (2018). The effect of life events on personality change across the adult lifespan. *Journal of Personality and Social Psychology*. [EPub ahead of print]

Denissen, J. A., van Aken, M. A., Penke, L., & Wood, D. (2013). Self-regulation underlies temperament and personality: An integrative developmental framework. *Child Development Perspectives, 7*, 255–260.

Eid, M., & Diener, E. (Eds.). (2006). *Handbook of multimethod measurement in psychology*. Washington, DC: American Psychological Association.

Eisenberg, N., & Morris, A. S. (2004). Moral cognitions and prosocial responding in adolescence. In R. M. Lerner & L. Steinberg (Eds.), *Handbook of adolescent psychology* (2nd ed., pp. 155–188). Hoboken, NJ: Wiley.

Erikson, E. H. (1959). Identity and the life cycle. *Psychological Issues, 1,* 18–164.

Erikson, E. H. (1968). *Identity: Youth and crisis.* New York: Norton.

Ferguson, C. J. (2010). A meta-analysis of normal and disordered personality across the life span. *Journal of Personality and Social Psychology, 98,* 659–667.

Fraley, R. C., & Roberts, B. W. (2005). Patterns of continuity: A dynamic model for conceptualizing the stability of individual differences in psychological constructs across the life course. *Psychological Review, 112,* 60–74.

Harris, J. R. (1995). Where is the child's environment?: A group socialization theory of development. *Psychological Review, 102,* 458–489.

Harter, S. (2006). The self. In W. Damon & R. M. Lerner (Series Eds.) & N. Eisenberg (Vol. Ed.), *Handbook of child psychology: Vol. 3. Social, emotional, and personality development* (6th ed., pp. 505–570). Hoboken, NJ: Wiley.

Hartup, W. W. (1996). The company they keep: Friendships and their developmental significance. *Child Development, 67,* 1–13.

Henrich, J., Heine, S. J., & Norenzayan, A. (2010). The weirdest people in the world? *Behavioral and Brain Sciences, 33,* 61–83.

Hopwood, C. J., Donnellan, M. B., Blonigen, D. M., Krueger, R. F., McGue, M., Iacono, W. G., et al. (2011). Genetic and environmental influences on personality trait stability and growth during the transition to adulthood: A three-wave longitudinal study. *Journal of Personality and Social Psychology, 100,* 545–556.

Hopwood, C. J., Morey, L. C., Donnellan, M. B., Samuel, D. B., Grilo, C. M., McGlashan, T. H., et al. (2013). Ten-year rank-order stability of personality traits and disorders in a clinical sample. *Journal of Personality, 81,* 335–344.

Hutteman, R., Hennecke, M., Orth, U., Reitz, A. K., & Specht, J. (2014). Developmental tasks as a framework to study personality development in adulthood and old age. *European Journal of Personality, 28,* 267–278.

Inhelder, B., & Piaget, J. (1958). *The growth of logical thinking from childhood to adolescence.* New York: Basic Books.

John, O. P., Naumann, L. P., & Soto, C. J. (2008). Paradigm shift to the integrative Big Five trait taxonomy: History, measurement, and conceptual issues. In O. P. John, R. W. Robins, & L. A. Pervin (Eds.), *Handbook of personality: Theory and research* (3rd ed., pp. 114–158). New York: Guilford Press.

Jokela, M., Hakulinen, C., Singh-Manoux, A., & Kivimäki, M. (2014). Personality change associated with chronic diseases: Pooled analysis of four prospective cohort studies. *Psychological Medicine, 44,* 2629–2640.

Kandler, C. (2012). Nature and nurture in personality development: The case of neuroticism and extraversion. *Current Directions in Psychological Science, 21,* 290–296.

Kandler, C., Bleidorn, W., Riemann, R., Angleitner, A., & Spinath, F. M. (2012). Life events as environmental states and genetic traits and the role of personality: A longitudinal twin study. *Behavior Genetics, 42,* 57–72.

Kandler, C., Kornadt, A. E., Hagemeyer, B., & Neyer, F. J. (2015). Patterns and sources of personality development in old age. *Journal of Personality and Social Psychology, 109,* 175–191.

Keating, D. P. (2004). Cognitive and brain development. In R. M. Lerner & L. Steinberg (Eds.), *Handbook of adolescent psychology* (2nd ed., pp. 45–84). Hoboken, NJ: Wiley.

Klimstra, T. A., Hale, W. W., III, Raaijmakers, Q. A., Branje, S. J., & Meeus, W. H. (2009). Maturation of personality in adolescence. *Journal of Personality and Social Psychology, 96,* 898–912.

Lachman, M. E. (2001). Development in midlife. *Annual Review of Psychology, 55,* 305–331.

Lucas, R. E., & Donnellan, M. B. (2011). Personality development across the life span: Longitudinal analyses with a national sample from Germany. *Journal of Personality and Social Psychology, 101,* 847–861.

Lüdtke, O., Roberts, B. W., Trautwein, U., & Nagy, G. (2011). A random walk down university avenue: Life paths, life events, and personality trait change at the transition to university life. *Journal of Personality and Social Psychology, 101,* 620–637.

Luhmann, M., Orth, U., Specht, J., Kandler, C., & Lucas, R. E. (2014). Studying changes in life circumstances and personality: It's about time. *European Journal of Personality, 28,* 256–266.

Markon, K. E., Krueger, R. F., & Watson, D. (2006). Delineating the structure of normal and abnormal personality: An integrative hierarchical approach. *Journal of Personality and Social Psychology, 88,* 139–157.

McAdams, D. P. (2001). Generativity in midlife. In M. E. Lachman (Ed.), *Handbook of midlife development* (pp. 395–443). New York: Wiley.

McAdams, D. P., & Olson, B. D. (2010). Personality development: Continuity and change over the life course. *Annual Review of Psychology, 61,* 517–542.

McCrae, R. R., & Costa, P. (2008). The five-factor theory of personality. In O. P. John, R. W. Robins, & L. A. Pervin (Eds.), *Handbook of personality: Theory and research* (3rd ed., pp. 1–58). New York: Guilford Press.

McCrae, R. R., Costa, P. T. J., Ostendorf, F., Angleitner, A., Hrebickova, M., Avia, M. D., et al. (2000). Nature over nurture: Temperament, personality, and life span development. *Journal of Personality and Social Psychology, 78,* 173–186.

Moffitt, T. E. (1993). Adolescence-limited and life-course-persistent antisocial behavior: A developmental taxonomy. *Psychological Review, 100,* 674–701.

Moksnes, U. K., & Espnes, G. A. (2013). Self-esteem and life satisfaction in adolescents: Gender and age as potential moderators. *Quality of Life Research, 22,* 2921–2928.

Mõttus, R., Johnson, W., & Deary, I. J. (2012). Personality traits in old age: Measurement and rank-order stability and some mean-level change. *Psychology and Aging, 27,* 243–249.

Mueller, S., Wagner, J., Drewelies, J., Duezel, S., Eibich, P., Specht, J., et al. (2016). Personality development in old age relates to physical health and cognitive performance: Evidence from the Berlin Aging Study II. *Journal of Research in Personality, 65,* 94–108.

Nasby, W., & Read, N. W. (1997). The life voyage of a solo circumnavigator: Integrating theoretical and methodological perspectives. *Journal of Personality, 65,* 785–1068.

Neugarten, B. L. (1968). *Middle age and aging: A reader in social psychology.* Chicago: University of Chicago Press.

Neyer, F. J., & Lehnart, J. (2007). Relationships matter in personality development: Evidence from an 8-year longitudinal study across young adulthood. *Journal of Personality, 75,* 535–568.

Pickles, A., & Rutter, M. (1991). Statistical and conceptual models of "turning points" in developmental processes. In D. Magnusson, L. R. Bergman, G. Rudinger, & B. Törestad (Eds.), *Problems and methods in longitudinal research: Stability and change* (pp. 133–165). Cambridge, UK: Cambridge University Press.

Plomin, R., DeFries, J. C., & Loehlin, J. C. (1977). Genotype–environment interaction and correlation in the analysis of human behavior. *Psychological Bulletin, 84,* 309–322.

Reitz, A. K., Zimmermann, J., Hutteman, R., Specht, J., & Neyer, F. J. (2014). How peers make a difference: The role of peer groups and peer relationships in personality development. *European Journal of Personality, 28,* 279–288.

Roberts, B. W., & DelVecchio, W. F. (2000). The rank-order consistency of personality traits from childhood to old age: A quantitative review of longitudinal studies. *Psychological Bulletin, 126,* 3–25.

Roberts, B. W., & Mroczek, D. (2008). Personality trait change in adulthood. *Current Directions in Psychological Science, 17,* 31–35.

Roberts, B. W., Walton, K. E., & Viechtbauer, W. (2006). Patterns of mean-level change in personality traits across the life course: A meta-analysis of longitudinal studies. *Psychological Bulletin, 132,* 1–25.

Roberts, B. W., & Wood, D. (2006). Personality development in the context of the neo-socioanalytic model of personality. In D. K. Mroczek, T. D. Little, D. K. Mroczek, & T. D. Little (Eds.), *Handbook of personality development* (pp. 11–39). Mahwah, NJ: Erlbaum.

Roberts, B. W., Wood, D., & Caspi, A. (2008). The development of personality traits in adulthood. In O. P. John, R. W. Robins, & L. A. Pervin (Ed.), *Handbook of personality: Theory and research* (3rd ed., pp. 375–398). New York: Guilford Press.

Roberts, B. W., Wood, D., & Smith, J. L. (2005). Evaluating five factor theory and social investment perspectives on personality trait development. *Journal of Research in Personality, 39,* 166–184.

Robins, R. W., Fraley, R. C., Roberts, B. W., & Trzesniewski, K. H. (2001). A longitudinal study of personality change in young adulthood. *Journal of Personality, 69,* 617–640.

Schaie, K. W. (1977). Quasi-experimental research designs in the psychology of aging. In J. E. Birren & K. W. Schaie (Eds.), *Handbook of the psychology of aging* (pp. 39–69). New York: Van Nostrand Reinhold.

Schwaba, T., & Bleidorn, W. (2018). Personality trait development across the transition to retirement. *Journal of Personality and Social Psychology.* [Epub ahead of print]

Schwaba, T., Luhmann, M., Denissen, J. J. A., Chung, J. M., & Bleidorn, W. (2018). Openness to experience and culture-openness transactions across the lifespan. *Journal of Personality and Social Psychology, 15,* 118–136.

Shiner, R., & Caspi, A. (2003). Personality differences in childhood and adolescence: Measurement, development, and consequences. *Journal of Child Psychology and Psychiatry, 44,* 2–32.

Soto, C. J. (2016). The Little Six personality dimensions from early childhood to early adulthood: Mean-level age and gender differences in parents' reports. *Journal of Personality, 84,* 409–422.

Soto, C. J., John, O. P., Gosling, S. D., & Potter, J. (2008). The developmental psychometrics of Big Five self-reports: Acquiescence, factor structure, coherence, and differentiation from ages 10 to 20. *Journal of Personality and Social Psychology, 94,* 718–737.

Soto, C. J., John, O. P., Gosling, S. D., & Potter, J. (2011). Age differences in personality traits from 10 to 65: Big Five domains and facets in a large cross-sectional sample. *Journal of Personality and Social Psychology, 100,* 330–348.

Soto, C. J., & Tackett, J. L. (2015). Personality traits in childhood and adolescence: Structure, development, and outcomes. *Current Directions in Psychological Science, 24,* 358–362.

Specht, J., Bleidorn, W., Denissen, J. J., Hennecke, M., Hutteman, R., Kandler, C., et al. (2014). What drives adult personality development?: A comparison of theoretical perspectives and empirical evidence. *European Journal of Personality, 28,* 216–230.

Specht, J., Egloff, B., & Schmukle, S. C. (2011). Stability and change of personality across the life course: The impact of age and major life events on mean-level and rank-order stability of the Big Five. *Journal of Personality and Social Psychology, 101,* 862–882.

Srivastava, S., John, O. P., Gosling, S. D., & Potter, J. (2003). Development of personality in early and middle adulthood: Set like plaster or persistent change? *Journal of Personality and Social Psychology, 84,* 1041–1053.

Stephan, Y., Sutin, A. R., & Terracciano, A. (2014). Physical activity and personality development across adulthood and old age: Evidence from two longitudinal studies. *Journal of Research in Personality, 49,* 1–7.

Tackett, J. L., Balsis, S., Oltmanns, T. F., & Krueger, R. F. (2009). A unifying perspective on personality pathology across the life span: Developmental considerations for the fifth edition of the *Diagnostic and Statistical Manual of Mental Disorders. Development and Psychopathology, 21,* 687–713.

Tackett, J. L., Kushner, S. C., De Fruyt, F., & Mervielde, I. (2013). Delineating personality traits in childhood and adolescence: Associations across measures, temperament, and behavioral problems. *Assessment, 20,* 738–751.

Van den Akker, A. L., Deković, M., Asscher, J., & Prinzie, P. (2014). Mean-level personality development across childhood and adolescence: A temporary defiance of the maturity principle and bidirectional associations with parenting. *Journal of Personality and Social Psychology, 107,* 736–750.

van Scheppingen, M. A., Jackson, J. J., Specht, J., Hutteman, R., Denissen, J. J., & Bleidorn, W. (2016). Personality trait development during the transition to parenthood: A test of social investment theory. *Social Psychological and Personality Science, 7,* 452–462.

Wagner, J., Ram, N., Smith, J., & Gerstorf, D. (2016). Personality trait development at the end of life: Antecedents and correlates of mean-level trajectories. *Journal of Personality and Social Psychology, 111,* 411–429.

Wichstrøm, L. (1999). The emergence of gender difference in depressed mood during adolescence: The role of intensified gender socialization. *Developmental Psychology, 35,* 232–245.

Wortman, J., Lucas, R. E., & Donnellan, M. B. (2012). Stability and change in the Big Five personality domains: Evidence from a longitudinal study of Australians. *Psychology and Aging, 27,* 867–874.

Wrosch, C., & Heckhausen, J. (1999). Control processes before and after passing a developmental deadline: Activation and deactivation of intimate relationship goals. *Journal of Personality and Social Psychology, 77,* 415–427.

Wrzus, C., Hänel, M., Wagner, J., & Neyer, F. J. (2013). Social network changes and life events across the life span: A meta-analysis. *Psychological Bulletin, 139,* 53–80.

Zimmermann, J., & Neyer, F. J. (2013). Do we become a different person when hitting the road?: Personality development of sojourners. *Journal of Personality and Social Psychology, 105,* 515–530.

PART III

MOTIVATED AGENTS
The Development of Goals and Values

Developmental psychologists have long been fascinated with the question of *intentionality*. How do members of the *Homo sapiens* species come to see themselves as intentional agents in the world? How do we become, in our own minds at least, self-determined, goal-directed organisms who formulate plans and strategies in order to achieve valued ends? While even newborns exhibit goal-directed behavior, it likely takes many years before human beings fully come to terms with the idea that desires, beliefs, plans, and goals reside in their own minds, and that each motivated agent develops his or her own unique goal agenda. By the time children reach kindergarten, most of them have implicitly formulated, or come to discover, the central axioms of *theory of mind*. They now know, or at least believe, that people do things *because they want to do them,* out of desire and belief, and other psychological constructs that reside in the mind. Over time it will become increasingly clear to them, moreover, that each mind is different—seeing the world in a different way; harboring different desires, plans, and values; and striving, therefore, for different things.

Whereas theory of mind represents a major step forward in human cognition, it may also signal an important landmark in the development of personality. Once human beings realize that their own desires and beliefs are the source of motivation, they may reflexively begin to work on those desires and beliefs, and formulate explicit goals and plans to achieve them, whether they be short-term goals, such as remembering to take one's lunch to school each day, or (eventually) long-term goals, such as becoming a physician, or finding a life partner. Going back to Freud, personality psychologists have paid special attention to the problem of human motivation, and they have often (though not always) distinguished this realm of inquiry from the study of dispositional personality traits. As with traits, human beings display remarkable diversity and variation in the kinds of goals they value, and in their strategies for pursuing their goals. We may imagine, therefore, a second line of development in personality that tracks the emergence of motivated agency in childhood and the eventual articulation of goals, values, plans, strategies, and other features of an intricate motivational infrastructure, unique to each human life.

In the first year of life, human babies do *not* develop conscious goals to establish secure attachment bonds with their caregivers. But the evolved attachment adaptation for *Homo sapiens* creates what John Bowlby long ago described as a goal-corrected system that organizes various attachment behaviors, from eye contact to sucking, in order to achieve the predictable outcome of caregiver–infant proximity. From the beginning, attachment theory has been about human motivation. In Chapter 15, Jeffry A. Simpson and Rachael E. Jones build on Bowlby's original

253

insights to describe contemporary research and thinking on the normative developmental course for attachment and important individual differences. Drawing on life-history theory, they explain how and why people follow different evolved trajectories of personality development as a function of differences in life experience, which themselves shape differences in attachment orientation.

Kennon M. Sheldon and Julia Schüler put motivation front and center in Chapter 16, as they aim to integrate contemporary self-determination theory (SDT), which prioritizes the fulfillment of intrinsic human needs (autonomy, competence, and relatedness), with David McClelland's classic approach to assessing individual differences in achievement, power, and affiliation motivation. They argue that people seek out different kinds of satisfying end states as a function of learning and experience, and they pay special attention to those situations in which one's goal agenda can be hijacked by extrinsic circumstances, resulting in unbalanced motivational states. In Chapter 17, Amanda M. Durik and K. Ann Renninger pick up the SDT theme of competence as they explore the vast literature on the development of achievement strivings. Whereas McClelland theorized about an implicit, even unconscious, achievement motive, subsequent formulations have focused on explicit achievement goals, their utility value and cost, the person's sense of his or her own abilities and weaknesses as they apply to achievement striving, and instances wherein implicit and explicit strivings come together to express a deep and specific *interest* in a particular achievement domain.

The salience of the motivated agent in personality development may be most apparent in Chapter 18, wherein Alexandra M. Freund, Christopher M. Napolitano, and Joshua L. Rutt lay out a goal-based framework for the study of adult personality development. They point out that goals are more than the desired end states that exist in the mind of the agent; they are also the cognitive representations of the association between the desired end states and the means by which to achieve them. Among the most consequential changes that occur in adult lives are those that involve how psychological goals are selected and pursued, how agents disengage themselves from goals that no longer seem attainable or no longer serve deeper values and needs, and the processes of compensation and optimization that adults adopt in their efforts to promote their own unique motivational agendas. As William James observed over 100 years ago, the extent to which an agent experiences success in attaining goals, or what James called "pretensions," goes a long way in determining *self-esteem*. In Chapter 19, Ulrich Orth and Richard W. Robins examine the development of self-esteem across the human life course. Reviewing a broad swath of literature, including recent longitudinal studies, they discuss how self-esteem first arises in childhood, the temporal stability of individual differences in self-esteem, developmental trends in mean levels of self-esteem, cohort differences, and the extent to which having high or low self-esteem really matters for a person's adaptation to life.

Motivated agency is as much about values as it is about goals. Not only do human beings, as motivated agents, pursue *valued* goals, but they also typically hold—and sometimes cherish—abstract *values* regarding what is good, what is true, and what ideal ends a good person *should* pursue and promote. In Chapter 20, Darcia Narvaez takes up the issue of moral values, bringing a multidisciplinary perspective to the study of moral development, focusing a great deal of attention on the neurobiological and familial forces that shape a moral sensibility in the early years of life. In Chapter 21, Paul Wink, Michele Dillon, and Dan Farina examine reglious values, spirituality, and the like, focusing on religion and religious values in the context of American society. They argue that the American sociocultural environment tends to favor personal agency in religion, encouraging young people and adults to take initiative in all matters religious and to fashion their own unique, self-determined spiritual destinies. Adopting a life-course perspective, they discuss the relationships between religion and personality, and consider how developmental contexts and transitions impact religious and spiritual engagement.

In Chapter 22, Gary S. Gregg aims to contextualize the entire psychological infrastructure for motivated agency—what he terms *goals, values,* and *social selves*—within the frame of culture. Whereas the cultural framing of psychological agency often contrasts the norms of individualistic and collectivist cultures, Gregg shifts perspective to consider the "other cultural psychology," delving deep into classic studies of traditional societies, and how they differ from modern societies. He spotlights research on Japanese and Arab-Muslim cultures to consider the contrast between traditionalism and modernity. A full understanding of motivated agency within cultures may require, Gregg argues, a shift away from broad national cultures (e.g., Chinese culture, American culture) to focus more on specific and variegated cultural niches in the globalizing world.

CHAPTER 15

Attachment and Social Development within a Life-History Perspective

Jeffry A. Simpson
Rachael E. Jones

Claire has been a participant in a longitudinal study her entire life. When she was born, her mother had already dropped out of high school and was not living with Claire's biological father. For most of the first 18 months of Claire's life, her mother and father were unemployed, had a conflict-ridden relationship, struggled with major money problems, and moved several times. Despite the fact that Claire's mother said she loved her and enjoyed being a parent, Claire was classified as insecurely attached to her mother based on their behavior together. When Claire became upset, for example, her mother could not comfort her, so Claire—a mere 1-year-old—had to learn to comfort herself.

Between ages 2 and 5, Claire and her family experienced even more life stress. Her biological father provided little assistance and died unexpectedly at a very young age. When Claire was 3, trained observers coded Claire's mother acting unsupportive and hostile toward her. At preschool, Claire's teachers described her as immature, fearful, and angry compared to her peers.

During elementary school, Claire's life improved somewhat, but unpredictable and stressful events continued to crop up. One of her relatives, for example, was charged with killing someone, and her mother had a string of short-term boyfriends. Things became better, however, at school. Claire was smart; her focus on schoolwork and her grades gradually improved, and she developed a new group of friends.

But early in adolescence, Claire started engaging in high-risk behaviors. For example, she began abusing alcohol and drugs, and she had several different sexual partners by the time she was 16 years old. When she was 19, Claire got pregnant, without a job or steady boyfriend. Early in adulthood, she moved back in with her mother, remained chronically unemployed, had trouble maintaining romantic relationships, and worried about the quality of her parenting.

How can the trajectory of Claire's life be understood? How did her early life experiences shape the person she became as an adult? What role did being insecurely attached play in her personality and social development across time? In recent years, psychologists have learned a great deal about the way in which certain early life experiences and the attachment orientations that emerge from them typically affect how people develop as their lives unfold. In this chapter, we answer these and other questions by turning to theory and research on personality and social development over time, linking several key principles to Claire and her unique developmental trajectory.

The chapter is organized around six sections. In the first section, we describe the primary evolutionary tenets of attachment theory, including key normative and individual-difference principles underlying the theory. In the second section, we describe a broad theory of personality and social development—life-history theory—which explains how and why people follow different evolved developmental trajectories as their lives unfold, depending in large part on the events and experiences they encounter across their lives. In the third section, we present a model anchored on life-history principles—the evolutionary model of social development proposed by Belsky, Steinberg, and Draper (1991). This influential model explains how and why certain events that occur during specific stages of life typically affect personality and developmental outcomes at later points in life. As we shall see, the psychological construct that connects early life experiences with later outcomes is whether individuals develop secure or insecure attachment orientations in relation to significant others during their lives, beginning with their caregivers. In the fourth section, we summarize findings from a recent longitudinal study that tests key stages and components of the evolutionary model of social development. In the fifth section, we discuss how some of the specific events in Claire's life offer complementary idiographic evidence that is largely consistent with the Belsky and colleagues model. In the final section, we return to a core theme of the chapter—why many of the thoughts, feelings, and behaviors that Claire displayed at different stages of her development reflect her attachment orientation and can be construed as "adaptive" in terms of promoting her reproductive fitness, particularly in light of her very challenging and unpredictable life course.

Evolutionary Principles of Attachment Theory

According to Bowlby (1969, 1973, 1980), humans—especially young children—evolved to maintain close physical and emotional proximity to stronger, older, and/or wiser attachment figures, which would have increased their chances of surviving the perils of childhood and eventually reproducing in evolutionary history. The specific constellation of cognitive, behavioral, and emotional tendencies that evolved to promote proximity and regulate feelings of security is known as the *attachment system,* which is activated when individuals—both children

and adults—feel ill, distressed, vulnerable, or overwhelmed (Bowlby, 1973).

Attachment theory has two basic components: (a) a normative component, which explains modal (species-typical) patterns and stages of attachment in humans, such as why attachment bonds form, and (b) an individual-difference component, which explains deviations from modal patterns and stages, such as why children and adults have different attachment patterns/orientations.

Normative Features of Attachment

Three normative features of attachment have direct ties to evolutionary principles (Simpson & Belsky, 2016): (1) the synchronization of infant–parent behaviors evident during the opening months of a child's life; (2) the strong motivation of children to maintain close contact with, and seek proximity to, their caregivers (attachment figures); and (3) the four early developmental stages in which attachment reactions and behaviors emerge.

Synchronized Capabilities

Human infants are born in an underdeveloped, premature state compared to infants in most species (Kaplan, Lancaster, & Hurtado, 2000). Nonetheless, they are well equipped to bond with their caregivers from the very moment they are born. This preparedness to bond is synchronized with their mothers' natural tendency to respond in ways that are well suited to infants' developing abilities, which in turn facilitates infant–caregiver bonding (Simpson & Belsky, 2008). Mothers, for example, usually exaggerate their facial expressions, change them more slowly, and maintain longer eye contact when interacting with their infants than with others (Eibl-Eibesfeldt, 1989). When talking to their infants, mothers slow their speech, accentuating certain syllables, and speaking one octave higher normal speech (Grieser & Kuhl, 1988). Infants prefer these behaviors, which mesh well with their developing visual and auditory capacities.

Contact Maintenance and Proximity Seeking

Attachment behaviors ostensibly evolved to promote and maintain physical proximity between vulnerable children and their attachment figures (Bowlby, 1969). Young children accomplish this by enacting three broad types of behaviors. Signaling behaviors, such as vocalizing and smiling, usually draw caregivers toward their child, often to participate in positive interactions. Aversive behaviors, such as crying and screaming, motivate caregivers to attend to their child, typically to quell these aversive reactions. Active behaviors, such as approaching and following, keep children close to their caregivers. In all likelihood, each of these behaviors served the same evolutionary function—to draw and keep vulnerable infants in close physical proximity to their caregivers, thereby increasing their chances of survival enroute to eventual reproduction (Marvin, Britner, & Russell, 2016).

Phases of Development

Bowlby (1969) claimed that attachment propensities develop during four developmental phases. During Phase 1 (typically between birth and 2–3 months), infants respond well to a variety of people, not showing a preference for any one attachment figure. This propensity should have facilitated survival in difficult ancestral environments in which the probability of early maternal death was much greater than it is today.

During Phase 2 (typically between 2–3 months and 7 months), infants become more discriminating in their social responsiveness. For example, they start to distinguish caregivers and family members from strangers, prefer certain people over others, and direct more of their attachment behavior toward certain individuals, usually those who most often care for them. Such refined discrimination at this age would have helped infants sustain care and attention from their primary caregivers, also facilitating their survival enroute to reproduction.

During Phase 3 (typically from 7 months to 3 years), children assume a more proactive role in seeking proximity and initiating social contact. During this phase, they also start developing internal working models—schemas composed of beliefs, expectancies, attitudes, and emotions reflecting what relationships tend to be like based on their experiences with attachment figures (Bowlby, 1973). Phase 3 is also when the three primary functions of attachment begin to appear in behavior: (1) proximity maintenance (staying near to, and resisting separations from, the attachment figure), (2) safe haven (turn-

ing to the attachment figure for comfort and support when distressed), and (3) secure base (using the attachment figure as a safe foundation from which to engage in nonattachment behaviors). These tendencies should also have promoted survival and eventual reproduction in ancestral environments.

During Phase 4 (which typically begins around age 3), behaviors that facilitate goal-corrected partnerships with others start to emerge. Given their blossoming language skills and theory-of-mind capabilities, children begin to view the world from the perspective of their interaction partners rather than just themselves. These abilities allows children to incorporate the goals, plans, and desires of their partners into their own decision making, which in turn facilitates joint plans and activities. These unique abilities should have further promoted the formation and maintenance of pair-bonds in evolutionary history.

As children become toddlers, their need for physical proximity is gradually supplanted by the desire to maintain psychological proximity (i.e., *felt security*; Sroufe & Waters, 1977). Early in adolescence, observable indicators of attachment bonds with parents continue to wane as proximity maintenance, safe haven, and secure base functions are slowly transferred to first peers and then to romantic partners, who often become primary attachment figures in adulthood (Furman & Simon, 1999). The attachment mechanisms that bonded children to their parents are then used in adulthood to facilitate the strong, long-term attachment bonds that are needed for mates to successfully coparent, which should have promoted the long-term survival of offspring in ancestral environments (Zeifman & Hazan, 2016).

In summary, humans are born to bond with their caregivers, with mothers' and infants' behaviors being naturally synchronized, and with infants' behaviors drawing and keeping caregivers close by. The attachment orientations that develop from early caregiving experiences then guide individuals' expectations and behaviors in later friendships and adult romantic relationships.

Individual Differences in Attachment

Although human infants evolved to form attachment bonds with their caregivers, the type of bond they form depends on the nature and quality of their early caregiving environment

(Ainsworth, Blehar, Waters, & Wall, 1978). Needless to say, infants do not have the cognitive ability to appraise conditions in their local environment, such as whether it is safe, plentiful, and rich in resources or threatening, harsh, and impoverished. However, they can determine the degree to which their caregivers are sensitive, responsive, and attentive to their needs. This information should provide critical cues about the nature and quality of the current and perhaps future environmental conditions (Chisholm, 1996; Frankenhuis, Gergely, & Watson, 2013). If, during evolutionary history, caregivers could devote the time, effort, and energy necessary to be sensitive, responsive, and attentive to their children, the local environment was most likely safe and had sufficient resources. Caregivers, therefore, could focus on their children rather than having to deal with external threats. If, on the other hand, caregivers were insensitive, unresponsive, and devoted little attention to their children, the local environment was probably less resource-rich and perhaps dangerous.

The Strange Situation is well suited to identify different attachment patterns in young children because it exposes them to two common danger cues in our evolutionary past: being left alone, and being left with a stranger. Examining reunions between mothers and their 12- to 18-month-old infants, Ainsworth and her colleagues (1978) documented three primary attachment patterns in young children: secure, anxious–ambivalent, and anxious–avoidant. When reuniting with their mothers after being left alone or waiting with a stranger, securely attached children use their caregivers to regulate and reduce their distress, which allows them to resume other activities (e.g., exploration, play). Anxious–avoidant children, by comparison, ignore or withdraw from their caregivers upon being reunited with them, attempting to control and abate their negative affect in an independent, self-reliant fashion. Anxious–ambivalent children make inconsistent, conflicted attempts to glean comfort and support from their caregivers upon reunion, intermixing clinginess with outbursts of anger at their caregivers (see Fearon & Belsky, 2016).

These attachment patterns are believed to be different behavioral strategies that would have solved adaptive problems posed by different kinds of rearing environments during evolutionary history (Belsky, 1997; Chisholm, 1996). Mothers of securely attached infants do tend to be available and responsive to the needs of their children (De Wolff & van IJzendoorn, 1997). As a result, secure children need not worry about the availability and responsiveness of their caregivers, which allows them to regulate their emotions and engage in other important life tasks.

Anxious–ambivalent children have caregivers who routinely behave in an inconsistent or unpredictable manner (Ainsworth et al., 1978). The persistent demandingness of anxious–ambivalent children may, therefore, be a strategy designed to obtain, retain, or improve parental attention and care (Cassidy & Berlin, 1994), which should have improved an anxious child's chances of survival leading toward reproduction.

Avoidant children typically have caregivers who are cold and rejecting (Ainsworth et al., 1978). Bowlby (1980) conjectured that avoidance allows infants to disregard cues that might trigger their attachment systems. If such cues were fully processed, avoidant infants might recognize the actual inaccessibility of their caregivers, which could prove incapacitating. Offering perhaps a more plausible evolutionary explanation, Main (1981) surmised that the distant, self-reliant behavior of avoidant children allows them to maintain sufficiently close proximity to their belligerent or poorly motivated caregivers without driving them away.

When children enter adolescence, new relationship experiences are assimilated into their internal working models, which are continuously being updated and revised (Bowlby, 1973). Working models now, however, represent the degree to which individuals (1) believe they are worthy of love and affection, and (2) view significant others as loving, affectionate, and likely to stay (Mikulincer & Shaver, 2016). Moreover, unlike in childhood, the attachment system in adulthood becomes integrated with the mating and caregiving systems (Shaver, Hazan, & Bradshaw, 1988).

In adulthood, romantic partners become the central attachment figures. Securely attached adults have learned how to regulate their emotions more constructively and effectively (Mikulincer & Shaver, 2003), work to build greater intimacy with their romantic partners (Mikulincer & Shaver, 2016), and thus have higher quality, more stable romantic relationships (Feeney, 2016). In addition, these attributes should lead secure individuals to develop better self-regulation abilities, which allows them to forge better, more meaningful, and more stable interpersonal ties across most life domains (e.g., family, work, leisure). Anxiously attached adults, in contrast, regulate their emotions more poorly (relying on hyperactivating strategies; Mikulincer & Shaver, 2003), yearn to feel more secure in their romantic relationships (Mikulincer & Shaver, 2016), but have lower quality and more conflict-prone relationships (Feeney, 2016). Avoidantly attached adults also regulate their emotions rather poorly (using deactivating strategies; Mikulincer & Shaver, 2003), strive to achieve and maintain a high degree of personal autonomy and control (Mikulincer & Shaver, 2016), and also have lower quality romantic relationships that are more vulnerable to dissolution (Feeney, 2016).

Life-History Theory

Having reviewed the evolutionary foundations of attachment theory, we now turn to life-history theory (LHT; Del Giudice, Gangestad, & Kaplan, 2016; Kaplan & Gangestad, 2005; see also Del Giudice, Chapter 2, this volume), which actually encompasses attachment theory (Simpson, 1999). LHT is a metatheory that explains why certain traits and behaviors typically emerge when certain kinds of events occur across the lifespan. The amount of time, effort, and resources that an organism can expend at any point during development is finite. Because of this fact, all organisms—including human beings—must make *trade-offs* in how they allocate the limited amount of time, effort, and resources they have at each life stage enroute to eventually reproducing. Since individuals cannot simultaneously maximize each component that comprises their overall reproductive fitness (which entails surviving to reproductive age, successfully reproducing, then caring for offspring and/or kin), they have to prioritize the specific life-domains into which they make investments. Broadly speaking, LHT specifies the primary selection pressures in our evolutionary past that should have governed when, and the environmental conditions under which, individuals devoted more versus less time, energy, and resources to their physical development, growth, mating, and parenting.

All individuals must make three trade-offs when deciding (typically unconsciously or outside of awareness) how to partition their resources at each stage of development in order to increase their reproductive fitness: (1) whether

to invest more in current (immediate) reproduction versus future (delayed) reproduction; (2) whether to invest more in higher quantity versus higher quality offspring; and (3) whether to invest more in mating versus parenting. Individuals cannot invest large amounts of time, energy, or resources to one side of these trade-offs (e.g., mating or having a large number of children) without investing less in the other (e.g., parenting or having fewer children).

Consider, for example, the trade-off that Claire had to make between current reproduction (having her first child at the relatively young age of 19) versus future reproduction (having her first child later in life). By investing in immediate reproduction, Claire could not invest as much time, effort, and resources in future reproduction (e.g., having children at a slightly older age, when more resources might be available to raise them). Indeed, in contemporary Western societies, people who have children as teenagers usually do not have the time, money, or energy to obtain further education or valuable job experiences, which could allow them to attract better mates and invest more time, effort, and resources in a smaller number of children somewhat later in life (Griskevicius et al., 2013).

An Evolutionary Model of Social Development

The first and most influential evolutionary model of personality and social development was proposed by Belsky and colleagues (1991; see also Belsky, 1997). According to their evolutionary model of social development, one primary evolutionary function of early social experience is to prepare children for the social and physical environments they will most likely inhabit during their lifetimes. The model focuses mainly on the trade-off that must be made between offspring quantity versus quality. Certain types of information contained in the early environment should help a child adopt an appropriate reproductive strategy later in life—one that should have increased his or her reproductive fitness, on average, in similar environments during our ancestral past. For example, harsh or unpredictable environments in which competition for limited resources is intense should lead most parents to behave in a more demanding or rejecting manner toward their children, and offspring who themselves are more aggressive and less cooperative should have higher reproductive fitness as adults compared to offspring who lack these traits. Conversely, offspring reared in less stressful environments with more plentiful or better resources could have increased their reproductive fitness by adopting a more cooperative, communal orientation in adulthood (see Hinde, 1986).

The Belsky and Colleages Model

The Belsky and colleagues (1991) model, which is displayed in Figure 15.1, has five developmental stages. It proposes that (1) early contextual factors in the family of origin (e.g., the amount of stress, spousal harmony, financial resources) affect (2) early childrearing experiences (e.g., the amount of sensitive, supportive, and/or responsive caregiving). These experiences then affect (3) psychological and behavioral development (e.g., the child's attachment orientation, trust, opportunism), which influence (4) somatic development (e.g., how quickly sexual maturation is reached) and eventually (5) the adoption of specific reproductive strategies (e.g., the timing of first sexual intercourse, the stability and quality of romantic pair-bonds, the amount of parental investment). Although these stages are sequentially linked, earlier stages may statistically interact with later ones to predict downstream outcomes. For example, early contextual factors in Claire's family of origin (e.g., the instability of her early home life) could interact with some of her later childrearing experiences (e.g., the quality of caregiving she received from her mother) to predict later outcomes in Claire's life (e.g., her propensity for taking risks as a teenager).

Belsky and his colleagues (1991) also surmised that two developmental trajectories (pathways) should exist, with each one reflecting a distinct reproductive strategy. As shown on the left side of Figure 15.1, one strategy entails a fast, short-term, opportunistic orientation toward relationships, especially mating and parenting relationships. In this strategy, sexual intercourse happens relatively early in life, romantic pair-bonds tend to be short-lived and unstable, and parental investment is reduced. This orientation ought to have increased the quantity (total number) of offspring in most ancestral environments. The second strategy, depicted on the right of Figure 15.1, entails a slow, long-term, investing orientation toward relationships in which sexual intercourse occurs later, romantic pair-bonds tend to be stable and more endur-

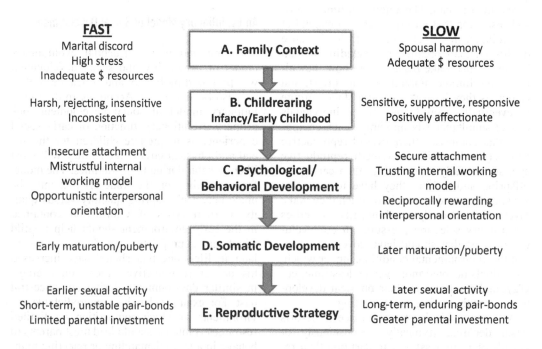

FIGURE 15.1. Developmental pathways of divergent reproductive strategies. Based on the evolutionary model of social development by Belsky, Steinberg, and Draper (1991).

ing, and parental investment is higher. This orientation should have enhanced the quality of offspring (the quality of their phenotypic traits) in most ancestral environments.

Nomothetic Evidence for the Model

A considerable amount of *nomothetic evidence,* most of it cross-sectional, supports the evolutionary model of social development (for reviews, see Belsky, 2012; Simpson & Belsky, 2016). Nomothetic evidence comes from information collected across many people, whereas *idiographic evidence* focuses on specific individuals. Nomothetic evidence is used to test predictions derived from models, which assume that most people are influenced by the same basic physical and biological laws of nature. With respect to the evolutionary model of social development, for example, higher levels of socioemotional stress in families are strongly associated with more insensitive, harsh, rejecting, and inconsistent parenting styles. Greater economic hardship (McLoyd, 1990), more occupational stress (Bronfenbrenner & Crouter, 1982), and higher marital discord (Belsky, 1981; Emery, 1988) are also clearly related to more hostile or withdrawn parenting styles. Greater social support and more economic resources, on the other hand, are reliably linked with warmer, more sensitive parenting practices (Lempers, Clark-Lempers, & Simons, 1989), mainly because less burdened parents tend to be more patient with and tolerant of their children (Belsky, 1984).

The link between parental sensitivity and the psychological and behavioral development of children is also well documented, and it functions through the attachment system. During the first year of life, more insensitive and less responsive caregiving results in insecure attachment orientations in young children (De Wolff & van IJzendoorn, 1997), which in turn forecast behavior problems later in development. Insecurely attached preschoolers, for instance, typically are more socially withdrawn (Waters, Wippman, & Sroufe, 1979), less sympathetic with distressed peers (Waters et al., 1979), and less well liked by peers (LaFreniere & Sroufe, 1985). During elementary school, insecure children also manifest more severe behavior problems, including aggression and disobedience (Lewis, Fiering, McGuffog, & Jaskir, 1984). All of these behaviors are driven by their insecure working

models, which prepare insecure children for environments in which most people are likely to be more opportunistic and less communal.

The most novel feature of the model centers on the hypothesized predictors of the rate of physical development (i.e., sexual maturity). Belsky and colleagues (1991) hypothesized that children exposed to higher amounts of socioemotional stress should develop insecure attachments to their parents, have more behavioral problems, and reach puberty—and thus reproductive capacity—sooner than children who do not have this developmental trajectory. According to LHT (Kaplan & Gangestad, 2005), environments in which resources are scarce or difficult to obtain, relationships are typically unstable, and the risk of early death is high, should motivate people to divert more energy to accelerated physical development, earlier mating, and shorter-term pair-bonds. This developmental strategy would have improved the odds of reproducing before dying at a relatively young age in our evolutionary past. Conversely, environments in which resources are plentiful and relationship ties tend to be reciprocal and communal should motivate individuals to shift their energy, effort, and resources to delayed physical development, later mating, and longer-term pair-bonds that should have fostered greater parental investment. In these environments, individuals could have increased their reproductive fitness by waiting to reproduce until they had acquired the skills and resources necessary to maximize the quality of each child. Each child could thus benefit maximally from all of the embodied capital (e.g., socialization, training, education) invested in him or her.

The findings of several lines of research support most of these predictions (see Belsky, 2012, for a review). For example, greater parent–child warmth and cohesion predict delayed pubertal development in both prospective longitudinal studies (e.g., Ellis, McFadyen-Ketchum, Dodge, Pettit, & Bates, 1999; Graber, Brooks-Gunn, & Warren, 1995) and retrospective or concurrent ones (e.g., Kim, Smith, & Palermiti, 1997; Miller & Pasta, 2000). Moreover, greater parent–child conflict and coercion, which are associated with harsh and unpredictable environments, forecast earlier pubertal timing in both prospective longitudinal studies (e.g., Ellis & Essex, 2007; Moffitt, Caspi, Belsky, & Silva, 1992) and retrospective or concurrent ones (e.g., Kim et al., 1997). In addition, spouses who have happier, less conflictual marriages tend to have daughters who reach pubertal maturation later, as confirmed by both prospective longitudinal studies (e.g., Ellis et al., 1999; Ellis & Garber, 2000) and nonprospective ones (e.g., Kim et al., 1997). Finally, girls who are insecurely attached early in life (at 15 months) tend to experience both onset and completion of pubertal development earlier in life (Belsky, Houts, & Fearon, 2010), whereas being securely attached at 15 months buffers (protects) girls who were exposed to higher levels of stress early in life from experiencing earlier menarche (Sung et al., 2016).

A few studies have not found puberty-related effects. Steinberg (1988), for instance, did not find a relation between the amount of family conflict/coercion and pubertal timing in girls. However, family experience/pubertal developmental effects have been documented in studies that consider possible genetic confounds (e.g., biological reasons for earlier menarche) that might be due to the shared genes of mothers and their daughters in sibling design studies (Tithers & Ellis, 2008) and in natural experiments (Pesonen et al., 2008). It is important to note that all of these puberty-related effects are confined to girls. No such effects have been found for boys.

Empirical support for the last stages of the Belsky and colleagues (1991) model comes from research linking adult attachment styles to mating and romantic relationship functioning, and from research relating adult attachment orientations with parenting behavior. Women and men who report being more securely attached to their romantic partners are less likely to have promiscuous sexual attitudes and engage in extrapair sex (Brennan & Shaver, 1995) and more likely to want a single sexual partner during the next 30 years (Miller & Fishkin, 1997). Women who are securely attached in romantic relationships typically have first sexual intercourse at a later age (Bogaert & Sadava, 2002). Securely attached men and women have more satisfying romantic relationships (Feeney, 2016), experience less negative affect (Simpson, 1990), and engage in more constructive conflict resolution tactics (Simpson, Rholes, & Phillips, 1996). In light of these tendencies, secure adults are less prone to divorce or separate (Feeney, 2016), and both partners are more committed to and trusting of each other (Fuller & Fincham, 1995).

To date, virtually all of the studies that have tested segments of the Belsky and colleagues (1991) model have relied on cross-sectional

or short-term longitudinal methods. Very few studies have followed individuals from birth over their lives. In the next section, we report recent findings from a study that prospectively assessed many of the key constructs in this model over the first 23 years of life in a well-known longitudinal sample.

The Development of Mating Strategies: A Prospective Longitudinal Approach

According to Belsky and colleagues' (1991) model, a slow (restricted) reproductive strategy entails a slower pace of development and reproduction, which should be associated with greater investment in fewer but higher-quality offspring. A fast (unrestricted) reproductive strategy, on the other hand, involves a faster pace of development and reproduction, often resulting in more offspring but less investment in each one. Slow strategists should, therefore, invest more time and effort in maintaining long-term, committed relationships that facilitate greater investment in fewer offspring, whereas fast strategists should put more time and effort into multiple, short-term mating opportunities.

Harsh, Predictable, and Unpredictable Conditions

As discussed earlier, the adaptive value of a given life-history strategy, whether slow or fast, should depend on the environment in which it develops. Two key environmental factors ought to be the amount of morbidity/mortality (harshness) in the local area and the quality of parental care that children receive (Belsky et al., 1991; Simpson & Belsky, 2008). However, another key environmental factor needs to be considered—the extent to which the environment is predictable versus unpredictable (Ellis, Figueredo, Brumbach, & Schlomer, 2009). Unpredictability is typically indexed by the frequency of changes in the immediate family environment that directly affect parents and their children (e.g., Belsky, Schlomer, & Ellis, 2012; Simpson, Griskevicius, Kuo, Sung, & Collins, 2012). The distinction between harshness and unpredictability is important to make because environments may be harsh *or* unpredictable, both, or neither. A harsh environment, for example, may be characterized by consistent poverty that still allows for survival. Although living in poverty is very stressful, it is predictable, so individuals can learn to prepare for and cope with such harshness-related events. In unpredictable environments, however, stressful events occur unexpectedly, meaning that individuals cannot necessarily prepare for them. The resulting stress is therefore more difficult to manage because events are often sudden and uncontrollable. Unpredictability can, as a result, have more lasting effects on people, especially when it occurs early in life (see Simpson et al., 2012).

The costs and benefits of initiating and then maintaining long-term romantic relationships should be influenced by the degree to which the local environment is predictable versus unpredictable. In predictable environments, parents can increase the survival and well-being of their children through supportive biparental care and higher investment, which requires the devoted help of long-term, committed mates in most instances. Taking the time to invest in long-term relationships that produce fewer but perhaps higher-quality offspring makes sense when individuals can be reasonably confident that their long-term investments will result in good outcomes. In unpredictable environments, in contrast, long-term investments may result in catastrophic outcomes, especially if environmental conditions change and become dire. Unexpected increases in juvenile mortality rates, for example, might lead slow strategists to lose their entire investment in offspring. In these unstable, unpredictable environments, it makes more sense from an evolutionary standpoint to start reproducing at an earlier age and have more offspring in order to improve the odds that some offspring will survive and eventually reproduce as adults (Ellis et al., 2009). This strategy can also diversify the genetic material of one's offspring through mating with different partners (Donaldson-Matasci, Lachmann, & Bergstrom, 2008). Thus, fast strategists who enact an unrestricted sociosexual orientation—such as Claire—should have higher reproductive fitness in unpredictable environments, whereas slow strategists who enact a restricted sociosexual orientation ought to have higher reproductive fitness in more stable, predictable environments.

Importance of the Early Environment

According to Ellis and colleagues (2009), exposure to unpredictable environments early in life should lead people to adopt faster reproductive

strategies (unrestricted sociosexuality), whereas exposure to predictable environments should yield slower reproductive strategies (restricted sociosexuality). Such patterns have been documented in a few prospective longitudinal studies. For example, exposure to more predictable environments in the opening years of life uniquely predicts having fewer sexual partners by age 15 (Belsky et al., 2012) and being older at first pregnancy (Nettle, Coall, & Dickins, 2011). Moreover, exposure to more predictable adolescent environments indirectly predicts engaging in restricted sociosexual behaviors and being more likely to use contraception in early adulthood (Brumbach, Figueredo, & Ellis, 2009). Furthermore, exposure to more predictable environments during the first 5 years of life in particular forecasts fewer sexual partners by age 23 (Simpson et al., 2012), above and beyond the effects of both environmental harshness across the first 16 years of life and the effects of unpredictability experienced after age 5.

Parental Support and Attachment as Mediators

The information contained in early environments must be detected by children in order to shape their future development. Most young children, however, are not aware of the conditions that exist in the wider environment. Belsky and his colleagues (1991) suggest that parents provide their children with *critical information* about the local environment through the quality and sensitivity of their parenting practices. A great deal of research has confirmed that it is more difficult to provide good, high-quality care in stressful conditions (Belsky & Jaffee, 2006; Crnic & Low, 2002). Thus, the quality of parental care should be a particularly valid cue indexing conditions in the local environment (Del Giudice & Belsky, 2011; Simpson, 1999).

According to a life-history account, harsh and/or unpredictable early-life environments should reduce the quality of care that children receive, eventually resulting in fast reproductive strategies (unrestricted sociosexuality; Belsky et al., 1991; Chisholm, 1993; Ellis, 2004). The few prospective longitudinal studies that have investigated whether and how disruptive parenting is associated with girls' sexual development have supported this prediction. Disruptive parenting has been indexed by father absence (Ellis & Essex, 2007), maternal separation and lack of paternal involvement (Nettle et al., 2011), and maternal depression (Belsky et al., 2012). Parental disruption also predicts becoming involved in lower-quality romantic relationships (Conger, Cui, Bryant, & Elder, 2000; Cui & Fincham, 2010). These findings therefore provide preliminary evidence that the quality of parental care might be one route through which early environmental conditions start shaping adult reproductive strategies.

We know surprisingly little, however, about *how* early parental care shapes the development of reproductive strategies as individuals move into adulthood. One possibility is that the quality and/or consistency of early parental care instills beliefs and expectations in children regarding what their future interactions with others will be like, which in turn affects their later psychological and behavioral adjustment (Del Giudice, 2009; Simpson & Belsky, 2008). If so, this process should be governed by the attachment system, which motivates individuals to seek and maintain close proximity to supportive others, especially when they are stressed, afraid, or feel overly challenged (Bowlby, 1969; Simpson & Rholes, 1994).

Bowlby (1969, 1973, 1980) proposed that when a potential threat is detected, the attachment system generates a sequence of psychological, physiological, and behavioral responses designed to elicit support from caregivers, which, if successful, restores a sense of emotional safety and felt security. Early caregiving experiences influence the beliefs and expectations that individuals have about the support they are likely to get from attachment figures in threatening situations, which also provides valuable information about the safety and predictability of the current environment. Caregivers who can be counted on to provide good, reliable support tend to instill positive expectations about the availability of support from other people (i.e., secure attachment representations), whereas caregivers who provide inconsistent or poor support usually instill negative expectations about the availability of support from others (i.e., insecure attachment representations). Once formed, attachment representations tend to guide an individual's thoughts, feelings, and behaviors within close relationships over the lifespan (Bowlby, 1973).

Research has also confirmed that securely attached individuals not only prefer long-term relationships, but they also function better in them (Mikulincer & Shaver, 2016). For example, individuals who are securely attached in infancy display better conflict resolution skills and

more positive emotions in their adult romantic relationships (Simpson, Collins, Tran, & Haydon, 2007), and they also have higher-quality relationships (Roisman, Collins, Sroufe, & Egeland, 2005). In addition, priming attachment security experimentally increases the desire for long-term relationships in most people (Gillath & Schachner, 2006). And cross-sectional studies have shown that securely attached adults are more committed to and supportive in their romantic relationships (e.g., Collins & Feeney, 2000; Simpson, 1990), whereas avoidantly attached adults (who represent one of two types of attachment insecurity) prefer short-term relationships and are less emotionally involved when they are involved in longer-term relationships (Birnbaum, 2010; Schachner & Shaver, 2004).

In summary, consistent with the Belsky and colleagues (1991) model, these findings suggest that attachment representations should mediate the connection between exposure to predictable versus unpredictable early environments and reproductive strategies in early adulthood. More specifically, exposure to predictable early-life environments should facilitate more reliable, higher-quality parenting, which should generate secure attachment representations, leading to slower, more restricted sociosexual orientations.

The Minnesota Longitudinal Study of Risk and Adaptation

To test these ideas prospectively and longitudinally, we (Szepsenwol et al., 2017) analyzed data from the Minnesota Longitudinal Study of Risk and Adaptation (MLSRA; Sroufe, Egeland, Carlson, & Collins, 2005). The MLSRA has followed approximately 180 individuals from before they were born into middle adulthood. All of the participants were born in the mid-1970s to first-time mothers who were living below the poverty line when their children were born. At multiple points of development across the lifespan, the MLSRA has excellent measures of each participant's early-life environment (e.g., coder-rated measures of the predictability and harshness of each environment), coder-rated observational measures of parenting quality/support based on videotaped mother–child interactions early in life, and interview measures (coded by observers) of attachment representations and markers of restricted (slow) versus unrestricted (fast) sociosexuality from late adolescence and early adulthood.

Measures

What makes this study unique is the nature and quality of the measures, particularly those relevant to certain components and stages of the Belsky and colleagues (1991) model (see Figure 15.1). *Early predictability* was assessed by three items from the Life Events Schedule (LES; Egeland, Breitenbucher, & Rosenberg, 1982). These interview-based items ask each mother to report and discuss the disruptive nature of three types of changes in her life during the preceding year: (1) changes in employment status (e.g., periods of unemployment), (2) changes in residence (e.g., moving to a different house or apartment), and (3) changes in cohabitation status (e.g., whether and how often romantic partners moved in or out of the home). Each item was then rated by coders for the degree of disruption associated with each event on a scale of 0 (*no disruption*) to 3 (*severe disruption*). This measure encompassed the first 4 years of each participant's life when the LES was administered (when he or she was 12, 18, and 48 months old). Consistent with earlier studies (e.g., Simpson et al., 2012; Szepsenwol, Simpson, Griskevicius, & Raby, 2015), we first created an unpredictability measure by summing the three items from each of the three assessments. We then subtracted this score from the maximum possible score to create a composite predictability score, which was then divided by three to form a 0 (*highly unpredictable*) to 9 (*highly predictable*) scale.

Early harshness was assessed by participants' socioeconomic status (SES) during the first year of life. SES is a good marker of harshness in Western societies because it is linearly related to morbidity and mortality (Adler, Boyce, Chesney, Folkman, & Syme, 1993; Chen, Matthews, & Boyce, 2002). The first SES assessment (collected at 42 months) was based on mothers' educational attainment and the revised version of the Duncan Socioeconomic Index (SEI; Duncan, 1961; Stevens & Featherman, 1981). The second assessment (collected at 54 months) was based on only mothers' SEI. SES scores were transformed to t scores within each assessment period in order to remove negative values, and the average of the 42-month and 54-month scores were treated as our composite measure of early harshness.

Early maternal support was assessed by videotaped social interactions between each mother and her child (participant). When participants were 24 and 42 months old, they and

their mothers were observed doing a set of problem-solving and teaching tasks. The tasks were designed to increase in complexity until they became too difficult for any child to solve without some help. Mothers were told to allow their child to attempt each task independently, but to offer help if/when they thought it was appropriate to do so. Each videotaped session was then rated by coders for mothers' quality of support on 7-point scales. Mothers who showed interest and were attentive to the needs of their child, responded contingently to their child's emotional signals, and reinforced their child's success were given high scores. Mothers who were distant, hostile, and/or unsupportive were given low scores. The average of the 24- and 42-month scores served as our measure of early maternal support.

When participants were age 19, their *attachment representations* were measured by the Adult Attachment Interview (AAI; George, Kaplan, & Main, 1985), a semistructured interview that assesses the degree to which individuals have a coherent narrative about their early experiences with caregivers (parents), primarily between ages 5 and 12. Participants were asked to describe their early relationships with their caregivers and to discuss periods of separation, rejection, abuse, and loss. The transcribed AAIs were then rated by coders on 9-point scales using Main and Goldwyn's (1998) coding system. We used the Coherence of Mind scale, which assesses each individual's ability to freely explore his or her feelings about childhood experiences in an organized/emotionally well-regulated versus a nonorganized/emotionally dysregulated manner, as our measure of attachment security (see Raby, Cicchetti, Carlson, Egeland, & Collins, 2013; Roisman, Madsen, Hennighausen, Sroufe, & Collins, 2001).

Sociosexuality in early adulthood was assessed from an interview participants completed at age 23. The sociosexuality coding was based on participants' responses to 14 interview items that asked about their current romantic relationship, their relationship history in the prior 2 years, and their ideal romantic relationship. Coders rated participants' responses to all 14 items for evidence of restricted versus unrestricted sociosexuality on a 5-point scale. High scores were given to participants who displayed no evidence of short-term dating or sexual promiscuity, who wanted to be in a romantic relationship with just one person, and/or who were currently in a long-term romantic relationship (or had been in one recently). Low scores were given to those who reported multiple dating and sexual partners (most or all of which were short-term), and who were interested in dating multiple people. The averaged ratings of the coders was our measure of sociosexuality in early adulthood.

We also assessed the *current predictability* of each participant's environment at age 23. Current predictability was measured with the same items used to assess early predictability (i.e., changes in employment status, changes in residence, and changes in cohabitation status during the past year). Specifically, coders rated each interview-based item for level of disruption on a scale ranging from 0 (*no disruption*) to 3 (*severe disruption*). A current predictability measure was then calculated by summing the ratings and subtracting the sum from the maximum possible sum to create a 0 (*highly unpredictable*) to 9 (*highly predictable*) scale. This measure was used to determine whether the effects of early-life predictability continued to be significant once current predictability was statistically controlled.

Findings

To determine whether early predictability uniquely (independently) predicted greater restricted sociosexuality at age 23, we conducted a series of hierarchical regression analyses. Consistent with our central hypothesis, greater early-life predictability forecasted more restricted sociosexuality at age 23. Framed another way, individuals like Claire who experienced more unpredictability early in life were more likely to have a fast, unrestricted mating orientation at age 23. The level of predictability in the current environment at age 23 was also uniquely associated with greater restricted sociosexuality, but the effects of early predictability remained significant. As expected, men were more unrestricted than women on average, but gender did *not* moderate the effects of either early or current predictability in predicting sociosexuality at age 23.

Following this, we examined whether receiving more supportive parenting early in life (based on behavioral observations of maternal supportive presence when participants were 2 and 3.5 years old) and whether secure attachment representations in adolescence (based on AAI scores at age 19) mediated the link between exposure to predictability early in life and re-

stricted sociosexuality at age 23. The model we tested is shown in Figure 15.2. Consistent with our hypothesis, exposure to more predictable environments early in life was associated with receiving better parental support during the same time period, controlling for the effects of early harshness. Higher-quality early parental support, in turn, predicted having more secure attachment representations of one's childhood at age 19, which in turn predicted being more restricted at age 23. Cast another way, individuals like Claire who grew up in more unpredictable environments were more likely to receive poorer parental support, which led them to develop insecure attachment representations by adolescence, which then predicted a faster, more unrestricted sociosexuality orientation at age 23.

Considered as a whole, these recent findings show that the impact of early predictability on restricted sociosexuality in early adulthood partially flows through the quality of early parental support and then attachment security in adolescence. These findings provide novel, prospective longitudinal support for several key components of the Belsky and colleagues (1991) model.

Claire's Life: An Idiographic Examination

To this point, we have reviewed nomothetic evidence relevant to various components of Belsky and colleagues' (1991) evolutionary model of social development. To date, the only developmental stage for which nomothetic evidence has *not* been found is reproductive timing (sexual maturation) in boys. Unlike girls, boys who experience higher levels of stress or are insecurely attached to their parents early in life do not mature faster physically than boys exposed to less stress or who are securely attached.

There is, however, another form of evidence one can use to evaluate theoretical models—*idiographic evidence.* Idiographic information comes from studying specific individuals who are viewed as unique agents with a unique life history, some of whom may experience life events or have attributes that distinguish them from other people. Claire's rather unique developmental history provides just this sort of evidence, and her fast developmental trajectory is remarkably consistent with the Belsky and colleagues (1991) model (see Figure 15.1).

During the first 2 years of her life, Claire's family context was highly stressful, containing a lot of unpredictability. Before her first birth-

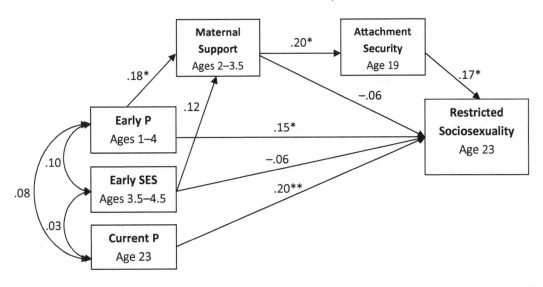

FIGURE 15.2. Mediation analysis (from Szepsenwol et al., 2017): Standardized direct and indirect effects (betas) of early predictability (P) on restricted sociosexuality in early adulthood. Effects are estimated using full information maximum likelihood. $N = 155$. $*p < .05$; $**p < .01$.

day, Claire's on again–off again parents—both of whom were unemployed—moved four times. Her parents also reported having numerous heated arguments in Claire's presence, most of which centered on their chronic unemployment and associated money, alcohol, and drug issues. When interviewed about her life during this period of time, Claire's mother stated that her main problem in life was "putting too much trust in other people."

When Claire was 12 and 18 months old, she and her mother completed the Strange Situation task to assess the attachment pattern that characterized their relationship. Once again, the Strange Situation involves a series of short separations and reunions, during which the parent (usually the mother) leaves her child in a room (both alone and with a stranger), then returns shortly thereafter. Most young children find this task distressing, but what distinguishes securely attached parent–child pairs from insecurely attached pairs is how the child reacts when his or her parent reenters the room. Claire was classified by observers as insecurely attached in both Strange Situation assessments, being rated as anxiously attached at 12 months but then avoidantly attached at 18 months.

One likely reason for her insecurity was the sustained unpredictable stress that pervaded her early life, which most likely affected the quality

of care she received during infancy and early childhood. Between ages 2 and 5, for example, Claire's father had repeated run-ins with the law, then suddenly died in a freak accident. Her home life was further complicated by the birth of a sister during a time when Claire's mother lived alone and continued to be chronically unemployed. When Claire was 2 and 3½ years old, she and her mother were videotaped engaging in a series of tasks that started out easy for Claire to complete, but became much more difficult, making the interactions stressful for both Claire and her mother. During these tasks, Claire's mother was rated as being unsupportive and even hostile, berating Claire for her inability to complete the more difficult tasks. Claire's mother was also abusive toward her at home, although this information did not come to light until Claire reported it many years later. These negative caregiving experiences are likely to have affected Claire's demeanor at preschool, where her teachers described her as irritable, worried, distressed, hypersensitive, fearful of new situations, and not liked by her preschool peers. On the positive side, the chaos in Claire's home life subsided some, partly because she finally had her own bedroom that contained her own books and toys.

During middle childhood (the elementary school years), the level of unpredictability within her home declined some, but the amount of unpredictability in the surrounding environment remained high. One of her relatives was charged with committing a major violent crime, there were more alcohol problems with other members of her extended family, her mother continued to have different live-in boyfriends (some of whom treated Claire badly), and one of her playmates died of cancer. Fortunately, Claire was bright and wanted to have friends, so her school grades and friendship ties gradually improved over elementary school. Nevertheless, she started to display more psychological vulnerabilities. In first grade, for example, Claire's teachers reported that she worried about dying and being abandoned. By the end of elementary school, she scored high on standard measures of depression and having suicidal thoughts. Her teachers indicated that Claire was stubborn and defiant in the classroom, displayed little motivation to do well in school, had difficulties with several of her peers, had low self-esteem, and was "emotionally unresponsive" much of the time.

According to the Belsky and colleagues (1991) model, this cascade of early life events should have accelerated Claire's physical and sexual maturation, which it did. Claire had her first menstrual period at age 10, approximately 3 years sooner than the average girl. She first engaged in sexual intercourse at age 12, and reported having more than 10 sexual partners by the time she was only 16 years old. During early adolescence, Claire reported using alcohol or drugs almost daily, started engaging in petty (minor) criminal activities, was suspended from school multiple times, and eventually dropped out of high school before graduating.

When she was 19, Claire completed the AAI, which asks people to think back to when they were growing up (between ages 5 and 12) and answer a series of questions about their parents, how they remember being treated as a child, whether or not certain traumatic events happened to them in childhood, and how their caregivers responded when such events happened. Individuals who are rated as dismissive/avoidant on the AAI remember their parents and upbringing as normal or even ideal, but they cannot support these claims with specific, episodic memories of significant childhood events. Dismissive/avoidant people also disregard the importance of attachment figures and related emotions early in life. Individuals who are rated as preoccupied/anxious discuss their

childhood experiences with attachment figures extensively during the interview. Their interviews typically reveal deep-seated, unresolved anger toward one or both parents, which taints their descriptions and interpretations of past experiences. Individuals who are rated as secure present a clear, well-supported description of their past relationship with both parents. Their episodic memories of childhood are clear and coherent, and they have no difficulty recalling important childhood experiences, even if their childhood or upbringing was difficult. Claire was classified as unresolved/preoccupied on the AAI, revealing a high level of incoherence during the interview. She had not worked through and set aside some of the difficult experiences she remembered having with her mother and the string of quasi step-fathers she had, and she rambled on about these experiences in a poorly organized, angry manner during the AAI interview, consistent with the Belsky and colleagues (1991) model.

As Claire entered early adulthood, the quality and support of her romantic relationships and friendships based on interviews were rated as below average. She had her first baby at age 19 all on her own, without any financial or social support from the biological father. During the first year of her son's life, she completed her high school equivalency degree, moved back into a more stable home environment with her mother, and began looking for a steady, better paying job. When her son was 12 months old, they completed the Strange Situation task, just as Claire and her mother had done approximately 20 years earlier. The relationship between Claire and her son was classified as secure. Thus, unlike Claire when she was an infant, her son was able to use Claire as a source of comfort and security to reduce his distress upon reuniting with her in the Strange Situation. One likely source of his security was Claire's parenting behavior. Indeed, when Claire participated in teaching tasks with her son when he was 2 and 3½—the same tasks she had completed with her mother 20 years earlier—she was rated as being supportive and completely nonhostile.

By age 23, Claire was no longer living at her mother's home, she had moved around a lot, and there were periods of time when she was homeless. She continued to have a string of short-term boyfriends but never maintained a serious romantic relationship for more than a few months. During this time, she received some help parenting her son from one set of his grandparents, but she worried about the quality of her parenting. She was still drinking and taking drugs on occasion and found it difficult to sustain the motivation it took to remain gainfully employed. At age 26, she started having debilitating panic attacks, which further undermined her ability to work and develop anything more than short-term romantic affairs. By age 28, Claire and her son had moved back in with her mother once again, where they spent several more years.

In summary, this more fine-grained idiographic glimpse of Claire's life trajectory fits the Belsky and colleagues (1991) model in most, but not all, ways. For example, it strongly supports Belsky and colleagues' accelerated somatic development prediction in light of the early age at which Claire started sexual maturity (age 10) and began having sex (age 12). At the same time, this idiographic information also reveals some departures from what the model predicts. Unlike Claire, for example, her son was securely attached in the Strange Situation, perhaps because Claire gained sufficient insight *not* to replicate the unsupportive, hostile care that she received as a child. In addition, due to her use of contraception, Claire had only one child by the time she reached her late 20s, which is not characteristic of many people who are following a fast reproductive strategy. This highlights an important point: Life trajectories can and sometimes do change in meaningful ways, either within the life of a person as he or she has new experiences and encounters new life events, and/or at intergenerational transmission points between the lives of two people, such as Claire and her son.

Conclusion

LHT provides a powerful theoretical lens through which different events in the lives of different people can be interpreted and understood. The linchpin that connects what happens early in life with how individuals think, feel, and behave interpersonally as adults is the attachment orientations and underlying working models they carry in their heads during their lifetimes. Attachment orientations and working models can and sometimes do change as people enter new relationships and have new experiences (Fraley & Roisman, 2015), especially those that contradict the working models they have developed (Simpson, Rholes, Campbell,

& Wilson, 2003). This may be partially true of Claire, who did not "transmit" her insecure attachment tendencies to her son, at least, not early in his life.

From the standpoint of her mental and physical health, Claire's life appears to be maladaptive and replete with negative outcomes. Her mental and physical state at most periods of her life were objectively worse than most people at similar ages. From an evolutionary standpoint, however, Claire made the best of a very difficult series of life events by reproducing before she could have died at a young age. Individuals in evolutionary history who were exposed to similar unpredictable, risky environments early in life would have achieved higher reproductive fitness by being wary of other people and not trusting them (reflecting insecure attachment), rapidly taking advantage of opportunities when they arose, reaching reproductive age sooner, and reproducing at a younger age, even without long-term mates. Thus, the genes associated with the development of these characteristics should have remained in the gene pool during evolutionary history. Consistent with this notion, recent prospective research examining attachment early in life (assessed in the Strange Situation) and adult personality has revealed that individuals who were insecurely attached as children have lower scores on the metatrait known as "stability" in adulthood. Specifically, individuals who were insecurely attached as children are less agreeable, less conscientious, and more neurotic in adulthood than individuals who were securely attached as children (Young, Simpson, Griskevicius, Huelsnitz, & Fleck, 2017). It is believed that this constellation of traits—being more disagreeable, less conscientious, and more emotionally unstable—should have facilitated the enactment of a fast life-history strategy, including its many behavioral outcomes (Simpson, Griskevicius, Szepsenwol & Young, 2017).

The evolutionary model of social development depicts just one possible way to construe the intricate patterning of lives through time. There are other models, including many nonevolutionary ones, that also explain how life experiences might be interconnected to reveal different kinds of life trajectories. The Belsky and colleagues (1991) model, however, has some unique selling points. It is anchored in a major theoretical perspective that has been supported by a vast amount of data collected on many different species; it makes novel predictions that other models did not anticipate or cannot make (e.g., the accelerated sexual development hypothesis, which exists for girls); and it has garnered a considerable amount of support in both cross-sectional and prospective studies on humans. Many of the details of Claire's complicated life provide further idiographic support for key predictions in the model.

REFERENCES

Adler, N. E., Boyce, W. T., Chesney, M. A., Folkman, S., & Syme, S. L. (1993). Socioeconomic inequalities in health: No easy solution. *Journal of the American Medical Association, 269,* 3140–3145.

Ainsworth, M. D. S., Blehar, M. C., Waters, E., & Wall, S. (1978). *Patterns of attachment: A psychology study of the Strange Situation.* Hillsdale, NJ: Erlbaum.

Belsky, J. (1981). Early human experience: A family perspective. *Developmental Psychology, 17,* 3–23.

Belsky, J. (1984). The determinants of parenting: A process model. *Child Development, 55,* 83–96.

Belsky, J. (1997). Attachment, mating, and parenting: An evolutionary interpretation. *Human Nature, 8,.* 361–381.

Belsky, J. (2012). The development of human reproductive strategies: Progress and prospects. *Current Directions in Psychological Science, 21,* 310–316.

Belsky, J., Houts, R. M., & Fearon, R. M. P. (2010). Infant attachment security and the timing of puberty: Testing an evolutionary hypothesis. *Psychological Science, 21,* 1195–1201.

Belsky, J., & Jaffee, S. (2006). The multiple determinants of parenting. In D. Cicchetti & D. Cohen (Eds.), *Developmental psychopathology: Vol. 3. Risk, disorder and adaptation* (2nd ed., pp. 38–85). New York: Wiley.

Belsky, J., Schlomer, G. L., & Ellis, B. J. (2012). Beyond cumulative risk: Distinguishing harshness and unpredictability as determinants of parenting and early life history strategy. *Developmental Psychology, 48,* 662–673.

Belsky, J., Steinberg, L., & Draper, P. (1991). Childhood experience, interpersonal development, and reproductive strategy: An evolutionary theory of socialization. *Child Development, 62,* 647–670.

Birnbaum, G. E. (2010). Bound to interact: The divergent goals and complex interplay of attachment and sex within romantic relationships. *Journal of Social and Personal Relationships, 27,* 245–252.

Bogaert, A. F., & Sadava, S. (2002). Adult attachment and sexual behavior. *Personal Relationships, 9,* 191–204.

Bowlby, J. (1969). *Attachment and loss: Vol. 1. Attachment.* New York: Basic Books.

Bowlby, J. (1973). *Attachment and loss: Vol. 2. Separation: Anxiety and anger.* New York: Basic Books.

Bowlby, J. (1980). *Attachment and loss: Vol. 3. Loss: Sadness and depression.* New York: Basic Books.

Brennan, K. A., & Shaver, P. R. (1995). Dimensions of adult attachment, affect regulation, and romantic relationship functioning. *Personality and Social Psychology Bulletin, 21,* 267–283.

Bronfenbrenner, U., & Crouter, A. (1982). Work and family through time and space. In S. Kamerman & C. Hayes (Eds.), *Families that work* (pp. 39–83). Washington, DC: National Academy Press.

Brumbach, B. H., Figueredo, A. J., & Ellis, B. J. (2009). Effects of harsh and unpredictable environments in adolescence on development of life history strategies: A longitudinal test of an evolutionary model. *Human Nature, 20,* 25–51.

Cassidy, J., & Berlin, L. J. (1994). The insecure/ambivalent pattern of attachment: Theory and research. *Child Development, 65,* 971–991.

Chen, E., Matthews, K. A., & Boyce, W. T. (2002). Socioeconomic differences in children's health: How and why do these relationships change with age? *Psychological Bulletin, 128,* 295–329.

Chisholm, J. S. (1993). Death, hope, and sex: Life-history theory and the development of reproductive strategies. *Current Anthropology, 34,* 1–24.

Chisholm, J. S. (1996). The evolutionary ecology of attachment organization. *Human Nature, 7,* 1–38.

Collins, N. L., & Feeney, B. C. (2000). A safe haven: An attachment theory perspective on support seeking and caregiving in intimate relationships. *Journal of Personality and Social Psychology, 78,* 1053–1073.

Conger, R. D., Cui, M., Bryant, C. M., & Elder, G. H. (2000). Competence in early adult romantic relationships: A developmental perspective on family influences. *Journal of Personality and Social Psychology, 79,* 224–237.

Crnic, K., & Low, C. (2002). Everyday stresses and parenting. In M. H. Bornstein (Ed.), *Handbook of parenting: Vol. 5. Practical issues in parenting* (2nd ed., pp. 243–267). Mahwah, NJ: Erlbaum.

Cui, M., & Fincham, F. D. (2010). The differential effects of parental divorce and marital conflict on young adult romantic relationships. *Personal Relationships, 17,* 331–343.

De Wolff, M., & van IJzendoorn, M. (1997). Sensitivity and attachment: A meta-analysis on parental antecedents of infant attachment. *Child Development, 68,* 571–591.

Del Giudice, M. (2009). Sex, attachment, and the development of reproductive strategies. *Behavioral and Brain Sciences, 32,* 1–67.

Del Giudice, M., & Belsky, J. (2011). The development of life history strategies: Toward a multi-stage theory. In D. M. Buss & P. H. Hawley (Eds.), *The evolution of personality and individual differences* (pp. 154–176). New York: Oxford University Press.

Del Giudice, M., Gangestad, S. W., & Kaplan, H. S. (2016). Life history theory and evolutionary psychology. In D. M. Buss (Ed.), *The handbook of evolution-*

ary psychology (2nd ed., pp. 88–114). Hoboken, NJ: Wiley.

Donaldson-Matasci, M. C., Lachmann, M., & Bergstrom, C. T. (2008). Phenotypic diversity as an adaptation to environmental uncertainty. *Evolutionary Ecology Research, 10*, 493–515.

Duncan, O. (1961). A socioeconomic index for all occupations. In A. J. Reiss, Jr. (Ed.), *Occupations and social status* (pp. 109–138). New York: Free Press.

Egeland, B. R., Breitenbucher, M., & Rosenberg, D. (1982). Prospective study of the significance of life stress in the etiology of child abuse. *Journal of Consulting and Clinical Psychology, 48*, 195–205.

Eibl-Eibesfeldt, I. (1989). *Human ethology.* New York: de Gruyter.

Ellis, B. J. (2004). Timing of pubertal maturation in girls. *Psychological Bulletin, 130*, 920–958.

Ellis, B. J., & Essex, M. J. (2007). Family environments, adrenarche, and sexual maturation: A longitudinal test of a life history model. *Child Development, 78*, 1799–1817.

Ellis, B. J., Figueredo, A. J., Brumbach, B. H., & Schlomer, G. L. (2009). Fundamental dimensions of environmental risk: The impact of harsh versus unpredictable environments on the evolution and development of life history strategies. *Human Nature, 20*, 204–268.

Ellis, B. J., & Garber, J. (2000). Psychosocial antecedents of variation in girls' pubertal timing. *Child Development, 71*, 485–501.

Ellis, B. J., McFadyen-Ketchum, S., Dodge, K. A., Pettit, G. S., & Bates, J. E. (1999). Quality of early family relationships and individual differences in the timing of pubertal maturation in girls. *Journal of Personality and Social Psychology, 77*, 387–401.

Emery, R. (1988). *Marriage, divorce, and children's adjustment.* Beverly Hills, CA: SAGE.

Fearon, R. M. P., & Belsky, J. (2016). Precursors of attachment security, In J. Cassidy & P. R. Shaver (Eds.), *Handbook of attachment: Theory, research, and clinical applications* (3rd ed., pp. 291–313). New York: Guilford Press.

Feeney, J. A. (2016). Adult romantic attachment: Developments in the study of couple relationships. In J. Cassidy & P. R. Shaver (Eds.), *Handbook of attachment: Theory, research, and clinical applications* (3rd ed., pp. 435–463). New York: Guilford Press.

Fraley, R. C., & Roisman, G. I. (2015). Early attachment experiences and romantic functioning: Developmental pathways, emerging issues, and future directions. In J. A. Simpson & W. S. Rholes (Eds.), *Attachment theory and research: New directions and emerging themes* (pp. 9–38). New York: Guilford Press.

Frankenhuis, W. E., Gergely, G., & Watson, J. S. (2013). Infants may use contingency analysis to estimate environmental states: An evolutionary, life-history perspective. *Child Development Perspectives, 7*, 115–120.

Fuller, T. L., & Fincham, F. D. (1995). Attachment style in married couples: Relation to current marital functioning, stability over time, and method of assessment. *Personal Relationships, 2*, 17–34.

Furman, W., & Simon, V. A. (1999). Cognitive representations of adolescent relationships. In W. Furman, B. B. Brown, & C. Feiring (Eds.), *The development of romantic relationships in adolescence* (pp. 75–98). New York: Cambridge University Press.

George, C., Kaplan, N., & Main, M. (1985). *The Adult Attachment Interview.* Unpublished protocol, Department of Psychology, University of California, Berkeley, CA.

Gillath, O., & Schachner, D. A. (2006). How do sexuality and attachment interrelate?: Goals, motives, and strategies. In M. Mikulincer & G. S. Goodman (Eds.), *Dynamics of romantic love: Attachment, caregiving, and sex* (pp. 337–355). New York: Guilford Press.

Graber, J., Brooks-Gunn, J., & Warren, M. (1995). The antecedents of menarcheal age. *Child Development, 66*, 346–359.

Grieser, D. L., & Kuhl, P. K. (1988). Maternal speech to infants in a tonal language: Support for universal prosodic features in motherese. *Developmental Psychology, 24*, 14–20.

Griskevicius, V., Ackerman, J. M., Cantú, S. M., Delton, A. W., Robertson, T. E., Simpson, J. A., et al. (2013). When the economy falters do people spend or save?: Responses to resource scarcity depend on childhood environments. *Psychological Science, 24*, 197–205.

Hinde, R. A. (1986). Some implications of evolutionary theory and comparative data for the study of human prosocial and aggressive behaviour. In D. Olweus, J. Block, & M. Radke-Yarrow (Eds.), *Development of anti-social and prosocial behaviour* (pp. 13–32). Orlando, FL: Academic Press.

Kaplan, H. S., & Gangestad, S. W. (2005). Life history theory and evolutionary psychology. In D. M. Buss (Ed.), *The handbook of evolutionary psychology* (pp. 68–95). Hoboken, NJ: Wiley.

Kaplan, H. S., Lancaster, J., & Hurtado, A. M. (2000). A theory of human life history evolution. *Evolutionary Anthropology, 9*, 156–185.

Kim, K., Smith, P. K., & Palermiti, A. L. (1997). Conflict in childhood and reproductive development. *Evolution and Human Behavior, 18*, 109–142.

LaFreniere, P. J., & Sroufe, L. A. (1985). Profiles of peer competence in the preschool: Interrelations between measures, influence of social ecology, and relation to attachment history. *Developmental Psychology, 21*, 56–69.

Lempers, J., Clark-Lempers, D., & Simons, R. (1989). Economic hardship, parenting, and distress in adolescence. *Child Development, 60*, 25–49.

Lewis, M., Feiring, C., McGuffog, C., & Jaskir, J. (1984). Predicting psychopathology in six-year-olds from early social relations. *Child Development, 55*, 123–136.

Main, M. (1981). Avoidance in the service of attachment: A working paper. In K. Immelmann, G. Barlow, M. Main, & L. Petrinovich (Eds.), *Behavioral development: The Bielefeld Interdisciplinary Project* (pp. 651–693). New York: Cambridge University Press.

Main, M., & Goldwyn, R. (1998). *Adult Attachment Rating and Classification Systems* (Version 6). Unpublished manuscript, University of California, Berkeley, CA.

Marvin, R. S., Britner, P. A., & Russell, B. S. (2016). Normative development: The ontogeny of attachment in childhood. In J. Cassidy & P. R. Shaver (Eds.), *The handbook of attachment: Theory, research, and clinical applications* (3rd ed., pp. 273–290). New York: Guilford Press.

McLoyd, V. C. (1990). The declining fortunes of black children: Psychological distress, parenting, and socioemotional development in the context of economic hardship. *Child Development, 61,* 311–346.

Mikulincer, M., & Shaver, P. R. (2003). The attachment behavioral system in adulthood: Activation, psychodynamics, and interpersonal processes. In M. P. Zanna (Ed.), *Advances in experimental social psychology* (Vol. 35, pp. 53–152). New York: Academic Press.

Mikulincer, M., & Shaver, P. R. (2016). *Attachment in adulthood: Structure, dynamics, and change* (2nd ed.). New York: Guilford Press.

Miller, C., & Fishkin, S. A. (1997). On the dynamics of human bonding and reproductive success. In J. A. Simpson & D. T. Kenrick (Eds.), *Evolutionary social psychology* (pp. 197–235). Mawah, NJ: Erlbaum.

Miller, W. B., & Pasta, D. J. (2000). Early family environment, reproductive strategy and contraceptive behavior. In J. L. Rodgers, D. C. Rowe, & W. B. Miller (Eds.), *Genetic influences on human fertility and sexuality* (pp. 183–230). Boston: Kluwer.

Moffitt, T. E., Caspi, A., Belsky, J., & Silva, P. A. (1992). Childhood experience and the onset of menarche: A test of a sociobiological model. *Child Development, 63,* 47–58.

Nettle, D., Coall, D. A., & Dickins, T. E. (2011). Early-life conditions and age at first pregnancy in British women. *Proceedings of the Royal Society B, 278,* 1721–1727.

Pesonen, A., Raikkonen, K., Heinonen, K., Kajantie, E., Forsen, T., & Eriksson, J. G. (2008). Reproductive traits following a parent–child separation trauma during childhood: A natural experiment during World War II. *American Journal of Human Biology, 20,* 345–351.

Raby, K. L., Cicchetti, D., Carlson, E. A., Egeland, B., & Collins, W. A. (2013). Genetic contributions to continuity and change in attachment security: A prospective, longitudinal investigation from infancy to young adulthood. *Journal of Child Psychology and Psychiatry, 54,* 1223–1230.

Roisman, G. I., Collins, W. A., Sroufe, L. A., & Egeland, B. (2005). Predictors of young adults' representations of and behavior in their current romantic relationship: Prospective tests of the prototype hypothesis. *Attachment and Human Development, 7,* 105–121.

Roisman, G. I., Madsen, S. D., Hennighausen, K. H., Sroufe, L. A., & Collins, W. A. (2001). The coherence of dyadic behavior across parent–child and romantic relationships as mediated by the internalized representation of experience. *Attachment and Human Development, 3,* 156–172.

Schachner, D. A., & Shaver, P. R. (2004). Attachment dimensions and sexual motives. *Personal Relationships, 11,* 179–195.

Shaver, P. R., Hazan, C., & Bradshaw, D. (1988). Love as attachment: The integration of three behavioral systems. In R. J. Sternberg & M. L. Barnes (Eds.), *The psychology of love* (pp. 68–99). New Haven, CT: Yale University Press.

Simpson, J. A. (1990). Influence of attachment styles on romantic relationships. *Journal of Personality and Social Psychology, 59,* 971–980.

Simpson, J. A. (1999). Attachment theory in modern evolutionary perspective. In J. Cassidy & P. R. Shaver (Eds.), *Handbook of attachment: Theory, research, and clinical applications* (pp. 115–140). New York: Guilford Press.

Simpson, J. A., & Belsky, J. (2008). Attachment theory within a modern evolutionary framework. In J. Cassidy & P. R. Shaver (Eds.), *Handbook of attachment: Theory, research, and clinical applications* (2nd ed., pp. 131–157). New York: Guilford Press.

Simpson, J. A., & Belsky, J. (2016). Attachment theory within a modern evolutionary framework. In J. Cassidy & P. R. Shaver (Eds.), *Handbook of attachment: Theory, research, and clinical applications* (3rd ed., pp. 91–116). New York: Guilford Press.

Simpson, J. A., Collins, W. A., Tran, S., & Haydon, K. C. (2007). Attachment and the experience and expression of emotions in adult romantic relationships: A developmental perspective. *Journal of Personality and Social Psychology, 92,* 355–367.

Simpson, J. A., Griskevicius, V., Kuo, S. I., Sung, S., & Collins, W. A. (2012). Evolution, stress, and sensitive periods: The influence of unpredictability in early versus late childhood on sex and risky behavior. *Developmental Psychology, 48,* 674–686.

Simpson, J. A., Griskevicius, V., Szepsenwol, O., & Young, E. S. (2017). An evolutionary life history perspective on personality and mating strategies. In A. T. Church (Ed.), *The Praeger handbook of personality across cultures: Vol. 3. Evolutionary, ecological, and cultural contexts of personality* (pp. 1–29). Santa Barbara, CA: Praeger.

Simpson, J. A., & Rholes, W. S. (1994). Stress and secure base relationships in adulthood. In K. Bartholomew & D. Perlman (Eds.), *Advances in personal relationships: Attachment processes in adulthood* (Vol. 5, pp. 181–204). London: Jessica Kingsley.

Simpson, J. A., Rholes, W. S., Campbell, L., & Wilson, C. L. (2003). Changes in attachment orientations across the transition to parenthood. *Journal of Experimental Social Psychology, 39,* 317–331.

Simpson, J. A., Rholes, W. S., & Phillips, D. (1996). Conflict in close relationships: An attachment perspective. *Journal of Personality and Social Psychology, 71,* 899–914.

Sroufe, L. A., Egeland, B., Carlson, E. A., & Collins, W. A. (2005). *The development of the person: The Minnesota Study of Risk and Adaptation from Birth to Adulthood.* New York: Guilford Press.

Sroufe, L. A., & Waters, E. (1977). Attachment as an organizational construct. *Child Development, 48,* 1184–1199.

Steinberg, L. (1988). Reciprocal relation between parent–child distance and pubertal maturation. *Developmental Psychology, 24,* 122–128.

Stevens, G., & Featherman, D. L. (1981). A revised socioeconomic index of occupational status. *Social Science Research, 10,* 364–395.

Sung, S., Simpson, J. A., Griskevicius, V., Kuo, S. I., Schlomer, G. L., & Belsky, J. (2016). Secure infant–mother attachment buffers the effect of early-life stress on age of menarche. *Psychological Science, 27,* 667–674.

Szepsenwol, O., Griskevicius, V., Simpson, J. A., Young, E. S., Fleck, C., & Jones, R. E. (2017). The effect of predictable early childhood environments on sociosexuality in early adulthood. *Evolutionary Behavior Sciences, 11,* 131–145.

Szepsenwol, O., Simpson, J. A., Griskevicius, V., & Raby, K. L. (2015). The effect of unpredictable early childhood environments on parenting in adulthood. *Journal of Personality and Social Psychology, 109,* 1045–1067.

Tithers, J. M., & Ellis, B. J. (2008). Impact of fathers on daughters' age of menarche: A genetically and environmentally controlled sibling study. *Developmental Psychology, 44,* 1409–1420.

Waters, E., Wippman, J., & Sroufe, L. A. (1979). Attachment, positive affect, and competence in the peer group: Two studies in construct validation. *Child Development, 50,* 821–829.

Young, E. S., Simpson, J. A., Griskevicius, V., Huelsnitz, C. O., & Fleck, C. (2017). Childhood attachment and adult personality: A life history perspective. *Self and Identity.* [Epub ahead of print]

Zeifman, D. M., & Hazan, C. (2016). Pair bonds as attachments: Mounting evidence in support of Bowlby's hypothesis. In J. Cassidy & P. R. Shaver (Eds.), *Handbook of attachment: Theory, research, and clinical applications* (3rd ed., pp. 416–434). New York: Guilford Press.

CHAPTER 16

Needs, Motives, and Personality Development
Unanswered Questions and Exciting Potentials

Kennon M. Sheldon
Julia Schüler

In this chapter we apply two major theories of basic psychological needs—self-determination theory (SDT; Deci & Ryan, 1985, 2000) and motive disposition theory (MDT; McClelland, 1985; Schultheiss, 2008)—in an attempt to understand the nature of successful personality development and healthy personality functioning more generally. SDT and MDT are perhaps the two most prominent and well-developed theories of motivation in the world today; thus, it is striking that they have rarely been considered together. Recent findings and theoretical innovations (Schüler, Brandstätter, & Sheldon, 2013; Sheldon, 2011; Sheldon & Schüler, 2011, 2015) have opened a way for such an inquiry, and we follow the path wherever it takes us, as we try understand the nature of personality development from a motivational perspective (Sheldon, 2009b).

In the process, we repeatedly turn to the example of "Martha," a hypothetical young woman discussed at length in Sheldon and Schüler (2015). In that chapter, Martha is portrayed as a quiet 30-year-old tech worker, driven to succeed, who rarely socializes with others. Despite her aloofness, Martha is mostly respected and liked by coworkers, and she is even being considered for management by her supervisors because of her penetrating intuition. In her personal life, Martha cares for

seven cats and organizes a subscriber-based YouTube channel hosting "cute kitten" videos. Also in her personal life, Martha is quiet, rather inconspicuous, and helpful, which might be the reason that the old woman on the first floor once called her the "perfect neighbor." Martha's father is a successful lawyer, whose love for Martha seems to be strictly contingent on her success in tasks that he considers important (e.g., school and work performance). Martha's mother is a successful, independent entrepreneur, whose life motto is "You can reach every goal if you just try hard enough." Martha's life so far has been anything but a spontaneous, easygoing affair. She has struggled hard over the years to prevail against competitive colleagues and to earn respect and recognition in her job. On the positive side, she achieved a good position in an influential insurance company on her own. Concerning this matter, her mother's motto has worked well.

Because she feels a little lonely sometimes, Martha tries on occasion to establish closer contacts with a few other people. Martha's attempt to get to know new people by attending a running group results in her creating a detailed training plan, which ultimately leads to success in the city marathon. As she passes the finish line, Martha's original goal (to meet new people) is now long forgotten. Her rigorous training regimen has cost her the last free minutes in her already crowded weekly schedule. No time has been left for social interactions—a fact that doesn't now seem to bother her in the slightest. She feels autonomous and competent. This source of satisfaction ends abruptly, however, when Martha hurts her left knee. The injury keeps her from continuing as a long-distance runner. Initially, she tries to ignore the physician's instructions, and she keeps running ("Try hard enough, Martha!"). But her pain ultimately overrides her mother's motto. Her mother's motto also fails to make room for the costs of ambitious goal striving at work. Things go wrong here, too.

In the Sheldon and Schüler (2015) chapter, Martha was depicted as being trapped in a downward spiral of negative well-being because recent changes in her job description had required her to demonstrate more interpersonal concerns and skills, capabilities she did not currently have in her repertoire. The downward spiral began after Martha received a negative job review that criticized her ability to work with or manage others. Unfortunately, Martha was overreliant on obtaining feelings of job-related competence within her life, without enough alternative avenues for finding satisfaction. In this chapter, we speculate on what Martha's life was like during her childhood and attempt to identify the roots of her age-30 dilemmas. In the process, the reader will learn much about contemporary motivation theory. The reader will also come to appreciate the many unanswered questions that remain in this fascinating research area, and we hope, be inspired to conduct his or her own research to address these questions!

To begin, surely most readers would agree that certain kinds of experiences are especially rewarding and satisfying for nearly anybody: experiences such as learning and mastering an exciting new skill; feeling understood, supported, and loved by cherished others; and, finally, deciding for oneself what course to chart in one's life. Indeed, some such experiences may be *universally* rewarding to all human beings, and this "rewardingness" may even be an evolved feature of basic human nature (as we discuss below). If this is so, then it seems a short leap to the idea that all people should be trying to get as many such experiences as possible. To use an analogy, if ice cream tasted good and were good for everyone, then everybody should be trying to get ice cream.

However, a focus of this chapter is to explain why this is not the case. In fact, there are wide individual differences in how much people seek out different kinds of satisfying experiences, differences presumably based on childhood learning and development. Consider a dedicated careerist (like Martha), with a life concentrated around success, winning, and accomplishment, and much less attention given to social relationships and connections. This person lives a completely different life (in terms of goals, behavior, and experiences) than a dedicated caretaker, for whom friends and family are the most important things. This second person builds his or her life around establishing and deepening harmonious social relationships, whereas achievement and success are secondary or insignificant for him or her. How did the careerist and the caretaker get to be the way they are? Also, can both individuals be said to be equally happy and healthy in their particular ways of living their lives? Or is it necessary to have a balance between various types of satisfactions, in order to be a fully functioning human being?

The larger theoretical question we want to consider is "How do individual differences in motivation emerge from a basic (or universal) human nature?" If we assume that all humans have the same basic psychological needs (as does SDT), then why do people become asymmetrical and imbalanced in their pursuit and experience of these needs, such that each person develops his or her own unique motive profile? Also, how do some people (like Martha) become so unbalanced that they are vulnerable to depression, after their only (or primary) source of satisfaction dries up? We also consider some very interesting related questions. For example, is it possible to develop an imbalance in one's motives for only a temporary period in one's life, in order to work intensively for particular life-stage goals (e.g., "getting tenure" or "mothering my newborn")? Indeed, might such imbalances be temporarily functional and even necessary? But then might one get permanently "stuck" in an unbalanced state, due to an unhealthy addiction to only one type of satisfaction, at the expense of other types?

In order to address these and related questions, this chapter has a five-part structure. First, we consider the *multidimensional personality in context* (MPIC) model proposed by Sheldon, Cheng, and Hilpert (2011; see also Sheldon, 2004), as a way to think about personality universals and individual differences in the same broad picture. The MPIC also provides a way to consider the wide variety of possible influences on people's motivational development across the lifespan, including social influences, cognitive influences, and biological and physiological influences. Having presented this big-picture framework, we become more specific and focus on *self-determination theory* (SDT; Deci & Ryan, 1985, 2000), which provides theoretical background for considering the universal positive effects of having certain types of basic experiences. Third, we introduce MDT (McClelland, 1985), which provides theoretical background for considering why people develop individual differences in how much they actually seek out these basic experiences. Both SDT and MDT, from different angles, make assumptions about the origin of human needs and motives. We present in the fourth part of the chapter the recently proposed *two-process model of psychological needs* (TPM; Sheldon, 2011), which attempts to answer the question of how universal needs and varying motives can be fit together in one picture. The TPM does this by proposing a dynamic process model of the temporal relations among needs, behaviors, experiences, and motives, and by proposing a positive, reinforcement-based explanation of how motive dispositions are acquired. Finally, in the fifth part of the chapter, we apply SDT, MDT, and the TPM to speculate further on the motivational development of personality. As

will be seen, far more questions than answers exist in this area.

The MPIC: A Useful Big-Picture Framework

According to the MPIC model (Sheldon, 2011; Sheldon et al., 2011), a person's behavior at any moment in time ("time *t*") is a combined function of nested processes occurring simultaneously at many different levels of organization (see Figure 16.1). Human personality and consciousness are built on and constrained by physical reality (atoms nested within molecules, nested within cells, nested within organ tissues), but they also emerge as somewhat independent from these lower-level processes, deriving causal potentials of their own that are irreducible to mere physics or chemistry. Moreover, the emergent nesting of organization and causality do not stop with personality but instead extend beyond the body to relations with other personalities, and with the larger cultural matrix in which the person finds him or herself.

Consider a person at a sporting event who stands up as the national anthem is sung; his behavior at that moment ("time *t*") is largely governed by a group-level process, as everybody stands in unison. Next, he buys a bucket of popcorn. His behavior at that moment is largely governed by the hunger pangs caused by low glucose levels in his bloodstream, a much

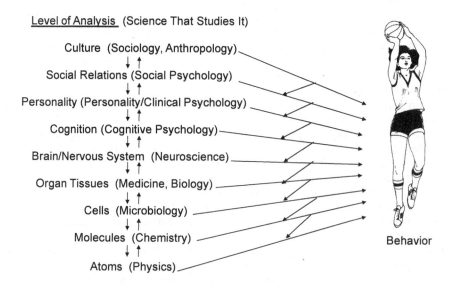

FIGURE 16.1. A multilevel perspective on the organization of behavior.

lower-level process. Thus, the MPIC depicts the causation of behavior as moving up and down the hierarchy of organization, at different time t's. Of course, behavior can be affected by not only one but also by multiple levels of organization at once; also, behavior can be affected by interactions between different levels. As an example of one such cross-level interaction, Colin Kaepernick, an American football quarterback, is attracting notoriety (as this chapter is written) by refusing to stand for the national anthem before games, instead kneeling as a protest against persistent racism in the United States. The interaction of personality principles he holds dear and a particular social context in which he is nested (the collective singing of the anthem) produces a behavior in him at time t (kneeling) that is quite different from that of most players and fans (standing up).

Again, the MPIC purports to depict the complete set of causal forces that can act on a person at time t, as located on a nested vertical hierarchy of levels of organization. In principle, time t could be extended indefinitely on a *horizontal* axis, to cover the entire lifespan of a person. At this time scale, the influences on personality development can include very broad forces, such as age-graded norms or role expectations which act "down" on people at particular times in their lives. But behavior and personality development can also be affected by physical processes indexed to the lifespan, such as hormonal shifts at adolescence, or endocrinologi-

cal responses to pregnancy. Space precludes a more thorough presentation of the MPIC model, but the reader is referred to Sheldon (Sheldon, 2004; Sheldon et al., 2011).

For our purposes in this chapter, it is useful to consider a restricted version of the MPIC, focusing on the four "levels" of personality shown in Figure 16.2, as well as the influences located above this level, in the social surround. The four levels of personality include the "three tiers" of personality that were described by McAdams (1996; McAdams & Manczak, 2011; Sheldon, 2004), namely, the tiers of traits/dispositions, goals/motives, and narratives/self-experience.

Notably, McAdams, Shiner, and Tackett are using a very similar "three-tier" framework to organize this very book! Our own chapter fits into the book's section on the development of goals/motives (depicted as Level 3 in Figure 16.2), although it also addresses lower-level issues of nonconscious traits/dispositions by considering implicit motives (depicted as Level 2). As Figure 16.2 illustrates, the MPIC also proposes a Level 1 or *foundational* level, of human universals existing "beneath" the many individual differences manifested by people (Sheldon, 2004). There are many kinds of human universals that have been proposed, ranging from physiological needs to social-cognitive mechanisms to socially evoked ritual and group processes (Malinowski, 1944; Sheldon, 2004). The explanation for universals generally rests on

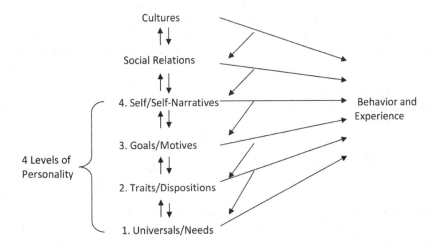

FIGURE 16.2. The MPIC model, which expands the personality level.

an evolutionary argument, in which some adaptations were so important and beneficial that over time they became represented within the genome of every human being (Geary & Huffman, 2002; Tooby & Cosmides, 1990); lacking genetic variation, they were no longer subject to selection pressure.

In this chapter we focus on one type of universal, that is, basic psychological needs, that are said to be shared by all human beings, no matter what their culture or developmental upbringing (Deci & Ryan, 2000). We assume that individual differences in motivation nevertheless emerge from this common matrix, such that people come to favor acquiring some needs more than other needs. Importantly, needs are what is *needed,* but motives are what is *sought,* and these do not have to be the same thing. We further assume that as long as a person gets an overall minimally sufficient amount of need satisfaction, he or she can perhaps function and feel well, even with an unbalanced motive profile and unbalanced need satisfaction scores (Sheldon & Niemiec, 2006).

The SDT Perspective on Basic Psychological Needs

Before beginning this section, we should point out that SDT is complex, consisting of several "minitheories," all of which have potential relevance to developmental processes and outcomes. These minitheories include the organismic integration minitheory, the causality orientations minitheory, the goal contents minitheory, the cognitive evaluation minitheory, and the basic psychological needs minitheory (Vansteenkiste, Niemiec, & Soenens, 2010). In this chapter, we focus only on the developmental relevance of the basic psychological needs minitheory and leave the reader to find information on the other minitheories elsewhere (Kasser, 2002; Ryan, 1995; Sheldon, 2009a).

The term *basic psychological need* already indicates that among the many physiological commodities that are essential for survival, such as the needs for food, air, and water, human beings have psychological needs that are similarly important for their psychological survival. Specifically, SDT (Deci & Ryan, 1985) proposes that there are three essential needs for psychological well-being and growth: autonomy, competence, and relatedness. These are types or qualities of evolved experience that

humans enjoy and benefit from, experiences that replenish people's energies and support their health and development. The *need for autonomy* means that it is essential for individuals to experience volition (i.e., the feeling that they are doing what they choose to be doing); that is, people need to experience a sense of psychological freedom that enables them to take ownership of, and responsibility for, their own behavior (see also deCharms, 1968). The *need for competence* is based on White's (1959) idea that it is crucial for individuals to feel effectance in goal striving; that is, people need to feel some sense of competence and success as they strive to develop their skills, so that such striving will be reinforced and sustained. The *need for relatedness* refers to the perception of caring for others, and being cared for by them. People need to be part of a social environment in which they are treated respectfully and in which they support and are supported by important others (Baumeister & Leary, 1995).

If autonomy, competence, and relatedness are indeed innate basic needs, akin to psychological vitamins, then their satisfaction should lead to positive consequences. And this is what empirical research has convincingly shown in the last two decades. Basic psychological needs satisfaction, as measured by survey as or instantiated experimentally within situations, leads to physical and psychological well-being (for a summary, see Ryan & Deci, 2008; Sheldon, 2004), promotes health-conducive behavior (Williams, Niemiec, Patrick, Ryan, & Deci, 2009), and fosters intrinsic motivation (Illardi, Leone, Kasser, & Ryan, 2009). This is true across different life domains (e.g., family, school, workplace, sports), for women as well as men (Ryan, La Guardia, Solky-Butzel, Chirkov, & Kim, 2005), and across different cultures (Lynch, La Guardia, & Ryan, 2009; Sheldon et al., 2011; for a summary of the many positive effects of need satisfaction, see Vansteenkiste et al., 2010). However, the dark side of the "basic" character of needs is that their frustration leads to negative consequences, including motivational undermining, alienating and pathogenetic effects (Ryan & Deci, 2000), controlling regulatory styles, needs substitutes, and rigid behavior patterns.

Let us consider Martha's current plight at age 30, using the SDT perspective on basic needs and their crucial role for well-being. Although Martha used to get many feelings of competence from her work, since receiving her negative performance review, she has not felt very competent at all. Also, she never did have many close friends, and still does not, so her need for relatedness is not met either. She also feels somewhat nonautonomous at present because she feels helpless and does not know how to take charge of the situation to improve it. As described in Sheldon and Schüler (2015), her downward spiral is manifestly evident in her maladaptive attempts to compensate for absent needs satisfaction, by drinking too much, and by getting involved in short-term sexual relationships that do not last, or are even masochistic.

In view of the importance of basic needs satisfaction, it is important to discuss the conditions that *support* needs satisfaction at the "social relations" level of the MPIC. *Competence* is supported in achievement contexts that are structured and predictable, rather than chaotic and arbitrary (Hsu, Wang, Hsiao, & Wu, 2013; Sierens, Vansteenkiste, Goossens, Soenens, & Dochy, 2009; Skinner & Belmont, 1993). This means that the setting provides transparent performance expectations, clearly defined goals and objectives, opportunities and means to move towards these goals, and informative feedback along the way. For example, Skinner and Belmont (1993) found that optimal structure (in which teachers clearly conveyed their expectations and consistently gave information about to how to achieve outcomes) predicted children's motivation across the school year, and Sierens and colleagues (2009) also showed that the provision of structure and order in the classroom predicted motivation. For Martha, it might have been helpful if there were systems in place requiring her to regularly discuss major job projects with colleagues and superiors, thereby getting earlier feedback and a heads-up on emerging difficulties. *Relatedness* is assumed to be supported in contexts that promote a warm and respectful atmosphere (Patrick, Knee, & Canevello, & Lonsbary, 2007; Rohner, 2004). This means that there is concern for equality and a norm of reciprocal involvement and caring, such that people feel they can trust, and even come to love, others. In a study by Patrick and colleagues (2007), feelings of relatedness (e.g., "When I am with my partner, I feel loved and cared about") were the strongest predictors of positive romantic functioning. In Martha's case, a friendlier and less competitive working atmosphere might have invited her to become more interested in her colleagues as persons, and to share herself with others.

Autonomy is supported by contexts (family, school, the workplace, sports, friendship and leisure time) that foster people's choice and self-determination (Chirkov & Ryan, 2001; Deci, La Guardia, Moller, Scheiner, & Ryan, 2006; Gagne, Ryan, & Bargmann, 2003; Niemiec et al., 2006; Reinboth, Duda, & Ntoumanis, 2004). This means that authorities (i.e., teachers, parents, bosses, coaches, doctors) are interested in subordinates' perspectives, provide subordinates with choice whenever possible, and offer meaningful rationales when requesting that subordinates do things they don't want to. In contrast, controlling authorities use threat, coercion, punishment, monetary rewards, and deadlines, and do not care how these are experienced (Sheldon, Williams, & Joiner, 2003). In Martha's case, she had up to this point felt relatively autonomous, and able to work as she pleased; however, she now fears that her supervisors are trying to manipulate and control her, perhaps in service of their own political ends, not her best interests.

Again, Deci and Ryan (2000, p. 229) conceptualized basic psychological needs as "innate psychological nutriments that are essential for the ongoing psychological growth, integrity, and well-being . . . of all people." This applies to young and old, and it applies regardless of one's cultural upbringing. In other words, everybody "needs" the needs to the same extent. The only thing that meaningfully varies, according to SDT, is *how much satisfaction people are actually getting*. There are two main factors that affect the amount of needs satisfaction people get; as mentioned earlier, the social environment provides conditions that foster or thwart basic needs satisfaction, as some contexts or cultures may be less satisfying than others. The second factor lies in the choices and personality of the person. Martha herself chose to focus predominantly on career, correspondingly neglecting other domains of her life (e.g., friendships). Regardless, given its theoretical focus on *levels* of satisfactions, SDT researchers do not focus at all on individual differences in needs *strength*. To the extent that needs are considered as behavioral motives (rather than as experiential requirements), it is generally assumed that they are equally motivating for everyone. But now we turn to MDT, which is all about individual differences in the behavioral motives that people develop.

The MDT Perspective on Basic Needs and Motives

Although MDT sometimes uses the term *need* to describe its motivational constructs (i.e., need for achievement, need for affiliation, need for power), the more accurate term is *motive* (although we use the abbreviations nAch, nAff, and nPow, below). Motives are viewed as relatively stable preferences to approach certain kinds of incentives and to avoid certain kind of disincentives (Atkinson, 1957; McClelland, Koestner, & Weinberger, 1989; Murray, 1938; Schultheiss, 2008). MDT research focuses on three particular motives that are assumed and found to be critical for adaptation. These are the *achievement motive,* the *power motive,* and the *affiliation motive,* defined as dispositional preferences to seek out particular kinds of incentives, preferences that drive, orient, and select behavior (McClelland, 1987).

Specifically, individuals with a strong *achievement motive* have a concern for doing well according to a standard of excellence (McClelland, Atkinson, Clark, & Lowell, 1953). They seek out challenge and competition in order to test and improve their competence, to win, and to feel proud and competent. Their goal setting is characterized by moderately difficult tasks (Brunstein & Maier, 2005) that are challenging but feasible, and are therefore the best option for measuring progress in the development of their skills. Those high in need for achievement (nAch) aim to receive performance feedback based on their own previous performance, and are relatively uninterested in comparing their performance with others (Brunstein & Heckhausen, 2008). More recent studies extend the range of correlates of the achievement motive showing, for example, that it predicts persistence in behavior, such as regular engagement in sport activities (Gröpel, Wegner, & Schüler, 2016), and psychophysiological responses, such as increased cortisol release when achievement-related incentives are present (Yang, Ramsay, Schultheiss, & Pang, 2015).

Individuals with a strong *affiliation motive* have "a desire to establish and/or maintain warm and friendly interpersonal relations" (French & Chadwick, 1956, p. 296). The affiliation motive is incentivized by the pleasure of being with other people and communicating with them (McClelland, 1987). People with a high affiliation motive strive for interpersonal situations characterized by harmony and equal relationships, and dislike and avoid conflict situations and even contrary discussions. In accordance with this propensity, individuals high in the affiliation motive interact more and make more eye contact with others who seem to be friendly, but look away from people who are dissimilar to themselves or express different opinions (Exline, 1963; Lansing & Heyns, 1959). Hagemeyer, Dufner, and Denissen (2016) replicated the classic finding by McAdams, Jackson, and Kirshnit (1984) that the implicit affiliation motive predicts high levels of nonverbal socializing behavior such as eye contact and smiling, and Wegner, Bohnacker, Mempel, Teubel, and Schüler (2014) confirmed these findings for the specific domain of sports (nonverbal pleasant behavior toward opponents in raquet sports team competitions; for further correlates of the affiliation motive, see Sokolowski, 2008).

Individuals with a strong *power motive* have the desire to have an impact on others and influence others in order to gain and maintain reputation and prestige (Winter, 1973). This category includes not only aggressive and irresponsible behavior (Winter, 1988) but also behavior that is better accepted and even desired by the social environment, such as convincing others through reasoned arguments (Schultheiss & Brunstein, 2002), striving for and reaching influential leading positions in hierarchically-organized corporations (McClelland & Boyatzis, 1982) and guiding, helping and educating other people (e.g., as teachers, psychotherapists). For example, Baumann, Chatterjee, and Hank (2016) showed that people high in implicit power motivation are more apt to engage in prosocial behavior if they have an ability to self-regulate positive emotion (for further correlates of the power motive, see Schmalt & Heckhausen, 2008).

Martha's implicit motive scores, derived from thematic codings of stories she was asked to write about ambiguous pictures (picture story exercises; see Schultheiss & Pang, 2007), indicate that she has a very strong implicit achievement motive, a fact that is also reflected in her own self-concept ("I'm a driven person"). She is slightly below the norm in the implicit power motive. However, Martha has an implicit affiliation motive score considerably above the population mean, but, oddly, she does not think of herself as a relationally oriented person; instead, she thinks of herself as a bit of a loner, and in fact, as described earlier, Martha does not really seek people out.

Implicit versus Explicit Motivation

This leads us to the primary dynamic concept employed by MDT researchers, namely, the distinction between implicit motives and explicit motives. This distinction starts from the well-known fact that motives measured with picture story exercises (in which imaginative thoughts are coded from stories written to pictures) such as the Thematic Apperception Test (TAT; Morgan & Murray, 1935) and its derivates (Schultheiss & Pang, 2007), tend to be uncorrelated with motives measured with participants' self-reports (e.g., questionnaires). To explain this, McClelland and colleagues (1989) developed a model of two motivational systems, which operate relatively independent of each other. The *implicit motivational system* is based on primary affects such as shame and pride, and is associated with evolutionary older parts of the brain that operate outside a person's conscious awareness. In contrast, the *explicit motivational system* (explicit motives and goals) is based on a person's conscious reflections about his or her values and goals, and represents an important part of the self-concept. Rather than being based on affective processes (as are implicit motives), the explicit system is based on cognitive processes (e.g., conscious goal setting, processes of consideration and reflection, cognitive beliefs) taking place within evolutionarily younger parts of the brain.

This assumed duality of the motivational system is supported by studies showing that implicit and explicit motives indeed differ in important aspects. For example, they predict different types of behavior (implicit motives predict situation–choice behavior over time, whereas explicit motives predict verbal behavior in well-structured situations); are aroused by different incentives (implicit by activity-inherent incentives, explicit by social-evaluative incentives); are supposedly based on different developmental histories (McClelland argued that implicit motives are formed, starting in the first few years, whereas explicit motives are formed, starting in middle childhood); and have to be measured differently (implicit motives by projective testing; explicit motives by self-report) (Brunstein, 2008; McClelland et al., 1989).

Implicit–Explicit Motive Discrepancies

It is generally considered to be adaptive for people to pursue the same basic motivational targets within both their implicit and explicit systems. Implicit motives provide a general orientation toward certain classes of goals (e.g., *doing something better* goals), and therewith have an *energizing function,* based on the positive emotions the person anticipates feeling after action is taken. Explicit motives, however, are based on cognizance of social norms and represent the adaptive need to adjust one's wishes and needs to the social reality (within limits). Explicit motives have a *directive function* in behavioral regulation. When the implicit and explicit motivational systems work in coalition, they are highly functional and support goal attainment. For example, a person like Martha with a high implicit achievement motive benefits from thinking about herself as being achievement oriented (explicit achievement motive), and from setting explicit achievement goals in different life domains (career goals, ambitious aims in sports).

Still, the essential duality of motivational systems can also lead to a maladaptive discordance between implicit and explicit motives. A person (like Martha) can, for example, have a substantial implicit affiliation motive but a weak explicit affiliation motive, perhaps because she works in a job that demands that she treat people in an impersonal way, such that she comes to view herself as a distant person. Or a person might have a strong implicit achievement motive but a weak explicit achievement motive because she thinks of herself as a stay-at-home mother. A variety of studies (also across different cultures; Hofer & Busch, 2013), have revealed that such "motivational incongruence" causes emotional problems, whereas motive congruence fosters emotional well-being (Brunstein, Schultheiss, & Maier, 1999). To name but a few examples, motive incongruence cause negative and reduced positive affect (Langens, 2006; Schüler, Job, Fröhlich, & Brandstätter, 2008), leads to psychosomatic complaints (Baumann, Kaschel, & Kuhl, 2005) and is associated with unhealthy eating behavior (Job, Oertig, Brandstätter, & Allemand, 2010). We return to the notion of implicit–explicit noncongruence later in the chapter.

Origin and Development of Implicit Motives

To explain the relatively small set of motives considered by MDT researchers, McClelland focused on a small set of "natural incentives." These incentives are (at least at first) equally attractive to every human being, in part because they are accompanied by *primary positive emotions*. Referring to Ekman (1971) and his research on the universality of facial expressions, McClelland suggested three central natural incentives that are associated with positive emotions. The natural incentive of *variety* is accompanied by interest–surprise and the associated subjective states are feeling curious or exploratory. Later, McClelland (1985, p. 228) referred to the variety incentive as the natural incentive of *doing something better. Contact* goes hand in hand with the primary emotion of joy–happiness–pleasure and is subjectively experienced as feeling loved and loving others, feeling peaceful and happy. The natural incentive of *having impact* leads to the primary emotion of anger–excitement and can subjectively be experienced as feeling strong and excited. The self is experienced as a causal agent. Notably, the primary emotions do not *motivate* behavior in the strict sense of the word; instead they provide the "affective charge that makes motivational systems so powerful and persistent in shaping behavior" (McClelland, 1987, p. 128). They amplify the effects of motives on behavior.

How do people acquire individual differences in their motivational preferences? McClelland (1985) referred to the principles of learning as suggested by behaviorists. Implicit motives—and their different strengths in individuals—are "built on affective experiences with natural incentives early in life" (McClelland et al., 1989, p. 697). Early childhood experiences with the natural incentive *doing something better* lead to the development of a strong *achievement motive*; experiences with *contact* foster the development of a strong *affiliation motive*; and a social environment that rewards behavior associated with *having impact* leads to a strong *power motive*. Notably, however, studies that examine the developmental precursors of motives in detail are still very rare (McClelland & Pilon, 1983). In fact, it is fair to say that McClelland's developmental ideas remain largely untested, despite their foundational influence within MDT.

Let us again consider Martha's current plight, this time from a McClelland-esque MDT perspective. Again, she has very strong implicit and explicit achievement motives that are currently being thwarted, and a somewhat strong implicit affiliation motivation that is currently being ignored, in part because of her self-belief that

she is "not a people person" and does not much like to mix with others. How did she arrive at this condition of having both unmet implicit achievement motives and discrepant implicit and explicit affiliation motives? The roots perhaps may be found in her childhood: Martha's somewhat strong implicit affiliation motive developed in the first 2 years of her life, when she experienced warmth and security from her mother, was the "pet" of her older siblings, and was also well loved at her day care center. Her even stronger implicit achievement motive also emerged early in childhood, when her demanding father withheld love and attention, providing these only when she did very well at learning the tasks of life (e.g., when learning to walk, talk, and function).

Martha's low explicit affiliation motive emerged only later, as a result of often feeling unacceptable to not only her father but also the other children in her school, who were less driven and perfectionistic than she. She developed a belief that she does not really need social contacts, consistent with her father's frequent comment that "being successful in school is more important than spending time with friends." Even today, although Martha is an interesting and ultimately likable person, her own self-concept as a loner tends to stand in the way of her making real friends. Furthermore, she experiences some internal incoherence and stress because the belief "I am a loner" does not seem to accord with the desires for connection and companionship that linger at the fringes of her consciousness. Obviously, the situation is complex; Martha's thwarted relatedness needs in childhood caused her to consciously reject sociality, thereby denying herself what she needs, as assumed by both dispositional (MDT) and universalist (SDT) perspectives. Her father had quite a negative impact on her! This illustrates the vital importance of the social relations level of analysis within the MPIC, in part because it is the level at which young personalities are socialized.

Readers should be aware that the previous account relies completely on learning history to explain the origin of individual differences, and ignores both genetic factors (given that we know all traits and motives are at least somewhat heritable) and possible gene–situation interaction–transaction factors (i.e., epigenetics). These kinds of perspectives have, for the most part, not made their way into MDT, and constitute a different class of questions awaiting future research.

Differences and Similarities between SDT and MDT

Summing up the most striking differences between the needs concepts in SDT and MDT: SDT assumes that needs are innate and universal (Level 1 of the MPIC), whereas MDT assumes that needs develop in early childhood due to learning processes based on differential experiences with innate natural incentives (Level 2 of the MPIC). However, Deci and Ryan (2000, p. 229) stated that "there are not instances of optimal, healthy development in which a need for autonomy, relatedness, or competence was neglected, whether or not individuals consciously valued these needs." Thus, from a strict SDT perspective, developing a relative disinclination to pursue certain needs (i.e., intimacy or relatedness) may be a maladaptive process rather than a process of normal personality differentiation, as MDT assumes. In brief, SDT views basic needs are *experiential requirements* that all people need to get, just as plants need certain nutrients (Sheldon, 2011), whereas MDT assumes that people can differ in the way they select, orient, and energize their behavior, with no ill effects as long as their explicit motives concur with their implicit motives.

Still, the two needs concepts in SDT and MDT share some common characteristics. The most striking one is that SDT and MDT identify nearly the same three motivational themes or contents as crucial within human life. SDT's "basic need for competence" maps clearly onto MDT's "need for achievement," and SDT's "basic need for relatedness" maps clearly onto MDT's "need for affiliation" (or intimacy; McAdams, 1980). Also, SDT's "basic need for autonomy" bears a small degree of similarity to MDT's "need for power," although the basic need for autonomy typically refers to "power over oneself," that is, trying to influence and control oneself, whereas the need for power (nPow) is typically construed as a social motive involving "power over others" (Winter, 1973; see Schüler, Sheldon, & Fröhlich, 2010). Further common ground is provided by the fact that SDT and MDT both assume that these three basic types of needs/motives are innate and are somehow functional for human adaptation.

The Two-Process Model of Psychological Needs

Why, then, do MDT and SDT researchers rarely use each other's measures, or cite each other? Is there a way to combine SDT and MDT motivational accounts given their focus on the same basic themes and experiences, to create a single integrated theory? More generally, can both *desires to get the experience of* X and *actual experiences of* X be contained within the same process framework? This is the goal of the TPM (Sheldon, 2011).

TPM research began with the SDT-based question, "Can a thwarted basic need give rise to a motive to obtain the missing experience?" (Sheldon & Gunz, 2009). It certainly seems logical that a person who feels lonely on Friday night might call up a friend, that a person who feels incompetent in school might study harder, or that a person who feels controlled at work might seek opportunities for self-expression. Indeed, this might seem to be the whole point of having an evolved motivational need! However, conventional SDT has had a difficult time accounting for this situation because unsatisfied people are (by definition) operating from a position of deficiency, and their functioning should therefore be impaired and degraded rather than focused and enhanced. In other words, construing needs-satisfying experiences as nutrients that enable agency makes it difficult to explain how an agent can take action to rectify the *absence* of satisfaction. The TPM, in contrast, assumes that, at least in the short term, unmet needs can give rise to corresponding motives or wishes (Sheldon & Gunz, 2009), although in the long term, chronically unmet needs are likely to give rise to helplessness and ill health.

Figure 16.3 illustrates the dynamic provisions of the TPM (Sheldon, 2011), showing that states of dissatisfaction or thwarting can give rise to motives to procure the missing experiences, giving rise to goal-based behaviors (enacted via discrepancy-reduction processes), giving rise, ideally, to the desired experiences. These, in turn, can positively reinforce the behavioral operations that procured the desired experiences, making it more likely those behaviors will be enacted again (i.e., a disposition toward such behaviors develops). The "two process" terminology merely references the two main parts of this dynamic sequence: the "front end," in which behavioral motives are activated (either chronically, or acutely within a given situation), and the "back end," in which such behaviors give rise to particular experiences that may or may not be satisfying to the person.

Let us return to the question of how to integrate SDT and MDT. MDT, we argue, has traditionally focused on the front part of the TPM, by measuring people's motive dispositions (by coding their written responses to ambiguous pictures) and using these scores as predictors of various types of behaviors and outcomes. In contrast SDT, we argue, has traditionally focused on the back part of the TPM, by asking what kinds of experiences are most universally satisfying for people. Notice, however, that each theory also in some way references the other half of the model. Motive dispositions are reinforced by experiences, that is, via the positive primary emotions they evoke (McClelland, 1985; although SDT researchers would suggest that it is needs-satisfying experiences, rather than emotions, that reinforce the behaviors [Sheldon, 2011]). In SDT, needs satisfaction is viewed as an essential support for motivated behavior (Deci & Ryan, 2000), which is, of course, necessary to help bring about the conditions for further needs satisfaction. The TPM merely gives an explicit way to "close the loop" between the initial and later stages of a behavioral sequence, enabling SDT and MDT to be construed as addressing two different aspects of the very same process.

There are some initial data concerning the closing of this loop. Sheldon (2011) argued that motive dispositions persist because they successfully obtain the types of satisfaction toward which they aim; they procure their own reinforcements. Sheldon and Schüler (2011) found direct evidence to support this, as explicit nAch predicted competence satisfaction measured over time, and explicit need for affiliation (nAff) predicted relatedness satisfaction over time.

Extrapolating from these findings, we may speculate that individual differences in motive dispositions arise in childhood due to exposure to developmental environments that selectively reinforce some activities (via corresponding needs satisfaction) rather than others, causing the person to come to become reliant on those activities and types of satisfaction, perhaps even throughout the lifespan. Simply put, those who get a lot of competence needs satisfaction as children may become disposed to seek out achievement as a dominant mode of living; receiving much relatedness needs satisfaction may create a disposition to orient toward affiliation and relationships; and receiving much autonomy support may cause people to orient toward autonomy and self-determination. These considerations are in line with the definition of implicit motives as learned preferences for certain kinds of emotional experiences, and with the basic principles of learning. The more often these experiences (e.g., feeling competent, socially related, and autonomous) occur, the stronger becomes the associated motivational system. However, no data currently exist, to our knowledge, to support this picture that links early needs satisfaction (SDT) to childhood motive disposition acquisition (MDT).

The TPM also provides a way to understand how a person might get "out of touch" with him- or herself, with an account that is somewhat different from MDT's concept of implicit–explicit motive incongruence: Namely, a person may be missing a needed experience but not be motivated to get it; that is, the two parts of the dynamic process can become uncoupled, so that absent needs do not spur relevant behavior, or so that a selected behavior is irrelevant to meeting absent needs. Martha, psychologically overcompensating for her distressed state, drinks heavily and has maladaptive short-term relationships. Why, if she is moderately strong in implicit affiliation motivation *and* is missing relatedness needs satisfaction, does she not go after high-quality relatedness directly? Why are her needs and motives uncoupled?

This is where MDT's conception of implicit–explicit noncongruence can help; as suggested

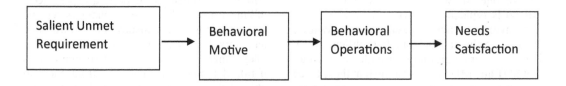

FIGURE 16.3. A regulatory process linking needs as requirements and needs as motives.

earlier, Martha is limited by inaccurate self-beliefs ("I'm just not a people person"), beliefs that prevent her from fully recognizing the signals of her own loneliness, and from acknowledging her own subliminal impulses to break the cycle. Consciously, she believes that success at work is the only thing that really matters. In terms of the "organismic integration minitheory" of SDT, not covered in this chapter, this belief is an "introject" left over from childhood, a guilt-based motivation associated with her father that is only partially internalized and partially assimilated. Unfortunately, this idea keeps Martha "stuck" and has stalled her development in this crucial part of life.

Theoretical Questions, Developmental Speculations, and Thought Experiments

Earlier, we focused mainly on the question of how and why individuals come to differ in their dominant motives and motive dispositions (Levels 2 and 3 in the MPIC), despite sharing a basic human nature (Level 1 in the MPIC). The reader might have noticed that the answer to this question is both simple and complex. First, the simple answer: Human beings need to experience competence, social relatedness, and autonomy in order to feel well, to make the most of themselves in terms of personal growth, personal life satisfaction, and being a valuable part of society. In these terms, the *universal distal goal of motivation* (i.e., basic needs satisfaction) is very well defined and fixed by our biological heritage. What is more variable, and more modifiable by the social environment and our reciprocal shaping of that environment, is *the way we proximally strive to satisfy these universal constraints*. Being on a relatively long leash to get psychological satisfaction (as long as basic biological needs are met), human beings have a variety of possibilities to set proximate goals, to take action, to benefit emotionally or suffer from goal striving, to develop personally (or not) and, in the end, to be more or less successful in attaining the distal goal of basic needs satisfaction.

Beyond this simple answer, many more complex questions remain *un*answered in this field of research. For us, one of the most pressing questions is: How do the two halves of the TPM become uncoupled, such that states of dissatisfaction do not manage to give rise to appropriate remedial motives, or motives that do

not provide satisfaction manage to persist nevertheless? Also, is decoupling *always* negative? For example, what if motive–need decoupling is sometimes functional, providing people with enough degrees of freedom that they can adaptively choose to forego present satisfaction, in the interest of achieving greater satisfaction in the future?

Can "Decoupling" Lead to Positive Long-Term and Developmental Effects?

In Martha's case, a strong implicit achievement motive, in combination with an almost exclusive focus on achievement goals and a belief that she is a loner, led to an unbalanced portfolio of basic needs satisfaction. In particular, her implicit affiliation motive has become "decoupled" from her behavior. However, Martha only really began to suffer from this situation when she began failing in her job—it is risky to "put all one's eggs in one basket" (Linville, 1985) because changes in the social environment (e.g., changing expectations at the workplace, or a new supervisor who sees only our weaknesses) can easily pull the basket out from under us.

But what would have happened if Martha's job environment ("above" personality, at Level 5 in the version of the MPIC in Figure 16.2) had instead supported her, via a supervisor who recognized that she might need to develop some new skills as he assigned her the new responsibilities, and arranged for relevant help and coaching along the way? From an enlightened managerial perspective, perhaps the way to maximize Martha's career potential would be to encourage her tendency to become unbalanced at first, as she developed critical work skills and organizational knowledge. Later on, she could be groomed for management, rectifying the initial imbalance and thereby enabling her to pass her hard-won skills on to mentees and subordinates. In other words, it is possible that a temporary imbalance of motives and needs, with the right supports, can be highly functional for development. We consider this idea in more detail below.

Development is a process. This becomes particularly clear when considering "developmental tasks" (Havighurst, 1953). We have "developmental deadlines" (Heckhausen, 1999), such as limited time available for becoming (relatively) independent from our parents (in early adulthood), for starting a family, for finding a satisfying job (in young and middle adulthood), and then, in later life, for maintaining and developing our skills and personality in the face of a more limited future time perspective. We suggest that the successful attainment of such age-graded life tasks is an important source of basic needs satisfaction: Becoming more and more independent from one's parents is a good thing in terms of feeling autonomous, obtaining an enjoyable and challenging job is a good context in which to experience competence, and it is easier to feel social connectedness when one cultivates a close network of family and friends. Thus, behaviors that lead to success in striving for these tasks are highly adaptive, both in the present and the future (see, e.g., Jutta Heckhausen's lifespan theory of control [Heckhausen & Schulz, 1995]; see also Masten and colleagues' conception of "developmental cascades" [Masten, Desjardins, McCormick, Kuo, & Long, 2010]).

In accordance with Heckhausen's (2000) assumption that individuals can actively organize their own development, Wrosch and Heckhausen (1999) showed that when approaching a developmental deadline (e.g., the biological clock that determines the timing of childbearing), people tend to manifest higher commitment to corresponding goals (i.e., they respond to the deadline). Notably, however, Heckhausen's considerations focus on an individual's *conscious* enactment of goal-directed action rather than on his or her implicit motives and basic needs. But can people's *nonconscious* motives be changed, by changing developmental necessities?

From a developmental perspective, it would seem to be highly adaptive if people could alter their implicit motives in response to important transitions in their lives. This is because implicit motives can produce strong emotional responses that support and shape the required behavior (McClelland, 1985). For example, it might be good to have boosted implicit affiliation motivation at a time when one is attempting to woo a life partner and start a family, whereas boosted implicit achievement motivation might be highly adaptive in the first phases of establishing a career. In other words, either life phase might elicit a temporary imbalance in one's motives and corresponding basic needs satisfaction, at a possible short-term cost. However, such motivational fluctuations might also help people to lay the foundation for future states in which needs are better met, overall, or are in better balance with each other (Sheldon & Niemiec, 2006).

One problem with this scenario is that currently, implicit motives are conceptualized as being highly stable and largely unchanging aspects of an individual's personality, developed in the very first years of life (McClelland, 1985). In this view, we would not expect implicit motives to change across the lifespan, nor to be responsive to the changing demands that people face at different times of life. However, as with many of the other issues we discuss in this chapter, there are few extant data. The few longitudinal studies that exist have revealed inconsistent results with regard to changes in motive dispositions, either in terms of mean-level continuity or rank-order continuity. Veroff, Reuman, and Feld (1984) found that the affiliation and achievement motives decrease with age in women, and that young and old men have lower power motive scores than do middle-aged men. Franz (1994) showed that the power motive remained stable across the lifespan, whereas the achievement and affiliation motives increased with age for both men and women. Valero, Nikitin, and Freund (2015) found evidence that implicit motives in general (aggregated across nAch, nAff, and nPow) are stronger for older than for younger adults, due to a decrease in future time perspective. In contrast, Denzinger, Backes, Job, and Brandstätter (2016) argued that age-dependent changes in affective and neuroendocrinology reactivity should lead to reduced responsiveness to motive-specific incentives and therewith to reduced motive-specific behavior. The authors empirically supported the hypothesized reduction in motive strength across age for all three motives (achievement, affiliation, power).

We suggest that what is needed are studies that measure implicit motive strength in exactly the life phases in which important developmental transitions and deadlines occur; these assessments should be precisely targeted. However, these studies should also examine such fluctuations in the context of the whole lifespan, including early childhood, when motives are formed. Unfortunately, such studies would be difficult and expensive to conduct, and would require decades to unfold. Thus, the question of whether implicit motives can change in response to varying life tasks across the lifespan remains open. Our hypothesis, based on our own life experiences, is that they can, although explicit motives may have to lead the way (discussed below). What is most difficult, perhaps, is if such life-transitions occur *simultaneously,* for example, in an academic career when the labor-intensive postdoctoral phase and the family formation phase take place almost simultaneously in a relatively brief period of time (as happened for one of the two authors of this chapter).

Can Even Implicit–Explicit Motive Incongruence Sometimes Be Beneficial for Basic Needs Satisfaction?

Earlier, we showed that implicit–explicit motive incongruence can reflect the decoupling of implicit and explicit motives, leading to a deficit of basic needs satisfaction. Martha experiences low (or compromised) relatedness needs satisfaction because she consciously defines herself as a loner and doesn't value social relationships as important (low explicit affiliation motive), interfering with her fairly strong implicit affiliation motive. However, we can surmise that her implicit affiliation motive still expresses itself, one way or another. Maybe she watches a lot of romantic comedies, or posts a lot on Facebook. But what if she had a weak *implicit* affiliation motive, as well as a weak explicit affiliation motive? How could she *ever* get her basic need for relatedness satisfied, with neither implicit nor explicit affiliation motivation to draw on? Notice that from an MDT perspective, this represents a case of *congruence* between implicit and explicit motives (they are both low), and therefore should not be a problem. However the SDT perspective suggests that this *is* a problem because there is no motivation to get what is needed.

How could the problem be solved? One possible answer is that an explicit motive could develop in response to the absent needs satisfaction, which helps to boost needs satisfaction, and perhaps even boost implicit motivation (since implicit motives are learned, in response to positive reinforcements). In terms of the TPM and the dynamic sequence in Figure 16.3, a deficiency of a universally required experience (of relatedness) could give rise to a conscious intention to get the missing experience, finally resulting in the actual experiences—despite the person's current personality structure, which works against having the experiences. In SDT and MPIC terms, a maladaptive personality organization can always be rectified, potentially, because the basic psychological need always remains within the core foundation of all human personalities.

Although the TPM does not distinguish between implicit and explicit motivations, it seems likely that explicit motives are more easily or quickly changeable via this route than implicit ones, since implicit motives are built on long-term learning, and explicit motives are built on more easily modifiable self-beliefs and cognitions. Thus, one very plausible model is that Martha could come to consciously realize, perhaps through therapy, that she really does care about relationships with others. With some work, this could enable her to "recouple" the two parts of the TPM, such that in her daily life, she comes to recognize feelings of loneliness when they arise, and to use such feelings as a signal to reach out to somebody. In this model, conscious cognition leads the way to development and positive change, once the conscious self has been alerted to the problem, and has elected to set relevant goals.

Notice that the MPIC (see Figure 16.2) allows for this possibility, by allowing self-experience to (at least at times) play a causal role with respect to behavior. Again, explicit motives have a *directive* function, and to the extent they can climb onto a reliable energy source (i.e., a relevant implicit motive), they can create a truly harmonious arrangement within the personal motivational system. Martha's problems could perhaps be resolved relatively quickly with the right modifications to her self-concept and life given the platform of strong implicit affiliation motive that she already possesses. We suggest that the existence of two independent motivational systems (implicit and explicit; McClelland et al., 1989) can be highly functional to reach basic needs satisfaction, in essence providing people with two different routes to satisfaction: one route that is "pushed" by subliminal urges, and another that is "pulled" by conscious goals and self-beliefs. What has been missing from this MDT perspective, which is supplied by the SDT perspective, is the idea that all people may really need certain experiences, regardless of how their personalities are now organized with respect to those experiences.

Can People Vary in How Satisfying Particular Needs Are for Them?

But let us push back the other way yet again, to discuss yet one more example of how SDT, MDT, and the TPM can not only mutually reinforce but also extend each other. Again, the TPM assumes basic needs satisfaction rewards and strengthens the corresponding implicit motives that prompted the need-relevant behavior in the first place, and SDT assumes that everybody "needs" the needs to an equal extent. However, from a MDT perspective, it may be more complex: Individuals likely differ in their capacity to experience certain kinds of incentives as rewarding. If so, then some people may "need" some experiences more than others. Individuals with a strong achievement motive might benefit to a greater extent from feelings of competence, and those with a strong affiliation motive might benefit more from feelings of relatedness.

Such an interaction or "matching" hypothesis has been empirically supported (Hofer & Busch, 2013; Schüler & Brandstätter, 2013; Schüler et al., 2010; Schüler, Sheldon, Prentice, & Halusic, 2016) when predicting domain-specific and short-term types of mood. However, when it comes to the prediction of domain-*general* and longer-term well-being, the effects of need satisfaction seem "universal," in the sense that implicit motives do not moderate the effects of needs satisfaction on these broader outcomes (Schüler et al., 2013). The authors concluded that implicit motives determine how people regulate their momentary emotions and behavior, and derive satisfaction from certain incentives, but that basic needs satisfaction is responsible for global and long-term subjective well-being.

Broader Theoretical Questions

In this final section, we try to sum up our main points and also point out what knowledge is still missing. Currently, the field knows very little about a host of important issues, many of which have already been alluded to within this chapter. One of the most important is: What is the relationship between explicit and motive systems, beyond the simple idea that when they disagree, there may be problems? Can conflict between the explicit and implicit motive systems sometimes be adaptive, at least for a short period of time? Might this adaptiveness occur in cases where implicit–explicit motive incongruence serves a higher distal goal (basic needs satisfaction), at least in the long term, even though the incongruence might cause temporary problems at a more proximal level (e.g., via conflicts between conscious self-beliefs and nonconscious urges)?

The previous paragraph concerned conflicts between conscious and nonconscious motives. But what about conflicts between different *motives* themselves, for example, between achievement and affiliation (as in a graduate student with a new baby *and* the first week of studies to deal with), or between other motives such as affiliation and power, or relatedness and autonomy? These kinds of conflicts reflect the difficult balances that need to be achieved between agency and communion Bakan (1966), self-centeredness versus prosociality, and individualism versus collectivism, and may have influence regardless of whether the motives are implicit or explicit.

We also need to know more about cases in which differing motives (i.e., achievement vs. affiliation) conflict *across* platforms (i.e., implicit vs. explicit). Suppose Martha had, in addition to her strong implicit achievement motive, a strong explicit affiliation motive. Would this be a problem? For example, would a belief that "I am a people person," in conjunction with being an obsessive achievement striver (behaviorally), lead to conflict in a person's life or psyche? Or perhaps such conflict could actually a *good* thing, as in the temporal sequence suggested earlier, in which Martha eventually developed a stronger explicit affiliation motive, which helped her learn to recognize her own feelings of loneliness and isolation when they occur, which helped her to take action to remedy these feelings?

Yet another very broad issue, which further expands the potential complexity of any "final" process model of motivation, concerns the potential to differentiate "hope" and "fear" as distinct components of both implicit and explicit motives (achievement = fear of failure and hope of success; affiliation = fear of rejection and hope for closeness; power = fear of weakness and hope of power; McClelland, 1985). "Fear" and "hope" are closely aligned with the classic "avoidance" versus "approach" dimension of motivation (Elliot & Dweck, 2005). For example, does fear of failure spur behavior that is relevant for *avoiding* the *thwarting* of the basic need for competence, and is this kind of striving in turn helpful or harmful for obtaining positive feelings of competence *satisfaction*? That is, can avoidance motivation, based on a strong fear motive, be beneficial in terms of generating basic needs satisfaction, or is it inappropriate from the start?

Let's imagine that Martha's implicit affiliation motive score in a picture story exercise is mainly attributable to a strong fear of rejection (in scoring manuals that are used to analyze picture stories, the hope and fear subcomponents are often added together and form an overall motive score) (Pang, 2010; Winter, 1994). She learned this fear of rejection from social interactions with her father in childhood. The reason for not valuing friendships, for not trying to make friends and establish stable social relationships might then be a strategy to avoid being socially rejected. This might be an effective short-term strategy to avoid negative feelings, but in the end, it makes the satisfaction of basic need for relatedness impossible. This is another example of a successful short-term regulation of emotion and behavior that in the long run may not lead to the desired results (e.g., long-term and stable basic needs satisfaction). These speculations can also be located on the list of unanswered research questions that require future research.

Beyond all these questions, a personality developmental perspective requires us to additionally ask: How would all of the previously discussed processes and relationships tend to vary or change across the lifespan, in response to either socially prescribed tasks or roles, or to the person's internal impulses toward greater health, happiness, and maturity? How might all of these motivational processes and potential conflicts be mapped onto the MPIC's horizontal time dimension, as both outcomes of influences acting at particular levels of the causal hierarchy, and as potential causes of what happens next?

For example, consider the effects of unbalanced needs satisfaction. How bad is it to be unbalanced? After all, Martha was doing pretty well, or at least okay, before her job demands changed. It is possible that only a certain *minimum* of total satisfaction, averaged across the three needs, is really necessary; in this scenario, a person (like Martha) might get lots of satisfaction of one need (competence), which is enough to partially, or even mostly, compensate for absent satisfactions of the relatedness need. A "5, 2, 2" needs satisfaction configuration may be nearly as good as a "3, 3, 3" configuration (they both sum to 9; Sheldon & Niemiec, 2006)—perhaps Martha could have gone on like that for decades!

However, from a developmental perspective, at this time of her life, Martha was surely missing out on important influences and experiences relevant to the full unfolding of her personality potentials. Suppose that, with the help and support of sensitive supervisors, Martha manages to adapt to the new interpersonal challenges of her job. After having rectified the imbalances that plagued Martha in her early 30s, suppose that her strong implicit affiliation motivation helps her to become a wise leader in her 40s and 50s, and even CEO of her company in her 60s. Surely this would be a more desirable outcome for everyone, including Martha, than if she had simply kept on valuing professional accomplishments alone, divorced from the feelings and needs of others! In this long-term view, SDT is correct after all: Everybody *does* need all three needs, even if they can wait for years, or even decades, to reach the full complement of potential satisfaction—or even if they never really get there. To achieve one's full potential may require creating a life and personality in which all three needs are fully satisfied, as well as the needs of those around one within the network of selves at Level 5 of the MPIC model.

In conclusion, much more research is needed to understand the intersections (i.e., the synergies and conflicts) between various motivations (i.e., affiliation and achievement) within different motivational systems (i.e., implicit and explicit), of different types (approach vs. avoidance), at different portions of the lifespan (i.e., young adult vs. middle age), with regard to basic needs satisfaction (of autonomy, competence, and relatedness), in relation to positive developmental outcomes (happiness, self-actualization, family well-being, etc.). Doubtless, there are many different ways for people to navigate these many intersections, ways that remain to be identified and explored. However, we suggest that there is a criterion for identifying the "best" resolution of the problem, namely, the sum total of needs satisfaction that is experienced over the course of the lifespan. Testing this bold but plausible conjecture will require far better data than we currently possess.

REFERENCES

Atkinson, J. W. (1957). Motivational determinants of risk-taking behavior. *Psychological Review, 64*(6), 359–372.

Bakan, D. (1966). *The duality of human existence: An essay on psychology and religion.* Chicago: Rand McNally.

Baumann, N., Chatterjee, M. B., & Hank, P. (2016). Guiding others for their own good: Action orientation is associated with prosocial enactment of the implicit power motive. *Motivation and Emotion, 40,* 56–68.

Baumann, N., Kaschel, R., & Kuhl, J. (2005). Striving for unwanted goals: Stress dependent discrepancies between explicit and implicit achievement motives reduce subjective well-being and increase psychosomatic symptoms. *Journal of Personality and Social Psychology, 89*(5), 781–799.

Baumeister, R. F., & Leary, M. R. (1995). The need to belong: Desire for interpersonal attachments as a fundamental human motivation. *Psychological Bulletin, 117*(3), 497–529.

Brunstein, J. C. (2008). Implicit and explicit motives. In J. Heckhausen & H. Heckhausen (Eds.), *Motivation and action* (pp. 221–246). Cambridge, UK: Cambridge University Press.

Brunstein, J. C., & Heckhausen, H. (2008). Achievement motivation. In J. Heckhausen & H. Heckhausen (Eds.), *Motivation and action* (pp. 137–183). Cambridge, UK: Cambridge University Press.

Brunstein, J. C., & Maier, G. W. (2005). Implicit and self-attributed motives to achieve: Two separate but interacting needs. *Journal of Personality and Social Psychology, 89*(2), 205–222.

Brunstein, J. C., Schultheiss, O. C., & Maier, G. W. (1999). The pursuit of personal goals: A motivational approach to well-being and life adjustment. In V. Brandstätter & R. M. Lerner (Eds.), *Action and self-development: Theory and research through the life span* (pp. 169–196). London: SAGE.

Chirkov, V. I., & Ryan, R. M. (2001). Parent and teacher autonomy support in Russian and U.S. adolescents: Common effects on wellbeing and academic motivation. *Journal of Cross-Cultural Psychology, 32,* 618–635.

deCharms, R. (1968). *Personal causation.* New York: Academic Press.

Deci, E. L., La Guardia, J. G., Moller, A. C., Scheiner, M. J., & Ryan, R. M. (2006). On the benefits of giving as well as receiving autonomy support: Mutuality in close friendships. *Personality and Social Psychology Bulletin, 32,* 313–327.

Deci, E. L., & Ryan, R. M. (1985). *Intrinsic motivation and self-determination in human behavior.* New York: Plenum Press.

Deci, E. L., & Ryan, R. M. (2000). The "what" and "why" of goal pursuits: Human needs and the self-determination of behavior. *Psychological Inquiry, 11,* 227–268.

Denzinger, F., Backes, S., Job, J., & Brandstätter, V. (2016). Age and gender differences in implicit motives. *Journal of Research in Personality, 65,* 52–61.

Ekman, P. (1971). Universal and cultural differences in facial expression of emotion. In J. K. Kole (Ed.), *Nebraska Symposium on Motivation* (Vol. 19, pp. 207–283). Lincoln: University of Nebraska Press.

Elliot, A. J., & Dweck, C. S. (Eds.). (2005). *Handbook of competence and motivation.* New York: Guilford Press.

Exline, R. V. (1963). Explorations in the process of person perception: Visual interaction in relation to competition, sex, and need for affiliation. *Journal of Personality, 31*(1), 1–20.

Franz, C. E. (1994). Does thought content change as individual age?: A longitudinal study of midlife adults. In T. F. Heatherton & J. L. Weinberger (Eds.), *Can personality change?* (pp. 227–249). Washington, DC: American Psychological Association.

French, E. G., & Chadwick, I. (1956). Some characteristics in affiliation motivation. *Journal of Abnormal and Social Psychology, 52*(3), 296–300.

Gagne, M., Ryan, R. M., & Bargmann, K. (2003). Autonomy support and need satisfaction in the motivation and well-being of gymnasts. *Journal of Applied Sport Psychology, 15*(4), 372–390.

Geary, D. C., & Huffman, K. J. (2002). Brain and cognitive evolution: Forms of modularity and functions of mind. *Psychological Bulletin, 128,* 667–698.

Gröpel, P., Wegner, M., & Schüler, J. (2016). Achievement motive and sport participation. *Psychology of Sport and Exercise, 27,* 93–100.

Hagemeyer, B., Dufner, M., & Denissen, J. J. A. (2016). Double dissociation between implicit and explicit affiliative motives: A closer look at socializing behavior in dyadic interactions. *Journal of Research in Personality, 65,* 89–93.

Havighurst, R. J. (1953). *Human development and education.* London: Longman.

Heckhausen, J. (1999). *Developmental regulation in adulthood: Age normative and sociostructural constraints as adaptive challenges.* New York: Cambridge University Press.

Heckhausen, J. (Ed.). (2000). *Motivational psychology of human development: Developing motivation and motivating development.* Oxford, UK: Elsevier.

Heckhausen, J., & Schulz, R. (1995). A life-span theory of control. *Psychological Review, 102,* 284–304.

Hofer, J., & Busch, H. (2013). Living in accordance with one's implicit motives: Cross-cultural evidence for beneficial effects of motive-goal congruence and motive satisfaction. In A. Efklides & D. Moraitou (Eds.), *A positive psychology perspective on quality of life* (pp. 51–56). New York: Springer.

Hsu, W. T., Wang, Y. C., Hsiao, C. H., & Wu, H. C. (2013). Autonomy and structure can enhance motivation of volunteers in sport organizations. *Perceptual and Motor Skills, 117*(3), 709–719.

Illardi, B. C., Leone, D., Kasser, R., & Ryan, R. M. (2009). Employee and supervisor ratings of motivation: Main effects and discrepancies associated with job satisfaction and adjustment in a factory setting. *Journal of Applied Social Psychology, 23,* 1789–1805.

Job, V., Oertig, D., Brandstätter, V., & Allemand, M. (2010). Discrepancies between implicit and explicit motivation and unhealthy eating behaviour. *Journal of Personality, 78*(4), 1209–1238.

Kasser, T. (2002). *The high price of materialism.* Cambridge, MA: MIT Press.

Langens, T. A. (2006). Congruence between implicit and explicit motives and emotional well-being: The moderating role of activity inhibition. *Motivation and Emotion, 31*(1), 49–59.

Lansing, J. B., & Heyns, R. W. (1959). Need affiliation and frequency of four types of communication. *Journal of Abnormal and Social Psychology, 58*(3), 365–372.

Linville, P. (1985). Self-complexity and affective extremity: Don't put all of your eggs in one cognitive basket. *Social Cognition, 3,* 94–120.

Lynch, M. F., La Guardia, J. G., & Ryan, R. M. (2009). On being yourself in different cultures: Ideal and actual self-concept, autonomy support and well-being in China, Russia and the United States. *Journal of Positively Psychology, 4,* 290–304.

Malinowski, B. (1944). *A scientific theory of culture.* Chapel Hill: University of North Carolina Press.

Masten, A. S., Desjardins, C. D., McCormick, C. M., Kuo, S. L., & Long, J. D. (2010). The significance of childhood competence and problems for adult success in work: A developmental cascade analysis. *Developmental Psychopathology, 22,* 679–694.

McAdams, D. P. (1980). A thematic coding system for the intimacy motive. *Journal of Research in Personality, 14*(4), 413–432.

McAdams, D. P. (1996). Personality, modernity, and the storied self: A contemporary framework for studying persons. *Psychological Inquiry, 7,* 295–321.

McAdams, D. P., Jackson, R. J., & Kirshnit, C. (1984). Looking laughing, and smiling in dyads as a function of intimacy motivation. *Journal of Personality, 52,* 261–273.

McAdams, D. P., & Manczak, E. (2011). What is a "level" of personality? *Psychological Inquiry, 22,* 40–44.

McClelland, D. C. (1985). *Human motivation.* Glenview, IL: Scott, Foresman.

McClelland, D. C. (1987). *Human motivation.* New York: Cambridge University Press.

McClelland, D. C., Atkinson, J. W., Clark, R. A., & Lowell, E. L. (1953). *The achievement motive.* New York: Appleton-Century-Crofts.

McClelland, D. C., & Boyatzis, R. E. (1982). The leadership motive pattern and long term success in management. *Journal of Applied Psychology, 67,* 737–743.

McClelland, D. C., Koestner, R., & Weinberger, J. (1989). How do self-attributed and implicit motives differ? *Psychological Review, 96*(4), 690–702.

McClelland, D. C., & Pilon, D. A. (1983). Sources of adult motives in patterns of parent behavior in early childhood. *Journal of Personality and Social Psychology, 44*(3), 564–574.

Morgan, C., & Murray, H. A. (1935). A method for investigating fantasies: The thematic apperception test. *Archives of Neurology and Psychiatry, 34,* 289–306.

Murray, H. A. (1938). *Explorations in personality.* New York: Oxford University Press.

Niemiec, C. P., Lynch, M. F., Vansteenkiste, M., Bernstein, J., Deci, E. L., & Ryan, R. M. (2006). The antecedents and consequences of autonomous self-regulation for college: A self-determination theory perspective on socialization. *Journal of Adolescence, 29,* 761–775.

Pang, J. S. (2010). Content coding methods in implicit motive assessment: Standards of measurement and best practices for the picture story exercise. In O. C. Schultheiss & J. C. Brunstein (Eds.), *Implicit motives* (pp. 119–150). Oxford, UK: Oxford University Press.

Patrick, H., Knee, C. R., & Canevello, A., & Lonsbary, C. (2007). The role of need fulfillment in relationship functioning and well-being: A self-determination theory perspective. *Journal of Personality and Social Psychology, 92,* 434–457.

Reinboth, M., Duda, J. L., & Ntoumanis, N. (2004). Dimensions of coaching behavior, need satisfaction, and the psychological and physical welfare of young athletes. *Motivation and Emotion, 28*(3), 297–313.

Rohner, R. P. (2004). The parental "acceptance–rejection syndrome": Universal correlates of perceived rejection. *American Psychologist, 59,* 830–840.

Ryan, R. M. (1995). Psychological needs and the facilitation of integrative processes. *Journal of Personality, 63*(3), 397–427.

Ryan, R. M., & Deci, E. L. (2000). The darker and brighter sides of human existence: Basic psychological needs as a unifying concept. *Psychological Inquiry, 11*(4), 319–338.

Ryan, R. M., & Deci, E. L. (2008). Self-determination theory and the role of basic psychological needs in personality and the organization of behavior. In O. P. John, R. W. Robins, & L. A. Pervin (Eds.), *Handbook of personality psychology: Theory and research* (3rd ed., pp. 654–678). New York: Guilford Press.

Ryan, R. M., La Guardia, J. G., Solky-Butzel, J., Chirkov, V. I., & Kim, Y. (2005). On the interpersonal regulation of emotions: Emotional reliance across gender, relationships, and cultures. *Personal Relationships, 12,* 145–163.

Schmalt, H.-D., & Heckhausen, H. (2008). Power motivation. In J. Heckhausen & H. Heckhausen (Eds.), *Motivation and action* (pp. 202–226). Cambridge, UK: Cambridge University Press.

Schüler, J., & Brandstätter, V. (2013). How basic need satisfaction and dispositional motives interact in predicting flow experience in sport. *Journal of Applied Social Psychology, 43*(4), 687–705.

Schüler, J., Brandstätter, V., & Sheldon, K. M. (2013). Do implicit motives and basic psychological needs interact to predict well-being and flow?: Testing a universal hypothesis and a matching hypothesis. *Motivation and Emotion, 37*(3), 480–495.

Schüler, J., Job, V., Fröhlich, S. M., & Brandstätter, V. (2008). A high implicit affiliation motive does not always make you happy: A corresponding explicit motive and corresponding behavior are further needed. *Motivation and Emotion, 32*(3), 231–242.

Schüler, J., Sheldon, K. M., & Fröhlich, S. M. (2010). Implicit need for achievement moderates the relationship between competence need satisfaction and subsequent motivation. *Journal of Research in Personality, 44*(1), 1–12.

Schüler, J., Sheldon, K. M., Prentice, M., & Halusic, M. (2016). Do some people need autonomy more than others?: Implicit dispositions toward autonomy moderate the effects of felt autonomy on well-being. *Journal of Personality, 84*(1), 5–20.

Schultheiss, O. C. (2008). Implicit motives. In O. P. John, R. W. Robins, & L. A. Pervin (Eds.), *Handbook of personality: Theory and research* (3rd ed., pp. 603–633). New York: Guilford Press.

Schultheiss, O. C., & Brunstein, J. C. (2002). Inhibited power motivation and persuasive communication: A lens model analysis. *Journal of Personality, 70*(4), 553–582.

Schultheiss, O. C., & Pang, J. S. (2007). Measuring implicit motives. In R. W. Robins, R. C. Fraley, & R. F. Krueger (Eds.), *Handbook of research methods in personality psychology* (pp. 322–344). New York: Guilford Press.

Sheldon, K. M. (2004). *Optimal human being: An integrated multi-level perspective.* Mahwah, NJ: Erlbaum.

Sheldon, K. M. (2009a). *Current directions in motivation and emotion.* London: Pearson.

Sheldon, K. M. (2009b). Goal-striving across the lifespan: Do people learn to select more self-concordant goals as they age? In M. C. Smith & T. G. Reio (Eds.), *The handbook of research on adult development and learning* (pp. 553–569). New York: Routledge.

Sheldon, K. M. (2011). Integrating behavioral-motive and experiential-requirement perspectives on psychological needs: A two process model. *Psychological Review, 118,* 552–569.

Sheldon, K. M., Cheng, C., & Hilpert, J. (2011). Understanding well-being and optimal functioning: Applying the multilevel personality in context (MPIC) model. *Psychological Inquiry, 22,* 1–16.

Sheldon, K. M., & Gunz, A. (2009). Psychological needs as basic motives, not just experiential requirements. *Journal of Personality, 77,* 1467–1492.

Sheldon, K. M., & Niemiec, C. (2006). It's not just the amount that counts: Balanced need-satisfaction also affects well-being. *Journal of Personality and Social Psychology, 91,* 331–341.

Sheldon, K. M., & Schüler, J. (2011). Wanting, having, and needing: Integrating motive disposition theory and self-determination theory. *Journal of Personality and Social Psychology, 101,* 1106–1123.

Sheldon, K. M., & Schüler, J. (2015). Agency and its discontents: A two-process perspective on basic psychological needs and motives. In M. Mikulincer & P. R. Shaver (Eds.), *Handbook of personality and social psychology* (Vol. 4, pp. 167–187). Washington, DC: American Psychological Association.

Sheldon, K. M., Williams, G., & Joiner, T. (2003). *Self-determination theory in the clinic: Motivating physical and mental health.* New Haven, CT: Yale University Press.

Sierens, E., Vansteenkiste, M., Goossens, L., Soenens, B., & Dochy, F. (2009). The synergistic relationship of perceived autonomy support and structure in the prediction of self-regulated learning. *British Journal of Educational Psychology, 79*(1), 57–68.

Skinner, E. A., & Belmont, M. J. (1993). Motivation in the classroom: Reciprocal effects of teacher behavior and student engagement across the school year. *Journal of Educational Psychology, 85,* 571–581.

Sokolowski, K. (2008). Social bonding: Affiliation motivation and intimacy motivation. In J. Heckhausen & H. Heckhausen (Eds.), *Motivation and action* (pp. 184–201). Cambridge, UK: Cambridge University Press.

Tooby, J., & Cosmides, L. (1990). On the universality of human nature and the uniqueness of the individual: The role of genetics and adaptation. *Journal of Personality, 58,* 17–67.

Valero, D., Nikitin, J., & Freund, A. (2015). The effect of age and time perspective on implicit motives. *Motivation and Emotion, 39,* 175–181.

Vansteenkiste, M., Niemiec, C., & Soenens, B. (2010). The development of the five mini-theories of self-determination theory: An historical overview, emerging trends, and future directions. In T. Urdan & S. Karabenick (Eds.), *Advances in motivation and achievement: The decade ahead* (Vol. 16, pp. 105–166). Bingley, UK: Emerald Group.

Veroff, J., Reuman, D., & Feld, S. (1984). Motives in American men and women across the adult life span. *Developmental Psychology, 20*(6), 1142–1158.

Wegner, M., Bohnacker, V., Mempel, G., Teubel, T., & Schüler, J. (2014). Explicit and implicit affiliation motives predict verbal and nonverbal social behavior in sports competition. *Psychology of Sport and Exercise, 15,* 588–595.

White, R. W. (1959). Motivation reconsidered: The concept of competence. *Psychological Review, 66,* 297–333.

Williams, G. C., Niemiec, C. P., Patrick, H., Ryan, R. M., & Deci, E. L. (2009). The importance of supporting autonomy and perceived competence in facilitating long-term tobacco abstinence. *Annals of Behavioral Medicine, 37,* 315–324.

Winter, D. G. (1973). *The power motive.* New York: Free Press.

Winter, D. G. (1988). The power motive in women and men. *Journal of Personality and Social Psychology, 54,* 510–519.

Winter, D. G. (1994). *Manual for scoring motive imagery in running text (version 4.2).* Ann Arbor: University of Michigan.

Wrosch, C., & Heckhausen, J. (1999). Control processes before and after passing a developmental deadline: Activation and deactivation of intimate relationship goals. *Journal of Personality and Social Psychology, 77*(2), 415–427.

Yang, F., Ramsay, J. E., Schultheiss, O. C., & Pang, J. S. (2015). Need for achievement moderates the effect of motive-relevant challenge on salivary cortisol changes. *Motivation and Emotion, 39,* 321–334.

CHAPTER 17

Achievement Strivings

Motives and Goals That Promote Competence

Amanda M. Durik
K. Ann Renninger

In this chapter we describe the development of *achievement strivings,* a person's motives and goals to be competent, to acquire the skills and knowledge needed to work with some content, such as mathematics or tennis (White, 1959). We consider these topics in relation to McAdams's (2013) description of the three layers of psychological selfhood: the *actor self* (responsive to particular content in the situation), the *agent self* (aware of explicit goals), and the *author self* (thoughtful about prior experiences for identifying meaning). This approach complements and extends recent discussions of the history and refinement of achievement goal constructs over time (Senko, 2016), constructs and processes involved in competence motivation (Elliot, Dweck, & Yeager, 2017), pursuit of achievement goals in the context of other valued goals (Hofer & Fries, 2016), and beliefs about capabilities, including their origins and consequences (Usher, 2016). Specifically, we explain that consideration of selfhood, and its relation to individuals' ages, experiences, and interest, have implications for working theory and measurement of achievement motivation. Content may be necessary for engagement of the self at all three levels in order to foster sustained and meaningful engagement, even though achievement strivings at the level of the agent self can operate independent of particular content.

McAdams (2013) describes three layers of selfhood: actor, agent, and author. These layers help clarify how explicit achievement strivings might be facilitated by implicit strivings, and vice versa. Selfhood begins to develop in early childhood, beginning with the self as *actor,* evolves in middle childhood to include the self as *agent,* and following this, to also include the self as *author.* For example, toddlers engage the actor self. They are responsive to situations, including others' expectations, but are not yet self-aware, and they cannot reason abstractly. As such, achievement strivings among toddlers are promoted by a ball that is out of reach, piano keys that can be pressed to make noise, or wooden blocks that can be stacked until the tower falls over. These strivings emerge in direct contact with the environment and specific content. A person's agent self emerges in middle childhood, along with an increased capacity for self-awareness and abstract thought. For example, a fifth grader might construct a skateboarding ramp in the driveway, plan to join a youth soccer league, or try out for a role in the school play. Achievement strivings that emerge for the agent self are a consequence of explicit goals and values associated with those goals. Finally, the author self that develops during adolescence can reflect on prior experiences and find coherence in past choices. For example, an adult can describe the events that led to returning to school to finish college, becoming a biologist, or quitting a job in order to start a business. Achievement strivings that emerge for the author self are a consequence of reflecting on past achievement opportunities in order to clarify what has been personally rewarding (or not) and what is worth pursuing in the future.

The analogy of self as an agent is prominent in research on achievement motivation because most contemporary research has focused on the benefits of adopting explicit goals (e.g., Ames, 1992; Dweck & Leggett, 1988; Locke & Latham, 1990; Nicholls, 1984), and the explicit values that fuel those goals, such as weighing costs and benefits (e.g., Eccles et al., 1983; Feather, 1988). This is a rational perspective, in that people are assumed to know what they can and want to accomplish and are expected to exert effort to move toward those ends through deliberate behaviors and choices. This set of premises provides a basis for research on self-concept of ability, achievement goals, utility value, and cost (e.g., Flake, Barron, Hulleman, McCoach, & Welsh, 2015; Gniewosz, Eccles, & Noack, 2015; Yeager et al., 2016).

Although recent research on achievement strivings has focused heavily on explicit goals, which we associate with the agent self, this was not always the case. Early conceptualizations of achievement motivation focused on implicit motives (e.g., McClelland, Clark, Roby, & Atkinson, 1949; Tomkins, 1947). These perspectives suggested that as individuals respond to situations that afford opportunities for skills development, they are likely to engage in activities that support the development of competence without explicit goals. For example, individuals might work toward understanding a particular content, such as biology, because their interest is triggered, without a specific sense of what is possible. The extent to which achievement strivings are explicit for the agent self may be influenced by both the self as actor and agent in relation to particular content. Specifically, when people are interested in content, implicit and explicit achievement strivings may be coordinated to direct people toward what they want. This is consistent with research from neuroscience indicating that the brain circuitry associated with reward is activated once interest is triggered and begins to develop (Panksepp, 1998; see Renninger & Hidi, 2016). As such, discussion of meaningful and sustained achievement strivings for competence needs to account for

whether and how much interest a person has for particular content.

Interest

Developed interest is characterized by repeated, voluntary, and independent perseverance to engage the challenges of particular content (e.g., ecology, mathematics, birds; Hidi & Renninger, 2006; Renninger & Hidi, 2016). Defined as a variable that is malleable and can be supported to develop, *interest* describes both a person's psychological state during engagement with particular content and the motivation to reengage with that content over time (Hidi & Renninger, 2006; Krapp, 2002; Schiefele, 1991; Silvia, 2006). Interest requires consideration of achievement strivings beyond the agent self. Specifically, the actor self may be especially relevant to the experience of interest, and the author self may be especially relevant for understanding past successes and failures in a larger context. As such, striving is a product of the actor self (e.g., being caught up in watching a hummingbird), which later may facilitate the identification of explicit goals (e.g., planning a vacation to learn about birds) and contribute to the sense of having a valued identity (see related discussions in Krapp, 2002; Renninger, 2009).

We describe the case of a person whom we refer to as Jason. His case provides an illustration of the layered psychological self and how he integrates the achievement strivings associated with his job as an academic ecologist and his hobby of birding, which he does in his free time.

Meet Jason, Ecologist and Birder

Jason is an ecologist, who grew up in the outskirts of Indianapolis. His parents met in college, where his dad studied engineering and his mom studied history. They took family vacations every summer to a little cabin in a rural part of their state to unwind and to appreciate nature. Now, as a grownup, Jason is a faculty member in a biology department at a university. He has developed interest in both ecology and watching birds. His interest in each overlaps, but he pursues them in different ways. Although he is interested in ecology and believes it is valuable, he also sees it as what he is committed to do in his career, which carries certain responsibilities. He is deliberate in setting goals that further his competence and career success, and feels satisfaction when he achieves those goals. His interest in ecology helps him to sustain deep engagement in his work and allows him to continue to find new things to understand. As such, it also helps him continue to identify ways in which he can further his competence.

In contrast, Jason sees birding as a hobby. It is what he does in his free time. Although he does not experience pressure to perform at a particular level of competence, exercising and developing competence in birding clearly contributes to his continued interest in it. Moreover, Jason sees the benefits of using his ecology knowledge while bird watching. It enables him to seek out and appreciate rare birds. This also means that he continues to develop knowledge relevant to ecology.

Research on achievement motivation tends to focus on the types of goals and contexts that are reflected in Jason's activities as an ecologist. He knows what he wants and needs to do to be competent in ecology. In this sense, he is an agent as he navigates his career, doing research, publishing, and working with and teaching students. He is also working with a reasonably defined and socially accepted definition of competence for academics, which can help him identify and set goals that will lead to his success. Within this context, his interest in ecology supports his engagement and shapes the trajectory of his career development.

Although birders have many formal ways to evaluate their accomplishments, this kind of involvement is not Jason's. From his perspective, even though achievement strivings are critical to his engagement in the activity, the achievement context for birding does not have a clear definition of competence. Thus, Jason's goals as a birder are less explicit. His emphasis is on doing birding itself, even though he has a desire to achieve in the sense that he likes to sight rare birds and to gain knowledge of what other birders have seen. He is an actor while watching birds, and he may not realize the goals that he (as actor) sets for himself while birding (see related discussion in Renninger, Bachrach, & Posey, 2008). In other words, the actor self is central to the experience of interest, although, of course, the agent self also plays a role at times (e.g., when Jason actively sets aside time on a Saturday morning to watch birds). Finally, the author self makes sense of both of these domains and helps him understand how these different activities fit together—the decisions and trade-offs that are made along the way—and the satisfaction Jason gains from both.

Achievement Strivings

Early psychologists studying achievement strivings focused on *achievement* as a general tendency to desire success that varies and could be generalized to a person's activity across domains (e.g., McClelland et al., 1949; Murray, 1938). They also recognized that it varied between people and that it could be influenced by situations. However, unlike most contemporary discussions (see review by Schultheiss & Brunstein, 2005, for an exception), earlier psychologists thought that people were not able to accurately report on their achievement motives. Therefore, they used projective measures that relied on individuals' interpretations of situations along achievement-related dimensions, rather than asking them to self-report them (e.g., Tomkins, 1947). For example, McClelland and colleagues (1949) asked participants to generate narratives about people and events in ambiguous pictures (e.g., a picture of a pensive boy in the foreground with a mural of a surgical procedure in the background), and coded their responses for achievement themes (e.g., stories about future career success). The researchers also manipulated the extent to which the study context emphasized achievement and evaluation (e.g., a relaxed context or a testing context), in order to identify the themes that emerged when achievement was made salient. In this way, they identified themes about challenges, goals, and obstacles that were elicited by the more achievement-oriented context of evaluation.

Over time, achievement strivings came to be viewed as reflecting beliefs about possibility, and motives were thought to be subjectively accessible. Researchers began using explicit measures of achievement strivings that asked individuals to reflect and report on achievement motives and behaviors (see review by Fineman, 1977), and self-reported measures became more widely accepted. For example, Jackson (1974) developed a self-report measure that asked participants to report on their behaviors related to achievement and failure, with the assumption that some individuals desire achievement more than others, and that their responses will reflect these tendencies. Similar expectations continue to inform stand-alone measures of achievement motivation (e.g., Spence & Helmreich, 1983), and they are embedded in measures of higher-order personality constructs such as conscientiousness (e.g., McCrae & Costa, 1997). The general emphasis in such studies is on the intensity of strivings as a feature of individuals, not on how the strivings of a person vary within a person from one domain to another (e.g., from ecology to birding), or how achievement strivings in new domains might be developed.

In using explicit measures almost exclusively, many researchers have narrowed their consideration of achievement strivings to focus primarily on explicit achievement strivings. This highlights the self as the agent of future outcomes and beliefs about competence, and values are understood to guide explicit goals for selecting activities that cultivate competence (e.g., Elliot & McGregor, 2001; Locke & Latham, 2002; Simpkins, Davis-Kean, & Eccles, 2006). Some investigators assess motivations within domains, recognizing that beliefs about competence and value can be dramatically different from one domain to the next, and that beliefs are more predictive of behavior when the belief and the behavior are assessed within the same domain (e.g., Bandura, 1986; Eccles et al., 1983; see discussion in Urdan & Schoenfelder, 2006). In fact, social-psychological interventions based on this premise have demonstrated that individuals' achievement strivings are influenced by changes in feelings of belonging (e.g., Walton, Cohen, Cwir, & Spencer, 2012), perceptions of science as a "chilly climate" (e.g., Walton, Logel, Peach, Spencer, & Zanna, 2015), performance expectations (Hulleman, Godes, Hendricks, & Harackiewicz, 2010), cultural values (Shechter, Durik, Miyamoto, & Harackiewicz, 2011) and utility value (e.g., Harackiewicz et al., 2016).

In summary, achievement strivings were initially conceptualized as being implicit and therefore not part of individuals' beliefs about themselves. More recently, conceptualizations of achievement strivings have been shifted to focus on the self as an agent of future outcomes and have been studied at both the broad level of personality and within particular domains. Although this approach has allowed researchers to gain traction on how explicit achievement strivings work, and accentuates the role of what we consider the agent self, it is critical not to forget the role of the implicit self, described in earlier work.

McClelland, Koestner, and Weinberger (1989) noted that both explicit and implicit motives operate simultaneously and may capture qualitatively different and relatively independent constructs. In this chapter, we suggest the importance of returning to this insight. Achievement strivings that naturally occur when interest is developed can be implicit and cannot be overlooked. Jason's case provides an illustration. Jason's enjoyment of birding led him to immerse himself in environments on the weekends that can help him think about ecology, and his strivings in ecology were triggered and continue to be propelled by his enjoyment as he develops his knowledge of rare birds in particular. A complete account of achievement strivings needs to acknowledge explicit goals, as well as nonconscious goals, or implicit motives that enable Jason to seize opportunities that add to his possibilities (McClelland, 1985). We further note that whereas explicit achievement strivings are captured in the achieving self as an agent, implicit achievement strivings may be more accurately captured by considering the achieving self as an actor. Both are important and can be mutually supportive.

Development of the Agent Achieving Self

The agent self relies on several aspects of self-knowledge in order to assess, plan, and act on achievement strivings. These include beliefs about competence, achievement goals, utility value, and cost. We discuss these separately because they become relevant at different stages of development, but they function together, are typically correlated, and inform each other (see Wigfield & Cambria, 2010).

Beliefs about Competence

Answers to questions such as "Can I play tennis?", "How good am I at drawing?", "Can I improve my public speaking skills?", and "How well could I answer more complex math problems?" are beliefs about one's competence. The beliefs are central to explicit achievement strivings. There are several constructs that describe individuals' beliefs about competence, including self-concept of ability (Eccles & Wigfield, 1995, 2002; Marsh, 1989), self-efficacy (Bandura, 1986, 1997), perceived competence (Harackiewicz & Sansone, 1991), theories of intelligence (mindset; Dweck & Leggett, 1988), and expectancies for success (Atkinson, 1974; Eccles et al., 1983; Tolman, 1932; Vroom, 1964). They share a focus on people's beliefs about their current and future capabilities. A developmental analysis of explicit achievement strivings begins with beliefs about competence because they orient the achieving agent self toward what is possible.

Even very young children have the capacity to understand competence, and they care about it. They know, for example, whether they can add and subtract, say the alphabet, and so forth. In assessing their own capacities, children tend to focus on what they can do, defining competence at an intrapersonal level. As such, young children have positive (perhaps even overly optimistic) beliefs about their competence and tend to believe that they are competent in many different domains (Nicholls, 1979; Pajares, 1996; Schunk, 1995; Stipek & Mac Iver, 1989). These feelings have been described as a fundamental desire to be effective in the environment (White, 1959), and a foundation for core beliefs about the self as valuable (Covington, 1984, 1999; Harter, 1999). Along these lines, incompetence feels bad even to preschoolers, who expressed shame if they performed poorly on a task (Stipek, Recchia, & McClintic, 1992).

Over time, children's perspectives on competence shift from focusing only on the self to comparing themselves with others, and they also come to understand that their competence varies across different activities and subjects. Feedback from tasks and from people contributes to their perceptions about their abilities (Covington, 1984; Harter, 1999, 2006), and children can be supported to develop an interest in new content (Renninger & Hidi, 2016) and recognize that they can learn (e.g., Bempechat, London, & Dweck, 1991). Wigfield and colleagues (1997; see also Wigfield & Cambria, 2010) note that individuals are acutely aware of their competence and how they are evaluated by other people. Although there is evidence that self-concept of ability becomes more individualized with age, even young children show different beliefs in different domains (Marsh, 1989; Marsh, Craven, & Debus, 1991). For example, preschool-aged children showed domain specificity of self-concept of ability for math versus verbal activities (Marsh, Ellis, & Craven, 2002).

Children's perspectives on competence widen further when they begin to engage in self–other comparison around ages 8–10 years. Children in this age range are increasingly sensitive to performance feedback from the environment and use this feedback to judge themselves (Harter, 2003; Möller, Pohlmann, Köller, & Marsh, 2009). This developmental shift occurs as children come to understand their own capacities in relation to other people, and as they increase their ability to hold multiple beliefs about the self that may seem contradictory (e.g., feeling competent at mathematics but not reading, see Harter, 1986). It also affects their readiness to develop new interests and what educators can do to support them to do so (Renninger, 2009). It is not surprising that as children get older and begin to use multiple sources to evaluate their competence, their beliefs about their abilities tend to decrease (De Fraine, Van Damme, & Onghena, 2007; Liu, Wang, & Parkins, 2005). If they are to develop new areas of competence (some of which may become interests), they need different types of supports (encouragement, modeling, opportunities to practice) than they did as younger children.

Achievement Goals

Beliefs about what is possible are supported by beliefs about competence (Schunk & Pajares, 2002; Wigfield & Eccles, 2002), as well as interest and willingness to engage (Renninger, 2009; Renninger et al., 2008), which can ultimately support the adoption of explicit goals. A *goal* is a representation of a desired end state (Elliot, 2005; Elliot & Fryer, 2008; Locke & Latham, 1990). In order to set an explicit goal, an individual needs to be able to comprehend at least a rudimentary sense of time (i.e., the end state is presumed to occur at some time point beyond the present), care about the end state (i.e., the end state is valuable), and recognize him- or herself as an agent in the pursuit (Bandura, 1986; Elliot & Fryer, 2008). Articulation of explicit achievement goals relies on individuals having the capacity to identify and integrate these ideas. As children experience the world, they see that certain behaviors precede other events. This allows for the possibility of anticipation, which ultimately develops into an understanding of time, and how things can change from the past to the future (Nuttin & Lens, 1985). With a sense of time, children can imagine how their own efforts might bring about certain outcomes, which leads to the identification of explicit goals, some of which are related to achievement and competence.

Achievement goals are focused on a desired end state for competence, and depending on how competence is defined, they are often categorized as being either mastery or performance goals (Ames, 1992; Dweck & Leggett, 1988; Nicholls, 1984), even though these are not mutually exclusive (e.g., Barron & Harackiewicz, 2001; Pintrich, 2000). When individuals set *mastery goals,* they define competence based on either task-specific criteria (e.g., performing the task optimally) or improvement across time (e.g., developing skills). As such, these goals are not inherently social, in the sense that mastery goals define competence in relation to a particular task or within the person. In contrast, *performance goals* define competence in relation to social criteria. When individuals set performance goals, they define competence based on the performance of other people (e.g., being better than other students) or in terms of the desire to demonstrate high ability (e.g., showing high ability relative to others; see reviews by Huang, 2012; Hulleman, Schrager, Bodmann, & Harackiewicz, 2010). As such, these goals require an understanding and recognition of the achievements of others in relation to the self (Möller et al., 2009). In addition, each goal to approach competence can be paired with its negatively valenced complement—to avoid incompetence (Elliot & Church, 1997; Elliot & Harackiewicz, 1996 [based on earlier conceptualizations by McClelland, 1951]). Whereas *mastery-avoidance* goals are focused on preventing skills from dwindling or not missing opportunities to learn, *performance-avoidance* goals are focused on not performing poorly relative to other people (Elliot & McGregor, 2001). Individuals with higher expectancies for success are more likely to adopt approach goals, whereas those with lower expectancies for success are more likely to adopt avoidance goals (Cury, Elliot, Da Fonseca, & Moller, 2006).

The work of Dweck and her colleagues shows that people's beliefs about their abilities can change their goals (Cury et al., 2006; Dweck & Leggett, 1988). When people believe that their abilities are malleable, they are more likely to believe that effort and hard work will result in competence, so they are focused on mastery and can be said to have a growth mindset, whereas, those who believe abilities do not change are more likely to be focused on demonstrating their competence relative to others (e.g., Cury et al., 2006), and/or to seek out information that lets them know how much ability they have

(e.g., Dweck & Leggett, 1988), so they focus on performance goals. Individuals who focus on performance may be more likely to believe that abilities are fixed (and not changeable). When abilities are perceived as fixed, then individuals are focused on demonstrating that they are competent rather than developing competence. Their fixed mindset can become a liability when they face difficulty (Kamins & Dweck, 1999). Research also indicates that beliefs about mindset are associated with the feedback that individuals receive from the environment. For example, children whose caregivers praised them for hard work (rather than for them being smart) were more willing to take on difficult tasks (Kamins & Dweck, 1999).

Given these promising effects, classroom interventions have been developed to encourage students to believe that their abilities can change. In addition, meta-analytic results support the idea that beliefs about the malleability of abilities is associated with more effective self-regulation and goal pursuit (Burnette, O'Boyle, VanEpps, Pollack, & Finkel, 2013). That said, scaling up laboratory manipulations to real-world settings can be challenging. One recent study showed that an online mindset intervention delivered to high school students affected achievement only among students who had a history of low performance (Paunesku et al., 2015). This is an important point for two reasons. First, a mindset intervention might not affect achievement for everyone; however, these data are also consistent with the theory: When students struggle, it is most important they believe their abilities are malleable.

The adoption of achievement goals is usually measured with self-report scales, in which people are asked the extent to which their goals in a given situation reflect the desire to develop skills and to master the activity and/or the desire to perform better than other people. In these studies, goals have been compared across different age groups. In one cross-sectional study, Bong (2009) reported on the assessment of achievement goals among students from first grade through middle school with regard to the domain of math. Overall, these data indicated that elementary school children reported higher levels of achievement goals than did middle school children. There was also variation in the relative level of certain achievement goals over other goals. Specifically, although both younger and older students reported higher approach than avoidance goals, younger students reported mastery-approach goals (e.g., wanting to learn as much as possible) at a higher level than performance approach goals (e.g., demonstrating high performance relative to other students), and older students showed the opposite pattern. Bong also found that achievement goals were more highly correlated with each other for the younger rather than the older students, suggesting that the younger students may have a general desire to be competent, but also have imprecise ideas about how competence is defined.

It has been suggested that performance goals may peak in middle and high school (Anderman, Austin, & Johnson, 2002) given the increased evaluative focus of higher grade levels in schooling, and the importance of peers and self–other comparisons during adolescence (e.g., Coleman, 1961; Steinberg & Silverberg, 1986). Yet, it turns out that patterns of goal adoption are somewhat idiosyncratic. For example, Anderman and Midgley (1997) reported a decrease in goals focused on mastery from fifth to sixth grade in the domains of both English and math, but a small increase in performance goals in English only, and another study indicated a small decline in all goals from sixth to seventh grade (Middleton, Kaplan, & Midgley, 2004).

Individuals' achievement strivings have been found to vary a lot depending on the content. As children get older, their achievement goals in different subjects become more independent (Bong, 2001), which suggests that they are coming to understand that their desire to be competent in one domain is separate from their desires to be competent in other domains. This is especially pronounced in patterns of mastery goals (Anderman & Midgley, 1997), which are strongly related to interest in specific content. For example, in a study of the relationships among achievement goals in middle school and high school students, the correlations among mastery-approach goals across domains were considerably lower than correlations among performance goals across domains (Bong, 2001). In other words, students who adopted mastery-approach goals in math may or may not have set similar goals in English; meanwhile, those who adopted performance-approach goals in math were quite likely to also adopt performance-approach goals in English.

The desire for mastery (i.e., to learn and to develop skills) in a given subject depends on the content, which may explain why mastery goals vary by domain to a greater extent than do performance goals. More specifically, the adoption of mastery goals in a given domain may reflect the value of and/or interest in the knowledge and skills that are unique to it (Harackiewicz, Durik, Barron, Linnebrink-Garcia, & Tauer, 2008; Renninger et al., 2008). This has implications for how the achieving self as an agent perceives value and sets goals. When individuals recognize that particular domain content is valuable, they are likely to adopt goals that lead toward the development of knowledge, values, and related skills (Harackiewicz et al., 2008; Hidi & Renninger, 2006; Renninger, 2000).

In summary, the self as an achieving agent is aware of capacities and potential with regard to competence, can recognize desired states of competence that have not yet been attained, and can set goals to move toward those ends. These beliefs and plans can operate across domains, such that general measures of need for achievement as a personality variable predict the adoption of achievement goals in various situations (e.g., Elliot & Church, 1997; Harackiewicz et al., 2008).

Utility Task Value and Cost

Eccles and her colleagues (e.g., Eccles et al., 1983; Eccles & Wigfield, 2002) identify three values that clarify the ways in which task engagement is believed to be worthwhile: utility value, intrinsic value, and attainment value (Eccles et al., 1983; Eccles & Wigfield, 2002).[1] *Utility value* refers to people's perceptions that a task can be instrumental to their ability to achieve other goals. *Intrinsic value* refers to the extent that a given achievement task is enjoyable during task engagement. Finally, *attainment value* refers to the extent that a task is important for an individual's developing identity. Eccles and colleagues' (1983) model has also specified the role of cost in predicting achievement behavior. Examples of cost include effort, anticipated negative emotion, and loss of time for other activities. Whereas the values increase perceptions that task engagement is worthwhile, cost defines the investment required for task en-

---

[1] Whereas initial formulations of the value of achievement directly implicated the likelihood of success (Atkinson, 1974), subsequent models have expanded the view to include qualitatively different values that are related to the task content (Eccles et al., 1983; Feather, 1988).

gagement, which decreases perceptions that engagement is worthwhile. These processes work in opposition and are considered in turn.

This section on the developing achievement self as an agent features utility value and cost because both involve awareness of the goals and constraints that surround task engagement (McAdams, 2013). Although the task values are typically thought of together, as variations of the kinds of value (and cost) that tasks offer, they correlate with each other highly (Eccles & Wigfield, 1995), and are sometimes even combined to reflect general value about a domain (e.g., Simpkins, Fredricks, & Eccles, 2012), these values are distinct. The distinctions are brought into focus by the layered self as actor, agent, and author.

Whether a task is perceived to be useful for achieving goals, its utility value, can directly implicate the self as an agent. Perceived utility emerges as a meaningful construct as children develop through elementary school, in part because it requires an understanding of time, which is fairly complex (Wigfield & Cambria, 2010).[2] As the understanding of time develops, the capacity to realize and follow through to attain goals for the future becomes possible. As Wigfield (1994) pointed out, younger children have difficulty conceptualizing whether a given domain is useful or important to them. It is not surprising therefore that utility of math and science as measured in fifth grade was a weaker predictor of future course taking than was intrinsic value (enjoyment) measured at the same time (Simpkins et al., 2006). By 10th grade, both utility and intrinsic value predicted course taking (Simpkins et al., 2006).

The content of achievement domains is also important. For example, researchers have compared the effectiveness of utility statements that reflect goals that are more intrinsic to the person (i.e., building community) versus extrinsic (e.g., making money; Vansteenkiste et al.,

2004). Utility for internalized goals tends to reveal task engagement that is more sustained and adaptive (Tabachnick, Miller, & Relyea, 2008; Vansteenkiste et al., 2004).

Similarly, individuals who have a deep or well-developed interest in a domain may have a clearer understanding of the practices that are useful for building competence over time (Renninger et al., 2008). Although the ability to consider utility for longer-term goals may emerge in middle childhood, individuals may also recognize and begin setting such goals for themselves earlier in relation to developed interest (Renninger & Hidi, 2002; Renninger et al., 2008), and/or may become more effective at selecting, engaging, and sustaining behaviors that can contribute to goal attainment in the longer term (de Bilde et al., 2011; De Volder & Lens, 1982; Duckworth, Kirby, Tsukayama, Berstein, & Ericsson, 2011; Lens & Gailly, 1980). This additionally suggests that they develop the ability to make effective use of opportunities, or choices (Flowerday & Schraw, 2003; Tabachnick et al., 2008).

Given the promise of utility value, classroom interventions have been developed to encourage students to recognize utility in what they are learning (see review by Durik, Hulleman, & Harackiewicz, 2015). For example, students who have been presented with testimonials from (supposed) peers about the utility of science report that they have more interest in science than those who did not receive information about utility (Gaspard et al., 2015). Students also have been prompted to generate the utility for themselves (e.g., Hulleman & Harackiewicz, 2009), an approach that enables college students from groups that are underrepresented in science to continue enrollment in science classes (e.g., Harackiewicz, Canning, Tibbetts, Priniski, & Hyde, 2016). In general, learners who have lower expectancies for success benefit more from utility value interventions than those with higher expectancies (e.g., Hulleman, Godes, et al., 2010). The interventions rely on the capacity of individuals to identify goals, and to see learning content as a means to achieve them. These effects have emerged among students who are at least high school age, but the effects appear to vary among younger populations (Durik, Schwartz, Schmidt, & Shumow, 2018). It is not yet clear why younger students responded differently to these kinds of manipulations, but it may reflect less clarity in their views of themselves and their futures.

[2]Understanding of behavior in relation to time increases with age. Future time perspective is an individual difference variable that reflects the extent to which individuals think about their futures, and has been found to change with age (see review by Husman & Lens, 1999). In general, older adolescents are more oriented toward the future than are younger adolescents and better able to understand how choices lead to benefits in the longer term (Ferrari, Nota, & Soresi, 2010; see review by Nurmi, 1991). In contrast, younger adolescents tended to make decisions in the present, with more spontaneity (de Bilde, Vansteenkiste, & Lens, 2011).

The achieving self as an agent considers how choosing a path comes with constraints (McAdams, 2013). *Cost* refers to potential negative consequences that are anticipated as a consequence of engaging in a particular task, a consideration that involves understanding one set of goals can facilitate or hinder progress on other goals. For example, individuals can anticipate negative consequences when tasks require effort (e.g., homework will be difficult), lost opportunities to do other things (e.g., homework takes time away from leisure activities), and negative feelings (e.g., homework can be frustrating) (Flake et al., 2015), which can have a negative influence on engagement (Eccles et al., 1983). In this sense, the achieving self as an agent both acknowledges constraints and makes decisions about whether the value of tasks outweighs their cost.

How individuals think about the value of the tasks in which they engage has been shown to be important. A task that is useful for a valued goal that extends far into the future may be thought as involving a *higher level of construal* (Trope & Liberman, 2010). When tasks are at higher levels of construal, their primary features are salient, which can help to overcome consideration of costs. For example, research on late adolescents and young adults has shown that higher levels of construal yield more effective self-regulation: likelihood of selecting tasks that have long-term benefits, delaying gratification, and persisting through difficulty (Freitas, Gollwitzer, & Trope, 2004). Similarly, college students who viewed school tasks as important, or instrumental, for achieving personally valued future goals were likely to have more effective strategies for self-regulating (Tabachnick et al., 2008). In other words, individuals who identify the utility of long-term goals can also be expected to self-regulate on related tasks in order to achieve.

Although older children have better developed cognitive capacities to understand present and future value, decline in mean levels of utility value are usually observed with increasing age. For example, students' subjective value for various school subjects were found to decline from first through 12th grade (Jacobs, Lanza, Osgood, Eccles, & Wigfield, 2002; Watt, 2004) and perceptions of difficulty have been shown to increase as students progress through high school (Watt, 2004). The pattern of these effects varies somewhat by subject area. Whereas students' perceptions of math as important declined as they progressed through elementary school and then leveled off, perceptions that sports are important remained high throughout elementary school and then declined as students progressed through middle and high school (Fredricks & Eccles, 2002). These patterns suggest both that task value decreases across adolescence, and that with increasing age, perceptions and/or beliefs become more differentiated. By adolescence, students are likely to report value, or interest, in one subject and also to recognize a reduction of value in another subject (Frenzel, Pekrun, Dicke, & Goetz, 2012; Renninger, Kensey, Stevens, & Lehman, 2015).

In summary, the achieving self as an agent sets relatively explicit goals in striving for competence. With age, individuals are increasingly able to assess their own competencies, define their desired levels of future competence, and understand the utility value and cost associated with choice. As their capacities develop, the self as an achieving agent becomes more able to identify and self-regulate to become competent.

In the sections that follow, we further suggest that the accomplishments of the achieving self as an agent are facilitated by the achieving self as both an actor and author. Specifically, we note that accomplishment is coordinated with the individual's developing interest in the content.

Development of the Actor Achievement Self

With all of the focus on the agent self, it is important not to forget the actor self. The actor self relies on challenges (e.g., figuring out how to be effective in the immediate environment), which in turn enables the continued development of competence regardless of age. For example, both toddlers and expert basketball players might try to grab a ball without accidentally knocking it away. The actor self is responsive to and energized, but may not be deliberate about setting explicit goals—he or she is busy with attempts at being effective. Evidence for this in part comes from early work that assumed that achievement motives are not consciously accessible (a conceptualization that has been revived more recently; Schultheiss & Brunstein, 2005).

The role of the self as an actor is central to discussion of the development of achievement strivings across the lifespan. Achievement strivings are present in young children's development, before meta-awareness of the self as an agent is even possible. Interest has been observed in infants and young children, for example, when they repeatedly attend to and reach for objects (e.g., Langsdorf, Izard, Rayias, & Hembree, 1983; Renninger, 1990). Their interactions with the environment contribute to developing competence (e.g., language and motor skills development), even though their achievement goals are not articulated in an explicit fashion. Bertenthal (1996) describes young learners as having very basic sensory and motor tendencies. These tendencies have been described as being fueled by *effectance motivation,* the self-rewarding motive to have an impact on the environment (McClelland et al., 1989; White, 1959). Feelings of competence that initially are considered to be implicit and later become more explicit support the experience of interest (Deci & Ryan, 1985; Vallerand & Reid, 1984). This is similar to discussion of exploration as an initial approach to understanding new content (Renninger, 2010).

Interest inherently engages the self as an actor (Renninger & Hidi, 2016), which may mean that during engagement a person is not reflectively aware of the self (as an agent; Plant & Ryan, 1985). Even adults can become so immersed in activity that they lose track of more abstract concepts such as time and the self (Dietrich, 2004), as occurs when intrinsically motivated behavior reaches the state of psychological flow (Csikszentmihalyi, 1990). As such, achievement strivings that involve the actor self may not be captured directly in measures that ask individuals to reflect on their experience and report on it. Researchers have directly observed individuals' choices to engage in activities, and when other reasons for engagement were not present, have suggested that the experience itself was inherently rewarding or interesting (e.g., Deci & Ryan, 1985; Lepper, Greene, & Nisbett, 1973).

Considerable research has tracked individuals' reports about their interest during task engagement (see review in Renninger & Hidi, 2016), and suggests that while the phenomena of interest characterizes individuals of a wide range of ages, there are differences across the lifespan as well. For example, using self-reported measures of task value, Wigfield and Cambria (2010) report that intrinsic value (individuals' recognition that they like a subject, and find it interesting and not boring) may be more salient to young children than are other task values, such as utility. Younger children tend to focus on enjoyment and fun when describing activities that are meaningful to them. For example, fifth graders were more likely to mention emotional experiences when discussing their interest in math relative to ninth graders, who reflected more on their behaviors and their recognition of choosing these activities for autonomous reasons (Frenzel et al., 2012).

Although interest, as both a psychological state and motivational variable, informs the agent, actor, and author selves, the agent self may not be self-aware when engaged. Interested individuals may engage in achievement strivings even though their goals are not explicit, and may underreport their interest if asked about it—especially if their interest is new and their interest is not yet developed. Once engaged, those with interest in the task are likely to regulate and persist in the activity, despite its cost (Sansone, 2009).

In summary, the actor self is relevant when individuals respond to challenges and become involved in content in the moment of task engagement. The agent self may guide individuals back to these situations as they become aware of feeling competent, setting explicit goals, and perceiving the value of what they are doing. Although these achievement strivings are different, they can work in concert. Finally, as individuals develop an interest in content, the author self may help individuals realize the importance of content for identity (Renninger, 2009).

Jason's Layered Self

Jason's interests in both ecology as a career and birding as a hobby are mutually reinforcing (Azevedo, 2013). His implicit and explicit achievement strivings facilitate his engagement in both and allow him to weave a coherent sense of self.

Jason as an Achieving Agent

Jason is aware of his competence as an ecologist, sets achievement goals, and perceives his work in ecology as including both utility and certain costs. When asked about his goals as an ecologist, Jason indicated that he wanted to understand how communities of organisms interact with each other and their environments. He wants to know why certain species exist where they do, and why they cannot be found in other places. As he observed, he is asking the same basic questions about ecology that intrigued him when he was a teenager. His goals for research reflected a desire for mastery, as well as performance. He is interested in particular questions (although it is increasingly nuanced versions of these questions) and his position as an ecologist allows him to continue seeking deeper understanding.

He also wants to publish in reputable journals and be known as an expert. These achievements are useful for his continued development; he sees it as helping him be in contact with people who are doing interesting things, which facilitates his learning and also provides opportunities for his students. As a researcher, he values contributing to science, although he also recognizes an avoidance goal (the goal of not leaving out an important chunk of the literature in publications and presentations). Yet the value comes with certain costs and the need to generate strategies to minimize them. As he explained, "The field component of my work is often hot and uncomfortable, and you're covered in bugs and getting wet. If I'm doing fieldwork, I do as much as I can in the shortest time possible."

As a young scholar, he sees his career as being on track, but he still has many goals for himself. He wants to make a larger contribution to the field and feels as though growing his laboratory and working with more students will help make this happen. He wants to develop a network of students with whom he can collaborate and who can collaborate with each other.

Jason as an Achieving Actor

Jason's goals for birding are different from his goals as an ecologist. His main goal is to be able to go birding more often. When prompted to explain his goals for a particular birding outing, he describes them as tied to what the environment could offer and the strategies he planned to use. He said that birding in the autumn is different from birding in the summer because the strategies he uses to find rare birds vary depending on the season. Changes in the environment and the need to be sensitive to these changes are part of the challenge, and also what he loves, about birding. Although his planning for the trip constitutes explicit goals, once he is out bird watching, he says that he just "uses his eyes and

ears." In other words, his goals during birding are more implicit; they are not planned ahead of time. Rather, he engages the rewards that accompany his interest in the pursuit of rare birds, which enables engagement with challenges that are absorbing and satisfying, and possibly the absence of an agent self.

Jason recalls his early experiences with birding as a child. He says that he "got into" birds just by picking up binoculars and a field guide when he was 8 years old. He described this almost as though it was not a deliberate decision, but instead something that seemed to just happen. He remembers that his interest was triggered by a male hummingbird that used to perch on a tree just outside the window of the cabin that his family used to visit during the summer. He said that he would drag a child-size folding chair outside to sit and watch the bird. He became so absorbed in his observations that he got lost in time. He described himself as watching the bird for hours.

Jason's interest in birding led him to spend time outside, learning about species and the environment, and he also spent time reading about birds and bird habitats. Without question, these are achievement behaviors, but in these moments, he was an actor. The activity and environment guided his interactions and responses. It also appears that the knowledge he acquired not only provided a foundation for his continued interest in birds but also laid the groundwork for his later interest in and career in ecology.

Jason as an Achieving Author

Jason reflected on how his interest in birding and his career in ecology were related. He indicated that he was interested in birding from a very young age, but as he moved through high school, he realized that science might be a direction for his career. He first considered the possibility of becoming an ecologist when, as a high school student, he participated in field research on bird ecology at summer camp. He recounts realizing that his interest in birds might also be a meaningful career as a "bridge moment." Later, however, he discovered that his interest in ecology was not well suited for studying birds. The research questions that interested him in ecology (e.g., why certain species live in some habitats and not others) were better studied in species besides birds (i.e., species that do not migrate huge distances). As such, he now studies why certain insects (e.g., beetles) are attracted to certain sections of a habitat and not others, and considers ecology his career and birding his hobby.

In summary, Jason is interested in both birding and ecology. When interacting with domain content, he becomes deeply absorbed and engaged, highlighting the experience of the achieving self as an actor. In addition, and over time, with environmental supports, he has come to recognize his commitment to and aspirations within these content areas. This has allowed him to set explicit goals, as an agent, and to perceive opportunities for continued development in each. Finally, Jason as an author self is in a position to report on choices and goals that were in service of the cultivation of these interests, and to realize how these strivings shaped the years and decades that make up a life.

Individual Interest: The Coherent Self as Agent, Actor, and Author

The three layers of psychological selfhood can be understood to operate independently. For example, an individual might set a goal as an agent that does not engage the actor self or contribute meaning to the author self. It also appears that coordination of achievement strivings is also possible, and that there may be benefits to coordination (see Sheldon & Elliot, 1999).

The benefits come into focus when considering the opposite: achievement strivings as an agent without the presence of interest at the layers of actor and author. Individuals who strive for achievement in domains (e.g., the goal of becoming a nurse) in which they do not get deeply involved as an actor (e.g., disliking biology and chemistry) are going to find it very difficult to stay on track. They will need to invest extensive self-regulatory resources in order to persist and attain their goals (Renninger, Sansone, & Smith, 2004; Sansone & Thoman, 2005). Although it might be possible to achieve explicit goals in the absence of interest, the experience of interest can help individuals to initiate goal-directed behavior and remain task-focused once engaged (Lipstein & Renninger, 2007; O'Keefe & Linnenbrink-Garcia, 2014; Sansone & Harackiewicz, 1996; Sansone, Thoman, & Fraughton, 2015; Sansone, Weir, Harpster, & Morgan, 1992). In general, goals that are not accompanied by the experience of interest at the actor level are likely to be abandoned if individuals do not have sufficient motivation for achievement and self-control at a general level (e.g., McCrae & Costa, 1997; Murray, 1938). The absence of the recognition of an interest at the author level also presents a vulnerability. For example, even if individuals manage to achieve the goals set by the agent self, if they lack the passion or perceived meaning, they might reflect on the time invested as fruitless.

People are hardwired for interest; the triggering of interest activates the reward circuitry (see review in Renninger & Hidi, 2016). As an actor, interest is central to a coherent sense of self and meaning. However, the experience of interest is not sufficient. Individuals who experience interest in the moment and get deeply involved in content as an actor may be especially likely in the long term to set goals. However, if individuals never engage the agent self, they may not recognize the implications of success (e.g., high school students so immersed in video games might not know where their lives are headed) (Covington, 1984; Harter, 1999). Recognizing one's own agency in bringing about success may be an important contributor to feelings of self-worth and satisfaction (Covington, 1984; Harter, 1999).

Jason's interests in bird watching and in ecology illustrate this coordination. For example, Jason's interest in birding allows him to recognize that he can set goals, and to have knowledge about why he likes birding and how he goes about doing it. In response to the question, "What do you like about birds?" he first reformulated the question to clarify an important difference to him: the difference between birds and birding. He first clarified that birds, as objects, are amazing creatures. Then, he went on to say that what he really liked was the experience of finding them. He liked using his knowledge of birds and ecology in order to predict where they might be, then to see what could be observed. In this sense, he had a very clear understanding of his goals.

Jason also sees how his hobby is informed by his training as an ecologist. While out watching birds, he remembers what he sees, then goes home and enters his sightings into a huge, public database. He likes to be contributing data that will be useful for people like himself, but who are more bird-focused in their research. He values this because it is not only a way for him to keep track of what he has seen, but it also affirms the scientist in him. Similarly, his interest in birds can help him to self-regulate despite the costs he associates with fieldwork. Jason notes that when he is working in the field and covered with bugs, he sometimes notices "a nice little bird nearby singing" at him, and this makes the bugs involved in collecting field data more tolerable.

Jason's achieving self as an author can also be identified. He describes himself as having a general hope of what he might find when he goes out to watch birds, and explains that sometimes this is thwarted. He says it can be disappointing, although as he has aged, he also has come to appreciate that even though he might not have seen the bird he was hoping to see, he may still have gotten a better look at another species.

As these examples suggest, understanding the achieving self in relation to interest and its development is critical. Interest is a psychological state during engagement and the actor, agent, and/or author's experiences (the knowledge building and coordinated valuing) of interest influence implicit as well as explicit goals, across multiple ages. The actor self gets deeply engaged repeatedly across time, the agent self can organize efforts and goals for future opportunities, and then the author self makes meaning from these otherwise fragmented experiences and strivings.

Concluding Thoughts

In this chapter, using McAdams's (2013) framework of the layered psychological self, we have provided an overview of what is presently understood about how achievement strivings develop and change across the lifespan. We explain that achievement strivings historically have been examined as both explicit (agent self) and implicit (actor self) because competence develops in both ways. The framework of the layered psychological self suggests that considering implicit along with explicit goals provides a more nuanced and broader description of achievement strivings.

It appears that competence strivings co-occur somewhat differently based on age, experience, and interest. Even though the agent self emerges later in development than the actor self, the actor self can emerge spontaneously at any point, if the content is of interest. The actor self may be especially relevant when the content is new for individuals, and if an individual is deeply engaged, interest may obscure explicit goals, which means that connections to the self as an author may not be predictable.

Strivings toward competence are both implicit and explicit, all of which move individuals toward being more effective in their environments. This analysis suggests that the same explicit goal might be engaged very differently, depending on the presence or absence of interest. We suggest that researchers may gain traction in being able to predict achievement behavior by considering its relation to interest and the ways in which the aspects of the psychological self are coordinated around particular content.

REFERENCES

Ames, C. (1992). Classrooms: Goals, structures, and student motivation. *Journal of Educational Psychology, 84*(3), 261–271.

Anderman, E. M., Austin, C. C., & Johnson, D. M. (2002). The development of goal orientation. In A. Wigfield & J. S. Eccles (Eds.), *Development of achievement motivation* (pp. 197–220). San Diego, CA: Academic Press.

Anderman, E. M., & Midgley, C. (1997). Changes in achievement goal orientations, perceived academic competence, and grades across the transition to middle-level schools. *Contemporary Educational Psychology, 22*, 269–298.

Atkinson, J. W. (1974). The mainsprings of achievement-oriented activity. In J. W. Atkinson & J. O. Raynor (Eds.), *Motivation and achievement* (pp. 11–39). Washington, DC: Winston.

Azevedo, F. S. (2013). Knowing the stability of model rockets: An investigation of learning in interest-based practices. *Cognition and Instruction, 31*, 345–374.

Bandura, A. (1986). *Social foundations of thought and action: A social cognitive theory.* Englewood Cliffs, NJ: Prentice-Hall.

Bandura, A. (1997). *Self-efficacy: The exercise of control.* New York: Freeman.

Barron, B. (2006). Interest and self-sustained learning as catalysts of development: A learning ecology perspective. *Human Development, 49*, 193–224.

Barron, K. E., & Harackiewicz, J. M. (2001). Achievement goals and optimal motivation: Testing multiple goal models. *Journal of Personality and Social Psychology, 80*, 706–722.

Bempechat, J., London, P., & Dweck, C. S. (1991). Children's conceptions of ability in major domains: An interview and experimental study. *Child Study Journal, 21*, 11–36.

Bertenthal, B. I. (1996). Origins and early development of perception, action, and representation. *Annual Review of Psychology, 47*, 431–459.

Bong, M. (2001). Between- and within-domain relations of academic motivation among middle and high school students: Self-efficacy, task-value, and achievement goals. *Journal of Educational Psychology, 93,* 23–34.

Bong, M. (2009). Age-related differences in achievement goal differentiation. *Journal of Educational Psychology, 101,* 879–896.

Burnette, J. L., O'Boyle, E. H., VanEpps, E. M., Pollack, J. M., & Finkel, E. J. (2013). Mind-sets matter: A meta-analytic review of implicit theories and self-regulation. *Psychological Bulletin, 139,* 655–701.

Coleman, J. (1961). *The adolescent society.* Glencoe, IL: Free Press.

Covington, M. V. (1984). The self-worth theory of achievement motivation: Findings and implications. *Elementary School Journal, 85,* 5–20.

Covington, M. V. (1999). Caring about learning: The nature and nurturing of subject matter appreciation. *Educational Psychologist, 34,* 127–136.

Csikszentmihalyi, M. (1990). *Flow: The psychology of optimal experience.* New York: Harper & Row.

Cury, F., Elliot, A. J., Da Fonseca, D., & Moller, A. C. (2006). The social-cognitive model of achievement motivation and the 2 × 2 achievement goal framework. *Journal of Personality and Social Psychology, 90*(4), 666–679.

de Bilde, J., Vansteenkiste, M., & Lens, W. (2011). Understanding the association between future time perspective and self-regulated learning through the lens of self-determination theory. *Learning and Instruction, 21,* 332–344.

De Fraine, B., Van Damme, J., & Onghena, P. (2007). A longitudinal analysis of gender differences in academic self-concept and language achievement: A multivariate multilevel latent growth approach. *Contemporary Educational Psychology, 32,* 132–150.

De Volder, M. L., & Lens, W. W. (1982). Academic achievement and future time perspective as a cognitive–motivational concept. *Journal of Personality and Social Psychology, 42,* 566–571.

Deci, E. L., & Ryan, R. M. (1985). *Intrinsic motivation and self-determination in human behavior.* New York: Plenum Press.

Dietrich, A. (2004). Neurocognitive mechanisms underlying the experience of flow. *Consciousness and Cognition, 13,* 746–761.

Duckworth, A. L., Kirby, T., Tsukayama, E., Berstein, H., & Ericsson, K. A. (2011). Deliberate practice spells success: Why grittier competitors triumph at the National Spelling Bee. *Social Psychological and Personality Science, 2,* 174–181.

Durik, A. M., Hulleman, C. S., & Harackiewicz, J. M. (2015). One size fits some: Instructional enhancements to promote interest. In K. A. Renninger & M. Nieswandt (Eds.), *Interest, the self, and K–16 mathematics and science learning* (pp. 49–62). Washington, DC: American Educational Research Association.

Durik, A. M., Schwartz, J., Schmidt, J. A., & Shumow, L. (2018). Age differences in effects of self-generated utility among black and Hispanic adolescents. *Journal of Applied Developmental Psychology, 54,* 60–68.

Dweck, C. S., & Leggett, E. L. (1988). A social-cognitive approach to motivation and personality. *Psychological Review, 95,* 256–273.

Eccles, J., Adler, T. F., Futterman, R., Goff, S. B., Kaczala, C. M., Meece, J. L., et al. (1983). Expectancies, values, and academic behaviors. In J. T. Spence (Ed.), *Achievement and achievement motives: Psychological and sociological approaches* (pp. 75–146). San Francisco: Freeman.

Eccles, J. S., & Wigfield, A. (1995). In the mind of the actor: The structure of adolescents' achievement task values and expectancy-related beliefs. *Personality and Social Psychology Bulletin, 21,* 215–220.

Eccles, J. S., & Wigfield, A. (2002). Motivational beliefs, values, and goals. *Annual Review of Psychology, 53,* 109–132.

Elliot, A. J. (2005). A conceptual history of the achievement goal construct. In A. J. Elliot & C. S. Dweck (Eds.), *Handbook of competence and motivation* (pp. 52–72). New York: Guilford Press.

Elliot, A. J., & Church, M. A. (1997). A hierarchical model of approach and avoidance achievement motivation. *Journal of Personality and Social Psychology, 72,* 218–232.

Elliot, A. J., Dweck, C. S., & Yeager, D. S. (2017). Competence and motivation: Theory and application. In E. J. Elliot, C. S. Dweck, & D. S. Yeager (Eds.), *Handbook of competence and motivation: Theory and application* (2nd ed., pp. 3–8). New York: Guilford Press.

Elliot, A. J., & Fryer, J. (2008). The goal construct in psychology. In J. Y. Shah & W. L. Gardner (Eds.), *Handbook of motivation science* (pp. 235–250). New York: Guilford Press.

Elliot, A. J., & Harackiewicz, J. M. (1996). Approach and avoidance achievement goals and intrinsic motivation: A mediational analysis. *Journal of Personality and Social Psychology, 70,* 461–475.

Elliot, A. J., & McGregor, H. A. (2001). A 2 × 2 achievement goal framework. *Journal of Personality and Social Psychology, 80,* 501–519.

Feather, N. T. (1988). Values, valences, and course enrollment: Testing the role of personal values within an expectancy-value framework. *Journal of Educational Psychology, 80,* 381–391.

Ferrari, L., Nota, L., & Soresi, S. (2010). Time perspective and indecision in young and older adolescents. *British Journal of Guidance and Counselling, 38,* 61–82.

Fineman, S. (1977). The achievement motive construct and its measurement: Where are we now? *British Journal of Psychology, 68,* 1–22.

Flake, J. K., Barron, K. E., Hulleman, C., McCoach, B. D., & Welsh, M. E. (2015). Measuring cost: The forgotten component of expectancy-value theory. *Contemporary Educational Psychology, 41,* 232–244.

Flowerday, T., & Schraw, G. (2003). Effect of choice on

cognitive and affective engagement. *Journal of Educational Research, 96,* 207–215.

Fredricks, J. A., & Eccles, J. S. (2002). Children's competence and value beliefs from childhood through adolescence: Growth trajectories in two male-sex-typed domains. *Developmental Psychology, 38,* 519–533.

Freitas, A. L., Gollwitzer, P., & Trope, Y. (2004). The influence of abstract and concrete mindsets on anticipating and guiding others' self-regulatory efforts. *Journal of Experimental Social Psychology, 40,* 739–752.

Frenzel, A. C., Pekrun, R., Dicke, A., & Goetz, T. (2012). Beyond quantitative decline: Conceptual shifts in adolescents' development of interest in mathematics. *Developmental Psychology, 48,* 1069–1082.

Gaspard, H., Dicke, A.-L., Flunger, B., Brisson, B. M., Häfner, I., Nagengast, B., et al. (2015). Fostering adolescents' value beliefs for mathematics with a relevance intervention in the classroom. *Developmental Psychology, 51,* 1226–1240.

Gniewosz, B., Eccles, J. S., & Noack, P. (2015). Early adolescents' development of academic self-concept and intrinsic task value: The role of contextual feedback. *Journal of Research on Adolescence, 25,* 459–473.

Harackiewicz, J. M., Canning, E. A., Tibbetts, Y., Priniski, S. J., & Hyde, J. S. (2016). Closing achievement gaps with a utility-value intervention: Disentangling race and social class. *Journal of Personality and Social Psychology, 111,* 745–765.

Harackiewicz, J. M., Durik, A. M., Barron, K. E., Linnenbrink-Garcia, L., & Tauer, J. M. (2008). The role of achievement goals in the development of interest: Reciprocal relations between achievement goals, interest and performance. *Journal of Educational Psychology, 100*(1), 105–122.

Harackiewicz, J. M., & Sansone, C. (1991). Goals and intrinsic motivation: You can get there from here. In M. Maehr & P. Pintrich (Eds.), *Advances in motivation and achievement* (Vol. 7, pp. 21–49). Greenwich, CT: JAI Press.

Harter, S. (1986). Cognitive-developmental processes in the integration of concepts about emotions and the self. *Social Cognition, 4,* 119–151.

Harter, S. (1999). *The construction of the self: A developmental perspective.* New York: Guilford Press.

Harter, S. (2003). The development of self-representations during childhood and adolescence. In M. R. Leary & J. P. Tangney (Eds.), *Handbook of self and identity* (pp. 610–642). New York: Guilford Press.

Harter, S. (2006). The self. In N. Eisenberg (Ed.) & W. Damon & R. M. Lerner (Series Eds.), *Handbook of child psychology: Vol. 3. Social, emotional, and personality development* (pp. 505–570). New York: Wiley.

Hidi, S., & Renninger, K. A. (2006). The four-phase model of interest development. *Educational Psychologist, 41*(2), 111–127.

Hofer, M., & Fries, S. (2016). A multiple goals perspective on academic motivation. In K. R. Wentzel & D. B. Miele (Eds.), *Handbook of motivation at school* (2nd ed., pp. 440–458). New York: Routledge

Huang, C. (2012). Discriminant and criterion-related validity of achievement goals in predicting academic achievement: A meta-analysis. *Journal of Educational Psychology, 104,* 48–73.

Hulleman, C. S., Godes, O., Hendricks, B. L., & Harackiewicz, J. M. (2010). Enhancing interest and performance with a utility value intervention . *Journal of Educational Psychology, 102,* 880–895.

Hulleman, C. S., & Harackiewicz, J. M. (2009). Promoting interest and performance in high school science classes. *Science, 326,* 1410–1412.

Hulleman, C. S., Schrager, S. M., Bodmann, S. M., & Harackiewicz, J. M. (2010). A meta-analytic review of achievement goal measures: Different labels for the same constructs or different constructs with similar labels? *Psychological Bulletin, 136,* 422–449.

Husman, J., & Lens, W. (1999). The role of the future in student motivation. *Educational Psychologist, 34,* 113–125.

Jackson, D. N. (1974). *Personality Research Form manual.* Goshen, NY: Research Psychologists Press.

Jacobs, J. E., Lanza, S., Osgood, D. W., Eccles, J. S., & Wigfield, A. (2002). Changes in children's self-competence and values: Gender and domain differences across grades one through twelve. *Child Development, 73,* 509–527.

Kamins, M. L., & Dweck, C. S. (1999). Person versus process praise and criticism: Implications for contingent self-worth and coping. *Developmental Psychology, 35,* 835–847.

Krapp, A. (2002). An educational-psychological theory of interest and its relation to SDT. In E. L. Deci & R. M. Ryan (Eds.), *Handbook of self-determination research* (pp. 405–427). Rochester, NY: University of Rochester Press.

Langsdorf, P., Izard, C. E., Rayias, M., & Hembree, E. A. (1983). Interest expression, visual fixation, and heart rate changes in 2- to 8-month-old infants. *Developmental Psychology, 19,* 375–386.

Lens, W., & Gailly, A. (1980). Extension of future time perspective in motivational goals of different age groups. *International Journal of Behavioral Development, 3,* 1–17.

Lepper, M. R., Greene, D., & Nisbett, R. E. (1973). Undermining children's intrinsic interest with extrinsic reward: A test of the "overjustification" hypothesis. *Journal of Personality and Social Psychology, 28,* 129–137.

Lipstein, R., & Renninger, K. A. (2007). "Putting things into words": The development of 12–15-year-old students' interest for writing. In P. Boscolo & S. Hidi (Eds.), *Motivation and writing: Research and school practice* (pp. 113–140). New York: Elsevier.

Liu, W. C., Wang, C. K. J., & Parkins, E. J. (2005). A longitudinal study of students' academic self-concept in a streamed setting: The Singapore context. *British Journal of Educational Psychology, 75,* 567–586.

Locke, E. A., & Latham, G. P. (1990). *A theory of goal setting and task performance.* Upper Saddle River, NJ: Prentice Hall.

Locke, E. A., & Latham, G. P. (2002). Building a practically useful theory of goals setting and task motivation. *American Psychologist, 37,* 705–717.

Marsh, H. W. (1989). Age and sex effects in multiple dimensions of self-concept: Preadolescence to early-adulthood. *Journal of Educational Psychology, 81,* 417–430.

Marsh, H. W., Craven, R. G., & Debus, R. (1991). Self-concepts of young children aged 5 to 8: Their measurement and multidimensional structure. *Journal of Educational Psychology, 83,* 377–392.

Marsh, H. W., Ellis, L. A., & Craven, R. G. (2002). How do preschool children feel about themselves?: Unraveling measurement and multidimensional self-concept structure. *Developmental Psychology, 38,* 376–393.

McAdams, D. P. (2013). The psychological self as actor, agent, and author. *Psychological Science, 8,* 272–295.

McClelland, D. C. (1951). Measuring motivation in phantasy: The achievement motive. In H. Guetzkow (Ed.), *Groups, leadership, and men* (pp. 191–205). Pittsburgh, PA: Carnegie Press.

McClelland, D. C. (1985). *Human motivation.* Glenview, IL: Scott, Foresman.

McClelland, D. C., Clark, R. A., Roby, T. B., & Atkinson, J. W. (1949). The projective expression of needs: IV. The effect of the need for achievement on thematic apperception. *Journal of Experimental Psychology, 39,* 242–255.

McClelland, D. C., Koestner, R., & Weinberger, J. (1989). How do self-attributed and implicit motives differ? *Psychological Review, 96,* 690–702.

McCrae, R. R., & Costa, P. T., Jr. (1997). Personality trait structure as a human universal. *American Psychologist, 52,* 509–516.

Middleton, M. J., Kaplan, A., & Midgley, C. (2004). The change in middle school students' achievement goals in mathematics over time. *Social Psychology of Education, 7,* 289–311.

Möller, J., Pohlmann, B., Köller, O., & Marsh, H. W. (2009). Meta-analytic path analysis of the internal/external frame of reference model of academic achievement and academic self-concept. *Review of Educational Research, 79,* 1129–1167.

Murray, H. A. (1938). *Explorations in personality.* New York: Oxford University Press.

Nicholls, J. G. (1979). Development of perception of own attainment and causal attributions for success and failure in reading. *Journal of Educational Psychology, 71,* 94–99.

Nicholls, J. G. (1984). Achievement motivation: Conceptions of ability, subjective experience, task choice, and performance. *Psychological Review, 91,* 328–346.

Nurmi, J. E. (1991). How do adolescents see their future?: A review of the development of future orientation and planning. *Developmental Review, 11,* 1–59.

Nuttin, J., & Lens, W. (1985). *Future time perspective and motivation: Theory and research method.* Leuven, Belgium/Hillsdale, NJ: Leuven University Press/Erlbaum.

O'Keefe, P. A., & Linnenbrink-Garcia, L. (2014). The role of interest in optimizing performance and self-regulation. *Journal of Experimental Social Psychology, 53,* 70–78.

Pajares, F. (1996). Self-efficacy beliefs in academic settings. *Review of Educational Research, 66,* 543–578.

Panksepp, J. (1988). *Affective neuroscience: The foundations of human and animal emotion.* New York: Oxford University Press.

Paunesku, D., Walton, G. M., Romero, C., Smith, E. N., Yeager, D. S., & Dweck, C. S. (2015). Mind-set interventions are a scalable treatment for academic underachievement. *Psychological Science, 26,* 784–793.

Pintrich, P. R. (2000). Multiple goals, multiple pathways: The role of goal orientation in learning and achievement. *Journal of Educational Psychology, 92,* 544–555.

Plant, R. W., & Ryan, R. M. (1985). Intrinsic motivation and the effects of self-consciousness, self-awareness, and ego-involvement: An investigation of internally controlling styles. *Journal of Personality, 53*(3), 435–449.

Renninger, K. A. (1990). Children's play interests, representation, and activity. In R. Fivush & K. Hudson (Eds.), *Knowing and remembering in young children* (pp. 127–165). New York: Cambridge University Press.

Renninger, K. A. (2000). Individual interest and its implications for understanding intrinsic motivation. In C. Sansone & J. M. Harackiewicz (Eds.), *Intrinsic and extrinsic motivation: The search for optimal motivation and performance* (pp. 373–404). San Diego, CA: Academic Press.

Renninger, K. A. (2009). Interest and identity development in instruction: An inductive model. *Educational Psychologist, 44,* 105–118.

Renninger, K. A. (2010). Working with and cultivating the development of interest, self-efficacy, and self-regulation. In D. Preiss & R. Sternberg (Eds.), *Innovations in educational psychology: Perspectives on learning, teaching and human development* (pp. 107–138). New York: Springer.

Renninger, K. A., Bachrach, J. E., & Posey, S. K. E. (2008). Learner interest and achievement motivation. In M. L. Maehr, S. A. Karabenick, & T. C. Urdan (Eds.), *Advances in motivation and achievement: Vol. 15. Social psychological perspectives* (pp. 461–491). Derby, UK: Emerald Group.

Renninger, K. A., & Hidi, S. (2002). Student interest and achievement: Developmental issues raised by a case study. In A. Wigfield & J. S. Eccles (Eds.), *De-*

velopment of achievement motivation (pp. 173–195). San Diego, CA: Academic Press.

Renninger, K. A., & Hidi, S. E. (2016). *The power of interest for motivation and engagement.* New York: Routledge.

Renninger, K. A., Kensey, C. C., Stevens, S. J., & Lehman, D. L. (2015). Perceptions of science and their role in the development of interest. In K. A. Renninger, M. Nieswandt, & S. Hidi (Eds.), *Interest in mathematics and science learning* (pp. 93–110). Washington, DC: American Educational Research Association.

Renninger, K. A., Sansone, C., & Smith, J. L. (2004). Love of learning. In C. Peterson & M. E. P. Seligman (Eds.), *Character strengths and virtues: A classification and handbook* (pp. 161–179). New York: Oxford University Press.

Sansone, C. (2009). What's interest got to do with it?: Potential trade-offs in the self-regulation of motivation. In J. P. Forgas, R. Baumiester, & D. Tice (Eds.), *Psychology of self-regulation: Cognitive, affective, and motivational processes* (pp. 35–51). New York: Psychology Press.

Sansone, C., & Harackiewicz, J. M. (1996). I don't feel like it: The function of interest in self-regulation. In L. Martin & A. Tesser (Eds.), *Striving and feeling: The interaction of goals and affect* (pp. 203–228). Hillsdale, NJ: Erlbaum.

Sansone, C., & Thoman, D. B. (2005). Interest as the missing motivator in self-regulation. *European Psychologist, 10,* 175–186.

Sansone, C., Thoman, D., & Fraughton, T. (2015). The relation between interest and self-regulation in mathematics and science. In K. A. Renninger, M. Nieswandt, & S. Hidi, (Eds.), *Interest in mathematics and science learning* (pp. 111–131). Washington, DC: American Educational Research Association.

Sansone, C., Weir, C., Harpster, L., & Morgan, C. (1992). Once a boring task always a boring task?: Interest as a self-regulatory mechanism. *Journal of Personality and Social Psychology, 63,* 379–390.

Schiefele, U. (1991). Interest, learning, and motivation. *Educational Psychologist, 26,* 299–323.

Schultheiss, O. C., & Brunstein, J. C. (2005). An implicit motive perspective on competence. In A. J. Elliot & C. S. Dweck (Eds.), *Handbook of competence and motivation* (pp. 31–51). New York: Guilford Press.

Schunk, D. H. (1995). Self-efficacy and education and instruction. In J. E. Maddux (Ed.), *Self-efficacy, adaptation, and adjustment: Theory, research, and application* (pp. 281–303). New York: Plenum Press.

Schunk, D. H., & Pajares, F. (2002). The development of academic self-efficacy. In A. Wigfield & J. S. Eccles (Eds.), *Development of achievement motivation* (pp. 15–31). San Diego, CA: Academic Press.

Senko, C. (2016). Achievement goal theory: A story of early promises, eventual discords, and future possibilities. In K. Wentzel & D. Miele (Eds.), *Handbook*

of motivation at school (Vol. 2, pp. 75–95). New York: Routledge.

Shechter, O. G., Durik, A. M., Miyamoto, Y., & Harackiewicz, J. M. (2011). The role of utility value in achievement behavior: The importance of culture. *Personality and Social Psychology Bulletin, 37,* 303–317.

Sheldon, K. M., & Elliot, A. J. (1999). Goal striving, need satisfaction, and longitudinal well-being: The self-concordance model. *Journal of Personality and Social Psychology, 76,* 482–497.

Silvia, P. J. (2006). *Exploring the psychology of interest.* New York: Oxford University Press.

Simpkins, S. D., Davis-Kean, P. E., & Eccles, J. S. (2006). Math and science motivation: A longitudinal examination of the links between choices and beliefs. *Developmental Psychology, 42,* 70–83.

Simpkins, S. D., Fredricks, J. A., & Eccles, J. S. (2012). Charting the Eccles' Expectancy–Value Model from mothers' beliefs in childhood to youths' activities in adolescence. *Developmental Psychology, 48,* 1019–1032.

Spence, J. T., & Helmreich, R. L. (1983). Achievment-related motives and behaviors. In J. T. Spence (Ed.), *Achievmeent and achievement motives: Psychological and sociological approaches* (pp. 7–74). San Francisco: Freeman.

Steinberg, L., & Silverberg, S. B. (1986). The vicissitudes of autonomy in early adolescence. *Child Development, 57,* 841–851.

Stipek, D. J., & Mac Iver, D. M. (1989). Developmental changes in children's assessment of intellectual competence. *Child Development, 60,* 521–538.

Stipek, D. J., Recchia, S., & McClintic, S. (1992). Self-evaluation in young children. *Monograph of the Society for Research in Child Development, 57*(1, Serial No. 226), 1–98.

Tabachnick, S. E., Miller, R. B., & Relyea, G. E. (2008). The relationships among students' future-oriented goals and subgoals, perceived task instrumentality, and task-oriented self-regulation strategies in an academic environment. *Journal of Educational Psychology, 100,* 629–642.

Tolman, E. C. (1932). *Purposive behavior in animals and men.* New York: Appleton-Century.

Tomkins, S. S. (1947). *The Thematic Apperception Test.* New York: Grune & Stratton.

Trope, Y., & Liberman, N. (2010). Construal-level theory of psychological distance. *Psychological Review, 117,* 440–442.

Urdan, T., & Schoenfelder, E. (2006). Classroom effects on student motivation: Goal structures, social relationships, and competence beliefs. *Journal of School Psychology, 44,* 331–349.

Usher, E. L. (2016). Personal capability beliefs. In L. Corno & E. M. Anderman (Eds.), *Handbook of educational psychology* (3rd ed., pp. 146–159). New York: Routledge.

Vallerand, R. J., & Reid, G. (1984). On the causal effects of perceived competence on intrinsic motivation: A test of cognitive evaluation theory. *Journal of Sport Psychology, 6,* 94–102.

Vansteenkiste, M., Simons, J., Lens, W., Soenens, B., Matos, L., & Lacante, M. (2004). Less is sometimes more: Goal content matters. *Journal of Educational Psychology, 96,* 755–764.

Vroom, V. H. (1964). *Work and motivation.* New York: Wiley.

Walton, G. M., Cohen, G. L., Cwir, D., & Spencer, S. J. (2012). Mere belonging: The power of social connections. *Journal of Personality and Social Psychology, 102,* 513–532.

Walton, G. M., Logel, C., Peach, J. M., Spencer, S. J., & Zanna, M. P. (2015). Two brief interventions to mitigate a "chilly climate" transform women's experience, relationships, and achievement in engineering. Journal of Educational Psychology, 107, 468–485.

Watt, H. M. G. (2004). Development of adolescents' self-perceptions, values, and task perceptions according to gender and domain in 7th through 11th grade Australian students. *Child Development, 75,* 1556–1574.

White, R. H. (1959). Motivation reconsidered: The concept of competence. *Psychological Review, 66,* 297–333.

Wigfield, A. (1994). Expectancy–value theory of achievement motivation: A developmental perspective. *Educational Psychology Review, 6,* 49–78.

Wigfield, A., & Cambria, J. (2010). Students' achievement values, goal orientations, and interest: Definitions, development, and relations to achievement outcomes. *Developmental Review, 30,* 1–35.

Wigfield, A., & Eccles, J. S. (2002). The development of competence beliefs, expectancies for success, and achievement values from childhood through adolescence. In A. Wigfield & J. S. Eccles (Eds.), *Development of achievement motivation* (pp. 92–120). San Diego, CA: Academic Press.

Wigfield, A., Eccles, J. S., Yoon, K. S., Harold, R. D., Arbreton, A. J. A., Freedman-Doan, C., et al. (1997). Change in children's competence beliefs and sujective task value across the elementary school years: A 3-year study. *Journal of Educational Psychology, 89,* 451–469.

Yeager, D. S., Romero, C., Paunesku, D., Hulleman, C. S., Schneider, B., Hinojosa, C., et al. (2016). Using design thinking to improve psychological interventions: The case of the growth mindset during the transition to high school. *Journal of Educational Psychology, 108,* 374–391.

CHAPTER 18

Personality Development in Adulthood
A Goal Perspective

Alexandra M. Freund
Christopher M. Napolitano
Joshua L. Rutt

Having been said to be over the hill at age 35 after various injuries, Swiss tennis pro Roger Federer had a glorious comeback in the summer of 2017, winning Wimbledon's men's singles tournament—his first grand-slam victory in 5 years. That Federer won in Wimbledon may not have been surprising to some; after all, he has prevailed in 19 major tournaments (to date) and is widely considered among the greatest tennis players of all time. What is more surprising is that *this* Federer (after having taken off much of the prior year), at *this* age (a geriatric for professional tennis—35) won the tournament in *this* fashion (without dropping a single set across the fortnight). In addition to Federer's great talent for tennis, how could one have predicted his ability to overcome injuries and health-related problems several times and reclaim his place at the very top of this sport?

To phrase the question differently, imagine that you are approached by representatives of a tennis institute who wish to identify the next Federer-type tennis champion. Their institute is full of extraordinarily gifted adolescent players. "As a psychologist," they ask you, "how can you predict which of our players will go on to succeed in the junior circuit? How can you predict which of our players will continue to succeed into their mid-30s, and become the next Roger Federer? How will they fare off the court?"

Some of you might argue that one should mainly consider the personality traits of the young athletes to predict their success (e.g., the "Big Five"; e.g., Judge, Higgins, Thoresen, & Barrick, 1999). In fact, most likely it will help to know how emotionally stable (neurotic), extraverted, open, conscientious, and agreeable a young player is when predicting whether he or she is likely to make it in the highly competitive arena of professional tennis. Moreover, as personality traits are highly stable over time (Roberts & DelVecchio, 2000; but see Roberts & Mroczek, 2008), they allow for a fairly good prediction of the young athletes' level of neuroticism, extraversion, openness, conscientiousness, and agreeableness over time and across different situations. However, this level will not provide a very good account of how differently the young athletes' lives may develop over time. McAdams (1996) describes traits—Level 1 in his three-level personality model—as the "dispositional signature for personality description" (p. 301) that provides little more than a broad and decontextualized view of a person. The predictive power of the individual "Big Five" traits for major life goals is fairly low (see the low or nonsignificant associations in the systematic review by Roberts & Robins, 2000).

Turning to another trait, some researchers might argue that, generally, the most potent predictor of future success in life is intelligence. Although general intelligence may strongly predict general and particularly job-related success later on in life (Ree & Earles, 1992; but see Sternberg, 1997), it is doubtful that intelligence will tell us much about the life paths that these young athletes will take. Importantly for pursuits that require high levels of persistence and the ability to delay gratification and forego temptations, research by Mischel, Shoda, and Rodriguez (1989) and Moffit and colleagues (2011) has demonstrated that, over and above intelligence, success (here, health and wealth) is predicted by how well people can regulate and control themselves in relation to goal pursuits. In other words, we argue that although Roger Federer—and many other highly successful tennis players such as Steffi Graf, to pick just one female champion—is likely quite intelligent, it is not the intelligence that mainly predicts his success. Instead, we maintain that the kinds of goals people set for themselves and the way they pursue these goals is one of the important building blocks of personality (Freund & Riediger, 2006). Thus, complementing the trait perspective, in this chapter, we approach *personality*—defined as the way people prototypically view themselves and interact with their environment—and the development of personality across adulthood from a *goal perspective*.

Following this perspective, we distinguish (1) processes concerning the setting and commitment to personal goals from (2) processes concerning goal pursuit and maintenance over time and across situations. We maintain that these processes of goal setting on the one hand, and goal pursuit on the other, are essential for understanding who we are at any given point in time, and who we will become.

Goals as Building Blocks of Personality

What are goals? Unlike lay conceptions of goals, current motivational psychology conceives of *goals* as not only the desired end states one would like to achieve but also the cognitive representation of the association between the desired end states and the means by which one achieves them (Kruglanski et al., 2002). Cognitive representations of desired end states without the associated means are better defined as dreams, wishes, or positive fantasies. Conversely, representations of behaviors without the associated desired end states are just that,

behaviors. Thus, goals denote the association of means and ends.

As we elaborate below, we view goals as both the *product* of the developmental history of a person and important drivers or *producers* of a person's development (Freund & Riediger, 2006). In our view, goals are the most useful theoretical construct when attempting to understand who a person will become in the future, as goals direct and guide cognition, emotion, motivation, and behavior over time and across situations. Goals organize, structure, and integrate perception, thought, emotions, and behavior into meaningful action units (e.g., Freund, 2007).

In other words, we hold that a person's goals, and how these goals change, are central for understanding personality development across adulthood. Thus, in order to predict who among the young athletes might become the next Federer-type tennis pro, we would ask what his or her aspirations and goals are (i.e., how clear is his or her goal of becoming a tennis champion, and how committed is he or she to this compared to other goals (e.g., having close friendships, school achievement). These questions concern goal setting. Regarding goal pursuit, we would want to know how much time and effort the player is willing to invest into optimizing his or her performance, as well as his or her persistence when confronted with setbacks or failures.

Taking a goal perspective to approach personality development across adulthood, we focus mostly on the "doing" side of personality (Allport, 1937), elaborating how goals guide behavior across situations and over time. This focus is largely in line with what McAdams (1996) terms the second level in his personality model, which comprises personal concerns or characteristic adaptations that constitute a person's goals and beliefs. Personality on the second level invokes "personal strivings, life tasks, defense mechanisms, coping strategies, domain-specific skills and values, and a wide assortment of other motivational, developmental, or strategic constructs that are contextualized in time, place, or role" (McAdams, 1996, p. 301).

We consider this second level of personality as particularly helpful for understanding personality from an adult development perspective. Models of adult development have long stressed the importance of the selection, pursuit, and maintenance of personal goals for development (Baltes & Baltes, 1990; Freund & Baltes, 2002), and empirical evidence has indeed demonstrated that selecting goals, and investing in their pursuit and in compensatory efforts when faced with losses are positively associated with psychological well-being and other subjective indicators of successful development throughout all phases of adulthood (e.g., Freund & Baltes, 2002), particularly for those with fewer available resources (e.g., Lang, Rieckmann, & Baltes, 2002; Young, Baltes, & Pratt, 2007).

To explore adult personality development from this perspective, we describe in this chapter (1) *what* kinds of goals we develop at certain points in our life and how this changes across adulthood (i.e., goal setting), and (2) *how* we go about pursuing them across adulthood (i.e., goal pursuit). Taking a lifespan perspective (e.g., Baltes, 1997), we will show that the experience of a changing ratio of potential gains and losses across adulthood strongly affects our goal selection, as well as our goal pursuit and maintenance, and, in turn, that the selection, as well pursuit and maintenance of goals, affects the gains and losses we experience. In this way, goals can be considered as building blocks of personality (Freund & Riediger, 2006).

The Role of Goal Setting and Pursuit in Personality Development

One of the basic assumptions underlying our perspective on personality development is that people proactively shape who they are and who they become (Lerner & Busch-Rossnagel, 1981). According to Baltes (1997), the active role of the individual for development is embedded in the interplay of the three central factors impacting development across the entire lifespan: (1) *biology* (e.g., brain maturation in youth, menopausal hormonal changes in middle adulthood), (2) *culture/society* (e.g., social norms that provide guidelines of the timing for developmental transitions such as retirement), and (3) the *individual* (e.g., choosing, committing to, and pursuing a set of goals). These three factors interact with each other in complex and dynamic ways. For instance, personal goals (e.g., whether and when to start a family) are supported and constrained by societal expectations (e.g., about the appropriate age for starting a family and the acceptable forms of cohabitation), which, in turn, are at least partly rooted in biology (e.g., age range of fertility). However,

persons also place themselves into certain societal and cultural contexts (e.g., by moving to a different city, country, or even continent) and may also influence society and culture to a certain degree.

Due to the complexity of the interaction of these factors in shaping development, it is impossible to determine their exact relative impact on each given behavior. However, a simplified theoretical assumption of a compensatory relation between the three factors would suggest that the less development is under the control of societal and biological influences, the more degrees of freedom a person has to influence his or her development by selecting and pursuing personal goals.

According to the lifespan perspective (e.g., Baltes, 1997), development is considered a lifelong process; rather than being a "fixed" entity by adulthood, a person develops until death. Second, development is multidirectional (i.e., all phases of the lifespan are characterized by gains and losses). However, the ratio of gains to losses varies across the lifespan. Third, development is not just a product of genetic/biological and environmental factors; he or she also plays an active role in who he or she will become through setting, pursuing, and maintaining goals (e.g., Brandtstädter, 2006; Lerner & Busch-Rossnagel, 1981).

Another important characteristic of the lifespan perspective, and one that provides the structure for discussing goal selection in adulthood (i.e., the "what" of adult goals), is what has been termed the macro model of developmental influences (Baltes, Cornelius, Nesselroade, 1979; Baltes, Reese, & Lipsitt, 1980). This heuristic model holds that development is shaped by three factors: (1) *age-graded*, (2) *history-graded*, and (3) *non-normative*. We elaborate more on these factors impacting development and how they affect personality development below.

Goal Setting: The "What" of Goals across Adulthood

If we want to know more about what path a person's life will take, it is important to find out *what* goals this person pursues. Clearly, someone who has the goal to become a kindergarten teacher will acquire different skills, get to know different people, and have a different everyday life than a person who has the goal to become the next Roger Federer. The experiences these two persons will make during their education and their professional lives, the fact that the life of a tennis pro requires not only extensive training but also a lot of traveling to various tournaments whereas the life of a kindergarten teacher does not, the different sets of skills they will acquire and enhance, as well as their likely different social environments, all come together to shape how they will think about themselves and interact with the world. The kinds of goals we set and pursue regulate who we become. In this sense, then, goals are central aspects of our personality.

In this section, we describe *what* goals adults pursue—and how these goals change across adulthood—by characterizing goals as being shaped by age-graded, history-graded, and non-normative influences. This provides the first component of understanding personality development in adulthood in addressing the questions (1) What are the goals that adults typically pursue, and (2) how do their goals change across adulthood?

Age-Graded Influences on Adults' Goals

In this section, we move beyond the specific example of tennis champions and address more generally which goals adults generally adopt. One way to think about which goals adults pursue is to consider the goals that people try to achieve in order to be generally viewed as "successful adults," tapping into the normative social expectations, as well as biological and historical factors influencing development (e.g., Freund, 2007; Havighurst, 1953/1972; Heckhausen, 1999). In many societies, indicators of successful development include markers for success like completing education, moving away from parents, starting a relationship or family, financial independence, career development, maintaining healthy and adult relationships, maintaining health, or planning for and successfully navigating retirement. These goals are all shaped by *age-graded* influences, which can be defined as aspects of biology or context that normatively influence people as a function of their chronological age (Baltes et al., 1979). For example, although we may hear the occasional story of the free-spirited "retired" 30-year-old, Western adults normatively aim for a successful retirement beginning sometime during their seventh decade.

Stage theories posit that people move through a succession of goals that hierarchically build

on each other, and that achieving these goals is essential for successful development. Building on Erikson (1950), who held that development occurs in response to normative crises humans face and have to solve at a certain age, Havighurst's work on developmental tasks (e.g., 1953/1972) provides a classic, stage-based template from which we can understand the age-graded goals that people typically pursue at certain points in the life course, and further, how these goals tend to shift systematically across the lifespan. To Havighurst, achieving these tasks during the normative age period is imperative for successful development. He defined developmental tasks as goals that arise "at or about a certain period in the life of the individual, successful achievement of which leads to his happiness and to success with later tasks, while failure leads to unhappiness in the individual, disapproval by the society, and difficulty with later tasks" (p. 2).

For adulthood, Havighurst (1953/1972) described more than 20 developmental tasks occurring across three age groups (early adulthood, middle age, and late maturity). A subset of these developmental tasks is presented in Table 18.1. Space considerations limit our ability to explore each of these developmental tasks in this chapter, but even a glance suggests that people adopt goals largely in line with the central life domains suggested by Havighurst to be central at a given age (see also Hutteman, Hennecke, Orth, Reitz, & Specht, 2014).

Acknowledging the importance of age-graded demands on development across the lifespan but without assuming a stage model, Cantor (1990) coined the term *life tasks*. According to Cantor, *universal* life tasks denote a set of goals that are rooted in *evolution* and have significance for survival (e.g., group cohesion), and have *developmental significance* (e.g., normative turning points such as entering adulthood) as well as *sociocultural significance* (e.g., timing for entering and leaving the workforce). Cantor assumes that, in any given society or subculture, there is substantial shared knowledge about the content and timing of certain tasks, and that they serve as guideposts for individual development when the universal life tasks are translated into *individual* life tasks or goals.

Shift in Goal Orientation across Adulthood

Going beyond the specific content of developmental or life tasks, we propose that the devel-

TABLE 18.1. Havighurst's (1953/1972) Developmental Tasks in Early, Middle, and Old Adulthood

Age period	Developmental tasks
Early adulthood (18–30 years)	Selecting a mate Learning to live with a partner Starting a family Rearing children Managing a home Getting started in an occupation Taking on civic responsibility Finding a congenial social group
Middle adulthood (30–60 years)	Assisting teenage children to become responsible and happy adults Achieving adult social and civic responsibility Reaching and maintaining satisfactory performance in one's occupational career Developing adult leisure time activities Relating to one's spouse as a person Accepting and adjusting to the physiological changes of middle age Adjusting to aging parents
Old adulthood (60 years and older)	Adjusting to decreasing physical strength and health Adjusting to retirement and reduced income Adjusting to the death of a spouse Establishing an explicit affiliation with one's age group Adopting and adapting social roles in a flexible way Establishing satisfactory living arrangements

opmental shift in goal orientation across adulthood, from maximizing gains to minimizing losses (e.g., Freund, Hennecke, & Mustafic, 2012), is also essential for understanding how personality develops across this period.

Perhaps the most dramatic change that occurs across adulthood concerns the ratio of developmental gains to losses (Baltes, 1997; Baltes, Lindenberger, & Staudinger, 2006). During young adulthood, *gains* are abundant. Young adults acquire new knowledge and skills, increase their autonomy (both in financial/material and psychological terms), expand their social networks, enter a professional career, and (often) begin a family. However, once one has reached middle adulthood, a time in life when many are the height of their functioning (e.g., regarding social power, being established in one's career as well as family), has accumulated material belongings, and has built a social network with friends and colleagues, *maintenance* of these valued achievements becomes more important. Moving into old age, losses threatening our functioning become more likely (e.g., general physical, health-related, and certain cognitive declines, as well as losing social status through retirement). This change in the ratio of gains to losses is also reflected in age-related social ex-

pectations about development across adulthood (Heckhausen, Dixon, & Baltes, 1989; Mustafic & Freund, 2012b).

Given that people are highly sensitive to changes in their functioning and resources (e.g., Hobfoll, 1989), we assume that experiencing or expecting decreasing gains and increasing losses profoundly affects the goals adults select. In line with this assumption, research suggests that adults' goals shift from a primary orientation toward maximizing gains in young adulthood to the maintenance of functioning and resources in middle adulthood, and finally the minimization of losses in older adulthood (Ebner, Freund, & Baltes, 2006; Freund, 2006; Heckhausen, 1999). Clearly, with professional athletes, goals in the athletic domain operate in a compressed time frame. We argue that Roger Federer's recent success at, for tennis, an advanced age was in part due to his adoption of loss-minimizing techniques such as reducing the number of tournaments he played and adopting adjusted practice techniques and strokes suitable for decreased mobility and increased recovery time.

The developmental tasks as outlined by Havighurst (1953/1972) align largely with the assumption of a stronger gain orientation in young adulthood, a maintenance orientation in middle adulthood, and a loss avoidance orientation in old age (see Table 18.2). Young adults' developmental tasks largely consist of goals motivated by the maximization of gains. Whether selecting a partner, getting started in a career, or becoming a member of a social group, young adults are tasked with achieving age-related goals that set a foundation for long-term gains. As these adults progress toward middle age, the developmental tasks begin to reflect goals in which the motivation revolves around maintaining those achievements. For example, a middle-aged adult may attempt to achieve the developmental task of adjusting to the physiological changes associated with slower metabolic rate by increasing exercise, adjusting diet, or adapting his or her current lifestyle. Finally, older adults are tasked with achieving developmental goals that largely reflect the motivation to minimize losses. For example, adjusting for retirement may involve not only skillful financial planning to account for a diminished, fixed retirement income but also the selection of retirement activities consistent with new physiological limitations (see Wang & Shi, 2014, for a detailed review).

History-Graded Influences on Adults' Goals

In addition to age-graded factors impacting personality in the form of what goals adults of different ages are likely to pursue, history-graded factors play an important role in what people typically try to achieve. There are at least two aspects of history-graded influences on development: A first, common approach is to study how events or periods shape developmental trajectories. A clear example of such work comes from Elder (1974), who studied the developmental trajectories of children of the Great Depression. Other examples include work on the influence of the 9/11 attacks (e.g., Bonanno, Galea, Bucciarelli, & Vlahov, 2007), or German reunification (e.g., Pinquart, Juang, & Silbereisen, 2004). Although such work is useful, we focus in this chapter on a second aspect of history-graded influences on adults' goals, namely, how the general social-historical milieu and gradual historical shifts shape adults' goals.

Historical forces shape the contexts within which adults develop and set goals. For example, Arnett's notion of emerging adulthood (2000), a period of extended exploration and identity development, is perhaps only possible within a specific stratum of contemporary Western society, and within a specific historical period providing people in their 20s with the educational opportunities and financial supports necessary to undertake identity explorations (Côté, 2014). If we had assessed individuals of the same chronological age who grew up 80 years ago, during the Great Depression (as

TABLE 18.2. A Taxonomy of Example Adult Goals within the Career Domain, Organized by Two Main Influences: Motivational Orientation and Influence Type (Age–Graded, History–Graded, and Non–Normative)

Prototypical goal orientation toward maximizing gains	
Young adult age-graded	Establish first position within career field of choice
Young adult history-graded	Attend online classes for graduate degree to advance
Young adult non-normative	Change careers after serendipitous encounter
Prototypical goal orientation toward maintaining resources	
Middle adult age-graded	Achieve stability and autonomy in career
Middle adult history-graded	Maintain financial resources during market fluctuations
Middle adult non-normative	Move for new job opportunities to maintain lifestyle
Prototypical goal orientation toward minimizing loss	
Older adult age-graded	Adjust spending after moving to fixed income
Older adult history-graded	With no pension, actively manage retirement funds
Older adult non-normative	Educate self to avoid financial scams

Elder did), their goals would likely differ from today's "emerging adults." Far fewer young adults from that earlier era could afford extended periods of identity development, as their goals often turned toward the economic (Elder, 1974). To make the point again, but later in the lifespan, contemporary younger adults in many countries (including the United States and Switzerland) must often actively manage their retirement plans through investments, whereas young adults from decades ago, hired on a system of generous retirement pensions, likely conceive of their retirement goals in a different way. Thus, historical forces clearly shape the content of the content of goals.

History-graded influences interact with age-related shifts in goal orientation to shape adults' goals. Just as with age-graded goals, we posit that the history-graded goals that adults pursue also prototypically change across adulthood as a function of adults' shifting goal orientation. In other words, while some goals are predominantly shaped by social-historical forces, the goal orientation also changes as a function of age. Take, for example, a common contemporary history-graded goal: learning to use social media websites or applications (e.g., Facebook or Twitter). For middle-aged and older adults, clear maintenance or loss-minimization goals emerge from social media proficiency, such as reconnection with lost contacts, maintaining relationships with distant family members, or reducing loneliness (Chopik, 2016). Younger adults, in contrast, may be more prototypically motivated to become proficient with social network sites to maximize their potential gains by, for instance, networking with potential future employers (Gerard, 2012). Or, returning to tennis, young players may use social media to connect with potential playing partners or coaches to maximize gains, whereas Federer and other stars might use social media to maintain their prominent advertising portfolios.

Interestingly, history-graded factors may at times override age-graded factors, such as when young adults adopt the loss-minimizing goal of adjusting career expectations in light of global recession (Blumenthal, Silbereisen, Pastorelli, & Castellani, 2015) or when, due to technological advances, as well as increased longevity, older adults adopt the gain-maximizing goal of finding a new romantic partner through the use of Internet dating platforms (McWilliams & Barrett, 2014).

Non-Normative Influences on Adults' Goals

In the lifespan framework, the third factor impacting development is non-normative events. Adult development, just like any other period in the lifespan, is an idiosyncratic experience. If age-graded and history-graded goals provide the normative markers for adulthood, the shared experiences of what it means to be adult at this age and during this particular era, then non-normative goals provide the "spice of life"; they are the goals that inform what it means to be one particular, unique adult. This uniqueness is an essential element of adulthood, the period of the lifespan when we are most differentiated (Werner, 1957), when our accumulated triumphs, failures, decisions, and experiences coalesce.

One way that to think about non-normative influences on adult goals is to imagine them as the "twists" or "turning points" in one's life story (McAdams, 2008). Some non-normative life events, such as freak accidents, largely "happen" to people and are not necessarily brought about by adults' goal setting. Regardless of their origin, people vary in the degree to which they can adapt to these events (Luhmann, Orth, Specht, Kandler, & Lucas, 2014), and this adaptation, in the face of negative events, is one way to define resilience (see Masten & Cicchetti, 2016, for a detailed review).

However, agency may also play a role in bringing about non-normative events that impact the setting and pursuit of goals in adulthood. Bandura (1998) argued that non-normative events can be key determinants of life paths: "People can make chance happen by pursuing an active lifestyle that increases the number of fortuitous encounters they are likely to experience" (p. 98). Recently, Napolitano (2013) proposed the concept of *serendipitous relations* to denote an integration of such chance encounters with serendipity (Merton & Barber, 2004). According to this conceptualization, serendipity does not simply occur but is instead created by a person's active, curious, and committed goal pursuits. In other words, adults earlier-set goals may bring about serendipitous situations that may influence the setting of later goals.

The concept of serendipitous relations provides a possible approach to further understand the impact of non-normative events on adult personality development (Napolitano, 2013). Given their goal orientation toward gains, young adults may be best suited to maximize any unexpected, non-normative opportunity that may come their way if it offers the possibility for growth and gains. In contrast, middle-aged and older adults may be less likely to engage with unexpected opportunities for gains, especially if they might also result in losses pertinent to important life domains. In other words, the unexpected event that younger adults see as the beginning of an opportunity, older adults might see as a distraction. Alternatively, middle-aged and older adults might be better than younger adults in spotting and exploring unforeseen opportunities that serve the maintenance or avoidance of losses of functioning. For instance, a tennis student might attend a camp, hoping to meet a coach who will catapult him or her to new success, whereas the ears of an established pro may "perk up" upon a chance encounter with a well-known rehabilitation specialist. Most generally, then, we posit that adults' changing goal orientation also changes the non-normative events that their actions bring about, and it also changes the goals that adults set after such chance events.

The "what" of goals addresses the first component of personality development across adulthood. The second component is the question "how" adults typically strive for their goals, and how this striving changes across adulthood.

Goal Pursuit: The "How" of Adult Goals

The "doing" aspect of personality involves not only what adults at different ages try to achieve, maintain, or avoid, but also *how* they pursue their goals. As in the previous section on goal setting, we again maintain that the shift in developmental gains and losses is central to understanding the development of processes of goal pursuit across adulthood. Therefore, we specifically address the following questions: What are the consequences of the shift in the ratio of gains and losses across adulthood that affect the availability of resources for goal pursuit? How do adults of different ages decide among the multiple ways a given goal can be pursued? In the following section, we elaborate on goal focus as one central goal dimension (Freund & Hennecke, 2015).

Age-Related Changes in Goal Focus

Goal setting mainly concerns a decision about which ends one wants to achieve (the "what"

of goals). However, during goal pursuit, people necessarily also have to attend to the means with which they will achieve the desired ends. The concept of *goal focus* denotes the relative salience of the destination (*outcome focus*) and path to get there (*process focus*) (Freund & Hennecke, 2015). Before we turn to age-related changes in goal focus, let us introduce the concept of goal focus.

According to action identification theory (e.g., Vallacher & Wegner, 1985), people have a tendency to represent actions on the highest level possible (i.e., as the "why" of an action) rather than how to implement an action because the "why" tends to be more meaningful to a person than the more concrete means. According to Vallacher and Wegner, action representations shifts to lower, more concrete representations if the higher-order goals are blocked and means for overcoming obstacles need to be identified and implemented. On this basis, one might argue that people have a general tendency to represent their goals in terms of superordinate outcomes rather than the more concrete, lower-level means of goal pursuit. In this sense, imagine young Federer setting the prescient goal of becoming the world's greatest male tennis player.

However, as elaborated in *construal level theory* (Trope & Liberman, 2003), temporal distance of an event (or goal) plays a central role in how people represent these events (or goals). The greater the distance, the more likely it is that events are represented in terms of abstract features that capture their perceived essence. In contrast, the shorter the temporal distance, the more likely it is that events are represented in more concrete and detailed terms. This suggests that although people might have a general bias toward representing goals on the more abstract, superordinate level of outcomes, the shorter the future time perspective, the more people should focus on the concrete, detailed level of goal-relevant means. In other words, Federer's goal of winning a specific tournament involves very concrete details on means, whereas the early goal to be best in the world lacks these specifics.

Moreover, goals related to maintenance or avoidance of loss (e.g., "I want to maintain a close and positive relationship with my partner") are not reached at any point in time and thus require continuous goal pursuit. For this reason, maintenance and avoidance of loss goals lend themselves more easily to a process focus than do gain-oriented goals (Mustafic & Freund, 2012a) that typically specify an endpoint (e.g., "I want to pass the exam"). Therefore, maintenance goals should be more likely—and have been shown—to be associated with a process focus, whereas goals involving the achievement of new outcomes (i.e., gains) should be more likely to invoke an outcome focus. As a first step to test this hypothesis, Mustafic and Freund (2012a) asked adults of different ages to report their personal goals and rate them regarding the degree to which they aimed at achieving gains or maintaining a current state, as well as how much they focused on the process of goal pursuit or the attainment of the end state (outcome focus). As in previous research, being older was positively associated with adopting a maintenance orientation, as well as a stronger process focus. Importantly, maintenance orientation was significantly associated with a process focus. Moreover, there was statistical evidence indicating that maintenance orientation mediates the association between age and process focus.

As elaborated earlier, research on age-related differences in focusing on achieving growth or gains in one's personal goals versus maintaining functioning or avoiding losses suggest that, compared to older adults, younger adults are more motivated to enhance their performance and optimize their gains (Ebner et al., 2006; Freund, 2006). This result can be interpreted as indicating that younger adults are more motivated to achieve a certain outcome, such as higher performance. In this way, younger adults ensure the accumulation of resources that might be important for their further development. Middle-aged adults might hold an equally strong process and outcome focus because, on the one hand, they are starting to experience a shift in resources toward decline and are, in many areas, at the peak regarding their performance, making achievement of new outcomes less likely. This should lead to a stronger focus on the process than the outcome of goal pursuit. On the other hand, middle-aged adults typically still experience their resources such as life time and vigor as plentiful and further gains as possible, likely resulting in an equally strong outcome focus. This changes in old age, when resources decline (Baltes et al., 2006). Given the shift in goal orientation in response to the changing availability of resources, it is not surprising that goal focus shifts from a higher outcome focus to an increasingly higher process focus in old adults (e.g., Freund, Hennecke, & Riediger, 2010).

Adaptiveness of Goal Focus

Is it more adaptive to adopt a process focus or an outcome focus when pursuing one's goals? Does it help to focus more on the means of goal pursuit (i.e., keep one's nose to the grindstone) or on the outcomes (i.e., keep one's eyes on the prize) (Houser-Marko & Sheldon, 2008) when pursuing difficult goals that require a high degree of self-control, such as exercising regularly or dieting? Empirical evidence suggests that a process focus might be more beneficial than an outcome focus. For instance, in one study Freund and Hennecke (2012) found that younger, middle-aged, and older adults who all followed the same diet over the period of 6 weeks were more successful in their goal to lose weight and also in maintaining a positive mood while dieting when they had a stronger process focus than outcome focus. Similarly, Freund and colleagues (2010) showed that exercise beginners are more likely to engage in regular exercise over time when they adopt a process focus, and they experience higher affective well-being over time. Again returning to tennis, a focus on form and repeatable motions may be better associated with success than a focus on a particular point, game, or match.

An important aspect of successful goal pursuit involves how a person reacts to barriers or failures. Investigating the role of goal focus for successful goal pursuit, Hennecke and Freund (2014) found that in response to failures in their dieting efforts, adults who adopted a stronger process focus persisted more in their diet and showed behaviors aimed at repairing the diet failures. In contrast, an outcome focus was associated with difficulties in "getting back on the wagon" after a lapse in keeping the diet. Not surprisingly, the higher persistence and repair in dieting was related to more success in the goal of dieting, namely, to lose weight. As was found in the case of exercising regularly, a stronger process focus was related to positive mood during the dieting phase. The positive mood associated with process focus, in turn, might help people to persist in such difficult long-term goals as dieting or exercising.

Goal Disengagement

Assuming the resources to attain our goals (e.g., time, money, social support) are limited, it is essential for successful development to use them efficiently (Freund, 2008). Therefore, we need to identify not only the goals that we best pursue in order to foster our development, but also those goals from which we best disengage if the likelihood of actually achieving them is very low or too costly when considering other, more promising goals for which there might not be sufficient resources left. In fact, empirical evidence suggests that disengaging from goals can be adaptive in some situations but not in others. For example, women who did not disengage from the goal to have a child after having passed the developmental deadline experienced declines in mental health (Heckhausen, Wrosch, & Fleeson, 2001). However, for goals that may actually be attainable and not futile, persistence may be better. In a similar study, adults who disengaged prematurely from the goal to get married when it was still statistically probable that they could find a partner also experienced mental health decline (Wrosch & Heckhausen, 1999). Given the decline in resources across adulthood that are necessary for achieving one's goals, it is not surprising that older adults are also more likely to disengage from goals (Haase, Heckhausen, & Wrosch, 2013). In this way, goal disengagement can be considered one important way of managing resource losses in old age, but it might be detrimental to younger adults whose resources are still plentiful.

Managing Multiple Goals in the Face of Limited Resources

Given the limitation of resources that humans encounter at any point in their lives, how do we manage the pursuit of multiple goals that compete for these finite resources? Resource limitations are the primary cause of goal conflict across adulthood (Riediger & Freund, 2004). Goal conflict, in turn, is associated with negative outcomes such as lower psychological well-being and psychosomatic complaints (e.g., Freund, Knecht, & Wiese, 2014).

How does goal conflict develop across adulthood? On the one hand, taking into account the multiple demands that adults face at different ages, one might expect that middle-aged adults are at the highest risk of experiencing goal conflict. After all, middle adulthood can be characterized as the "rush hour of life" (Bittman & Wajcman, 2000) with the normative developmental tasks of getting ahead in one's professional career, raising one's children, and, in order to be considered a well-rounded person, also engaging in leisure and social activities.

The demands of developmental tasks are much lower in younger and then again in older adulthood. On the other hand, given the decreasing availability of resources across adulthood, one would expect older adults to be particularly prone to experience goal conflicts.

The existing research on multiple goals suggests that older adults experience lower goal conflict and select goals that are more facilitative than do younger adults, and that this helps them to stay highly involved in the pursuit of their goals (e.g., Riediger, Freund, & Baltes, 2005). Furthermore, there is evidence that everyday motivational conflicts of feeling that one wants to or should do something else instead of what one is actually doing are less prevalent in older than in younger adults, and that this is among the processes that contribute to a higher level of day-to-day emotional well-being in older as compared to younger adults (Riediger & Freund, 2008). One of the mechanisms underlying this age-related difference seems to be that older adults focus more on the goals that are most important to them (Riediger & Freund, 2006). This might be due to the fact that older adults are confronted with fewer social expectations of the goals they pursue compared to younger and middle-aged adults. An alternative explanation is that due to the increasing limitation of resources, older adults are more used to prioritizing one goal over the other when faced with goal conflicts, thereby focusing their limited resources. The hypothesis of age-related differences in prioritizing is consistent with empirical evidence of an age-related increase in disengagement from difficult or even unattainable goals (e.g., Wrosch, Heckhausen, & Lachman, 2000). Again turning to tennis, Federer disengaged from playing tournaments throughout the year to focus only on the four "major" events. Taken together, then, the research on the management of multiple goals suggests that despite the increasing limitation of resources, motivational competence increases across adulthood.

Time Perspective and Self-Control

We consider a final aspect of goal pursuit, which, as with other topics reviewed earlier, may change across adulthood. Empirical findings suggest that time perspective plays an important role in how we pursue our goals because the way we think about our goals with respect to time—our future, the events we anticipate, who we want to become—can influence goal pursuit. Goals necessarily require thinking about the future, and recent evidence suggests that certain specific ways of viewing our future may enhance self-control and thus promote successful goal pursuit.

Future self-continuity, for example, refers to the extent to which people feel similar to, or connected with, their future conceptions of themselves (Parfit, 1971). Empirically, future self-continuity has been linked to self-control: People who report stronger future self-continuity were better able to resist immediate gratification and also showed better financial habits (i.e., saving money for their future; Ersner-Hershfield, Garton, Ballard, Samanez-Larkin, & Knutson, 2009). Similarly, adults who viewed computer-rendered pictures of themselves as older allocated a greater percentage of their income to retirement savings (in a hypothetical scenario) than did adults who did not view age-altered pictures of themselves (Hershfield et al., 2011). They also reported greater future self-continuity. Thus, when adults thought about themselves in relation to who they would become, they were better able to delay gratification, a cornerstone of self-control and successful goal pursuit (Mischel et al., 1989). In a recent study by Rutt and Löckenhoff (2016), older adults reported greater future self-continuity than younger adults. Thus, older adults might show better goal pursuit because they not only focus more on the process than the outcome of goal pursuit, but they also view themselves as being more connected to who they will become in the future compared to younger adults.

What drives the age differences in future self-continuity? One prime candidate for explaining age-related differences in constructs such as counterfactual thinking (which is required when thinking of oneself as being very different from oneself in the present) are age-related cognitive declines. However, Löckenhoff and Rutt (2017) noted that across multiple studies, cognitive decline did not explain age-related differences in future self-continuity. Considering motivational factors, changes in perceived self-continuity may be due to the age-related shifts toward striving for maintenance rather than growth and, thereby, change: Self-continuity may reflect a motivation for older adults to maintain a continuous sense of identify, especially as age-related changes to their health and physical functioning become prominent. Further supporting this possibil-

ity is the finding that age-related increases in self-continuity extended to the past, as well as the future, suggesting that older adults perceive higher self-continuity over time in general rather than just the future (Rutt & Löckenhoff, 2016). Another factor that might contribute to age-related increases in future self-continuity is that older adults' may find that their personality dispositions (e.g., the Big Five) have remained fairly stable over the past years, and extrapolate the stability into the future. In contrast, young adults who have probably experienced more changes in the transition from childhood to adolescence and into young adulthood may, on this basis, expect the same rate of change in the coming years.

Some Methodological Comments

Before we conclude this chapter, let us add some methodological remarks. Lifespan developmental research is faced with various challenges beyond those facing all of psychology (e.g., developing reliable measures of personality): First, describing and explaining adult development requires truly long-term longitudinal designs, optimally spanning the entire adult age span from entering adulthood to death. Such studies are extremely rare, as they go beyond the typical time frame of a researcher's career, and they pose formidable challenges to the research logistic (e.g., keeping track of participants over decades without compromising their anonymity and data management, sticking to the same constructs and their assessment over time). Second, in order to avoid the confounding of age, cohort, and historical time, one needs to combine cross-sectional and longitudinal designs with multiple cohorts (Baltes, Reese, & Nesselroade, 1977). Such designs are even more costly than simple longitudinal designs and even rarer (a notable exception is the Seattle Longitudinal Study, e.g., Schaie & Hertzog, 1983).

Third, despite their potency in describing development over time, such designs are correlational and do not allow a strong test of developmental processes and of causality. This problem is not solved by intensive data assessments that are now possible, thanks to the recent technological advances regarding portable devices that allow assessment of large amounts of data from one person (e.g., experience-sampling methods, measurement burst designs). Establishing causality regarding the processes driving age-related differences or change requires experimental designs. Given that age cannot be manipulated, researchers have to be very creative in finding ways to manipulate developmental processes. One example of such an experimental design is provided by Ebner and colleagues (2006), who manipulated the subjective availability of resources in order to test whether the age-differences in goal orientation are causally related to the perceived availability of resources.

A fourth challenge is that the meaning (i.e., validity) of stimuli (including items on a questionnaire) might change with age (for an elaboration of this issue, see Freund & Isaacowitz, 2013). For instance, asking older adults whether they enjoy trying out different kinds of new food might indicate a robust stomach and health more than the openness to new experiences it signals for younger adults. Thus, when including multiple age groups, it is imperative to carefully establish the equivalence of the measures.

A comprehensive discussion of the methodological challenges of research on the development of personality across adulthood goes beyond the scope of this brief chapter. Suffice it here to mention just these four challenges facing this field.

Summary and Conclusions

Conceiving of personal goals as building blocks of personality, we have investigated personality development across adulthood on the level of what McAdams (1996) called personal concerns, distinguishing (1) *what* people typically want to achieve, maintain, or avoid at a certain time in their lives and (2) *how* they go about pursuing these goals. Together, processes of goal setting and pursuit help to describe and predict how people interact with their world, react to internal and external age-related changes, and proactively shape who they will become in the future.

The kinds of goals people set for themselves have an important impact on their life paths: They regulate which skills and goal-relevant means people acquire in order to pursue their goals, their social environment, as well as the everyday experiences that contribute significantly to how they view themselves and interact with the world. We combined two concepts from the lifespan developmental perspective. First, adopting Baltes and colleagues' (1980) metamodel of developmental influences, we

argued that adult goals are largely shaped by either normative age-graded or history-graded influences, or instead non-normative, idiosyncratic influences. Second, we posited that the character of these goals is informed by adults' shifting goal orientation, from aiming for gains earlier in adulthood to minimizing losses in older adulthood. Taken together, then, adults pursue goals based on age-graded, history-graded, or idiosyncratic non-normative influences, and the character of these goals changes across adulthood based on the nature of their goal orientation.

The second aspect of goals we consider vital for describing personality development across adulthood concerns the "how" of goal strivings. How do people allocate their resources to pursue their goals, and how do they manage multiple goals in the face of a changing ratio of gains and losses across adulthood? One of the goal dimensions that seems to change in tandem with the availability of resources and goal orientation from gains toward the avoidance of losses, is the salience of the process or the outcome of goal pursuit. Paralleling the shift in goal orientation, younger adults—whose goals mainly concern achievement of gains—focus more on the outcomes, whereas older adults—whose goals are more strongly oriented toward maintenance and the avoidance of loss—focus more on the process of goal pursuit. Adopting a stronger process focus seems to be adaptive regardless of age, by helping people to successfully pursue challenging goals over longer periods of time and to recover from failure. Regarding goal focus, then, older adults seem to demonstrate a higher motivational competence (for an overview see Freund et al., 2012).

The increasing motivational competence across adulthood is also evident in the management of multiple goals. With increasing age, adults select goals that converge on central life domains and experience less goal conflict (Riediger & Freund, 2006). This effect might be due to the stronger social expectations regarding the goals that younger and middle-aged adults ought to pursue, such that they have less autonomy to choose those goals that facilitate rather than conflict with each other.

Finally, we have discussed how the amount of change that adults expect for themselves decreases across adulthood: Older adults perceive themselves as more similar to who they will become in the future than do younger adults. Importantly, in the current context, self-continuity increases the ability to delay gratification. Delay of gratification, in turn, is an important predictor of successful development (Mischel et al., 1989; Moffitt et al., 2011).

Returning to our opening scenario and the question of who among the young, talented tennis players might become a Federer-type champion, we believe that knowing these young athletes' goals; which age-graded, history-graded, and non-normative factors apply to them; what goal focus they adopt when going about pursuing their goals; and how they manage the pursuit of multiple goals will help us to predict their life paths to some degree and also how successful they will be in pursuing them. We argue that the study of adult goals is essential to the study of adult personality development.

REFERENCES

Allport, G. W. (1937). *Personality: A psychological interpretation.* New York: Holt.

Arnett, J. J. (2000). Emerging adulthood: A theory of development from the late teens through the twenties. *American Psychologist, 55,* 469–480.

Baltes, P. B. (1997). On the incomplete architecture of human ontology: Selection, optimization, and compensation as foundation of developmental theory. *American Psychologist, 52,* 366–380.

Baltes, P. B., & Baltes, M. M. (1990). Psychological perspectives on successful aging: The model of selective optimization with compensation. In P. B. Baltes & M. M. Baltes (Eds.), *Successful aging: Perspectives from the behavioral sciences* (pp. 1–34). New York: Cambridge University Press.

Baltes, P. B., Cornelius, S. W., & Nesselroade, J. R. (1979). Cohort effects in developmental psychology. In J. R. Nesselroade & P. B. Baltes (Eds.), *Longitudinal research in the study of behavior and development* (pp. 61–87). New York: Academic Press.

Baltes, P. B., Lindenberger, U., & Staudinger, U. M. (2006). Life span theory in developmental psychology. In R. M. Lerner & W. Damon (Eds.), *Handbook of child psychology: Vol. 1. Theoretical models of human development* (6th ed., pp. 569–664). Hoboken, NJ: Wiley.

Baltes, P. B., Reese, H. W., & Lipsitt, L. P. (1980). Life-span developmental psychology. *Annual Review of Psychology, 31,* 65–110.

Baltes, P. B., Reese, H. W., & Nesselroade, J. R. (1977). *Life-span developmental psychology: An introduction to research methods.* Monterey, CA: Brooks/Cole.

Bandura, A. (1998). Exploration of serendipitous determinants of life paths. *Psychological Inquiry, 9,* 95–99.

Bittman, M., & Wajcman, J. (2000). The rush hour: The character of leisure time and gender equity. *Social Forces, 79,* 165–189.

Blumenthal, A., Silbereisen, R. K., Pastorelli, C., & Castellani, V. (2015). Academic and social adjustment during adolescence as precursors of work-related uncertainties in early adulthood. *Swiss Journal of Psychology, 74,* 159–168.

Bonanno, G. A., Galea, S., Bucciarelli, A., & Vlahov, D. (2007). What predicts psychological resilience after disaster?: The role of demographics, resources, and life stress. *Journal of Consulting and Clinical Psychology, 75,* 671–682.

Brandtstädter, J. (2006). Action perspectives on human development. In R. Lerner & W. Damon (Eds.), *The handbook of child psychology: Vol 1. Theoretical models of human development* (6th ed., pp. 516–568). New York: Wiley.

Cantor, N. (1990). From thought to behavior: "Having" and "doing" in the study of personality and cognition. *American Psychologist, 45,* 735–750.

Chopik, W. J. (2016). The benefits of social technology use among older adults are mediated by reduced loneliness. *Cyberpsychology, Behavior, and Social Networking, 19,* 551–556.

Côté, J. E. (2014). The dangerous myth of emerging adulthood: An evidence-based critique of a flawed developmental theory. *Applied Developmental Science, 18,* 177–188.

Ebner, N. C., Freund, A. M., & Baltes, P. B. (2006). Developmental changes in personal goal orientation from young to late adulthood: From striving for gains to maintenance and prevention of losses. *Psychology and Aging, 21,* 664–678.

Elder, G. H., Jr. (1974). *Children of the Great Depression: Social change in life experience.* Chicago: University of Chicago Press.

Erikson, E. H. (1950). *Childhood and society.* New York: Norton.

Ersner-Hershfield, H., Garton, M. T., Ballard, K., Samanez-Larkin, G. R., & Knutson, B. (2009). Don't stop thinking about tomorrow: Individual differences in future self-continuity account for saving. *Judgment and Decision Making, 4,* 280–286.

Freund, A. M. (2006). Age-differential motivational consequences of optimization versus compensation focus in younger and older adults. *Psychology and Aging, 21,* 240–252.

Freund, A. M. (2007). Differentiating and integrating levels of goal representation: A life-span perspective. In B. R. Little, K. Salmela-Aro, J. E. Nurmi, & S. D. Phillips (Eds.), *Personal project pursuit: Goals, action and human flourishing* (pp. 247–270). Mahwah, NJ: Erlbaum.

Freund, A. M. (2008). Successful aging as management of resources: The role of selection, optimization, and compensation. *Research in Human Development, 5,* 94–106.

Freund, A. M., & Baltes, P. B. (2002). Life-management strategies of selection, optimization and compensation: Measurement by self-report and construct validity. *Journal of Personality and Social Psychology, 82,* 642–662.

Freund, A. M., & Hennecke, M. (2012). Changing eating behaviour vs. losing weight: The role of goal focus for weight loss in overweight women. *Psychology and Health, 27,* 25–42.

Freund, A. M., & Hennecke, M. (2015). On means and ends: The role of goal focus in successful goal pursuit. *Current Directions in Psychological Science, 24,* 149–153.

Freund, A. M., Hennecke, M., & Mustafic, M. (2012). On gains and losses, means and ends: Goal orientation and goal focus across adulthood. In R. M. Ryan (Ed.), *The Oxford handbook of human motivation* (pp. 280–300). New York: Oxford University Press.

Freund, A. M., Hennecke, M., & Riediger, M. (2010). Age-related differences in outcome and process goal focus. *European Journal of Developmental Psychology, 7,* 198–222.

Freund, A. M., & Isaacowitz, D. M. (2013). Beyond age comparisons: A plea for the use of a modified Brunswikian approach to experimental designs in the study of adult development and aging. *Human Development, 56,* 351–371.

Freund, A. M., Knecht, M., & Wiese, B. S. (2014). Multidomain engagement and self-reported psychosomatic symptoms in middle-aged women and men. *Gerontology, 60,* 255–262.

Freund, A. M., & Riediger, M. (2006). Goals as building blocks of personality and development in adulthood. In D. K. Mroczek & T. D. Little (Eds.), *Handbook of personality development* (pp. 353–372). Mahwah, NJ: Erlbaum.

Gerard, J. G. (2012). Linking in with LinkedIn(R): Three exercises that enhance professional social networking and career building. *Journal of Management Education, 36,* 866–897.

Haase, C. M., Heckhausen, J., & Wrosch, C. (2013). Developmental regulation across the life span: Toward a new synthesis. *Developmental Psychology, 49,* 964–972.

Havighurst, R. J. (1972). *Developmental tasks and education.* New York: McKay. (Original work published 1953)

Heckhausen, J. (1999). *Developmental regulation in adulthood: Age-normative and sociostructural constraints as adaptive challenges.* Cambridge, UK: Cambridge University Press.

Heckhausen, J., Dixon, R. A., & Baltes, P. B. (1989). Gains and losses in development throughout adulthood as perceived by different adult age groups. *Developmental Psychology, 25,* 109–121.

Heckhausen, J., Wrosch, C., & Fleeson, W. (2001). Developmental regulation before and after a developmental deadline: The sample case of "biological clock" for childbearing. *Psychology and Aging, 16,* 400–413.

Hennecke, M., & Freund, A. M. (2014). Identifying success on the process level reduces negative effects of prior weight loss on subsequent weight loss during

a low-calorie diet. *Applied Psychology: Health and Well-Being, 6,* 48–66.

Hershfield, H. E., Goldstein, D. G., Sharpe, W. F., Fox, J., Yeykelis, L., Carstensen, L. L., et al. (2011). Increasing saving behavior through age-progressed renderings of the future self. *Journal of Marketing Research, 48,* 23–37.

Hobfoll, S. E. (1989). Conservation of resources: A new attempt at conceptualizing stress. *American Psychologist, 44,* 513–524.

Houser-Marko, L., & Sheldon, K. (2008). Eyes on the prize or nose to the grindstone: The effects of level of goal evaluation on mood and motivation. *Personality and Social Psychology Bulletin, 34,* 1556–1569.

Hutteman, R., Hennecke, M., Orth, U., Reitz, A. K., & Specht, J. (2014). Developmental tasks as a framework to study personality development in adulthood and old age: Developmental tasks in personality development. *European Journal of Personality, 28,* 267–278.

Judge, T. A., Higgins, C. A., Thoresen, C. J., & Barrick, M. R. (1999). The Big Five personality traits, general mental ability, and career success across the life span. *Personnel Psychology, 52,* 621–653.

Kruglanski, A. W., Shah, J. Y., Fishbach, A., Friedman, R., Chun, W. Y., & Sleeth-Keppler, D. (2002). A theory of goal systems. In M. P. Zanna (Ed.), *Advances in experimental social psychology* (Vol. 34, pp. 331–378). San Diego, CA: Academic Press.

Lang, F. R., Rieckmann, N., & Baltes, M. M. (2002). Adapting to aging losses: Do resources facilitate strategies of selection, compensation, and optimization in everyday functioning? *Journals of Gerontology B: Psychological Sciences and Social Sciences, 57,* 501–509.

Lerner, R. M., & Busch-Rossnagel, N. A. (1981). Individuals as producers of their development: Conceptual and empirical bases. In R. M. Lerner & N. A. Busch-Rossnagel (Eds.), *Individuals as producers of their development: A life-span perspective* (pp. 1–36). New York: Academic Press.

Löckenhoff, C. E., & Rutt, J. L. (2017). Age differences in self-continuity: Converging evidence and directions for future research. *The Gerontologist, 57,* 396–408.

Luhmann, M., Orth, U., Specht, J., Kandler, C., & Lucas, R. E. (2014). Studying changes in life circumstances and personality: It's about time. *European Journal of Personality, 28,* 257–267.

Masten, A. S., & Cicchetti, D. J. (2016). Resilience in development: Progress and transformation. In R. Lerner & W. Damon (Eds.), *Developmental psychopathology: Vol. 4. Risk, resilience, and intervention* (6th ed., pp. 1–63). Hoboken, NJ: Wiley.

McAdams, D. P. (1996). Personality, modernity, and the storied self: A contemporary framework for studying persons. *Psychological Inquiry, 7,* 295–321.

McAdams, D. P. (2008). Personal narratives and the life story. In O. P. John, R. W. Robins, & L. A. Pervin (Eds.), *Handbook of personality: Theory and re-*

search (3rd ed., pp. 241–261). New York: Guilford Press.

McWilliams, S., & Barrett, A. E. (2014). Online dating in middle and later life: Gendered expectations and experiences. *Journal of Family Issues, 35*(3), 411–436.

Merton, R. K., & Barber, E. (2004). *The travels and adventures of serendipity.* Princeton, NJ: Princeton University Press.

Mischel, W., Shoda, Y., & Rodriguez, M. L. (1989). Delay of gratification in children. *Science, 244,* 933–938.

Moffitt, T. E., Arseneault, L., Belsky, D., Dickson, N., Hancox, R. J., Harrington, H., et al. (2011). A gradient of childhood self-control predicts health, wealth, and public safety. *Proceedings of the National Academy of Sciences of the USA, 108,* 2693–2698.

Mustafic, M., & Freund, A. M. (2012a). Means or outcomes?: Goal orientation predicts process and outcome focus. *European Journal of Developmental Psychology, 9,* 493–499.

Mustafic, M., & Freund, A. M. (2012b). Multidimensionality in developmental conceptions across adulthood. *GeroPsych, 25,* 57–72.

Napolitano, C. M. (2013). More than just a simple twist of fate: Serendipitous relations in developmental science. *Human Development, 56,* 291–318.

Parfit, D. (1971). Personal identity. *Philosophical Review, 80,* 3–27.

Pinquart, M., Juang, L. P., & Silbereisen, R. K. (2004). The role of self-efficacy, academic abilities, and parental education in the change in career decisions of adolescents facing German unification. *Journal of Career Development, 31,* 125–142.

Ree, M. J., & Earles, J. A. (1992). Intelligence is the best predictor of job performance. *Current Directions in Psychological Science, 1,* 86–89.

Riediger, M., & Freund, A. M. (2004). Interference and facilitation among personal goals: Differential associations with subjective well-being and persistent goal pursuit. *Personality and Social Psychology Bulletin, 30,* 1511–1523.

Riediger, M., & Freund, A. M. (2006). Focusing and restricting: Two aspects of motivational selectivity in adulthood. *Psychology and Aging, 21,* 173–185.

Riediger, M., & Freund, A. M. (2008). Me against myself: Motivational conflicts and emotional development in adulthood. *Psychology and Aging, 23,* 479–494.

Riediger, M., Freund, A. M., & Baltes, P. B. (2005). Managing life through personal goals: Intergoal facilitation and intensity of goal pursuit in younger and older adulthood. *Journal of Gerontology B: Psychological Sciences, 60,* P84–P91.

Roberts, B. W., & DelVecchio, W. F. (2000). The rank-order consistency of personality traits from childhood to old age: A quantitative review of longitudinal studies. *Psychological Bulletin, 126,* 3–25.

Roberts, B. W., & Mroczek, D. (2008). Personality trait change in adulthood. *Current Directions in Psychological Science, 17,* 31–35.

Roberts, B. W., & Robins, R. W. (2000). Broad dispositions, broad aspirations: The intersection of personality traits and major life goals. *Personality and Social Psychology Bulletin, 26,* 1284–1296.

Rutt, J. L., & Löckenhoff, C. E. (2016). From past to future: Temporal self-continuity across the life span. *Psychology and Aging, 31,* 631–639.

Schaie, K. W., & Hertzog, C. (1983). Fourteen-year cohort-sequential studies of adult intelligence. *Developmental Psychology, 19,* 531–543.

Sternberg, R. J. (1997). The concept of intelligence and its role in lifelong learning and success. *American Psychologist, 52,* 1030–1037.

Trope, Y., & Lieberman, N. (2003). Temporal construal. *Psychological Review, 110,* 403–421.

Vallacher, R. R., & Wegner, D. M. (1985). *A theory of action identification.* Hillsdale, NJ: Erlbaum.

Wang, M., & Shi, J. (2014). Psychological research on retirement. *Annual Review of Psychology, 65,* 209–233.

Werner, H. (1957). The concept of development from a comparative and organismic point of view. In D. B. Harris (Ed.), *The concept of development: An issue in the study of human behavior* (pp. 125–148). Minneapolis: University of Minnesota Press.

Wrosch, C., & Heckhausen, J. (1999). Control processes before and after passing a developmental deadline: Activation and deactivation of intimate relationship goals. *Journal of Personality and Social Psychology, 77,* 415–427.

Wrosch, C., Heckhausen, J., & Lachman, M. E. (2000). Primary and secondary control strategies for managing health and financial stress across adulthood. *Psychology and Aging, 15*(3), 387–399.

Young, L. M., Baltes, B. B., & Pratt, A. K. (2007). Using selection, optimization, and compensation to reduce job/family stressors: Effective when it matters. *Journal of Business and Psychology, 21,* 511–539.

CHAPTER 19

Development of Self–Esteem across the Lifespan

Ulrich Orth
Richard W. Robins

In the *Up* series of documentary films, directors Paul Almond and Michael Apted have followed the lives of 14 British children since they were 7 years old, interviewing them every 7 years as they grew up and traversed the challenges and opportunities of adolescence, young adulthood, and middle age (Apted, 2012). The series was inspired by the Jesuit motto "Give me a child until he is seven and I will give you the man." The in-depth portrayals of the participants, although shaped by the unique lens through which they are viewed by the directors, provide an interesting set of biographies to explore patterns and mechanisms in the development of self and identity.

Self-esteem is a particularly salient issue in the life of Suzy, one of the participants in the *Up* series. At age 7, Suzy comes across as an effusive little girl who is excited about fashion and dolls. Just 7 years later, at age 14, she has become shy and withdrawn, retreating into an adolescent shell devoid of the interests and activities that excited her as a child. After enduring a somewhat tumultuous life, Suzy, at age 49, expresses regret that she failed to take responsibility for herself earlier in life and develop a stronger sense of her self-worth, concluding, "Maybe now is the first time that I actually feel happy within my own skin. It's taken me a long time to do it, but I actually feel that I can accept decisions, wrong decisions, that I have made

in the past. I am comfortable with it now, I can live with it" (Apted, 2009). A central life transition for Suzy was the beginning of a committed and satisfying romantic relationship in her early 20s, which seemed to bolster her life satisfaction and self-esteem. Suzy's life story provides a compelling portrayal of how self-esteem can wax and wane over the course of development, and how social relationships—in particular, romantic relationships—can serve to enhance self-esteem, a topic to which we return later in this chapter.

Researchers have long been interested in understanding stability and change in self-esteem (e.g., Block & Robins, 1993; Demo, 1992; Huang, 2010; Wylie, 1979). In this chapter, we address several interrelated questions: How does self-esteem first emerge in childhood? How stable are individual differences in self-esteem? Does self-esteem show systematic changes across the lifespan? Do people from different generations (e.g., "baby boomers" vs. "millennials") vary in their average level of self-esteem? Which factors influence the development of self-esteem? Does self-esteem matter for people's lives? These issues have been debated in the literature for decades, with little progress toward resolution. Recently, however, a growing number of longitudinal studies has moved the field toward some consensus about many of the abiding questions in the study of self-esteem development. Our goal in this chapter is to describe this emerging consensus by providing an overview of the major findings in the field.

Before we address these issues, we first turn to the definition of self-esteem. *Self-esteem* refers to an individual's subjective evaluation of his or her worth as a person (e.g., Donnellan, Trzesniewski, & Robins, 2011; MacDonald & Leary, 2012). Here, we use the term *worth* very broadly to simply mean a positive evaluation of any and all aspects of the self. Thus, *self-esteem* is, by definition, a subjective construct and does not necessarily reflect a person's objective characteristics and competencies, or how a person is evaluated by others. It is therefore important to distinguish self-esteem from narcissism, as both constructs involve positive self-evaluations (Orth, Robins, Meier, & Conger, 2016; Paulhus, Robins, Trzesniewski, & Tracy, 2004). Whereas *self-esteem* refers to feelings of self-acceptance and self-respect, *narcissism* is characterized by feelings of superiority, grandiosity, self-centeredness, entitlement, and lack of empathy (Ackerman et al., 2011; Bosson et al., 2008). Thus, although high self-esteem is compatible with a prosocial, positive attitude toward others, narcissism is linked to antisocial tendencies (Donnellan, Trzesniewski, Robins, Moffitt, & Caspi, 2005; Paulhus et al., 2004; Tracy, Cheng, Robins, & Trzesniewski, 2009). The definition of self-esteem as a subjective evaluation is consistent with how self-esteem is typically assessed, that is, using self-report measures (for a review, see Donnellan, Trzesniewski, & Robins, 2015). For example, the Rosenberg Self-Esteem Scale (Rosenberg, 1965), the most commonly used measure, includes statements such as "I take a positive attitude toward myself" and "I feel that I am a person of worth, at least on an equal plane with others." To take another example, the Lifespan Self-Esteem Scale by Harris, Donnellan, and Trzesniewski (2018)—a measure that has been developed for surveying participants of all ages, beginning with children as young as 5 years—includes questions such as "How do you feel about yourself?" and "How do you feel about the kind of person you are?"

Researchers often distinguish between global and domain-specific self-esteem. Whereas *global self-esteem* refers to an individual's overall evaluation of his or her worth, *domain-specific self-esteem* refers to an individual's evaluation of his or her worth in specific domains such as peer relationships, intellectual ability, and physical appearance. Wherever possible in this chapter, we discuss findings for both global and domain-specific self-esteem.

How Does Self-Esteem Emerge Early in Life?

An important but insufficiently understood question is how children first develop a global sense of their worth. Behavioral genetics research suggests that both genetic and environmental factors influence global self-esteem, but that environmental factors account for more variance than do genetic factors, with the heritability of self-esteem estimated to be about 40% (Kendler, Gardner, & Prescott, 1998; McGuire, Neiderhiser, Reiss, Hetherington, & Plomin, 1994; Neiss, Sedikides, & Stevenson, 2002; Neiss, Stevenson, Legrand, Iacono, & Sedikides, 2009). However, as yet, there is little evidence about the specific mechanisms that account for the emergence of self-esteem early in life. In the following, we outline two possible models.

To subjectively experience low or high self-esteem, children must have developed a *self-concept,* that is, a set of mental representations that include at least basic beliefs about who they are physically, psychologically, and socially (Coughlin & Robins, 2017). The literature suggests that children's domain-specific self-evaluations can be assessed at an earlier age than can global self-esteem (Donnellan, Trzesniewski, & Robins, 2015). Whereas domain-specific self-evaluations (e.g., "I am good at counting") have been assessed beginning at about age 4 years, researchers traditionally have assumed that global self-esteem cannot be measured reliably before about age 8 (Harter & Pike, 1984; but see Harris et al., 2017). Thus, a first model of the emergence of global self-esteem (which we call the *bottom-up model*) includes the proposition that, as young children develop their self-concept, they form beliefs about their abilities, talents, and stable characteristics in specific domains (e.g., sports, academic abilities, appearance, and peer relationships), based on their experiences in these domains, as well as feedback they receive from caregivers, teachers, and peers. The bottom-up model states that later, at about age 7 or 8, children begin to aggregate their self-evaluations across domains, leading gradually to the development of global feelings of self-esteem. However, empirical studies do not generally support the assumption that domain-specific self-evaluations are the basis for global self-esteem (Harris, Wetzel, Robins, Donnellan, & Trzesniewski, 2018; Marsh & Yeung, 1998). Moreover, when predicting people's global self-esteem on the basis of their domain-specific self-evaluations, a large part of the variance remains unexplained, suggesting that global self-esteem is more than the sum of domain-specific self-evaluations (Luciano & Orth, 2016; Pelham & Swann, 1989).

Given that the bottom-up model is difficult to reconcile with empirical findings, we now consider a second, fundamentally different model, which we call the *internalization of early social experiences model*. This model suggests that a child's global sense of self-esteem does not evolve from domain-specific self-evaluations but rather is shaped by early experiences in important interpersonal relationships. This model has its roots in a diverse range of theoretical perspectives, including attachment theory (Bowlby, 1969) and symbolic interactionism (Cooley, 1902; Mead, 1934). Attachment theory suggests that secure attachment to the caregiver leads to the construction of a positive internal working model of the self, that is, the representation that the self is valuable and deserving of love and care from close others (Bretherton & Munholland, 2008; Marvin & Britner, 2008). Even if children are not able to verbally express their general feelings of self-worth at age 4 or 5 years, children's global self-esteem might be an automatic and preconscious reflection of the quality of their experiences with their primary caregivers.

Similarly, symbolic interactionism suggests that children's relationship experiences with their parents and "significant others" influence the development of their self-esteem (Cooley, 1902). Specifically, the impressions of our early caregivers serve as a "looking glass," reflecting back an image of ourselves that is then internalized and serves as the basis for self-esteem. Although symbolic interactionists viewed the internalization of other's views as a lifelong process of self-construction, both attachment theory and symbolic interactionism share the view that early experiences of social evaluation and connection are particularly critical for the development of a child's general tendency to feel valuable versus worthless. More generally, these perspectives suggest that global self-esteem is co-constructed through relational processes that first emerge in childhood but persist across the lifespan (Harris et al., 2017).

Supporting the internalization of early social experiences model, research suggests that the quality of parenting is a key factor that influences the development of self-esteem. For example, longitudinal studies indicate that parental warmth, parental support, and support of children's autonomy predict higher self-esteem among children (Allen, Hauser, Bell, & O'Connor, 1994; Amato & Fowler, 2002; Brummelman et al., 2015; but see Harris et al., 2015). Longitudinal evidence also suggests that the effect of parenting quality experienced during the first years of life persists as children grow up and become adults (Orth, 2018). In that study, which used data from a national sample from the United States, interviews with mothers and behavioral observation were used to gain information about the family environment during children's first years of life. Later, children's self-esteem was assessed biannually from ages 8–27 years. The most important predictor of later self-esteem was the quality of the home environment, including quality of parenting and cognitive stimulation. Although the predictive effect became smaller as children grew older, the effect was still present during young adulthood, and statistical modeling indicated that it should persist into midlife and perhaps even old age. Moreover, quality of the home environment partially accounted for the effects of other features of the early childhood family environment, such as quality of the parental relationship, maternal depression, and poverty. These findings suggest that the family environment in early childhood shapes the long-term development of individual differences in self-esteem. In future research, it would be interesting to test models of the emergence of global self-esteem early in life in more detail. The importance of early family environment is also apparent in the case of Suzy, whose parents divorced when she was in her early teenage years, around the time her troubles with self-esteem first emerged. When talking about the environment that she created for her own children, Suzy said, "We were lucky. We had a very good family unit with them growing up, and that meant an awful lot to me that I was able to do that for them, because I never had it for myself" (Apted, 2012).

How Stable Are Individual Differences in Self-Esteem?

One question that comes to mind while watching the *Up* series is the degree to which the participants who appear insecure as children grow up to become adolescents and adults who are similarly plagued by self-doubts; and conversely, whether those brimming with self-confidence as children remain self-assured later in life. More specifically, we can ask whether participants who had high (or low) self-esteem (compared to the other participants) when they were age 7 or 14, still have high (or low) self-esteem (compared to the other participants) at ages 21, 28, or even 56. This question can be addressed by examining the degree to which individuals maintain their rank ordering over time, which is typically assessed using test–retest correlations.

Although some have argued that self-esteem fluctuates from situation to situation, like our emotions (Heatherton & Polivy, 1991), research suggests that the rank-order stability of self-esteem is quite high, even across long periods of time. In a meta-analysis of longitudinal studies and in analyses with several large, representative samples, the rank-order stability of self-esteem was estimated as .64, corrected for measurement error (Trzesniewski, Donnellan, & Robins, 2003), which is comparable to the rank-order stability of basic personality traits. Moreover, Trzesniewski and colleagues (2003) found that the rank-order stability of self-esteem varies as a function of age; it is relatively low in childhood, increases across adolescence, peaks in adulthood, then decreases in old age. Overall, this developmental pattern in the rank-order stability of self-esteem corresponds to findings on other personality characteristics, such as the Big Five domains (Lucas & Donnellan, 2011; Roberts & DelVecchio, 2000; Specht, Egloff, & Schmukle, 2011).

However, although test–retest correlations provide important information, more sophisticated statistical models are needed to fully understand the stability of individual differences in self-esteem. For example, we know that test–retest correlations typically decrease as the time lag between assessments increases, but a key question is whether the stability of a construct ever approaches zero. If stability asymptotes at a nonzero level, this suggests that an underlying "trait" factor (or some other constant factor; e.g., genetics or a nonchanging environment) accounts for stable individual differences in the construct. Using data from a large sample assessed six times across almost 30 years, Kuster and Orth (2013) found that the long-term stability of self-esteem approached an asymptotic value of about .40. Thus, as the time interval increased, test–retest correlations first quickly decreased but then leveled off at a medium-size value for intervals of several decades (instead of dropping to zero). This value, which replicated for women and men, is similar in magnitude to that found for the Big Five personality traits (Anusic & Schimmack, 2016; Fraley & Roberts, 2005). In other words, the evidence suggests that individual differences in self-esteem are relatively stable, even if these differences are tracked over long periods, such as from young adulthood to midlife or even to old age. Thus, self-esteem, like other aspects of personality, is best conceptualized as a trait-like construct. It should be noted that the study by Kuster and Orth (2013) did not include participants younger than age 14 years and that it is unknown whether the findings apply also to child samples. Evidence from Trzesniewski and colleagues (2003) and Fraley and Roberts (2005) suggests that the long-term stability of individual differences in self-esteem may be significantly lower in childhood compared to later developmental periods.

Another way to assess the rank-order stability of a construct is by using latent trait–state models, which partition interindividual variance into stable (trait) and unstable (state) components (Cole, 2012; Kenny & Zautra, 1995, 2001). Three longitudinal studies have used latent trait–state models to examine the stability of self-esteem across long periods (Donnellan, Kenny, Trzesniewski, Lucas, & Conger, 2012; Kuster & Orth, 2013; Wagner, Lüdtke, & Trautwein, 2016). The results of the three studies converged in showing strong trait effects (70–85% of the interindividual variance), and relatively weak state effects (15–30% was pure state variance or measurement error). Overall, then, the evidence reviewed in this section supports the notion that self-esteem is an enduring personality characteristic.

Does Self-Esteem Show Systematic Changes across the Lifespan?

Although individual differences in self-esteem are relatively stable—as reviewed in the previous section—the average level of self-esteem might change systematically across the life course. Thus, with regard to the *Up* series, it is possible that the 14 participants maintained their ordering relative to each other, but, as a group, their self-esteem tended to increase or decrease from one developmental period to the next. This type of change is referred to as *mean-level* or *normative change.*

For a long time, the literature has suggested that people's self-esteem does not show normative changes in any developmental period from childhood to old age (Wylie, 1979). The first study that significantly challenged this notion was based on analyses of cross-sectional data from more than 320,000 individuals who had completed a self-esteem questionnaire on the Internet (Robins, Trzesniewski, Tracy, Gosling, & Potter, 2002). The findings suggested that, on average, self-esteem decreases from childhood to adolescence, recovers slightly in young adulthood, increases during middle adulthood, reaches a peak at about age 65 years, and declines sharply in old age. However, as is true for all cross-sectional analyses, the findings provide only a snapshot of age differences at a given point in time. Consequently, an important methodological problem is that the observed age differences may reflect cohort differences (i.e., differences based on when a person was born) not changes due to growing older. For example, participants who were 65 years old when the data were collected, and who reported the highest self-esteem scores of all adult participants, may have had high self-esteem all along because of differing sociocultural conditions when they were young (e.g., because of favorable economic or parenting conditions). Thus, it is possible that the observed increase in self-esteem scores from adolescence to middle adulthood does not reflect developmental change (i.e., aging), but differences in the cohorts being studied at these ages. To resolve this problem, longitudinal data are needed. This is one reason why the *Up* series is so powerful—one can see the participants aging from one film to the next, across five decades of life.

To date, three longitudinal studies have tracked the trajectory of self-esteem across the lifespan (Orth, Maes, & Schmitt, 2015; Orth, Robins, & Widaman, 2012; Orth, Trzesniewski, & Robins, 2010). All three studies included large samples assessed multiple times across periods ranging from 4 to 16 years. The participants ranged in age from adolescence to old age in two studies, and from young adulthood to old age in the third. The analyses were based on *latent growth modeling,* using the information from all participants simultaneously to model a single trajectory across the entire observed age range (Duncan, Duncan, & Strycker, 2006; Preacher, Wichman, MacCal-

lum, & Briggs, 2008). All studies tested competing growth models, including models with no change, and models with linear, quadratic, and cubic change. All three studies provided evidence for an inverted U-shaped trajectory, in which self-esteem increases from adolescence to midlife, peaks at about age 50–60, and decreases in old age. Across studies, the increase from adolescence to midlife had an effect size ranging from about 0.30 to 0.50 (expressed as *d*; Cohen, 1992), and the decrease from midlife to old age corresponded to an effect size ranging from about −0.20 to −0.70 (thus, varying more strongly across studies). This pattern is also supported by longitudinal studies that focused on self-esteem development during specific developmental stages, such as adolescence and young adulthood (Birkeland, Melkevik, Holsen, & Wold, 2012; Chung, Hutteman, van Aken, & Denissen, 2017; Chung et al., 2014; Erol & Orth, 2011; Kiviruusu, Huurre, Aro, Marttunen, & Haukkala, 2015; Wagner, Lüdtke, Jonkmann, & Trautwein, 2013; Zeiders, Umaña-Taylor, & Derlan, 2013) and old age (von Soest, Wagner, Hansen, & Gerstorf, 2018; Wagner, Gerstorf, Hoppmann, & Luszcz, 2013; Wagner, Hoppmann, Ram, & Gerstorf, 2015; Wagner, Lang, Neyer, & Wagner, 2014).

With regard to the self-esteem trajectory in childhood and early adolescence, however, the evidence from longitudinal studies is less clear. Although some studies have found that self-esteem decreases during childhood and the transition into adolescence (Eccles, Wigfield, Harold, & Blumenfeld, 1993; Marsh, 1989; Marsh, Barnes, Cairns, & Tidman, 1984)—for example, it seems that Suzy's self-esteem declined from ages 7–14—others have failed to find the self-esteem drop from childhood to adolescence (Cole et al., 2001; Huang, 2010; Kuzucu, Bontempo, Hofer, Stallings, & Piccinin, 2014), and still others have found that self-esteem decreases for girls but increases for boys (Block & Robins, 1993). To help reconcile these conflicting findings, Orth, Erol, and Luciano (2018) conducted a meta-analysis of all longitudinal studies to date and did not find support for the hypothesis that self-esteem declines during childhood. Instead, the meta-analytic findings suggest that mean levels of self-esteem increase slightly from the preschool years to middle childhood, are stable (but do not decline) during early and middle adolescence, then begin to increase around age 15 and continue to increase into adulthood, a pattern that did not differ by gender. Future research should test whether this pattern holds for the childhood trajectory of domain-specific self-esteem.

Why does self-esteem show a steady uptrend from late adolescence to middle age? To date, no theories that focus specifically on the development of self-esteem during adulthood have been proposed. However, important background is provided by theory from the broader context of personality development (Specht et al., 2014). In particular, neo-socioanalytic theory suggests that adults typically develop in the direction of mature personality traits, especially during young adulthood (Roberts & Wood, 2006; see also Roberts & Nickel, 2021). The reason is that adult individuals assume many social roles, such as relationship partner, parent, and employee, and that social roles involve expectations about appropriate behavior. For most social roles, these expectations include agreeableness, conscientiousness, assertiveness, and emotional stability (i.e., mature personality traits). Given that people are typically committed to satisfying these expectations, many adults gradually improve on these traits. Especially in young adulthood, individuals transition into many of these social roles, by entering into working life, committing to a stable romantic relationship, having a baby, and taking over additional social roles in the community (Hutteman, Hennecke, Orth, Reitz, & Specht, 2014). Given that mature personality traits are positively correlated with higher self-esteem (Robins, Hendin, & Trzesniewski, 2001; Watson, Suls, & Haig, 2002), neo-socioanalytic theory suggests that adults gradually improve in their self-esteem, especially during young adulthood.

More research is needed regarding old age. Although most studies have found that self-esteem declines in old age, especially in very old age, the magnitude of the decline differs considerably across studies (Orth et al., 2010, 2012, 2015; von Soest, Wagner, Hansen, & Gerstorf, 2018; Wagner, Gerstorf, Hoppmann, & Luszcz, 2013; Wagner, Hoppmann, et al., 2015; Wagner et al., 2014). This issue is highly relevant because if many elderly adults experience profound drops in self-esteem and serious self-doubts at the end of life, these changes may contribute to declining levels of well-being and the emergence of depressive symptoms (Orth & Robins, 2013; Sowislo & Orth, 2013). This may be particularly true for an individual like Suzy, who has struggled with self-esteem issues throughout her life but seems to be doing well at midlife—is she someone who may be particularly likely to lose some of her hard-earned self-worth as she enters old age?

The example of Suzy illustrates the importance of understanding not only the typical magnitude of the old-age decline in self-esteem but also the conditions that ameliorate or exacerbate the decline. It is possible that some of the variability in the observed effect sizes reflect cultural, social, and economic differences between the countries in which the data were collected. For example, attitudes toward older people, pension schemes, and the quality of the health care system could influence whether people maintain their self-esteem, experience a benign reduction, or suffer a significant loss in self-worth as they grow old. In fact, research suggests that differences in socioeconomic status, physical health, cognitive abilities, and perceived control over one's life account for at least some differences in the self-esteem trajectory in old age (Orth et al., 2010; Wagner, Gerstorf, et al., 2013; Wagner, Hoppmann, et al., 2015). More precisely, the self-esteem decline was very small when older adults did not experience negative changes in their income, health, and cognitive abilities, and control over their lives (Orth et al., 2010). In future research, it will be important to gain a better understanding of the individual, social, and cultural factors that influence the old-age trajectory.

In addition to chronological age (i.e., age in years since birth), Wagner and colleagues found that the time remaining in a person's life (i.e., the temporal distance to death) predicts the old-age decline in self-esteem (Wagner, Gerstorf, et al., 2013; Wagner, Hoppmann, et al., 2015), perhaps because some of the factors that influence self-esteem are adversely affected by declines in cognitive and physical functioning during the last years of life (Gerstorf et al., 2008). Although such analyses can be conducted only retrospectively, that is, using data from individuals who are deceased, when available, both chronological age and distance to death should be examined in studies of self-esteem in old age.

A question that has rarely been explored in the literature is whether other aspects of self-esteem besides its level (i.e., high vs. low) vary as a function of age. People differ in not only their level of self-esteem but also the degree to which their self-esteem fluctuates over time and is contingent on external feedback. Notably, Suzy's life seems like a roller coaster of ups and downs in self-esteem, whereas other participants in the *Up* series seem to have maintained a more consistent level. Findings based on data from a large diary study suggest that self-esteem not only increases from adolescence to middle adulthood, but it also becomes more stable and less contingent (Meier, Orth, Denissen, & Kühnel, 2011). We note, however, that this finding was based on a cross-sectional study, and only longitudinal research can demonstrate that the increase in stability and decline in contingency reflect developmental change rather than cohort differences.

Another neglected question is whether domain-specific and global self-esteem show a similar developmental trajectory across the lifespan. For the adolescent period, the evidence is inconsistent. Whereas some studies have found similar domain-specific and global self-esteem trajectories (Steiger, Allemand, Robins, & Fend, 2014; von Soest, Wichstrøm, & Kvalem, 2016), other studies suggest that the trajectories differ, in part because the various domains sometimes follow different trajectories (Cole et al., 2001; Harris, Wetzel, Robins, Donnellan, & Trzesniewski, 2018; Kuzucu et al., 2014). For example, Harris, Wetzel, and colleagues (2018) found decreases in physical appearance and academic self-esteem, no change in same-sex peer relationships, and a slight increase in opposite-sex peer relationship self-esteem. The studies by Cole and colleagues (2001) and Kuzucu and colleagues (2014) suggest that self-esteem in the domain of behavioral conduct declines significantly during adolescence, whereas academic and social self-esteem increase.

Regarding adulthood, researchers have mostly ignored the development of domain-specific self-esteem. In a recent study on age differences from 16 to 90 years, academic self-esteem showed a trajectory similar to global self-esteem (increasing in young and middle adulthood, decreasing in old age), whereas self-esteem in the domains of physical appearance and physical ability decreased continuously (Luciano & Orth, 2016). Moreover, whereas academic self-esteem was strongly correlated with global self-esteem across the whole life course, for physical appearance and physical ability, the correlations with global self-esteem decreased significantly with age. However, more research is needed to clarify how domain-specific self-esteem develops across the lifespan and the ways in which it is linked to the development of global self-esteem. Despite some gaps in the literature, the

field is converging on the view that global self-esteem generally increases from adolescence through adulthood, then declines in old age, and that contingent and unstable self-esteem shows a similar trajectory from adolescence to adulthood.

Do People from Different Generations Vary in Self-Esteem?

The *Up* series focuses on a cohort of children who were born in the late 1950s and thus largely grew up in the 1960s. To what extent did their generation influence the lives they led and the people they became? This is the kind of question that researchers ask when they study whether people born in different generations show systematic differences in their average level of self-esteem. Twenge (2006) has advanced the provocative claim that "Generation Me"—the cohort of individuals born in the 1970s–1990s—are exceptionally confident and even narcissistic compared to previous generations. Although Twenge's hypotheses on Generation Me focus mainly on narcissism (for the debate, see, e.g., Twenge, Konrath, Foster, Campbell, & Bushman, 2008; Wetzel, Donnellan, Robins, & Trzesniewski, 2018), Twenge and her collaborators have also proposed that there have been secular changes in self-esteem (Gentile, Twenge, & Campbell, 2010; Twenge & Campbell, 2001). Interestingly, in *49 Up*, Suzy reflects about her children and their generation, commenting: "I think what I admire about the young today is their confidence and that's what I wished I'd had. They just seem to take life and deal with it" (Apted, 2009).

In fact, some sociocultural changes beginning around the 1970s raise the possibility that more recent generations might exhibit higher self-esteem than older generations (Gentile et al., 2010). For example, self-esteem has become a more prominent topic in the public and media, leading parents, child care workers, and teachers to focus more strongly on the promotion of self-esteem among children and adolescents. Moreover, grade inflation in the educational system and increasing possibilities for self-presentation in social media such as Facebook, Twitter, and YouTube might alter the typical way members of more recent generations (who use these websites and services more frequently than members of older generations) perceive themselves. All of these secular changes might alter the average self-esteem trajectory characterizing a particular generational cohort.

Fortunately, cohort-sequential longitudinal studies, in which multiple cohorts of individuals are followed over time, provide a way to determine whether generational cohorts differ in their overall level of self-esteem and in the shape of the lifespan trajectory of self-esteem. In summary, the findings from four cohort-sequential longitudinal studies suggest that neither the overall level nor the shape of the self-esteem trajectory has changed across the cohorts born during the 20th century (Erol & Orth, 2011; Orth et al., 2010, 2012, 2015; but see Twenge, Carter, & Campbell, 2017). Three of the studies covered large parts of the lifespan, whereas the study by Erol and Orth (2011) focused on adolescence and young adulthood. The null results on cohort effects are meaningful given the large samples (ranging from 1,800 to 7,100 participants), which provide ample statistical power. Moreover, two of the samples were nationally representative, strengthening the generalizability of the findings. Thus, with regard to self-esteem, cohort-sequential findings do not support the hypotheses about "Generation Me." Studies with other research designs likewise suggest that more recent generations do not have higher self-esteem compared to older generations (Hamamura & Septarini, 2017; Trzesniewski & Donnellan, 2010). More generally, the findings suggest that it matters little whether Suzy, or anyone else, was born in the 1950s, or a generation before or after; her level of self-esteem, and the changes in self-esteem she exhibits during her life, are likely to be quite similar.

Which Factors Influence the Development of Self-Esteem?

People differ significantly in the way their self-esteem changes over time. While Suzy declined in self-esteem during the transition to adolescence, then increased after entering young adulthood, the other members of the *Up* series exhibited quite different patterns. The variability in patterns of self-esteem development raises the question of which factors shape the individual trajectory of self-esteem. In this section, we review evidence on the following sets of possible factors: (1) gender and ethnicity, (2) social relationships, (3) socioeconomic status, (4) work success, (5) stressful life events, and (6) cultural context.

Longitudinal research has frequently tested for gender differences in the self-esteem trajectory. Corresponding to meta-analyses of cross-sectional data (Kling, Hyde, Showers, & Buswell, 1999; Major, Barr, Zubek, & Babey, 1999; Zuckerman, Li, & Hall, 2016), the longitudinal evidence suggests that the gender difference in self-esteem development is small but robust, with boys and men reporting slightly higher self-esteem than girls and women, respectively (Erol & Orth, 2011; Orth et al., 2010, 2012, 2015; von Soest et al., 2016; Wagner, Lüdtke, et al., 2013). Moreover, the meta-analytic evidence suggests that the gender difference increases during childhood, peaks in adolescence (albeit at an overall small effect size, as reported earlier), and is again smaller in adulthood (Kling et al., 1999; Major et al., 1999; Zuckerman et al., 2016). However, even if gender accounts for a small difference in self-esteem, it is likely that gender does not influence self-esteem directly, but that correlated factors (e.g., lower status of women in some cultural contexts; differential treatment of men and women in school and work contexts; women's awareness of gender discrimination) account for the effect (Zuckerman et al., 2016).

Similarly, using data from U.S. samples, longitudinal research has identified ethnic differences, that is, differences in the self-esteem trajectories of Americans of European, Hispanic, African, Asian, or Native descent (Erol & Orth, 2011; Orth et al., 2010; Shaw, Liang, & Krause, 2010). For example, the results suggested that African Americans, when compared to European Americans, experienced a stronger self-esteem increase in young adulthood but also a stronger decrease in old age. Again, it is likely that the self-esteem effect is not directly due to ethnicity, but rather reflects social or economic factors that differ systematically across ethnic groups. A promising avenue for future research is to move beyond these between-group comparisons in self-esteem and explore ethnocultural variables that predict *within-group* variability in self-esteem. For example, Hernández, Robins, Widaman, and Conger (2017) studied ethnic pride in Mexican-origin youth and found that fifth-grade boys who were particularly proud of their ethnic heritage showed subsequent increases in self-esteem as they transitioned into adolescence.

Theoretical perspectives suggest that social relationships are a key factor influencing self-esteem. In addition to attachment theory and symbolic interactionism (discussed previously in the section on the emergence of self-esteem in early childhood), sociometer theory extends symbolic interactionism by postulating that self-esteem is an internal monitor of the degree to which the individual's need for social inclusion is satisfied or threatened (Leary, 2004, 2012; Leary & Baumeister, 2000). Longitudinal studies support central propositions of sociometer theory, suggesting that being socially included and valued by others leads to increases in self-esteem (Gruenenfelder-Steiger, Harris, & Fend, 2016; Reitz, Motti-Stefanidi, & Asendorpf, 2016; Srivastava & Beer, 2005). Moreover, longitudinal research suggests that romantic relationships might be particularly relevant in explaining self-esteem change in adulthood (Mund, Finn, Hagemeyer, Zimmermann, & Neyer, 2015; Schaffhuser, Wagner, Lüdtke, & Allemand, 2014). For example, two studies found that relationship transitions, such as beginning a romantic relationship, significantly influenced people's self-esteem (Luciano & Orth, 2017; Wagner, Becker, Lüdtke, & Trautwein, 2015). Importantly, these two studies used the statistical method of *propensity score matching*. This technique provides for relatively strong conclusions about causality because the treatment group (i.e., individuals who experienced the transition) and control group (i.e., individuals who did not experience the transition) are matched on a large number of covariates, thus mimicking the random assignment employed in experimental designs, and ruling out the possibility of selection effects (e.g., individuals with high vs. low self-esteem might differ in their propensity to have particular relationship experiences). In the study by Luciano and Orth (2017), the effect of beginning any romantic relationship was significant in the first year after the transition, but not in the second and third years. However, when comparing matched samples of participants who began a relationship that lasted for at least 1 year (a presumably more stable and fulfilling relationship) versus participants who remained single, the effect was much larger and persisted across the entire study period. Moreover, a recent study indicated that the context of romantic relationships—that is, the environment shared and partly created by both partners, such as size of social network, family characteristics, stressful life events, and financial conditions—influences both partners' self-esteem (Orth, Erol, Ledermann, & Grob,

2018). Thus, research to date strongly suggests that social relationships influence self-esteem.

The case of Suzy offers a nice illustration of the impact of transitioning into a stable, satisfying romantic relationship. Whereas Suzy seemed uneasy and dissatisfied with herself when interviewed at age 21, by age 28, she was much more relaxed and had found some peace of mind after having entered into a stable relationship with Rupert, to whom she has been married ever since (Apted, 2012). When asked by the interviewer at age 28, "When I last saw you at 21, you were nervous, you were chain-smoking, you were uptight, and now you seem happy. What's happened to you over these last seven years?" she responds, "I suppose Rupert. I give him some credit" (Apted, 2009). The empirical evidence suggests that Rupert does indeed deserve some credit.

Socioeconomic status is also associated with self-esteem. Longitudinal studies show that individuals with higher income, education level, and occupational prestige tend to have higher self-esteem at all ages across the lifespan (Orth et al., 2010, 2012, 2015; Wagner, Gerstorf, et al., 2013; Wagner et al., 2014), replicating meta-analytic findings based on cross-sectional data (Twenge & Campbell, 2002). However, because these longitudinal studies used socioeconomic status as a covariate of mean-level change in self-esteem, the findings are mute with regard to the hypothesized causal relation between the constructs. Two studies examined the possible effects of socioeconomic status more directly, by testing prospective effects and controlling for prior levels of the variables; however, neither income nor occupational prestige prospectively predicted change in self-esteem (Kuster, Orth, & Meier, 2013; Orth et al., 2012). Thus, the available evidence does *not* suggest that socioeconomic status has a causal effect on self-esteem.

Similarly, extant research does not suggest that work success causally influences self-esteem, although the constructs are positively correlated (Judge & Bono, 2001). Two longitudinal studies have tested for prospective effects of work outcomes—subjective measures such as job satisfaction and work stress, as well as objective measures such as employment status and supervisor status—but found small, and mostly nonsignificant, effects on self-esteem (Kuster et al., 2013; Orth et al., 2012).

Stressful life events such as experiencing a serious accident, contracting a chronic disease, and suffering from criminal victimization may entail loss of self-esteem, as suggested by longitudinal studies (Orth & Luciano, 2015; Pettit & Joiner, 2001; Tetzner, Becker, & Baumert, 2016). Importantly, these studies controlled for theoretically relevant third variables, such as gender and socioeconomic status, increasing the validity of the conclusions. Moreover, a longitudinal study tested whether the birth of the first child—a life event that has positive connotations but is also considered a stressful event—affected self-esteem among new mothers and fathers (Bleidorn, Buyukcan-Tetik, et al., 2016). The findings suggested that self-esteem declined in the first year after childbirth (particularly among mothers) and continued to decrease gradually in the following years. These results were replicated in a recent study with a representative sample of Norwegian mothers, showing that the pattern of effects held not only for first-time mothers but also for mothers having their second, third, or later baby (van Scheppingen, Denissen, Chung, Tambs, & Bleidorn, 2018). This study also showed that the decrease in self-esteem after childbirth was preceded by an increase during pregnancy, and that changes in self-esteem were associated with changes in mothers' relationship satisfaction. Moreover, as reviewed earlier, evidence suggests that a relationship breakup worsens people's self-esteem, even when researchers control for a large number of covariates (Luciano & Orth, 2017).

Research suggests that cultural contexts influence the prototypical self-concept among their members (Heine, Lehman, Markus, & Kitayama, 1999; Markus & Kitayama, 1991), potentially affecting the development of self-esteem. However, there is still a lack of longitudinal evidence on self-esteem development outside of westernized countries. Cross-sectional studies suggest that, overall, the general pattern of self-esteem development replicates in many countries (Bleidorn, Arslan, et al., 2016; Robins et al., 2002). Nevertheless, there is evidence of cross-cultural variability in self-esteem development. Using data from nearly 1 million participants from about 50 countries, Bleidorn, Arslan, and colleagues (2016) found that socioeconomic and cultural-value characteristics of countries moderated the normative trajectory during young adulthood. Their findings suggested, for example, that women from countries with greater gender equality show larger increases in self-esteem during young adulthood compared to women from countries with more traditional gender roles. However, the causal status of the relation between culture and self-esteem is unclear due to the cross-sectional nature of the data.

Taken together, the available evidence suggests that social relationships and stressful life events influence people's self-esteem. Moreover, given the methodological characteristics of many of the relevant studies (e.g., controlling for prior levels of the variables, controlling for third variables, and using propensity score matching), the research provides relatively strong support for a causal interpretation of the effects. Nevertheless, there are many gaps in our knowledge of the personal, relational, social, and cultural influences on self-esteem development, and whether there are critical developmental windows when presumed causal factors are particularly consequential.

Does Self-Esteem Matter?

The research we have reviewed in this chapter suggests that individual differences in self-esteem emerge early in life and become increasingly stable as children grow up and go through life. Thus, the findings suggest that self-esteem is a personality trait. But is it a trait that truly matters for people's lives? This question is critically important given that an earlier review concluded that due to a lack of longitudinal studies at the time, self-esteem is "not a major predictor or cause of almost anything" (Baumeister, Campbell, Krueger, & Vohs, 2003, p. 37) and that, subsequently, researchers have hotly debated whether self-esteem exerts any influence on important life outcomes (Krueger, Vohs, & Baumeister, 2008; Swann, Chang-Schneider, & McClarty, 2007, 2008). Since Baumeister and colleagues' (2003) review, an increasing number of longitudinal studies have provided evidence that self-esteem does have consequences for a broad set of outcomes in people's lives (for a review, see Orth & Robins, 2014). Specifically, researchers have examined the implications of self-esteem for social and romantic relationships (Johnson & Galambos, 2014; Marshall, Parker, Ciarrochi, & Heaven, 2014; Mund et al., 2015; Orth et al., 2012), education (Hernández et al., 2017; Trzesniewski et al., 2006; von Soest et al., 2016), work (Kuster et al., 2013; Orth et al., 2012; Trzesniewski et al., 2006; von Soest et al., 2016), crime and delinquency (Donnellan et al., 2005;

Trzesniewski et al., 2006), and health (Orth et al., 2012; Trzesniewski et al., 2006). Moreover, a large body of research suggests that low self-esteem contributes to the development of depression (Orth et al., 2016; Orth, Robins, & Roberts, 2008; Rieger, Göllner, Trautwein, & Roberts, 2016; Sowislo & Orth, 2013; Steiger et al., 2014; Wouters et al., 2013; for a review, see Orth & Robins, 2013).

Importantly, the studies cited allow for strong conclusions about the consequences of self-esteem because many of them used large representative samples (often with more than 1,000 participants), aggregated the estimates across several waves of data, and controlled for prior levels of the constructs. Moreover, many studies controlled for theoretically relevant third variables (e.g., gender, socioeconomic status, intelligence, popularity among peers, and life events), ruling out alternative hypotheses about confounding effects of other influential factors. Thus, contrary to the conclusion of Baumeister and colleagues (2003), the findings suggest that high versus low self-esteem are not mere epiphenomena of success versus failure in important life domains, but that self-esteem plays a causal role in people's experiences in social and romantic relationships, in their school and work life, and in the health domain. Note, however, that the prospective effects of self-esteem were typically of small to medium size. This is not surprising because, clearly, a multitude of factors influence success and well-being in life domains such as peer and romantic relationships, work, and health. However, it is theoretically and practically important to know that self-esteem is one of these factors. If self-esteem has real-world consequences, then interventions aimed at strengthening people's self-esteem should prove beneficial for the individual and, ultimately, society. In fact, meta-analytic evidence indicates that psychological interventions can improve people's self-esteem, and that effective interventions result in improvements in not only self-esteem but also other areas of functioning (Haney & Durlak, 1998; O'Mara, Marsh, Craven, & Debus, 2006).

Conclusion

Over the past few decades, research on self-esteem development has made considerable progress toward clarifying previously unresolved issues and reaching consensus about

long-debated questions. The research reviewed in this chapter suggests that (1) individual differences in self-esteem are relatively stable across decades of life, indicating that self-esteem is a trait-like construct; (2) self-esteem has a genetic component, but environmental factors during early childhood explain, at least partially, individual differences in self-esteem that persist into adulthood; (3) despite its trait-like character, self-esteem shows normative change across the whole life course, increasing across large parts of the lifespan, peaking at about ages 60–65 years, then decreasing in old age; (4) people from different generations do not differ in their average level of self-esteem or in the way their self-esteem changes across the lifespan; (5) social relationships, stressful life events, and important life transitions influence the development of self-esteem at all developmental periods; and (6) self-esteem is a causal force that influences people's lives in the domains of relationships, work, and health.

We believe that the evidence accumulated in the field of self-esteem development is relatively strong given the abundance of studies using longitudinal designs, large and representative samples (often from archival data sets openly available to the research community), and sophisticated statistical methods, such as growth curve modeling, latent trait–state modeling, and propensity score matching. Nevertheless, much work remains to be done. For example, at the beginning of this chapter, we discussed two possible models of how self-esteem emerges early in life. However, due to a lack of empirical research, these models are almost untested, and numerous additional models could be derived from other theoretical perspectives. Thus, future research should seek to better understand the emergence of self-esteem in early childhood. Moreover, although our review suggests that social relationships and major life events are factors influencing the development of self-esteem, the available evidence with regard to other factors such as work success and cultural context is scarce and inconsistent. For example, many theoretical perspectives predict that work experiences should have a causal effect on self-esteem given their relevance for people's pretensions (James, 1890), their self-perceived competence (Tafarodi & Swann, 1995) and their odds for social inclusion versus exclusion (Leary, 2012). However, more research on the potential self-esteem effect of work experiences is needed. Finally, research reviewed in this chapter suggests that self-esteem influences important life outcomes. However, the mechanisms by which self-esteem exerts its influence are insufficiently understood. Some of these mediating processes might operate on the intrapersonal level. For example, research suggests that low self-esteem strengthens the tendency to ruminate about failures and negative social feedback, which compromises the person's well-being (Kuster, Orth, & Meier, 2012). However, other mediating processes might occur at the interpersonal level. For example, individuals with low self-esteem tend to withdraw in relationship conflicts, increasing the likelihood of relationship breakups (Murray, Rose, Bellavia, Holmes, & Kusche, 2002). Thus, an important task for future research is to examine the mechanisms through which self-esteem influences people's lives.

In summary, the research reviewed in this chapter provides a clear counterpoint to the adage that inspired the *Up* series, "Give me a child until he is seven and I will give you the man." Instead, we see evidence of both consistency and change. Although self-esteem shows some degree of stability across decades of life, its long-term stability is far from perfect. People's self-esteem continues to change in meaningful and consequential ways from childhood through old age. A particularly poignant example is the case of Suzy, whose confidence and exuberance at age 7 hardly foretold the ups and downs in self-esteem she would experience over the course of her life.

REFERENCES

Ackerman, R. A., Witt, E. A., Donnellan, M. B., Trzesniewski, K. H., Robins, R. W., & Kashy, D. A. (2011). What does the Narcissistic Personality Inventory really measure? *Assessment, 18,* 67–87.

Allen, J. P., Hauser, S. T., Bell, K. L., & O'Connor, T. G. (1994). Longitudinal assessment of autonomy and relatedness in adolescent–family interactions as predictors of adolescent ego development and self-esteem. *Child Development, 65,* 179–194.

Amato, P. R., & Fowler, F. (2002). Parenting practices, child adjustment, and family diversity. *Journal of Marriage and Family, 64,* 703–716.

Anusic, I., & Schimmack, U. (2016). Stability and change of personality traits, self-esteem, and well-being: Introducing the meta-analytic stability and change model of retest correlations. *Journal of Personality and Social Psychology, 110,* 766–781.

Apted, M. (2009). *7-49 Up* [6 DVDs]. London: Granada Ventures.

Apted, M. (2012). *56 Up* [DVD]. London: Granada Ventures.

Baumeister, R. F., Campbell, J. D., Krueger, J. I., & Vohs, K. D. (2003). Does high self-esteem cause better performance, interpersonal success, happiness, or healthier lifestyles? *Psychological Science in the Public Interest, 4,* 1–44.

Birkeland, M. S., Melkevik, O., Holsen, I., & Wold, B. (2012). Trajectories of global self-esteem development during adolescence. *Journal of Adolescence, 35,* 43–54.

Bleidorn, W., Arslan, R. C., Denissen, J. J. A., Rentfrow, P. J., Gebauer, J. E., Potter, J., et al. (2016). Age and gender differences in self-esteem: A cross-cultural window. *Journal of Personality and Social Psychology, 111,* 396–410.

Bleidorn, W., Buyukcan-Tetik, A., Schwaba, T., van Scheppingen, M. A., Denissen, J. J. A., & Finkenauer, C. (2016). Stability and change in self-esteem during the transition to parenthood. *Social Psychological and Personality Science, 7,* 560–569.

Block, J., & Robins, R. W. (1993). A longitudinal study of consistency and change in self-esteem from early adolescence to early adulthood. *Child Development, 64,* 909–923.

Bosson, J. K., Lakey, C. E., Campbell, W. K., Zeigler-Hill, V., Jordan, C. H., & Kernis, M. H. (2008). Untangling the links between narcissism and self-esteem: A theoretical and empirical review. *Social and Personality Psychology Compass, 2,* 1415–1439.

Bowlby, J. (1969). *Attachment and loss: Vol. 1. Attachment.* New York: Basic Books.

Bretherton, I., & Munholland, K. A. (2008). Internal working models in attachment relationships: Elaborating a central construct in attachment theory. In J. Cassidy & P. R. Shaver (Eds.), *Handbook of attachment: Theory, research, and clinical applications* (2nd ed., pp. 102–127). New York: Guilford Press.

Brummelman, E., Thomaes, S., Nelemans, S. A., Orobio de Castro, B., Overbeek, G., & Bushman, B. J. (2015). Origins of narcissism in children. *Proceedings of the National Academy of Sciences of the USA, 112,* 3659–3662.

Chung, J. M., Hutteman, R., van Aken, M. A. G., & Denissen, J. J. A. (2017). High, low, and in between: Self-esteem development from middle childhood to young adulthood. *Journal of Research in Personality, 70,* 122–133.

Chung, J. M., Robins, R. W., Trzesniewski, K. H., Noftle, E. E., Roberts, B. W., & Widaman, K. F. (2014). Continuity and change in self-esteem during emerging adulthood. *Journal of Personality and Social Psychology, 106,* 469–483.

Cohen, J. (1992). A power primer. *Psychological Bulletin, 112,* 155–159.

Cole, D. A. (2012). Latent trait–state models. In R. H. Hoyle (Ed.), *Handbook of structural equation modeling* (pp. 585–600). New York: Guilford Press.

Cole, D. A., Maxwell, S. E., Martin, J. M., Peeke, L. G., Seroczynski, A. D., Tram, J. M., et al. (2001). The development of multiple domains of child and adolescent self-concept: A cohort sequential longitudinal design. *Child Development, 72,* 1723–1746.

Cooley, C. H. (1902). *Human nature and the social order.* New York: Scribner's Sons.

Coughlin, C., & Robins, R. W. (2017). Self-concept development. In A. Wenzel (Ed.), *SAGE encyclopedia of abnormal and clinical psychology* (pp. 3026–3030). Thousand Oaks, CA: SAGE.

Demo, D. H. (1992). The self-concept over time: Research issues and directions. *Annual Review of Sociology, 18,* 303–326.

Donnellan, M. B., Kenny, D. A., Trzesniewski, K. H., Lucas, R. E., & Conger, R. D. (2012). Using trait–state models to evaluate the longitudinal consistency of global self-esteem from adolescence to adulthood. *Journal of Research in Personality, 46,* 634–645.

Donnellan, M. B., Trzesniewski, K. H., & Robins, R. W. (2011). Self-esteem: Enduring issues and controversies. In T. Chamorro-Premuzic, S. von Stumm, & A. Furnham (Eds.), *The Wiley-Blackwell handbook of individual differences* (pp. 718–746). Chichester, UK: Wiley-Blackwell.

Donnellan, M. B., Trzesniewski, K. H., & Robins, R. W. (2015). Measures of self-esteem. In G. J. Boyle, D. H. Saklofske, & G. Matthews (Eds.), *Measures of personality and social psychological constructs* (pp. 131–157). London: Elsevier.

Donnellan, M. B., Trzesniewski, K. H., Robins, R. W., Moffitt, T. E., & Caspi, A. (2005). Low self-esteem is related to aggression, antisocial behavior, and delinquency. *Psychological Science, 16,* 328–335.

Duncan, T. E., Duncan, S. C., & Strycker, L. A. (2006). *An introduction to latent variable growth curve modeling: Concepts, issues, and applications.* Mahwah, NJ: Erlbaum.

Eccles, J., Wigfield, A., Harold, R. D., & Blumenfeld, P. (1993). Age and gender differences in children's self- and task perceptions during elementary school. *Child Development, 64,* 830–847.

Erol, R. Y., & Orth, U. (2011). Self-esteem development from age 14 to 30 years: A longitudinal study. *Journal of Personality and Social Psychology, 101,* 607–619.

Fraley, R. C., & Roberts, B. W. (2005). Patterns of continuity: A dynamic model for conceptualizing the stability of individual differences in psychological constructs across the life course. *Psychological Review, 112,* 60–74.

Gentile, B., Twenge, J. M., & Campbell, W. K. (2010). Birth cohort differences in self-esteem, 1988–2008: A cross-temporal meta-analysis. *Review of General Psychology, 14,* 261–268.

Gerstorf, D., Ram, N., Estabrook, R., Schupp, J., Wagner, G. G., & Lindenberger, U. (2008). Life satisfaction shows terminal decline in old age: Longitudinal evidence from the German Socio-Economic Panel Study (SOEP). *Developmental Psychology, 44,* 1148–1159.

Gruenenfelder-Steiger, A. E., Harris, M. A., & Fend, H. A. (2016). Subjective and objective peer approval evaluations and self-esteem development: A test of reciprocal, prospective, and long-term effects. *Developmental Psychology, 52,* 1563–1577.

Hamamura, T., & Septarini, B. G. (2017). Culture and self-esteem over time: A cross-temporal meta-analysis among Australians, 1978–2014. *Social Psychological and Personality Science, 8,* 904–909.

Haney, P., & Durlak, J. A. (1998). Changing self-esteem in children and adolescents: A meta-analytic review. *Journal of Clinical Child Psychology, 27,* 423–433.

Harris, M. A., Donnellan, M. B., Guo, J., McAdams, D. P., Garnier-Villarreal, M., & Trzesniewski, K. H. (2017). Parental co-construction of 5–13-year-olds' global self-esteem through reminiscing about past. *Child Development, 88,* 1810–1822.

Harris, M. A., Donnellan, M. B., & Trzesniewski, K. H. (2018). The Lifespan Self-Esteem Scale: Initial validation of a new measure of global self-esteem. *Journal of Personality Assessment, 100,* 84–95.

Harris, M. A., Gruenenfelder-Steiger, A. E., Ferrer, E., Donnellan, M. B., Allemand, M., Fend, H., et al. (2015). Do parents foster self-esteem?: Testing the prospective impact of parent closeness on adolescent self-esteem. *Child Development, 86,* 995–1013.

Harris, M. A., Wetzel, E., Robins, R. W., Donnellan, M. B., & Trzesniewski, K. H. (2018). The development of global and domain self-esteem from ages 10 to 16 for Mexican-origin youth. *International Journal of Behavioral Development, 42,* 4–16.

Harter, S., & Pike, R. (1984). The Pictorial Scale of Perceived Competence and Social Acceptance for Young Children. *Child Development, 55,* 1969–1982.

Heatherton, T. F., & Polivy, J. (1991). Development and validation of a scale for measuring state self-esteem. *Journal of Personality and Social Psychology, 60,* 895–910.

Heine, S. J., Lehman, D. R., Markus, H. R., & Kitayama, S. (1999). Is there a universal need for positive self-regard? *Psychological Review, 106,* 766–794.

Hernández, M. M., Robins, R. W., Widaman, K. F., & Conger, R. D. (2017). Ethnic pride, self-esteem, and school belonging: A reciprocal analysis over time. *Developmental Psychology, 53,* 2384–2396.

Huang, C. (2010). Mean-level change in self-esteem from childhood through adulthood: Meta-analysis of longitudinal studies. *Review of General Psychology, 14,* 251–260.

Hutteman, R., Hennecke, M., Orth, U., Reitz, A. K., & Specht, J. (2014). Developmental tasks as a framework to study personality development in adulthood and old age. *European Journal of Personality, 28,* 267–278.

James, W. (1890). *The principles of psychology* (Vol. 1). New York: Holt.

Johnson, M. D., & Galambos, N. L. (2014). Paths to intimate relationship quality from parent–adolescent relations and mental health. *Journal of Marriage and Family, 76,* 145–160.

Judge, T. A., & Bono, J. E. (2001). Relationship of core self-evaluations traits—self-esteem, generalized self-efficacy, locus of control, and emotional stability—with job satisfaction and job performance: A meta-analysis. *Journal of Applied Psychology, 86,* 80–92.

Kendler, K. S., Gardner, C. O., & Prescott, C. A. (1998). A population-based twin study of self-esteem and gender. *Psychological Medicine, 28,* 1403–1409.

Kenny, D. A., & Zautra, A. (1995). The trait–state–error model for multiwave data. *Journal of Consulting and Clinical Psychology, 63,* 52–59.

Kenny, D. A., & Zautra, A. (2001). Trait-state models for longitudinal data. In L. M. Collins & A. G. Sayer (Eds.), *New methods for the analysis of change* (pp. 243–263). Washington, DC: American Psychological Association.

Kiviruusu, O., Huurre, T., Aro, H., Marttunen, M., & Haukkala, A. (2015). Self-esteem growth trajectory from adolescence to mid-adulthood and its predictors in adolescence. *Advances in Life Course Research, 23,* 29–43.

Kling, K. C., Hyde, J. S., Showers, C. J., & Buswell, B. N. (1999). Gender differences in self-esteem: A meta-analysis. *Psychological Bulletin, 125,* 470–500.

Krueger, J. I., Vohs, K. D., & Baumeister, R. F. (2008). Is the allure of self-esteem a mirage after all? *American Psychologist, 63,* 64–65.

Kuster, F., & Orth, U. (2013). The long-term stability of self-esteem: Its time-dependent decay and nonzero asymptote. *Personality and Social Psychology Bulletin, 39,* 677–690.

Kuster, F., Orth, U., & Meier, L. L. (2012). Rumination mediates the prospective effect of low self-esteem on depression: A five-wave longitudinal study. *Personality and Social Psychology Bulletin, 38,* 747–759.

Kuster, F., Orth, U., & Meier, L. L. (2013). High self-esteem prospectively predicts better work conditions and outcomes. *Social Psychological and Personality Science, 4,* 668–675.

Kuzucu, Y., Bontempo, D. E., Hofer, S. M., Stallings, M. C., & Piccinin, A. M. (2014). Developmental change and time-specific variation in global and specific aspects of self-concept in adolescence and association with depressive symptoms. *Journal of Early Adolescence, 34,* 638–666.

Leary, M. R. (2004). The sociometer, self-esteem, and the regulation of interpersonal behavior. In R. F. Baumeister & K. D. Vohs (Eds.), *Handbook of self-regulation* (pp. 373–391). New York: Guilford Press.

Leary, M. R. (2012). Sociometer theory. In P. A. M. Van Lange, A. W. Kruglanski, & E. T. Higgins (Eds.), *Handbook of theories of social psychology* (pp. 141–159). Thousand Oaks, CA: SAGE.

Leary, M. R., & Baumeister, R. F. (2000). The nature and function of self-esteem: Sociometer theory. In M. P. Zanna (Ed.), *Advances in experimental social psychology* (Vol. 32, pp. 1–62). San Diego, CA: Academic Press.

Lucas, R. E., & Donnellan, M. B. (2011). Personality development across the life span: Longitudinal analyses with a national sample from Germany. *Journal of Personality and Social Psychology, 101,* 847–861.

Luciano, E. C., & Orth, U. (2016). *The life-span development of domain-specific self-esteem and its relation with global self-esteem.* Manuscript submitted for publication.

Luciano, E. C., & Orth, U. (2017). Transitions in romantic relationships and development of self-esteem. *Journal of Personality and Social Psychology, 112,* 307–328.

MacDonald, G., & Leary, M. R. (2012). Individual differences in self-esteem. In M. R. Leary & J. P. Tangney (Eds.), *Handbook of self and identity* (pp. 354–377). New York: Guilford Press.

Major, B., Barr, L., Zubek, J., & Babey, S. H. (1999). Gender and self-esteem: A meta-analysis. In W. B. Swann, J. H. Langlois, & L. A. Gilbert (Eds.), *Sexism and stereotypes in modern society: The gender science of Janet Taylor Spence* (pp. 223–253). Washington, DC: American Psychological Association.

Markus, H. R., & Kitayama, S. (1991). Culture and the self: Implications for cognition, emotion, and motivation. *Psychological Review, 98,* 224–253.

Marsh, H. W. (1989). Age and sex effects in multiple dimensions of self-concept: Preadolescence to early adulthood. *Journal of Educational Psychology, 81,* 417–430.

Marsh, H. W., Barnes, J., Cairns, L., & Tidman, M. (1984). Self-Description Questionnaire: Age and sex effects in the structure and level of self-concept for preadolescent children. *Journal of Educational Psychology, 76,* 940–956.

Marsh, H. W., & Yeung, A. S. (1998). Top-down, bottom-up, and horizontal models: The direction of causality in multidimensional, hierarchical self-concept models. *Journal of Personality and Social Psychology, 75,* 509–527.

Marshall, S. L., Parker, P. D., Ciarrochi, J., & Heaven, P. C. L. (2014). Is self-esteem a cause or consequence of social support?: A 4-year longitudinal study. *Child Development, 85,* 1275–1291.

Marvin, R. S., & Britner, P. A. (2008). Normative development: The ontogeny of attachment. In J. Cassidy & P. R. Shaver (Eds.), *Handbook of attachment: Theory, research, and clinical applications* (2nd ed., pp. 269–294). New York: Guilford Press.

McGuire, S., Neiderhiser, J. M., Reiss, D., Hetherington, E. M., & Plomin, R. (1994). Genetic and environmental influences on perceptions of self-worth and competence in adolescence: A study of twins, full siblings, and step-siblings. *Child Development, 65,* 785–799.

Mead, G. H. (1934). *Mind, self and society from the standpoint of a social behaviorist.* Chicago: University of Chicago Press.

Meier, L. L., Orth, U., Denissen, J. J. A., & Kühnel, A.

(2011). Age differences in instability, contingency, and level of self-esteem across the life span. *Journal of Research in Personality, 45,* 604–612.

Mund, M., Finn, C., Hagemeyer, B., Zimmermann, J., & Neyer, F. J. (2015). The dynamics of self-esteem in partner relationships. *European Journal of Personality, 29,* 235–249.

Murray, S. L., Rose, P., Bellavia, G. M., Holmes, J. G., & Kusche, A. G. (2002). When rejection stings: How self-esteem constrains relationship-enhancing processes. *Journal of Personality and Social Psychology, 83,* 556–573.

Neiss, M. B., Sedikides, C., & Stevenson, J. (2002). Self-esteem: A behavioural genetic perspective. *European Journal of Personality, 16,* 351–367.

Neiss, M. B., Stevenson, J., Legrand, L. N., Iacono, W. G., & Sedikides, C. (2009). Self-esteem, negative emotionality, and depression as a common temperamental core: A study of mid-adolescent twin girls. *Journal of Personality, 77,* 327–346.

O'Mara, A. J., Marsh, H. W., Craven, R. G., & Debus, R. L. (2006). Do self-concept interventions make a difference?: A synergistic blend of construct validation and meta-analysis. *Educational Psychologist, 41,* 181–206.

Orth, U. (2018). The family environment in early childhood has a long-term effect on self-esteem: A longitudinal study from birth to age 27 years. *Journal of Personality and Social Psychology, 114,* 637–655.

Orth, U., Erol, R. Y., Ledermann, T., & Grob, A. (2018). Co-development of well-being and self-esteem in romantic partners: Disentangling the effects of mutual influence and shared environment. *Developmental Psychology, 54,* 151–166.

Orth, U., Erol, R. Y., & Luciano, E. C. (2018). Development of self-esteem from age 4 to 94 years: A meta-analysis of longitudinal studies. *Psychological Bulletin, 144,* 1045–1080.

Orth, U., & Luciano, E. C. (2015). Self-esteem, narcissism, and stressful life events: Testing for selection and socialization. *Journal of Personality and Social Psychology, 109,* 707–721.

Orth, U., Maes, J., & Schmitt, M. (2015). Self-esteem development across the life span: A longitudinal study with a large sample from Germany. *Developmental Psychology, 51,* 248–259.

Orth, U., & Robins, R. W. (2013). Understanding the link between low self-esteem and depression. *Current Directions in Psychological Science, 22,* 455–460.

Orth, U., & Robins, R. W. (2014). The development of self-esteem. *Current Directions in Psychological Science, 23,* 381–387.

Orth, U., Robins, R. W., Meier, L. L., & Conger, R. D. (2016). Refining the vulnerability model of low self-esteem and depression: Disentangling the effects of genuine self-esteem and narcissism. *Journal of Personality and Social Psychology, 110,* 133–149.

Orth, U., Robins, R. W., & Roberts, B. W. (2008). Low self-esteem prospectively predicts depression in adolescence and young adulthood. *Journal of Personality and Social Psychology, 95,* 695–708.

Orth, U., Robins, R. W., & Widaman, K. F. (2012). Life-span development of self-esteem and its effects on important life outcomes. *Journal of Personality and Social Psychology, 102,* 1271–1288.

Orth, U., Trzesniewski, K. H., & Robins, R. W. (2010). Self-esteem development from young adulthood to old age: A cohort-sequential longitudinal study. *Journal of Personality and Social Psychology, 98,* 645–658.

Paulhus, D. L., Robins, R. W., Trzesniewski, K. H., & Tracy, J. L. (2004). Two replicable suppressor situations in personality research. *Multivariate Behavioral Research, 39,* 303–328.

Pelham, B. W., & Swann, W. B. (1989). From self-conceptions to self-worth: On the sources and structure of global self-esteem. *Journal of Personality and Social Psychology, 57,* 672–680.

Pettit, J. W., & Joiner, T. E. (2001). Negative life events predict negative feedback seeking as a function of impact on self-esteem. *Cognitive Therapy and Research, 25,* 733–741.

Preacher, K. J., Wichman, A. L., MacCallum, R. C., & Briggs, N. E. (2008). *Latent growth curve modeling.* Los Angeles: SAGE.

Reitz, A. K., Motti-Stefanidi, F., & Asendorpf, J. B. (2016). Me, us, and them: Testing sociometer theory in a socially diverse real-life context. *Journal of Personality and Social Psychology, 110,* 908–920.

Rieger, S., Göllner, R., Trautwein, U., & Roberts, B. W. (2016). Low self-esteem prospectively predicts depression in the transition to young adulthood: A replication of Orth, Robins, and Roberts (2008). *Journal of Personality and Social Psychology, 110,* e16–e22.

Roberts, B. W., & DelVecchio, W. F. (2000). The rank-order consistency of personality traits from childhood to old age: A quantitative review of longitudinal studies. *Psychological Bulletin, 126,* 3–25.

Roberts, B. W., & Nickel, L. B. (2021). Personality development across the life course: A neo-socioanalytic perspective. In O. P. John & R. W. Robins (Eds.), *Handbook of personality: Theory and research* (4th ed., pp. 259–283). New York: Guilford Press.

Roberts, B. W., & Wood, D. (2006). Personality development in the context of the neo-socioanalytic model of personality. In D. K. Mroczek & T. D. Little (Eds.), *Handbook of personality development* (pp. 11–39). Mahwah, NJ: Erlbaum.

Robins, R. W., Hendin, H. M., & Trzesniewski, K. H. (2001). Measuring global self-esteem: Construct validation of a single-item measure and the Rosenberg Self-Esteem Scale. *Personality and Social Psychology Bulletin, 27,* 151–161.

Robins, R. W., Trzesniewski, K. H., Tracy, J. L., Gosling, S. D., & Potter, J. (2002). Global self-esteem across the life span. *Psychology and Aging, 17,* 423–434.

Rosenberg, M. (1965). *Society and the adolescent self-image.* Princeton, NJ: Princeton University Press.

Schaffhuser, K., Wagner, J., Lüdtke, O., & Allemand,

M. (2014). Dyadic longitudinal interplay between personality and relationship satisfaction: A focus on neuroticism and self-esteem. *Journal of Research in Personality, 53,* 124–133.

Shaw, B. A., Liang, J., & Krause, N. (2010). Age and race differences in the trajectory of self-esteem. *Psychology and Aging, 25,* 84–94.

Sowislo, J. F., & Orth, U. (2013). Does low self-esteem predict depression and anxiety?: A meta-analysis of longitudinal studies. *Psychological Bulletin, 139,* 213–240.

Specht, J., Bleidorn, W., Denissen, J. J. A., Hennecke, M., Hutteman, R., Kandler, C., et al. (2014). What drives adult personality development?: A comparison of theoretical perspectives and empirical evidence. *European Journal of Personality, 28,* 216–230.

Specht, J., Egloff, B., & Schmukle, S. C. (2011). Stability and change of personality across the life course: The impact of age and major life events on mean-level and rank-order stability of the Big Five. *Journal of Personality and Social Psychology, 101,* 862–882.

Srivastava, S., & Beer, J. S. (2005). How self-evaluations relate to being liked by others: Integrating sociometer and attachment perspectives. *Journal of Personality and Social Psychology, 89,* 966–977.

Steiger, A. E., Allemand, M., Robins, R. W., & Fend, H. A. (2014). Low and decreasing self-esteem during adolescence predict adult depression two decades later. *Journal of Personality and Social Psychology, 106,* 325–338.

Swann, W. B., Chang-Schneider, C., & McClarty, K. L. (2007). Do people's self-views matter? *American Psychologist, 62,* 84–94.

Swann, W. B., Chang-Schneider, C., & McClarty, K. L. (2008). Yes, cavalier attitudes can have pernicious consequences. *American Psychologist, 63,* 65–66.

Tafarodi, R. W., & Swann, W. B. (1995). Self-liking and self-competence as dimensions of global self-esteem: Initial validation of a measure. *Journal of Personality Assessment, 65,* 322–342.

Tetzner, J., Becker, M., & Baumert, J. (2016). Still doing fine?: The interplay of negative life events and self-esteem during young adulthood. *European Journal of Personality, 30,* 358–373.

Tracy, J. L., Cheng, J. T., Robins, R. W., & Trzesniewski, K. H. (2009). Authentic and hubristic pride: The affective core of self-esteem and narcissism. *Self and Identity, 8,* 196–213.

Trzesniewski, K. H., & Donnellan, M. B. (2010). Rethinking "Generation Me": A study of cohort effects from 1976–2006. *Perspectives on Psychological Science, 5,* 58–75.

Trzesniewski, K. H., Donnellan, M. B., Moffitt, T. E., Robins, R. W., Poulton, R., & Caspi, A. (2006). Low self-esteem during adolescence predicts poor health, criminal behavior, and limited economic prospects during adulthood. *Developmental Psychology, 42,* 381–390.

Trzesniewski, K. H., Donnellan, M. B., & Robins, R. W.

(2003). Stability of self-esteem across the life span. *Journal of Personality and Social Psychology, 84,* 205–220.

Twenge, J. M. (2006). *Generation Me: Why today's young Americans are more confident, assertive, entitled—and more miserable than ever before.* New York: Free Press.

Twenge, J. M., & Campbell, W. K. (2001). Age and birth cohort differences in self-esteem: A cross-temporal meta-analysis. *Personality and Social Psychology Review, 5,* 321–344.

Twenge, J. M., & Campbell, W. K. (2002). Self-esteem and socioeconomic status: A meta-analytic review. *Personality and Social Psychology Review, 6,* 59–71.

Twenge, J. M., Carter, N. T., & Campbell, W. K. (2017). Age, time period, and birth cohort differences in self-esteem: Reexamining a cohort-sequential longitudinal study. *Journal of Personality and Social Psychology, 112,* e9–e17.

Twenge, J. M., Konrath, S., Foster, J. D., Campbell, W. K., & Bushman, B. J. (2008). Egos inflating over time: A cross-temporal meta-analysis of the Narcissistic Personality Inventory. *Journal of Personality, 76,* 875–901.

van Scheppingen, M. A., Denissen, J. J. A., Chung, J. M., Tambs, K., & Bleidorn, W. (2018). Self-esteem and relationship satisfaction during the transition to motherhood. *Journal of Personality and Social Psychology, 114,* 973–991.

von Soest, T., Wagner, J., Hansen, T., & Gerstorf, D. (2018). Self-esteem across the second half of life: The role of socioeconomic status, physical health, social relationships, and personality factors. *Journal of Personality and Social Psychology, 114,* 945–958.

von Soest, T., Wichstrøm, L., & Kvalem, I. L. (2016). The development of global and domain-specific self-esteem from age 13 to 31. *Journal of Personality and Social Psychology, 110,* 592–608.

Wagner, J., Becker, M., Lüdtke, O., & Trautwein, U. (2015). The first partnership experience and personality development: A propensity score matching study in young adulthood. *Social Psychological and Personality Science, 6,* 455–463.

Wagner, J., Gerstorf, D., Hoppmann, C., & Luszcz, M. A. (2013). The nature and correlates of self-esteem trajectories in late life. *Journal of Personality and Social Psychology, 105,* 139–153.

Wagner, J., Hoppmann, C., Ram, N., & Gerstorf, D. (2015). Self-esteem is relatively stable late in life: The role of resources in the health, self-regulation, and social domains. *Developmental Psychology, 51,* 136–149.

Wagner, J., Lang, F. R., Neyer, F. J., & Wagner, G. G. (2014). Self-esteem across adulthood: The role of resources. *European Journal of Ageing, 11,* 109–119.

Wagner, J., Lüdtke, O., Jonkmann, K., & Trautwein, U. (2013). Cherish yourself: Longitudinal patterns and conditions of self-esteem change in the transition to young adulthood. *Journal of Personality and Social Psychology, 104,* 148–163.

Wagner, J., Lüdtke, O., & Trautwein, U. (2016). Self-esteem is mostly stable across young adulthood: Evidence from latent STARTS models. *Journal of Personality, 84,* 523–535.

Watson, D., Suls, J., & Haig, J. (2002). Global self-esteem in relation to structural models of personality and affectivity. *Journal of Personality and Social Psychology, 83,* 185–197.

Wetzel, E., Donnellan, M. B., Robins, R. W., & Trzesniewski, K. H. (2018). Generational changes in self-esteem and narcissism. In V. Zeigler-Hill & T. K. Shackelford (Eds.), *The SAGE handbook of personality and individual differences* (pp. 132–145). Thousand Oaks, CA: SAGE.

Wouters, S., Duriez, B., Luyckx, K., Klimstra, T., Colpin, H., Soenens, B., et al. (2013). Depressive symptoms in university freshmen: Longitudinal relations with contingent self-esteem and level of self-esteem. *Journal of Research in Personality, 47,* 356–363.

Wylie, R. C. (1979). *The self-concept.* Lincoln: University of Nebraska Press.

Zeiders, K. H., Umaña-Taylor, A. J., & Derlan, C. L. (2013). Trajectories of depressive symptoms and self-esteem in Latino youths: Examining the role of gender and perceived discrimination. *Developmental Psychology, 49,* 951–963.

Zuckerman, M., Li, C., & Hall, J. A. (2016). When men and women differ in self-esteem and when they don't: A meta-analysis. *Journal of Research in Personality, 64,* 34–51.

CHAPTER 20

Moral Development and Moral Values

Evolutionary and Neurobiological Influences

Darcia Narvaez

Morality covers the gamut of life—every action is governed by values—whether those we have chosen or those we have implicitly absorbed. Our morality is shaped by multiple factors: what we inherit, where we habitually put our attention, what actions we choose, and the perceptual sensitivities and capacities we develop from how we were raised. All these shape our values and character. As a result, the study of moral development requires a transdisciplinary and transmethodological approach. Disciplinary contributions from evolutionary systems theory, clinical studies, and developmental and personality research each provide insight into the moral development of humanity. Methodologies of study must also be broad and address both a universalist and an individual-difference approach. The former seeks to find basic patterns across humanity—individuals and societies—whereas the latter takes into account the diversity of influences on the development of an individual's moral dispositions. In this chapter, contributions from multiple disciplines and methods are included in an examination of the development of moral values.

The Study of Moral Valuing

To begin, let's examine a little history, from moral judgment research to values lists, then delve more pointedly into the underlying nature and development of moral values.

Most research in moral developmental psychology has focused on isolated aspects of moral functioning in individuals, such as moral reasoning and decision making in the face of hypothetical dilemmas (e.g., Kohlberg, 1984; Haidt, 2001; Turiel, 1983). For some decades, under the influence of moral philosophical concerns, moral developmental psychology focused on moral reasoning development under the theoretical direction of Lawrence Kohlberg and his (mis)interpretation of Jean Piaget (i.e., "hard stage" theory; Lapsley, 2006). Kohlberg (1984) studied the development of justice-based valuing through the assessment of moral judgment and reasoning, emphasizing a deontological framing of morality—what comprised one's duty according to logical rationality (Kant, 1949). But Kohlberg was also keen to distinguish among different sets of values and, in particular, to defeat moral relativism. He wanted to demonstrate empirically the moral superiority of the lawbreaking actions of civil rights leaders such as Martin Luther King, Jr., and the moral inferiority of the law-upholding actions of an Adolf Hitler. His system assessed the developmental shifts from preconventional to conventional to postconventional reasoning (where Martin Luther King, Jr.'s reasoning is categorized). Empirical studies of Kohlberg and the neo-Kohlbergian orientations that followed show, with little doubt, that cognitive maturation in interaction with intensive and variable social experience leads to greater sophisticated reasoning, especially when measured in tacit ways, such as with recognition measures, instead of with measures dependent on verbal fluency (Rest, 1979; Rest, Narvaez, Bebeau, & Thoma, 1999). We might say that Kohlberg's work was intended to measure moral values of intellectual thought—as measured by rationales given for preferred actions in response to hypothetical moral dilemmas. Kohlberg assumed that at the highest stage, an individual's thought and action would align. But empirical evidence was thin for a relation between reasoning capacities and actual action. Noting the gap between making a judgment about what should be done and action taken, broader conceptualizations of the propellants of moral behavior, such as moral personality, were proposed (e.g., Blasi, 1983). Indeed, subsequent research has demonstrated that self-reported second-order desires (Frankfurt, 1988), desires about what desires to have—one's moral identity—influence one's behavior beyond moral reasoning or judgment (Aquino & Reed, 2002).

In another line of research examining the types of values individuals profess, Rokeach (1979) identified lists of terminal values (e.g., a world of beauty, wisdom) and instrumental values (e.g., love, obedience), and determined that individuals prioritize them differently. More recently and more systematically, Schwartz (1992, 2005) identified a set of 10 values, tested them in 67 countries, and found similar distinctive structures across nations, and different cultural motivational patterns. The values are placed into four main categories: *openness to change* includes self-direction and stimulation; *self-enhancement* includes hedonism, achievement, and power; *conservation* is described by security, conformity, and tradition; *self-enhancement* embraces benevolence and universalism. Also interested in cultural differences and based on Shweder's (1993) earlier work contrasting the United States and India, Haidt (2012) focused attention on group differences in five (then six) values that he called moral foundations: Though most ethical traditions emphasize *fairness* and *caring* for others, values of *liberty, purity, hierarchy,* and *ingroup* over outgroup are also highly prized by some individuals and groups. In fact, the latter values have been associated with American political conservatives (Gra-

ham, Haidt, & Nosek, 2009); however it is notable that the content of such items are shaped according to the particular interests of Christian conservatives (Suhler & Churchland, 2011).

Values list studies demonstrate that individual differences in value priority vary by nationality and political orientation. However, just because particular values are favorably *endorsed* does not mean that individuals *act* on those values in particular situations. Similar to the judgment–action gap, there is often a value–action gap. For example, social desirability inflates self-reports of religious service attendance (Presser & Stinson, 1998), reflecting prescriptive values rather than being descriptive of actual behavior, which is much lower, when time diaries are used in data collection (Brenner, 2011). This value–action gap is well described by J. D. Vance in his book *Hillbilly Elegy* (2016), in which he chronicles his upbringing in Kentucky. There, values of hard work, church attendance, and Christian behavior are widely espoused by community members yet also widely absent in those same people's behavior.

As mentioned, Kohlberg's (1984) enterprise was driven by philosophical frames of explicit reasoning and moral intention as fundamental to an individual's moral functioning. Values list prioritization studies are explicit tasks as well. The study of explicit, verbalizable discourse has shown its limitations with the discoordination between advocacy and actual behavior. This is not a surprise, as psychology research has shifted paradigms from a focus on the explicit to a focus on the implicit, understanding that most human functioning emerges from automatic tacit processes not accessible to verbal explanation or, sometimes, awareness (Bargh & Chartrand, 1999; Reber, 1993). Which tacit processes guide behavior, including moral behavior, can change by situation in a unique person-by-context signature (Lapsley & Narvaez, 2004; Narvaez & Lapsley, 2005). Let's bear these issues in mind as we examine morality in more detail.

What Influences Moral Values?

What is a moral value? In this chapter, a moral value is a perceptual–action feature of our behavior, which can change situation by situation and moment by moment. Our actions are always guided by what we perceive to be good in the moment. For example, if someone we like makes a joke at our expense, we take it as friendly teasing, but if someone we don't like does the same thing, we are insulted. Or, if we become upset after someone cuts us off in traffic, lashing out in anger can feel like a fair or just action—tit for tat—a common reaction in a culture of honor, in which feelings that one was disrespected incite retaliatory behavior (Nisbett & Cohen, 1996; Vance, 2016). In contrast, when we maintain a mood of gratitude, we are more likely to help others (Moore & Isen, 1990; Morris, 1989). Strikingly, within an Amish community with cultural practices of humility and grace, community leaders swiftly forgave the actions of a neighbor who held their daughters hostage, executed five and seriously wounded five others (before killing himself; Kraybill, Nolt, & Weaver-Zercher, 2008). Values are reflected in the moods and mindsets we bring to a situation. Actions are guided by not only momentary valuing but also our habitual choices about what looks good and feels right, by the schemas we develop to filter events and guide expectations (Taylor & Crocker, 1981). For example, if we were brought up in a religious tradition, we likely learned to express gratitude before a meal. We learned to expect thankfulness in our own behavior and that of others. Then, when thankfulness is not forthcoming in self or others, we sense a violation of morals. In this way, our cultural upbringing influences the moral values and expectations we carry with us.

Like all animals, we operate in a flow of action (Bogdan, 1994; Varela, Thompson, & Rosch, 1991). Most of these guiding forces are implicitly held. Hence the importance of how well cultivated one's habits, characteristic dispositions and intuitions are (Hogarth, 2001). Many human decisions and actions are carried out automatically and without conscious control, based on social–perceptual habits and environmental press (e.g., Bargh & Chartrand, 1999), with many neurobiological layers that influence tacit conceptions but are not available to explicit description (Keil & Wilson, 2000). The subconscious mind, which guides our actions most of the time, has its own associative rationality, responding to familiar situational patterns (Damasio, 1999). This "adaptive unconscious" (Hassin, Uleman, & Bargh, 2005; Wilson, 2004) is rooted in subcortical emotion systems that we inherit as adaptations from our ancestors, which, to be good guides, must be shaped well by early experience with our caregivers (Panksepp & Biven, 2011). In other words, as I discuss

further below, individual moral development is initially shaped by the community. Through our experience with caregivers and the caregiving environment as babies and small children, we develop the sensorimotor and neurobiological intelligence that undergird our social and self-habits that we carry forward into the rest of life (Siegel, 1999; Stern, 1985). In early life, these experiences actually mold the very plastic but immature neurobiology humans arrive with at birth, a neurobiology that expects particular supports to develop well. These neurobiological foundations continue to shape preferences and values, undergirding social and moral life. Below, I examine these ideas more fully.

Influences on Moral Values

Let's examine two general sets of influences on the development of moral values. These comprise aspects of *ethogenetic theory,* which uses an evolutionary developmental systems perspective to describe how moral dispositions are rooted in neurobiological structures that are biosocially shaped by early experience and how those structures influence later moral orientations and behavior (Narvaez, 2014, 2016, 2018). See Figure 20.1 for a summary of both sets of influences. One I call *vertical* influences—how a certain person's life is shaped. Most of the time, psychology researchers focus here, on understanding how moral values emerge or change through childhood or what kinds of influences engrave the life of the individual. The second set of influences on moral values concerns the *horizontal* influences (across generations). Horizontal influences are inherited through evolutionary processes occurring over millions of years, including both genetic and nongenetic inheritances (e.g., capacities for self-organization), as well as ancestral history (e.g., one's grandparents' experiences influences on one's genetic expression or phenotype) (Gluckman & Hanson, 2005). Research in anthropology, biological, and evolutionary sciences provide insights here. For example, the field of behavioral epigenetics has demonstrated that some traits considered genetic (e.g., anxiety) are often epigenetic, effected by one's own early experience or the experience of recent ancestors (Dias & Ressler, 2013; Meaney, 2001).

Both types of influences, vertical and horizontal, interact within the life course of an individual to create the nature of the person. We

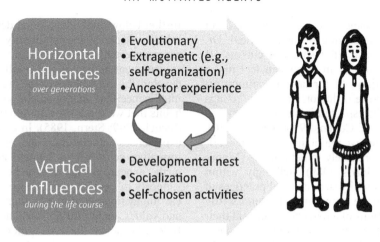

FIGURE 20.1. Ethogenetic theory: Horizontal and vertical influences on an individual's development.

start with the horizontal, the inheritances from ancestors.

Horizontal Influences

In this section, I examine evolutionary inheritances that humanity receives. These include a deeply cooperative natural world, the evolved moral sense and the evolved nest.

Human beings live on a planet of beings that are highly interdependent, where many entities evolved to give and take in an endless, ever-renewing cycle of mutualism (Bronstein, 2015; Worster, 1994). "Genes cooperate in genomes; cells cooperate in tissues; individuals cooperate in societies" (Rubenstein & Kealey, 2010, p. 78). (Yes, as Darwin [1859/1962] noted, there is competition in nature—a common focus of male scholars [Gross & Averill, 2003]—but it plays a relatively minor role in the everyday workings of the biosphere that is largely symbiotic [Margulis, 1998].) One animal sloughs off its skin or other matter and another animal uses it for homebuilding or nourishment. The extensive cooperation within biological systems is of ongoing research interest. For example, in forests, old trees nourish the young—even of other species (Wohlleben, 2016); in soil, a dynamic heterogenous environment, there is greater biodiversity than among the life forms that live above the soil (Ohlson, 2014). Cooperation is so fundamental that in the natural world, very little changes across generations—most of what exists in one generation is conserved into the next

(Margulis, 1998). Indeed, humans are part of the tree of life, sharing characteristics with species that emerged billions of years ago. For example, as Neil Shubin points out in *Your Inner Fish: A Journey into the 3.5-Billion-Year History of the Human Body* (2009), the spinal column that humans share with other vertebrates evolved more than 500 million years ago (humans have been around for about 2 million years). Human bodies are themselves communities of cooperation, whose genetic material consists primarily (90–99%) of the genes of the trillions of microorganisms that form the microbiota that keep a human body alive (Collen, 2015; Dunn, 2011). In other words, we emerged *from* cooperative systems and we *are* cooperative systems. "Within our cells, the mitochondria that provide energy are descended from free-living bacteria that gave up their autonomy for a cooperative existence" (Denison & Muller, 2016, p. 41).

Humans are assumed to have emerged from evolutionary processes taking place over billions of years, inheriting many things beyond genes (Jablonka & Lamb, 2005). Based on ethological and evolutionary sciences that gather and compare observations, *evolutionary systems theory* offers a comprehensive list of human inheritances that include culture, the ecological landscape, and self-organization (Griffiths & Gray, 2001; Oyama, 2000a, 2000b). Within a lifespan, the individual will self-organize around the opportunities and supports provided. A key inheritance directly related to moral values is the "moral sense."

The Evolved Moral Sense

Darwin (1871/1981) came to the idea of the moral sense because he sought to counter theorists who argued that humans evolved to be selfish. Instead, he identified components of a "moral sense" through the tree of life in order to show that morality was *not contrary but fundamental to* human nature. The set of characteristics—empathy, social pleasure, concern for the opinion of others, memory for plans and outcomes in relation to pleasing the community, and intentional self-control to fit in socially—can be seen here and there in other animals. Recent experiments support Darwin's observation of animals. For example, rats will help a trapped peer instead of eating their favorite snack, chocolate (Ben-Ami Bartal, Decety, & Mason, 2011). But Darwin contended that the moral sense culminates in human beings. If we understand that it is normal, based on ethological evidence, for humans to display the moral sense described, then we should ask why some people act with an "immoral sense." How does a group of humans *lose* the moral sense?

Unfortunately, the opposite assumptions and questions have been asked by scholars. As Ho (2010, p. 67) points out, contrary to Darwin's views, neo-Darwinian theory emphasizes the competitive selfishness of humanity (which was presumably constructed by sociopolitical attitudes: "Victorian English society preoccupied with competition and the free market, with capitalist and imperialist exploitation"). Others have pointed out the androcentric nature of neo-Darwinian theory as well (Longino, 1990). The neo-Darwinian view, grounded in unverified assumptions, resulted in the presumably paradoxical question "How could altruistic behavior evolve (given that genes and the behavior they control are fundamentally selfish)?" Instead, based on evidence across nature, including humanity, the question should be inverted: "Why do humans compete, given their natural sociality?" And, one could extend the question: "Why do humans behave in selfish, aggressive ways when the moral sense is part of their heritage?" Moreover, when we look more closely, we see that across societies, the moral sense seems to vary in scope: Some societies show moral concern only for a subset of humans or, in many First Nations societies, include more-than-human entities (e.g., animals, plants, rivers). If the moral sense evolved, why such variability?

An answer is emerging. It now appears that the moral sense is largely developed *after* birth and requires particular kinds of experience, specifically humanity's evolved nest. I discuss this in the next sections.

We can think of moral development like Leo Tolstoy's discussion of happy and unhappy families in his novel *Anna Karenina*. He noted, to paraphrase, that happy families are all alike but unhappy families are all unique. Similarly, moral flourishing looks similar across individuals as a form of dynamic, high-minded, self-controlled, flexible, selfless sociality with resilience (e.g., making amends) when setbacks occur. Harry Potter is a fictional exemplar of these capacities. Nelson Mandela exemplified a real person who characterized this type of moral resilience. For example, he was able to move past his anger and reconcile with his enemies even while spending 27 years as a political prisoner in his country of South Africa. In contrast, as with unhappy families, there are multiple ways for individual moral development to "go wrong" (which perhaps makes them more interesting as characters). There are individuals who do not display the evolved moral sense. They are habitually low-minded, caught in fleshly pursuits (Al Bundy in *Married with Children*), impulsively lacking self-control (Homer Simpson from *The Simpsons*), rigidly hierarchical in social relations (Archie Bunker from *All in the Family*), or unable to forgive (George Costanza from *Seinfeld*). In the discussion ahead, I focus on Sheldon Cooper (*The Big Bang Theory*), intellectually gifted but almost asocial, and Francis Underwood (*House of Cards*), ruthless in treatment of others for his own desire for power. You might have noticed that all the characters are male. It turns out that boys are particularly affected by early life care, when neurobiological systems are shaped because they mature more slowly physically, socially, and linguistically, and because they are affected more negatively by early life stress than are girls. As a result, boys are more vulnerable to neuropsychiatric disorders that appear developmentally such as autism, early-onset schizophrenia, attention-deficit/hyperactivity disorder (ADHD), and conduct disorders (Schore, 2017). This may be the reason that boys make for more variable and interesting characters in fiction.

Sheldon Cooper (*The Big Bang Theory*) seems to lack Darwin's moral sense. In terms of behavioral economic theory, his basic social orientation was set to be more egoistic than em-pathic (Cory, 2016). He is not known for desir-ing or displaying its components—empathy, so-cial pleasure, concern for the opinion of others or for pleasing the community. Sheldon displays few social skills and instead shows extensive difficulties with human relationships (and ani-mal relationships for that matter). He is unable to intuitively pick up the emotional signaling of others. Instead, he requires instructed memori-zation of social scripts. He has been told rules for life by his mother and others, and has com-mitted many to memory, but they do not match up with his own anti- or nonsocial intuitions and reactions. Sheldon shows an obsessive–compul-siveness in needing to follow rigid scripts (e.g., where to sit, how to knock on a door) and be-comes discombobulated when interrupted. His sense of superiority, along with his lack of com-mon sense make him an entertaining character, though his self-centeredness make him an irri-tating companion. What might have gone wrong with Sheldon's upbringing? The roots for moral disarray often begin in early childhood, when toxic stress or poor care have greatest impact. Early experience initially shapes moral values by engraving one's neurobiology, influencing one's deep moral values, setting one on a bet-ter or worse trajectory in terms of social–moral development. Enduring states in early life, such as unmitigated distress, become traits—e.g., stress reactivity (Lupien McEwen, Gunnar, & Heim, 2009), and the stress response necessar-ily puts attention on oneself.

Let's start by looking at species-typical de-velopment. Every animal has a nest that opti-mizes development of its young. Humans do too. In fact, one of the most important inheri-tances for the development of moral values (and Darwin's moral sense) may be the evolved nest.

The Evolved Nest

As ethological observation has noted, all ani-mals provide a nest that matches up with the maturational schedule of their young in order to optimize normal development (Gottlieb, 2002; West-Eberhard, 2003). Humans are no different. Humans evolved a particular nest to provide the intensive care that human offspring need (Kon-ner, 2005). Humans are born highly immature compared to other hominids (and should be in the womb at least another 18 months!) (Treva-than, 2011). As a result, most brain development occurs *after* birth. Thus, humans evolved to ex-

pect a particular type of early care (Greenough & Black, 1992). Child well-being requires an in-tense level of support on the part of the mother and community (Bronfenbrenner, 1979), a situ-ation that was available throughout most of hu-manity's existence (Hrdy, 2009).

How do we know what humanity's evolved nest looks like? Substantive evidence comes from extant studies of nomadic foraging com-munities around the world, the type of society in which the human genus spent 99% of its history (Fry, 2006; Hrdy, 2009; Konner, 2005). Nomad-ic foragers raise their children in a similar way wherever they have been observed around the world (Hewlett & Lamb, 2005). Anthropolo-gists summarize the communal caregiving that infants and young children experience across these groups:

> Young children in foraging cultures are nursed frequently; held, touched, or kept near others al-most constantly; frequently cared for by individu-als other than their mothers (fathers and grand-mothers, in particular) though seldom by older siblings; experience prompt responses to their fusses and cries; and enjoy multiage play groups in early childhood. (Hewlett & Lamb, 2005, p. 15)

To this list can be added soothing perinatal experiences and positive social support (Nar-vaez, 2013). How much do these characteristics matter for development? A great deal. It may be best illustrated this way. Think about raising a wolf in a human family: You will end up with a wolf. But if you raise a human in a wolf family, you end up with a wolf-child (as has happened), an individual missing many characteristic human attributes such as walking on their feet instead of all fours, language, and social skills. In other words, humans are greatly affected by their experiences after birth. Though the focus here is on the evolved nest in early life, it should be understood that the evolved developmental system for human beings lasts for several de-cades, as human beings need several decades to mature and need models and mentors along the way.

The evolved nest can be taken as a cross-cultural *baseline* for optimizing normal human development. We should not be surprised that when a child is missing some aspect of the evolved nest, he or she turns out more self-centered or unwell. I discuss the moral develop-mental effects of the evolved nest in following sections.

Vertical Influences
(during an Individual's Life Course)

Vertical influences are those that occur within an individual's life—what the individual experiences him- or herself or creates (after early childhood shapes a self). In this section, I examine how an individual is influenced by experience, especially by the evolved nest. The components of the nest interact with horizontal influences to shape the individual's moral propensities.

But first, like a tourist guide, let me alert you to a couple of issues. Virtually all psychological and neurobiological studies are performed in civilized nations (settled and dependent on forcibly extracting resources from places outside where they live) where rewards and punishments are used to socialize children. The studies are also typically performed in Western-educated populations (those who know how to participate in the games of schooling and of psychological experiments), typically in rich, industrialized nations with some degree of democracy (Henrich, Heine, & Norenzayan, 2010). It turns out that the fact that most studies are performed in *civilized* nations may be the most important fact for our attention here. Most of human history (99%) occurred before history was recorded. It was spent in "unsettled" societies (i.e., small nomadic bands that forage for food [some of which still exist today]; Lee & Daly, 2005). As noted earlier, these societies provided the evolved nest and are immensely different in their assumptions about life, their practices, and attitudes toward one another—all of which interrelate (for a review, see Narvaez, 2013). In these societies, most early learning occurs informally through immersed experience, observation, and practice. Adults are not coercive and everyone is considered to be his or her own person, yet children need no external motivation to follow the practices of those older than they (e.g., Endicott & Endicott, 2014; Morelli, Ivey Henry, & Foerster, 2014).

Before examining what influences moral development, we must ask: What do children bring to their life course? What is innate? It is hard to sort out what moral characteristics are innate in human beings because of the largely unknown effects of conception and gestation on psychological traits, though we do know that maternal depression and stress during pregnancy have epigenetic effects on the child's temperament, increasing irritability (Davis et al.,

2007), as well as on many biological systems, particularly in boys, that influence later psychological functioning (e.g., greater stress reactivity and anhedonia; Mueller & Bale, 2008).

In terms of innate predispositions, socioemotional sensitivity specifically, researchers have observed empathic response to crying peers in neonates, a type of empathy. Hoffman (2000) has mapped the development of empathy from this physiological resonance to graduated awareness of the feelings and states of others through childhood, along with their interest in alleviating others' distress (for a review, see Dunn, 2014). Beyond these early observations of children's empathic responsivity, children's moral value development becomes an interaction between horizontal influences and vertical influences, that is, among evolved needs, biological capacities, prior and ongoing experience. Although studies of babies' moral judgment have indicated that babies have a measurable sense of justice, generally preferring puppets that help others to puppets that hinder others (Bloom, 2013), Jessica Sommerville's (2015) research program demonstrates that although infants generally show a preference for fairness and fair actors, individual differences are related to the degree of the parent's dispositional empathy.

Turning to the evolved nest, we know from animal research that when animals are deprived of an expected experience and sensitive periods are not supported properly, opportunities for expected alterations close (e.g., Harlow, 1958; Meaney, 2001). Complex behaviors (e.g., social skills) are hierarchical and have sequences of sensitive periods for multiple subsystems. "Experience-dependent shaping of high-level circuits cannot occur until the computations being carried out by lower-level circuits have become reliable" (Knudsen, 2004, p. 1414). A particular, sensitive period opens up when there is sufficiently reliable and precise information, when the circuit has adequate connectivity (excitatory and inhibitory) to process information, and mechanisms are activated that allow plasticity. If all these factors are not in place, there will be no effect on the circuit.

Three things are known to occur during a sensitive period. (a) Axons are elaborated, and synapses are formed. (b) Axons and synapses are eliminated based on usage. (c) Synapse consolidation also occurs through cell adhesion mechanisms. A sensitive period ends when "the circuit's landscape becomes resistant to change," which is a permanent feature of *critical* periods (Knudsen, 2004, p. 1417). With the passing of a sensitive period that is not critical, change may occur later but require much more energy (sustained enriched experience). With deprivation, circuits developed during maturational sensitive periods are formed abnormally; unable mechanistically to acquire typical patterns of connectivity, "they never respond appropriately to social signals offered by members of their own species" (Knudsen, 2004, p. 1420). Behavior analysis is typically unable to detect these neuronal deficiencies because higher functions tend to mask lower level abnormalities in information processing, and because often the brain will use an alternative route to make up for deficiencies as much as possible.

What functions are scheduled to develop in early life that undergird morality later? Psychologist Daniel Stern (2010) wondered why babies are not ready to learn to speak until after the first year. He answered his question by noting that babies

> have too much to learn about the basic processes and structures of interpersonal exchange. *In particular, they have to learn the forms of dynamic flow that carry social behavior.* In addition, they have to learn this before language arrives to mess it all up. The basic structures are all non-verbal, analogic, dynamic Gestalts that are not compatible with the discontinuous, digital, categorical nature of words. (p. 110, emphasis added)

Note that initially what is developed is the *implicit* mind, the mind that guides most of human behavior, undergirding dispositional traits and characteristic values and goals. We can see that the implicit mind is initially shaped in early life, shaping social capacities.

Assessments of attachment represent one indicator of how well neurobiological systems were established (Bowlby, 1969/1982, 1988). Schore's (2003b) *regulation theory* contends that attachment represents the right-brain hemisphere's capacities, which develop more rapidly in the first years of life, for regulating biological synchronicity between organisms. Secure attachment is a signal of well-developed, socially significant neurobiology (e.g., vagus nerve function: good vagal tone allows for intimate relationships; Porges, 2011). Insecure attachment signals that neurobiological development has gone awry in some way. The insecurely attached individual has difficulty regulating the

intensity and duration of emotional states (for more detail, see Schore, 2002, 2003b). Dispositions toward social anxiety or avoiding others are reflective of poorly developed vagal tone, stress response, and other self-regulatory systems.

In other words, sociality and morality are rooted in biology—in how well basic biological systems develop, all of which are influenced by the evolved nest (for more detail, see Narvaez, 2014). For example, in early life, the brain's right hemisphere is the formative seat of various systemic forms of self-regulation, such as vagal tone (Porges, 2011; Schore, 2001, 2003a, 2003b). If the evolved nest of support is not provided when expected, these systems can be underdeveloped or malformed, influencing behavior regulation and sociality. Sheldon Cooper of *The Big Bang Theory* shows the type of incapacities that are apparent with right-hemisphere underdevelopment or dysfunction: the inability to quickly pick up nonverbal social cues, awkward social interactions, feeling threatened by intimacy, distress when the unexpected occurs and scripts are not followed (matching the "stiffness of mind" evident in patients with prefrontal lobe damage [Goldberg, 2002], an area that has significant development in the first year of life [Schore, 1994]).

How do the components of the evolved nest influence moral values? As Darwin (1871/1981) noted, adults in "less civilized" societies (than Britain in the 19th century) exhibited the components of the moral sense (societies Darwin encountered on his voyages followed the practices of nomadic foragers). If adult personalities are a measure of cultivated moral values (an integration of bottom-up shaping and top-down cultural values), we can examine the recurring patterns among adults from nomadic foraging societies in which the evolved nest is commonplace. A word of warning: Some modern scholars collapse nomadic foraging data into other types of preindustrial societal data (e.g., complex hunter–gatherers, tribes, chiefdoms), misleading readers about the characteristics of nomadic foragers (e.g., Fry & Söderberg, 2014; Pinker, 2011; see Fry, 2013, for multiple rebuttals). Also, one should remember that most societies are and have been collectivistic rather than individualistic, like the United States and other countries where most psychological research has taken place (Henrich et al., 2010). In collectivistic or communal societies, the emphasis is on maintaining harmonious connection with others, including with young children. Returning to nomadic foraging data, the findings are remarkable. Similar characteristics are noted among the adults when we examine accounts of first- and early-contact diarists (e.g., Spaniards like Columbus) in response to meeting indigenous peoples of the Americas (Siepel, 2015; Turner, 1994), as well as anthropological studies of nomadic foragers in the last century or so (e.g., Fry & Soulliac, 2017; Gowdy, 1998; Ingold, 2005; see Narvaez, 2013, for a review). Across nomadic foraging societies, adult personalities on average are reported to be generous, social, cooperative, egalitarian, and content, with high sense of both communalism and autonomy. In terms of behavior economics theory, their personalities have been set to a more *empathic* than *egoistic* orientation (Cory, 2016). In a recent study of forager–horticulturalists (a non-nomadic people called the Tsimane, who likely provide components of the evolved nest) using Big-Five personality theory (Gurven, von Rueden, Kaplan, & Massenkoff, 2013), researchers found a "big two"—communally oriented factors of prosociality and industry. It appears then that the species-typical development system, the evolved nest, supports the development of prosociality and the evolved moral sense. I examine this linkage further below.

The evolved nest maintains close connection between the child and the caring community. The components of the evolved nest influence all that the child becomes, from physiology to sociality and morality, largely not only because humans are so immature at birth but also because humans are much more shapeable than any other animal through general plasticity and multiple epigenetic effects (mechanisms for activating genes, such as turning them "on" or "off"; Gómez-Robles, Hopkins, Schapiro, & Sherwood, 2015). Neurobiological capacities shaped in early life infuse personality and moral values. When one has an inflexible, easily distressed psychobiology, one is less likely to be openminded or openhearted toward ideas and people who are different. One will be more closed off emotionally or easily shut down by perceived threats (Schore, 2003b). Sheldon Cooper appears to have this type of psychobiology, which I have noted is more likely among boys stressed prenatally and/or postnatally. In contrast, with a flexible, agile neurobiology, one will be socially oriented and maintain calm, or quickly restore it, in the face of new experiences and people.

The neurobiological effects of each nest component on an individual's health and well-being are discussed in detail elsewhere (e.g., Narvaez, Panksepp, Schore, & Gleason, 2013). Our laboratory has been collecting correlational data on the relation of nest components to child well-being and morality using standardized measures of (3- to 5-year-old) children's moral development (Kochanska, 1994) along with validated measures of parenting attitudes and behaviors (Narvaez, Gleason, Lefever, Wang, & Cheng, 2016; Narvaez, Wang, et al., 2013). Here are a couple of examples of what we found using a longitudinal data set of mothers and children observed and tested several times from 4 to 36 months (Narvaez, Gleason, et al., 2013). After controlling for age, income, and education, as well as maternal responsivity (which is routinely correlated with all positive child outcomes), greater affectionate touch throughout the early years was correlated with the development of empathy, self-regulation, conscience, and intelligence. Perhaps most surprising to a modern audience, breastfeeding *initiation* correlated with conscience and intelligence, while breastfeeding *length* correlated with the development of conscience and self-control. These results are not surprising if one understands the content of breast milk—thousands of ingredients tailored to the particular child at the time of ingestion (Karra, Shobha, Udipi, Kirksey, & Roepke, 1986), with building blocks for the immune system and other major systems of the body/brain (Goldman, Goldblum, & Hanson, 1990). The results conform with findings regarding breastfeeding generally. For example, in a study of 14,000 infants, general developmental milestones were reached more quickly the longer exclusive breastfeeding occurred, or to put it another way: the more infant formula consumed instead of breastmilk, the greater the developmental delays (Sacker, Quigley, & Kelly, 2006). Neurobiological research is demonstrating the causal underpinnings of breast milk's effects on neurobehavioral organization and maturation, such as greater myelination among breast-fed children (e.g., Hart, Boylan, Carroll, Musick & Lampe, 2003; Khedr, Farghaly, Sel-D, & Osman, 2004; see Gaber Rizk, 2014, for a review). The effects of breast milk on brain size and white matter were pronounced among boys participating in a randomized feeding trial at preterm birth and brain-scanned in adolescence (Isaacs et al., 2010). Again, boys are more influenced by early experience.

It is not a surprise that components of the evolved nest might have such effects because multiple epigenetic effects take place in the early life of mammals, especially humans, who evolved to expect the intensive care their evolved nest provides (Gómez-Robles et al., 2015; Gudsnuk & Champagne, 2012; Kuzawa & Quinn, 2009). In short, early life experience shapes temperament and dispositions based on the plasticity of the brain–body in early life.

Longitudinal observational studies show that children who experience mutually responsive care in early life are more likely to demonstrate the development of a (prosocial) moral self at 5.5 years old, which includes committed compliance to parental values (demonstrated by following those values when the child is alone); this moral self in turn mediates socially engaged, competent, and prosocial behavior at age 6.5 (Kochanska, Koenig, Barry, Kim, & Yoon, 2010). Thus, we can see how dispositional traits are shaped initially implicitly, with neurobiological engravings of trust or distrust (Erikson, 1950), according to the nature of early care, and then elaborated with more deliberate family and cultural practices. These dispositions include implicit schemas of self (e.g., good–bad), relationships (trustworthy or not) and the nature of the world (safe–unsafe) (Narvaez, 2014). The moral self emerges from the habitual activation of moral schemas through reciprocal social experience, habitual family practices, and from attention-drawing discussions that co-construct autobiographical memories.

With language development, children are able to discuss feelings with family members, so that causes of inner states are linked to actions and outcomes, facilitating direct instruction from parents on these matters (Thompson, 2006). Caregiver verbal interactions have various effects. For example, even with toddlers, caregivers help the child review, structure, and consolidate their memories in a script-like fashion by how and what they elaborate in conversations with the child (Fivush, Kuebli, & Clubb, 1992; Nelson & Gruendel, 1981). These conversations help structure the child's own self and moral narratives (Lapsley & Hill, 2009). So, for example, whether the caregiver talks and asks questions about feelings and actions or about clothes and looking good, he or she is guiding the child to develop conceptual structures that form memories about the self.

In adolescence, identity and purpose become more salient (Damon, 2008). Identity and sense of purpose continue to be guided by these implicit notions of, for example, social trust or distrust, personal competence or incompetence (Erikson, 1968). The empirical linkages between childhood traits and characteristic adaptations and adolescent identity and narratives still need to be specified (Lapsley, 2015). We can perform some theoretical linkages here.

Moral Orientations

We can see that explicit measures of moral reasoning cannot capture the type of neurobiological development we've been discussing. *Triune ethics metatheory* (*TEM*; Narvaez, 2008, 2014, 2016) attempts to integrate the neurobiological and psychological literatures to explain the different types of moral orientations we can have. Measures of triune ethics orientations represent a combination of what others perceive one to be like (the implicit self) and what one is aiming for (moral identity) in social situations. An *engagement* ethic or relational attunement, representing the type of moral sense Darwin identified, indicates well-functioning psychosocialneurobiology. Self-protectionist ethics such as *social opposition* and *social withdrawal* represent forms of social behavior noted by clinicians when neurobiological systems have been toxically stressed. A variety of imagination ethics that use abstracting capabilities are based on these basic forms and are mentioned below.

All of us are born with survival systems to keep us alive. They include the emotion systems located in the extrapyramidal action nervous system: fear, anger, panic/grief, and basic lust—all well mapped in mammalian brains and integrated with the stress response (Panksepp, 1998). When toxic stress takes place in early childhood, survival systems are enhanced and become dominant, while prosociality networks are underdeveloped (Niehoff, 1999). Survival systems kick in under stress and promote things such as territoriality, imitation, deception, struggles for power, maintenance of routine, and following precedent (MacLean, 1990). When survival systems take over the mind, they change perception of what seems good in the moment (Sapolsky, 2004), and if they trump other values and guide behavior, we can call them a *self-protectionist ethic* (Narvaez, 2008, 2014, 2016). Protectionist ethics indicate a hierarchical orientation (dominance or submission) to which survival systems are oriented to promote self-safety. Self-protectionism becomes apparent as a mindset when individuals hold themselves apart from others, unable to relationally attune as an equal to others (Laing, 1959/1990). When the stress response is active, blood flow shifts toward mobilization for safety and away from higher order thinking (Arnsten, 2009; Sapolsky, 2004). The shift can occur by situation and happen so quickly that it is not apparent to the individual. Individuals can dispositionally favor aggressing or withdrawing, or shift between them opportunistically. Someone can shift quickly into aggression under particular circumstances, as with road rage (Deffenbacher, Deffenbacher, Lynch, & Richards, 2003). George Costanza (*Seinfeld*) offers a good illustration. When at a day care, he suddenly felt in danger from a perceived fire in the building. He starts to run out of the building, impulsively pushing out of his way anyone on his path, including children and an elderly woman. Most aggression in mammals obtains from reactive self-defense, a dynamic intermixture of fear and anger (Blanchard, Blanchard, & Takahashi, 1977; Panksepp, 1998). People who are dispositionally stress reactive will spend more time in a protectionist mindset and feel slights when there are none, such as when they are accidentally bumped (Dodge & Somberg, 1987). This implicitly driven behavior will be rationalized by the explicit mind (Taber & Lodge, 2006) as occurs with violent criminals (Gilligan, 1997). My collaborators and I have shown that individuals whose childhoods were more inconsistent with the evolved nest, which increases chances for dispositional stress reactivity (Lupien et al., 2009), were more likely to have protectionist ethics and behaviors (Narvaez, Wang, & Cheng, 2016); they also were more distrustful, behaved less prosocially, and had lower integrity scores (Narvaez, Thiel, Kurth, & Renfus, 2016). This conforms with neurobiological findings that stress reactivity decreases emotional intelligence (Singh & Sharma, 2012).

Let's return to our two fictional characters. Francis Underwood (*House of Cards*, novel and Netflix show) is a manipulative politician, a coldhearted, ruthless pragmatist out for power. He was traumatized by an abusive father. Francis Underwood is not as autistic (socially awkward in perception, sensitivity and behavior) as Sheldon Cooper, but he has similar antisocial attitudes. Neither cares much about other people, except instrumentally, using them to help him get what he wants. It appears that when they were babies, they were smart enough to "go into their heads" when their needs were not met, as a defense against early trauma/neglect (Winnicott, 1965). Like those with avoidant attachment, they took a cognitive (i.e., emotionally disconnected) route to getting along in life, suppressing emotion, which at the same time thwarted the development of emotional intelligence during the early sensitive periods of development (Crittenden, 1995). They both show how a person can learn rules from explicit instruction that don't match up with implicit understandings of the world. While such a person may comply with others' moral values when necessary, he has not internalized the values—does not believe/understand/know them. What kinds of moral orientations are Sheldon and Francis exhibiting?

Both Sheldon and Francis demonstrate protectionist ethics. Sheldon displays *social withdrawal* enhanced by intellect into what I call *detached imagination,* which represents emotionally detached intellectualism, a type of moral disengagement (Bandura, 1999). It does not attend to relational connections to others, lacks a sense of responsibility to others, and makes plans without a sense of long-term consequences on the web of life (a common criticism of Western society's emphasis on intellect; e.g., MacMurray, 1935/1999; McGilchrist, 2009). Our studies have found that detached imagination correlates with personal distress and social distrust (Narvaez, Thiel, et al., 2016). Recent real-life examples of this mindset include the bankers and mortgage brokers who caused the 2008 U.S. financial crash (illustrated in *The Big Short* [2010] by Michael Lewis).

Social opposition is a common outcome for insecurely attached children, displayed in aggression and noncompliance (Sroufe, Egeland, Carlson, & Collins, 2005). Francis Underwood displays social opposition enhanced by intellect, a *vicious imagination,* which represents planful control or harm of others. It can take various forms such as not only revenge but also pathological altruism (Oakley, Madhavan, & Wilson, 2012). In our studies, we found that vicious imagination strongly correlated with insecure attachment and trait aggression (Narvaez, Thiel, et al., 2016).

In summary, we have multiple ethical mindsets that can shift and change our moral orientation in the circumstance or become dispositional. Propensity for different ethical mindsets are founded on how well one's neurobiological structures work, enhanced by personal choices and cultural press.

What happens when early life goes well? In our studies with multiple-age adults, the *engagement ethic* is related to all around good functioning, as represented by secure attachment, mental health, perspective taking, empathy, self-regulation, and prosocial behavior, and, when abstracting capabilities are involved, a *communal imagination* is related strongly to forgiveness, prosocial action, and integrity (Narvaez & Hardy, 2016; Narvaez, Thiel, et al., 2016). I discuss optimal functioning more in the next section.

Adult Lives

Moral functioning involves the interrelation of several components: perception, sensitivity, and interpretation of situations; reasoning, judgment, and reflection; motivation and focus; implementation of action and follow through (Rest, 1983). Morally mature adults have honed their moral capacities and demonstrate the practical wisdom to coordinate them in ways that young people typically lack (Hursthouse, 1999). What do we see in wise elders? Wise people display an engagement ethic, the ability to attune to others in face-to-face encounters with an egalitarian, open manner, showing Darwin's full moral sense, built on a well-functioning visceral–emotional nervous system on the hypothalamic–limbic axis (Panksepp, 1998) as well as a well-functioning right hemisphere (Schore, 1994). Data from adults who report a childhood more consistent with the evolved nest fit path models linking secure attachment, mental health (anxiety and depression), perspective taking, and relational attunement with others in both negative and positive pathways (Narvaez, Wang, et al., 2016). Such capacities are confirmed by studies conducted by the Berlin Wisdom Project, in which, for example, those with higher scores on wisdom-related knowledge demonstrate other-enhancing values and a preference for cooperative social orientations rather than protective ones (submission, withdrawal, dominance) (Kunzmann & Baltes, 2003). In studies of general wisdom, moral reasoning development was necessary but not sufficient for the highest scores on wisdom, whose combination was more typical of older participants (Pasupathi & Staudinger, 2001). Nevertheless,

wisdom is not necessarily age related (Smith & Baltes, 1990).

Narratives guide our lives, from cultural to personal to biological narratives. Biological "narratives" have deep neurobiological foundations in the implicit worldview a person carries from patterns of experience in childhood (unless changed from later impactful experience), reflected in a basic (dis)trust toward self and sense of (un)safety in the world (Narvaez, 2011). Just like deep cultural assumptions, these are difficult to uncover through explicit narratives. However, in an individual whose early experiences were *inconsistent* with the evolved nest, neurobiological systems will be less regulated, leading to a disconnect between the individual's natural inclinations and moral values learned explicitly. The focus of explicit life narratives will be on the self or on issues of self-control, such as following rules, because, under conditions of poor self-regulation, explicit attention to rules is needed (Niehoff, 1999). This state is reflective of Aristotle's *incontinence* (in contrast to *virtue,* in which desires and behavior align without temptation). Individuals will be more oriented to punishment, and more threat reactive toward unscripted situations, outsiders, and the unfamiliar, as they did not learn the social agility that comes with evolved nest provision. As noted earlier, they are more likely to show mental rigidity and the splitting (us-against-them or black-and-white thinking) noted by clinicians in patients with early trauma (e.g., Fairbairn, 1952; Lanius, Vermetten, & Pain, 2010).

In contrast, early experience *consistent* with the evolved nest results in good self-regulation and coordination of neurobiological systems for sociality (e.g., vagus nerve; Porges, 2011). In a well-fostered individual, stress reactivity did not develop to routinely draw attention to self concerns, so prosocial moral valuing and behavior come naturally most of the time. Indeed, rescuers of Jews in World War II tended to report warm relationships with their parents (Oliner & Oliner, 1988). A well-developed individual bends his or her life toward prosociality and communality, and these are reflected in the narratives he or she believes and discusses about his or her life. Topics of his or her narratives will be on the needs of others.

The research of Anne Colby and Bill Damon (1992) shows what a communally oriented adult life looks like. In an attempt to study moral commitment, they systematically solicited nominations of moral exemplars, who demonstrated a sustained commitment to moral ideals that included a respect for humanity, a disposition to act according to those ideals, and a willingness to risk self-interest for them. They also had to be inspirational to others and humble about their importance, while contributing significantly to their community. Colby and Damon summarized the characteristics of the 23 people they interviewed. Exemplars were clear about what they thought was right and what their moral responsibilities were. It wasn't that the exemplars had exceptional moral reasoning or judgment—their moral commitment was much more than intellectual. Moral responsibility was central to their self-identity, which was grounded in a meaning greater than the self. Exemplars were positive and optimistic about their work, demonstrating not only courage but also openness to personal growth throughout life. Most importantly, they exhibited a unity of personal and moral goals, which has been confirmed by other studies showing a blending of personal agency and communalism (Frimer, Walker, Dunlop, Lee, & Riches, 2011); that is, moral goals were not viewed as a sacrifice or even a choice but became the means to attaining personal goals. As for everyone, moral actions were everyday occurrences, but for the exemplars, the *range* of concerns and *depth* of engagement were exceptional; that is, their moral concerns had greater scope, intensity, and breadth than those of non-exemplars.

Colby and Damon (1992) also documented moral transformation. They discussed a case in which peers influenced a change in moral values. Southerner Virginia Durr described how she changed after she went to college when, for the first time, she encountered "colored" people treated as equals. Over time, she made friends and learned to care for them as equals, eventually becoming a civil rights activist. This aligns with a more recent case in the news, the conversion of Derek Black (Saslow, 2016). Derek was raised as a white supremacist and, as a child, started the white supremacist website for kids called Stormfront. But then he went to college (against his family's wishes), made diverse friends who, after they found out who he really was paused their relationships. But then they came back to him and initiated friendly dialogue about his beliefs, which over months brought him to renounce white supremacism. Thus, characteristic values and goals, as well as life narratives, may be altered by an individual's choices and relationships, even though these might have been initially molded by familial and cultural press. Moral values can change top-down from therapeutic efforts or transformative experiences.

Conclusion

Each person is an embodied story—integrating the tale of not only human evolution but also their own lived experience. Moral learning, like all learning, is biosocial and embodied in our neurobiological systems. We are first constructed by the community of care (or undercare), including our biological and genetic functions, *within immersed relationships* (Ingold, 2013). Thus, precursors to adult moral capacities are shaped by community caregiving practices. Morality, including components of moral sensitivity, judgment, motivation, and action, is initially bottom-up learning from relational immersion in early life (Kochanska, 2002). Implicit social-procedural knowledge that underlies conscious thought and action is shaped by environments with caregiver relations in which cognitive and emotional capacities develop together (Greenspan & Shanker, 2004; Stern, 1985).

The evolved nest emerges from our cooperative history as a species and undergirds a relational epistemology or worldview. Babies and children rely on a caring community to provide for their needs, which thereby fosters the evolved moral sense: Experience becomes internalized culture (Hall, 1976)—all the way down to neurobiological structures. In other words, moral development is highly communal in construction and in execution. When the evolved nest is provided, matching the maturational schedule of the child, it influences the trajectory and type of moral development, affecting dispositional traits, characteristic values and goals, and integrative life narratives. The evolved moral sense is supported. However, when early life does not include the evolved nest, leading to self-protectionist ethics, there is still hope. Life experiences can intervene and have the power to transform moral values and behavior.

ACKNOWLEDGMENT

I acknowledge the Templeton Religion Trust for its funding of the Self, Motivation and Virtue project and the John Templeton Foundation for its funding of the Virtue, Happiness and the Meaning of Life project.

REFERENCES

Aquino, K., & Reed, A., II. (2002). The self-importance of moral identity. *Journal of Personality and Social Psychology, 83,* 1423–1440.

Arnsten, A. F. T. (2009). Stress signaling pathways that impair prefrontal cortex structure and function. *Nature Reviews Neuroscience, 10*(6), 410–422.

Bandura, A. (1999). Moral disengagement in the perpetration of inhumanities. *Personality and Social Psychology Review, 3*(3), 269–275.

Bargh, J. A., & Chartrand, T. L. (1999). The unbearable automaticity of being. *American Psychologist, 54,* 462–479.

Ben-Ami Bartal, I., Decety, J., & Mason, P. (2011). Empathy and pro-social behavior in rats. *Science, 334,* 1427–1430.

Blanchard, R. J., Blanchard, D. C., & Takahashi, L. K. (1977). Reflexive fighting in the albino rat: Aggressive or defensive behavior? *Aggressive Behavior, 3,* 145–155.

Blasi, A. (1983). Moral cognition and moral action: A theoretical perspective. *Developmental Review, 3,* 178–221.

Bloom, P. (2013). *Just babies: The origins of good and evil.* New York: Crown.

Bogdan, R. J. (1994). *Grounds for cognition: How goal-guided behavior shapes the mind.* New York: Psychology Press.

Bowlby, J. (1982). *Attachment and loss: Vol. 1. Attachment* (2nd ed.). New York: Basic Books. (Original work published 1969)

Bowlby, J. (1988). *A secure base: Parent–child attachment and healthy human development.* New York: Basic Books.

Brenner, P. S. (2011). Exceptional behavior or exceptional identity?: Overreporting of church attendance in the U.S. *Public Opinion Quarterly, 75,* 19–41.

Bronfenbrenner, U. (1979). *The ecology of human development.* Cambridge, MA: Harvard University Press.

Bronstein, J. L. (Ed.). (2015). *Mutualism.* New York: Oxford University Press.

Colby, A., & Damon, W. (1992). *Some do care: Contemporary lives of moral commitment.* New York: Free Press.

Collen, A. (2015). *10% human: How your body's microbes hold the key to health and happiness.* London: WilliamCollins.

Cory, G. A., Jr. (2016). Physiology and behavioral economics: The new findings from evolutionary neuroscience. In M. Altman (Ed.), *Handbook of contemporary behavioral economics* (pp. 24–49). New York: Routledge.

Crittenden, P. M. (1995). Attachment and psychopathology. In S. Goldberg, R. Muir, & J. Kerr (Eds.), *Attachment theory: Social, developmental, and clinical perspectives* (pp. 367–406). Hillsdale, NJ: Analytic Press.

Damasio, A. (1999). *The feeling of what happens.* New York: Harcourt & Brace.

Damon, W. (2008). *The path to purpose: Helping our children find their calling in life.* New York: Free Press.

Darwin, C. (1962). *The origin of species.* New York: Collier Books. (Original work published 1859)

Darwin, C. (1981). *The descent of man.* Princeton, NJ: Princeton University Press. (Original work published 1871)

Davis, E. P., Glynn, L. M., Schetter, C. D., Hobel, C., Chicz-Demet, A., & Sandman, C. A. (2007). Prenatal exposure to maternal depression and cortisol influences infant temperament. *Journal of the American Academy of Child and Adolescent Psychiatry, 46,* 737–746.

Deffenbacher, J. L., Deffenbacher, D. M., Lynch, R. S., & Richards, T. L. (2003). Anger, aggression and risky behavior: A comparison of high and low anger drivers. *Behaviour Research and Therapy, 41*(6), 701–718.

Denison, R. F., & Muller, K. (2016). The evolution of cooperation. *The Scientist, 30*(1), 40–46.

Dias, B. G., & Ressler, K. J. (2013). Implications of memory modulation for post-traumatic stress and fear disorders. *Nature Neuroscience, 16*(2), 146–153.

Dodge, K. A., & Somberg, D. R. (1987). Hostile attributional biases among aggressive boys are exacerbated under conditions of threats to the self. *Child Development, 58*(1), 213–224.

Dunn, J. (2014). Moral development in early childhood and social interaction in the family. In M. Killen & J. Smetana (Eds.), *Handbook of moral development* (2nd ed., pp. 135–159). New York: Psychology Press.

Dunn, R. (2011). *The wild life of our bodies: Predators, parasites, and partners that shape who we are today.* New York: Harper.

Endicott, K., & Endicott, K. (2014). Batek childrearing and morality. In D. Narvaez, K. Valentino, A. Fuentes, J. McKenna, & P. Gray (Eds.), *Ancestral landscapes in human evolution: Culture, childrearing and social wellbeing* (pp. 108–125). New York: Oxford University Press.

Erikson, E. H. (1950). *Childhood and society.* New York: Norton.

Erikson, E. H. (1968). *Identity: Youth and crisis.* New York: Norton.

Fairbairn, W. R. D. (1952). *An object-relations theory of the personality.* New York: Basic Books.

Fivush, R., Kuebli, J., & Chubb, P. A. (1992). The structure of event representations: A developmental analysis. *Child Development, 63,* 188–201.

Frankfurt, H. G. (1988). *The importance of what we care about: Philosophical essays.* New York: Cambridge University Press.

Frimer, J. A., Walker, L. J., Dunlop, W. L., Lee, B. H., & Riches, A. (2011). The integration of agency and communion in moral personality: Evidence of enlightened self-interest. *Journal of Personality and Social Psychology, 101*(1), 149–163.

Fry, D. P. (2006). *The human potential for peace: An anthropological challenge to assumptions about war and violence.* New York: Oxford University Press.

Fry, D. P. (Ed.). (2013). *War, peace and human nature.* New York: Oxford University Press.

Fry, D. P., & Söderberg, P. (2014). Myths about hunter–gatherers redux: Nomadic forager war and peace. *Journal of Aggression, Conflict and Peace Research, 6,* 255–266.

Fry, D. P., & Souillac, G. (2017). The original partnership societies: Evolved propensities for equality, prosociality, and peace. *Interdisciplinary Journal of Partnership Studies, 4*(1), Article 4.

Gaber Rizk, T. M. (2014). Breast milk versus formula milk and neuropsychological development and sleep. *Journal of Pediatrics and Neonatal Care, 1*(2), Article No. 00005.

Gilligan, J. (1997). *Violence: Reflections on a national epidemic.* New York: Vintage.

Gluckman, P. D., & Hanson, M. A. (2005). *Fetal matrix: Evolution, development and disease.* New York: Cambridge University Press.

Goldberg, E. (2002). *The executive brain: Frontal lobes and the civilized brain.* New York: Oxford University Press.

Goldman, A. S., Goldblum, R. M., & Hanson, L. A. (1990). Anti-inflammatory systems in human milk. *Advances in Experimental Medicine and Biology, 262,* 69–76.

Gómez-Robles, A., Hopkins, W. D., Schapiro, S. J., & Sherwood, C. C. (2015). Relaxed genetic control of cortical organization in human brains compared with chimpanzees. *Proceedings of the National Academy of Sciences of the USA, 112,* 14799–14804.

Gottlieb, G. (2002). On the epigenetic evolution of species-specific perception: The developmental manifold concept. *Cognitive Development, 17,* 1287–1300.

Gowdy, J. (1998). *Limited wants, unlimited means: A reader on hunter–gatherer economics and the environment.* Washington, DC: Island Press.

Graham, J., Haidt, J., & Nosek, B. A. (2009). Liberals and conservatives rely on different sets of moral foundations. *Journal of Personality and Social Psychology, 96,* 1029–1046.

Greenough, W., & Black, J. (1992). Induction of brain structure by experience: Substrate for cognitive development. In M. R. Gunnar & C. A. Nelson (Eds.), *Minnesota Symposia on Child Psychology: Developmental behavioral neuroscience* (Vol. 24, pp. 155–200). Hillsdale, NJ: Erlbaum.

Greenspan, S. I., & Shanker, S. I. (2004). *The first idea.* Cambridge, MA: Da Capo Press.

Griffiths, P. E., & Gray, R. D. (2001). Darwinism and developmental systems. In S. Oyama, P. E. Griffiths, & R. D. Gray (Eds.), *Cycles of contingency: Developmental systems and evolution* (pp. 195–218). Cambridge, MA: MIT Press.

Gross, M., & Averill, M. (2003). Evolution and patriarchal myths of scarcity and competition. In S. Hardin & M. Hintikka (Eds.), *Discovering reality: Feminist perspectives on epistemology, metaphysics, methodology and philosophy of science* (2nd ed., pp. 71–95). Dordrecht, The Netherlands: Kluwer Academic.

Gudsnuk, K., & Champagne, F. A. (2012). Epigenetic influence of stress and the social environment. *Institute for Laboratory Animal Research Journal, 53*(3–4), 279–288.

Gurven, M., von Rueden, C., Kaplan, H., & Massenkoff, M. (2013). How universal is the Big Five?: Testing the five-factor model of personality variation among forager–farmers in the Bolivian Amazon. *Journal of Personality and Social Psychology, 104,* 354–370.

Haidt, J. (2001). The emotional dog and its rational tail: A social intuitionist approach to moral judgment. *Psychological Review, 8,* 814–834.

Haidt, J. (2012). *The righteous mind.* New York: Penguin/Random House.

Hall, E. T. (1976). *Beyond culture.* Garden City, NY: Anchor.

Harlow, H. (1958). The nature of love. *American Psychologist, 13,* 673–685.

Hart, S., Boylan, L. M., Carroll, S., Musick, Y. A., & Lampe, R. M. (2003). Brief report: Breast-fed one-week-olds demonstrate superior neurobehavioral organization. *Journal of Pediatric Psychology, 28*(8), 529–534.

Hassin, R. R., Uleman, J. S., & Bargh, J. A. (Eds.). (2005). *The new unconscious.* New York: Oxford University Press.

Henrich, J., Heine, S. J., & Norenzayan, A. (2010). The weirdest people in the world? *Behavioral and Brain Sciences, 33*(2–3), 61–83.

Hewlett, B. S., & Lamb, M. E. (2005). *Hunter–gatherer childhoods: Evolutionary, developmental and cultural perspectives.* New Brunswick, NJ: Aldine.

Ho, M. W. (2010). Development and evolution revisited. In K. E. Hood, C. Tucker Halper, G. Greenberg, & R. M. Lerner (Eds.), *Handbook of developmental science, behavior, and genetics* (pp. 61–109). Chichester, UK: Wiley-Blackwell.

Hoffman, M. L. (2000). *Empathy and moral development: Implications for caring and justice.* Cambridge, UK: Cambridge University Press.

Hogarth, R. M. (2001). *Educating intuition.* Chicago: University of Chicago Press.

Hrdy, S. (2009). *Mothers and others: The evolutionary origins of mutual understanding.* Cambridge, MA: Belknap Press.

Hursthouse, R. (1999). *On virtue ethics.* Oxford, UK: Oxford University Press.

Ingold, T. (2005). On the social relations of the hunter–gatherer band. In R. B. Lee & R. Daly (Eds.), *The Cambridge encyclopedia of hunters and gatherers* (pp. 399–410). New York: Cambridge University Press.

Ingold, T. (2013). Prospect. In T. Ingold & G. Palsson

(Eds.), *Biosocial becomings: Integrating social and biological anthropology* (pp. 1–21). Cambridge, UK: Cambridge University Press.

Isaacs, E. B., Fischl, B. R., Quinn, B. T., Chong, W. K., Gadian, D. G., & Lucas, A. (2010). Impact of breast milk on IQ, brain size and white matter development. *Pediatric Research, 67*(4), 357–362.

Jablonka, E., & Lamb, M. J. (2005). *Evolution in four dimensions: Genetic, epigenetic, behavioral, and symbolic variation in the history of life.* Cambridge, MA: MIT Press.

Kant, I. (1949). *Fundamental principles of the metaphysics of morals.* New York: Liberal Arts Press.

Karra, M. V., Shobha, M. S., Udipi, A., Kirksey, A., & Roepke, J. L. B. (1986). Changes in specific nutrients in breast milk during extended lactation. *American Journal of Clinical Nutrition, 43,* 495–503.

Keil, F. C., & Wilson, R. A. (2000). Explaining explanations. In F. C. Keil & R. A. Wilson (Eds.), *Explanation and cognition* (pp. 1–18). Cambridge MA: Bradford/MIT Press.

Khedr, E. M., Farghaly, W. M., Sel-D, A., & Osman, A. A. (2004). Neural maturation of breastfed and formula-fed infants. *Acta Paediatrica, 93*(6), 734–738.

Knudsen, E. I. (2004). Sensitive periods in the development of the brain and behavior. *Journal of Cognitive Neuroscience, 16*(8), 1412–1425.

Kochanska, G. (1994). Beyond cognition: Expanding the search for the early roots of internalization and conscience. *Developmental Psychology, 30*(1), 20–22.

Kochanska, G. (2002). Mutually responsive orientation between mothers and their young children: A context for the early development of conscience. *Current Directions in Psychological Science, 11*(6), 191–195.

Kochanska, G., Koenig, J. L., Barry, R. A., Kim, S., & Yoon, J. E. (2010). Children's conscience during toddler and preschool years, moral self and a competent, adaptive developmental trajectory. *Developmental Psychology, 46,* 1320–1332.

Kohlberg, L. (1984). *Essays on moral development: Vol. 2. The psychology of moral development.* San Francisco: Harper & Row.

Konner, M. (2005). Hunter–gatherer infancy and childhood: The !Kung and others. In B. Hewlett & M. Lamb (Eds.), *Hunter–gatherer childhoods: Evolutionary, developmental and cultural perspectives* (pp. 19–64). New Brunswick, NJ: Transaction.

Kraybill, D. B., Nolt, S. M., & Weaver-Zercher, D. L. (2008). *Amish grace: How forgiveness transcended tragedy.* San Francisco: Jossey-Bass.

Kunzmann, U., & Baltes, P. B. (2003). Wisdom-related knowledge: Affective, motivational, and interpersonal correlates. *Personality and Social Psychology Bulletin, 29,* 1104–1119.

Kuzawa, C. W., Quinn, E. A. (2009). Developmental origins of adult function and health: Evolutionary hypotheses. *Annual Review of Anthropology, 38,* 131–147.

Laing, R. D. (1990). *The divided self.* London: Penguin. (Original work published 1959)

Landis, D., & Bhagat, R. S. (Eds.). (1996). *Handbook of intercultural training* (2nd ed.). Thousand Oaks, CA: SAGE.

Lanius, R. A., Vermetten, E., & Pain, C. (Eds.). (2010). *The impact of early life trauma on health and disease: The hidden epidemic.* New York: Cambridge University Press.

Lapsley, D. K. (2006). Moral stage theory. In M. Killen & J. Smetana (Eds.), *Handbook of moral development* (pp. 37–66). Mahwah, NJ: Erlbaum.

Lapsley, D. (2015). Moral identity and developmental theory. *Human Development, 58,* 164–171.

Lapsley, D. K., & Hill, P. (2009). The development of the moral personality. In D. Narvaez & D. K. Lapsley (Eds.), *Personality, identity and character: Explorations in moral psychology* (pp. 185–213). New York: Cambridge University Press.

Lapsley, D. K., & Narvaez, D. (2004). A social-cognitive view of moral character. In D. K. Lapsley & D. Narvaez (Eds.), *Moral development: Self and identity* (pp. 189–212). Mahwah, NJ: Erlbaum.

Lee, R. B., & Daly, R. (Eds.). (2005). *The Cambridge encyclopedia of hunters and gatherers.* New York: Cambridge University Press.

Lewis, M. (2010). *The big short: Inside the doomsday machine.* New York: Norton.

Longino, H. E. (1990). *Science as social knowledge: Values and objectivity in scientific inquiry.* Princeton, NJ: Princeton University Press.

Lupien, S. J., McEwen, B. S., Gunnar, M. R., & Heim, C. (2009). Effects of stress throughout the lifespan on the brain, behaviour and cognition. *Nature Reviews Neuroscience, 10*(6), 434–445.

MacLean, P. D. (1990). *The triune brain in evolution: Role in paleocerebral functions.* New York: Plenum Press.

MacMurray, J. (1999). *Reason and emotion.* New York: Humanity Books. (Original work published 1935)

Margulis, L. (1998). *Symbiotic planet: A new look at evolution.* Amherst, MA: Sciencewriters.

McGilchrist, I. (2009). *The master and his emissary: The divided brain and the making of the Western World.* New Haven, CT: Yale University Press.

Meaney, M. J. (2001). Maternal care, gene expression, and the transmission of individual differences in stress reactivity across generations. *Annual Review of Neuroscience, 24,* 1161–1192.

Moore, B., & Isen, A. (1990). *Affect and social behavior.* New York: Cambridge University Press.

Morelli, G., Ivey Henry, P., & Foerster, S. (2014). Relationships and resource uncertainty: Cooperative development of Efe hunter–gatherer infants and toddlers. In D. Narvaez, K. Valentino, A. Fuentes, J. McKenna, & P. Gray (Eds.), *Ancestral landscapes in human evolution: Culture, childrearing and social wellbeing* (pp. 69–103). New York: Oxford University Press.

Morris, W. (1989). *Mood: The frame of mind.* New York: Springer-Verlag.

Mueller, B. R., & Bale, T. L. (2008). Sex-specific programming of offspring emotionality following stress early in pregnancy. *Journal of Neuroscience, 28*(36), 9055–9065.

Narvaez, D. (2008). Triune ethics: The neurobiological roots of our multiple moralities. *New Ideas in Psychology, 26,* 95–119.

Narvaez, D. (2011). The ethics of neurobiological narratives. *Poetics Today, 32*(1), 81–106.

Narvaez, D. (2013). The 99%—Development and socialization within an evolutionary context: Growing up to become "a good and useful human being." In D. Fry (Ed.), *War, peace and human nature: The convergence of evolutionary and cultural views* (pp. 643–672). New York: Oxford University Press.

Narvaez, D. (2014). *Neurobiology and the development of human morality: Evolution, culture and wisdom.* New York: Norton.

Narvaez, D. (2016). *Embodied morality: Protectionism, engagement and imagination.* New York: Palgrave-Macmillan.

Narvaez, D. (2018). Ethogenesis: Evolution, early experience and moral becoming. In K. Gray & J. Graham (Eds.), *The atlas of moral psychology* (pp. 451–464). New York: Guilford Press.

Narvaez, D., Gleason, T., Lefever, J. B., Wang, L., & Cheng, A. (2016). Early experience and ethical orientation. In D. Narvaez (Ed.), *Embodied morality: Protectionism, engagement and imagination* (pp. 73–98). New York: Palgrave-Macmillan.

Narvaez, D., Gleason, T., Wang, L., Brooks, J., Lefever, J., Cheng, A., et al. (2013). The evolved development niche: Longitudinal effects of caregiving practices on early childhood psychosocial development. *Early Childhood Research Quarterly, 28*(4), 759–773.

Narvaez, D., & Hardy, S. (2016). Measuring triune ethics orientations. In D. Narvaez (Ed.), *Embodied morality: Protectionism, engagement and imagination* (pp. 47–72). New York: Palgrave-Macmillan.

Narvaez, D., & Lapsley, D. K. (2005). The psychological foundations of everyday morality and moral expertise. In D. K. Lapsley & C. Power (Eds.), *Character psychology and character education* (pp. 140–165). Notre Dame: IN: University of Notre Dame Press.

Narvaez, D., Panksepp, J., Schore, A., & Gleason, T. (Eds.). (2013). *Evolution, early experience and human development: From research to practice and policy.* New York: Oxford University Press.

Narvaez, D., Thiel, A., Kurth, A., & Renfus, K. (2016). Past moral action and ethical orientation. In D. Narvaez (Ed.), *Embodied morality: Protectionism, engagement and imagination* (pp. 99–118). New York: Palgrave-Macmillan.

Narvaez, D., Wang, L., & Cheng, A. (2016). Evolved developmental niche history: Relation to adult psychopathology and morality. *Applied Developmental Science, 4,* 294–309.

Narvaez, D., Wang, L., Gleason, T., Cheng, A., Lefever, J., & Deng, L. (2013). The evolved developmental niche and sociomoral outcomes in Chinese three-year-olds. *European Journal of Developmental Psychology, 10*(2), 106–127.

Nelson, K., & Gruendel, J. (1981). Generalized event representations: Basic building blocks of cognitive development. In M. Lamb & A. Brown (Eds.), *Advances in developmental psychology* (pp. 131–158). Hillsdale, NJ: Erlbaum.

Niehoff, D. (1999). *The biology of violence: How understanding the brain, behavior, and environment can break the vicious circle of aggression.* New York: Free Press.

Nisbett, R., & Cohen, D. (1996). *Culture of honor.* New York: Westview Press.

Oakley, B., Madhavan, G., & Wilson, D. S. (Eds.). (2012). *Pathological altruism.* New York: Oxford University Press.

Ohlson, K. (2014). *The soil will save us: How scientists, farmers, and foodies are healing the soil to save the planet.* New York: Rodale Books.

Oliner, S. P., & Oliner, P. M. (1988). *The altruistic personality: Rescuers of Jews in Nazi Europe.* New York: Free Press.

Oyama, S. (2000a). *Evolution's eye: A systems view of the biology–culture divide.* Durham, NC: Duke University Press.

Oyama, S. (2000b). *The ontogeny of information: Developmental systems and evolution* (2nd ed.). Cambridge, UK: Cambridge University Press.

Panksepp, J. (1998). *Affective neuroscience: The foundations of human and animal emotions.* New York: Oxford University Press.

Panksepp, J., & Biven, L. (2011). *The archaeology of mind: Neuroevolutionary origins of human emotions.* New York: Norton.

Pasupathi, M., & Staudinger, U. M. (2001). Do advanced moral reasoners also show wisdom?: Linking moral reasoning and wisdom-related knowledge and judgement. *International Journal of Behavioral Development, 25,* 401–415.

Pinker, S. (2011). *The better angels of our nature.* New York: Viking.

Porges, S. W. (2011). *The polyvagal theory: Neurophysiological foundations of emotions, attachment, communication, self-regulation.* New York: Norton.

Presser, S., & Stinson, L. (1998). Data collection mode and social desirability bias in self-reported religious attendance. *American Sociological Review, 63*(1), 137–145.

Reber, A. S. (1993). *Implicit learning and tacit knowledge: An essay on the cognitive unconscious.* New York: Oxford University Press.

Rest, J. R. (1979). *Developing in judging moral issues.* Minneapolis: University of Minnesota Press.

Rest, J. (1983). Morality. In P. H. Mussen (Series Ed.) & J. Flavell & E. Markman (Vol. Eds.), *Handbook of child psychology: Vol. 3. Cognitive development* (4th ed., pp. 556–629). New York: Wiley.

Rest, J., Narvaez, D., Bebeau, M. J., & Thoma, S. J.

(1999). *Postconventional moral thinking: A neo-Kohlbergian approach.* Mahwah, NJ: Erlbaum.

Rokeach, M. (1979). Some unresolved issues in theories of beliefs, attitudes and values. In H. E. Howe, Jr. & M. M. Page (Eds.), *Nebraska Symposium on Motivation* (Vol. 27, pp. 261–304). Lincoln: University of Nebraska Press.

Rubenstein, D., & Kealey, J. (2010). Cooperation, conflict, and the evolution of complex animal societies. *Nature Education Knowledge, 3*(10), 78.

Sacker, A., Quigley, M. A., & Kelly, Y. J. (2006). Breastfeeding and developmental delay: Findings from the Millennium Cohort Study. *Pediatrics, 118*(3), e682–e689.

Sapolsky, R. (2004). *Why zebras don't get ulcers* (3rd ed.). New York: Holt.

Saslow, E. (2016, October 15). The white flight of Derek Black. *Washington Post.* Retrieved January 5, 2017, from *www.washingtonpost.com/national/the-white-flight-of-derek-black/2016/10/15/ed5f906a-8f3b-11e6-a6a3-d50061aa9fae_story.html?utm_term=.8dfbc631bb92&wpisrc=nl_most-draw8&wpmm=1.*

Schore, A. N. (1994). *Affect regulation the origin of the self: The neurobiology of emotional development.* Mahwah, NJ: Erlbaum.

Schore, A. N. (2001). The effects of early relational trauma on right brain development, affect regulation, and infant mental health. *Infant Mental Health Journal, 22*, 201–269.

Schore, A. N. (2002). Dysregulation of the right brain: A fundamental mechanism of traumatic attachment and the psychopathogenesis of posttraumatic stress disorder. *Australian and New Zealand Journal of Psychiatry, 36*, 9–30.

Schore, A. N. (2003a). *Affect dysregulation and disorders of the self.* New York: Norton.

Schore, A. N. (2003b). *Affect regulation and the repair of the self.* New York: Norton.

Schore, A. N. (2017). All our sons: The developmental neurobiology and neuroendocrinology of boys at risk. *Infant Mental Health Journal, 38*, 15–52.

Schwartz, S. H. (1992). Universals in the content and structure of values: Theory and empirical tests in 20 countries. In M. Zanna (Ed.), *Advances in experimental social psychology* (Vol. 25, pp. 1–65). New York: Academic Press.

Schwartz, S. H. (2005). Robustness and fruitfulness of a theory of universals in individual human values. In A. Tamayo & J. B. Porto (Eds.), *Valores e comportamento nas organizações* [Values and behavior in organizations] (pp. 56–95). Petrópolis, Brazil: Vozes.

Shubin, N. (2009). *Your inner fish: A journey into the 3.5-billion-year history of the human body.* New York: Vintage.

Shweder, R. (1993). *Thinking through cultures.* Cambridge, MA: Harvard University Press.

Siegel, D. J. (1999). *The developing mind: How relationships and the brain interact to shape who we are.* New York: Guilford Press.

Siepel, H. (2015). *Conquistador voices: The Spanish conquest of the Americas as recounted largely by the participants, Vol. I: Christopher Columbus, Hernan Cortes.* Angola, NY: Spruce Tree Press.

Singh, Y., & Sharma, R. (2012). Relationship between general intelligence, emotional intelligence, stress levels and stress reactivity. *Annals of Neuroscience, 19*(3), 107–111.

Smith, J., & Baltes, P. B. (1990). Wisdom-related knowledge: Age/cohort differences in responses to life planning problems. *Developmental Psychology, 26*, 494–505.

Sommerville, J. A. (2015). The emergence of moral character in infancy: Developmental change and individual differences in fairness concerns and prosocial behavior during the first two years of life. In C. B. Miller, R. M. Furr, A. Knobel, & W. Fleeson (Eds.), *Character: New directions from philosophy, psychology and theology* (pp. 445–466). New York: Oxford University Press.

Sroufe, L. A., Egeland, B., Carlson, E. A., & Collins, W. A. (2005). *The development of the person: The Minnesota Study of Risk and Adaptation from Birth to Adulthood.* New York: Guilford Press.

Stern, D. N. (1985). *The interpersonal world of the infant.* New York: Basic Books.

Stern, D. (2010). *Forms of vitality: Exploring dynamic experience in psychology, the arts, psychotherapy, and development.* New York: Oxford University Press.

Suhler, C. L., & Churchland, P. M. (2011). Can innate, modular "foundations" explain morality?: Challenges for Haidt's moral foundations theory. *Journal of Cognitive Neuroscience, 23*(9), 2103–2116.

Taber, C. S., & Lodge, M. (2006). Motivated skepticism in the evaluation of political beliefs. *American Journal of Political Science, 50*, 755–769.

Taylor, S. E., & Crocker, J. (1981). Schematic bases of social information processing. In E. T. Higgins, C. P. Herman, & M. P. Zanna (Eds.), *Social cognition: The Ontario Symposium* (Vol. 1, pp. 89–134). Hillsdale, NJ: Erlbaum.

Thompson, R. A. (2006). The development of the person: Social understanding, relationships, self, conscience. In W. Damon & R. M. Lerner (Eds.), *Handbook of child psychology: Vol. 3. Social, emotional, and personality development* (6th ed., pp. 24–98). New York: Wiley.

Trevathan, W. R. (2011). *Human birth: An evolutionary perspective* (2nd ed.). New York: de Gruyter.

Turiel, E. (1983). *The development of social knowledge: morality and convention.* Cambridge, UK: Cambridge University Press.

Turner, F. (1994). *Beyond geography: The Western spirit against the wilderness.* New Brunswick, NJ: Rutgers University Press.

Vance, J. D. (2016). *Hillbilly elegy: A memoir of a family and culture in crisis.* New York: HarperCollins.

Varela, F. J., Thompson, E., & Rosch, E. (1991). *The embodied mind: Cognitive science and human experience.* Cambridge, MA: MIT Press.

West-Eberhard, M. J. (2003). *Developmental plasticity and evolution.* New York: Oxford University Press.

Wilson, T. D. (2004). *Strangers to ourselves.* New York: Belknap.

Winnicott, D. W. (1965). *The maturational processes and the facilitating environment.* London: Hogarth Press/Institute of Psycho-Analysis.

Wohlleben, P. (2016). *The hidden life of trees: What they feel, how they communicate* (J. Billinghurst, Trans.). Vancouver: Greystone Books.

Worster, D. (1994). *Nature's economy: A history of ecological ideas* (2nd ed.). Cambridge, UK: Cambridge University Press.

CHAPTER 21

Religion, Spirituality, and the Agential Self

Paul Wink
Michele Dillon
Dan Farina

The study of religion and spirituality is well suited to exemplifying the agency of the psychological self (McAdams, 2013). We illustrate in this chapter why this is the case. We first highlight how the American sociocultural environment favors individual agency in religious and spiritual engagement. We then discuss the relationship between religion and personality, and turn to consider how lifespan contexts and transitions impact religious and spiritual engagement. Cases of individual lives over time help illustrate these various dynamics.

Agency in American Religion

Today, the dynamic nature of religious belief and behavior is especially pronounced in Western society. It is driven on the one hand by secularization processes and, on the other, by the increased prevalence of new forms of spiritual engagement. Though broad-based, the dynamics in play underscore the actualization of the self as an agent who explores and prioritizes various options and goals (McAdams, 2013). Such agency is abetted by the denominational pluralism within the United States and by the concomitant cultural emphasis on religious freedom and the ethos of individual choice long institutionalized in American religion.

Since the 1960s, rates of religious participation have plummeted across Western Europe, with just 18% of individuals attending a place of worship monthly in the United Kingdom or France (Pew Research Center, 2018). Although religion is more resilient in the United States, one of the most significant transformations in contemporary American society is the ongoing exponential decline in religious affiliation. For much of the 20th century, from the 1940s, when national opinion surveys first began, until the late 1980s, a small minority of American adults, approximately 7%, expressed no religious affiliation (Glenn, 1987). By the late 1990s, this figure had doubled (Hout & Fischer, 2002), and by 2016 it had more than tripled, with 25% indicating no religious preference. Thus, the unaffiliated currently comprise the single largest religious group in America, followed by Catholics (21%) and white evangelical Protestants (16%) (Jones, Cox, Cooper, & Lienesch, 2016).

Spiritual Seeking

Another major, though more long-term, development has been the emergence of spiritual seeking and new spiritual practices independent of institutionalized religion. The expansion of immigration from Asia as a result of new legislation enacted in 1965 brought immigrants to the United States whose Eastern religious and spiritual practices found a receptive hold on the imagination of many young baby boomers, who were then college-age students experimenting with a range of innovative cultural mores (Roof, 1999). For some baby boomers—and subsequently their children—spiritual seeking entailed the abandonment of church or institutionalized Christian religion and the exploration of Buddhist meditation, yoga, Shaman journeying, and other nature- or earth-centered worship practices reminiscent of the early Transcendentalists. Others maintained engagement in a specific Christian denomination but also incorporated various elements from these spiritual and other denominational traditions. Today, between one-fourth and one-third of Americans, whether Christian or unaffiliated, believe in non-Christian, New Age spirituality, such as reincarnation, in yoga not just as a physical exercise but as a spiritual practice, and that there is spiritual energy in rocks, mountains, and other physical things (Pew Research Center, 2009). Some such spiritual beliefs are also apparent in some of the most highly secularized Western European countries (e.g., Houtman & Aupers, 2007).

Reflecting the ambiguities in how individuals construe the religious–spiritual self, three-fourths of religiously affiliated Americans describe themselves as "religious," but 15% describe themselves as "spiritual but not religious," and another 8% reject either label. And among the unaffiliated, 18% describe themselves as religious, and 37% as "spiritual but not religious" (Pew Research Center, 2012, p. 44). Such findings point to the nuanced character in the subjective construal of contemporary religion–spirituality. They also point to the range of meanings that may go undocumented in studies of religion whose measures rely on church attendance or belief in a personal God.

The subtle way in which individuals author an individualized religious–spiritual narrative is well illustrated in the comments of Kate, a California-born, lifelong Episcopalian, whose strong faith sustained her through many ups and downs. A retired social worker who never married, in her early 70s, Kate was attending church weekly, was active in its community life, and also participating in a couple of non-church women's spiritual groups. Despite the centrality of church attendance and traditional religious belief in her life, Kate was hesitant to describe herself as religious, instead preferring

a self-narrative that emphasized her spiritual strivings. She remarked:

> The word *religion* is a really, really wretched term. I look upon it negatively now. It's a system of beliefs, and even though I'm a churchgoer, I'm totally unorthodox in any Christian beliefs. I take the good things. I don't believe in original sin or in any particular theology but there are many good things to be exemplified and utilized in Christianity. . . . And I feel the same way about Buddhism. I find many tenets of Buddhism to be excellent dictums by which to live. . . . I would say that I'm a spiritual person, or I strive to be a spiritual person, not necessarily a religious person. I make a distinction there. I am very much a spiritual person—that's something growing in me. (Dillon & Wink, 2007 pp. 135–136)[1]

This was not a new self-understanding. As an articulate, candid, and introspective adolescent, she had told an interviewer, at age 16: "I've been pondering over what I believe this year, and can't quite take the Bible and the sermons. I'm not an atheist, but I'm not a believer. I can't decide if I am religious. I believe in the spirit of religion, but I can't believe in the details" (Dillon & Wink, 2007, p. 132).

Both spiritual seeking and religious disaffiliation add to the variegated complexity and fluidity of the contemporary religious–spiritual environment. (They also complicate the conceptualization, measurement, and meanings of religion and spirituality as discrete constructs [e.g., Wink, 2011], which for the purposes of this chapter we tend to set aside.) Although disaffiliation is an important secular trend, it is not indicative of a lack of religious or spiritual belief. Rather, again pointing to individual agency, there is much variation in how individuals construe and act on their religious–spiritual identity. Only a small proportion of the unaffiliated describe themselves as atheist (3.1%) or

---

[1]The illustrative, individual case data from Kate and others in this chapter come from Dillon and Wink's (2007) longitudinal study of men and women born in Oakland or Berkeley, California, in the early or late 1920s. The sample was a representative community sample; participants came from an even mix of middle- and working-class backgrounds, most were Protestant, and almost all were white. The study was initiated by researchers at the Institute of Human Development (IHD) as the University of California, Berkeley; the participants were studied intensively in childhood and adolescence, and interviewed in depth in early (1958), middle (1970), late-middle (1982), and late adulthood (1997–2000).

agnostic (4.0%), and many of them, moreover, express conventional religious beliefs that are closely aligned with mainstream Christianity (Pew Research Center, 2015). Furthermore, among the affiliated, there is a lot of diffuseness in the religious beliefs of those who self-identify as Catholic or Protestant (Pew Research Center, 2015). Further underscoring the agency of the religious–spiritual self, many U.S. Christians report occasionally attending religious services at multiple places of diverse worship (Pew Research Center, 2009).

Religion and Personality

Before discussing the ebb and flow of religion over the life course, we consider its relationship with personality. This framing enhances the understanding of religiousness and spirituality as psychological constructs, and also provides an overarching framework for how these two constructs change over time. Religion shares a number of characteristics with personality development. In general terms, there is relative stability in some of its components over the life course, it is moderately correlated with predictable everyday goals and ways of being, and it has well-defined implications for psychosocial functioning. There is, moreover, a robust correlation between the personality traits of conscientiousness and agreeableness and conventional measures of religiousness (Saroglou, 2010; Wink, Ciciolla, Dillon, & Tracy, 2007).

Religiousness and Personality

In numerous studies, traditional religiousness has been found to be positively related to the five-factor model's (Big Five) personality dimensions of agreeableness and conscientiousness but not extroversion, neuroticism, or openness (Saroglou, 2010). This means that individuals who identify as high in religiousness (i.e., emphasizing the importance of God and prayer in their daily lives and regularly attend church) tend to be giving or altruistic, compliant, modest, straightforward, and trusting (facets of agreeableness), and, at the same time, self-disciplined, competent, achievement-oriented, and valuing of order (facets of conscientiousness). The relationship between religiousness is stable over time with adolescent conscientiousness and agreeableness associated with religiousness in late adulthood (ages

70–79; Wink et al., 2007). Because both agreeableness and conscientiousness have a genetic component, there is, not surprisingly, a mild to moderate genetic influence on religious behavior (Bouchard, 2004). Nevertheless, life stages, sociocultural context, and specifically, religious denomination are critical factors shaping the religious goals and behavior of individuals. As indeed Bouchard (2004, p. 150) acknowledges, "Membership in a specific religious denomination is largely due to environmental factors."

Evidence of agreeableness and conscientiousness is found in how high scorers on religiousness describe themselves on self-report scales and projective measures, and in how they are viewed by others (friends, parents, expert raters). Although women tend to be more religious than men (Pew Research Center, 2016), the association between religiousness and agreeableness and conscientiousness is true of both genders, and it applies across the different stages of adulthood, as well as across diverse cultures and religions (e.g., Protestantism, Catholicism, Judaism, and Islam) (Saroglou, 2010). Religiousness also correlates with other measures of personality, such as Eysenck's construct of psychoticism (indicative of conformity, consideration, tender-mindedness, and good impulse control), and communion (the valuing of meaning, warmth, relatedness, nurturance and the need to "get along" with others) (Gebauer, Paulhus, & Neberich, 2013).

The Big Five correlates of religiousness are also reflected in the relation between religion and social values. In terms of Schwartz's circumplex model (Roccas & Elster, 2014), highly religious individuals tend to endorse values associated with conservatism as opposed to openness to change, and to emphasize the importance of security, conformity, and tradition in their lives. Religious individuals also favor the value of self-transcendence, involving an extension of the self to include a concern for others, as opposed to the value of self-enhancement (e.g., the desire for power), though there are some important nuances in this relation (Roccas & Elster, 2014). Again, the association of religiousness with social values appears to be robust, though with some variation, across different cultures and religions (e.g., Saroglou, Delpierre, & Dernelle, 2004).

The personality correlates of religiousness are reflected in the behavior of highly religious individuals. Reflecting a connection with conscientiousness, highly religious individuals tend to drink and smoke less, engage in less sexually permissive behavior and petty crime, and, in college, receive better grades. As expected from its association with agreeableness, religiousness has been found to be positively related to altruism (e.g., Dillon & Wink, 2007).

Spirituality and Personality

Despite the variability in the operationalization and assessment of spirituality, it has been consistently linked to the Big Five dimension of openness. This means that spiritual individuals tend to seek out new and emotionally charged experiences, embrace complexity, and demonstrate artistic interests (Saroglou, 2010). These personality characteristics are evident among self-described spiritual persons and in how they are viewed by others who know them well, as well as by ratings of experts with access to in-depth interview material (e.g., Wink et al., 2007). Once again, this relationship is stable over time, with adolescent spirituality predictive of spirituality in late adulthood (Wink et al., 2007). Findings on the association between spirituality and the other Big Five dimensions are less consistent. Whereas some studies provide evidence suggesting that, like religiousness, spirituality is positively related to agreeableness and conscientiousness (Saroglou, 2010), other studies do not find such a connection (Wink et al., 2007). This discrepancy may be a function of how spirituality is operationalized. The positive association between spirituality and agreeableness and conscientiousness may be found in studies using a broad definition inclusive of individuals whose spirituality is embedded in both traditional and nontraditional religious beliefs and practices, in contrast to a stricter operationalization of spirituality that is independent of church religion. In any case, it is important to note that the absence of a relation does not imply a negative association but simply suggests that characteristics such as compliance, tender-mindedness, self-discipline, and achievement striving are not of central concern to highly spiritual individuals.

There is also evidence that contemporary variants of spirituality tend to be related to healthy narcissism—the self-investment marked by a sense of personal autonomy and independence, intellectual curiosity, and an emphasis on personal growth—rather than to a more pathological self-absorption (Wink, Dillon, & Fay, 2005). Finally, in terms of values, both religiousness and spirituality share a positive association with benevolence, signifying an emphasis on extension of the self through caring for others. Highly spiritual individuals, however, in contrast to their religious counterparts, appear to embrace more strongly the value of universalism, implying a concern for all people irrespective of their religious affiliation, beliefs, or cultural background. In summary, both religiousness and spirituality are associated with a relatively stable, well-defined, and distinct cluster of personality characteristics, notwithstanding overlap and nuances in the nature of these associations in particular individual lives and social contexts.

Lifespan Contexts

A lifespan perspective illuminates how personality traits and social context interrelate in shaping individuals' religious and spiritual development. It also points to how the intertwining of period, cohort, and age effects complicate religious–spiritual identities, beliefs, and practices. All of these effects are typically stronger in the case of religion–spirituality than are found in the study of personality development. An added complexity is introduced by the potential divergence between various dimensions of religion at any one time in an individual's life. This is the case because religious affiliation and/or belief are not necessarily predictive of church attendance, and church attendance is not necessarily reflective of religious identity or of a consistent set of beliefs. In other words, any one dimension of religiousness may exhibit a different trajectory of change over the life course, as will become evident below. Furthermore, such trajectories tend to be mediated or moderated by gender, ethnicity, and, in American society, migration/nativity (generational) status (i.e., whether the individual and/or parents were born in the United States).

Adolescence and Emerging Adulthood

In surveying how religion and spirituality develop over time, we begin with adolescence. We decided on this starting point because this is a time of increased autonomy from parental control. Regardless of how permissive the parents, the adolescent years coinciding with high school are a critical turning point, when young people's religious behavior starts to slip away from parental control. Early adolescent behavior begins to reflect a growing sense of agency in the person's own choice of values, a shift from childhood, in which religious practices are invariably determined by family habits and parental control. Indeed, the critical developmental significance of the adolescent years is underscored today amid the accelerated societal shift away from religion; the fact is that "most Americans who leave their childhood religious identity to become unaffiliated generally do so before their 18th birthday" (Jones at al., 2016, p. 6).

Despite the new freedoms afforded by contemporary culture, adolescent religious agency is not a new phenomenon. Rather, it has long been part of American life. The narrative of a middle-class Protestant woman captures such agency. When Lillian Sinnott was interviewed as a young mother in the 1950s, she recounted how as a 13-year-old in Northern California in the 1940s, she had embarked with her parents' blessing on an exploration of her religious options:

> We always went as a family until [I was] thirteen, and then my parents said we could go to anyplace we wanted and choose. So my older brother quit, and my sister tapered off, and I went hunting. I went to the Presbyterian Church for a while because of the youth group, and then, during the war, a very Fundamentalist soul-saving church and a youth center there—I worked as hostess. Then I tried the Catholic Church for a while and learned as much as I could. In college [I] had a friend who was a reformed Jew, and I went a lot with her. When it came time for [my husband and me] to marry, we picked, on the basis of the right-sized chapel, Episcopalian. Then I got acquainted with the Unitarian and liked it, and since then we have either gone to that or to First Christian, which I was raised in. (in Dillon & Wink, 2007, p. 65).

Given the interaction between the identity tasks of adolescence (Erikson, 1968) and a culture of religious freedom, it is not surprising that there is a well-established decline in religiousness during late adolescence and early adulthood. This pattern has been documented since the beginnings of academic psychology at the dawn of the 20th century (Starbuck, 1911). More recently, research dating from the early 1980s onward confirms this pattern (e.g., Hunsberger & Brown, 1984; Willits & Crider, 1989). Importantly, the decline is evident in both cross-sectional (e.g., Twenge, Exline, Grubbs,

Sastry, & Campbell, 2015) and longitudinal (Chan, Tsai, & Fuligni, 2015; Lopez, Huynh, & Fuligni, 2011; Uecker, Regnerus, & Vaaler, 2007) studies. This convergence therefore rules out the possibility that decreased religiousness in early or emerging adulthood is a cohort effect resulting from accelerated secularization processes that may affect cohorts of students born even just 7 years or so apart. However, although the general effect is robust, the factors underlying the decline are more complicated.

Change in Dimensions

Changes in religiousness from late adolescence (high school years) to early adulthood (mid-20s) are typically investigated using measures of religious affiliation, personal religious beliefs (e.g., belief in a personal or impersonal God), the importance or intensity of religion in the person's life, and frequency of participation at a place of religious worship. The transition to adulthood has relatively little effect on religious affiliation and intensity of religious identity (e.g., Stoppa & Lefkowitz, 2010). Less than one-fifth of young adult participants in the National Longitudinal Study of Adolescent Health report change in their affiliation. And when it occurs, it usually involves a shift from a religious denomination to being religiously unaffiliated (Uecker et al., 2007), a shift accentuated in recent years by the exponential rise in the religiously unaffiliated more generally. Similar to the affiliation decline, approximately one-fifth of young men and women report a significant decline in intensity of religious identity (i.e., "How important is religion to you?") (Uecker et al., 2007). There is also a decline, though small in magnitude, in the importance of religious beliefs in everyday life (e.g., using religion to solve personal problems). This pattern is more frequent among men than women, and less likely among Evangelicals and black Protestants (Stoppa & Lefkowitz, 2010). The relative stability in the importance of religious beliefs in a person's life and its centrality to personal identity is a significant finding. As we discuss later, it is one of the mechanisms that is conducive to the decision of parents to resume religious participation after a pause in their religious activity in early adulthood.

Among the dimensions of religious affiliation, participation, and belief, it is religious attendance that sees the most precipitous decline. Approximately 60–70% of young adults report a decrease, beginning with the high school years, in religious involvement, including attendance at a place of worship and participation in other organized religious activities (Uecker et al., 2007). The average rate of attendance among college sophomores is less than once a month (Stoppa & Lefkowitz, 2010). This decline is pervasive; it is characteristic of all demographic groups and religious affiliations, including college students who identify as born-again Christians attending a Christian college (Hall, Edwards, & Wang, 2016). A large-scale, California-based longitudinal study tracing changes in religiousness from senior year in high school to 4 years after graduation focused primarily on Latin Americans, Asian Americans, and European Americans (Chan et al., 2015). In this study, contrary to expectations, the decline in religious participation was not affected by generational status (whether participants or their parents were born outside of the United States), parental education, or whether the participant attended college. At the outset of the study (grade 12), girls exhibited greater religious attendance than boys—a robust pattern of gender difference evident across many studies concurrently (e.g., Smith & Denton, 2005) and in American youth in the 1940s (e.g., Dillon & Wink, 2007). There were, however, no gender differences in the rate of decline. Those of Latin American ancestry experienced a sharper decline in religious participation than other ethnic groups, but this was due to their initial higher rates of church attendance (Chan et al., 2015).

Patterns of Decline

Although religious attendance in early adulthood tends to decrease uniformly across all demographic categories, the pattern of the decline varies by denomination and early religious socialization. Using a representative sample drawn from the National Longitudinal Survey of Youth (ages 18–25), Petts (2009) found that being raised in a religiously active family predicted subsequent religiousness in young adulthood, as well as a less precipitous decline in engagement. In contrast, an early pattern of decline in church attendance characterized adolescents brought up in religiously heterogeneous families (i.e., families in which parents differed in their religious denominational affiliation) and was more characteristic of mainline Protestants as opposed to their evangelical counterparts. In addition, by age 25, whereas

cohabitation decreased church participation, marriage increased it, but only among the moderately religious respondents (Petts, 2009).

The fact that individuals with stronger religious backgrounds decline less in their religious participation or experience a more delayed decline is in accord with long-term longitudinal findings (e.g., Dillon & Wink, 2007; Mc-Cullough, Enders, Brion, & Jain, 2005). There is quite a bit of stability in individual religiousness over time; although mean (or group) levels of religiousness fluctuate, individuals tend to retain their relative standing vis-à-vis their peers. In other words, although most young adults are likely to experience a decline in religious participation, individuals who are comparatively more religiously involved in early adolescence are also more likely to be religiously active in early adulthood than their peers who were less religiously engaged before entering late adolescence (showing an intercorrelation of .54). This pattern of relative stability tends to continue across adulthood—with an intercorrelation of .67 between early and late adulthood—and underscores the significance of early religious socialization and church participation in predicting subsequent religiosity even 50 years later in late adulthood (Dillon & Wink, 2007, p. 103). From a methodological standpoint, it is important to note that any change in religiousness at a group level is independent of whether individuals retain the same rank vis-à-vis their peers. This is the case because rank-order stability is assessed using the correlation coefficient. This statistic is not affected by mean-level change over time but is influenced, rather, by whether individuals retain their relative position vis-à-vis others. We see a similar pattern in personality development. All of the Big Five personality traits show considerable rank-order stability in adulthood, but that does not preclude mean-level fluctuations with time (e.g., Roberts & DelVecchio, 2000).

Explanations of Religious Decline in Emerging Adulthood

The decline in religious participation that begins in high school and extends into the early to mid-20s is a function of the newfound freedom given to teenagers and young adults as they forge a sense of identity independent of their family of origin. In Eriksonian (Erickson, 1968) terms, these years provide a moratorium for identity exploration before taking on the tasks and responsibilities of adulthood. What is it about this freedom that accounts for the drop in overt religious behavior? A widely accepted view associates religious decline with college attendance. In the 1970s, the college environment was described as "a breeding ground for apostasy" (Caplovitz & Sherrow, 1977), an ecology no doubt abetted by the new cultural permissiveness of the 1960s and 1970s. Yet, beyond any specific cultural moment, college education is expected to have a "liberalizing" impact, as students are exposed to new and more critical and analytical ways of thinking. As Hunter (1983) argues, it is a "well-established fact that education, even Christian education, secularizes" (p. 132). Indeed, actively engaged American Catholics, who are the most critical of official church teachings on sex and gender, are likely to have been educated in Catholic colleges (e.g., Dillon, 2018).

Despite its appeal, the thesis that young adults are turned off religion by the purportedly secular character of the (secular or religious) college environment does not stand empirical scrutiny for two reasons. First, the drop in religious participation in the early to mid-20s is more precipitous among those who do not go to college, and among those who do, it is not affected by attendance at either a 2-year or 4-year institution (Uecker et al., 2007). This is a surprise because one might expect that the 4-year college experience would heighten the probability of being exposed to secular forces. Second, if college education is responsible for a decline in religiousness, its effect should include both religious beliefs and attendance. However, whereas religious attendance declines among college students, religious beliefs do not. Thus, college attendance in and of itself does not appear to affect religious belief systems as postulated by those who argue for the secularizing impact of higher education.

The decline in religious participation has been linked to increases during early adulthood in drug use, premarital sex, and cohabitation, behaviors that are frowned upon by religious institutions and, therefore, likely to inhibit religious attendance (Uecker et al., 2007). Yet this link is tenuous because the available findings make it hard to determine whether it is "counternormative" behavior that leads to a drop in religiousness or whether an initial decline in religiousness promotes the behavior. A more persuasive explanation for the early adult decline in religiousness is the simple fact that, as

argued by Smith and Denton (2005), teenagers lose their interest in going to church, a shift in behavior that is attributable to being "too busy" with a host of other responsibilities (e.g., work, school) and distractions (Hoge, Johnson, & Luidens, 1993).

Furthermore, among current cohorts of young Americans, the pull away from religion is driven by not only the broader societal increase in religious disaffiliation (e.g., Hout & Fischer, 2014) and declining church attendance (Pew Research Center, 2012) but also more long-term secularization. Because parental religiosity is a robust predictor of children's religious engagement (Dillon & Wink, 2007), the less intense religious commitment of current and recent cohorts of parents has a discernible ripple effect. Today's emerging adults—including those who still identify with a religious denomination and/or who go to church—have in general been exposed to weaker religious socialization as a result of having parents who themselves were relatively weak in their religious commitments (e.g., Smith, Longest, Hill, & Christoffersen, 2014; Uecker et al., 2007). The secularizing role of parents is further reflected in the fact that among the unaffiliated, young adults (36%) are more likely than those in their 60s (23%) to say that being raised in a family that was "not that religious" is a major reason why they are no longer affiliated (Jones et al., 2016).

Family Formation and Return to the Fold

Notwithstanding cultural change, family formation is associated with increased religious participation (e.g., Myers, 1996; Stolzenberg, Blair-Loy, & Waits, 1995; Thornton, Axinn, & Hill, 1992). This is particularly true of "traditional families" with two parents and children (Chaves, 2011). Whether this increased participation is due to marriage—particularly among individuals of the same religious affiliation—having children, or having children of a certain age is unclear. Given the well-established link between family formation and increased church attendance, Wuthnow (2007) attributes the contemporary American societal decline in religiousness to the prevalence of delayed or postponed marriage evident among current and recent cohorts of emerging adults. Others associate the resurgence in individual religious behavior with parenthood in general (Baker & Smith, 2009; Sandomirsky & Wilson, 1990; Uecker et al., 2007) or, more specifically, with the timing of when one becomes a parent. Stolzenberg and colleagues (1995), for example, found increased church attendance only among parents who had their first child while in their 20s.

In a recent study, Schleifer and Chaves (2014) attempted to disentangle the causal effect of marriage and parenthood on religious attendance, using longitudinal data from the General Social Survey collected three times over a 4-year period. Cross-sectionally, marriage and parenthood were positively associated with religious service attendance. However, once account was taken of how each individual changed over time, attendance was only significantly associated with having preteen children (ages 6–12). There was no association when the children were younger (preschool) or older (teenagers) (Schleifer & Chaves, 2014). This pattern suggests that parents increase their involvement in order to provide their children with religious socialization coinciding with, and anticipating, the religious rites of passage, including First Communion, Confirmation, and Bar/Bat Mitzvah. Once these rites are accomplished, however, the commitment of parents and of their teenage children declines.

In a further refinement of the family formation thesis, Uecker, Mayrl, and Stroope (2016) found that the increase in religious attendance associated with having children is due to parents returning to the fold (i.e., highly religious youth becoming reengaged with organized religion after a decline during their early 20s). This pattern characterized single mothers and married parents, with both groups scoring higher than their childless peers. Uecker and colleagues speculate that the religious reengagement of both single mothers and married parents might be motivated by the desire to transmit culturally salient norms and behavior scripts to their offspring. And for single parents, there may also be a practical motivation to avail themselves of the social and material support (e.g., babysitting services, parenting classes, discussion groups, day care) frequently provided by religious congregations (Becker & Hofmeister, 2001). In contrast to church attendance, which remained low overall, despite the return to the fold of parents with children, Uecker and colleagues found continued high levels of religious affiliation throughout early adulthood. This suggests that many Americans remain attached to their religious identity even if they do not translate it into active practice. By the same token, it is important to note that there is also stability in the long-term effect of a religiously unaffiliated background; Americans raised without a religion are more likely to remain unaffiliated as they age (Hout & Fischer 2014; Jones et al., 2016).

Middle Adulthood

Little is known about changes in individual religiousness during middle adulthood, a long age interval that stretches from the early 40s to the early 60s. This dearth in knowledge is partly explained by the fact that few normative events or life-course turning points (e.g., marriage, parenthood) occur for the first time during this phase. Certainly, divorce and/or remarriage, the empty nest, and menopause, in the case of women, could serve as anchors for research studies that might also explore the place of religion and spirituality in middle adulthood. Given the responsiveness of religiousness to external factors such as marriage and parenting, one would not expect much change in religious attendance when people are in their 40s and 50s. If anything, a modest decline in religious attendance might be hypothesized given that middle adulthood is a time of diminished child socialization pressures. At the same time, there is typically an increase in a person's career responsibilities and community engagement. Support for this hypothesis comes from the IHD longitudinal study (see footnote 1; Dillon & Wink, 2007). Following the anticipated decline in religiousness from adolescence to early adulthood (ages 30–39), individuals showed an additional modest, but significant, decrease from their 30s to their 40s, before reaching a plateau in their 40s to their late 50s/early 60s (before significantly increasing in the postretirement years).

The family/life-course context conducive to a midlife decline in religious involvement is captured by Ian Logan. An engineer, and lifelong Methodist, who spent a few years living outside the United States, he exemplified the conscientiousness that is characteristic of the personality of conventionally religious individuals (e.g., Wink et al., 2007). Ian was highly active in his church's worship and other religious activities continuously throughout childhood, adolescence, and early adulthood. At age 42, however, with two adolescent children, there was a discernible decline in his level of religious engagement. Though his belief in God had not changed, he himself commented on his weakened church commitment. Remarking that he was somewhat "remiss" in prioritizing the religious dimension of his own children's lives, he explained that the "hectic pace at which we [as a family] operate [made] involvement in church activities not as much as it should be." As is true of many others, there was subsequently a resurgence in Ian's religious participation that was evident in his case in his early 50s, and especially in his 60s, when church activities were again a focal point of his weekly routine (Dillon & Wink, 2007, pp. 85–88). His case illustrates, however, that for even the most highly committed religious individuals, the practical context of family and everyday life can dampen—just as in the family formation phase it may motivate—religious involvement.

The life-course religious trajectory identified by Dillon and Wink (2007) finds additional partial support from a 34-year study following up religiousness among four generations of family members originally recruited in Los Angeles in 1971 (Bengtson, Copen, Putney, & Silverstein, 2009). Aggregated data across the different generations indicated an overall stability in religious attendance between ages 26 and 65 (Hayward & Krause, 2013). As expected, between ages 15 and 25, the sample exhibited a decline, followed by an upswing in religious attendance, and a reverse pattern for ages 65–95. The fact that the study assessed church attendance in middle adulthood at only two time periods—ages 25 and 65 (a span of 40 years)—did not allow for investigating whether religiousness dipped when individuals were in their 30s and 40s. In a separate analysis using the same data, Bengtson, Putney, Silverstein, and Harris (2015) confirmed the absence of change in religious attendance in middle adulthood. This stability in religious behavior was accompanied, however, by modest increases over adulthood in the strength with which participants regarded themselves as religious (irrespective of participation and the importance they placed on having religion in public life and literal interpretation of biblical teachings). The latter finding once again demonstrates the relative independence of religious attendance from the perceived centrality of religion in a person's life. At the same time, it also points to the continued relevance of religion to the personal identity of successive generations of Americans, including millennials, notwithstanding the transformation in the place of religion in American society more generally.

Late Adulthood

An increase in religiousness in older adulthood is well established by both cross-sectional (Hout & Greely, 1987; Levin & Taylor, 1997; Schwadel, 2011) and longitudinal studies (Bengtson et al., 2015; Dillon & Wink, 2007; Hayward & Krause, 2013). An upswing in religious participation typically occurs when individuals are in their mid-60s, coinciding with the postretirement period's increased leisure time and a mix of other social and existential factors (e.g., Dillon & Wink, 2007) that we discuss below. Heightened levels of participation tend to remain stable until individuals are in their 80s, when a gradual decline occurs primarily as a result of physical disabilities that restrict the mobility of the very old (Bengtson et al., 2015; Hayward & Krause, 2013). This decline does not, however, affect religious beliefs or religious intensity; these remain unchanged for people well into their 90s (Bengtson et al., 2015).

The relatively settled nature of religious involvement across an individual's life and how it helps to anchor the routines and goals associated with its different phases is illustrated by Janice. When she was in her 30s, married and with young children, Janice was actively involved in church, attending almost weekly and also taught Sunday School. She talked then about her great faith in the power of prayer, but she also commented that her church involvement was also perhaps reflective of "wanting to belong to a social group." Forty years later, widowed and in her mid-70s, she still identified as a Presbyterian and, like many Americans, frequently attended different denominational churches on any given Sunday. Social connection, clearly, still mattered to her; her choice of church varied depending on which of her religiously diverse friends she accompanied. Yet, at the same time, she was adamant that it was faith that guided her life and gave it purpose. "My faith. My religion if you will. It's been part of my life all through my seventy-five years. . . . In the book I read it says 'There's a time to die, a time to be born, and a time to love and a time to hate'" (in Dillon & Wink, 2007, pp. 115–116).

Given increased secularization and the potential impact of associated cohort effects on the pattern of change, it is vital to confirm the presence of a link between religiousness and aging using longitudinal data. These data, of necessity, however, come from relatively small studies that are not representative of the population at large and are susceptible to nonrandom patterns of attrition (Hayward & Krause, 2014). The generalizability of longitudinal findings therefore is enhanced by cross-sectional studies that can assess large samples of individuals varying in age. The obvious weakness of cross-sectional studies is that they cannot disentangle the effects of age from the effects of cohort (e.g., changes in religiousness between individuals born one generation or 15 years apart) and historical period (e.g., the influence of the turbulent 1960s or of 9/11 on individuals irrespective of their age). Contemporary analytical techniques allow for the investigation of all three of these effects in a single statistical model, while partially controlling for their interrelations. Nevertheless, any cross-sectional study, no matter how statistically sophisticated, can only disentangle the conjoint effect of two of the three variables (age, cohort, period) with the third necessarily held constant (Luo, 2013).

Religion, Aging, and Cultural Variation

In this section, we describe in some detail Hayward and Krause's (2015) study for two reasons. First, the study broadens our understanding of the relationship between religiousness and aging by using cross-sectional data from the World Values Survey (WVS)/European Values Study that contains data from over 700,000 individuals from 80 countries. The data were collected in six assessment waves between 1981 and 2014, spanning more than 30 years. Second, it allows for cross-national comparisons that shed light on important mechanisms that may account for the age-related increases in religiousness. The WVS includes two questions assessing *organized* religiousness (i.e., church attendance: "Apart from weddings and funerals, how often do you attend religious services these days?"), and *private* religiosity ("How important is God in your life?").

In analyzing the WVS data, Hayward and Krause (2015) found an overall significant positive association between the study's measures of both organized and private religiosity and aging. These relationships varied, however, by geographic/cultural region. Church attendance and private religiosity increased with age in Western Europe (both in Catholic and Protestant countries), Latin America, and the Confucian Zone (e.g., Japan, Korea, and Taiwan). No such age-related changes were noted in Africa. Mixed results were found for the Islamic and

Southeast Asian zones (e.g., India, Pakistan, and the Philippines), where an age-related increase in worship attendance, but not in the importance of God, was noted, and in the Orthodox zone (e.g., Russia), where the opposite pattern was observed. These findings challenge the view that religion provides a universal, and hence a culturally invariant, panacea for concerns about the meaning of life (e.g., Hogg, Adelman, & Blagg, 2010) and fear of death (e.g., Vail et al., 2010), concerns that are themselves purported to be universal and to increase in salience with age. According to terror management theory (TMT; Vail et al., 2010), for example, religious beliefs provide the best antidote to the dread of death because of the promise of literal immortality (life after death, or transformation of the human spirit) rather than symbolic immortality (continuation of one's being through creative achievements or through the life of one's offspring). Because the prospect of mortality becomes more salient with age, proponents of TMT argue that elderly adults increasingly require management of it and therefore turn to religion as the most effective means to that end.

While Hayward and Krause's (2015) findings challenge the universality of the connection between religion and fear of death–aging, they do not necessarily invalidate the basic premise of TMT postulating the universality of the terror of mortality. Terror management would be consonant, for example, with Hayward and Krause's findings if feelings about death were held to be culturally relative rather than universal. For example, Western societies might inculcate a fear of death through a taboo about discussing issues of mortality and aging. These factors might result in Westerners anticipating death with terror and thus, in old age, turning to religion. In contrast, traditional African cultures might normalize death and deny its emotional charge, obviating the need to manage death terror. A stronger argument against TMT is provided by growing evidence that the fear of death declines rather than increases with age, as older Americans are much more afraid of the process of dying than of death itself (Wink & Scott, 2005). Fear of death, moreover, appears to be highest among older individuals who are moderately religious; it is especially characteristic of those who believe in an afterlife but who tend not to attend church or pray very often (e.g., Wink & Scott, 2005). And it is lowest among those who are either highly religious or not religious at all. In short, as this latter finding suggests, it is the consistency in an individual's beliefs or worldview that matter; irrespective of whether this is a sacred or secular outlook, the alignment of belief and practice provides the strongest buffer against fear of death.

Additionally, an alternative mechanism to TMT may explain the cultural differences Hayward and Krause (2015) found in the relation between age and religion. As is well documented, elderly (and other) churchgoing Americans receive emotional support from members of their congregation (e.g., Hayward & Krause, 2013). This support, in turn, is associated positively with self-rated health and excitement about life and negatively with depressive feelings (Idler, McLaughlin, & Kasl, 2009). Therefore, for older adults living in societies that, like the United States, emphasize individualism, the social networks and social support provided by organized religion appears to be beneficial for psychosocial functioning. As a corollary, it may be the case that in cultures, such as those of Southeast Asia or the Islamic world, where age had a weak positive relationship to religiousness, older people might receive sufficient emotional support outside of religious organizations from larger and tighter family units that emphasize care for older adults, and where these individuals tend to live with their adult offspring and their children.

Another important issue highlighted by Hayward and Krause's (2015) WVS study involves period effects. Because the WVS comprised six assessments conducted over a period of more than 30 years, it allows, albeit still cross-sectionally, for an assessment of the influence of growth in societal wealth (as measured by national GDP [gross domestic product]) on religiousness. Compared to poor nations, wealthy nations, with the notable exception of the United States, showed lower, and declining, mean levels of both religious attendance and personal importance of God. Hayward and Krause (2015) argue that this pattern fits better with the secularization hypothesis—that economic modernization buffers against existential insecurity and thus propels declining religiosity—than with the postmaterial hypothesis that economic development shifts religious values more toward individualized spiritual seeking (Inglehart, 1997).

Hayward and Krause (2015) argue that because the postmaterial hypothesis predicts that increased GDP will correspond with dips in organizational religiousness but not in personal religious belief, it does not fit with their finding of religious decline across the board. Their argument, however, hinges on the assumption that the WVS's measure of personal religiosity— "How important is God in your life?"—assesses the kind of spiritual turn that the postmaterial hypothesis associates with spiritual seekers. But this construal is at odds with the more diffuse sense of transcendence that characterizes the beliefs and self-understanding of contemporary spiritual seekers (e.g., Arnett, 2004; Smith & Denton, 2005). Therefore, because the WVS's concept of God implies a traditional, monotheistic understanding of religion, the decline of this belief as a function of material wealth does not appear to invalidate the postmaterial hypothesis.

Spirituality over the Life Course

Despite the rise in forms of spirituality that are independent of either religious affiliation or church participation, little is known about how spiritual seeking changes across the life course.

The only data on age-related changes in spiritual seeking come from Wink and Dillon's (2002) longitudinal study using data from the IHD longitudinal study. These analyses indicate that individuals' spirituality remained stable from early adulthood (ages 30–39) to middle adulthood (ages 40–49), and then increased significantly from individuals' 40s to their 50s (late middle adulthood), and again from their 50s to their 70s (late adulthood). Although this pattern of increase was true of men and women, the changes were more pronounced for women. The prototypical spiritual seeker was an older woman who was introspective as an adolescent and who, in her 30s and 40s, experienced a stressful event (e.g., divorce, conflict with children) (Dillon & Wink, 2007; Wink & Dillon, 2002).

The growth of spiritual seeking in the second half of adulthood can be interpreted in two ways. From a psychological perspective, it offers support to Carl Jung's (1953) theory that conceptualizes spirituality as a postmidlife phenomenon and the outcome of the maturational processes associated with aging. According to Jung, the first part of adulthood tends to be devoted to establishing oneself in the adult world, a task that requires the individual to draw on his or her existing personal resources and adapt to conventional social roles (e.g., marriage, becoming a parent, establishing a career). By contrast, the second part of adulthood affords the individual an opportunity to begin the process of finding a more individuated or socially autonomous place in the world. This shift, Jung argues, leads to spiritual development that is independent of traditional religious beliefs and practices. In a somewhat similar vein, Tornstam (2005) argues that cumulative life experiences nurture a shift in how individuals view the world, one that specifically pushes them toward what might be labeled as a postmaterial understanding of the self. In this construal, a postmaterial self is one marked by gerotranscendence. This developmental turn assumes that individuals in old age show less interest in self-oriented material security and rationality, and instead give greater priority to the development of spiritual connections, meditation, universal intergenerational values, and wisdom.

Wink and Dillon's (2002) findings on spiritual growth over the life course can be interpreted as reflecting both period and cohort effects. This is because the timing of the increase in spiritual seeking among the study participants coincided with the 1970s, a time of spiritual ferment in the United States. The fact that the younger cohort of study participants (individuals born in the late 1920s) increased in spirituality more than their older counterparts (born in the early 1920s) suggests cohort effects. The sociological and the psychological–maturational explanations for observed life-course changes in individuals' spirituality do not exclude each other; rather, they point to the fact that personal development invariably takes place in a particular sociohistorical context.

The interaction between psychological motives and cultural resources is illustrated in the case of Kate (quoted earlier). In her early 30s, when she was living and working in a northeastern city, she experienced depression, brought on by the sudden death of the man whom she loved and expected to marry. Three years of psychotherapy, by her own account, "completely changed [her] whole life direction" and gave her "a way to grow and develop." This commitment to self-growth and openness to diverse experiences—personality traits characteristic of spiritual seekers more generally (Wink et al., 2007)—continued to drive her life narrative. Trained as a social worker, Kate not only worked with disadvantaged youth but also chose to live in their impoverished inner-city neighborhood.

Spiritual seeking, already emergent in her adolescent views (as noted earlier), came to assume a much more central place for Kate starting in her 40s. Importantly, the inner psychological motives driving her quest were well matched with the expanded cultural opportunities available. Having returned to California, she "felt the spiritual nudging again," prompting her initially to get involved with the then-resurgent Catholic Charismatic movement, before rediscovering a progressive Episcopal church, as well as participating in a small "house-church," where participants meditated and talked about spiritual issues and their own journeys. Kate maintained and further expanded these religious and spiritual activities well into her 70s, though, as noted earlier, she resisted calling herself religious). What is clear, however, is that notwithstanding her psychological strengths, it is unlikely that Kate could have fulfilled her self-driven spiritual desires and aspirations into the spiritual experiences that became central to her identity absent the sort of sociocultural environment in which such practices flourished.

Age-Related Changes in the Meaning of Religiousness

Looked at from the perspective of McAdams's (2013) theory of the self, both Jung's (1953) and Tornstam's (2005) views of religious development entail a shift from being an agent to becoming an author. In this framing, the individual creates his or her own religious narrative, a narrative that is at least partly independent of the conventionality entailed in the self as an actor or agent. A shift in construal of the relationship between the self and a transcendent being is particularly apparent in cases of individual conversion. When atheists become Southern Baptists, for example, there is a clearly a major change in their personal goals, how they construe questions of meaning (e.g., Paloutzian, 2005), and how they reorient the self and goals in response to their newly acquired "spiritual strivings" and "ultimate concerns" (e.g., Emmons 1999).

Irrespective of conversion, changes in the narrative of the self are, from a life-course perspective, applicable to both spiritual seekers and those who are more conventionally religious. The notion of a process of faith development that is compatible with traditional religious beliefs and practices is central to Fowler's (1981) thesis. He adopts a cognitive-structural stage model of faith development. Among other characteristics, it assumes growth in the individual's perspective taking, in complexity of moral judgment and social awareness, and in a more individuated approach to authority. Central to Fowler's model is the assumption that the meaning of an individual's religiousness may change or evolve independently of church attendance, religious affiliation, or the importance of religious beliefs to the person's identity. In other words, as people age, they may, for example, continue their weekly church attendance or Bible reading, and continue to identify as Methodist or Baptist. Yet this does not preclude a significant shift in the meanings they derive from or inject into religion.

Recent advances in developmental psychology challenge the notion of invariant developmental stages that assume uniform changes across various domains of functioning. Influenced by this work, Streib, Hood, and Klein (2010) argued for the abandonment of a stage theory of faith development in favor of one recognizing uneven development across various religious domains. According to Paloutzian (2005), meaning serves as an independent dimension of religiousness. Many Americans explain their construal of what it means to be religious by invoking the Golden Rule. Yet how people interpret its meaning—and what goals it requires of them—can vary with age. We see this in the case of Martha Wilson, a highly agential, upper-class, married woman who was born and lived all of her life in the San Francisco Bay Area. An actively engaged Presbyterian, who described herself as "deeply religious," the Golden Rule was one dimension of her broader religious profile—weekly church attendance, teaching Sunday School, serving as an Elder— that, in its outward appearance, did not vary much across her life. Yet, over time, she showed a deeper understanding of the meaning of the Golden Rule. When she was in her 30s, "Love thy neighbor" summarized her moral philosophy. She also readily acknowledged that she didn't always follow this dictum and spontaneously admitted to having prejudicial feelings toward others, including toward her fundamentalist sister-in-law and Jehovah's Witnesses. Forty years later, the reflections she offered in articulating her beliefs and values expressed a more internalized appreciation of the depth and practical scope of the Golden Rule's meaning:

> I think it really is true that you do have to love your neighbor. I do believe that God really did create us all equal, although we haven't figured that out quite yet. I believe you really, really have

to love one another. You don't have to like everybody but you do—if we're ever going to live in this world in peace—you do have to love everybody. I think that people have got to quit worrying about sexual preference God made us the way we are; and if you're gay or lesbian, that's the way you were made, unless you strayed off the track somewhere and you're a voyeur or whatever. I believe that you have to accept people, truly accept them. And as I said, I don't think you have to like everybody—I don't think that's possible. But I do think you have to love everyone. And this includes the criminals and everybody—no matter how hard that is. There are a lot of people who are not very lovable. (in Dillon & Wink, 2007, p. 114)

Thus, with age, Martha developed a deeper and more internalized apprehension of the meaning of God's love for all people, even as her outward religious behavior remained relatively unvaried over time.

Conclusion

Religion and spirituality are conceptually separate, multidimensional constructs whose empirical manifestation provides a dynamic field of research and one characterized by much evidence of the agential self. Both religion and spirituality are highly correlated with discrete personality traits, and are highly responsive to macro societal change, as well as to the changing tasks and opportunities associated with different life stages. Consequently, each has a different developmental trajectory affected both by the psychological motives and needs of the individual and changes in family formation and public culture.

The relationship between personality and religiousness and spirituality raises questions about which comes first: Do individuals who are agreeable and conscientious, for example, tend to gravitate toward religion, or is it that being religious is conducive to the acquisition of these personality characteristics? Longitudinal findings showing that personality predicts increases in religiousness over time, rather than the reverse, lend support to the former hypothesis (Wink et al., 2007). New research, however, would do well to explore the interaction among personality, family socialization, religiousness, and spirituality. Such research could investigate, for example, whether individuals who grow up in families that emphasize traits such as agreeableness and conscientiousness are likely to gravitate toward religion over their life course, independent of early religious socialization, compared to their counterparts with different personality traits.

The delayed social roles (e.g., postponed marriage and parenthood) associated with emergent adulthood also beg research attention to whether and how changes in life-course patterns may impact religious and spiritual engagement, at both the individual and societal levels. By the same token, it will be important to track whether personality traits and the religious outlets for the self-realization of personal goals at particular life-course stages will be impacted, and how, by the increased trend toward religious disaffiliation. In America, religion has long served as both foreground and background for the individual's self-construal as actor, author, and agent. This current time of societal transition may nuance these relations in ways that will illuminate new insights about both the self and culture.

ACKNOWLEDGMENTS

We thank Dan McAdams and Rebecca Shiner for helpful comments and suggestions on an earlier draft of this chapter.

REFERENCES

Arnett, J. J. (2004). *Emerging adulthood: The winding road from the late teens through the twenties.* New York: Oxford University Press.

Baker, J. O., & Smith, B. G. (2009). The nones: Social characteristics of the religiously unaffiliated. *Social Forces, 87,* 1251–1263.

Becker, P. E., & Hofmeister, H. (2001). Work, family, and religious involvement for men and women. *Journal for the Scientific Study of Religion, 40,* 707–722.

Bengtson, V. L., Copen, C. E., Putney, N. M., & Silverstein, M. (2009). A longitudinal study of the intergenerational transmission of religion. *International Sociology, 23,* 325–345.

Bengtson, V. L., Putney, N. M., Silverstein, M., & Harris, S. C. (2015). Does religiousness increase with age?: Age changes and generational differences over 35 year. *Journal for the Scientific Study of Religion, 54,* 363–379.

Bouchard, T. J. (2004). Genetic influence on human psychological traits: A survey. *Current Directions in Psychological Science 13,* 148–151.

Caplovitz, D., & Sherrow, F. (1977). *The religious drop outs: Apostasy among college graduates.* Thousand Oaks, CA: SAGE.

Chan, M., Tsai, K. M., & Fuligni A. J. (2015). Changes in religiosity across the transition to young adulthood. *Journal of Youth and Adolescence, 44,* 1555–1566.

Chaves, M. (2011). *American religion: Contemporary trends.* Princeton, NJ: Princeton University Press.

Dillon, M. (2018). *Postsecular Catholicism: Relevance and renewal.* New York: Oxford University Press.

Dillon, M., & Wink, P. (2007). *In the course of a lifetime: Tracing religious belief, practice, and change.* Berkeley: University of California Press.

Emmons, R. A. (1999). *The psychology of ultimate concerns: Motivation and spirituality in personality.* New York: Guilford Press.

Erikson, E. H. (1968). *Identity: Youth and crisis.* New York: Norton.

Fowler, J. (1981). *Stages of faith.* New York: Harper & Row.

Gebauer, J. E., Paulhus, D. L., & Neberich, W. (2013). Big two personality and religiosity across cultures: Communals as religious conformists and agentics as religious contrarians. *Social Psychological and Personality Science, 4,* 21–30.

Giddens, A. (1991). *Modernity and self-identity: Self and society in the late modern age.* Stanford, CA: Stanford University Press.

Glenn, N. (1987). The trend in "No religion" respondents to U.S. national surveys, late 1950s to early 1980s. *Public Opinion Quarterly, 51,* 292–314.

Hall, T. W., Edwards, E., & Wang, D. C. (2016). The spiritual development of emerging adults over the college years: A 4-year longitudinal investigation. *Psychology of Religion and Spirituality, 8,* 206–217.

Hayward, R. D., & Krause, N. (2013). Changes in church-based social support relationships during older adulthood. *Journals of Gerontology B: Psychological Sciences and Social Sciences, 68,* 85–96.

Hayward, R. D., & Krause, N. (2014). Forms of attrition in a longitudinal study of religion and health in older adults and implications for sample bias. *Journal of Religion and Health, 55,* 50–66.

Hayward, R. D., & Krause, N. (2015). Aging, social developmental, and cultural factors in changing patterns of religious involvement over a 32-year period: An age–period–cohort analysis of 80 countries. *Journal of Cross-Cultural Psychology, 46,* 979–995.

Hoge, D. R., Johnson, B., & Luidens, D. A. (1993). Determinants of church involvement of young adults who grew up in Presbyterian churches. *Journal for the Scientific Study of Religion, 32,* 242–255.

Hogg, M. A., Adelman, J. R., Blagg, R. D. (2010). Religion in the face of uncertainty: An uncertainty–identity theory account of religiousness. *Personality and Social Psychology Review, 14,* 72–83.

Hout, M., & Fischer, C. (2002). Why More Americans have no religious preference: Politics and generations. *American Sociological Review, 67,* 165–190.

Hout, M., & Fischer, C. (2014). Explaining why more Americans have no religious affiliation: Political backlash and generational succession, 1972–2012. *Sociological Science, 1,* 423–447.

Hout, M., & Greeley, A. (1987). The center doesn't hold: Church attendance in the United States, 1940–1984. *American Sociological Review, 52,* 325–345.

Houtman, D., & Aupers, S. (2007). The spiritual turn and the decline of tradition: The spread of post-Christian spirituality in fourteen Western countries, 1981–2000. *Journal for the Scientific Study of Religion, 46,* 305–320.

Hunsberger, B., & Brown, L. B. (1984). Religious socialization, apostasy, and the impact of family background. *Journal for the Scientific Study of Religion, 23,* 239–251.

Hunter, J. D. (1983). *American evangelicalism: Conservative religion and the quandary of modernity.* New Brunswick, NJ: Rutgers University Press.

Idler, E. L., McLaughlin, J., & Kasl, S. (2009). Religion and the quality of life in the last year of life. *Journals of Gerontology B: Psychological and Social Sciences, 64,* 528–537.

Inglehart, R. (1997). *Modernization and postmodernization: Cultural, economic, and political change in 43 societies.* Princeton, NJ: Princeton University Press.

Jones, R., Cox, D., Cooper, B., & Lienesch, R. (2016). *Exodus: Why Americans are leaving religion—and why they're unlikely to come back.* Washington, DC: Public Religion Research Institute.

Jung, C. (1953). On the psychology of the unconscious. In H. Read, M. Fordham, & G. Adler (Eds.), *The collected works of C. G. Jung* (pp. 3–119). Princeton, NJ: Princeton University Press.

Levin, J. S., & Taylor, R. J. (1997). Age differences in patterns and correlates of the frequency of prayer. *The Gerontologist, 37,* 75–89.

Lopez, A. B., Huynh, V. W., & Fuligni, A. J. (2011). A longitudinal study of religious identity and participation during adolescence. *Child Development, 82,* 1297–1309.

Luo, L. (2013). Assessing validity and application scope of the intrinsic estimator approach to the age–period–cohort problem. *Demography, 50,* 1945–1967.

McAdams, D. P. (2013). The psychological self as actor, agent, and author. *Perspectives on Psychological Science, 8,* 272–295.

McCullough, M., Enders, C., Brion, S., & Jain, A. (2005). The varieties of religious development in adulthood. *Journal of Personality and Social Psychology, 89,* 78–89.

Myers, S. (1996). Families and the inheritance of religiosity. *American Sociological Review, 61,* 858–866.

Paloutzian, R. (2005). Religious conversion and spiritual transformation. In R. F. Paloutzian & C. Park (Eds.), *Handbook of the psychology of religion and spirituality* (pp. 331–347). New York: Guilford Press.

Petts, R. (2009). Trajectories of religious participation from adolescence to young adulthood. *Journal for the Scientific Study of Religion, 48,* 552–571.

Pew Research Center. (2009). *Many Americans mix multiple faiths.* Washington, DC: Author.

Pew Research Center. (2012). *"Nones" on the rise: One-in-five adults have no religious affiliation.* Washington, DC: Author.

Pew Research Center. (2015). *U.S. public becoming less religious.* Washington, DC: Author.

Pew Research Center. (2016). *The gender gap in religion around the world.* Washington, DC: Author.

Pew Research Center. (2018). *Being Christian in Western Europe.* Washington, DC: Author.

Roberts, B., & DelVecchio, W. (2000). The rank-order consistency of personality from childhood to old age: A quantitative review of longitudinal studies. *Psychological Bulletin, 126,* 3–25.

Roccas, S., & Elster, A. (2014). Values and religiosity. In V. Saroglou (Ed.), *Religion, personality, and social behavior* (pp. 213–229). New York: Psychology Press.

Roof, W. C. (1999). *Spiritual marketplace: Baby boomers and the remaking of American religion.* Princeton, NJ: Princeton University Press.

Sandomirsky, S., & Wilson, J. (1990). Processes of disaffiliation: Religious mobility among men and women. *Social Forces, 68,* 1211–1229.

Saroglou, V. (2010). Religiousness as a cultural adaptation of basic traits: A five-factor model perspective. *Personality and Social Psychology Review, 14,* 108–125.

Saroglou, V., Delpierre, V., & Dernelle, R. (2004). Values and religiosity: A meta-analysis of studies using Schwartz's model. *Personality and Individual Differences, 37,* 721–734.

Schleifer, C., & Chaves, M. (2014). Family formation and religious service attendance: Untangling marital and family effects. *Sociological Methods and Research, 46,* 125–152.

Schwadel, P. (2011). Age, period, and cohort effects on religious activities and beliefs. *Social Science Research, 40,* 181–192.

Smith, C., & Denton, M. L. (2005). *Soul searching: The religious and spiritual lives of American teenagers.* New York: Oxford University Press.

Smith, C., Longest, K., Hill, J., & Christoffersen, K. (2014). *Young Catholic America.* New York: Oxford University Press.

Starbuck, E. D. (1911). *The psychology of religion.* New York: Walter Scott.

Stolzenberg, R. M., Blair-Loy, M., & Waits, L. J. (1995). Religious participation in early adulthood: Age and family life cycle effects on church membership. *American Sociological Review, 60,* 84–103.

Stoppa, T. M., & Lefkowitz, E. S. (2010). Longitudinal changes in religiosity among emerging adult college students. *Journal of research on adolescence, 20,* 23–38.

Streib, H., Hood, R. W., & Klein, C. (2010). The Religious Schema Scale: Construction and initial validation of a quantitative measure for religious styles. *International Journal for the Psychology of Religion, 20,* 152–172.

Thornton, A., Axinn, W. G., & Hill, D. H. (1992). Reciprocal effects of religiosity, cohabitation, and marriage. *American Journal of Sociology, 98,* 628–651.

Tornstam, L. (2005). *Gerotranscendence: A developmental theory of positive aging.* New York: Springer.

Twenge, J. M., Exline, J. J., Grubbs, J. B., Sastry, R., & Campbell, W. K. (2015). Generational and time period differences in American adolescents' religious orientation, 1966–2014. *PLOS ONE, 10*(5), e0121454.

Uecker, J. E., Mayrl, D., & Stroope, S. (2016). Family formation and returning to institutional religion in young adulthood. *Journal for the Scientific Study of Religion, 55,* 384–406.

Uecker, J. E., Regnerus, M., & Vaaler, M. (2007). Losing my religion: The social sources of religious decline in early adulthood. *Social Forces, 85,* 1667–1692.

Vail, K. E., Rothschild, Z. K., Weise, D. R., Solomon, S., Pyszczynski, T., & Greenberg, J. (2010). A terror management analysis of the psychological functions of religion. *Personality and Social Psychology Review, 14,* 84–94.

Willits, F. K., & Crider, D. M. (1989). Church attendance and traditional religious beliefs in adolescence and young adulthood: A panel study. *Review of Religious Research, 31,* 68–81.

Wink, P. (2011). Trouble with spirituality. *Research in the Social Scientific Study of Religion, 21,* 49–69.

Wink, P., Ciciolla, L., Dillon, M., & Tracy, A. (2007). Religiousness, spiritual seeking, and personality: Findings from a longitudinal study. *Journal of Personality, 75,* 1051–1070.

Wink, P., & Dillon, M. (2002). Spiritual development across the life-course: Findings from a longitudinal study. *Journal of Adult Development, 9,* 79–94.

Wink, P., Dillon, M., & Fay, K. (2005). Spirituality, narcissism and psychotherapy: How are they related? *Journal for the Scientific Study of Religion, 44,* 143–158.

Wink, P., & Scott, J. (2005). Does religiousness buffer against the fear of death and dying in late adulthood?: Findings from a longitudinal study. *Journals of Gerontology B: Psychological Sciences, 60,* P207–P214.

Wuthnow, R. (2007). *After the baby boomers: How twenty- and thirty-somethings are shaping the future of American religion.* Princeton, NJ: Princeton University Press.

CHAPTER 22

Culture and the Development
of Motives, Values, and Social Selves

Gary S. Gregg

In this chapter I discuss cultural influences on motives, values, interpersonal styles, systems of self-care, and social selves—characteristics that loosely fall within McAdams's (1995, 2015) Level II personality organization. These tend to be more flexible and develop more from experience than the temperament-based Level I traits (e.g., the Big Five), but they are more broadly shared within a culture than are Level III identities rooted in individualizing life stories. The chapter begins with a brief review of the last three decades' findings on differences between individualist and collectivist cultures. Then I shift perspective to the "other" cultural psychology, based not on comparisons of the globe's contemporary cultures, but on studies of more "traditional" societies, many of them conducted 40–80 years ago. To illustrate some of the ways that "traditional" cultures differed from each other, I compare Japanese and Arab-Muslim cultures, then use these examples to discuss key differences between "traditional" and "modern" societies in general. I conclude by arguing that many of the individualism versus collectivism contrasts have resulted from the process of "modernization," and need to be reinterpreted in light of the changed living conditions and lifestyles that modernization brings. The chapter ends with some suggestions about how cultural psychology might now focus less

on national cultures, and more on niches within the globalizing world.

Individualism and Collectivism

Cultural psychology has grown dramatically in recent decades, and converged on a set of key findings. First, the "Big Five" personality traits—extraversion, agreeableness, conscientiousness, openness, and neuroticism—appear to be universal (Heine & Buchtel, 2009), with some minor but still important variations. Second, the "Big Six" emotions—happiness, sadness, fear, anger, surprise, and disgust—also appear to be universal, with each culture having display rules that shape when and how they are expressed, so that the emotional life shared by all humans takes on a distinctive style within each culture. Third, the most important differences between the world's cultures appear to derive from "individualist" versus "collectivist" (IND vs. COL) values that shape contrasting "egocentric" versus "sociocentric" selves. Studies by Hofstede (1980), Markus and Kitayama (1991), Nisbett (2004), Triandis (1995), and others have shown that cultural values emphasizing individualism or collectivism shape a wide array of psychological characteristics, including perception, motivation, family and group loyalties, self-concepts, and self-esteem. Each creates an ingrained worldview that can make it difficult for people from individualist cultures (mostly modern Western societies) to understand and interact with those from collectivist cultures—and vice versa.

Takeo Doi (1973) wrote about feeling bewildered at his first social gathering in the United States when the host invited him to "help himself" to snacks and drinks because a high-COL Japanese host would have researched his tastes and offered him those he likes. A Moroccan friend of mine returned shaken from a job interview with an American agency because the director began with the high-IND question, "So Mohammed, tell us about yourself." He had prepared to talk about his skills, but fumbled his response because he didn't have a capsule life story ready to showcase his distinctiveness. Many programs that prepare Westerners to study or work abroad now use the IND–COL studies to help them recognize cultural differences and avoid misunderstandings such as these.

Scores of studies show the IND versus COL differences to be broad and deep (for fuller reviews and references, see Heine, 2008; Keith, 2011; Matsumoto & Juang, 2016; Triandis, 1995). They affect basic perception: People in IND cultures perceive objects and people to be separate from their contexts, while those in COL cultures attend to the relations among them. As they look at a drawing of fish in a pond, members of IND cultures zero in on the largest fish, while those from COL cultures take in the whole underwater scene. In IND cultures, people tend to remember events from their own viewer's perspective, while those in COL cultures tend to remember them as seen from an outsider's point of view. When asked to group two items that go together of *man–woman–child* or *dog–carrot–rabbit,* members of IND cultures group man and woman because they are adults and dog and rabbit because they are animals, while those from COL cultures tend to group woman with child and rabbit with carrot because of the relationships between them. People in IND cultures tend to use more state verbs—"He is a salesman"—that emphasize objects in categories, while those in COL cultures tend to use more action verbs—"He sells cars"—that emphasize relationships. IND languages tend to use separate pronouns for "I" and "you," while COL languages tend to convey these by verb conjugations or other grammatical features. Of special importance, members of IND cultures perceive people as having fixed personality traits that cause their behavior, while those in COL cultures tend to view personality as flexible and behavior as caused by situations or relationships.

IND–COL is associated with—and perhaps based on—differences in group dynamics. In IND societies, people tend to belong to many groups but have weak commitments to each; in COL societies, they tend to have one or two groups to which they make strong commitments. Replications of Asch's (1955) famous conformity experiment have found greater conformity in COL societies than in IND societies, especially when the group consists of members of a person's ingroup. Whereas people in IND cultures tend to see events as caused by the actions of individuals, those in COL cultures more often see groups as actors. There is some evidence that people in IND societies work better on their own, while those in COL societies work best in cooperative groups. This carries into the important area of motivation, with achievement motivation in IND cultures associated with individual success, and in COL cultures more strongly associated with group success. In the 1960s, DeVos (1973) found the need for achievement to be negatively correlated with the need for affiliation (bonds with others) in the United States, but positively correlated in Japan, where a desire to bring honor and repay the "debt" to one's family (see below) often motivates striving.

Perhaps the most studied differences between IND and COL societies concern self-concepts and self-esteem. In IND cultures, people tend to think of themselves in terms of their fixed inner dispositions and traits in ways that emphasize their independence and separateness from others. In COL cultures, people tend to define themselves by their network of relationships and roles, emphasizing their interdependence. In addition, members of IND cultures tend to engage in "self-enhancement," using a variety of strategies to raise their self-esteem (e.g., remembering successes more readily than failures), while those in COL cultures either do not self-enhance or they use "self-criticism" strategies in accordance with an ethic of modesty. IND cultures foster greater expression of positive emotions, and happiness tends to be correlated with positive feelings; in COL cultures, happiness tends to be more strongly associated with respect from others.

Therefore, IND and COL cultures show associations with a wide array of basic psychological processes, from perception and "holistic" versus "analytic" thinking to group dynamics, emotion, and self-conception. High-COL cultures clearly foster the development of more relationally focused values, motives, and goals—McAdams's Level II characteristics. Greenfield, Keller, Fuligni, and Maynard (2003) argue that the IND versus COL contrast sets up "independent" versus "interdependent" pathways of personality development, and concur with Triandis and Suh (2002) that they create individualistic and collectivistic "personality types."

But studies of IND versus COL also have found unexpected complexities. Some of the differences have turned out to depend more on the situation in which people find themselves than on their culture's values, and increasing evidence shows that people can behave as individualists or collectivists depending on how a situation frames the task. More importantly, in their meta-analysis of 83 studies, Oyserman, Coon, and Kemmelmeier (2002) found only modest support for the IND versus COL dimension, and only small differences between Japan (the archetypal COL culture) and the United States (the archetypal IND culture), with the United States being actually more collectivist (p. 18). Kagitçibasi (2007) argues that researchers have confounded IND versus COL values—what people *should* do—with *actual* relationships, and that the terms need to be redefined to recognize that "interdependence" (COL) and "autonomy" (IND) coexist within all cultures. A consensus appears to be emerging around the position that Triandis (1995) long has taken: that cultural values vary on a single IND versus COL dimension, but for individuals, IND and COL form separate dimensions, so that people may be high or low on either. Later I consider the evidence that the most important differences between COL and IND cultures result from "modernization": changes in life expectancy, affluence, and comfort; in economics, family structure, and childrearing styles; and in literacy and media use.

Two Cultural Psychologies

Psychologists came late to "culture." With important exceptions, they waited until university systems developed to provide collaborators and student participants, and digital communications made it possible for studies to be done quickly enough to meet their publication demands. As a result, psychologists have tended to compare the most modern sectors of both Western and non-Western societies, mainly college students, employees in multinational corporations, and schoolteachers. This "new" cultural psychology has mostly sought to identify trait-like dimensions on which all cultures can be scaled—like the Big Five and IND versus COL. In fact, Oyserman, Kemmelmeier, and Coon (2002) insist that cultural psychology's goal is "not to provide a rich description of a specific culture" (p. 116).

Anthropologists, by contrast, have tended to study characteristics that are distinctive of single cultures, and to seek out the most "traditional" communities they could find. A handful of psychologists also have continued to study single cultures in depth, and their work converges with efforts by non-Western researchers to develop "indigenous psychologies" based on concepts drawn from their own traditions (Allwood & Berry, 2006; Kagitçibasi, 2000; Kim & Berry, 1993; Kim, Yang, & Hwang, 2006; Sinha, 2003). Studies by Hsu (1971) of China, Doi (1973) of Japan, Kakar (1978) of India, and Ammar (1964) of Egypt can be seen as early formulations of indigenous psychologies in that they offer culturally specific accounts of personality development. More recently, Chao's (1994) and Fung's (1999) studies of childrearing and Peng and Nisbett's (1999; Nisbett, 2004) studies of cognition represent investigations of China's indigenous psychology. Lebra (1976, 2004) provides a summary of this research on Japan, Bond (1987, 2010) on China, and Gregg (2005) on Arab-Muslim societies. As Kim and Berry (1993) argue, cultural psychology needs to be built from both knowledge of single cultures and multicultural studies of universal dimensions. But we currently have two cultural psychologies: studies of indigenous psychologies conducted in the more traditional sectors of societies (mostly) before the 1980s, and studies of dimensions of cultural variation conducted in the most modern sectors of societies (mostly) after the 1980s. We face the challenge of uniting these two cultural psychologies.

A Theoretical Model

Based on studies of indigenous psychologies, LeVine (1973) proposed a two-level model of personality organization. The first level develops from the interaction of inherited temperament and early experience, and consolidates around ages 5–7. The second develops largely in response to deliberate socialization, consolidates with the entrance to adulthood, and includes values and motives enacted in overt behavior and one's personal identity as theorized by Erikson (1950). LeVine believes this distinction is crucial to accounting for important discontinuities: An adult's personality may require both active suppression of childhood characteristics that run against culture's norms, and effortful development of characteristics that have no foundation in early development. Child care in many traditional societies set up three potentially important discontinuities that often posed developmental challenges. The first occurred around the time of weaning, which frequently coincided with "displacement" by a new baby and exposure to nutrition and health hazards; the second occurred between ages 5 and 7, when "indulgent" care often shifted to more demanding and harsher training; and the third occurred in adolescence, typically marked by rites of passage for boys and marriage and motherhood for girls.

Studies of indigenous psychologies in fact indicate that a third level of organization needs to be added to LeVine's (1973) model, "between" early childhood and adulthood. This level consolidates in early adolescence as children master their culture's interpersonal etiquettes, religious beliefs, and self-care practices. It corresponds to McAdams's Level II, encompassing the formation of values, motives, and interpersonal scripts, and also of a "social self" or "persona" as described by G. H. Mead (1934): a self-image built by imagining one's self seen from the perspective of society as a whole, or of the "generalized other." It is the provisional consolidation of motives, goals, and a social persona in early adolescence that triggers the task of identity development: As Erikson (1950) theorizes, the transition to adulthood raises fundamental challenges, even in COL cultures:

"Can I live up to society's expectations for me? Must I accept society's script for me?"

The resulting three-level model closely parallels McAdams's (1995, 2015) model. Adopting the apprenticeship–competence–mastery conception of development, we can diagram cultural influences on personality as shown in Figure 22.1 (Gregg, 2005).

This model recognizes the two main transitions in bodily growth, brain development, and cognitive maturation that all cultures appear to treat as transition points—the first at roughly ages 5–7 (Rogoff, Sellers, Pirottqa, Fox, & White, 1975; Sameroff & Haith, 1996) and the second around puberty (Schlegel & Barry, 1991)—as consolidating the previous level and making possible development of the succeeding level. It recognizes discontinuities in development and abiding tensions in adult personality that may result from them.

Indigenous Psychologies: Japan and Arab-Muslim Societies

With this model in mind, let us briefly compare the indigenous psychologies of two "traditional" cultures. According to Hofstede's (2001) data, Japan and Arab-Muslim societies (represented by Morocco) are about equally "collectivist" and not much different on his dimension of "power distance."[1] Neither were studied when they were "truly" traditional, but between the 1930s and the 1970s, researchers sought out more traditional communities, and their descriptions largely agree with histori-

---

[1] See data for Morocco at *http://geert-hofstede.com/morocco.html*. Other MENA (Middle East and North Africa) countries score a little higher than Japan on collectivism. Studies of the MENA region are mixed and perhaps not of high quality: Oyserman, Coon, and colleagues' (2002) data show Egypt to be *more* collectivist and *less* individualist than Japan, but Turkey to be *less* collectivist and *more* individualist.

	Infancy	Early Childhood	Late Childhood	Adolescence and Early Adulthood	Mature Adulthood
I. Core Personality	Apprenticeship	Competence	Mastery		
II. Motives and Social Persona		Apprenticeship	Competence	Mastery	
III. Identity			Apprenticeship	Competence	Mastery

FIGURE 22.1. Three-level model of cultural influences on personality.

cal accounts. In premodern Japan, a disarmed peasantry was closely surveilled by a small samurai class that could kill them at will, and that held groups of families responsible for the behavior of individual members. This intensified inhibitions on aggression among commoners and buttressed conformity to the family and village "collective." Historical accounts and early Western travelers (Kojima, 1986; Lewis, 1996; Valignano, 1962), as well as 20th-century anthropologists, have noted that Japanese parental authorities relied mainly on cultivating a sense of indebtedness, inducing shame and guilt, and threats of exclusion—rather than physical threats and blows—to socialize their children to "harmonious" familial roles and loyalties.[2]

In premodern Arab-Muslim societies, by contrast, much of the population lived beyond all but the most determined reach of governments, in segmentary lineage, clan, and tribal groupings that often feuded over scarce and shifting resources. In these areas, most boys were raised to fight, in accordance with an intimidating and aggressive code of masculine "honor." Observers there have noted that parental authorities often used physical threats and blows in addition to shaming to socialize their children, which for boys was part of their toughening to become fighters. Both Japan and Arab-Muslim societies were patriarchies, in which women showed at least public deference to men, but they sharply contrasted in terms of gender relations and sexuality. With some exceptions, Arab-Muslim societies strongly emphasized women's chastity, seclusion, and veiling,[3] while most scholars concur that among non-Samurai, Japan afforded much greater gender equality, evident in the nearly equal sex ratios that reflect equal treatment of male and female babies (Skinner, 1993). Women were not secluded or veiled, mixed-gender celebrations with heavy drinking were common, and there was little cultural emphasis on premarital chastity or postmarital fidelity (Smith & Wiswell, 1982). In addition, the beliefs and

self-care practices associated with "folk" Islam hardly could have differed more from Japan's Buddhist-Shinto religiosity.

Japan

Accounts of development in Japan generally converge on (1) the cultivation in infancy and toddlerhood of *amae* "indulged dependence" and *omoiyari* "empathy," (2) that were socialized in middle childhood toward "harmonious" *oyabun-kobun* (parentlike–childlike) and *sempai-kohai* (senior–junior) relationships. This was fostered by a combination of the security and freedom enjoyed within the extended family and the cultivation of a sense of *on* indebtedness to parents and ancestors, reinforced by threats of exclusion from the family's protection and exposure to the dangers of the outside world. This in turn fostered interpersonal styles suited to Japan's pervasive "vertical" senior–junior relationships, and an identity-anchoring loyalty to the *ie* "stem" household as an entity that existed generation after generation and had mythic–spiritual meanings. (For references on Japan, see Bachnik & Quinn, 1994; Doi, 1973, 1985; Kondo, 1990; Lebra, 1976, 2004; Rosenberger, 1992; Shimizu & LeVine, 2001; Yamaguchi & Arizumi, 2006.)

Descriptions of the resulting "relational self" emphasize a tension between *ninjo* "human feelings" that can be freely expressed in some settings and *giri* "social obligations" that prescribe etiquette-governed behavior in more formal contexts. *Amae*-ing (indulging dependence) often operated at the core of the *ninjo* "human feelings" that were expressed in intimate family relations, and one could fulfill one's *giri* "social obligations" and build a self only to the extent that he or she learned *enryo,* to restrain the desire to be indulged in dependence and thereby develop *kejime,* the knowledge or maturity required to manage emotional expression in shifting social contexts. Japanese culture then valued overcoming "selfishness" in order to attain a "selfless heart" that enables people to recruit "human feelings" to motivate the "harmonious" fulfillment of their social obligations—an ideal that permeated Buddhist-Shinto ethics, aesthetics, and spirituality.

Children also grew up in continual relations with invisible beings and forces, some protective, others malevolent. There were *kami* spirits living in mountains, forests, springs, and fields; ancestral spirits, ghosts, and sorcerers; Bud-

---

[2]Though the government-fostered dissemination of Bushido ethics and creation of an education system based on military models of discipline appear to have increased the use of threats and beatings—at least for boys—in the first half of the 20th century.

[3]These actually were circum-Mediterranean values, and spread through the "purdah zone" (Papanek, 1982) across northern India.

dhist deities and demons; dangerous pollutants (especially blood, diseases, death), purificatory substances and rites; and protective/empowering *ki* energies. Villages, urban neighborhoods, and the interiors of households were dense with force fields emanating from the spirit beings, pollutants, and Shinto and Buddhist shrines. Infants were enmeshed in these spirit fields from birth, and children between roughly ages 7 and 14 learned to continually monitor and manage them as an integral aspect of safeguarding their health, controlling their emotions, and maintaining harmonious social relations; that is, they learned a hybrid Shinto-Buddhist religiosity that integrated (mostly Chinese origin) "folk" medical beliefs. Health and illness were caused by robust versus weakened flows of *ki* spiritual energies that were influenced by the balance of *yin* and *yang* forces. Specific diseases resulted from five "external" climates (wind, heat, moisture, dryness, cold), five "internal" emotions (anger, joy, worry, grief, fear), and from exposure to pollutants (Caudill, 1976). (Repeatedly disobedient children often were regarded as ill, and treated with acupuncture or *moxibustion*—burning of artemesia powder on the skin—to improve the flow of *ki,* as a treatment rather than a punishment.) Together, emotional orientations, interpersonal etiquettes, and "self" developed to harmoniously enact traditional society's networks of vertical (senior–junior) relationships, and the religious self-care system aimed to maintain the body's harmony with natural and spirit forces, creating an indigenous psychology and trajectory of development distinctive to Japan.

However "sociocentric" or "collectivist" this development may have been, individual life histories reflected variation in Level II motives and created Level III individuation. Life histories collected by Plath (1980) in the 1970s and Morris-Suzuki (1985) in the 1980s illustrate the struggles of adolescents and young adults with conflicts between their inner feelings and their outer obligations. Soji told Plath he grew up dreaming of becoming a soldier and idolizing a martyred Samurai folk hero. He enlisted at the beginning of the war, and was assigned to a suicide squadron but was spared by Japan's surrender. He said becoming a suicide soldier fulfilled his identity: "We volunteered, we wanted to fight. The highest goal of life was to die in action. I gave myself to it totally." The training base was his "utopia . . . a pure joy for me," and he told Plath (1980, p. 58) that his postwar

life as a real estate agent and father had been a disappointment, saying he had "died" in 1945. Iida also was drafted at the war's beginning, but read Lenin's *Imperialism* on the train to the induction center, and told Morris-Suzuki (1985, p. 167) that "quite suddenly, it seemed as though a great dark mist which had surrounded me vanished and in an instant everything became crystal clear." He concluded that the war was an imperialist adventure and at his draft physical, he alone took the step forward to declare himself unfit to serve, and tricked the doctor into believing he had tuberculosis. After the war, he joined the Communist party and became a successful novelist.

Women's lives also diverged. Goryohan enjoyed a couple of years' freedom after the war, when she and her girlfriends embraced Western fashions, had "lots and lots of boyfriends," and "did what we felt like doing" (Plath, 1980, pp. 146–147). Then she accepted an arranged marriage and became a mother and the caretaker of her mother-in-law. "I snuffed out my sense of self, my opinions, tried not to think about what I wanted," she told Plath, "I gave up all my hobbies and lessons, became a maidservant" (p. 149). At 43, she said she "hasn't grown up yet." Tsutsumi was a teen when the war began, and told Morris-Suzuki (1985) that she dreamed of sacrificing herself for the nation and emperor. She volunteered for the army's nursing corps, but was rejected and worked as an army clerk instead. After the war she accepted an arranged marriage and stayed home with her baby. Then a correspondence course inspired her to become an artist, and after reading a biography of Beethoven—"In his twenties, now a young man, he suddenly abandons his town, his friends and family, and sets course for the great cultural centre of his time, Vienna" (p. 229)—she left her family and went to Tokyo to study art. At 29, after a divorce and many jobs, she was accepted into an art school and by 1980 had achieved a national reputation as a ceramic artist—interestingly, preserving an ancient Japanese style.

These life histories show that Japan's indigenous psychology, with its Level I fostering of interdependence, indebtedness, and emotional attunement, socialized at Level II to a highly "relational" social persona rooted in the value of "selfless" harmony and anchored in identification with one's *ie* household, hardly precluded the development of distinctive personal identities in early adulthood (Gregg, 2010).

Arab-Muslim Societies

Parents in Arab-Muslim societies followed a model of infant care similar to that in Japan (and most "traditional" societies) in fostering *amae*-like interdependence. This served as a foundation for etiquettes of hierarchical family–kin relations and for identification with a multigenerational household that had mythic–spiritual meanings as did the *ie* in Japan: the *dar* "house of . . . " or *ahl* "people of . . . " or *nas* "people of . . . " or *bani* "children of. . . . " In middle childhood, however, socialization to honor–modesty values and Muslim religiosity charted sharply contrasting courses of development (see Gregg, 2007, for additional detail and references).

Honor was enacted as a performance of *rujula* manliness in a sporadic and sometimes deadly "game of challenge and riposte" (Bourdieu, 1966, p. 197). As one Bedouin explained to Abu-Lughod (1986), "A real man stands alone and fears nothing. He is like a falcon (*shahin*). A falcon flies alone. If there are two in the same territory, one must kill the other" (p. 88). Courage in fights especially built honor, but honor also required controlling, protecting, and provisioning the women and junior men in one's household, and displaying generous hospitality to guests. It was enacted in the postures, gestures, tones of voice, dress, seating arrangements, and so forth, that convey an imposing presence tempered by humility in prayer and acts of generosity.

Women and boys could not achieve this kind of manly honor, but they built honor by *tahashsham*-ing: displaying "modesty" in the form of compliance, self-control, and deference (Abu-Lughod, 1986) that displayed their *c aqel* social maturity and built the reputation of the household. Modesty for women included virginity before marriage and veiling and seclusion after it. But beyond buttressing men's prowess, these practices articulated the value of femaleness and anchored women's social selves or personae. Clusters of metaphors and theories of sexuality and conception powerfully associated females with the fecundity—and also with the wildness—of Nature (Delaney, 1991). "Idioms of enclosure" made fecundity sacred. Women's precious but fragile reproductive power was protected and made *haram* "sacred" by concentric enclosures: within their bodies, within their household compounds, within their *hajba* "veiled" full-body covering, within the endogamous (in-marrying) kinship system,

and within the nomad's camp, the farmer's village, and the urban dweller's kin-based alley of houses (Boddy, 1989). God's two most important names—*al Rahman* "The Compassionate" and *al Rahim* "The Merciful"—are built from the *r * h * m* root meaning "womb" and "uterine kin," echoing the sacred character of fecundity and nurturance. The "syntax" of social life (Bourdieu, 1966) thus consisted of the complementarity of male honor won mainly by prowess, courage, and protection/provisioning of dependent women and boys, with female honor won by reproductive success and the etiquettes of modesty; that is, the cultural codes of honor and modesty formed the core of men's and women's Level II social personas and defined cardinal values and motives.

Islam provided a second value system, with a universal vision of one's community—the "House of Islam" that extends brotherhood to all Muslims—and a counterethics to the honor-based values of kin solidarity and feuding. It also provided a religious–"supernatural" system of self-care by which people monitored and managed their bodies and psyches. In middle childhood, children learned to monitor, appease, and ward off the *jinn* spirits that saturated their surroundings, and *the evil eye*, a glance of envy that can harm or destroy its object. They learned that their environments and foods contain "hot" and "cold" substances that must be balanced to strengthen rather than weaken their health, and they learned that empowering *baraka* "divine blessedness" flows through water, sugar, grain, meats, sacrificial animals, and saints and their tombs. They learned to regard their sinful, angry, and deviant thoughts as whisperings of the devil, and to combat them with purification and prayer. They learned to weave references to God and Quranic phrases through their speech, making God and *baraka* always present. They also learned to monitor their own states of pollution and purity. Any substance that leaves the body—urine, sweat, tears, menstrual blood, semen, and so forth—increases one's pollution and renders one increasingly vulnerable to *jinn* spirits, the evil eye, sorcery, and the whisperings of Satan. The performance of washing rites before prayers restores a state of purity that protects one from the array of "supernatural" threats, and the Ramadan fast provides a yearly purification of both body and soul. Together, the honor–modesty system and Muslim spirituality fostered the development of a pair of Level II social personas that sometimes converged and sometimes conflicted, with the tension between them providing material for folktales and great literary works, much as did the conflict of "human feelings" (*ninjo*) and "social obligations" (*giri*) in Japan.

Life-history interviews I conducted with young adult Moroccans living in relatively traditional settings in the pre-Saharan region show that everyone internalized both the honor–modesty system and the Islamic self-care system as central to their Level II values, motives, and social personas (Gregg, 2007). But they differed in how they lived them, and especially in their Level III identities. Hussein repeatedly cast himself in the role of a vulnerable junior in need of a protector/empowerer figure, which he attributed to a lifelong fear "inscribed" in him by beatings from his father and teachers. He sought an honorable life as a protector of threatened juniors himself: as a defense attorney who would defend the falsely accused from corrupt officials and businessmen—with his work "witnessed by God," whom he perceived as his main empowerer. By contrast, Mohammed described how he became a quick-to-fight tough guy like his *rajel kabir* "Big Man" grandfather who had been killed in a village feud. But he couldn't keep his aggression within honorable bounds, and he turned into an "ignorant/rabid" delinquent who fought, smoked, drank, and visited prostitutes until he experienced a religious reconversion and turned to a fundamentalist piety to rein himself in and become an honorable adult.

The women I interviewed also internalized Muslim religiosity and modesty-centered versions of the honor system, but their lives too diverged. Rachida became devoutly religious as a teen but threatened suicide to resist her parents' arrangement of a marriage for her and stay in school. She became the first woman teacher in her community, living in self-chosen seclusion in her parents' home: She went out only veiled, but her family treated her with almost a man's respect because she was its main breadwinner. Khadija accepted and then fled an arranged marriage, began dangerously living the "French-style" free life whose appeal she had tried unsuccessfully to suppress with religious devotion (saying she felt she was both "Khadija" and "Christine"), and by a series of unlikely coincidences emigrated to Belgium, attended college and married there. Beyond Level II values, motives, and social personas that were distinctively Arab-Muslim, these life

histories—like those of the Japanese recorded by Morris-Suzuki (1985) and Plath (1980)—defined individualized Level III identities.

Japan and Arab-Muslim societies thus shared some aspects of infant care that they also shared with most "traditional" cultures (see below). But development took sharply different courses in middle childhood, with Japan emphasizing values associated with "pure-hearted," "selfless," and "harmonious" fulfillment of one's senior–junior social obligations, and MENA emphasizing competitive–dominating assertions of manly honor for men and deferential modesty for women and juniors. Their contrasting treatments of gender and sexuality alone would make personality development in Japan and MENA markedly different, as would their interpersonal etiquettes and their Buddhist versus Muslim religiosity and systems of self-care. Similar scores on "IND versus COL" may reflect real similarities, but conceal crucial differences in their indigenous psychologies. And when one turns to other traditional societies—like India with its caste system and "Hindu" spirituality, or like the Sambia of New Guinea (Herdt, 1990), where years of ritual homosexuality accompanied the training of boys to be masculine warriors and led to heterosexual marriage—the variation in indigenous psychologies and personality development becomes truly impressive.

Personality Development in "Traditional" and "Modern" Societies

Building on these descriptions of Japan and Arab-Muslim societies, let us consider the key differences *between* "traditional" and "modern" societies. We need the quotes around "tradition" and "modernity," because both have been entangled with Western and colonial values. I use "traditional" to refer to preindustrial societies, and specifically to conditions in which most people lived (1) by subsistence, barter, and trading; (2) in hunter–gatherer bands, nomadic tribes, or agricultural villages; (3) in social structures built around extended family households and lineages; and (4) with childhood mortality rates of 25–35% and life expectancies around 40.

I use the term "modern" to refer to societies that resemble the Organization for Economic Cooperation and Development (OECD) nations, with industrial–service economies in which most people live in towns and cities and work for wages or salaries; that have bureaucratically organized schools, governments, police, and militaries; and that have close to 100% schooling and literacy rates, childhood mortality under 1%, and life expectancies approaching 80. It is crucial to emphasize that modernization does not guarantee societal *development* as Sen (1999) defines this in terms of a populace's *capabilities* and *freedoms*. Some modern infrastructures support dictatorships and police states. Some nations have dual economies in which a "modern" sector coexists with a portion of the populace that continues to live in "traditional" subsistence sectors, often in rural villages. And most modern nations have large "underdeveloped" sectors in which people live lives that are no longer traditional but not modern, mostly in urban slums—fully one-third of the world's city dwellers. Even the United States has sectors of rural poverty in which people rely heavily on subsistence and barter, and urban ghettos, with life expectancies similar to those in "developing" societies.

Modernization brings utterly profound changes in psychological development and personality organization that seldom have been considered in the last decades' cultural psychology. Three changes especially shape Level II motives, goals, and social personas.

Traditional Cultures I: Care of the Self

First and foremost, modernization increases life expectancy from about 40 years to nearly 80 years and decreases childhood mortality from roughly one-third to about 0.5%. In premodern conditions, bacterial, viral, and parasitic infections are prevalent and often debilitating, and their discomforts, like the discomforts of injuries, are rarely alleviated by treatment or medications. Traditional cultures center around religious–mythic–"supernatural" belief systems and practices designed to monitor, protect, heal, and strengthen the body, and to give meaning to physical sufferings and frequent losses. These serve as systems of self-care for the psyche as well: People rely on them to interpret and manage their emotions, desires, attachments, and anxieties. They tend to be woven into (1) beliefs about gods, spirits, demons, ghosts, and flows of power; (2) daily, seasonal, and lifecycle rites; (3) personal grooming, dress, and adornment; (4) the processing of foods, principles of cuisine, and sharing of meals; (5) the design and architecture of dwellings and the layouts of villages;

and (6) the verbal, postural, and gestural etiquettes of daily social interaction. These embed the psyche in fields of invisible forces whose existence modern science denies. "Becoming modern" typically entails rejecting these beliefs as superstitions: Science replaces worlds densely alive with spirit beings, forces, and meanings with a world of dead matter obeying impersonal laws of nature—the process Max Weber (1946) described as the "disenchantment of the world."

The disenchantment remains far from complete, as some people in fully modern societies continue to believe in gods and in "superstitions" about their diets, astrological signs, and health risks. But the creation of psychology in the late 19th and early 20th centuries corresponded to the modernizing shift from viewing our thoughts and feelings as caused by spirit forces and beings to viewing them as emerging from within—from a mysterious but enchanting "unconscious" or, more recently, from the no-longer-mysterious firing of neurons. This aspect of modernization produces a profound shift in socialization and personality development. In traditional societies, parents took it as an urgent matter to teach their children how to manage the spirit beings and forces that threaten and protect their health. They also invoked spirit beings and forces to instill fear and enforce obedience, which can be especially effective after children have experienced illnesses, injuries, and deaths of loved ones that are attributed to them. While some modern parents teach their children about God and Satan, most reassure them that there are no bogey-men in their closets, that cooties are not real, and that people die of "natural causes" rather than demons, evil thoughts, sorcery, poorly performed rites, or punitive gods.

A significant part of personality development in late childhood and early adolescence entailed mastering "supernatural" beliefs and practices such that they became second nature: the largely automatic *syntax* of social life and self-care. Experiences of physical discomfort, loss of loved ones, and mastery of self-care beliefs and practices also shaped important values and motives that no doubt could have been studied as trait-like individual differences: People varied in the strength of their "need for purity," "witchcraft anxiety," and so forth, as modern individuals differ in their "need for achievement." And their mastery of these systems constructed a self or *persona* within a matrix of invisible beings and forces—within the imagined gaze of a spiritual

Generalized Other. In modern societies, by contrast, children and adolescents are socialized to deploy their imaginations to construct a self within the "reenchanted" matrix of subcultures and media characters—Harry Potter, Star Wars, World of Warcraft, athletes, celebrities, and so forth—that forms an ever shifting *virtual* Generalized Other. This yields a profoundly different Level II personality organization than did immersion of the psyche in a *real* world of spirits that must be continually managed by "magical" practices.

Traditional Cultures II: Hierarchical Family–Kin Relations

In traditional societies, most people lived their entire lives within networks of family and extended kin, often in the networks into which they were born. Households, lineages, clans, and villages served as the school and the employer, and often as the police, the judiciary, the medical clinic, and the army. They provided the resources to subsist and dwell, a vocation and a spouse, and care in illness and old age. In every traditional society studied, these networks were patriarchal in that elders and men exerted authority over juniors and women, whom they also "protected." Juniors and women obeyed and displayed deference toward their seniors—though degrees and forms of patriarchy varied greatly. Psychologically, these relationships can best be termed *interdependent*: Seniors exerted authority over juniors, and recognizing (or creating) their dependence, they provisioned and protected them; juniors performed their dependence by etiquettes of subordination, modesty, and respect, and expected provisioning and protection in return. Traditional societies regarded these patriarchal relations as "natural," and often as central to the cosmological order and/or religious laws, so that deferential "filial piety" and the responsibility of seniors to command and protect "their" juniors became religious duties. In addition to learning systems of self-care, then, socialization in late childhood and early adolescence focused on mastering the etiquettes of hierarchical interdependence, initially as juniors to everyone but increasingly as seniors to other juniors, so that juniorhood served as an apprenticeship to seniorhood.

In most traditional societies, peer groups were rare: Children and adolescents did not grow up with agemates, but with older and younger siblings and aunts and uncles within kin-based neighborhoods, and so always within networks of senior–junior dyads (Schlegel & Berry, 1991). Sibling caretaking—with children from the age of 7 or 8 caring for infants and toddlers—created a foundation for these relationships, and as B. Whiting and J. Whiting (1975) found, they provided strong socialization to "responsibility" for the caretakers. Many cultures represented all senior–junior dyads as similar to the "natural" parent–child relation, or to elder-younger sibling relations. As children learned their networks of extended family and kin and internalized the etiquettes for interacting with them, the networks formed a Generalized Other that by mirroring-back their positions and roles constructed a *relational, interdependent, sociocentric* social persona or self.

This persona often centered on the "household," which more or less coincided with one's extended family or band or lineage or clan: Many traditional cultures celebrated the "House" (or sometimes the lineage or clan) as a mythic–religious entity greater than the individuals making it up, whose living members owe deep debts to ancestors and to maintaining its power and reputation. Hsu's (1971) account of growing up, *Under the Ancestor's Shadow,* in 1930s village China describes the process of forging loyalty to the project of building and maintaining a "Big House." Roland (1988) follows Kakar (1978) and others in seeing "empathic attunement" by multiple caretakers in India as fostering an identification with the household as a "we self," with the household's reputation coming to serve as an anchoring "self-object." Chaouite (1987) argues that the family caretakers' rallying around at weaning establishes the household as the child's main transitional object, and begins the formation of a household reputation-centered "we self" in Arab-Muslim societies. LeVine and LeVine (1991) described a similar "symbolic identity" with the household and physical house in the Kenyan Gusii. In most traditional societies, it was imperative that by the age of 10 or 12, children master the etiquettes of interaction to operate within their extended family/lineage network, and that by puberty they act as representatives of their household/lineage within the wider village or tribal community—anchoring a household-centered social persona.

Like the religious–"supernatural" system, the network of hierarchical interdependent relations entailed a set of *values*—associated with Confucian ethics and "face" in China, with *on* indebtedness to parents and *giri* social obligations in Japan, with *dharma, karma,* and *jati* ("caste") in Hindu India, and with an honor–modesty "code" in Arab-Muslim societies. It also shaped a cluster of social *motives*: if one could turn back the clock and study truly traditional communities, then trait-like motives of "indebtedness to parents," "shame sensitivity," "need for *karma,*" "honor motivation," and so forth, could be defined in indigenous terms and measured as personality characteristics. The key point for psychologists is that the mastery of "patriarchal" relations and etiquettes—rather than classroom achievement and peer popularity—was the crucial developmental task of late childhood and early adolescence, along with mastery of a religious–spirit system of self-care, and a loyalty-sustaining identification with the "house." Internalization of these as a kind of second- ature shaped culturally specific Level II values, motives, and social personae.

Traditional Cultures III: Infant and Child Care

Based on his studies in Kenya and other African societies, LeVine and colleagues (1994) identified two broad cultural models of infant care that appear to hold for most traditional and modern societies, respectively. Traditional Kenyan mothers (and other caretakers) tend to hold or carry infants on their bodies and sleep next to them at night, and to nurse them on demand and to soothe any hints of distress, often dozens of times a day. Videotaped samples of interaction show that mothers avoid and dampen their babies' excitement: They engage in little face-to-face communication, preferring soothing body-contact communication. Mothers (and other caretakers) appear highly attentive to signs of distress, and try to keep their infants as calm and content as possible, which many observers have seen as "indulgent" caretaking and as fostering a "symbiotic" attachment. LeVine believes this model evolved in (nondeliberate) adaptation to conditions of chronic malnutrition and high infant mortality: It delayed the mother's next pregnancy and maximized the infant's nutrition and minimized its caloric expenditure, as distressful crying burns through precious calories.

LeVine and colleagues (1994) term this a *pediatric* style of infant care because it appears to be designed to maximize the baby's chances of surviving its first years. They contrast it to the *pedagogic* style prevalent in the sample of American mothers they studied. With good nutrition and survival nearly assured, modern caretakers actively play with their babies: They engage in a great deal of face-to-face communication and play talk, try to make their babies smile and giggle, excite them with tickling and toys, and get them interested in exploring the world around them. They term this style "pedagogic" because parents are (mostly nondeliberately) preparing their children for schooling by encouraging their active exploration and social interaction. They also found that the Americans' pedagogic style elicited nearly three times the distressful crying of the Kenyan babies.

LeVine and many researchers who have studied child care in Japan, China, India, and the Arab-Muslim region note another important developmental consequence of the pediatric style. In addition to fostering secure attachment, it typically built a strong interdependent relationship with the mother and with other caretakers who "indulged" the infant's dependence: meeting its needs with a minimum of distress or even before the infant communicates them. Toddlers tended to be fed when hungry and allowed to sleep when tired, and were subjected to few restrictions or demands. Whiting and Child's (1953) comparison of 72 cultures with an American working-middle-class sample found that non-Western societies also tended to be relaxed and gentle about toilet training and tolerant of sexual exploration by comparison. Extended families typically rallied around sick or injured toddlers to comfort, soothe, and distract them. If all went according to the "pediatric" cultural model, the interdependent attachment widened from the mother to the household, building a relational foundation for lifelong attachment, loyalty, and "we-self" identification with the family–kin "House" or lineage (Greenfield et al., 2003).

After ages 5–7, most cultures began more deliberate, demanding, and sometimes harsh socialization, and childrearing shifted to what LeVine and colleagues (1994) term a "respect–obedience" model, as children began contributing to the household's work and learning its interpersonal etiquettes. Children rarely were segregated from adult activities, and by ages 3–5 began helping with work, usually with closely "scaffolded" guidance, and by ages 8–10 were making significant contributions to their households, gaining a sense of competence and autonomy rare in modern societies. Rogoff (2003) notes that Central African Aka children "know most of the skills needed for survival when they are 7 to 12 years old" (p. 136). The seniors who guided, commanded, and disciplined also provisioned and protected, and they typically did so in the style and rhetoric of earlier caretaking, so the emotional interdependence ideally was sustained.

This pattern has been described for Japan, China, India, Arab-Muslim societies, and numerous other cultures—though with important variations in family arrangements, rewards, and coercion. In all of these societies, it was imperative for adults to expand their family–kin relationships through networks of "reciprocity" or "patron–client" relations with non-kin: *oyabun/ kobun* relations in Japan, *jajmani* relations in India, *guanxi* relations in China, *wasta* and fictive kin relations in Arab-Muslim societies. These dyadic relations between people with greater and lesser wealth or higher and lower status entailed reciprocal exchanges of favors and gifts—usually labor or services from the client and goods or influence from the patrons. A significant portion of the economic activity in a traditional village or town neighborhood took place through such reciprocity or patron– client relations, and the frequent use of fictive kin terms could blur the boundaries between real kin and non-kin.

The point for psychologists is that most traditional social orders consisted of networks of hierarchical dyadic relations—family–kin and patron–client—that were enacted via etiquettes of authority and deference. They entailed elements of "parent-like" authority, protection, and provisioning and "child-like" compliance, dependence, and modesty. Same-age peer relations were relatively rare. During late childhood and early adolescence, socialization to religious-"supernatural" self-care systems and to the etiquettes of authority and deference— combined with development of competence at the household's subsistence work—ideally built on a foundation of early childhood interdependence, and shaped Level II values, motives, and self-representations. Socialization during this period tended to combine nurturance, closely scaffolded apprenticeship learning (Rogoff, 1990, 2003), and sometimes harsh coercion and rites of passage. With "pediatric model" interdependent attachment as its foundation, the nexus of family–kin relations—often buttressed by the mythic–religious character of the "house"—provided a source of security against

continual threats of sickness, suffering, and death, and to threats of despoliation by landlords or princes in some societies and to attacks by rival bands, clans, or tribes in others.

Modernization

Modernization destroys these worlds, their developmental pathways, and their forms of personality organization. The experience of health and comfort, and the expectation of an 80-year life alone create an entirely new ecology of human development. In addition, families shrink from large, extended households to nuclear and part-nuclear forms—and children become an economic cost to their parents rather than an essential resource. Children go to school, now usually starting at age 3 or 4, where they are socialized in age-matched peer groups. Children, adolescents, and adults live much of their lives in bureaucratic organizations that operate by supposedly meritocratic principles, and outside of them, they socialize in groups of same-age friends. Parents raise their children to achieve in school and acquire their own vocation, friends, and spouses rather than to sustain lifelong loyalty to their ancestral family "house." Authority-deference kin and patron–client relations nearly disappear as the social order shifts from face-to-face control to bureaucratic institutions and peer pressures.

Around the globe, parents are choosing smaller families and adopting pedagogic styles of infant care and "authoritative" mentoring rather than command-and-obedience styles of socializing their children and adolescents—to prepare them to go forth into the world and achieve their own lives, and to choose their own friends and spouses. Patriarchal gender relations are being rejected, and all forms of recreational as well as reproductive sexuality cultivated. As Giddens (1991) points out, once family members no longer depend on each other as a production unit that jointly holds rights to resources and unites as a political and sometimes military unit, marriage and parenthood come to be "pure relationships," entered solely for their emotional satisfactions—and therefore highly romanticized and highly fragile. And as science debunks "superstitions" and disenchants the world of spirit beings and forces, religion becomes a personal lifestyle choice rather than a shared cosmology, and humans' imaginations are absorbed in the virtual reenchantments of mass entertainment.

Contemporary Cultural Psychology

Together, the differences *among* traditional cultures (e.g., Japanese vs. Arab-Muslim) and the differences *between* traditional and modern societies raise two key questions. First, to what extent do the broad dimensions of cultural variation—especially IND versus COL—capture these profound differences in personality development? Second, how should the IND versus COL dimension be interpreted?

There currently are several lines of research on dimensions of cultural variation. The best known are those studying the IND versus COL contrast, especially Hofstede's (1980) survey of IBM employees that identified IND versus COL and five other dimensions, and Triandis's (1995) studies that supported the centrality of IND versus COL.[4] But there also are . . .

- Schwartz's (2004) studies of values, which identified dimensions of *conservatism* versus *openness to change* and *self-transcendence* versus *self-enhancement.*
- Bond's studies of "social axioms" (Bond et al., 2004), which identified a dimension of *dynamic externality* associated with a mix of collectivism, hierarchy, and conservatism, and a second dimension of *societal cynicism.*
- Inglehart's (1997) World Values Survey, which identified dimensions of *survival* versus *self-expression* and *traditional* versus *secular–rational* values.

Several studies compared these dimensions (Hofstede, 2001; Ng, Lee, & Soutar, 2007; Schwartz, 1994; Smith, Peterson, & Schwartz, 2002; Steenkamp, 2001), and found that the central dimension of each approximates IND versus COL.[5] It remains unclear whether the approaches have identified importantly different values or have yielded slightly different ways of measuring and labeling a single underlying

IND versus COL cluster of values. Most importantly, all show strong correlations with measures of "modernity," and these raise the question of how they should be interpreted: Are they the central characteristics of human *cultures* in general? Or are they the main features of culture that are changing due to *modernization*?

Interpreting Dimensions of Cultural Variation

Most cultural psychologists appear to follow Nisbett (2004) and Kitayama (Kitayama & Uskul, 2011) in believing they are studying deep cultural differences that pre-date industrialization. For Nisbett (2004; Peng & Nisbett, 1999), these date back millennia to the Greek and Confucian traditions, and for Kitayama and Uskul (2011) to centuries of residential stability (Japan) versus movement to frontiers (United States). Triandis (1995) believed that variation in IND versus COL originated in hunter–gatherer versus pastoralist versus agricultural ways of life, and in different family systems. Both he and Hofstede (2001) rejected the notion that individualism is just a feature of modernity (Triandis, 2001), but they did believe that urbanization, smaller families, affluence, education, and media all promote a shift toward individualism.

All of these approaches indicated that the core dimensions have strong associations with indicators of "modernization," especially gross national product/gross domestic product (GNP/GDP), literacy, and life expectancy. Hofstede's (2001) individualism has been found to correlate $r = .80$ to $r = .90$ with measures of national wealth, and $r = .50$ to $r = .80$ with other major indicators of development (Gouveia & Ros, 2000).[6] Values associated with *autonomy* (openness + self-enhancement) and *conservatism* in Schwartz's model correlate $r = .40$ to $r = .75$ with the main indicators of development. Hofstede (2001) believes his data support the conclusion that wealth increases individualism, rather than that individualism promotes economic growth (p. 253), and noting how strongly GNP predicts values, he wrote, "I consistently controlled for differences in GNP/capita in all correlations with culture indices . . . [because] if I can explain phenomena across societies by differences in wealth, I don't need culture" (Hofstede, 2004, p. 277).

---

[4] Debate continues about the importance and similarities of the dimensions other than I versus C such as Hofstede's "power distance" and "masculinity" (both correlated with IND vs. COL), Triandis's tightness versus looseness and simplicity versus complexity (see Vinken, Soeters, & Ester, 2004, for discussions of these issues and the relationships between cultural and individual values and selves).

[5] Schwartz (2004) initially rejected this conception, but more recently noted that his autonomy/embeddedness dimension overlaps "to some degree" with Hofstede's IND versus COL.

---

[6] His power distance dimension showed correlations of $r = .40$ to $r = .70$ with those indicators.

Inglehart saw *survival* versus *self-expression* values as closely equivalent to COL versus IND and to Schwartz's *conservatism* versus *autonomy*,[7] but he regarded the core dimensions mainly as products of modernization. Inglehart and Baker (2000) presented evidence that the transition from agricultural to industrial society promotes a secularization of values (accompanying the world's "disenchantment"), and that the transition from industrial to a service-based society then brings a crucial shift from *survival/security* toward *self-expression* values that accompany improved health and lengthening lifespans. It isn't wealth alone that brings change, they believed, but the broader development of health, education, and rights—as shown by the strong association ($r = .84$) of individualist *self-expression* values with the United Nations (UN) Human Development Index (Inglehart & Oyserman, 2004).[8] Greenfield and colleagues (2003) also saw the contrasting IND versus COL pathways of personality development as deriving from modernization: "The interdependent pathway appears to be an adaptive response to small face-to-face communities and a subsistence economy. . . . The independent pathway, in contrast, appears to be an adaptive response to large, anonymous, urban communities and a commercial economy" (pp. 465–466).

What do these strong associations of cultural values–motives–personalities with indices of "modernization" mean? First, IND versus COL and similar dimensions clearly capture real differences among contemporary societies. Second, these differences should be interpreted not as indicating the primordial choices the world's cultures have made, but as their state of modernization. Third, IND versus COL likely does not capture many of the most important characteristics of traditional cultures' indigenous psychologies—like those that made Japanese and Arab-Muslim societies so distinctive and different. COL and IND become salient in comparisons of societies that are less and more "modernized," but this may not have been a central dimension of variation *among* premodern societies. Fourth, even when interpreted as reflecting degrees of modernization, the focus on sociocentric COL versus egocentric IND neglects some of the most important psychological aspects of the Great Transformation to modernity, especially because they compare the most modernized segments of societies—corporate employees, teachers, and college students—and miss those living in more traditional or underdeveloped areas.

Here, Inglehart takes an important step in arguing that the critical psychological effects of modernization derive from the great decline in *existential anxiety*: in insecurity and fear about hunger, disease, despoliation, suffering, and death. The implications of retheorizing the central dimension of cultural variation from COL versus IND to *security* versus *self-expression* are huge. The dimension labeled IND versus COL may be partly about valuing social "connectedness" versus "autonomy," but even more importantly about the fragility and hardship of premodern lives and their immersion in hierarchical, kin-centered networks and realms of spirit beings and forces. Inglehart's *security* versus *self-expression* conception may not be ideal—especially about whether "self-expression" correctly names the pole opposed to "security." But it at least recognizes the momentous psychological differences between premodern societies with 25+% childhood mortality, a life expectancy of 40 years, near-continual disease and discomfort, and often chronic feuding–warfare or despoliation by landowners, warlords, and emperors, and the conditions of health, comfort, and "lifestyle" choice that prevail in the most modernized and developed societies.

The broad contrast between pediatric and pedagogic styles of child care derives from these differing conditions of nutrition, disease, and family size, along with the centrality of schooling and "meritocratic" achievement in modern societies. Modernization ends the anchoring of personality in identification with a household "we-self" endowed with spiritual qualities. Add to this modernity's pervasive same-age peer relations; young adults' selection of their vocations, spouses, and friends; the liberation of sexuality from reproduction; the trend toward full gender equality; and the acceptance of homosexuality and other lifestyle-defining sexualities. These completely transform interpersonal relationships from any known traditional family–kin hierarchy. In addition, the "modern"

---

[7] Inglehart and Oyserman (2004) reported that the correlations between these range from $r = .62$ to $r = .70$, and $r = .88$ with Triandis's measure of individualism, showing that they measure a single dimension.

[8] In addition to the homogenizing evolution toward individualist *self-expression*, Inglehardt and Baker (2000) found evidence of multiple pathways associated with religious and political heritages, and perhaps of multiple modernities.

psyche is no longer enmeshed in realms of invisible spirit beings and forces that are taken to
be the real reality behind the visible world, but
in media entertainments and spectacles viewed
through screens that are taken as windows
opening onto "virtual" worlds. Any of these
three aspects of "modernization" alone would
make psychological development utterly and
profoundly different than it was in preindustrial
societies. Together they present psychologists
with the fascinating challenge of investigating
just how "modernity" transforms personality
development.

Conclusion

The evidence is strong that the IND versus COL
dimension of values, egocentric versus sociocentric self-conceptions, and independent versus interdependent pathways of personality development describe important variation among
contemporary societies. The evidence also is
strong that this should be interpreted primarily
as reflecting differences in economic development and modernization, and not as the main
dimension of variation that once existed among
the globe's hundreds of traditional cultures,
none of which remotely resembled any modern
society.

It may be disconcerting for psychologists
to realize that by coming late to culture, they
largely missed their opportunity to study the
world's traditional cultural variation. But they
can study the rich literature on indigenous
psychologies and embrace the last 25 years'
findings about IND versus COL as forming
the foundation for a theory of psychological
"modernization." And they can build on this
foundation by investigating important aspects
of modernization beyond IND versus COL, especially those associated with differing forms
of existential anxiety, and with culturally distinctive strategies for "coping" with them. As
Hijazi (1970) pointed out after studying the civil
war in Lebanon, the psychological experience
of helplessness before the forces of nature differs profoundly from vulnerability to political intimidation and violence—as do people's
psychological adaptations to them. Cultural
psychologists might now turn from comparing
national cultures to studying ecological niches
created by the globalized world system, especially in the more difficult-to-access niches that
researchers currently neglect:

1. The mostly rural communities that to varying extents have been "left behind" by
   modernization, in which disease, suffering, and loss remain high, and in which
   kin-centered social organizations and religious–spirit self-care systems remain partly intact.
2. The nearly one-third of the world's city
   dwellers who live in slum conditions, often
   with near premodern disease and mortality
   rates, and often high rates of violence.
3. Communities chronically affected by political intimidation and corruption.
4. The 10% global elite who are dispropor-
   tionately shaping our modernity, but grow
   up and live in social worlds that bear little
   resemblance to those of "ordinary" people.

Finally, cultural psychologists can build on
recent decades' work to tackle the Big Question
of the psychological character of modernity.
Seen against the backdrop of the traditional societies in which humans lived until the previous
century or two, "modernity" looks highly exot-
ic, and neither natural nor inevitable. We know
surprisingly little about modernity as one ecology of human development among the hundreds
that historically comprised the planet's cultural
variation. But in addition to the profound changes in life expectancy, social relations, self-care,
and individual choice of lifestyles, three characteristics of modernity appear to be especially
consequential for Level II personality development:

1. The seemingly "meritocratic" sorting of individuals into increasingly segregated "socioeconomic status" strata, and the related
   use of school success and failure as the crucial means of reward and coercion.
2. The raising of children in age-graded peer
   groups, and resulting heavy dependence of
   attachment and self-worth on peer popularity.
3. The immersion of the psyche in cyber-
   digital realms of entertainment, spectacle,
   and social networks—a structuring of
   the imagination that forms a distinctively
   modern system of emotional/motivational
   self-management and a virtual Generalized
   Other.

All of these are entirely new in human history, and together form the ecology of modernity's indigenous psychology.

REFERENCES

Abu-Lughod, L. (1986). *Veiled sentiments.* Berkeley: University of California Press.

Allwood, C., & Berry, J. (2006). Origins and development of indigenous psychologies. *International Journal of Psychology, 41*(4), 243–268.

Ammar, H. (1964). *Fi bina' al-bashar* [On building human character]. Cairo: Sirs al-Layan.

Asch, S. (1955). Opinions and social pressure. *Scientific American, 193*(5), 31–35.

Bachnik, J., & Quinn, C. (Eds.). (1994). *Situated meaning: Inside and outside in Japanese self, society, and language.* Princeton, NJ: Princeton University Press.

Boddy, J. (1989). *Wombs and alien spirits.* Madison: University of Wisconsin Press.

Bond, M. (1987). *The psychology of the Chinese people.* New York: Oxford University Press.

Bond, M. (Ed.). (2010). *The Oxford handbook of Chinese psychology.* New York: Oxford University Press.

Bond, M., Leung, K., Au, A., Tong, K., deCarrasquel, S., Murakami, F., et al. (2004). Culture-level dimensions of social axioms and their correlates across 41 cultures. *Journal of Cross-Cultural Psychology, 35*(5), 548–570.

Bourdieu, P. (1966). The sentiment of honor in Kabyle society. In J. Peristiany (Ed.), *Honor and shame* (pp. 191–241). Chicago: University of Chicago Press.

Caudill, W. (1976). The cultural and interpersonal context of everyday health in Japan and America. In C. Leslie (Ed.), *Asian medical systems* (pp. 159–177). Berkeley: University of California Press.

Chao, R. (1994). Beyond parental control and authoritarian parenting style. *Child Development, 65,* 1111–1119.

Chaouite, A. (1987). L'enfant marocain [The Moroccan child]. In M. Dernouny & A. Chaouite (Eds.), *Enfance Maghrebines [Childhood in North Africa]* (pp. 41–66). Casablanca: Afrique Orient.

Delaney, C. (1991). *The seed and the soil.* Berkeley: University of California Press.

DeVos, G. (1973). *Socialization for achievement.* Berkeley: University of California Press.

Doi, T. (1973). *The anatomy of dependence* (J. Bester, Trans.). New York: Harper & Row.

Doi, T. (1985). *The anatomy of self.* Tokyo: Kodansha.

Erikson, E. (1950). *Childhood and society.* New York: Norton.

Fung, H. (1999). Becoming a moral child. *Ethos, 27*(2), 180–209.

Giddens, A. (1991). *Modernity and self-identity.* Stanford, CA: Stanford University Press.

Gouveia, V., & Ros, M. (2000). Hofstede and Schwartz's models for classifying individualism at the cultural level. *Psicothema, 12,* 25–33.

Greenfield, P., Keller, H., Fuligni, A., & Maynard, A. (2003). Cultural pathways through universal development. *Annual Review of Psychology, 54,* 461–490.

Gregg, G. (2005). *The Middle East: A cultural psychology.* New York: Oxford University Press.

Gregg, G. (2007). *Culture and identity in a Muslim society.* New York: Oxford University Press.

Gregg, G. (2010). Culture and self. In J. Hall, L. Grindstaff, & M. Lo (Eds.), *Handbook of cultural sociology* (pp. 223–232). New York: Routledge.

Heine, S. (2008). *Cultural psychology.* New York: Norton.

Heine, S., & Buchtel, E. (2009). Personality: The universal and the culturally specific. *Annual Review of Psychology, 60,* 369–394.

Herdt, G. (1990). Sambia nosebleeding rites and male proximity to women. In J. Stigler, R. Shweder, & G. Herdt (Eds.), *Cultural psychology* (pp. 366–400). Cambridge, UK: Cambridge University Press.

Hijazi, M. (1970). *Al-takhaluf al-ijtima^c i* [Underdeveloped Society]. Beirut: Ma'had al-Inma' al-Arabi.

Hofstede, G. (1980). *Culture's consequences.* Beverly Hills, CA: Sage.

Hofstede, G. (2001). *Culture's consequences* (2nd ed.). Thousand Oaks, CA: SAGE.

Hofstede, G. (2004). Epi-dialogue. In H. Vinken, J. Soeters, & P. Ester (Eds.), *Comparing cultures* (pp. 270–278). Boston: Brill.

Hsu, F. (1971). *Under the ancestor's shadow.* Stanford, CA: Stanford University Press.

Inglehart, R. (1997). *Modernization and postmodernization.* Princeton, NJ: Princeton University Press.

Inglehart, R., & Baker, W. (2000). Modernization, cultural change, and the persistence of traditional values. *American Sociological Review, 65*(1), 19–51.

Inglehart, R., & Oyserman, D. (2004). Individualism, autonomy, self expression. In H. Vinken, J. Soeters, & P. Ester (Eds.), *Comparing cultures* (pp. 74–96). Boston: Brill.

Kagitçibasi, C. (2000). Indigenous psychology and indigenous approaches to developmental research. *International Society for the Study of Behavioral Development Newsletter, 37,* 6–9.

Kagitçibasi, C. (2007). *Family, self, and human development across cultures: Theory and applications* (2nd ed.). New York: Taylor & Francis.

Kakar, S. (1978). *The inner world.* Delhi: Oxford University Press.

Keith, K. (Ed.). (2011). *Cross-cultural psychology.* Singapore: Wiley-Blackwell.

Kim, U., & Berry, J. (1993). *Indigenous psychologies.* Newbury Park, CA: SAGE.

Kim, U., Yang, K.-S., & Hwang, K.-K. (Eds.). (2006). *Indigenous and cultural psychology.* New York: Springer.

Kitayama, S., & Uskul, A. (2011). Culture, mind, and the brain: Current evidence and future directions. *Annual Review of Psychology, 62,* 419–449.

Kojima, H. (1986). Child rearing concepts as a belief–value system of the society and the individual. In H. Stevenson, H. Azuma, & K. Hakuta (Eds.), *Child development and education in Japan* (pp. 39–54). New York: Freeman.

Kondo, D. (1990). *Crafting selves.* Chicago: University of Chicago Press.

Lebra, S. (2004). *The Japanese self in cultural logic.* Honolulu: University of Hawaii Press.

Lebra, T. (1976). *Japanese patterns of behavior.* Honolulu: University of Hawaii Press.

LeVine, R. (1973). *Culture, behavior, and personality.* Chicago: Aldine.

LeVine, R., Dixon, S., LeVine, S., Richman, A., Leiderman, P., Keefer, C., et al. (1994). *Child care and culture.* New York: Cambridge University Press.

LeVine, R., & LeVine, S. (1991). Home design and the self in an African culture. *Psychoanalytic Study of Society, 16,* 87–109.

Lewis, C. (1996). The contributions of Betty Lanham. In D. Shwalb & B. Shwalb (Eds.), *Japanese childrearing* (pp. 125–138). New York: Guilford Press.

Markus, H., & Kitayama, S. (1991). Culture and the self. *Psychological Review, 98,* 224–253.

Matsumoto, D., & Juang, L. (2016). *Culture and psychology.* Boston: Cengage.

McAdams, D. (1995). What do we know when we know a person? *Journal of Personality, 63*(3), 365–396.

McAdams, D. (2015). Three lines of personality development. *European Psychologist, 20,* 252–264.

Mead, G. H. (1934). *Mind, self, and society.* Chicago: University of Chicago Press.

Morris-Suzuki, T. (1985). *Showa.* New York: Schocken.

Ng, S., Lee, J., & Soutar, G. (2007). Are Hofstede's and Schwartz's value frameworks congruent? *International Marketing Review, 24*(2), 164–180.

Nisbett, R. (2004). *The geography of thought.* New York: Farrar, Straus & Giroux.

Oyserman, D., Coon, H., & Kemmelmeier, M. (2002). Rethinking individualism and collectivism. *Psychological Bulletin, 128*(1), 3–72.

Oyserman, D., Kemmelmeier, M., & Coon, H. (2002). Cultural psychology: A new look. *Psychological Bulletin, 128*(1), 110–117.

Papanek, H. (1982). *Separate worlds: Studies of Purdah in South Asia.* Amherst, NY: Prometheus.

Peng, K., & Nisbett, R. (1999). Culture, dialectics, and reasoning about contradiction. *American Psychologist, 54,* 741–754.

Plath, D. (1980). *Long engagements: Maturity in Japan.* Stanford, CA: Stanford University Press.

Rogoff, B. (1990). *Apprenticeship in thinking.* London: Oxford University Press.

Rogoff, B. (2003). *The cultural nature of human development.* New York: Oxford University Press.

Rogoff, B., Sellers, M., Pirottqa, S., Fox, N., & White, S. (1975). Age of assignment of roles and responsibilities to children: A cross-cultural survey. *Human Development, 18,* 353–369.

Roland, A. (1988). *In search of self in India and Japan.* Princeton, NJ: Princeton University Press.

Rosenberger, N. (Ed.). (1992). *Japanese sense of self.* Cambridge, UK: Cambridge University Press.

Sameroff, A., & Haith, M. (Eds.). (1996). *The five to seven year shift.* Chicago: University of Chicago Press.

Schlegel, A., & Barry, H. (1991) *Adolescence.* New York: Free Press.

Schwartz, S. (1994). Beyond individualism/collectivism. In K. Uichol, H. Triandis, C. Kagitcibasi, S.-C. Choi, & G. Yoon (Eds.), *Individualism and collectivism* (pp. 85–119). Thousand Oaks, CA: SAGE.

Schwartz, S. (2004). Mapping and interpreting cultural differences around the world. In H. Vinken, J. Soeters, & P. Ester (Eds.), *Comparing cultures* (pp. 43–73). Boston: Brill.

Sen, A. (1999). *Development as freedom.* New York: Knopf.

Shimizu, H., & Levine, R. (Eds.). (2001). *Japanese frames of mind.* Cambridge, UK: Cambridge University Press.

Sinha, J. B. P. (2003). Trends towards indigenization of psychology in India. In K. S. Yang, K. K. Hwang, P. Pederson, & I. Diabo (Eds.), *Progress in Asian psychology: Conceptual and empirical contributions* (pp. 11–28). Westport, CT: Praeger.

Skinner, G. (1993). Conjugal power in Tokugawa Japanese families. In B. Miller (Ed.), *Sex and gender hierarchies* (pp. 236–270). Cambridge, UK: Cambridge University Press.

Smith, P., Peterson, M., & Schwartz, S. (2002). Cultural values, sources of guidance, and their relevance to managerial behavior. *Journal of Cross-Cultural Psychology, 33,* 188–208.

Smith, R., & Wiswell, E. (1982). *The women of Suye Mura.* Chicago: University of Chicago Press.

Steenkamp, J.-B. (2001). The role of national culture in international marketing research. *International Marketing Review, 18*(1), 30–44.

Triandis, H. (1995). *Individualism and collectivism.* Boulder, CO: Westview Press.

Triandis, H. (2001). Individualism and collectivism. In D. Matsumoto (Ed.), *Handbook of culture and psychology* (pp. 35–50). New York: Oxford University Press.

Triandis, H., & Suh, E. (2002). Cultural influences on personality. *Annual Review of Psychology, 53,* 133–160.

Valignano, A. (1962). Alessandro Valignano's sumario of 1580. In B. Silberman (Ed.), *Japanese character and culture* (pp. 286–288). Tucson: University of Arizona Press.

Vinken, H., Soeters, J., & Ester, P. (Eds.). (2004). *Comparing cultures: Dimensions of culture in a comparative perspective* (pp. 5–27). Boston: Brill.

Weber, M. (1946). Politics as a vocation. In H. Gerth & C. Mills (Eds.), *From Max Weber: Essays in sociology* (pp. 77–128). New York: Oxford University Press.

Whiting, B., & Whiting, J. (1975). *Children of six cultures.* Cambridge, MA: Harvard University Press.

Whiting, J., & Child, I. (1953). *Child training and personality.* New Haven, CT: Yale University Press.

Yamaguchi, S., & Arizumi, Y. (2006). Close interpersonal relationships among Japanese. In U. Kim, K. Yang, & K. Hwang (Eds.), *Indigenous and cultural psychology* (pp. 163–174). New York: Springer.

PART IV

AUTOBIOGRAPHICAL AUTHORS
Life Stories and the Search for Meaning

Storytelling is a cardinal feature of human nature. Wherever members of the *Homo sapiens* species congregate today, from foraging societies in the Amazon basin to the great cities of China and Europe, people tell stories. We tell stories—and listen to them, watch them, perform them, and experience them in a range of venues and media—for the purposes of entertainment, instruction, persuasion, healing, and sometimes simply to pass the time. Whereas we do (and should) resort to scientific explanations, logical proof, empirical verification, and rational analysis when we try to sort out the material world around us and try to predict events, human beings often operate in a *narrative* mode when making sense of individual human lives. Ask a person questions like these: "Who are you?"; "How did you come to be?"; "What gives your life unity and purpose?" If the person is 5 years old, she may look at you as if you are crazy. But if she is 25, she will probably tell you a story.

Ever since Erik Erikson made famous the concept of an identity crisis, developmental psychologists have interpreted the late-adolescence and early-adult years as a time when human beings, especially those living in modern societies, struggle to figure out who they are and how they are to fit into an emerging adult world. The identity challenge has profound implications for personality development at the levels of the social actor and the motivated agent. Dispositional traits are stretched and challenged to accommodate the new role demands that emerging adults face, as they seek to perform emotion and engage the social world in an authentic, consistent, and more or less responsible manner. Moreover, identity development nearly always involves some kind of assessment, and often a reorganization, of a motivated agent's goal agenda: What do I want to strive for as an adult? What do I value? Complicating the scenario even further is the new identity demand for temporal continuity of the self. The emerging adult sees something that a child can rarely see—that once upon a time, I was something, and now I am something *else*. I was a child, but now I am (almost) an adult. And I will be something different yet again in the future. How do I make sense of this? How do I come to an integrated understanding of myself that explains how the self of yesteryear came to be the self of today—the very same self who will eventually become a different (but in some sense similar) self in the years to come?

This is when the autobiographical author, at long last, enters the scene. The author needs to tell a story about the self to explain how *I came to be the person I am becoming.* Personality and developmental psychologists who study this sort of thing call it *narrative identity.* As autobiographical authors, we reconstruct the past and imagine the future in such a way as to create an integrative narrative of self, a life story that aims to provide our random lives with some semblance of unity, purpose, and temporal continuity. The internalized and evolving life stories that we create become part and parcel of our personalities. In a metaphorical sense, life stories are layered over the goals and values of the motivated agent, which are layered over the social actor's dispositional personality traits.

The five chapters grouped together in Part IV of the *Handbook of Personality Development* all center on the concept of narrative identity. In Chapter 23, Robyn Fivush, Elaine Reese, and Jordan A. Booker trace the development of narrative identity back to the stories that young children and their parents share. Adopting a sociocultural perspective, they show how autobiographical memory develops in everyday social interactions in which families share past experiences, and parents help children learn how to narrate and evaluate these experiences. Parents draw children into reminiscing almost as soon as children begin to talk. The different styles of reminiscing that parents exhibit, shaped as they are by cultural norms, have significant downstream effects on how children learn to think about their own experiences and tell stories about the self.

Chapters 24 and 25 follow the development of narrative identity across the human lifespan, while providing close-up methodological snapshots of life-story research in action. In Chapter 24, Kate C. McLean and Jennifer P. Lilgendahl survey research on narrative identity in adolescence and young adulthood, while considering the different approaches that researchers have employed in collecting narrative data. They introduce the idea of differential trajectories in the development of narrative identity in the emerging adulthood years. In Chapter 25, Jonathan M. Adler examines the relationship between dimensions of narrative identity on the one hand and indices of happiness, psychological well-being, and mental health on the other. In so doing, he focuses attention on different procedures that narrative researchers employ to code and categorize narrative content. His research review suggests that narrative themes of redemption, contamination, agency, and communion tend to be deeply implicated in well-being.

In Chapter 26, Ruthellen Josselson mines her 45-year longitudinal study of women's identity to illustrate the value of a purely qualitative life-narrative approach that aims to preserve context and the multilayered complexity of human lives. Both told and lived, life stories are about personal meanings, she writes, and those meanings are likely to change substantially over time, even for adults who seem to show relatively stable or quiescent trajectories of personality development. Josselson adopts the metaphor of a kaleidoscope for depicting the development of narrative identity: Elements in identity may remain the same, though new ones are sometimes added; but over time, the arrangement of the items frequently changes to assume new and strikingly different patterns.

Finally, in Chapter 27, Phillip L. Hammack and Erin E. Toolis contextualize narrative identity within the broad domains of culture, society, politics, and history. They argue that human beings are fundamentally *dialogic* creatures—we exist in dialogue with ourselves and with a polyphonic cultural world. People draw on their own collective social identities—as white Americans, as Muslims, as black American women, as gay or lesbian individuals, as Palestinians or Israelis, and so on—in constructing the stories they tell and live by. But they do more, for the development of narrative identity involves making meaning of social ecologies that typically command engagement with multiple, and often competing, cultural narratives. Through a process of master narrative engagement, autobiographical authors confront a dizzying array of compelling stories about how to live a worthy life. The challenge is to make personal meaning out of it all, but the process is always constrained by social forces, economic opportunities, historical contingencies, and a host of factors outside the narrating self, and over which we may have little control.

CHAPTER 23

Developmental Foundations of the Narrative Author in Early Mother–Child Reminiscing

Robyn Fivush
Elaine Reese
Jordan A. Booker

When asked about a low point in her life, 16-year-old Anna (pseudonym) responded (interviewer responses in parentheses):

"Um, it's the fight that I had (yeah) and it was last year I think. Um, I don't really know what happened it just like suddenly everyone started hating each other and you know what girls are like. (yeah) Um, and I had this one best friend since I was like you know, tiny because we were born around the same time and our parents were friends, and just like all of a sudden everything just, went really bad and we started saying really horrible things to each other and I don't really know why (mmm) like specifically but everything added up and it got to the point where I just couldn't talk to her and it was really horrible. And um, that's why I have different friends now. (a few intervening comments before interviewer asks 'How did you feel?') Pretty horrible. I, like I was really upset about what she was saying to me but I also felt really bad cos I thought, I don't really think I said anything like that bad back, but I felt really guilty because like, yeah, (yeah) felt like it was my fault, wasn't really (several intervening interviewer comments) I have different friends now and I feel way better with them, like cos they're more like me (yeah) so I don't feel like I have to, you know hide (yeah) from what I actually want to do (okay) and it's nicer."

From this short narrative about a challenging time in her life (from Reese, 2013), it is clear that Anna is already well on her way to becoming an author of her own life story. She places this specific event, the fight with her friend, within a broader life narrative of growing up, and struggles with trying to understand how and why this particular event occurred. Anna fully explores the negative aspects of the experience, but then ends the narrative by noting the good to come out of the experience ("I have different friends now and I feel way better with them"). She interprets the event insightfully for her age, reflecting that with her new friends she doesn't "feel like I have to, you know, hide from what I actually want to do, and it's nicer," suggesting a sense of emerging self that is reflected and reinforced in these new friendships. Authoring an autobiography is clearly a critical task in modern industrialized societies (McAdams, 2001; 2015; Nelson, 2003), and in this short excerpt we see how one young woman is beginning to present her self; through creating a story of conflict and communion, Anna narrates a story that is very much about who she is and what she values.

Narratives are a critical layer of personality, as articulated by McAdams (2013a). Before youth develop into authors capable of narrating complex, yet coherent, life stories, they build two earlier layers of self-construction: the self as actor and the self as agent. Across early childhood, children interact with the world as actors with behaviors and emotions that others can interpret and respond to. During this period, children use aspects of social performance in engaging with others (i.e., self-regulating behaviors and emotions) to adapt to surrounding cultural norms, but their behaviors and emotions are heavily grounded in the present moment. Children rely on more experienced partners to engage in reminiscing and storytelling during this time (Nelson & Fivush, 2004). As children progress into middle and later childhood, they take on roles as agents capable of forming goals (e.g., personal achievements, belonging with others). As agents, children form enduring commitments to personally meaningful behaviors and activities. These commitments direct their daily interactions with others—what events and interactions they will approach and those they will avoid. Experienced agents who are transitioning into adolescence begin to reflect on these goals and the implications of successes and setbacks for the self (i.e., self-esteem). Such reflections establish the foundation for more complex reflections on life's many experiences and their connections to one's broader life story.

Thus, authoring one's autobiography is a complex process that develops gradually across childhood and adolescence, and, of course, continues to develop across the lifespan (Fivush & Zaman, 2015; McAdams, 2015). In this chapter, we explicate this developmental process through a sociocultural framework, highlighting how this process both unfolds within and is shaped by social interactions. To foreshadow, we show how the ability to author a coherent and compelling autobiography develops in everyday social interactions in which family members share their past experiences, and parents help children learn how to narrate and evaluate these experiences. We begin, as with any good story, at the beginning, with infancy and, using two case studies from a longitudinal data set collected by Reese (2013), show how early mother–child reminiscing interactions relate to children's emerging ability to narrate their own past in ways that shape self-understanding. In the first section, we provide a general theoretical and empirical overview before turning, in the second section, to the case studies. We follow two children, Anna and Tom, from early mother–child reminiscing conversations at 19 months of age through the transition into adolescence, culminating in the emergence of self-authorship at age 16. We developmentally trace differences in how these two mothers structure

reminiscing, and how these children participate in these early conversations. We show how these differences are expressed in recurring forms and themes across childhood, and are then integrated into the adolescents' own life narratives. After presenting these case studies, we take a step back to tell the larger story of how individual life narratives are initially coauthored in family interactions, and how children learn to become authors in their own right in these early conversations. Importantly, for some children, this process results in a fully voiced reflective self-authorship, whereas for other children, self-authorship seems flat and nonreflective.

Sociocultural Developmental Theory of Narrative Identity

Narratives are fundamentally the way we understand the world, other people, and ourselves (Bruner, 1990; Fivush, 2010; McLean, Pasupathi, & Pals, 2007; Sarbin, 1986). As Hutto (2007) argues, to understand a person, you must understand his or her story. And stories are more than descriptions of what happened. Good stories place events in context, in terms of both the world ("It was a dark and stormy night") and of the narrator ("It was my first year in college"), and integrate what Bruner (1990) has called the *landscape of actions* with the *landscape of consciousness*—actions in the world with inner thoughts, reactions, motivations and intentions, creating a human drama. Personal stories of exploits and disappointments, adventures and mishaps, are individually interesting and personally significant. Even more so, as we coalesce these stories into an overarching life narrative that links these disparate events together through personal themes and values, we create a continuous and coherent sense of self (Conway, Singer, & Tagini, 2004; Habermas & Reese, 2015; Ricoeur, 1991). It is in this sense that narratives define our identity (McAdams, 2001, 2015). The stories of our lives embody who we are in the world and in relation to other people.

Critically, narratives are social. We share the events of our day and of our lives in countless interactions on a daily basis. Narratives of specific events that are routinely shared are used to frame, understand, and place value on impactful or widely held stories in families (e.g., parents' first date or wedding day, a previous birthday party; Merrill & Fivush, 2016) and broader cultures (e.g., the events of 9/11, the assassination of John F. Kennedy; McLean & Syed, 2016). Within these events, discussions of major actors and goals are woven into evaluative frameworks that reinforce shared worldviews between storytellers and the audience. Instances of storytelling in the household occur multiple times within an hour (such as around the dinner table), and highly emotional events are more likely to be shared among family members (see McLean & Syed, 2016). These shared events maintain connections among family members and contribute to self-understanding as families make sense of and derive meaning from shared stories.

Provocatively, family storytelling begins at birth. Infants are born into storied worlds; parents and grandparents begin to tell newborns stories of the family, and weave this new member into the family narrative (Fiese, Hooker, Kotary, Schwagler, & Rimmer, 1995). Parents draw children into reminiscing about their personal experiences virtually as soon as children begin to talk, and, across the preschool years, children become more active and competent participants in these co-constructed narratives (Farrant & Reese, 2000; Reese, 1999; Reese, Haden, & Fivush, 1993; see Fivush, Haden, & Reese, 2006, for a review). In this way, stories of self are deeply embedded in family and cultural practices of storytelling (Fivush & Merrill, 2016). Based on Vygotsky's (1978) developmental theories, Nelson and Fivush (2004) outlined a sociocultural developmental model of autobiographical memory, delineating how personal narratives are socially constructed, and Habermas and Reese (2015) and Fivush, Habermas, Waters, and Zaman (2011) extended these arguments to the development of narrative identity. In brief, cultural practices foreground activities that will be important for children to become competent members of their culture. For example, in literate cultures, infants are immediately exposed to letters and numbers on their clothing, toys and books, and adults begin singing and rhyming games emphasizing letters and words. Well before they can possibly understand these symbols, infants are already learning that these symbols are important. With development, parents expect their children to participate more and more in activities that will culminate in becoming a literate adult. Similarly, being able to tell coherent and compelling personal narratives is a critical cultural skill, at least in industrialized cultures

(Fivush, 2010; McAdams, 2001; Nelson, 2003). Whether sitting in story circle at school, applying for college or a job, or meeting new friends or a possible romantic partner, one must be able to tell a compelling story about who one is. Beginning very early in development, parents structure everyday interactions around telling personal stories in ways that shape children's developing narrative identity. This is a long developmental process, beginning as children are just learning to use language, and culminating in the creation of a nascent life story in adolescence. Adolescence is a crucial time in the development of the life story because it is in adolescence that newfound reflective capabilities coalesce with social concerns, resulting in a period of intense identity exploration (Erikson, 1968; Habermas & Bluck, 2000). Adolescents' life stories provide a window onto their emerging identities.

Maternal Reminiscing Style

As expected by a sociocultural perspective, the form of life stories is culturally variable, depending on culturally mediated values, such as independence and interdependence (for a review, see Wang, 2013a, 2013b), cultural life scripts that provide prototypical sequences of life events such as schooling and marriage (Berntsen & Rubin, 2004), and cultural narrative frames that provide evaluative frameworks for interpretation and meaning such as redemption sequences (McAdams, Reynolds, Lewis, Patten, & Bowman, 2001; McLean & Syed, 2016). Much of this is considered in other chapters in this handbook. In addition to cultural variability, sociocultural theory also posits individual variability, in that the individual ways in which parents structure the early socialization environment will have long-lasting impact on children's developing skills set. For the creation of personal narratives, the way in which parents structure early reminiscing conversations with their children helps children learn both the forms and functions of these narratives.

Assessing Maternal Reminiscing

Family reminiscing is an aspect of daily life that spans mealtime conversations, chats during car rides, and bedtime storytelling. Given the ubiquitousness of such stories, studies of family reminiscing have used multiple naturalistic and laboratory-based methods to observe how parents and children co-construct event narratives. This includes recordings of spontaneous dinnertime conversations, seminaturalistic home visits, and more structured laboratory visits, during which parents and children are asked to reminisce together about various types of events (e.g., shared and unshared experiences, or specific emotional experiences, such as a time the child was happy or sad) (for overviews, see Fivush et al., 2006; Reese, 2013). The majority of research has focused on mothers with preschoolers, with fewer studies that include fathers, or children in middle childhood or adolescence (but for some exceptions, see Fivush, Marin, McWilliams & Bohanek, 2009; Fivush & Zaman, 2013; McLean, 2015; Recchia & Wainryb, 2014). Studies have been both cross-sectional and longitudinal, with the majority of longitudinal studies assessing development across the preschool years (but for longitudinal data that cross from preschool to adolescence, see Bauer & Larkina, 2014; Reese, Jack, & White, 2010; Reese, Yan, Jack, & Hayne, 2010). In addition, a few studies have used an experimental design, in which mothers are trained to reminisce in specific ways and child outcomes are assessed after days, months, or years (Hedrick, Haden, & Ornstein, 2009; Peterson, Jesso, & McCabe, 1999; Reese & Newcombe, 2007; van Bergen, Salmon, Dadds, & Allen, 2010).

Although studies of family reminiscing have examined various narrative dimensions, the most robust body of research has focused on elaboration (Fivush et al., 2006). Initial coding schemes were based on coding each proposition, defined as a subject–verb clause, as an elaboration or a repetition (Reese et al., 1993). In this propositional coding scheme, elaborations are conceptualized as statements or questions that introduce new information into the ongoing narratives through asking open-ended questions (e.g., "What did we do at the park?" coded as a memory question elaboration), providing new details (e.g., "We went on the swings, remember?", coded as a contextual statement elaboration) and confirming and extending information the child provides (e.g., if the child recalls "swings" and the mother responds, "Yes, that's right, we went on those swings, and we swung so high", coded as a statement elaboration on the information provided by the child). In contrast, repetitions were coded when the mother simply repeated information she had previously provided (e.g., "What did we do at the park?" and when the child does not respond, the mother simply repeats, "What did we do?" rather than elaborating with something like "We went on the swings, didn't we?"). In this initial scheme, elaborations on evaluative and emotional information (e.g., "It was so much fun, wasn't it?" or "You were so upset") are not distinguished from elaborations about factual information. In some later studies, elaborations on facts and on emotions were coded separately, both in terms of number of emotion words used and in the exploration of emotions in the reminiscing conversations (e.g., "Yes, you were sad. Why were you so sad? Was it because no one would play with you?"). When factual and emotional information are coded separately, there are high correlations between elaborating on facts and elaborating on emotions (see Fivush, Berlin, McDermott-Sales, Menuti-Washburn, & Cassidy, 2003, for a full discussion of these different forms of coding), which suggests that highly elaborative mothers elaborate on all aspects of an event.

Indeed, much of the most recent literature has used a single global dimensional coding scheme, coding level of maternal elaboration from 1 (*low*) to 5 (*high*), and these schemes correlate moderately with the more labor-intensive propositional coding schemes (Leyva et al., 2018), suggesting that the key aspect of an elaborative style is simply a high number of maternal questions and comments that add new information to the unfolding narrative. Thus, overall, some mothers reminisce in highly elaborative ways, providing rich detail, whereas other mothers are less elaborative, having fewer and sparser reminiscing conversations with their children (for reviews, see Fivush, 2013; Reese, 2013). Importantly, it is not simply that some mothers are more talkative than others; mothers who are more highly elaborative during reminiscing are not necessarily more talkative in other contexts such as book reading or free play (Haden & Fivush, 1996; Hoff-Ginsburg, 1991). Furthermore, mothers are highly stable in how elaboratively they reminisce, both across time with the same child, and across siblings (Haden, 1998; Reese et al., 1993). These patterns indicate that maternal reminiscing style reflects implicit and explicit goals of helping children understand their past, create coherent narratives, and create emotional bonds through creating a shared history across time (Kulkofsky, Wang, & Koh, 2009).

Factors Associated with Maternal Reminiscing

Given the stability of individual differences in maternal reminiscing style, it is perhaps not surprising that both longitudinal and training intervention studies indicate that more highly elaborative mothers have children who come to tell more detailed, coherent, and emotionally rich narratives about their own personal experiences than do children of less elaborative mothers (see Salmon & Reese, 2016, for a review). Moreover, when mothers reminisce more elaboratively, especially about the causes and consequences of emotions, their children subsequently have more consistent views of self (Bird & Reese, 2006) and more advanced understanding of emotions—both others' emotions and their own (Laible, Panfile Murphy, & Augustine, 2013; van Bergen et al., 2009). Emotional understanding is critical for establishing the meaning of the event for the self during adolescence (Booker & Dunsmore, 2017; Habermas & Reese, 2015). Of course, as laid out by Nelson and Fivush (2004), there are multiple factors that contribute to children's autobiographical narrative skills, including children's language skills, self-awareness and episodic memory skills, all dynamically interacting with the social context in iterative ways across development. Three factors are especially important when thinking about relations to adolescents' personality: child temperament, attachment security, and theory of mind.

Child temperament is an obvious factor to examine in shaping mother–child reminiscing, both because temperament is a precursor to adult personality traits (Caspi & Silva, 1995), and because children's characteristic approaches to people and to the world could shape mothers' ability to engage in highly elaborative reminiscing with them. Yet the research on child temperament has produced limited and inconsistent relations with maternal reminiscing (see Laible et al., 2013, for a review). Perhaps the most robust finding is that mother–child reminiscing is of higher quality when young children have higher levels of effortful control (Bird, Reese, & Tripp, 2006; Laible et al., 2013). Children high in effortful control may be more willing to sustain attention during a quiet activity such as a conversation. This link has weakened by later in the preschool years, and is superceded by the mother's positive representations of the caregiving relationship with the child (Laible et al., 2013). Yet by ages 5–6 years, children high-

er in effortful control are now supplying more emotional content themselves to the reminiscing conversations (Bird et al., 2006).

In contrast, the links between attachment security and mother–child reminiscing are stronger and more consistent. *Attachment* refers to the early established emotional bond between parent and child, in particular, to the way the child is able to rely on the parent, physically and emotionally (Ainsworth, Blehar, Waters, & Wall, 1978). Early in development, children who are more securely attached to their mothers, reflecting a more responsive and sensitive caregiving environment, have mothers who are more elaborative when reminiscing, especially about difficult emotional experiences (Fivush & Reese, 2002; Laible & Thompson, 2000; Newcombe & Reese, 2004). Likewise, mothers' own attachment security is linked positively to highly elaborative reminiscing with their young children (Reese, 2008). Thus, elaborative reminiscing both reflects and reinforces more secure mother-child attachment bonds (Fivush & Reese, 2002). Children's early attachment status as secure or insecure lays the foundation for adult attachment status (Main, Kaplan, & Cassidy, 1985). Adults who are secure with respect to their early attachment relationships have more successful and satisfying intimate relationships (Young & Acitelli, 1998) and are better able to cope with life's inevitable difficult moments through creating coherent explanatory narratives (Graci & Fivush, 2017).

Finally, *theory of mind* refers to the idea that people have desires, thoughts, and emotions that may or may not be the same as one's own, or that one can have changing desires, thoughts, and emotions over time, as well as the insight that human behavior reflects internal intentions and motivations of the actor (see Wellman, 2014, for a review). Elaborative maternal reminiscing is related to children's developing theory of mind. In an experimental study, when mothers were taught to reminisce more elaboratively when their children were toddlers, those children subsequently displayed more advanced theory of mind (specifically for their understanding of the origins of knowledge), and more accurate and voluminous memories than children whose mothers did not receive special training in reminiscing (Reese & Newcombe, 2007; Taumoepeau & Reese, 2013). The benefit of maternal elaborative reminiscing for children's theory of mind was only present for children with lower language skills, suggesting a buffering effect of elaborative reminiscing for this metarepresentational skill when children's own language skill is less developed.

Long-Term Impact of Maternal Reminiscing Style

Even when accounting for multiple social and cognitive factors, maternal reminiscing style in early childhood uniquely predicts autobiographical narratives across the preschool years (Fivush, et al., 2006) and is the best predictor of young adolescents' insights when narrating life stories (Reese et al., 2010). A primary reason why maternal reminiscing strongly predicts adolescents' narrative insights into self is likely to be the exploration of emotions that takes place during early maternally scaffolded elaborative conversations about the past (see Salmon & Reese, 2016). Through engaging in richer, more complex reminiscing with their mothers, children of more elaborative mothers come to develop a more complex theory of mind and understanding of emotion, and thus develop a more subjective perspective on their own experiences (Fivush, 2012; Fivush & Nelson, 2006). This early understanding of subjective perspective is related to how one develops authorship over his or her life (Reese et al., 2010), in that it provides the foundation for an authorial standpoint. In the remainder of this chapter, we focus on two case studies from a longitudinal data set collected in New Zealand by Elaine Reese (see Reese, 2013, for an overview) to illustrate individual developmental trajectories. By focusing on families from the same culture, one highly elaborative mother and her child, and one less elaborative mother and her child, we are able to show how individual variability in the early sociocultural reminiscing environment continues to influence children's autobiographical narratives as they transition into becoming authors of their own life stories.

Case Studies: Profiles of Anna and Tom

Our two case studies are selected from Elaine Reese's longitudinal data set examining multiple aspects of memory, narrative, self, and identity (e.g., Bird & Reese, 2006; Farrant & Reese, 2000; Harley & Reese, 1999; Reese et al., 2010). The sample comprised largely European New Zealand ethnicity, reflecting the demographics of the South Island of New Zealand. At the start of the study, about half of the mothers had completed some post-high school education at a university or polytechnic institute, or held a bachelor's degree. Families enrolled when children were 19 months of age, and researchers visited them in their homes six times over the early childhood period (ages 19–65 months). Adolescent visits took place in a university laboratory at ages 12 and 16. We selected these two cases from adolescents who were functioning well at age 16 in terms of their self-reported well-being. To highlight the role of maternal reminiscing style in adolescents' insights into life events, we selected from that group of well-functioning adolescents one (Anna) whose mother was among the top five most highly elaborative reminiscers at 19 months, and another (Tom) whose mother was among the five least elaborative reminiscers at 19 months. We note that selecting one child of each gender might raise some additional issues, and we return to the issue of gender later in the chapter. Thus, we selected cases that were likely to differ in their narrative identities but were similar in most other respects, including traits and coping strategies, as well as overall functioning. In a separate sample of New Zealand adolescents, we showed that the trait and narrative layers of personality are weakly related yet distinct (Reese et al., 2014).

We present excerpts for these two dyads from three critical developmental points: early childhood, the transition to adolescence, and adolescence. We note that this longitudinal study did not have a middle childhood time point. During early childhood, we set the stage by presenting the initial mother–child reminiscing conversation collected at 19 months of age, when the child is barely able linguistically to participate in such conversations, to provide a sense of how mothers are beginning to scaffold narrative interactions that allow their child to enter this cultural practice. Our next examples come from near the end of early childhood, the 51-month data point, when children are easily able to participate in reminiscing and are making the transition to providing their own perspective and evaluation on their experiences (Fivush, 2012; Fivush & Nelson, 2006). These two early childhood data points take place when the self as actor is being developed and while children are forming a basic sense of self by fulfilling readily interpretable social roles (McAdams, 2015). Next we highlight mother–child conversations at 12 years of age, the transition between middle childhood and adolescence, as children are consolidating and articulating their sense of self as intentional agent, and moving into developing an authorial voice (McAdams, 2015). Finally, we present the adolescents' own personal narratives at 16 years of age, as adolescents navigate the transition from selecting and incorporating specific self-actualizing goals to being authors of their broader life stories. As we will demonstrate, the foundations laid in early childhood echo across childhood and into adolescence in terms of the ability to deeply evaluate and understand self. To place these narratives in a larger context, we first present a brief description of each family.

The Families

Anna

Anna lives with her mother and father, and older brother, Nick. Both parents are of European New Zealand ethnicity and have university degrees. When Anna was 19 months old, she was classified as securely attached, and her vocabulary score was above the mean (1.3 SD). Her temperament scores on sociability, emotionality, activity, and inhibition were all within 1 SD of the sample mean. Anna was not yet displaying recognition of self in a mirror, but she did recognize herself in a photo. At age 16, Anna's vocabulary remains above average (1.6 SD) for the sample. In terms of personality traits and coping strategies, Anna scores below average (1.1 SD) on extraversion and above average (1.3 SD) on openness. Her agreeableness, conscientiousness, and neuroticism scores are all within 1 SD of the sample means, as are her reported rumination, externalizing, social support-seeking, and problem-solving coping strategies. In terms of well-being, Anna's self-esteem and her life satisfaction are within 1 SD of the sample mean.

Tom

Tom lives part time with his mother and part time with his father, who separated when he was in primary school. He has an older sister. Both parents are of New Zealand European ethnicity, and Tom's mother has a university degree (she did not report his father's education level). When Tom was 19 months, he was classified as insecurely attached, and his language score was the lowest in the sample. Tom's sociability score was 1.1 SD above the sample mean, and

his other temperament scores were all within 1 SD of the mean. He was not yet recognizing himself in mirrors or photos. At age 16, Tom's vocabulary had improved to slightly above average for the sample (1 SD). Tom's personality trait scores are all within 1 SD of the sample mean, as are his rumination, externalizing, social support-seeking, and problem-solving coping strategies. In terms of well-being, his self-esteem and life satisfaction are both within 1 SD of the sample mean.

Anna therefore represents the classic profile of a child of a highly elaborative mother (see Farrant & Reese, 2000; Newcombe & Reese, 2004; Reese et al., 2010): She is securely attached to her mother and has good language skills in early childhood. Tom instead represents the classic profile of a child of a low elaborative mother: He is insecurely attached to his mother and has low language skills in early childhood. These characteristics set the stage for the resulting different styles of maternal reminiscing, although it is important to bear in mind that mothers' reminiscing styles are not purely in response to children's language skill or the lack thereof. Even when accounting for children's language, self-awareness, theory of mind, and attachment security, mothers' elaborative reminiscing predicts and supports children's memory and narrative skills in early childhood (Farrant & Reese, 2000; Peterson et al., 1999; Reese & Newcombe, 2007) and adolescents' insight into life events (Reese et al., 2010; see Habermas & Reese, 2015, for a review).

Early Childhood Reminiscing Conversations: Foundations of the Narrative Author

The two early time points, 19 and 51 months of age, illustrate children's nascent traits of self-expression and disclosure, as well as their emerging abilities to create narratives that describe and explain who they are; as we will see, at this early developmental point, it is the mother who provides the structure and guides the content for these stories, setting the foundational building blocks for children's nascent abilities to narrate self. We start with Anna and her mother when Anna was 19 months of age. In this excerpt, from a 55-turn conversation, Anna and her mother are reminiscing about a family outing to a farm, where Anna got to feed baby lambs. In this, and in all the mother–child conversations, we place the conversation itself on the left and commentary on the right:

M: How many lambs were there?	It is unclear if Anna is actually responding to her mother, but her mother interprets this as a correct response and "restates" and elaborates that there were two baby lambs, and names them, giving the narrative textual detail.
C: [Coughs.] Do do do.	
M: Two of the little baby lambs.	
M: Gertie and George.	
C: Heee.	
M: And they had little tails, didn't they?	Anna takes a conversational turn without content, but her mother uses this to elaborate further about the tails, and extends to another question that Anna can answer.
M: What did their tails do?	
C: Wave.	
C: Ah.	
M: Yeah, they wiggled and wiggled.	The mother then confirms and elaborates on Anna's response, before asking another question that extends the narrative further.
M: And what did Anna give to the lambs?	
C: Fayah.	
M: Baby lambs.	Anna may or may not be responding accurately, but is involved, and the mother takes Anna's babbles and weaves them into the narrative.
M: What did you give to the lambs?	
C: Is a baa a ah.	
M: Baby lamb.	
M: Did you give them a bottle?	The narrative ends by turning from the baby lambs to what Anna did, bringing Anna in as an active participant in the event.
C: Ayes.	
M: You did!	

In this short excerpt, we see that Anna is barely able to contribute information to this conversation. Yet Anna is engaged, and Anna's mother pulls Anna into the reminiscing context, actually turning Anna's babbles into meaningful responses. With each turn, Anna's mother elaborates and extends the narrative such that, by the end, we have a sweet story about visiting and feeding the baby lambs. Note also that Anna's mother construes Anna as an actor on her world; this is not something that is simply described, but something that Anna actively participated in and did.

At age 51 months, we see that Anna is better able to participate in the reminiscing, and Anna and her mother truly reconstruct Anna's visit with the hairdresser, each contributing information, and even negotiating what happened:

M: What did you do, when y—when you got your hair cut?	The mother starts with an open-ended question, allowing Anna to decide what part of the event she wants to discuss. Anna immediately chimes in.
M: What happened?	
C: I only had a short turn though.	The mother follows up on Anna's contribution, by asking her to expand, moving beyond what happened to think about why the event unfolded this way.
M: Mm.	
M: Why was that?	
C: Cos I had longer hair and we only wanted a wee bit off cos I liked having long hair.	Anna is easily able to provide an explanation, which the mother implicitly acknowledges as correct and then elaborates on.
M: Mm, it's made the ends look really nice, hasn't it?	
C: Mm.	In order to keep the conversation going, the mother asks another open-ended question, to which Anna responds.
M: So what did the lady do, when she was going to cut your hair?	

C: She cutted it.

M: Did you have to wear anything?

C: I had a picture with all the things they need for a hairdresser.

M: I'd forgotten about that picture.

M: All the things that the hairdresser needed.

M: It was fun, wasn't it?

M: And because you were such a good girl, what happened at the end?

C: I got a lollipop.

M: Mm.

M: Cos you were very good.

C: Cos I was very shy as well.

M: She said that you sat very still.

M: She was quite pleased with you.

Anna recalls something the mother had forgotten about; in acknowledging this, the mother is helping Anna understand that her memory is her own, that not everyone will remember events in the same way. The mother then moves to an evaluation of shared emotion, creating a sense of communion between them.

The 32-turn conversation ends with a focus on who Anna is as a person—the mother focusing on Anna being good, and Anna offering her own interpretation of her behavior as being shy. So this event is not just about Anna getting her hair cut, but very much about an enjoyable, shared experience that helps define who Anna is as a person, a good girl, perhaps sometimes shy, whom other people like.

Even at this early age, we see Anna owning her story. Her mother allows Anna to move through the story, asking questions that allow Anna to elaborate and extend the narrative. Her mother also helps Anna in integrating evaluative information into the story. Most interesting, at the end of the narrative, the mother turns to the fun they had together, creating a communal theme to the event, and they both end by connecting this specific occurrence to the type of person that Anna is, not only "good" but also "shy."

In contrast to Anna and her mother, Tom and his mother engage in sparse, almost difficult, reminiscing conversations. Here, when he is 19 months old, Tom and his mother reminisce about a recent visit from his cousin; note that the entire conversation is included because it was so brief (three conversational turns).

M: Do you miss Antonia now she's gone?

M: Do ya?

M: Do you miss your cousin?

M: She flew home yesterday, didn't she?

M: Hey?

C: Mmmm.

M: Yeah, there is someone in the hall, but you don't need to worry about them.

M: No.

M: So do you miss your cousin?

M: [pause] Hmm.

The mother begins with a yes–no question, asking Tom if he misses his cousin after her visit. Tom is not responsive, and the mother simply repeats and cajoles Tom into answering (Hey?).

Tom barely acknowledges the questions, and gets distracted by the researcher waiting in the hallway.

The mother tries to bring his attention back to the conversation but is unable to.

The conversation feels uncomfortable. It is not simply that Tom is not interested or unable to participate, it is that his mother does not seem able to connect to him in any way. This is even more evident in the conversation when Tom is 51 months old, in which they discuss Tom's grandfather's operation and hospital stay. Again, the entire conversation is included (four conversational turns).

M: What about Grandad, what happened to Grandad when he went to um, hospital?	The mother tries to get Tom to respond to her question about the grandfather's operation by simply repeating it three times.
M: What'd what was his operation on?	
M: What was his operation on, mate?	
C: Don't want to tell you.	Tom refuses to talk about it. The mother pushes this a bit, and Tom confirms he does not want to talk.
M: You don't want to tell me?	
C: No.	

These two dyads present a stark contrast in the preschool years. Whereas Anna is engaged even before she can really participate in these conversations, Tom seems uninterested in reminiscing with his mother at all. Anna and her mother tell coherent, elaborated, evaluative narratives about Anna's experiences, focusing on what Anna did, and interpreting Anna's behavior in terms of who she is in the world. Even at this young age, Anna and her mother engage in some back-and-forth negotiation of what occurred in a way that facilitates building a shared memory and a shared history, and there is a clear sense of enjoyment in this sharing. In contrast, Tom and his mother simply never engage. Tom's mother asks direct, repetitive questions, and Tom presents himself as unwilling or unable to respond. There is no narrative that emerges, and certainly no discussion of who Tom is as a person, or who Tom and his mother are as a family building a shared history. We note that Anna's mother adopts many of the conversational features that are known to promote children's language and positive behavior in clinical samples, such as praise and repetition of children's utterances (e.g., parent–child interaction therapy [PCIT]; see Garcia, Bagner, Pruden, & Nichols-Lopez, 2015). In contrast, Tom's mother adopts some of the conversational strategies that parents in a therapeutic setting are taught to limit, such as directive questions. PCIT, however, does not include a specific focus on past events or emotions, or open-ended questions to encourage children's speech, which are all key features of elaborative reminiscing. How might these early childhood conversations play out as families develop?

Reminiscing Conversations at the Transition to Adolescence: Agency and Communion

Narratives collected at 12 years of age illustrate children's roles as intentional agents in the world. According to McAdams (2015), by this age, children have a well-developed sense of themselves as intentional agents. Through shared stories with social partners, such as parents, children display their desires, values, means of coping with setbacks, as well as meaningful, well-articulated goals for the self. These goals reflect basic and universal needs of personal achievement and affiliation with others (Winter, John, Stewart, Klohnen, & Duncan, 1998), and may reflect two major dimensions of the life story: *agency* (i.e., achievement, responsibility, status) and *communion* (i.e., love, community, care for others) (McAdams, Hoffman, Mansfield, & Day, 1996). The ways children discuss and value *getting ahead* and *getting along* become more prominent across childhood, and these motivating drives can be further reinforced by parents' elaboration of values and validation of children's goals (e.g., Suizzo, 2007). To illustrate this, we select specific sections of mother–child reminiscing that touch on these themes.

For 12-year-old Anna and her mother, reminiscing continues to be a highly elaborative and co-constructed conversational context that explores both the facts of what happened and evaluative perspective, what this event means, and what it illustrates more broadly about who Anna is as a person. The first excerpt is from a conversation about a highly positive event, a family trip to Australia and a theme park there, where they spent time with cousins. This is an extremely long conversation with 144 conversational turns, and these few exchanges occur right at the beginning:

C: And it was the week we went to Dream World. And it rained really hard.	Anna is highly engaged right from the beginning of the conversation, providing many details and evaluations.

M: It was freezing, wasn't it?

C: Yeah, a lot of the rides were closed.

M: Yeah.

C: Like the roller coaster, but it was okay because there wasn't as many people there and I got to hold a koala and that was fun. And we saw my cousins and I haven't seen them since I was eight. And we went shopping and I got some jandals and clothes and went to Australia Zoo.

The mother is supportive, validating Anna's perspective. Note that in talking about what was fun, Anna includes seeing her cousins, whom she has not seen in many years, expressing at least a passing interest in family and communion.

Later in the conversation, after elaborating in great detail about the various activities and adventures the family had during the week, they talk about the last day of the vacation:

M: It didn't rain there that day.

C: No, it didn't rain that day, it was . . .

M: It was our nice day.

C: [simultaneous with "it was"] Saturday, the day before we went home

M: Yeah.

C: And, wasn't that Josh's sister? [unclear word] about something? I don't know.

M: You stayed in Grace's room.

C: Yeah, but I was just not talking.

M: You sometimes get a bit shy in new places.

C: Yeah and then I went for a walk and then I felt better.

M: Yeah.

Still, talking about the weather, the conversation shifts to Anna's interactions with her cousins on the last day of the trip. Note that Anna and her mother are still very much in sync, finishing each other's sentences.

Anna brings up that she was not talking to her cousin, and her mother expands by explaining how Anna sometimes gets shy in these situations, which Anna acknowledges and then talks about what she did to regulate her emotions, which her mother validates. The end of this conversation is very much about the kind of person Anna is. Note that "shy" was also referenced in the preschool conversation, creating an impressively consistent view of Anna across childhood.

In these two brief excerpts from an extremely extended reminiscing conversation, we see many of the same themes echoing Anna and her mother's preschool conversations: the sense of a shared history, and the sense of enjoyment in reminiscing about this shared event, as well as the connections made between single occurrences in Anna's life, and who she is as a person. The conversation also alludes to the importance of family, spending time with infrequently seen cousins, thus at least peripherally bringing in themes of communion. But what about more negative experiences? Negative events are more difficult to discuss, for obvious reasons, but may be especially important because they often challenge the self, and require more active meaning making in order to resolve (Laible, 2011; Mansfield, Pasupathi, & McLean, 2015). In mother–child conversations, highly elaborative mothers often provide a more constructive perspective on negative experiences, helping their child create a different narrative arc to the event (Fivush et al., 2003; Fivush & Sales, 2006), as we see in this excerpt in which Anna and her mother discuss Anna's loss at a tennis tournament (coincidentally, their conversation, once again, was 144 conversational turns):

C: Yeah, and then I didn't win any of the others and then I won the last one.

Anna states that she lost multiple matches, and her mother immediately begins to discuss how difficult this was, but that Anna should talk about it.

M: And you may be, it's not easy to talk about those really bad things is it? But do you want to say what happened in the middle? It's like a meltdown. Really wasn't it?	
C: Yeah, kind of.	The mother actually exaggerates the event by calling it a meltdown, which Anna acknowledges, and her mother elaborates on.
M: And there were tears.	
C: Yeah.	
M: There were tears because it just wasn't a good day at all was it?	
C: No, not really.	The mother frames the difficulty of the event and Anna's motivation to just walk away, but then the mother turns the conversation to how the mother did not let her do this.
M: And you didn't want to do it.	
C: No.	
M: And did your mum say that's okay, Anna, you don't have to do it?	
C: No. [Laughs].	The conversation now becomes a recounting of the conversation between the mother and Anna about why Anna had to finish the tournament.
M: What did mum say?	
C: She said, what did you say?	
M: That you had to finish.	
C: You have to finish and so I did and then I got a present cos I kept going.	The mother uses this example to make the larger point about having to keep going in the face of adversity, and Anna finishes the mother's sentence, completing it with the word *persevering*.
M: It's really important we thought to have, acknowledge the fact that you kept going on it was really . . .	
C: Persevering.	
M: Perseverance in the face of extreme difficulty. It was a really great thing to do.	The mother validates this lesson and praises Anna for her accomplishment.

In this excerpt, the mother really pushes Anna into some uncomfortable spaces, including a comment on not letting Anna simply walk away from her losses. As the lengthy conversation progresses, it becomes apparent that the mother sees this as a life lesson for Anna, to learn to persevere in the face of difficulty, and both end up talking about the importance of this value. In fact, it is Anna who uses this word for the first time, suggesting that they have talked about this before and Anna has internalized this perspective. Anna is clearly portrayed by both herself and her mother as highly agentic, persevering in the face of failure in order to build strength of character. Her mother ends this part of the conversation by praising Anna for what she did.

Contrast this with conversational excerpts from 12-year-old Tom and his mother, first when discussing a highly positive event. This 33-turn conversation is one of the longest that Tom and his mother had over the course of the study. Yet, once again, Tom and his mother have difficulty connecting.

M: Okay so what's a positive event that's happened in your life, Tom?	Tom readily supplies an event to discuss. Like Anna, his positive event was going on a family trip to see cousins. His mother follows up with an open-ended question, to which Tom responds. However, she doesn't ask for further elaboration about the skiing; instead she immediately switches the topic to meals.
C: Going to, going to Queenstown, to see my cousins.	
M: What did you do?	
C: Um skiing.	

M: And what di— wh— di— what sort of meals did you have?	As in early childhood, the conversation seems stilted and uncomfortable, and Tom and his mother fail to connect.
[several intervening questions about food]	
M: What sort of things did Charlie do? Your cousin. What did you do together? Did you play PlayStation?	
C: Not that much.	
M: Oh, okay, did he have some PlayStation games that you don't?	Tom's mother persists in inquiring about Tom's activities with his cousins but mostly gets one-word answers in return. Despite the potential of this event for exploring communal and agentic themes, the conversation ends with a description of his cousin's cellphone.
C: No.	
M: Okay. What about ahhh Antonia? What did Antonia have?	
C: Cellphone.	
M: A cellphone. Was it a nice cellphone?	
C: Yes.	
M: Did she show you how to use it?	
C: No.	

However, it is the dyad's discussion of a negative event that is particularly revealing. Tom nominates his parents' divorce as the negative event he'd like to discuss. In so many ways, this is a more difficult event to tackle than a loss at a tennis tournament, and given the history of reminiscing between Tom and his mother, it is not surprising that the discussion is unsuccessful. We are able to include the 12-turn conversation in its entirety because of its brevity.

M: . . . that's happened in your life?	Tom's mother bravely asks an open-ended question about why the divorce was negative, to which Tom responds with a relatively long answer. Note the repetition of the passive construction "wasn't allowed"—Tom is careful here not to state that it was his mother who wasn't allowing his dad in the house.
C: Your divorce.	
M: And why was it negative?	
C: Cos dad wasn't allowed back in our home and yeah. Dad wasn't allowed back in our home, yeah. And he wasn't allowed to like help us in the backyard and all that.	
M: Oh, okay. But did your relationship change with your father?	Tom's mother accepts the response but doesn't elaborate or validate it. Instead she uses closed-ended questions that do not provide Tom a platform on which to elaborate on his negative feelings. Indeed, she implicitly suggests that perhaps things are even better since the divorce. Tom shuts down entirely and refuses to continue the conversation, so his negative feelings about the divorce are not even discussed, much less resolved.
C: No.	
M: Um what else may have changed?	
C: Nothing.	
M: Was it better that Dad doesn't come into the house now or not?	
C: Yep.	
M: Why is it better?	
C: I don't know. I'm not doing this.	

These excerpts clearly illustrate enduring differences between a mother who reminisces in highly elaborative ways and one who does not. The excerpts also illustrate that these reminiscing conversations are bidirectional even from the earliest point in development; children are differentially engaged in reminiscing, and mothers are both scaffolding and responding. Still, it is also obvious that Anna's mother is more skillful than Tom's mother at eliciting her child's participation. Tom's mother does not seem to be able to ask questions in ways that allow Tom to elaborate on his actions or his emotions, whereas Anna's mother is highly skilled at both. Moreover, even when Anna was a young child, her mother constructed clear connections between Anna's experiences and her sense of self, and Anna, herself, is making these connections as well. Even in these brief excerpts between Anna and her mother, the reader can sense the give and take in these conversations and the co-construction of who Anna is as an actor and agent in the world, and in relation to other people. All of this is sparse, if present at all, in the conversations between Tom and his mother. There is no sense of connection or meaning making in these conversations, and no construction of Tom's individuality. How might these themes be internalized and integrated into adolescents' emerging construction of their own narrative identity?

Adolescence: The Emergence of the Narrative Author

It is obvious from these examples, particularly from Anna, that children can be adept at narrating events from their lives well before adolescence. The research on autobiographical narratives shows that by middle childhood, children are capable of competently narrating single events in a canonical narrative structure, replete with evaluations and orienting information (Bohn & Berntsen, 2008; Pasupathi & Wainryb, 2010; Peterson & McCabe, 1983). Yet what separates children from adolescents in their life narratives is the ability to integrate across events—to bind the past self to the present self, and to create those narrative connections anew when confronted with a challenging turn of events (see McAdams, 2013b, 2015). Habermas and colleagues (Habermas & Köber, 2015; Habermas & Reese, 2015) term this a *bridging of biographical ruptures.* The key development, they argue, is the advent of *autobiographical reasoning,* or the use of language to connect past events and past self to the present and future self. Although simple forms of autobiographical reasoning start to appear in late middle childhood, it is not until midadolescence that individuals show robust evidence of

autobiographical reasoning in their life narratives, and even then, there are individual differences among adolescents and adults (Köber, Schmiedek, & Habermas, 2015). Habermas and Reese (2015, p. 178) argue that this newfound capability is the result of the development of autobiographical memory and self coalescing into a qualitatively different "cognitive–communicative format." This proposal is supported by the longitudinal data discussed earlier, in which maternal reminiscing style, along with children's language, self-awareness, and attachment security, support the development of children's autobiographical memory and self, and ultimately of adolescents' insight into life events (Reese et al., 2010).

For instance, in the example from the beginning of this chapter, 16-year-old Anna uses autobiographical reasoning when she contrasts her friends before with the new friends she now has, and remarks on the change: "I feel way better with them, like cos they're more like me . . . so I don't feel like I have to, you know hide . . . from what I actually want to do . . . and it's nicer." Anna thus contrasts her past friends and her present friends, but more importantly, she contrasts the way she feels with her new friends compared to her former friends, and the reasons for those feelings.

In contrast, when 16-year-old Tom was given an identical prompt to talk about a low point in his life, he responded by nominating the death of his grandmother (again, interviewer comments in parentheses):

"Um, probably when Nana died. (Okay, when Nana died, so what would you like to tell me about that?) Um, she had a heart attack and it was a quite a really, it was a really sad funeral. (Mmm hmm, anything else.) No, not really. (Mmm hmm, and how did you feel?) Sad. (Were there any other people there?) There was about a hundred people there. (Mmm hmm, and how did the other people feel?) I think they would be having a mixture of emotions, like sad, grief, anger you know. (Um, and why is this a low point in your life?) Because I really liked my Nana. (Yeah, has this event changed your life?) Not really."

Tom is describing what is arguably a much greater loss than Anna's, and he acknowledges his own emotions and those of others, but he does not show any evidence of autobiographical reasoning in this excerpt. Although Tom's language skills are now perfectly adequate for expressing complex thoughts, he does not narrate life events with a similar sophistication. In fact, Tom is quite able to articulate the complexity of others' emotions, but barely acknowledges his own! We argue that one primary reason for Tom's lack of autobiographical reasoning is the limited exploration of past experiences in reminiscing with his mother over the years. Whereas Anna's mother is scaffolding a form of autobiographical reasoning from the earliest excerpts on, explicitly linking actions in the world with the internal landscape of consciousness, Tom's mother provides little of this connective tissue in creating their shared narratives. Thus, these case studies illustrate both the consistency of maternal reminiscing across preschool and childhood, and the internalization of the maternal reminiscing style into adolescents' personal identity narratives.

Caveats

Of course, in selecting two case studies, there are many factors that we did not address. The most obvious is gender, not only that Anna and Tom are of different genders, but also that we only examined maternal reminiscing and did not address other possibly significant reminiscing partners, such as fathers, siblings, or other family members. Gender has emerged as an important consideration in the family reminiscing literature. Although not all studies find differences in reminiscing with daughters compared to sons, when differences emerge, they favor daughters (for reviews, see Fivush, 2007; Fivush et al., 2006; Fivush & Zaman, 2013). Mothers are more elaborative when reminiscing with daughters than with sons, and even more consistently, mothers are more emotionally expressive when reminiscing with daughters as compared to sons. In the few studies that compare mothers to fathers, mothers are more elaborative and emotionally expressive than fathers, and both mothers and fathers tend to be more elaborative and emotionally expressive with daughters as compared to sons (Reese, Haden, & Fivush, 1996; Zaman & Fivush, 2013). Thus, Anna's and Tom's mothers mirror gender differences found in the literature. In addition, we see gender differences in certain aspects of personal narratives beginning fairly early in development. By age 7, girls are telling more detailed and more emotionally expressive narratives than are boys (Buckner & Fivush, 1998). In the larger sample from which Anna's and Tom's cases were drawn, gender differenc-

es in the length of the children's memory narratives with a researcher had already emerged by age 5½ years, with girls supplying memory narratives about recent events that were nearly twice as long as boys' narratives (Cleveland & Reese, 2008). This gender difference was not a function of the children's current expressive language skills, and it continues through middle childhood and adolescence (Fivush, Bohanek, Zaman, & Grapin, 2012; Pasupathi & Wainryb, 2010). As adults, women tell more detailed and emotionally expressive autobiographical narratives than do men (see Grysman & Hudson, 2013, for a review). Gender differences in autobiographical reasoning, or in narrative meaning making more generally, are less consistent (McLean, 2015; Reese et al., 2017).

Perhaps more important for our arguments, gender is not an explanatory variable. Even if the differences we observe between Anna and her mother and Tom and his mother are related to gender, we are still in need of an explanation of why mothers (and fathers) might reminisce differently with daughters than with sons, and how and why this matters for individual autobiography. The sociocultural perspective provides a theoretical framework within which gender becomes one of many individual-difference variables (along with language skills, self-awareness, temperament, attachment status, and others already mentioned in this chapter) that contribute to and are affected by reminiscing interactions. There are myriad reasons why some mothers may be more elaborative than others, but the outcome of elaborative reminiscing for their children is clear—more elaborated and insightful autobiographical narratives. Our two case studies illustrate how this process unfolds across development.

Conclusions: Becoming an Author

Clearly, becoming an autobiographical author is a complex developmental process that is influenced and mediated by multiple factors. There is no single developmental trajectory to narrative identity, nor is any single factor alone sufficient in this process. Rather, we argue, as discussed by many of the authors of chapters in this volume, developing narrative identity involves multiple individual, social, and cultural factors dynamically interacting across the lifespan. But, importantly, as we have shown here, these individual factors unfold within, and are influenced by, the social interactions within which the individual is embedded. By closely examining individual differences in how mothers structure early narrative interactions that help children learn the forms and functions of recalling their personal past, we have identified one critical factor in becoming a self-reflective author. Children of mothers who are more elaborative when reminiscing develop a more authorial voice in adolescence. Of course, this is a reciprocal developmental process; children are, at all points, active agents in creating their own socialization environment (Rosa & Tudge, 2013). Individual differences in temperament, attachment, language skills, episodic memory skills, and gender, among others, influence both individual developmental trajectories and how mothers engage in reminiscing interactions with their children. Still, even accounting for multiple individual child differences, how mothers reminisce with their young children uniquely predicts adolescent narrative insight and identity.

We end with a beginning. We have shown how one important early relationship, the mother–child relationship, influences the development of an authorial autobiographical voice. But this relationship itself is embedded in layers of relationships and contexts (Fivush & Merrill, 2015; McLean, 2015). Reminiscing with other family members—fathers, siblings, grandparents and peers—has barely been explored. And thus far the research has mostly focused on the child reminiscing about personal experiences. How might stories of others' experiences also influence how children come to understand their own stories? Research on intergenerational narratives, stories adolescents know about their parents' childhoods, suggest that these kinds of stories are also important for developing identity (McLean, 2015; Merrill, & Fivush, 2016). Families themselves are embedded in layers of social and cultural structures replete with myths and stories that define the shape of a life and provide shared evaluative frameworks for understanding self and others (McLean & Syed, 2016). Humans are embedded in stories within stories within stories. How an individual authorial voice emerges from and contributes to these multiple layers is a story to be continued.

ACKNOWLEDGMENTS

This chapter was written while Robyn Fivush was a Senior Fellow at the Fox Center for Humanistic Inquiry at Emory University, and Jordan A. Booker was a Postdoctoral Fellow in the Fellowships in Research and Science Teaching program at Emory University. The research described in this chapter was supported by a grant from the Marsden Fund of the Royal Society of New Zealand to Elaine Reese. We thank Amy Bird, Keryn Harley, Kate Farrant, D'Neal Leroux, Rhiannon Newcombe, Joanna Parry, Sarah-Jane Robertson, Sandra Sullivan, Hilary Watson, and Naomi White for their work on the Origins of Memory study.

REFERENCES

Ainsworth, M. D. S., Blehar, M. C., & Waters, E., & Wall, S. (1978). *Patterns of attachment: A psychological study of the Strange Situation*. Hillsdale, NJ: Erlbaum.

Bauer, P. J., & Larkina, M. (2014). The onset of childhood amnesia in childhood: A prospective investigation of the course and determinants of forgetting of early-life events. *Memory, 22*, 907–924.

Berntsen, D., & Rubin, D. C. (2004). Cultural life scripts structure recall from autobiographical memory. *Memory and Cognition, 32*, 427–442.

Bird, A., & Reese, E. (2006). Emotional reminiscing and the development of an autobiographical self. *Developmental Psychology, 42*, 613–626.

Bird, A., Reese, E., & Tripp, G. (2006). Parent–child talk about past emotional events: Associations with child temperament and goodness-of-fit. *Journal of Cognition and Development, 7*, 189–210.

Bohn, A., & Berntsen, D. (2008). Life story development in childhood: The development of life story abilities and the acquisition of cultural life scripts from late middle childhood to adolescence. *Developmental Psychology, 44*, 1135–1147.

Booker, J. A., & Dunsmore, J. C. (2017). Affective social competence in adolescence: Current findings and future directions. *Social Development, 26*, 3–20.

Bruner, J. (1990). *Acts of meaning*. Cambridge, MA: Harvard University Press.

Buckner, J. P., & Fivush, R. (1998). Gender and self in children's autobiographical narratives. *Applied Cognitive Psychology, 12*, 407–429.

Caspi, A., & Silva, P. A. (1995). Temperamental qualities at age three predict personality traits in young adulthood: Longitudinal evidence from a birth cohort. *Child Development, 66*, 486–498.

Cleveland, E. S., & Reese, E. (2008). Children remember early childhood: Long-term recall across the offset of childhood amnesia. *Applied Cognitive Psychology, 22*, 127–142.

Conway, M. A., Singer, J. A., & Tagini, A. (2004). The self in autobiographical memory: Correspondence and coherence. *Social Cognition, 22*, 491–529.

Erikson, E. H. (1968). *Identity*. New York: Norton.

Farrant, K., & Reese, E. (2000). Maternal style and children's participation in reminiscing: Stepping stones in children's autobiographical memory development. *Journal of Cognition and Development, 1,* 193–225.

Fiese, B. H., Hooker, K. A., Kotary, L., Schwagler, J., & Rimmer, M. (1995). Family stories in the early stages of parenthood. *Journal of Marriage and the Family, 57,* 763–770.

Fivush, R. (2007). Maternal reminiscing style and children's developing understanding of self and emotion. *Clinical Social Work Journal, 35,* 37–46.

Fivush, R. (2010). The development of autobiographical memory. *Annual Review of Psychology, 62,* 2.1–2.24.

Fivush, R. (2012). Subjective perspective and personal timeline in the development of autobiographical memory. In D. Bernsten & D. Rubin (Eds.), *Theories of autobiographical memory* (pp. 226–245). Cambridge, UK: Cambridge University Press.

Fivush, R. (2013). Maternal reminiscing style: The sociocultural construction of autobiographical memory across childhood and adolescence. In P. J. Bauer & R. Fivush (Eds.), *The Wiley handbook on the development of children's memory* (pp. 568–585). Chichester, UK: Wiley-Blackwell.

Fivush, R., Berlin, L. J., McDermott-Sales, J., Menuti-Washburn J., & Cassidy, J. (2003). Functions of parent–child reminiscing about emotionally negative events. *Memory, 11,* 179–192.

Fivush, R., Bohanek, J. G., Zaman, W., & Grapin, S. (2012). Gender differences in adolescent's autobiographical memories. *Journal of Cognition and Development, 13,* 295–319.

Fivush, R., Habermas, T., Waters, T. E. A., & Zaman, W. (2011). The making of autobiographical memory: Intersections of culture, narratives, and identity. *International Journal of Psychology, 46,* 321–345.

Fivush, R., Haden, C. A., & Reese, E. (2006). Elaborating on elaborations: The role of maternal reminiscing style in cognitive and socioemotional development. *Child Development, 77,* 1568–1588.

Fivush, R., Marin, K., McWilliams, K., & Bohanek, J. G. (2009). Family reminiscing style: Parent gender and emotional focus in relation to child well-being. *Journal of Cognition and Development, 10,* 210–235.

Fivush, R., & Merrill, N. (2015). The personal past as historically, culturally and socially constructed. *Applied Cognitive Psychology, 28,* 301–303.

Fivush, R., & Merrill, N. (2016). An ecological systems approach to family narratives. *Memory Studies, 9,* 305–314.

Fivush, R., & Nelson, K. (2006). Parent–child reminiscing locates the self in the past. *British Journal of Developmental Psychology, 24,* 235–251.

Fivush, R., & Reese, E. (2002). Reminiscing and relating: The development of parent–child talk about the past. In J. D. Webster & B. K. Haight (Eds.), *Critical advances in reminiscence work: From theory to application* (pp. 109–122). New York: Springer.

Fivush, R., & Sales, J. M. (2006). Coping, attachment and mother–child narratives of stressful events. *Merrill–Palmer Quarterly, 52,* 125–150.

Fivush, R., & Zaman, W. (2013). Gender differences in elaborative parent–child emotion and play narratives. *Sex Roles, 68,* 591–604.

Fivush, R., & Zaman, W. (2015). Gendered narrative voices: Sociocultural and feminist approaches to emerging identity in childhood and adolescence. In K. C. McLean & M. U. Syed (Eds.), *The Oxford handbook of identity development* (pp. 33–52). New York: Oxford University Press.

Garcia, D., Bagner, D. M., Pruden, S. M., & Nichols-Lopez, K. (2015). Language production in children with and at risk for delay: Mediating role of parenting skills. *Journal of Clinical Child and Adolescent Psychology, 44,* 814–825.

Graci, M. E., & Fivush, R. (2017). Narrative meaning making, attachment, and psychological growth and stress. *Journal of Social and Personal Relationships, 34,* 486–509.

Grysman, A., & Hudson, J. A. (2013). Gender differences in autobiographical memory: Developmental and methodological considerations. *Developmental Review, 33,* 239–272.

Habermas, T., & Bluck, S. (2000). Getting a life: The emergence of the life story in adolescence. *Psychological Bulletin, 126,* 748–769.

Habermas, T., & Köber, C. (2015). Autobiographical reasoning in life narratives buffers the effect of biographical disruptions on the sense of self-continuity. *Memory, 23,* 664–674.

Habermas, T., & Reese, E. (2015). Getting a life takes time: The development of the life story in adolescence, its precursors and consequences. *Human Development, 58,* 172–201.

Haden, C. A. (1998). Reminiscing with different children: Relating maternal stylistic consistency and sibling similarity in talk about the past. *Developmental Psychology, 34,* 99–114.

Haden, C. A., & Fivush, R. (1996). Contextual variation in maternal conversational styles. *Merrill–Palmer Quarterly, 42,* 200–227.

Harley, K., & Reese, E. (1999). Origins of autobiographical memory. *Developmental Psychology, 35,* 1338–1348.

Hedrick, A. M., Haden, C. A., & Ornstein, P. A. (2009). Elaborative talk during and after an event: Conversational style influences children's memory reports. *Journal of Cognition and Development, 10,* 188–209.

Hoff-Ginsburg, E. (1991). Mother–child conversations in different social classes and communicative settings. *Child Development, 62,* 782–796.

Hutto, D. D. (2007). The narrative practice hypothesis: Origins and applications of folk psychology. *Royal Institute of Philosophy Supplement, 60,* 43–68.

Köber, C., Schmiedek, F., & Habermas, T. (2015). Characterizing lifespan development of three aspects of coherence in life narratives: A cohort-sequential study. *Developmental Psychology, 51,* 260–275.

Kulkofsky, S., Wang, Q., & Koh, J. B. K. (2009). Functions of memory sharing and mother–child reminiscing behaviors: Individual and cultural variations. *Journal of Cognition and Development, 10,* 92–114.

Laible, D. (2011). Does it matter if preschool children and mothers discuss positive vs. negative events during reminiscing?: Links with mother-reported attachment, family emotional climate, and socioemotional development. *Social Development, 20,* 394–411.

Laible, D., Panfile Murphy, T., & Augustine, M. (2013). Constructing emotional and relational understanding: The role of mother–child reminiscing about negatively valenced events. *Social Development, 22,* 300–318.

Laible, D. J., & Thompson, R. A. (2000). Mother–child discourse, attachment security, shared positive affect, and early conscience development. *Child Development, 71,* 1424–1440.

Leyva, D., Reese, E., Laible, D., Schaughency, E., Das, S., & Clifford, A. (2018). *The art of elaboration: Differential links of parents' elaboration to child autobiographical memory and socioemotional skills.* Manuscript under review.

Main, M., Kaplan, N., & Cassidy, J. (1985). Security in infancy, childhood, and adulthood: A move to the level of representation. *Monographs of the Society for Research in Child Development, 50,* 66–104.

Mansfield, C. D., Pasupathi, M., & McLean, K. C. (2015). Developing through difficulty: Does narrating growth of self in stories of transgressions promote self-acceptance and self-compassion. *Journal of Research in Personality, 58,* 69–83.

McAdams, D. P. (2001). The psychology of life stories. *Review of General Psychology, 5,* 100–122.

McAdams, D. P. (2013a). The psychological self as actor, agent, and author. *Perspectives on Psychological Science, 8,* 272–295.

McAdams, D. P. (2013b). *The redemptive self: Stories Americans live by* (rev. expanded ed.). New York: Oxford University Press.

McAdams, D. P. (2015). *The art and science of personality development.* New York: Guilford Press.

McAdams, D. P., Hoffman, B. J., Mansfield, E. D., & Day, R. (1996). Themes of agency and communion in significant autobiographical scenes. *Journal of Personality, 64,* 339–377.

McAdams, D. P., Reynolds, J., Lewis, M., Patten, A. H., & Bowman, P. J. (2001). When bad things turn good and good things turn bad: Sequences of redemption and contamination in life narrative and their relation to psychosocial adaptation in midlife adults and in students. *Personality and Social Psychology Bulletin, 27,* 474–485.

McLean, K. C. (2015). *The co-authored self: Family stories and the construction of personal identity.* New York: Oxford University Press.

McLean, K. C., Pasupathi, M., & Pals, J. L. (2007). Selves creating stories creating selves: A process model of self-development. *Personality and Social Psychology Review, 11,* 262–278.

McLean, K. C., & Syed, M. U. (2016). Personal, master, and alternative narratives: An integrative framework for understanding identity development in context. *Human Development, 58,* 318–349.

Merrill, N., & Fivush, R. (2016). Intergenerational narratives and identity across development. *Developmental Review, 40,* 72–92.

Nelson, K. (2003). Narrative and self, myth and memory: Emergence of the cultural self. In R. Fivush & C. Haden (Eds.), *Autobiographical memory and the construction of a narrative self: Developmental and cultural perspectives* (pp. 3–28). Mahwah, NJ: Erlbaum.

Nelson, K., & Fivush, R. (2004). The emergence of autobiographical memory: A social cultural developmental model. *Psychologica Review, 111,* 486–511.

Newcombe, R., & Reese, E. (2004). Evaluations and orientations in mother–child narratives as a function of attachment security: A longitudinal investigation. *International Journal of Behavioral Development, 28,* 230–245.

Pasupathi, M., & Wainryb, C. (2010). On telling the whole story: Facts and interpretations in autobiographical memory narratives from childhood through midadolescence. *Developmental Psychology, 46,* 735–746.

Peterson, C., Jesso, B., & McCabe, A. (1999). Encouraging narratives in preschoolers: An intervention study. *Journal of Child Language, 26,* 49–67.

Peterson, C., & McCabe, A. (1983). *Developmental psycholinguistics: Three ways of looking at a child's narrative.* New York: Plenum Press.

Recchia, H., & Wainryb, C. (Eds.). (2014). *Talking about right and wrong: Parent–child conversations as contexts for moral development.* Cambridge, UK: Cambridge University Press.

Reese, E. (1999). What children say when they talk about the past. *Narrative Inquiry, 9,* 215–241.

Reese, E. (2008). Maternal coherence in the Adult Attachment Interview is linked to maternal reminiscing and to children's self concept. *Attachment and Human Development, 10,* 451–464.

Reese, E. (2013). *Tell me a story: Sharing stories to enrich your child's world.* New York: Oxford University Press.

Reese, E., Chen, Y., McAnally, H., Myftari, E., Neha, T., Wang, Q., et al. (2014). Narratives and traits in personality development among New Zealand Māori, Chinese, and European adolescents. *Journal of Adolescence, 37,* 727–737.

Reese, E., Haden, C. A., & Fivush, R. (1993). Mother–child conversations about the past: Relationships of style and memory over time. *Cognitive Development, 8,* 403–430.

Reese, E., Haden, C. A., & Fivush, R. (1996). Mothers, fathers, daughters, sons: Gender differences in autobiographical reminiscing. *Research on Language and Social Interaction, 29,* 27–56.

Reese, E., Jack, F., & White, N. (2010). Origins of adolescents' autobiographical memories. *Cognitive Development, 25,* 352–367.

Reese, E., Myftari, E., McAnally, H. M., Chen, Y.,

Neha, T., Wang, Q., et al. (2017). Telling the tale and living well: Adolescent narrative identity, personality traits, and well-being across cultures. *Child Development, 88,* 612–628.

Reese, E., & Newcombe, R. (2007). Training mothers in elaborative reminiscing enhances children's autobiographical memory and narrative. *Child Development, 78,* 1153–1170.

Reese, E., Yan, C., Jack, F., & Hayne, H. (2010). Emerging identities: Narrative and self from early childhood to early adolescence. In K. C. McLean & M. Pasupathi (Eds.), *Narrative development in adolescence: Creating the storied self* (pp. 23–44). New York: Springer-Verlag.

Ricoeur, P. (1991). Life in quest of narrative. In D. Wood (Ed.), *On Paul Ricoeur: Narrative and interpretation* (pp. 20–33). London: Routledge.

Rosa, E. M., & Tudge, J. (2013). Urie Bronfenbrenner's theory of human development: Its evolution from ecology to bioecology. *Journal of Family Theory and Review, 5,* 243–258.

Salmon, K., & Reese, E. (2016). The benefits of reminiscing with young children. *Current Directions in Psychological Science, 25,* 233–238.

Sarbin, T. R. (1986). *Narrative psychology: The storied nature of human conduct.* London: Praeger/Greenwood Publishing Group.

Suizzo, M.-S. (2007). Parents' goals and values for children: Dimensions of independence and interdependence across four U.S. ethnic groups. *Journal of Cross-Cultural Psychology, 38,* 506–530.

Taumoepeau, M., & Reese, E. (2013). Maternal reminiscing, elaborative talk, and children's theory of mind: An intervention study. *First Language, 33,* 388–410.

van Bergen, P., Salmon, K., Dadds, M. R., & Allen, J. (2009). The effects of mother training in emotion-rich, elaborative reminiscing on children's shared recall and emotion knowledge. *Journal of Cognition and Development, 10,* 162–187.

Vygotsky, L. S. (1978). *Mind in society: The development of higher psychological processes.* Cambridge, MA: Harvard University Press.

Wang, Q. (2013a). The cultured self and remembering. In P. J. Bauer & R. Fivush (Eds.), *The Wiley handbook on the development of children's memory* (pp. 605–625). New York: Wiley.

Wang, Q. (2013b). *The autobiographical self in time and culture.* New York: Oxford University Press.

Wellman, H. M. (2014). *Making minds: How theory of mind develops.* New York: Oxford University Press.

Winter, D. G., John, O. P., Stewart, A. J., Klohnen, E. C., & Duncan, L. E. (1998). Traits and motives: Toward an integration of two traditions in personality research. *Psychological Review, 105,* 230–250.

Young, A. M., & Acitelli, L. K. (1998). The role of attachment style and relationship status of the perceiver in the perceptions of romantic partner. *Journal of Social and Personal Relationships, 15,* 161–173.

Zaman, W., & Fivush, R. (2013). Gender differences in elaborative parent–child emotion and play narratives. *Sex Roles, 68,* 591–604.

CHAPTER 24

Narrative Identity in Adolescence and Adulthood

Pathways of Development

Kate C. McLean
Jennifer P. Lilgendahl

As we embark on a discussion of narrative identity development, we ask our readers to consider a young man whom we call Stephen,[1] a participant in our longitudinal study of identity and personality development in the college context. We have thus far collected nine waves of survey data from Stephen, beginning just before he started college. In this study, one of our foci is career identity, particularly for those interested in science/technology/engineering/mathematics (STEM) majors, and who come from underrepresented backgrounds. Stephen is biracial (black and white), and just before beginning college reported a desire to major in chemistry as part of his goal of becoming a physician. As we have followed him, he has indeed remained committed to his goal of entering the medical field and has indeed majored in chemistry. His survey measures show a well-adjusted young man who is quite normative for his cohort, scoring within 1 standard deviation of the mean for multiple measures of well-being, personality traits, and identity exploration and commitment over the first 2 years of our study. However, something changes at the beginning of the third year of college, and the steady, normative pathway suggested by his scale scores takes a dramatic turn.

All of a sudden he begins to explore his identity deeply, along with a large dip in his commitments (moving him outside of 1 standard deviation from the mean for his cohort); these changes seem to be particularly prominent in the domain of ethnic identity. Thus, seemingly out of nowhere, Stephen moves from a place of relatively normativity and stability, to a unique and unstable place. Although we have gained all of this information from his survey measures, we still don't really know what happened. What has prompted this shift? What does this change in his self-views look like?

Luckily, Stephen completed not only survey measures of well-being, personality traits, and identity processes, but also multiple narrative assessments during each year of college, data that tell a much more elaborated story. These narratives not only include some explanation for why we see this shift in his identity during his third year of college, but also point us to how Stephen actually develops over those 3 years, despite the general stability in his survey measures of development. These narrative data begin to tell us about the experiences that underlie relatively abstract processes of exploration and commitment, the shifts we see in these processes, and they also tell us about the content of identity—*what it is that is actually developing*. With these data, we see that a narrative

---

[1] Stephen is a pseudonym, and we have changed some details of his case to protect privacy.

approach highlights how someone who seems relatively average, like most other people in his cohort at least, is an individual with experiences worthy of study as they help to illuminate how and what develops as young people come to understand who they are.

We tantalize our readers with this abstract rendition of Stephen's case, to which we return in more detail after a discussion of the extant research on narrative identity development. We begin with a brief comment on the history of the field and a theoretical overview, followed by methodological considerations. We then highlight the most up-to-date findings and elaborate on Stephen's case, and what it reveals about narrative identity development.

Historical Context and Theoretical Considerations

As is articulated in the opening to this handbook, the fields of personality and developmental psychology have historically existed as separate disciplines, and narrative identity is a particularly good example of this division. But it is also an example of the potential for the integration between these fields. Indeed, beginning around the same time, in the mid-1980s, developmental and personality psychologists began to consider the importance of stories, albeit in very different ways.

The current iteration of the study of stories within the discipline of personality was largely driven by the motivation to return greater breadth and depth to the study of individual differences beyond traits, which were the focus of the field of personality in the 1980s. Motivated by this emphasis on broader, more holistic definitions of persons, researchers began to examine individual differences in life stories, or in the construction of in-depth personally defining autobiographical memory narratives (e.g., McAdams, 1985). This work led to a new framework for the study of personality that included multiple levels of personality, one of which was narrative identity (McAdams, 1995; McAdams & Pals, 2006; see also McAdams, 2015; Singer, 2004; Singer & Salovey, 1993; Thorne, 2000). Though conceptualized as a framework for *personality,* McAdams's (1985) original work was both personological *and* developmental. McAdams emphasized the Eriksonian roots of his framework, offering this approach to identity as an alternative to Marcia's (1966) status approach to identity (see also McLean & Syed, 2015a; Syed & McLean, 2015). McAdams argued that the narrative approach was more closely aligned with Erikson's (1968) emphasis on temporal integration, as a part of the development of personal continuity (for more recent iterations of this approach, see McAdams 2015). Thus, in this area, *narrative identity* is defined as an integrative story that explains how one came to be the person one is, a story that provides unity and purpose to the individual. Not surprisingly then, variations in the construction of this story are associated with psychological functioning in predictable ways.

In a parallel empirical universe, developmentalists, largely driven by the motivation to understand childhood amnesia, began to examine the development of autobiographical memory in early childhood (e.g., Fivush & Fromhoff, 1988; see also Nelson & Fivush, 2004). Researchers identified past-event conversations between parent and child as a location for the development of self and autobiography, as children learn to tell stories about themselves through time with the help of their parents, or storytelling experts. Therefore, the focus of this line of research is on the inherent social action and activity of narrative, which creates a link between self and other, and the individual and his or her larger culture (e.g., Bruner, 1990; Hammack, 2008; McLean & Syed, 2015b; Nelson & Fivush, 2004). Through storytelling practices, children learn not only about the structure of a story but also the content—what kinds of stories are valued, and how should they be shared. As children gain narrative skills, they continue to construct the stories of their lives in conversation with others (see Fivush, Haden, & Reese, 2006 for a review), and in light of the larger cultural messages and pressures to which they are exposed. Adolescents and adults begin to wrestle with these master narratives as they negotiate a place of individual self-understanding within a larger cultural and social context that can both encourage and impinge on personal identity (Hammack, 2011; McLean & Syed, 2015b). This theoretical perspective broadens the lens of empirical study beyond the individual to other people and broader cultural structures connected to that individual, with the emphasis on the coauthorship of the self (McLean, 2015).

Thus, these two strains of work led to quite different emphases—the latter focused on conversations between parents and children about specific past events as a mechanism of narrative development, and the former focused on how patterns in these much larger stories are associated with psychological functioning. Around the turn of the century, these literatures began to find connection (e.g., McAdams, 2001; Pasupathi, 2001; Thorne, 2000), and the past 15 years have seen a flourishing conversation between these researchers, nicely represented in this section of the current volume (see also Fivush & Zaman, 2015; McAdams & Zapata-Gietl, 2015).

As is often the case when disciplines merge, the intersection of these two fields creates a far more comprehensive understanding of the construct of narrative identity. The developmental focus brings an emphasis on skills development and normative changes that are linked to other shifts, such as cognitive development. A developmental lens also highlights the contextually relevant mechanisms of development, such as the emphasis on relational contexts and conversations as drivers of skills development and narrative elaboration (Fivush et al., 2006; McLean et al., 2007). For example, McLean and colleagues (2007) proposed that *situated stories* are stories told in particular proximal and distal contexts to particular audiences, by individuals with particular needs and goals. The repeated process of situated storytelling is a mechanism by which selves develop, both in terms of the maintenance of stable aspects of selves, as well as for growth and change in narrative identity. Similarly, personality psychologists address mechanisms, but from a different lens, as with the examination of how traits may set the stage for certain components of autobiographical reasoning within narratives, or in how autobiographical reasoning may contribute to changes in personality over time (Lilegendahl, Helson, & John, 2013; Pals, 2006). Personality psychologists also emphasize variability rather than normative trends, opening the possibility for thinking about *trajectories* of development, on which we elaborate with Stephen's case.

Given this now robust literature, there is also some agreement about some of the basic narrative features that are reliably associated with important outcomes. Broadly, these features of narrative may be thought of as capturing motivational themes, affective themes, coherence or structural elements of narrative, and processes of autobiographical reasoning, or integrative meaning. We bring the reader's attention to Adler (Chapter 25, this volume) for a more intensive review of the primary constructs in

the field (see also Adler, Lodi-Smith, Philippe, & Houle, 2015; McAdams & McLean, 2013). However, pertinent to the work we describe in this chapter is the construct of autobiographical reasoning. This feature of narrative centers on the degree to which an individual has engaged in reflection on the past and what it means to his or her current self-understanding (see Habermas & Bluck, 2000; McLean & Pratt, 2006; Pals, 2006; Pasupathi, Mansour, & Brubaker, 2007), representing a critical process for developing a more integrative identity. Finally, we note that narrative methods, to which we turn next, are especially generative, and researchers need not be constrained by examining only the constructs we list here. There are many ways to examine personal narratives, which is one of the benefits of this approach.

Methodological Considerations

In general, narrative psychologists who take a quantitative approach do so by eliciting narratives via written, interview, or conversational assessments, which are then coded by third parties for a variety of dimensions, some of which we listed earlier (e.g., coherence, emotional valence). These narrative codes are often then examined in relation to constructs such as well-being, personality traits, and the like (see Adler, Chapter 25, this volume). We do not review coding processes here, as these issues are well covered in the literature (see Adler et al., 2017; Syed & Nelson, 2015). Instead we draw attention to three particularly relevant issues for the study of narrative identity *development*. First, we address the issue of capturing the entire life story versus specific memory narratives, in terms of what prompts are most appropriate at different developmental stages. Second, we discuss the choice of using specific versus open-ended narrative prompts, which brings attention to capturing identity-relevant content, as well as identity processes. Finally, we discuss the issue of repeated narration, or story development over time, of obvious developmental interest. We elaborate on each of these below.

The Life Story versus Memory-Specific Prompts

The first concern is the decision of whether to assess the entire life story or specific memory narratives. Although there are a number of reasons why one may consider one or the other; a significant factor is stage of development. The life story is a comprehensive (but not necessarily all-encompassing or veridical) account of how one has come to be the person one is today (see Adler, Chapter 25, this volume). The full life story has typically been assessed with McAdams's (1993) Life Story Interview, which includes a set of prompts that invite the participant to divide his or her life into chapters and identify many qualities of the life story, including themes, high points and low points, and significant interpersonal influences. To construct meaningful responses to such prompts may take years of practice at storytelling, learning about oneself and the culture in which that self is defined, as well as employing the cognitive skills and motivation to understand and communicate who one is. Thus, although the precursors to its construction begin in early childhood and continue to develop throughout adolescence (for a review, see Habermas & Reese, 2015; Reese, Jack, & White, 2010), it is not until adulthood that the full and comprehensive assessment of the life story, as assessed with the Life Story Interview, is likely to be most valuable and appropriate. It is not surprising that this interview has primarily been used with middle-aged, or older, adults who have reached a point in life when identity has fully formed, and providing an integrative account of one's life is a meaningful exercise.

In contrast, adolescents and emerging adults typically do not yet have a fully constructed life story or narrative identity; in this case, the collection of more specific memories, such as turning points and self-defining memories, can help to uncover patterns of narration that may be important to linking together a fuller life story as development progresses (but for a developmentally appropriate life-story measure for adolescents, see Reese, Chen, Jack, & Hayne, 2010). Studies using specific memory narratives have fruitfully focused on one highly significant memory narrative (e.g., McLean & Pratt, 2006) or several memory narratives selected for their self-defining qualities (Blagov & Singer, 2004). These specific prompts can tell us about the relevant concerns to those at different developmental stages (e.g., school, romance, work), as well as processes used to understand those more specific experiences, without requiring participants to construct an entire life story. Recently Syed (2017) has suggested that these prompt-specific narratives, which do not require the kind of integrative work of a full

life story, may better reflect the second level of personality, as they concern developmental tasks and concerns.

Open- versus Closed-Ended Prompts

A second methodological distinction to consider is between broad, open-ended prompts that give participants a wide range of latitude with respect to memory content (e.g., self-defining memories, high points), and prompts that are tailored to specific identity contents, such as social identities (e.g., ethnicity: Syed, 2010a; gender: McLean, Shucard, & Syed, 2017); or other domains of identity (e.g., relationships, religion, or values: McLean, Syed, & Shucard, 2016). Both have value for the study of narrative identity development. At the broad, open-ended level, participants are unconstrained and able to share from the domains of identity and experience that are the most emotionally salient and authentically connected to current self-understanding (see McLean, Syed, Yoder, & Greenhoot, 2014). In contrast, prompting participants to narrate experiences relevant to specific identity domains and contexts allows the researcher to tailor the narrative approach to specific developmental concerns and challenges (Syed, 2017). For example, in our longitudinal study of narrative identity development during college, we prompt for academic and romantic high points and low points at the end of each school year. In this way, we have adapted the classic high-point and low-point prompts to be specific to two domains that are central to self-exploration and identity development during college, with the goal of tapping into active narrative identity processes as they are unfolding in context. As we will demonstrate with Stephen's case, our aim with this study is to make effective use of combining broad and context-specific prompts in order to elicit the fullest picture of narrative identity development during emerging adulthood.

Prompts targeting specific events and identity contents have also been useful for research on narrative identity development throughout adulthood. In particular, several studies have demonstrated the usefulness of prompting for identity-challenging and difficult life experiences (Pals, 2006), such as divorce or having a child with a disability (King & Raspin, 2004; King, Scollon, Ramsey, & Williams, 2000). In this context, the narrative approach has proven to be useful in revealing how adults attempt to make sense of disruptive experiences and rebuild their identities in the aftermath. Nevertheless, the use of prompts about specific identity contents has not been particularly common in research on adult narrative identity development, and we suggest that this is an underutilized methodological approach that researchers should consider more often for midlife and aging samples (e.g., parenting, retirement, health). Regardless of developmental stage, researchers who have relied solely on traditional quantitative approaches to study domain-specific aspects of identity development may benefit from adding narrative prompts to their studies. The qualitative richness and open-ended nature of narratives often reveals unpredicted new insights about the experience of identity development within specific contexts. For example, narratives allow participants to describe identity-relevant experiences holistically, which can reveal how, and where, different identity contents intersect (see McLean et al., 2014); we also explore this in our case study.

Repeated Narration

Finally, it may be argued that the narrative approach to personality and identity is especially well suited for studying how the self is constructed, maintained, and transformed through *time*. This makes it quite surprising that so few studies of narrative identity and its development have involved the repeated measurement of narrative, that is, how, or if, stories are repeated over time. Even when studies have been longitudinal, it has typically been the case that qualities coded from narratives at one point in time are used to predict outcomes and changes over time in other measures, such as ego development or well-being (e.g., King & Raspin, 2004; Pals, 2006). However, this is starting to change with recent longitudinal studies (Dunlop, Guo, & McAdams, 2016; Lilgendahl & McLean, 2015). For example, in our current longitudinal study, we collect narratives three times during each year of college in order to track patterns of both stability and change in self-narration and predict patterns of change in personality and identity measures from those pathways of narration. The value of examining repeated narration is that we can see not only where the stability lies in narrative identity but also what changes and how, as we expect normative growth and evolution in stories (e.g., McAdams, 1993). The value of repeated narration for advancing our

understanding of narrative identity development is also a theme of our case study.

Narrative Identity Development: Normative Trends and Individual Differences

One might almost say that the beginning of one's narrative identity is *in utero*. As parents anticipate the child they will have, they may begin to have ideas about characteristics of this child, and even create stories about the developing being. Arguably, the first big story (perhaps beyond conception) is birth, an experience that, of course, is not remembered by the main character but is often narrated with frequency to the child, becoming a part of the "narrative ecology" in which the child is raised (McLean, 2015; McLean & Breen, 2014; Reese, Hayne, & MacDonald, 2008; see also Zaman & Fivush, 2011). Thus, as parents tell stories to and about their children, the seeds of narrative identity are planted.

Beginning in very early childhood, around two or three years of age, parents and children begin the process of engaging in 'past-event conversations,' the kinds of conversations that can seem mundane—what did you did at Grandma's, or what you had for breakfast—but that lay the foundation for learning the skill of narration, as well as for learning about developing self. The vast literature on narrative development in early childhood is well covered in this volume (see Fivush, Reese, & Booker, Chapter 23; see also Fivush et al., 2006), so suffice it to say that parents play a large role in scaffolding the skills for telling stories, the interest in doing so, as well as early individual differences in narration, such as how elaborative a child is when telling stories.

Adolescence and emerging adulthood are heightened times of identity development, as we see increases in autobiographical reasoning processes used to construct that larger story (e.g., Habermas and de Silveira, 2008; McLean, Breen, & Fournier, 2010). For example, normative gains are made, especially between ages 12 and 20, in forming causal links between time periods, and between events and the broader self, as well as providing broader biographical understanding and context to one's life story (Habermas & de Silveira, 2008). These increases are likely due to continued development and refinement of cognitive skills that allow for the careful reflective and analytical work of constructing a life story, and the responses to the many changes that occur during this time period that need sense making. During the college years, the narration of major life-story scenes shows normative increases in emotional positivity and self-differentiation, which is consistent with continued gains in identity development during this period (McAdams et al., 2006).

Another press for the emergence of identity development is the social and cultural demand to define oneself. Erikson (1968) emphasized the need for individuals to define themselves in relation to the larger culture, or to find their place in their communities (see also Syed & McLean, 2016). More recently, various researchers have proposed refinement on these ideas, refinements that center on the understanding of the life course (Arnett, 2016); the cultural concept of biography (Habermas, 2007), the life script (Rubin & Bernsten, 2003), and the biographical master narrative (McLean & Syed, 2015b). The common thread across these proposals is that there are culturally normative events that should occur in people's lives (e.g., marriage and childbearing), depending on the culture they are in, as well as culturally normative timing of those events (e.g., marriage before childbearing). It is now clear that this knowledge about the normative biography for given cultures is acquired beginning in late middle childhood, and into adolescence (e.g., Bohn & Berntsen, 2008, 2013; Habermas, 2007). In sum, there are various internal and external pressures that make adolescence and emerging adulthood a time ripe for identity development.

Although these earlier stages play a special role in identity development, identity continues to be relevant across the lifespan (Erikson, 1968; Kroger, 2015; Lilgendahl, 2015; McAdams, 2015; Syed & McLean, 2018). As new events are experienced, such as marriage, divorce, childrearing, and retirement, new chapters or interpretations of one's life story may emerge. Indeed, the research on adulthood has also found normative changes, such as the increased reflection and integrative meaning making that continues through midlife, and the increase in stable understandings of self in later adulthood (McLean, 2008; McLean & Lilgendahl, 2008; Pasupathi & Mansour, 2006; Singer, Rexhaj, & Baddeley, 2007). However, there is a rather significant gaping hole in the narrative identity literature on adults in their later 20s and those in their 30s, and even 40s (for exceptions, see Carlsson, Wängqvist, & Frisén, 2015; Dunlop,

Hanley, McCoy, & Harake, 2017; Habermas & Köber, 2015). Research on personality traits has shown that the important developmental transitions that take place during those years include the transition out of school and into the workforce, transitions between jobs or careers, transitions into and out of romantic relationships, and the onset of parenting and children leaving the home (e.g., Neyer & Asendorpf, 2001; Roberts, Caspi, & Moffitt, 2003). Given the extent to which such experiences may transform identity and require sense making and narrative integration, it is notable that there has not been substantial empirical (or theoretical) work in the field of narrative identity on these topics.

Along with the differences in processes of autobiographical reasoning at different life stages, it is likely that there are differences in the content of identity at different life stages. Identity content, as opposed to process, has been relatively neglected in the field of identity development (see Galliher, McLean, & Syed, 2017). However, as we just noted, we would expect that the contents of identity may shift in developmentally normative ways from the intensity of schooling and romance in adolescence and emerging adulthood to the intensity of work life and parenting in midlife. Examining what contents individuals are working on not only provides us the necessary descriptive information about the phenomenon under study, but also shows that individuals reason in different ways about different kinds of content. For example, there appears to be more reasoning among emerging adults about contents that involve some degree of choice or volition, such as politics and religion, compared to contents that are more ascribed, or for which their personal importance is culturally obvious, such as family (McLean, Syed, & Shucard, 2016).

Much of the work we have reviewed here has focused on normative developments, such as the increase in autobiographical reasoning skills, consistent with many developmental approaches. However, there are also individual differences in development. Much of the work has been on how individual differences at the first and second levels, and primarily the first level, are associated with narratives. For example, extant research has demonstrated how narrative identity may be involved in both the continuity and development of personality. On the side of continuity, research has shown that the basic Big Five traits, which are relatively stable over time (e.g., Roberts, Walton, & Viechtbauer, 2006), are correlated with predictable qualities in narratives. For example, the traits of extraversion and agreeableness are associated with more themes of love and friendship in life stories, the trait of openness is associated with greater complexity and self-differentiation, and the trait of neuroticism manifests itself with muted positive affect and more negative conclusions in narratives of past events (Lilgendahl & McAdams, 2011; McAdams et al., 2004).

Longitudinal research suggests that such findings may reflect more than mere trait expressions, and that narrative processes may play an active causal role in continuity by mediating the influence of traits on later life outcomes (e.g., Pals, 2006; Sutin & Robins, 2005). Furthermore, under some circumstances, narrative processes may also be the agents of personality growth and change, particularly in the context of narrating difficult and identity-challenging life events. Specifically, several studies have shown that narrating life's challenges in adulthood with an emphasis on accommodative or exploratory processing (i.e., examining the ways those events may transform the self) is predictive of increases in ego development over time (King et al., 2000; Lilgendahl et al., 2013).

Our review of the current state of the field brings us to the conclusion that combining developmental and personality approaches is a fruitful avenue. What is relatively lacking in the existing literature is an examination of *individual differences in the trajectories of narratives themselves,* an approach we have taken in a recently launched longitudinal project.

Trajectories of Development in Emerging Adulthood: The Identity Pathways Project

" . . . After my first study participation I remember being so excited because I knew exactly what I wanted to do. As I was hooked up to an EEG machine and asked several questions, I remember being in awe by the whole process and all the equipment. It made me want to do research, and the more I thought about it the rest of the day I re-alized I wanted to do research in medicine which has sculpted my life since then. . . . It felt so good to have a direction, a goal to work towards. . . . "

"Last semester was the first time in my life that I legitimately failed any exam. . . . I remember picking up my exam and just crying for about ten minutes. It did then and still does cause me to question my academic interests and whether I even have the capability to excel in organic chemistry—whether I even have the capacity to think in the specific way that organic chemistry requires. I know I am really interested in chemistry, but I have doubted my major and future plans ever since."

" . . . I remember when my boyfriend and I broke up, it was really hard for me. He was my first time love, my first serious boyfriend; he taught me a lot about people, relationships and myself. . . . Then one night about two weeks after it happened, I called him up and things were o.k. at first, we were just talking, and then it got serious. . . . I totally lost it. All he could say was 'listen to yourself!' And I did in that moment, I stopped and heard myself and heard how pathetic I was, how I had lost all self-respect. I think it really made me realize how ridiculous it is to invest all of your happiness into a relationship. . . . I knew after that, I had to find happiness in myself. . . . I have been stronger in myself and in relationships ever since."

The preceding memory narratives come from emerging adults in the midst of their college years. We use these narratives to demonstrate the close-up snapshot they offer of the typical emotional ups and downs of college life, which commonly revolve around academics/career and relationships. The underlined portions also vividly illustrate active engagement with the dynamic process of narrative identity development, via processes of autobiographical reasoning. These narratives provide a glimpse of the utility of narrative for understanding identity development in terms of content, context, and process; however, alone, they provide only one relatively static snapshot of narrative identity. With our new longitudinal study, the Identity Pathways Project, we are aiming to further enrich what is so valuable about the narrative identity approach by capitalizing on the value of repeated narration over many points in time (see also Dunlop, Guo, & McAdams, 2016). Furthermore, our goal in this study is to use a variety of different types of narrative prompts, both broad and domain-specific, to examine how individual differences in pathways of identity development differentiate between those who make a successful transition into adult life and those who struggle. Our outcomes include personality maturity, well-being, and career identity achievement, outcomes linked to role-related success in adulthood, such as occupational attainment and relationship stability (e.g., Neyer & Asendorpf, 2001; Roberts et al., 2006). As mentioned earlier, we are also particularly interested in understanding issues of persistence in STEM majors in college. Stephen's case allows us to highlight how some of these empirical goals are well served with a narrative approach.

The Case of Stephen

As we briefly reviewed in our opening, Stephen is a biracial male (black and white) who is premed, majoring in chemistry. Although there are layers of richness to Stephen's case, we focus primarily on issues related to his choice of major, as this particular aspect of his identity development is illustrative of the richness and unique value of a narrative approach. In this case, his academic trajectory and his ethnic identity become intricately linked in meaningful ways, and in ways that are not clearly visible from other types of data.

Stephen reports that his father is a doctor, which seems to be the main reason he has chosen this career path. For example, just before beginning college, he writes about why he is interested in being a doctor: "My dad is a doctor and he took our family on medical mission trips around the world. Seeing him help those in need was really cool and I want to do the same." In the middle of his second year, he wrote, "The fact that my father is a doctor probably has something to do with my desire to become a physician, but the reason for this is that I have grown up watching what he does and it looks more like fun than work." Thus, Stephen is very stable in linking his father's work and his own career goals, but they are not particularly developed or reflective goals, and there is also little evidence in his narratives at these assessments points of serious exploration of other career possibilities; thus, Stephen initially provides an excellent example of apparent identity foreclosure (see Schwartz, 2001).

Early in college, Stephen also seems to compartmentalize his ideas about academics and career from other parts of himself. He does not connect his goals to relationships (besides the relatively surface-level connection to his father), to his larger value system, or really to any other part of himself. When asked about his academic high and low points at the end of his freshman and sophomore years of college, he talks about his struggles in classes and study habits, but not much else. Given the work on ethnic minorities and identity in relation to STEM fields (see Syed, Azmitia, & Cooper, 2011 for a review), it

is interesting that Stephen never talks about his ethnicity in the context of his academic and career goals. It is possible that growing up with an African American father who is a doctor gives him a sense of belongingness in his science courses that many ethnic/minority students do not feel (e.g., Syed, 2010b).

In fact, Stephen's ethnic identity appears only twice in our assessments so far; however, it does so in particularly vivid ways. In his first assessment, just before beginning college, he reported an experience with racism in response to a self-defining memory prompt, which means that for Stephen, this is a vivid, emotional, important event that he has thought about many times, and that he thinks defines an important part of who he is. The event is the birthday party of a friend in fourth grade. Stephen writes:

"We were in the middle of a Nerf battle and I was one of the last people who had not been hit. Suddenly, I heard one of the kids who I did not know scream, 'Get the darkie!' It took me a while to realize that he was referring to me because I was half black, didn't really consider myself to be very dark, and had never experienced anyone singling me out as different before that moment. This was the first time that I realized that my skin color and hair really were 'defining' parts of who I was or what other people thought I was. I brushed the comment off, and didn't even tell it to my parents for the worry that they would call the boy's parents and embarrass me. Now I realize that this is one of the first memories that I have of people treating me differently because of my ethnicity. After not talking to the boy about why his comment was an awful one or not discussing that moment with my parents I have come to learn that my response to the situation was the wrong one. I do not believe that I should have started a fight over it, for that could only result in the wrongful propagation of a false stereotype, but I do believe that I should have explained to the boy why what he said was so inappropriate. Thankfully, this memory has helped me learn from the past and now whenever I experience racism or stereotyping, I am sure to call it out in order to try to dwindle racism down so that my children's memories contain none such as this one."

There are many levels of analysis that we might target here. But let's begin with the underlined portions of the narrative, which display autobiographical reasoning. Here, Stephen has taken this event and has drawn some kind of meaning from it, meaning that not only changes his behavior but also allows him a deeper form of self-understanding. Stephen decides to combat racism, and feels that his behavior can be one way to do that—both in what he does not do (fight) and what he does do (call it out).

After we read this first narrative, we assumed that ethnicity was central to Stephen's identity, and that we would see him continue to reason about it and bring it into reasoning about other aspects of his identity through the college years. This is a time of heightened reflection on one's self, perhaps especially for those emerging adults who must begin to think about how their ethnic identities interact with other parts of themselves, such as major and occupational choice. Indeed, Moin Syed has shown that college is a time of heightened ethnic identity exploration and questioning for ethnic/minority students (Syed & Azmitia, 2008), and also that ethnic/minority students tend to gravitate toward majors that allow exploration of this aspect of their identities, such as those majors in the social sciences or humanities (Syed, 2010a). Would Stephen lose interest in premed, instead finding room for exploration in psychology or politics?

Well, no. We hear nothing about Stephen's ethnic identity, or ethnicity *at all,* for almost 2½ years (we also did not ask). He writes about classes and dating in ways that are relatively typical of college students, not particularly unique or notable. Then ethnicity reemerges. In the beginning of his junior year, he again responds to a self-defining memory prompt, though this time the prompt was shifted to focus on a self-defining memory that has a significant impact on his *ideal future self.* Stephen writes:

"My racial identity. This is something that I have been trying to figure out how it fits into my life for, well, my whole life, but in the past year and really past couple months, it has really exploded. I am half black and half white—or at least that is what I used to say. I've recently been saying 'My dad's black and my mom's white' because I'm not really sure what I am. I think I have been losing part of my white identity. I don't know if this is a good or bad thing, but it sure has been fucking with me and I can assure that it has contributed to the depression that I have been feeling lately. I feel lost. However, I have finally allowed myself to open my eyes to the fucked up racist world that we live in. I think that I used to try to hide it from myself because I don't know how to deal with the fact that half of who I am has been, and will be for the foreseeable future, the oppressor of my other identity. I have darker skin than almost everyone

in my classes. I have the black hair, large lips, wide nose. I am seen as black. However, I grew up in a predominately white neighborhood and had mostly white friends. I could never talk about race like I do now. I couldn't even address it with my parents—or at least my mom because I was scared of hurting her feelings. But these are not things that I learned suddenly as a result of some instance, but putting all of my life experiences together has happened so suddenly that I feel like I am in shock and I feel in a daze most days, thinking about every interaction that I have had with my white friends, professors, and even mom, trying to piece together what they all mean. I am becoming an angry black man. I hope to learn something from all of this and I hope to be able to learn to love all parts of myself, but honestly, I have some hate for myself—at least the white part—which I need to channel into something productive."

Like his first narrative, Stephen is forced into considering his ethnic identity from experiences with racism. Unlike his first narrative, however, he does not know what to make of his experiences. He is in a state of confusion, uncertainty, and anger. He has not yet drawn meaning, or a full understanding, of these events. But he is working on it.

First, Stephen is beginning to draw links *between* the parts of himself, something he had done little of in his previous assessments. He sees his ethnic identity as tightly connected to his family, to his friends, and to the culture in which he lives. This process of constructing an identity is not a process that involves introspection on isolated parts of the self. This process involves reconstructing and revealing the links between various parts of the self (Syed & McLean, 2016), some of them impossible to ignore—such as the ethnicities of his parents, as well as the societal structure that might require confrontation of these issues, as he intimates in his comments about "a fucked up world" and how he is "seen as black."

Because Stephen still appears to be working on this integration and has not yet articulated it to us (or perhaps to himself), we offer some speculations about what these links might look like. In the other narratives he reported, we see a repeated mention of his high school friends, friends that he let go of quickly, and with some apparent anger. In his first year, he calls them "childish." In the second year, they are "immature, elitist brats." They are not even mentioned in the third year. Based on what he says in the self-defining memory narrative above about his white friends, perhaps they did not allow for, or embrace, his full expression of himself; it seems that he did not even want to try to express that part of himself with them.

Another speculation involves the timing of this narrative. It was written at a time when the preceding year saw the events in Ferguson, Missouri, followed by the deaths of Freddie Gray in Baltimore, Tamir Rice in Cleveland, two police officers in Brooklyn, and Sandra Bland in Texas. This was (and still is) a time of extreme heightened attention to being a black male in America; it may have been a time when it would have been near impossible to *not* examine this aspect of self—both at the distal level of a national movement, for example, as well as in proximal daily experiences of being a black man. Thus, the cultural context of his identity development is intertwined with how he begins to think about himself, as he makes links to the stereotype of the angry black man, the implied meaning of his physical features, the history of oppression that has such a painful intersection within his family, and understandable self-hatred connected to his white self. This is a very vivid example of the link between the individual and the culture as it plays out in a very specific context, in a very specific life.

We have drawn some possible conclusions about what is going on with Stephen, but in his narrative, he portrays himself as in a state of disarray, with so many components of himself to understand and to link together, knowing that he needs to find some meaning, some peace, and some integration of his self. And we are left in some disarray, too. What happens to Stephen?

Thank goodness this is not his last narrative.

At the end of this same school year, spring of junior year, he reports on the academic high point of his year.

"A high point of my academic life was when I applied for a program that I thought was going to be another year doing more hard science research internship [and it] turned out to be the most amazing internship opportunity I have ever had. While I thought I wanted to do clinical research this summer to add to my Medical School apps, the program I had applied to, informed me DURING MY INTERVIEW that this was not going to be benchwork at all and that they have a focus on social science research. I had to keep the shock off of my face. Turns out, the program is centered on research to improve health equity among minorities which I had not yet known was the perfect thing

that I needed in my life at the time. I was already worried I would burn out from the research if I didn't have a break and I have always been interested in social justice but I didn't fully know how much bias comes into play in health care. This was the perfect thing for me and especially because I want to go into the health care field, I can take what I learned with me and work within the system to make progression. So far it's a pretty dope internship."

Although Stephen does not (yet) make an explicit connection to his own ethnic identity (and we eagerly await the coming narratives), this seems an event ripe for possible integration and meaning making in understanding his career goals and trajectories as linked to, and as a part of, his ethnic identity. He has not mentioned social justice explicitly before, but he stories this as a relatively stable part of himself. Did he just neglect to mention it, or is this something new that he reconstructs as having some continuity? Or perhaps he has not made the explicit links that might be there implicitly. In his very first narrative, Stephen writes about standing up to racism, to "call it out." This suggests that he *has* thought about issues of social justice, so perhaps as his story evolves, Stephen will create these links across the events in his life to create a greater sense of personal continuity and coherence.

We also see other, more recent, hints that the internship experience was an event in the making. Stephen's academic high and low points from the end of sophomore year show that his interests in the "hard" sciences are being challenged, and social sciences are becoming more interesting to him, much as Syed (2010b) would have predicted. For example, he struggles in a Physics course, but finds great inspiration in a Sociology course, which "was the most influential class I have ever taken . . . ever." Stephen wants to switch majors to sociology but cannot do it because of the credit requirements, but he does write, "It did make me start considering more of a social science route in terms of down the road and after graduation." Thus, the internship comes at a very opportune moment in his life. Perhaps this is an event that allows him to start finding some integration in the various parts of himself that began to come to the fore during this third year of college.

Indeed, it can take time for events to find their place with each other, and for parts of the self to find their place with each other. In Stephen's case, this time may have been lengthened by the level of untroubled identity foreclosure he exhibited as he entered college. He was confident and unreflective about being premed, and he also seemed to have ethnicity all figured out, in that he had learned the positive (but perhaps overly simplistic and optimistic) lesson from the fourth grade birthday party that he should always stand up to racism. Thus, it seems to have taken some challenging and unsettling experiences—struggling with and not truly enjoying the hard sciences, along with increasingly difficult experiences with racism—to break through that foreclosed identity and push Stephen into a more open and exploratory state (see also Neville & Cross, 2017). This more exploratory identity state may be part of what allows some new and positive experiences such as the Sociology class and the internship to take root and have an impact on his identity development. In the internship narrative, we see how these two critical pieces of his identity—career and ethnicity—starting to deepen as they intersect. In developing a vision of himself as someone who will work within the health care system to eliminate racial bias in the delivery of health care, we simultaneously see Stephen's career identity and interest in social justice (arguably closely related to his ethnic identity) transform from underdeveloped simplicities to concrete meaning and purpose.

Will this new direction in Stephen's career plans be a catalyst for resolving the difficult questioning he has recently experienced with respect to his biracial identity? We do not know, and only time will tell. It is worth noting that career and race/ethnicity are fundamentally different aspects of identity in one important way. While one's major and career plans are relatively chosen components of identity, ethnicity is an *ascribed* identity, and is therefore a fundamentally unchangeable part of the person that some would argue *must* be addressed in some way, at least if one is of minority status in the United States, particularly in the current climate. Race is also a fundamentally social identity that is intertwined with many other aspects of identity in complex ways, including family, religion, culture, politics, sexuality, peer relations, and so forth, and may therefore be informed by a variety of events that are unplanned and unfold nonlinearly (e.g., encounters with racism). Race is always there, but it may float in and out of the forefront of identity depending on life circumstances. Thus, it makes sense that ethnic

identity may take a great deal of time and effort to construct, as we see so vividly in Stephen's narrative.

In summary, in our analysis of Stephen, in which we have gone beyond the typical measures of personality and identity development, we have gained some real insights. We have learned that despite the stability in his major choice, there has been an incredible change in his attitude about that major, the meaning of it, and the possibilities that it holds for his future self. It becomes more of his own, not just linked to his father's career. We see how some issues become more or less salient over time within one person. We see how experiences accumulate into moments of seemingly sudden insight. We see how various components of the self do or do not work together. All of these insights are exceedingly difficult to "see" with survey measures (Syed & McLean, 2016).

New Lines of Inquiry Arising from Stephen's Case

The observations we have made about Stephen's unique pathway of narrative identity development point to several broader conclusions that illuminate important new lines of inquiry for the field. First, Stephen's pattern of narration shows the nonlinear ebb and flow of identity over time, something only intense repeated measures can truly reveal. We see how the explanation of why Stephen wants to be a doctor remains quite stable, and foreclosed, until new experiences open up exploration. We also see how the compartmentalization of the various aspects of his identity, in particular, ethnicity and occupational contents, may stifle exploration. When he starts to consider himself more deeply, the possibility arises for creating more coherent spaces of intersection. We also gain some insights about identity foreclosure and the dangers of staying on the STEM path simply because it is encouraged by family and has a long history of personal commitment (beginning before college). Stephen's commitment to a premed major may have closed him off to exploring other interests in the first 2 years of college, something he is only fully understanding now. In summary, Stephen's case suggests many possibilities for how repeated narration can be used in future research to examine not only the presence or absence of identity processes, as has typically been the focus, but also how events and life circumstances can serve to dynamically suppress or trigger identity processes over time, in sometimes nonlinear and intersecting ways (see McLean & Pasupathi, 2012, for a discussion of this issue in the context of combining status and narrative approaches to identity).

Second, we also see that not only the difficult and challenging events inspire identity work, an implicit and sometimes explicit argument in research on narrative identity (e.g., Pals, 2006), but also positive events can affirm self or stimulate exploration, change, and meaning, which may be especially important in emerging adulthood when identity is first forming (Lilgendahl, 2015). The class in sociology revealed a new aspect of Stephen's self that prompted exploration based on his excitement about possibilities for different areas of study. That opening up and excitement may have been what allowed him to embrace the opportunity that unfolded in his internship. Without that positive experience in class, the internship may not have been received with such enthusiasm. Still, these positive events may have been so influential in that particular moment of Stephen's life because they were occurring in parallel with difficult ones, namely, struggles in premed courses and encounters with racism. Thus, an examination of various types of events and the dynamic relations between them seems critical for a full understanding of identity development.

Finally, as we discussed earlier, like many developmentally oriented research programs (see Galliher et al., 2017), the extant research on narrative identity has primarily focused on processes of narrative identity development. We see an area ripe for investigation to be the *content* of identity development, as connected to those processes (see McLean et al., 2014, 2016, 2017; Syed & McLean, 2015). A recent framework suggests four levels of content: culture, social roles, domains, and everyday experiences (Galliher et al., 2017). All of these aspects of content are critical to understanding *what* is developing, something important to consider before we target *how* these aspects of identity are developing (i.e., process). In Stephen's case, we see his identity content situated in contemporary American *culture,* a context of heightened attention to race-related violence. We see his *role* as the son of a white and black parent, complicating the cultural context. We see the *domain* content of identity in the intersection of his ethnic and occupational identities as he begins to lean toward social justice in his pursuit of a career in medicine. And we see how

the *everyday experiences* of taking a class in college and getting an exciting internship can reveal identity developments. Across all of these levels of content, Stephen must construct a coherent self that holds all of these levels and makes sense of them in one person. This new framework and Stephen's case make a compelling argument for the consideration of identity content to better understand the processes of identity development.

Perhaps most critical for a field such as identity development, which has focused almost exclusively on the individual (see McLean & Syed, 2015b), the lesson from Stephen is that identity development *cannot* be understood outside of a cultural context; in fact, identity development cannot *exist* outside of a culture because it is the culture that gives that identity the meaning it holds for the person and for others. Stephen says this explicitly when he talks about becoming an angry black man, a cultural stereotype, and being part oppressor and part oppressed, part of the history of the culture in which he is now defining himself. Recent calls for putting culture at the forefront of identity development research suggest an analysis of not only *personal* narratives but also cultural *master* narratives to understand the ways in which individuals and cultures interact in constituting themselves (Hammack, 2008; McLean & Syed, 2015b). In line with this reasoning, we concur that narrative approaches allow for the kinds of data that facilitate an examination of these cultural and individual processes in a way that is limited with other kinds of data. With narratives we can see how personal reconstruction is set within a proximal and distal context that give meaning to that reconstruction. In Stephen's case specifically, we see how being biracial gives rises to tensions between more than one master narrative operating within oneself. Although there is a large literature on biracial identity, little of it if any has taken an explicitly narrative approach. We argue that narratives are especially well suited to reveal how people negotiate the kinds of intense identity conflicts produced by competing master narratives imposed by the broader sociohistorical context.

In conclusion, we hope to have provided a review of the history, theory, methods, and current state of the field in the study of narrative identity development. We hope to have shown the reader the rich history of the field, the innovative methodology that reveals a person's development unlike many other methods in psychology, the returns on this type of method with the extant, robust findings, and how the individual case can reveal the complexities of identity development and the fruitfulness of such an approach. Narrative can be best understood as a highly generative method, one that can offer answers to important and complex questions, and provide many new questions with each story that is read.

ACKNOWLEDGMENTS

We thank Moin Syed and the editors of this volume for helpful comments on earlier drafts of this chapter, and the National Science Foundation (Award No. 1528433) and Haverford College for funding this project.

REFERENCES

Adler, J. M., Dunlop, W. L, Fivush, R., Lilgendahl, J. P., Lodi-Smith, J., McAdams, D. P., et al. (2017). Research methods for studying narrative identity: A primer. *Social Psychology and Personality Science, 8,* 519–527.

Adler, J. M., Lodi-Smith, J., Philippe, F. L., & Houle, I. (2015). The incremental validity of narrative identity in predicting well-being: A review of the field and recommendations for the future. *Personality and Social Psychology Review, 20,* 142–175.

Arnett, J. J. (2016). Life stage concepts across history and cultures: Proposal for a new field on indigenous life stages. *Human Development, 59,* 290–316.

Blagov, P. S., & Singer, J. A. (2004). Four dimensions of self-defining memories (specificity, meaning, content, and affect) and their relationships to self-restraint, distress, and repressive defensiveness. *Journal of Personality, 72,* 481–511.

Bohn, A., & Berntsen, D. (2008). Life story development in childhood: The development of life story abilities and the acquisition of cultural life scripts from late middle childhood to adolescence. *Developmental Psychology, 44,* 1135–1147.

Bohn, A., & Berntsen, D. (2013). The future is bright and predictable: The development of prospective life stories across childhood and adolescence. *Developmental Psychology, 49,* 1232–1241.

Bruner, J. S. (1990). *Acts of meaning.* Cambridge, MA: Harvard University Press.

Carlsson, J., Wängqvist, M., & Frisén, A. (2015). Identity development in the late twenties: A never ending story. *Developmental Psychology, 51*(3), 334–345.

Dunlop, W. L., Guo, J., & McAdams, D. P. (2016). The autobiographical author through time: Examining the degree of stability and change in redemptive and contaminated personal narratives. *Social Psychological and Personality Science, 7,* 428–436.

Dunlop, W. L., Hanley, G. E., McCoy, T. P., & Harake, N. (2017). Sticking to the (romantic) script: An examination of love life scripts, stories, and self-reports of normality. *Memory, 25*(10), 1444–1454.

Erikson, E. (1968). *Identity, youth and crisis.* New York: Norton.

Fivush, R., & Fromhoff, F. (1988). Style and structure in mother–child conversations about the past. *Discourse Processes, 11,* 337–355.

Fivush, R., Haden, C. A., & Reese, E. (2006). Elaborating on elaborations: Role of maternal reminiscing style in cognitive and socioemotional development. *Child Development, 77,* 1568–1588.

Fivush, R., & Zaman, W. (2015). Gendered narrative voices: Sociocultural and feminist approaches to emerging identity in childhood and adolescence. In K. C. McLean & M. Syed (Eds.), *The Oxford handbook of identity development* (pp. 33–52). New York: Oxford University Press.

Galliher, R., McLean, K. C., & Syed, M. (2017). An integrated model for studying identity content in context. *Developmental Psychology, 53*(11), 2011–2022.

Habermas, T. (2007). How to tell a life: The development of the cultural concept of biography across the lifespan. *Journal of Cognition and Development, 8,* 1–31.

Habermas, T., & Bluck, S. (2000). Getting a life: The development of the life story in adolescence. *Psychological Bulletin, 126,* 748–769.

Habermas, T., & de Silveira, C. (2008). The development of global coherence in life narratives across adolescence: Temporal, causal, and thematic aspects. *Developmental Psychology, 44,* 707–721.

Habermas, T., & Köber, C. (2015). Autobiographical reasoning in life narratives buffers the effect of biographical disruptions on the sense of self-continuity. *Memory, 23,* 664–674.

Habermas, T., & Reese, E. (2015). Getting a life takes time: The development of the life story in adolescence, its precursors and consequences. *Human Development, 58,* 172–201.

Hammack, P. L. (2008). Narrative and the cultural psychology of identity. *Personality and Social Psychology Review, 12*(3), 222–247.

Hammack, P. L. (2011). *Narrative and the politics of identity: The cultural psychology of Israeli and Palestinian youth.* New York: Oxford University Press.

King, L. A., & Raspin, C. (2004). Lost and found possible selves, subjective well-being, and ego development in divorced women. *Journal of Personality, 72,* 603–632.

King, L. A., Scollon, C. K., Ramsey, C., & Williams, T. (2000). Stories of life transition: Subjective well-being and ego development in parents of children with Down syndrome. *Journal of Research in Personality, 34,* 509–536.

Kroger, J. (2015). Identity development through adulthood: The move toward "wholeness." In K. C. McLean & M. Syed (Eds.), *The Oxford handbook of identity development* (pp. 65–80). New York: Oxford University Press.

Lilgendahl, J. P. (2015). The dynamic role of identity processes in personality development: Theories, patterns, and new directions. In K. C. McLean & M. Syed (Eds.), *The Oxford handbook of identity development* (pp. 490–507). New York: Oxford University Press.

Lilgendahl, J. P., Helson, R., & John, O. P. (2013). Does ego development increase during midlife?: The effects of openness and accommodative processing of difficult events. *Journal of Personality, 81*, 403–416.

Lilgendahl, J. P., & McAdams, D. P. (2011). Constructing stories of self-growth: How individual differences in patterns of autobiographical reasoning relate to well-being in midlife. *Journal of Personality, 79*, 391–428.

Lilgendahl, J. P., & McLean, K. C. (2015, October). *Academic and romantic highs and lows: A contextualized narrative approach to identity development and well-being in the transition to college.* Presented at the annual meeting of the Society for the Study of Emerging Adulthood, Miami, FL.

Marcia, J. E. (1966). Development and validation of ego-identity status. *Journal of Personality and Social Psychology, 3*(5), 551–558.

McAdams, D. P. (1985). *Power, intimacy, and the life story: Personological inquiries into identity.* New York: Guilford Press.

McAdams, D. P. (1993). *The stories we live by: Personal myths and the making of the self.* New York: Guilford Press.

McAdams, D. P. (1995). What do we know when we know a person? *Journal of Personality, 63*, 363–396.

McAdams, D. P. (2001). The psychology of life stories. *Review of General Psychology, 5*, 100–122.

McAdams, D. P. (2015). *The art and science of personality development.* New York: Guilford Press.

McAdams, D. P., Anyidoho, N. A., Brown, C., Huang, Y. T., Kaplan, B., & Machado, M. A. (2004). Traits and stories: Links between dispositional and narrative features of personality. *Journal of Personality, 72*, 761–784.

McAdams, D. P., Bauer, J. J., Sakaeda, A. R., Anyidoho, N. A., Machado, M. A., Magrino-Failla, K., et al. (2006). Continuity and change in the life story: A longitudinal study of autobiographical memories in emerging adulthood. *Journal of Personality, 74*, 1371–1400.

McAdams, D. P., & McLean, K. C. (2013). Narrative identity. *Current Directions in Psychological Science, 22*, 233–238.

McAdams, D. P., & Pals, J. L. (2006). A new Big Five: Fundamental principles for an integrative science of personality. *American Psychologist, 61*, 204–217.

McAdams, D. P., & Zapata-Gietl, C. (2015). Three strands of identity development across the human life course: Reading Erik Erikson in full. In M. Syed & K. C. McLean (Eds.), *The Oxford handbook of identity development* (pp. 81–96). New York: Oxford University Press.

McLean, K. C. (2008). Stories of the young and the old:

Reflections on self-continuity. *Developmental Psychology, 44*, 254–264.

McLean, K. C. (2015). *The co-authored self: Family stories and the construction of personal identity.* New York: Oxford University Press.

McLean, K. C., & Breen, A. V. (2014). Selves in a world of stories. In J. A. Arnett (Ed.), *The Oxford handbook of emerging adulthood* (pp. 385–400). New York: Oxford University Press.

McLean, K. C., Breen, A., & Fournier, M. A. (2010). Adolescent identity development: Narrative meaning-making and memory telling. *Journal of Research on Adolescence, 20*, 166–187.

McLean, K. C., & Lilgendahl, J. P. (2008). Why we recall our highs and lows: Reactions between memory function, age, and well-being. *Memory, 16*, 751–762.

McLean, K. C., & Pasupathi, M. (2012). Looking forwards and looking backwards: Two approaches to identity development [Special issue]. *Identity, 12*, 8–28.

McLean, K. C., Pasupathi, M., & Pals, J. P. (2007). Selves creating stories creating selves: A process model of self-development. *Personality and Social Psychology Review, 11*, 262–280.

McLean, K. C., & Pratt, M. W. (2006). Life's little (and big) lessons: Identity statuses and meaning-making in the turning point narratives of emerging adults. *Developmental Psychology, 42*, 714–722.

McLean, K. C., Shucard, H., & Syed, M. (2017). Applying the master narrative framework to gender identity development in emerging adulthood. *Emerging Adulthood, 5*, 93–105.

McLean, K. C., & Syed, M. (2015a). The field of identity development needs an identity: An introduction to *The Oxford Handbook Of Identity Development.* In K. C. McLean & M. Syed (Eds.), *The Oxford handbook of identity development* (pp. 1–10). New York: New York: Oxford University Press.

McLean, K. C., & Syed, M. (2015b). Personal, master, and alternative narratives: An integrative framework for understanding identity development in context. *Human Development, 58*(6), 318–349.

McLean, K. C., Syed, M., & Shucard, H. (2016). Bringing identity content to the fore: Links to identity development processes. In J. A. Arnett (Ed.), *The Oxford handbook of emerging adulthood.* New York: Oxford University Press.

McLean, K. C., Syed, M., Yoder, A., & Greenhoot, A. F. (2014). Identity integration: The importance of domain content in linking narrative and status approaches to emerging adult identity development. *Journal of Research on Adolescence, 26*, 61–76.

Nelson, K., & Fivush, R. (2004). The emergence of autobiographical memory: A social cultural–developmental theory. *Psychological Review, 111*, 486–511.

Neville, H. A., & Cross, W. E. (2017). Racial awakening: Epiphanies and encounters in black racial identity. *Cultural Diversity and Ethnic Minority Psychology, 23*, 102–108.

Neyer, F. J., & Asendorpf, J. B. (2001). Personality–relationship transaction in young adulthood. *Journal of Personality and Social Psychology, 81,* 1190–1204.

Pals, J. L. (2006). Narrative identity processing of difficult life experiences: Pathways of personality development and positive self-transformation in adulthood. *Journal of Personality, 74,* 1079–1110.

Pasupathi, M. (2001). The social construction of the personal past and its implications for adult development. *Psychological Bulletin, 127,* 651–672.

Pasupathi, M., & Mansour, E. (2006). Adult age differences in autobiographical reasoning in narratives. *Developmental Psychology, 42,* 798–808.

Pasupathi, M., Mansour, E., & Brubaker, J. R. (2007). Developing a life story: Constructing relations between self and experience in autobiographical narratives. *Human Development, 50,* 85–110.

Reese, E., Chen, Y., Jack, F., & Hayne, H. (2010). Emerging identities: Narrative and self from early childhood to early adolescence. In K. McLean & M. Pasupathi (Eds.), *Narrative development in adolescence* (pp. 23–43). New York: Springer.

Reese, E., Hayne, H., & MacDonald, S. (2008). Looking back to the future: Māori and Pakeha mother–child birth stories. *Child Development, 79,* 114–125.

Reese, E., Jack, F., & White, N. (2010). Origins of adolescents' autobiographical memories. *Cognitive Development, 25,* 352–367.

Roberts, B. W., Caspi, A., & Moffitt, T. E. (2003). Work experiences and personality development in young adulthood. *Journal of Personality and Social Psychology, 84,* 582–593.

Roberts, B. W., Walton, K. E., & Viechtbauer, W. (2006). Patterns of mean-level change in personality traits across the life course: A meta-analysis of longitudinal studies. *Psychological Bulletin, 132,* 1–25.

Rubin, D. C., & Berntsen, D. (2003). Life scripts help to maintain autobiographical memories of highly positive, but not highly negative, events. *Memory and Cognition, 31,* 1–14.

Schwartz, S. J. (2001). The evolution of Eriksonian and neo-Eriksonian identity theory and research: A review and integration. *Identity, 1,* 7–58.

Shih, M., & Sanchez, D. T. (2005). Perspectives and research on the positive and negative implications of having multiple racial identities. *Psychological Bulletin, 131,* 569–591.

Singer, J. A. (2004). Narrative identity and meaning making across the adult lifespan: An introduction. *Journal of Personality, 72,* 437–460.

Singer, J., Rexhaj, B., & Baddeley, J. (2007). Older, wiser, and happier?: Comparing older adults' and college students' self-defining memories. *Memory, 15,* 886–898.

Singer, J. A., & Salovey, P. (1993). *The remembered self: Emotion and memory in personality.* New York: Simon & Schuster.

Sutin, A. R., & Robins, R. W. (2005). Continuity and correlates of emotions and motives in self-defining memories. *Journal of Personality, 73,* 793–824.

Syed, M. (2010a). Developing an integrated self: Academic and ethnic identities among ethnically-diverse college students. *Developmental Psychology, 46*(6), 1590–1604.

Syed, M. (2010b). Memorable everyday events in college: Narratives of the intersection of ethnicity and academia. *Journal of Diversity in Higher Education, 3*(1), 56–69.

Syed, M. (2017). Advancing the cultural study of personality and identity: Models, methods, and outcomes. *Current Issues in Personality Psychology, 5,* 65–72.

Syed, M., & Azmitia, M. (2008). A narrative approach to ethnic identity in emerging adulthood: Bringing life to the identity status model. *Developmental Psychology, 44*(4), 1012–1027.

Syed, M., Azmitia, M., & Cooper, C. R. (2011). Identity and academic success among underrepresented minorities: An interdisciplinary review and integration. *Journal of Social Issues, 67*(3), 442–468.

Syed, M., & McLean, K. C. (2015). The future of identity development research: Reflections, tensions, and challenges. In K. C. McLean & M. Syed (Eds.), *The Oxford handbook of identity development* (pp. 562–574). New York: Oxford University Press.

Syed, M., & McLean, K. C. (2016). Understanding identity integration: Theoretical, methodological, and applied issues. *Journal of Adolescence, 47,* 109–118.

Syed, M., & McLean, K. C. (2018). Erikson's theory of psychosocial development. In E. Braaten (Ed.), *The SAGE encyclopedia of intellectual and developmental disorders* (pp. 577–581). Thousand Oaks, CA: SAGE.

Syed, M., & Nelson, S. C. (2015). Guidelines for establishing reliability when coding narrative data. *Emerging Adulthood, 3*(6), 375–387.

Thorne, A. (2000). Personal memory telling and personality development. *Personality and Social Psychology Review, 4*(1), 45–56.

Zaman, W., & Fivush, R. (2011). When my mom was a little girl . . . : Gender differences in adolescents' intergenerational and personal stories. *Journal of Research on Adolescence, 21,* 703–716.

CHAPTER 25

Narrative Identity Development across the Lifespan and Psychological Well-Being

Jonathan M. Adler

The field of personality development is centrally concerned with a pair of big questions: Who are you, and how did you get to be that way? As this handbook demonstrates, the broad, interdisciplinary field has brought a variety of scientific approaches to bear on answering those questions. Yet, when stepping back from the science of personality development to ask individual people those same questions, they answer in the form of a story. For any given person, his or her personality development is a narrative about the key moments that have shaped his or her maturation. *Narrative identity* is the internalized, evolving story of the self that weaves together the reconstructed past, perceived present, and imagined future; it is the story that answers the big questions: Who are you and how did you get to be that way (McAdams, 2001; McAdams & McLean, 2013)? The field of research on narrative identity development privileges the voices and subjective perspectives of individuals describing their own development, and a science of narrative identity seeking to unpack the power of these stories has blossomed.

The primary psychological functions of narrative identity are to provide the individual with a sense of unity, purpose, and meaning (e.g., McAdams, 2001; McAdams & McLean, 2013). Whereas our dispositional traits inform our behavior as social actors and our goals and values capture our contextualized motivation, narra-

tive identity tells us what it all means and why (e.g., McAdams, 2015). As contemporary Western culture in industrialized nations pushes individuals toward increasing fragmentation and bite-size, microexpressions of self (e.g., Gergen, 2000; Manago, 2014), a coherent internal narrative persists, synthesizing the disparate parts of the self into a unified narrative (Hammack, 2008; McAdams, 1997). Individuals express a sense of purpose and meaning that transcends the specific situations and domains of their strivings (e.g., McAdams & Olson, 2010; McAdams & Pals, 2006). Fundamentally, these functions of narrative identity—unity, purpose, and meaning—serve another end: supporting the psychological well-being of the individual. The sense that one has a coherent self and that that self has a purpose and a sense of meaning feels good, and incoherent, purposeless, and meaningless selves feel bad (e.g., Adler, 2012; Heintzelman & King, 2014; Lysaker, Wickett, Campbell, & Buck, 2003; McAdams, 2006a). So in the service of their psychological well-being, individuals pursue a number of narrative strategies that take different shape over the life course.

This chapter demonstrates how narrative identity development does—and does not—support psychological well-being across development (at least in the modern, Western contexts in which it has primarily been studied). I open with

433

a high-level overview of the milestones in narrative identity development during each stage of the life course (see Table 25.1 for a summary). I devote special attention to the characteristics of narrative identity that have been found to have especially robust associations with psychological well-being. Next, I briefly introduce one dominant approach to narrative methodology that supports many of the findings discussed in this chapter. I then ground the theory and empirical research in the story of one individual, named Carlo. I present Carlo's story, then analyze the ways in which it embodies the principles of narrative identity development and their relationship with psychological well-being.

Childhood Antecedents of Narrative Identity

Children do not have identity, at least not in the integrated, narrative sense. As I describe in the next section, there are a variety of reasons that narrative identity emerges in adolescence, including the cognitive maturation necessary for this complex psychological task. Nevertheless, children certainly tell stories about their experiences and these stories—and the interactions that shape their telling—lay the foundation for the later development of narrative identity.

The first key milestone in the early development of narrative identity is the emergence of autobiographical memory in early childhood, typically between ages 1 and 3. This is the point when children first begin to remember personal events as things that have happened to them (e.g., Fivush, Gray, & Fromhoff, 1987). This self-knowledge is heavily scaffolded by parents and other adult caregivers, who prompt this type of autobiographical remembering and keep the focus of conversation on topic (Habermas & Bluck, 2000). This scaffolding predicts the later amount and complexity of children's remembering (Haden, Haine, & Fivush, 1997), as well as directing what is socially appropriate to recall (Snow, 1990).

The second key milestone in the early development of narrative identity is the development of theory of mind, typically around ages 3–4. At this point, children become capable of populating their autobiographical memories with characters that have motivations and beliefs different from their own. Children at this stage begin to initiate discussion of the past and shift from recounting single-event memories to developing generalized scripts of common sequences of experience (Nelson, 1993).

Practice with scripts leads to the third key milestone in the early development of narrative identity, the acquisition of a story grammar around ages 5–6. By this time, children have an implicit understanding of how stories typically unfold in their cultural context, following a chronological order that mimics their actual sequence, and including some kind of initiating event and its resolution (Stein & Glenn, 1979).

TABLE 25.1. Milestones in Narrative Identity Development across the Lifespan and Psychological Well–Being

Rough age	Developmental milestone	Consequence for psychological well-being
1–3 years	Emergence of autobiographical memory	Social interactions shape what gets remembered
3–4 years	Development of theory of mind	Include distinct characters other than the self, introduces motivational themes
5–6 years	Acquisition of a story grammar	Internalize cultural templates for basic story elements (temporality, causality)
10–14 years	Internalization of cultural scripts	Expand facility with extended accounts of human lives, begin to grapple with master narratives
Adolescence	Emergence of narrative identity	Autobiographical reasoning leads to thematic meaning making
Adulthood	Mature narration of one's life experiences	The differentiation of thematic elements of narrative identity are associated with psychological well-being
Old age	Life review	Individual shifts to play the roles of audience and critic of one's own story

By later childhood, ages 10–14, children's and early adolescents' stories deepen in their emphasis on causality and acquire an understanding of cultural scripts, marking the fourth key milestone in the early development of narrative identity (Reese, Jack, & White, 2010). The skills needed to structure a story temporally reach adult levels of competence by ages 9 to 11 and begin to focus on causal explanations for the sequence of events (Habermas & Bluck, 2000; Reese, Yan, Jack, & Hayne, 2010). In addition, children and early adolescents come to understand what more extended accounts of human lives typically look like in their cultural context, marked by different stages, with different central concerns (McAdams, 2015).

Yet, even with the acquisition of cultural scripts, it is not until adolescence that people begin to construct truly integrated life stories (Habermas & Bluck, 2000; Habermas & Reese, 2015; Reese, Jack, et al., 2010).

The Emergence of Narrative Identity in Adolescence

Based on the foundation laid in childhood, narrative identity truly emerges in adolescence. Three major forces come together at this developmental moment to prompt the launch of an integrated story of the self.

First, as the literature on childhood antecedents of narrative identity makes clear, crafting a life story is a sophisticated cognitive task, dependent on sufficiently complex abilities that take time to mature. Habermas and Bluck (2000) reviewed the range of cognitive tools necessary to achieve competence at life-story narration, including temporal sequencing, the ability to articulate causal connections between events and between events and the self, inferential abilities to discern patterns via self-reflection, and an internalization of cultural concepts of biography. It is not until adolescence that individuals master these cognitive skills sufficiently to approach the task of weaving separate biographical stories together into an integrated narrative of self.

Second, the biological transformation of the body that occurs with the onset of puberty raises the question: How am I the same person when I look so different than I used to? This question is fundamentally about unity—the coherence of the self over time—one of the key functions of narrative identity. At about the same time, adolescents' brains have matured enough to tackle the complex cognitive task of narrating their lives, their bodily changes make this challenge especially salient.

Third, social pressures to articulate a sense of self begin to mount during adolescence. While we might ask children what they want to be when they grow up, we do not expect them to mean it with any enduring conviction. In contrast, we do expect adolescents to begin to describe a future self that indicates the meaning and purpose that inform present-day choices. Conventional social structures both demand and support this self-articulation, from preparing college and job applications to the sorting of people into everyday social affiliation groups (e.g., athletes, artists, "nerds," post-Confirmation or post-Bar/Bat Mitzvah members of religious groups). The developing individual is contextualized within an array of *master narratives* (i.e., Hammack, 2008; McLean & Syed, 2016), the dominant stories available to members of a given culture that serve as systemic structures with which they must interact and negotiate. Master narratives become especially salient in adolescence, as the task of identity formation puts the individual in active conversation with social scripts.

Thus, cognitive maturation, biological transformation, and social expectation conspire to cue the emergence of narrative identity in adolescence. The major developmental task of adolescence is the exploration and eventual commitment to an identity (Erikson, 1959), and during this time, individuals begin to narrate their lives, with an emphasis on unity, purpose, and meaning. These are initial provisional articulations, but they serve as the first true draft of narrative identity.

Narrative Identity Development in Adulthood

Unlike childhood and adolescence, the extended developmental stage of adulthood is not marked by predictable milestones or a straightforward typology of forces shaping its progression. But narrative identity continues to develop across the adult life course. While adolescence and emerging adulthood (Arnett, 2000) are primarily concerned with identity development, individuals continue to grapple with their evolving sense of self even when other developmental concerns, such as generativity, dominate.

In the majority of instances, new life experiences can be assimilated into one's existing life story. Promotions may be seen as the next chapter in a coherently unfolding story of one's career. While a wedding may be a turning point for some individuals, for others, it is simply a moment to recognize and formalize a long-standing relationship that is not fundamentally transformed by the act of getting married. Yet the adult life course is also marked by moments of discontinuity, both chosen and unanticipated. Some of these experiences may be primarily positive, such as the transition to parenthood (e.g., Dunlop, 2017), career changes (Bauer & McAdams, 2004), or religious conversions (Bauer & McAdams, 2004). But often the experiences that cue an accommodative change in one's life story are difficult experiences, those that pose "biographical disruptions" (e.g., Bury, 1982; Habermas & Köber, 2014). Such experiences pose a challenge to the unity, purpose, and meaning that are supported by an existing life story and often demand a substantial revision.

Empirical research has demonstrated that during these moments of transition in adulthood, individuals use their narrative identity as a foundation for making meaning of their new experiences and also that narrative identity itself develops during the experience. For example, one of the most common identity challenges faced during the adult lifespan is the experience of physical illness. Many diseases, both acute and chronic, are diagnosed during the adult years, in addition to the normative physical decline of this period. Such experiences can challenge unity, purpose, and meaning, the overarching functions of narrative identity, as the individual grapples with the implications of bodily change. In the face of such experiences, narrative identity serves as a foundation for maintaining psychological well-being.

In one study (Adler et al., 2015, Study 2), my colleagues and I tracked a set of late-midlife adults (people in their early 60s) over the course of several years. Our sample was drawn from a much larger sample, which allowed us to single out participants with a unique trajectory over the course of the study. We selected those participants who had been mostly healthy up through the first assessment point, when they shared their life story, and then received a major physical illness diagnosis in the following 6 months (and did not receive any additional significant diagnoses for the remainder of the study). We were interested in whether the themes in participants' life stories would relate to the trajectory of their psychological well-being following the illness diagnosis. Indeed,

we found that among these people who got sick, differences in the way they told their life stories before the illness were significantly associated with the trajectory of their psychological well-being in the years following diagnosis. This relationship remained significant when we statistically controlled for their physical health status, which suggests that the way these participants made sense of their lives was associated with their psychological well-being regardless of their physical health status. These data suggest that narrative identity may serve as a foundation that people use when new, difficult experiences crop up, as a way of maintaining unity and purpose, and therefore psychological well-being.

Narrative identity itself also changes over the course of challenging experiences in adulthood. In another study (Adler, 2012), I tracked adults as they underwent psychotherapy for a wide variety of issues, ranging from divorce and the transition to parenthood to significant psychopathology. I enrolled participants before they began treatment—they had contacted a clinic to say they would like to see a therapist but had not yet had their first session—and followed them for several months. Participants wrote narratives about their experiences in treatment and how they were thinking about their lives and also completed standardized measures of mental health over 12 assessment points. Modeling the trajectories of both participants' narrative identity and their mental health over the course of treatment, I found that changes in narrative identity preceded changes in mental health. In other words, participants' stories changed before their mental health changed, suggesting that the development of narrative identity may itself fuel changes in mental health.

Narrative Identity and Psychological Well-Being in Adulthood

So, what are the characteristics of narrative identity that are most strongly associated with psychological well-being in adulthood? My colleagues and I recently published a review article that weighs in on this central question (Adler, Lodi-Smith, Philippe, & Houle, 2016). We collected every study that has systematically compared narrative identity variables to other variables (demographic, dispositional traits, etc.) in their relationship with psychological well-being and identified four major categories of themes that demonstrate incremental validity; that is, they are associated with psychological well-being, above and beyond the impact of other variables. (It is important to note that the four categories themselves were not quantitatively derived, and we did not offer them as an overarching empirical structure of narrative variables; rather, they were a framework for organizing the research that has been conducted thus far on the topic of narrative's incremental validity.)

The first category is *motivational themes*. These are individual-difference variables that are fundamentally concerned with what the protagonist is seeking or has achieved. Two motivational themes in particular, agency and communion, stand out as emblematic of this group. *Agency* is the extent to which the protagonist is portrayed as motivated to influence his or her circumstances autonomously, as opposed to following the whims of external forces. *Communion* is the extent to which the protagonist is portrayed as motivated toward interpersonal connection. Both agency and communion, as well as other motivational themes, show strong and robust associations with psychological well-being, above and beyond the explanatory power of other variables.

The second category is *affective themes*. Almost all narratives include an affective component, even if it is a simple positive or negative tone. Just as agency and communion are signature motivational themes, there are two signature affective themes that have received extensive attention in the empirical literature: redemption and contamination. In *redemption* sequences, scenes that start out bad have positive endings. In *contamination* sequences, the opposite pattern is observed: Scenes that begin well end negatively. Redemption and contamination (as well as other affective themes) have been associated with a range of psychological well-being outcomes, even accounting for the impact of the overall emotional tone of the narrative or the dispositional traits of neuroticism and extraversion, which have strong affective components.

The third category includes themes of *integrative meaning*. This category captures narrative elements related to the extent to which narrators make an interpretative evaluation of their experiences, or work to explicitly connect their experiences to their developing sense of self. Themes in this category cluster into two subcategories which we labeled *assimilative*

and *accommodative* (following Block, 1982). Assimilative themes capture the ways in which narrators weave new experiences into their existing worldview, enhancing unity and purpose. Accommodative themes capture the ways in which narrators transform their worldviews in light of new experiences, sometimes disrupting unity but often leading to a greater sense of purpose and meaning. The empirical literature suggests that these two types of integrative meaning are both associated with psychological well-being, but in somewhat different ways. Assimilative themes seem more strongly associated with *hedonic well-being* (Ryan & Deci, 2001)—the presence of positive affect and the absence of negative affect—above and beyond the impact of dispositional traits and other variables. Accommodative themes seem more strongly associated with *eudiamonic well-being* (Ryan & Deci, 2001)—the presence of psychological maturity and complexity—above and beyond the impact of dispositional traits and other variables.

The fourth category includes *structural elements* of narratives. This category is concerned less with the thematic content of narratives and more with the way the story is told. Narrative *coherence* is a key structural element of narratives, comprising several dimensions related to the narrator's success in orienting his or her audience, conveying a temporally and causally consistent plot, and indicating the meaning of the story being shared. While the association between structural elements of narratives, such as coherence, have been associated with psychological well-being, comparatively fewer studies have examined their incremental association compared to the other categories.

As noted earlier, the literature on psychological well-being indicates two different dimensions of well-being, a hedonic dimension focused on affective experience and a eudiamonic one focused on a sense of meaningfulness and complex processing of one's experience (e.g., Ryan & Deci, 2001). A robust literature indicates that there are two distinct narrative pathways to these different dimensions of psychological well-being (e.g., Bauer & McAdams, 2004; King, 2001; King & Raspin, 2004; Pals, 2006).

On the one hand, a variety of narrative variables from all four categories have demonstrated concurrent correlations and temporally precedent associations with hedonic well-being outcomes. Principal among these themes are redemption and agency. Redemption sequences have been shown to be associated with high levels of happiness and life satisfaction and low levels of psychopathology (e.g., Adler et al., 2015; Dunlop & Tracy, 2013; McAdams & Guo, 2015). While all lives have positive and negative experiences, thematically deriving positive outcomes from negative experiences feels good. Redemption sequences also form the affective core of a particular configuration of narrative identity that McAdams (2006b) has called "the redemptive self." Indeed, McAdams and Guo (2015) demonstrated that redemption sequences and the broader system of narrative themes that constitute the redemptive self provide a foundation for especially high levels of generativity among midlife American adults. In addition, the motivational theme of agency has also been associated with positive hedonic well-being, both concurrently and prospectively (e.g., Adler, 2012; Adler et al., 2015; McAdams, Hoffman, Mansfield, & Day, 1996).

On the other hand, a distinct set of narrative variables has demonstrated associations with eudiamonic well-being outcomes. For example, as noted earlier, exploratory processing is a theme of integrative meaning that is associated with increases in ego development and a sense of meaningfulness (e.g., King, 2001; Pals, 2006). When individuals deeply explore the potential meanings of their experiences, it does not necessarily lead to happiness, but it does enhance the complexity and nuance of the lens through which one understands his or her life. Following a cohort of women over 40 years, Pals (2006) found that exploratory processing in life narratives collected at age 52 mediated the relationship between dispositional personality traits at age 21 and psychological maturity at age 61. Likewise, King and Raspin (2004) found that following divorce after long-term (average 22 years) of marriage, women who narrated their experience with a greater sense of elaboration experienced increases in ego development over the following 2 years.

In integrating the findings pertaining to these two narrative pathways, King (2001) described the unique configuration of high hedonic and high eudiamonic psychological well-being as "the good life." Different approaches to narrating one's experience provide distinct routes to different well-being outcomes. However, it is possible to narrate one's life in a way that both deeply explores one's experiences and features a redemptive arc or high levels of agency. This narrative approach may produce a life story that supports King's notion of "the good life."

In summary, narrative identity plays two key roles in adulthood: serving as a foundation of meaning which people draw on when new experiences challenge their sense of unity and purpose, and dynamically unfolding itself in response to new experiences. Individual differences in the thematic and structural elements of narrative identity are associated with psychological well-being, often above and beyond the explanatory power of other variables, including dispositional traits (Adler et al., 2016), and different approaches to narrating one's life lead to different psychological well-being outcomes.

Narrative Identity Development in Old Age

Compared to the other stages of the life course, there is substantially less research on narrative identity in old age. Unlike the other life stages, the stories of elderly adults need to grapple more explicitly with how the story will end. Erikson (1959) suggested that the final stage of psychosocial development is concerned with a tension between ego integrity and despair. Thus, life stories at this stage must grapple with acceptance and gratitude, or with regret and dissatisfaction. McAdams (2015) writes that "from the standpoint of narrative identity, ego integrity shifts the older person's focus somewhat from author to reader (and critic). In a sense, the person becomes the audience for his or her own life story" (p. 305). Thus, narrative identity tends to move away from the kind of specific, rich description of key events and more toward a reflection on key relationships and values, painted with broader brush strokes.

With the many age-normative challenges to psychological well-being—physical decline, the death of loved ones, the loss of autonomy, and so forth—the goals of unity, purpose, and meaning take on a somewhat different shade in old age. Storytelling serves to draw broader themes of continuity and reflect meaning making in primarily retrospective ways. Bohlmeijer, Roemer, Cuijpers, and Smit (2007) contrasted reminiscence with life review. *Reminiscence* is a more general term for reflecting on the past, whereas *life review* is a more structured appraisal of the whole life, with an explicitly evaluative component. In a meta-analysis of studies examining the relationship between reminiscence, life review, and psychological well-being in older adults, both processes showed positive associations with well-being, though the association with life review was much stronger than that with reminiscence. In other words, older adults who engaged in a process of reflecting on their entire lives, with an eye toward assessing its meaning, experienced substantial gains in their psychological well-being as a result. Thus, while the task of continuing to articulate one's narrative identity remains no less important in old age, the specific methods and functions of doing so may shift as individuals near the end of their story.

Narrative Methodology

Studying narrative identity scientifically involves the collection of personal stories in a way that facilitates their comparison. From adolescence through old age, this process generally requires that decisions be made regarding study design, the collection of narratives, and the assessment of narratives. (Given the absence of a fully formed narrative identity in childhood, alternative approaches are required for assessing the development of narrative skills.) My colleagues and I have written a detailed primer on narrative methods (Adler et al., 2017), but I will touch on the high-level issues here.

Two principle issues related to narrative study design are the development of hypotheses that narratives are appropriately situated to address and the crafting of prompts to adequately elicit narrative data. Research questions focused on narrative identity are fundamentally concerned with meaning making. Narratives are not good ways of collecting veridical reports about individuals' objective history, since they are psychological constructions that serve the current needs of the narrator. If a researcher is primarily interested in what really happened in a participant's life, he or she should find alternative ways of investigating that topic, but if the research question centrally concerns the way individuals have come to understand their past, narratives are excellent tools.

Likewise, the prompts chosen to elicit narratives from participants ought to be carefully crafted to best collect data relevant to the research questions. There is a substantial body of research that has used the Life Story Interview (McAdams, 2008) as a semistructured tool for eliciting complete life stories. Even when the research questions do not concern the entire life story, the format of the prompts on the Life Story Interview offers an excellent template (the prompt for eliciting self-defining memories [Blagov & Singer, 2004] also serves as a good example). These prompts were designed to ensure that responses take a fundamentally narrative form, compared with just listing information, as might be obtained by a free-response survey item. In order to assess the kinds of variables that narrative identity scholars have traditionally examined, the data must be stories (e.g., it is difficult to imagine assessing the thematic qualities of a list).

Narratives may be collected from participants either orally or in written format. Each approach is supported by a robust literature, and few studies offer direct comparisons between the modalities. Interviews may produce more elaborated narratives that present a broader array of interpretive options and also offer researchers the opportunity to pose follow-up questions or ensure that participants have responded to the prompt fully. In contrast, written narratives may be briefer, less susceptible to interviewer effects, and offer participants a stronger feeling of anonymity for sharing sensitive information (e.g., Grysman & Denny, 2017; McCoy & Dunlop, 2016).

Before they can be analyzed, oral narratives need to be transcribed. This process is absolutely critical for data integrity and is often conducted by professional transcribers. For hypothesis-testing research, narratives should be randomized and disconnected from other data before they can be coded by raters. Raters ought to be trained to a high standard of interrater reliability before proceeding with coding the bulk of the data (see Syed & Nelson, 2015, for an excellent overview of issues related to interrater reliability).

The scientific analysis of narrative data typically focuses on the quantitative assessment of narrative content and structure. A broad array of narrative variables have received attention in previous research. As described earlier, motivational themes, affective themes, themes of integrative meaning, and structural aspects of narratives have all been common foci (Adler et al., 2016). For each variable, established coding systems have been developed or new ones may be created.

For example, McAdams and Guo (2015) describe the most common approach to operationalizing redemption sequences. These sequences, scored with a presence–absence code for each narrative prompt, are identified when the narrative presents a shift from a demonstrably negative beginning to a linked positive ending. The shift may occur in the plot of the narrative or be based on a positive insight or lesson gleaned from a negative experience, formulated after the episode occurred. Dunlop and Tracy (2013) assessed redemption sequences among people attending Alcoholics Anonymous. Here is an example of a narrative coded for the presence of redemption from their sample: "I was feeling useless, unloved, lonely, depressed, ashamed, that I fell through on my recovery plan, and after losing seven months you almost lose hope, right? But I found my own strength again, through God, and through the NA and AA program, 11 days clean, I feel like the obsession has been lifted from me again" (p. 581). This individual describes the shift from shame and depression to personal strength and liberation that is at the core of many redemptive recovery narratives.

As another example, I have examined the theme of agency in a variety of personal narratives using a dimensional approach. In this coding system (presented in Adler et al., 2015), the theme is scored along a 4-point continuum, where very low scores characterize a protagonist who is batted around at the mercy of external forces, and very high scores characterize a protagonist who is able to meaningfully influence the direction of his or her life, making active choices and proactively responding to unexpected events. The following is an example of a narrative excerpt that scored high on agency (from Adler et al., 2015, p. 481): "I think that was a big point in my life where I saw how important it was to be my own person and create my own identity even to the point when I got married, I didn't want to give up my maiden name because I felt like, no, I don't want to lose this. This is who I am, and I will add on my married experience to it." This participant describes a commitment to setting her own course in life that indicates high levels of agency.

Researchers use coding systems such as these to assess narrative data for its thematic and structural aspects. Once narrative coding is complete, narrative data may be linked to psychological well-being data for inductive analysis.

Carlo: An Illustrative Case Study

Having summarized the development of narrative identity across the lifespan and describing

the ways in which it is associated with psychological well-being (especially in adulthood), I now turn to an individual life story to ground the theoretical assertions. It is not possible to illustrate every aspect of narrative identity development using a single case without data collected from across the entire lifespan. Instead, I have selected Carlo[1] (age 34) as a case that demonstrates the relationship between narrative identity development in adulthood and psychological well-being. Carlo participated in a Life Story Interview (McAdams, 2008) in my laboratory and completed a battery of self-report questionnaires as part of a broader project on narrative identity and disability (Adler, 2018). Although I focus on his life story in this account, I highlight thematic elements of the story that resonate with the themes noted earlier and conclude by formally discussing the relationship between his narrative and his psychological well-being, as assessed by the questionnaires.

* * *

When Carlo was a young child—5 or 6—he snuck away from his house, traversing the yard and absconding to the house next door. He remembers carefully lifting a metal panel behind the neighbor's house and discovering treasure. Buried in the clandestine compartment were twigs, leaves, and small plastic toys, along with a "note" from his friend, the girl who lived in the house who was about his same age and had left them there for Carlo to discover. He remembers the "wonder and excitement and awe" in the shared secret and the special connection it signified. At age 34, the memory stands out to Carlo as an emblematic one from his childhood because the theme of revelation runs throughout his work as an artist. Indeed, in many ways it is the theme of his life.

In another memory from childhood, Carlo is standing on his parents' patio in suburban Vancouver on a warm summer night with his mother. Young Carlo was deep into an obsession with outer space, and his mom suggested they go outside to gaze at the stars. He rushed out in excitement but found that when he cast his eyes to the night sky, he could not see them. Carlo's mom pointed up at the sky and eventually took Carlo's head in her hands to orient it

---

[1] This is a pseudonym. Following common ethical practices in qualitative research (e.g., Haverkamp, 2005; Tracey, 2010), I invited Carlo to review the first draft of this chapter and incorporated his feedback.

correctly, but despite her efforts, the stars just wouldn't come into focus. He remembers disappointment, but the emotions that loom even larger in his memory are anxiety and guilt that his inability to see the stars was profoundly worrying to his mother. Even as a young child, Carlo had issues with his physical health, but this moment crystallized the fact that he was indeed losing his vision. Carlo said:

> "I didn't want to upset her, to have her worry about me, and I think she was. I mean, she still does sometimes. But I think that was something that I was even worrying about as a kid, about how to protect my parents. . . . And I still do that. They worry about me, but I wish they didn't. And I think it has to do with a lot of social and cultural conditions relating to disability. That's the stuff that's really hard to unlearn."

While this was not the moment when Carlo's family first grappled with his declining vision, it is an emblematic one, one that distills the ways in which his vision presented a biographical disruption, with deep psychological ramifications (e.g., Bury, 1982; Habermas & Köber, 2014).

Carlo had low vision throughout his childhood, with particularly poor night vision. He remembers the ways in which this isolated him from his peers, making him feel "like an outsider." Sports like baseball, in which the visual tracking of the ball was key to playing well, just wouldn't work for him, so he pursued independent sports, such as martial arts. These early experiences set up a trajectory for Carlo whereby his physical difference led to an interpersonal separation, a sense of disconnection and *low communion* with which he would struggle well into adulthood. He also had other physical health issues, including sickle-cell anemia, which punctuated his adolescence with periods of crisis. Mundane experiences, such as dehydration or catching a cold, could lead to immense pain and emergency hospitalizations.

As an adolescent, Carlo fell in love with animation. He was pulled toward classical approaches, in which images were hand-drawn on transparent celluloid sheets ("cels") and then sequenced. Despite missing substantial periods of 12th grade due to hospitalizations, Carlo worked hard to graduate on time and was accepted into a competitive college program in animation. "I was able to draw and do whatever I needed to do," he said, "but when it came to being in these dimly lit film studios and editing rooms, I felt like my body was working against the practice that I had to participate in." It was a sadly ironic situation: Carlo's red blood cells, the focus of sickle-cell disease, had been the source of so much pain in his life and now his low vision was preventing his work with animation cels from succeeding. Carlo had a girlfriend, but they didn't really talk about his experiences. "I think she knew she felt uncomfortable inviting me out with her friends to do stuff at night that would happen in dimly lit situations, but it was just something that we didn't have the language for or a system in place for." They stayed together for 3 years, but Carlo had the sense that she was not the right partner for him. During this period, Carlo's story is marked by themes of *low agency* and *low communion*. He is stymied in his efforts to become an animator, and his romantic relationship is marked by an uncomfortable distance that Carlo felt unable to span.

Carlo left his program and switched his major to English. He delved into poetry and started publishing a magazine with some friends. But during college, his vision began worsening, and he started to have trouble reading text. He was diagnosed with retinitis pigmentosa, a degenerative condition that typically leads to blindness. Carlo said, "Little pockets of vision were disappearing. It was as if termites were eating through my visual field." His mentor in his English program was visually impaired and encouraged Carlo to pursue support services through the Canadian National Institute for the Blind. He had begun a new relationship, and his girlfriend similarly encouraged him to get help. Carlo's response was to think, "Okay, I better just help myself. You know, if this is going to be a reality, I have to figure out how to support myself and advocate for myself." In being referred to support services by people who cared about him, Carlo saw an opportunity to exert his own agency in caring for himself; he framed his help seeking as being in the pursuit of agency. It is important to note that this quest, while *highly agentic*, was also a lonely one that he chose to embark upon on his own and therefore *low in communion*.

Carlo was given a white cane and taught how to use it to navigate the world. "I was very resistant when I started using [it]," Carlo said. "I didn't like using it and I think it was because of the institutional symbol of it." For many people with disabilities, assistive devices, whether a white cane, a wheelchair, or a hearing aid, become physical manifestations of difference and exclusion (Mitchell & Snyder, 1997). These devices may themselves eclipse an individual's authority over their own identity, conferring what Garland-Thomson (2014) refers to as an "ascribed identity." Speaking about the Canadian National Institute for the Blind, Carlo said,

> "They had ideas about how I should reintegrate into society. . . . I could hold this thing, but it would separate me as being in a totally separate group from my peers. . . . People would look at me, and people would ask me questions, and it was really like a lightning rod for attention that I didn't want."

The cane not only served as a beacon for navigating the world, it was also a bright, white symbol of false helplessness.

Yet, rather than choosing to accept this arrangement, Carlo decided to actively resist it. He had his girlfriend paint an eyeball on the rolling ball tip of the cane. Carlo said, "It was just this little funny thing that I did so I could feel better about using this thing I don't like using." It was his first experiment with societal conventions of disability and an effort to reclaim his sense of *agency* from the cane itself. Modifying and even replacing the white cane is a practice Carlo continues to this day, though he is currently more focused on the social institutions that surround disability than the artifacts.

Carlo adopted the label "visually impaired person" and became interested in hearing other people's stories of sight loss. He was struck by the common experience of grief, something he hadn't felt. He had intellectualized his experience, exploring the neurological processes he was undergoing and writing about his unique visual experiences. Then, Carlo's body once again forced him to acknowledge the unanticipated ways his physical experience could suddenly change.

He had been hospitalized with a sickle-cell crisis, and the doctors detected something unusual on a routine x-ray. Follow-up tests revealed an aggressive tumor on Carlo's thyroid that had to be removed immediately. "It was a huge shock," Carlo said, "I kind of like, I stopped. . . . I felt like I was going to die. . . . I has been in and out of the hospital my whole life, but it felt like the most serious thing that had happened to me at that point." He withdrew from his classes at university, and had the surgery and radiation treatment.

But Carlo didn't psychologically process the experience. He and his best friend had been planning a 3-month backpacking trip in Europe for over a year, and Carlo stayed laser-focused on being able to go. Just weeks after treatment ended, he went off to Europe, with his 70-pound backpack. Carlo said he felt so weak at the beginning of the trip that he might have toppled over if he got pushed the wrong way. But months of shouldering the backpack made him stronger.

When he returned home, however, he discovered that his repressed feelings of fear and sadness from the cancer experience were much closer to the surface than he had realized.

> "I would just be in situations, just having conversations with my parents, and realize that there's this sinking feeling in my stomach and I would just start crying. . . . It just ended up making me feel like I was not in control of my body, but again it was something that I didn't share with many people. It was something that I didn't have language around."

It was as though returning home, and especially being with his parents, opened Carlo up to years of unprocessed feelings about his lack of power over his body. The raw emotions bubbled out, but he still didn't have the ability to make sense of them. It was as though he could not yet find *a coherent structure* for his experience, a way of comprehending the cancer on top of everything else he had been through.

As Carlo finished university, his long-term girlfriend broke up with him, and his much-beloved grandmother passed away. It was a dark time, and Carlo decided that he needed a change. He applied to graduate school and moved to Portland, Oregon, which he sees as a pivotal turning point in his life. He was pursuing a Master's in Fine Arts and focused his artwork on the cultural stigma of disability. He said, "I started digging deep into those dynamics that I really felt were problematic in my position as a disabled person." Carlo also found a community of fellow artists who were exploring similar themes in their work, and the isolation he had felt in adolescence and after his vision deteriorated in college was transformed into a sense of kinship. Through this newfound sense of community and the language of art, Carlo was finally able to process many of his thoughts and feelings about his relationship with his body and the way it interacted with his societal contexts. He used his work to explore these personal experiences and to communicate about them in new ways. In this way, increases in Carlo's *sense of communion* led him to *increases in agency and coherence* as well.

This also led to a shift in Carlo's self-conception:

> "I started thinking of myself not as a visually impaired person or a blind person, but as someone who learns through my non-visual senses. . . . I started not using vision as the goal, and not using as the thing I was always trying to reference."

Here, Carlo embodies a central theory from the interdisciplinary field of disability studies. Scholars working in this tradition contrast traditional medical models of disability, which view the disabled body as something to be treated or normalized, with relational/political models of disability (e.g., Kafer, 2013). From this perspective, "the problem of disability no longer resides in the minds or bodies of individuals, but in built environments and social patterns that exclude or stigmatize particular kinds of bodies, minds, and ways of being" (p. 6). This approach neither rejects nor valorizes medical intervention, but recognizes its ideological aspects and its power to define normality and deviance (Davis, 2017). Carlo's reframing of his identity as a "non-visual learner" shifts his definition of self from a deficit-oriented frame to an active, empowered one. The *enhanced sense of communion* that he experienced in graduate school provided Carlo with the sufficient psychological foundation to make an accommodative change in his self-understanding, one that resulted in a *more agentic* identity.

Carlo was invited to an artist residency in Pennsylvania, where his life changed in two important ways. First, he remembers finding his sense of mission in life:

> "There was this moment where I was just sitting out one night on this beautiful farm. . . . I mean, it was a beautiful place, but also people were engaged in what they were doing and I felt like I was a part of that. I didn't feel like I was just observing. . . . I felt like I'm a part of this thing. And that's when I realized that doing art wasn't just going to be a pastime; it was going to be a lifestyle for me. Living through my art practice was possible and this is what it looks like. And it was really good, you know."

In a nice counterpoint to his childhood memory of not being able to see the stars, being outside at night at this retreat was the context for articulating a newfound sense of purpose. Ironically,

Carlo uses visual metaphors to speak about this revelation. As a nonvisual learner, Carlo shifts from an "observer" status to being a practitioner. He could envision a future as a working artist.

He also fell in love. Katherine,[2] a fellow artist at the residency, lived on the East Coast. They stayed in touch when Carlo went back to Portland, and when they began an artistic collaboration, they also started dating. Carlo said,

> "She's the person that I was really wanting to be with the whole time that I was in relationships that I wasn't quite keen on, but was in and was just kind of okay with. It was with her that I started being able to get really deep into some of the difficulty that I was repressing. . . . I'm able to feel through the difficulty of my past experiences and have someone who understands me and can support me."

Katherine, who identifies as able-bodied, nevertheless shared an emotional vocabulary with Carlo that allowed them to be in conversation about their struggles, past and current. The *theme of communion* is especially strong in this passage, reflecting the close connection Carlo feels with Katherine. They got married earlier this year.

Carlo continued to experience struggles, but he relates to them differently now. He was recently invited to speak about his art in Dublin, Ireland. Carlo told the story this way:

> "I went from this high point of giving a successful talk back to my hotel. . . . I turn out of the elevator and I hit a wall. And, okay, I kind of reposition myself and start walking, and I hit another wall. And then I do this about five times in a row. And it just totally made me feel really bad and feel disabled. I felt completely disabled. I told [my friend who had invited me to speak], 'This is the part that people don't get to see. This is the part I don't bring into my art practice.' And that was the point where we started a conversation about it and since then I have brought vulnerability and difficulty into my art practice. It's still not something that I feel like I've figured out, but it's something that I really want to continue to think through and work through. . . . How do I approach disability and difficulty in a way that doesn't feel like pity? . . . I ended up making this video that gets at some of the complexity of that experience in a really productive way."

Carlo is able to take a deeply disempowering experience, one that threw him out of his preferred self-conception into one of being "com-

---

[2] Also a pseudonym.

pletely disabled," and transform it into an opportunity for engaging with vulnerability more deeply in his work. He found that the walls in the hotel made literal the social and political walls he had been metaphorically bumping into as he navigated the world. The video he produced showed him walking down a city street using a megaphone to perform the social functions of the ubiquitous white cane, with Carlo's own voice speaking for himself, rather than letting the cane speak for him. In doing so, Carlo narrates a classic *redemption sequence,* wherein a negative beginning yields to a more positive end, as well as one of *enhanced personal agency.* For Carlo, this is not just a feature of his story, he translated it into action as well. Today, Carlo's art is primarily focused on communicating the complexity of the contemporary social arrangements of disability. He creates immersive pieces, in which the audience actively participates and experiences an authentic way of engaging differently. He is clear that his art is not meant to simulate blindness or serve primarily as an empathy exercise. Instead, he wants to alert people to alternative ways of experiencing their world and to play with the interdependence that we all share. "I want to interrupt the signal that [the white cane] sends out, which is 'This person needs help! This person needs help!' I do, and I don't. We all do." In a certain way, Carlo's artwork is a more complex, mature version of the sticks and small plastic toys that he and his friend next door would hide for each other in childhood. Carlo uses his work to show people facets of their experience that they cannot readily see because of their overreliance on their vision. When they close their eyes, and take the leap of trust that doing so requires, they open themselves up to hidden treasures.

* * *

Carlo's life story illustrates each of the four categories of narrative characteristics my colleagues and I outlined and demonstrated to have an incremental association with psychological well-being, when compared to other demographic and personality variables (Adler et al., 2016).

His story is rich with motivational themes. Early on, Carlo struggles with both agency and communion. His sickle-cell anemia interfered with his initial career path, and his low vision kept him isolated from peers and distant in ro-

mantic relationships. Throughout his life, he has chosen to purse an agentic response to adversity, but ultimately the sense of communion he experiences at the artist's residency and with Katherine allows him to satisfy the universal needs for autonomy, competence, and relatedness (e.g., Ryan & Deci, 2001).

Carlo also narrates key moments in his life using the affective theme of redemption. His story about bringing vulnerability into his art practice begins with a contamination sequence, in which his successful talk is followed by his disempowering experience back at his hotel. But Carlo quickly transforms this episode by citing it as the seed of a major revelation about his approach to his work. He chooses to funnel his negative experience into a new phase of creative practice that more fully embraces his sense of vulnerability and the complexity of difference and disability. In doing so, Carlo redeems the negative experience with a positive outcome. This is the most poignant among many redemption sequences in his life story.

There is evidence of both assimilative and accommodative approaches to making integrative meaning in Carlo's story. For example, in the immediate wake of his cancer diagnosis, Carlo seems to employ an assimilative approach. He does not engage with the potentially devastating implications of this experience and instead heads off to Europe with his 70-pound backpack and his best friend. While Carlo certainly undertook a good deal of denial and repression in making this choice, maintaining his current view of himself did allow him to experience the growth that came from simply escaping his current context and doing something different for a while.

In contrast, Carlo's reframing of his identity from being a disabled or blind person to being a nonvisual learner is evidence of accommodative processing. Here, Carlo reshapes his worldview in a way that fundamentally alters his basic structures of meaning making. This new way of thinking about himself opens Carlo up to a different way of being in the world and pursuing his art work.

Unlike the motivational, affective, and integrative meaning thematic aspects of narrative identity, its structural aspects are often more challenging to identify explicitly. As a narrator, Carlo certainly met a threshold criterion of coherence; his story was not hard to follow, as the lengthy quote about his experience in Ireland demonstrates. Narrative coherence may have the strongest ramifications for psychological well-being when it is markedly low (e.g, Freeman, 2010; Lysaker et al., 2003; McAdams, 2006a) and Carlo's story is perfectly legible. Nevertheless, Carlo's experience of returning from his trip to Europe and finally coming to terms with his cancer diagnosis demonstrates the ways in which experiences of incoherence plagued Carlo's psychological well-being at moments in his life.

As discussed earlier, and elsewhere (Adler et al., 2016), the literature on narrative identity demonstrates that themes of agency, communion, redemption, and integrative meaning making, as well as moderate to high levels of coherence are each associated with positive psychological well-being. It is therefore no surprise that Carlo enjoys positive mental health, as indicated by his scores on the self-report scales. Carlo scored 32 out of a possible 35 on the Satisfaction with Life Scale (Diener, Emmons, Larsen, & Griffin, 1985). He scored 4.6 out of 5 on the Positive Affectivity scale of the Positive and Negative Affectivity Schedule (Watson, Clark, & Tellegen, 1988) and a 1.8 out of 5 on the Negative Affectivity scale. He also scored extremely low on the Beck Depression Inventory (Beck, Steer, & Brown, 1996; a score of 1, placing him well below the threshold for even mild depression), and relatively low on the Pennsylvania State Worry Questionnaire, a measure of generalized anxiety (Brown, Antony, & Barlow, 1992; a score of 36 out of 80). Finally, he also scored quite high on each of the six subscales in Ryff and Keyes's (1995) Psychological Well-Being measure, including the highest possible score on the Personal Growth subscale (38/42 on Autonomy; 39/42 on Environmental Mastery; 42/42 on Personal Growth; 41/42 on Positive Relations; 41/42 on Purpose in Life; 41/42 on Self-Acceptance). This profile represents one especially high in psychological well-being, broadly conceived. Carlo experiences high levels of positive affect, low levels of negative affect, a heightened sense of life satisfaction, and a deep sense of personal growth.

In addition to these measures, Carlo also completed Loevinger's measure of ego development (Hy & Loevinger, 1996). Ego development represents the degree of nuance and complexity that individuals use when making meaning of themselves and the world, and has been referred to as psychological maturity (Hy & Loevinger, 1996). Carlo's score placed him at Stage 7 (out

of 9), which is a score well above the population mean. Hy and Loevinger describe this stage: "Although a concern for the problems of dependence and independence is a recurrent one, at this stage the person distinguishes physical, financial, and emotional dependence" (p. 6). This sense of differentiation was evident in Carlo's life story, as he grappled with the different ways he is independent, dependent, and inter-dependent on others. The combination of a high level of ego development and high scores on other psychological well-being measures is a particularly privileged psychological profile, one that has been referred to as "the good life" (e.g., King, 2001).

Thus, Carlo's story illustrates the ways in which narrative identity in adulthood serves as a foundation for psychological well-being. His particular approach to narrating the many challenges in his life shows many of the themes that have been empirically connected to mental health, and Carlo embodies this research tradition.

Conclusion

Crafting the story of one's life provides the individual with a sense of unity, purpose, and meaning, which further support psychological well-being. The ability to narrate one's life develops over the course of key milestones during childhood and blossoms into maturity during adolescence. Across the adult lifespan, narrative identity both serves as a foundation for psychological functioning and continues to develop itself. Key moments of discontinuity or "biographical disruption" (e.g., Bury, 1982; Habermas & Köber, 2014) serve as cues for adult individuals to revisit and potentially revise their stories. But when it comes to psychological well-being, not all stories are created equal. Stories rich in the motivational themes of agency and communion, the affective theme of redemption, assimilative and accommodative approaches to integrative meaning making, and high levels of narrative coherence are associated with positive mental health. As Carlo's story makes clear, these narrative characteristics give rise to an identity that is well situated for responding to life's challenges and supporting well-being in the face of them.

REFERENCES

Adler, J. M. (2012). Living into the story: Agency and coherence in a longitudinal study of narrative identity development and mental health over the course of psychotherapy. *Journal of Personality and Social Psychology, 102,* 367–389.

Adler, J. M. (2018). Bringing the (disabled) body to personality psychology: A case study of Samantha. *Journal of Personality, 86*(5), 803–824.

Adler, J. M., Dunlop, W. L., Fivush, R., Lilgendahl, J. P., Lodi-Smith, J., McAdams, D. P., et al. (2017). Research methods for studying narrative identity: A primer. *Social Psychological and Personality Science, 8*(5), 519–527.

Adler, J. M., Lodi-Smith, J., Philippe, F. L., & Houle, I. (2016). The incremental validity of narrative identity in predicting well-being: A review of the field and recommendations for the future. *Personality and Social Psychology Review, 20*(2), 142–175.

Adler, J. M., Turner, A. F., Brookshier, K. M., Monahan, C., Walder-Biesanz, I., Harmeling, L. H., et al. (2015). Variation in narrative identity is associated with trajectories of mental health over several years. *Journal of Personality and Social Psychology, 108*(3), 476–496.

Arnett, J. J. (2000). Emerging adulthood: A theory of development from the late teens through the twenties. *American Psychologist, 55*(5), 469–480.

Bauer, J. J., & McAdams, D. P. (2004). Personal growth in adults' stories of life transitions. *Journal of Personality, 72,* 573–602.

Beck, A. T., Steer, R. A., & Brown, G. K. (1996). *Manual for Beck Depression Inventory.* San Antonio, TX: Psychological Corporation.

Blagov, P., & Singer, J. A. (2004). Four dimensions of self-defining memories (specificity, meaning, content, and affect) and their relationship to self-restraint, distress, and repressive defensiveness. *Journal of Personality, 72*(3), 481–511.

Block, J. (1982). Assimilation, accommodation, and the dynamic of personality development. *Child Development, 53,* 281–295.

Bohlmeijer, E., Roemer, M., Cuijpers, P., & Smit, F. (2007). The effects of reminiscence on psychological well-being in older adults: A meta-analysis. *Aging and Mental Health, 11*(3), 291–300.

Brown, T. A., Antony, M. M., & Barlow, D. H. (1992). Psychometric properties of the Penn State Worry Questionnaire in a clinical anxiety disorders sample. *Behaviour Research and Therapy, 30*(1), 33–37.

Bury, M. (1982). Chronic illness as biographical disruption. *Sociology of Health and Illness, 4*(2), 167–182.

Davis, L. J. (2017). Introduction: Disability, normality, and power. In L. J. Davis (Ed.), *The disability studies reader* (5th ed., pp. 1–16). New York: Routledge.

Diener, E., Emmons, R. A., Larsen, R. J., & Griffin, S. (1985). The Satisfaction with Life Scale. *Journal of Personality Assessment, 49,* 71–76.

Dunlop, W. L. (2017). Studying the motivated agent through time: Personal goal development during the adult life span. *Journal of Personality, 85*(2), 207–219.

Dunlop, W. L., & Tracy, J. L. (2013). Sobering stories: Narratives of self-redemption predict behavioral change and improved health among recovered alcoholics. *Journal of Personality and Social Psychology, 104,* 576–590.

Erikson, E. (1959). *Identity and the life cycle.* New York: Norton.

Fivush, R., Gray, J. T., & Fromhoff, F. A. (1987). Two year olds talk about the past. *Cognitive Development, 2,* 393–409.

Freeman, M. (2010). "Even amidst": Rethinking narrative coherence. In M. Hyvarinen, L. C. Hyden, M. Saarenheimo, & M. Tamboukou (Eds.), *Beyond narrative coherence* (pp. 167–186). Philadelphia: Benjamins.

Garland-Thomson, R. (2014). The story of my work: How I became disabled. *Disability Studies Quarterly, 34*(2), np.

Gergen, K. J. (2000). *The saturated self: Dilemmas of identity in contemporary life.* New York: Basic Books.

Grysman, A., & Denney, A. (2017). Gender, experimenter gender and medium of report influence the content of autobiographical memory report. *Memory, 25,* 132–145.

Habermas, T., & Bluck, S. (2000). Getting a life: The emergence of the life story in adolescence. *Psychological Bulletin, 128,* 748–769.

Habermas, T., & Köber, C. (2014). Autobiographical reasoning is constitutive for narrative identity: The role of the life story for personal continuity. In K. C. Mclean & M. Syed (Eds.), *The Oxford handbook of identity development* (pp. 149–165). Oxford, UK: Oxford University Press.

Habermas, T., & Reese, E. (2015). Getting a life takes time: The development of the life story in adolescence, its precursors and consequences. *Human Development, 58,* 172–201.

Haden, C., Haine, R., & Fivush, R. (1997). Developing narrative structure in parent–child reminiscing across the preschool years. *Developmental Psychology, 33,* 295–307.

Hammack, P. L. (2008). Narrative and the cultural psychology of identity. *Personality and Social Psychology Review, 12,* 222–247.

Haverkamp, B. E. (2005). Ethical perspectives on qualitative research in applied psychology. *Journal of Counseling Psychology, 52,* 146–153.

Heintzelman, S. J., & King, L. A. (2014). Life is pretty meaningful. *American Psychologist, 69*(6), 561–574.

Hy, L. X., & Loevinger, J. (1996). *Measuring ego development* (2nd ed.). Hillsdale, NJ: Erlbaum.

Kafer, A. (2013). *Feminist, queer, crip.* Bloomington: Indiana University Press.

King, L. A. (2001). The hard road to the good life: The happy, mature person. *Journal of Humanistic Psychology, 41,* 51–72.

King, L. A., & Raspin, C. (2004). Lost and found possible selves, well-being, and ego development in divorced women. *Journal of Personality, 72,* 603–631.

Lysaker, P. H., Wickett, A. M., Campbell, K., & Buck, K. D. (2003). Movement towards coherence in the psychotherapy of schizophrenia: A method for assessing narrative transformation. *Journal of Nervous and Mental Diseases, 191,* 538–541.

Manago, A. M. (2014). Identity development in a digital age: The case of social networking sites. In K.C. McLean & M. Syed (Eds.), *The Oxford handbook of identity development* (pp. 508–524). New York: Oxford University Press.

McAdams, D. P. (1997). The case for unity in the (post) modern self: A modest proposal. In R. Ashmore & L. Jussim (Eds.), *Self and identity* (pp. 46–78). New York: Oxford University Press.

McAdams, D. P. (2001). The psychology of life stories. *Review of General Psychology, 5,* 100–122.

McAdams, D. P. (2006a). The problem of narrative coherence. *Journal of Constructivist Psychology, 19,* 109–125.

McAdams, D. P. (2006b). *The redemptive self: Stories Americans live by.* New York: Oxford University Press.

McAdams, D. P. (2008). *The Life Story Interview.* Evanston, IL: Foley Center for the Study of Lives, Northwestern University. Retrieved from *www.sesp.northwestern.edu/foley/instruments/interview.*

McAdams, D. P. (2015). *The art and science of personality development.* New York: Guilford Press.

McAdams, D. P., & Guo, J. (2015). Narrating the generative life. *Psychological Science, 26,* 475–483.

McAdams, D. P., Hoffman, B. J., Mansfield, E. D., & Day, R. (1996). Themes of agency and communion in significant autobiographical scenes. *Journal of Personality, 64,* 339–378.

McAdams, D. P., & McLean, K. C. (2013). Narrative identity. *Current Directions in Psychological Science, 22,* 233–238.

McAdams, D. P., & Olson, B. D. (2010). Personality development: Continuity and change. In S. Fiske, D. Schacter, & R. Sternberg (Eds.), *Annual review of psychology* (Vol. 61, pp. 517–542). Palo Alto, CA: Annual Reviews.

McAdams, D. P., & Pals, J. L. (2006). A new Big Five: Fundamental principles for an integrative science of personality. *American Psychologist, 61,* 204–217.

McCoy, T., & Dunlop, W. (2016). Contextualizing narrative identity: A consideration of assessment settings. *Journal of Research in Personality, 65,* 16–21.

McLean, K. C., & Syed, M. (2016). Personal, master, and alternative narratives: An integrative framework for understanding identity development in context. *Human Development, 58*(6), 318–349.

Mitchell, D. T., & Snyder, S. L. (1997). *The body and physical difference: Discourses of disability.* Ann Arbor: University of Michigan Press.

Nelson, K. (1993). The psychological and social origins of autobiographical memory. *Psychological Science, 4,* 7–14.

Pals, J. L. (2006). Narrative identity processing of difficult life experiences: Pathways of personality development and positive self-transformation in adulthood. *Journal of Personality, 74,* 1079–1110.

Reese, E., Jack, F., & White, N. (2010). Origins of adolescents' autobiographical memories. *Cognitive Development, 25,* 352–367.

Reese, E., Yan, C., Jack, F., & Hayne, H. (2010). Emerging identities: Narrative and self from early childhood to early adolescence. In K.C. McLean & M. Pasupathi (Eds.), *Narrative development in adolescence* (pp. 23–43). New York: Springer.

Ryan, R. M., & Deci, E. L. (2001). On happiness and human potentials: A review of research on hedonic and eudaimonic well-being. *Annual Review of Psychology, 52,* 141–166.

Ryff, C. D., & Keyes, C. L. M. (1995). The structure of psychological well-being revisited. *Journal of Personality and Social Psychology, 69,* 719–727.

Snow, C. E. (1990). Building memories: The ontogeny of autobiography. In D. Cicchetti & M. Beeghly (Eds.), *The self in transition: Infancy to childhood* (pp. 213–242). Chicago: University of Chicago Press.

Stein, N., & Glenn, C. (1979). An analysis of story c:omprchension in elementary school children. In R. Freedle (Ed.), *New directions in discourse processing* (Vol. 2). Hillsdale, NJ: Ablex.

Syed, M., & Nelson, S. C. (2015). Guidelines for establishing reliability when coding narrative data. *Emerging Adulthood, 3*(6), 375–387.

Tracey, S. J. (2010). Qualitative quality: Eight "big tent" criteria for excellent qualitative research. *Qualitative Inquiry, 16*(10), 837–851.

Watson, D., Clark, L. A., & Tellegen, A. (1988). Development and validation of brief measures of positive and negative affect: The PANAS Scales. *Journal of Personality and Social Psychology, 54,* 1063–1070.

CHAPTER 26

Narrative, Identity, and Identity Statuses
Reflections on the Kaleidoscopic Self

Ruthellen Josselson

"I coulda been a contender, I coulda been somebody"—these famous lines spoken by Marlon Brando in *On the Waterfront* rather sum up a life in just nine words. They give us a sense of the character's identity and allude to a central theme in a life history. In nine words, with no measurement, we know quite a lot about this person.

McAdams's (2001a, 2001b) model of personality development includes, as a third level of analysis and integration, an autobiographical author who creates a story of his or her life, organizing events and inner experiences into some more or less coherent whole that links past, present, and future. The emphasis here is on meanings that the individual constructs, explanations for who the person is, and how he or she is living a particular life (and where he or she might be headed).

Ideas about narrative and about identity have converged in recent decades; both are somewhat fuzzy concepts that aim to encompass the complexity and multiple layers of human experience. Both narrative and identity integrate meaningful aspects of experience into some communicable shape that is both expressed and lived. How can we model the intricacy of dynamic processes that continually flow and change over time? (Consider how many layers of self experience and of time are present in the statement, "I coulda been a contender.")

In this chapter, I begin by setting out the premise that identity is best understood in a narrative framework that preserves context. I then try to summarize Erikson's ideas about identity, which were grounded in narratives, and then show how these ideas have been reflected in identity status research. After broadly reviewing the empirical findings of identity status research, I explore aspects of identity and narrative as I have understood them in a 45-year longitudinal study of women's identity development. Integrating these various streams of work and theory, I wish to develop the idea that in the evolution of identity, over time are elements of both stability and change that may be understood as kaleidoscopic in the sense that elements may be stable (although new elements may be added) but their arrangement changes to create quite different patterns. In order to demonstrate the utility of the kaleidoscope metaphor, I use examples of people who have integrated fairly stable identities that nevertheless change over time, and a very detailed illustration of a woman with a fragmented identity.

Narrative

The so-called "narrative turn" has marked all of the social sciences. Over the last three decades, narrative research and the concepts of narrative and life story have become increasingly prominent in a wide area of human or social sciences—psychology, education, sociology, and history, to name just a few. Besides being used to explore specific topics, narrative studies are flourishing as a means of understanding personal identity, life-course development, culture, and the historical world of the narrator.

In contemporary psychology, Jerome Bruner (1990) has most championed the legitimization of what he calls "narrative modes of knowing" that, in contrast to paradigmatic modes of knowing that privilege hypothesis testing and measurement, instead privilege the particulars of lived experience within their social and cultural context. Meanings are generated by the linkages the participant makes between aspects of the life he or she is, was, or hopes to be living.

Within the growing narrative research tradition, the approach is interpretive and hermeneutic; methods are largely focused on describing and understanding rather than measuring and predicting, concerned with meaning rather than causation and frequency, and recognition of the importance of language and discourse rather than reduction to numerical representation. These approaches are holistic rather than atomistic, concern themselves with particularity rather than universals, are interested in the cultural context rather than trying to be context-free and give overarching significance to subjectivity rather than questing for some kind of objectivity (Giddens, 1991; Polkinghorne, 1988; Smith, Harré, & Van Langenhove, 1995).

The stories people tell about their lives are presumed to have narrative rather than historical truth (Spence, 1984). In lieu of precisely accurate representation of the reality of one's past or present life, these narratives are viewed as constructions assembled from fragments of experience, thoughts, and feelings at a certain moment in time. They are constructions produced under quite singular circumstances (e.g., an interview) that must be taken into account reflexively. Yet despite their indeterminacy, which facts, ideas, or events are selected and formulated into a story may teach us something about the narrators' central concerns in life and the meanings they make of themselves in their social context and the progression of their lives (McAdams, Josselson, & Lieblich, 2006). Identity and the self have been reconceptualized as life narratives (Cohler, 1982; Brockmeier & Carbaugh, 2001; Lieblich & Josselson, 2013; Polkinghorne 1988; Singer, 2004). We *are* the

stories we live by (McAdams, 1993; Randall, 2014).

Given that identity is a synthesizing, largely unconscious process, it cannot be described directly. Instead, we create narratives that construct and reconstruct our sense of self in the world, narratives that preserve continuity, provide some semblance of coherence, and link inner experience with sociocultural realities.

The stories we tell about ourselves and our personal experiences grow in complexity and detail as we move through childhood into the adolescent and young adult years. According to developmental research, it is not until adolescence that people are able and motivated to conceive of their lives as a full-fledged, integrative narrative of the self (Habermas & Bluck, 2000). Life-history narration requires enough reflexivity to separate narrator from protagonist; people need to have the cognitive and emotional capacity to take a view of themselves from outside the plot. Once the capacity to create a life history emerges (just before the psychosocial crisis of identity), people may produce and reproduce their life stories in a number of circumstances that require or motivate them to do so, as well as create an internal life history that describes the march of the self through social reality. The balance of past, present, and future events in one's life story changes as life goes on, and memories of the past are reworked to be consistent with evolving identity (Josselson, 2009).

Identity

Although many scholars over the past century have written about identity, Erik Erikson's (1968) effort to detail identity as a fundamental aspect of personality and as a developmental process has been most heuristic. Erikson described the construction of a coherent and purposeful self-concept, which he called "identity," as a psychosocial process (and frequently turned to case examples and narrative to demonstrate his meanings). Young people in modern societies are faced with the psychological challenge of constructing a self that provides their lives with unity, purpose, and meaning. They are challenged with the dual questions: "Who am I?" and "How do I fit into my society as an adult?" Identity is at the juncture of biological, psychological, and social dimensions of the individual, and although its challenges come to the fore during late adolescence, identity development continues throughout adult life as it intersects with, influences, and integrates adult tasks of intimacy, generativity, and integrity (Kroger, 2015).

Identity is, as Erikson underscored, a complex concept, and identity formation and revision are elusive processes to study. Identity is ongoing, he emphasized: It is "always changing and developing . . . never . . . static or unchangeable" (1968, pp. 23–24), yet it is also marked by "two simultaneous observations: the perception of the selfsameness and continuity of one's existence in time and space and the perception of the fact that others recognize one's sameness and continuity" (p. 50). At the same time, it also includes, on a different level, "the *style of one's individuality,* and that this style coincides with the sameness and continuity of one's *meaning for significant others* in the immediate community" (p. 50, emphasis in the original). Erikson thus stresses the psychosocial nature of the identity concept: One can only have a workable identity if it is recognized by others.

Erikson (1968) returned again and again over his career to refining and reformulating his understanding of the identity stage, changing his mind (unlike with any of the other developmental stages) about whether its negative pole ought to be called "role confusion," "role diffusion," or "identity confusion." Although he offered many attempts to "define" identity, one of his clearest statements of the complexity of the process of identity formation is the following:

> In psychological terms, the process of identity formation employs a process of simultaneous reflection and observation, a process . . . by which the individual judges himself in the light of what he perceives to be the way in which others judge him in comparison to themselves and to a typology significant to them; while he judges their way of judging him in the light of how he perceives himself in comparison to them and to types that have become relevant to him. The process is . . . for the most part unconscious except where inner conditions and outer circumstances combine to aggravate a painful, or elated, "identity-consciousness. (pp. 22–23).

Identity, in other words, is fully recursive and only conscious when there is some mismatch between inner experience and outer reality. Barring that, the unconscious functioning of the identity structure leaves us taking our identity for granted, both in terms of who we are in the world and in the conviction that we will be the same tomorrow.

Identity reflects the meanings we are making of our lives, our sense of unity and purpose, and this is expressed in narrative form (see especially Bruner, 1990; Lieblich & Josselson, 2013; McAdams & McLean, 2013; Polkinghorne, 1988, Singer, 2004). As Kierkegaard famously said, we live life forwards and understand it backwards. Our life narrative, which encompasses our identity, both directs us forward and provides us a (more or less) coherent look back. Living involves continually constructing and reconstructing stories, revising the plot as new events are added, without knowing the outcome. Life progresses—the self and identity are not finalized—until our story ends and others fashion a story of who we were.

Viewing identity as a narrative marks its dynamic nature. It is a process, not an entity. Identity, as an ongoing story, evolves to encompass what comes into a life and omits what no longer seems at play in that life. The unity of the individual life resides in a construction of its narrative, a form in which hopes, dreams, despairs, doubts, plans, and emotions are all phrased.

To say that identity is organized narratively, though, doesn't imply that people "have" a life story that can be downloaded like a file on a computer. The synthetic work of identity is largely unconscious, holding all of the parts together, although we can usually create some chain of causation if called upon to do so (as in "How come you did *that*!?") People construct a more elaborate life story for someone else only rarely, and this is always tailored to the moment of the telling. We might tell our life story in segments to a new friend—in segments because few people have the patience to listen to an extended account; we may create one for a job interview—only including what may appear favorable in the eyes of the evaluator. Yet we have an internal life story that we don't tell, a set of memories of experiences that are meaningfully linked to one another, so that we have a sense of having started somewhere, lived through inner and outer events, and arrived at where we are, headed somewhere else. Life stories vary among people as to how much they reflect unity, coherence, and sense of purpose in a life. Some people construct life stories for themselves and for others, with clearly marked paths, as though the present were the inevitable outcome of the past, where all that led up to this moment in time was prologue. Others have a fragmented life story, a story with threads that never unite and its fragmentation may or may not be recognized by the narrator, who may not expect that his or her life "adds up" or has consistent themes. And many people's stories lie between these extremes, with aspects of the story that have coherent threads over time and others with important subplots that seem to belong to some other story, that are not integrated into a central narrative.

Narrative, like identity, is a concept that refers to some kind of unity of the self, a unity that integrates past, present, and future, inner and outer reality, and the primary investments and experiences of the self. "Identity is a life story—an internalized and evolving narrative of the self" (McAdams, 2001a, p. 644). Identity can only be expressed in narration, and all personal narratives, whether small stories (Bamberg, 2006; Bamberg & Georgakopoulou, 2008) or whole life stories, always denote identity. Narratives, like identity, are embedded in the social and relational context in which both are rooted.

The Identity Statuses

The complexity of the identity concept seemed to elude measurement and instead necessitates some approach that would invite late adolescents to describe their experiences making (or not making) identity commitments during the college years. Jim Marcia (2007) took on the challenge to "measure the unmeasurable" (p. 4) by using a semistructured interview in which college students were asked to narrate their efforts to create an identity. From this, he observed patterns that eventually became the *identity status model* (Marcia, 1966), a model that has provided a conceptual platform for hundreds of studies. Recognizing that one cannot directly assess the internal configuration that Erikson called *identity,* Marcia was in search of indicators of its nature. In Marcia's reading of Erikson, and in his analysis of the interviews he conducted, two independent dimensions seemed to be at the heart of both Erikson's discussions of identity and the phenomenological experience of the participants: exploration (crisis in the earliest formulation) and commitment (see Figure 26.1). That is, some young people (Foreclosures), simply carry forth ideological, relational, and occupational commitments be-

queathed to them by significant others in their lives, thus foreclosing, without consideration of other possibilities, indicating a fairly rigid identity structure. Other people make commitments following a period in which they have considered, even experimented with, other ways of being or believing, and these Marcia called Identity Achievements (even while recognizing that Erikson did not think that identity could ever be finally "achieved"). Still other young people were found to be in periods of flux in identity (Moratoriums), without commitments but trying to forge them, still in the midst of the psychosocial period that Erikson called the "moratorium period," a time society allots for such exploration. Yet others were without commitments and seemed not to be trying to create them (Diffusions), indicating an identity structure without discernible boundaries. These latter individuals were close to what Erikson described as people diffuse (or confused) in regard to their identity formation. Hundreds of studies (in many Western and non-Western countries [Kroger, 2015]) have developed construct validity for the identity statuses by demonstrating that the statuses behaved in theoretically consistent ways on other indicators of personality development (Kroger, 2015; for a review, see Kroger & Marcia, 2011).

Both interview-based and psychometric studies making use of the identity statuses continue to strengthen our understanding that consolidating identity during the late adolescent years (i.e., being classified as Identity Achieved) is adaptive and indicative of general well-being and healthy development (Kroger & Marcia, 2011). Meta-analyses show that those who are Identity Achieved are higher in ego development (Jespersen, Kroger, & Martinussen, 2013), and that this is maintained over time. Both cross-sectional and longitudinal studies show, though, that relatively large proportions of young adults have not formulated an independent identity (i.e., become Identity Achieved) by age 36 (Kroger, Martinussen, & Marcia, 2010).

Individual studies, as well as meta-analyses, have shown that Foreclosure seems to be a more adaptive status than envisioned by Erikson or Marcia, although somewhat less so than Achievement. Foreclosures ground their identity in identification and look to authority figures for direction and security (e.g., Marcia, 1966; Marcia, Waterman, Matteson, Archer, & Orlofsky, 1993). and they base their moral reasoning on conventional thinking and are not open

		EXPLORATION: *Yes*	EXPLORATION: *No*
COMMITMENT	*Yes*	*Pathmakers* (Identity Achievement)	*Guardians* (Foreclosure)
	No	*Searchers* (Moratorium)	*Drifters* (Diffusion)

FIGURE 26.1. Identity status classification. Names in italics are the renamed statuses (Josselson, 1996) but are conceptually the same as the original names that appear in parentheses.

to new experiences (Marcia et al., 1993; Skoe & Marcia, 1991). Short-term longitudinal studies (most longitudinal studies average about 3 years [Kroger, 2015]) indicate that people can return from other statuses to Foreclosure, a process still hard to theorize from Erikson's model. Josselson (1987) has suggested—and demonstrated—that for at least some late adolescent women, the searching they seemed to be doing during college evaporates if they return to their home and reintegrate themselves into their precollege familial and community environments.

The emerging portraits of those in Moratorium and Diffusion classifications in young adulthood crystallize around the description of these statuses as composed of people in more or less distress. We still don't know whether the distress is caused by the lack of identity resolution or whether distress not related to identity becomes a barrier to making identity commitments (see Marcia, 2006). In Erikson's theory, successful resolution of the identity versus identity confusion stage involves a positive *balance* between commitment and confusion. Identity formation always implies both consolidation of aspects of self-in-society that feel meaningful and purposeful, as well as aspects that are unformed, confused, labile, changeable, or inconstant. Erikson would likely assert that it is the very tension between what one feels committed to and what one feels uncertain about that fuels further growth. Marcia (2007) reminds us that in both his and Erikson's conceptualizations, individuals are admixtures of statuses, not necessarily fitting into just one.

The most general statement I can make about the nearly 600 studies of the identity statuses over 50 years is that they illustrate how complex identity processes are. Some scholars assess the statuses categorically, using interviews, as did Marcia (1966) in the original design; others have devised and utilized paper-and-pencil scales to assess statuses, then either assigned participants to categories or regarded scores on each status dimension in a linear fashion. These differences in assessment approach have made generalizations across studies difficult, if not impossible. And there are many intervening variables; gender perhaps is the most outstanding. Identity status is also sensitive to economic conditions (Fadjukoff, Kokko, & Pulkkinen, 2010). At the most simplistic level, one can say that, overall, Identity Achievement reflects and portends the highest functioning and psychological well-being, while Identity Diffusion, with the vast individual differences within this category, portends the least desirable psychological functioning. Moratorium, being an unstable period of exploration, is one that people generally move out of into one of the other three statuses, but MAMA cycles of Moratorium followed by Achievement and then other periods of exploration have been noted (Stephen, Fraser, & Marcia, 1992). The Foreclosure status seems to comprise "firm" Foreclosures, authoritarian in personality structure, who stay in this status indefinitely and "developmental" Foreclosures, who eventually, often because of external challenges, undergo exploration and change (Kroger, 1995).

Identity and the Life Cycle

Scholars are increasingly recognizing that the investigation of identity requires some phenomenological approach in the form of narrative (see Habermas & Köber, 2015; Hammack, 2015; McAdams & Zapata-Gietl, 2015), in which we may witness identity as a dynamic system that relates internal experience and the social world. To witness identity in its inception and development requires listening to, then interpreting, stories that people tell about their own becoming. Although identity develops within the individual, it is always evolving within a relational world, in which response from others is necessary to securing recognition that one is who one supposes oneself to be. As Jane Kroger (1993) detailed in a very insightful retrospective interview study, people choose a context consistent with their identity structure. She demonstrated how Foreclosures chose or created "insulated vocational, ideological and social contexts for themselves within whatever broader climate of social attitudes existed at the time" (p. 143). Moratoriums, by contrast, found contexts that expanded their range of opportunities or experiences. Over time, the Identity Achievements sought possibilities in their social world and chose contexts that supported their need for autonomy.

Identity, Erikson said, is the integrator that moves one toward wholeness (Hoare, 2001; Kroger, 2007). Identity is the overall pattern that results from arrangement of the elements of the self. Witnessing its changes over time is much like looking into a kaleidoscope: The elements rearrange, sometimes new ones are added, and some previous important elements seem to disappear. In some patterns, most likely the committed, stable statuses of Foreclosure and Achievement, there is predictability and incremental change; in others, Moratoriums and Diffusions, the configurations may change wildly, with patterns that seem unstable.

Identity as a "crisis" period moves from center stage at the close of adolescence and gives way to the challenges of adulthood, the later stages of "intimacy versus isolation," "generativity versus stagnation" and "integrity versus despair" in Erikson's model of development. Identity, however, continues to evolve and influence these later stages, while, in a mutual patterning, intimacy, generativity, and integrity all have implications for identity.

In Erikson's model of adult development, resolutions of the identity stage scaffold the next stage: the search for intimacy, the making of a deep commitment to another person with whom to share one's life. Having a sense of who one is and wants to be in life leads to a need to partner, and the society also presses with this expectation. Successful resolution of the intimacy stage yields the ability to love, to experience mutual devotion and respect toward a partner or selected others. The "I" enlarges to a particular "We."

Following resolution of intimacy issues, around midlife, generativity comes to the fore in Erikson's model. At this stage, adults turn their attention away from the self toward care of the next generation. This may mean care of children or the next generation more broadly construed, such as mentoring younger people, contributing to one's community or taking care of the environment for those yet to be born. The negative pole of this stage is stagnation and self-absorption. The virtue derived from successful resolution of the stage of generativity is that of "care." If these stages of identity, intimacy, and generativity are successfully traversed, the later life stage of integrity versus despair is likely to be resolved in favor of a sense that one's life has had meaning (Marcia, 2014).

Although each of these issues—intimacy, generativity, and integrity—are the focus of progressive life stages, identity continues its integrative function, shaping and being reshaped. Identity influences how one is generative, for example, and how one is generative becomes part of identity. Each later stage involves a reformulation of identity as one responds to the demands and rewards of each developmental era (Erikson, Erikson, & Kivnick, 1989; Marcia, 2010). Although there are sometimes dramatic transformations of identity, more often identity evolves slowly. Over time, identity broadens and deepens as the identity structure subsumes newly developed or newly realized aspects of the person. Other long-term longitudinal studies have similarly shown that well-formulated identity in late adolescence predicts healthy later adulthood (Helson, Soto, & Cate, 2006; Stewart & Ostrove, 1998). Difficulties in resolution of the challenges of the identity stage, however, may presage, or even create, difficulties in managing the ensuing stages of adult development (Marcia & Josselson, 2013).

To understand and conceptualize the *evolution* of identity requires longitudinal studies that would detail how a person's identity transforms over time. Erikson (1969, 1962) attempted to detail these processes by turning to psychobiography, recognizing that identity could best be understood by analyzing the complexities of a life.

A Longitudinal Study of Women's Identity

My own work began with my enchantment with Erikson and my disappointment that his analyses of identity focused solely on men. In 1970, I initiated what has become a 45-year longitudinal study of 26 randomly chosen women whom I categorized into Marcia's identity statuses when they were college seniors and have interviewed intensively each decade since. I now have interviews at ages 21, 33, 43, 56, and 67 that narrate the development of each woman, with focus on her identity. The research method has relied on narrative analysis, an approach that thematically analyzes each interview, finds the links (or changes) between interviews of the same person at different ages, then makes cross-case comparisons (Josselson, 1996, 2017).

The women I have followed represent a diverse range of college-educated women from disparate backgrounds. Some grew up in large urban areas, others in small cities, towns, and rural areas—and there remains diversity in where they live now. Some were from well-to-do families; others put themselves through college by working while studying. Some had immigrant parents and are embedded in ethnicities that feel to them separate from the American mainstream. There is religious diversity—people who were raised as Catholics, Protestants, or Jews, although their religious affiliation and commitment has declined enough over the years that many now do not make religious identity very important. Many were the first in their families to go to college, getting themselves there either by forming their own dream or fulfilling their parents' hopes for them. In midlife, most of them feel comfortable materially, part of the middle- or upper-middle class, most of them having a higher standard of living than their families of origin.

Graduating from college in the early 1970s, these women were at the forefront of the changes in life possibilities for women and well aware of the opportunities they had to take meaningful roles in the workforce. When I first met them,

when they were 21, about to take their college degrees, all envisioned the same outlines for the future. They would marry, have children, and work. But the particularities of the work they would do, the husbands they would marry, and the children they might mother remained obscure, as the future always is. By the time they were in their early 30s, the shape of the identities they would live out was firmer than it had been at the end of college, with some of the details filled in. By their early 40s, they were actively revising what was in place—in their work, their marriages, and themselves. And in their mid-50s, they were reaping the fruits of the dreams they had been striving to realize in their lives.[1] All but one of them has spent most of her life in the work world, either in professional careers or having a series of jobs. All but one married at least once and most, in their mid-50s, were still married to their first husband; just over half had children. In their mid-60s, they were either retired, thinking about retiring, or just figuring out identity commitments that had eluded them for decades. The nature of their relationships with their families continued to evolve and shape their sense of identity.

In terms of the identity status categories, although there is no reliable way to assess identity status in adulthood, the pathways of identity were clear. (In the early 1990s, reporting on this study, I changed the names of the statuses to make them less pejorative. I renamed the Foreclosures Guardians because they were guarding their past selves; Pathmakers replaced Identity Achievers, as identity is never "achieved," and these are people who were making their own paths. I called the Moratoriums Searchers to distinguish the status name from the developmental phase and to indicate that they were involved in searching for identity, while I renamed the Diffusions Drifters. (The names have changed but still denote Marcia's identity status model.) The six women who had been Pathmakers in college continued to make their own paths except for one who lost her way and began to drift. Of the five Guardians, three remained so,

---

[1] In a study that included both cross-sectional and longitudinal data about women 12 years older than those I have studied, researchers found the early 50s to be women's "prime of life," in that life satisfaction was highest in this period (Mitchell & Helson, 1990). Increases in positive emotions over the course of midlife, using large samples, have been well documented (see Helson et al., 2006, for review).

while two had later crises that led them to create an identity on their own terms. The Searchers, whom we would expect to make changes, either forged an identity of their own and became Pathmakers (five women), went back to a previous way of being after college ended (two women), or began to drift and continued to do so (two women). Of the six college-age Drifters, all continued to drift except for one, who forged a workable identity in her early 50s.

These generalizations give an overview of the group of people I have been studying but do not engage the intricacies of identity configuration and reconfiguration over time. The very detailed and rich life histories, told and retold, offer us the opportunity to examine closely the kaleidoscopic nature of identity processes. In the remainder of this chapter, I wish to develop the idea that, when assessed through life narratives, identity is kaleidoscopic in that patterns remain stable and also change. What most changes over time are the meanings that are assigned to events and aspects of the self, and these meanings are the conscious and direct manifestation of the underlying identity. The metaphor of the kaleidoscope signifies the dynamic and integrative nature of identity and cautions us against reifying in time those we study.

The Kaleidoscopic Self

In reviewing what I've learned from my 45-year longitudinal study of women's identity, I came to the conclusion that identity and the self are kaleidoscopic. Parts of the self and its experiences are arranged in a pattern, a pattern that shifts over time. One can, perhaps, still find most of the elements of previous configurations, but they have different positions over time, and the overall pattern looks different. A kaleidoscope works on the principle of multiple reflections and, in terms of a life, central elements are indeed reflected in a variety of ways—these are what appear as overriding themes or values in a life. (When one assesses a life via questionnaire, the researcher is choosing an element to ask the participant to report on, but its positioning in the life is obscured.)

New experiences or social roles may lead to a quite different picture as events such as motherhood or chronic illness are included in the overall patterning of elements. The unforeseen happenings in life, sometimes called "accommodative challenge" in the literature (Helson & Roberts, 1994), often require adjustment and rearrangement. The particularities of these become central. Several of the women I have followed over time had, for example, children or a husband with special needs or stable jobs with companies that collapsed. Betty, a Pathmaker, in her late 30s, had to become expert in learning disabilities and mental health to help manage her seriously challenged son. This was a new identity element, previously unimagined, that she had to integrate into her ongoing identity configuration.

At age 21, Betty's identity was centered on becoming a physical therapist and living close to nature. Being "outdoorsy" and using her body were important to her. Her favorite daydream was to someday build her own home. (Betty was classified in college as a Pathmaker.) When I met her at age 33, her husband had become quite wealthy and retired; they were organizing a life in which Betty could work part of the year as a physical therapist (something she very much wanted to do) and travel for adventure the rest of the year, taking along their two young children. By age 43, Betty had recognized the serious problems of her younger child, and finding resources and help for him was a central concern, although she managed to maintain her pattern of working part of the year and traveling the rest.

When I met her at age 56, Betty's life was a kaleidoscopic arrangement of many of the elements that had been present all along. Her son was settled and needed less of her attention, so she was devoting herself to working as a physical therapist and traveling for philanthropic purposes. In addition, she now had the space to take up art projects, her art having taking a minor role when other concerns were more pressing. But these are still only some of the primary elements of the pattern of Betty's identity. Another set of pieces involved where the family would live. A major crisis occurred when Betty was in her mid-30s and her husband found some beautiful land in Maine on which he wanted to build a house. But the land, though Betty loved it, seemed too far from the medical services they needed for their son, so Betty made the decision to turn down this plan. Instead, they built—themselves—a house in the woods nearer to a city, and Betty was very proud of this house as an important expression of herself (and her husband) and a life accomplishment. I could not capture the essence of Betty's life and identity without discussing this house (which I visited). It is also important to note that the philanthropic work that Betty and her husband do at age 56 involves helping others build houses. From the earliest interview, the elements of Betty's life are foreshadowed: Living close to nature, being of service to others as a physical therapist, and raising a family are the themes that reverberate throughout Betty's life. But at age 21, the aspects of life that are most prominent in Betty's later identity arrangement are yet to be—her disabled son, the wealth her husband created, the focus on travel. These are choices and constraints that she could not have imagined would be in her life story, but she integrates them into the emerging pattern of her life and identity. One can see stability here and also change, the pattern evolving kaleidoscopically in the sense of shifting arrangements.

Meanings of earlier selves or identities also change over time as the present reimagines and determines the personal past (Josselson, 2009). Maria, a Pathmaker, as a college senior was a conscientious and determined young woman whose identity struggles centered on a relationship she had with an African American boy she planned to marry despite the objections of her traditional Italian family. At this age, her identity was dominated by her sense of being principled and value-oriented, ready to stand up to conformity and racism. By age 33, when she had married someone else and had two children, she described her earlier self as misguided, someone who was overlooking her boyfriend's problems. He would not have made a good father, Maria said, and having a family was most important to her at this age. When she was 43, struggling with her daughter, who was dating someone Maria didn't approve of, Maria again narrated her late-adolescent self, now depicting her as being in rebellion against her strict family. And by age 56, the memory of her boyfriend had come to be cherished as a time of passion, which Maria was lacking in her current life. Thus, over time, Maria the narrator reshapes her story of Maria the protagonist, sequentially depicting herself as independent and principled, practical and goal-directed, rebellious, and passionate, and she uses these identity elements to define her relationship with her husband, then her daughter, and ultimately with herself.

In Maria's case, what changes is not the facts of the episode, but her interpretation of it and her perspective on the aspects of self that "lived" the experience. She was, perhaps, at one and the same time, principled and rebellious, idealizing her boyfriend and suspicious of him, excited by the intensity of her sexuality and fearful of it. Over time, she reworks the narrative to highlight aspects of all these partial selves, and the shifting arrangement of parts defines her current identity. Like a kaleidoscope, the same elements are recombined to show a different pattern. There are shifts in interior voices and therefore the experience of self, reflecting the "dynamics of inconsistency and tension" (Bakhtin, 1981, p. 34) in the multilayered self. The personal past is reconfigured not so much to be consistent with the present, but to make it into a meaningful (though "unfinalized," in Bakhtin's terms) whole, the parts adequately justaposed. Discarded or disused selves *may* oppose the current self by forming counterpoints, but they may also exist on different dimensions or in different realms of experience from the contemporary self, neither consistent nor orthogonal. Hermans (1995) argues that memory is the wellspring of emergent selves, and this is often clear in longitudinal retellings. Discarded selves may eventually find a new place and will then be narrated to *seem* consistent with the present. But memory is also a container of selves that serve by staying in the wings, either witnessing or commenting on the action.

Deadends or disappointments in relationships or occupational commitments lead to changes that overlay (but don't erase) earlier syntheses of hopes or goals. The kaleidoscopic self can change dramatically, but most often it evolves—much like turning a kaleidoscope, in which the parts subtly rearrange until a new pattern is discernible. In some instances, especially in states of identity confusion or diffusion, the pieces are strewn somewhat haphazardly without unifying principles, leaving the person vulnerable to being blown about by the winds of fortune, with short-term agency perhaps, but little synthesizing direction.

We can, then, learn a great deal about identity when it does not cohere into an organized narrative, when, over time, the parts readjust even though causation is largely foregone. Things happen. Things are how they are because that's how they are. There is no organizing center to the self. This is the identity situation of the Drifters (Diffusions). For them, these issues of patterning of identity elements are most visible because the elements seem to be in a perpetual process of motion, never quite settling into a stable pattern. Donna's narratives over 45 years, at 10-year intervals, are an instance of refractions and shuffling of elements. Such instances help us better understand the importance of the synthetic and integrative function of identity over time as it (flexibly) anchors the person in the social world.

Donna

I present Donna's repeated life narratives in a good deal of detail so that we can follow the kaleidoscopic elements—the ones that emerge, those that disappear, and the shifts in their balance over time. I am, of course, choosing a great deal to omit, shards that *I* didn't think were particularly important or necessary to how I tell her story, but still, I thereby interfere with her kaleidoscopic arrangement.

Donna was a particularly smart and talented young woman who excelled in a small elite women's college when I first met her in 1970. The first in her family to go to college, she took pride in her academic abilities. She had some interest in art conservation but felt that she could do anything she wanted and hadn't yet really figured out what she most wanted to do. She stood out for me among my participants at the time because of her personal life—she had eloped and married after her freshman year, divorced a year later, then moved in with another man to whom she was engaged as a college senior.

In her college interview, Donna could only describe herself in relation to what others wanted of her and whether she complied with or rebelled against their wishes. She married out of rebellion and then regretted doing so. She was drawn to her (ex-)husband because he had clear ideas about how she should be in their marriage. "I just fitted into his desires," she said, then she left him when she realized she didn't want to be the traditional wife he wanted. I was astonished that, although it was only 2 years later, she seemed to remember little of this marriage. Her memory was vague about most of her life experiences. She valued her fiancé, Dan, because he gave her "space" and also fit in with her family. She often spoke of her decisions in terms of what her mother, to whom she was very close but desperately trying to separate from, had told her. I was struck by her earliest memory: "In the third grade, my teacher asked us to write

a poem and I was convinced I couldn't write a poem, so I went and copied a poem from somewhere and when she confronted me with it, I denied it." I thought that was a theme of what Donna was doing at this age—trying to copy an identity from somewhere else, all the while denying that she was doing so—and not being comfortable with any possibilities that had so far presented themselves. At this point, though, Donna said that she wanted the freedom to try new things, whatever they might be. I had become accustomed, with the Drifters, even back then, to the folly of my wish for them to give a coherent account of themselves.

By age 33, Donna was quite settled but recounted a complex and confused journey. What steadied her was her engagement with a spiritual advisor who led a somewhat cult-like community that she and Dan (to whom she was now married) had joined. They found this community after their marriage almost collapsed following 6 years in their 20s, in which drugs, alcohol, and a philosophy of open marriage were driving them apart. During this time, Donna had been working in photography and for several years was commuting between Miami and Key West, where Dan was working in his family's construction business. She had learned to fly her own plane back and forth. When she decided to move back to live full time with Dan, she felt she had to give up a good job, a great apartment, and a good salary. "Giving up all these things was not because of any marital problems, but as a result of soul searching and realizing that I ought to get on with the more important aspects of growing together as a couple and a family." Their spiritual leader taught a path of meditation, prayer, chastity, and vegetarianism, and these became the central pillars of Donna's identity in her early 30s. I noted as she spoke that Donna did not say that she wanted a family, instead that "I ought to get on with it."

Donna had two young children when I saw her at age 33, and she was trying to be a full-time mother because this is what she felt her babies needed. Still, she tried to grab what time she could to work on her photography and still accepted a few assignments, finding her work in photography quite fulfilling. She hoped to devote more time and attention to her work once her children were older. She stressed the way in which her marriage was an anchor stabilizing her and credited her husband with supporting all of her endeavors. Motherhood, she felt, was stretching her, teaching her to respond to others' needs and helping her learn about herself. "It exposes you to the good and bad within yourself." Donna was struggling with the demands of being a mother and having "days of not accomplishing anything tangible."

In her interview at age 33, Donna spoke about herself in the language of spirituality, inner peace, and karma, none of which connected very directly with what she was doing in the world—at least I couldn't make these connections. Karma explained many of her decisions. She had been in quest of feelings, of expressing herself, and although she tried many things, nothing quite sufficed except for short periods of time. Her new religious awareness had created a lot of guilt about an abortion she had had in her early 20s, and no amount of prayer relieved her of that burden. Still, despite a lot of contradictions, Donna seemed quite settled in her early 30s, enlightened by her spirituality and her confidence in the wisdom of her spiritual advisor, as well as bound to the demands of motherhood, commitment to her marriage, and her frustrated wishes to return to her work. I might have thought of her at this age as having found the somewhat packaged identity, defined by others, that she had been ambivalently seeking while in college.

When I saw her at age 43, Donna told me that the last decade had been difficult and she seemed to me to have returned to her earlier turmoil. She was still primarily involved in raising her now early adolescent children but not enjoying them or motherhood very much. From time to time, she had home-schooled her daughter. Her most recent passion had been learning to play the *viola da gamba* and she was spending a great deal of time practicing and playing with an ensemble.

Reflecting on her life, she felt that she had lost everything to motherhood. She described herself at this age as "really trying to get to focus on who I am." She found herself revisiting her past and trying to make sense of who she had been, asking herself a lot of questions. Why had she married her first husband? Why had she divorced? She could remember so little of this time, as though she had left the happy home of childhood and been thrust into a fog. Why had she had an abortion? And how could she come to terms with a recent miscarriage? "I'm looking at things now with a different consciousness and can't reconcile them with

my belief system now. Life just propelled me." She seemed to feel that accepting herself in the present involved coming to terms with a past that she couldn't specifically remember. I thought that she was experiencing and expressing the fragmentation of self that Drifters so often struggle with, a fragmentation that precludes forging a workable, integrated identity. The pieces of a self were there, but she wasn't very sure how some of them got there or how they fit together.

Donna was active in her life, but felt disconnected from what she was doing. When she stopped to think about what she was doing, she got mired in confusion. The story of the previous 10 years that Donna told me at age 43 contained continuing disjointed episodes. At some point, she had abruptly moved with the children to Italy for 6 months but could give no account that I could understand of why she had done this. Her response to my question about this gives the flavor of how Donna thought about her choices in life: "It was more the flow into something—more of an intuitive thing. I felt it and moved on it and pieces fell into place and it happened." While there, she spent some time studying the *viola da gamba* and looking at art. She told me that her husband, who was wonderful about giving her space, supported her doing this.

Over these years, she had also trained as a yoga instructor and an energy therapist, but hadn't done anything with these skills beyond the certification. Donna had taken membership for the family in a traditional church even though her spiritual life remained with her spiritual community. Home schooling "hadn't worked out." When the children were both in school, she had largely given up photography and wasn't sure what she wanted to do. Then, unexpectedly, she became pregnant. Donna didn't say she wanted another child, but she was "crushed" by the miscarriage. Around the same time, her husband's business was teetering and they were, for the first time, having financial worries. She had to help her husband in his work in her nonmothering time. Then she had a cancer scare. Donna was clearly quite stressed and somewhat depressed at this interview. The calm place was her *viola da gamba*. She was also directing the youth choir at church and building each year an elaborate Christmas village as a fundraiser. But when I asked her what had been the major good experiences in her life in the last 10 years, she told me that "there weren't any." She felt she was still struggling with the question of "what do I really want to do? I just go on doing this and that." The last few years, she told me, had been years of feeling her feelings more intensely—anger and sadness particularly. "I never stopped doing things long enough to know what really makes me happy or feeds me on a deeper level." She thought she might like to reground herself in work, perhaps take on more photography projects. She knew she wanted to feel creative and artistic.

Donna felt that her marriage was a success, glued by their shared spiritual commitment, which still involved meditation, chastity, and vegetarianism, as well as intermittent spiritual retreats. I could not find a way to ask how she got pregnant if they were practicing chastity, but as with all such contradictions, Drifters live with them. Thinking back on the turbulence in their marriage when they were in their early 20s, Donna said, "We followed the times into something we didn't understand very well." Like so much in Donna's past, it was ancient history, poorly grasped, a faded episode of life quite disconnected from the present.

Dominating Donna's concerns at this age were her frustrations with herself as a mother. She felt she had chosen to stay home with her children out of her "perfectionistic" belief that that was the right way, but she felt that she had no training to be a mother and wasn't feeling that she had been very good at it.

Donna also told me of an intense relationship with her *viola da gamba* teacher, a relationship "of many levels and a lot of love," that ended when this woman abruptly distanced herself and rejected Donna. At 43, Donna was aware of a need to ground herself and still cautiously hopeful of doing so. She was exploring her inner world, trying to connect to her past and make sense of her life. While she was doing what she needed to do as a wife and a mother, she was feeling emotionally disconnected from these roles, and while her spiritual life gave her structure and moral stability, she was at a loss to know what to do with her sense of fragmentation.

Age 53

When I saw her at age 53, Donna was in pieces, alone and afraid, barely holding herself together. "Every way in which I had been attempting to provide myself the context to define myself,

went," she told me. Donna was now divorced, and both of her children were in college. She was not working, and all she had left was the large home in which she had lived most of her adult life. Oddly, this left her in the position of being both wealthy and poor, living in a very valuable property but having no income beyond some minimal alimony. Donna's recounting of the past 10 years was fractured by her distress, her wish to tell me all the details, and her hesitance to do so. Donna herself seemed not to quite understand just what had happened to her.

She could no longer find a connection to doing photography and, for most of the previous decade, was primarily using her time to help out in her husband's failing business. Although she had dabbled in a number of activities over the years, "I knew that I wanted to go to finding myself but I didn't have a clue and so I know I've kind of entered upon different relationships or fell into things."

Over the past decade, Donna had had a series of affairs, with men and women, hoping to find someone who would help her define herself. These intense relationships preoccupied her over these years, and all ended in heartache. "I was just totally raw and vulnerable, but really was looking for who I was." Through this time she had tried a number of therapies to help her understand what was happening to her as she became deeply enmeshed in one relationship after another.

In her mid-50s, without family or work, Donna found her life "excruciating." "There's just no, there is no, there's no place for me to go and gain my context from somebody or some other situation." The divorce was particularly painful, but it too was shrouded in fog. My best understanding of what Donna described is that she was involved with a woman and her husband began living with another woman part of each week, and it somehow all just came apart. "I never in a million years would have thought that I would not spend the rest of my life with Dan. That's who I was."

Listening closely to Donna's words, we hear that she felt "consumed," felt she was "giving myself over" and " trying to gain my context from somebody." She was well aware that she looked inside and couldn't find a reliable sense of self, but she couldn't find someone to create an identity for her.

Amid all the upheaval, Donna was still fulfilling her responsibilities as a mother. She arranged tuition for her daughter's college and drove her there—then came back to an empty house, alone for the first time in her life. She filled her days taking care of the house and gardens, trying at least to preserve her property, the only asset she could salvage from her marriage.

"I could do anything. I'm a person that really doesn't do well with choices. And also just the not knowing, and feeling I'm not in a strong enough place, and I'm not in a place where I want to add any more regrets. I do regret the loss of family, I do regret being alone. . . . I've applied for a few jobs here and there, but it hasn't happened, and I guess my heart hasn't been pulled strong enough to really go after anything."

When Donna looked back at her life from the vantage point of age 53, she recalled being a good child who suppressed "any kind of connection with my own self or my own needs." Going to college was "escape" from the demands of being good, but she did so many things she now regrets, referring here to her first marriage and then the abortion in her 20s. For Donna, the best time was her 20s, when she went to graduate school and got an MFA and "did some amazing projects." And there was clarity in deciding to leave her job, live in Key West with Dan and become a mother. Through this time, in retrospect, she regards herself as having been a strong person.

"My very strong sense of knowing exactly what I wanted for the children in their upbringing in terms of everything from music, diapers, just committed to all these things that I don't know where they came from. Things in terms of—we were strongly vegetarian, we have a strong spiritual discipline. . . . I was so immersed in . . . really providing teachers and people and experiences for them and really into listening to who they were as individuals and recognizing both as individuals. So even from the birth, studying and doing my own home birth, I just knew what was right and what wasn't, what was good and what was wrong. The whole home environment for them."

And then, in Donna's telling, came the "shadow self," the confused, frightened, emotionally overwhelmed and lonely self that asserted itself in her early 40s.

As always, Donna narrated mixed images of herself.

"Some of what I love about where I am is the child-like innocence about life and possibility and mixing in elements of faith and spontaneity and synchronicity. I want to be flexible enough to allow the magical in life to happen. I can be so incredibly enthusiastic. Giving up possibility is painful and at the other end is too much possibility and I know there are too many things I can do. . . . The greatest fear of my life is that I will reach the end of my life and I will not have come to express who I am and I will have just wasted. . . . "

Age 67

At age 67, Donna's kaleidoscopic picture had settled into one dominated by her work as a photographer and her quest for "creative expression." Her spiritual path and her children were still present but as backdrop. In her late 50s, Donna had decided to return to school to study advanced techniques of digital photography and electronic media, and she moved across the country for 3 years to do so. Unfortunately, she graduated with a new degree in 2008, when the recession began, so it was difficult to find work. When I met her in 2016, she was still exploring, trying to find the right projects to work on, but she had some employment working with others. Donna was more content that I had ever seen her, having relegated the family and relationship struggles to the background. She felt, for the first time, that she could define herself— as a photographer. It was of no interest to her that she was starting out when others her age were retiring.

Donna had distant relationships with her children but was trying to be a good grandmother to her daughter's children, who lived far away. It was still a painful process to come to terms with the divorce and to make sense of why losing a marriage of 30 years was part of her karma. The romantic affairs of her 50s now seemed like "not me" and "How could you?" and she wondered how she could trust herself. She was no longer playing the *viola da gamba,* but she was still pursuing her spiritual path through meditation groups, vegetarianism, and prayer. Some elements of the earlier pictures were still there but were now repositioned, all in relation to the dominating focus on her work. For the first time since I have known her, Donna seemed focused and relatively content.

Looking back from age 67, Donna saw herself as waylaid from a career she had always wanted by the necessity of helping her husband in his business. At age 43, she had seen herself as having been pulled away from her career goals by motherhood, and at age 57, thoughts of career had vanished altogether. So Donna's narrative of her past was continually revised as she reinvented herself at each age period. She thought of her decision to return to school at age 55 as a first marker of her capacity to make a decision for herself.

At age 67, most of the consistently important elements of her kaleidoscopic pattern have their place—spiritual life and photography at the center, friendship present but secondary, children at the periphery, with music (a center of her identity at age 43) and the quest for intimate relationships (which had dominated her sense of self at age 56) barely discernible in the pattern.

Identity is always in motion. For Donna, enthusiasm, conscientiousness, and openness to experience have been the dynamic forces that have lighted and moved her kaleisoscopic patterns, even though it took a long time for a consistent and satisfying arrangment to emerge. And Donna's story is not yet finished; I don't know where she might find herself years hence. Perhaps she will not be able to do the work she wants to do and will give it up; perhaps she will find a new partner and organize her life around him or her. These elements are present in her kaleidoscopic picture and could well reappear as prominent.

* * *

Of the nine women I classified as Drifters/ Diffusions at the end of college, eight remained so into late midlife. Of all the groups, they were most likely to experience regret (in their mid-50s) and to continue to feel that they hadn't yet settled on who or how they wished to be in their lives. As a group, the Drifters were among the most talented and privileged women I followed. More than half of the women in this group were attending a highly respected private women's college, which means that they came from families wealthy enough to send them there and were academically outstanding enough to be accepted. Their "drifting" in college was not for lack of talent or skill or resources. They were women of promise, who had the opportunity to choose their future.

Their college-age interviews revealed an inner world that didn't hold together, that was made up of pieces that didn't seem to fit, and a lack of concern about this inner fragmentation. The sense of their childhood or their parents was distant from them, irrelevant. But in abolishing their past, these women obliterated a core part of themselves, leaving only a space, an emptiness, a receptacle to be filled with whatever they might find. They were living "free"— either out of choice or anger. Few at this time could say much about what their parents were like. Their parents seemed to be shadow figures, ghosts without qualities, there only to be fled. For many different reasons, they were unable to identify with their parents or make use of them as templates for their own identities.

Over time, the Drifters' narratives, particularly of their early lives, shifted dramatically, which makes it impossible to say which early experiences may have been formative. Their development remains shrouded because, at each point in their lives that I have talked to them, they tell a different version of their histories. Even the facts of their early lives are transformed as they experience themselves differently at different phases of their lives.

The identity problem is difficult for them because they seem to internalize so little that felt good from their childhood, some good that felt foundational. Thus, they were starting from a blank slate, hoping that good things for them would appear in the future. From what I knew of them in college, the task before them seemed to be inventing themselves rather than reshaping bit by bit. With so much possible in the absence of valued existing structure, nothing was very realizable. With so little that felt solid taken in from the past, the building blocks were not there. The Drifters got stuck in the sense that they *could* be anything at all. There was little inside that felt fundamental or core against which to match or test external possibility. Being one thing or another, believing this philosophy or following that religion, all were equally likely. "Instinct" and "feeling" seemed to be reasonable sources of action. As a result, the self remained at the mercy of inner impulses and external claims.

These dramatic fluctuations in the kaleidoscopic pattern, typical of the Drifters, are counterpoints to the steady, slowly evolving identity that is seen in those who have been Pathmakers. For them, identity shifts in the sense that the kaleidoscope pieces rearrange or enlarge under the necessity of the developmental tasks of intimacy and generativity—and these shifts take place gradually. With these people, who have well-formulated identities, we are more likely to see the pattern as a whole at any given time rather than disconnected pieces that constitute the pattern.

The function of both identity and narrative is the integration of parts into a recognizable, reasonably coherent, relatively stable whole. It is perhaps when this synthetic work is compromised, as I showed in Donna's case, that we can best appreciate the complexity of the integrative process. The identity structure is largely unconscious and cannot be narrated directly, but it is manifest in the conscious integration of the various aspects of experience including roles, values, wishes, beliefs, feelings, worldview, and relational ties. Identity as a psychological structure relates the disparate parts of the self into some more or less coherent organization, leaving room for different kinds of self-experience, even contradictory ones. The stability of identity, which grows over time, reflects a relatively secure and affirmed awareness of a place in the world that is recognized by others; at the same time, identity changes. All of the major longitudinal studies have wrestled with the difficulties of keeping in focus simultaneously both stability and change (Block, 1971; Elder, 1974; Vaillant, 1995, 2008). Yet that is the nature of human life: People change and they also stay the same. The kaleidoscope metaphor is a way of containing both at the same time.

When we study identity narratively, preserving its kaleidoscopic, patterned nature, we see identity in its essential, dynamic form. We can then witness its multiplicity and multilayeredness (some notable studies that do this are Gregg, 2007; Halbertal & Koren, 2006; and Singer, 2016) and its place in the later stages of adult development. As Bakhtin (1981) detailed, the self is unfinalizable; it is continually evolving.

REFERENCES

Bakhtin, M. (1981). *The dialogical imagination: Four essays.* Austin: University of Texas Press.

Bamberg, M. (2006). Stories: Big or small: Why do we care? *Narrative Inquiry, 16*(1), 139–147.

Bamberg, M., & Georgakopoulou, A. (2008). Small stories as a new perspective in narrative and identity analysis. *Text & Talk: An Interdisciplinary Journal of Language, Discourse and Communication Studies, 28*(3), 377–396.

Block, J. (1971). *Lives through time.* Berkeley, CA: Bancroft.

Brockmeier, J., & Carbaugh, D. (2001). *Narrative and identity: Studies in autobiography, self, and culture.* Amsterdam, The Netherlands: Benjamins.

Bruner, J. (1990). *Acts of meaning: Four lectures on mind and culture* (reprint ed.). Cambridge, MA: Harvard University Press.

Cohler, B. J. (1982). Personal narrative and the life course. In P. Baltes & O. G. Brim (Eds.), *Life span development and behavior* (Vol. 4, pp. 205–241). New York: Academic Press.

Elder, G. H., Jr. (1974). *Children of the Great Depression: Social change in life experience.* Chicago: University of Chicago Press.

Erikson, E. H. (1962). *Young man Luther: A study in psychoanalysis and history.* New York: Norton.

Erikson, E. H. (1968). *Identity and the life cycle.* New York: Norton.

Erikson, E. H. (1969). *Gandhi's truth: On the origins of militant nonviolence.* New York: Norton.

Erikson, E. H., Erikson, J. M., & Kivnick, H. Q. (1989). *Vital involvement in old age.* New York: Norton.

Fadjukoff, P., Kokko, K., & Pulkkinen, L. (2010). Changing economic conditions and identity formation in adulthood. *European Psychologist, 15,* 293–303.

Giddens, A. (1991). *Modernity and self-identity: Self and society in the Late Modern Age.* Stanford, CA: Stanford University Press.

Gregg, G. S. (2007). *Culture and identity in a Muslim society.* New York: Oxford University Press.

Habermas, T., & Bluck, S. (2000). Getting a life: The emergence of the life story in adolescence. *Psychological Bulletin, 126,* 748–769.

Habermas, T., & Köber, C. (2015). Autobiographical reasoning is constitute for narrative identity: The role of the life story for personal continuity. In K. McLean & M. Syed (Eds.), *The Oxford handbook of identity development* (pp. 149–166). New York: Oxford University Press.

Halbertal, T., & Koren, I. (2006). Between "being" and "doing": Conflict and coherence in the identity formation of gay and lesbian orthodox Jews. In D. P. McAdams, R. Josselson, & A. Lieblich (Eds.), *Identity and story: Creating self in narrative* (pp. 37–61). Washington, DC: American Psychological Association.

Hammack, P. (2015). Theoretical foundations of identity. In K. McLean & M. Syed (Eds.), *The Oxford handbook of identity development* (pp. 11–33). New York: Oxford University Press.

Helson, R., & Roberts, B. W. (1994). Ego development and personality change in adulthood. *Journal of Personality and Social Psychology, 66*(5), 911–920.

Helson, R., Soto, C. J., & Cate, R. A. (2006). From young adulthood through the middle ages. In In D. K. Mroczek & T. D. Little (Eds.), *Handbook of personality development* (pp. 337–352). Mahwah, NJ: Erlbaum.

Hermans, H. (1995). Voicing the self: From information processing to dialogical interchange. *Psychological Bulletin, 119*(1), 31–50.

Hoare, C. (2001). *Erikson on development in adulthood: New insights from the unpublished papers.* New York: Oxford University Press.

Jespersen, K., Kroger, J., & Martinussen, M. (2013). Identity status and ego development: A meta-analysis. *Identity, 13*(3), 228–241.

Josselson, R. (1987). *Finding herself: Pathways to identity development in women.* San Francisco: Jossey-Bass.

Josselson, R. (1996). *Revising herself: The story of women's identity from college to midlife.* New York: Oxford University Press.

Josselson, R. (2009). The present of the past: Dialogues with memory over time. *Journal of Personality, 77*(3), 647–668.

Josselson, R. (2017). *Paths to fulfillment: Women's search for meaning and identity.* New York: Oxford University Press.

Kroger, J. (1993). Identity and context: How the identity statuses choose their match. In R. Josselson & A. Lieblich (Eds.), *The narrative study of lives* (Vol. 1, pp. 130–162). Thousand Oaks, CA: SAGE.

Kroger, J. (1995). The differentiation of "firm" and "developmental" foreclosure identity statuses: A longitudinal study. *Journal of Adolescent Research, 10,* 317–337.

Kroger, J. (2007). Why is identity achievement so elusive? *Identity: An International Journal of Theory and Research, 7*(4), 331–348.

Kroger, J. (2015). Identity development in adulthood: The move toward "wholeness." In K. McLean & M. Syed (Eds.), *The Oxford handbook of identity development* (pp. 65–80). New York: Oxford University Press.

Kroger, J., & Marcia, J. E. (2011). The identity statuses: Origins, meanings, and interpretations. In S. J. Schwartz, K. Luyckx, & V. L. Vignoles (Eds.), *Handbook of identity theory and research* (pp. 31–53). New York: Springer.

Kroger, J., Martinussen, M., & Marcia, J. E. (2010). Identity status change during adolescence and young adulthood: A meta-analysis. *Journal of Adolescence, 33*(5), 683–698.

Lieblich, A., & Josselson, R. (2013). Identity and narrative as root metaphors of personhood. In J. Martin & M. Bickhard (Eds.), *The psychology of personhood: Philosophical, historical, social-development and narrative perspectives* (pp. 203–222). New York: Cambridge University Press.

Marcia, J. E. (1966). Development and validity of ego-identity status. *Journal of Personality and Social Psychology, 3,* 551–558.

Marcia, J. E. (2006). Ego identity and personality disorders. *Journal of Personality Disorders, 20*(6), 577–596.

Marcia, J. (2007). Theory and measure: The identity status interview. In M. Watzlawik & A. Born (Eds.), *Capturing identity: Quantitative and qualitative methods* (pp. 1–14). Lanham, MD: University Press of America.

Marcia, J. E. (2010). Life transitions and stress in the context of psychosocial development. In T. W. Miller (Ed.), *Handbook of stressful transitions across the lifespan* (pp. 19–34). New York: Springer Science + Business Media.

Marcia, J. (2014). From industry to integrity. *Identity, 14*(3), 165–176.

Marcia, J., & Josselson, R. (2013). Eriksonian personality research and its implications for psychotherapy. *Journal of Personality, 81*(6), 617–629.

Marcia, J. E., Waterman, A. S., Matteson, D. R., Archer, S. L., & Orlofsky, J. L. (1993). *Ego identity: A handbook for psychosocial research.* New York: Springer-Verlag.

McAdams, D. P. (1993). *The stories we live by: Personal myths and the making of the self.* New York: Guilford Press.

McAdams, D. P. (2001a). *The person: An integrated introduction to personality psychology* (3rd ed.). Fort Worth, TX: Harcourt.

McAdams, D. P. (2001b). The psychology of life stories. *Review of General Psychology, 5*(2), 100–122.

McAdams, D. P., Josselson, R., & Lieblich, A. (2006). Introduction. In D. P. McAdams, R. Josselson, & A. Lieblich (Eds.), *Identity and story: Creating self in narrative* (pp. 3–11). Washington, DC: American Psychological Association.

McAdams, D., & McLean, K. (2013). Narrative identity. *Current Directions in Psychological Science, 22*(3), 233–238.

McAdams, D. P., & Zapata-Gietl, C. (2015). Three strands of identity development across the human life course: Reading Erik Erikson in full. In K. McLean & M. Syed (Eds.), *The Oxford handbook of identity development* (pp. 81–97). New York: Oxford University Press.

Mitchell, V., & Helson, R. (1990). Women's prime of life: Is it the 50s? *Psychology of Women Quarterly, 14*(4), 451–470.

Polkinghorne, D. E. (1988). *Narrative knowing and the human sciences.* Albany: State University of New York Press.

Randall, W. (2014). *The stories we are: An essay on self-creation* (2nd ed.). Toronto: University of Toronto Press.

Singer, J. A. (2004). Narrative identity and meaning making across the adult lifespan: An introduction. *Journal of Personality, 72*(3), 437–460.

Singer, J. A. (2016). *The proper pirate: Robert Louis Stevenson's quest for identity.* New York: Oxford University Press.

Skoe, E. E., & Marcia, J. E. (1991). A measure of care-based morality and its relation to ego identity. *Merrill-Palmer Quarterly, 37*(2), 289–304.

Smith, J. A., Harré, R., & Van Langenhove, L. (Eds.). (1995). *Rethinking methods in psychology.* London: SAGE.

Spence, D. P. (1984). *Narrative truth and historical truth: Meaning and interpretation in psychoanalysis.* New York: Norton.

Stephen, J., Fraser, E., & Marcia, J. E. (1992). Moratorium-achievement (Mama) cycles in lifespan identity development: Value orientations and reasoning system correlates. *Journal of Adolescence, 15,* 283–300.

Stewart, A. J., & Ostrove, J. M. (1998). Women's personality in middle age: Gender, history, and midcourse corrections. *American Psychologist, 53*(11), 1185–1194.

Vaillant, G. E. (1995). *The wisdom of the ego.* Cambridge, MA: Harvard University Press.

Vaillant, G. E. (2008). *Aging well: Surprising guideposts to a happier life from the landmark study of adult development.* Boston: Little, Brown.

CHAPTER 27

The Dialogic Development of Personality

Narrative, Culture, and the Study of Lives

Phillip L. Hammack
Erin E. Toolis

A personality is a full Congress of orators and pressure-groups, of children, demagogues, communists, isolationists, war-mongers, mugwumps, grafters, log-rollers, lobbyists, Caesars and Christs, Machiavels and Judases, Tories and Promethean revolutionists. And a psychologist who does not know this in himself [*sic*] . . . should be encouraged to make friends . . . with the various members of his [*sic*] household.

—MURRAY (1940, pp. 160–161)

The Story of Three Palestinian Breakfasts[1]

The strong Mediterranean sun starts to creep into shuttered windows in the cramped village house. The sound of roosters and diesel engines signal the start to another day in Qadas,[2] a small Palestinian village in the Israeli-occupied West Bank. A woman in her 60s, wearing a colorful green *hijab* and accompanying dress that is distinct to the village, stands above a pot of dark, rich, cardamom-infused coffee. She watches carefully as it starts to bubble. It must be removed quickly so as not to overcook it and spoil it for the American

guest seated at the table. Her 16-year-old daughter, Adara, finishes frying the eggs—fresh from the family chicken coop just outside the kitchen door—in a generous amount of olive oil, produced from the family's nearby olive grove, poured from a jug. The American man watches intently, studying every detail of the women and the meal preparation. The older woman looks up and notices. "*Inshallah* [God willing], we will get through this," she says, referring to the recent spate of Israeli military incursions that have made it difficult for the family to leave the village. "Maybe Hamas will save us," she adds. The man looks at Adara and locks eyes, just for a moment. She quickly returns her gaze to the eggs. Neither woman will sit with the American man until the men of the house arrive and are seated at the table.

Three days later in Israeli-occupied East Jerusalem, the same American man sits at the kitchen table with 16-year-old Mohammed as his mother, her striking black hair flowing (she only wears the *hijab* when outside the home), stands above

[1]Ethnographic accounts described in this chapter are from a study conducted by Phillip L. Hammack in Israel and the occupied Palestinian territories from 2003 to 2007. All names of research participants are pseudonyms.

[2]Qadas is the name of a Palestinian village that was destroyed in the 1948 Arab–Israeli War. It is used here as a pseudonym for a Palestinian village in the Israeli-occupied West Bank.

465

the electric kettle, waiting for the water to boil. She fills the three cups of Nescafe instant coffee. Over Kellogg's Corn Flakes and instant coffee, the three talk about the family's long connection to Jerusalem and Mohammed's aspirations for university study in engineering. Talk turns inevitably to politics. The American man listens intently. Mohammed's mother looks down at the table in defeat. Mohammed closes the conversation, "One day, we'll have our country back." The American man and the mother lock eyes.

One week later and a short train ride up Israel's stunning Mediterranean coast, the American man sits at the breakfast table with Sami and his family in Haifa. Sami's father stands proudly over the meal he spent the previous night preparing. The beans for fresh *hummus* and *foul* have been soaking ever since. Sami's mother prepares the Arabic coffee and a pot of fresh mint tea. Her hair is short, her eye liner a stunning green that draws attention to her strong, nurturing eyes. There is laughter and warmth. There is optimism. A crucifix and liquor cabinet are in sight just next to the piano in the next room, reminding the American man he is in a Christian home. "He must study to become a doctor," Sami's mother says, with the warm but dominant energy she always exudes. "It's the only way. They can't discriminate against him [for being Arab] if he's a doctor." Sami and the American man lock eyes.

The stories of three different Palestinian breakfasts and their casts of characters challenge monolithic notions of "culture" as a concept that indexes patterns or habits broadly shared by members of a collective identity. These distinct breakfasts reveal that even the most mundane of daily activities—breakfast with a foreign visitor—vary according to other salient indicators of identity. Adara, Mohammed, and Sami inhabit profoundly different social and political worlds based on gender, religion, social class, and locality. *Yet they are all Palestinian.* Mohammed is angry and fatalistic, as one might expect of a young Palestinian Muslim during the second *intifada* (uprising), yet his family's simple breakfast more closely resembles those experienced by the American guest in the homes of *Jewish Israelis.* Sami and his family are happy and optimistic, yet they are deeply aware of their subordinate status as a minority in an ethnonational state.

The stories of Adara, Mohammed, and Sari are shaped not just by their membership in a collective social identity as young Palestinians,

inhabiting a context of continued Israeli military occupation or subordinate status. Rather, these three young people are developing their personalities, crafting personal narratives, and making meaning of their social ecologies in a context that commands engagement with multiple, sometimes competing narratives. Adara's village is covered in posters of *shahid* (martyrs) from militant Palestinian groups, resisting Israel's military occupation. She and her family possess green identification cards issued by Israel that prohibit them from entering Israel. Adara has never been to Jerusalem, a journey less than an hour by car. By contrast, Mohammed and his family possess a blue identification card issued by Israel that indicates "permanent resident" status and allows them to travel anywhere in Israel and the occupied Palestinian territories. They take great advantage of this status. Sami and his family are citizens of Israel. They have an Israeli passport that grants them the ability to travel much of the world. These three young people share the same sense of cultural identity, *yet their possibilities for narrative identity development diverge dramatically.* Will Adara ever leave her village? Will Mohammed choose to join the resistance "to get his country back," or will his story be shaped by his mother's fatalism? Will Sami become a doctor and avoid discrimination based on his minority status?

The possibilities of personality development for these young Palestinians highlights Murray's contention that the personality is fundamentally *populated* by a "full Congress of orators," that our personalities appropriate the discourses, ideologies, and cast of characters to which we have been exposed in the course of development. In this chapter, we present a view of narrative, culture, and personality grounded in the *personological* tradition of Henry Murray (1938/2008) and the *person-centered* view of cultural psychology (e.g., Gjerde, 2004; Hammack, 2010a). Our theoretical influences expand to perspectives that emphasize the meaning and significance of *social identity* (e.g., Tajfel & Turner, 1986), *power and subjectivity* (e.g., Foucault, 1982), and *social activity or practice* (e.g., Vygotsky, 1978) as a site in which minds are "produced" (e.g., Mead, 1934) and hence narratives are navigated and negotiated. We view the person as a fundamentally *dialogic* entity (Bakhtin, 1981) whose being is shaped by the *polyphonic* nature of culture (Bakhtin, 1984/1992) and membership in some *verbal-ideological community* (Volosinov, 1929/1973).

Our view of culture, then, is far from static and far from neutral with regard to considerations of social structure. *Culture is a set of practices that creates meaning and coherence through language and shared understanding. The agency presumed to exist in this process is always constrained by social forces of opportunity* (see Hammack & Toolis, 2015, 2016). Power, identity, and meaning are negotiated in the social act, and the history of these acts creates for the person a narrative identity: a story that provides meaning and coherence in the midst of life's inevitable ruptures and discontinuities (Cohler, 1982; McAdams, 1988, 2001, 2011). *Personality,* then, cannot simply be described according to patterns or traits within a person or across people. A complete picture of personality considers the *life story* as "an internalized and evolving structure of the mind—an integrative story about who I am, how I came to be, and where my life may be going" (McAdams & Manczak, 2015, p. 425). McAdams and Pals (2006) conceive of the life story and its cultural particularity as a key component in a "new Big Five" approach to personality. Simply put, *"Personality is (in part) a life story"* (McAdams & Guo, 2017, p. 185, original emphasis).

Understood in their complete form, then, personalities are the stories we construct about ourselves and our lives. They are heavily shaped by *the cultural process*—the socially mediated experience of engagement with master narratives of group history and identity (Hammack, 2008). In the remainder of this chapter, we develop this thesis and explore empirical examples that assume the principles of the uniquely *personological* approach we outline here. We hope to generate new lines of inquiry in personality and social psychology that embody this perspective.

Personality Development as Narrative Engagement: A Framework for the Study of Lives

Adara, Mohammed, and Sami each inhabit distinct social ecologies of development—the underdeveloped village under military occupation (Qadas), the divided and heavily symbolic city at the epicenter of conflict (Jersualem), the peaceful seaside "model of coexistence" (Haifa). If we are to understand the development of these three young personalities, we must consider not just the experiential content of their life stories but also the voices that might populate their personal narratives: parents, teachers,

political leaders, imams, priests, *shahid*. This perspective on personality development considers the *press* created by various social forces and activating particular psychological *needs* of both the individual and the collective (Murray, 1938/2008)—needs for security, recognition, achievement, and the like. To really know Adara, Mohammed, and Sami, we have to know not only their life stories but also how and why these stories provide a sense of meaning, unity, and coherence in the midst of adversity (Cohler, 1991; McAdams, 1990, 1995).

Our framework is anchored in three core assumptions about culture and human development. First, we view culture not as a static concept but rather as a dynamic one characterized chiefly by a *polyphonic set of power-related discourses, always in states of dialogue.* This view of culture allows us to posit the existence of both *master,* or dominant/hegemonic, narratives and *counter,* or resistance, narratives (see Bamberg & Andrews, 2004). Furthermore, this view ascribes primacy to both language and power in ways that capture the dynamism of the culture process.

Second, we view a core social and cognitive task of human development as the construction of a personal narrative of identity that provides meaning and coherence in a complex social world (e.g., McAdams, 2011). Hence, we see the person as embedded in the culture process and as a vehicle for both social reproduction and resistance (e.g., Hammack, 2010b, 2011). Here we see the person as both agentic in response to an inherited social system and matrix of social identities and highly constrained by the way that inherited system has been configured (Hammack & Toolis, 2016). The personal narrative is thus a "document" of a life, even as its construction brings with it implications for the endurance of a particular social structure. (Consider Mohammed's decision to either resist the Israeli occupation through militant resistance or his own personal education and development as an engineer.) *The personal narrative is the momentary product of the culture process.* It tells us about not only the person but also the culture as it dynamically evolves.

Finally, and already implied by our first two assumptions, we view a critical feature of human development as the process of *master narrative engagement* in which the individual, through a social process, is confronted with multiple narratives of history and identity, and makes decisions—conscious or otherwise—

about which to appropriate or assimilate into the personal narrative (Hammack & Cohler, 2009; Hammack & Toolis, 2016). The idea of "engagement" is meant to capture the attunement to a social world of discourse that individuals undertake as they navigate this polyphony of voices. Engagement results in processes of internalization and appropriation that then reveal the endurance of various narratives and ideologies. (Consider the reprise of white nationalism under the United States regime of Donald Trump: Racist discourses internalized and appropriated could then be given a socially legitimate platform with the permission of the leader.) In the remainder of this section, we develop each of these core assumptions in turn.

Culture and the Narrative Ecology of Development

As she walks around Qadas, the quiet Palestinian village, Adara leads a group of children, showing the American visitor all the sights. "This beautiful park here, this was funded through the generosity of Hamas." Posters of the *shahid* hang throughout the village, including in the marquee outside the crumbling movie theater. The year is 2004, and the second Palestinian *intifada* continues. These key components of the material world of Qadas tell a story about Palestinian history and identity. For individuals developing in this particular social ecology, they are a constant reminder that they live in a context of ongoing conflict and armed resistance.

"I believe there should be two states, Israel and Palestine, side by side, respecting one another in peace. I do not believe we should have a religious state, even though I am religious myself." These are the words of Adara when asked specifically about her views on the Israeli–Palestinian conflict. Although the material world of Qadas at first appeared to be strongly oriented toward a *particular* narrative of Palestinian identity—a narrative emphasizing armed resistance, martyrdom, and a religious brand of national identity favored by Hamas—Adara's narrative suggested a different goal for conflict resolution. Although she herself was religious—always covered in a fashionable *hijab,* never alone with the American man in order to respect the taboo against unmarried women and men together—and although Qadas itself was at that time a stronghold for Hamas, Adara's perspective more closely resembled the secular nationalist narrative of Palestinian aspirations promulgated by Fatah, Hamas' political and cultural rival.

The story of Adara and her engagement with a *polyphony* of voices related to the political and cultural nature of contemporary Palestinian identity speaks to our view of culture and narrative. Culture is not best understood as a static set of rituals, practices, or beliefs. Nor is culture simply a matter of material reality, comprised of artifacts. Culture is best understood as a dynamic *process* in which persons and settings co-constitute social, material, and psychological reality through narrative engagement. The stuff of the material world assumes a storied form: Adara's mother wears around her neck the antique key to her ancestors' home in a Palestinian village destroyed in the 1948 war that Palestinians call *al-Nakba* ("the Catastrophe") but Israelis celebrate as their "War of Independence" (Bar-On, 2006; Hammack & Pilecki, 2012; Jawad, 2006). Adara has heard the story time and time again.

It is no coincidence that Adara's life story assumes a tragic form, unlike that of Sami, whose narrative takes that of a classic redemptive one. In Haifa, the place where Sami's family has lived uninterrupted for generations, there are no antique keys or *shahid* posters. In Haifa, Palestinians stroll the beautifully illuminated Ben-Gurion Boulevard at night, smoking cigarettes or eating ice cream. It is rare to see women wearing the *hijab*. The street is lined with upscale cafes, restaurants, and bars. Unmarried men and women mingle.

Our view of culture thus rejects the notion that culture creates "patterns" of meaning among distinct groups (cf. Benedict, 1934), or that culture creates some kind of psychological uniformity in perception or cognition (see Gjerde, 2004). The case of Palestinian identity reveals that members of a shared social identity can diverge considerably in their lived experience and their ideologies with variations in regional or local experience, gender, social class, and religious affiliation. And yet there is a "press" we feel in relation to the needs and experiences of the collective, a psychological experience we may call the *press of culture*.

In Murray's (1938/2008) formulation, the press speaks to an effect that a particular situation exerts upon the person. For young Palestinians, the situation of collective insecurity and lack of independence likely exerts a press to identify strongly with the collective, appropriating some version of nationalist identity into the personal narrative (Hammack, 2010a, 2011). Mohammed is quick to assert the need for armed resistance to Israel's military occupation, even as his educational aspirations suggest his ultimate goal is to escape the region (a taboo move in Palestinian society, since the Israeli–Palestinian conflict is deeply rooted in a battle of demography). Ali, another Muslim Jersualemite Palestinian, espouses strong support for suicide bombers in the second Palestinian *intifada*:

"It makes me happy to see all these Palestinians fighting for their country. Every kind of fighting, suicide bombings too. It's like I am happy and sad because—sad because it's the only way we can fight, and I'm happy because I see Palestinians willing to die for their country. . . . It makes me happy because Israel has a problem."

When asked to lead the call to prayer at a session the next day, Ali admits he is not religious and not capable of such a task.

Young men like Ali and Mohammed are responding to hegemonic narratives of Palestinian identity that, in the early 21st century, inculcated a strong commitment to armed resistance. These young men were highly educated, with little to no political aspirations, and little to no desire to actually participate in political violence. (Indeed, 15 years later, one has emigrated to North America and the other works directly with Jewish Israelis in business.) In their adolescence, they were exposed to a story of Palestinian identity that emphasized historic and contemporary dispossession, the legitimacy of armed resistance, and existential insecurity of the Palestinian people (Hammack, 2010a). *They felt compelled to reproduce this narrative as participants in Palestinian culture.*

Our view of narrative, culture, and human development thus presumes that the person is deeply embedded in a social ecology of development in which *master narratives are constantly circulating,* calling for individual appropriation to secure the reproduction of a given social system, with its particular matrix of power and social identities. It is best, in our view, to think of culture as a dynamic process in which social structures are challenged or reproduced. Culture is an *activity,* not a product (e.g., Gutierrez & Rogoff, 2003; Rogoff, Baker-Sennett, Lacasa, & Goldsmith, 1995). We are participants in the culture process when we engage in social interaction and practice, and the key source of

psychological mediation in this process is *narrative engagement.*

The Personal Narrative as Cultural Product

In his landmark essay on personal narrative and the life course, Bert Cohler (1982) proclaimed, "There are no events or facts regarding lives which are independent of interpretations which are made of them" (p. 228). The personal narrative is not, then, an accounting of the "facts" of one's life. Rather, it is an interpretive document of meaning making at any given point in time. And this document, we suggest, is best viewed as a cultural product itself—an artifact of a life lived at a particular historical moment, in a particular time and place. When viewed as historical artifact, the personal narrative becomes a tool for the cultural psychologist to *access the culture process as it is unfolding.* The stories of Adara, Mohammed, and Sami are not stories about Palestinian culture or identity in any kind of timeless sense. Rather, they are stories of lives in context—in this case, the context of the second Palestinian *intifada.*

Consistent with McAdams's theory of personality, we view the personal narrative (or *life story*) as a key component of personality development (e.g., McAdams, 2011, 2015; McAdams & Guo, 2017; McAdams & Manczak, 2015; McAdams & McLean, 2013; McAdams & Olson, 2010; McAdams & Pals, 2006). The personal narrative is the cognitive creation in which the person makes sense of lived experience in a documentary form, regardless of whether it is formally narrated. The mind is a site in which this personal narrative is always in a state of formation and revision. As Cohler (1982) argued and narrative psychologists have since demonstrated (e.g., Josselson, 2017), the personal narrative has a development. It is a psychological tool for personal meaning making in the face of disruption and discontinuity: Lives are interrupted by losses and unexpected gains—divorces, deaths, births, marriages, conflicts, estrangements. When considered through the lens of society and culture, however, the personal narrative is also a *social* tool.

In his theory of self-presentation and stigma management, Goffman (1963) argued that the *biography* (akin to our view of the personal narrative) is a key tool for *information control.* In basic social interactions, we determine the features of the personal narrative to be shared. Will we admit, in this particular social interaction with a family member with divergent political views, who we voted for in the 2016 U.S. presidential election? Will we admit, in this interaction with a foreigner in a sexually conservative society, that we are gay or lesbian? To the extent that we produce personal narratives in interaction, we participate in the process of social and cultural development itself. If we hide our sexual minority identity, do we tolerate homophobia? If we avoid discussing Trump, do we condone his support for white nationalism? If we disclose our sexual minority status far and wide (as Harvey Milk once insisted), do we participate in the gradual process of social change toward greater acceptance of sexual diversity?

Our point is that the development of a personal narrative—an account of one's life that provides a sense of meaning, coherence, and continuity—is not solely a process for individual psychology. Rather, because the person is always embedded in a multilevel social ecology (e.g., Bronfenbrenner, 1979), the development of a personal narrative is a cultural process that either reproduces or repudiates dominant discourses and ideologies. *The content of our life stories is a document of the culture process.* As such, it calls for close interrogation among social and personality psychologists and other social scientists, *but not as a static product.* The charting of personal narratives over time, using longitudinal, qualitative methods, is vital to the science of personality development.

The Theory of Master Narrative Engagement

The idea of master narrative engagement is that we make meaning of our identities and experiences through dialogue with existing, shared cultural discourses that circulate through speech and cultural artifacts (Hammack & Toolis, 2016). We define a *master narrative* as a dominant discourse that prescribes certain beliefs, values, and behaviors. Although the social realm is *polyphonic*—that is, characterized by competing and often conflicting narratives— master narratives work to reduce this plurality and present themselves as singular, universal, essential, and natural (McLean & Syed, 2016). Most important, they are typically perceived as *compulsory* and thus can be considered hegemonic in relation to the politics of social identities (Hammack & Toolis, 2016). Bakhtin (1984/1992) refers to this phenomenon as *monologism,* in which the ruling class propagates a hegemonic story that portends to be "the ulti-

mate word" in order to maintain the prevailing social order and prevent change.

Individuals must contend with master narratives as they develop their identities. Our framework for this process is informed by cultural–historical activity theory (CHAT), largely based on the work of Bakhtin (1981, 1984/1992, 1990), Volsinov (1929/1973), and Vygotsky (1978). CHAT conceives of human development as fundamentally social, dialogic, and culturally mediated. CHAT's concept of *linguistic mediation* is central to our theory, which posits that language is a symbolic tool that we use to selectively engage with and transform our environment. This theory regards the role of language in human development as central. Vygotsky (1978) theorizes that as infants, children learn about meaning in the material world through everyday social practice with the guidance of a caregiver, using symbols such as pointing and later language to guide their attention.

Early in development, language is primarily an interpersonal process as the child's means of social contact, but eventually it is transformed into an intrapersonal process as *social speech* is internalized or "turned inward" and becomes *inner speech* (Vygotsky, 1978). Speech is critical in the development of higher psychological functions as children use language not just to reflect the world but to guide their activity in the world, thus allowing children to become both the subjects and objects of their own behavior (Vygotsky, 1978). In Vygotsky's (1978) words, "The internalization of socially rooted and historically developed activities is the distinguishing feature of human psychology" (p. 57).

In this view, individuals develop within a verbal–ideological community in constant contact with the language of others (Bakhtin, 1981; Volosinov, 1929/1973). This perspective describes the psychological process of how the outer becomes inner, as we assimilate the speech of others into our own language. The thoughts we think, the identities we construct, the words we utter, and the actions we take are permeated with the meaning of others (Bakhtin, 1981). As such, narrative is not an isolated, individual, mental representation disconnected from the external material world. Rather, we are born into a world already populated with meaning. Bakhtin (2010) refers to this process as *assimilation,* in which we take in the words of others and rework them for our own use. Hence, there is no neat and clean boundary between the psyche and the social; rather, they co-constitute one another in a process of dialectical synthesis. Individuals construct their identities in dialogue with these greater cultural narratives. This process reveals the *dialogic development* of personality.

The process of master narrative engagement is not only fundamentally social but also *political,* with implications for power and status (Hammack & Toolis, 2015, 2016). One of the primary functions of master narratives is to make meaning of social categories. Master narrative engagement theory draws from Tajfel and Turner's (1986) *social identity theory,* which claims that the social categories or groups to which one belongs deeply shape an individual's beliefs, values, norms, and behavior. Social identity theory and the rich line of empirical work it has spawned illustrates the way in which mere categorization into (even arbitrary) social groups can activate ingroup bias, and Tajfel and Turner suggest that individuals are fundamentally motivated to enhance the status of their social identities through various strategies. Social identity theory thus foregrounds notions of power and status in a larger matrix of social categories.

Integrating social identity theory and narrative theory, our perspective highlights the way in which individuals and groups use stories to make meaning of their social category membership and potentially enhance the status of the group. Social identity theory allows us to understand personal narratives as highly variable yet patterned by their cultural, historical, and social location. Thus, the idea of master narrative engagement avoids overdetermining the self and asserts that meaning is dialogic, and that human development happens not *within* people but *between* people (Prawat, 1999; Stetsenko & Arievitch, 2004). This holistic, contextualized approach allows us to transcend dichotomies and to link outer and inner processes, and to examine the intersection of the personal and social (Hammack & Toolis, 2016).

Even as individuals draw from master narratives to make sense of social reality, it is important to acknowledge that this process is characterized by active negotiation, which may involve an appropriation or repudiation of dominant cultural narratives. Here, we highlight the centrality of *engagement* to master narrative engagement theory. We emphasize the dynamic and bidirectional nature of our theory, which helps to explain how meaning is constantly reinterpreted across generations in the face of complex and shifting social and political forces such as globalization and postcolonialism (Bhatia, 2011; Hammack & Pilecki, 2012). Such an approach has implications for social justice by avoiding the dangerous tendency to reify social categories and by illuminating the capacity for collective mobilization and social change (Reicher, 2004). As Vygotsky (1978) argued, this "dialectical materialist approach to analysis of human history" (p. 60) enables us to understand not only how one's context shapes human development but also how humans transform their context.

Personology and Narrative: Epistemology and the Study of Lives

As we have suggested, a notion of culture and personality anchored in the concept of narrative offers us a theoretically rich and nuanced approach to the study of lives in context. It allows us to directly interrogate the "Congress of orators" Murray (1940) once argued comprise personality. How does one implement a uniquely *personological* approach to this issue? How does one rigorously study the dynamic intersection between self and society, realized through an analysis of both master and personal narratives? In this section, we elaborate on the activity of the social scientist who is motivated to take these theoretical notions into the field, into the world of culture.

First, it seems axiomatic that such inquiry best occurs in the field and not in the laboratory. The psychological laboratory as a site of empirical inquiry has always been concerned more with internal rather than external validity, at the cost often of producing knowledge whose value beyond the rarefied setting of the laboratory is suspect (see Moghaddam & Harré, 1982). We do not shun knowledge produced in the laboratory. Rather, we take the position of one of psychological science's founders, Wilhelm Wundt, that psychology seeks to answer different types of questions, some of which are best addressed using the methods of experimental science and others of which are better addressed using the methods of "naturalistic" science. Wundt (1916) famously argued for two distinct branches of psychological science: *experimental* and *cultural* (or *folk*) psychology. Cultural psychology, he suggested, requires the methods of history, anthropology, and the like because it is chiefly concerned with documenting human lives in context (see Danziger, 1983). Matters of sensation, perception, and physiology are the stuff of experimental psychology, in Wundt's vision (e.g., Wundt, 1904, 1907). Later iterations of cultural psychology have emphasized the way in which the empirical task is not to produce universal knowledge but rather to directly interrogate particularity and variability (e.g., Shweder, 1990); that is, the scientist of culture does not produce timeless knowledge but rather serves as a documentarian of a particular social reality and its accompanying lived experience at a specific time and place (see also Gergen, 1973; Mishler, 2004; Sampson, 1978).

Second, the personological approach to narrative and culture is anchored in a *hermeneutic* or *interpretive* epistemology that emphasizes the study of meaning making in context. Here, again, it is useful to briefly visit the history of psychological science. In the late 19th century, a number of great minds sought to carve out a disciplinary identity for psychology. In contrast to the positivist vision of William James (1890), who argued that psychology be considered a "natural science" concerned chiefly with the mechanics of the brain, Wilhelm Dilthey (1894/1977) argued that psychology be viewed as a hermeneutic science concerned with human understanding and meaning making. Dilthey (1923/1988) argued that psychology ought to be considered not a *natural* science but a *human* science, more closely allied with fields such as history and anthropology. This epistemological emphasis is vital to understand, for the positivist quest for universal laws of the mental life necessarily leads us away from the study of *individual persons* and toward the study of *variables* and *aggregates* (see Danziger, 1990; Lamiell, 1987; Shweder, 1973, 1990). Personology privileges a person-centered, *idiographic* (Allport, 1937) approach to the study of individual lives in context, maintaining its lens on the whole person as a being-in-culture (Gjerde, 2004; Hammack, 2010a). Personological analysis thus considers the analytic levels of the person and the setting in tandem.

Psychology's tendency to emulate the natural sciences has predisposed the field to a postpositivist epistemology, with a goal of prediction and the discovery of objective and universal law-based facts, leading to an overreliance on nomothetic, deductive methods (Schiff, 2017). The dominant approach to studying personality has focused on variables rather than persons

(Schiff, 2017). This phenomenon is reflected in the abundance of personality studies on the Big Five personality traits, which necessitate averaging across participants (e.g., McCrae & Costa, 1997; McCrae & Terracciano, 2005; Ozer & Benet-Martínez, 2006; Schmitt, Allik, McCrae, & Benet-Martínez, 2007; Yamagata et al., 2006). When culture is discussed, it is treated as simply another predictor or moderator in the equation—in short, a static independent variable.

Even among narrative scholars, postpositivist approaches to identity and culture are often used to reduce and quantify narrative data so as to aggregate across participants and test hypotheses (e.g., McLean, Wood, & Breen, 2013; Syed & Azmitia, 2008, 2010). In these studies, narrative data are seen as merely "exploratory" or are used to complement quantitative findings (e.g., McLean et al., 2013). McLean and Syed (2016) have even suggested that narrative psychology move away from an interpretive, person-centered paradigm, implying that a postpositivist approach is more scientific and rigorous. We believe this stance is problematic, as it privileges the historically hegemonic paradigm in psychological science (see Sampson, 1978) and fails to appreciate the value of a person-centered, qualitative method in the study of lived experience (Hammack & Toolis, 2016; see also Schiff, 2017).

We contend that the study of personality development, narrative, and culture must attend to four key considerations: *meaning, context, variability,* and *particularity*. First, grounded in Murray's (1938/2008) personological approach, we aim to further psychology as a human science that is primarily concerned with *meaning making* (see also Bruner, 1990). This humanistic approach relies on an interpretive or social constructionist epistemology that conceives of truth as locally, dialogically constructed through social interaction (Gergen, 1985). Such an interpretive approach is rooted in the work of hermeneutic scholars including Heidegger (1962) and Ricouer (1984) and can be traced to Dilthey's (1894/1977) argument to take up *understanding* as the main goal of psychology, rather than the *prediction and control* of human thought and behavior.

In alignment with this humanistic, interpretive epistemology, the personological approach advances an active, dynamic theory of mind, emphasizing purposive, directional activity and self-expression as a major function of personality (Murray, 1938/2008). Murray's personological theory, in which motives play a central role, was significant in rejecting the narrow focus on observable, overt behaviors and the mechanistic conception of the mind espoused during the reign of stimulus–response (S-R) behaviorism, seeking to restore meaning and a focus on internal conscious and unconscious processes to the field of psychology (Epstein, 1979; McAdams, 2008).

> One of the many incongruent representations of reality which have resulted from our fixation on the old stimulus response formula has been the notion of a personality as a more or less inert aggregate of reaction patterns, which requires a stimulus to start it going, instead of conceiving of a matrix of incessant functional processes . . . a brain seething with fantasies, programs, and projects, with tentative goals, expectations, and hopes, with fears and dreads, which lead on to actions which select certain regions and constituents of the environment and which apprehensively avoid others. (Murray & Kluckhohn, 1967, p. 38)

In Murray's (1938/2008) view, the person is not a *tabula rasa* passively written upon by experience, overdetermined by habit or childhood or environmental stimuli, but an imaginative, creative, constantly evolving being navigating conflicting needs and presses, capable of change and growth (Schneidman et al., 1982). Methodologically, this view entails an interrogation of how the person actively and intersubjectively constructs meaning of their/his/her lived experiences (Kral, 2008). As such, our data of interest are the stories or histories as produced by the subject, with the "text" rather than the variable as the main unit of analysis (Dilthey, 1894/1977; see also Ricoeur, 1984). As Murray remarked, "The history of the organism is the organism" (p. 39).

The second key consideration in the personological approach is *context*. While acknowledging the importance of creativity and agency for constructing and transforming self and society, a personological approach to the study of lives is equally characterized by a focus on context, demonstrating a careful balance between attention to agency and structure. Murray (1938/2008) himself argued strongly for the consideration of context, positing that the person cannot be understood in isolation but as "an emergent entity of and in a physical, social, and cultural milieu" (p. 6), illustrating that all persons must be understood as dynamically situ-

ated within a physical and social environment. Although context has been given more attention in recent decades (Mischel, 2004), it is still the case that cultural and historical influences are often neglected in mainstream personality psychology.

The personologist in the field attends to context by carefully examining the influence of macrocultural factors such as social institutions, artifacts, values, and norms when collecting and interpreting participants' stories and histories (Kral, 2008; Murray, 1938/2008; Ratner, 2008; Shweder, 1990). Doing so makes it possible to link individual experience to cultural, historical, and social structures (e.g., Hammack, 2011). Zilber, Tuval-Mashiach, and Lieblich (2008) suggest that there are three spheres of context to consider in understanding life stories: the *intersubjective,* or the immediate relationships in which the narrative is co-constructed; the *social field,* or the sociohistorical structure in which the life is lived; and *master narratives,* or the broad cultural meaning systems that impart form and meaning onto a life story. Analysis of life narratives requires a systematic exploration of themes and their connection to social institutions, cultural concepts, and artifacts (Ratner, 2008). It may also involve the use of ethnographic methods to capture a "thick description" (Geertz, 1973) of participants' lived experience (Shweder, 1996).

It is critical to note that social structures and ideologies impose constraints on an individual's agency (Ratner, 2008). Vygotsky (1926/1997) notes these limitations in writing, "Life becomes creation only when it is finally freed of all the social forms that distort and disfigure it. . . . Not in the narrow confines of his [*sic*] personal life and his [*sic*] own affairs will one become a true creator of the future" (p. 350; cited in Ratner, 2008). As participants are not always aware of the ways in which their narratives shape and are shaped by their historical and cultural context, such an approach often requires utilizing what Josselson (2004) refers to as a "hermeneutics of suspicion." Rather than accept a narrative at its word, relying solely upon a "hermeneutics of faith," the researcher must reflect on the individual's social identities and locations and "decode" or "demystify" elements of the text that may be disguised, distorted, or unsayable (Josselson, 2004; see Hammack & Toolis, 2016).

The third key consideration of the personological approach is *particularity,* which is best addressed with the use of inductive, idiographic methods. Kluckhohn and Murray (1967) observed, "There is uniqueness in each inheritance and uniqueness in each environment, but, more particularly, uniqueness in the number, kinds, and temporal order of critically determining situations encountered in the course of life" (p. 55). The goal of psychology, they argued, should be to understand the ways in which "every man [*sic*] is in certain respects (a) like all other men [*sic*], (b) like some other men [*sic*], and (c) like no other man [*sic*]" (p. 53). Yet psychology has historically privileged questions and methods that aim to discover how every human is like all other humans. As Schiff (2017) observes:

> Placing our emphasis on averages and variables, we ignore the particular. We can talk a lot about what happens to the average individual, but when it comes to talking about you, me, or the person in front of us, there is precious little to say. We can say that on average, these processes are connected in the population. But this is of little value for studying the real world, or confronting real-world problems in which there are no imaginary average individuals but only actual ones. (p. 20)

Multiple critiques have been launched against this tendency to privilege the aggregate in our scientific practice. Rooted in the ideals of the Enlightenment, this approach seeks ever higher levels of abstraction and takes the stories out of the person, severing meaning from context and social position (Schiff, 2017). In treating individuals as interchangeable, we risk losing sight of our subject matter (Epstein, 1979; Runyan, 1983). Nomothetic (i.e., concerned with aggregates and general laws; see Allport, 1937, 1962) research often lacks reproducibility or temporal stability, frequently failing to produce generalizable, replicable results (Open Science Collaboration, 2015). Furthermore, traditional laboratory studies are often decontextualized and lack ecological validity (Epstein, 1979; Moghaddam & Harré, 1982). While it is important to conduct research to understand universals and groups, if psychology aims to be able to truly understand patterns *within a particular person's lived experience* (which, we argue, it should), it is critical that we move beyond a trait-based or variable-centered psychology that aggregates across people and strips individuals of context to a *person-centered* psychology that takes the life history as its "long unit" of analysis (Gjerde, 2004; Hammack, 2010a; Murray, 1938/2008; Smith, 2005; Thorne & Nam, 2009).

This humanizing, holistic approach restores the person to psychology.

Personology's emphasis on particularity points to our final key methodological consideration: attention to cultural *variability*. If we are to take difference seriously and avoid the dangers of overgeneralization, it is critical that psychological research is conducted with diverse samples. As Henrich, Heine, and Norenzayan (2010) and Arnett (2008) have observed, the overwhelming majority of psychological research continues to be conducted with WEIRD (individuals from Western, educated, industrialized, rich, and democratic nations) samples, which are highly unrepresentative of most of the world's population. Psychology's historical tendency to conduct research for and with a privileged subsection of the population, and to eschew considerations of history, culture, race, sexuality, gender, and class, has harmed the discipline and society by limiting our understanding of the fullness of humanity and producing knowledge that supports the status quo (Gone, 2011; Pickren, 2009; Prilleltensky, 1989). We argue that the master narrative or "monologism" of positivism and universalism in our own field has come at a cost—reduction, the erasure of difference and variability, the neglect of resistance (Hammack, 2018; Haslam & Reicher, 2012; Reicher, 2004), and the displacement and decontextualization of meaning (see also Schiff, 2017). By using inductive, interpretive tools with diverse samples, a person-centered qualitative approach to psychological inquiry can help to disrupt this master narrative and contribute to a more pluralist, inclusive, liberatory research agenda (Gone, 2011). Bhatia (2018) has called for the use of interpretive methods to *decolonize* psychology, proposing "an alternative psychology that goes beyond the mechanistic, universalizing, essentializing, and ethnocentric dimensions that make up the hegemony of Euro-American psychological science."

In summary, our approach to the study of the person in culture is grounded in an interpretive epistemology and calls for methods that are sensitive to meaning, context, particularity, and variability. We do not claim that the type of knowledge this approach produces is somehow "superior" to that produced in the psychological laboratory and anchored in a positivist or postpositivist epistemology. We seek to explicitly avoid establishing new hierarchies in the knowledge production industry. Rather, we argue that the epistemology and methodology we advocate is ideally suited to the *question* of how persons and settings are co-constituted through narrative. Hence a more holistic science of personality development benefits from inclusion (and legitimation) of empirical inquiry grounded in the personological tradition.

Personological Inquiry on Narrative and Culture

Although nomothetic, variable-centered, decontextualized methods continue to dominate mainstream psychology, there is a growing body of narrative scholarship that exemplifies the study of the whole person, with attention to meaning, context, particularity, and cultural variability. This literature explores how individuals make sense of their identities in dialogue with broader cultural meaning systems. In this section, we briefly review this literature.

Collective and Personal Narratives

The first set of studies we review has broadly examined the relationship between the form and content of individual life stories and narratives that circulate at the collective level—whether they be about history or national identity. A leader in psychology's "narrative turn," McAdams's theoretical approach to narrative and culture conceives of an agentic storyteller who slowly and deliberately crafts a story of self by selecting from a "menu" of cultural scripts, images, and characters (e.g., McAdams, 2001, 2015; McAdams & Olson, 2010; McAdams & Pals, 2006). Personal narratives, it stands to reason, can often mirror collective narratives in both form and content. For example, McAdams's (2006) research on the narratives of generative U.S. adults explored the ways in which the structure and content of their stories were shaped by the dominant cultural narrative of the "American Dream." His findings demonstrated that the language of *redemption,* rooted in cultural values of autonomy, individual achievement, and progress, was reflected in participants' tendency to structure their life stories in an ascending or descent-and-gain pattern (from bad to good; see Lieblich, Tuval-Mashiach, & Zilber, 1998), thereby granting a positive meaning to suffering and life challenges. McAdams (2006) demonstrated the way in which this language is anchored in canonical cultural texts and historical figures in U.S. history, thus high-

lighting the co-constitution of persons and cultures through life-story construction.

In a dramatically different cultural context (i.e., Israel and Palestine) with individuals at a much earlier point in their development (i.e., adolescence), Hammack (2011) revealed a similar link between dominant stories of the collective and the construction of personal narratives. Life stories collected during the second Palestinian *intifada* (2000–2005) suggested that Jewish Israelis tended to construct personal narratives that assumed a redemptive form that mirrored the national narrative of Israel as a foil to Jewish identity in Europe and to the devastation of the Holocaust in particular (Hammack, 2009, 2011). By contrast, life stories of Palestinians assumed a tragic or contaminated form that mirrored the national Palestinian narrative of historic loss and dispossession, as well as fatalism about possibilities for independence (Hammack, 2010a, 2011). Illustrating *particularity* and *variability* among members of a collective identity, Hammack's research revealed the way in which Israelis and Palestinians appropriated thematic content that indicated within-group heterogeneity. For example, he found that some young Palestinians appropriated a master narrative of Palestinian identity grounded in secular nationalism (the foundational ideology of Palestinian nationalism), while others appropriated a narrative of religious nationalism that had become increasingly popular during the second *intifada* (Hammack, 2010a, 2011). The life stories of Palestinian citizens of Israel also demonstrated considerable variability, as youth engaged with diverse narratives depending on factors such as religious identity and local ecology of development (Hammack, 2010c, 2011). This research reveals the way in which personal narratives appropriate content of master narratives, but in a manner that illustrates the polyphonic nature of discourse (Bakhtin, 1984/1992).

Gregg's (2007, 2012, 2013) interviews with young adults in Morocco similarly reveal variability in the ways in which individuals engage with collective narratives in a polyphonic manner in the course of their personality development. His findings demonstrate how participants navigated between competing dominant narratives of "modernity" imposed by Western, colonial influences and dominant narratives of "tradition" imparted by parents and religious teachings. His interviewees shifted between multiple, often contradictory identities, which they integrated through the reconfiguration of key symbols and metaphors (Gregg, 2012). Gregg (2013) linked this internal multiplicity to power relations within a globalizing, postcolonial context, stating, "The duality of identity discourses in the Moroccan narratives clearly represents an internalization of the power differential between the Western societies that colonized North Africa and the North Africans who remain 'backwards' and poor by comparison to Europe" (p. 96). This analysis complicates the conception of culture as monolithic and uniform, critiquing simplistic contrasts between collectivist and individualist cultures. Importantly, it integrates consideration of power and discourse into personal narrative construction (Gjerde, 2004).

Narrative research with urban Indian youth by Bhatia (2018) also demonstrates the variable and inherently political nature of self and culture as understood through individuals' lived experiences, rather than through an essentializing Eurocentric lens. Bhatia explicated the ways in which Indian youth constructed their identities within the rapidly shifting cultural context of globalization and neoliberalization. His analysis employed the concept of ventriloquation (Valsiner, 2000) to illuminate the ways that workers in newly emerging call centers create a "third position" to navigate tensions between newly circulating narratives of growing autonomy and Westernized conceptions of self and work, and traditional cultural scripts and the desire to maintain their "Indianness." Like the theory of master narrative engagement (Hammack, 2011), the concept of ventriloquation sheds light on the meaning of personal narratives by linking them to larger social and cultural values and concerns. Bhatia's analysis illustrates how youth confront the inherited meaning systems of previous generations and colonial meaning systems introduced by globalization in making sense of their identities and social locations, in ways that both reproduce and challenge the social order. By attending to cultural variability in psychological processes, Bhatia's work points to the ways in which an inductive, person-centered inquiry can help to expose many often-studied, taken-for-granted psychological concepts (e.g., the individual, autonomous, neoliberal self) as cultural constructs rather than universals.

Researchers have also examined the way in which individual narratives are linked to collective narratives of historical trauma, as illustrated by narrative studies of Holocaust survivors.

In interviews conducted by Schiff, Skilingstead, Archibald, Arasim, and Peterson (2006), Holocaust survivors demonstrated remarkable stability in the retelling of narratives over time, suggesting that stories of identity serve to connect the past to the present and provide a sense of self-continuity. In another study with Holocaust survivors, Schiff, Noy, and Cohler (2001) examined the ways in which participants integrated the stories of others into their own life narratives. These "collected stories" helped participants to locate their lives in relation to others and to mark their cultural and historical context, highlighting the intersection between the collective and the individual. Personological approaches thus uncover the way in which individuals make meaning of historical trauma, sometimes appropriating narratives that are salient at the collective level.

Cultural and historical context shapes not only the *how* and *why* particular narratives are told, but *if* and *when* such narratives are told. Lieblich's (2014a) life-story interviews with two separate groups of aged Israeli Jewish adults examined the historical and cultural factors that shaped the meaning made of their experiences, as well as their willingness to share their life stories. In the first study, conducted with survivors from a *kibbutz* devastated by the 1948 Arab–Israeli War, participants were highly motivated to share their life stories. For these adults, who were highly educated, religious, and born in the territory that became Israel in 1948, the past was given meaning by a shared desire to preserve the historical memory of their community and by beliefs in God's will and the fate of the Jewish people (Lieblich, 2007, 2014a). In the second study, involving seaside community members who identified as working-class immigrants living in Israel, participants were much less willing to construct life stories and focused more on the present (Lieblich, 2014a, 2014b). The richly contextualized narratives presented in Lieblich's research demonstrate the ways in which participants' willingness to construct life narratives, and the meaning made of life experiences, were shaped by a host of social, developmental, cultural, religious, and historical factors related to collective narratives.

Narrative and Social Identity: Gender and Sexual Identity

Another set of studies that exemplifies the personological approach to narrative and culture documents the way in which individuals engage with narratives of social categories related to gender and sexuality. Josselson's (1996, 2017) research on American women's identities explores the retelling of narratives as women grow and change over time. Her study was originally motivated by the observation that identity development research has often neglected the lived experiences of women, pointing to the danger of obscuring group differences—especially for marginalized groups—that has historically accompanied the pursuit of uniform, universal psychological laws. Josselson (2017) has conducted interviews with a cohort of women every 10 years for the past 35 years, beginning when they were seniors in college. Her study displays the strength of a personological approach—the ability to holistically examine the multiplicity and evolution of identity *within* a single life (Josselson, 2009). By examining each woman's life in cultural and historical context, Josselson's (1996) analysis revealed the complexity, diversity, and nonlinearity of women's stories, which failed to fit neatly into androcentric psychological models such as Erikson's (1959) traditional stage theory.

Person-centered narrative inquiry has also been used to better understand how men negotiate their gender identities in dialogue with dominant narratives of masculinity. White's (2006a, 2006b, 2006c) research on the narratives of feminist-identified, African American men examined the ways in which participants rejected master narratives of hegemonic masculinity and instead appropriated feminist discourses and ideologies, creating "new" masculine identities characterized by equity, nonviolence, and open-mindedness. In a similar vein, Hurtado and Sinha (2008, 2016) investigated how young, feminist Latino men engaged with master narratives of masculinity and manhood, and the concept of *machismo* in particular, in constructing their identities and experiences. Their analyses probed the plurality of Latino men's experiences and the ways in which their intersecting social identities, including cultural background, race, social class, and sexuality, shaped their meaning-making processes. This research highlights the merit of emphasizing *particularity* and *context* in psychological processes by uncovering the multidimensional and intersectional nature of identity, showing how individuals are shaped by their unique social location.

In his analysis of memoirs of gay men writing over a 60-year period, Cohler (2007) found

that the thematic content of personal narratives varied across generations. Integrating this analysis with a study of young sexual- and gender-identity minorities, Hammack and Cohler (2011) link the thematic content of life stories with the social policy context related to sexual and gender diversity during critical periods of development. For example, men who experienced early adulthood in the 1950s integrated themes of shame, stigma, and negative encounters with mental health professionals, mirroring the cultural and political context of criminalization and extreme pathologization of homosexuality of the era. The narratives of these men contained many sequences of "contamination" (McAdams & Bowman, 2001) on account of the hostile social context, redeemed only by immersion into the sexual-minority community. By contrast, men who experienced early adulthood in the 1990s integrated themes of resilience through "coming out" young (typically in high school) and an increasing sense of "normality" with regard to life-course possibilities. Youth experiencing early adulthood in the late 2000s revealed an especially dynamic range of narrative engagement, with some internalizing the redemptive storyline of sexual-minority identity (i.e., "struggle and success" through coming out; see Cohler & Hammack, 2007), while others eschewed traditional sexual-minority labels, constructing "emancipation" narratives from the perceived constraints of prior labels (Cohler & Hammack, 2007; Hammack & Cohler, 2011; see also Davis, 2015; Hammack, Thompson, & Pilecki, 2009; Westrate & McLean, 2010). This line of research highlights the way in which human development is bound not only by the particularity of *place* and the "menu" of cultural scripts in a given setting (McAdams & Pals, 2006) but also the particularity of *time*, as membership in a generation-cohort appears to impact the way in which sexual minorities construct personal narratives. This temporal contingency has implications not only for identity development but also for health, as gay men's understanding of health has historically been shaped by the trauma of the AIDS epidemic and its disproportionate impact on them (e.g., Hammack, Frost, Meyer, & Pletta, 2018).

Because a narrative approach allows scholars to integrate multiple levels of analysis, narrative research is well positioned not only to understand the ways in which context and social structures affect individual lives but also to change these social structures (Frost, 2018;

Frost & Ouellette, 2004). Frost (2011) employed a narrative approach to explore the relationship stories of 99 U.S. adults in same-sex relationships, examining the meaning-making strategies used by participants to negotiate the relationship between stigma and intimacy. Frost's analysis explicated the variety of meaning-making strategies used by participants to frame the impact of stigma on their romantic relationships, ranging from constructions of stigma as having a contaminating effect to stigma as a generative experience that strengthened the bond between partners. This analysis exemplifies a contextualized approach by considering the role played by cultural scripts about sexuality, as well as social structures such as marriage laws, in the construction of participants' narratives. Furthermore, this line of research puts forth a case for the utility of narrative evidence to inform policy decisions and contribute to efforts for social change (Frost, 2018).

The Politics of Narrative

How individuals engage with and appropriate discourse related to specific political events provides a window into the course of social and political change (see Hammack & Pilecki, 2012). Some researchers have studied narratives of political activists to examine this process. In interviews with aging British activists, for example, Andrews (1991) examined how individuals made sense of their lives in regards to their lifelong political commitment. This research was conducted in the vein of psychology's interpretive turn, seeking not generalizability or universal laws, but to construct rich biographical sketches of each participant's whole life course, understood in relation to cultural narratives about aging (Andrews, 1991). Andrews (2007) has also examined the stories of antiwar activists in the United States, revolution leaders in East Germany in the 1990s (Andrews, 1997, 1998), and individuals who testified in South Africa's Truth and Reconciliation Commission (Andrews, 1999, 2003). Andrews's case studies explore the intersection between personal meaning and circulating collective discourses, investigating how life stories shape and are shaped by the particular context in which they occur (Andrews, 2007).

Similarly, Grabe and Dutt (2015; Dutt & Grabe, 2014; Grabe, 2017) studied the narratives of women engaged in political movements

to understand the psychosocial processes by which marginalized individuals resist oppression and create social change. In one study, Dutt and Grabe (2014) conducted an idiographic narrative analysis on the lives of three women from diverse cultural and geographic backgrounds archived in the Global Feminisms Project, including Grace Lee Boggs of the United States, Matilde Lindo of Nicaragua, and D. Sharifa of India. In their analysis, they examine each woman's unique experiences and trajectory in context, while highlighting similar themes in how women broadly engaged with marginalized identity statuses, developed critical consciousness, and sustained a commitment to social justice. Grabe (2017) presents full *testimonios* of women involved in an autonomous movement in Nicaragua to explore participants' development of critical consciousness and identities as "citizen subjects" who mobilize for liberation. By attending to individual meaning-making processes, this work illuminates the voices and agency of marginalized women in constructing counternarratives and working to create societal change.

Dutta's research utilizes a narrative approach to examine how ethnic conflict shapes people's everyday lives, feelings of belonging, and social identities. Dutta's (2015) autoethnography provides a nuanced, rich, embodied narrative account of her particular lived experiences growing up as an "ethnic outsider" in a region in Northeast India experiencing ethnic violence, and the meaning she made of home and belonging in the midst of trauma and displacement. In interrogating the role of race, ethnicity, and gender in the construction of her narrative, and reflexively exploring the relationship among her identity, environment, participants, and social location, Dutta examines how her story has been shaped by greater political and national relations, complicating the notion of culture as essential, static, or monolithic. This work highlights the strength of a person-centered approach to allow researchers to access the internally heterogeneous, constantly evolving, and inherently political nature of cultural narratives. Whereas nomothetic methods often rely on aggregation with the goal of generalization, idiographic methods can reveal "new ways of knowing and being in the world" with "an emphasis on exploring possibilities of reworking rigid ethnic boundaries that have come to be taken for granted" (Dutta, 2015, p. 161).

Narrative, Stigma, and Social Meaning

A personological approach to narrative and culture has also been applied to the study of stigmatized social categories, such as immigrants, racial and ethnic minorities, and the unhoused. Toolis and Hammack's (2015a) work with homeless youth in the United States explored the ways in which participants made meaning of social identity categories in conversation with hegemonic cultural narratives that portray them as criminal or incompetent. They presented four case studies describing the ways in which youth navigated economic injustice and stigmatizing dominant narratives stemming from the American dream, which attributes poverty to individual failure (Bullock, 2013). Using the theoretical concept of master narrative engagement (Hammack & Cohler, 2009), Toolis and Hammack highlighted the ways in which youths' life narratives were heavily constrained by structural barriers and material hardship, yet also demonstrated agency in constructing counternarratives that resisted the blame and stigma accompanied by homelessness, instead constructing their identities, knowledge, and experiences as valuable. Further work by Toolis and Hammack (2015b) on dominant narratives about homelessness in the United Statees points to the utility of narrative research in uncovering counternarratives and examining the polyphonic, contested nature of community narratives. Their analysis of the narratives of housed and unhoused community members revealed a dominant narrative that justified excluding and criminalizing homeless individuals, as well as narratives that resisted exclusion as unjust and unsafe. This work highlights the ways in which individuals engage with competing discourses about stigmatized social identity categories to negotiate boundaries between "insiders" and "outsiders."

The ways in which social identity categories come to bear on individuals' life narratives is also discussed in Hurtado's (2003) work with young Chicanas in the United States. Hurtado's interviews, which explored how feminist consciousness was expressed in participants' everyday lived experience, attended to the diverse ways in which young Chicanas constructed their stories as they contended with difference and moved between multiple social contexts. Their stories were undoubtedly shaped by their racial, ethnic, gender, and sexual identity categories.

Hurtado observed, "My respondents had to understand that the negative judgements of their stigmatized group memberships were socially constructed and therefore could be refuted and not accepted as absolute fact. At the same time, they had to become comfortable in predominantly white institutions in social contexts that did not necessarily reflect the values and norms they had grown up with" (p. xvii). Hurtado's analysis illuminated the ways in which young Chicanas navigated these tensions and resisted stigmatizing dominant narratives to interpret their experiences in their own words.

In their research, Bhatia (2007) and Sirin and Fine (2008) endeavor to link individual identity to dominant narratives of national identity by documenting the diasporic stories of immigrant individuals with hyphenated identities. Bhatia's analysis traces the ways in which middle-class, suburban Indian immigrants living in the United States constructed their lives and identities in a new country in which they were labeled as a racial "other." Sirin and Fine utilized a variety of methods, including in-depth interviews and focus groups, to explore how Muslin American youth integrate the diverse aspects of their identities in a post-9/11 United States, where they often face stigma and marginalization. Both studies attend to meaning making in social and historical context, skillfully explicating the active, dynamic, contested negotiation of identity formation.

Conclusion

The American man stands at the frenetic corner of 16th Street and Valencia in San Francisco's Mission District, pacing a bit, nervous with anticipation. His appearance has changed. It has been an entire decade since he sat at the kitchen table in Jerusalem, sipping Nescafe as Mohammed narrated a tragic life story of collective dispossession, fatalism, and support for political violence in the ongoing Israeli–Palestinian conflict. Would the two even recognize each other? What is Mohammed doing here? The message was brief: "In San Francisco and would love to see you again!"

> "To make it in this world, you've gotta swallow your pride sometimes. Now I'm working with Jews, and Americans, and whoever it takes. The important thing is to succeed in life, to do my

best, to make my family proud. My family needs me to do what's right. There's nothing I can do about the conflict, but I can make things good for myself and for my family. I'm going places. I'll do what I need to get there."

The American man tries to avoid the raising of his eyebrows and the dropping of his jaw. It is not a formal life-story interview, but Mohammed's voice has changed. There is fatalism and cynicism, to be sure, but there is also pragmatism and hope. The voice of the Palestinian collective, so strongly amplified a decade ago, is muted. The voice of the family is strong. The man knew Mohammed's family well. The man knew Mohammed, *the whole person*. There was the pragmatic and nurturing voice of his older brother, always imploring Mohammed to focus on his schoolwork, think about the world beyond Jerusalem, and make something for himself. But Mohammed had found his own voice, and it was a far more optimistic and expansive one now at age 26 than it had been at age 16.

In this chapter, we have outlined an approach to the study of personality development anchored in concepts of narrative, culture, and the "study of lives" tradition pioneered by Henry Murray (1938/2008). Consistent with contemporary theoretical approaches in personality science (e.g., McAdams, 2015), we have argued that a core component of personality is the life story, developed over time and in a particular social and cultural milieu. Our view of culture is dynamic, and we have argued that cultures and persons are co-constitutive in the process of life-story construction. As individuals appropriate and repudiate the voices that proliferate in their social ecologies of development—voices of dominant political parties, voices of family members, voices of peers, teachers, and so forth—they participate in the culture process. Palestinian culture has fundamentally changed in the decade between encounters with Mohammed. Mohammed's current narrative reveals this change in its more pragmatic tone and content. Mohammed's dialogic journey has led him here as a young adult: to a place of newfound optimism, possibility, and concern for himself and his family *over and above* the collective.

In this conclusion, we briefly highlight our key theoretical claims and methodological prescriptions, and we offer concrete suggestions for empirical work using the approach we advocate here. We conceive of the person as an integrated whole, existing in social and histori-

cal time, actively making meaning through a *dialogic* process as a cultural participant, emboldened and constrained by the relative power or privilege conferred by the social structure and its matrix of social identities. This view of persons emphasizes meaning, context, particularity, and variability, consistent with Murray's (1938/2008) personological approach, the interpretive approach to narrative psychology (e.g., Hammack, 2008, 2011; Hammack & Toolis, 2016; Josselson, 2017), and the fundamental premises of a person-centered cultural psychology (e.g., Gjerde, 2004). It also integrates insights about power and identity from social identity theory (Tajfel & Turner, 1986), viewing persons not only as individuals but also as members of particular social categories (e.g., gender, race, nationality, sexual identity), the configuration of which brings implications for life-story construction, as social categories confer relative status and meaning (Reicher, 2004). The context of development creates *press* on individuals to engage with certain narratives over others, and through a process of narrative identity development, they assert their roles as makers of culture. Undoubtedly, how individuals experience the press of particular contexts depends on both individual and collective *needs* established in the course of development. Thus our framework centers concepts at the center of Murray's personological approach to the study of lives.

Our framework seeks a new narrative for the science of personality development in culture—a shift away from nomothetic approaches grounded in a positivist or postpositivist epistemology (Schiff, 2017) and toward approaches that can "decolonize" psychological theory and methods (Bhatia, 2018). For too long, mainstream psychology has been limited by a reductionistic, essentializing, Eurocentric approach to studying thought and behavior (Bhatia, 2018; Gone, 2011; Schiff, 2017). Psychological science is in desperate need of restoring attention to meaning making, context, particularity, and variability if it is to truly further understanding of how humans interpret their experiences in the world (e.g., Henrich et al., 2010). Personality science, like psychological science more broadly, benefits from a recognition of the way in which our knowledge can be used for more critical, liberatory ends through description and understanding rather than the historic aim to predict and control human behavior (Bhatia, 2018; Hammack, 2018; Schiff, 2017). As both concept and method, narrative offers the tool through which we access personality development in context in just such a manner. Narrative provides the window into the process of both individual and collective meaning making. Narrative *engagement* takes us away from a monologic conception of culture and personality, as we assume that individuals make meaning in ways that are inherently dialogic. *This dialogic process is not politically neutral*: The voices about Palestinian identity with which Mohammed, Adara, and Sami were engaging during the second *intifada* positioned them ideologically within the larger Israeli–Palestinian conflict at the time.

The research we have reviewed here is representative of the type of empirical work our framework advocates. For scholars interested in pursuing inquiry in the framework we suggest here, we offer four concrete recommendations. First, we recommend the embrace of an explicit *interpretive* epistemology in which the key research question is not about universals of personality development but rather concerns *meaning, particularity,* and *variability* in the course of development. This epistemology necessitates a concern with *context* that benefits from field, rather than laboratory, methods. Researchers approach data not with the aim to discover some ultimate truth about personality development but rather to understand how personality unfolds in myriad ways—a concern with what is *unique* rather than *general* about persons (see Allport, 1962).

Second, we recommend the use of *multilevel qualitative methods* to systematically examine narrative at both cultural and personal levels. Master narratives, for example, are accessible through analysis of discourse that circulates at the collective level: in art, literature, film, educational textbooks, political speeches, and so forth (see Hammack, 2011). This discourse is the source of *press* upon individual lives in the course of life-story development. Scholars of personality development benefit from expanding—in a systematic way—their lens beyond the individual to the world of cultural products, artifacts, and discourses. Personal narratives are accessible through formal and informal interviews, as well as analysis of conversational data (e.g., Pilecki & Hammack, 2014). Qualitative methods have now received formal legitimacy within psychological science, with the absorption of the Society for Qualitative Inquiry in Psychology (SQIP) into Division 5 of the American Psychological Association (APA) and the emergence of an APA-published journal, *Qualitative Psychology*. Standards for reporting and reviewing qualitative work are gradually emerging (e.g., Levitt, Motulsky, Wertz, Morrow, & Ponterotto, 2017; Levitt et al., 2018; see also Gergen, Josselson, & Freeman, 2015), not to create methodological uniformity but to clarify the ways in which the evaluation of qualitative and quantitative inquiry diverge. As qualitative methods continue to move from the margins to the center of psychological science, the vision of a personological approach to narrative, culture, and human development is given full legitimacy. Researchers (especially young investigators) need no longer consider the politics of method or epistemology but rather can focus on the appropriate approach and tools to address questions about meaning making in context.

Third, and related to our suggestion to privilege qualitative inquiry, we recommend the explicit embrace of an *idiographic* approach to the study of personality. As Allport (1937) argued, the idiographic approach stands in contrast to the nomothetic approach that aggregates across individuals to produce general knowledge. The idiographic approach maintains the analytic lens on the *whole person* and maintains the *person,* rather than the *variable,* as the unit of analysis. Thus, personological inquiry of the kind we advocate here may involve the coding of qualitative data across individual cases, *but the analysis and presentation of data maintain an emphasis on the person.*

Finally, to the extent that we want to seriously understand personality *development* in cultural context, we recommend the use of *longitudinal* methods that chart an individual's trajectory over time. Life stories, rather than being static, are always dynamically evolving as persons and settings change over time. Consider the case of Mohammed. To understand the course of his narrative identity development, away from the contamination of the collective during adolescence toward the possibility of redemption during young adulthood, we have to understand the nuances of his social ecology of development: not just that he grew up in occupied East Jerusalem lacking citizenship in any sovereign state, experienced marginalization for his Palestinian identity, and was confronted daily with the tragic discourse (and material reality) of the Palestinian master narrative and its calls for resistance. We also need to know about Mohammed's family, about the influence of his brother and mother, about his experiences in university in the politically polarized, Israeli-occupied West Bank and in graduate school with numerous Jews in Israel.

To return to Murray's (1940) claim that the personality represents a "full Congress of orators and pressure-groups," we cannot know the person in culture absent consideration of the *dialogue* between a person and this "full Congress." Our epistemology and our methodological practices benefit from attunement to this dialogue, for our value and import as social scientists stems from our contributions toward not just universal laws and principles of human behavior but also our ability to describe, explain, and contextualize the unfolding of individual lives over time.

ACKNOWLEDGMENTS

Preparation of this chapter was supported by a William T. Grant Scholar Award and a fellowship from the Center for Advanced Study in the Behavioral Sciences at Stanford University, both awarded to Phillip L. Hammack.

REFERENCES

Allport, G. W. (1937). *Personality: A psychological introduction.* New York: Holt.

Allport, G. W. (1962). The general and the unique in psychological science. *Journal of Personality, 30*(3), 405–422.

Andrews, M. (1991). *Lifetimes of commitment: Aging, politics, psychology.* Cambridge, UK: Cambridge University Press.

Andrews, M. (1997). Life review in the context of acute social transition: The case of East Germany. *British Journal of Social Psychology, 36*(3), 273–290.

Andrews, M. (1998). Criticism/self-criticism in East Germany: Contradictions between theory and practice. *Critical Sociology, 24*(1–2), 130–153.

Andrews, M. (1999). The politics of forgiveness. *International Journal of Politics, Culture, and Society, 13*(1), 107–124.

Andrews, M. (2003). Grand national narratives and the project of truth commissions: A comparative analysis. *Media, Culture and Society, 25*(1), 45–65.

Andrews, M. (2007). *Shaping history: Narratives of political change.* Cambridge, UK: Cambridge University Press.

Arnett, J. J. (2008). The neglected 95%: Why American psychology needs to become less American. *American Psychologist, 63*(7), 602–614.

Bakhtin, M. M. (1981). *The dialogic imagination* (C.

Emerson & M. Holquist, Trans.). Austin: University of Texas Press.

Bakhtin, M. M. (1990). *Art and answerability: Early philosophical essays.* Austin: University of Texas Press.

Bakhtin, M. M. (1992). *Problems of Dostoevsky's poetics* (C. Emerson, Trans.). Minneapolis: University of Minnesota Press. (Original work published 1984)

Bakhtin, M. M. (2010). *Speech genres and other late essays.* Austin: University of Texas Press.

Bamberg, M., & Andrews, M. (Eds.). (2004). *Considering counter-narratives: Narrating, resisting, making sense.* Amsterdam, The Netherlands: Benjamins.

Bar-On, M. (2006). Conflicting narratives or narratives of a conflict: Can the Zionist and Palestinian narratives of the 1948 war be bridged? In R. I. Rotberg (Ed.), *Israeli and Palestinian narratives of conflict: History's double helix* (pp. 142–173). Bloomington: Indiana University Press.

Benedict, R. (1934). *Patterns of culture.* Boston: Houghton Mifflin.

Bhatia, S. (2007). *American karma: Race, culture, and identity in the Indian diaspora.* New York: New York University Press.

Bhatia, S. (2011). Narrative inquiry as cultural psychology: Meaning-making in a contested global world. *Narrative Inquiry, 21*(2), 345–352.

Bhatia, S. (2018). *Decolonizing psychology: Globalization, social justice and Indian youth identities.* New York: Oxford University Press.

Bronfenbrenner, U. (1979). *The ecology of human development: Experiments by nature and design.* Cambridge, MA: Harvard University Press.

Bruner, J. (1990). *Acts of meaning.* Cambridge, MA: Harvard University Press.

Bullock, H. E. (2013). *Women and poverty: Psychology, public policy, and social justice.* Boston: Wiley-Blackwell.

Cohler, B. J. (1982). Personal narrative and life course. In P. Baltes & O. G. Brim (Eds.), *Life span development and behavior* (Vol. 4, pp. 205–241). New York: Academic Press.

Cohler, B. J. (1991). The life story and the study of resilience and response to adversity. *Journal of Narrative and Life History, 1,* 169–200.

Cohler, B. J. (2007). *Writing desire: Sixty years of gay autobiography.* Madison: University of Wisconsin Press.

Cohler, B. J., & Hammack, P. L. (2007). The psychological world of the gay teenager: Social change, narrative, and "normality." *Journal of Youth and Adolescence, 36,* 47–59.

Danziger, K. (1983). Origins and basic principles of Wundt's *Volkerpsychologie. British Journal of Social Psychology, 22*(4), 303–313.

Danziger, K. (1990). *Constructing the subject: Historical origins of psychological research.* New York: Cambridge University Press.

Davis, B. R. (2015). Harmomy, dissonance, and the gay community: A dialogical approach to same-sex desiring men's sexual identity development. *Qualitative Psychology, 2*(1), 78–95.

Dilthey, W. (1977). *Descriptive psychology and historical understanding* (R. M. Zaner & K. L. Heiges, Trans.). The Hague, The Netherlands: Martinus Nijhoff. (Original work published 1894)

Dilthey, W. (1988). *Introduction to the human sciences: An attempt to lay a foundation for the study of society and history* (R. J. Betanzos, Trans.). Detroit, MI: Wayne State University Press. (Original work published 1923)

Dutt, A., & Grabe, S. (2014). Lifetime activism, marginality, and psychology: Narratives of lifelong feminist activists committed to social change. *Qualitative Psychology, 1*(2), 107–122.

Dutta, U. (2015). The long way home: The vicissitudes of belonging and otherness in Northeast India. *Qualitative Inquiry, 21*(2), 161–172.

Epstein, S. (1979). Explorations in personality today and tomorrow: A tribute to Henry A. Murray. *American Psychologist, 34*(8), 649–653.

Erikson, E. H. (1959). *Identity and the life cycle.* New York: Norton.

Foucault, M. (1982). The subject and power. *Critical Inquiry, 8,* 777–795.

Frost, D. M. (2011). Stigma and intimacy in same-sex relationships: A narrative approach. *Journal of Family Psychology, 25*(1), 1–10.

Frost, D. M. (2018). Narrative approaches within a social psychology of social justice: The potential utility of narrative evidence. In P. L. Hammack (Ed.), *The Oxford handbook of social psychology and social justice* (pp. 83–93). New York: Oxford University Press.

Frost, D. M., & Ouellette, S. C. (2004). Meaningful voices: How psychologists, speaking as psychologists, can inform social policy. *Analyses of Social Issues and Public Policy, 4,* 219–226.

Geertz, C. (1973). *The interpretation of cultures: Selected essays.* New York: Basic Books.

Gergen, K. J. (1973). Social psychology as history. *Journal of Personality and Social Psychology, 26*(2), 309–320.

Gergen, K. J. (1985). The social constructionist movement in modern psychology. *American Psychologist, 40*(3), 266–275.

Gergen, K. J., Josselson, R., & Freeman, M. (2015). The promises of qualitative inquiry. *American Psychologist, 70*(1), 1–9.

Gjerde, P. F. (2004). Culture, power, and experience: Toward a person-centered cultural psychology. *Human Development, 47,* 138–157.

Goffman, E. (1963). *Stigma: Notes on the management of spoiled identity.* New York: Simon & Schuster.

Gone, J. P. (2011). Is psychological science a-cultural? *Cultural Diversity and Ethnic Minority Psychology, 17*(3), 234–242.

Grabe, S. (2017). *Narrating a psychology of resistance: Voices of the Compañeras in Nicaragua.* New York: Oxford University Press.

Grabe, S., & Dutt, A. (2015). Counter narratives, the psychology of liberation, and the evolution of a women's social movement in Nicaragua. *Peace and Conflict: Journal of Peace Psychology, 21*(1), 89–105.

Gregg, G. S. (2007). *Culture and identity in a Muslim society.* New York: Oxford University Press.

Gregg, G. S. (2012). Multiple identities and their organization. In R. Josselson & M. Harway (Eds.), *Navigating multiple identities: Race, gender, culture, nationality, and roles* (pp. 13–38). New York: Oxford University Press.

Gregg, G. S. (2013). Religious voices and identity in the life-narratives of young adult Moroccans. In M. Buitelaar & H. Zock (Eds.), *Religious voices in self-narratives: Making sense of life in times of transition* (pp. 83–102). Berlin: de Gruyter.

Gutierrez, K. D., & Rogoff, B. (2003). Cultural ways of learning: Individual traits or repertoires of practice. *Educational Researcher, 32*(5), 19–25.

Hammack, P. L. (2008). Narrative and the cultural psychology of identity. *Personality and Social Psychology Review, 12*(3), 222–247.

Hammack, P. L. (2009). Exploring the reproduction of conflict through narrative: Israeli youth motivated to participate in a coexistence program. *Peace and Conflict: Journal of Peace Psychology, 15*(1), 49–74.

Hammack, P. L. (2010a). The cultural psychology of Palestinian youth: A narrative approach. *Culture and Psychology, 16*(4), 507–537.

Hammack, P. L. (2010b). Identity as burden or benefit?: Youth, historical narrative, and the legacy of political conflict. *Human Development, 53,* 173–201.

Hammack, P. L. (2010c). Narrating hyphenated selves: Intergroup contact and configurations of identity among young Palestinian citizens of Israel. *International Journal of Intercultural Relations, 34*(4), 368–385.

Hammack, P. L. (2011). *Narrative and the politics of identity: The cultural psychology of Israeli and Palestinian youth.* New York: Oxford University Press.

Hammack, P. L. (2018). Social psychology and social justice: Critical principles and perspectives for the twenty-first century. In P. L. Hammack (Ed.), *The Oxford handbook of social psychology and social justice* (pp. 3–39). New York: Oxford University Press.

Hammack, P. L., & Cohler, B. J. (2009). Narrative engagement and sexual identity: An interdisciplinary approach to the study of sexual lives. In P. L. Hammack & B. J. Cohler (Eds.), *The story of sexual identity: Narrative perspectives on the gay and lesbian life course* (pp. 3–22). New York: Oxford University Press.

Hammack, P. L., & Cohler, B. J. (2011). Narrative, identity, and the politics of exclusion: Social change and the gay and lesbian life course. *Sexuality Research and Social Policy, 8,* 162–182.

Hammack, P. L., Frost, D. M., Meyer, I. H., & Pletta, D. (2018). Gay men's health and identity: Social change and the life course. *Archives of Sexual Behavior,* *47*(1), 59–74.

Hammack, P. L., & Pilecki, A. (2012). Narrative as a root metaphor for political psychology. *Political Psychology, 33*(1), 75–103.

Hammack, P. L., Thompson, E. M., & Pilecki, A. (2009). Configurations of identity among sexual minority youth: Context, desire, and narrative. *Journal of Youth and Adolescence, 38,* 867–883.

Hammack, P. L., & Toolis, E. (2015). Identity, politics, and the cultural psychology of adolescence. In L. Jensen (Ed.), *The Oxford handbook of human development and culture* (pp. 396–409). New York: Oxford University Press.

Hammack, P. L., & Toolis, E. E. (2016). Putting the social into personal identity: The master narrative as root metaphor for psychological and developmental science. *Human Development, 58*(6), 350–364.

Haslam, S. A., & Reicher, S. D. (2012). When prisoners take over the prison: A social psychology of resistance. *Personality and Social Psychology Review, 16*(2), 154–179.

Heidegger, M. (1962). *Being and time* (J. Macquarrie & E. Robinson, Trans.). New York: Harper & Row.

Henrich, J., Heine, S. J., & Norenzayan, A. (2010). The weirdest people in the world? *Behavioral and Brain Sciences, 33*(2–3), 61–83.

Hurtado, A. (2003). *Voicing Chicana feminisms: Young women speak out on sexuality and identity.* New York: New York University Press.

Hurtado, A., & Sinha, M. (2005). Restriction and freedom in the construction of sexuality: Young Chicanas and Chicanos speak out. *Feminism and Psychology, 15*(1), 33–38.

Hurtado, A., & Sinha, M. (2008). More than men: Latino feminist masculinities and intersectionality. *Sex Roles, 59*(5–6), 337–349.

Hurtado, A., & Sinha, M. (2016). *Beyond machismo: Intersectional Latino masculinities.* Austin: University of Texas Press.

James, W. (1890). *The principles of psychology.* New York: Holt.

Jawad, S. A. (2006). The Arab and Palestinian narratives of the 1948 war. In R. I. Rotberg (Ed.), *Israeli and Palestinian narratives of conflict: History's double helix* (pp. 72–114). Bloomington: Indiana University Press.

Josselson, R. (1996). *Revising herself: The story of women's identity from college to midlife.* New York: Oxford University Press.

Josselson, R. (2004). The hermeneutics of faith and the hermeneutics of suspicion. *Narrative Inquiry, 14,* 1–28.

Josselson, R. (2009). The present of the past: Dialogues with memory over time. *Journal of Personality, 77*(3), 647–668.

Josselson, R. (2017). *Paths to fulfillment: Women's search for meaning and identity.* New York: Oxford University Press.

Kluckhohn, C., & Murray, H. A. (1967). Personality

formation: The determinants. In C. Kluckhohn & H. A. Murray (Eds.), *Personality in nature, society, and culture* (2nd ed., pp. 53–67). New York: Knopf.

Kral, M. J. (2008). Psychology and anthropology: Intersubjectivity and epistemology in an interpretive cultural science. *Journal of Theoretical and Philosophical Psychology, 28*(1), 257–275.

Lamiell, J. T. (1987). *The psychology of personality: An epistemological inquiry.* New York: Columbia University Press.

Levitt, H. M., Bamberg, M., Creswell, J. W., Frost, D., Josselson, R., & Suárez-Orozco, C. (2018). Journal article reporting standards for qualitative primary, qualitative meta-analytic, and mixed methods research in psychology: The APA Publications and Communications Board Task Force Report. *American Psychologist, 73*(1), 26–46.

Levitt, H. M., Motulsky, S. L., Wertz, F. J., Morrow, S. L., & Ponterotto, J. G. (2017). Recommendations for designing and reviewing qualitative research in psychology: Promoting methodological integrity. *Qualitative Psychology, 4*(1), 2–22.

Lieblich, A. (2007). The second generation of Kfar Etzion: A study of collective memory. In D. Mendels (Ed.), *On memory: An interdisciplinary approach* (pp. 213–230). Oxford, UK: Peter Lang.

Lieblich, A. (2014a). Narrating your life after 65 (or: To tell or not to tell, that is the question). *New Directions for Child and Adolescent Development, 145,* 71–83.

Lieblich, A. (2014b). *Narratives of positive aging: Seaside stories.* New York: Oxford University Press.

Lieblich, A., Tuval-Mashiach, R., & Zilber, T. (1998). *Narrative research: Reading, analysis, and interpretation.* Thousand Oaks, CA: SAGE.

McAdams, D. P. (1988). *Power, intimacy, and the life story: Personological inquiries into identity.* New York: Guilford Press.

McAdams, D. P. (1990). Unity and purpose in human lives: The emergence of identity as a life story. In A. I. Rabin, R. A. Zucker, R. A. Emmons, & S. Frank (Eds.), *Studying persons and lives* (pp. 148–200). New York: Springer.

McAdams, D. P. (1995). What do we know when we know a person? *Journal of Personality, 63*(3), 365–396.

McAdams, D. P. (2001). The psychology of life stories. *Review of General Psychology, 5,* 100–122.

McAdams, D. P. (2006). *The redemptive self: Stories Americans live by.* New York: Oxford University Press.

McAdams, D. P. (2008). Foreword. In H. A. Murray, *Explorations in personality* (70th anniversary ed., pp. vii–xlvi). New York: Oxford University Press.

McAdams, D. P. (2011). Narrative identity. In S. J. Schwartz, K. Luyckx, & V. L. Vignoles (Eds.), *Handbook of identity theory and research* (Vol. 1, pp. 99–115). New York: Springer.

McAdams, D. P. (2015). *The art and science of personality development.* New York: Guilford Press.

McAdams, D. P., & Bowman, P. J. (2001). Narrating

life's turning points: Redemption and contamination. In D. P. McAdams, R. Josselson, & A. Lieblich (Eds.), *Turns in the road: Narrative studies of lives in transition* (pp. 3–34). Washington, DC: American Psychological Association Press.

McAdams, D. P., & Guo, J. (2017). The cultural shaping of life stories. In A. T. Church (Ed.), *The Praeger handbook of personality across cultures* (Vol. 2, pp. 185–210). Santa Barbara, CA: Praeger.

McAdams, D. P., & Manczak, E. (2015). Personality and the life story. In M. Mikulincer, P. R. Shaver, M. L. Cooper, & R. J. Larsen (Eds.), *APA handbook of personality and social psychology: Vol. 4. Personality processes and individual differences* (pp. 425–446). Washington, DC: American Psychological Association Press.

McAdams, D. P., & McLean, K. C. (2013). Narrative identity. *Current Directions in Psychological Science, 22,* 233–238.

McAdams, D. P., & Olson, B. D. (2010). Personality development: Continuity and change over the life course. *Annual Review of Psychology, 61,* 517–542.

McAdams, D. P., & Pals, J. L. (2006). A new Big Five: Fundamental principles for an integrative science of personality. *American Psychologist, 61,* 204–217.

McCrae, R. R., & Costa, P. T. (1997). Personality trait structure as a human universal. *American Psychologist, 52*(5), 509–516.

McCrae, R. R., & Terracciano, A. (2005). Personality profiles of cultures: Aggregate personality traits. *Journal of Personality and Social Psychology, 89*(3), 407–425.

McLean, K. C., & Syed, M. (2016). Personal, master, and alternative narratives: An integrative framework for understanding identity development in context. *Human Development, 58*(6), 318–349.

McLean, K. C., Wood, B., & Breen, A. V. (2013). Reflecting on a difficult life: Narrative construction in vulnerable adolescents. *Journal of Adolescent Research, 28*(4), 431–452.

Mead, G. H. (1934). *Mind, self and society.* Chicago: University of Chicago Press.

Mischel, W. (2004). Toward an integrative science of the person. *Annual Review of Psychology, 55,* 1–22.

Mishler, E. G. (2004). Historians of the self: Restorying lives, revising identities. *Research in Human Development, 1,* 101–121.

Moghaddam, F., & Harré, R. (1982). Rethinking the laboratory experiment. *American Behavioral Scientist, 36*(1), 22–38.

Murray, H. A. (1940). What should psychologists do about psychoanalysis? *Journal of Abnormal and Social Psychology, 35,* 150–175.

Murray, H. A. (2008). *Explorations in personality* (70th anniversary ed.). New York: Oxford University Press. (Original work published 1938)

Murray, H. A., & Kluckhohn, C. (1967). Outline of a conception of personality. In C. Kluckhohn & H. A. Murray (Eds.), *Personality in nature, society, and culture* (2nd ed., pp. 3–49). New York: Knopf.

Open Science Collaboration. (2015). Estimating the reproducibility of psychological science. *Science, 249,* aac4716-1–aac4716-8.

Ozer, D. J., & Benet-Martínez, V. (2006). Personality and the prediction of consequential outcomes. *Annual Review of Psychology, 57,* 401–421.

Pickren, W. E. (2009). Liberating history: The context of the challenge of psychologists of color to American psychology. *Cultural Diversity and Ethnic Minority Psychology, 15*(4), 425–433.

Pilecki, A., & Hammack, P. L. (2014). "Victims" versus "righteous victims": The rhetorical construction of social categories in historical dialogue among Israeli and Palestinian youth. *Political Psychology, 35*(6), 813–830.

Prawat, R. S. (1999). Social constructivism and the process–content distinction as viewed by Vygotsky and the pragmatists. *Mind, Culture, and Activity, 6*(4), 255–273.

Prilleltensky, I. (1989). Psychology and the status quo. *American Psychologist, 44*(5), 795–802.

Ratner, C. (2008). Cultural psychology and qualitative methodology: Scientific and political considerations. *Culture and Psychology, 14*(3), 259–288.

Reicher, S. (2004). The context of social identity: Domination, resistance, and change. *Political Psychology, 25*(6), 921–945.

Ricoeur, P. (1984). The model of the text: Meaningful action considered as a text. *Social Research, 51,* 185–218.

Rogoff, B., Baker-Sennett, J., Lacasa, P., & Goldsmith, D. (1995). Development through participation in sociocultural activity. In J. Goodnow, P. Miller, & F. Kessel (Eds.), *Cultural practices as contexts for development* (pp. 45–65). San Francisco: Jossey-Bass.

Runyan, W. M. (1983). Idiographic goals and methods in the study of lives. *Journal of Personality, 51*(3), 413–437.

Sampson, E. E. (1978). Scientific paradigms and social values: Wanted—A scientific revolution. *Journal of Personality and Social Psychology, 36*(11), 1332–1343.

Schiff, B. (2017). *A new narrative for psychology.* New York: Oxford University Press.

Schiff, B., Noy, C., & Cohler, B. J. (2001). Collected stories in the life narratives of Holocaust survivors. *Narrative Inquiry, 11*(1), 159–194.

Schiff, B., Skillingstead, H., Archibald, O., Arasim, A., & Peterson, J. (2006). Consistency and change in the repeated narratives of Holocaust survivors. *Narrative Inquiry, 16*(2), 349–377.

Schmitt, D. P., Allik, J., McCrae, R. R., & Benet-Martínez, V. (2007). The geographic distribution of Big Five personality traits: Patterns and profiles of human self-description across 56 nations. *Journal of Cross-Cultural Psychology, 38*(2), 173–212.

Shneidman, E., Barron, F., Sanford, N., Smith, M. B., Tomkins, S., & Tyler, L. (1982). Aspects of the personological system of Henry A. Murray. *Personality and Social Psychology Bulletin, 8*(4), 604–623.

Shweder, R. A. (1973). The between and within of cross-cultural research. *Ethos, 1*(4), 531–545.

Shweder, R. A. (1990). Cultural psychology—What is it? In J. W. Stigler, R. A. Shweder, & G. Herdt (Eds.), *Cultural psychology: Essays on comparative human development* (pp. 1–46). New York: Cambridge University Press.

Shweder, R. A. (1996). True ethnography: The lore, the law, and the lure. In R. Jessor, A. Colby, & R. A. Shweder (Eds.), *Ethnography and human development: Context and meaning in social inquiry* (pp. 15–52). Chicago: University of Chicago Press.

Sirin, S. R., & Fine, M. (2008). *Muslim American youth: Understanding hyphenated identities through multiple methods.* New York: New York University Press.

Smith, M. B. (2005). "Personality and social psychology": Retrospections and aspirations. *Personality and Social Psychology Review, 9*(4), 334–340.

Stetsenko, A., & Arievitch, I. M. (2004). The self in cultural–historical activity theory: Reclaiming the unity of social and individual dimensions of human development. *Theory and Psychology, 14*(4), 475–503.

Syed, M., & Azmitia, M. (2008). A narrative approach to ethnic identity in emerging adulthood: Bringing life to the identity status model. *Developmental Psychology, 44*(4), 1012–1027.

Syed, M., & Azmitia, M. (2010). Narrative and ethnic identity exploration: A longitudinal account of emerging adults' ethnicity-related experiences. *Developmental Psychology, 46*(1), 208–219.

Tajfel, H., & Turner, J. (1986). The social identity theory of intergroup behavior. In W. G. Austin & S. Worchel (Eds.), *The social psychology of intergroup relations* (pp. 7–24). Chicago: Nelson-Hall.

Thorne, A., & Nam, V. (2009). The storied construction of personality. In P. Corr & G. Matthews (Eds.), *The Cambridge handbook of personality psychology* (pp. 491–505). Cambridge, UK: Cambridge University Press.

Toolis, E. E., & Hammack, P. L. (2015a). The lived experience of homeless youth: A narrative approach. *Qualitative Psychology, 2*(1), 50–68.

Toolis, E. E., & Hammack, P. L. (2015b). "This is my community": Reproducing and resisting boundaries of exclusion in contested public spaces. *American Journal of Community Psychology, 56*(3–4), 368–382.

Valsiner, J. (2000, June). *Making meaning out of mind: Self-less and self-ful dialogicality.* Paper presented at the First International Conference of the Dialogical Self, University of Nijmegen, The Netherlands.

Volosinov, V. N. (1973). *Marxism and the philosophy of language* (L. Matejka & I. R. Titunik, Trans.). Cambridge, MA: Harvard University Press. (Original work published 1929)

Vygotsky, L. S. (1978). *Mind in society: The development of higher psychological processes.* Cambridge, MA: Harvard University Press.

Vygotsky, L. S. (1997). *Educational psychology.* Boca Raton, FL: St. Lucie Press. (Original work published 1926)

Westrate, N. M., & McLean, K. C. (2010). The rise and fall of gay: A cultural–historical approach to gay identity development. *Memory, 18*(2), 225–240.

White, A. M. (2006a). African American feminist fathers' narratives of parenting. *Journal of Black Psychology, 32*(1), 43–71.

White, A. M. (2006b). African American feminist masculinities: Personal narratives of redemption, contamination, and peak turning points. *Journal of Humanistic Psychology, 46*(3), 255–280.

White, A. M. (2006c). "You've got a friend": African American men's cross-sex feminist friendships and their influence on perceptions of masculinity and women. *Journal of Social and Personal Relationships, 23*(4), 523–542.

Wundt, W. (1904). *Principles of physiological psychology* (E. Titchener, Trans.). New York: Macmillan.

Wundt, W. (1907). *Outlines of psychology* (C. H. Judd, Trans.). New York: Stechert.

Wundt, W. (1916). *Elements of folk psychology: Outlines of a psychological history of the development of mankind* (E. L. Schaub, Trans.). New York: Macmillan.

Yamagata, S., Suzuki, A., Ando, J., Ono, Y., Kijima, N., et al. (2006). Is the genetic structure of human personality universal?: A cross-cultural twin study from North America, Europe, and Asia. *Journal of Personality and Social Psychology, 90*(6), 987–998.

Zilber, T. B., Tuval-Mashiach, R., & Lieblich, A. (2008). The embedded narrative navigating through multiple contexts. *Qualitative Inquiry, 14*(6), 1047–1069.

PART V

APPLICATIONS AND INTEGRATIONS

The scientific study of personality development expands outward to inform many other domains of inquiry, ranging from molecular genetics to cultural anthropology. Within the psychological sciences, personality development is implicated in a broad array of research topics traditionally studied by social, cognitive, clinical, and health psychologists, among others. In Part V of the *Handbook of Personality Development,* we gather together chapters that explore six of these topics, illustrating applications of ideas on personality development to other domains as well as integrations of concepts across domains.

In Chapter 28, Sarah E. Hampson provides an authoritative review of the scientific literature on relationships between personality and health, working within a developmental framework. She examines how personality development can influence health and how health can influence personality development. The literature is dominated by studies relating Big Five dispositional traits to health outcomes and processes, but Hampson also shows how health issues play out for the motivated agent and the autobiographical author, too. Moving from the physical to the purely psychological, in Chapter 29, which focuses on the development of subjective well-being (SWB) across the human lifespan, Nathan W. Hudson, Richard E. Lucas, and M. Brent Donnellan begin by clarifying exactly what SWB is and what it isn't. Then, they discuss reasons why one might expect stability or change in well-being, before focusing specifically on what the empirical evidence shows regarding the extent to which SWB changes or remains relatively stable over time.

Chapters 30–32 shift the focus to clinical psychology and the study of mental disorders. In Chapter 30, C. Emily Durbin examines the relationship between personality development and internalizing psychopathology. The relationship is tricky and subtle, she writes, because internalizing disorders (e.g., anxiety, depression, phobias, and posttraumatic stress disorders) may feel like they "befall" a person (they come upon a person from another place, like an illness or an invasion) or like the disorder itself is what the person "becomes." Durbin reviews research addressing differences in personality characteristics as a function of particular internalizing disorders, and she considers what these differences may tell us about the causes of these disorders.

In Chapter 31, Michelle M. Martel, Tess E. Smith, and Christine A. Lee discuss relationships between personality development and externalizing disorders, such as conduct disorders, substance abuse, and the like. They show that personality traits may serve as markers of longitudinal pathways to externalizing psychopathology. They also consider aspects of externalizing psychopathology that relate to motivational processes and narrative meaning making. In Chapter

32, Andrew M. Chanen and Katherine N. Thompson examine personality disorders per se—such as those grouped into three clusters in DSM-5 (e.g., schizotypal personality disorder, borderline personality disorder, narcissistic personality disorder, avoidant personality disorder)—from a developmental perspective. Research suggests that signs of incipient personality disorders can be recognized in childhood, that such pathology is common and clinically significant, and that certain interventions can support more adaptive development in childhood, adolescence, and the emerging adulthood years.

The last chapter in the *Handbook of Personality Development* considers personality development and close (i.e., romantic) interpersonal relationships, a topic that is central to social psychology. Jennifer M. Senia and M. Brent Donnellan begin Chapter 33 by underscoring the fact that the establishment of a happy and stable romantic relationship is an important life goal for many, if not most, adult members of the species *Homo sapiens*. Indeed, relationship satisfaction is strongly correlated with overall life satisfaction in the adult years. Senia and Donnellan consider the state of empirical evidence regarding how personality characteristics are associated with relationships, and how relationship processes and events are associated with personality development. Their chapter takes us back to themes foregrounded in the beginning of our volume. Human beings have evolved to be exquisitely social creatures, oriented toward forming close relationships with other members of our groups. The different ways in which we involve ourselves in close relationships are reflective of consequential personality characteristics, and shaped by the development of personality across the human life course.

CHAPTER 28

Personality Development and Health

Sarah E. Hampson

It is health that is real wealth and not pieces of gold and silver.
—MAHATMA GANDHI

When it comes right down to it, health is everything: "Without health life is not life" (attributed to the Buddha). The overwhelming significance of staying healthy may not be uppermost in our minds when we are young, unless we have the misfortune to fall seriously ill in childhood or youth. Ill-health often seems to strike, meteor-like, from out of nowhere. Yet modern science tells us that the seeds of many diseases may be found in our genes, our lifestyles, and our personalities. The idea that our personalities can influence our health has a long history, but it's only recently that strong scientific evidence for this link has accumulated. It is a complex association, with numerous intervening links forming a chain from personality to health or illness through several intermediate steps such as stress and behavior. Making the connection between personality and health does not mean that we are to blame for our diseases, but it does give us insights into how we might be able to alter our health trajectory.

In this chapter, I examine how personality development can influence health, and how health can influence personality development. In McAdams's integrative theory of personality and self, a child develops from being a social actor to a motivated agent and an autobiographical author, to eventually become an adult who integrates all three of these components into the self (Hooker & McAdams, 2003; Mc-

Adams, 2013). Much of the evidence for the link between personality and health is based on personality trait research (personality as actor), but I also consider goals (personality as agent, agentic personality), and the relation between health and autobiography (personality as author). Personality trait research is dominated by the five-factor model (McCrae & Costa, 2008), also referred to as the Big Five framework (John, Naumann, & Soto, 2008), for assessing personality in terms of broad and relatively independent domains: extraversion, agreeableness, conscientiousness, emotional stability (vs. neuroticism), and openness to experience (also called intellect/imagination). Other traits have been studied in relation to health, including optimism, pessimism, sensation seeking, and various measures of self-control that are similar to conscientiousness. These traits can be conceptually related to the five-factor framework, which has proved to be a valuable organizing tool in personality and health research (Turiano, Chapman, Gruenwald, & Mroczek, 2015).

When studying the link between personality traits and health, it is important to consider that both sides of the equation are moving targets. Health changes can be sudden, but the onset of chronic diseases such as Type 2 diabetes are usually the result of metabolic changes taking place over years or decades. Similarly, personality traits change across the life course. We are learning that personality development seems to parallel other areas of human development. Just like our physical development, personality traits undergo dramatic changes in childhood and youth, then stabilize somewhat in adulthood before changing more rapidly again in old age (Specht et al., 2014). The comparison is so pronounced that normative personality development across childhood and youth has been described as following the "maturity" principle (Hogan & Roberts, 2004; Roberts, Wood, & Caspi, 2008). In their meta-analysis, Roberts, Walton, and Viechtbauer, (2006) compared mean levels of traits in samples that differed by age and found that the maturational trend over the first 30 or so years of adulthood is for people to become less neurotic, and more dominant (a part of extraversion), agreeable, and conscientious, whereas in old age, they become less open to experience and have less social vitality (another extraversion facet).

As with traits, the goals and motives of agentic personality also change across the lifespan (Heckhausen & Wrosch, 2016). Health goals become more central with age, particularly with the onset of chronic disease, and older people's goals are likely to become less ambitious. Having a health goal, such as to exercise more, implies that one has control over one's action. The importance of belief in control is at the heart of Heckhausen, Wrosch, and Schulz's (2010) lifespan theory of control, in which they argue that we are motivated to exert control over the developmental challenges that come with aging. We do so through a range of control strategies, some designed to help us achieve specific goals, such as directing resources to the goal (joining a health club), whereas other strategies may involve self-protective goal disengagement (e.g., no longer aiming to complete a half marathon but settling for the 5K run instead). Similarly, the autobiographical self changes with time as a result of experiences and reevaluation. The onset of illness can be a life-changing event that causes a major reappraisal of one's identity.

The causal relation between personality and health runs in both directions: Personality influences health, and health influences personality. Studies generally cannot yield definitive findings about the direction of the association, but some study designs permit stronger inferences than others. Cross-sectional studies have uncovered many interesting associations between personality and health, but they cannot lead to strong conclusions about the direction of causality. Longitudinal studies are more compelling and are used exclusively in this chapter. When significant associations are found between personality measured some time prior to the assessment of health status, after controlling for obvious confounds (e.g., gender and education), then a stronger inference can be made that personality has had an effect on health. Similarly, if personality is assessed after a significant health event, it may suggest that the event influenced personality. Given that both personality and health change over the lifespan, a more sophisticated design is to measure them both on multiple occasions and investigate the relation between change in one and change in the other. Nevertheless, all of these study designs are observational, not experimental, so they cannot provide unambiguous answers about the direction of causality. In addition, there is always the possibility that personality change and health change are the result of an underlying influence not included in the study (the so-called "third variable" explanation) that gives rise to a spurious association, in which case there would be no causal relation between personality and health.

The selection of findings on personality development and health presented here emphasizes studies relating personality traits to objective assessments of physical health. Self-reported disease status and general health are also widely used in personality and health research. However, self-reports can be less accurate than more objective measures, such as a medical diagnosis or the results of a laboratory test. Self-reports are subject to biases, including personality biases. For example, people who are more neurotic tend to report more symptoms (Costa & McCrae, 1987). Objective assessments of health refer to measures such as blood pressure, heart rate, height, and weight taken by a qualified clinician; they also include laboratory assays of biological materials such as blood and urine. These measurements are commonly referred to as "biomarkers." An undisputable objective indicator of health is vital status (alive or dead), and longevity is used as a health outcome in some longitudinal studies of personality and health.

The chapter is organized as follows. The first sections sum up findings on the prospective association between personality assessed at one stage in life and health assessed at a later stage. Next, studies of personality change in relation to health, and health change in relation to personality, are considered. Then I look at whether there are interventions to change the course of personality development to lead to better health outcomes. Finally, I draw some conclusions about the possibilities offered by the changing nature of personality to improve health.

Personality in Childhood and Adolescence in Relation to Later Health

The idea that a child's personality is linked, perhaps causally, to his or her health as an adult may seem quite a stretch. To illustrate with an extreme but, sadly, all too real example, we may remember a classmate in elementary school who was a rule-breaker, always getting into trouble and doing risky things. How did life turn out for that classmate? In personality terms, we could describe him or her as sensation seeking: someone who seeks out thrills and adventure, and acts impulsively. On the Big Five dimensions, he or she might be high on extraversion, low on conscientiousness, and perhaps emotionally unstable. Based on research on predictors of substance use, we know that he or she was at increased risk of smoking cigarettes and drinking alcohol as a preteen, using marijuana in his or her early teens, and possibly going on to hard drug use. Tragically, as a young adult, he or she may have died in a drunk-driving accident, or from a drug overdose. If the classmate survived these youthful hazards, he or she may have developed lung cancer later in life, caused by a lifetime addiction to cigarettes, or liver disease from heavy drinking. This is an extreme example. Childhood personality pathways to adult health outcomes are likely to be less dramatic. Over time, modest personality influences may be associated with the development of more or less healthy habits, and personality traits may interact with environmental factors, such as exposure to stress, leading to slow but insidious effects on later health.

In childhood, roughly defined as elementary school grades 1–6 (ages 6–12 years), children's personalities are typically assessed by observers such as teachers or parents because children's self-reflective capacity is limited. At this age, personality undergoes changes, as has been shown by comparing trait stability measured by rank-order correlations within different age groups. The rank-order correlation coefficient measures the degree of similarity between the relative standing of members of a sample on a trait at one time compared to another. Rank-order stability indicates the extent to which an individual maintains his or her position in a group: Is the most talkative kid in the class in elementary school the most talkative teen in high school? These correlations are lower for children than for adults across the same time interval, but they are far from negligible. In their analysis of 152 studies, Roberts and DelVecchio (2000) reported a rank-order stability correlation for children ages 6–12 years between .40 and .50, whereas for adults ages 50–59, it was over .70. Rank-order stability is different from the mean-level stability, which describes the extent to which the average level of a trait in a population changes across times of measurement and is indicative of normative, maturational trends. Given that childhood personality traits are undergoing maturational and idiosyncratic change, is it possible that trait levels assessed on one occasion in childhood can tell us anything about future health? The surprising answer is "yes."

Two studies demonstrated that childhood personality traits assessed in elementary school predict clinical health status in young adulthood (Moffitt et al., 2011) and middle age (Hampson, Edmonds, Goldberg, Dubanoski, & Hillier, 2013). In both studies, health status was measured by combinations of biomarkers indicative of cardiovascular and metabolic disease risk, such as lipid levels, blood glucose, and waist size. Childhood traits even predict longevity (Friedman et al., 1993). Childhood personality scores were derived in different ways across these studies: by a comprehensive assessment of parent-, teacher-, and self-reports combined across multiple assessments (Moffitt et al., 2011); by combined parent and teacher ratings (Friedman et al., 1995); and by teachers' impressions of the child formed over an entire school year (Hampson et al., 2013). Nevertheless, the strongest and most consistent associations with health outcomes found in these studies were for traits of childhood conscientiousness. The broad domain of personality labeled *conscientiousness* includes important characteristics such as self-control, persistence in the face of challenges, planning ahead, and being organized. Such qualities promote a range of positive life outcomes, including health.

These studies demonstrated associations across decades between childhood traits in the Big Five domain of conscientiousness and health in adulthood, after controlling for confounding variables such as educational attainment and gender. Importantly, childhood conscientiousness predicts health outcomes even after removing the influence of adult conscientiousness. At least two independent studies have demonstrated that regardless of their level of conscientiousness in adulthood, conscientious children are more likely to be healthier adults, as indicated by a combination of cardiovascular and metabolic biomarkers (Hampson et al., 2013), and by longevity (Martin, Friedman, & Schwartz, 2007). The maturational trend (mean level change) suggests a decline in conscientiousness in childhood and adolescence followed by increases in adulthood (Soto, John, Gosling, & Potter, 2011). However, conscientiousness shows modest rank-order stability across time. In the Hawaii Longitudinal Study of Personality and Health, the correlation between conscientiousness measured in childhood at about age 10 and 40 years later was $r =$ .25 (Edmonds, Goldberg, Hampson, & Barckley, 2013; Hampson & Goldberg, 2006). Using data from the ongoing Dunedin Multidisciplinary Health and Development Study, Moffitt and colleagues (2011) obtained a slightly higher correlation of $r = .30$ for self-control assessed across a shorter time span from childhood to young adulthood, and Martin and colleagues (2007) observed a somewhat lower correlation of $r = .15$ for participants in the Terman Life Cycle study between child and adult conscientiousness averaged across measures 18 and 28 years later. These comparatively low levels of rank-order stability reflect the length of time between assessments and the age span, which encompassed the period of maximum developmental change (i.e., childhood to adulthood).

The long-lasting influence of childhood conscientiousness on health, regardless of later conscientiousness, suggests that there may be something special about this trait during the elementary school years. Epidemiologists describe this type of time-limited effect as a critical or sensitive period for exposure to a particular risk factor (Lynch & Davey Smith, 2005). They are typically concerned with an external influence such as poverty. Here, we can extend the idea to an internal influence, namely, the level of a particular personality trait. It may be the case that childhood is a critical period for laying down patterns of behavior and their biological effects that endure into adulthood. Childhood conscientiousness may foster healthy habits, such as participating in active hobbies, and practicing dental hygiene. On the other hand, personality traits such as lack of self-control may result in behaviors that increase the probability of exposure to dangerous or traumatic situations and adversely affect health through long-lasting biological consequences of stress. Investigating these kinds of links in the chain from childhood personality to adult health outcomes is one current direction in personality and health research (Shanahan, Hill, Roberts, Eccles, & Friedman, 2014).

A somewhat different approach to studying childhood personality and health is illustrated by the Cardiovascular Risk in Young Finns (CRYF) study, which is an ongoing investigation of risk factors for cardiovascular disease in a representative sample ages 3–18 at recruitment. The investigators combined a variety of environmental and individual psychosocial risk factors, including parent's ratings of their child's self-regulation, into a summary score. In effect, this score collapsed a series of variables that could be seen as related in a causal chain into a single index. The summary score predicted a composite measure of cardiovascular health assessed by self-report and clinical measures 27 years later (Pulkki-Råback et al., 2015). In addition, children's self-regulation alone predicted cardiovascular health, consistent with other studies that have measured the related concepts of self-control and conscientiousness.

Adult Personality in Relation to Later Health

Young Adulthood

Young or "emerging" adulthood (roughly ages 18–30) is a period of continuing physical and psychological development that has been singled out as a development period in its own right that lies between adolescence and adulthood (Arnett, 2000). Young adults in this age group explore relationships and career choices with varying degrees of success, and their experience in these roles may lead to personality changes. Investment in social roles such as marriage and parenthood has been associated with normative personality development in some (e.g., Roberts & Wood, 2006) but not all studies (e.g., van Scheppingen et al., 2016).

Despite personality change in young adulthood, personality measured during this time can predict later health outcomes. College students have long provided a ready sample for psychological research, including studies of personality and health. In the middle of the previous century, the Grant Longitudinal Study was initiated with a sample of healthy and successful male Harvard undergraduates. They were first assessed as undergraduates between 1938 and 1942, then followed up repeatedly with self-report and objective assessments of physical and psychological health. This classic study is well described in Vaillant's (1977, 2012) engaging books. The Harvard study, like the Terman Life Cycle Study, continues to offer rich opportunities for researchers, who can conduct new analyses on these old and valuable data to test current hypotheses. For example, Peterson, Seligman, and Vaillant (1988) measured pessimistic explanatory style by content analysis of reports of their World War II experiences obtained from a subset of the Harvard men. They related this measure of pessimism to the men's physical health assessed by doctors every 5 years until age 60. Those who were more pessimistic had worse health in later life, controlling for baseline health. Moreover, pessimistic style predicted decreases in health from one assessment to the next. This is one of the first studies to show that a personality characteristic measured at one time was associated with subsequent health change measured over a series of assessments. In the Big Five framework, the dimension of optimism is probably associated with aspects of all of the Big Five except openness/intellect (Sharpe, Martin, & Roth, 2011).

More recent studies of young adults also emphasize the significance of predicting health change from personality characteristics. The Dunedin Study demonstrated the influence of personality traits measured during young adulthood on later health change (Israel et al., 2014). Lower levels of conscientiousness and openness measured by observer ratings at age 26 were associated with decreases in clinically assessed health (a combination of biomarkers) from ages 26 to 38, controlling for numerous other risk factors. As the researchers noted, this is a powerful demonstration of the influence of personality on health because these traits prospectively predicted health change, similar to the findings for pessimism in the Harvard study. In a comparable design, in the CRYF, two personality traits of young Finns ages 24–39 at baseline predicted their weight gain over the subsequent 6 years (Hintsanen et al., 2012). Higher novelty seeking predicted weight gain for men and women, and lower reward dependence (i.e., being less empathic, sentimental, and sensitive to social cues) predicted weight gain for women

only. The latter finding is somewhat surprising, but it might be that those women with lower reward dependence were less concerned with the social rewards of maintaining their weight.

Studying the long-term implications for health of personality assessed in children, youth, and young adults requires a major investment of resources, so, not surprisingly, there are relatively few such studies. Although these studies inevitably did not include personality measures that are now considered state of the art, their data can either be reanalyzed to provide measures aligned with the five-factor model (Martin & Friedman, 2000), or their measures can be interpreted within this framework (Peterson et al., 1988). By reanalyzing these valuable data to address contemporary research questions, they continue to provide insights into the association between early personality and later health (Kern, Hampson, Goldberg, & Friedman, 2014).

Adulthood

The period from around ages 30–60 is when there is comparatively little personality development and rank-order stability of personality traits reaches its peak (Specht et al., 2014). Based on the hypothesis that personality exerts a sustained, prospective influence on health outcomes, studies limited to this age range are expected to yield the strongest associations between personality and health. A stable level on a trait such as conscientiousness over years or decades may have cumulative benefits for the individual through, for example, the maintenance of good health practices that provide high levels of cardiovascular and metabolic protection.

Mortality is the ultimate hard endpoint for longitudinal studies of adult health. There is by now compelling evidence to indicate that the personality trait of conscientiousness is a prospective predictor of longevity: Adults who are more conscientious are likely to live longer than those who are less conscientious. This evidence for adults confirms the dramatic findings for childhood conscientiousness in the Terman Life Cycle Study first reported by Friedman and colleagues (1993) over 20 years ago. The evidence for adults comes from individual studies (e.g., Hagger-Johnson et al., 2012; Terracciano, Löckenhoff, Zonderman, Ferrucci, & Costa, 2008), and meta-analyses that combine findings across multiple studies. A meta-analysis of 20 independent samples including nearly 9,000 people established a pooled correlation of $r = .11$ between conscientiousness and mortality (Kern & Friedman, 2008). This effect may not seem high, but it is greater than the effect of aspirin on reducing the risk of heart disease, and the effect of intelligence on mortality risk (Roberts, Kuncel, Shiner, Caspi, & Goldberg, 2007). Another meta-analysis of over 76,000 individuals from seven different cohort studies, with a mean age of 50.9 years at the time of personality measurement, found that conscientiousness was the only one of the Big Five traits to predict all-cause mortality (Jokela et al., 2013). Those in the lowest tertile for conscientiousness had a 34% increased risk of dying compared to those in the top two tertiles. Other Big Five traits that have been associated with mortality risk, but less consistently, are neuroticism and hostility (low agreeableness), and a few studies have found extraversion to increase and openness to experience to decrease mortality risk (Ferguson & Bibby, 2012; Roberts, Kuncel, Shiner, Caspi, & Goldberg, 2007; Turiano, Spiro, & Mroczek, 2012).

Personality Development and Personality–Health Mechanisms

Personality and health researchers are investigating mechanisms that may explain the association between personality traits and health outcomes that have been observed across the lifespan (Hampson, 2012; Hill, Turiano, Hurd, Mroczek, & Roberts, 2011; Turiano et al., 2015). For example, a conscientious person may be more likely to have a healthy lifestyle than an unconscientious person. The conscientious person will take the steps that are necessary to exercise regularly and have healthful food available at home. He or she will have sufficient perseverance to stick with exercise goals, and enough self-control to resist those high-fat, high-sugar, high-salt foods deliberately designed to tempt us. Healthful habits sustained over adult life reduce the likelihood of developing chronic, life-threatening conditions such as diabetes and heart disease, and childhood conscientiousness appears to set us on the path to acquiring and maintaining those habits and enjoying the ensuing health benefits (Hampson, Edmonds, Goldberg, Dubanoski, & Hillier, 2015).

Health-behavior mechanisms only provide a partial explanation for the association between personality and health, leaving room for other possible processes to be involved. Stress is one

such process through which personality influences may operate (Hampson et al., 2016). Luo and Roberts (2015) found that changes in conscientiousness, stress, and self-reported health studied over 3 years were associated. These changes suggested a stress mechanism in which higher conscientiousness protected a person from experiencing stress, which in turn protected his or her health. More research relating changes on traits, health outcomes, and potential mechanisms can be expected in the future as investigators try to pinpoint more precisely the possible causal relations among these variables.

The studies described so far have suggested that regardless of the age at which personality was measured, the trait of conscientiousness, and ones conceptually similar to it, have been the most consistently related to later morbidity and mortality. This reliable and replicable prospective finding suggests that conscientiousness may be causally related to health, and mechanisms for this influence have been examined. However, these studies do not fully consider the possible impact of personality development on health. They demonstrated that being more conscientious at a certain age conferred a future health benefit, but they do not consider the effects of personality change on health. If a trait is indeed causally related to a health outcome, then changes on the trait should be associated with corresponding changes on that outcome. I consider in the next part of this chapter studies that offer the possibility for stronger causal inferences because they have examined personality change.

Personality Change and Health

Change in Adulthood

Developmental changes in the direction of personality maturation (increasing agreeableness, conscientiousness, and extraversion, and decreasing neuroticism) may be beneficial for health. These maturational changes in the socially desirable direction may result in better health because of greater conformity to good health practices, and less stress resulting from negative social interactions or other events precipitated by undesirable traits.

A study of over 11,000 Australians indicated that socially desirable personality change is associated with health improvements (Magee, Heaven, & Miller, 2013). The Big Five personality traits and self-reported health were measured on two occasions, 4 years apart. Increases in extraversion and conscientiousness, and decreases in neuroticism were associated with better health. A strength of this study was that personality and health were each measured at the two time points, so that both personality change and health change could be examined. In a study that had a longer follow-up period of 10 years, Turiano, Pitzer, and colleagues (2012) used data from the Midlife in the United States (MIDUS) study to relate personality change to self-reported health. Big Five personality traits were assessed on two occasions 10 years apart, and health was assessed by self-report on the second occasion. As in the study by Magee and colleagues (2013), becoming more conscientious and less neurotic was associated with better health but, in addition, becoming more agreeable was associated with poorer health. This finding indicates that socially desirable changes in personality may not necessarily translate into health benefits. For example, a person who becomes more agreeable over time may be more willing to provide care for a family member with developmental disability or dementia. Caregivers are at higher risk of developing their own physical and mental health problems (Schulz & Sherwood, 2008). In a similar vein, more empathic parents caring for adolescent children had higher levels of inflammation than less empathic parents (Manczak, DeLongis, & Chen, 2016). Empathy is a personality trait that overlaps with agreeableness and conscientiousness (Melchers et al., 2016).

Researchers are only beginning to study the mechanisms by which personality changes are related to health changes. If traits influence health through behaviors, then trait change may be related to behavior change and, hence, health change. In a study conducted with a community sample over 3 years, Takahashi, Edmonds, Jackson, and Roberts (2012) observed that increases in conscientiousness were associated with increases in health-enhancing behaviors and self-reported health. However, a recent meta-analysis produced different results. Data from seven longitudinal studies indicated that individuals' health-enhancing behavior did not increase and decrease in concert with increases and decreases in their conscientiousness (Jokela, 2016). There are several possible reasons for this null finding, such as differences in the measures of conscientiousness across the different studies, but this analysis is a reminder of how

much more there is to discover about mechanisms of personality, behavior, and health change over the life course.

If desirable trait change can be associated with poor health, then personality change per se may be related to health outcomes. Is it possible that absolute trait change in adulthood is damaging for health? Another study using MIDUS data illustrates this possibility. Human and colleagues (2013) related personality change over two assessments 10 years apart, to self-reported health, and to the metabolic syndrome objectively assessed at the time of the second personality assessment. The metabolic syndrome is a constellation of biomarkers such as waist circumference, blood pressure, and fasting blood glucose, which indicates risk of cardiovascular disease and diabetes. Trait change in the undesirable direction was associated with worse self-reported health. However, the most striking finding from this study was that absolute personality change was associated with having more biomarkers meeting the cutoff for metabolic syndrome. This study also found that absolute change (either increases or decreases) in agency, which measured empowerment and the sense of control over one's environment, was associated with poorer metabolic health. The biomarkers were only measured at the second assessment, so it is unknown how much health change occurred over the follow-up. It is possible that changing health over 10 years led to the observed changes in personality, so causal inferences from these findings are tempered by this limitation. Nevertheless, it is a provocative idea that personality change in either direction can have negative consequences for health. In adulthood, personality is typically relatively stable (both rank-order and mean-level stability), so when personality change does occur, it may be related to a life event or stressor, which could affect health. Perhaps trait change in adulthood threatens one's coherent sense of self. In adults, traits, motives, and autobiographical narrative are integrated to form a sense of self, so changes in any one of these components may weaken that sense of self, which may have negative health consequences.

Change in Old Age

We still have much to learn about personality in old age, but it does appear to be a time when maturational personality change becomes more likely after a period of relative stability in adulthood (Specht et al., 2014). Findings vary across studies as to what may be normative developmental trends for this age group. One study showed decreased conscientiousness and increased agreeableness in those ages 61–99 years, termed the "dolce vita" effect (Marsh, Nagengast, & Morin, 2013), whereas others have not obtained similar results (Allemand, Zimprich, & Hendriks, 2008; Soto et al., 2011). These days, old age, if defined as over age 60, may last for several decades, and studies that include the oldest-old may yield different results from those that do not.

Personality change in old age has been related to health outcomes. Mroczek and Spiro (2007) related changes in neuroticism to mortality risk among older men in the Normative Aging Study. At the beginning of the study, their participants ranged in age from 43 to 91 years, and they were followed for 12 years. Changes in neuroticism were modeled as growth trajectories, which provide a measure of the trait's initial level and change over time. They found that the men with the highest initial levels of neuroticism in combination with the highest increases in neuroticism had the highest mortality risk. Studying octogenarians, Mõttus, Johnson, Starr, and Deary (2012) investigated personality change for all the Big Five traits in the ninth decade, measured over two assessments from ages 81 to 87. Unlike Mroczek and Spiro's study, emotional stability (i.e., neuroticism) remained stable over the two assessments, whereas the remaining Big Five traits declined. Declines in conscientiousness were associated with declines in physical fitness. As people live longer but not necessarily healthier lives, understanding the association between personality change and health change in the oldest-old is becoming increasingly relevant.

Health Change and Personality

It may be intuitively easier to believe that changes in health lead to personality change, than to believe that changes in personality lead to changes in health. Stressful life events appear to have effects on aspects of personality, such as making a person more neurotic (Riese et al., 2014), and the onset of a life-changing disease is surely one kind of major stressful event. Illness leads to multiple changes with potential to alter personality. The experience of having a disease affects a person's biology, which may affect their personality. A person diagnosed with a disease may also acquire a new social identity and a new social role: the "sick" role (Goffman, 1990). When a person becomes a "cancer patient," a "diabetic," or he or she "has the flu," the person must change aspects of his or her lifestyle and be treated differently by others because of this new identity. The person may come to see him- or herself differently as a result. It seems highly plausible, therefore, to expect some personality change as a consequence of illness.

Literature and real life abound with examples of illness affecting people's lives and, by extension, their personalities. I enjoy Jane Austen's novels, and my favorite is *Persuasion*. One of the more dramatic moments in the book is when Louisa Musgrove impetuously jumps off a wall, surprising her gallant companion, who fails to catch her. She suffers a fairly serious concussion. During her convalescence, she falls in love with a thoughtful, poetry-loving young man with a tendency toward melancholy. Prior to her accident, she was not much of a reader or a deep thinker. How could these two fall in love? We are told they fell in love over poetry. He was a constant presence during her recovery and doubtless taught her to appreciate the poetry he loved. Not much more explanation is offered, but we can fill in the blanks. The injury may have left her frightened, chastened even, as well as weak, confused, and in pain. In this susceptible state, she underwent a change of values and perhaps a reappraisal of her life to date. Doubtless, in the future, she would see her accident as a key turning point in her autobiography.

A more contemporary and real-life illustration of the life-changing impact of illness was provided by Laura Hillenbrand, author of a best-selling book about an initially unpromising race horse called Seabiscuit, who eventually became American Horse of the Year in 1938. In a *New Yorker* Personal History article, she gave a vivid account of the sudden onset of chronic fatigue syndrome and its subsequent effects on her life (Hillenbrand, 2003). She had to make enormous compromises to accommodate this debilitating illness. She dropped out of college and rarely left the house. For years, she was unable to travel in a car because of severe vertigo. In the broader sense of personality as the combination of traits, motives/goals, and autobiography, this illness led to dramatic changes and was a major event in her personal narrative.

A challenge for studying the effects of illness on personality is that, ideally, personality should be measured prior to the onset of illness, as well as afterward. A retrospective report of personality before the illness is likely to be less accurate than measures obtained before the illness occurred. Fortunately, some recent studies have collected these measures. A study of young adults in Finland demonstrated that the onset of a chronic illness by age 20, or between ages 20 and 23, was related to increased neuroticism from ages 20 to 23 (Liekas & Salmela-Aro, 2015). In addition, those who were diagnosed with a chronic disease by age 20 had greater increases in conscientiousness between ages 20 and 23 than those with no such diagnosis. This study suggests that disease onset in emerging adulthood, which is already a time of considerable personality change, may have both negative and positive consequences for personality change. Increases in neuroticism may be the result of health-related anxiety and vigilant disease monitoring, whereas increases in conscientiousness may be the result of improved health behavior leading to changes in self-perception. A study of older participants drawn from three large-scale cohort studies, spanning young adulthood to old age, found that conscientiousness decreased after the onset of chronic illness (Jokela, Hakulinen, Singh-Manoux, & Kivimäki, 2014). In contrast to these studies, using data from the Baltimore Longitudinal Study of Aging, which includes multiple assessments of personality and disease over time, Sutin, Zonderman, Ferrucci, and Terracciano (2013) observed that personality remained largely unchanged in response to disease onset. Based on the limited research so far, it is not clear whether illness onset is linked to changes that deviate from or enhance the pattern of normative trait development for a particular age. In addition, there is still much to discover about the effects of specific illnesses on trait change.

Intentional Personality Change

Personality change is assumed to be triggered by a number of influences, including biological maturation, the influence of social milestones such as going to college, and events such as disease onset (Lodi-Smith & Roberts, 2007). Most people would like to change some aspect of their personality (Hudson & Roberts, 2014). I have an acquaintance who told me she decided as a teenager to change from being an introvert to an extravert because extraverts were happier

and had more fun. I would say she succeeded, so some of us can indeed make intentional personality changes.

A question that is difficult to answer, however, is whether personality change is the result or cause of behavior change (Hudson & Fraley, 2015). Landmark life events necessitate behavior changes that over time may become consolidated in the form of trait change and change in identity (Roberts & Jackson, 2008). Alternatively, life events may impose new roles and social identities that require changes in traits and behaviors (Lodi-Smith & Roberts, 2007). These contrasting mechanisms of trait change have been described, respectively, as bottom-up (i.e., behavior-driven) versus top-down approaches (i.e., trait-driven), (Magidson, Roberts, Collado-Rodriguez, & Lejuez, 2014).

A health event is one motivator of behavior change that may lead to bottom-up trait change. An accident, or the onset of a serious chronic illness, can be a powerful wake-up call to adopt a healthier lifestyle. In my work on illness beliefs among people with type 2 diabetes, it was not uncommon for people to say that the onset of this disease made them take better care of themselves (Hampson, Glasgow, & Toobert, 1990). Leading a healthier lifestyle as a result of their illness might have had a bottom-up effect of increasing their level of conscientiousness. There is evidence for this kind of personality change. Healthy living at baseline, particularly higher levels of physical exercise and more modest alcohol consumption, was associated with positive trait change, including increased conscientiousness, over the subsequent 4 years in a nationally representative sample of Australian adults (Allen, Vella, & Laborde, 2015). Even more marked effects might be observed when healthy living is prompted by a change in health status.

It is also possible to change personality using a top-down approach that aims to change personality traits, and therefore behavior. Psychotherapeutic interventions have been shown to be associated with trait changes on the Big Five, such as extraversion and neuroticism (for reviews, see Chapman, Hampson, & Clarkin, 2014; Magidson et al., 2014; Roberts et al., 2017). Top-down trait change, aided by an intervention to help with implementing intentions to change, has also been demonstrated with undergraduates (Hudson & Fraley, 2015).

Intentional personality change includes changing goals and motivations, as well as traits. *Agency,* the capacity to consciously shape the direction of one's life, is an essential human quality that is not adequately addressed in trait research (Heckhausen et al., 2010). To maximize success in life, it is necessary not only to choose goals wisely and pursue them vigorously, but also to know when it is time to let go. Heckhausen and colleagues identify two kinds of control that are involved in successful development. *Primary control processes* are directed at changing one's world to bring the environment into line with one's wishes. For example, an older woman may choose to move to a senior-living community when she finds she no longer wishes to have the responsibilities of independent living. *Secondary control processes* (motivation) support primary control by helping one to stay committed to a goal in the face of challenges, for example, by seeking social support from others. It is important to take a lifespan perspective when studying human agency because goals change with age. Among older adults, it is necessary to disengage from goals that were more relevant in youth. For those with chronic illness, goals must be modified to adapt to limitations (Saajanaho et al., 2016). Primary control strategies are associated with better health outcomes, less depression, and less functional disability (Heckhausen et al., 2010), and conflict between primary and secondary processes leads to poorer health outcomes (Hamm, Chipperfield, Perry, Heckhausen, & Mackenzie, 2014). These findings suggest that the agentic aspects of personality are important for health. Supporting the development of adaptive primary control strategies and the motivation to stay committed to one's health-related goals are ways in which we can stay on more healthful trajectories.

Summary and Conclusions

At the beginning of this chapter, I suggested that a greater understanding of the relation between personality development and health would provide insights into how we might be able to alter our health trajectory. As we have seen, although personality development continues across the lifespan, some personality traits, particularly conscientiousness, measured at one point in life predict later health. This holds true for personality measured during life stages characterized by more change (i.e., childhood, youth, and old age), as well as the relatively

stable period of life during adulthood. Personality change also predicts health change, and health change predicts personality change. The implication of these findings is that at any time in life, it may be valuable to attempt personality change in the health-enhancing direction. However, childhood seems to be an especially promising time to encourage the development of greater conscientiousness through actions such as school-based interventions and parental modeling.

Nevertheless, it is important not to paint an overly straightforward picture of the association between personality development and health, and what it implies. As we have seen, while many studies suggest that personality assessed at one point in life predicts later health, these observations are only suggestive of a causal relation, and much remains to be learned about the mechanisms that underlie this association, especially when considered developmentally. As personality and health develop and change over time, the processes relating the two are also changing. While we have begun to study these changes, more longitudinal data with multiple measures are needed, as well as sophisticated analytic techniques to reach a better understanding of these complex associations. Until we have a more complete grasp on mechanisms of personality and health over the lifespan, we should proceed cautiously with interventions intended to improve health by changing personality.

The focus on personality development and change across the lifespan now prevalent in trait research contradicts our personal experience of a fairly consistent sense of self over time. Our personal narratives, or autobiographical selves, may be punctuated by major turning points that reflect marked changes in our lives, but we are probably not so aware of more modest changes in ourselves over time. We may under- or overestimate the degree of actual change. Consider a classic study in which participants were asked to recall how well adjusted they were 25 years earlier, when they were 19 years olds (Woodruff & Birren, 1972). The investigators were fortunate enough to have the self-ratings of adjustment from their participants when they were 19 to compare with the 25-year retrospective ratings. They found a discrepancy: Participants remembered themselves as being less well adjusted at 19 than they had described themselves at the time. They recalled more self-change than was apparently the case, perhaps to be consistent with their personal narratives of becoming mature adults. Despite the evidence that childhood personality appears to direct people onto pathways to later health outcomes, it seems unlikely that people would accurately recall their level of conscientiousness as children or attribute their health at midlife to this childhood trait (although this would be an interesting question to research). While the stories that we live by may not be completely accurate, they provide meaning and coherence (McAdams, 1993). Findings from studies of personality development and health, such as those reviewed here, may provide insights that people can incorporate into their autobiographies and perhaps use to make desired changes in their lives.

As this chapter has illustrated, the majority of research on personality development and health has been focused on traits, ignoring the agentic and autobiographical aspects of the self. Trait research has revealed some remarkable findings about the relation between personality and health outcomes across the lifespan. Nevertheless, a more complete understanding of how personality change is related to health may be achieved if personality researchers go beyond traits. By incorporating the subjective experience of growing and changing over the lifespan, we may achieve a more complete picture of the relation between personality and health.

ACKNOWLEDGMENTS

Preparation of this chapter was supported by Grant No. R01AG020048. I am grateful to Patrick L. Hill for his comments on an earlier draft.

REFERENCES

Allemand, M., Zimprich, D., & Hendriks, A. J. (2008). Age differences in five personality domains across the life span. *Developmental Psychology, 44*(3), 758–770.

Allen, M. S., Vella, S. A., & Laborde, S. (2015). Health-related behavior and personality trait development in adulthood. *Journal of Research in Personality, 59*, 104–110.

Arnett, J. J. (2000). Emerging adulthood. *American Psychologist, 55*(5), 469–480.

Chapman, B. P., Hampson, S. E., & Clarkin, J. (2014). Personality-informed interventions for healthy aging: Conclusions from a National Institute on Aging work group. *Developmental Psychology, 50*(5), 1426–1441.

Costa, P. T., & McCrae, R. R. (1987). Neuroticism, so-

matic complaints, and disease: Is the bark worse than the bite? *Journal of Personality, 55*, 299–316.

Edmonds, G. W., Goldberg, L. R., Hampson, S. E., & Barckley, M. (2013). Personality stability from childhood to midlife: Relating teachers' assessments in elementary school to observer- and self-ratings 40 years later. *Journal of Research in Personality, 47*, 505–513.

Ferguson, E., & Bibby, P. A. (2012). Openness to experience and all-cause mortality: A meta-analysis and $r_{equivalent}$ from risk ratios and odds ratios. *British Journal of Health Psychology, 17*, 85–102.

Friedman, H. S., Tucker, J. S., Schwartz, J. E., Tomlinson-Keasey, C., Martin, L. R., Wingard, D. L., et al. (1995). Psychosocial and behavioral predictors of longevity: The aging and death of the "termites." *American Psychologist, 50*(2), 69–78.

Friedman, H. S., Tucker, J. S., Tomlinson-Keasey, C., Schwartz, J. E., Wingard, D. L., & Criqui, M. H. (1993). Does childhood personality predict longevity? *Journal of Personality and Social Psychology, 65*(1), 176–185.

Goffman, E. (1990). *The presentation of self in everyday life*. London: Penguin Books.

Hagger-Johnson, G., Sabia, S., Nabi, H., Brunner, E., Kivimaki, M., Shipley, M., et al. (2012). Low conscientiousness and risk of all-cause, cardiovascular and cancer mortality over 17 years: Whitehall II cohort study. *Journal of Psychosomatic Research, 73*, 98–103.

Hamm, J. M., Chipperfield, J. G., Perry, R. P., Heckhausen, J., & Mackenzie, C. S. (2014). Conflicted goal engagement: Undermining physical activity and health in late life. *Journals of Gerontology B: Psychological Sciences and Social Sciences, 69*(4), 533–542.

Hampson, S. E. (2012). Personality processes: Mechanisms by which personality traits "get outside the skin." *Annual Review of Psychology, 63*, 315–339.

Hampson, S. E., Edmonds, G. W., Goldberg, L. R., Barckley, M., Klest, B., Dubanoski, J. P., et al. (2016). Lifetime trauma, personality traits, and health: A pathway to midlife health status. *Psychological Trauma, 8*(4), 447–454.

Hampson, S. E., Edmonds, G. W., Goldberg, L. R., Dubanoski, J. P., & Hillier, T. A. (2013). Childhood conscientiousness relates to objectively measured adult physical health four decades later. *Health Psychology, 32*(8), 925–928.

Hampson, S. E., Edmonds, G. W., Goldberg, L. R., Dubanoski, J. P., & Hillier, T. A. (2015). A life-span behavioral mechanism relating childhood conscientiousness to adult clinical health. *Health Psychology, 34*(9), 887–895.

Hampson, S. E., Glasgow, R. E., & Toobert, D. J. (1990). Personal models of diabetes and their relations to self-care activities. *Health Psychology, 9*(5), 632–646.

Hampson, S. E., & Goldberg, L. R. (2006). A first large cohort study of personality trait stability over the

40 years between elementary school and midlife. *Journal of Personality and Social Psychology, 91*(4), 763–779.

Heckhausen, J., & Wrosch, C. (2016). Challenges to developmental regulation across the life course: What are they and which individual differences matter? *International Journal of Behavioral Development, 40*(2), 145–150.

Heckhausen, J., Wrosch, C., & Schulz, R. (2010). A motivational theory of life-span development. *Psychological Review, 117*(1), 32–60.

Hill, P. L., Turiano, N. A., Hurd, M. D., Mroczek, D. K., & Roberts, B. W. (2011). Conscientiousness and longevity: An examination of possible mediators. *Health Psychology, 30*(5), 536–541.

Hillenbrand, L. (2003, July). A sudden illness. *The New Yorker*, pp. 56–59.

Hintsanen, M., Jokela, M., Cloninger, C. R., Pulkki-Råback, L., Hintsa, T., Elovainio, M., et al. (2012). Temperament and character predict body-mass index: A population-based prospective cohort study. *Journal of Psychosomatic Research, 73*, 391–397.

Hogan, R., & Roberts, B. W. (2004). A socioanalytic model of maturity. *Journal of Career Assessment, 12*(2), 207–217.

Hooker, K., & McAdams, D. P. (2003). Personality reconsidered: A new agenda for aging research. *Journals of Gerontology B: Psychological Sciences and Social Sciences, 58*(6), P296–P304.

Hudson, N. W., & Fraley, R. C. (2015). Volitional personality trait change: Can people choose to change their personality traits? *Journal of Personality and Social Psychology, 109*(3), 490–507.

Hudson, N. W., & Roberts, B. W. (2014). Goals to change personality traits: Concurrent links between personality traits, daily behavior, and goals to change oneself. *Journal of Research in Personality, 53*, 68–83.

Human, L. J., Biesanz, J. C., Miller, G. E., Chen, E., Lachman, M. E., & Seeman, T. E. (2013). Is change bad?: Personality change is associated with poorer psychological health and greater metabolic syndrome in midlife. *Journal of Personality, 81*(3), 249–260.

Israel, S., Moffitt, T. E., Belsky, D. W., Hancox, R. J., Poulton, R., Roberts, B., et al. (2014). Translating personality psychology to help personalize preventive medicine for young adult patients. *Journal of Personality and Social Psychology, 106*(3), 484–498.

John, O. P., Naumann, L. P., & Soto, C. J. (2008). Paradigm shift to the integrative Big Five trait taxonomy. In O. P. John, R. W. Robins, & L. A. Pervin (Eds.), *Handbook of personality: Theory and research* (3rd ed., pp. 114–158). New York: Guilford Press.

Jokela, M. (2016, July). *Is low conscientiousness a causal risk factor for poor health?* Paper presented at the 18th European Conference on Personality, Timisoara, Romania.

Jokela, M., Batty, G. D., Nyberg, S. T., Virtanen, M., Nabi, H., Singh-Manoux, A., et al. (2013). Personality and all-cause mortality: Individual-participant

meta-analysis of 3,947 deaths in 76,150 adults. *American Journal of Epidemiology, 178*, 667–675.

Jokela, M., Hakulinen, C., Singh-Manoux, A., & Kivimäki, M. (2014). Personality change associated with chronic diseases: Pooled analysis of four prospective cohort studies. *Psychological Medicine, 44*(12), 2629–2640.

Kern, M. L., & Friedman, H. S. (2008). Do conscientious individuals live longer?: A quantitative review. *Health Psychology, 27*(5), 505–512.

Kern, M. L., Hampson, S. E., Goldberg, L. R., & Friedman, H. S. (2014). Integrating prospective longitudinal data: Modeling personality and health in the Terman Life Cycle and Hawaii Longitudinal Studies. *Developmental Psychology, 50*(5), 1390–1406.

Leikas, S., & Salmela-Aro, K. (2015). Personality trait changes among young Finns: The role of life events and transitions. *Journal of Personality, 83*(1), 117–126.

Lodi-Smith, J., & Roberts, B. W. (2007). Social investment and personality: A meta-analysis of the relationship of personality traits to investment in work, family, religion, and volunteerism. *Personality and Social Psychology Review, 11*, 68–86.

Luo, J., & Roberts, B. W. (2015). Concurrent and longitudinal relations among conscientiousness, stress, and self-perceived physical health. *Journal of Research in Personality, 59*, 93–103.

Lynch, J., & Davey Smith, G. (2005). A life course approach to chronic disease epidemiology. *Annual Review of Public Health, 26*, 1–35.

Magee, C. A., Heaven, P. C. L., & Miller, L. M. (2013). Personality change predicts self-reported mental and physical health. *Journal of Personality, 81*(3), 324–334.

Magidson, J. F., Roberts, B. W., Collado-Rodriguez, A., & Lejuez, C. W. (2014). Theory-driven intervention for changing personality: Expectancy value theory, behavioral activation, and conscientiousness. *Developmental Psychology, 50*(5), 1442–1450.

Manczak, E. M., DeLongis, A., & Chen, E. (2016). Does empathy have a cost?: Diverging psychological and physiological effects within families. *Health Psychology, 35*(3), 211–218.

Marsh, H. W., Nagengast, B., & Morin, A. S. (2013). Measurement invariance of Big-Five factors over the life span: ESEM tests of gender, age, plasticity, maturity, and la dolce vita effects. *Developmental Psychology, 49*(6), 1194–1218.

Martin, L. R., & Friedman, H. S. (2000). Comparing personality scales across time: An illustrative study of validity and consistency in life-span archival data. *Journal of Personality, 68*(1), 85–110.

Martin, L. R., Friedman, H. S., & Schwartz, J. E. (2007). Personality and mortality risk across the life span: The importance of conscientiousness as a biopsychosocial attribute. *Health Psychology, 26*(4), 428–436.

McAdams, D. P. (1993). *The stories we live by: Personal myths and the making of the self.* New York: Guilford Press.

McAdams, D. P. (2013). The psychological self as actor, agent, and author. *Perspectives on Psychological Science, 8*(3), 272–295.

McCrae, R. R., & Costa, P. T. (2008). The five-factor theory of personality. In O. P. John, R. W. Robins, & L. A. Pervin (Eds.), *Handbook of personality: Theory and research* (3rd ed., pp. 159–181). New York: Guilford Press.

Melchers, M. C., Li, M., Haas, B. W., Reuter, M., Bischoff, L., & Montag, C. (2016). Similar personality patterns are associated with empathy in four different countries. *Frontiers in Psychology, 7,* Article 290.

Moffitt, T. E., Arseneault, L., Belsky, D., Dickson, N., Hancox, R. J., Harrington, H., et al. (2011). A gradient of childhood self-control predicts health, wealth, and public safety. *Proceedings of the National Academy of Sciences of the USA, 108*(7), 2693–2698.

Mõttus, R., Johnson, W., Starr, J. M., & Deary, I. J. (2012). Correlates of personality trait levels and their changes in very old age: The Lothian Birth Cohort 1921. *Journal of Research in Personality, 46,* 271–278.

Mroczek, D. K., & Spiro, A. (2007). Personality change influences mortality in older men. *Psychological Science, 18*(5), 371–376.

Peterson, C., Seligman, M. E., & Vaillant, G. E. (1988). Pessimistic explanatory style is a risk factor for physical illness: A thirty-five-year longitudinal study. *Journal of Personality and Social Psychology, 55*(1), 23–27.

Pulkki-Råback, L., Elovainio, M., Hakulinen, C., Lipsanen, J., Hintsanen, M., Jokela, M., et al. (2015). Cumulative effect of psychosocial factors in youth on ideal cardiovascular health in adulthood: The Cardiovascular Risk in Young Finns study. *Circulation, 131,* 245–253.

Riese, H., Snieder, H., Jeronimus, B. F., Korhonen, T., Rose, R. J., Kaprio, J., et al. (2014). Timing of stressful life events affects stability and change of neuroticism. *European Journal of Personality, 28,* 193–200.

Roberts, B. W., & DelVecchio, W. F. (2000). The rank-order consistency of personality traits from childhood to old age: A quantitative review of longitudinal studies. *Psychological Bulletin, 126*(1), 3–25.

Roberts, B. W., & Jackson, J. J. (2008). Sociogenomic personality psychology. *Journal of Personality, 76,* 1523–1544.

Roberts, B. W., Kuncel, N. R., Shiner, R., Caspi, A., & Goldberg, L. R. (2007). The power of personality: The comparative validity of personality traits, socioeconomic status, and cognitive ability for predicting important life outcomes. *Perspectives on Psychological Science, 2*(4), 313–345.

Roberts, B. W., Luo, J., Briley, D. A., Chow, P. I., Su, R., & Hill, P. L. (2017). A systematic review of personality trait change through intervention. *Psychological Bulletin, 143*(2), 117–141.

Roberts, B. W., Walton, K. E., & Viechtbauer, W. (2006). Patterns of mean-level change in personality traits across the life course: A meta-analysis of longitudinal studies. *Psychological Bulletin, 132*(1), 1–25.

Roberts, B. W., & Wood, D. (2006). Personality development in the context of the neo-socioanalytic model of personality. In D. K. Mroczek & T. D. Little (Eds.), *Handbook of personality development* (pp. 11–39). Mahwah, NJ: Erlbaum.

Roberts, B. W., Wood, D., & Caspi, A. (2008). Personality development. In O. P. John, R. W. Robins, & L. A. Pervin (Eds.), *Handbook of personality: Theory and research* (3rd ed., pp. 375–398). New York: Guilford Press.

Saajanaho, M., Viljanen, A., Read, S., Eronen, J., Kaprio, J., Jylhä, M., et al. (2016). Mobility limitation and changes in personal goals among older women. *Journals of Gerontology B: Psychological Sciences and Social Sciences, 71*(1), 1–10.

Schultz, R., & Sherwood, P. R. (2008). Physical and mental health effects of family caregiving. *American Journal of Nursing, 108*(9, Suppl.), 23–27.

Shanahan, M. J., Hill, P. L., Roberts, B. W., Eccles, J., & Friedman, H. S. (2014). Conscientiousness, health, and aging: The life course of personality model. *Developmental Psychology, 50*(5), 1407–1425.

Sharpe, J. P., Martin, N. R., & Roth, K. A. (2011). Optimism and the Big Five factors of personality: Beyond Neuroticism and Extraversion. *Personality and Individual Differences, 51*(8), 946–951.

Soto, C. J., John, O. P., Gosling, S. D., & Potter, J. (2011). Age differences in personality traits from 10 to 65: Big Five domains and facets in a large cross-sectional sample. *Journal of Personality and Social Psychology, 100*(2), 330–348.

Specht, J., Bleidorn, W., Denissen, J. A., Hennecke, M., Hutteman, R., Kandler, C., et al. (2014). What drives adult personality development?: A comparison of theoretical perspectives and empirical evidence. *European Journal of Personality, 28*(3), 216–230.

Sutin, A. R., Zonderman, A. B., Ferrucci, L., & Terracciano, A. (2013). Personality traits and chronic disease: Implications for adult personality development. *Journals of Gerontology B: Psychological Sciences and Social Sciences, 68*(6), 912–920.

Takahashi, Y., Edmonds, G. W., Jackson, J. J., III, & Roberts, B. W. (2012). Longitudinal correlated changes in conscientiousness, preventative health-related behaviors, and self-perceived physical health. *Journal of Personality, 81*(4), 417–427.

Terracciano, A., Löckenhoff, C. E., Zonderman, A. B., Ferrucci, L., & Costa, P. T. (2008). Personality predictors of longevity: Activity, emotional stability, and conscientiousness. *Psychosomatic Medicine, 70*(6), 621–627.

Turiano, N. A., Chapman, B. P., Gruenewald, T. L., & Mroczek, D. K. (2015). Personality and the leading behavioral contributors of mortality. *Health Psychology, 34*(1), 51–60.

Turiano, N. A., Pitzer, L., Armour, C., Karlamangla, A., Ryff, C. D., & Mroczek, D. K. (2012). Personality trait level and change as predictors of health outcomes: Findings from a national study of Americans (MIDUS). *Journals of Gerontology B: Psychological Sciences and Social Sciences, 67*(1), 4–12.

Turiano, N. A., Spiro, A. I., & Mroczek, D. K. (2012). Openness to experience and mortality in men: Analysis of trait and facets. *Journal of Aging and Health, 24*(4), 654–672.

Vaillant, G. E. (1977). *Adaptation to life.* Boston: Little, Brown.

Vaillant, G. E. (2012). *Triumphs of experience: The men of the Harvard Grant study.* Cambridge, MA: Belknap Press of Harvard University.

van Scheppingen, M. A., Jackson, J. J., Specht, J., Hutteman, R., Denissen, J. A., & Bleidorn, W. (2016). Personality trait development during the transition to parenthood: A test of social investment theory. *Social Psychological and Personality Science, 7*(5), 452–462.

Woodruff, D. S., & Birren, J. E. (1972). Age changes and cohort differences in personality. *Developmental Psychology, 6*(2), 252–259.

CHAPTER 29

The Development of Subjective Well-Being across the Lifespan

Nathan W. Hudson
Richard E. Lucas
M. Brent Donnellan

Throughout life, individuals are constantly required to make decisions about how to spend their time and where to engage their efforts. Which career should I pursue? Which relationship partner is right for me? Should I continue following this diet and eat this apple or splurge for a bit with the chocolate cake? Each of these decisions—from the minor and inconsequential to the life-defining—requires us to consider our idiosyncratic goals and attempt to predict the ways in which our actions allow us to achieve these goals. And ultimately, many of us believe that if we make the right decisions—and have a little bit of luck—the final outcome will be a satisfying life full of happiness. Indeed, people seem to make decisions large and small based on the assumption that their choices will promote or maintain their happiness. Indeed, most people believe that the achieving a happy and satisfying life is a goal worth pursuing—and it might even be the ultimate goal in life for many people (Adler, Dolan, & Kavetsos, 2017; Diener, 2000; Gilbert, 2006).

But what is this state of happiness that seems to motivate much of what people do in life? Is "happiness" just a superficial feeling of mindless pleasure, or is it something deeper and more fulfilling? Does happiness actually im-prove when good things happen (and drop when misfortune occurs)—or is happiness relatively stable, with lasting changes difficult to achieve? We all know those people who seem able to maintain their cheerful disposition despite repeated, severe setbacks; do these cases reflect a broader pattern where stable tendencies toward happiness or misery persist despite changing life circumstances? These and other questions motivate researchers who study what is colloquially referred to as "happiness" and more precisely described as "subjective well-being" (SWB; Diener, Suh, Lucas, & Smith, 1999) in the psychological literature.

In this chapter, we discuss the concept of SWB, paying particular attention to people's intuitions about it and the specific research questions that are motivated by these intuitions. We start with an overview of the definitions of SWB, focusing both on what it is and what it is *not*. We then move to a discussion of questions that are especially relevant when considering SWB in the context of lifespan development. For instance, we discuss reasons why one might expect stability or change in well-being over time, focusing specifically on the empirical evidence about the extent to which SWB actually changes. Next, we review evidence about the development of SWB over the lifespan. Finally, we discuss areas for future research on stability and change in SWB.

What Is SWB?

SWB reflects a person's overall, subjective evaluation of the quality of his or her life as a whole. According to Diener (1984), three characteristics distinguish SWB from other, potentially similar constructs. First, the judgments of interest are *subjective*. They reflect a person's own evaluation of his or her life. Thus, SWB can be distinguished from more objective evaluations of quality of life (Diener, Lucas, Schimmack, & Helliwell, 2009). For example, some philosophical approaches to understanding the "good life" attempt to derive objective lists of characteristics that make up and define the good life, such as dedication to a particular cause or living according to a certain moral code. Relatedly, many psychologists focus on a set of constructs that fall under the umbrella of "psychological well-being" (Keyes, Shmotkin, & Ryff, 2002; Ryff, 1989). This approach uses expert opinion and psychological theory to derive a list of critical dimensions that define psychological well-being. A potentially thorny problem with these more objective approaches (both philosophical and psychological) is that it is difficult, if not impossible, to come up with an uncontroversial list of characteristics that unambiguously define the good life. It may, at first blush, seem that some amount of consensus is possible; for instance, most models of the good life posit that strong social bonds are a necessity. However, it quickly becomes apparent that deep disagreement exists, and few criteria are available for resolving differences in what boils down to opinions about how one should lead a life. Furthermore, even if a comprehensive list of important characteristics could be compiled, different people might weight different life domains differently. For some, sacrifices to the quality of their personal relationships may be justified by the sense of purpose that they find in their jobs. For others, close family ties are more important than career advancement. The fact that different people value agency and communion to differing degrees attests to the complexity of objective approaches. Fortunately, the subjective element of SWB allows different people to weight different domains and experi-

ences in ways that match their own views about their lives and foregoes the need to impose some external definition of a satisfying life.

A second defining feature of SWB is that it is a global evaluation of one's life as a whole. There are many domains of life that could be evaluated, including health, occupational success, and personal relationships. SWB researchers assume that the positive and negative features of one's life add up to an overall sense of whether life is going well or going poorly. As noted earlier, different individuals may weight different domains differently, and positive circumstances in one domain can balance negative life circumstances in another to create an overall sense that life is going well. Accordingly, SWB measures typically focus on overall levels of well-being that reflect this idiosyncratic differential weighting of different life domains.

An important component of this second criterion is that the object that is being evaluated— the thing that is *going well*—is the person's life as a whole. Psychologists study all kinds of evaluations: evaluations of one's social relationships, of one's competence, of one's intelligence, and so on. Each of these may contribute to an overall sense of happiness and subjective feelings of well-being; but they do not replace evaluations of one's life as a whole.

Finally, SWB measures focus on *positive* aspects of the evaluation of life. Rather than emphasizing constructs such as depression and anxiety—topics that have typically been the focus of clinical psychology—SWB researchers usually provide a balanced focus on the positive and negative evaluations. Thus, research on SWB extends beyond clinical psychology to involve social, personality, and developmental psychologists, as well as researchers from related fields such as economics, sociology, and political science.

So why don't well-being researchers simply use the term *happiness* to capture what they mean by this global evaluation? Why would they replace a simple, widely understood term with a much more cumbersome bit of jargon? The answer primarily lies in the fact that there are multiple meanings of the term *happiness*. In one use of the term, *happiness* captures precisely what well-being researchers hope to assess with their measures of SWB. When people say that someone lived a "happy life" or that they themselves "just hope to be happy," they are typically referring to this broad evaluation of one's life as a whole. Yet happiness has another common meaning, one that refers to a very specific affective experience that happens over a short period of time, such as being happy while taking a long bike ride or watching a funny movie. These latter experiences may not reflect the broader and deeper form of evaluation that SWB researchers hope to assess. For this reason, well-being researchers often rely on the term SWB. We discuss these issues in more detail below when overviewing the measurement of SWB.

Measuring SWB

It seems intuitive that if we want to know how happy someone is with his or her life as a whole, we should just ask. Indeed, given the importance of subjectivity to the construct, self-report methods are sometimes seen as the only method—or at least the "gold standard" method—for assessing SWB. However, this simple intuition does not reflect the complexity of assessing SWB. Namely, there are reasons to be skeptical of self-reports. People might not have perfect memory for all the relevant criteria by which a life could be judged, they may misunderstand the question we pose to them, or they may simply be unwilling to provide an honest answer. For these reasons, measurement is a central issue in the study of SWB, and one that has proven to be particularly contentious. In the sections that follow, we first cover standard self-report measurement approaches—but we also discuss concerns about these measures and alternative measurement techniques.

Many different approaches for obtaining self-reports exist (Diener, 1984). First, it is possible to ask people quite directly how happy or satisfied they are with their lives overall, using a small set of face valid items. This approach, which is typified by measures of life satisfaction or happiness (Diener, Emmons, Larsen, & Griffin, 1985; Lyubomirsky & Lepper, 1999), assumes that people can reflect on the various life domains that they consider to be important, weight the domains by some internal scheme, and then aggregate across domains to derive an overall evaluation. Diener and others have referred to these judgments as "cognitive" evaluations of well-being because these kinds of judgments seemingly require respondents to explicitly consider and report an overall evaluation of their lives.

Cognitive judgments can be contrasted with affective evaluations of well-being. Presumably, people whose lives are going well experience frequent and perhaps somewhat intense positive emotions, and they experience infrequent or relatively mild negative emotions. Thus, one could get a sense of a person's SWB by assessing that person's typical emotional experiences. Importantly, positive and negative emotional experiences are somewhat independent, which means that they should be assessed separately to obtain a comprehensive picture of a persons's affective well-being (Schimmack, 2008).

A second issue that must be considered when assessing SWB concerns the time frame over which assessments are made. Recent research suggests that important differences emerge when well-being is assessed in a reflective, retrospective manner, as opposed to assessing it "online" as the experience of life circumstances is happening (Kahneman & Riis, 2005). For instance, when asked to evaluate his or her life as a whole, a respondent must consider a wide range of life domains, weight each by importance, then aggregate across all domains to derive an overall evaluation, at least if the report is to be considered valid (Schwarz & Strack, 1999). Because this task can be difficult (Schwarz, 1999), and because respondents typically provide responses to global life satisfaction questions too quickly to search their memory for all relevant information (Robinson & Clore, 2002a, 2002b), some researchers have suggested that respondents rely on a variety of heuristics that can negatively impact the validity of the responses that they provide (Kahneman, 1999; Schwarz & Strack, 1999). For example, Schwarz, Strack, and their colleagues suggested that broad life satisfaction judgments can be influenced by the weather at the time of judgment (Schwarz & Clore, 1983), preceding questions in a survey (Schwarz, Strack, & Mai, 1991), or whether one's favorite soccer team has recently won a game (Schwarz, Strack, Kommer, & Wagner, 1987). The large size of the effects found in these studies led the authors to suggest that well-being measures have problematic levels of validity (Schwarz & Strack, 1999).

Partly in response to these concerns, some scholars have suggested that studies should not rely on respondents to remember and accurately aggregate across experiences. Instead, these researchers believe it might be more valid to ask respondents relatively simple questions about how they are feeling at one particular moment, then to aggregate many responses over time (Kahneman, 1999). For instance, ecological momentary assessment or experience sampling methods can be administered repeatedly throughout the day using participants' own mobile phones or specialized handheld devices. These methods can be used to track well-being over time (Mehl & Conner, 2012).

Despite well-cited concerns about global survey methods, empirical evidence for the superiority of online experiential measures of well-being over global, retrospective reports is surprisingly hard to find. First, the initial research showing that retrospective reports were highly malleable were based on studies with extremely small samples, and more recent attempts to replicate the original effects have consistently found much smaller effects, if those effects can be reproduced at all (Lucas & Lawless, 2013; Yap et al., 2017). In addition, research suggests that repeatedly asking respondents the same question over and over again (as is required in more intensive, online [i.e., in vivo] assessment strategies) can create unique measurement problems that negatively affect the validity of the resulting measures (Baird & Lucas, 2011; Baird, Lucas, & Donnellan, 2017; Watson & Tellegen, 2002). Finally, recent research shows that when the two types of measures are explicitly pitted against one another in tests of criterion validity, the global retrospective measures typically perform as well or better than the aggregated online measures (Hudson, Lucas, & Donnellan, 2016). Thus, the concerns about the validity of global reports of SWB are not consistently supported by empirical evidence.

As noted earlier, the subjective nature of SWB might make it seem as though self-reports are the only option for assessing the construct. However, alternatives do exist. For instance, it seems likely that happy people will emit signs of their happiness to others who know them well, and indeed, research shows that informant reports tend to correlate moderately with self-reports of SWB (Schneider & Schimmack, 2009). In addition, there may be cognitive or behavioral signs that a person is happy, and measures that tap these signals may be used to supplement and validate the self-report measures that exist. Although the details of these methods are outside the scope of the present chapter, these alternatives to self-report may be used to assess SWB.

The Stability of SWB

Now that issues of measurement have been considered, we turn to more substantive research focused on testing people's intuitions about the nature of SWB. Most importantly, we focus on questions about whether SWB changes over time. Early research on SWB focused on identifying reliable predictors of well-being measures. One common theme that emerged from this early research was that the many factors that people might expect to impact happiness—factors such as income, health, and life events—exhibited surprisingly weak associations with SWB measures (Diener et al., 1999). This robust empirical finding, when combined with additional evidence that scores on SWB measures are moderately to strongly heritable (Lykken & Tellegen, 1996; Roysamb, Nes, & Vitterso, 2014) and consistently correlated with stable personality traits (Lucas & Diener, 2015) led some to question whether change in SWB is even possible. Specifically, some researchers proposed that people are stuck on a "hedonic treadmill," where events may impact well-being in the short term—but that people inevitably adapt over time, resulting in no lasting impact of major life circumstances over time (Brickman & Campbell, 1971; Headey & Wearing, 1991). Thus, the individual differences in happiness that people notice are attributable not to the effects of different life circumstances, but rather to differences in underlying personality traits between people. In other words, some people are just born happy, whereas others are far less sanguine by nature.

In recent years, this somewhat pessimistic view of the possibility for change has been challenged by research on the change that occurs in SWB measures over time. In this chapter, we focus on two types of change. The first is rank-order change, which reflects the extent to which those who are especially high in well-being at one point in time maintain that relatively high level over time. The second form is mean-level change, which reflects the extent to which people change in similar ways after similar experiences (e.g., major life events) or across the lifespan, and whether there are normative trends in the typical levels of well-being that are reported at different periods. In this section, we focus on rank-order stability and change.

Evidence about the long-term rank-order stability or consistency of SWB measures has accumulated quickly over the past decades. This is due, in part, to the fact that global measures of life satisfaction have been included in many long-running panel studies, in which the same participants were followed year after year for many years of their lives. These studies provide important evidence regarding the short- and long-term stability of well-being measures. For instance, Lucas and Donnellan (2007, 2012) used data from up to four different nationally representative panel studies to examine stability over intervals up to and beyond 20 years. They showed that year-to-year consistency is quite high—around .50 to .60. These stability coefficients are especially impressive given the fact that single-item measures with limited reliability were used. Importantly, however, these stability coefficients declined systematically within increasing intervals. Indeed, after 20 years, the predicted stability was closer to .20 or .25 across studies—a figure that is much lower than the 1-year stability estimates. Furthermore, the decline in stability appeared to asymptote at this lower level, suggesting that with even longer intervals, some degree of stability remains.

Together, these patterns of results provide a more nuanced view of rank-order stability and change in SWB measures. First, the high year-to-year stability suggests that scores are reasonably consistent over time. Information about an individual's level of SWB at one time point is useful for predicting future scores. There is little reason to believe that SWB is an ephemeral individual difference. Second, the fact that stability coefficients weaken with increasing intervals suggests that real change does occur. Finally, the fact that stability coefficients asymptote near .20 or .25 suggests that there may be a temperament-based core to well-being. Notably, the empirical evidence from panel studies is supported by meta-analytic summaries of stabilities from many different studies that vary in interval length (Anusic & Schimmack, 2016; Schimmack & Oishi, 2005).

Changes in SWB Following Life Events

Research on the rank-order stability of SWB shows that respondents' scores on these measures can change over time. This finding alone does not clarify whether any changes occur in systematic and predictable ways following major changes in life circumstances. However, just as the inclusion of well-being measures in long-running panel studies allowed research-ers to evaluate the long-term stability of SWB, the availability of long-term follow-up data has allowed researchers to examine whether SWB changes after the experience of major life events. This research confirms that such changes in life circumstances are associated with corresponding changes in well-being scores, and that, at least for some people and some events, the changes that occur can last a long time or perhaps even be permanent.

In one of the earliest studies to examine this question, Lucas, Clark, Georgellis, and Diener (2003) used data from the long-running German Socio-Economic Panel (GSOEP) study to examine how life satisfaction changed before and after the experience of marriage and widowhood. This study showed that the pattern of changes varies across the two events. For marriage, participants experienced small increased in life satisfaction as they approached the year of the event, followed by relatively quick returns to original baseline levels of life satisfaction within a few years. In other words, individuals (on average) tended to show adaptation to marriage, but the observed increase appeared to be temporary. For widowhood, on the other hand, respondents reported sharp declines in life satisfaction, with slow adaptation. Life satisfaction levels never returned to their baseline levels, even many years after the event. Thus, widowhood appeared to alter trajectories of well-being for individuals (on average). Subsequent research has tended to replicate these results in other panel studies (Anusic, Yap, & Lucas, 2014a, 2014b; Yap, Anusic, & Lucas, 2012).

These analyses have also been conducted with other life events, and these studies confirm that there is no single answer to the question of whether life satisfaction and other forms of well-being change following major life events; that answer depends on the specific event being studied (see Luhmann, Hofmann, Eid, & Lucas, 2012, for a meta-analytic review). Lucas (2007) showed that lasting disabilities appear to be associated with moderate to large drops in life satisfaction, whereas divorce is associated with, at most, small changes following the event (though those who divorce seem to be lower in life satisfaction even long before the event of divorce occurs; Lucas, 2005).

Collectively, there is support for the claim that mean levels of life satisfaction can exhibit lasting changes after life events, depending on the event. An additional conclusion that may be drawn from these studies, however, is that the specific pattern of changes that occurs also varies across individuals. For most events studied, there is a great deal of variability in the patterns of observed changes. For instance, Lucas and colleagues (2003) showed that although on average people quickly adapted to the event of marriage, some people experienced large and lasting boosts in life satisfaction after the event, and these were balanced by a group of respondents that actually declined in life satisfaction following what many would expect to be a positive event. Thus, an important goal for future research is to identify individual-level factors that can explain when and why more or less complete adaptation occurs (Anusic & Lucas, 2014; Yap, Anusic, & Lucas, 2014).

Research on Age and Well-Being

In addition to evaluating how well-being is related to life events, researchers are also interested in documenting normative levels of well-being across the lifespan. This work helps to answer the fascinating basic question of when (or even if) individuals experience a "prime" of their lives (i.e., the period of peak happiness for most people). This work on age-graded patterns in well-being may also help elucidate the psychological processes that underlie people's subjective assessments of their well-being. For instance, early scholars believed that well-being likely follows a similar trajectory to physical prowess: peaking in young adulthood and declining thereafter (Banham, 1951; Bühler, 1935). This prediction is rooted in the notion that subjective well-being is a relatively accurate reflection of the objective conditions of people's lives, which, in several important ways, tend to worsen with age (Diener & Suh, 1998; Wilson, 1967). For example, older adults tend to have worse health outcomes (e.g., Idler, 1993) and more restricted social engagement (Carstensen, 1992) compared with their younger counterparts.

In contrast to classic predictions about declines in happiness with age, contemporary scholars have emphasized that the psychological maturity that accompanies age may lead to *increases* in SWB. For example, biologically predetermined emotional maturation—analogous to physical maturation—may produce increases in individuals' emotional stability as they age, facilitating an enhanced sense of well-being (e.g., fewer negative emotions) (Bleidorn

et al., 2010; Roberts, Wood, & Caspi, 2008). Beyond biology, social-psychological factors, such as an increasing awareness of limited time left to live, may also lead older individuals to engage in strategies designed to maximize positive emotions and minimize negative ones (Carstensen, 1995; Carstensen, Isaacowitz, & Charles, 1999). For example, socioemotional selectivity theory posits that older adults select into situations that foster positive affect and mitigate negative affect—and when such selection is not possible, they engage in emotional regulation to a greater degree than do younger persons (Charles & Carstensen, 2008; Charles & Piazza, 2009; Charles, Piazza, Luong, & Almeida, 2009).

Of course, the idea that well-being is determined by the objective circumstances of people's lives as well as by intrapersonal factors (e.g., emotional maturity) are not mutually exclusive. And as we discuss below, the empirical associations between age and well-being seem to support both perspectives. That said, as we described in greater detail earlier in this chapter, global well-being (people's top-down evaluations of the quality of their lives and affective experiences) and experiential well-being (actual *in vivo* experiences of well-being) are at least partially separable (e.g., Hudson, Lucas, & Donnellan, 2017; Lucas, Diener, & Suh, 1996). As a consequence, global and experiential well-being could potentially exhibit differential associations with age (Hudson, Lucas, & Donnellan, 2016). Moreover, one might expect life circumstances and psychological maturity to have different implications for global and experiential well-being. For example, the greater emotional maturity that accompanies age might positively bias individuals' global evaluations of their well-being, even given equivalent experiential well-being (Charles et al., 2016). Stated differently, even if the positivity of people's emotional experiences does not vary with age, differences in mental perspective might nevertheless cause older adults to report more positive overall impressions of their lives. For these reasons, we discuss age trajectories in global and experiential well-being separately in the following sections.

Age Trajectories in Life Satisfaction

Historically, the majority of research examining age trajectories in well-being has focused on simple linear trends in life satisfaction (i.e., does life satisfaction increase or decrease with age?). The empirical literature based on simple linear models has been considerably mixed, with studies variously finding that life satisfaction increases with age (Lucas & Gohm, 2000; Prenda & Lachman, 2001; Vaux & Meddin, 1987), that it decreases with age (Freund & Baltes, 1998; Mroczek & Spiro, 2005), or that adults express similar levels of life satisfaction irrespective of age (Diener & Suh, 1998; Hamarat, Thompson, Steele, Matheny, & Simons, 2002).

Within the past 15 years, however, a growing body of literature has begun to question whether a simple linear model is adequate and has instead suggested that life satisfaction follows a quadratic—U-shaped—trajectory across adulthood, such that life satisfaction tends to decline throughout young adulthood and perhaps middle adulthood, before rebounding in advanced age (e.g., Blanchflower & Oswald, 2008; Stone, Schwartz, Broderick, & Deaton, 2010). Although several studies have converged on the basic shape of this quadratic trajectory, they diverge with respect to when life satisfaction reaches its nadir—with estimates ranging from people's mid-30s (Clark & Oswald, 1994; Shields & Wheatley Price, 2005) or 40s (Blanchflower & Oswald, 2004; Frijters, Haisken-De-New, & Shields, 2004), to their mid-50s (Stone et al., 2010) or even 60s (Blanchflower, 2001). Likewise, some studies suggest age is unrelated to levels of well-being, at least until around age 70 (Baird, Lucas, & Donnellan, 2010).

Nevertheless, it is useful to consider whether the U-shaped curve for life satisfaction is consistent with the ideas that both objective life circumstances and psychological maturity contribute to people's overall sense of well-being. For example, drops in life satisfaction across young adulthood may reflect transitions into increasing amounts of time at work versus leisure, in addition to adopting more generative (and sometimes stressful) roles, such as caring for children, partners, and aging parents—which may, on occasion, foster reductions in positive affect and elevations in negative affect (e.g., Kahneman, Krueger, Schkade, Schwarz, & Stone, 2004). In contrast, late-life gains in life satisfaction are consistent with differences in mental perspective (e.g., awareness of a limited time left to live) spurring older adults to select into more positive situations and to otherwise engage in strategies designed to maximize positive affect and minimize negative feelings

(Carstensen, 1995; Carstensen et al., 1999). Collectively, these findings may indicate that, at least in terms of life satisfaction, individuals do not experience a "prime" of their lives so much as a midlife nadir—and moreover, the notion of "midlife crises" may contain perhaps the trappings of a kernel of truth.

Four caveats regarding the body of literature supporting a U-shaped association between age and life satisfaction are worth highlighting. First, cross-sectional correlational studies examining age-related differences in well-being may be susceptible to cohort effects. Namely, the associations between age and life satisfaction may not represent true developmental effects, but may rather be an artifact of people of different ages within one sample being born during especially prosperous or trying times (e.g., older adults may have greater well-being simply because they lived through more prosperous economic times). Somewhat mitigating this concern, several studies provide support for the idea that the quadratic age pattern in life satisfaction is robust to cohort effects. Specifically, the quadratic pattern has emerged in multiple cohorts within single cultures, and it has also robustly replicated across more than 70 countries with diverse histories (Blanchflower & Oswald, 2008), including America (Blanchflower & Oswald, 2004; Stone et al., 2010), Western European countries (Baird et al., 2010; Blanchflower, 2001; Blanchflower & Oswald, 2004; Clark & Oswald, 1994; Frijters et al., 2004; Shields & Wheatley Price, 2005), and South Africa (Powdthavee, 2005).

Second, the extent to which the U-shaped age pattern in life satisfaction generalizes across cultures—especially less-developed ones—remains poorly understood. Specifically, few studies have examined age patterns in life satisfaction within poorer, less-developed countries. And the limited evidence currently available is somewhat mixed with respect to whether late-life rebounds in life satisfaction occur only in wealthier, more developed nations (Deaton, 2008), or whether the quadratic trajectory is more or less universal across cultures (Blanchflower & Oswald, 2008). To the extent that middle- to late adulthood is associated with gains in well-being only in wealthier countries (Deaton, 2008)—and life satisfaction therefore drops relatively linearly with age for those in less developed nations—this may suggest that late-life difficulties in less developed countries (e.g., health problems without adequate medical care) overwhelm the positive effects of greater psychological maturity.

Third, several studies have failed to replicate the U-shaped pattern. For example, although one study found evidence for a U-shaped pattern in life satisfaction among Germans (Frijters et al., 2004), at least three other large-sample studies did not find statistically significant quadratic associations between age and life satisfaction in Germany (Baird et al., 2010; Hudson et al., 2016; Winkelmann & Winkelmann, 1998). Nevertheless, the general preponderance of current evidence suggests the existence of a quadratic association between age and life satisfaction: thus, the lack of findings in these studies may represent sampling error.

Last, studies vary with respect to whether they modeled the literal, observed age trends in life satisfaction (e.g., Baird et al., 2010), versus the semipartial associations between age and well-being, controlling other relevant variables, such as income, health, and/or demographics (e.g., Blanchflower & Oswald, 2008). Notably, although the inclusion of covariates might help isolate the mechanisms responsible for age-graded changes in life satisfaction, this also has the potential to shift the interpretation of the studies' findings to represent hypothetical counterfactuals (e.g., what would we expect to observe in a hypothetical world where younger and older adults did not differ in terms of health?; Hudson et al., 2016). At least one study, however, suggests that the quadratic association between age and well-being emerges regardless of whether control variables are included in the models (Stone et al., 2010). Nevertheless, it remains possible that the apparent empirical consensus regarding the U-shaped association between age and life satisfaction in the current literature is exaggerated by "researcher degrees of freedom" regarding the specific models used in various studies and covariates included (Simmons, Nelson, & Simonsohn, 2011).

Terminal Decline

In addition to evidence about the average levels of life satisfaction across the lifespan, there is evidence that levels of well-being, including life satisfaction, may fall sharply prior to death (Gerstorf et al., 2008; Mroczek & Spiro, 2005). This effect is called *terminal decline* in the literature. At least two interrelated explanations help to reconcile the finding that life satisfac-

tion stays either stable or increases in late adulthood with the existence of a terminal decline. First, in the words of Gerstorf and colleagues (2008), terminal decline occurs as a function of "distance to death rather than distance from birth (i.e., chronological age)" (p. 1149). In other words, the circumstances associated with dying contribute to declines in well-being, irrespective of a person's age when those circumstances occur. One consequence of this distinction is that it is possible that older individuals may experience increasing life satisfaction throughout the lattermost years of their lives, until health or other problems become so severe as to be imminently life threating (which may occur at different ages for different individuals).

Second, and relatedly, the older adults who provide data in most ongoing studies are not representative of their age group more generally (Baird et al., 2010; Hudson et al., 2016). The explanation is that they have often lived longer than what is typical for a member of their birth cohort. Thus, the older adults present in most studies may be those who are healthy enough to enjoy late-life, age-graded increases in well-being sans any imminently terminal issues. Moreover, individuals with greater well-being may live longer than those with poorer well-being (Carstensen et al., 2011). Thus, those who survive to provide data in advanced old age may be a biased sample and only represent the most well-off individuals from their cohorts—which would produce an apparent, albeit ultimately misleading advanced-old age increase in well-being in cross-sectional studies. The concern is that the oldest participants in many studies are often highly selective members of their birth cohorts.

Age Trajectories in Affect

For the remainder of this chapter, we discuss empirical evidence for cross-sectional age patterns in people's affective well-being. It is important to differentiate global affect (people's top-down assessments of their typical patterns of positive and negative emotions) and experiential affect (people's actual *in vivo* experiences of positive and negative emotions) because a variety of factors can bias people's top-down perceptions of their global affect, holding their actual affective experiences constant. For example, older adults may be biased toward remembering positive events over negative ones. If this is the case, they may not differ from younger adults in terms of experienced affect, but they may nevertheless report more positive global affect (Charles et al., 2016).

In terms of operationalization, when individuals are asked to summarize their affective experiences over long periods of time (e.g., several weeks), research suggests that people are unable to accurately recall emotional information across such large timespans, which forces them to rely upon their top-down beliefs and expectations regarding their typical levels of affect (Robinson & Clore, 2002a, 2002b, 2007). In other words, when people are asked to summarize their affect across extended windows of time, they tend to report their beliefs about their typical affective experiences rather than their actual experienced affect. Thus, when discussing affect, we consider any studies that asked participants to summarize their typical affect over long periods of time (e.g., weeks, months) to have measured global affect. In contrast, when reviewing research on experiential affect, we include studies that measured affect via the experience sampling method (ESM; Shiffman, Stone, & Hufford, 2008), the day reconstruction method (DRM; Kahneman et al., 2004), or by asking participants to summarize their affective experiences from the previous day.

Beyond the distinction between global and experiential affect, research suggests that positive and negative affect are at least partially independent of one another (Watson, Clark, & Tellegen, 1988). Although a few studies have examined only "affective balance" (i.e., positive emotions minus negative ones; e.g., Ryff, 1989), most studies have separately estimated the associations between age and positive affect and age and negative affect. Therefore, in the sections that follow, we discuss global negative affect, global positive affect, experiential negative affect, and experiential positive affect separately.

Global Affect

Negative Affect

A large body of research has examined the correlations between age and global affect. Generally, these studies have converged on the finding that negative affect tends to decline with age (Barrick, Hutchinson, & Deckers, 1989; Charles et al., 2016; Charles, Reynolds, & Gatz, 2001; Costa et al., 1987; Gross et al., 1997; Hudson et al., 2016; Lawton, Kleban, & Dean, 1993;

Lucas & Gohm, 2000; Mroczek & Kolarz, 1998; Vaux & Meddin, 1987). Indeed, very few studies have contradicted this general consensus by finding that age is unrelated to negative affect (Malatesta & Kalnok, 1984; Smith & Baltes, 1993), or that negative affect increases with age (e.g., Pinquart, 2001, meta-analyzed 142 studies and found a small negative correlation between negative affect and age, which reversed when covariates were included). The finding that negative affect tends to decrease with age is consistent with theories positing that biologically driven maturation processes promote emotional stability (Bleidorn et al., 2010; Roberts et al., 2008) and also that social-psychological factors, such as increasing awareness of limited time left to live, may encourage older adults to maximize positive emotions and minimize negative ones (Carstensen, 1995).

Despite the fact that research generally suggests that global negative affect decreases with age, an emerging body of research has begun to indicate that different discrete negative emotions may follow disparate trajectories across adulthood. Specifically, preliminary evidence suggests that most negative emotions—and especially anger—decrease across adulthood, whereas sadness appears to increase as a function of age (Hudson et al., 2016; Kunzmann, Kappes, & Wrosch, 2014; Kunzmann, Richter, & Schmukle, 2013). Further supporting this notion, several studies have found U-shaped quadratic associations between age and depression, such that depression is minimized in middle-age before escalating into old age (Gatz, Johansson, Pedersen, Berg, & Reynolds, 1993; Kessler, Foster, Webster, & House, 1992).

Why might sadness defy the general trend of negative affect decreasing with age? One potential explanation is that despite the fact that older adults appear to experience more success in regulating negative emotions, the incidence of sadness-provoking experiences (e.g., death of loved ones and other losses) may increase with advanced age. Moreover, it may be easier for adults to select out of anger- or frustration-promoting situations (e.g., social conflict) than to select out of sadness-promoting circumstances (e.g., experiences of loss) (Carstensen, 1995; Kunzmann et al., 2014).

Positive Affect

In contrast to research on global negative affect, which has generally converged on the notion that negative affect ebbs with age, research on global positive affect has produced mixed findings. Specifically, several studies have found that positive affect increases as a function of age (Lucas & Gohm, 2000; Mroczek & Kolarz, 1998; Ryff, 1989; Vaux & Meddin, 1987). Others have found no association between age and positive affect (Barrick et al., 1989; Charles et al., 2001; Malatesta & Kalnok, 1984). Still others have found that positive affect *declines* as a function of age—either consistently across adulthood (Costa et al., 1987; Hudson et al., 2016; Kunzmann, 2008; Kunzmann, Little, & Smith, 2000; Pinquart, 2001)—or that it remains stable across most of life before declining in advanced old age (Charles et al., 2001). In one study, controlling for health reversed the negative association between age and positive affect (Kunzmann et al., 2000)—potentially suggesting that, holding health constant, older adults experience greater positive affect than do younger adults, and it is only failing health that counteracts and even overwhelms this effect. However, in another study, controlling health did not alter the negative association between age and positive affect (Hudson et al., 2016).

Unfortunately, there does not appear to be a simple explanation for the mixed findings regarding positive affect. One possibility is that global positive affect follows a quadratic trajectory across adulthood (Hudson et al., 2016; cf. Pinquart, 2001), and existing studies may not cover the lifespan long enough to observe this pattern. Thus, it may be the case that the mixed linear trends observed in prior studies are due to an underlying curvilinear effect. However, it remains an open question whether such a quadratic pattern would replicate in future studies.

Clearly additional research is needed to clarify how positive affect changes as a function of age. For example, it may simply be the case that positive affect does not vary across adulthood—and that the discrepant correlations between age and positive affect in the literature represent sampling error around an ultimately null effect. Alternatively, it may be the case that different mechanisms have counteracting effects on positive affect as individuals age. For example, meta-analyses suggest that certain facets of extraversion—which includes positive affect—may decline with age (Roberts, Walton, & Viechtbauer, 2006). This may counteract older adults' attempts to up-regulate positive

affect (Carstensen, 1995), producing a net zero effect. Ultimately, these and other possibilities should be explored and disentangled in future research.

Experiential Measures of Affect

Negative Affect

In contrast to research on global affect, far fewer studies have examined age-graded patterns in experiential measures of affect. Nevertheless, aligning with research on global negative affect, these studies have almost universally converged on the idea that experiential measures of negative affect tend to decline as a function of age—irrespective of whether it is measured via ESMs (Carstensen, Pasupathi, Mayr, & Nesselroade, 2000; Riediger, Schmiedek, Wagner, & Lindenberger, 2009), the DRM (Hudson et al., 2016), or as a self-report summary of the prior day's affect (Charles et al., 2016). Only one study has found that negative affect, as measured via ESM, is invariant with respect to age (Charles & Pasupathi, 2003).

Once again aligning with research on global negative affect, the limited body of available research may indicate that sadness in particular defies the general pattern for negative affect by increasing with age. For example, one study based on DRM measures found that experiences of anger decreased with age, whereas experiential sadness increased across adulthood (Hudson et al., 2016). Similarly, in experimental contexts, as compared with younger persons, older adults report greater fear and sadness—but not anger or disgust—in response to emotionally evocative stimuli (Haase, Seider, Shiota, & Levenson, 2012). Thus, specific negative feelings may show distinct age trajectories.

Positive Affect

Paralleling research regarding global positive affect, studies have produced mixed findings with respect to the association between age and experiential measures of positive affect. For example, one study found that positive affect, as measured via ESM, increases with age (Riediger, Schmiedek, Wagner, & Lindenberger, 2009). Somewhat more ambiguously, another study found that the *difference* between positive and negative affect increased with age (Carstensen et al., 2011). In contrast, another study found that DRM affect decreased with age (Hudson et al., 2016). Still other studies have found no association between experiential positive affect and age (Charles & Pasupathi, 2003; Carstensen, Pasupathi, Mayr, & Nesselroade, 2000). As with global positive affect, these studies may point to the idea that the true association between age and positive affect is close to zero.

Potentially reconciling the mixed findings with respect to experiential positive affect, one study recently found support for the notion that older adults may attempt to minimize *high-arousal* positive emotion (e.g., excitement) in lieu of low-arousal emotion (e.g., contentment) (Scheibe, English, Tsai, & Carstensen, 2013). This phenomenon might cause studies that use aggregate measures containing both high- and low-arousal positive emotions to find null effects. However, at least one other study failed to find support for the proposition that low-arousal emotions increase with age—instead finding that positive affect generally decreased with age, and satisfaction (a low-arousal positive emotion) was unrelated to age (Hudson et al., 2016).

Summary of Age Trends

In summary, the existing literature provides some indication that average levels of life satisfaction decrease across young adulthood before reaching a nadir sometime between people's 30s and 60s, and subsequently rebounding in old age. In contrast, both global and experiential negative affect appear to decline in a relatively linear fashion across adulthood—with the exception that sadness appears to increase with age. Finally, the current literature is mixed and inconclusive with respect to positive affect, as both experiential and global positive affect have been variously found to be positively correlated, negatively correlated, or unrelated to age. These findings are collectively consistent with the notions that both objective life circumstances and intrapersonal factors contribute to individuals' SWB given what is known about trajectories of life circumstances and personality traits across the lifespan. Nevertheless, future research is needed to understand particularly the associations between age and positive affect. Moreover, future research is needed to test the cross-cultural generalizability of these findings.

Conclusion

Researchers and laypeople alike are concerned about the extent to which happiness, or SWB, changes across the lifespan and whether well-being changes in response to life events. For those who seek to improve their lives, it is often important to know whether their substantial efforts will pay off; and one way to evaluate this is to assess whether their efforts at self-improvement co-occur with corresponding changes in the ways these people evaluate their lives. Presumably, those who are able to achieve important goals, to obtain the job they have been working toward for many years, or to develop the stable and supportive romantic relationships that they believe are valuable will be happier than those who fail at these tasks.

Initially, early research on SWB suggested there was a limit to people's ability to change. However, studies that use high-quality data from a wide range of sources suggest that these early conclusions needed amendment. The emerging view is that SWB shows some consistency across time, but levels can and do change with age and life events. The correlation between scores at two time points is far from unity, and there are individual differences in change over time. The experience of certain major life events such as widowhood or disability may disrupt people's happiness, causing lasting changes, at least for some people. Furthermore, research shows that the different components of well-being change in predictable ways over the lifespan; future research is needed to explain these changes and to determine whether they are due to biological maturation or to systematic changes in circumstances that occur as people age. Regardless of the causes of change, existing research on stability and change in SWB suggests the SWB is a developmental construct much the way personality traits are viewed as developmental constructs in contemporary theorizing about trait development. This perspective has important practical and theoretical implications for our understanding of people's evaluations of the success of their lives. Well-being is perhaps more stable and consistent than predicted by early models, but it is far from an immutable entity that stays perfectly constant across the lifespan. Researchers are actively working to address several inconsistencies in the literature and to document the processes that explain both stability and change in well-being.

REFERENCES

Adler, M., Dolan, P., & Kavetsos, G. (2017). Would you choose to be happy?: Tradeoffs between happiness and the other dimensions of life in a large population survey. *Journal of Economic Behavior and Organization, 139,* 60–73.

Anusic, I., & Lucas, R. E. (2014). Do social relationships buffer the effects of widowhood?: A prospective study of adaptation to the loss of a spouse. *Journal of Personality, 82*(5), 367–378.

Anusic, I., & Schimmack, U. (2016). Stability and change of personality traits, self-esteem, and well-being: Introducing the meta-analytic stability and change model of retest correlations. *Journal of Personality and Social Psychology: Personality Processes and Individual Differences, 110*(5), 766–781.

Anusic, I., Yap, S. C. Y., & Lucas, R. E. (2014a). Does personality moderate reaction and adaptation to major life events?: Analysis of life satisfaction and affect in an Australian national sample. *Journal of Research in Personality, 51,* 69–77.

Anusic, I., Yap, S. C. Y., & Lucas, R. E. (2014b). Testing set-point theory in a Swiss national sample: Reaction and adaptation to major life events. *Social Indicators Research, 119*(3), 1265–1288.

Baird, B. M., & Lucas, R. E. (2011). " . . . And how about now?": Effects of item redundancy on contextualized self-reports of personality. *Journal of Personality, 79*(5), 1081–1112.

Baird, B. M., Lucas, R. E., & Donnellan, M. B. (2010). Life satisfaction across the lifespan: Findings from two nationally representative panel studies. *Social Indicators Research, 99,* 183–203.

Baird, B. M., Lucas, R. E., & Donnellan, M. B. (2017). The role of response styles in the assessment of intraindividual personality variability. *Journal of Research in Personality, 69,* 170–179.

Banham, K. M. (1951). Senescence and the emotions: A genetic theory. *Pedagogical Seminary and Journal of Genetic Psychology, 78,* 175–183.

Barrick, A. L., Hutchinson, R. L., & Deckers, L. H. (1989). Age effects on positive and negative emotions. *Journal of Social Behavior and Personality, 4,* 421–429.

Blanchflower, D. G. (2001). Unemployment, well-being, and wage curves in Eastern and Central Europe. *Journal of the Japanese and International Economies, 15,* 364–402.

Blanchflower, D. G., & Oswald, A. J. (2004). Well-being over time in Britain and the USA. *Journal of Public Economics, 88,* 1359–1386.

Blanchflower, D. G., & Oswald, A. J. (2008). Is well-being U-shaped over the life cycle? *Social Science and Medicine, 66,* 1733–1749.

Bleidorn, W., Kandler, C., Hülsheger, U. R., Riemann, R., Angleitner, A., & Spinath, F. M. (2010). Nature and nurture of the interplay between personality traits and major life goals. *Journal of Personality and Social Psychology, 99,* 366–379.

Brickman, P., & Campbell, D. (1971). Hedonic relativism and planning the good society. In M. Appley (Ed.), *Adaptation-level theory: A symposium* (pp. 287–305). New York: Academic Press.

Bühler, C. (1935). The curve of life as studied in biographies. *Journal of Applied Psychology, 19,* 405–409.

Carstensen, L. L. (1992). Social and emotional patterns in adulthood: Support for socioemotional selectivity theory. *Psychology and Aging, 7,* 331–338.

Carstensen, L. L. (1995). Evidence for a life-span theory of socioemotional selectivity. *Current Directions in Psychological Science, 4,* 151–156.

Carstensen, L. L., Isaacowitz, D. M., & Charles, S. T. (1999). Taking time seriously: A theory of socioemotional selectivity. *American Psychologist, 54,* 165–181.

Carstensen, L. L., Pasupathi, M., Mayr, U., & Nesselroade, J. R. (2000). Emotional experience in everyday life across the adult life span. *Journal of Personality and Social Psychology, 79,* 644–655.

Carstensen, L. L., Turan, B., Scheibe, S., Ram, N., Ersner-Hershfield, H., Samanez-Larkin, G. R., et al. (2011). Emotional experience improves with age: Evidence based on over 10 years of experience sampling. *Psychology and Aging, 26,* 21–33.

Charles, S. T., & Carstensen, L. L. (2008). Unpleasant situations elicit different emotional responses in younger and older adults. *Psychology and Aging, 23,* 495–504.

Charles, S. T., & Pasupathi, M. (2003). Age-related patterns of variability in self-descriptions: Implications for everyday affective experience. *Psychology and Aging, 18,* 524–536.

Charles, S. T., & Piazza, J. R. (2009). Age differences in affective well-being: Context matters. *Social and Personality Psychology Compass, 3,* 711–724.

Charles, S. T., Piazza, J. R., Luong, G., & Almeida, D. M. (2009). Now you see it, now you don't: Age differences in affective reactivity to social tensions. *Psychology and Aging, 24,* 645–653.

Charles, S. T., Piazza, J. R., Mogle, J. A., Urban, E. J., Sliwinski, M. J., & Almeida, D. M. (2016). Age differences in emotional well-being vary by temporal recall. *Journals of Gerontology B: Psychological Sciences and Social Sciences, 71*(5), 798–807.

Charles, S. T., Reynolds, C. A., & Gatz, M. (2001). Age-related differences and change in positive and negative affect over 23 years. *Journal of Personality and Social Psychology, 80,* 136–151.

Clark, A. E., & Oswald, A. J. (1994). Unhappiness and unemployment. *Economic Journal, 104,* 648–659.

Costa, P. T., Zonderman, A. B., McCrae, R. R., Huntley, J. C., Locke, B. Z., & Barbano, H. E. (1987). Longitudinal analyses of psychological well-being in a national sample: Stability of mean levels. *Journal of Gerontology, 42,* 50–55.

Deaton, A. (2008). Income, health, and well-being around the world: Evidence from the Gallup World Poll. *Journal of Economic Perspectives, 22,* 53–72.

Diener, E. (1984). Subjective well-being. *Psychological Bulletin, 95*(3), 542–547.

Diener, E. (2000). Subjective well-being: The science of happiness and a proposal for a national index. *American Psychologist, 55*(1), 34–43.

Diener, E., Emmons, R. A., Larsen, R. J., & Griffin, S. (1985). The Satisfaction with Life Scale. *Journal of Personality Assessment, 49,* 71–75.

Diener, E., Lucas, R. E., Schimmack, U., & Helliwell, J. (2009). *Well-being for public policy.* New York: Oxford University Press.

Diener, E., & Suh, E. M. (1998). Subjective well-being and age: An international analysis. In K. W. Schaie & M. P. Lawton (Eds.), *Annual review of gerontology and geriatrics: Vol. 17. Focus on emotion and adult development* (pp. 304–324). New York: Springer.

Diener, E., Suh, E. M., Lucas, R. E., & Smith, H. L. (1999). Subjective well-being: Three decades of progress. *Psychological Bulletin, 125,* 276–302.

Freund, A. M., & Baltes, P. B. (1998). Selection, optimization, and compensation as strategies of life management: Correlations with subjective indicators of successful aging. *Psychology and Aging, 13,* 531–543.

Frijters, P., Haisken-DeNew, J. P., & Shields, M. A. (2004). Investigating the patterns and determinants of life satisfaction in Germany following reunification. *Journal of Human Resources, 39,* 649–674.

Gatz, M., Johansson, B., Pedersen, N., Berg, S., & Reynolds, C. (1993). A cross-national self-report measure of depressive symptomatology. *International Psychogeriatrics, 5,* 147–156.

Gerstorf, D., Ram, N., Estabrook, R., Schupp, J., Wagner, G. G., & Lindenberger, U. (2008). Life satisfaction shows terminal decline in old age: Longitudinal evidence from the German Socio-Economic Panel Study (SOEP). *Developmental Psychology, 44,* 1148–1159.

Gilbert, D. T. (2006). *Stumbling on happiness.* New York: Knopf.

Gross, J. J., Carstensen, L. L., Pasupathi, M., Tsai, J., Götestam Skorpen, C., & Hsu, A. Y. (1997). Emotion and aging: Experience, expression, and control. *Psychology and Aging, 12,* 590–599.

Haase, C. M., Seider, B. H., Shiota, M. N., & Levenson, R. W. (2012). Anger and sadness in response to an emotionally neutral film: Evidence for age-specific associations with well-being. *Psychology and Aging, 27,* 305–317.

Hamarat, E., Thompson, D., Steele, D., Matheny, K., & Simons, C. (2002). Age differences in coping resources and satisfaction with life among middle-aged, young-old, and oldest-old adults. *Journal of Genetic Psychology, 163,* 360–367.

Headey, B., & Wearing, A. (1991). *Understanding happiness: A theory of subjective well-being.* Cheshire, UK: Longman.

Heller, D., Watson, D., & Ilies, R. (2004). The role of person versus situation in life satisfaction: A critical examination. *Psychological Bulletin, 130,* 574–600.

Hudson, N. W., Lucas, R. E., & Donnellan, M. B. (2016). Getting older, feeling less?: A cross-sectional and longitudinal investigation of developmental patterns in experiential well-being. *Psychology and Aging, 31,* 847–861.

Hudson, N. W., Lucas, R. E., & Donnellan, M. B. (2017). Day-to-day affect is surprisingly stable: A two-year longitudinal study of well-being. *Social Psychological and Personality Science, 8*(1), 45–54.

Idler, E. L. (1993). Age differences in self-assessments of health: Age changes, cohort differences, or survivorship? *Journal of Gerontology, 48,* S289–S300.

Kahneman, D. (1999). Objective happiness. In D. Kahneman, E. Diener, & N. Schwarz (Eds.), *Well-being: The foundations of hedonic psychology* (pp. 3–25). New York: Russell Sage Foundation.

Kahneman, D., Krueger, A. B., Schkade, D. A., Schwarz, N., & Stone, A. A. (2004). A survey method for characterizing daily life experience: The day reconstruction method. *Science, 306,* 1776–1780.

Kahneman, D., & Riis, J. (2005). Living, and thinking about it: Two perspectives on life. In F. A. Huppert, N. Baylis, & B. Keverne (Eds.), *The science of well-being* (pp. 285–304). New York: Oxford University Press.

Kessler, R. C., Foster, C., Webster, P. S., & House, J. S. (1992). The relationship between age and depressive symptoms in two national surveys. *Psychology and Aging, 7,* 119–126.

Keyes, C. L., Shmotkin, D., & Ryff, C. D. (2002). Optimizing well-being: The empirical encounter of two traditions. *Journal of Personality and Social Psychology, 82*(6), 1007–1022.

Kunzmann, U. (2008). Differential age trajectories of positive and negative affect: Further evidence from the Berlin Aging Study. *Journals of Gerontology B: Psychological Sciences and Social Sciences, 63,* P261–P270.

Kunzmann, U., Kappes, C., & Wrosch, C. (2014). Emotional aging: A discrete emotions perspective. *Frontiers in Psychology, 5,* 380.

Kunzmann, U., Little, T. D., & Smith, J. (2000). Is age-related stability of subjective well-being a paradox?: Cross-sectional and longitudinal evidence from the Berlin Aging Study. *Psychology and Aging, 15,* 511–526.

Kunzmann, U., Richter, D., & Schmukle, S. C. (2013). Stability and change in affective experience across the adult life span: Analyses with a national sample from Germany. *Emotion, 13,* 1086–1095.

Lawton, M. P., Kleban, M. H., & Dean, J. (1993). Affect and age: Cross-sectional comparisons of structure and prevalence. *Psychology and Aging, 8,* 165–175.

Lucas, R. E. (2005). Time does not heal all wounds. *Psychological Science, 16*(12), 945–950.

Lucas, R. E. (2007). Long-term disability is associated with lasting changes in subjective well-being: Evidence from two nationally representative longitudinal studies. *Journal of Personality and Social Psychology, 92*(4), 717–730.

Lucas, R. E., Clark, A., Georgellis, Y., & Diener, E. (2003). Reexamining adaptation and the set point model of happiness: Reactions to changes in marital status. *Journal of Personality and Social Psychology, 84*(3), 527–539.

Lucas, R. E., & Diener, E. (2015). Personality and subjective well-being: Current issues and controversies. In M. Mikulincer, P. R. Shaver, M. L. Cooper, & R. J. Larsen (Eds.), *APA handbook of personality and social psychology: Vol. 4. Personality processes and individual differences* (pp. 577–599). Washington, DC: American Psychological Association.

Lucas, R. E., Diener, E., & Suh, E. (1996). Discriminant validity of well-being measures. *Journal of Personality and Social Psychology, 71*(3), 616–628.

Lucas, R. E., & Donnellan, M. B. (2007). How stable is happiness?: Using the STARTS model to estimate the stability of life satisfaction. *Journal of Research in Personality, 41,* 1091–1098.

Lucas, R. E., & Donnellan, M. B. (2012). Estimating the reliability of single-item life satisfaction measures: Results from four national panel studies. *Social Indicators Research, 3,* 323–331.

Lucas, R. E., & Gohm, C. L. (2000). Age and sex differences in subjective well-being across cultures. In E. Diener & E. M. Suh (Eds.), *Culture and subjective well-being* (pp. 291–317). Cambridge, MA: MIT Press.

Lucas, R. E., & Lawless, N. M. (2013). Does life seem better on a sunny day?: Examining the association between daily weather conditions and life satisfaction judgments. *Journal of Personality and Social Psychology, 104*(5), 872–884.

Luhmann, M., Hofmann, W., Eid, M., & Lucas, R. E. (2012). Subjective well-being and adaptation to life events: A meta-analysis. *Journal of Personality and Social Psychology, 102*(3), 592–615.

Lykken, D., & Tellegen, A. (1996). Happiness is a stochastic phenomenon. *Psychological Science, 7*(3), 186–189.

Lyubomirsky, S., & Lepper, H. S. (1999). A measure of subjective happiness: Preliminary reliability and construct validation. *Social Indicators Research, 46*(2), 137–155.

Malatesta, C. Z., & Kalnok, M. (1984). Emotional experience in younger and older adults. *Journal of Gerontology, 39,* 301–308.

Mehl, M. R., & Conner, T. S. (Eds.). (2012). *Handbook of research methods for studying daily life.* New York: Guilford Press.

Mroczek, D. K., & Kolarz, C. M. (1998). The effect of age on positive and negative affect: A developmental perspective on happiness. *Journal of Personality and Social Psychology, 75,* 1333–1349.

Mroczek, D. K., & Spiro, A., III. (2005). Change in life satisfaction during adulthood: Findings from the veterans affairs normative aging study. *Journal of Personality and Social Psychology, 88,* 189–202.

Pinquart, M. (2001). Age differences in perceived positive affect, negative affect, and affect balance in middle and old age. *Journal of Happiness Studies, 2,* 375–405.

Powdthavee, N. (2005). Unhappiness and crime: Evidence from South Africa. *Economica, 72,* 531–547.

Prenda, K. M., & Lachman, M. E. (2001). Planning for the future: A life management strategy for increasing control and life satisfaction in adulthood. *Psychology and Aging, 16,* 206–216.

Riediger, M., Schmiedek, F., Wagner, G. G., & Lindenberger, U. (2009). Seeking pleasure and seeking pain: Differences in prohedonic and contra-hedonic motivation from adolescence to old age. *Psychological Science, 20,* 1529–1535.

Roberts, B. W., Walton, K. E., & Viechtbauer, W. (2006). Patterns of mean-level change in personality traits across the life course: A meta-analysis of longitudinal studies. *Psychological Bulletin, 132,* 1–25.

Roberts, B. W., Wood, D., & Caspi, A. (2008). The development of personality traits in adulthood. In O. P. John, R. W. Robins, & L. A. Pervin (Eds.), *Handbook of personality: Theory and research* (3rd ed., pp. 375–398). New York: Guilford Press.

Robinson, M. D., & Clore, G. L. (2002a). Belief and feeling: Evidence for an accessibility model of emotional self-report. *Psychological Bulletin, 128*(6), 934–960.

Robinson, M. D., & Clore, G. L. (2002b). Episodic and semantic knowledge in emotional self-report: Evidence for two judgment processes. *Journal of Personality and Social Psychology, 83,* 198–215.

Robinson, M. D., & Clore, G. L. (2007). Traits, states, and encoding spped: Support for a top-down view of neuroticism/state relations. *Journal of Personality, 75,* 95–120.

Roysamb, E., Nes, R. B., & Vitterso, J. (2014). Well-being: Heritable and changeable. In K. M. Sheldon & R. E. Lucas (Eds.), *Stability of happiness: Theories and evidence on whether happiness can change* (pp. 9–31). Amsterdam, The Netherlands: Academic Press.

Ryff, C. D. (1989). Happiness is everything, or is it?: Explorations on the meaning of psychological well-being. *Journal of Personality and Social Psychology, 57*(6), 1069–1081.

Scheibe, S., English, T., Tsai, J. L., & Carstensen, L. L. (2013). Striving to feel good: Ideal affect, actual affect, and their correspondence across adulthood. *Psychology and Aging, 28,* 160–171.

Schimmack, U. (2008). The structure of subjective well-being. In M. Eid & R. J. Larsen (Eds.), *The science of subjective well-being* (pp. 97–123). New York: Guilford Press.

Schimmack, U., & Oishi, S. (2005). The influence of chronically and temporarily accessible information on life satisfaction judgments. *Journal of Personality and Social Psychology, 89*(3), 395–406.

Schneider, L., & Schimmack, U. (2009). Self-informant agreement in well-being ratings: A meta-analysis. *Social Indicators Research, 94*(3), 363–376.

Schwarz, N. (1999). Self-reports: How the questions shape the answers. *American Psychologist, 54*(2), 93–105.

Schwarz, N., & Clore, G. L. (1983). Mood, misattribution, and judgments of well-being: Informative and directive functions of affective states. *Journal of Personality and Social Psychology, 45*(3), 513–523.

Schwarz, N., & Strack, F. (1999). Reports of subjective well-being: Judgmental processes and their methodological implications. In D. Kahneman, E. Diener, & N. Schwarz (Eds.), *Well-being: The foundations of hedonic psychology* (pp. 61–84). New York: Russell Sage Foundation.

Schwarz, N., Strack, F., Kommer, D., & Wagner, D. (1987). Soccer, rooms, and the quality of your life: Mood effects on judgments of satisfaction with life in general and with specific domains. *European Journal of Social Psychology, 17*(1), 69–79.

Schwarz, N., Strack, F., & Mai, H.-P. (1991). Assimilation and contrast effects in part-whole question sequences: A conversational logic analysis. *Public Opinion Quarterly, 55*(1), 3–23.

Shields, M. A., & Wheatley Price, S. (2005). Exploring the economic and social determinants of psychological well-being and perceived social support in England. *Journal of the Royal Statistical Society A (Statistics in Society), 168,* 513–537.

Shiffman, S., Stone, A. A., & Hufford, M. R. (2008). Ecological momentary assessment. *Annual Review of Clinical Psychology, 4,* 1–32.

Simmons, J. P., Nelson, L. D., & Simonsohn, U. (2011). False-positive psychology: Undisclosed flexibility in data collection and analysis allows presenting anything as significant. *Psychological Science, 22,* 1359–1366.

Smith, J., & Baltes, P. B. (1993). Differential psychological ageing: Profiles of the old and very old. *Ageing and Society, 13,* 551–587.

Stone, A. A., Schwartz, J. E., Broderick, J. E., & Deaton, A. (2010). A snapshot of the age distribution of psychological well-being in the United States. *Proceedings of the National Academy of Sciences of the USA, 107,* 9985–9990.

Vaux, A., & Meddin, J. (1987). Positive and negative life change and positive and negative affect among the rural elderly. *Journal of Community Psychology, 15,* 447–458.

Watson, D., Clark, L. A., & Tellegen, A. (1988). Development and validation of breif measures of positive and negative affect: The PANAS scales. *Journal of Personality and Social Psychology, 54,* 1063–1070.

Watson, D., & Tellegen, A. (2002). Aggregation, acquiescence, and the assessment of trait affectivity. *Journal of Research in Personality, 36*(6), 589–597.

Wilson, W. (1967). Correlates of avowed happiness. *Psychological Bulletin, 67,* 294–306.

Winkelmann, L., & Winkelmann, R. (1998). Why are the unemployed so unhappy?: Evidence from panel data. *Economica, 65,* 1–15.

Yap, S. C. Y., Anusic, I., & Lucas, R. E. (2012). Does personality moderate reaction and adaptation to major life events?: Evidence from the British Household Panel Survey. *Journal of Research in Personality, 46*(5), 477–488.

Yap, S. C. Y., Anusic, I., & Lucas, R. E. (2014). Does happiness change?: Evidence from longitudinal studies. In K. M. Sheldon & R. E. Lucas (Eds.), *Stability of happiness: Theories and evidence on whether happiness can change* (pp. 127–145). Amsterdam, The Netherlands: Elsevier.

Yap, S. C. Y., Wortman, J., Anusic, I., Glenn, S., Scherer, L. D., Donnellan, M. B., et al. (2017). The effect of mood on judgments of subjective well-being: Nine tests of the judgment model. *Journal of Personality and Social Psychology, 113,* 939–961.

CHAPTER 30

Personality Development
and Internalizing Psychopathology

C. Emily Durbin

Why do some people become seriously depressed or anxious, while others are free of these challenges or face different psychological problems? If major depression and obsessive–compulsive disorder are diseases, why is there so much variability in how these conditions manifest and how they affect the lives of those who experience them? Are anxiety and depression conditions that befall a person and temporarily wreak havoc with his or her psychology, or do they emerge from within, a part of a person's psychological makeup? If someone recovers from depression or anxiety, how does this change other parts of his or her psychology afterward?

Internalizing disorders (anxiety and mood problems, including the psychiatric categories of major depressive disorder (MDD) and persistent depressive disorder, social anxiety disorder, separation anxiety disorder, specific phobias, panic disorder, agoraphobia, generalized anxiety disorder (GAD), posttraumatic stress disorder (PTSD), and obsessive–compulsive disorder) are characterized by broad alterations across many psychological domains—mood, cognitions, motivation, and behavior. They can have a correspondingly profound impact on many aspects of psychological functioning, including a person's sense of self. Depending on when and for how long these syndromes are active during people's lives, they may become

an important part of a people's understanding of themselves and their life stories, or they may be viewed as an unwelcome but temporary aberration that interrupts a very different view of the self. The novelist William Styron seemed to experience depression in this way—it befell him. He described his depression in the following way in his memoir *Darkness Visible: A Memoir of Madness*:

> That the word "indescribable" should present itself is not fortuitous, since it has to be emphasized that if the pain were readily describable most of the countless sufferers from this ancient affliction would have been able to confidently depict for their friends and loved ones (even their physician) some of the actual dimensions of their torment, and perhaps elicit a comprehension that has been generally lacking; such incomprehension has usually been due not to a failure of sympathy but to the basic inability of healthy people to imagine a form of torment so alien to everyday experience. (1990, pp. 16–17)

By contrast, others seem to experience internalizing problems not as inexpressable, foreign visitors, but as part of the scenery of their internal lives, inseparable from their memories of the past self and difficult to imagine being absent from the future self. For example, the cartoonist Roz Chast depicts characters with a quivering, scratchy line, lit with anxiety that pervades even the most mundane activities. Her characters fret over prosaic concerns that they magnify with a neurotic style, such as selecting a greeting card from among progressively more nihilistic and pessimistic sentiments, agonizing over the time lost returning to one's apartment to collect a sweater, and reading an obituary page in which the age of each deceased person is compared to that of the reader. Her characters find threat everywhere, and cause for concern and monitoring of possible disasters are a way of life. They seem less mentally ill than characterologically neurotic. This view of internalizing problems fits classic models of descriptive psychopathology that emphasized the disproportionate burden of anxiety and depression among those whose temperamental style is not dissimilar from the symptoms of these conditions. As Kraepelin argued, depressive episodes frequently "rise like mountain peaks from a structurally similar pain" (in Mayer-Gross, Slater, & Roth, 1969).

The modern lay narrative about mood and anxiety disorders has long been dominated by a biological disease metaphor (i.e., depression is caused by a "chemical imbalance" in the brain) that falls firmly within the "befall" camp. These neurochemical aberrations are like pathogens that infect a healthy person and need to be eradicated through medical intervention, or an inborn quirk of biology that can be corrected through benevolent tinkering with the building blocks of that biology. With effective treatment, "balance" is restored, both metaphorically and psychologically. As appealing as this narrative is, it is a poor representation of the complex neurobiological processes implicated in these conditions, for which a "chemical imbalance" provides little toehold for understanding the actual causal processes.

Moreover, the modern lay narrative is strikingly different from older lay conceptual models of internalizing problems, many of which expressly described depressive and anxiety disorders as being firmly located within the character of the sufferer. Robert Burton's (1621/2001) treatise, *The Anatomy of Melancholy,* described melancholy (depression) as being "either in disposition or in habit [characterological]," of which, "what cannot be cured must be endured." Many of these characterological depictions of internalizing problems were demonstrably wrong and harmful to those suffering, in that they minimized empathy by ascribing moral failings to those with these problems, and

encouraged the use of unhelpful treatments. But they also captured something essential to the experience of many people with anxiety or depression. Specifically, some have the strong sense that elements of their internalizing condition are hard to separate from more enduring aspects of their psychological makeup.

The precise ways in which clinical syndromes of anxiety and depression overlap with or are causally related to more general and temporally persistent individual differences are challenging to identify empirically, but the relevance of these two domains to one another has been repeatedly borne out. In the broadest brushstrokes, those who do and do not (or have vs. have not ever) met diagnostic criteria for a mood or anxiety disorder typically differ from one another in systematic ways in many components of personality. The words *depressed* and *anxious,* their synonyms, and other aspects of clinical internalizing syndromes appear in many measures of normal-range personality traits, and we use these terms colloquially to describe the dispositions of people we know. The major scientific challenges for the field are to bring clarity to these observations and to the descriptive language we use to capture them in lay terms (*a neurotic, a nervous Nelly, a Debbie downer*). Why might the personalities of those with and without internalizing problems differ? What can these differences tell us about the causes of internalizing disorders? Is it possible for anxiety and depression to shape a personality? What befalls us, and what do we become?

The iconic actor Humphrey Bogart died relatively young, leaving behind a masterful body of work and a beautiful younger wife, the only slightly less iconic Lauren Bacall. He was wealthy and respected for his fierce integrity and an urbane cool that was an aspirational version of midcentury American manhood. He also had a painful path in life, late to success and burdened by insecurities from a neglected childhood that no amount of comfort in adulthood could ease. He was melancholic, frequently depressed, and dangerously alcoholic, particularly when acutely depressed. These problems recurred throughout his family—both his parents and siblings had very serious substance use problems and internalizing disorders. At his worst, he "retreated slowly into gloom and silence and Scotch" (Sperber & Lax, 1997, p. 68). His drinking and insecurities shaped a disastrous pattern of relationship choices that defined his adulthood and posed a challenge to his career advancement. His life provides rich examples of the tight connections between personality and internalizing problems, both the genetic luck that can befall us and the ways our dispositions are difficult to separate from infelicitous circumstances both in our pasts and futures. I return to aspects of his psychology throughout this chapter to illustrate some of the major points.

A critical insight of modern science on personality–internalizing disorder associations is that one must not only consider the overlap of the personality domain and those of anxiety and depression but also place these constructs and their interrelationship within the framework of time, or more precisely, development. Processes within each domain are not static; they are both moving along their own trajectory within each person and being influenced by the person's developmental status and their context, and in turn shaping the developmental contexts that will follow for the person. It is impossible to understand how anxiety matters to a person and impacts his or her life without taking into account where the person is in his or her life and where he or she is trying to go, and individual differences in personality lose their meaning when one loses a sense of place within his or her own history. Once one acknowledges that each domain is dynamic, it is obvious that personality and mood and anxiety problems may have more than one type of relationship to one another, so that there will not be one answer to why they are related. It also follows that the influence of these domains on one another can change across the lifespan, and given that each domain broadly shapes critical components of human functioning, they may operate in tandem to impact other aspects of development.

Therefore, I attempt to use a broader developmental perspective to review what we know about the interrelationship of individual differences in personality and internalizing problems, and how we can try to learn more in a way that acknowledges the complexity of the psychological processes. I focus primarily on trait levels of individual differences in personality for the sake of brevity and cohesiveness, but they are by no means the only layer of personality that is relevant for understanding internalizing problems. I first describe some basic findings on how these domains are related, outline the theoretical approaches developed to explain these data, and articulate how modern

personality science has produced findings that call for more explicitly developmentally informed models.

How Is Personality Related to Internalizing Disorders?

Most work on the relationships between personality and internalizing psychopathology has conceptualized these domains at rather general levels of abstraction. Most studies collect measures of broad individual differences in traits, usually higher-order traits of the kind that populate the five-factor model (McCrae & Costa, 1999) and Big Three model (Tellegen, 1985). The advantages of these broad conceptualizations have been well described and include expansive coverage of "the first cut" of many personality elements (i.e., the most basic and obvious distinctions that can be made across persons), greater statistical reliability, and ecological validity, in that broad dimensions are part of how people perceive others with whom they are acquainted. Similarly, psychopathologists have found considerable benefits to higher-order dimensions of psychiatric problems. These models efficiently summarize clinical definitions of psychopathology (e.g., social phobia vs. major depression) by modeling their overlap as a function of two global spectra—internalizing (mood and anxiety) and externalizing (substance use and disruptive behavior) problems. Internalizing and externalizing dimensions are placed at the top of a hierarchy as broad liabilities, and individual disorders at lower levels of the hierarchy represent more specific manifestations of those liabilities (Eaton et al., 2013; Hicks, Krueger, Iacono, McGue, & Patrick, 2004; Krueger et al., 2002; Krueger, Markon, Patrick, Benning, & Kramer, 2007).

This formulation enables a "unified" model of multiple domains of individual differences (e.g., Krueger & Markon, 2006) in which psychopathology dimensions can be explored for their relationship with personality trait models. The framework allows one to step back from voluminous findings at a narrow level (e.g., relationships between a trait facet, such as the social dominance piece of extraversion, and a specific disorder, such as social phobia) and to appreciate the degree to which highly similar findings regarding trait correlates of different internalizing disorders recur throughout the literature.

Personality Traits Implicated in Internalizing Disorders

There are several well-replicated findings that need to be explained by any theory of how personality and anxiety and depression are related. First, both the general internalizing dimension and specific internalizing disorders are associated with elevated neuroticism or negative emotionality (NE). A meta-analysis of 175 studies (Kotov, Gamez, Schmidt, & Watson, 2010) demonstrated large associations between NE and all internalizing disorders. However, the specificity of this link is weak, as externalizing disorders also had large associations with NE (the mean effect size of NE's association with externalizing disorders was smaller than that for internalizing disorders, but the confidence intervals overlapped, suggesting they do not differ greatly in magnitude). NE may reflect a general demoralization factor, a gauge of the emotional upset and reactivity in the face of stress common to many psychiatric conditions, not something unique to depression and anxiety. More specificity can be observed at the level of trait facets. Anxiety and depression are most tightly associated with stress reaction elements of NE, whereas externalizing problems are more related to aggression and anger (e.g., Krueger, Caspi, Moffitt, Silva, & McGee, 1996). The second major finding confirmed by meta-analyses is large, specific associations between internalizing disorders and low levels of extraversion/positive emotionality (PE; Clark & Watson, 1991; Kotov et al., 2010; Mineka, Watson, & Clark, 1998). Low PE is a modest indicator of risk for later anxiety and depression (Khazanov & Ruscio, 2016). Findings for high NE and low PE dovetail with theoretical models of internalizing disorders (Clark, 2005; Clark, Watson, & Mineka, 1994) that emphasize their core abnormalities as comprising basic processes of emotional reactivity.

Importantly, emotionality traits do not tell the full story. In their meta-analysis, Kotov and colleagues (2010) found that low conscientiousness had a large and nonspecific association with internalizing and externalizing disorders. The importance of impulsivity, lack of planning, poor persistence, and general failure to "get it together" are obvious for substance abuse and disruptive behavior problems. They have not featured prominently in descriptions of the personality of anxious and depressed persons. However, the role of low conscientiousness makes sense when viewed in light of experimental psychopathology and affective science work that has identified executive functioning/effortful control processes as important moderators of emotional experience (Bush, Luu, & Posner, 2000; Rothbart & Rueda, 2005). Early in life, emotional processes are integrated with "top-down" functions of reflection, attention allocation, and inhibition, and modulation of behavior (including emotion) is coordinated with environmental demands (Diamond, 2013). These effortful control processes can be strategic or overlearned, and are likely involved in behaviors described in models of conscientiousness. Markers of conscientiousness (e.g., planfulness, responsibility, persistence) may help to explain why internalizing problems are so commonly associated with problems in relationships and work functioning.

Models of Personality–Internalizing Disorder Associations

Most studies exploring associations between personality and psychopathology frame their findings with respect to one or more of an influential list of theoretical models, first articulated as a set 25 years ago to describe potential causes of overlap between personality and depressive disorders (Klein, Wonderlich, & Shea, 1993; Watson & Clark, 1995). They include spectrum, precursor, predisposition, common cause, concomitants, scar, and pathoplasty models. Work in the ensuing years to test these models has shown they are more useful as heuristics for considering processes than as opposing theories that make sufficiently novel predictions allowing one model to outperform another. One way to approach this complexity is to recognize the etiological heterogeneity of internalizing disorders. Scientists have spent many decades trying to identify the causes of each of these conditions and have failed to identify any single factor that explains more than a small amount of why some people develop these problems. We must conclude then that there are many pathways by which different people may arrive at similar clinical manifestations. Some of these pathways may be more "saturated" with personality-relevant processes, and even among those for whom personality is relevant, the nature of the causal associations may still differ across persons.

In the next section, I describe these "classic" models and highlight how they have been useful for making sense of empirical findings. In the subsequent section, I describe more modern proposals that will help not just to organize existing findings, but to shape research designs that will provide new and hopefully more illuminating findings.

The spectrum or continuity model eliminates all conceptual distinctions between the trait and disorder in question—they are alternative terms describing the same phenomena. Behaviors, cognitions, and motivations that make up the trait and those that appear on symptom lists for internalizing disorders are presumed to reflect individual differences in the same underlying psychological dimension(s). Symptoms lie on the extreme end of the same dimension as the trait; extreme trait levels shade continuously into and, in some cases, overlap with symptoms. Normal social reticence shades into the extreme discomfort with meeting others that is described in the diagnostic criteria for social phobia; neurotic worries reach their apex in the all-consuming, repetitive concerns of the chronic worrier with GAD. If the spectrum model is correct and personality traits and disorders are fundamentally the same, measures of the trait and of the disorder should be strongly associated. However, if one accepts statistically significant or even moderately sized associations as supporting evidence, this model becomes barely falsifiable, particularly for cross-sectional designs using self-report assessment of both constructs. There are important questions that cannot be answered by invoking a spectrum of internalizing that encompasses the full normal range of NE, and mood and anxiety symptoms. For example, why do some people with PTSD feel that their personality changed substantially after experiencing the traumatic event that precipitated their PTSD? Why is there still variability in clinical presentation of depression even among those with similarly high levels of NE? Such knowledge requires different designs and approaches that focus on illuminating processes, rather than patterns of covariance.

Despite the simplicity this model offers, its power fades a bit when we consider what might be lost with this simplification and whether the evidence supporting it justifies eliminating distinctions between personality traits and internalizing disorders. The kinds of evidence marshaled to support the conclusion that personality traits and internalizing disorders are fundamentally the same come from studies that are excellent at summarizing the quantitative overlap between personality and internalizing problems, but cannot distinguish among potential causes of that overlap. Specifically, most of the relevant studies are ones in which people complete self-reports of their personality and their internalizing problems at the same time; having the same source of information, the same means of collecting it, and the same time point generally inflates the overlap between the domains. Analyses of concurrent associations are not informative about how the associations were established (they are "after the fact").

The *precursor/prodrome model* proposes that extreme levels of personality traits are a weaker or incipient version of the disorder's symptoms that emerges developmentally before the expression of a full-blown version of the disorder. Not everyone who has the prodromal signs will go on to develop the disorder, just as a scratchy throat can presage the onset of a cold or might resolve without worsening. In contrast to the spectrum model, precursor/prodrome hypotheses do not assume that the trait and disorder are entirely overlapping either conceptually or etiologically, as this model requires other causal factors to be invoked to explain why some people with relevantly extreme levels of the trait go on to manifest the disorder, whereas other people with similar trait levels do not.

The *common cause model* maintains a distinction between personality traits and disorders, but explains their intercorrelations by proposing that the trait of interest and internalizing problems are caused by shared factors. Under the strongest version of this model, the trait and disorder do not have any direct causal relationship with one another after accounting for their shared etiology. Presumably, these shared etiological factors also account for any overlap in the external correlates of the trait and disorder. In this model, the causes of each domain are viewed as primary, and there is little left of interest to explore that connects traits and internalizing problems after these causally prior factors are considered. The common cause model is consistent with evidence for overlapping genetic contributions to NE and depression (Kendler, Gatz, Gardner, & Pedersen, 2006), although these data are also consistent with many of the other theoretical models as well.

The predisposition, pathoplasty, concomitants, and scar models suggest there are direct causal connections between traits and disorders. Trait constellations produce distinctive patterns of trait-like behavior that set into motion downstream effects that ultimately result in the disorder. For example, people low in PE may fail to develop a deep bench of social connections that would ordinarily buffer them from the depressogenic effects of stressful life events.

In the *pathoplasty or exacerbation model,* personality traits do not cause someone to develop the disorder, but they shape how the disorder is manifested and its course (e.g., the pattern or severity of symptoms, course, or treatment response). Consistent with this model, high NE predicts poorer course and treatment response among those with depression (Quilty et al., 2008; Tang et al., 2009). However, such evidence is also consistent with other explanations, namely traits may predict treatment response or another outcome because people who have more severe variants of the disorder likely also have more extreme preexisting trait levels.

Under the *concomitants or state model,* trait-disorder associations are measurement artifacts caused by the impact of symptoms of the disorder on the assessment of trait-relevant behaviors. For example, acute depression is associated with more negative self-perceptions that can bias self-reports of negatively evaluative traits, as depressed persons describe themselves more harshly than other would. Within-subjects analyses show self-reported NE is elevated when people are depressed compared with when they are not (Kendler, Neale, Kessler, Heath, & Eaves, 1993; Ormel, Oldehinkel, & Vollebergh, 2004). These negative self-perceptions are part of a general negativity bias in depression sometimes referred to as *depressive realism,* an observation that depression is associated with modestly more accurate judgments, largely because depressed people have a weaker bias towards positivity (Moore & Fresco, 2012). Humphrey Bogart was an excellent example of this, and this cognitive style was a defining feature of his onscreen appeal. Warner Brothers studio marketed his melancholy demeanor, "a wryness born of experience, hints of a troubled past not shared with the audience, and an essentially dark view of the world appropriately in keeping with the times" (Sperber & Lax, 1997, p. 210). For the post–World War II era, Bogart's style suggested an honorable cynicism that suited the cultural moment. For Bogart himself, his pessimism cut deeply and darkened even his greatest personal and professional successes. The cruelest parts of depression and anxiety can be the

way they warp self-perceptions and convince the sufferer that these biased versions in fact reveal a deeper truth about the self.

The *scar/complication model* proposes that the experience of having an internalizing disorder changes not just one's view of the self, but one's actual personality, such that traits are different after the disorder onsets than before and remain in their changed state after the disorder remits (i.e., a scar). They capture how something that befalls us can change who we become. For example, one study found that major depression predicted higher NE at a later time point, controlling for NE at an earlier time point (Fanous, Neale, Aggen, & Kendler, 2007; Kendler et al., 1993). However, three other studies have failed to find scar effects of MDD on NE (Duggan, Sham, Lee, & Murray, 1991; Ormel et al., 2004; Zeiss & Lewinsohn, 1988).

Critique of Traditional Models

While it is appealing to think that we can identify the model that best captures the relationship between a personality trait and an internalizing disorder, none of these models has been disconfirmed or uniquely supported. This is partly because many models predict the same findings equally well, and partly because very few studies use research designs that can distinguish among predictions of the various models. Furthermore, traits are descriptions of a person's standing relative to others on a construct; they are not within-person drivers of behavior (Molenaar, 2004). A person's level of NE is a summary of observations about him or her, not an explanation for why he or she behaves in particular ways, and we mistake the trait's scientific status when we presume otherwise. Recognizing this state of affairs helps us to think about this problem in a more process-oriented way to generate more dynamic research.

Perhaps most importantly, traditional models of the association between traits and internalizing disorders are largely adevelopmental. Even those that suggest a temporal ordering of traits and disorders do not consider the dynamic nature of either traits or disorders, nor the likelihood that the broader developmental context impacts how they are related to one another. They are snapshots of an unfolding process, often mixing in images taken at different points in the process as if timing were irrelevant. The traditional models do not take into account normative lifespan changes in traits, which makes it difficult to interpret the relevant data. For example, if a trait is a precursor for panic disorder but mean levels of the trait increase in the population during specific developmental intervals, should we expect greater vulnerability for panic disorder during those intervals? Or would risk be limited to those who had elevated levels at an earlier period?

Taking a developmental perspective on these issues allows for a more explicit focus on processes that may explain correlational data and can motivate more causally informative studies. Developmental psychopathology conceptualizes psychiatric problems as deviation from normative developmental pathways (Cicchetti, 1993). This perspective is most powerful when coupled with an understanding of the normative trajectory of the processes of interest (so that deviations can be more precisely defined) and an appreciation of the factors that shape these normative changes. The past 20 years of personality science have provided just such data. We now know quite a lot about age-related changes in mean levels of traits, and large-scale epidemiological studies have documented the prevalence rates of disorders across much of the lifespan. Following these data and the logic of developmental psychopathology, one can articulate several principles to understand existing data and spur new work, as outlined by Durbin and Hicks (2014).

These principles derive from a model of codevelopment of personality and psychopathology. Traits and disorders are not static; therefore, the processes that link them cannot be revealed using designs that assume they are unchanging. In fact, their patterns of change may in fact reveal some of the causal processes. Both traits and internalizing problems are responsive to the actions of other forces, including developmental pressures that may cause traits and anxiety or depression to change in similar ways. Research designs that allow us to study how within-person changes in personality processes influence within-person change in onset, maintenance, and recovery from disorders will be particularly useful.

Codevelopment Principles to Inform Trait-Internalizing Disorder Research

Normative change and normative differences bring precision to links between traits and in-

ternalizing problems. As background, personality changes over the lifespan open avenues for exploring causes of interrelationships between traits and internalizing disorders and whether these causes change across development. Rank-order stability of traits is lowest in childhood (Roberts & DelVecchio, 2000), which suggests that associations between traits and internalizing problems may be different in childhood than later in the lifespan. A childhood trait that longitudinally predicts a disorder in adulthood (i.e., an effect typically interpreted as evidence for predisposition) may not exhibit a cross-sectional association with that disorder in either childhood or adulthood. This could occur for two reasons. The functional correlates of traits may vary in the context of different developmental pressures, or the enduring vulnerability indexed by that trait may change in manifestation over the lifespan. There is evidence that childhood-onset depression and adult-onset depression differ in their correlates, such that the former is associated with greater overall psychiatric symptomatology and more comorbidity with externalizing problems (Hill, Pickles, Rollinson, Davies, & Byatt, 2004; Jaffee et al., 2002).

One simple heuristic for concretizing this principle is to utilize data on lifespan changes to identify individuals whose developmental trajectories are non-normative. For example, it would be informative to study those who fail to exhibit personality change similar to their peers and those with disorders whose courses are unusual relative to others with the same conditions (e.g., an early onset). Study designs that include multiple assessments of both traits and disorders during key developmental periods when significant normative change occurs (e.g., adolescence through early adulthood) are essential, and those that measure personality prior to disorder onset provide additional power for disconfirming causal hypotheses.

Non-normative developmental trait trajectories relevant to internalizing problems can be expressed in two patterns: *stagnation* and *recovery*. The stagnation hypothesis (Durbin & Hicks, 2014) is that the presence of internalizing problems stunts personality development, particularly when the disorder is active during a period of expected normative change. In this way, something that befalls a person can then be what he or she becomes. One possible mechanism of stagnation concerns goals and goal-directed behavior. A person's change in goals can prompt new behavioral processes meant to bring about the new desired outcomes, including selecting in or out of different environmental contexts, structuring the environment in new ways to make goal achievement more likely, or adopting new cognitive approaches to engaging with aspects of the environment. Internalizing problems that alter one's goals or the perception that one can achieve them, such as depressive pessimism, might lead to a stagnation of personality change—what befalls us impacts whom we become.

The recovery hypothesis posits that symptom remission frees personality to change toward the developmental norm. One hallmark of internalizing disorders is a lack of behavioral and cognitive flexibility (Kashdan & Rottenberg, 2010); thus, resolution of disorder may allow someone to explore new behavioral repertoires in a way that is more responsive to environmental demands. Evidence consistent with a recovery mechanism would include rate of personality change following recovery that is greater than the normative trend over a similar time span, consistent with a catching-up effect. For example, Ormel and colleagues (2004) reported that measures of NE, low self-esteem, and low mastery were elevated during major depressive episodes (MDEs) but returned to their premorbid levels after remission. Harkness, Bagby, Joffe, and Levitt (2002) found that after 3 months of antidepressant treatment, patients with MDD reported lower levels of NE, and higher levels of PE and conscientiousness (CN) in comparison with their intake scores.

Another important normative finding from the personality development literature is the existence of sex differences in mean trait levels and their trajectories of change. These have seldom been considered in studies testing models of internalizing disorder–trait associations, despite sex differences in the prevalence of internalizing disorders (Kessler et al., 2005). Meta-analytic data from adults (Costa, Terracciano, & McCrae, 2001; Lynn & Martin, 1997) reveal sex differences in NE (higher in women), especially its anxiety/stress reaction components (those most closely associated with internalizing problems), and social potency facets of extraversion (higher in men). Similar effects have emerged in adolescent samples, with additional findings of higher aggression and lower in CN in boys (Blonigen et al., 2008; Donnellan, Conger, & Burzette, 2007; Roberts, Caspi, & Moffitt, 2001). Some of these differences are

evident as early as childhood, including that for elevated fear/stress reaction in girls and lower CN in boys (Else-Quest, Hyde, Goldsmith, & Van Hulle, 2006; Olino, Durbin, Klein, Hayden, & Dyson, 2013). Sex differences in trait change are not as well replicated; there is evidence that some sex differences narrow and others widen during the transition from adolescence to adulthood (Blonigen et al., 2008; Donnellan et al., 2007; Durbin et al., 2016; Roberts et al., 2001).

Internalizing disorders are about twice as common in females than in males. For depression, this sex difference does not appear until midadolescence (Costello, Erklani, & Angold, 2006; Hankin & Abramson, 2001), after which it does not change in magnitude across the remainder of the lifespan. This observation is consistent with girls' higher mean levels of some NE traits and increases in these traits for girls (but not boys) in midadolescence (Durbin et al., 2016). Sex differences in anxiety disorder prevalence are quite similar to that for depression (McLean, Asnaani, Litz, & Hofmann, 2011). Sex differences in anxiety and depression may occur because of differences in the type, intensity, or meaning of developmental pressures experienced by males and females across the life course, or the supports that cultures provide to each gender for navigating both normative and non-normative transitions. Sex differences in personality development may also point to the existence of different developmental pressures or adaptations to those pressures in males and females that might account for sex-differentiated risks for anxiety and depression.

Considering specific developmental periods and contexts can yield greater precision in identification of causal processes. The processes that link traits and internalizing disorders play out in the broader context of lifespan development, namely, the tasks, goals, and relationships that wax and wane as they emerge and shift in importance to the person over time (Baltes, 1987; Masten et al., 1995, 2004; Roisman, Masten, Coatsworth, & Tellegen, 2004). Personality traits coalesce, stabilize, and change in concert with the roles, tasks, and relationships that people live in and strive for. Symptoms of mood and anxiety disorders are also contextualized. People with depression are anhedonic about their typical activities, those with GAD worry excessively about the particulars of their life circumstances, and rituals of obsessive–compulsive disorder are experienced differently if one is a schoolchild or a mother. Individual differences in adaptation central to both internalizing problems and personality are revealed in how people navigate these life circumstances. Some challenges recur across the lifespan; we will always need to find a way to make connections with others, both to advance our goals and to find meaning in close relationships. Personality profiles and internalizing problems may emerge as recurrent blocks to successfully navigating these challenges. However, some challenges do not arise or become salient until particular developmental periods; therefore, they present new occasions in which personality may change in negative ways, and difficulties with anxiety or depression may emerge. For example, during middle childhood, children are exposed to more frank, explicit feedback regarding how their abilities and achievements stack up relative to their peers. This contrasts earlier periods in which children are given more regular, reassuring, and globally positive feedback, thus setting the stage for children to experience new feelings questioning their competence and self-esteem during middle childhood. Similarly, as people age and the time horizon for accomplishing certain highly valued life goals looms, symptoms of hopelessness and avolition may be more readily experienced.

Because developmental conditions can shape opportunities and costs for pursuing valued goals, investing in personally relevant domains, and for making behavioral changes, the processes that link traits and disorders may vary across developmental periods that are characterized by different developmental pressures. For example, high NE may be a predisposition for anxiety disorder early in childhood but a scar of prior depression later in the lifespan. Early in childhood, when key developmental transitions require navigating novel and uncertain changes that one is expected to make with little chance for escape (e.g., transitioning to formal schooling), children with high NE are more likely to develop problems with anxiety as they experience these transitions as stressful and lack the agency to avoid or even substantially alter the terms of the transitions. Someone who experiences depression for the first time as an emerging adult may have difficulty accomplishing goals owing to his or her depression, such as establishing a romantic partnership or advancing in a career; even after the depression lifts, disappointment regarding one's life circumstances and negative self-regard may persist in the form of elevated anxiety, self-doubt, and worry.

Life domains knit together causal interplay between traits and disorder. A codevelopment framework predicts that internalizing disorders and personality traits may become more intertwined over time because of accumulation processes that originate with the trait or disorder. If individual differences in internalizing problems or a trait impact functioning in other life domains (e.g., academics/work, health, or relationships), the life circumstances and psychological structures that result from these outcomes will then constrain or provide affordances for change in the other domain. The net result is a tighter relationship between traits and the disorder, as they collude together via the life structures they helped create to influence subsequent change in both domains. For example, someone whose trait structure of low PE and CN causes them to rub coworkers the wrong way will make fewer career advances, and thus lose opportunities to develop leadership and interpersonal skills in a position of authority, and to accumulate financial resources. These may in turn make it more likely that the person develops a mood disorder. An internalizing disorder can create psychological processes that make growth and change more difficult, such as by producing longer-term changes in the person's relationships. For example, in her blog, *Hyperbole and a Half,* Allie Brosch (2013) described how her depression changed her interpersonal outlook and distanced her from others:

"I gradually came to accept that maybe enjoyment was not a thing I got to feel anymore. I didn't want anyone to know, though. I was still sort of uncomfortable about how bored and detached I felt around other people and I was still holding out hope that the whole thing would spontaneously work itself out. As long as I could manage to not alienate anyone, everything might be okay!. . . . It's weird for people who still have feelings to be around depressed people. They try to help you have feelings again so things can go back to normal, and it's frustrating for them when that doesn't happen. . . . So they try harder to make you feel hopeful and positive about the situation. You explain it again, hoping they'll try a less hope-centric approach, but re-explaining your total inability to experience joy inevitably sounds kind of negative; like maybe you WANT to be depressed. The positivity starts coming out in a spray—a giant, desperate happiness sprinkler pointed directly at your face. And it keeps going like that until you're having this weird argument where you're trying to convince the person that you are far too hopeless for hope so they'll just give up on their optimism crusade and let you go back to feeling bored and lonely by yourself."

Roberts and Caspi's (2003) corresponsive principle of personality development proposes that the features of personality that cause people to encounter particular experiences are the very ones that will be changed or deepened by those same experiences, as the experiences tend to reinforce those traits. If this is true, then personality processes have more than one role—they are starting points in exposure to a developmental press, mechanisms that process the meaning of the press, and behavioral patterns that can change as a result of it. Personality processes include the means by which what we have become creates what befalls us, and how what befalls us deepens what we become.

Unsuccessful responses to a *developmental pressure* contribute to the onset or severity of internalizing problems, as well as to deviations in personality development. Developmental pressures are evident during periods of normative transition or upon occurrence of stressful events that tax the person's capabilities. First, normal transitions (e.g., moving from middle to high school, puberty, and dating) are more taxing when they occur simultaneously rather than singly (Simons, Burgeson, & Carlton-Ford, 1987). Second, stressful life events may also be considered developmental pressures if the nature of the stressor results in new psychological demands. People whose responses to the pressures do not meet the challenge or that do so by creating new problems tend to have negative outcomes that may contribute to onset or severity of a disorder or deterioration of personality functioning.

The predictive validity of personality for internalizing problems is heightened during times of developmental press—individual differences are most important for determining who will worsen or develop a new episode of anxiety or depression when the stakes are high for change. It is well established that high NE predicts MDD in the context of stressful life events (e.g., Kendler, Kuhn, & Prescott, 2004; Van Os & Jones, 1999). In contrast to stressful life events that may occur at any point in the lifespan, normative transitions are windows during which many traits bear upon the ability to successfully navigate the relevant choice points. Personality

processes shape how these pressures are interpreted and guide individual responses to them, creating links between traits and disorder that are less evident during quiescent developmental periods. For example, low extraversion will be more consequential for children's depression when making a transition from middle school to high school, which requires establishing new friendships, than it is for beginning a new term at the same school. Thus, periods of developmental press or transition represent moments during which the connections between personality and disorder are both especially tight and potentially changeable, and therefore are windows for especially informative empirical studies. Stressful life events whose primary characteristic is threat may tend to elicit narrow responses that draw chiefly on the person's well-practiced mechanisms for negative affect and coping, whereas normative transitions carry both threat and opportunity, as well as cultural scripts for how they are "meant" to be navigated.

Considering personality in the limited framework of traits alone will not fully account for these mechanisms. A person's trait profile may conflict with the "developmental projects" (i.e., the new goals perceived as important to defining success at this point in their lives) that arise during a time of developmental pressure (Freund & Riediger, 2006). Whether personality change occurs is dependent on how important these goals or strivings are, and the extent of a person's psychological resources to enact behaviors and cognitions consistent with their developmental projects rather than their traits (McAdams & Olson, 2010). It is much easier to continue on as one typically does, and much harder to try new patterns. Given the inflexibility associated with internalizing disorders, persons with anxiety or depression may have more difficulty overriding trait dispositions to change their behavior in pursuit of their developmental projects. This may be why many with internalizing problems describe themselves as feeling "inauthentic," in that they struggle to follow their values and goals fully because of the strong pull of dispositions they have difficulty overriding. For those who can engage authentically with their developmental tasks and enact behaviors new to their repertoire or counter to their existing trait structure, their risk for subsequent anxiety and depression may decrease. Others with internalizing problems may have ambivalent feelings about their values and accomplishments, and denigrate what they have accomplished. In later life, Humphrey Bogart "would depict his career as an accident, a job he'd simply fallen into, a part of his self-mythologizing in keeping with a rugged code that saw acting as not quite fit for a real man" (Sperber & Lax, 1997, p. 16).

The impacts of life transitions may vary by their nature (volitional or involuntary), or by the person's personality structure or the presence of disorder at the time of the transition. Compared with involuntary transitions (e.g., puberty), volitional transitions are open to greater influence in timing and quality from prior traits and disorders. Given the importance of a perception of lack of control to anxiety, involuntary transitions may be sensitive periods for the development of anxiety problems. For volitional transitions, personality traits have another potential causal route—they can guide people into certain environments, a process referred to as "selection." Selection can heighten or minimize the likelihood that a transition will result in changes in traits or disorders. Internalizing problems may have similar selection effects. Depression in adolescence predicts subsequent sexual risk behaviors (Lehrer, Shrier, Gortmaker, & Buka, 2006), thus heightening the likelihood that a normative transition may result in problematic life outcomes and enhancing the risk for further psychopathology, including persistent depression and anxiety. In adulthood, internalizing problems are associated with mate characteristics, especially psychopathology in romantic partners (Maes et al., 1998; Mathews & Reus, 2001) and marital/couple discord (e.g., Whisman, 2001); selecting into these relationships can create further stressors that make recovery from depression and anxiety less likely. Bogart's depressive resignation helped select him into repeated bad marriages, characterized by intense conflict, which fueled further his alcoholism, anger, and black moods.

In other cases, behavioral responses to time-limited developmental pressures may become more permanent fixtures of personality if they become consolidated into one's identity, particularly during the formative narrative identity development period of late adolescence and early adulthood (Habermas & Bluck, 2000). Narrative identity is an internalized story of oneself, one's past, and one's future, which serves to affirm one's choices and prepares for new challenges. It is distinct from traits (McAdams & Pals, 2006), and its development is a primary task of emerging adulthood (McAdams, 1985). When maladaptive patterns that have become habitual enough to be organized as traits are accompanied by a personal narrative consistent with these traits, subsequent person–environment interplay stabilizes these processes and close off avenues for adaptive change (i.e., via cumulative continuity; Roberts, Wood, & Caspi, 2008). Internalizing disorders that occur during this formative period may be particularly troublesome if they gain traction as a part of this narrative (e.g., "I am a person who can't handle stress"; "I am a depressive").

Humphrey Bogart was known for his outward confidence and cool, but his internal psychology was shaped by a fear of failure. Even at the height of his professional success, he was uncomfortable with praise and "his past rejections were more vivid than his current success" (Sperber & Lax, 1997, p. 332). He had terrible difficulty in intimate relationships with women, recreating the tense and conflictual relationship with his mother, a famous children's artist who was so emotionally cold toward her children that he could not recall ever being hugged or kissed. They were cared for by servants who were so emotionally and physically abusive to the children that neighboring families were concerned for their well-being. Duty was the only bond that held Bogart's mother to them, and Bogart's romantic relationships recreated this halfhearted obligation. He seemed reluctant to enter both his second and third marriages and refused to leave them out of a sense of duty. He selected partners who were anything but affectless toward him, women who demonstrated the intensity of their feelings for him in bouts of intense anger, jealousy, and physical violence. Even in his happiest and mutually affectionate marriage to Bacall, Bogart struggled with his wife's career aspirations, fearing that she would neglect him and his children. His worldview was captured by fellow actor Mary Astor: "Bogey looked at the world, at his place in it, at movies, at life in general, and these was something in it that made him sick, contemptuous, bitter" (Sperber & Lax, 1997, pp. 156–157). His life story—from privileged but emotionally hollow beginning, through success well after he thought he deserved it—shaped many of the decisions that brought torment, insecurity, and sadness to his life.

Consider theories accounting for normative personality change and individual differences in change when seeking to understand

associations between traits and internalizing disorders. The large mean-level changes in self-reported traits toward maturation observed during the transition into adulthood can be conceptualized as resulting from a developmental "press" in which the normative tasks of this period recruit particular personality processes (Durbin & Hicks, 2014). Salient developmental tasks that characterize this period reflect evolutionarily relevant goals (Denissen, van Aken, & Roberts, 2011) such as achieving an independent financial and living situation, obtaining stable employment, and establishing an intimate partner relationship and family (Masten et al., 2004; Roisman et al., 2004). Compared to the developmental tasks of earlier periods, these are much more complex. They require greater coordination of behaviors, more deft deployment of emotional skills, and carry greater societal expectations for individual responsibility. The burden of navigating these tasks falls on the person; thus, the blame or praise for failure or success more clearly reflects on the self. Given the centrality of self-perceptions of agency and competence in internalizing disorders, the pressures of this period could provoke new anxiogenic and depressogenic processes.

The term *competence* has been used to describe success in performing these tasks, wherein success is defined with reference to the guidelines and values of a given sociocultural context (Masten et al., 1995, 2004). One hypothesis is that relatively competent individuals also exhibit personality profiles characterized as "mature," that is, low NE and high CN relative to age-related norms (Durbin & Hicks, 2014; Hicks, Durbin, Blonigen, Iacono, & McGue, 2012; Johnson, Hicks, McGue, & Iacono, 2007). A period of relative immaturity as people enter the early stages of a new developmental period and struggle with its developmental pressures may be normative precursors to ultimate maturation, as the new behaviors and cognitions required for success in these tasks take time to develop (Denissen, van Aken, Penke, & Wood, 2013). During this time, self-perceived competence may decline. This is consistent with evidence that self-esteem exhibits a nonlinear pattern of change, with decreases in middle adolescence that are bracketed by increases in early adolescence and later adolescence/early adulthood (Baldwin & Hoffman, 2002). In fact, new onsets of depression are quite common in this period relative to other periods in the lifespan (Zisook et al., 2007).

One observation consistent with the idea that mean-level trait changes may be prompted by a mismatch between the capabilities afforded by one's personality profile and the challenges of a new development period is that individual differences in trait change are dependent on initial personality structure. People who exhibit the most trait change through the transition into adulthood are those who had the highest NE and lowest CN in adolescence (Blonigen et al., 2008; Donnellan et al., 2007; Roberts et al., 2001). Adolescents with low NE and high CN are not sufficiently mature to take on adult responsibilities, but they are better prepared to navigate them than are their prepared peers, as some of the necessary behaviors, skills, and attitudes are already in their personality repertoires. Consequently, adolescents with a more mature personality structure probably feel more efficacious about successfully meeting the new demands, which might reduce their risk for psychopathology. Less mature individuals, however, likely experience more uncertainty, more feedback and pressure from their environment to change, and a greater urgency to "catch up" in order to successfully complete the tasks of adulthood. Those who fail to mature or show changes away from the maturational trend would be expected to be at highest risk for psychopathology, including internalizing problems. Depression and anxiety may reflect a manifestation of broader processes related to struggles accommodating to normative developmental pressures.

Conclusions about the Codevelopment of Personality and Internalizing Disorders

We can move beyond traditional, static models of how anxiety and depression are related to personality, building on modern knowledge of personality development. Trait–disorder associations are dynamic. The same disorder and same trait may be linked by different mechanisms depending on developmental contexts, and within persons, based on the idiographic histories of their traits and experience with disorder. It is highly unlikely that any one of the traditional models (e.g., spectrum, predisposition, and scar) can account for all or even most of the processes driving associations observed between traits and disorders over the life course and across the population. Rather than there being one "model" that accurately captures how a personality construct and an internalizing disorder are related, there are probably many different processes capable of producing such a link, and these various processes may vary in their salience at different points in the lifespan or in the history of a disorder. Rather than focusing on participants within age periods (e.g., late adolescence), it will be more illuminating to choose participants who are approaching and living through environmental contexts and developmental transitions of importance (regardless of age). These transitions may represent moments when individual differences in personality become very important for shaping adjustment, and when the importance of achieving these milestones and consequences for failure to do so may produce heightened risk for internalizing disorders for those with personality profiles poorly matched for these milestones.

Conclusions

The study of personality–internalizing disorder relationships is at somewhat of a crossroads. The basic facts of how strongly individual differences in traits (but not yet other aspects of personality, which have been relatively neglected) relate to these conditions have been known for some time. What has proven much more difficult is moving beyond these descriptive facts toward an understanding of what these findings mean because, although these constructs are straightforward at a descriptive level, they are highly complex in their causes, their history within persons, and their deep connections to other processes within persons in their environments, and in the transactions that occur between persons and environments. It seems that, for some people, depression and anxiety are things that befall them and whose effects can fade with recovery. It also seems that depression and anxiety can hit those with particular personality constellations harder than others. For the most chronic forms of internalizing problems, particularly those that begin earlier in life, depression and anxiety may play a critical role in shaping dispositional traits.

Modern personality science recognizes the dynamic nature of these constructs and a foundation of new findings regarding personality development is bringing more richness to our understanding of how and why personality operates as it does. Empirical approaches that allow us to pin down part of these dynamics and that trace the contours of human development with more fidelity will provide a new set of core findings regarding individual differences and will allow us to understand these problems in more sophisticated ways. Theoretical approaches that help us to wrestle with causal processes that involve multiple sources, feedback, and constructs that change in their influences and impacts over time, and that help to incorporate different levels of personality, will also be critical. Altogether, these advances are guiding us as we move beyond "the usual suspects" and move toward a greater understanding of not just what befalls us and what we become, but *how* we become and how our becoming beckons what befalls us.

REFERENCES

Baldwin, S. A., & Hoffman, J. P. (2002). The dynamics of self-esteem: A growth-curve analysis. *Journal of Youth and Adolescence, 31*(2), 101–113.

Baltes, P. B. (1987). Theoretical propositions of life-span developmental psychology: On the dynamics between growth and decline. *Developmental Psychology, 23*(5), 611–626.

Blonigen, D. M., Carlson, M. D., Hicks, B. M., Krueger, R. F., & Iacono, W. G. (2008). Stability and change in personality traits from late adolescence to early adulthood: A longitudinal twin study. *Journal of Personality, 76,* 229–266.

Brosch, A. (2013, May 9). Depression: Part two [Blog]. Retrieved from *http://hyperboleandahalf.blogspot. com/2013/05/depression-part-two.html.*

Burton, R. (2001). *The anatomy of melancholy* (J. Holbrook, Ed.). New York: New York Review Books. (Original work published 1621)

Bush, G., Luu, P., & Posner, M. (2000). Cognitive and emotional influences in anterior cingulate cortex. *Trends in Cognitive Sciences, 4*(6), 215–222.

Cicchetti, D. (1993). Developmental psychopathology: Reactions, reflections, projections. *Developmental Review, 12,* 471–502.

Clark, L. A. (2005). Temperament as a unifying basis for personality and psychopathology. *Journal of Abnormal Psychology, 114,* 505–521.

Clark, L. A., & Watson, D. (1991). Tripartite model of anxiety and depression: Psychometric evidence and taxonomic implications. *Journal of Abnormal Psychology, 100,* 316–336.

Clark, L. A., Watson, D., & Mineka, S. (1994). Temperament, personality, and the mood and anxiety disorders. *Journal of Abnormal Psychology, 103*(1), 103–116.

Costa, P., Jr., Terracciano, A., & McCrae, R. R. (2001). Gender differences in personality traits across cultures: Robust and surprising findings. *Journal of Personality and Social Psychology, 81*(2), 322–331.

Costello, E. J., Erkanli, A., & Angold, A. (2006). Is there an epidemic of child or adolescent depression? *Journal of Child Psychology and Psychiatry, 47,* 1263–1271.

Denissen, J. J. A., van Aken, M. A. G., Penke, L., & Wood, D. (2013). Self-regulation underlies temperament and personality: An integrative developmental framework. *Child Development Perspectives, 7*(4), 255–260.

Denissen, J. A., van Aken, M. A., & Roberts, B. W. (2011). Personality development across the lifespan. In T. Chamorro-Premuzic, S. von Stumm, & A. Furnham (Eds.), *The Wiley–Blackwell handbook of individual differences* (pp. 75–100). Chichester, UK: Wiley.

Diamond, A. (2013). Executive functions. *Annual Review of Psychology, 64,* 135–168.

Donnellan, M. B., Conger, R. D., & Burzette, R. G. (2007). Personality development from late adolescence to young adulthood: Differential stability, normative maturity, and evidence for the maturity-stability hypothesis. *Journal of Personality, 75,* 237–263.

Duggan, C. F., Sham, P., Lee, A. S., & Murray, R. M. (1991). Does recurrent depression lead to a change in neuroticism? *Psychological Medicine, 21,* 985–990.

Durbin, C. E., & Hicks, B. M. (2014). Personality and psychopathology: A stagnant field in need of development. *European Journal of Personality, 28*(4), 362–386.

Durbin, C. E., Hicks, B. M., Blonigen, D. M., Johnson, W., Iacono, W. G., & McGue, M. (2016). Personality trait change across late childhood to young adulthood: Evidence for nonlinearity and sex differences in change. *European Journal of Personality, 30*(1), 31–44.

Eaton, N. R., Krueger, R. F., Markon, K. E., Keyes, K. M., Skodol, A. E., Wall, M., et al. (2013). The structure and predictive validity of internalizing disorders. *Journal of Abnormal Psychology, 122,* 86–92.

Else-Quest, N. M., Hyde, J. S., Goldsmith, H. H., & Van Hulle, C. A. (2006). Gender differences in temperament: A meta-analysis. *Psychological Bulletin, 132*(1), 33–72.

Fanous, A. H., Neale, M. C., Aggen, S. H., & Kendler, K. S. (2007). A longitudinal study of personality and major depression in a population-based sample of male twins. *Psychological Medicine, 37,* 1163–1172.

Freund, A. M., & Riediger, M. (2006). Goals as building blocks of personality and development in adulthood. In D. K. Mrozek & T. D. Little (Eds.), *Handbook of personality development* (pp. 353–372). Mahwah, NJ: Erlbaum.

Habermas, T., & Bluck, S. (2000). Getting a life: The emergence of the life story in adolescence. *Psychological Bulletin, 126,* 748–769.

Hankin, B. L., & Abramson, L. Y. (2001). Development of gender differences in depression: An elaborated cognitive vulnerability–transactional stress theory. *Psychological Bulletin, 27,* 773–796.

Harkness, K. L., Bagby, R. M., Joffe, R. T., & Levitt, A. (2002). Major depression, chronic minor depression, and the five-factor model of personality. *European Journal of Personality, 16,* 271–281.

Hicks, B. M., Durbin, C. E., Blonigen, D. M., Iacono, W. G., & McGue, M. (2012). Relationship between personality change and the onset and course of alcohol dependence in young adulthood. *Addiction, 107,* 540–548.

Hicks, B. M., Krueger, R. F., Iacono, W. G., McGue, M., & Patrick, C. J. (2004). Family transmission and heritability of externalizing disorders: A twin-family study. *Archives of General Psychiatry, 61,* 922–928.

Hill, J., Pickles, A., Rollinson, L., Davies, R., & Byatt, M. (2004). Juvenile- versus adult-onset depression: Multiple differences imply different pathways. *Psychological Medicine, 34,* 1483–1493.

Jaffee, S. R., Moffitt, T. E., Caspi, A., Fombonne, E., Poulton, R., & Martin, J. (2002). Differences in early childhood risk factors for juvenile-onset and adult-onset depression. *Archives of General Psychiatry, 58,* 215–222.

Johnson, W., Hicks, B. M., McGue, M., & Iacono, W. G. (2007). Most of the girls are alright, but some aren't: Personality trajectory groups from ages 14 to 24 and some associations with outcomes. *Journal of Personality and Social Psychology, 93,* 266–284.

Kashdan, T. B., & Rottenberg, J. (2010). Psychological flexibility as a fundamental aspect of health. *Clinical Psychology Review, 30*(7), 865–878.

Kendler, K. S., Gatz, M., Gardner, C. O., & Pedersen, N. L. (2006). Personality and major depression: A Swedish longitudinal, population-based twin study. *Archives of General Psychiatry, 63,* 1113–1120.

Kendler, K. S., Kuhn, J., & Prescott, C. A. (2004). The interrelationship of neuroticism, sex, and stressful life events in the prediction of episodes of major depression. *American Journal of Psychiatry, 161*(4), 631–636.

Kendler, K. S., Neale, M. C., Kessler, R. C., Heath, A. C., & Eaves, L. J. (1993). A longitudinal twin study of personality and major depression in women. *Archives of General Psychiatry, 50,* 853–862.

Kessler, R. C., Berglund, P., Demler, O., Jin, R., Merikangas, K. R., & Walters, E. E. (2005). Lifetime prevalence and age-of onset distributions of DSM-IV disorders in the National Comorbidity Survey Replication. *Archives of General Psychiatry, 62,* 593–602.

Khazanov, G. K., & Ruscio, A. M. (2016). Is low positive emotionality a specific risk factor for depression?: A meta-analysis of longitudinal studies. *Psychological Bulletin, 142*(9), 991–1015.

Klein, M. H., Wonderlich, S., & Shea, M. T. (1993). Models of relationships between personality and depression: Toward framework of theory and research. In M. H. Klein, S. Wonderlich, & M. T. Shea (Eds.), *Personality and depression: A current view* (pp. 1–54). New York: Guilford Press.

Kotov, R., Gamez, W., Schmidt, F., & Watson, D. (2010). Linking "big" personality traits to anxiety, depressive, and substance use disorders: A meta-analysis. *Psychological Bulletin, 136,* 768–821.

Krueger, R. F., Caspi, A., Moffitt, T. E., Silva, P. A., & McGee, R. (1996). Personality traits are differentially linked to mental disorders: A multitrait–multidiagnosis study of an adolescent birth cohort. *Journal of Abnormal Psychology, 105,* 299–312.

Krueger, R. F., Hicks, B. M., Patrick, C. J., Carlson, S. R., McGue, M., & Iacono, W. G. (2002). Etiological relationships among substance dependence, antisocial behavior, and personality: Modeling the externalizing spectrum. *Journal of Abnormal Psychology, 111,* 411–424.

Krueger, R. F., & Markon, K. E. (2006). Reinterpreting comorbidity: A model-based approach to understanding and classifying psychopathology. *Annual Review of Clinical Psychology, 2,* 111–133.

Krueger, R. F., Markon, K. E., Patrick, C. J., Benning, S. D., & Kramer, M. D. (2007). Linking antisocial behavior, substance use, and personality: An integrative quantitative model of the adult externalizing spectrum. *Journal of Abnormal Psychology, 116,* 645–666.

Lehrer, J. A., Shrier, L. A., Gortmaker, S., & Buka, S. (2006). Depressive symptoms as a longitudinal predictor of sexual risk behaviors among US middle and high school students. *Pediatrics, 118*(1), 189–200.

Lynn, R., & Martin, T. (1997). Gender differences in extraversion, neuroticism, and psychoticism in 37 nations. *Journal of Social Psychology, 137*(3), 369–373.

Maes, H. H., Neale, M. C., Kendler, K. S., Hewitt, J. K., Silberg, J. L., Foley, D. L., et al. (1998). Assortative mating for major psychiatric diagnoses in two population-based samples. *Psychological Medicine, 28*(6), 1389–1401.

Masten, A. S., Burt, K. B., Roisman, G. I., Obradovic, J., Long, J. D., & Tellegen, A. (2004). Resources and resilience in the transition to adulthood: Continuity and change. *Development and Psychopathology, 16,* 1071–1094.

Masten, A. S., Coatsworth, J. D., Neemann, J., Gest, S. D., Tellegen, A., & Garmezy, N. (1995). The structure and coherence of competence from childhood through adolescence. *Child Development, 66,* 1635–1659.

Mathews, C. A., & Reus, V. I. (2001). Assortative mating in the affective disorders: A systematic review and meta-analysis. *Comprehensive Psychiatry, 42*(4), 257–262.

Mayer-Gross, W., Slater, E., & Roth, M. (1969). *Clinical psychiatry.* Baltimore: Williams & Wilkins.

McAdams, D. P. (1985). *Power, intimacy, and the life story: Personological inquiries into identity.* New York: Guilford Press.

McAdams, D. P., & Olson, B. D. (2010). Personality development: Continuity and change over the life course. *Annual Review of Psychology, 61,* 517–542.

McAdams, D. P., & Pals, J. L. (2006). A new Big Five: Fundamental principles for an integrative science of psychology. *American Psychologist, 61*(3), 204–217.

McCrae, R. R., & Costa, P. T., Jr. (1999). A five-factor theory of personality. In L. A. Pervin & O. P. John (Eds.), *Handbook of personality: Theory and research* (pp. 139–153). New York: Guilford Press.

McLean, C. P., Asnaani, A., Litz, B. T., & Hofmann, S. G. (2011). Gender differences in anxiety disorders: Prevalence, course of illness, comorbidity and burden of illness. *Journal of Psychiatric Research, 45*(8), 1027–1035.

Mineka, S., Watson, D. W., & Clark, L. A. (1998). Psychopathology: Comorbidity of anxiety and unipolar mood disorders. *Annual Review of Psychology, 49,* 377–412.

Molenaar, P. C. M. (2004). A manifesto on psychology as idiographic science: Bringing the person back into scientific psychology, this time forever. *Measurement: Interdisciplinary Research and Perspectives, 2,* 201–218.

Moore, M. T., & Fresco, D. M. (2012). Depressive realism: A meta-analytic review. *Clinical Psychology Review, 32*(6), 496–509.

Olino, T. M., Durbin, C. E., Klein, D. N., Hayden, E. P., & Dyson, M. W. (2013). Gender differences in young children's temperament traits: Comparisons across observational and parent-report methods. *Journal of Personality, 81*(2), 119–129.

Ormel, J., Oldehinkel, A. J., & Vollebergh, W. (2004). Vulnerability before, during, and after a major depressive episode: A 3-wave population-based study. *Archives of General Psychiatry, 61,* 990–996.

Quilty, L. C., De Fruyt, F., Rolland, J.-P., Kennedy, S. H., Rouillon, P. F., & Bagby, R. M. (2008). Dimensional personality traits and treatment outcome in patients with major depressive disorder. *Journal of Affective Disorders, 108,* 241–250.

Roberts, B. W., & Caspi, A. (2003). The cumulative continuity principle of personality development: Striking a balance between continuity and change in personality traits across the lifecourse. In R. M. Staudinger & U. Lindenberger (Eds.), *Understanding human development: Lifespan psychology in exchange with other disciplines* (pp. 183–214). Dordrecht, The Netherlands: Kluwer Academic.

Roberts, B. W., Caspi, A., & Moffitt, T. (2001). The kids are alright: Growth and stability in personality development from adolescence to adulthood. *Journal of Personality and Social Psychology, 81,* 670–683.

Roberts, B. W., & DelVecchio, W. F. (2000). The rank-order consistency of personality traits from childhood to old age: A quantitative review of longitudinal studies. *Psychological Bulletin, 126,* 3–25.

Roberts, B. W., Wood, D., & Caspi, A. (2008). The development of personality traits in adulthood. In O. P. John, R. W. Robins, & L. A. Pervin (Eds.), *Handbook of personality: Theory and research* (3rd ed., pp. 375–398). New York: Guilford Press.

Roisman, G. I., Masten, A. S., Coatsworth, J. D., & Tellegen, A. (2004). Salient and emerging developmental tasks in the transition to adulthood. *Child Development, 75,* 123–133.

Rothbart, M., & Rueda, M. R. (2005). The development of effortful control. In U. Mayr, E. Awh, & S. W. Steele (Eds.), *Developing individuality in the human brain: A tribute to Michael I. Posner* (pp. 167–188). Washington, DC: American Psychological Association.

Simons, R. G., Burgeson, R., & Carlton-Ford, S. (1987). The impact of cumulative change in early adolescence. *Child Development, 58,* 1220–1234.

Sperber, A. M., & Lax, E. (1997). *Bogart.* New York: Morrow.

Styron, W. (1990). *Darkness visible: A memoir of madness.* New York: Random House.

Tang, T. Z., DeRubeis, R. J., Hollon, S. D., Amsterdam, J., Shelton, R., & Schalet, B. (2009). Personality change during depression treatment. *Archives of General Psychiatry, 66,* 1322–1330.

Tellegen, A. (1985). Structures of mood and personality and their relevance to assessing anxiety, with an emphasis on self-report. In A. H. Tuma & J. D. Maser (Eds.), *Anxiety and the anxiety disorders* (pp. 681–706). Hillsdale, NJ: Erlbaum.

Van Os, J., & Jones, P. B. (1999). Early risk factors and adult person–environment relationships in affective disorder. *Psychological Medicine, 29,* 1055–1067.

Watson, D., & Clark, L. A. (1995). Depression and the melancholic temperament. *European Journal of Personality, 9,* 351–366.

Whisman, M. A. (2001). The association between depression and marital dissatisfaction. In S. R. H. Beach (Ed.), *Marital and family processes in depression: A scientific foundation for clinical practice* (pp. 3–24). Washington, DC: American Psychological Association.

Zeiss, A. M., & Lewinsohn, P. M. (1988). Enduring deficits after remissions of depression: A test of the scar hypothesis. *Behaviour Research and Therapy, 26,* 151–158.

Zisook, S., Lesser, I., Stewart, J. W., Wisniewski, S. R., Balasubramani, G. K., Fava, M., et al. (2007). Effect of age at onset on the course of major depressive disorder. *American Journal of Psychiatry, 164,* 1539–1546.

CHAPTER 31

Personality Development and Externalizing Psychopathology

Michelle M. Martel
Tess E. Smith
Christine A. Lee

John's mother is concerned about him. Over the last 2 years, he has been truant from school multiple times, was caught vandalizing property twice, and has been in three physical fights with boys at school. Furthermore, at home, he always seems angry and oppositional; he has been arguing, talking back, and lying even over minor issues. He is a 13-year-old in seventh grade; John's mother knows that his behavior is normal in some ways, but she is worried about him, particularly given the fact that his school recently suspended him for his third physical fight. John's mother is also worried about the group of teenagers with which John has been hanging out; she thinks they might be drinking and doing drugs. She shares all of this with a therapist at their initial clinical intake appointment.

When the therapist asks John's mother about his history, she says that he was always a good kid, quiet and compliant, until his father left the family when he was 11 years old. John and his mother have had no contact with his father since that time. Since then, John has become sullen and withdrawn.

When the therapist meets with John alone toward the end of the appointment, John is sullen and silent. He shrugs when the therapist asks him questions. Finally, he tells the therapist that he has no idea what his mother is talking about and says he is just being a normal teenager. When

the therapist asks him if he can see any negative consequences of his behavior, John shrugs and says, "Not really."

The therapist now has quite a bit of behavioral, social, and developmental information about John, and can now use this information to classify John's current problem behaviors, formulate some hypotheses about what has led to them, identify underlying markers and mechanisms of these problems, and finally—and perhaps most importantly—determine how most effectively to intervene.

Externalizing Psychopathology

As a well-trained clinician, the therapist has been extensively trained in diagnostic classification, knowing that externalizing psychopathology is an overarching category or spectrum of psychopathology that includes disorders characterized by "acting-out" behaviors, such as aggression, noncompliance, and impulsivity. This grouping encompasses a variety of disorders, with frequently overlapping symptoms and high diagnostic comorbidity, or co-occurrence, including two more narrow categories of disorders in DSM-5: (1) disruptive, impulse-control, and conduct disorders and (2) substance-related and addictive disorders (Achenbach & Edelbrock, 1978; American Psychiatric Association, 2013; Krueger et al., 2002; Krueger, Markon, Patrick, Benning, & Kramer, 2007).

Disruptive, Impulse-Control, and Conduct Disorders

DSM-5 disruptive, impulse-control, and conduct disorders are conditions characterized by difficulty controlling emotions and behaviors that are disruptive to others or conflict with societal rules and expectations (American Psychiatric Association, 2013). They include oppositional defiant disorder (ODD), conduct disorder (CD), antisocial personality disorder (ASPD), intermittent explosive disorder, pyromania, kleptomania, and other specified and unspecified disruptive, impulse-control, and conduct disorders. ODD, CD, and ASPD are often considered the "core" of the externalizing spectrum of psychopathology and have been the focus of most existing research to date; therefore, they are our major focus in this chapter, although other, related disorders are also reviewed when relevant literature is available.

ODD is defined by symptoms of angry/irritable mood, argumentative/defiant behavior, and vindictiveness (American Psychiatric Association, 2013) that, based on recent research, are often grouped into emotional versus behavioral domains (Burke et al., 2014; Lavigne, Bryant, Hopkins, & Gouze, 2015). ODD often manifests early and can be identified as early as preschool (Egger & Angold, 2006). ODD is a relatively common disorder with an estimated lifetime prevalence between 2 and 16% for males and 2 and 9% for females (American Psychiatric Association, 2013; Nock, Kazdin, Hiripi, & Kessler, 2007).

CD, defined by more serious rule-breaking and aggressive behavior, is slightly less common, with prevalence rates estimated between 6 and 16% for males and between 2 and 9% for females (American Psychiatric Association, 2013; Nock, Kazdin, Hiripi, & Kessler, 2006). CD can further be distinguished into subtypes according to whether symptoms arise in childhood (i.e., prior to 10 years of age) or, more commonly, in adolescence (American Psychiatric Association, 2013; Moffitt, 1993). Age of onset is associated with different patterns of symptoms, with childhood-onset being associated with more aggressive behaviors, and adolescent-onset being associated with more delinquent, rule-breaking behaviors (Lahey, Goodman, et al.,

1999). Furthermore, CD includes a specifier of "limited prosocial emotions," which indicates lack of remorse or guilt, callousness (i.e., lack of empathy), lack of concern about performance, and shallow affect. These "limited prosocial emotions" are seen as a precursor to adult psychopathy (Frick & Nigg, 2012).

ASPD, long considered an adulthood disorder given that DSM-5 states problem behaviors must have been present since the age of 15 years, is defined as a pattern of disregard for and violation of the rights of others, including a failure to conform to social norms, deceitfulness, impulsivity, irritability, aggressiveness, disregard for safety, irresponsibility, and a lack of remorse (American Psychiatric Association, 2013). These symptoms are related to, but are broader than, psychopathy (Cleckley, 1976). This disorder has a prevalence rate of approximately 2–3% in community samples and is also much more common in males than in females (Moran, 1999).

Externalizing Disorders across the Lifespan

ODD, CD, and ASPD are prime examples of how externalizing disorders may manifest in different ways over time and across individuals, or—in other words—heterotypic continuity and discontinuity and intra- and interindividual heterogeneity. ODD symptoms often first appear in preschool and precede the development of CD, whereas CD develops in a subset of children with ODD during middle childhood through middle adolescence, and only some of these individuals go on to develop ASPD. Individuals with externalizing disorders in childhood are at greater risk of developing adult-onset externalizing disorders, and those with childhood-onset problems exhibit worse trajectories and outcomes (Moffitt, 1993). Furthermore, these problems are highly comorbid with substance-related and addictive disorders (Krueger et al., 2002, 2007).

Substance-Related and Addictive Disorders

Substance-related and addictive disorders also appear to form part of the externalizing spectrum based on high levels of comorbidity and advanced statistical and mathematical work (Krueger et al., 2002, 2007). These disorders are characterized by a problematic pattern of use, including increased tolerance necessitating higher doses to achieve desired effects, withdrawal symptoms, and a failure to fulfill major role obligations and problems stemming from use, all of which lead to clinically significant distress or impairment (American Psychiatric Association, 2013). Like the other externalizing disorders, substance use disorders are two to three times as common in males compared to females, and estimates of prevalence are at least 8% (Substance Abuse and Mental Health Services Administration, 2001). Models of substance-related and addictive disorders suggest that individuals can be at risk through deviance proneness and/or stress and negative affect routes (Sher, 1991; Sher, Grekin, & Williams, 2005).

Other Externalizing Disorders

There are several other disorders that, while not currently considered part of the externalizing spectrum, have been considered highly related to externalizing psychopathology due to high levels of comorbidity and/or overlapping symptoms. One prime example is attention-deficit/hyperactivity disorder (ADHD) which, although currently placed within the DSM-5 neurodevelopmental disorder category, has an approximately 50% comorbidity rate with ODD (Egger & Angold, 2006), likely largely due to its behavioral symptoms of hyperactivity-impulsivity (vs. inattention) (APA, 2013; Carragher et al., 2014; Witkiewitz et al., 2013). This disorder has a prevalence rate of 3 to 5% during childhood (Polanczyk, de Lima, Horta, Biederman, & Rohde, 2007). Another related disorder, currently categorized as a depressive disorder within DSM-5, is disruptive mood dysregulation disorder (DMDD), defined by irritable–angry mood and temper outbursts, with a prevalence rate of approximately 3% (American Psychiatric Association, 2013; Leibenluft, 2011). This disorder, like ADHD, highly co-occurs with ODD at a rate of approximately 25% (Brotman et al., 2006; Copeland, Angold, Costello, & Egger, 2013). Therefore, these disorders may merit consideration as part of the externalizing spectrum, particularly during childhood.

Looking back at the case study, John's argumentative and temperamental behavior with his mother seems in line with ODD. However, his more severe aggression (i.e., physical fights), property damage, and rule violations (i.e., truancy), may be better characterized as CD. Despite John's deviant behavior, there is

no indication that that he is displaying lack of remorse or lack of empathy, consistent with a "limited prosocial emotions" specifier. John is too young for a diagnosis of ASPD and though John's mother suspects substance use, there is not enough information to diagnose a substance use disorder. Last, neither John nor his mother appears to endorse hyperactivity/impulsivity, consistent with ADHD, or frequent temper outbursts, consistent with DMDD. So, at present, the best diagnosis for John would seem to be CD with an adolescent onset.

Traits and Externalizing Psychopathology

John's therapist routinely sees externalizing psychopathology in clinical practice characterized by high neuroticism, or negative affect; low conscientiousness, or effortful control; and high disagreeableness, with inhibition seemingly the key unifying factor cutting across disorders. This is exemplified in John's case. Yet somewhat more distinct associations for particular problems are sometimes also apparent with high disagreeableness related to callous–unemotional traits, severe CD, ASPD, and psychopathy.

In conducting a literature search, the therapist realizes that temperament and personality traits are increasingly gaining attention as possible mechanisms explaining externalizing spectrum comorbidity. Traits exhibit well-replicated associations with externalizing psychopathology that map onto comorbidity patterns within and across the externalizing and internalizing domains of psychopathology (e.g., Krueger & Tackett, 2003; Markon, Krueger, & Watson, 2005; Nigg, 2006; Tackett, 2006). Although historically, temperament and personality traits were examined separately, with temperament being used to describe traits in younger children and personality being used to describe traits in adolescents and adults, these two kinds of traits are increasingly viewed as overlapping with neuroticism related to negative affect or emotionality, extraversion related to surgency or approach, and conscientiousness related to effortful control (Shiner, 1998). In line with this idea, similar patterns of associations have been found across both types of traits in relation to externalizing problems in general; that is, preschoolers with externalizing problems exhibit higher negative affect, higher surgency, or approach, and lower effortful control (Martel, Gremillion, & Roberts, 2012). Similarly, children with externalizing problems display more neuroticism, or negative emotionality; higher extraversion; less conscientiousness, or effortful control; and lower agreeableness than their non-externalizing peers (Huey & Weisz, 1997; Martel & Nigg, 2006). Likewise, adolescents and college students with externalizing problems are characterized by high neuroticism (particularly anger/frustration), low agreeableness, and low conscientiousness (DeYoung, Peterson, Séguin, & Tremblay, 2008; Huey & Weisz, 1997; Lynam et al., 2005). Furthermore, negative affect and effortful control appear to interact to predict externalizing problems (Eisenberg et al., 2009; Martel & Nigg, 2006; Muris, Meesters, & Blijlevens, 2007). Overall, high neuroticism, high extraversion, low conscientiousness, and low agreeableness appear to characterize individuals with externalizing problems across all ages, with interactive associations between negative affect and effortful control.

Traits and ODD

Present theory has suggested that ODD may primarily be a disorder of negative affect, or irritability (Burke et al., 2014; Stringaris & Goodman, 2009; Stringaris, Maughan, & Goodman, 2010). In line with this idea, prior empirical research indicates that children with disruptive behavior problems exhibit higher negative affect and related traits, such as irritability, compared to children without disruptive behavior problems (Dougherty et al., 2011; Ezpeleta, Granero, de la Osa, Penelo, & Domènech, 2012; Lahey, Waldman, & McBurnett, 1999; Martel & Nigg, 2006). ODD also exhibits associations with low effortful control, disinhibition, and low agreeableness (Gjone & Stevenson, 1997b; Hirshfeld-Becker et al., 2007; Kim et al., 2010). Finally, Zastrow, Martel, and Widiger (2016) found more nuanced associations with traits at the level of ODD symptom domains. High negative affect was associated with all three ODD symptom domains, while low agreeableness was specifically associated with the angry/irritable ODD symptom domain, and high surgency was specifically associated with the argumentative/defiant and vindictive ODD symptom domains. Negative affect and surgency interacted with agreeableness to predict impairment: low agreeableness was associated with high impair-

ment, regardless of other trait levels, while high negative affect and high surgency predicted high impairment in the presence of high agreeableness. Therefore, similar to general externalizing problems, high negative affect, high surgency, low effortful control, and low agreeableness are associated with childhood ODD.

Traits and CD

Low conscientiousness appears to exhibit general and well-replicated associations with CD and delinquency (Anderson, Tapert, Moadab, Crowley, & Brown, 2007; John, Caspi, Robins, Moffitt, & Stouthamer-Loeber, 1994). Similarly, the related construct of behavioral disinhibition predicts delinquency and related externalizing problems in adolescence (Hirshfeld-Becker et al., 2007; Pitzer, Esser, Schmidt, & Laucht, 2009; White, Bates, & Buyske, 2001) and young adulthood (Caspi, Moffitt, Newman, & Silva, 1996). Lack of control and low constraint have been identified as specific predictors of early-onset persistent CD relative to adolescent onset (Moffitt, Caspi, Dickson, Silva, & Stanton, 1996; Taylor & Iacono, 2007).

Callous–unemotional traits refer to a lack of guilt, absence of empathy, and shallow or constricted emotions, and are a downward extension of adult psychopathy (Cleckley, 1976; Frick, 1995; Frick & White, 2008). Frick and Morris (2004) suggest that the presence of callous–unemotional traits may damage a child's interpersonal style and conscience development, thus leading to later proactive aggression (Frick, Ray, Thornton, & Kahn, 2014a, 2014b; Frick & Viding, 2009). Such traits are hypothesized to make it easier for one to engage in future conduct problems, such as law breaking or deceit. Accordingly, high callous–unemotional traits have been linked to conduct problems and higher rates of delinquency (Frick, Cornell, Barry, Bodin, & Dane, 2003; Frick, Stickle, Dandreaux, Farrell, & Kimonis, 2005; Stadler et al., 2011).

Overall, low effortful control and callous–unemotional traits exhibit primary associations with conduct problems. Furthermore, theory suggests that a small percentage of those with conduct problems exhibit high callous–unemotional traits, whereas the remaining subgroup experiences low effortful control and possibly high negative affect (Frick, 2012; Frick & Morris, 2004).

Traits and ASPD/Psychopathy

Little personality work on adult externalizing psychopathology has focused on ASPD, instead choosing to focus on psychopathy (Crego & Widiger, 2015). Yet psychopathy is present in only a subset of those with ASPD, in line with the idea that only a subset of children and adolescents with CD are characterized by callous–unemotional traits. Cluster B personality disorders, including ASPD, are characterized by impulsivity, aggressiveness, and novelty seeking (Fossati et al., 2007). Work on the adult externalizing spectrum, including ASPD, suggests that ASPD and other adult externalizing problems, such as substance use disorders, may share a core disinhibition component (Krueger et al., 2007).

Yet in regard to the more substantial work on psychopathy, Cleckley's list of traits that seem most characteristic of psychopaths include superficial charm, dishonesty, shallow affect, self-centeredness, interpersonal unresponsiveness, and no clear or strong life plan (reviewed by Crego & Widiger, 2016). Other important traits include boldness, low anxiousness, explorativeness, manipulative behavior, criminal behavior, lack of empathy, insincerity, and rebelliousness (Crego & Widiger, 2016). Consensus descriptions of psychopathy describe it as high interpersonal antagonism, pan-impulsivity, the absence of self-directed affect, angry hostility, and interpersonal assertiveness (Lynam & Widiger, 2007). Psychopathy has been theorized to consist of a triarchic conceptualization of disinhibition, or problems with impulsive control; boldness, or social dominance, emotional resiliency, and sensation seeking; and meanness, or aggressive resource seeking (Patrick, Fowles, & Krueger, 2009; Strickland, Drislane, Lucy, Krueger, & Patrick, 2013). A two-domain distinction is sometimes used, wherein boldness and meanness are lumped together in an interpersonal–affective dimension and disinhibition and other externalizing problems are considered an impulsive–antisocial dimension (Skodol et al., 2011).

Studies examining Big Five personality associations with psychopathy consistently identify low agreeableness and high (or low) conscientiousness as core characteristics (Crego & Widiger, 2015; Lilienfeld, Watts, Francis Smith, Berg, & Latzman, 2015; Lynam & Miller, 2015; Ross, Lutz, & Bailley, 2004). In addition, some facets of low neuroticism (low self-consciousness, vulnerability, anxiousness), high neuroticism (impulsivity), high extraversion (assertiveness, activity, and excitement seeking), and openness to action are associated with psychopathy (Crego & Widiger, 2016; Lilienfeld et al., 2015; Lynam & Miller, 2015). Therefore, disagreeableness, impulsivity, low anxiety, and high excitement-seeking traits seem to particularly characterize psychopathy.

Traits and Substance Use Disorders

Work on personality and substance use disorders finds similar associations as work on other externalizing disorders. Individuals with substance use disorders appear to be characterized by high neuroticism (or negative emotionality), low conscientiousness (or low constraint, or disinhibition), and high disagreeableness (Kotov, Gamez, Schmidt, & Watson, 2010; Littlefield & Sher, 2014; McGue, Slutske, Taylor, & Iacono, 1997). Disinhibition and sensation seeking in particular seem potently associated with substance use disorders (Sher, Bartholow, & Wood, 2000). Negative emotionality may be particularly related to alcohol use disorders, while disinhibition may be more specific to other drug use disorders (McGue, Slutske, & Iacono, 1999). Thus, overall, high neuroticism and low conscientiousness seem particularly associated with substance use disorders.

Traits and Other Externalizing Problems

Similar to other externalizing psychopathology, ADHD has been found to be primarily associated with low effortful control, as well as possibly high extraversion, or surgency, and high negative affect (reviewed by Martel, 2009). Specifically, inattentive symptoms are associated with low effortful control, and hyperactivity–impulsivity appears to be associated with high extraversion with high negative affect associated with both symptom domains (Martel & Nigg, 2006). DMDD is associated with high negative affect, particularly frustration (Leibenluft, 2011).

Consistent with this work, based on his mother's report, John appears to display both low agreeableness and low conscientiousness. John is argumentative and disrespectful with his mother and engages in physical altercations with peers, consistent with low agreeableness. John's school truancy and rule-breaking behaviors, such as vandalism, are suggestive of low conscientiousness. Further information is needed to learn about John's level of extraversion or impulsivity. For instance, John's risky behavior could be related to high impulsivity or sensation seeking. Overall, John's history is consistent with known trait–psychopathology associations.

Traits as Markers of Longitudinal Pathways to Externalizing Psychopathology

Highlighting the importance of understanding trait–psychopathology associations in clinical cases such as John's, high negative affect, disinhibition, and high surgency appear to predict externalizing psychopathology in general. High negative affect may be particularly predictive of ODD, while disinhibition may be more strongly predictive of CD, ASPD, and substance use disorders. Finally, low fear may be particularly predictive of more severe CD, ASPD, and substance use problems. Such information might be able to inform early assessment of externalizing problems so as to identify youth at risk for later severe problems early in development, when they might be more amenable to intervention or even prevention strategies. Furthermore, teasing apart whether such traits are markers of vulnerability or a core part of the externalizing spectrum requires etiology-informed designs, described next.

Theory of Traits as Markers of Longitudinal Pathways to General Externalizing Psychopathology

Research suggests traits may be part of the pathway to psychopathology, including the externalizing spectrum (Martel, 2009). However, the nature of associations between traits and psychopathology is still debated (Nigg, 2006; Tackett, 2006). To date, a number of different models of these associations have been proposed, with two particularly prominent: the vulnerability model and the spectrum model (De Bolle, Beyers, De Clercq, & De Fruyt, 2012; Van Leeuwen, Mervielde, De Clerq, & De Fruyt, 2007). The vulnerability model theorizes that traits might make individuals more vulnerable to psychopathology. In contrast, the spectrum model suggests that psychopathology and traits lie on the same continuum, with psychopathology being synonymous with extreme temperament-based traits (Nigg, 2006; Shiner

& Caspi, 2003; Tackett, 2006). Regardless of the particular model endorsed, the substantial work we reviewed earlier suggests that traits relate to psychopathology in a meaningful way, such that they can predict the onset of psychopathology in young children. This can be viewed as consistent with either vulnerability or spectrum models. In line with this idea, longitudinal research suggests that low levels of effortful control, or disinhibition, high negative affect, low reactive control, and impulsivity in early childhood predict later externalizing behaviors and disorders in general (reviewed by Eisenberg et al., 2005; Olson, Sameroff, Kerr, Lopez, & Wellman, 2005; Tackett, 2006; Valiente et al., 2003). Yet, more specific relations can also be seen, as described below.

Traits as Markers of Longitudinal Pathways to ODD

Longitudinal work examining trait relations with ODD suggests differential trait associations with ODD in terms of concurrent comorbidity and prediction of other disorders over time. Negative emotionality and activity, related to surgency, both predict later development of ODD (Stringaris et al., 2010). Furthermore, these traits show differential associations with comorbidity, with individuals with high emotionality at age 3 being more likely to exhibit comorbid ODD and internalizing problems 4 years later, and individuals with high activity levels being more prone to later comorbid ODD and ADHD (Stringaris et al., 2010). Therefore, high negative affect and high surgency both appear to predict ODD and differentially relate to the common comorbidities of internalizing problems and ADHD, respectively.

Traits as Markers of Longitudinal Pathways to CD

Longitudinal work examining trait pathways to CD suggests two distinct pathways. Low withdrawal, more specifically, low fear response, appears to predict later development of CD (reviewed by Nigg, 2006) through low guilt and empathy (Blair, 2001). The second pathway emphasizes high levels of negative affect and low reactive or effortful control (reviewed by Nigg, 2006) through high anger reactivity, irritability, and high sensation seeking, which lead to the development of behaviors and symptoms consistent with CD (Frick & Morris, 2004). Thus, it appears that children can arrive at CD through either low fear or high negative affect.

More information about John's history is needed to better understand how traits may have influenced John's current externalizing behavior. However, at present, his high negative affect, as shown through irritability and angry reactivity, suggests this might be the pathway characterizing his vulnerability to CD. It is useful to know that negative emotionality is a common trait marker of externalizing behaviors, including substance use disorders.

Traits as Markers of Longitudinal Pathways to ASPD

Longitudinal research examining trait pathways in relation to antisocial behaviors indicates that early impulsivity and negative affect predict later antisocial behavior (reviewed by Tackett, 2006). Impulsivity at age 3 and later is predictive of later antisocial behaviors (Caspi, 2000). This predictive pattern of impulsivity continues throughout middle childhood and adolescence (White et al., 2001). Additionally, high negative affect in childhood followed by low disinhibition during adolescence is predictive of antisocial behaviors continuing into later adulthood (Moffit et al., 1996). Therefore, high negative affect and disinhibition predict the development of ASPD.

Traits as Markers of Longitudinal Pathways to Substance Use Disorders

Longitudinal work further suggests similar trait pathways to substance abuse as ASPD. Overall, disinhibition and negative emotionality predict both adolescent and adult substance abuse (reviewed by Tackett, 2006). Specifically, research shows low self-control and high novelty seeking, as well as traits such as boldness, predict adolescent substance use (Hicks et al., 2014). Other studies have shown that early childhood traits, including urgency and conscientiousness, predict addictive behaviors in adolescence (Guller, Zapolski, & Smith, 2015).

Traits as Spectrum-Based Markers of Etiology for General Externalizing Psychopathology

To date, multiple studies of childhood and adolescence have found support for shared genetic influences on the traits of conscientiousness/constraint and/or negative emotionality with CD/ODD-related externalizing problems, consistent with a spectrum conceptualization of trait–psychopathology relations. For instance, Krueger and colleagues (2007) found support for a biometric model of concurrent substance dependence, antisocial behavior and disinhibitory personality traits, suggesting that this co-occurrence is largely due to a shared underlying genetic factor. Longitudinal twin studies found similar results of negative emotionality and externalizing behavior accounted for by shared genetic influences (Blonigen, Hicks, Krueger, Patrick, & Iacono, 2005; Gjone & Stevenson, 1997b; Schmitz et al., 1999; Singh & Waldman, 2010). In fact, Littlefield and Sher (2014) suggest that high neuroticism and disinhibition may almost completely explain associations between genetic factors and substance use disorders.

Other investigators have examined evidence for a spectrum association between callous–unemotional traits and antisocial behavior in children and adolescents. Results from a twin study of psychopathy revealed that the association between callous–unemotional traits and antisocial behavior in childhood was primarily due to shared genetic influence (Viding, Blair, Moffitt, & Plomin, 2005). A subsequent study suggests that the heritability of antisocial behavior is greater among children with callous–unemotional traits compared to those without callous–unemotional traits, and that this difference was even more pronounced after controlling for hyperactive symptoms (Viding, Jones, Frick, Moffitt, & Plomin, 2008). Overall, shared genetic influences may underlie the association between temperamental traits and externalizing problems, thus supporting the spectrum model.

Other endogenous factors may also support spectrum associations between traits and youth antisocial behavior. Research has demonstrated that certain psychophysiological functions (e.g., autonomic arousal) have been associated with the covariance of several temperamental–personality dimensions, such as negative emotionality and disinhibition, and disruptive behavior disorders (Beauchaine, 2001; Beauchaine, Katkin, Strassberg, & Snarr, 2001). In addition, reduced activity in the anterior cingulate cortex in response to negative affective pictures was predicted by novelty seeking in boys with CD versus healthy controls (Stadler et al., 2007). These results provide encouragement for future studies of the shared genetic, psychophysiological, and neurological factors underlying trait dimensions and CD/ODD that might provide support for a spectrum explanation.

Theory, in fact, suggests that negative emotionality and disinhibition are likely candidates for spectrum explanations of externalizing psychopathology. Therefore, these traits may do more than just increase vulnerability for externalizing psychopathology; they may—in extreme form—be synonymous with externalizing psychopathology. Therefore, vulnerability and spectrum theories of trait–psychopathology relations may not be mutually exclusive and may operate conjointly. Thus, negative emotionality and disinhibition in particular may merit inclusion in assessment batteries.

Traits and Treatment for Externalizing Psychopathology

Now that the therapist is aware of trait characteristics of externalizing psychopathology and their possible assessment applications, he or she wonders if they can be put to good use as treatment targets. The clinician knows that externalizing behavior in children is commonly treated with parent training and behavior modification programs (Eyberg, Nelson, & Boggs, 2008). These treatments typically focus on the reduction of overall symptoms or related impairment. However, based on work suggesting interindividual heterogeneity in markers and etiology of externalizing psychopathology, recent work has focused on whether treatment efficacy might be impacted by child trait profiles such as callous-unemotional traits. In addition, recent research has examined whether traits themselves might be useful treatment targets.

Callous–Unemotional Traits as a Moderator of Treatment Effects

Callous–unemotional traits have typically been seen as indicators of severe externalizing behaviors and as more resistant to treatment. For example, Frick and colleagues (2014a, 2014b) found that 18 out of 20 treatment studies showed that children and adolescents with high levels of callous–unemotional traits had worse treatment outcomes, including being less likely to participate in treatment, requiring more physical restraint, and being more likely to reoffend. These results remained significant after the researchers controlled for conduct problems and deficits in social skills and problem-solving behaviors. Moreover, Hawes and Dadds (2005, 2007) found that after parent training, those

with higher levels of callous–unemotional traits did not show improvement when parents used effective discipline techniques and time-out procedures, though there were no differences between how parents implemented treatment based on child callous–unemotional traits. Finally, Högström, Enebrink, and Ghaderi (2013) found that treatment outcomes were moderated by callous–unemotional traits, such that children with high callous–unemotional traits exhibited poorer treatment outcomes after parent management training.

Yet children with high callous–unemotional traits do show some improvement following treatment, indicating that those with high callous–unemotional traits are not completely resistant to treatment. A 10-week parent training intervention for parents of elementary-age boys found that some boys did show decreases in levels of callous–unemotional treatment throughout treatment (Hawes & Dadds, 2005). Additionally, a multisystemic approach that combined aspects of behavior training, cognitive-behavioral therapy, problem-solving behaviors, and crisis management found a moderate effect size for the reduction of callous–unemotional traits pre- and posttreatment in a sample of elementary-age children (Kolko et al., 2009). In this study, callous–unemotional traits did not predict poorer treatment outcome in a sample of elementary-age children (Kolko & Pardini, 2010). Last, a parent–child interaction therapy approach led to reductions in conduct problems for those with high callous–unemotional traits (Kimonis, Bagner, Linares, Blake, & Rodriguez, 2014). Overall, individuals with high callous–unemotional traits seem more resistant to treatment, particularly parental discipline techniques. Therefore, recent treatment recommendations suggest that those with callous–unemotional traits may respond better to parenting strategies that emphasize positive rewards for good behavior rather than negative consequences for misbehavior.

Traits as Targets of Interventions

Innovative treatment research has evaluated whether targeting particular personality traits might offer an efficacious and time-efficient way to treat externalizing psychopathology and, most particularly, substance use in adolescents and adults. In these studies, participants complete personality profiles (i.e., anxiety sensitivity, hopelessness, sensation seeking, impulsivity) and are matched to a brief intervention focused on that specific trait. Each unique intervention takes place over two sessions and provides psychoeducation about that trait and differential behavioral and cognitive coping skills specific to each trait (Conrod, Stewart, Comeau, & Maclean, 2006). Such individualized treatment has been found to reduce chances of marijuana, cocaine, and other drug use in youth over a 2-year period compared to a placebo condition (Conrod, Castellanos-Ryan, & Strang, 2010). Similar success for personality-targeted interventions was found for reducing the onset and severity of problematic and risky alcohol use in youth when compared to no treatment or treatment as usual (i.e., drug education in class; Conrod, Castellanos, & Mackie, 2008, 2011; Conrod et al., 2013), with these effects persisting over time. Moreover, these results replicated in an adult substance-using sample, with success apparent only when given the personality-matched intervention, but not when given a mismatched intervention (Conrod et al., 2000). Thus, the targeting of personality traits in brief substance use interventions appears to be efficacious and possibly time-efficient in adolescents. An important future direction is examining whether such an approach could be extended to other types of externalizing psychopathology. In particular, it would be useful to know whether negative affect could be targeted in John's treatment for CD.

Important Future Directions with Clinical Implications

Despite such work on trait characteristics of externalizing psychopathology, there remain many unanswered questions. For example, there is limited empirical evidence evaluating how those with externalizing behaviors and disorders may act as "motivated agents." This information could provide even more nuanced information about individual goals and treatment targets for individuals like John. Luckily, current general knowledge suggests several hypotheses.

Motivations, Goals, and Values

The role of the "motivated agent" (McAdams, 2013) has received little attention in theory of externalizing psychopathology. Perhaps the most studied areas in this domain are attachment and moral development. Meta-analysis in-

dicates that disorganized attachment increases risk for externalizing behavior in children with smaller effects for insecure avoidant and resistant attachment (Fearon, Bakermans-Kranenburg, van IJzendoorn, Lapsley, & Roisman, 2010). Work on moral development and values suggests that at least some children, adolescents, and adults with externalizing psychopathology do not develop empathy and moral values like others do, which increases their risk for disruptive and externalizing behavior problems (Frick, 2012; Kerr, Lopez, Olson, & Sameroff, 2004; Kochanska, Barry, Aksan, & Boldt, 2008; Miller & Eisenberg, 1988). Furthermore, there is some suggestion that adolescents who are less religious than their parents are at risk for externalizing problems (Kim-Spoon, Longo, & McCullough, 2012), and that low self-esteem is associated with aggression, antisocial behavior, and delinquency in adolescents and college students in the United States and New Zealand (Donnellan, Trzesniewski, Robins, Moffitt, & Caspi, 2005).

Also, general research about traits can be used to guide hypotheses of what potential goals and values those with externalizing behaviors may prioritize, and this information may prove useful as assessment and treatment targets. Based on the prior review, one might hypothesize that those with externalizing psychopathology will often be motivated by a desire for immediate rewards (i.e., delay discounting) and novel experiences (i.e., sensation seeking).

Delay Discounting

One particularly salient goal for those with externalizing psychopathology might be the desire for immediate rewards, as supported by delay discounting research. *Delay discounting* measures one's preference for a smaller, immediate reward versus a larger, delayed reward (Kirby, Petry, & Bickel, 1999). Previous research has indicated that higher rates of delay discounting, or the preference for smaller but immediate versus larger but delayed rewards, are significantly related to increased externalizing behaviors, including, but not limited to, substance use, aggression, and criminal behavior (Cherek & Lane, 1999; Cherek, Moeller, Dougherty, & Rhoades, 1997; Miller, Lynam, & Jones, 2008; Nagin & Pogarsky, 2004; Stein & Madden, 2013). More specifically, those who engage in substance use, such as cigarettes, alcohol, and opioids, reported higher rates of discounting (Bobova, Finn, Rickert, & Lucas, 2009; MacKillop et al., 2011; Ohmura, Takahasi, & Kitamura, 2005; Robles, Huang, Simpson, & McMillan, 2011; Stein & Madden, 2013), a relationship with an overall moderate effect size (MacKillop et al., 2011). Relatedly, adolescents who displayed higher rates of delay discounting committed more property crimes (Nagin & Pogarsky, 2004), and parolees who had a history of violent crime had higher rates of delay discounting than parolees without such a history (Cherek & Lane, 1999; Cherek et al., 1997; Nagin & Pogarsky, 2004). These findings suggest the robust relationship between higher rates of delay discounting and externalizing behaviors. Perhaps those who desire immediate hypothetical monetary rewards may similarly desire the immediate gratification obtained through substance use and violence. Therefore, many externalizing behaviors appear to be motivated by the goal of immediate gratification.

Delay discounting is also connected to a variety of externalizing psychopathologies. Individuals with both alcohol dependence and childhood CD had higher rates of discounting than those with either disorder alone, suggesting a possible additive effect of externalizing disorders (Bobova et al., 2009). Similarly, Petry (2002) found that those with comorbid substance use disorders and ASPD discounted more than substance users alone. Finally, adolescents and adults with ADHD displayed higher discounting rates than those without ADHD (Barkley, Edwards, Laneri, Fletcher, & Metevia, 2001; Jackson & MacKillop, 2016). The significant relationship between delay discounting and externalizing psychopathology affirms the saliency of reward immediacy as a relevant goal.

Sensation Seeking

A high desire for *sensation seeking,* or the search for novel experiences that may be risky or dangerous (Whiteside & Lynam, 2001), might also serve as motivation for those with externalizing psychopathology. Those with externalizing psychopathology may create goals or make decisions based on novelty or excitement. Unsurprisingly, sensation seeking has been found to be significantly related to externalizing behaviors such as risky drinking, alcoholism, antisocial behavior, and pathological gambling (Adams, Kaiser, Lynam, Charnigo, & Milich, 2012; Magid & Colder, 2007; Whiteside & Lynam, 2009; Whiteside, Lynam, Miller, &

Reynolds, 2005). Thus, sensation seeking may guide those with externalizing psychopathology to prioritize new and exciting experiences, despite any associated risk.

These possible motivations provide more insight into John's behavior. Perhaps John is acting out due to attachment difficulties related to the loss of his father. It is also possible that John is motivated by short-term rewards, such as the immediate gratification from exacting revenge through physical violence. Last, John could be seeking new and fun experiences. The risky behavior, such as vandalism, may be positively reinforcing and goal-consistent for John. The possible motivations provide future direction for assessment and treatment targets for John's upcoming treatment.

Making Meaning

There is also no previous research that directly examines how those with externalizing psychopathology create an autobiographical narrative or what common themes may emerge throughout such a narrative. However, research about children with ADHD and story comprehension suggests that children with ADHD, and perhaps other externalizing problems as well, may struggle overall in creating a cohesive narrative of their life story. In particular, previous work has indicated that when children with ADHD retell stories, they construct poorer quality stories compared to children without ADHD (Berthiaume, Lorch, & Milich, 2010; Flory et al., 2006; Freer, Hayden, Lorch, & Milich, 2011; Leonard, Lorch, Milich, & Hagans, 2009; Lorch, Milich, Flake, Ohlendorf, & Little, 2010). Children with ADHD do not recall as many important events of the narrative, do not have as coherent a narrative, and are less able to make important inferences about the narrative. When children retell the stories or create a story to match wordless picture books, they do not focus on the important events of the story, such as the goals of the characters, how the characters attempt to meet these goals, and the outcomes of these events (Flory et al., 2006; Freer et al., 2011; Lorch et al., 2010). Their narratives are less cohesive, meaning that their recall may omit the overall goal or outcome, story events may be in the wrong order, and/or transitions are lacking (Flake, Lorch, & Milich, 2007; Lorch et al., 2010). Therefore, if children with ADHD struggle with retelling or creating understandable narratives when listening to others' stories, they may struggle with creating a cohesive narrative for their own autobiographies. While this research is currently limited to children with ADHD, future work may examine how those with other externalizing behaviors or disorders create narratives and whether similar deficits apply.

Story comprehension deficits may have implications for John's self-report of his own life narrative. Beyond being sullen, John may have difficulty constructing a clear and structured narrative of his past history. He may struggle with identifying important events in his own life and making inferences about his and others' behavior. Therefore, even if John is cooperative during treatment, it may be difficult to comprehend John's life history based on his self-report. This would be important information to know for assessment and treatment of John.

Future Directions and Clinical Implications for Motivation and Meaning

A critically important future direction is to conduct research on motivation and meaning perspectives in externalizing psychopathology across the lifespan. An important first step for such work would be to ask children and adults with externalizing psychopathology about their motives (e.g., immediate reward, desire for novel experiences) for specific behaviors and their emerging life narratives as part of the assessment process. Such information would likely lead to a more nuanced understanding of the individual and more personalized treatment targets.

Conclusion

In summary, externalizing psychopathology is characterized by high neuroticism, or negative affect; low conscientiousness, or effortful control; and high disagreeableness, with disinhibition as a key unifying feature. Such associations, at present, seem best captured by vulnerability and spectrum models suggesting that traits at least increase risk for externalizing psychopathology. In line with this idea, treatment targeted or differentially applied to such traits appears to be efficacious and efficient. Yet a critically important future direction for work in this area is to evaluate motivation and meaning perspectives of personality to further advance understanding of externalizing psychopathology and to assessment and intervention for these problems.

Knowing the information detailed in this chapter, John's therapist decides that John is likely to meet criteria for CD. He likely developed these problems as a way to vent his negative emotions about his father's abandonment through acting-out behavior, rejection of authority, and sensation seeking. John does not seem to be thoughtful about the consequences of his actions. Therefore, the therapist characterizes him as high in negative affect, disagreeableness, and sensation seeking, as well as low in conscientiousness. Based on this information, the therapist decides that a successful therapeutic approach will likely need to incorporate work on identification of anger and sadness over his father's abandonment, teaching of emotion regulation strategies, problem solving and adaptive coping skills, and building healthy social support and peer relationships.

The therapist remains curious about the motivation and meaning of John's behaviors and traits. The therapist suspects that John's acting-out behaviors are based on his motivation to distract himself from negative feelings and thoughts about his father, getting back at or rejecting his father, and having low self-esteem because of his father's abandonment. John might shrug and indicate that he has no life narrative at present, that he is "winging it." Such information would suggest useful targets for treatment, such as alternative coping skills, processing of thoughts and feelings about his father, and planning and problem solving for the future. In addition, generation of a life narrative might be important for giving John adaptive and positive goals to work toward in the future. The clinician looks forward to having a better research base upon which to evaluate such ideas.

ACKNOWLEDGMENT

We would like to thank Joshua Wilt, PhD, for helpful comments on a draft of this chapter.

REFERENCES

Achenbach, T. M., & Edelbrock, C. S. (1978). The classification of child psychopathology: A review and analysis of empirical efforts. *Psychological Bulletin, 85*(6), 1275–1301.

Adams, Z. W., Kaiser, A. J., Lynam, D. R., Charnigo, R. J., & Milich, R. (2012). Drinking motives as mediators of the impulsivity–substance use relation: Pathways for negative urgency, lack of premeditation, and sensation seeking. *Addictive Behaviors, 37,* 848–855.

American Psychiatric Association. (2013). *Diagnostic and statistical manual of mental disorders* (5th ed.). Arlington, VA: Author.

Anderson, K. G., Tapert, S., Moadab, I., Crowley, T. J., & Brown, S. A. (2007). Personality risk profile for conduct disorder and substance use disorders in youth. *Addictive Behaviors, 32,* 2377–2382.

Barkley, R. A., Edwards, G., Laneri, M., Fletcher, K., & Metevia, L. (2001). Executive functioning, temporal discounting and sense of time in adolescents with attention deficit hyperactivity disorder (ADHD) and oppositional defiant disorder (ODD). *Journal of Abnormal Child Psychology, 29,* 541–556.

Beauchaine, T. (2001). Vagal tone, development, and Gray's motivational theory: Toward an integrated model of autonomic nervous system functioning in psychopathology. *Development and Psychopathology, 13,* 183–214.

Beauchaine, T. P., Katkin, E. S., Strassberg, Z., & Snarr, J. (2001). Disinhibitory psychopathology in male adolescents: Discriminating conduct disorder from attention-deficit/hyperactivity disorder through concurrent assessment of multiple autonomic states. *Journal of Abnormal Psychology, 110,* 610–624.

Berthiaume, K. S., Lorch, E. P., & Milich, R. (2010). Getting clued in: Inferential processing and comprehension monitoring in boys with ADHD. *Journal of Attention Disorders, 13,* 31–42.

Blair, R. J. R. (2001). Neurocognitive models of aggression, the antisocial personality disorders, and psychopathy. *Journal of Neurology, Neurosurgery, and Psychiatry, 71,* 727–731.

Blonigen, D. M., Hicks, B. M., Krueger, R. F., Patrick, C. J., & Iacono, W. G. (2005). Psychopathic personality traits: Heritability and genetic overlap with internalizing and externalizing psychopathology. *Psychological Medicine, 35,* 637–648.

Bobova, L., Finn, P. R., Rickert, M. E., & Lucas, J. (2009). Disinhibitory psychopathology and delay discounting in alcohol dependence: Personality and cognitive correlates. *Experimental and Clinical Psychopharmacology, 17,* 51–61.

Brotman, M. A., Schmajuk, M., Rich, B. A., Dickstein, D. P., Guyer, A. E., Costello, E. J., et al. (2006). Prevalence, clinical correlates, and longitudinal course of severe mood dysregulation in children. *Biological Psychiatry, 60,* 991–997.

Burke, J. D., Boylan, K., Rowe, R., Duku, E., Stepp, S. D., Hipwell, A. E., et al. (2014). Identifying the irritability dimension of ODD: Application of a modified bifactor model across five large community samples of children. *Journal of Abnormal Psychology, 123,* 841–851.

Carragher, N., Krueger, R. F., Eaton, N. R., Markon, K. E., Keyes, K. M., Blanco, C., et al. (2014). ADHD and the externalizing spectrum: Direct comparison of categorical, continuous, and hybrid models of liability in a nationally representative sample. *Social Psychiatry and Psychiatric Epidemiology, 49,* 1307–1317.

Caspi, A. (2000). The child is father of the man: Personality continuities from childhood to adulthood. *Journal of Personality and Social Psychology, 78,* 158–172.

Caspi, A., Moffitt, T. E., Newman, D. L., & Silva, P. A. (1996). Behavioral observations at age 3 years predict adult psychiatric disorders: Longitudinal evidence from a birth cohort. *Archives of General Psychiatry, 53,* 1033–1039.

Cherek, D. R., & Lane, S. D. (1999). Laboratory and psychometric measurements of impulsivity among violent and nonviolent female parolees. *Biological Psychiatry, 46,* 273–280.

Cherek, D. R., Moeller, G., Dougherty, D. M., & Rhoades, H. (1997). Studies of violent and nonviolent male parolees: II. Laboratory and psychometric measurements of impulsivity. *Biological Psychiatry, 41,* 523–529.

Cleckley, H. (1976). *The mask of sanity* (5th ed.). St. Louis, MO: Mosby.

Conrod, P. J., Castellanos, N., & Mackie, C. (2008). Personality-targeted interventions delay the growth of adolescent drinking and binge drinking. *Journal of Child Psychology and Psychiatry, 49,* 181–190.

Conrod, P. J., Castellanos-Ryan, N., & Mackie, C. (2011). Long-term effects of a personality-targeted intervention to reduce alcohol use in adolescents. *Journal of Consulting and Clinical Psychology, 79,* 296–306.

Conrod, P. J., Castellanos-Ryan, N., & Strang, J. (2010). Brief, personality-targeted coping skills interventions and survival as a non-drug user over a 2-year period during adolescence. *JAMA Psychiatry, 67,* 85–93.

Conrod, P. J., O'Leary-Barrett, M., Newton, N., Topper, L., Castellanos-Ryan, N., Mackie, C., et al. (2013). Effectiveness of a selective, personality-targeted prevention program for adolescent alcohol use and misuse: A cluster randomized controlled trial. *JAMA Psychiatry, 70,* 334–342.

Conrod, P. J., Stewart, S. H., Comeau, N., & Maclean, A. M. (2006). Efficacy of cognitive-behavioral interventions targeting personality risk factors for youth alcohol misuse. *Journal of Clinical Child and Adolescent Psychology, 35,* 550–563.

Conrod, P. J., Stewart, S. H., Pihl, R. O., Côté, S., Fontaine, V., & Dongier, M. (2000). Efficacy of a brief coping skills interventions that match personality profiles of female substance abusers. *Psychology of Addictive Behaviors, 14,* 231–242.

Copeland, W. E., Angold, A., Costello, E. J., & Egger, H. (2013). Prevalence, comorbidity, and correlates of DSM-5 proposed disruptive mood dysregulation disorder. *American Journal of Psychiatry, 170,* 173–179.

Crego, C., & Widiger, T. A. (2015). Psychopathy and the DSM. *Journal of Personality, 83,* 665–677.

Crego, C., & Widiger, T. A. (2016). Cleckley's psychopaths: Revisited. *Journal of Abnormal Psychology, 125,* 75–87.

De Bolle, M., Beyers, W., De Clercq, B., & De Fruyt, F. (2012). General personality and psychopathology in referred and nonreferred children and adolescents: An investigation of continuity, pathoplasty, and complication models. *Journal of Abnormal Psychology, 121,* 958–970.

DeYoung, C. G., Peterson, J. B., Séguin, J. R., & Tremblay, R. E. (2008). Externalizing behavior and the higher order factors of the Big Five. *Journal of Abnormal Psychology, 117,* 947–953.

Donnellan, M. B., Trzesniewski, K. H., Robins, R. W., Moffitt, T. E., & Caspi, A. (2005). Low self-esteem is related to aggression, antisocial behavior, and delinquency. *Psychological Science, 16*(4), 328–335.

Dougherty, L. R., Bufferd, S. J., Carlson, G. A., Dyson, M., Olino, T. M., Durbin, C. E., et al. (2011). Preschoolers' observed temperament and psychiatric disorders assessed with a parent diagnostic interview. *Journal of Clinical Child and Adolescent Psychology, 40,* 295–306.

Egger, H. L., & Angold, A. (2006). Common emotional and behavioral disorders in preschool children: Presentation, nosology, and epidemiology. *Journal of Child Psychology and Psychiatry, 47,* 313–337.

Eisenberg, N., Sadovsky, A., Spinrad, T., Fabes, R. A., Losoya, S., Valiente, C., et al. (2005). The relations of problem behavior status to children's negative emotionality, effortful control, and impulsivity: Concurrent relations and prediction of change. *Developmental Psychology, 41,* 193–211.

Eisenberg, N., Valiente, C., Spinrad, T. L., Cumberland, A., Liew, J., & Reiser, M. (2009). Longitudinal relations of children's effortful control, impulsivity, and negative emotionality to their externalizing, internalizing, and co-occurring behavior problems. *Developmental Psychology, 45,* 988–1008.

Eyberg, S. M., Nelson, M. M., & Boggs, S. R. (2008). Evidence-based psychosocial treatments for children and adolescents with disruptive behavior. *Journal of Clinical Child and Adolescent Psychology, 37,* 215–237.

Ezpeleta, L., Granero, R., de la Osa, N., Penelo, E., & Domènech, J. M. (2012). Dimensions of oppositional defiant disorder in 3-year-old-preschoolers. *Journal of Child Psychology and Psychiatry, 53,* 1128–1138.

Fearon, R. M. P., Bakermans-Kranenburg, M. J., van IJzendoorn, M. H., Lapsley, A. M., & Roisman, G. I. (2010). The significance of insecure attachment and disorganization in the development of children's externalizing behavior: A meta-analytic study. *Child Development, 81*(2), 435–456.

Flake, R. A., Lorch, E. P., & Milich, R. (2007). The effects of thematic importance on story recall among children with attention deficit hyperactivity disorder and comparison children. *Journal of Abnormal Child Psychology, 35,* 43–53.

Flory, K., Milich, R., Lorch, E. P., Hayden, A. N.,

Strange, C., & Welsh, R. (2006). Online story comprehension among children with ADHD: Which core deficits are involved? *Journal of Abnormal Child Psychology, 34,* 853–865.

Fossati, A., Barratt, E. S., Borroni, S., Villa, D., Grazioli, F., & Maffei, C. (2007). Impulsivity, aggressiveness, and DSM-IV personality disorders. *Psychiatry Research, 149,* 157–167.

Freer, B. D., Hayden, A., Lorch, E. P., & Milich, R. (2011). The stories they tell: Story production difficulties of children with ADHD. *School Psychology Review, 40,* 352–366.

Frick, P. J. (1995). Callous–unemotional traits and conduct problems: A two-factor model of psychopathy in children. *Issues in Criminological and Legal Psychology, 24,* 47–51.

Frick, P. J. (2012). Developmental pathways to conduct disorder: Implications for future directions in research, assessment, and treatment. *Journal of Clinical Child and Adolescent Psychology, 41,* 378–389.

Frick, P. J., Cornell, A. H., Barry, C. T., Bodin, S. D., & Dane, H. E. (2003). Callous–unemotional traits and conduct problems in the prediction of conduct problem severity, aggression, and self-report of delinquency. *Journal of Abnormal Child Psychology, 31,* 457–470.

Frick, P. J., & Morris, A. S. (2004). Temperament and developmental pathways to conduct problems. *Journal of Clinical Child and Adolescent Psychology, 33,* 54–68.

Frick, P. J., & Nigg, J. T. (2012). Current issues in the diagnosis of attention deficit hyperactivity disorder, oppositional defiant disorder, and conduct disorder. *Annual Review of Clinical Psychology, 8,* 77–107.

Frick, P. J., Ray, J. V., Thornton, L. C., & Kahn, R. E. (2014a). Annual research review: A developmental psychopathology approach to understanding callous–unemotional traits in children and adolescents with serious conduct problems. *Journal of Child Psychology and Psychiatry, 55,* 532–548.

Frick, P. J., Ray, J. V., Thornton, L. C., & Kahn, R. E. (2014b). Can callous–unemotional traits enhance the understanding, diagnosis, and treatment of serious conduct problems in children and adolescents?: A comprehensive review. *Psychological Bulletin, 140,* 1–57.

Frick, P. J., Stickle, T. R., Dandreaux, D. M., Farrell, J. M., & Kimonis, E. R. (2005). Callous–unemotional traits in predicting the severity and stability of conduct problems and delinquency. *Journal of Abnormal Child Psychology, 33,* 471–487.

Frick, P. J., & Viding, E. (2009). Antisocial behavior from a developmental psychopathology perspective. *Development and Psychopathology, 21,* 1111–1131.

Frick, P. J., & White, S. F. (2008). The importance of callous–unemotional traits for the development of aggressive and antisocial behavior. *Journal of Child Psychology and Psychiatry, 49,* 359–375.

Gjone, H., & Stevenson, J. (1997a). The association between internalizing and externalizing behavior in childhood and early adolescence: Genetic or environmental common influences? *Journal of Abnormal Child Psychology, 25,* 277–286.

Gjone, H., & Stevenson, J. (1997b). A longitudinal twin study of temperament and behavior problems: Common genetic or environmental influences? *Journal of the American Academy of Child and Adolescent Psychiatry, 36,* 1448–1456.

Guller, L., Zapolski, T. B., & Smith, G. T. (2015). Personality measured in elementary school predicts middle school addictive behavior involvement. *Journal of Psychopathology and Behavioral Assessment, 37,* 523–532.

Hawes, D. J., & Dadds, M. R. (2005). The treatment of conduct problems in children with callous–unemotional traits. *Journal of Consulting and Clinical Psychology, 73,* 737–741.

Hawes, D. J., & Dadds, M. R. (2007). Stability and malleability of callous–unemotional traits during treatment for childhood conduct problems. *Journal of Clinical Child and Adolescent Psychology, 36,* 347–355.

Hicks, B. M., Johnson, W., Durbin, C. E., Blonigen, D. M., Iacono, W. G., & McGue, M. (2014). Delineating selection and mediation effects among childhood personality and environmental risk factors in the development of adolescent substance abuse. *Journal of Abnormal Child Psychology, 42,* 845–859.

Hirshfeld-Becker, D. R., Biederman, J., Henin, A., Faraone, S. V., Micco, J. A., van Grondelle, A., et al. (2007). Clinical outcomes of laboratory-observed preschool behavioral disinhibition at five-year follow-up. *Biological Psychiatry, 62,* 565–572.

Högström, J., Enebrink, P., & Ghaderi, A. (2013). The moderating role of child callous–unemotional traits in an Internet-based parent-management training program. *Journal of Family Psychology, 27,* 314–323.

Huey, S. J., Jr., & Weisz, J. R. (1997). Ego control, ego resiliency, and the five-factor model as predictors of behavioral and emotional problems in clinic-referred children and adolescents. *Journal of Abnormal Psychology, 106,* 404–415.

Jackson, J. N. S., & MacKillop, J. (2016). Attention-deficit/hyperactivity disorder and monetary delay discounting: A meta-analysis of case-control studies. *Biological Psychiatry: Cognitive Neuroscience and Neuroimaging, 1,* 316–325.

John, O. P., Caspi, A., Robins, R. W., Moffitt, T. E., & Stouthamer-Loeber, M. (1994). The "little five": Exploring the nomological network of the five-factor model of personality in adolescent boys. *Child Development, 65,* 160–178.

Kerr, D. C., Lopez, N. L., Olson, S. L., & Sameroff, A. J. (2004). Parental discipline and externalizing behavior problems in early childhood: The roles of moral regulation and child gender. *Journal of Abnormal Child Psychology, 32*(4), 369–383.

Kim, H. W., Cho, S. C., Kim, B. N., Kim, J. W., Shin, M. S., & Yeo, J. Y. (2010). Does oppositional defiant disorder have temperament and psychopathological

profiles independent of attention deficit/hyperactivity disorder? *Comprehensive Psychiatry, 51,* 412–418.

Kim-Spoon, J., Longo, G. S., & McCullough, M. E. (2012). Adolescents who are less religious than their parents are at risk for externalizing and internalizing symptoms: The mediating role of parent–adolescent relationship quality. *Journal of Family Psychology, 26*(4), 636–641.

Kimonis, E. R., Bagner, D. M., Linares, D., Blake, C. A., & Rodriguez, G. (2014). Parent training outcomes among young children with callous–unemotional conduct problems with or at-risk for developmental delay. *Journal of Child and Family Studies, 23,* 437–448.

Kirby, K. N., Petry, N. M., & Bickel, W. K. (1999). Heroin addicts have higher discount rates for delayed rewards than non-drug-using controls. *Journal of Experimental Psychology: General, 128,* 78–87.

Kochanska, G., Barry, R. A., Aksan, N., & Boldt, L. J. (2008). A developmental model of maternal and child contributions to disruptive conduct: The first six years. *Journal of Child Psychology and Psychiatry, 49*(11), 1220–1227.

Kochanska, G., Barry, R. A., Jimenez, A. L., Hollatz, A. L., & Woodard, J. (2009). Guilt and effortful control: Two mechanisms that prevent disruptive developmental trajectories. *Journal of Personality and Social Psychology, 97,* 322–333.

Kolko, D. J., Dorn, L. D., Bukstein, O. G., Pardini, D., Holden, E. A., & Hart, J. (2009). Community vs. clinic-based modular treatment of children with early-onset ODD or CD: A clinical trial with 3-year follow-up. *Journal of Abnormal Child Psychology, 37,* 591–609.

Kolko, D. J., & Pardini, D. A. (2010). ODD dimensions, ADHD, and callous–unemotional traits as predictors of treatment response in children with disruptive behavior disorders. *Journal of Abnormal Psychology, 119,* 713–725.

Kotov, R., Gamez, W., Schmidt, F., & Watson, D. (2010). Linking "big" personality traits to anxiety, depressive, and substance use disorders: A meta-analysis. *Psychological Bulletin, 136,* 768–821.

Krueger, R. F., Hicks, B. M., Patrick, C. J., Carlson, S. R., Iacono, W. G., & McGue, M. (2002). Etiologic connections among substance dependence, antisocial behavior, and personality: Modeling the externalizing spectrum. *Journal of Abnormal Psychology, 111,* 411–424.

Krueger, R. F., Markon, K. E., Patrick, C. J., Benning, S. D., & Kramer, M. D. (2007). Linking antisocial behavior, substance use, and personality: An integrative quantitative model of the adult externalizing spectrum. *Journal of Abnormal Psychology, 116,* 645–666.

Krueger, R. F., & Tackett, J. L. (2003). Personality and psychopathology: Working towards the bigger picture. *Journal of Personality Disorders, 17,* 109–128.

Lahey, B. B., Goodman, S. H., Walkman, I. D., Bird, H., Canino, G., Jensen, P., et al. (1999). Relation of age of onset to the type and severity of child and adolescent conduct problems. *Journal of Abnormal Child Psychology, 27,* 247–260.

Lahey, B. B., Waldman, I. D., & McBurnett, K. (1999). Annotation: The development of antisocial behavior: An integrative causal model. *Journal of Child Psychology and Psychiatry, 40,* 669–682.

Lavigne, J. V., Bryant, F. B., Hopkins, J., & Gouze, K. R. (2015). Dimensions of oppositional defiant disorder in young children: Model comparisons, gender, and longitudinal invariance. *Journal of Abnormal Child Psychology, 43,* 423–439.

Leibenluft, E. (2011). Severe mood dysregulation, irritability, and the diagnostic boundaries of bipolar disorder in youths. *American Journal of Psychiatry, 168,* 129–142.

Leonard, M. A., Lorch, E. P., Milich, R., & Hagans, N. (2009). Parent–child joint picture-book reading among children with ADHD. *Journal of Attention Disorders, 12,* 361–371.

Lilienfeld, S. O., Watts, A. L., Francis Smith, S., Berg, J. M., & Latzman, R. D. (2015). Psychopathy deconstructed and reconstructed: Identifying and assembling the personality building blocks of Cleckley's chimera. *Journal of Personality, 83,* 593–610.

Littlefield, A. K., & Sher, K. J. (2014). Personality and substance use disorders. In K. J. Sher (Ed.), *The Oxford handbook of substance use and substance use disorders* (pp. 351–374). New York: Oxford University Press.

Lorch, E. P., Milich, R., Flake, R. A., Ohlendorf, J., & Little, S. (2010). A developmental examination of story recall and coherence among children with ADHD. *Journal of Abnormal Child Psychology, 38,* 291–301.

Lynam, D. R., Caspi, A., Moffitt, T. E., Raine, A., Loeber, R., & Stouthamer-Loeber, M. (2005). Adolescent psychopathy and the Big Five: Results from two samples. *Journal of Abnormal Child Psychology, 33,* 431–443.

Lynam, D. R., & Miller, J. D. (2015). Psychopathy from a basic trait perspective: The utility of a five-factor model approach. *Journal of Personality, 83,* 611–626.

Lynam, D. R., & Widiger, T. A. (2007). Using a general model of personality to identify the basic elements of psychopathy. *Journal of Personality Disorders, 21,* 160–178.

MacKillop, J., Amlung, M. T., Few, L. R., Ray, L. A., Sweet, L. H., & Munafò, M. R. (2011). Delayed reward discounting and addictive behavior: A meta-analysis. *Psychopharmacology, 216,* 305–321.

Magid, V., & Colder, C. R. (2007). The UPPS Impulsive Behavior Scale: Factor structure and associations with college drinking. *Personality and Individual Differences, 43,* 1927–1937.

Markon, K. E., Krueger, R. F., & Watson, D. (2005). Delineating the structure of normal and abnormal personality: An integrative hierarchical approach. *Journal of Personality and Social Psychology, 88,* 139–157.

Martel, M. M. (2009). Research review: A new perspective on attention-deficit hyperactivity disorder: Emotion dysregulation and trait models. *Journal of Child Psychology and Psychiatry, 50,* 1042–1051.

Martel, M. M., Gremillion, M. L., & Roberts, B. (2012). Temperament and common disruptive behavior problems in preschool. *Personality and Individual Differences, 53,* 874–879.

Martel, M. M., & Nigg, J. T. (2006). Child ADHD and personality/temperament traits of reactive and effortful control, resiliency, and emotionality. *Journal of Child Psychology and Psychiatry, 47,* 1175–1183.

McAdams, D. P. (2013). The psychological self as actor, agent, and author. *Perspectives on Psychological Science, 8,* 272–295.

McGue, M., Slutske, W., & Iacono, W. G. (1999). Personality and substance use disorders: II. Alcoholism versus drug use disorders. *Journal of Consulting and Clinical Psychology, 67,* 394–404.

McGue, M., Slutske, W., Taylor, J., & Iacono, W. G. (1997). Personality and substance use disorders: I. Effects of gender and alcoholism subtype. *Alcoholism: Clinical and Experimental Research, 21,* 513–520.

Miller, J. D., Lynam, D. R., & Jones, S. (2008). Externalizing behavior through the lens of the five-factor model: A focus on agreeableness and conscientiousness. *Journal of Personality Assessment, 90,* 158–164.

Miller, P. A., & Eisenberg, N. (1988). The relation of empathy to aggressive and externalizing/antisocial behavior. *Psychological Bulletin, 103*(3), 324–344.

Moffitt, T. E. (1993). Adolescence-limited and life-course-persistent antisocial behavior: A developmental taxonomy. *Psychological Review, 100,* 674–701.

Moffitt, T. E., Caspi, A., Dickson, N., Silva, P., & Stanton, W. (1996). Childhood-onset versus adolescent-onset antisocial conduct problems in males: Natural history from ages 3 to 18 years. *Development and Psychopathology, 8,* 399–424.

Moran, P. (1999). The epidemiology of antisocial personality disorder. *Social Psychiatry and Psychiatric Epidemiology, 34,* 231–242.

Muris, P., Meesters, C., & Blijlevens, P. (2007). Self-reported reactive and regulative temperament in early adolescence: Relations to internalizing and externalizing problem behavior and "Big Three" personality factors. *Journal of Adolescence, 30,* 1035–1049.

Nagin, D. S., & Pogarsky, G. (2004). Time and punishment: Delayed consequences and criminal behavior. *Journal of Quantitative Criminology, 20,* 295–317.

Nigg, J. T. (2006). Temperament and developmental psychopathology. *Journal of Child Psychology and Psychiatry, 47,* 395–422.

Nock, M. K., Kazdin, A. E., Hiripi, E., & Kessler, R. C. (2006). Prevalence, subtypes, and correlates of DSM-IV conduct disorder in the National Comorbidity Survey Replication. *Psychological Medicine, 36,* 699–710.

Nock, M. K., Kazdin, A. E., Hiripi, E., & Kessler, R. C. (2007). Lifetime prevalence, correlates, and persistence of oppositional defiant disorder: Results from the National Comorbidity Survey Replication. *Journal of Child Psychology and Psychiatry, 48,* 701–713.

Ohmura, Y., Takahasi, T., & Kitamura, N. (2005). Discounting delayed and probabilistic monetary gains and losses by smokers of cigarettes. *Psychopharmacology, 182,* 508–515.

Olson, S. L., Sameroff, A. J., Kerr, D. C., Lopez, N. L., & Wellman, H. M. (2005). Developmental foundations of externalizing problems in young children: The role of effortful control. *Development and Psychopathology, 17,* 25–45.

Patrick, C. J., Fowles, D. C., & Krueger, R. F. (2009). Triarchic conceptualization of psychopathy: Developmental origins of disinhibition, boldness, and meanness. *Development and Psychopathology, 21,* 913–938.

Petry, N. M. (2002). Discounting of delayed rewards in substance abusers: Relationship to antisocial personality disorder. *Psychopharmacology, 162,* 425–432.

Pitzer, M., Esser, G., Schmidt, M. H., & Laucht, M. (2009). Temperamental predictors of externalizing problems among boys and girls: A longitudinal study in a high-risk sample from ages 3 months to 15 years. *European Archives of Psychiatry and Clinical Neuroscience, 259,* 458–459.

Polanczyk, G., de Lima, M. S., Horta, B. L., Biederman, J., & Rohde, L. A. (2007). The worldwide prevalence of ADHD: A systematic review and metaregression analysis. *American Journal of Psychiatry, 164,* 942–948.

Robles, E., Huang, B. E., Simpson, P. M., & McMillan, D. E. (2011). Delay discounting, impulsiveness, and addiction severity in opiod-dependent patients. *Journal of Substance Abuse Treatment, 41,* 354–362.

Ross, S. R., Lutz, C. J., & Bailley, S. E. (2004). Psychopathy and the five factor model in a noninstitutionalized sample: A domain and facet level analysis. *Journal of Psychopathology and Behavioral Assessment, 26,* 213–223.

Schmitz, S., Fulker, D. W., Plomin, R., Zahn-Waxler, C., Emde, R. N., & DeFries, J. C. (1999). Temperament and problem behaviour during early childhood. *International Journal of Behavioral Development, 23,* 333–355.

Sher, K. J. (1991). *Children of alcoholics: A critical appraisal of theory and research.* Chicago: University of Chicago Press.

Sher, K. J., Bartholow, B. D., & Wood, M. D. (2000). Personality and substance use disorders: A prospective study. *Journal of Consulting and Clinical Psychology, 68,* 818–829.

Sher, K. J., Grekin, E. R., & Williams, N. A. (2005). The development of alcohol use disorders. *Annual Review of Clinical Psychology, 1,* 493–523.

Shiner, R. L. (1998). How shall we speak of children's personalities in middle childhood?: A preliminary taxonomy. *Psychological Bulletin, 124*(3), 308–332.

Shiner, R., & Caspi, A. (2003). Personality differences in childhood and adolescence: Measurement, development, and consequences. *Journal of Child Psychology and Psychiatry, 44,* 2–32.

Singh, A. L., & Waldman, I. D. (2010). The etiology of associations between negative emotionality and childhood externalizing disorders. *Journal of Abnormal Psychology, 119,* 376–388.

Skodol, A. E., Bender, D. S., Morey, L. C., Clark, L. A., Oldham, J. M., Alarcon, R. D., et al. (2011). Personality disorder types proposed for DSM-5. *Journal of Personality Disorders, 25,* 136–169.

Stadler, C., Kroeger, A., Weyers, P., Grasmann, D., Horschinek, M., Freitag, C., et al. (2011). Cortisol reactivity in boys with attention-deficit/hyperactivity disorder and disruptive behavior problems: The impact of callous unemotional traits. *Psychiatry Research, 187,* 204–209.

Stadler, C., Sterzer, P., Schmeck, K., Krebs, A., Kleinschmidt, A., & Poustka, F. (2007). Reduced anterior cingulate activation in aggressive children and adolescents during affective stimulation: Association with temperament traits. *Journal of Psychiatric Research, 41,* 410–417.

Stein, J. S., & Madden, G. J. (2013). Delay discounting and drug abuse: Empirical, conceptual, and methodological considerations. In J. MacKillop & H. de Wit (Eds.), *The Wiley–Blackwell handbook of addiction psychopharmacology* (pp. 165–208). Malden, MA: Wiley.

Strickland, C. M., Drislane, L. E., Lucy, M., Krueger, R. F., & Patrick, C. J. (2013). Characterizing psychopathy using DSM-5 personality traits. *Assessment, 20,* 327–338.

Stringaris, A., & Goodman, R. (2009). Three dimensions of oppositionality in youth. *Journal of Child Psychology and Psychiatry, 50,* 216–223.

Stringaris, A., Maughan, B., & Goodman, R. (2010). What's in a disruptive disorder?: Temperamental antecedents of oppositional defiant disorder: Findings from the Avon longitudinal study. *Journal of the American Academy of Child and Adolescent Psychiatry, 49,* 474–483.

Substance Abuse and Mental Health Services Administration. (2001). *Summary of findings from the 2000 National Household Survey on Substance Abuse* (NHSDA Series H-13, DHHS Publication No. [SMA] 01-3549). Rockville, MD.

Tackett, J. L. (2006). Evaluating models of the personality–psychopathology relationship in children and adolescents. *Clinical Psychology Review, 26,* 584–599.

Taylor, J., & Iacono, W. G. (2007). Personality trait differences in boys and girls with clinical or sub-clinical diagnoses of conduct disorder versus antisocial personality disorder. *Journal of Adolescence, 30,* 537–547.

Valiente, C., Eisenberg, N., Smith, C. L., Reiser, M., Fabes, R. A., Losoya, S., et al. (2003). The relations of effortful control and reactive control to children's externalizing problems: A longitudinal assessment. *Journal of Personality, 71,* 1171–1196.

Van Leeuwen, K., Mervielde, I., De Clercq, B. J., & De Fruyt, F. (2007). Extending the spectrum idea: Child personality, parenting and psychopathology. *European Journal of Personality, 21,* 63–89.

Viding, E., Blair, R. J. R., Moffitt, T. E., & Plomin, R. (2005). Evidence for substantial genetic risk for psychopathy in 7-year-olds. *Journal of Child Psychology and Psychiatry, 46,* 592–597.

Viding, E., Jones, A. P., Frick, P. J., Moffitt, T. E., & Plomin, R. (2008). Heritability of antisocial behavior at 9: Do callous–unemotional traits matter? *Developmental Science, 11,* 17–22.

White, H. R., Bates, M. E., & Buyske, S. (2001). Adolescence-limited versus persistent delinquency: Extending Moffitt's hypothesis into adulthood. *Journal of Abnormal Psychology, 110,* 600–609.

Whiteside, S. P., & Lynam, D. R. (2001). The Five Factor Model and impulsivity: Using a structural model of personality to understand impulsivity. *Personality and Individual Differences, 30,* 669–689.

Whiteside, S. P., & Lynam, D. R. (2009). Understanding the role of impulsivity and externalizing psychopathology in alcohol abuse: Application of the UPPS Impulsive Behavior Scale. *Personality Disorders: Theory, Research, and Treatment, S*(1), 69–79.

Whiteside, S. P., Lynam, D. R., Miller, J. D., & Reynolds, S. K. (2005). Validation of the UPPS Impulsive Behavior Scale: A four-factor model of impulsivity. *European Journal of Personality, 19,* 559–574.

Witkiewitz, K., King, K., McMahon, R. J., Wu, J., Luk, J., Bierman, K. L., et al. (2013). Evidence for a multidimensional latent structural model of externalizing disorders. *Journal of Abnormal Child Psychology, 41,* 223–237.

Zastrow, B. L., Martel, M. M., & Widiger, T. (2016). Preschool oppositional defiant disorder: A disorder of negative affect, surgency, and disagreeableness. *Journal of Clinical Child and Adolescent Psychology.* [Epub ahead of print]

CHAPTER 32

The Development of Personality Disorders

Andrew M. Chanen
Katherine N. Thompson

The past three decades has seen significant advances in the study of individual differences from birth through to adulthood. Recognition of the reciprocal interaction of biological and environmental influences over the life course has informed and fundamentally reshaped our understanding of personality pathology. It is now acknowledged that personality pathology can be recognized early in life. Moreover, there is growing understanding that personality pathology is common and clinically significant throughout childhood, adolescence, and emerging adulthood, and is more plastic than previously believed. Recognition and management of personality pathology at the earliest possible age and developmental stage (early intervention) have become important clinical tasks and offer opportunities to intervene to support more adaptive development.

Personality Disorder in the Modern Era

The modern roots of personality pathology can be traced back to the European descriptive psychopathologists of the early 20th century (Berrios, 1993). Kraepelin, and later Kretschmer, proposed proto-spectrum models in which personality disturbances were seen as attenuated forms of the major psychoses (Berrios, 1993). By contrast, Jaspers made the distinction between personality developments (understood from the individual's previous personality) and disease processes (unpredictable from the premorbid state) (Berrios, 1993). The concept of personality disorder as we know it came into being with Schneider's description of distinct *psychopathic personalities,* published in 1923 (Berrios, 1993). Schneider described both *abnormal* personality (statistical deviance that was not inherently pathological) and *disordered* personality that was more extreme and impairing. Livesley (2001) notes that this contrast between personality spectra and personality types presaged the recurrent debate, which continues to this date, regarding dimensions and categories of personality disorder.

Psychoanalytic concepts were introduced into classificatory systems beginning with Freud's *character types,* associated with his psychosexual developmental model. Although enriching the field of psychopathology, Livesley (2000) credits the classificatory confusion associated with such psychoanalytic concepts with providing the impetus for the American Psychiatric Association's third edition of the *Diagnostic and Statistical Manual of Mental Disorders* (DSM-III; American Psychiatric Association, 1980) and the decision to place personality disorders on a separate axis (Axis II). The main purpose of DSM-III was to provide standardized and reliable diagnostic criteria for mental disorders. This marked a turning point for the field and led to an exponential rise in research publications about personality disorder (Blashfield & McElroy, 1987).

DSM-III introduced 10 personality disorder categories, divided into three clusters, based on clinical description. Cluster A included paranoid, schizoid, and schizotypal personality disorders. Cluster B included antisocial, borderline, histrionic, and narcissistic personality disorders, and Cluster C included, avoidant, dependent, and obsessive–compulsive personality disorders. This structure persists into DSM-5, despite general agreement in the field that it is conceptually and psychometrically flawed (Bernstein, Iscan, Maser, & Boards of Directors of the Association for Research in Personality Disorders International Society for the Study of Personality Disorders, 2007). Of these personality disorders, antisocial and borderline personality disorders have the largest research base.

Since the introduction of the DSM system in 1952 (American Psychiatric Association, 1952), personality disorders have been conceived of as stable disorders. DSM-III gave prominence to the notion that personality disorders could be distinguished from the more episodic mental state disorders. DSM-III introduced separate axes for *mental state* disorders (diagnosed on Axis I) and for personality and other *trait* disorders, such as intellectual disability (diagnosed on Axis II). The rationale for this has changed with each edition of the DSM. In DSM-III, it was to ensure that personality disorders would be considered separately and be given due attention during diagnostic assessment. This basis of this changed in DSM-III-R (American Psychiatric Association, 1987) to the persistence of the disorders. Personality disorders were believed to begin in childhood or adolescence and to persist in a stable form into adult life. In 1994, DSM-IV (American Psychiatric Association, 1994) returned to a rationale similar to that offered in the DSM-III (i.e., to give prominence to disorders that might otherwise be overlooked). Despite these changes, the DSM definition of personality disorder has consistently incorporated the conventional wisdom that personality disorders are enduring and stable over time.

The removal of the multiaxial system in DSM-5 (American Psychiatric Association, 2013) marked an important move toward recognizing the legitimacy of personality disorders among other forms of mental disorder. DSM-5 was intended to replace the categorical personality disorder system of DSM-IV with a dimensional model of personality disorder. However, infighting among the DSM-5 Personality and Personality Disorders Work Group and a political backlash led to its demise (Silk, 2016). Instead, an "alternative DSM-5 model for personality disorders" was published in Section III of the manual, reserved for emerging measures and models. This model was portrayed as a hybrid dimensional–categorical model for the assessment and diagnosis of personality pathology. It combined dimensional ratings of the severity of impairment in self and interpersonal personality functioning, with 25 pathological personality traits. When combined with other inclusion and exclusion criteria, this was proposed to create six diagnostic categories for specific personality disorders and a diagnosis of *personality disorder trait specified* for all other presentations of personality disorders (Skodol, 2014). However, this model has been trenchantly criticized as both clinically impractical and scientifically flawed. It has been argued that the claim to be an integrated model is false because the typal and domain diagnoses simply exist side by side, only connected by use of the same traits (Livesley, 2012).

Personality disorder is currently defined in DSM-5 as an enduring, pervasive, and inflexible pattern of thoughts, emotions, and behavior that markedly differs from societal expectations (American Psychiatric Association, 2013). It begins in adolescence or early adulthood.

Historically, the *International Classification of Diseases* (ICD) has followed, rather than led the field of classification. With the publication of ICD-10 (World Health Oranization, 1992), efforts were made to coordinate with DSM-IV (American Psychiatric Association, 1994) categories, but without operationally defined, polythetic criteria. This situation is likely to change with the forthcoming ICD-11, which is expected to fundamentally alter its approach by introducing a trait-based dimensional model of personality disorder (Tyrer, Reed, & Crawford, 2015).

Temperament, Personality, and Personality Disorder

Our understanding of personality across the normal–abnormal range has increased greatly over the past three decades. Normal and abnormal personality are now known to be continuous across the life course (O'Connor, 2002). However, historically, researchers interested in early individual differences often focused on the study of temperament traits, with less emphasis on normal-range personality traits in childhood (Rothbart & Bates, 2006; Tackett, Kushner, De Fruyt, & Mervielde, 2013). Even less attention has been paid to understanding the characteristics of personality pathology in early life. Yet existing research highlights substantial overlap in the content covered across the domains of temperament, normal-range child personality, and child personality pathology (De Clercq, De Fruyt, Van Leeuwen, & Mervielde, 2006; Shiner, 2009; Tackett, Kushner, et al., 2013).

The broader personality disorder literature has largely focused on adult and, to a lesser extent, adolescent populations. Findings consistently indicate that personality disorder is unitary but heterogeneous, comprised of core personality dysfunction and with variability characterized by adaptive and maladaptive personality trait dimensions (Bastiaansen, De Fruyt, Rossi, Schotte, & Hofmans, 2013; Krueger, Skodol, Livesley, Shrout, & Huang, 2007; Tyrer, Crawford, & Mulder, 2011). Also, normal and abnormal personality are now known to change trajectory across the lifespan (Cohen et al., 2008; Hallquist & Lenzenweger, 2013; Morey et al., 2007), rather than being highly stable. Personality pathology can also change with treatment, with acute manifestations being particularly responsive to intervention (Stoffers et al., 2012). Even characteristic traits can change over time, particularly when assisted by effective treatments, which might work partly by catalyzing delayed maturational processes (Newton-Howes, Clark, & Chanen, 2015).

Convergence between Models of Normal and Abnormal Personality across Developmental Periods

As demonstrated in this book, the study of normal-range personality has converged on the *Big Five,* a hierarchical five-factor model (FFM) of personality traits (Markon, Krueger, & Watson, 2005). The strong psychometric properties of measures of these factors are well documented, and they account for a significant amount of the variance in both normal-range personality and personality pathology (Kushner, Quilty, Tackett, & Bagby, 2011; Samuel & Widiger, 2008).

Studies have demonstrated a similar higher-order structure to these personality dimensions in children, adolescents, and adults (Mervielde, De Clercq, De Fruyt, & Van Leeuwen, 2005; Tackett et al., 2012), and specific measures of personality pathology in children, adolescents, and adults yield consistent findings (Kushner, Tackett, & De Clercq, 2013; Livesley, 1998). Until recently, most pathological personality trait measures were developed for adults and adapted for use in younger age groups (De Fruyt & De Clercq, 2014; Kushner et al., 2013). Several studies have demonstrated similar associations between normal and pathological personality traits from adolescence through to adulthood (and old age), supporting an overarching structural framework across the lifespan (De Fruyt & De Clercq, 2014). Importantly, these shared structures suggest many layers of continuity by demonstrating connections between adult and child trait covariance (Markon et al., 2005; Tackett et al., 2012), connections between normal and pathological personality trait covariance (Markon et al., 2005; Samuel & Widiger, 2008), and overlap between different personality pathology trait measures (Kushner et al., 2013). This set of findings also highlights a major advantage of dimensional approaches to personality pathology, which is to facilitate communication across age and development.

The Big Five traits are observable in early childhood (Tackett et al., 2012) and provide a useful framework for understanding the interrelations between personality disorder and other forms of mental disorder across the lifespan (De Clercq & De Fruyt, 2012; Tackett et al., 2012; see "Precursor Signs and Symptoms," below). For example, conduct disorder is linked to antisocial personality in adulthood, and neuroticism in childhood is associated with avoidant personality disorder, social phobia, and generalized anxiety disorder (De Clercq & De Fruyt, 2012). A link is also observed between low conscientiousness and agreeableness and high neuroticism and attention-deficit/hyperactivity disorder, which might be related to later paranoid, borderline, and antisocial personality disorders (De Clercq & De Fruyt, 2012). When operationalized, it becomes clear that it is difficult to distinguish between temperament and personality (De Clercq & De Fruyt, 2012; De Fruyt & De Clercq, 2014). This has provided impetus for using trait description in childhood clinical assessment (De Clercq & De Fruyt, 2012). The description of Chelsea as a child (p. 554) suggests that she might be high in neuroticism and conscientiousness but low in agreeableness.

Factor-analytic studies have indicated that personality disorder traits in childhood overlap substantially with those reported in adults and have similar rank-order stability (Shiner, 2009). The Dimensional Personality Symptom Item Pool (DIPSI) has been used to investigate personality traits in children (De Clercq et al., 2006; Decuyper, De Clercq, & Tackett, 2015). Personality traits have been found to be grouped into externalizing and internalizing factors, which can then be broken down further into four factors that include disagreeableness, emotional instability, compulsivity, and introversion (De Clercq et al., 2006; Kushner et al., 2013). When the factor structure of the Structured Interview for DSM-IV Personality was investigated in adolescents with borderline personality disorder, two main factors were found, one internally oriented (affective instability, paranoid ideation, emptiness, avoidance of abandonment) and the other externally oriented (inappropriate anger, impulsivity, suicidal or self-mutilating behavior, unstable relationships) (Speranza et al., 2012). These findings are comparable to those in studies in adults using the Dimensional Assessment of Personality Pathology—Basic Questionnaire (DAPP-BQ), which yielded a four-factor structure. They included emotional dysregulation, dissocial behavior, inhibitedness, and compulsivity (Livesley, 1998). Livesley suggested that this phenotypic approach to personality disorder is advantageous because it results in a large number of building blocks that have specific effects and a few factors with widespread effects, and can explain the complex variation in the structure of personality and personality disorder (Livesley, 1998).

Chelsea is the eldest of Brenda's three children. Chelsea's father, Ray, abused alcohol and was violent toward Brenda and his children. He was also described as deceitful and exploitative. He left the family home when Chelsea was 5 years old, and Chelsea saw him rarely during her childhood. Brenda was described as impulsive and emotionally unstable by those who knew her well. She had little family support and worked full time at a supermarket, often leaving Chelsea to care for her younger siblings, Joel and Lauren.

As a child, Chelsea was intelligent, attractive, and achieved well in sports. She remembers her mother Brenda "claiming responsibility" for these attributes. However, when it came to the actual tasks of parenting, she experienced Brenda as unreliable, neglecting, and often cruel and violent. By the time Chelsea was 11 years old, Brenda would not come home for several days at a time, leaving Chelsea "in charge." At other times, Brenda brought home male partners, who mistreated Chelsea and her siblings.

Chelsea's preschool teachers described her as sensitive, anxious, and emotional. She had severe difficulty separating from her mother and would cry and become so distressed that the teacher would have to take her out of class. She formed intense relationships with her peers and was prone to becoming excessively angry with them, especially when she feared that a friend might reject her. Nonetheless, she was able to form a small circle of friends. Chelsea had little time for play or for her own pursuits throughout her childhood, believing that her only choice was to step into the parenting role to care for her siblings. She also believed that she should somehow compensate her siblings for their parents' misdeeds and felt quite special when praised by others for her precocious capacity to care for her siblings. Later in her teenage years, Chelsea described feeling "robbed" of her childhood. She said that the worst aspect of her parents' neglect was their failure to protect her and her siblings. Consequently, Chelsea refused to go to foster care, so that she could stay to protect her siblings. This exposed her to more abuse and neglect, which made her increasingly angry. Yet she never really allowed herself to express this anger.

Stability and Change

Longitudinal studies (Caspi & Silva, 1995) support the continuity of individual differences from early childhood to young adulthood in the general population, although the strength of associations between individual differences in early childhood and adulthood are only weak to moderate. Traits become consistent through genetic influences, psychological makeup, exposure to a consistent environment, the goodness of fit between individuals and their environment, and a strong sense of identity (Roberts & DelVecchio, 2000).

The historical separation of the literature examining normal personality development from that examining personality disorder has hampered a lifespan–developmental clinical perspective. More recently, studies across the normal–abnormal range of personality have found that personality traits evident in childhood stabilize throughout life, including into later adulthood (De Fruyt et al., 2006; Roberts & DelVecchio, 2000). Such traits are approximately 50% heritable, with little variance accounted for by shared environmental influences. Chelsea's story (pp. 554, 556, and 557) suggests that her mother was high in neuroticism and that both were low in agreeableness and conscientiousness. The remainder is attributable to each individual's unique experiences and the interaction between an individual's biology and his or her environment (Roberts & DelVecchio, 2000). Genetic factors and environmental consistencies are likely to reinforce the continuity of personality, whereas variable environmental influences are likely to lead to malleability and, consequently, to the opportunity for clinical intervention (Newton-Howes et al., 2015).

Also critical for understanding the development of personality disorder is a better understanding of normal-range personality development, covered in detail in other chapters in this book. For example, large-scale investigations, particularly in adulthood, have demonstrated that personality trait change tends to develop toward greater maturity with age (i.e., increases in social dominance, conscientiousness, emotional stability, and agreeableness, and decreases in social vitality and openness) (Roberts, Walton, & Viechtbauer, 2006). However, this pattern looks somewhat different across studies of youth development, some of which have demonstrated a shift toward less maturity (e.g., lower conscientiousness) from childhood to adolescence, with a subsequent increase in regulation in later adolescence (Soto, John, Gosling, & Potter, 2011). Emotional tendencies and self-regulation capacities are critical for many forms of personality pathology and by understanding their normal-range development, we are better able to identify pathways to maladaptive personality development.

Consistency in individuals' relative trait levels increases monotonically, beginning in infancy, although the causes of these changes are not clearly understood. Recent meta-analytic data show that personality across the normal–abnormal range is moderately stable during childhood and adolescence. Rather than "setting like plaster" (James, 1890/1950), personality becomes more "viscous" over time (Ferguson, 2010; Srivastava, John, Gosling, & Potter, 2003). Personality stability increases from the teenage years through to emerging adulthood;

then the rate of change slows after age 30. Particularly, the "Big Five" dimensions of personality already show substantial stability across community (De Fruyt et al., 2006) and clinical (De Bolle et al., 2009) samples of children and adolescents. Importantly, for the assessment of personality pathology in adolescence, there is no sudden increase in the stability of traits across the normal–abnormal range during the transition from the teenage years to young adulthood (Roberts & DelVecchio, 2000). Rank-order stability of pathological personality traits is largely identical in adolescence and adulthood (De Clercq, De Fruyt, & Widiger, 2009; Johnson, Cohen, Smailes, et al., 2000), dispelling earlier notions that personality disorder was too changeable in adolescence to warrant diagnosis, scientific study, or treatment.

Much of the evidence that personality pathology appears to change from childhood through to adulthood in similar ways to normal-range personality is based on the work of the Children in Community study (CIC; Cohen, Crawford, Johnson, & Kasen, 2005), which requires replication. The early phases of this study have important methodological limitations with regard to personality disorder assessment, which suggest cautious interpretation of the findings. Remarkably, no well-designed study, using validated measures, has followed the course of personality pathology from childhood to later life. The CIC identified that personality disorder features peak in the early teens and decline linearly from ages 14 to 28 years (Johnson, Cohen, Kasen, et al., 2000). This decline reflects, in part, normative decreases in impulsivity, attention seeking, and dependency, and normative increases in social competence and self-control. Personality disorder features in the CIC were moderately stable, which is remarkably similar to comparable studies in adults over similar time intervals. The adolescents in the CIC with diagnosed personality disorder tended to have elevated personality disorder features during early adulthood (similar to Chelsea in our case study). These findings suggest continuity of personality disorder from adolescence to adulthood. Notably, one-fifth of participants experienced increases in personality pathology during this period. Overall, the CIC's findings show that child and adolescent personality pathology is the strongest predictor, over and above common mental state disorders, of young adult personality disorder. It is also notable that decreases in personality disorder features are more rapid in individuals who initially had lower levels of personality disorder symptoms (Crawford et al., 2005; De Clercq, Van Leeuwen, van den Noortgate, De Bolle, & De Fruyt, 2009), giving rise to an increasing gap between individuals scoring high and those scoring low in personality disorder features across adolescent development.

Although traits are largely consistent, they also remain dynamic throughout life. Mean levels of personality traits change across the life course, with the greatest magnitude of change during early to midadulthood (ages 20–40 years), not childhood or adolescence (Roberts et al., 2006). Individuals with personality pathology tend to show greater change, which is usually, but not always, in the direction of improvement over time. Despite this waxing and waning picture of acute disturbances (e.g., Chelsea's declining suicidality and self-harm) in individuals with personality disorder, psychosocial functioning (e.g., occupational and interpersonal functioning) tends to be poor and relatively stable (Skodol, 2008; Skodol et al., 2005). Chelsea was still experiencing difficulties in relationships and vocational pathways even into her 20s. Significantly, change in personality traits predicts change in personality pathology, but not vice versa (Warner et al., 2004), making it likely that traits more closely resemble the underlying personality disorder (Newton-Howes et al., 2015). It also underscores the importance of devoting greater attention to research on normative childhood personality development, as it forms a foundational knowledge base on which a better understanding of personality pathology development must be built.

The onset of puberty brought with it increasingly unmanageable and overwhelming feelings, especially anger, shame, and despair following sexual assaults perpetrated by several of Brenda's partners. Chelsea would try to bottle these feelings up but increasingly found herself in physical fights or turning to self-cutting to manage her feelings. The self-cutting increased during Chelsea's teenage years but she kept it, and the associated shame, secret. She also began using alcohol and marijuana. This usually involved unplanned binges, despite Chelsea's recognition that she felt more anxious and depressed afterward. Chelsea described being beleaguered by a nagging sense that she only lived for others and had little sense of herself as a whole person. She continued to feel powerless to effectively express her anger or her needs, and

this seemed to leave her vulnerable to being exploited, which only nourished her anger. Her relationships became even more tumultuous, entering into intense intimate relationships that broke down rapidly and were often marked by violence. Following the breakdown of one of these relationships, Chelsea took her first of many overdoses of painkillers, but she did not seek any medical help at this time.

Chelsea became pregnant at age 16, following an impulsive sexual encounter. She received little support from her school, which pressured her to leave. Following the birth of her son, she became socially isolated. Chelsea believed that talking about problems and asking for help was "weak" and, desperate to "avoid turning out like [her] parents," she entered into a prolonged period of soldiering on, caring for her son and evading or fighting with Child Protective Services, who questioned her parenting capacity. This left her feeling that she could never do enough for others, especially her son, which intensified her feelings of guilt, depression, and anger. Simultaneously, she would neglect her own needs, often resorting to alcohol and marijuana to numb herself. At times of crisis, she would become intensely suicidal and continued to take overdoses of prescribed and over-the-counter medications. This brought her into contact with hospital emergency departments, where she was often met with derision, contempt, and hostility, exacerbating her feelings of anger and shame.

Poor Social and Occupational Functioning

In addition to poor personality functioning, individuals with personality disorder have poor adaptive (social and occupational) functioning, which tends to be more pervasive and present across the life course. When placed in the context of normal adolescent development, this suggests young people with personality disorder are at risk of failing to achieve appropriate developmental milestones in the transition from childhood to adulthood. For example, as illustrated by Chelsea, their education might be incomplete, and they might struggle to learn self-care, build intimate and peer relationships, obtain employment, and begin to build financial independence. Although, personality disorder features wax and wane over time, adaptive functioning tends to remain persistently poor (Gunderson et al., 2011; Zanarini, Frankenburg, Hennen, Reich, & Silk, 2005). While Criterion

C of the general definition of personality disorder in DSM-5 outlines the presence of enduring poor social and occupational functioning, this feature is not described among the individual personality disorder categories (American Psychiatric Association, 2013).

Poor functioning is already present in young people in the early phase of personality disorder. Fifteen- to 18 year-old psychiatric patients with personality disorder have significantly poorer social and occupational functioning compared to psychiatric patients with no personality disorder (Chanen, Jovev, & Jackson, 2007). Compared with patients without personality disorder, those with personality disorder have significantly more days off school due to truancy, poorer peer relationships, and worse self-care and family relationships.

To date, relatively little is known about functional trajectories from childhood to adulthood among individuals with personality disorder. This is compounded by lack of consensus and inconsistency regarding the definition and measurement of adaptive functioning. It has been suggested that it comprises three components: well-being, social and interpersonal functioning, and basic functioning (Ro & Clark, 2013), and that personality functioning should be incorporated into general functioning (Clark & Ro, 2014). An alternative to this conceptualization is to split functioning into personality functioning and adaptive functioning (social and occupational functioning). Those functioning measures that are commonly available to researchers, namely, the Social and Occupational Functioning Assessment Scale (SOFAS; Goldman, Skodol, & Lave, 1992) and the Global Assessment of Functioning (GAF; American Psychiatric Association, 2000), do not specifically assess maladaptive social and occupational functioning or capture the nature of functional impairment associated with personality disorder in a comprehensive way. These issues require further research.

Remarkably, throughout these difficulties, Chelsea continued to care for her younger siblings, who themselves were facing increasing difficulties in their own relationships, and with drug and alcohol use and offending behavior. Following an overdose, Chelsea was required by a court to undergo a parenting capacity assessment, which concluded that she was indeed capable of meeting her son's needs. This validation of her capacities seemed to mark a turning point for Chelsea. By her mid-20s, Chelsea had markedly reduced her self-cutting and medication overdoses. She began to reflect on her own needs and seemed more able to recognize the potential for harmful intimate relationships. She reasoned that it was better to refrain from relationships than to continue to experience violence and abuse. However, this came at the considerable cost of loneliness and isolation. Chelsea found it difficult to maintain employment and had numerous low-skill jobs. She decided to return to study and gained entry into college to study nursing. However, she found the social interaction that accompanied her studies to be too intense. One evening, she impulsively became intoxicated with alcohol and cut herself. Recognizing the intensely overwhelming patterns of the past, Chelsea decided to seek treatment.

Risk Factors and Precursor Signs and Symptoms

Until the late 1990s, most developmental studies of personality disorder focused on early childhood experiences and how they influence later (adult) psychopathology (Newton-Howes et al., 2015). Such childhood effects are important, but they might be mediated and even reversed by later experiences (Schulenberg, Sameroff, & Cicchetti, 2004). A restricted focus on distal factors is arguably "nondevelopmental," because it assumes that the causes of mental health and ill health do not change across the lifespan. Possible mediating mechanisms that might contribute to the continuity or discontinuity in psychopathology between childhood and adult life include genetic mediation, "kindling" effects, environmental influences, coping mechanisms, and cognitive processing of experiences (Rutter, Kim-Cohen, & Maughan, 2006). For example, negative parent–child relationships in youth can exacerbate both internalizing and externalizing symptoms (as illustrated by Chelsea), if an individual is already emotionally dysregulated, whereas warm and accepting parenting might shield a child from negative outcomes (Stepp, Whalen, Pilkonis, Hipwell, & Levine, 2012).

Little is known about perinatal factors associated with personality disorder, except for schizotypal and schizoid personality disorders, where links have been found with influenza and with prenatal exposure to malnutrition and stress (Raine, 2006).

The CIC study (Cohen, Crawford, et al., 2005) is the only study that has identified "true" environmental risk factors (i.e., those that prospectively predict personality disorder) for the full range of personality disorders. Many of these factors are illustrated in Chelsea's story. These include "distal" factors such as low family-of-origin socioeconomic status, being raised by a single parent, family welfare support, numerous parental conflicts, and parental illness or death (Cohen, 2008; Cohen, Crawford, et al., 2005). Parental dynamics, such as maladaptive family functioning and parenting, including low emotional closeness between parent and child, use of harsh punishment during childhood, maternal overcontrol, and parental psychopathology, have also been found to precede later development of personality disorder (Bezirganian, Cohen, & Brook, 1993; Cohen, 2008; Cohen, Crawford, et al., 2005; Johnson, Cohen, Kasen, & Brook, 2006), along with adverse childhood experiences such as sexual, physical, and verbal abuse and childhood neglect (Cohen, 2008; Johnson, Cohen, Kasen, Smailes, & Brook, 2001; Moran et al., 2011). Other strong predictors were poor achievement, school expulsion, lack of goals, and low IQ (Cohen, Crawford, et al., 2005).

In addition, studies also indicate that certain temperamental characteristics and early-onset mental state or behavioral problems prospectively predict personality disorder (Chanen & McCutcheon, 2013). These include maternal reports of anxiety, and depressive symptoms and conduct problems, along with not only substance use disorders (especially alcohol use), depression, anxiety disorder, disruptive behavior disorders, especially conduct disorder, but also attention-deficit/hyperactivity disorder and oppositional defiant disorder (Bernstein, Cohen, Skodol, Bezirganian, & Brook, 1996; Cohen, 2008; Cohen, Crawford, et al., 2005; Kasen, Cohen, Skodol, Johnson, & Brook, 1999; Kasen et al., 2001; Lewinsohn, Rohde, Seeley, & Klein, 1997; Stepp, Burke, Hipwell, & Loeber, 2012; Thatcher, Cornelius, & Clark, 2005; Zoccolillo, Pickles, Quinton, & Rutter, 1992). Although DSM-5 antisocial personality disorder requires a diagnosis of conduct disorder before the age of 15, the evidence does not support a unique or specific developmental pathway to antisocial personality disorder (Frick & Viding, 2009; Rutter, 2012). Rather, conduct disorder is prospectively linked to a range of mental state and personality disorders (Burke, Waldman, & Lahey, 2010; Helgeland, Kjelsberg, & Torgersen, 2005). Overall, these findings suggest that similar or identical phenomena (e.g.,

impulsivity and aggression) might be misleadingly characterized as mental state pathology in children and, in later adult life, redefined as personality pathology (Chanen & Kaess, 2012). In fact, after adjusting for common mental state pathology (e.g., disruptive behavior disorders, anxiety and depression), personality disorder features in childhood and adolescence are the strongest long-term predictor of personality disorder diagnoses in adulthood (Cohen, Chen, et al., 2005; Crawford et al., 2005).

In the CIC, when the cumulative risk of these factors was calculated, risk for borderline personality disorder was associated with low socioeconomic status combined with cumulative trauma, stressful life events, low IQ, paternal and maternal parenting problems (Cohen et al., 2008). Comparatively, schizotypal personality disorder was associated with low socioeconomic status, being male, cumulative trauma, stressful life events, low IQ, and fathers' and mothers' parenting problems (Cohen et al., 2008). These parenting factors included low closeness to the mother and/or father, maternal control through guilt, "power assertive punishment," and parental antisocial behavior (Cohen, Chen, et al., 2005). Notably, both schizotypal and borderline personality features significantly contribute to the risk of having depression at any age (Cohen et al., 2008).

The CIC also found that a co-occurring mental state and personality disorder greatly increased the odds of young adult personality disorder relative to the odds of either a mental state or a personality disorder alone (Kasen et al., 1999). For example, when disruptive behavior disorder co-occurred with Cluster A personality disorder in adolescence, the odds ratio (OR) for persistence of this same personality disorder into adulthood was 24.6 times higher. The same pattern was also found for disruptive behavior co-occurring with Cluster B (OR = 12.5) or C (OR = 16.3) personality disorder, for anxiety disorder co-occurring with Cluster A (OR = 16.9), and for major depression co-occurring with Cluster A (OR = 20.5), B (OR = 19.1), or C (OR = 16.0) personality disorder.

Multilevel frameworks lend themselves particularly well to understanding the emergence and development of personality pathology over time. For example, Shiner and Tackett (2014) described the usefulness of a three-level framework for differentiating early risk and symptomatology, characteristics that reflect personality traits, characteristic adaptations (e.g., attachment and emotion regulation), and identity development. All levels are clearly relevant to personality disorder among youth and provide a helpful framework for organizing risk factors, correlates, and early manifestations, while allowing for the incorporation of development.

Discontinuities may also provide a window into the mechanisms operating across this period, along with clues for prevention and early intervention, by informing what might protect young people from personality disorder. An example of such research is a study in which positive maternal parenting behavior during an interaction task was associated with a reduction in borderline personality disorder pathology over time (Whalen et al., 2014). To date, there are few such studies about protective factors and little is known about the prospective developmental dynamics of resilience for personality disorder (Paris, Perlin, Laporte, Fitzpatrick, & DeStefano, 2014; Skodol et al., 2007).

Personality Disorder Begins in Childhood and Adolescence

There is general agreement that personality disorder has its roots in childhood and adolescence, and this was made explicit from the time of DSM-III (American Psychiatric Association, 1980). Nonetheless, the sections on disorders of childhood and adolescence in DSM-5 and ICD-10 still make no mention of personality disorder. Clinicians are often discouraged from diagnosing personality disorder in people under age 18 years, and diagnosing personality disorder prior to age 18 years remains controversial (Chanen & McCutcheon, 2008; De Clercq & De Fruyt, 2012). Accurate diagnosis is also hindered in DSM-5 and ICD-10 by the lack of developmentally appropriate personality disorder criteria or illustrations of such criteria (Chanen, Jovev, McCutcheon, Jackson, & McGorry, 2008). Although DSM-5 and ICD-10 use wording that effectively discourages the use of this diagnosis, it is clinical folklore that they prohibit personality disorder diagnosis in adolescence (except for antisocial personality disorder). In fact, DSM-5 only requires that personality disorder features be present for 1 year in those under age 18 years. This is likely to be too brief to accurately distinguish a mental state from a personality trait disorder (Newton-Howes et al., 2015). ICD-10 describes it as "highly unlikely" that personality disorder will be diagnosed before 16–17

years of age, but it offers no scientific justification for this.

While elevations in maladaptive personality traits are observable during childhood, personality disorder tends to appear clinically during the transition between childhood and adulthood, when children are cognitively, emotionally, and socially prepared for the developmental task of integrating knowledge and experience about themselves and others into a coherent whole. The late 20th and early 21st centuries have seen far-reaching changes in Western culture in the transition from childhood to adulthood (Arnett, 2000). Personality disorder has the potential to disrupt the complex developmental tasks associated with this phase of life and the achievement of adult role functioning. The past decade has seen significant advances in understanding the neural substrates underpinning cognitive, emotional, and social development (Nelson, Leibenluft, McClure, & Pine, 2005; Paus, 2005; Steinberg, 2005). This suggests an extended and coherent period of development from puberty to the middle 20s that lays groundwork for the establishment of adult role functioning. In particular, the latter part of this developmental phase is increasingly a period of role exploration and change, in which the goal is to become a self-sufficient person rather than focusing on achieving demographic transitions (Arnett, 2000). This distinct developmental phase of "youth" suggests that "adolescent" personality disorder is a relatively uninformative construct (Chanen, 2015), and that more natural developmental periods for consideration are childhood, youth (combining adolescence and emerging adulthood), adulthood, and old age (Tackett, Balsis, Oltmanns, & Krueger, 2009).

Despite the scientific evidence for the validity of personality disorder in childhood and adolescence, the diagnosis still remains off-limits in this age group for many clinicians (Chanen & McCutcheon, 2008). Clearly, the evidence presented here suggests that such views are no longer justified. However, many clinicians avoid the diagnosis on the grounds of "protecting" patients from the stigma associated with the label (Chanen & McCutcheon, 2013), particularly stigma that is common among health professionals (Newton-Howes, Tyrer, & Weaver, 2008). Although this stigma is undeniable, delaying appropriate diagnosis for this reason risks colluding with this stigma (Chanen, Sharp, & Hoffman, 2017). Delay also carries clinical risks because evidence is accumulating that many of the harms associated with personality disorder emerge early in the course of the disorder, and delay is likely to lead to worse outcomes (Chanen & Thompson, 2015). Moreover, delay in diagnosis restricts appropriate intervention and risks inappropriate and/or harmful intervention (Newton-Howes et al., 2015). Therefore, it is critical to provide clinicians with information that will help them to stop avoiding the diagnosis of personality disorder in adolescents.

Measurement of Personality Pathology

There have been advances in the measurement of early personality pathology in recent years. Researchers and clinicians hoping to assess early personality disorder characteristics have several questionnaire options available to them (e.g., De Clercq et al., 2006; Decuyper et al., 2015; Linde, Stringer, Simms, & Clark, 2013; Tromp & Koot, 2008). These measures capture both overlapping and distinct variance (e.g., Kushner et al., 2013), so attention should be paid to those facets covered in each measure prior to selection. In addition, researchers and clinicians working with youth are largely accustomed to collecting data from multiple informants, and assessment of personality pathology is no exception. Informant differences can also be quantified to better understand differences between reporters (Tackett, Herzhoff, Reardon, Smack, & Kushner, 2013). Another potential option to consider is utilizing a "thin-slice" assessment method to rate traits using available archival video data (Tackett, Herzhoff, Kushner, & Rule, 2016). Specifically, this method harnesses the power inherent in "snap judgments" made by unacquainted individuals (i.e., raters) to measure personality traits and has been shown to produce reliable and valid personality trait assessments in childhood across the normal–abnormal range (Tackett et al., 2016).

The DSM-5, Section III alternative personality disorder system has incorporated the evidence for personality disorder in young people, removing age-related caveats for its diagnosis, and the same is proposed for ICD-11 (Tyrer, Crawford, Mulder, et al., 2011). Both classifications recognize the dimensional nature of personality disorder across the lifespan, allowing for "subthreshold" personality pathology.

The semistructured interviews for DSM-IV (Structured Clinical Interview for DSM-IV

Axis II Personality Disorders [SCID II]; First, Gibbon, Spitzer, Williams, & Benjamin, 1997) and DSM-5 (Structured Clinical Interview for DSM-5 Personality Disorders [SCID-5-PD]; First, Williams, Benjamin, & Spitzer, 2016) are the mainstays for assessing personality disorder in clinical research studies (First et al., 2016). This interview comprehensively assesses each of the DSM-5 criteria. A diagnosis of personality disorder is given when the patient reaches the required number of features for a particular categorical personality disorder. It is common and normal for patients (youth and adults) who have one personality disorder to have other, co-occurring disorders (Kaess et al., 2012).

Measures of normal and maladaptive personality traits have been developed for use in children through to youth and adults. The DIPSI has been used in children (Decuyper et al., 2015). It was based on the Hierarchical Personality Inventory for Children (HiPIC; Mervielde & De Fruyt, 1999), and extended use of DSM-IV Axis II personality disorder items that were adapted to be age relevant. The facets are structured under four personality domains: disagreeableness, emotional instability, introversion, and compulsivity. Validity studies have used this measure in samples of children between 5 and 17 years of age (Decuyper et al., 2015), and compared this measure to Child Behavior Checklist (CBCL; Achenbach, 1991) and Youth Self Report (YSR; Achenbach, 1997). The DIPSI has recently been extended to include a further oddity factor that relates to schizotypal personality disorder, and was validated in a large sample of adolescents ages 11–17 years (Verbeke & De Clercq, 2014).

The Schedule for Nonadaptive and Adaptive Personality-2 (SNAP-2; Calabrese, Rudick, & Simms, 2012) has been developed in an attempt to integrate competing personality trait models, including the FFM, with personality disorder. This measure has been tested in a sample of 8,690 participants between ages 17 and 85 years, and 358 adolescents (ages 12–18 years), 474 adult psychiatric outpatients (ages 18–86 years), and 195 college students (ages 16–33 years). Items on this scale were consistent with the traits measured with other personality models, including the FFM (Calabrese et al., 2012]). This measurement instrument is a promising measure that can capture the continuum of personality traits from adaptive to maladaptive (Stepp, Yu, et al., 2012). Furthermore, a youth-specific version called the SNAP-Y has been developed for the 12- to 18-year-old age group (Linde et al., 2013).

The Personality Inventory for DSM-5 (PID-5; Krueger, Derringer, Markon, Watson, & Skodol, 2012), is the self-report personality pathology instrument included in Section III of DSM-5 (American Psychiatric Association, 2013). This measure contains 25 facets that are clustered into five higher-order domains: negative affectivity, detachment, antagonism, disinhibition and psychoticism. This questionnaire was originally developed for help-seeking adults (Krueger et al., 2012), but it has been validated in a clinical sample of adolescents (De Clercq et al., 2014). The PID-5 shows promise for measuring maladaptive personality traits, but it remains unclear how ratings on this measure can be translated into meaningful clinical data that guide diagnosis and treatment.

A summary of available structured clinical interview or self-report measures is outlined in Table 32.1. Most of these measures have been designed to assess borderline, antisocial, schizotypal, or narcissistic personality disorders because these disorders have generated the largest amount of research to date. It is important to note that many of these measures have largely been developed and validated in adult samples, and the type of respondent used in their development varies from university students to psychiatric patients. This might limit the generalizability of the assessment tools to children and adolescents.

Prevalence

Although there has been significant progress in the epidemiology of adult personality disorder, there are still limited data regarding the prevalence of personality disorder among children and youth. Methodological limitations, such as different sampling procedures and a lack of psychometrically valid assessment tools, restrict the conclusions that can be drawn from these studies.

The prevalence of DSM-5 personality disorder in adolescent community and primary care settings generally ranges from 6 to 17% across studies (Kongerslev, Chanen, & Simonsen, 2015), with the exception of one study (Lewinsohn et al., 1997), which reported the prevalence of any personality disorder diagnosis to be 2.8%. This finding was most likely due to methodological differences, which required

that a personality disorder feature be present for at least 5 years.

The CIC study (Bernstein et al., 1993; Cohen, Chen, et al., 2005) estimated the prevalence of DSM-III-R personality disorder (excluding antisocial personality disorder) to be 17.2%, with the most prevalent disorder being narcissistic disorder and the least prevalent being schizotypal disorder. The prevalence of personality disorder peaked at age 12 for boys and at age 13 for girls. Adding waves of data collected through to age 33 years, these researchers estimated the point prevalence of any current DSM-IV (American Psychiatric Association, 1994) personality disorder (including depressive and passive–aggressive personality disorders) to be between 12.7 and 14.6% through adolescence and young adulthood. At mean age 33, the estimated lifetime prevalence of personality disorder was 28.2%.

Prevalence estimates in clinical samples range from 41 to 64% (Feenstra, Busschbach, Verheul, & Hutsebaut, 2011; Grilo et al., 1998), and in youth justice samples from 36 to 88% (Gosden, Kramp, Gabrielsen, & Sestoft, 2003; Kongerslev et al., 2015; Kongerslev, Moran, Bo, & Simonsen, 2012). These prevalence estimates are similar to or slightly higher than those reported for adults (Zimmerman, Chelminski, & Young, 2008), ranking personality disorder among the most common disorders seen in clinical practice in child and youth mental health.

Personality Disorder Prevention and Treatment

The optimism brought about by naturalistic prospective studies that indicate personality disorder can improve over time without intervention, and the recognition that these disorders are emerging and most severe during adolescence, emphasizes both the importance of providing effective treatment and intervening early in the course of illness. Both of these forms of treatment and intervention aim to alter the life-course trajectory of personality disorder (Chanen & McCutcheon, 2013; Newton-Howes et al., 2015) and Chelsea's story highlights numerous opportunities for prevention from childhood through to young adulthood, as outlined below.

The Institutes of Medicine report (Mrazek & Haggerty, 1994) on the prevention of mental disorders described three levels of prevention, starting with *universal* (population based),

TABLE 32.1. Measures of Personality Disorder Diagnosis and Features

Measure	Authors	Type	No. of items/ structure	Rating	Comments
SCID II (DSM-IV and DSM-5)	First et al. (1997, 2016)	Structured interview	Covers all DSM-IV and DSM-5 personality disorder symptoms	0 = absent, 1 = subthreshold, 2 = threshold	Research focused
Dimensional Personality Symptom Item Pool (DIPSI)	De Clercq et al. (2006); Decuyper et al. (2015)	Self-report	172 items	5-point Likert scale	Validated in 5- to 17-year-olds
Schedule for Nonadaptive and Adaptive Personality–2 (SNAP-2)	Calabrese et al. (2012)	Self-report	375 items	True or false	Validated in 12- to 85-year-olds, including adolescents, university students, and psychiatric outpatients; available as SNAP-Y for 12- to 18-year-olds
Personality Inventory for DSM-5	Krueger et al. (2012)	Self-report	220 items	4-point Likert scale	Validated in a clinical sample of adolescents, and adults
Borderline Personality Disorder Structured Clinical Interview (BPDSI)	Arntz et al. (2003); Giesen-Bloo et al. (2010)	Structured interview	9 subsections corresponding to DSM-IV BPD criteria	Rated according to severity, 0–10 for all sections except Identity, which is rated 0–4.	Developed for use in adults
Borderline Personality Questionnaire (BPQ)	Poreh et al. (2006)	Self-report	80 items based on DSM-IV BPD criteria	True or false	Developed based on university-age samples from three countries with mean ~ 20 years
Zanarini Rating Scale for BPD (ZAN-BPD)	Zanarini et al. (2003b)	Structured Interview; self-report	Based on DSM-IV BPD criteria + four core areas: affective, cognitive, impulsive, interpersonal	Likert scale rated 0–4	Interview tested on 200 nonpsychotic adult psychiatric outpatients; self-report developed in adults ages 18–60 years, and based the original ZAN-PD interview

(*continued*)

TABLE 32.1. (*continued*)

Measure	Authors	Type	No. of items/ structure	Rating	Comments
Borderline Symptom List (BSL-23)	Bohus et al. (2009)	Self-report	23 items based on DSM-IV BPD criteria	Likert scale rated 0–4	Also available as BSL-95; developed in 379 psychiatric outpatient adults
McLean Screening Instrument for BPD (MSI-BPD)	Zanarini et al. (2003a)	Screening self-report instrument	10 items based on DSM-IV criteria, where criterion 9 is split into paranoia and dissociation	True or false	Developed in 200 adult psychiatric outpatients
International Personality Disorder Examination	Loranger et al. (1994)	Structured interview	67 items based on ICD-10 personality disorder criteria	True or false	Developed in 716 psychiatric outpatients in 14 different countries
Personality Disorder Questionnaire	Hyler et al. (1990)	Self-report	152 items based on DSM-III-R criteria	True or false	Developed in 87 adult psychiatric inpatients
Schizotypal Personality Questionnaire	Raine (1991)	Self-report	74 items; 9 subscales based on DSM-III-R schizotypal personality disorder criteria	Yes or no	Developed based on university-age samples
Narcissistic Personality Inventory–16 (NPI-16)	Ames et al. (2006)	Self-report	16 items	0 = narcissistic, 1 = not narcissistic	Developed in 776 university students across different academic disciplines
Pathological Narcissism Inventory	Pincus et al. (2009)	Self-report	52 items covering 7 dimensions of narcissism	0–5 Likert scale	Developed in 796 and 2,801 university students
Antisocial Personality Questionnaire	Blackburn & Fawcett (1999)	Self-report	125 items	Yes or no	Developed in 499 male mentally disordered offenders, and 238 male nonoffenders
Psychopathy Checklist— Revised (PCL-R)	Hare & Neumann (2005)	Self-report	20 items	Scored 1, 2, or 3	Refer to Blackburn, Logan, Donnelly, & Renwick (2008) for a review of this measure.

selective (risk factors), and *indicated* prevention (early or precursor signs and symptoms), together with *early intervention* for first-onset disorders. This approach to the onset of mental disorders emphasizes identifying risk factors for the persistence of symptoms or deterioration of problems, rather than just focusing on the initial onset of disorder. This framework has been applied to prevention and early intervention for personality disorder in children and youth (Chanen, Jovev, et al., 2008).

Universal and selective prevention programs for children have focused on preschool and primary school programs, and wider community interventions. These programs have produced a range of positive child and maternal outcomes, and reduced offending and other behavioral problems (Hawkins, Kosterman, Catalano, Hill, & Abbott, 2005; National Collaborating Centre for Mental Health, 2010; Olds, Sadler, & Kitzman, 2007). The Communities That Care System is one example of a universal prevention program to target delinquency and antisocial behavior. The program has shown that when intervention is provided to fifth-grade students, there is a decrease in the incidence of delinquent and violent behavior that is sustained through to grade 10 (Hawkins et al., 2012), although by grade 12, after 3 years from cessation of intervention, these differences were not longer significant (Hawkins, Oesterle, Brown, Abbott, & Catalano, 2014). One might imagine in Chelsea's case that a comprehensive community-based program might have been able to compensate for the parenting deficits and lack of social support available to her family.

A selective intervention program might have specifically targeted Chelsea's family, based on the history of parental personality and mental state disorder. Such an approach has been used to target low-income mothers and their newborn to 2-year-old children. The Nurse–Family Partnership program has shown sustained improvement in crime rate and employment for both mothers and their children (Olds, 2008). The National Institute of Health and Care Excellence (National Collaborating Centre for Mental Health, 2010) in the United Kingdom has similarly recommended selective intervention for children who have parents with a history of mental illness, substance use, and residential care, who are under age 18 years, or who have had contact with the criminal justice system. The type of intervention recommended for these children was nonmaternal care for children younger than 1 year, or parenting skills provision to parents who have children under the age of 3 years.

Indicated prevention and early intervention programs have been developed for both antisocial and borderline personality disorders. Chelsea's story illustrates numerous opportunities for indicated prevention, such as when presenting to hospital following acts of self-harm, or during her pregnancy, or when Child Protective Services identified parenting difficulties. Existing programs for antisocial personality disorder target children with conduct disorder or other externalizing problems (Sawyer, Borduin, & Dopp, 2015). These interventions focus on either parents or children, and are family systems based. The Fast Track Program has been used in kindergarten-age children who have been assessed either by teachers or parents to have conduct disorders. This intervention spanned 10 years, and follow-up data showed that at the age of 25 years, the children who participated had lower rates of violent crime, substance use convictions, and antisocial personality disorder (Dodge et al., 2015). A second program called multisystemic therapy targets youth who have had criminal involvement. This therapy has shown improved outcomes into adulthood for both these youth and their siblings (Dopp, Borduin, Wagner, & Sawyer, 2014).

Prevention and early intervention for borderline personality disorder among adolescents is in its infancy. In one study, the combination of manualized individual cognitive analytic therapy (CAT) in combination with a manualized comprehensive service model, called the Helping Young People Early (HYPE) program (Chanen, Jackson, et al., 2008; Chanen et al., 2009), demonstrated faster improvement in borderline personality disorder features than standardized good clinical care (Chanen et al., 2009). Other treatments that have targeted adolescents with borderline personality disorder include dialectical behavior therapy for adolescents (DBT-A; Mehlum et al., 2014), mentalization-based treatment for adolescents (MBT-A; Rossouw & Fonagy, 2012), and emotion regulation training (ERT; Schuppert et al., 2009, 2012). These other trials have failed to distinguish the phase and stage of disorder among their participants. Nonetheless, overall, the findings of these trials support the effectiveness of treating borderline personality pathology in young people. These treatments demonstrated improvement in internalizing and externalizing psychopathology, borderline personality symptoms, depression, quality of life, and suicidal ideation and self-harm. Structured treatments generally performed better than control treatments, except in the case of ERT.

These studies challenge the widely held view that personality disorders should not be diagnosed in adolescents due to the stigma attached to these labels (Chanen & McCutcheon, 2013) and demonstrate proof of concept for the early treatment of severe personality disorder among young people. However, prevention and early intervention programs would benefit from a broader focus on all severe personality pathology, along with recognition of the broad array of adverse psychopathological and functional outcomes of personality disorder (Chanen & McCutcheon, 2013; Cohen, Crawford, et al., 2005; Newton-Howes et al., 2015), measured using psychometrically valid instruments.

Conclusion

There is now a broad evidence-based consensus that personality disorder is reliable, valid, and common among young people, with adverse personal, social, and economic consequences. Prevention and early intervention aim to ameliorate these consequences and to improve the lives of young people with personality disorder, thereby reducing the long-term impact.

REFERENCES

Achenbach, T. M. (1991). *Manual for the Child Behavior Checklist/4–18 and 1991 Profile.* Burlington: University of Vermont Department of Psychiatry.

Achenbach, T. M. (1997). *Manual for the Young Adult Self-Report and Young Adult Behavior Checklist.* Burlington: University of Vermont Department of Psychiatry.

American Psychiatric Association. (1952). *Diagnostic and statistical manual of mental disorders.* Washington, DC: APA Mental Hospital Service.

American Psychiatric Association. (1980). *Diagnostic and statistical manual of mental disorders* (3rd ed.). Washington, DC: Author.

American Psychiatric Association. (1987). *Diagnostic and statistical manual of mental disorders.* (3rd ed., rev.). Washington, DC: Author.

American Psychiatric Association. (1994). *Diagnostic and statistical manual of mental disorders* (4th ed.). Washington, DC: Author.

American Psychiatric Association. (2000). *Diagnostic and statistical manual of mental disorders* (4th ed., text rev.). Washington, DC: Author.

American Psychiatric Association. (2013). *Diagnostic and statistical manual of mental disorders* (5th ed.). Arlington, VA: Author.

Ames, D. R., Rose, P., & Anderson, C. P. (2006). The NPI-16 as a short measure of narcissism. *Journal of Research in Personality, 40,* 440–450.

Arnett, J. J. (2000). Emerging adulthood: A theory of development from the late teens through the twenties. *American Psychologist, 55*(5), 469–480.

Arntz, A., van den Hoorn, M., Cornelis, J., Verheul, R., van den Bosch, W. M., & de Bie, A. J. (2003). Reliability and validity of the Borderline Personality Disorder Severity Index. *Journal of Personality Disorders, 17*(1), 45–59.

Bastiaansen, L., De Fruyt, F., Rossi, G., Schotte, C., & Hofmans, J. (2013). Personality disorder dysfunction versus traits: Structural and conceptual issues. *Personality Disorders, 4*(4), 293–303.

Bernstein, D. P., Cohen, P., Skodol, A., Bezirganian, S., & Brook, J. (1996). Childhood antecedents of adolescent personality disorders. *American Journal of Psychiatry, 153*(7), 907–913.

Bernstein, D. P., Cohen, P., Velez, C. N., Schwab-Stone, M., Siever, L. J., & Shinsato, L. (1993). Prevalence and stability of the DSM-III-R personality disorders in a community-based survey of adolescents. *American Journal of Psychiatry, 150*(8), 1237–1243.

Bernstein, D. P., Iscan, C., Maser, J., & Boards of Directors of the Association for Research in Personality Disorders International Society for the Study of Personality Disorders. (2007). Opinions of personality disorder experts regarding the DSM-IV personality disorders classification system. *Journal of Personality Disorders, 21*(5), 536–551.

Berrios, G. E. (1993). European views on personality disorders: A conceptual history. *Comprehensive Psychiatry, 34*(1), 14–30.

Bezirganian, S., Cohen, P., & Brook, J. S. (1993). The impact of mother–child interaction on the development of borderline personality disorder. *American Journal of Psychiatry, 150*(12), 1836–1842.

Blackburn, R., & Fawcett, D. (1999). The Antisocial Personality Questionnaire: An inventory for assessing personality deviation in offender populations. *European Journal of Psychological Assessment, 15*(1), 14–24.

Blackburn, R., Logan, C., Donnelly, J. P., & Renwick, S. J. (2008). Identifying psychopathic subtypes: Combining an empirical personality classification of offenders with the Psychopathy Checklist—Revised. *Journal of Personality Disorders, 22*(6), 604–622.

Blashfield, R. K., & McElroy, R. A. (1987). The 1985 journal literature on the personality disorders. *Comprehensive Psychiatry, 28*(6), 536–546.

Bohus, M., Kleindienst, N., Limberger, M. F., Stieglitz, R. D., Domsalla, M., Chapman, A. L., et al. (2009). The short version of the Borderline Symptom List

(BSL-23): Development and initial data on psychometric properties. *Psychopathology, 42*(1), 32–39.

Burke, J. D., Waldman, I., & Lahey, B. B. (2010). Predictive validity of childhood oppositional defiant disorder and conduct disorder: Implications for the DSM-V. *Journal of Abnormal Psychology, 119*(4), 739–751.

Calabrese, W. R., Rudick, M. M., & Simms, L. J. (2012). Development and validation of Big Four personality scales for the Schedule for Nonadaptive and Adaptive Personality—Second Edition (SNAP-2). *Psychological Assessment, 24*(3), 751–763.

Caspi, A., & Silva, P. A. (1995). Temperamental qualities at age three predict personality traits in young adulthood: Longitudinal evidence from a birth cohort. *Child Development, 66*(2), 486–498.

Chanen, A. M. (2015). Borderline personality disorder in young people: Are we there yet? *Journal of Clinical Psychology, 71*(8), 778–791.

Chanen, A. M., Jackson, H. J., McCutcheon, L., Dudgeon, P., Jovev, M., Yuen, H. P., et al. (2008). Early intervention for adolescents with borderline personality disorder using cognitive analytic therapy: A randomised controlled trial. *British Journal of Psychiatry, 193*(6), 477–484.

Chanen, A. M., Jackson, H. J., McCutcheon, L., Dudgeon, P., Jovev, M., Yuen, H. P., et al. (2009). Early intervention for adolescents with borderline personality disorder: A quasi-experimental comparison with treatment as usual. *Australian and New Zealand Journal of Psychiatry, 43*(5), 397–408.

Chanen, A. M., Jovev, M., & Jackson, H. J. (2007). Adaptive functioning and psychiatric symptoms in adolescents with borderline personality disorder. *Journal of Clinical Psychiatry, 68*(2), 297–306.

Chanen, A. M., Jovev, M., McCutcheon, L., Jackson, H. J., & McGorry, P. D. (2008). Borderline personality disorder in young people and the prospects for prevention and early intervention. *Current Psychiatry Reviews, 4*(1), 48–57.

Chanen, A. M., & Kaess, M. (2012). Developmental pathways toward borderline personality disorder. *Current Psychiatry Reports, 14*(1), 45–53.

Chanen, A. M., & McCutcheon, L. K. (2008). Personality disorder in adolescence: The diagnosis that dare not speak its name. *Personality and Mental Health, 2*(1), 35–41.

Chanen, A. M., & McCutcheon, L. K. (2013). Prevention and early intervention for borderline personality disorder: Current status and recent evidence. *British Journal of Psychiatry, 202*(s54), s24–s29.

Chanen, A. M., Sharp, C., & Hoffman, P. (Global Alliance for Prevention and Early Intervention for Borderline Personality Disorder). (2017). Prevention and early intervention for borderline personality disorder: A novel public health priority. *World Psychiatry, 16*(2), 215–216.

Chanen, A. M., & Thompson, K. (2015). Borderline personality and mood disorders: Risk factors, precursors and early signs in childhood and youth. In L. Choi-Kain & J. G. Gunderson (Eds.), *Borderline personality and mood disorders: Comorbidity and controversy* (pp. 155–174). New York: Springer.

Clark, L. A., & Ro, E. (2014). Three-pronged assessment and diagnosis of personality disorder and its consequences: Personality functioning, pathological traits, and psychosocial disability. *Personality Disorders: Theory, Research, and Treatment, 5*(1), 55–69.

Cohen, P. (2008). Child development and personality disorder. *Psychiatric Clinics of North America, 31*(3), 477–493.

Cohen, P., Chen, H., Gordon, K., Johnson, J., Brook, J., & Kasen, S. (2008). Socioeconomic background and the developmental course of schizotypal and borderline personality disorder symptoms. *Development and Psychopathology, 20*(2), 633–650.

Cohen, P., Chen, H., Kasen, S., Johnson, J. G., Crawford, T., & Gordon, K. (2005). Adolescent Cluster A personality disorder symptoms, role assumption in the transition to adulthood, and resolution or persistence of symptoms. *Development and Psychopathology, 17*(2), 549–568.

Cohen, P., Crawford, T. N., Johnson, J. G., & Kasen, S. (2005). The Children in the Community Study of developmental course of personality disorder. *Journal of Personality Disorders, 19*(5), 466–486.

Crawford, T. N., Cohen, P., Johnson, J. G., Kasen, S., First, M. B., Gordon, K., et al. (2005). Self-reported personality disorder in the Children in the Community sample: Convergent and prospective validity in late adolescence and adulthood. *Journal of Personality Disorders, 19*(1), 30–52.

De Bolle, M., De Clercq, B., Van Leeuwen, K., Decuyper, M., Rosseel, Y., & De Fruyt, F. (2009). Personality and psychopathology in Flemish referred children: Five perspectives of continuity. *Child Psychiatry and Human Development, 40*(2), 269–285.

De Clercq, B., & De Fruyt, F. (2012). A Five-Factor Model framework for understanding childhood personality disorder antecedents. *Journal of Personality, 80*(6), 1533–1563.

De Clercq, B., De Fruyt, F., De Bolle, M., Van Hiel, A., Markon, K. E., Krueger, R. F. (2014). The hierarchical structure and construct validity of the PID-5 trait measure in adolescence. *Journal of Personality, 82*(2), 158–169.

De Clercq, B., De Fruyt, F., Van Leeuwen, K., & Mervielde, I. (2006). The structure of maladaptive personality traits in childhood: A step toward an integrative developmental perspective for DSM-V. *Journal of Abnormal Psychology, 115*(4), 639–657.

De Clercq, B., De Fruyt, F., & Widiger, T. A. (2009). Integrating a developmental perspective in dimensional models of personality disorders. *Clinical Psychology Review, 29*(2), 154–162.

De Clercq, B., Van Leeuwen, K., van den Noortgate, W., de Bolle, M., & de Fruyt, F. (2009). Childhood personality pathology: Dimensional stability and change. *Development and Psychopathology, 21*(3), 853–869.

De Fruyt, F., Bartels, M., Van Leeuwen, K. G., De Clercq, B., Decuyper, M., & Mervielde, I. (2006). Five types of personality continuity in childhood and adolescence. *Journal of Personality and Social Psychology, 91*(3), 538–552.

De Fruyt, F., & De Clercq, B. (2014). Antecedents of personality disorder in childhood and adolescence: Toward an integrative developmental model. *Annual Review of Clinical Psychology, 10,* 449–476.

Decuyper, M., De Clercq, B., & Tackett, J. L. (2015). Assessing maladaptive traits in youth: An English-language version of the Dimensional Personality Symptom Itempool. *Personality Disorders, 6*(3), 239–250.

Dodge, K. A., Bierman, K. L., Coie, J. D., Greenberg, M. T., Lochman, J. E., McMahon, R. J., et al. (2015). Impact of early intervention on psychopathology, crime, and well-being at age 25. *American Journal of Psychiatry, 172*(1), 59–70.

Dopp, A. R., Borduin, C. M., Wagner, D. V., & Sawyer, A. M. (2014). The economic impact of multisystemic therapy through midlife: A cost–benefit analysis with serious juvenile offenders and their siblings. *Journal of Consulting and Clinical Psychology, 82*(4), 694–705.

Feenstra, D. J., Busschbach, J. J., Verheul, R., & Hutsebaut, J. (2011). Prevalence and comorbidity of Axis I and Axis II disorders among treatment refractory adolescents admitted for specialized psychotherapy. *Journal of Personality Disorders, 25*(6), 842–850.

Ferguson, C. J. (2010). A meta-analysis of normal and disordered personality across the life span. *Journal of Personality and Social Psychology, 98*(4), 659–667.

First, M. B., Gibbon, M., Spitzer, R. L., Williams, J. B. W., & Benjamin, L. S. (1997). *User's guide for the Structured Clinical Interview for DSM-IV Axis II Personality Disorders.* Washington, DC: American Psychiatric Press.

First, M. B., Williams, J. B. W., Benjamin, L. S., & Spitzer, R. L. (2016). *Structured Clinical Interview for DSM-5 Personality Disorders.* Washington, DC: American Psychiatric Association Press.

Frick, P. J., & Viding, E. (2009). Antisocial behavior from a developmental psychopathology perspective. *Development and Psychopathology, 21*(4), 1111–1131.

Giesen-Bloo, J. H., Wachters, L. M. Schouten, E., & Arntz, A. (2010). The Borderline Personality Disorder Severity Index-IV: Psychometric evaluation and dimensional structure. *Personality and Individual Differences, 49,* 136–141.

Goldman, H. H., Skodol, A. E., & Lave, T. R. (1992). Revising Axis V for DSM-IV: A review of measures of social functioning. *American Journal of Psychiatry, 149*(9), 1148–1156.

Gosden, N. P., Kramp, P., Gabrielsen, G., & Sestoft, D. (2003). Prevalence of mental disorders among 15–17-year-old male adolescent remand prisoners in Denmark. *Acta Psychiatrica Scandinavica, 107*(2), 102–110.

Grilo, C. M., McGlashan, T. H., Quinlan, D. M., Walker, M. L., Greenfeld, D., & Edell, W. S. (1998). Frequency of personality disorders in two age cohorts of psychiatric inpatients. *American Journal of Psychiatry, 155*(1), 140–142.

Gunderson, J. G., Stout, R. L., McGlashan, T. H., Shea, M. T., Morey, L. C., Grilo, C. M., et al. (2011). Ten-year course of borderline personality disorder: Psychopathology and function from the collaborative longitudinal personality disorders study. *Archives of General Psychiatry, 68*(8), 827–837.

Hallquist, M. N., & Lenzenweger, M. F. (2013). Identifying latent trajectories of personality disorder symptom change: Growth mixture modeling in the longitudinal study of personality disorders. *Journal of Abnormal Psychology, 122*(1), 138–155.

Hare, R. D., & Neumann, C. S. (2005). Structural models of psychopathy. *Current Psychiatry Reports, 7*(1), 57–64.

Hawkins, J. D., Kosterman, R., Catalano, R. F., Hill, K. G., & Abbott, R. D. (2005). Promoting positive adult functioning through social development intervention in childhood: Long-term effects from the Seattle Social Development Project. *Archives of Pediatrics and Adolescent Medicine, 159*(1), 25–31.

Hawkins, J. D., Oesterle, S., Brown, E. C., Abbott, R. D., & Catalano, R. F. (2014). Youth problem behaviors 8 years after implementing the Communities That Care prevention system: A community-randomized trial. *JAMA Pediatrics, 168*(2), 122–129.

Hawkins, J. D., Oesterle, S., Brown, E. C., Monahan, K. C., Abbott, R. D., Arthur, M. W., & Catalano, R. F. (2012). Sustained decreases in risk exposure and youth problem behaviors after installation of the Communities That Care prevention system in a randomized trial. *Archives of Pediatric and Adolescent Medicine, 166*(2), 141–148.

Helgeland, M. I., Kjelsberg, E., & Torgersen, S. (2005). Continuities between emotional and disruptive behavior disorders in adolescence and personality disorders in adulthood. *American Journal of Psychiatry, 162*(10), 1941–1947.

Hyler, S. E., Skodol, A. E., Kellman, H. D., Oldham, J. M., & Rosnick, L. (1990). Validity of the Personality Diagnostic Questionnaire—Revised: Comparison with two structured interviews. *American Journal of Psychiatry, 147*(8), 1043–1048.

James, W. (1950). *The principles of psychology.* New York: Dover. (Original work published 1890)

Johnson, J. G., Cohen, P., Kasen, S., & Brook, J. S. (2006). Personality disorders evident by early adulthood and risk for anxiety disorders during middle adulthood. *Journal of Anxiety Disorders, 20*(4), 408–426.

Johnson, J. G., Cohen, P., Kasen, S., Skodol, A. E., Hamagami, F., & Brook, J. S. (2000). Age-related change in personality disorder trait levels between early adolescence and adulthood: A community-based longitudinal investigation. *Acta Psychiatrica Scandinavica, 102*(4), 265–275.

Johnson, J. G., Cohen, P., Kasen, S., Smailes, E., & Brook, J. S. (2001). Association of maladaptive parental behavior with psychiatric disorder among parents and their offspring. *Archives of General Psychiatry, 58*(5), 453–460.

Johnson, J. G., Cohen, P., Smailes, E., Kasen, S., Oldham, J. M., & Skodol, A. E. (2000). Adolescent personality disorders associated with violence and criminal behavior during adolescence and early adulthood. *American Journal of Psychiatry, 157*(9), 1406–1412.

Kaess, M., von Ceumern-Lindenstjerna, I.-A., Parzer, P., Chanen, A. M., Mundt, C., Resch, F., et al. (2012). Axis I and II comorbidity and psychosocial functioning in female adolescents with borderline personality disorder. *Psychopathology, 46*(1), 52–62.

Kasen, S., Cohen, P., Skodol, A. E., Johnson, J. G., & Brook, J. S. (1999). Influence of child and adolescent psychiatric disorders on young adult personality disorder. *American Journal of Psychiatry, 156*(10), 1529–1535.

Kasen, S., Cohen, P., Skodol, A. E., Johnson, J. G., Smailes, E., & Brook, J. S. (2001). Childhood depression and adult personality disorder: Alternative pathways of continuity. *Archives of General Psychiatry, 58*(3), 231–236.

Kongerslev, M., Chanen, A. M., & Simonsen, E. (2015). Personality disorder in childhood and adolescence comes of age: A review of the current evidence and prospects for future research. *Scandinavian Journal of Child and Adolescent Psychiatry and Psychology, 3*(1), 31–48.

Kongerslev, M., Moran, P., Bo, S., & Simonsen, E. (2012). Screening for personality disorder in incarcerated adolescent boys: Preliminary validation of an adolescent version of the Standardised Assessment of Personality—Abbreviated Scale (SAPAS-AV). *BMC Psychiatry, 12*, 94.

Krueger, R. F., Derringer, J., Markon, K. E., Watson, D., & Skodol, A. E. (2012). Initial construction of a maladaptive personality trait model and inventory for DSM-5. *Psychological Medicine, 42*(9), 1879–1890.

Krueger, R. F., Skodol, A. E., Livesley, W. J., Shrout, P. E., & Huang, Y. (2007). Synthesizing dimensional and categorical approaches to personality disorders: Refining the research agenda for DSM-V Axis II. *International Journal of Methods in Psychiatric Research, 16*(Suppl. 1), S65–S73.

Kushner, S. C., Quilty, L. C., Tackett, J. L., & Bagby, R. M. (2011). The hierarchical structure of the Dimensional Assessment of Personality Pathology (DAPP-BQ). *Journal of Personality Disorders, 25*(4), 504–516.

Kushner, S. C., Tackett, J. L., & De Clercq, B. (2013). The joint hierarchical structure of adolescent personality pathology: Converging evidence from two approaches to measurement. *Journal of the Canadian Academy of Child and Adolescent Psychiatry, 22*(3), 199–205.

Lewinsohn, P. M., Rohde, P., Seeley, J. R., & Klein, D. N. (1997). Axis II psychopathology as a function of Axis I disorders in childhood and adolescence. *Journal of the American Academy of Child and Adolescent Psychiatry, 36*(12), 1752–1759.

Linde, J. A., Stringer, D., Simms, L. J., & Clark, L. A. (2013). The Schedule for Nonadaptive and Adaptive Personality for Youth (SNAP-Y): A new measure for assessing adolescent personality and personality pathology. *Assessment, 20*(4), 387–404.

Livesley, W. J. (1998). Suggestions for a framework for an empirically based classification of personality disorder. *Canadian Journal of Psychiatry, 43*(2), 137–147.

Livesley, W. J. (2000). Introduction to special feature: Critical issues in the classification of personality disorder, Part 1. *Journal of Personality Disorders, 14,* 1–2.

Livesley, W. J. (2001). Conceptual and taxonomic issues. In W. J. Livesley (Ed.), *Handbook of personality disorders: Theory, research, and treatment* (pp. 3–38). New York: Guilford Press.

Livesley, W. J. (2012). Disorder in the proposed DSM-5 classification of personality disorders. *Clinical Psychology and Psychotherapy, 19*(5), 364–368.

Loranger, A. W., Sartorius, N., Andreoli, A., Berger, P., Bucheim, P., Channavasavanna, S. M., et al. (1994). The International Personality Disorder Examination: The World Health Organization/Alcohol, Drug Abuse, and Mental Health Administration international pilot study of personality disorders. *Archives of General Psychiatry, 51*(3), 215–224.

Markon, K. E., Krueger, R. F., & Watson, D. (2005). Delineating the structure of normal and abnormal personality: An integrative hierarchical approach. *Journal of Personality and Social Psychology, 88*(1), 139–157.

Mehlum, L., Tormoen, A. J., Ramberg, M., Haga, E., Diep, L. M., Laberg, S., et al. (2014). Dialectical behavior therapy for adolescents with repeated suicidal and self-harming behavior: A randomized trial. *Journal of the American Academy of Child and Adolescent Psychiatry, 53*(10), 1082–1091.

Mervielde, I., De Clercq, B., De Fruyt, F., & Van Leeuwen, K. (2005). Temperament, personality, and developmental psychopathology as childhood antecedents of personality disorders. *Journal of Personality Disorders, 19*(2), 171–201.

Mervielde, I., & De Fruyt, F. (1999). Construction of the Hierarchical Personality Inventory for Children (HiPIC). In I. J. Deary, F. De Fruyt, & F. Ostendorf (Eds.), *Personality psychology in Europe.* Tilburg, The Netherlands: Tilburg University Press.

Moran, P., Coffey, C., Chanen, A. M., Mann, A., Carlin, J. B., & Patton, G. C. (2011). The impact of childhood sexual abuse on personality disorder: An epidemiological study. *Psychological Medicine, 41*(6), 1311–1318.

Morey, L. C., Hopwood, C. J., Gunderson, J. G., Skodol, A. E., Shea, M. T., Yen, S., et al. (2007). Comparison of alternative models for personality disorders. *Psychological Medicine, 37*(7), 983–994.

Mrazek, P. J., & Haggerty, R. J. (1994). *Reducing risks for mental disorders: Frontiers for preventive intervention research.* Washington, DC: National Academy Press.

National Collaborating Centre for Mental Health. (2010). *Antisocial personality disorder: Treatment, management and prevention.* Leicester, UK: British Psychological Society.

Nelson, E. E., Leibenluft, E., McClure, E. B., & Pine, D. S. (2005). The social re-orientation of adolescence: A neuroscience perspective on the process and its relation to psychopathology. *Psychological Medicine, 35*(2), 163–174.

Newton-Howes, G., Clark, L. A., & Chanen, A. M. (2015). Personality disorder across the life course. *Lancet, 385*(9969), 727–734.

Newton-Howes, G., Tyrer, P., & Weaver, T. (2008). Social functioning of patients with personality disorder in secondary care. *Psychiatric Services, 59*(9), 1033–1037.

O'Connor, B. P. (2002). The search for dimensional structure differences between normality and abnormality: A statistical review of published data on personality and psychopathology. *Journal of Personality and Social Psychology, 83*(4), 962–982.

Olds, D. L. (2008). Preventing child maltreatment and crime with prenatal and infancy support of parents: The Nurse–Family Partnership. *Journal of Scandinavian Studies in Criminology and Crime Prevention, 9*(Suppl. 1), 2–24.

Olds, D. L., Sadler, L., & Kitzman, H. (2007). Programs for parents of infants and toddlers: Recent evidence from randomized trials. *Journal of Child Psychology and Psychiatry, 48*(3–4), 355–391.

Paris, J., Perlin, J., Laporte, L., Fitzpatrick, M., & DeStefano, J. (2014). Exploring resilience and borderline personality disorder: A qualitative study of pairs of sisters. *Personal Mental Health, 8*(3), 199–208.

Paus, T. (2005). Mapping brain maturation and cognitive development during adolescence. *Trends in Cognitive Science, 9*(2), 60–68.

Pincus, A. L., Ansell, E. B., Pimentel, C. A., Cain, N. M., Wright, A. G., & Levy, K. N. (2009). Initial construction and validation of the Pathological Narcissism Inventory. *Psychological Assessment, 21*(3), 365–379.

Poreh, A. M., Rawlings, D., Claridge, G., Freeman, J. L., Faulkner, C., & Shelton, C. (2006). The BPQ: A scale for the assessment of borderline personality based on DSM-IV criteria. *Journal of Personality Disorders, 20*(3), 247–260.

Raine, A. (1991). The SPQ: A scale for the assessment of schizotypal personality based on DSM-III-R criteria. *Schizophrenia Bulletin, 17*(4), 555–564.

Raine, A. (2006). Schizotypal personality: Neurodevelopmental and psychosocial trajectories. *Annual Review of Clinical Psychology, 2*(1), 291–326.

Ro, E., & Clark, L. A. (2013). Interrelations between psychosocial functioning and adaptive- and mal-

adaptive-range personality traits. *Journal of Abnormal Child Psychology, 122*(3), 822–835.

Roberts, B. W., & DelVecchio, W. F. (2000). The rank-order consistency of personality traits from childhood to old age: A quantitative review of longitudinal studies. *Psychological Bulletin, 126*(1), 3–25.

Roberts, B. W., Walton, K. E., & Viechtbauer, W. (2006). Patterns of mean-level change in personality traits across the life course: A meta-analysis of longitudinal studies. *Psychological Bulletin, 132*(1), 1–25.

Rossouw, T. I., & Fonagy, P. (2012). Mentalization-based treatment for self-harm in adolescents: A randomized controlled trial. *Journal of the American Academy of Child and Adolescent Psychiatry, 51*(12), 1304–1313.

Rothbart, M. K., & Bates, J. E. (2006). Temperament. In N. Eisenberg, W. Damon, & R. M. Lerner (Eds.), *Handbook of child psychology* (Vol. 3, pp. 99–166). Hoboken, NJ: Wiley.

Rutter, M. (2012). Psychopathy in childhood: Is it a meaningful diagnosis? *British Journal of Psychiatry, 200*(3), 175–176.

Rutter, M., Kim-Cohen, J., & Maughan, B. (2006). Continuities and discontinuities in psychopathology between childhood and adult life. *Journal of Child Psychology and Psychiatry, 47*(3–4), 276–295.

Samuel, D. B., & Widiger, T. A. (2008). A meta-analytic review of the relationships between the five-factor model and DSM-IV-TR personality disorders: A facet level analysis. *Clinical Psychology Review, 28*(8), 1326–1342.

Sawyer, A. M., Borduin, C. M., & Dopp, A. R. (2015). Long-term effects of prevention and treatment on youth antisocial behavior: A meta-analysis. *Clinical Psychology Review, 42,* 130–144.

Schulenberg, J. E., Sameroff, A. J., & Cicchetti, D. (2004). The transition to adulthood as a critical juncture in the course of psychopathology and mental health. *Development and Psychopathology, 16*(4), 799–806.

Schuppert, H. M., Giesen-Bloo, J., van Gemert, T., Wiersema, H., Minderaa, R., Emmelkamp, P., et al. (2009). Effectiveness of an emotion regulation group training for adolescents—a randomized controlled pilot study. *Clinical Psychology and Psychotherapy, 16*(6), 467–478.

Schuppert, H. M., Timmerman, M. E., Bloo, J., van Gemert, T. G., Wiersema, H. M., Minderaa, R. B., et al. (2012). Emotion regulation training for adolescents with borderline personality disorder traits: A randomized controlled trial. *Journal of the American Academy of Child and Adolescent Psychiatry, 51*(12), 1314–1323.

Shiner, R. L. (2009). The development of personality disorders: Perspectives from normal personality development in childhood and adolescence. *Development and Psychopathology, 21*(3), 715–734.

Shiner, R. L., & Tackett, J. L. (2014). Personality and personality disorders. In E. J. Mash & R. A. Barkley (Eds.), *Child psychopathology* (3rd ed., pp. 848–896). New York: Guilford Press.

Silk, K. R. (2016). Personality disorders in DSM-5: A commentary on the perceived process and outcome of the proposal of the Personality and Personality Disorders Work Group. *Harvard Review of Psychiatry, 24*(5), e15–e21.

Skodol, A. E. (2008). Longitudinal course and outcome of personality disorders. *Psychiatric Clinics of North America, 31*(3), 495–503, viii.

Skodol, A. E. (2014). Personality disorder classification: Stuck in neutral, how to move forward? *Current Psychiatry Reports, 16*(10), 480.

Skodol, A. E., Bender, D. S., Pagano, M. E., Shea, M. T., Yen, S., Sanislow, C. A., et al. (2007). Positive childhood experiences: Resilience and recovery from personality disorder in early adulthood. *Journal of Clinical Psychiatry, 68*(7), 1102–1108.

Skodol, A. E., Gunderson, J. G., Shea, M. T., McGlashan, T. H., Morey, L. C., Sanislow, C. A., et al. (2005). The Collaborative Longitudinal Personality Disorders Study (CLPS): Overview and implications. *Journal of Personality Disorders, 19*(5), 487–504.

Soto, C. J., John, O. P., Gosling, S. D., & Potter, J. (2011). Age differences in personality traits from 10 to 65: Big Five domains and facets in a large cross-sectional sample. *Journal of Personality and Social Psychology, 100*(2), 330–348.

Speranza, M., Pham-Scottez, A., Revah-Levy, A., Barbe, R. P., Perez-Diaz, F., Birmaher, B., et al. (2012). Factor structure of borderline personality disorder symptomatology in adolescents. *Canadian Journal of Psychiatry, 57*(4), 230–237.

Srivastava, S., John, O. P., Gosling, S. D., & Potter, J. (2003). Development of personality in early and middle adulthood: Set like plaster or persistent change? *Journal of Personality and Social Psychology, 84*(5), 1041–1053.

Steinberg, L. (2005). Cognitive and affective development in adolescence. *Trends in Cognitive Sciences, 9*(2), 69–74.

Stepp, S. D., Burke, J. D., Hipwell, A. E., & Loeber, R. (2012). Trajectories of attention deficit hyperactivity disorder and oppositional defiant disorder symptoms as precursors of borderline personality disorder symptoms in adolescent girls. *Journal of Abnormal Child Psychology, 40*, 7–20.

Stepp, S. D., Whalen, D. J., Pilkonis, P. A., Hipwell, A. E., & Levine, M. D. (2012). Children of mothers with borderline personality disorder: Identifying parenting behaviors as potential targets for intervention. *Personality Disorders, 3*(1), 76–91.

Stepp, S. D., Yu, L., Miller, J. D., Hallquist, M. N., Trull, T. J., & Pilkonis, P. A. (2012). Integrating competing dimensional models of personality: Linking the SNAP, TCI, and NEO using item response theory. *Personality Disorders, 3*(2), 107–126.

Stoffers, J. M., Vollm, B. A., Rucker, G., Timmer, A., Huband, N., & Lieb, K. (2012). Psychological therapies for people with borderline personality disorder. *Cochrane Database of Systematic Reviews, 8,* CD005652.

Tackett, J. L., Balsis, S., Oltmanns, T. F., & Krueger, R. F. (2009). A unifying perspective on personality pathology across the life span: Developmental considerations for the fifth edition of the *Diagnostic and Statistical Manual of Mental Disorders*. *Development and Psychopathology, 21*(3), 687–713.

Tackett, J. L., Herzhoff, K., Kushner, S. C., & Rule, N. (2016). Thin slices of child personality: Perceptual, situational, and behavioral contributions. *Journal of Personality and Social Psychology, 110,* 150–166.

Tackett, J. L., Herzhoff, K., Reardon, K., Smack, A., & Kushner, S. K. (2013). The relevance of informant discrepancies for the assessment of adolescent personality pathology. *Clinical Psychology: Science and Practice, 20,* 378–392.

Tackett, J. L., Kushner, S. C., De Fruyt, F., & Mervielde, I. (2013). Delineating personality traits in childhood and adolescence: Associations across measures, temperament, and behavioral problems. *Assessment, 20*(6), 738–751.

Tackett, J. L., Slobodskaya, H. R., Mar, R. A., Deal, J., Halverson, C. F., Baker, S. R., et al. (2012). The hierarchical structure of childhood personality in five countries: Continuity from early childhood to early adolescence. *Journal of Personality, 80*(4), 847–879.

Thatcher, D. L., Cornelius, J. R., & Clark, D. B. (2005). Adolescent alcohol use disorders predict adult borderline personality. *Addictive Behaviors, 30*(9), 1709–1724.

Tromp, N. B., & Koot, H. M. (2008). Dimensions of personality pathology in adolescents: Psychometric properties of the DAPP-BQ-A. *Journal of Personality Disorders, 22*(6), 623–638.

Tyrer, P., Crawford, M., & Mulder, R. T. (2011). Reclassifying personality disorders. *Lancet, 377*(9780), 1814–1815.

Tyrer, P., Crawford, M., Mulder, R. T., Blashfield, R., Farnam, A., Fossati, A., et al. (2011). The rationale for the reclassification of personality disorder in the 11th revision of the *International Classification of Diseases* (ICD-11). *Personality and Mental Health, 5*(4), 246–259.

Tyrer, P., Reed, G. M., & Crawford, M. J. (2015). Classification, assessment, prevalence, and effect of personality disorder. *Lancet, 385*(9969), 717–726.

Verbeke, L., & De Clercq, B. (2014). Integrating oddity traits in a dimensional model for personality pathology precursors. *Journal of Abnormal Psychology, 123*(3), 598–612.

Warner, M. B., Morey, L. C., Finch, J. F., Gunderson, J. G., Skodol, A. E., Sanislow, C. A., et al. (2004). The longitudinal relationship of personality traits and disorders. *Journal of Abnormal Psychology, 113*(2), 217–227.

Whalen, D. J., Scott, L. N., Jakubowski, K. P., McMakin, D. L., Hipwell, A. E., Silk, J. S., et al. (2014). Affective behavior during mother–daughter conflict and borderline personality disorder severity across adolescence. *Personality Disorders, 5*(1), 88–96.

World Health Organization. (1992). *International classification of diseases, version 10.* Geneva, Switzerland: Author.

Zanarini, M. C., Frankenburg, F. R., Hennen, J., Reich, D. B., & Silk, K. R. (2005). The McLean Study of Adult Development (MSAD): Overview and implications of the first six years of prospective follow-up. *Journal of Personality Disorders, 19*(5), 505–523.

Zanarini, M. C., Vujanovic, A., Parachini, E. A., Boulanger, J. L., Frankenburg, F. R., & Hennen, J. (2003a). A screening measure for BPD: The McLean Screening Instrument for Borderline Personality Disorder (MSI-BPD). *Journal of Personality Disorders, 17*(6), 568–573.

Zanarini, M. C., Vujanovic, A. A., Parachini, E. A., Boulanger, J. L., Frankenburg, F. R., & Hennen, J. (2003b). Zanarini Rating Scale for Borderline Personality Disorder (ZAN-BPD): A continuous measure of DSM-IV borderline psychopathology. *Journal of Personality Disorders, 17*(3), 233–242.

Zimmerman, M. E., Chelminski, I., & Young, D. (2008). The frequency of personality disorders in psychiatric patients. *Psychiatric Clinics of North America, 31*(3), 405–420, vi.

Zoccolillo, M., Pickles, A., Quinton, D., & Rutter, M. (1992). The outcome of childhood conduct disorder: Implications for defining adult personality disorder and conduct disorder. *Psychological Medicine, 22*(4), 971–986.

CHAPTER 33

Personality Development and Relationships in Adulthood

Jennifer M. Senia
M. Brent Donnellan

Together, Patti and I'd made one and one equal three. That's rock 'n' roll.

This new life revealed that I was more than a song, a story, a night, an idea, a pose, a truth, a shadow, a lie, a moment, a question, an answer, a restless figment of my own and others' imagination. . . . Work is work . . . but life . . . is life . . . and life trumps art . . . always.

—BRUCE SPRINGSTEEN (2016, p. 369)

In his 2016 autobiography, Bruce Springsteen details a turning point in his life that occurred around the time he turned 40. He was finally able to accept the emotional complexities—the joys and frustrations—of intimacy and parenthood. Prior to that time, Bruce had convinced himself that he could not endure family life. His anxieties about relationships partially stemmed from his own childhood experiences and troubled relationship with his father (who was eventually diagnosed with paranoid schizophrenia), as well as his own struggles with anxiety and depression. Collectively, these factors would negatively impact his close relationships.

As a self-proclaimed serial monogamist, he confessed that 2 years in a relationship was his personal limit. He would eventually experience suffocating claustrophobia from the implications of commitment and responsibility. These chronic feelings of fear, distrust, and insecurity were especially salient surrounding his first marriage to Julianne Phillips, from 1985 to 1989. During this marriage, Springsteen recalls a series of severe anxiety attacks in which he

acknowledged being "emotionally stunted and secretly unavailable" with her (2016, p. 351). Springsteen confesses to failing her as a partner.

After Springsteen's relationship with Julianne Phillips dissolved, he entered into a lasting marriage to Patti Scialfa that endures as of the writing of this chapter (both are now in their 60s). Bruce and Patti have raised three children together and seem to have achieved a supportive and satisfying union. Springsteen had sporadically bumped into Scialfa over a 17-year period before she joined the E-Street Band (Springsteen's primary band) in 1984. During the course of her time in the E-Street Band, Scialfa and Springsteen formed a deep personal connection, and they eventually married on June 8, 1991. The marriage seems to have ushered an important change in Springsteen as he reflected that

she was confident in us and that gave me confidence that we would be all right. Patti had changed my life in a way that no one else ever had. She inspired me to be a better man, turned the dial way down on my running while still leaving me room to move. She gave me my motorcycle-canyon-running Sundays when I needed them and always honored who I was. She took care of me perhaps more than I deserved. (Springsteen, 2016, p. 381)

This autobiographical account illustrates the important role that relationships hold in human lives and highlights that relationships are both shaped by personal characteristics and potentially able to alter the course of individual personality development. It also speaks to potentially idiosyncratic impacts of relationship. The relationship between Springsteen and Phillips did not endure and seems not to have impacted Springsteen as powerfully as the bond between Springsteen and Scialfa. Why some relationships last and others terminate, as well as why personal changes happen because of one close relationship and not another, are critical questions facing researchers interested in transactions between relationships and personality trait development.

To be sure, relationships are central to human development from infancy to old age (Reis, Collins, & Berscheid, 2000), and the formation of a stable romantic relationship is considered to be a major developmental task of young adulthood (Hutteman, Hennecke, Orth, Reitz, & Specht, 2014). Individuals spend considerable amounts of time in the presence of romantic partners in adulthood: Genadek, Flood, and Garcia-Roman (2016) estimated that individuals spent about 4 hours per day with their partner in the early years of the 21st century. Accordingly, the formation of a happy and stable romantic relationship is an important life goal for most individuals (Arnett, Trzesniewski, & Donnellan, 2013; Karney & Bradbury, 2005; Roberts & Robins, 2000), and relationship satisfaction is a strong correlate of overall life satisfaction and well-being (Heller, Watson, & Ilies, 2004; Proulx, Helms, & Buehler, 2007).

In light of these considerations about the importance of romantic unions, our goal in this chapter is to consider how adult personality trait development is associated with experiences in romantic relationships (see also Mund, Finn, Hagemeyer, & Neyer, 2016). We first consider broad themes in the personality development literature and tie these themes to experiences in relationships. We then consider how relationships are associated with consequential life outcomes such as health and well-being. In this

review, we introduce critical issues of selection versus environmental causation (sometimes called *socialization effects* in the literature) that are perennially relevant when thinking about personality traits and relationships. We then directly consider the state of the evidence about how personality characteristics are associated with relationships, and how relationship processes and events are associated with personality development.

Personality Development and Relationships

Personality development is a vibrant subarea as attested to by the chapters in this handbook. In addition to this volume, there are book-length treatments (e.g., McAdams, 2015), as well as a number of other handbook chapters and reviews (Caspi, Roberts, & Shiner, 2005; McAdams & Olson, 2010; Roberts, Donnellan, & Hill, 2013; Roberts, Wood, & Caspi, 2008). Corker and Donnellan (in press) highlighted four key themes in this burgeoning literature, and we consider their relevance for this chapter in this section.

1. *Individuality exists at multiple levels from dispositions to characteristic adaptations to life narratives (e.g., McAdams & Pals, 2006).* Although much of the recent personality development literature focuses on dispositional traits, there is no reason that the basic principles and various kinds of person–situation transactions discussed in this literature should be limited to traits. Other kinds of personality constructs such as characteristic adaptions, which reflect narrower and more specialized individual differences that are linked to specific contexts of life (e.g., attachment styles; Fraley & Shaver, 2000) and identity might be especially relevant to relationships (e.g., Aron & Aron, 1997). Our own research focuses primarily on traits, so this is our lens on the topic; however, the transactional mechanisms and interpersonal connections inherent in relationships might be especially relevant for characteristic adaptations and identity. Characteristic adaptations and identity might be more proximal to relationship processes than are traits and, indeed, some of the associations between traits and relationships might be mediated by these kinds of constructs.

2. *Individuality is present early in the lifespan, and these early emerging individual dif-*

ferences are predictive of later outcomes (e.g., Shiner & Caspi, 2003). Temperamental qualities evident in children at age 3 are associated with adult relationship variables at age 21 (Newman, Caspi, Moffitt, & Silva, 1997). Likewise, Shiner, Masten, and Roberts (2003) found that personality attributes assessed in middle childhood predicted romantic relationship outcomes at age 30. Findings from long-term developmental studies bolster the case that personality attributes are potential causal factor in relationship processes because of temporal precedence. The individual differences were evident well before the individuals were involved in adult romantic relationships. Admittedly, the effect sizes were modest, but this is to be expected given that relationships are multiply determined outcomes involving two individuals (see, e.g., Donnellan, Larsen-Rife, & Conger, 2005; Robins, Caspi, & Moffit, 2000). Nonetheless, such findings help to strengthen inferences about whether personality attributes have a truly causal impact on relationships.

3. *Personality development is characterized by coherence across the lifespan and by multiple kinds of stability and change.* Although the specific behavioral manifestations of underlying personality traits and processes may change with development (e.g., expression of aggressiveness in toddlers vs. teenagers), attributes such as aggression and shyness show consistency over the lifespan (e.g., Caspi, Elder, & Bem, 1988). Personality becomes more consistent with age when viewed from the perspective of test–retest correlations or rank-order consistency (e.g., Roberts & DelVecchio, 2000), whereas there is also absolute change in the direction of increased maturity in adulthood when considering absolute levels of traits (Caspi et al., 2005). Young adulthood appears to be an important time for personality trait maturation (Donnellan, Conger, & Burzette, 2007; Hopwood et al., 2011; Roberts, Caspi, & Moffitt, 2001). Young adulthood is also a time when the formation of romantic partnerships is an important developmental task (e.g., Hutteman et al., 2014), suggesting perhaps that personality maturation co-occurs with involvement in romantic unions.

4. *Person–situation interaction processes promote personality consistency and change.* Wrzus and Roberts (2017) provide an important summary of the person–situation processes that promote stability and change in person-

ality attributes (see also Buss, 1987; Scarr & McCartney, 1983). For, example evocative person–situation transactions in which the traits of an individual evoke predictable environmental responses (e.g., aggressive tendencies in both children and adults; Anderson, Buckley, & Carnagey, 2008; Anderson, Lytton, & Romney, 1986) tend to promote stability because of self-perpetuating cycles. Aggression evokes aggressive reactions in others, thereby helping to reinforce an individual's own aggressive tendencies. Shyness contributes to awkward interpersonal encounters, and such interactions are likely to create heightened anxieties about social interactions in the future. Likewise, selection effects whereby individuals choose environments consistent with their personality tend to promote stability (e.g., Kandler, 2012). In contrast, life transitions into contexts marked by clear social norms, and a press for a particular pattern of behavior tends to promote personality changes (Caspi & Moffit, 1993). Committed romantic relationships might be such a context given that norms exist for how partners should behave in socially sanctioned unions such as marriages.

Relationships and Consequential Life Outcomes

D. W. Winnicott (1960) famously noted that there is no such thing as an infant to capture the reality that infant survival is inexorably linked to the presence of caregivers. The importance of relationships, however, continues throughout the lifespan as individuals move beyond their families of origin to form intimate bonds with romantic partners. Involvement in adult relationships facilitates physical health and longevity (see Robles, Slatcher, Trombello, & McGinn, 2014). For example, a meta-analysis drawing on 148 independent studies (involving 308,849 individuals followed for an average of 7.5 years) indicated that social relationships are associated with reduced mortality (Holt-Lunstad, Smith, & Layton, 2010). Participants who maintained adequate social relationships demonstrated a 50% greater likelihood of survival in contrast to participants without adequate relationships. The statistical associations persisted when the researchers controlled for initial health status, cause of death, sex, and age. The authors even concluded that "the magnitude of [the relationship] effect is comparable with quitting smoking and it exceeds many [leading] risk factors for mortality" such as obesity and physical inactivity (Holt-Lunstad et al., 2010, p. 14).

A potentially important caveat to research concerning relationships and health is the possibility that the qualities of the relationship itself might prove more important than simply being involved in a relationship or not. Involvement in unhappy and unsatisfying relationships such as conflictual marriages seems detrimental to health and psychological well-being (Hawkins & Booth, 2005; Kamp Dush, & Amato, 2005; Kamp Dush, Taylor, & Kroeger, 2008; Robles et al., 2014). Such findings suggest that qualities of the relationship are an important moderator when considering how involvement in relationships is associated with consequential life outcomes (Kiecolt-Glaser & Wilson, 2017; see also Hudson, Lucas, & Donnellan, 2017). Likewise, the qualities of the romantic union might matter for how the relationship is associated with personality development, a topic we mentioned in the context of Bruce Springsteen's autobiographical recollections, and we touch on in the concluding sections of this chapter.

In addition to its associations with physical health, relationship quality is also associated with well-being. In a meta-analysis of 93 studies, Proulx and colleagues (2007) found that higher levels of marital quality were associated with higher levels of well-being and reduced symptoms of psychological distress such as depression and anxiety. These conclusions are consistent with earlier meta-analytic work by Heller and colleagues (2004) pointing to a strong association between overall life satisfaction and relationships satisfaction. An interesting recent study used diary data from a nationally sample to evaluate how time spent with partners was associated with well-being variables (Flood & Genadek, 2016). Consistent with research using global assessments of interaction and well-being, individuals reported greater happiness in activities with their spouse relative to time spent apart. Individuals were 1.8 times more likely to report being very happy when they were with their spouse than when they were not. In addition, activities with a spouse were considered to be 1.5 times as meaningful relative to activities spent apart. These findings highlight the fact that time spent with romantic partners is associated with momentary reports of well-being and a sense of meaning in life. All told, the existing literature suggests that relationship experiences are important predictors of overall psychological health and functioning.

In summary, the literature about the correlates of relationships supports a blanket generalization that involvement in satisfying romantic relationships is associated with a number of positive outcomes. Some have even suggested that high-quality relationships can contribute to long-term thriving (e.g., Feeney & Collins, 2015). Indeed, adults in long-term committed relationships have greater social support, more financial resources, greater life satisfaction, increased longevity, and higher levels of both physical and mental health than do single adults (Waite & Gallagher, 2002). However, it is possible that gender moderates some of these associations, with some work suggesting that the benefits of relationships are stronger for women (Kiecolt-Glaser & Newton, 2001), others finding them stronger for men (Gardner & Oswald, 2004; Umberson, 1992), and still other studies reporting small or nonsignificant differences (Proulx et al., 2007; Robles et al., 2014). Accordingly, we revisit the issue of gender when considering how relationships might be associated with personality trait development.

The associations between relationships and outcomes naturally raise questions about causality. Two general perspectives are relevant when attempting to interpret the literature about relationships and outcomes. The *social experience hypothesis* suggests that relationship experiences cause health and well-being. Consider that married individuals tend to live longer than their single counterparts (Waite & Gallagher, 2002). This may be attributable to a number of mechanisms related to what happens within marital relationships. Married partners might encourage each other to lead healthier lives by promoting healthy activities and actively discouraging risky or unhealthy activities. Spouses may also monitor each other for signs of morbidity and may help to ensure compliance with instructions from health care providers. These experiential processes would likely promote longevity. On the other hand, individuals (and their partners) select themselves both into and out of relationships. Individuals with health risks (and therefore a propensity to die younger) may not get married or stay married. Thus, reported associations between relationships and outcomes such as longevity might be reflections of unmeasured preexisting differences that predict both involvement in relationships and the outcome in question. This is known as the *selection hypothesis* (e.g., Foster, 2010) and it is a major alternative explanation to any account that claims that relationship experiences simply cause better outcomes. Personality traits are relevant to these arguments as the same traits that are associated with satisfying and stable relationships are also associated with health, wealth, and well-being (see, e.g., Ozer & Benet-Martínez, 2006; Roberts, Kuncel, Shiner, Caspi, & Goldberg, 2007; see also Hampson, Chapter 28, this volume).

Empirical support is available for both explanations, and reviewers of the literature frequently note that the underlying causal dynamics deserve further scrutiny (Braithwaite & Holt-Lunstad, 2017). The big challenge boils down to design. Researchers can't simply assign participants to the married or single conditions for ethical and practical reasons. Fortunately, other options may help to constrain the kinds of causal inferences about the connections between relationships and outcomes.

The matched control groups design (e.g., van Scheppingen et al., 2016; Wagner, Becker, Lüdtke, & Trautwein, 2015) tries to equate groups on preexisting differences before considering how relationship experiences are associated with outcomes. The basic idea is to use statistical techniques to rule out possible "third variable" accounts. The major concern with this approach is whether adequate measures exist to account for all possible confounds. This concern is often unsurmountable given the limits of data collection and the myriad possible third variables. Fortunately, twin designs might prove especially useful for dealing with these concerns (see e.g., Bleidorn, Hopwood, & Lucas, 2018).

Indeed, twin designs are showing increasing promise for understanding how involvement in relationships might be causally related to behaviors, particularly externalizing-related problems. For example, Dinescu and colleagues (2016) analyzed 2,425 same-sex monozygotic (MZ) and dizygotic (DZ) twin pairs to compare alcohol consumption among married, single, divorced, and cohabiting twins. This design allowed researchers to test, for example, whether identical twins (i.e., individuals with the same genetic propensity for drinking) with different partnership status had different patterns of drinking. In many ways, this approach provides a comprehensive way to control preexisting differences given that identical twins reared in the same family of origin have the same genes and were exposed to similar developmental experiences (e.g., socioeconomic status [SES], neigh-

borhoods, qualities of the relationships of their parents).

Dinescu and colleagues (2106) found that preexisting group differences accounted for some of the differences in self-reported drinking frequency. Individuals who drank less frequently were more likely to be married; in contrast, the individuals who drank more frequently were more likely to remain single. However, their analyses also demonstrated that marriage had an independent, protective effect on drinking quantity ("How many drinks of alcohol do you have on a typical day when you are drinking?") and that effect was greater in men than in women (echoing our caveat about gender as a moderator of relationship effects). This study offers some of the best evidence to date that marriage is likely to have a causal effect on health behaviors (Dinescu et al., 2016). A conceptually similar result was reported by Burt and colleagues (2010), who used a twin design to study the association between marriage and antisocial behavior in young men. Consistent with selection effect accounts, they found that less antisocial men were more likely to marry than more antisocial men. However, they also found evidence that marriage itself seems to inhibit antisocial behavior in men given that unmarried twins were often more antisocial compared to their married co-twin.

These recent genetically informed studies provide hints that there is merit in both the social experience and selection perspectives. This is important when considering transactional dynamics between personality and relationships: Traits may help shape relationship processes (a selection type effect), and relationship experiences may influence trait development in adulthood (a social experience effect). We now turn to a review of the literature concerning the association between personality traits and relationships, as this association has been studied far more often in the literature than the idea that relationships are associated with trait development and change (e.g., Mund et al., 2016; Neyer, Mund, Zimmermann, & Wrzus, 2014).

Personality Traits Are Associated with Characteristics of Relationships

Classic research by Terman and Buttenweiser (1935) implicated personality traits in the development of marital satisfaction (see also Kelly & Conley, 1987), and interest in this topic has continued to the present day, particularly following the reinvigoration of the trait construct in personality research (e.g., Dyrenforth, Kashy, Donnellan, & Lucas, 2010; Humbad, Donnellan, Iacono, & Burt, 2010a; Karney & Bradbury, 1995; Malouff, Thorsteinsson, Schutte, Bhullar, & Rooke, 2010; Robins et al., 2000; Watson, Hubbard, & Wiese, 2000). Researchers typically distinguish between two kinds of associations in this literature: *actor effects* and *partner effects*. These terms originate from the terminology used in a popular statistical technique applied to data from couples—the actor–partner interdependence model (APIM; Kenny, Kashy, & Cook, 2006). An actor effect captures associations between an individual's personality attributes and *his or her own* thoughts, feelings, and behaviors in relationships. An actor effect would occur, for example, if dispositional tendencies toward high negative affectivity lead individuals to view their own relationship as relatively unstable and unsatisfying. Partner effects capture association between one individual's personality attributes and the thoughts, feelings, and behaviors of *his or her relationship partners*. Partner effects might represent evocative processes, for example, when high levels of negative affectivity create feelings of dissatisfaction in partners. We must emphasize that the term *effect* in the context of the APIM strictly refers to statistical effects and is not meant necessarily to imply causality.

Heller and colleagues (2004) conducted a meta-analysis of the associations between the Big Five trait domains and relationship satisfaction. This was essentially an analysis of actor effects given the designs of the underlying studies (e.g., self-reports of personality and self-reports of relationship satisfaction). Heller and colleagues reported that low neuroticism, high agreeableness, and high conscientiousness had the largest associations with relationship satisfaction among the Big Five domains (meta-analytic r's between .22 and .26). Other associations were below |.20| with extraversion being a stronger correlate of relationship satisfaction than openness. Malouff and colleagues (2010) specifically examined how the Big Five domains are related to partner effects using meta-analytic techniques and found that the strongest associations were for neuroticism, followed by agreeableness and conscientiousness.

Studies that use the APIM are generally consistent with the conclusions from these two meta-analytic reviews (e.g., Donnellan, Assad, Robins, & Conger, 2007; Dyrenforth et al., 2010; Humbad et al., 2010a; Orth, 2013). The Big Five traits that are most relevant to relationships are likely to be neuroticism/negative affectivity, agreeableness, and conscientiousness because these traits have the clearest conceptual linkages with interpersonal processes and distress. Interestingly, actor effects are often larger than partner effects in this literature (e.g., Dyrenforth et al., 2010). However, this conclusion might be a reflection that shared method biases often inflate the actor effects relative to partner effects in most designs (Orth, 2013). Most studies using the APIM also use self-reports to assess both personality traits and relationship satisfaction. Orth found that actor and partner effects were more similar in size when self- and partner reports of personality were used in latent variable models. Thus, conclusions about the relative size of actor and partner effects might need to be tempered until additional methodologically sophisticated studies involving multiple measures of personality traits have been published.

The existence of actor and partner effects for personality attributes and relationship satisfaction naturally raise questions about intervening processes; that is, how and why are the personality characteristics of individuals related to their global reports of relationship satisfaction? The vulnerability–stress–adaptation (VSA) model proposed by Karney and Bradbury (1995) is commonly invoked to explain how relatively distal personal characteristics are related to interpersonal couple processes such as day-to-day interactions and adaptations to factors such as economic difficulties, problematic children, or other stressors (e.g., Dyrenforth et al., 2010; Humbad et al., 2010a; Solomon & Jackson, 2014). According to the VSA model, personality attributes serve as either enduring vulnerabilities or protective factors depending on how the traits relate to interpersonal processes. Likewise, Huston and Houts (1998) suggested that personality is part of the so-called "psychological infrastructure" of relationships.

Consistent with the VSA and related accounts, a number of studies have indicated that personality traits predict variables reflecting interpersonal interactions within relationships, including observer reports of couple interactions (e.g., Bradbury & Fincham, 1988; Caughlin, Huston, & Houts, 2000; Donnellan, Conger, & Bryant, 2004; Donnellan et al., 2005; Hatton et al., 2008). Studies using observer reports typically record couple interactions and have trained research assistants code the observations for the presence of hostility and supportive exchanges. This provides a methodological rigorous test of hypotheses given that observer reports are an alternative method for assessing interactions. Traits may also influence the kinds of stressors that couples must face, as there are indications that traits are related to exposure to economic challenges (e.g., Donnellan, Conger, McAdams, & Neppl, 2009; Moffitt et al., 2011; Roberts, Caspi, & Moffitt, 2003) and risks for infidelity (e.g., Buss & Shackelford, 1997; Schmitt, 2004). In short, interpersonal processes and exposure to stressful conditions are potential mediators of the associations between personality traits and relationship quality and stability. Personality traits may then predict divorce because of how traits contribute to overall relationship quality (Solomon & Jackson, 2014).

A related issue that generates attention in the literature concerns how personality trait similarity is associated with relationship quality (e.g., Dyrenforth et al., 2010; Gonzaga, Campus, & Bradbury, 2007; Humbad, Donnellan, Iacono, McGue, & Burt, 2013; Luo et al., 2008; Robins et al., 2000). This topic also generates popular interest because it is related to claims made by online dating services about the importance of matching partners on personality attributes (Finkel, Eastwick, Karney, Reis, & Sprecher, 2012). Unfortunately, defining couple similarity in terms of personality raises a number of conceptual and statistical complexities (see e.g., Humbad et al., 2013; Kenny et al., 2006; Wood & Furr, 2016).

For example, when considering similarity, should it be defined as similar mean levels on particular traits (e.g., similarly low levels of agreeableness) or as a similar trait "profile" by considering congruence across a range of traits (e.g., similarity in Big Five profiles)? These considerations introduce analytic flexibility and contribute to inflated false-positive rates because researchers can perform many statistical tests by defining similarity in different ways and focusing attention on results that pass the so-called "statistical significance" filter (e.g., Gelman & Weakliem, 2009). Some of the positive findings in the field might be statistical artifacts related to insufficient controls for the actor and partner effects of traits (see Dyrenforth et al., 2010; Humbad et al., 2013) or to complexities when profile correlations are used to index personality profile similarity (Wood & Furr, 2016). There are also theoretical issues that

are important to consider. What does it mean psychologically for couples to have a similar (or dissimilar) trait profile, and why would that matter for relationships? Why would similarity for seemingly negative traits like antagonism (i.e., low agreeableness) matter for relationships instead of, say, interactive effects? These seemingly basic questions are not well addressed in the literature.

To be blunt, caution is needed when interpreting the existing literature about the role of personality trait similarity in relationships. Well-replicated and theoretically grounded findings are difficult to identify, and we are not optimistic that trait similarity is especially important once actor and partner effects of traits are taken into account (Dyrenforth et al., 2010). If there is an effect of similarity, it is likely to be quite small relative to actor and partner effects. Online dating services do not typically reveal their proprietary matching algorithms, so it is unclear whether their procedures are exceptions to this generalization. We are skeptical (see also Finkel et al., 2012).

Questions about the association between personality trait similarity and relationship quality also raise more foundational questions about just the degree of personality similarity within couples (e.g., assortative mating; Gattis, Berns, Simpson, & Christensen, 2004; McCrae & Costa, 2008; Rammstedt, Spinath, Richter, & Schupp, 2013; Watson, Beer, & McDade-Montez, 2014; Watson et al., 2004) and whether couples become more similar in their personalities over time (i.e., convergence; Caspi, Herbener, & Ozer, 1992; Gonzaga, Carter, & Buckwalter, 2010; Humbad, Donnellan, Iacono, McGue, & Burt, 2010b). There is some evidence of similarity in traits, but coefficients tend to fall below .35 at the level of the broad Big Five domains (see Watson et al., 2004). However, coefficients might be higher for certain personality facets, especially those related to the value domains of openness (McCrae & Costa, 2008; see also Humbad et al., 2010b). One tentative observation is that those trait domains that veer closer to measures of political and religious attitudes or values tend to have higher assortative mating coefficients than trait domains related to affective tendencies and general self-regulatory processes. Indeed, couple similarity for attitudes and values often produce coefficients above .60 (e.g., Watson et al., 2004).

In short, couples might be more matched on values and attitudes than broad personality dispositions. This possibility relates to our opening points about different levels of individuality. One way to think about different levels of individuality is by invoking the idea of an individual as both a social actor and a motivated agent drawing on distinctions in McAdams (2015). Under this model, traits characterize the social actor (how one behaves) and characteristic adaptations such as values, goals, and attitudes characterize the motivated agent because these attributes channel behavior toward specific expressions and end states. Individuals might consciously pair with other individuals with who share similar motivations and values but not necessarily with similar dispositions toward emotional expression and regulation. Similarity on values and goals might matter more to people than similarity on broad Big Five tendencies that are not strongly contextualized.

Indeed, it is likely that assortative mating coefficients reflect selection (i.e., similar people select each other as relationship partners) and sorting processes (people tend to interact with similar others) rather than experiential processes whereby individuals become more similar over time due to mutual influence or shared environmental effects. This conclusion is based on the fact the convergence of personality traits over time appears to be generally minimal for intact couples (e.g., Caspi et al., 1992; Gonzaga et al., 2010; Rammstedt et al., 2013; Senia, Donnellan, Clark, Neppl, & Wickrama, 2017); that is, more established couples do not seem to be appreciably more similar in terms in terms of individual differences than newly established couples. However, additional longitudinal research with large samples following long spans of time is needed to ensure that this is a robust conclusion.

In summary, personality traits appear to be a factor in whether romantic relationships are satisfying or dissatisfying and whether the overall union is stable. An individual's personality is related to how he or she acts toward a partner and his or her global judgments of relationship satisfaction. Likewise, an individual's personality is related to the behaviors and global judgments of romantic partners likely because traits can evoke responses in others. A hostile individual might evoke hostility from a partner. These partner effects are particularly interesting, as they suggest that personality attributes have interpersonal consequences. Interestingly, couples that stay together do not seem to grow more alike in terms of their personalities beyond

initial levels of similarity. These findings are generally well established in the literature and provide a firm foundation for concluding that personality is relevant for close relationships. We now turn to the flip side of the transactional perspective on personality and relationships by considering whether and how relationship experiences impact personality trait development.

Relationships and Personality Development

Before reviewing specific findings, it is important to be realistic about both the nature of the existing literature and the strength of the associations between relationships and personality trait development. Reviews of personality and relationship transactions often conclude that there is more empirical support in favor of personality effects on relationships than vice versa (e.g., Mund et al., 2016). Part of this imbalance may be due to prior assumptions that traits are so stable that it would pointless to include multiple assessments of traits in longitudinal studies of adults (see e.g., Roberts & Pomerantz, 2004). If traits don't change, it is hard to justify expending time and effort on multiple assessments. Such decisions naturally prevented researchers from testing whether relationship experiences predict trait development. This situation is changing, mostly because of accumulating evidence that personality traits can and do change across the lifespan (e.g., Roberts, Walton, & Viechtbauer, 2006; Roberts et al., 2017). Thus, more and more studies have begun to evaluate connections between traits and relationships (Lehnart, Neyer, & Eccles, 2010; Mroczek & Spiro, 2003; Neyer & Lehnart, 2007; Specht, Egloff, & Schmukle, 2011; Wagner et al., 2015). One complication, however, is that these recent studies often cover different phases of the lifespan and focus on different intervals of time. Given this heterogeneity, it can be difficult to draw clear conclusions from the existing literature because so few studies address the exact same issues.

There are also methodological reasons as to why it has been difficult to find consistent evidence that relationship experiences are related to personality development, ranging from issues of trait stability to concerns about measurement to modeling strategies. One issue is that traits are fairly stable in adulthood. Stability coefficients are often large compared to most effects in the literature, and changes can often take years to discern. This reality is behind the assumption that traits did not change. Indeed, Neyer and Asendorpf (2001) suggested that "personality traits of young adults are already so much stabilized that personality effects on relationships have a clear primacy over relationship effects on personality" (p. 1200). Finding evidence of relationship effects requires sample sizes large enough to detect what are likely to be small effect sizes. Beyond the reality that personality traits are relatively stable by adulthood, many existing studies often focus on the broad domains of the Big Five, whereas researchers might have more success finding relationship effects if they focused on narrower facets of personality (Mund & Neyer, 2014). These narrower dispositions probably have closer connections to relationship experiences than the broad trait domain.

A final consideration has to do with transitions and timing. It might be the case that transitions into and out of relationships (e.g., forming a relationship, marrying, or ending a relationship) have the strongest effects on personality trait development. Thus, research designs need to be sensitive to changes in partnership status and likely need to follow participants over long intervals (Finn, Mitte, & Neyer, 2015; Neyer et al., 2014). The complication is that people pair off and separate at different times, so large sample sizes are needed to provide enough transitions so that analyses have enough statistical power to prove informative.

In summary, there is increasing interest in considering how relationship experiences are related to personality development. Table 33.1 provides a brief overview. However, this is a relatively new area of research, and there are methodological complexities in the existing database. In light of these caveats, the conclusions and observations presented in this section of the chapter should be considered fairly tentative. We structure this review around four considerations: relationship quality and trait development, experiencing a first serious partnership, relationship status changes (e.g., separations and divorce), and personality trait development in the context of enduring relationships.

Relationship Quality

Although the topic is inherently interesting, there is limited empirical evidence to suggest that relationship quality may exert influences on personality development. Scollon and Die-

ner (2006) followed a sample of Australian participants (ages 16–70 at the first wave) across 8 years. They examined correlations between changes in personality traits (i.e., neuroticism and extraversion) and changes in role satisfaction (i.e., relationship satisfaction) among two groups (participants under age 30 vs. those over age 30) using latent growth modeling. Increased relationship satisfaction over the study period predicted decreases in neuroticism and marginal increases in extraversion. Moreover, the correlated changes were similar for both groups, suggesting that associations between relationship quality and personality held beyond the effects of age (Scollon & Diener, 2006). Few other studies have addressed this question with reasonable sample sizes.

First Serious Partnership Experiences

Much of the nascent empirical evidence about personality trait development and relationships centers on personality trait change after entering a first romantic partnership. Neyer and Asendorpf (2001) followed a sample of young German adults (ages 18–30 at time 1) for 4 years. They found that individuals who entered into a romantic partnership, relative to individuals who remained single, reported increases in conscientiousness, extraversion, and self-esteem, as well as decreases in their neuroticism and shyness. After collecting a third wave of additional data in the same longitudinal study, Neyer and Lehnart (2007) replicated many of these findings. Again, they found that those individuals who began a first romantic partnership had increases in self-reported extraversion and self-esteem, as well as lasting decreases in their neuroticism and shyness.

Lehnart and colleagues (2010) tested connections between relationships and trait development in a sample of adults from the United States. They found that individuals who entered a romantic partnership reported decreases in neuroticism-related traits (e.g., social anxiety and depressive symptoms), whereas participants who remained single over the study period showed fairly stable levels of neuroticism. However, they did not find evidence of effects for other aspects of neuroticism, such as anger and impulsivity. This further underscores the more recent suggestion (Mund & Neyer, 2014) that researchers should perhaps focus on narrower attributes rather than broad domains. The researchers also found that participants who re-

TABLE 33.1. Summary of Relationship Experiences and Personality Trait Development

First partnership	• Associated with decreases in neuroticism (Neyer & Asendorpf, 2001; Neyer & Lehnart, 2007; Wagner et al., 2015). • The statistical effects might be stronger for aspects of neuroticism related to depression and social anxiety than impulsivity and anger (Lehnart et al., 2010). • Increases in extraversion (Neyer & Asendorpf, 2001; Neyer & Lehnart, 2007; Wagner et al., 2015). • Personality changes (particularly lasting decreases in neuroticism) tend to persist even if first partnership dissolves.
Marriage	• Mixed findings. Might be associated with decreases in neuroticism (for men; Mroczek & Spiro, 2003) and decreases in extraversion, openness, agreeableness for married versus not married (Specht et al., 2011).
Separation and divorce	• Mixed findings for separation. Might be associated with increases in agreeableness (Specht et al., 2011) and increases in openness for men only (Specht et al., 2011). • Mixed findings for divorce. • The impact of relationship exits may depend upon the qualities of the dissolved relationship.
Widowhood	• Decreases in conscientiousness for women, increases in conscientiousness for men (Specht et al., 2011). • Increases in neuroticism, but the effects may mitigate with time (Mroczek & Spiro, 2003). • Many findings difficult to replicate (Chopik, 2018). • Widowhood might disrupt rank-order stability of personality (Chopik, 2018), perhaps by introducing environmental instability into an individual's life.

mained single over the entire study period reported declines in self-esteem (Lehnart et al., 2010). Such a finding may suggest that having no involvement in romantic relationships may impact feelings of self-worth.

Wagner and colleagues (2015) used propensity score matching techniques to test the effects of the first partnership experience on personality trait change and replicated some of the earlier findings in the literature. Specifically, participants who transitioned from being single to a first romantic partnership showed an increase in self-reported life satisfaction. In addition, participants who had their first partnership experience between the ages of 23 and 25 reported lower levels of neuroticism and higher levels of conscientiousness, extraversion, and self-esteem. However, these findings were not evident in individuals who established their first partnership between the ages of 21 and 23. This may suggest that the impact of first partnership experiences on personality development may depend itself on the timing of the partnership in the life course.

One of the interesting results that seems to emerge from the studies examining how first partnership is related to personality development is that the observed changes seem to persist even if the partnership was dissolved (Neyer & Asendorpf, 2001; Neyer & Lehnart, 2007). In other words, just having had the experience of involvement in a committed relationship may motivate personality maturation even if that particular union breaks up. Moreover, Neyer and Asendorpf compared the personality change of the young adults in their sample who eventually got married with those who stayed in a relationship without marrying. None of the comparisons were statistically significant, so they concluded that it was the partnership formation, not marriage specifically, that was predictive of personality development.

One qualification is that findings about the potential impact of marriage might be somewhat conditional based on the broader sociocultural context given that the meaning, timing, and norms regarding marriages differ across cultures (Dixon, 1971; Kalmijn, 2007). Marriage might be more or less influential depending on how it is constructed and supported by the larger culture. It might also take long intervals of time to detect the influence of marriage on personality trait development (Senia et al., 2017). An additional caveat is that the conclusions about the apparently positive impact of first partnership might not hold if the first committed relationship turns out to be emotionally or physically abusive.

Taken together, there are indications that involvement in the first committed partnership is associated with personality development, particularly with respect to decreases in some elements of neuroticism. It may be that involvement in a first partnership promotes relatively lasting psychological changes in terms of feeling accepted by another person, and this sense of security provides a context for acquiring further emotion regulation skills. A first union might also promote self-reflection and identity changes that promote longer-term emotional stability. These and other explanations need to be tested in subsequent studies. Likewise, as noted earlier, more work is needed to understand personality trait development for those individuals who find themselves in emotionally and physically abusive committed relationships.

Relationship Status Changes

Specht and colleagues (2011) examined how specific relationship events, such as getting married, separated, divorced, or widowed, were related to personality trait development in a large-scale German panel study covering a 4-year interval. Individuals who married experienced mean-level decreases in extraversion, openness, and agreeableness (Specht et al., 2011). Mroczek and Spiro (2003) found that getting married or remarried was associated with declines in neuroticism for middle-aged older men in the Normative Aging Study, a sample of veterans from World War II and the Korean War.

In terms of ending relationships, Specht and colleagues (2011) found that individuals who separated or divorced reported increases in agreeableness. Men who separated from their partner reported increases in openness; however, there were no such effects in women related to openness. Conscientiousness increased for both men and women who divorced. Costa, Herbst, McCrae, and Siegler (2000) used a large sample of participants in their 40s and found that divorced women exhibited modest increases in extraversion and openness relative to women who remained married. Divorced men showed

modest increases in dimensions of neuroticism, as well as decreases in conscientiousness. More recently, Allemand, Hill, and Lehmann (2015) tested the association between divorce and personality trait change in middle-aged German adults over a 12-year interval. Participants who experienced divorce tended to decrease in extraversion and in lower-order traits of extraversion (i.e., positive affect), as well as in a lower-order trait of conscientiousness (i.e., dependability), compared to nondivorced participants. They did not find evidence of an association between divorce and changes in neuroticism. Thus, there are indications that relationship endings are associated with trait changes. The caveat, again, is that that the impact of relationship dissolution is probably conditional, based on the characteristics of the union prior to its termination.

A few longitudinal studies have examined the effects of losing a spouse on personality trait change. Specht and colleagues (2011) found that following the death of a spouse, conscientiousness increased for men, whereas it decreased for women in their German sample. Mroczek and Spiro (2003) found that widowhood increased neuroticism shortly after the death of spouse in a longitudinal sample of men. However, there were also indications that some of the increase was transitory. A similar pattern was detected by Lucas, Clark, Georgellis, and Diener (2003), who found that widowhood is associated with long-term declines in life satisfaction but that the drop in life satisfaction was most pronounced immediately following the loss. A recent preregistered analysis of two panel studies suggested that there are no consistent mean-level changes associated with widowhood; however, rank-order trait consistency was lower for those who lost a spouse compared to those who did not (Chopik, 2018). This suggests that the loss of spouse might serve as an environmental disruption that contributes to personality instability. Some individuals increase on particular traits, whereas other decrease.

In summary, there are indications that relationship events are associated with personality trait changes when considering first partnership, marriage, divorce, and widowhood. The finding that neuroticism declines with the experience of first partnership appear to be the most robust. Such a finding might follow from social investment theory (SIT; e.g., Roberts & Wood, 2006). SIT proposes that investment in new social roles promotes personality changes because of the internalization of new ways of thinking, feeling, and behaving that accompany a specific role. The role of being a committed partner might entail expectations about emotional equanimity and maturity. Other kinds of relationship events might have more idiosyncratic consequences relative to personality that depend on the characteristics of the relationship itself (e.g., the impact of divorce, if any, may depend on the qualities of the marriage). This point is echoed in the opening vignette describing Springsteen's experiences in his second marriage.

Another relationship transition that deserves attention is becoming a parent. Parenthood would seem to involve particular role expectations, yet one of the more rigorous investigations of the effects of the transition to parenthood on personality change yielded largely null results (van Scheppingen et al., 2016; but see Bleidorn et al., 2016, for evidence of parenthood effects for self-esteem development in women). However, the transition to parenthood might also be complicated by characteristics of the child (some children are easier than others) and the relationship with the other parent. Thus, additional work is needed to determine how the transition to parenthood is related to trait development.

Personality Trait Development and Enduring Relationships

As we suggested in the section about relationships and outcomes, there is evidence that relationship experiences and partners themselves exert social control on the behaviors of partners when it comes to externalizing tendencies and substance use. There is also evidence that depression and cognitive vulnerabilities to depression can act like social contagion in dyads (e.g., Haeffel & Hames, 2014; Johnson, Galambos, Finn, Neyer, & Horn, 2017). Similar processes might extend to personality traits as some have speculated that social learning in dyads and related socialization processes might explain some adult personality changes (e.g., Roberts et al., 2013).

Senia and colleagues (2017) followed a sample of over 200 intact couples across an interval of 25 years. They replicated previous findings about adult personality trait development in this sample, in that the participants showed mean level increases in conscientiousness and decreases in neuroticism (similar to Roberts et al., 2006) and exhibited a high degree of

rank-order stability over a long interval of time (e.g., stability coefficients above .60; similar to those in Roberts & DelVecchio, 2000). They used a modified form of the APIM (Kenny et al., 2006) to test whether there were partner effects for personality. Specifically, they evaluated whether an individual's trait levels at the initial assessment related to his or her partner's personality traits 25 years in the future, controlling for baseline levels. They found evidence for partner effects for wives but not husbands for three traits—neuroticism, conscientiousness, and agreeableness. It appeared that the personality attributes of wives were related to the husband's future trait levels, but husbands did not have prospective influences on wives for the Big Five domains.

The Senia and colleagues (2017) results need to be replicated, but they offer some intriguing evidence for dyadic effects in terms of personality in long-term marriages. This finding might also fit with the spousal social control literature when conceptualizing relationships and health (August & Sorkin, 2010; Umberson, Crosnoe, & Reczek, 2010). *Spousal social control* occurs when one member attempts to regulate behaviors of his or her partner, directly or indirectly, by instilling social norms of healthy behavior and discouraging unhealthy behavior (Craddock, vanDellen, Novak, & Ranby, 2015). Neuroticism, conscientiousness, and agreeableness showed partner effects, and these three traits are the ones most consistently associated with success in adult roles (see Roberts et al., 2007). These three traits are also the indicators of the *stability or alpha metatrait* (DeYoung, Peterson, & Higgins, 2002; Digman, 1997), a higher-order construct that has been linked with effective social functioning. Interestingly, the social control literature suggests that wives are more likely to exert social control over husbands than vice versa (Lewis & Butterfield, 2007; Rook, August, Stephens, & Franks, 2011; Umberson, 1992). This might explain the gendered results observed in Senia and colleagues (2017). Nonetheless, it is important to emphasize that the effect sizes were small (e.g., standardized coefficients between .10 and .15) and the time span was long. The kinds of developmental effects on spousal traits might take years to accumulate. With such caveats in mind, we suspect that some personality trait development might occur in the context of long-term marriages, especially when considering effects from wives to husbands.

Conclusions

The personality development literature suggests that traits are relatively enduring attributes that show predictable patterns of stability and change across the lifespan. This literature highlights the importance of the interplay between people and their social contexts, such that personality helps to shape social contexts, and social contexts might also shape personality development. Relationships are a critical social context and, indeed, some writers suggest relationships are the most important context for human lives. Thus, personality–relationship transactions are an emerging topic of interest.

We have concluded that there are good reasons to suspect that personality traits influence the conditions of relationships largely by influencing how couples handle interpersonal stress and by the kinds of stressors that couples face. At the same time, relationship experiences might also influence personality development. The evidence that involvement in a first significant romantic union is related to declines in neuroticism seems especially robust. Other conclusions are more speculative because of the nature of the existing literature. Quite simply, more research is needed on these topics before firm conclusions may be drawn. However, we think there are good reasons to expect that relationships may influence personality development given related work about the general impact of relationships on life outcomes. Future research on transactional relations between personality and relationships should fine-tune *how* these effects occur (by testing for mediating and moderating mechanisms), *when* they occur developmentally, and for *whom* the effects are stronger.

We close by returning to the opening case study of Bruce Springsteen. It is clear that his own life story carves out an important role for his relationship with Patti Scialfa. He sees his marriage and the formation of a family with Patti as a major factor in the development of his own personality and sense of self. The narrative he provided underscores the centrality of close relationships for human development. His story also highlights an important consideration when thinking about relationships and personality development. Springsteen was married twice in a relatively short period of time, and these two relationships differed in terms of their qualities and longevity. These two relationship seem to have had a profoundly different influence on

his personality development and life story. This fact highlights the importance of understanding the ins and outs of particular close relationships when attempting to study why, how, and even whether romantic relationships are associated with personality trait development.

REFERENCES

Allemand, M., Hill, P. L., & Lehmann, R. (2015). Divorce and personality development across middle adulthood. *Personal Relationships, 22,* 122–137.

Anderson, C. A., Buckley, K. E., & Carnagey, N. L. (2008). Creating your own hostile environment: A laboratory examination of trait aggressiveness and the violence escalation cycle. *Personality and Social Psychology Bulletin, 34,* 462–473.

Anderson, K. E., Lytton, H., & Romney, D. M. (1986). Mothers' interactions with normal and conduct-disordered boys: Who affects whom? *Developmental Psychology, 22,* 604–609.

Arnett, J. J., Trzesniewski, K. H., & Donnellan, M. B. (2013). The dangers of generational myth-making rejoinder to Twenge. *Emerging Adulthood, 1,* 17–20.

Aron, A., & Aron, E. N. (1997). Self-expansion motivation and including other in the self. In W. Ickes (Section Ed.) & S. Duck (Ed.), *Handbook of personal relationships* (2nd ed., Vol. 1, pp. 251–270). London: Wiley.

August, K. J., & Sorkin, D. H. (2010). Marital status and gender differences in managing a chronic illness: The function of health-related social control. *Social Science and Medicine, 71,* 1831–1838.

Bleidorn, W., Buyukcan-Tetik, A., Schwaba, T., Van Scheppingen, M. A., Denissen, J. J., & Finkenauer, C. (2016). Stability and change in self-esteem during the transition to parenthood. *Social Psychological and Personality Science, 7,* 560–569.

Bleidorn, W., Hopwood, C. J., & Lucas, R. E. (2018). Life events and personality trait change. *Journal of Personality, 86,* 83–96.

Bradbury, T. N., & Fincham, F. D. (1988). Individual difference variables in close relationships: A contextual model of marriage as an integrative framework. *Journal of Personality and Social Psychology, 54,* 713–721.

Braithwaite, S., & Holt-Lunstad, J. (2017). Romantic relationships and mental health. *Current Opinion in Psychology, 13,* 120–125.

Burt, S. A., Donnellan, M. B., Humbad, M. N., Hicks, B. M., McGue, M., & Iacono, W. G. (2010). Does marriage inhibit antisocial behavior?: An examination of selection versus causation via a longitudinal twin design. *Archives of General Psychiatry, 67,* 1309–1315.

Buss, D. M. (1987). Selection, evocation, and manipulation. *Journal of Personality and Social Psychology, 53,* 1214–1221.

Buss, D. M., & Shackelford, T. K. (1997). Susceptibility to infidelity in the first year of marriage. *Journal of Research in Personality, 31,* 193–221.

Caspi, A., Elder, G. H., & Bem, D. J. (1988). Moving away from the world: Life-course patterns of shy children. *Developmental Psychology, 24,* 824–831.

Caspi, A., Herbener, E. S., & Ozer, D. J. (1992). Shared experiences and the similarity of personalities: A longitudinal study of married couples. *Journal of Personality and Social Psychology, 62,* 281–289.

Caspi, A., & Moffitt, T. E. (1993). When do individual differences matter?: A paradoxical theory of personality coherence. *Psychological Inquiry, 4,* 247–271.

Caspi, A., Roberts, B. W., & Shiner, R. L. (2005). Personality development: Stability and change. *Annual Review of Psychology, 56,* 453–484.

Caughlin, J. P., Huston, T. L., & Houts, R. M. (2000). How does personality matter in marriage?: An examination of trait anxiety, interpersonal negativity, and marital satisfaction. *Journal of Personality and Social Psychology, 78,* 326–336.

Chopik, W. J. (2018). Does personality change following spousal bereavement? *Journal of Research in Personality, 72,* 10–21.

Corker, K. S., & Donnellan, M. B. (in press). Person–situation transactions across the lifespan. In J. F. Rauthmann, R. A. Sherman, & D. C. Funder (Eds.), *Oxford handbook of psychological situations.* Oxford University Press.

Costa, P., Herbst, P., McCrae, R. R., & Siegler, I. (2000). Personality at midlife: Stability, intrinsic maturation, and response to life events. *Assessment, 7,* 365–378.

Craddock, E., vanDellen, M. R., Novak, S. A., & Ranby, K. W. (2015). Influence in relationships: A meta-analysis on health-related social control. *Basic and Applied Social Psychology, 37,* 118–130.

DeYoung, C. G., Peterson, J. B., & Higgins, D. M. (2002). Higher-order factors of the Big Five predict conformity: Are there neuroses of health? *Personality and Individual Differences, 33,* 533–552.

Digman, J. M. (1997). Higher-order factors of the Big Five. *Journal of Personality and Social Psychology, 73,* 1246–1256.

Dinescu, D., Turkheimer, E., Beam, C. R., Horn, E. E., Duncan, G., & Emery, R. E. (2016). Is marriage a buzzkill?: A twin study of marital status and alcohol consumption. *Journal of Family Psychology, 30,* 698–707.

Dixon, R. B. (1971). Explaining cross-cultural variations in age at marriage and proportions never marrying. *Population Studies, 25,* 215–233.

Donnellan, M. B., Assad, K. K., Robins, R. W., & Conger, R. D. (2007). Do negative interactions mediate the effects of negative emotionality, communal positive emotionality, and constraint on relationship satisfaction? *Journal of Social and Personal Relationships, 24,* 557–573.

Donnellan, M. B., Conger, R. D., & Bryant, C. M. (2004). The Big Five and enduring marriages. *Journal of Research in Personality, 38,* 481–504.

Donnellan, M. B., Conger, R. D., & Burzette, R. G. (2007). Personality development from late adolescence to young adulthood: Differential stability, normative maturity, and evidence for the maturity–stability hypothesis. *Journal of Personality, 75,* 237–264.

Donnellan, M. B., Conger, K. J., McAdams, K. K., & Neppl, T. K. (2009). Personal characteristics and resilience to economic hardship and its consequences: Conceptual issues and empirical illustrations. *Journal of Personality, 77,* 1645–1676.

Donnellan, M. B., Larsen-Rife, D., & Conger, R. D. (2005). Personality, family history, and competence in early adult romantic relationships. *Journal of Personality and Social Psychology, 88,* 562–576.

Dyrenforth, P. S., Kashy, D. A., Donnellan, M. B., & Lucas, R. E. (2010). Predicting relationship and life satisfaction from personality in nationally representative samples from three countries: The relative importance of actor, partner, and similarity effects. *Journal of Personality and Social Psychology, 99,* 690–702.

Feeney, B. C., & Collins, N. L. (2015). A new look at social support: A theoretical perspective on thriving through relationships. *Personality and Social Psychology Review, 19,* 113–147.

Finkel, E. J., Eastwick, P. W., Karney, B. R., Reis, H. T., & Sprecher, S. (2012). Online dating: A critical analysis from the perspective of psychological science. *Psychological Science in the Public Interest, 13,* 3–66.

Finn, C., Mitte, K., & Neyer, F. J. (2015). Recent decreases in specific interpretation biases predict decreases in neuroticism: Evidence from a longitudinal study with young adult couples. *Journal of Personality, 83,* 274–286.

Flood, S. M., & Genadek, K. (2016). Time for each other: Work and family constraints among couples. *Journal of Marriage and Family, 78,* 142–164.

Foster, E. M. (2010). Causal inference and developmental psychology. *Developmental Psychology, 46,* 1454–1480.

Fraley, R. C., & Shaver, P. R. (2000). Adult romantic attachment: Theoretical developments, emerging controversies, and unanswered questions. *Review of General Psychology, 4,* 132–154.

Gardner, J., & Oswald, A. (2004). How is mortality affected by money, marriage, and stress? *Journal of Health Economics, 23,* 1181–1207.

Gattis, K. S., Berns, S., Simpson, L. E., & Christensen, A. (2004). Birds of a feather or strange birds?: Ties among personality dimensions, similarity, and marital quality. *Journal of Family Psychology, 18,* 564–574.

Gelman, A., & Weakliem, D. (2009). Of beauty, sex and power: Too little attention has been paid to the statistical challenges in estimating small effects. *American Scientist, 97,* 310–316.

Genadek, K. R., Flood, S. M., & Garcia-Roman, J. (2016). Trends in spouses' shared time in the United States, 1965–2012. *Demography, 53,* 1801–1820.

Gonzaga, G. C., Campos, B., & Bradbury, T. (2007). Similarity, convergence, and relationship satisfaction in dating and married couples. *Journal of Personality and Social Psychology, 93,* 34–48.

Gonzaga, G. C., Carter, S., & Buckwalter, J. G. (2010). Assortative mating, convergence, and satisfaction in married couples. *Personal Relationships, 17,* 634–644.

Haeffel, G. J., & Hames, J. L. (2014). Cognitive vulnerability to depression can be contagious. *Clinical Psychological Science, 2,* 75–85.

Hatton, H., Donnellan, M. B., Maysn, K., Feldman, B. J., Larsen-Rife, D., & Conger, R. D. (2008). Family and individual difference predictors of trait aspects of negative interpersonal behaviors during emerging adulthood. *Journal of Family Psychology, 22,* 448–455.

Hawkins, D. N., & Booth, A. (2005). Unhappily ever after: Effects of long-term, low-quality marriages on well-being. *Social Forces, 84,* 451–471.

Heller, D., Watson, D., & Ilies, R. (2004). The role of person versus situation in life satisfaction: A critical examination. *Psychological Bulletin, 130,* 574–600.

Holt-Lunstad, J., Smith, T. B., & Layton, J. B. (2010). Social relationships and mortality risk: A meta-analytic review. *PLoS Medicine, 7,* e1000316.

Hopwood, C. J., Donnellan, M. B., Blonigen, D. M., Krueger, R. F., McGue, M., Iacono, W. G., et al. (2011). Genetic and environmental influences on personality trait stability and growth during the transition to adulthood: A three-wave longitudinal study. *Journal of Personality and Social Psychology, 100,* 545–556.

Hudson, N. W., Lucas, R. E., & Donnellan, M. B. (2017). *The highs and lows of love: Romantic relationship quality moderates whether spending time with one's partner predicts differences in individual well-being.* Manuscript submitted for publication.

Humbad, M. N., Donnellan, M. B., Iacono, W. G., & Burt, S. A. (2010a). Externalizing psychopathology and marital adjustment in long-term marriages: Results from a large combined sample of married couples. *Journal of Abnormal Psychology, 119,* 151–162.

Humbad, M. N., Donnellan, M. B., Iacono, W. G., McGue, M., & Burt, S. A. (2010b). Is spousal similarity for personality a matter of convergence or selection? *Personality and Individual Differences, 49,* 827–830.

Humbad, M. N., Donnellan, M. B., Iacono, W. G., McGue, M., & Burt, S. A. (2013). Quantifying the association between personality similarity and marital adjustment using profile correlations: A cautionary tale. *Journal of Research in Personality, 47,* 97–106.

Huston, T. L., & Houts, R. M. (1998). The psychological infrastructure of courtship and marriage: The role of personality and compatibility in romantic relationships. In T. N. Bradbury (Ed.), *The developmental course of marital dysfunction* (pp. 114–151). New York: Cambridge University Press.

Hutteman, R., Hennecke, M., Orth, U., Reitz, A. K., &

Specht, J. (2014). Developmental tasks as a framework to study personality development in adulthood and old age. *European Journal of Personality, 28,* 267–278.

Johnson, M. D., Galambos, N. L., Finn, C., Neyer, F. J., & Horne, R. M. (2017). Pathways between self-esteem and depression in couples. *Developmental Psychology, 53,* 787–799.

Kalmijn, M. (2007). Explaining cross-national differences in marriage, cohabitation, and divorce in Europe, 1990–2000. *Population Studies, 61,* 243–263.

Kamp Dush, C. M., & Amato, P. R. (2005). Consequences of relationship status and quality for subjective well-being. *Journal of Social and Personal Relationships, 22,* 607–627.

Kamp Dush, C. M., Taylor, M. G., & Kroeger, R. A. (2008). Marital happiness and psychological well-being across the life course. *Family Relations, 57,* 211–226.

Kandler, C. (2012). Nature and nurture in personality development: The case of neuroticism and extraversion. *Current Directions in Psychological Science, 21,* 290–296.

Karney, B. R., & Bradbury, T. N. (1995). The longitudinal course of marital quality and stability: A review of theory, method, and research. *Psychological Bulletin, 118,* 3–34.

Karney, B. R., & Bradbury, T. N. (2005). Contextual influences on marriage implications for policy and intervention. *Current Directions in Psychological Science, 14,* 171–174.

Kelly, E. L., & Conley, J. J. (1987). Personality and compatibility: A prospective analysis of marital stability and marital satisfaction. *Journal of Personality and Social Psychology, 52,* 27–40.

Kenny, D. A., Kashy, D. A., & Cook, W. L. (2006). *Dyadic data analysis.* New York: Guilford Press.

Kiecolt-Glaser, J. K., & Newton, T. L. (2001). Marriage and health: His and hers. *Psychological Bulletin, 127,* 472–503.

Kiecolt-Glaser, J. K., & Wilson, S. J. (2017). Lovesick: How couples' relationships influence health. *Annual Review of Clinical Psychology, 13,* 421–443.

Lehnart, J., Neyer, F. J., & Eccles, J. (2010). Long-term effects of social investment: The case of partnering in young adulthood. *Journal of Personality, 78,* 639–670.

Lewis, M. A., & Butterfield, R. M. (2007). Social control in marital relationships: Effect of one's partner on health behaviors. *Journal of Applied Social Psychology, 37,* 298–319.

Lucas, R. E., Clark, A. E., Georgellis, Y., & Diener, E. (2003). Reexamining adaptation and the set point model of happiness: Reactions to changes in marital status. *Journal of Personality and Social Psychology, 84,* 527–539.

Luo, S., Chen, H., Yue, G., Zhang, G., Zhaoyang, R., & Xu, D. (2008). Predicting marital satisfaction from self, partner, and couple characteristics: Is it me, you, or us? *Journal of Personality, 76,* 1231–1266.

Malouff, J. M., Thorsteinsson, E. B., Schutte, N. S., Bhullar, N., & Rooke, S. E. (2010). The five-factor model of personality and relationship satisfaction of intimate partners: A meta-analysis. *Journal of Research in Personality, 44,* 124–127.

McAdams, D. P. (2015). *The art and science of personality development.* New York: Guilford Press.

McAdams, D. P., & Olson, B. D. (2010). Personality development: Continuity and change over the life course. *Annual Review of Psychology, 61,* 517–542.

McAdams, D. P., & Pals, J. L. (2006). A new Big Five: Fundamental principles for an integrative science of personality. *American Psychologist, 61,* 204–217.

McCrae, R. R., & Costa, P. T., Jr. (2008). The five-factor theory of personality. In O. P. John, R. W. Robins, & L. A. Pervin (Eds.), *Handbook of personality: Theory and research* (3rd ed., pp. 159–180). New York: Guilford Press.

Moffitt, T. E., Arseneault, L., Belsky, D., Dickson, N., Hancox, R. J., Harrington, H., et al. (2011). A gradient of childhood self-control predicts health, wealth, and public safety. *Proceedings of the National Academy of Sciences of the USA, 108,* 2693–2698.

Mroczek, D. K., & Spiro, A. (2003). Modeling intraindividual change in personality traits: Findings from the Normative Aging Study. *Journals of Gerontology B: Psychological Sciences and Social Sciences, 58,* P153–P165.

Mund, M., Finn, C., Hagemeyer, B., & Neyer, F. J. (2016). Understanding dynamic transactions between personality traits and partner relationships. *Current Directions in Psychological Science, 25,* 411–416.

Mund, M., & Neyer, F. J. (2014). Treating personality–relationship transactions with respect: Narrow facets, advanced models, and extended time frames. *Journal of Personality and Social Psychology, 107,* 352–368.

Newman, D. L., Caspi, A., Moffitt, T. E., & Silva, P. A. (1997). Antecedents of adult interpersonal functioning: Effects of individual differences in age 3 temperament. *Developmental Psychology, 33,* 206–217.

Neyer, F. J., & Asendorpf, J. B. (2001). Personality–relationship transaction in young adulthood. *Journal of Personality and Social Psychology, 81,* 1190–1204.

Neyer, F. J., & Lehnart, J. (2007). Relationships matter in personality development: Evidence from an 8-year longitudinal study across young adulthood. *Journal of Personality, 75,* 535–568.

Neyer, F. J., Mund, M., Zimmermann, J., & Wrzus, C. (2014). Personality–relationship transactions revisited. *Journal of Personality, 82,* 539–550.

Orth, U. (2013). How large are actor and partner effects of personality on relationship satisfaction?: The importance of controlling for shared method variance. *Personality and Social Psychology Bulletin, 39,* 1359–1372.

Ozer, D. J., & Benet-Martínez, V. (2006). Personality and the prediction of consequential outcomes. *Annual Review of Psychology, 57,* 401–421.

Proulx, C. M., Helms, H. M., & Buehler, C. (2007). Marital quality and personal well-being: A meta-analysis. *Journal of Marriage and Family, 69,* 576–593.

Rammstedt, B., Spinath, F. M., Richter, D., & Schupp, J. (2013). Partnership longevity and personality congruence in couples. *Personality and Individual Differences, 54,* 832–835.

Reis, H. T., Collins, W. A., & Berscheid, E. (2000). The relationship context of human behavior and development. *Psychological Bulletin, 126,* 844–872.

Roberts, B. W., Caspi, A., & Moffitt, T. E. (2001). The kids are alright: Growth and stability in personality development from adolescence to adulthood. *Journal of Personality and Social Psychology, 81,* 670–683.

Roberts, B. W., Caspi, A., & Moffitt, T. E. (2003). Work experiences and personality development in young adulthood. *Journal of Personality and Social Psychology, 84,* 582–593.

Roberts, B. W., & DelVecchio, W. F. (2000). The rank-order consistency of personality traits from childhood to old age: A quantitative review of longitudinal studies. *Psychological Bulletin, 126,* 3–25.

Roberts, B. W., Donnellan, M. B., & Hill, P. L. (2013). Personality trait development in adulthood: Findings and implications. In H. Tennen & J. Suls (Eds.), *Handbook of psychology: Personality and social psychology* (2nd ed., pp 183–196). Hoboken, NJ: Wiley.

Roberts, B. W., Kuncel, N. R., Shiner, R., Caspi, A., & Goldberg, L. R. (2007). The power of personality: The comparative validity of personality traits, socioeconomic status, and cognitive ability for predicting important life outcomes. *Perspectives on Psychological Science, 2,* 313–345.

Roberts, B. W., Luo, J., Briley, D. A., Chow, P. I., Su, R., & Hill, P. L. (2017). A systematic review of personality trait change through intervention. *Psychological Bulletin, 143,* 117–141.

Roberts, B. W., & Pomerantz, E. M. (2004). On traits, situations, and their integration: A developmental perspective. *Personality and Social Psychology Review, 8,* 402–416.

Roberts, B. W., & Robins, R. W. (2000). Broad dispositions, broad aspirations: The intersection of personality traits and major life goals. *Personality and Social Psychology Bulletin, 26,* 1284–1296.

Roberts, B. W., Walton, K. E., & Viechtbauer, W. (2006). Patterns of mean-level change in personality traits across the life course: A meta-analysis of longitudinal studies. *Psychological Bulletin, 132,* 1–25.

Roberts, B. W., & Wood, D. (2006). Personality development in the context of the neo-socioanalytic model of personality. In D. Mroczek & T. D. Little (Eds.), *Handbook of personality development* (pp. 11–39). Mahwah, NJ: Erlbaum.

Roberts, B. W., Wood, D., & Caspi, A. (2008). The development of personality traits in adulthood. In O. P. John, R. W. Robins, & L. A. Pervin (Eds.), *Hand-*

book of personality: Theory and research (3rd ed., pp. 375–398). New York: Guilford Press.

Robins, R. W., Caspi, A., & Moffitt, T. E. (2000). Two personalities, one relationship: Both partners' personality traits shape the quality of their relationship. *Journal of Personality and Social Psychology, 79,* 251–259.

Robles, T. F., Slatcher, R. B., Trombello, J. M., & McGinn, M. M. (2014). Marital quality and health: A meta-analytic review. *Psychological Bulletin, 140,* 140–187.

Rook, K. S., August, K. J., Stephens, M. A. P., & Franks, M. M. (2011). When does spousal social control provoke negative reactions in the context of chronic illness?: The pivotal role of patients' expectations. *Journal of Social and Personal Relationships, 28,* 772–789.

Scarr, S., & McCartney, K. (1983). How people make their own environments: A theory of genotype → environment effects. *Child Development, 54,* 424–435.

Schmitt, D. P. (2004). The Big Five related to risky sexual behaviour across 10 world regions: Differential personality associations of sexual promiscuity and relationship infidelity. *European Journal of Personality, 18,* 301–319.

Scollon, C. N., & Diener, E. (2006). Love, work, and changes in extraversion and neuroticism over time. *Journal of Personality and Social Psychology, 91,* 1152–1165.

Senia, J. M., Donnellan, M. B., Clark, D. A., Neppl, T. K., & Wickrama, K. A. S. (2017). *Personality trait development in enduring marriages.* Unpublished manuscript, Michigan State University.

Shiner, R., & Caspi, A. (2003). Personality differences in childhood and adolescence: Measurement, development, and consequences. *Journal of Child Psychology and Psychiatry, 44,* 2–32.

Shiner, R. L., Masten, A. S., & Roberts, J. M. (2003). Childhood personality foreshadows adult personality and life outcomes two decades later. *Journal of Personality, 71,* 1145–1170.

Solomon, B. C., & Jackson, J. J. (2014). Why do personality traits predict divorce?: Multiple pathways through satisfaction. *Journal of Personality and Social Psychology, 106,* 978–996.

Specht, J., Egloff, B., & Schmukle, S. C. (2011). Stability and change of personality across the life course: The impact of age and major life events on mean-level and rank-order stability of the Big Five. *Journal of Personality and Social Psychology, 101,* 862–882.

Springsteen, B. (2016). *Born to run.* New York: Simon & Schuster.

Terman, L. M., & Buttenweiser, P. (1935). Personality factors in marital compatibility. *Journal of Social Psychology, 6,* 143–171.

Umberson, D. (1992). Gender, marital status and the social control of health behavior. *Social Science and Medicine, 34,* 907–917.

Umberson, D., Crosnoe, R., & Reczek, C. (2010). Social relationships and health behavior across the life course. *Annual Review of Sociology, 36,* 139–157.

van Scheppingen, M. A., Jackson, J. J., Specht, J., Hutteman, R., Denissen, J. J. A., & Bleidorn, W. (2016). Personality trait development during the transition to parenthood: A test of social investment theory. *Social Psychological and Personality Science, 7,* 452–462.

Wagner, J., Becker, M., Lüdtke, O., & Trautwein, U. (2015). The first partnership experience and personality development: A propensity score matching study in young adulthood. *Social Psychological and Personality Science, 6,* 455–463.

Waite, L., & Gallagher, M. (2002). *The case for marriage: Why married people are happier, healthier and better off financially.* New York: Random House.

Watson, D., Beer, A., & McDade-Montez, E. (2014). The role of active assortment in spousal similarity. *Journal of Personality, 82,* 116–129.

Watson, D., Hubbard, B., & Wiese, D., (2000). General traits of personality and affectivity as predictors of satisfaction in intimate relationships: Evidence from self- and partner-rating. *Journal of Personality, 68,* 413–449.

Watson, D., Klohnen, E. C., Casillas, A., Nus Simms, E., Haig, J., & Berry, D. S. (2004). Match makers and deal breakers: Analyses of assortative mating in newlywed couples. *Journal of Personality, 72,* 1029–1068.

Winnicott, D. W. (1960). The theory of the parent–infant relationship. *International Journal of Psychoanalysis, 41,* 585–595.

Wood, D., & Furr, R. M. (2016). The correlates of similarity estimates are often misleadingly positive: The nature and scope of the problem, and some solutions. *Personality and Social Psychology Review, 20,* 79–99.

Wrzus, C., & Roberts, B. W. (2017). Processes of personality development in adulthood: The TESSERA framework. *Personality and Social Psychology Review, 21,* 253–277.

Author Index

Subject Index

Note. *f*, *n*, or *t* following a page number indicates a figure, a note, or a table.